Why Do You Need This New Edition?

If you're wondering why you should buy this new edition of *The Struggle for Democracy*, here are 10 good reasons!

1. The entire book has been updated to offer coverage of the **2010 national elections**, with a special focus on Congress. The causes and likely consequences of the Republican Party's comeback from its defeats in 2006 and 2008 are included in this discussion.

2. **Economic trends and events** receive particular attention, including globalization and its effects, the mortgage and credit crises, rising gas prices, growing income and wealth inequality, and the ways in which these economic trends shape government action.

3. The ongoing wars in Iraq and Afghanistan; global environmental problems including global warming; ensuring energy supplies; the rise of China, India, and Brazil as major economic powers; nuclear weapons programs in North Korea, Pakistan, and Iran; and the threat posed by a newly resurgent and belligerent Russia highlight new coverage in **a greatly expanded chapter on foreign policy and national defense** (Chapter 19).

4. The ongoing—and extremely bitter—**partisanship that has defined American politics** since at least 1994 is examined and evaluated, with special attention to whether the 2010 national elections added to the partisan flavor of our politics or tamped it down.

5. **An updated chapter on the budget and economic policies** (Chapter 15) offers an overview of the policymaking process, as well as consideration of how the federal government collects revenues, what it spends these revenues on, and with what effects on the well-being of citizens; while **a revised and updated chapter on social safety nets** (Chapter 18) offers a thorough examination of domestic social insurance programs, health care, and need-based social welfare policies.

6. The massive BP **oil spill in the Gulf of Mexico** is examined closely because of the issues it raises about federalism, government regulation of business, and trust in government.

7. There is a deeper focus on **domestic public policy**, partly because of events and developments in the domestic and global economies that would have elicited new government responses no matter which party was in power, and partly because of the broad changes fashioned by President Barack Obama and the Democratic-led 111th Congress in 2009 and 2010.

8. Much of the narrative is revised with students in mind: **in-text explanations** have been expanded and revised for clarity, with **more key terms** highlighted and defined in the glossary. Figures and tables are completely updated.

9. Features throughout the textbook have been expanded and revised to promote **critical thinking.** Chapter opening elements, section headings, Critical Thinking questions, chapter summaries, and student self-testing features have been designed to enhance the overall learning experience.

10. The popular features **By the Numbers** and **Mapping American Politics** have been revised so that virtually every chapter within the textbook has them.

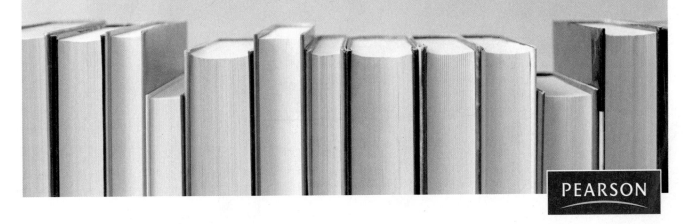

PEARSON

ELECTORAL COLLEGE VOTES IN THE 2008 ELECTION

THE UNITED STATES
A political map showing the number of electoral votes per state

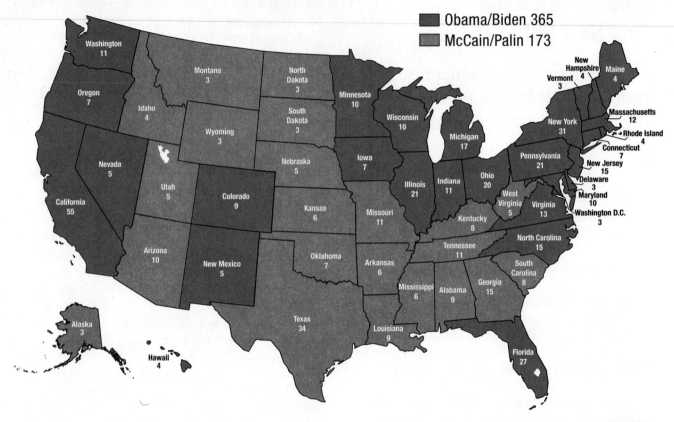

Obama/Biden 365
McCain/Palin 173

A political map with states drawn in proportion to the number of electoral votes

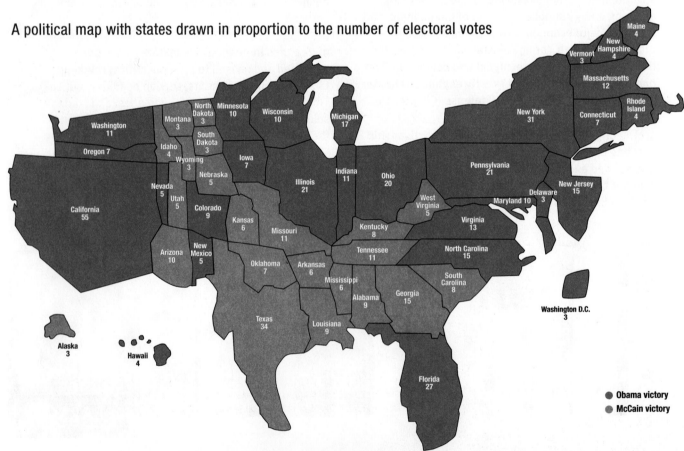

Obama victory
McCain victory

THE STRUGGLE FOR
DEMOCRACY

Tenth Edition

EDWARD S. GREENBERG
University of Colorado

BENJAMIN I. PAGE
Northwestern University

Longman

Boston Columbus Indianapolis New York San Francisco Upper Saddle River
Amsterdam Cape Town Dubai London Madrid Milan Munich Paris Montreal Toronto
Delhi Mexico City São Paulo Sydney Hong Kong Seoul Singapore Taipei Tokyo

Executive Editor: Reid Hester
Director of Development: Meg Botteon
Development Editor: Leslie Kauffman
Editorial Assistant: Elizabeth Alimena
Senior Marketing Manager: Lindsey Prudhomme
Supplements Editor: Donna Garnier
Production Manager: Savoula Amanatidis
Project Coordination and Text Design: Elm Street Publishing Services
Electronic Page Makeup: Integra Software Services, Pvt. Ltd.
Cover Design Manager: John Callahan
Cover Photo: © Kamisoka/iStockphoto
Photo Researcher: Connie Gardner
Manufacturing Manager: Mary Fischer
Printer and Binder: Quad/Graphics—Dubuque
Cover Printer: Lehigh-Phoenix Color Corporation—Hagerstown

For permission to use copyrighted material, grateful acknowledgment is made to the copyright holders on pp. C-1 and C-2, which are hereby made part of this copyright page.

Library of Congress Cataloging-in-Publication Data
Greenberg, Edward S.,
   The struggle for democracy / Edward S. Greenberg & Benjamin I. Page.—10th ed.
      p. cm.
   Includes bibliographical references and index.
   ISBN 978-0-205-77129-5—ISBN 978-0-205-77867-6
   1. United States—Politics and government—Textbooks.   2. Democracy—United States.   I. Page, Benjamin I.   II. Title.

JK276.G74 2011
320.473—dc22

Library of Congress Control Number: 2010024778

2 3 4 5 6 7 8 9 10—V042—13 12 11

Longman
is an imprint of

www.pearsonhighered.com

ISBN-13: 978-0-205-77129-5
ISBN-10:   0-205-77129-7

BRIEF CONTENTS

DETAILED CONTENTS

NOTE: Each chapter ends with the following sections: Summary, Test Yourself, MyPoliSciLab Exercises,
Internet Sources, and Suggestions for Further Reading.

PREFACE

Critical Thinking and *The Struggle for Democracy*

Through ten editions of *The Struggle for Democracy*, we have stayed true to our original vision for this book: to create a text that provides students not merely with an understanding or appreciation of the American political process, but with the tools for critically analyzing and evaluating that process. Our goal, all along, has been to create a textbook that treats students as adults, engages their intellectual and emotional attention, and encourages them to be active learners. Every element in this text is designed to promote the kind of critical thinking skills that we, as scholars and instructors, believe students need in order to become the engaged, active, and informed citizens so vital to any democracy. To this end, we have organized *The Struggle for Democracy* around two principal themes, both of which have been hallmarks of this text since its inception.

The Democracy Standard is a thematic thread that helps students come to grips with American government and politics in normative or value terms. Throughout the text and features, students are challenged to develop a strong understanding of what democracy is, the role that the democratic impulse has played in the American story, and how democracy is—or isn't—revealed in our government and politics. Throughout this textbook, we help students think about the system as a whole, as well as particular political practices and institutions, using a clearly articulated, evaluative democracy "yardstick" for reaching judgments about the degree to which we have become, or are becoming, more or less democratic.

The second theme is a **Framework for Analyzing and Understanding American Government and Politics**—a unique tool that helps students to understand the many influences at play in the American political process that shape what political leaders do and what sorts of government policies we have. This analytical framework makes clear that government, politics, and the larger society are deeply intertwined in recognizable patterns; that understanding what is going on requires a holistic focus; and that what might be called "deep structures"—the economy, society, political culture, and the constitutional rules—are particularly important for understanding how our system works. These deep structures have a great deal to do with the creation of the problems to which government must attend; the level of resources that are available to solve problems; the ideas that citizens and elected officials have in their heads as they go about using government to address problems; and the distribution of political power in society among individuals, groups, and organizations. Introduced in Chapter 1 and reflected in the overall organization of the

book, the framework is revisited in each chapter with a program of supporting features that encourage students to examine government processes as a product of tensions among these different levels of government. This simple visual tool helps students cut through the jumble of information about government and politics, and brings some order out of the confusion, to help students make sense of *why* things happen.

This framework also serves as the organizing framework for the book. Part 1 includes an introduction to the textbook, its themes, and the critical thinking tools used throughout the book. Part 2 covers the structural foundations of American government and politics addressing subjects such as America's economy, political culture, and place in the international system; the constitutional framework of the American political system; and the development of federalism. Part 3 focuses on what we call *political linkage* institutions, such as parties, elections, public opinion, social movements, and interest groups, that serve to convey the wants, needs, and demands of individuals and groups to public officials. Part 4 concentrates on the central institutions of the national government, including the presidency, Congress, and the Supreme Court. Part 5 describes the kinds of policies the national government produces and analyzes how effective government is in solving pressing social and economic problems.

What's New in This Edition

As always, we've striven to make this new edition completely up to date. Data and statistics have been updated throughout, and we've included thorough examinations of recent events. We've created policy chapters that focus on the most pressing issues facing American society today and expanded the critical thinking tools to help students process and evaluate all of this material.

- Critical thinking elements in each chapter are more numerous and more tightly integrated in this edition, with chapter-opening elements, section headings, critical thinking questions, chapter summaries, and student self-testing designed to work together to enhance the learning experience.

- There is an increased focus on matters of policy that is reflected in the reformulation of two chapters: Chapter 17, The Budget and Economic Policies, offers an overview of the policymaking process, as well as consideration of how the federal government collects revenues, what it spends these revenues on, and with what effects on the well-being of citizens, while Chapter 18, Social Safety Nets, offers a thorough examination of domestic social insurance programs and need-based social welfare policies, with a focus on the new health reform program.

- We've updated the entire book to offer coverage of the 2010 national elections, with a special focus on Congress. We examine the causes and likely consequences of the Republican Party's comeback from its bad defeats in 2006 and 2008.

- We pay more attention to economic trends and events, especially the various aspects of the Great Recession and jobless recovery that followed, spanning the years 2008–2010—including globalization and its effects, the mortgage and credit crises, rising gas prices, and economic downturns (Chapter 18), growing income and wealth inequality (Chapter 4), and the ways in which these economic trends shape government action, including new legislation to regulate the financial industry (Chapters 4, 17, and 18).

- We focus a great deal of attention on domestic public policy, partly because of events and developments in the domestic and global economies that would have elicited new government responses no matter which party has been in power, and partly because of the broad sweep of changes wrought by President Barack Obama and the Democratic-led 111th Congress in 2009 and 2010.

- We also have paid more attention to foreign and national defense affairs: the ongoing wars in Iraq and Afghanistan; problems of the global environment, including warming; what to do to ensure energy supplies; the rise of China, India, and Brazil as major economic powers; nuclear weapons programs in North Korea, Pakistan, and Iran; and the impact of a newly resurgent Russia highlight new coverage in a greatly expanded Chapter 19, Foreign Policy and National Defense.

- We evaluate and examine the ongoing—and extremely bitter—partisanship that has defined American politics since at least 1994, with special attention to whether the 2010 national elections added to the partisan flavor of our politics or tamped it down (Chapters 9, 10, and 11).

- We have increased the numbers of two features especially popular with instructors and their students; **By the Numbers** and **Mapping American Politics** now appear in virtually every chapter.

Hallmarks of the Text

Although all of the standard topics in the introductory course are covered in the text, our focus on using democracy as a measuring rod to evaluate our system of government, and on using an analytical framework for understanding how things work, allows us to take a fresh look at traditional topics and to give attention to topics that other textbooks do not:

- We pay much more attention than most other texts to *structural factors*—which include the American economy, social change in the United States, technological innovations and change, the American political culture, and changes in the global system—and examine how they affect politics, government, and public policy. These factors are introduced in Chapter 4—a chapter unique among introductory texts—and are brought to bear on a wide range of issues in subsequent chapters. In this edition, we offer more in-depth analysis of shifting structural factors, particularly in regard to globalization and its impact on Americans, and the growing economic divide between rich and poor.

- We attend very carefully to issues of *democratic political theory*. This follows from our critical thinking objective, which asks students to assess the progress of and prospects for democracy in the United States, and from our desire to present American history as the history of the struggle for democracy. For instance, we examine how the evolution of the party system has improved democracy in some respects in the United States but hurt it in others.

- We also include more *historical information* than is common among introductory texts, because the best way to understand the struggle for democracy and evaluate the progress of democracy in the United States is, in part, from a historical perspective. We show, for example, how the expansion of civil rights in the United States has been associated with important historical events and trends.

- We have integrated substantial *comparative information* because we believe that a full understanding of government and politics and the effect of structural factors on them is possible only through a comparison of developments, practices, and institutions in the United States with those in other nations. We understand better how our system of social welfare works, for example, when we see how other rich democratic countries deal with the problems of poverty, unemployment, and old age.

- Our approach also means that the subjects of *civil liberties* and *civil rights* are not treated in conjunction with the Constitution in Part 2, which is the case with many introductory texts, but in Part 5, on public policy. This is because we believe that the real-world status of civil liberties and civil rights, while partly determined by specific provisions of the Constitution, is better understood as the outcome of the interaction of structural, political, and governmental factors. Thus, the status of civil rights for gays and lesbians depends not only on constitutional provisions but also on the state of public opinion, degrees of support from elected political leaders, and the decisions of the Supreme Court. (Instructors who prefer to introduce their students to civil liberties and civil rights immediately after considering the Constitution can simply assign the liberties and rights chapters out of order.)

THINKING CRITICALLY...

The definition of democracy—introduced in Chapter 1—is broad and inclusive, built on the concepts of popular sovereignty, political equality, and liberty. Discussions of the relative democratic performance of the American political system—using the Chapter 1 definition as the evaluative yardstick—are laced throughout the text narrative, providing a unifying theme for the text as a whole. In addition, a number of features in each chapter prompt students to stop and consider the democratic implications of each topic, event, or concept, and challenge them to critically evaluate the quality of democracy in light of what they've learned.

- In the opening pages of each chapter, students are reminded about the democracy "yardstick" and how it might be used to think critically about the subject matter to follow.

> **THINKING CRITICALLY** About This Chapter
> This chapter is about public opinion, how it is formed, and what effect it has on American politics and government.
>
> Using the **FRAMEWORK**
> You will learn in this chapter how the structural-level factors we learned about in Chapter 4—including historical events, the political culture, economic and social change—as well as family and community socialization, shape public opinion. You will also learn how public opinion influences the behavior of political leaders and shapes many of the policies of the federal government.
>
> Using the **DEMOCRACY STANDARD**
> Based on the standard of democracy described in Chapter 1, public opinion should be one of the decisive factors in determining what government does. You will see in this chapter, however, that while the influence of public opinion is important, public officials must pay attention to other political forces as well. They sometimes pay close attention to public opinion; at other times, they pay only slight attention to it.

> prosecutions by officials because officials can recover damages only by showing that the medium has purposely reported untruths or has made no effort to find out if what is being reported is true.
>
> **?** In this age of instant, online publication, is prior restraint even an issue? Is there any way the government could prevent a story from being published today?

- Integrated critical thinking questions allow students to evaluate topics in terms of democracy in a way that both highlights the theme and integrates it into larger discussions.

- A chapter-ending conclusion, called **Using the Democracy Standard,** examines the issues in each chapter against the democracy standard laid out in Chapter 1.

> ## Using the **DEMOCRACY STANDARD**
>
> ### What role do the people play in foreign and defense policymaking?
>
> Democracy is less evident in the process of making military and foreign policies than in making domestic policies. For one thing, Americans generally care more about what is going on in the United States and how it affects them directly than they do about issues and developments in distant places. They also know more about what is going on in the United States—whether it be health care, living standards, or the environment—than they do about what is happening elsewhere, particularly in the poor countries that get very little media news coverage. Additionally, to be effective, many foreign and military policies must be made in secret, so citizens often do not have the information necessary to be politically effective. And political leaders have sometimes misled or ignored the public.[37] Given this, Americans are clearly more competent as citizens when faced with domestic matters than with military and foreign affairs and are more interested in playing a role in shaping domestic policies. The result is that Americans give political, diplomatic, and military leaders a relatively free hand in making foreign and military policy. This is very much what the framers had in mind when they fashioned the Constitution.

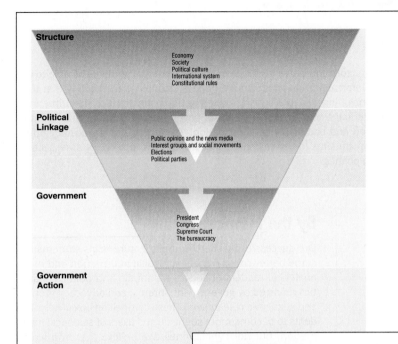

Structure

    Economy
    Society
    Political culture
    International system
    Constitutional rules

Political
Linkage

    Public opinion and the news media
    Interest groups and social movements
    Elections
    Political parties

Government

    President
    Congress
    Supreme Court
    The bureaucracy

Government
Action

FIGURE 1.1 The Analytical Framework

Various actors, institutions, and processes interact to influence
United States. Structural factors such as the economy, the p
system, and constitutional rules play a strong role in politica
the government directly, or, as is more often the case, throu
elections, parties, and interest groups. In a democratic soci
government should reflect these influences.

A Framework for Understanding American Government and Politics

- Our analytical framework, introduced in Chapter 1, provides students with a useful tool to help them make sense of *why* things happen. This simple, visual tool encourages students to take a holistic approach to examining the complexities of American government, helping them recognize patterns of influence and appreciate the role of what might be called "deep structures"—the economy, society, political culture, and the constitutional rules—in the political process.

- A **Using the Framework** box in each chapter then applies the framework to concrete questions, offering students the opportunity to examine crucial events, political trends, and specific policies as the result of tensions between and among various levels of government.

Using the **FRAMEWORK**

Why did we invade Iraq in 2003?

Background: Operation "Iraqi Freedom" began on March 20, 2003, when American and British forces, supported by very small contingents from other countries in the so-called coalition of the willing, launched aerial bombardments across Iraq with initial strikes aimed at air defenses and command and control facilities and an ill-fated attempt to kill Saddam Hussein in a pre-dawn bomb attack. (The stated goal was to shut down Iraq's weapons of mass destruction program, which was later shown not to have existed at the time.) After the initial air strikes, American and British ground forces struck from the south—Turkey had turned down a request to allow American troops to attack Iraq from Turkish territory—while Kurdish militias attacked

Iraq army units in the north. Baghdad fell on April 9. A Coalition Provisional Authority was put in place by the United States and the United Kingdom to govern Iraq until such time as the Iraqis could set up their own government. The rest, as they say, is history. Over the course of the next five years, a fierce insurgency and fierce conflicts between Sunni and Shiite militias raged, while member governments of the coalition of the willing gradually pulled out, with the British fielding only a token force by the end of 2008. So how did we get into this situation? Why did we invade in first place? Taking a look at how structural, political linkage, and governmental factors affect policymaking in Washington will help explain the outcome.

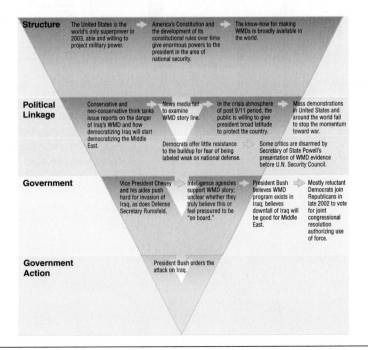

THINKING CRITICALLY...

As teachers of the introductory course, we find it deeply important that students be able to understand the statistical information on government, politics, economy, and society that they encounter every day—including statistics such as the gross domestic product, the crime rate, voting turnout in presidential elections, and the level of poverty in the United States—and to distinguish between good and bad statistical information. *The Struggle for Democracy* offers unique features that help students to better understand, interpret, and critically assess statistics and data that shape politics.

By the Numbers

Our successful **By the Numbers** feature helps students become better consumers of statistical information and more analytical readers of social, economic, and political statistics reported by government, interest and advocacy groups, and academic researchers. These compelling boxes help students to become more sophisticated users of statistical information, but not cynical ones. We believe that in a world increasingly described by numbers, students who are armed with these skills can be better and more effective citizens.

- Each box describes a particular statistic and tells why it is important—examples include voting turnout, the poverty line, the crime rate, the size of the federal government, interest group scoring of the performance of senators and representatives, and more.

- We then tell the story behind the statistic—why the statistic was first calculated, let us say, or what assumptions are embedded in it.

- We then show how the statistic is calculated and examine what critics and supporters say about its usefulness and validity.

- Finally, we ask students what they think, thus encouraging them to think in more depth about issues addressed by the statistic, whether it be party identification, voting turnout, or how the U.S. Census Bureau goes about doing the decennial census.

Tools for Understanding, Evaluating, Analyzing

Mapping American Politics

Cartograms—maps that display information that is organized on a geographical basis, with each unit (e.g., a county, state, or country) sized in various ways that are in proportion to the data being reported—further assist in helping students to visualize numeric information.

- The maps illuminate a broad range of issues, including how the geographic bases of the political parties are changing, how the states compare with one another on federal taxes paid and federal monies received, how well people are represented in the House and Senate, what the relationship is between violent crime incidence and capital punishment, and where American economic and military assistance dollars go. Cartograms comparing the United States with other countries have been added, including ones that map greenhouse gas emissions, participation in world trade, and spending on research and development.

- Comparisons help students visualize the relative impact of numbers.

- Thorough explanations show students where the numbers come from and how they are compared.

- Thoughtful assessments help students to understand the maps (and corresponding data) in light of the overall themes of the book.

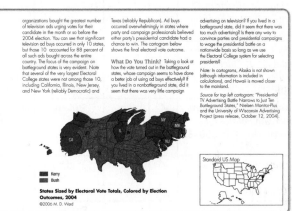

Timelines

Timelines appear throughout this book to help students develop a sense of historical context and assist students in keeping track of and mentally organizing materials that are described in depth and detail in the body of the text. Topics include federalism milestones, development of the U.S. census, a history of the Internet, the rise and fall of labor unions, a history of the nonviolent civil rights movement, party caucus and primary schedules, steps in the federal budgetary process, the creation of executive departments and agencies, a history of free expression, and U.S. military operations abroad.

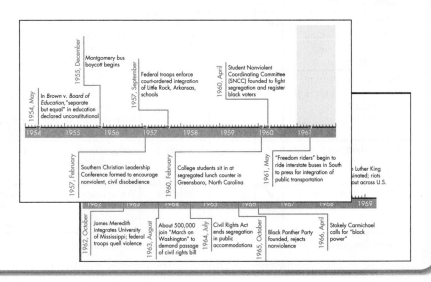

Resources In Print and Online

Name of Supplement	Print	Online	Available in Print	Description
MyClassPrep		✓	Instructor	This new resource provides a rich database of figures, photos, videos, simulations, activities, and much more that instructors can use to create their own lecture presentation. For more information visit www.mypoliscilab.com
Instructor's Manual 0205059805		✓	Instructor	Offers chapter overviews, lecture outlines, teaching ideas, discussion topics, and research activities. All resources hyperlinked for ease of navigation.
Test Bank 0205060447		✓	Instructor	Contains over 100 questions per chapter in multiple-choice, true-false, short answer, and essay format. Questions are tied to text Learning Objectives and have been reviewed for accuracy and effectiveness.
MyTest 0205059813		✓	Instructor	All questions from the Test Bank can be accessed in this flexible, online test generating software.
PowerPoint Presentation 0205059430		✓	Instructor	Slides include a lecture outline of the text, graphics from the book, and quick check questions for immediate feedback on student comprehension.
Transparencies 0205059449		✓	Instructor	These downloadable slides contain all maps, figures, and tables found in the text.
Pearson Political Science Video Program	✓		Instructor	Qualified adopters can peruse our list of videos for the American government classroom. Contact your local Pearson representative for more details.
Classroom Response System (CRS) 0205082289		✓	Instructor	A set of lecture questions, organized by American government topics, for use with "clickers" to garner student opinion and assess comprehension.
American Government Study Site		✓	Instructor/ Student	Online package of practice tests, flashcards and more organized by major course topics. Visit www.pearsonamericangovernment.com
You Decide! Current Debates in American Politics, 2011 Edition 020511489X	✓		Student	This debate-style reader by John Rourke of the University of Connecticut examines provocative issues in American politics today by presenting contrasting views of key political topics.
Voices of Dissent: Critical Readings in American Politics, Eighth Edition 0205697976	✓		Student	This collection of critical essays assembled by William Grover of St. Michael's College and Joseph Peschek of Hamline University goes beyond the debate between mainstream liberalism and conservatism to fundamentally challenge the status quo.
Diversity in Contemporary American Politics and Government 0205550363	✓		Student	Edited by David Dulio of Oakland University, Erin E. O'Brien of Kent State University, and John Klemanski of Oakland University, this reader examines the significant role that demographic diversity plays in our political outcomes and policy processes, using both academic and popular sources.
Writing in Political Science, Fourth Edition 0205617360	✓		Student	This guide, written by Diane Schmidt of California State University–Chico, takes students through all aspects of writing in political science step-by-step.
Choices: An American Government Database Reader		✓	Student	This customizable reader allows instructors to choose from a database of over 300 readings to create a reader that exactly matches their course needs. For more information go to www.pearsoncustom.com/database/choices.html.
Ten Things That Every American Government Student Should Read 020528969X	✓		Student	Edited by Karen O'Connor of American University. We asked American government instructors across the country to vote for the ten things beyond the text that they believe every student should read and put them in this brief and useful reader. Available at no additional charge when packaged with the text.
American Government: Readings and Cases, Eighteenth Edition 0205697984	✓		Student	Edited by Peter Woll of Brandeis University, this longtime best-selling reader provides a strong, balanced blend of classic readings and cases that illustrate and amplify important concepts in American government, alongside extremely current selections drawn from today's issues and literature. Available at a discount when ordered packaged with this text.
Penguin-Longman Value Bundles	✓		Student	Longman offers 25 Penguin Putnam titles at more than a 60 percent discount when packaged with any Longman text. Go to www.pearsonhighered.com/penguin for more information.
Longman State Politics Series	✓		Student	These primers on state and local government and political issues are available at no extra cost when shrink-wrapped with the text. Available for Texas, California, and Georgia.

* Visit the Instructor Resource Center to download supplements at www.pearsonhighered.com/educator

Save Time and Improve Results with

PEARSON

mypoliscilab™

The most popular online teaching/learning solution for American government, MyPoliSciLab moves students from studying and applying concepts to participating in politics. Completely redesigned and now organized by the book's chapters and learning objectives, the new MyPoliSciLab is easier to integrate into any course.

✔ STUDY A flexible learning path in every chapter.

Pre-Tests. See the relevance of politics with these diagnostic assessments and get personalized study plans driven by learning objectives.

Pearson eText. Navigate by learning objective, take notes, print key passages, and more. From page numbers to photos, the eText is identical to the print book.

Flashcards. Learn key terms by word, definition, or learning objective.

Post-Tests. Featuring over 50% new questions, the pre-tests produce updated study plans with follow-up reading, video, and multimedia

Chapter Exams. Also featuring over 50% new questions, test mastery of each chapter using the chapter exams.

✔ APPLY Over 150 videos and multimedia activities.

Video. Analyze current events by watching streaming video from the AP and ABC News.

Simulations. Engage the political process by experiencing how political actors make decisions.

Comparative Exercises. Think critically about how American politics compares with the politics of other countries.

Timelines. Get historical context by following issues that have influenced the evolution of American democracy.

Visual Literacy Exercises. Learn how to interpret political data in figures and tables.

MyPoliSciLibrary. Read full-text primary source documents from the nation's founding to the present.

✔ PARTICIPATE Join the political conversation.

PoliSci News Review. Read analysis of—and comment on—major new stories.

AP Newsfeeds. Follow political news in the United States and around the world.

Weekly Quiz. Master the headlines in this review of current events.

Weekly Poll. Take the poll and see how your politics compare.

Voter Registration. Voting is a right—and a responsibility.

Citizenship Test. See what it takes to become an American citizen.

✔ MANAGE Designed for online or traditional courses.

Grade Tracker. Assign and assess nearly everything in MyPoliSciLab.

Instructor Resources. Download supplements at the Instructor Resource Center.

Sample Syllabus. Get ideas for assigning the book and MyPoliSciLab.

MyClassPrep. Download many of the resources in MyPoliSciLab for lectures.

 The icons in the book and eText point to resources in MyPoliSciLab.

With proven book-specific and course-specific content, MyPoliSciLab is part of a better teaching/learning system only available from Pearson Longman.

✔ To see demos, read case studies, and learn about training, visit **www.mypoliscilab.com.**

✔ To order this book with MyPoliSciLab at no extra charge, use **ISBN 0-205-07876-1.**

✔ Questions? Contact a local Pearson Longman representative: **www.pearsonhighered.com/replocator.**

 Follow MyPoliSciLab on Twitter.

ACKNOWLEDGMENTS

Writing and producing an introductory textbook is an incredibly complex and cooperative enterprise in which many people, besides the authors, play roles. We would like to take the opportunity to thank them, one and all. Thanks to our development editor Leslie Kauffman for keeping us on track with our narrative and to Sue Nodine and her team at Elm Street for bringing all the parts together for final production. Thanks also to production manager Savoula Amanatidis, photo researcher Connie Gardner, and marketing manager Lindsey Prudhomme. Professor Michael Ward of Duke University created the **Mapping American Politics** feature in the eighth and ninth editions; Nancy Thorwardson updated several of the existing cartograms and created all the new ones for this edition. We thank both of them. Most of all, we want to thank the best social science editor in the business, Eric Stano, who always believed in this book project and in us, and whose guidance helped make the sixth, seventh, eighth, and ninth editions so successful. We hope that his wise counsel on revisions for the tenth edition will have a similar result. We wish him the best of luck with his new responsibilities at Pearson. We shall miss him.

We would also like to thank our students for helping to shape this book. The undergraduates in our introductory courses in American government and politics at the University of Colorado–Boulder and Northwestern University had much to say about what they liked and didn't like in the book, and they were more than willing to tell us how it might be improved. Our many graduate-student TAs in these introductory courses, moreover, were extremely helpful in advising us about how the ninth edition was working or not working as a teaching tool in the classroom. Special thanks for their help go to University of Colorado graduate students Bill Jaeger and Josh Ryan and undergraduate researchers Zach Franklin, Jeremy Speckhals, and Rachel Dane.

Over the years, Pearson Longman has enlisted the help of many political scientists on various aspects of this project. Their advice was especially valuable, and the final version of the book is far better than it would have been without their help. We would like to extend our appreciation to the following political scientists, who gave so generously of their time and expertise through the nine editions of *The Struggle for Democracy* and its supplements:

Ula Adeoye, *University of Illinois–Chicago*
Gordon Alexandre, *Glendale Community College*
John Ambacher, *Framingham State College*
Stephen P. Amberg, *University of Texas, San Antonio*
Sheldon Appleton, *Oakland University*
Thomas Clay Arnold, *University of Central Arkansas*
Jeffrey M. Ayres, *Lake Superior State University*
Ross K. Baker, *Rutgers University*
Manley Elliott Banks II, *Virginia Commonwealth University*
Ryan Barrilleaux, *University of Miami*
Ken Baxter, *San Joaquin Delta College*

Maria Bekafigo, *University of Georgia*
Todd Belt, *University of Hawaii*
Stephen Bennett, *University of Cincinnati*
Bill Bianco, *Duke University*
Joel Bloom, *University of Oregon*
Melanie J. Blumberg, *University of Akron*
Joseph P. Boyle, *Cypress College*
Richard Braunstein, *University of South Dakota*
Evelyn Brodkin, *University of Chicago*
James Bromeland, *Winona State University*
Barbara Brown, *Southern Illinois University–Carbondale*
Charles R. Brown, Jr., *Central Washington University*
Joseph S. Brown, *Baylor University*
Mark Byrnes, *Middle Tennessee State University*
David E. Camacho, *Northern Arizona University*
Mary Carns, *Stephen F. Austin University*
Cynthia Carter, *Florida Community College*
Jim Carter, *Sam Houston State University*
Gregory Casey, *University of Missouri*
Carl D. Cavalli, *North Georgia College and State University*
James Chalmers, *Wayne State University*
Paul Chardoul, *Grand Rapids Community College*
Mark A. Cichock, *University of Texas at Arlington*
Alan J. Cigler, *University of Kansas*
David Cingranelli, *State University of New York at Binghamton*
Natale H. Cipollina, *CUNY Baruch College*
Dewey M. Clayton, *University of Louisville*
John Coleman, *University of Wisconsin*
Ken Collier, *University of Kansas*
Lee Collins, *Monmouth College*
Edward Collins Jr., *University of Maine*
Richard W. Crockett, *Western Illinois University*
Lane Crothers, *Illinois State University*
Landon Curry, *University of Texas*
Paul B. Davis, *Truckee Meadows Community College*
Christine Day, *University of New Orleans*
Alan Draper, *St. Lawrence University*
David V. Edwards, *University of Texas, Austin*
Euel Elliott, *University of Texas*
Bob England, *Oklahoma State University*
Robert S. Erikson, *University of Houston*
Jasmine Farrier, *University of Louisville*
Thomas Ferguson, *University of Massachusetts, Boston*
M. Lauren Ficaro, *Chapman University*
Brian J. Fogarty, *University of North Carolina, Chapel Hill*
G. David Garson, *North Carolina State University*
John Geer, *Arizona State University*
Scott D. Gerber, *College of William and Mary*
Thomas Gillespie, *Seton Hall University*
Gregory Goldey, *Morehead State University*
Doris A. Graber, *University of Illinois*
John Green, *University of Akron*
Daniel P. Gregory, *El Camino Community College*
Eric E. Grier, *Georgia State University*

Mark F. Griffith, *The University of West Alabama*
Bruce E. Gronbeck, *University of Iowa*
Maria Guido, *Bentley College*
Robert Gumbrecht, *Merritt College*
Richard Haesly, *California State University–Long Beach*
Russell L. Hanson, *Indiana University*
Kevin R. Hardwick, *Canisius College*
Valerie Heitshusen, *University of Missouri*
Peter B. Heller, *Manhattan College*
Richard Herrara, *Arizona State University*
Roberta Herzberg, *Indiana University*
Seth Hirshorn, *University of Michigan*
Eugene Hogan, *Western Washington University*
John W. Homan, *Boise State University*
Marilyn Howard, *Columbus State Community College*
Ronald J. Hrebnar, *University of Utah*
David Hunt, *Triton College*
Jon Hurwitz, *University of Pittsburgh*
James Hutter, *Iowa State University*
Gary C. Jacobson, *University of California at San Diego*
William Jacoby, *University of South Carolina*
Willoughby Jarrell, *Kennesaw State College*
Jodi Jenkin, *Fullerton College*
Christopher B. Jones, *Eastern Oregon State University*
Mark R. Joslyn, *University of Kansas*
William Kelly, *Auburn University*
Fred Kramer, *University of Massachusetts*
Richard Lehne, *Rutgers University*
Jan E. Leighley, *Texas A&M University*
Joel Lieske, *Cleveland State University*
R. Philip Loy, *Taylor University*
Stan Luger, *University of Northern Colorado*
Maurice Mangum, *Southern Illinois University*
Dean E. Mann, *University of California*
Joseph R. Marbach, *Seton Hall University*
Michael D. Martinez, *University of Florida*
Peter Mathews, *Cypress College*
Louise Mayo, *County College of Morris*
Steve Mazurana, *University of Northern Colorado*
Michael W. McCann, *University of Washington*
Carroll R. McKibbin, *California Polytechnic State University*
William P. McLauchlan, *Purdue University*
Michael E. Meagher, *University of Missouri*
Stanley Melnick, *Valencia Community College*
Charles K. Menifield, *Murray State University*
Norma H. E. Miller, *South Carolina State University*
Neil Milner, *University of Hawaii*
Paul Moke, *Wilmington College*
Kristen R. Monroe, *Princeton University*
Mike Munger, *University of Texas*
Laurel A. Myer, *Sinclair Community College*
Albert Nelson, *University of Wisconsin, La Crosse*
Adam Newmark, *Appalachian State University*

David Nice, *Washington State University*
Charles Noble, *California State University at Long Beach*
Maureen Rand Oakley, *Mount St. Mary's College*
Colleen M. O'Connor, *San Diego Mesa College*
Daniel J. O'Connor, *California State University at Long Beach*
David J. Olson, *University of Washington*
Laura Katz Olson, *Lehigh University*
John Orman, *Fairfield University*
Marvin Overby, *University of Mississippi*
Elizabeth M. H. Paddock, *Drury College*
Kenneth T. Palmer, *University of Maine*
Toby Paone, *St. Charles Community College*
David Paul, *The Ohio State University–Newark*
Arthur Paulson, *Southern Connecticut State University*
Lisa Perez, *Austin Community College*
Joseph Peschek, *Hamline University*
Mark P. Petracca, *University of California*
Adeline Pierre, *College of Lake County*
Eric Plutzer, *Pennsylvania State University*
Vincent K. Pollard, *Kapiolani Community College*
Larry Pool, *Mountain View College*
Amy Pritchett, *Cypress College*
John D. Redifer, *Mesa State College*
Richard Reitano, *Dutchess Community College*
Curtis G. Reithel, *University of Wisconsin, La Crosse*
Russell D. Renka, *Southeast Missouri State University*
Richard C. Rich, *Virginia Polytechnic Institute and State University*
Leroy N. Rieselbach, *Indiana University*
Sue Tolleson Rinehart, *Texas Tech University*
Phyllis F. Rippey, *Western Illinois University*
David Robinson, *University of Houston–Downtown*
Pamela Rogers, *University of Wisconsin*
David W. Romero, *University of California*
Francis E. Rourke, *Johns Hopkins University*
David C. Saffell, *Ohio Northern University*
Donald L. Scruggs, *Stephens College*
Jim Seroka, *University of North Florida*
L. Earl Shaw, *Northern Arizona University*
John M. Shebb, *University of Tennessee*
Mark Silverstein, *Boston University*
Morton Sipress, *University of Wisconsin, Eau Claire*
Henry B. Sirgo, *McNeese State University*
David A. Smeltzer, *Portland State University*
Neil Snortland, *University of Arkansas, Little Rock*
George Wade Swicord, *South Florida Community College*
David Tabb, *San Francisco State University*
C. Neal Tate, *University of North Texas*
James Lance Taylor, *University of San Francisco*
Robert Thomas, *University of Houston*
Richard J. Timpone, *State University of New York at Stony Brook*
Eric Ulsaner, *University of Maryland*
José M. Vadi, *California State Polytechnic University, Pomona*

Elliot Vittes, *University of Central Florida*
Charles Walcott, *University of Minnesota*
Benjamin Walter, *Vanderbilt University*
Susan Weissman, *St. Mary's College of California*
Jonathan P. West, *University of Miami*
Nelson Wikstrom, *Virginia Commonwealth University*
Leonard A. Williams, *Manchester College*
Daniel Wirls, *Merrill College*
Eugene R. Wittkopf, *Louisiana State University*
James Woods, *University of Toledo*

Teresa Wright, *California State University–Long Beach*
Jay Zarowitz, *Muskegon Community College*
Michele Zebich-Knos, *Kennesaw State University*

Finally, we thank you, the instructors and students who use this book. May it bring you success.

EDWARD S. GREENBERG
BENJAMIN I. PAGE

PART 1 — INTRODUCTION: MAIN THEMES

In Part 1, we explain the overall plan of the book, describe the main themes you will see in each chapter, and suggest why these topics are important for the study of American government and politics. We introduce the central dramatic thread that ties the book together: the struggle for democracy. We make the point that American political life has always involved a struggle among individuals, groups, classes, and institutions over the meaning, extent, and practice of democracy. Finally, in this part, we suggest that although democracy has made great progress over the course of U.S. history, it remains only imperfectly realized and is threatened by new problems that only vigilant and active citizens can solve.

1

Democracy and American Politics

LEARNING OBJECTIVES

After reading this chapter, you should be able to:

1.1 Explain the meaning of democracy and its use as a standard to evaluate American government and politics

1.2 Outline a systematic framework for thinking about how government and politics work

ROBERT MOSES AND THE STRUGGLE FOR AFRICAN AMERICAN VOTING RIGHTS

The right to vote in elections is fundamental to democracy. But many Americans won the right to vote only after long struggles. It took more than 30 years from the adoption of the Constitution, for instance, for most states to allow people without property to vote. Women gained the right to vote in all U.S. elections only in 1920, and young people ages 18 to 20 did so only beginning in 1971. African Americans in the South were not able to vote in any numbers until after 1965, despite the existence of the Fifteenth Amendment—which says that the vote cannot be denied to American citizens on the basis of race, color, or previous condition of servitude—adopted in 1870.

In Mississippi in the early 1960s, only 5 percent of African Americans were registered to vote, and none held elective office, although they accounted for 43 percent of the population. In Walthall County, Mississippi, not a single black was registered, although roughly 3,000 were eligible to vote.[1] What kept them away from the polls was a combination of exclusionary voting registration rules, economic pressures, and violent intimidation directed against those brave enough to defy the prevailing political and social order. In Ruleville, Mississippi, civil rights

activist Fannie Lou Hamer was forced out of the house she was renting on a large plantation; fired from her job; and arrested, jailed, and beaten by police after she tried to register to vote.[2]

The Student Non-Violent Coordinating Committee (widely known by its initials, SNCC) launched its Voter Education Project in 1961 with the aim of ending black political isolation and powerlessness in the Deep South. Composed primarily of African American college students, SNCC worked to increase black voter registration, to challenge exclusionary rules like the poll tax and the literacy test, and to enter African American candidates in local elections. Its first step was to create "freedom schools" in some of the most segregated counties in Mississippi, Alabama, and Georgia to teach black citizens about their rights under the law. Needless to say, SNCC volunteers tended to attract the malevolent attentions of police, local officials, and vigilantes.

The first of the freedom schools was founded in McComb, Mississippi, by a remarkable young man named Robert Parris Moses. Despite repeated threats to his life and more than a few physical attacks, Moses traveled the back roads of Amite and Walthall counties, meeting with small groups of black

farmers and encouraging them to attend the SNCC freedom school. At the school, he showed them not only how to fill out the registration forms, but also how to read and interpret the constitution of Mississippi for the "literacy test" required to register to vote. Once people in the school gathered the courage to journey to the county seat to try to register, Moses accompanied them to lend support and encouragement.

Moses paid a price. Over a period of a few months in 1963, he was arrested several times for purported traffic violations; attacked on the main street of Liberty, Mississippi, by the county sheriff's cousin and beaten with the butt end of a knife; assaulted by a mob behind the McComb County courthouse; hit by police while standing in line at the voting registrar's office with one of his students, and dragged to the stationhouse; and jailed for not paying fines connected with his participation in civil rights demonstrations.

Despite the efforts of Moses and other SNCC volunteers, African American registration barely increased in Mississippi in the early 1960s. Black Americans there and in other states of the deep South would have to await the passage of the 1965 Voting Rights Act, which provided powerful federal government protections for all American citizens wishing to exercise their right to vote.[3] The Voter Education Project, nevertheless, is considered to have been a key building block of a powerful civil rights movement (see Chapters 8 and 16) that would eventually force federal action in the 1960s to support the citizenship rights of African Americans in the South. Robert Moses and many other African Americans were willing to risk all they had, including their lives, to gain full and equal citizenship in the United States. They surely would have been gratified and perhaps surprised by the election of African American Barack Obama in 2008 as the nation's 44th president.

The struggle for democracy is happening in many countries today, where people fight against all odds for the right to govern themselves and control their own destinies. Americans are participants in this drama, not only because American political ideas and institutions have often provided inspiration for democratic movements in other countries but also because the struggle for democracy continues in our own society. Although honored and celebrated, democracy remains an unfinished project in the United States. The continuing struggle to expand and perfect democracy is a major feature of American history and a defining characteristic of our politics today. It is a central theme of this book.

Democracy

1.1 Explain the meaning of democracy and its use as a standard to evaluate American government and politics

Why should there not be a patient confidence in the ultimate justice of the people? Is there any better, or equal, hope in the world?

—Abraham Lincoln, First Inaugural Address

With the exception of anarchists who believe that people can live in harmony without any form of authority, it is generally recognized that when people live together in groups and communities, an entity of some sort is needed to provide law and order; to protect against external aggressors; and to provide essential public goods such as roads, waste disposal, education, and clean water. If government is both necessary and inevitable, certain questions become unavoidable: Who is to govern? How are those who govern to be encouraged to serve the best interests of society? How can governments be induced to make policies and laws that citizens consider legitimate and worth obeying? In short, what is the best form of government? For most Americans the answer is clear: democracy.

Democracy's central idea is that ordinary people want to rule themselves and are capable of doing so. This idea has proved enormously popular, not only with Americans, but with people all over the world.[4] To be sure, some people would give top priority to other things besides self-government as a requirement for the good society, including such things as safety and security or the need to have religious law and values determine what government does. Nevertheless, the appealing notion that ordinary people can and should rule themselves has spread to all corners of the globe, and the number of people living in democratic societies has increased significantly over the past two decades.[5]

It is no wonder that a form of government based on the notion that people are capable of ruling themselves enjoys widespread popularity, especially compared with government by the few (e.g., the Communist Party rule in China and Cuba) or by a single person (e.g., the dictatorship of Kim Jung-il in North Korea). But there are many other reasons people have found it appealing. Some political thinkers think that democracy is the form of government that best protects human rights because it is the only one based on a recognition of the intrinsic worth and equality of human beings. Others believe that democracy is the form of government most likely to produce rational policies because it can count on the pooled knowledge and expertise of a society's entire population: a political version, if you will, of the wisdom of the crowds.[6] Still others claim that democracies are more stable and long-lasting because their leaders, elected by and answerable to voters, enjoy a strong sense of legitimacy among citizens. Many others suggest that democracy is the form of government most conducive to economic growth and material well-being, a claim that is strongly supported by research findings. (Though the historic economic expansionism in China may change thinking on this.) Others, finally, believe that democracy is the form of government under which human beings, because they are free, are best able to develop their natural capacities and talents.[7] There are many compelling reasons, then, why democracy has been preferred by so many people.

Americans have supported the idea of self-government and have helped make the nation more democratic over the course of our history.[8] Nevertheless, democracy remains an aspiration rather than a finished product. Our goal in this book is to help you think carefully about the quality and progress of democracy in the United States. We want to help you reach your own independent judgments about the degree to which politics and government in the United States make our country more or less democratic. We want to help you draw your own conclusions about which political practices and institutions in the

? Can societies function without some kind of government? What do you imagine would happen if the United States government were rendered powerless?

United States encourage and sustain popular self-rule and which ones discourage and undermine it. To do this, we must be clear about the meaning of democracy.

Democratic Origins

Many of our ideas about democracy originated with the ancient Greeks. The Greek roots of the word *democracy* are *demos,* meaning "the people," and *kratein,* meaning "to rule." Philosophers and rulers were not friendly to the idea that the *many* can and should rule themselves. Most believed that governing was a difficult art, requiring the greatest sophistication, intelligence, character, and training—certainly not the province of ordinary people. Aristotle expressed this view in his classic work *Politics,* where he observed that democracy "is a government in the hands of men of low birth, no property, and vulgar employments."

Instead, they preferred rule by a select *few* (such as an aristocracy, in which a hereditary nobility rules, or a clerical establishment as in Iran today, where religious leaders rule) or by an enlightened *one,* somewhat akin to the philosopher king described by Plato in his *Republic,* or a hereditary monarch as in England in the time of Elizabeth I. **Democracy,** then, is "rule by the people" or, to put it as the Greeks did, self-government by the many, as opposed to **oligarchy** (rule by the *few*) or **monarchy** (rule by the *one*). The idea that ordinary people might rule themselves represents an important departure from most historical beliefs.[9] In practice, throughout human history, most governments have been quite undemocratic.

Inherent in the idea of self-rule by ordinary people is an understanding that government must serve *all* its people and that ultimately none but the people themselves can be relied on to know, and hence to act in accordance with, their own values and interests.[10]

Interestingly, democracy in the sense described here is more a set of utopian ideas than a description of real societies. Athens of the fifth-century BCE is usually cited as the purest form of democracy that ever existed. There, all public policies were decided upon in periodic assemblies of Athenian citizens, though women, slaves, and immigrants were excluded from participation.[11] Nevertheless, the existence of a society in Athens where "a substantial number of free, adult males were entitled as citizens to participate freely in government"[12] proved to be a powerful example of what was possible for those who believed that rule by the people was the best form of government. A handful of other cases of popular rule kept the democratic idea alive across the centuries. Beginning in the fifth century BCE, for example, India enjoyed long periods marked by spirited and broadly inclusive public debate and discourse on public issues. In the Roman Republic, male citizens elected the consuls, the chief magistrates of the powerful city-state. Also, during the Middle Ages in Europe, some cities were governed directly by the people (at least by men who owned property) rather than by nobles, church, or crown. During the Renaissance, periods of popular control of government (again, limited to male property holders) occurred in the city-states of Venice, Florence, and Milan.

democracy

A system of government in which the people rule; rule by the many.

oligarchy

Rule by the few, where a minority group holds power over a majority, as in an aristocracy or a clerical establishment.

monarchy

Rule by the one, where power rests in the hands of a king or queen.

Direct Versus Representative Democracy

To the ancient Greeks, democracy meant rule by the common people exercised *directly* in open assemblies. They believed that democracy implied face-to-face deliberation and decision making about the public business. **Direct democracy** requires, however, that all citizens be able to meet together regularly to debate and decide the issues of the day. Such a thing was possible in fifth-century BCE Athens, which was small enough to allow all male citizens to gather in one place. In Athens, moreover, male citizens had time to meet and to deliberate because women provided household labor and slaves accounted for most production.

> What logistical and practical issues make direct democracy difficult, if not impossible, in a large society? Given the opportunity, do you think you would be able—or willing—to participate directly in governing your town, state, or nation?

Because direct, participatory democracy is possible only in small communities where citizens with abundant leisure time can meet on a face-to-face basis, it is an unworkable arrangement for a large and widely dispersed society such as the United States.[13] Democracy in large societies must take the representative form, since millions of citizens cannot meet in open assembly. By **representative democracy** we mean a system in which the people select others, called *representatives,* to act on their behalf.

Although representative (or indirect) democracy seems to be the only form of democracy possible in large-scale societies, some political commentators argue that the participatory aspects of direct democracy are

direct democracy

A form of political decision making in which the public business is decided by all citizens meeting in small assemblies.

representative democracy

Indirect democracy, in which the people rule through elected representatives.

RULE BY THE FEW President Mahmoud Ahmadinejab is the president of Iran—though his election in 2009 is widely regarded as fraudulent—and quite visible in defending the country's nuclear program and attacking the West, but real power in the country is exercised by an unelected clergy and the Revolutionary Guard. Here, the president receives a certificate of appreciation from Supreme Leader Ayatollah Ali Khamenei. Is a system that is responsive to the many in theory but run in reality by the few likely to retain its legitimacy over the long term? How might the people of Iran move their system to one where the majority rules rather than the few?

worth preserving as an ideal and that certain domains of everyday life—workplaces and schools, for instance—could be enriched by more direct democratic practices.[14] It is worth pointing out, moreover, that direct democracy can and does flourish in some local communities today. In many New England towns, for example, citizens make decisions directly at town meetings. At the state level, the initiative process allows voters in many states to bypass the legislature to make policies or amend state constitutions. Some observers believe that the Internet is empowering people to become more directly engaged and influential in the political process and that this process will accelerate in the future.[15] Increasingly, the Internet enables people to more easily gather information, deliberate with other citizens about important issues, organize political meetings and demonstrations, and directly communicate their interests and demands to political leaders at all levels of government.

Benchmarks of Representative Democracy

In large societies such as our own, then, democracy means rule by the people, exercised indirectly through representatives elected by the people. Still, this definition is not sufficiently precise to use as a standard by which to evaluate the American political system. It does not tell us what features indirect representative systems must have to ensure that those who govern do so on behalf of and in the interest of the people. You will see that this involves more than the existence of elections.[16] To help further clarify the definition of democracy, we add three additional benchmarks drawn from both the scholarly literature and popular understandings about democracy. These benchmarks are *popular sovereignty, political equality,* and *political liberty.* A society in which all three flourish, we argue, is a healthy representative democracy. A society in which any of the three is absent or impaired falls short of the representative democratic ideal. Let us see what each of them means.

RULE BY THE MANY   In small towns throughout New England, local policies and budgets are decided upon at regular town meetings, in which the entire town population is invited to participate. What are some advantages to such a system? What might be the drawbacks? What other kinds of forums might there be where direct democracy is possible?

Popular Sovereignty

Popular sovereignty means that people are the ultimate source of government authority and that what the government does is determined by what the people want. If ultimate authority resides not in the hands of the *many* but in the hands of the *few* (as in an aristocratic order), or of the *one* (whether a benevolent sovereign or a ruthless dictator), democracy does not exist. Nor does it exist if government consistently fails to follow the preferences and serve the interests of the people.

How can we recognize popular sovereignty when we see it? The following six conditions are especially important.

Government Policies Reflect the Wishes of the People

The most obvious sign of popular sovereignty is the existence of a close correspondence between what government does and what the people want it to do. It is hard to imagine a situation in which the people rule but government officials continuously make policies contrary to the expressed wishes of the majority of the people; sovereign people would most likely react by removing such officials from power.

But does the democratic ideal require that government officials always do exactly what the people want, right away, responding to every whim and passing fancy of the public? This question has troubled many democratic theorists, and most have answered that democracy is best served when representatives and other public officials respond to the people after the people have had the opportunity to deliberate among themselves about the issues.[17] We might, then, want to speak of democracy as a system in which government policies conform to what the people want over some period of time.

Government Leaders Are Selected in Competitive Elections

The existence of a close match between what the people want and what government does, however, does not necessarily prove that the people are sovereign. In a dictatorship, for example, the will of the people can be consciously shaped to correspond to the wishes of the leadership. For the direction of influence to flow from the people to the leadership, some mechanism must exist for forcing leaders to be responsive to the people's wishes and to be responsible to them for their actions. The best mechanism ever invented to achieve these goals is the contested election in which both existing and aspiring government leaders must periodically face the people for judgment. (See the "Mapping American Politics" feature on competition in U.S. presidential elections.)

Elections Are Free and Fair

If elections are to be useful as a way to keep government leaders responsive and responsible, they must be conducted in a fashion that is free and fair. By free, we mean that there is no coercion of voters or election officials and that virtually all citizens are able to run for office and vote in elections. By fair, we mean, among other things, that election rules do not favor some over others and that ballots are accurately counted.

People Participate in the Political Process

Although government leaders may be elected in a balloting process that is free and fair, such a process is useful in conveying the will of the people and keeping leaders responsive and responsible only if the people participate. If elections and other forms of political participation only attract a minority of the eligible population, they cannot serve as a way to understand what the broad public wants or as an instrument forcing leaders to pay attention to it. Widespread participation in politics—including voting in elections, contacting public officials, working with others to bring matters to public attention, joining associations that work to shape government actions, and more—is necessary to ensure not only that responsive representatives will be chosen, but that they will also have continuous incentives to pay attention to the people. Because widespread participation is so central to popular sovereignty, we can say that the less political participation there is in a society, the weaker the democracy.

High-Quality Information Is Available If people are to form authentic and rational attitudes about public policies and political leaders, they must have access to accurate political information, insightful interpretations, and vigorous debate. These are the responsibility of government officials, opposition parties, opinion leaders, and the news media. If false or biased information is provided, if policies are not challenged and debated, or if misleading interpretations of the political world (or none at all) are offered, the people cannot form opinions in accordance with their values and interests, and popular sovereignty cannot be said to exist.

WAITING TO VOTE IN SUDAN Although it remains unclear whether the 2010 elections in Sudan were free and fair, voters nevertheless lined up around the country to cast their ballots. These voters are waiting their turn in the town of Yambio. What other conditions need to be in place, in addition to ballot casting, to ensure that political leaders act as representatives of the people?

The Majority Rules How can the opinions and preferences of many individual citizens be combined into a single binding decision? Because unanimity is unlikely—so the insistence that new policies should require unanimous agreement for them to be adopted would simply enshrine the status quo—reaching a decision requires a decision rule of some sort. If the actions of government are to respond to all citizens, each citizen being counted equally, the only decision rule that makes sense is **majority rule,** which means that the government adopts the policy that the *most* people want.[18] The only alternative to majority rule is minority rule, which would unacceptably elevate the preferences and the interests of the *few* over the *many.*

Political Equality The second benchmark of representative democracy is **political equality,** the idea that each person, being of equal intrinsic value as other human beings, carries the same weight in voting and other political decision making.[19] Imagine, if you will, a society in which one person could cast 100 votes in an election, another person 50 votes, and still another 25 votes, while many unlucky folks had only 1 vote each—or none at all. Democracy is a way of making decisions in which each person has one, and only one, voice.

Most people know this intuitively. Our sense of what is proper is offended, for instance, when some class of people is denied the right to vote in a society that boasts the outer trappings of democracy. The denial of citizenship rights to African Americans in the South before the passage of the 1965 Voting Rights Act is such an example. We count it as a victory for democracy when previously excluded groups win the right to vote.

Political equality also involves what the Fourteenth Amendment to the Constitution calls "equal protection," meaning that everyone in a democracy is treated the same by government. Government programs, for example, cannot favor one group over another or deny benefits or protections to identifiable groups in the population, such as racial and religious minorities. Nor should people be treated better or worse than others by law enforcement agencies and the courts. Taken together, political equality and equal treatment are sometimes called **civil rights,** a subject we will address in more detail in Chapter 17.

But does political equality require that people be equal in ways that go beyond voice in decision making and treatment by government? In particular, does democracy require that inequalities in the distribution of income and wealth not be too extreme? While many do not think this to be the case, thinkers as diverse as Aristotle, Rousseau, and Jefferson

majority rule
The form of political decision making in which policies are decided on the basis of what a majority of the people want.

political equality
The principle that says that each person carries equal weight in the conduct of the public business.

civil rights
Guarantees by government of equal citizenship to all social groups.

MAPPING AMERICAN POLITICS

All the States Are Purple

Introduction Voting in elections in which people can choose among competing candidates and political parties is one of the hallmarks of democratic political systems. As we suggest in this chapter, democracy requires other things, such as political equality, civil liberties, and a free press, but competitive elections are essential. For the most part, at all levels of government in the United States, the most important public offices are filled by election, including that of the president. Both the map and the cartogram show the results from the 2008 presidential election won by Democrat Barack Obama over Republican John McCain, focusing on turnout and competition between the candidates.

Different Maps; Different Stories: The standard geographic map of the United States on this page shows states won by John McCain (in red) and Barack Obama (in blue). Election maps like this are widely distributed in newspapers, magazines, and television. However, they are misleading in a very fundamental way because they emphasize geographical space over people and overplay the partisan divisions in the country. They take no account of the relative populations of the states and exaggerate the political importance of large, under-populated spaces. This map suggests a

country that is mostly red, or Republican, yet we know that the Democrat candidate won a relatively decisive victory. So, is there a better way to visualize who voted and for whom in 2008?

The map on the next page is called a cartogram. We will be using cartograms throughout this book to learn more about American politics. A cartogram is a way to visually present information that is organized on a geographical basis, with

each unit (in this case, state) sized in proportion to the data being reported (in this case, number of voters). So rather than thinking of the cartogram as a "map," think of it as a figure displaying some aspect of American politics in a geographical fashion. Sometimes a cartogram shows geographical units in relation to one another in direct proportion to some simple measure, such as population size. Sometimes a cartogram shows

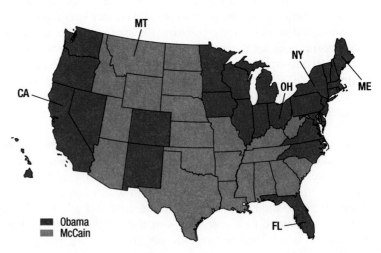

Standard U.S. Map, Blue for Obama States, Red for McCain States

thought so, believing that great inequalities in economic circumstances are almost always translated into political inequality.[20] Political scientist Robert Dahl describes the problem in the following way:

> If citizens are unequal in economic resources, so are they likely to be unequal in political resources; and political equality will be impossible to achieve. In the extreme case, a minority of rich will possess so much greater political resources than other citizens that they will control the state, dominate the majority of citizens, and empty the democratic process of all content.[21]

In later chapters, we will see that income and wealth are distributed in a highly unequal way in the United States and that this inequality is sometimes translated into great inequalities among people and groups in the political arena. In such circumstances, the norm of political equality is in danger of being violated.

geographical units drawn to reflect some measure on a per-capita basis (such as the distribution of homeland security defense dollars to states divided by population size). Sometimes a cartogram shows geographical units expanded or diminished from their "normal" geographical scale using mathematical transformations that enable the viewer to easily compare units (such as states and countries) while preserving the rough outlines of the normal shapes of these units. In each "Mapping American Politics" feature in this book, we will specify clearly what sort of cartogram we are using.

The cartogram here uses a simple and direct proportion; each state is sized according to the number of votes cast in the 2008 presidential election. By adjusting the size of the states to reflect the number of citizens who voted for president in 2008, this cartogram shows clearly that California, Florida, New York, Texas, and Ohio have lots of voters and Idaho, Wyoming, Montana, Nebraska, and Maine have relatively few.

Color is often used to convey additional information in cartograms, as we do here. The proportions of blue (for Democratic voters) and red (for Republican voters) in each state reflect the proportions of Democratic and Republican voters in that state. The result is a map with various shades of purple, because all states contain a mix of Democratic and Republican voters. The closer a state comes to the blue end of the spectrum, the more Democratic voters it has relative to Republicans; the closer a state comes to the red end of the spectrum, the more Republicans it has relative to Democrats. There are no pure red or blue states, no pure Republican or Democratic states. Even states that are deep purple (more blue), such as California, have many Republican voters, while states that are more red, such as Utah and Wyoming, have many Democratic voters.

What Do You Think? How does the cartogram convey more information than the conventional map about competition in the 2008 election and where the most voters are located? Do you see anything interesting in either the map or the cartogram that we have not mentioned here? How about your own state? What, if anything, about its portrayal in the cartogram surprises you?

Source: http://clerk.house.gov/members/electionInfo/2008/Table.htm. Details about methods for producing such cartograms can be found in the pioneering publication by Michael T. Gastner and Mark E. J. Newman, "Diffusion-Based Method for Producing Density-Equalizing Maps," *Proceedings of the National Academy of Sciences* 101 (May 18, 2004), pp. 7499–7504.

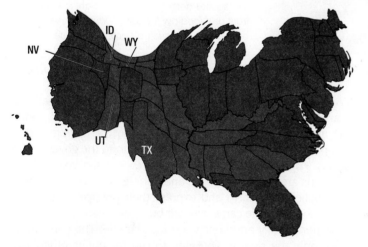

Size of States Adjusted to Reflect Voter Turnout; Each State is a Mix of Red and Blue Reflecting the Percentage of Obama and McCain Voters.

Standard US Map

Political Liberty

A third benchmark of democracy in indirect, representative systems is **political liberty.** Political liberty refers to basic freedoms essential to the formation and expression of majority opinion and its translation into public policies. These essential liberties include the freedoms of speech, of conscience and religion, of the press, and of assembly and association, embodied in the First Amendment to the U.S. Constitution. Philosopher John Locke thought that individual rights and liberty were so fundamental to the good society that their preservation was the central responsibility of any legitimate government and that their protection is the very reason people agreed to enter into a **social contract** to form government in the first place.

> **?** In what ways do you think technology might affect American democracy in the future? Could a society that governs itself through electronic participation meet all three criteria for democracy: equality, sovereignty, and liberty?

WOMEN DEMAND THE RIGHT TO VOTE Although political equality is a cornerstone of American democracy, the nation's understanding of who is entitled to equal status has changed over the years. The right to vote was granted to all men regardless of race in 1870, although stringent registration rules made it very difficult for nonwhites to exercise that right. It wasn't until 1920 that the Nineteenth Amendment extended the right to vote to women; in 1971, a constitutional amendment lowered the voting age from 21 to 18. Here, suffragettes demonstrate for the right to vote in front of Woodrow Wilson's White House. Why has voting been such a contentious issue in America's history?

Without these First Amendment freedoms, as well as those freedoms involving protections against arbitrary arrest and imprisonment, the other fundamental principles of democracy could not exist. Popular sovereignty cannot be guaranteed if people are prevented from participating in politics or if opposition to the government is crushed by the authorities. Popular sovereignty cannot prevail if the voice of the people is silenced and if citizens are not free to argue and debate, based on their own ideas, values, and personal beliefs, and form and express their political opinions.[22] Political equality is violated if some people can speak out but others cannot.

For most people today, democracy and liberty are inseparable. The concept of *self-government* implies not only the right to vote and to run for public office, but also the right to speak one's mind; to petition the government; and to join with others in political parties, interest groups, or social movements.

Over the years, a number of political philosophers and practitioners have viewed liberty as *threatened* by democracy rather than as essential to it. We will have more to say about this subject in the next section as we consider several possible objections to democracy. But it is our position that self-government and political liberty are inseparable, in the sense that the former is impossible without the latter.[23] It follows that a majority cannot deprive an individual or a minority group of its political liberty without violating democracy itself.

Objections to Liberal Democracy

What we have been describing—a system of representative government characterized by popular sovereignty, political equality, and liberty—commonly is called **liberal democracy.** Not everyone is convinced that liberal democracy is the best form of government. Following are the main criticisms that have been leveled against liberal democracy as we have defined it.

political liberty

The principle that citizens in a democracy are protected from government interference in the exercise of a range of basic freedoms, such as the freedoms of speech, association, and conscience.

social contract

The idea that government is the result of an agreement among people to form one, and that people have the right to create an entirely new government if the terms of the contract have been violated by the existing one.

liberal democracy

Representative democracy characterized by popular sovereignty, liberty, and political equality.

"Majority Tyranny" Threatens Liberty James Madison and the other Founders of the American republic feared that majority rule was bound to undermine freedom and threaten the rights of the individual. They created a constitutional system (as you will see in Chapter 2) that was designed to protect certain liberties against the unwelcome intrusions of the majority. The fears of the Founders were not without basis. What they called the "popular passions" have sometimes stifled the freedoms of groups and individuals who have dared to be different. In the 1950s, for example, many people in the movie industry, publishing, and education lost their jobs because of the anti-communist hysteria whipped up by Senator Joseph McCarthy and others.[24] For a time after the 9/11 attacks on the United States, Muslims in the United States became targets of popular hostility (see Chapter 15).

> **majority tyranny**
> Suppression of the rights and liberties of a minority by the majority.

Although there have been instances during our history of **majority tyranny,** in which the majority violated the citizenship rights of a minority—the chapter-opening story is a good example—there is no evidence that the *many* consistently threaten liberty more than the *few* or the *one.* To put it another way, the majority does not seem to be a special or unique threat to liberty. Violations of freedom seem as likely to come from powerful individuals and groups or from government officials responding to vocal and narrow interests as from the majority of the people.

Liberty is essential to self-government, and threats to liberty, whatever their origin, must be guarded against by all who value democracy. But we must firmly reject the view that majority rule inevitably or uniquely threatens liberty. Majority rule is unthinkable, in fact, without the existence of basic political liberties.[25]

The People Are Irrational and Incompetent Political scientists have spent decades studying the attitudes and behaviors of citizens in the United States, and some of the findings are not encouraging. For the most part, the evidence shows that individual Americans do not care a great deal about politics and are rather poorly informed, unstable in their views, and not much interested in participating in the political process.[26] These findings have led some observers to assert that citizens are

FEAR CAN UNDERMINE DEMOCRACY Political hysteria has periodically blemished the record of American democracy. Fear of domestic communism, and anarchism, captured in this editorial cartoon, was particularly potent in the twentieth century and led to the suppression of political groups by federal and state authorities acting, in their view, in the name of a majority of Americans. Why was such hysteria able to take hold in the United States? How likely is it that political hysteria will emerge today in the United States given the current economic troubles?

ill-equipped for the responsibility of self-governance and that public opinion (the will of the majority) should not be the ultimate determinant of what government does.

This is a serious charge and bears a great deal of attention, something we shall do in various places in this book. In Chapter 5, for example, we will see that much of the evidence about individual opinions often has been misinterpreted and that the American public is more informed, sophisticated, and stable in its views than it is generally given credit for.

Majoritarian Democracy Threatens Minorities   We have suggested that when rendering a decision in a democracy, the majority must prevail. In most cases, the minority on the losing side of an issue need not worry unduly about its well-being because many of its members are likely to be on the winning side in future decisions about other matters. Thus, people on the losing side of an issue such as welfare reform may be part of the majority and winning side on an issue such as how much to spend on education. What prevents majority tyranny over a minority in most policy decisions in a democracy is that the composition of the majority and the minority is always shifting, depending on the issue.

However, what happens in cases that involve race, ethnicity, religion, or sexual orientation, for example, where minority status is fixed? Does the majority pose a threat to such minorities? Many people worry about that possibility.[27] The worry is that unbridled majority rule leaves no room for the claims of minorities. This worry has some historical foundations, because majorities have trampled on minority rights with alarming frequency. Majorities long held, for instance, that Native Americans and African Americans were inferior to whites and undeserving of full citizenship. Irish, eastern European, Asian, and Latin American immigrants to our shores, among others, have been subjected to periods of intolerance on the part of the majority, as have Catholics and Jews. Gays and lesbians have been discriminated against in housing and jobs and have sometimes been violently victimized.

 How might majority rule override liberty or equality in defining a democracy? Must all be present if a democracy is to flourish?

As Robert Dahl points out, however, there is no evidence to support the belief that the rights of minorities are better protected under alternative forms of political government, whether rule by the *few* (note the persecution of the Christian minority in China by the Communist ruling party) or by the *one* (note the persecution of Shia Muslims under the rule of Saddem Hussein in Iraq), and that given the other benefits of majority rule democracy, it is to be preferred.[28]

In any case, democracy, as we have defined it, requires the protection of crucial minority rights. Recall that majority rule is only one of the defining conditions of popular sovereignty and that popular sovereignty is only one of the three basic benchmarks of democracy, the others being political equality and political liberty. The position of minorities is protected in a fully developed liberal democracy, in our view, by the requirements of equal citizenship (the right to vote, to hold public office, to be protected against violence, and to enjoy the equal protection of the law) and access to the full range of civil liberties (speech, press, conscience, and association). To the extent that a majority violates the citizenship rights and liberties of minorities, society falls short of the democratic ideal.

Democracy as an Evaluative Standard: How Democratic Are We?

After this discussion, it should be easy to see how and why the democratic ideal can be used as a measuring rod with which to evaluate American politics. (See the "By the Numbers" feature for ways of evaluating how the United States is doing compared with other countries.) We have learned that the fundamental attributes of a liberal representative democracy are popular sovereignty, political equality, and political liberty. Each suggests a set of questions that will be raised throughout this book to encourage critical thinking about American political life.

- *Questions about popular sovereignty.* Does government do what citizens want it to do? Do citizens participate in politics? Can citizens be involved when they choose to be, and are political leaders responsive? Do political linkage institutions, such as political parties, elections, interest groups, and social movements, effectively transmit what citizens want to political leaders? What is the quality of the public deliberation on the major public policy issues of the day? Do the news media and political leaders provide accurate and complete information?

- *Questions about political equality.* Do some individuals and groups have persistent and substantial advantages over other individuals and groups in the political process? Or is the political game open to all equally? Do government decisions and policies benefit some individuals and groups more than others?

- *Questions about political liberty.* Are citizens' rights and liberties universally available, protected, and used? Are people free to vote? Can they speak openly and form groups freely to petition their government? Do public authorities, private groups, or the majority threaten liberty or the rights of minorities?

These questions will help us assess where we are and where we are going as a democracy. They will help us go past superficial evaluations based on the existence or nonexistence of this institution or that institution—for example, an elected legislature—and allow us to raise questions about the quality of democracy in the United States and its prospects.[29] Popular sovereignty, political equality, and political liberty are benchmarks to help us in this evaluation. None are attainable, of course, in perfect form. They are, rather, ideals to which our nation can aspire and standards against which we can measure everyday reality.

A Framework for Understanding How American Politics Works

1.2 Outline a systematic framework for thinking about how government and politics work

In addition to helping you answer questions about the quality of democracy in the United States, our goal in this textbook is to help you understand how American government and politics work. To help you do so, we describe in this section a simple way to organize information and to think about how our political system works.

Organizing the Main Factors of Political Life

If we are to understand why things happen in government and politics—for example, the passage of the 1965 Voting Rights Act that Robert Moses and his SNCC colleagues did so much to bring about—we must begin with what biologists call *taxonomy:* placing things in their proper categories. We believe that each and every actor, institution, and process that influences what our politics are like and what our national government does can be placed into four main categories: structure, political linkage, government, and government action.

Is the United States the most democratic country in the world?

While this may surprise you, the answer is no, at least according to the leading measures used by scholars and journalists when addressing this question. We have suggested in this chapter that, while Americans admire democratic political arrangements, and while we have struggled for most of our history to make our society more democratic, democracy remains an unfinished project.

Why It Matters: People here and many people abroad may admire democracy but they also want other things for their societies. It may be the case, for example, that societies where very strong religious beliefs prevail may want government to ensure that religious practices are observed under the direction of religious authorities. Countries like Iran and Saudi Arabia come to mind, although one can observe democratic stirrings even there. Or, there may be societies where economic expansion and rapidly rising living standards are foremost in mind, with democracy taking a back seat. China comes to mind here. Even in the United States, some people might want other values maximized in society, perhaps security from terrorism even at the cost of personal liberties. For the most part, however, Americans say they like living in a democratic society and want it to remain vital. So, it matters for most Americans how we stack up to others and whether we are becoming more or less democratic.

Measuring Democracy: By far the most widely used measure of democracy is the one calculated by a nonprofit organization called Freedom House. It annually calculates a "freedom" score for every country in the world, then uses these scores to assign each of them to one of three categories: free, partly free, or not free.

The raw "freedom" score for determining into which category a country goes is actually made up of two separate sets of measures, one that focuses on political rights, the other on civil liberties. Each is scored by panels of regional experts and scholars. For political rights, they evaluate each country on such things as the degree to which free, fair, and competitive elections exist and whether all adults can vote on a nondiscriminatory basis. With respect to civil liberties, countries are rated on, among many other things, the extent to which the rule of law and an independent judiciary, free speech, press, and association, and protection of property rights exist. (For a full list of items used in the two measures, go to the Freedom House website at **www.freedomhouse.org**). Scores for political rights can go as high as 40; for civil liberties, the top score is 60. The United States scores very high on this measure at 93 (2008), but it is exceeded by Norway and Sweden (100), Canada (99), Australia and Denmark (98), Ireland (97), Germany and Spain (96), and France (94), and surpasses Italy (92) and Japan (88). The United States's total score is big enough, however, to comfortably fit within Freedom House's "free" category. The map shows which countries in the world Freedom House deems free, partly free, and not free.

The Economist magazine has created a measure it claims does a better job evaluating the quality of democracy, going beyond political rights and civil liberties (measured by Freedom House) to include evaluations of the transparency and efficiency of each nation's government, the degree to which people actually participate in a wide range of political activities, and the degree to which a nation's political culture values tolerance and active debate on the issues. Like Freedom House, *The Economist* uses

panels of experts to score each country, but it places them on a 10-point scale with 10 representing perfect democracy and 0 representing no democracy at all.

The United States scored 8.22 in 2008 on *The Economist* democracy scale, high enough to fit comfortably within the magazine's "full democracy" category (of which there were only 30 in the world in 2008), but with a rank of only 18th in the world. The top democratic nation on the scale was Sweden at a near perfect 9.88. Iceland, the Netherlands, Norway, Denmark, Finland, Australia, Canada, Switzerland, Ireland, and New Zealand all scored at 9.0 and above. The United States was ahead of such countries as Japan, Britain, and France in the "full democracy" grouping. The least democratic country in the world on *The Economist* measure was North Korea at 0.86.

Criticisms of the Democracy Measures: Although the Freedom House freedom measure is widely used by journalists and scholars, many criticize it for focusing only on competitive elections and civil liberties. One reason the editors of *The Economist* came up with an alternative measure was that they and others wanted a measure that does justice to the many processes, institutions, and behaviors that allow for popular self-government, including a tolerant and participative culture and an open and transparent government. Both measures might be faulted, of course, for depending on expert panels rather than clearly observable and easily measured political system attributes in their scoring systems.

What to Watch For: An expert panel is only as good as the experts who are on it. So try to pay attention to who is on the panel. Both Freedom House and

---

- *Structure.* Structural factors are enduring features of American life that play key roles in determining what issues become important in politics and government, how political power is distributed in the population, and what attitudes and beliefs guide the behavior of citizens and public officials. This category includes the economy and society, the constitutional rules, the

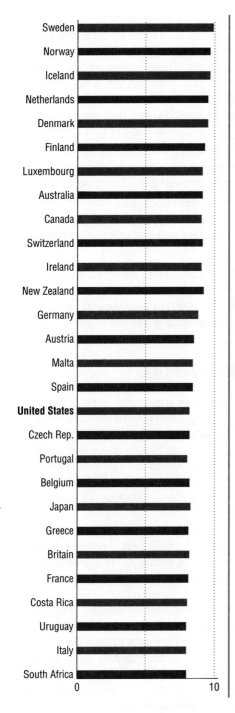

Sweden
Norway
Iceland
Netherlands
Denmark
Finland
Luxembourg
Australia
Canada
Switzerland
Ireland
New Zealand
Germany
Austria
Malta
Spain
United States
Czech Rep.
Portugal
Belgium
Japan
Greece
Britain
France
Costa Rica
Uruguay
Italy
South Africa

0   10

Source: Economist Intelligence Unit.

The Economist post the names and some information about their experts. Check that the experts have either academic

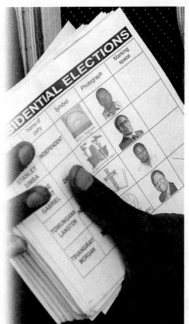

credentials or extensive field experience in the countries and regions they are asked to rate. Equally as important, check to see that the experts are not drawn from a single part of the world, say western Europe or the United States, but come from a large pool of qualified people from a broad range of countries and cultures so that as much bias as possible is taken out of a process that is inherently subjective.

What Do You Think? Does it matter to you how highly the United States is ranked on measures of democracy? Why or why not? What are some other values—perhaps security, economic growth, or the extent of religious freedom—that you find important as the basis for judging the quality of a society? If you care deeply about the quality of democracy in the United States but don't believe that the two democracy scores described here tell the full story, what other attributes of a political system would you try to measure? What would your democracy score look like?

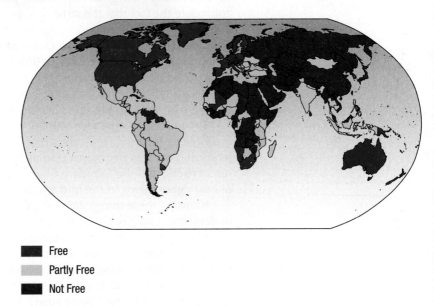

■ Free
▨ Partly Free
■ Not Free

Source: Freedom House. Map of Freedom 2007 from Freedom House Publications. Copyright © 2007. Reprinted by permission.

political culture, and the international system: the most fundamental and enduring factors that influence government and politics. They form the foundation upon which all else is built. They are the most enduring parts of the American system, the slowest to change.[30]

- *Political linkage.* Political linkage factors are all of those political actors, institutions, and processes that transmit the wants and demands of people and groups in our society to government officials and that together help shape what government officials do and what policies they adopt. These include public opinion, political parties, interest groups, the news media, and elections. While not a formal part of government, they directly influence what sorts of people are chosen to be government officials and what these officials do once they are in office.

- *Government.* Government factors include all public officials and institutions that have formal, legal responsibilities for making public policy for the United States. These include Congress, the president and the executive branch, the federal bureaucracy, and the federal courts, including the Supreme Court.

- *Government action.* This is about what government does. This category includes the wide range of actions carried out by government: making laws, issuing rules and regulations, waging war and providing national defense, settling civil disputes, providing order, and more.

This textbook is organized around these four categories. The chapters in Part 2 focus on structural factors. The chapters in Part 3 are about political linkage processes and institutions. The chapters in Part 4 attend to government institutions and leaders. Finally, the chapters in Part 5 examine what government does.

Connecting the Main Factors of Political Life

To understand how government and politics work in the United States, we must appreciate the fact that the structural, political linkage, and governmental categories interact with one another in a particular kind of way to determine what actions government takes (see Figure 1.1). One way to see this is to look at these categories in action, using the passage of the 1965 Voting Rights Act as an example. The main point of the exercise is to show how connecting and considering together the main factors of political life—structure, political linkage, and government—can help explain why government takes certain actions.

To understand passage of the landmark legislation, we might begin with *government,* focusing our attention on Congress and its members; President Lyndon Johnson (who was the most vigorous proponent of the voting rights legislation) and his advisers; and the Supreme Court, which was becoming increasingly supportive of civil rights claims in the mid-1960s.

Knowing these things, however, would not tell us all that we needed to know. To understand why Congress, the president, and the Court behaved as they did in 1965, we would want to pay attention to the pressures brought to bear on them by *political linkage* actors and institutions: public opinion (increasingly supportive of civil rights), the growing electoral power of African Americans in the states outside the South, and most important, the moral power of the civil rights movement inspired by people like Robert Moses and Martin Luther King.

Even knowing these things, however, would not tell us all that we needed to know about why the 1965 Voting Rights Act happened. Our inquiry would have to go deeper to include *structural* factors: economic, cultural, and social change; constitutional rules; and the international position of the United States. For example, economic changes in the nation over the course of many decades triggered a "great migration" of African Americans from the rural South to the urban North. Over the long run, this population shift to states with large blocks of Electoral College votes, critical to the election of presidents, increased the political power of African Americans. Cultural change increased the number of Americans bothered by the second-class citizenship of African Americans, even as combat service in World War II and the Korean War led many

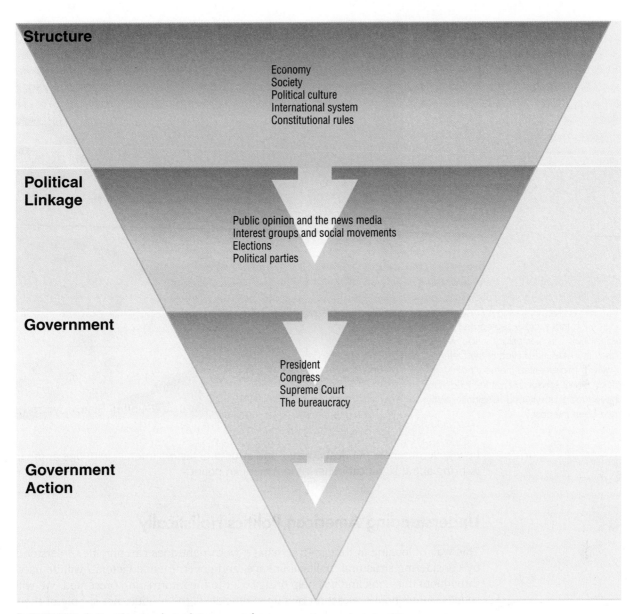

Structure

Economy
Society
Political culture
International system
Constitutional rules

Political Linkage

Public opinion and the news media
Interest groups and social movements
Elections
Political parties

Government

President
Congress
Supreme Court
The bureaucracy

Government Action

FIGURE 1.1 The Analytical Framework

Various actors, institutions, and processes interact to influence what government does in the United States. Structural factors such as the economy, the political culture, the international system, and constitutional rules play a strong role in political events. They may influence the government directly, or, as is more often the case, through political linkages such as elections, parties, and interest groups. In a democratic society, the policies created by the government should reflect these influences.

black Americans to insist on full citizenship rights. Finally, the Cold War struggle of the United States against the Soviet Union played an important role. Many American leaders, recognizing the contradiction between asking for the support of people of color in Third World countries in the struggle against communism while treating African Americans in the United States as second-class citizens, sought an end to the system of official segregation in the South (known as **Jim Crow**).[31]

We see, then, that a full explanation of why the 1965 Voting Rights Act happened (government action) requires that we take into account

Jim Crow

Popular term for the system of legally sanctioned racial segregation that existed in the American South until the middle of the twentieth century.

INTRODUCING THEMSELVES   Here, two young children meet on the first day of integration at a Fort Myers, Florida, elementary school in 1954 after the Supreme Court ruled that racially segregated schools were unconstitutional. The elementary school was on a military base under the jurisdiction of the Defense Department, which implemented the new policy relatively quickly. Local school districts in Florida and elsewhere moved more slowly and reluctantly. Why might this have been the case?

how governmental, political linkage, and structural factors interact with one another to bring about significant change in American politics.

Understanding American Politics Holistically

This way of looking at things—that what government does can only be understood by considering structural, political linkage, and governmental factors—will be used throughout this book and will help bring order to the information presented. We will suggest throughout that action by public officials is the product not simply of their personal desires (although these are important), but also of the influences and pressures brought to bear by other governmental institutions and by individuals, groups, and classes at work in the political linkage sphere. Political linkage institutions and processes, in turn, can often be understood only when we see how they are shaped by the larger structural context, including such things as the national and global economies and the political culture. This way of understanding how American government and politics work is illustrated in the "Using the Framework" feature on the next page. This feature appears in each chapter to explore why particular government actions happen.

You should also keep in mind that, as in all complex systems, feedback also occurs. That is to say, influences sometimes flow in the opposite direction, from government to political linkage actors and institutions to structural factors. For example, federal tax laws influence the distribution of income and wealth in society, government regulations affect the operations of corporations, and decisions by the courts may determine what interest groups and political parties are able to do. We will want to pay attention, then, to these sorts of influences in our effort to understand how the American political system works.

How was Southern resistance to black political participation overcome?

Background: The Voting Rights Act of 1965 transformed the politics of the American South. Under federal government protection, the Act permitted African Americans to vote and run for elected office in states where a combination of violence, economic pressure, and state and local government rules made political participation difficult if not impossible prior to 1965. We can understand how such a momentous transformation happened by examining structural, political linkage, and governmental factors.

Structure

Industrialization and the rise of large manufacturing corporations in the early 20th century spurred the "Great Migration" of African Americans from the South.

Relocation of African Americans to large states outside the Deep South improved their political, social, and economic standing.

World War II generated pressures to integrate the armed forces.

The struggle against the Soviet Union for the "hearts and minds" of Third World peoples made segregation problematic for the United States in world affairs.

Political Linkage

The votes of African Americans proved decisive in several large electoral vote states in the 1960 and 1964 presidential elections.

Dramatic civil rights demonstrations highlighted the denial of the vote to black Americans in the Deep South.

Public opinion and the mass media grew more supportive of demands by African Americans for full citizenship.

Unions and business organizations endorsed voting rights legislation.

Government

The Supreme Court prepared the ground by steadily expanding the reach of the "equal protection" clause of the Constitution's Fourteenth Amendment.

A pro–civil rights majority in Congress was responsive to the voting rights issue.

President Lyndon Johnson pushed hard for federal protection of African American voting rights.

Government Action

The Voting Rights Act of 1965

You need not worry about remembering exactly which actors and influences belong to which of the four categories. That will become obvious because the chapters of the book are organized into sections corresponding to them. Nor do you need to worry about exactly how the people and institutions in the different levels interact with one another. This will become clear as materials are presented and learned and as you become more familiar with the American political process.

SUMMARY

1.1 Explain the meaning of democracy and its use as a standard to evaluate American government and politics.

- Democracy is a system of rule by the people, rooted in three fundamental principles: popular sovereignty (meaning that the people ultimately rule), political equality (meaning that each person has equal say in determining what government does), and political liberty (meaning that the people are protected from government interference in exercising their rights).

- Ensuring that all three aspects of democracy are available and practiced has played an important role in American history, and remains an important theme in our country—as well as many other parts of the world—today.

- The United States is a liberal representative democracy—meaning that the people do not rule directly but through elected representatives, and have broad civil and political rights, but the majority does not always get its way.

- Because democracy holds a very special place in Americans' constellation of values and is particularly relevant to judging political processes, it is the standard used throughout this text to evaluate the quality of our politics and government.

1.2 Outline a systematic framework for thinking about how government and politics work.

- The organizing framework presented in this chapter visualizes the world of American politics as a set of interrelated *actors* and *influences*—institutions, groups, and individuals—that operate in three interconnected realms: the *structural, political linkage,* and *governmental* sectors. This way of looking at American political life as an ordered, interconnected whole will be used throughout the remainder of the book.

TEST YOURSELF

Answer key begins on page T-1.

1.1 Explain the meaning of democracy and its use as a standard to evaluate American government and politics.

1. Which of the following is the essence of democracy?
   a. Economic well-being
   b. Self-government
   c. Promotion of moral values
   d. Protection of human rights
   e. Creation of rational public policies

2. Which of the following is an essential component of a healthy representative democracy?
   a. Direct democracy
   b. Social equality
   c. Government policies that reflect the wishes of the people
   d. The selection of government leaders according to merit and experience
   e. The proliferation of uncontested elections

3. Some people claim that political actors such as politicians, interest groups, the media, and political parties propagate misleading or biased information about politics. If this claim has merit, why might it suggest that American democracy is unhealthy?
   a. Popular sovereignty requires the availability of high-quality information about politics.
   b. Misleading or biased information violates the principles of political liberty.
   c. Political decisions should be based on the principle of unanimity whenever possible.
   d. Political equality requires that the public be presented with all sides of an issue, with each side receiving equal representation.
   e. Misleading or biased information violates the bedrock principles of citizens' social contract with government.

1.2 Outline a systematic framework for thinking about how government and politics work.

4. Which of the following aspects of American politics is most durable?
   a. Legislative factors
   b. Structural factors
   c. Political linkage factors
   d. Government factors
   e. Government actions

5. Select a recent government action, and describe how it was influenced by structural, political linkage, and governmental factors.

PEARSON mypoliscilab EXERCISES

Apply what you learned in this chapter on MyPoliSciLab.

📖 **Read** on **mypoliscilab.com**

eText: Chapter 1

✔️ **Study** and **Review** on **mypoliscilab.com**

Pre-Test
Post-Test
Chapter Exam
Flashcards

👁️ **Watch** on **mypoliscilab.com**

Video: Mexico Border Security
Video: The Bailout Hearings
Video: Vaccines: Mandatory Protection

✴️ **Explore** on **mypoliscilab.com**

Simulation: You Are the Mayor and Need to Get a Town Budget Passed

INTERNET SOURCES

A number of sites on the Internet serve as "gateways" to vast collections of material on American government and politics. In subsequent chapters, we will indicate the location of sites on the Web to begin searches on the specific subject matter of the chapters. Here we concentrate on the general gateways, the starting points for wide-ranging journeys through cyberspace, geared to governmental and political subjects. Also included are gateways to the multitude of political Web logs (blogs). Here are the gateways:

About.com US Politics Blogs
http://uspolitics.about.com/od/blogs/

The Corner; National Review (conservative Web log)
http://corner.nationalreview.com

The Daily Kos (liberal Web log)
http://www.dailykos.com

The Internet Public Library
www.ipl.org/div/subject/browse/law00.00.00/

New York Times, Politics Navigator
www.nytimes.com/library/politics/polpoints.html

Political Index
www.politicalindex.com

Real Clear Politics
www.realclearpolitics.com

SUGGESTIONS FOR FURTHER READING

Bartels, Larry M. *Unequal Democracy: The Political Economy of the New Gilded Age.* New York and Princeton, NJ: The Russell Sage Foundation and Princeton University Press, 2008.
   An examination of rising income inequality and how it undermines several of the basic foundational requirements of political democracy.

Dahl, Robert A. *Democracy and Its Critics.* New Haven, CT: Yale University Press, 1989.
   A sweeping defense of democracy against its critics by one of the most brilliant political theorists of our time.

Dahl, Robert A. *On Democracy.* New Haven, CT: Yale University Press, 1998.
  A brief yet surprisingly thorough examination of classical and contemporary democracy, real and theoretical.

Putnam, Robert D. *Making Democracy Work: Civic Traditions in Modern Italy.* Princeton, NJ: Princeton University Press, 1993.
  A brilliant and controversial argument that the success of democratic government depends on the vitality of a participatory and tolerant civic culture.

Wolfe, Alan. *Does American Democracy Still Work?* New Haven, CT: Yale University Press, 2006.
  A pessimistic reading of trends in American politics, society, and economy that are diminishing the quality of American democracy.

Zakaria, Fareed. *The Future of Freedom: Illiberal Democracy at Home and Abroad.* New York: Norton, 2004.
  The author suggests that majority rule democracy can only happen and be sustained in societies where individual freedom and the rule of law already exist, suggesting that democracy is unlikely to take hold in places such as Russia and Iraq.

The chapters in Part 2 focus on structural influences on American government and politics. Structural influences are enduring features of American life that play key roles in determining what issues become important in politics and government, how political power is distributed in the population, and what attitudes and beliefs guide the behavior of citizens and public officials.

The constitutional rules are a particularly important part of the structural context of American political life. These rules are the subject matter of two of this part's chapters. Chapter 2 tells the story of the Constitution: why a constitutional convention was convened in Philadelphia in 1787, what the Founders intended to accomplish at the convention, and how specific provisions of the document have shaped our political life since the nation's founding. Chapter 3 examines federalism, asking what the framers intended the federal system to be and tracing how it has changed over the years.

The basic characteristics of American society also influence the workings of our political and governmental institutions, as well as the attitudes and behaviors of citizens and public officials. Chapter 4 looks in detail at the American economy, society, and political culture, as well as this country's place in the world, showing how these factors structure much of our political life.

2 | The Constitution

LEARNING OBJECTIVES

After reading this chapter, you should be able to:

2.1 Assess the enduring legacies of the American Revolution Declaration of Independence

2.2 Describe the governmental system established by the Constitution

2.3 Analyze the issues that led to the Constitutional Convention

2.4 Evaluate the framework that emerged from the Constitutional Convention

2.5 Explain the difficulties of ratifying the Constitution

2.6 Identify three processes by which the Constitution changes

DETAINEES, CHECKED AND BALANCED

Senator John McCain (R–AZ)—who had spent five years as a prisoner of war in Vietnam—offered an amendment to the 2005 Defense Department Authorization bill banning cruel, inhuman, and degrading treatment of detainees. President Bush threatened on several occasions to veto the bill if it contained the McCain "anti-torture" amendment, but the Senate and House voted overwhelmingly for it. During floor deliberations, senators and representatives from both parties cited their concerns about prevailing policies, noting the free-fall in America's international reputation after revelations about treatment of detainees at U.S. prisons at Guantanamo Bay (Cuba) and Abu Ghraib (Iraq), their sense that many of our detainee policies were at odds with basic American values, and that several were unconstitutional. Seeing the handwriting on the wall, the president reached an agreement with Senator McCain on some minor changes in language.[1] On January 30, Bush signed the bill.

End of the matter? According to most textbook renderings of "how a bill becomes a law" (see Chapter 11), a bill becomes law once it is passed by both houses of Congress and signed by the president.[2] All citizens and government officials, it is generally understood, are then obligated to abide by the law. Of course, in real life, in a constitutional system of separation of powers, the president and executive branch officials sometimes carry out the provisions of a law with less enthusiasm than Congress might have expected. President Bush went much further, in fact, essentially nullifying his bill-signing by issuing a signing statement afterward stating that "the executive branch shall construe [the law] in a manner consistent with the constitutional authority of the President...as Commander-in-Chief... [this] will assist in achieving the shared objective of the Congress and the President...of protecting the American people from further terrorist attacks."[3] The president seemed to be saying that he would not feel obliged to follow the provisions of the new law when he and he alone, acting in his constitutional capacity as commander-in-chief, deemed it necessary for the protection of the American people. As a senior administrative official put it to a *Boston Globe* reporter, "Of course the

president has the obligation to follow this law, [but] he also has the obligation to defend and protect the country … "[4]

President George W. Bush was not the first president to issue signing statements setting out his thinking on the meaning of the law. Presidents Andrew Jackson, Ulysses S. Grant, Teddy Roosevelt, Franklin Roosevelt, and Harry Truman, among others, issued signing statements during their terms, but usually sparingly. George W. Bush issued signing statements on sections of more than 1,200 bills during his eight years in office—far more than all presidents had issued collectively during the entire course of American history. A fair proportion of them fell into the category of "will not" or "cannot" carry out the law because of intrusions on the president's constitutional prerogatives and powers as commander-in-chief or as head of the executive branch.

During the 2008 election campaign, Barack Obama promised to end this practice if elected. On March 9, 2009, he issued an executive order that all executive branch officials must consult with the Attorney General before following any of the signing statements issued by President Bush, suggesting

that most of them would no longer be operative. Interestingly, however, President Obama also said that signing statements were legitimate if used properly and that he reserved the right to issue them when he deemed it to be appropriate, though he promised he would act with "caution and restraint."[5] And yet, in his first six months in office, he issued dozens of signing statements instructing executive officials to ignore portions of new laws he considered to be unconstitutional or damaging to presidential prerogatives. One even prompted a letter of protest from members of his own party in the House.[6] Apparently, President Obama was unwilling to reject entirely an important tool of presidential power.

In the Constitution, the framers designed a framework for a government of separated powers and checks and balances. By that we mean that the framers divided executive, legislative, and judicial powers and placed them into separate branches of the national government. While the framers situated a set of unique powers within each, they also gave each branch an important role in the affairs of the other branches in a bid at preventing any one of them from becoming too powerful. Giving legislative power to Congress but giving the president a central role in the legislative process, including the president's role in signing bills into law and having the ability to veto congressional enactments, is an example of this constitutional design. As you might suspect, a system of separation of powers and checks and balances is rife with potential conflict between the branches. It has been so since the beginning of the Republic. It is exactly the sort of thing the framers had in mind. This chapter is about the constitutional design of the American government, why the framers fashioned the sort of constitution they did, and how the Constitution shapes political life and government actions in the United States.

THINKING CRITICALLY About This Chapter

This chapter is about the founding of the United States (see Figure 2.1) and the formulation of the constitutional rules that structure American politics to this day.

Using the FRAMEWORK

You will see in this chapter how structural factors such as the American political culture, economic developments, and the composition of the Constitutional Convention shaped the substance of our Constitution. You will also see how the Constitution is itself an important structural factor that helps us understand how American government and politics work today.

Using the DEMOCRACY STANDARD

Using the conception of democracy you learned about in Chapter 1, you will be able to see how and why the framers were uneasy about democracy and created a republican form of government that, although based on popular consent, placed a number of roadblocks in the path of popular rule.

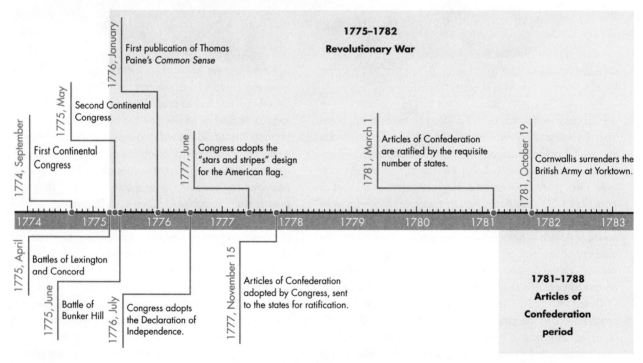

I FIGURE 2.1 Timeline of the Founding of the United States, 1774–1791

The American Revolution and the Declaration of Independence

2.1 Assess the enduring legacies of the American Revolution and the Declaration of Independence

Initially, the American Revolution (1775–1783) was waged more to preserve an existing way of life than to create something new. By and large, American colonists in the 1760s and 1770s were proud to be affiliated with Great Britain and satisfied with the general prosperity that came with participation in the British commercial empire.[7] When the revolution broke out, the colonists at first wanted only to preserve their traditional rights as British subjects. These traditional rights of life, liberty, and property seemed to be threatened by British policies on trade and taxation. Rather than allowing the American colonists to trade freely with whomever they pleased and to produce whatever goods they wanted, for instance, England was restricting the colonists' freedom to do either in order to protect its own manufacturers. To pay for the military protection of the colonies against raids by Native Americans and their French allies, England imposed taxes on a number of items, including sugar, tea, and stamps (required for legal documents, pamphlets, and newspapers). The imposition of these taxes without the consent of the colonists seemed an act of tyranny to many English subjects in America.

Although the initial aims of the Revolution were quite modest, the American Revolution, like most revolutions, did not stay on the track planned by its leaders. Although it was sparked by a concern for liberty—understood as the preservation of traditional rights against the intrusions of a distant government—it also stimulated the development of sentiments for popular sovereignty and political equality. As these sentiments grew, so did the likelihood that the American colonies would split from their British parent and form a system of government more to the liking of the colonists.

When the Second Continental Congress began its session on May 10, 1775—the First had met only briefly in 1774 to formulate a list of grievances to submit to the British Parliament—the delegates did not have independence in mind, even

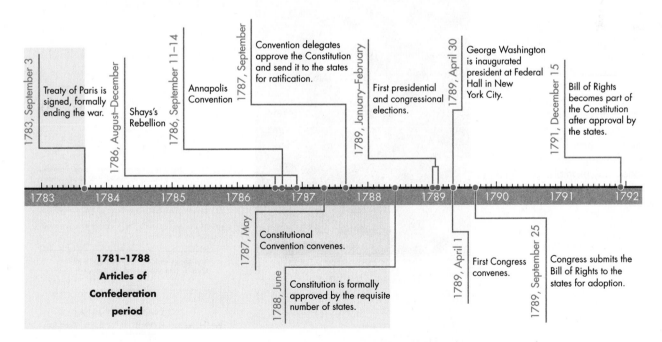

though armed conflict with Britain had already begun with the battles of Lexington and Concord. Pushed by the logic of armed conflict, an unyielding British government, and Thomas Paine's incendiary call for American independence in his wildly popular pamphlet *Common Sense,* however, the delegates concluded by the spring of 1776 that separation and independence were inescapable.[8] In early June, the Continental Congress appointed a special committee, composed of Thomas Jefferson, John Adams, and Benjamin Franklin, to draft a declaration of independence. The document, mostly Jefferson's handiwork, was adopted unanimously by the Second Continental Congress on July 4, 1776.

Key Ideas in the Declaration of Independence

The ideas in the Declaration of Independence are so familiar that we may easily miss their revolutionary importance. In the late eighteenth century, most societies in the world were ruled by kings with authority purportedly derived from God, subject to little or no control by their subjects. Closely following John Locke's ideas in *The Second Treatise on Government,* Jefferson's argument that legitimate government can be established only by the people, is created to protect inalienable rights, and can govern only with their consent, seemed outrageous at the time. However, these ideas sparked a responsive chord in people everywhere when they were first presented, and they remain extremely popular all over the world today. The argument as presented in the Declaration of Independence goes as follows:

- Human beings possess rights that cannot be legitimately given away or taken from them. *"We hold these truths to be self-evident, that all men are created equal, that they are endowed by their Creator with certain unalienable Rights, that among these are Life, Liberty, and the Pursuit of Happiness."*

CLARION CALL FOR INDEPENDENCE   American leaders were reluctant at first to declare independence from Great Britain. One of the things that helped change their minds was Thomas Paine's wildly popular—it is said that a higher proportion of Americans read it than any other political tract in U.S. history—and incendiary pamphlet *Common Sense,* which mercilessly mocked the institution of monarchy and helped undermine the legitimacy of British rule. What are some modern-day examples of Paine's pamphlet? Are influential bloggers good examples?

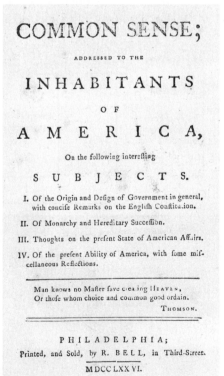

- People create government to protect these rights. *"That to secure these rights, Governments are instituted among Men, deriving their just powers from the consent of the governed."*

- If government fails to protect people's rights or itself becomes a threat to them, people can withdraw their consent from that government and form a new one, that is, void the existing **social contract** and agree to a new one. *"That whenever any Form of Government becomes destructive of these ends, it is the Right of the People to alter or to abolish it, and to institute new Government, laying its foundation on such principles, and organizing its powers in such form, as to them shall seem most likely to effect their Safety and Happiness."*

> **social contract**
> A philosophical device, used by Enlightenment thinkers, such as Locke, Rousseau, and Harrington, to suggest that governments are only legitimate if they are created by a voluntary compact among the people.
>
> **confederation**
> A loose association of states or territorial units without any or much power in a central authority.
>
> **constitution**
> The basic framework of law that prescribes how government is to be organized, how decisions are to be made, and what powers and responsibilities government shall have.

Important Omissions in the Declaration

The Declaration of Independence carefully avoided several controversial subjects, including what to do about slavery. Jefferson's initial draft denounced the Crown for violating human rights by "captivating and carrying Africans into slavery," but this was considered too controversial and was dropped from subsequent versions. The contradiction between the institution of slavery and the Declaration's sweeping claims for self-government, "unalienable" individual rights, and equality ("all men are created equal") was obvious to many observers at the time and is glaringly apparent to us today. The Declaration was also silent about the political status of women and the inalienable rights of Native Americans (referred to in the Declaration as "merciless Indian savages") and African Americans, even those who were not slaves. Indeed, it is safe to assume that neither Jefferson, the main author of the Declaration, nor the other signers of the document had women, Native Americans, free blacks, or slaves in mind when they were fomenting revolution and calling for a different kind of political society. Interestingly, free blacks and women would go on to play important roles in waging the Revolutionary War against Britain.[9]

The Articles of Confederation: The First Constitution

2.2 Describe the governmental system established by our first constitution

The leaders of the American Revolution almost certainly did not envision the creation of a single, unified nation. At most, they had in mind a loose **confederation** among the states. This should not be surprising. Most Americans in the late eighteenth century believed that a government based on popular consent and committed to the protection of individual rights was possible only in small, homogeneous republics, where government was close to the people and where fundamental conflicts of interest among the people did not exist. Given the great geographic expanse of the colonies, as well as their varied ways of life and economic interests, the formation of a single unified republic seemed unworkable.

Provisions of the Articles

Our first written **constitution**—a document specifying the basic organization, powers, and limits of government—passed by the Second Continental Congress in the

Articles of Confederation
The first constitution of the United States, adopted during the last stages of the Revolutionary War, created a system of government with most power lodged in the states and little in the central government.

midst of the Revolutionary War in 1777 (although it was not ratified by the requisite number of states until 1781), created a nation that was hardly a nation at all. The **Articles of Confederation** created in law what had existed in practice from the time of the Declaration of Independence: a loose confederation of independent states with little power in the central government, much like the United Nations today. Under the Articles, most important decisions were made in state legislatures.

The Articles provided for a central government of sorts, but it had few responsibilities and virtually no power. It could make war or peace, but it had no power to levy taxes (even customs duties) to pursue either goal. It could not regulate commerce among the states, nor could it deny the states the right to collect customs duties. It had no independent chief executive to ensure that the laws passed by Congress would be enforced, nor had it a national court system to settle disputes between the states. There were no means to provide a sound national money system. The rule requiring that all national laws be approved by 9 of the 13 states, with each state having one vote in Congress, made lawmaking almost impossible. And, defects in the new constitution were difficult to remedy because amending the Articles required the unanimous approval of the states.

Shortcomings of the Articles

The Articles of Confederation did what most of its authors intended: to preserve the power, independence, and sovereignty of the states and ensure that the central government would not encroach on the liberty of the people. Unfortunately, there were also many problems that the confederation was ill-equipped to handle.

Most important, the new central government could not finance its activities. The government was forced to rely on each state's willingness to pay its annual tax assessment. Few states were eager to cooperate. As a result, the bonds and notes of the confederate government became almost worthless, and the government's attempts to borrow were stymied.

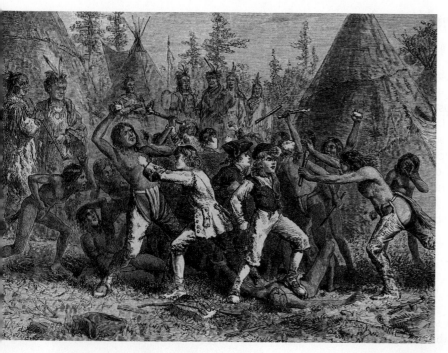

CLASHES ON THE FRONTIER As settlers moved west, they inevitably came into conflict with Native Americans already living there. Many of the settlers were angry and distressed when the national government under the Articles of Confederation proved unable to protect them against the people being displaced. This painting shows a battle waged between settlers and Native Americans on the Kentucky frontier in 1785. What weakness of the Articles led to such problems?

The central government was also unable to defend American interests in foreign affairs. Without a chief executive or a standing army, and with the states holding a veto power over actions of the central government, the confederation lacked the capacity to reach binding agreements with other nations or to deal with a wide range of foreign policy problems. These included the continuing presence of British troops in western lands ceded to the new nation by Britain at the end of the Revolutionary War, violent clashes with Native Americans on the western frontier, and piracy on the high seas.

The government was also unable to prevent the outbreak of commercial warfare between the states. As virtually independent nations with the power to levy customs duties, many states became intense commercial rivals of their neighbors and sought to gain every possible advantage against the products of other states. New York and New Jersey, for instance, imposed high tariffs on goods that crossed their borders from other states. This situation was an obstacle to the expansion of commercial activities and economic growth.

Factors Leading to the Constitutional Convention

2.3 Analyze the issues that led to the Constitutional Convention

Historians now generally agree that the failings of the Articles of Confederation led most of the leading citizens of the confederation to believe that a new constitution was desperately needed for the fledgling nation. What is left out of many accounts of the convening of the Constitutional Convention in Philadelphia, however, is the story of the growing concern among many of the most influential men in the confederation that the passions for democracy and equality among the common people set loose by the American Revolution were getting out of hand. During the American Revolution, appeals to the people for the defense of freedom and for the spread of the blessings of liberty were often translated by the people to mean their right to better access to the means of government and to the means of livelihood.[10] The common people were convinced that success would bring substantial improvements in their lives.[11]

The Eighteenth-Century Republican Beliefs of the Founders

This fever for popular participation and greater equality is not what most of the leaders of the American Revolution had in mind.[12] The Founders were believers in a theory of government known as **republicanism** (please note that we are not referring here to the Republican Party or its members and supporters).[13] Like all republicans of the eighteenth century, the framers were seeking a form of government that would not only be based on the consent of the governed but would prevent **tyranny**, whether tyranny came from the misrule of a single person (a king or military dictator, let us say), a small group of elites (an aristocracy, a clerical theocracy, or moneyed merchant class), or even the majority of the population. The solution to the problem of tyranny for eighteenth-century republican thinkers was threefold: to elect government leaders, limit the power of government, and place roadblocks in the path of the majority. The election of representatives to lead the government, in their view, would keep potentially tyrannical kings and aristocratic factions from power while ensuring popular consent. Limiting the power of government, both by stating what government could and could not do in a written

republicanism

A political doctrine advocating limited government based on popular consent, protected against majority tyranny.

tyranny

The abuse of the inalienable rights of citizens by government.

constitution and by fragmenting governmental power, would prevent tyranny no matter who eventually won control, including the majority of the people. Limiting the influence of the majority was further accomplished by making only one part of one branch of government subject to direct election of the people—the House of Representatives—leaving the other offices to indirect election (the Senate and the president) or lifetime appointment (the federal judiciary, including the Supreme Court).

Although eighteenth-century republicans believed in representative government—a government whose political leaders are elected by the people—they were not sympathetic to what we might today call popular democracy. For the most part, they thought that public affairs ought to be left to men from the "better" parts of society; the conduct of the public business was, in their view, the province of individuals with wisdom and experience, capacities associated mainly with people of social standing, substantial financial resources, and high levels of education. Nor did eighteenth-century republicans believe that elected representatives should be too responsive to public opinion. Once in office, representatives were to exercise independent judgment about how best to serve the public interest, taking into account the needs and interests of society rather than the moods and opinions of the people. They believed that such a deliberative approach would not only protect liberty but result in better government decisions and policies.[14]

> **?** How was majority tyranny a threat in the Founders' day? How, if at all, does the majority threaten minorities today?

Why the Founders Were Worried

Eighteenth-century republicans, then, did not believe that the people could or should rule directly. While they favored a system that allowed the common people to play a larger role in public life than existed in other political systems of the day, the role of the people was to be a far more limited one than we find acceptable today. They worried that too much participation by the people could only have a bad outcome. As James Madison put it in *The Federalist Papers,* "[Democracies] have ever been spectacles of turbulence and contention; have ever been found incompatible with personal security or the rights of property; and have in general been as short in their lives as they have been violent in their deaths."[15] (See Table 2.1 on the differences between democracy and eighteenth-century republicanism.)

An Excess of Democracy in the States
Worries that untamed democracy was on the rise were not unfounded.[16] In the mid-1780s, popular assemblies (called conventions) were created in several states to keep tabs on state legislatures and to issue instructions to legislatures concerning what bills to pass. Both conventions and instructions struck directly at the heart of the republican conception of the legislature as a deliberative body made up of representatives shielded from popular opinion.[17]

The constitution of the state of Pennsylvania was also an affront to republican principles. Benjamin Rush, a signatory to the Declaration of Independence, described it as "too much upon the democratic order."[18] This constitution replaced the property qualification to vote with a very small tax (thus allowing many more people to vote), created a **unicameral** (single-house) legislative body whose members were to be elected in annual elections, mandated that legislative deliberations be open to the public, and required that

> **unicameral**
> A legislative body with a single chamber.

TABLE 2.1 Comparing Eighteenth-Century Republicanism and the Democratic Ideal

18th-Century Republicanism	The Democratic Ideal
Government is based on popular consent.	Government is based on popular consent.
Rule by the people is indirect, through multiple layers of representatives.	Rule by the people may be direct or indirect through representatives.
The term *people* is narrowly defined (by education, property holding, and social standing).	The term *people* is broadly defined.
Office holding confined to a narrow and privileged stratum of the population.	Broad eligibility for office-holding.
Elected representatives act as "trustees" (act on their own to discover the public good).	Elected representatives act as "delegates" (act as instructed by the people; accurately reflect their wishes).
Barriers to majority rule exist.	Majority rule prevails.
Government is strictly limited in what it can do.	Government does what the people want it to do.
Government safeguards rights and liberties, with a special emphasis on property rights.	Government safeguards rights and liberties, with no special emphasis on property rights.

proposed legislation be widely publicized and voted on only after a general election had been held (making the canvassing of public opinion easier).

To many advocates of popular democracy, including Tom Paine, the Pennsylvania constitution was the most perfect instrument of popular sovereignty. To others, like James Madison, the Pennsylvania case was a perfect example of popular tyranny exercised through the legislative branch of government.[19]

The Threat to Property Rights in the States

One of the freedoms that republicans wanted to protect against the intrusions of a tyrannical government was the right of the people to acquire and enjoy private property. Developments toward the end of the 1770s and the beginning of the 1780s seemed to put this freedom in jeopardy. For one thing, the popular culture was growing increasingly hostile to privilege of any kind, whether of social standing, education, or wealth. Writers derided aristocratic airs; expressed their preference for unlettered, plain-speaking leaders; and pointed out how wealth undermined equal rights.[20] Legislatures were increasingly inclined, moreover, to pass laws protecting debtors. For example, Rhode Island and North Carolina issued cheap paper money, which note holders were forced to accept in payment of debts. Other states passed **stay acts**, which forbade farm foreclosures for nonpayment of debts. Popular opinion, while strongly in favor of property rights (most of the debtors in question were owners of small farms), also sympathized with farmers, who were hard-pressed to pay their debts with increasingly tight money, and believed—with some reason—that many creditors had accumulated notes speculatively or unfairly and were not entitled to full repayment.

What pushed American notables over the edge was the threat of insurrection represented by what came to be called Shays's Rebellion. Named after its leader Daniel Shays, the rebellion occurred in western Massachusetts in 1786 when armed men took over court houses in order to prevent judges from ordering the seizure of farms for nonpayment of state taxes and the incarceration of their owners in debtors prison. The crisis in western Massachusetts was the result of a near "perfect storm" of

stay acts
Laws postponing the collection of taxes or mortgage payments.

developments: plummeting prices for crops, a dramatic increase in state taxes to pay off Revolutionary War debts, and Governor James Bowdoin's insistence that note-holders be paid in full by the state (mostly financial speculators who had bought up the state debt for pennies-on-the-dollar). Unlike most other states in similar circumstances, Massachusetts did not take action to help its debt-ridden farmers. While other states, for example, passed legislation postponing tax and mortgage payments, it instead raised taxes and insisted upon full and timely payment with forfeiture of farms and jail the penalties for noncompliance. Although the state succeeded in putting down the rebellion and reopening the courts, it required the dispatch of the state militia, two pitched battles, and arrests of most of the leaders of the insurrection.

Most of the new nation's leading citizens were alarmed by the apparent inability of state governments to maintain public order under the Articles of Confederation.[21] Shays's Rebellion realized the worst fears of national leaders about the dangers of ineffective state governments and popular democracy spinning out of control, unchecked by a strong national government. As George Washington said, "If government cannot check these disorders, what security has a man?"[22] It was in this climate of crisis in 1786 that 12 delegates from five states meeting in Annapolis issued a call to the other states and Congress to convene a constitutional convention of all the states to correct the flaws in our first constitution. Rather than amend the Articles of Confederation, however, the delegates who gathered at the subsequent convention in Philadelphia in the summer of 1787 wrote an entirely new constitution.

The Constitutional Convention

2.4 Evaluate the framework that emerged from the Constitutional Convention

Most of America's economic, social, and political leaders were convinced by 1787 that the new nation and the experiment in self-government were in great peril. These concerns helped convince leaders in the states to select 73 delegates to attend the Constitutional Convention in Philadelphia (only 55 actually showed up for its deliberations). The goal was to create a new government capable of providing both energy and stability.

The convention officially convened in Philadelphia on May 25, 1787, with George Washington presiding. It met in secret for a period of almost four months. By the end of their deliberations, the delegates had hammered out a constitutional framework that has served as one of the structural foundations of American government and politics to the present day.

Who Were the Framers?

The delegates were not common folk. There were no common laborers, skilled craftspeople, small farmers, women, or racial minorities in attendance. Most delegates were wealthy men: holders of government bonds, real estate investors, successful merchants, bankers, lawyers, and owners of large plantations worked by slaves. They were, for the most part, far better educated than the average American and solidly steeped in the classics. The journal of the convention debates kept by James Madison of Virginia shows that the delegates were conversant with the great works of Western philosophy and political science; with great facility and frequency, they quoted Aristotle, Plato, Locke, Montesquieu, and scores of other thinkers. Finally, they were a group with broad experience in American politics—most had served in their state legislatures—and many were veterans of the Revolutionary War.[23]

Judgments about the framers, their intentions, and what they produced vary widely. Historian Melvin Urofsky wrote that "few gatherings in the history of this or any other country could boast such a concentration of talent."[24] Supreme Court Justice Thurgood Marshall, on the other hand, once claimed that the Constitution was "defective from the start" because the convention at which it was written did not include women or blacks.[25]

The most influential criticism of the framers and what they created was mounted in 1913 by the Progressive historian Charles Beard in his book *An Economic Interpretation of the Constitution.*[26] Beard boldly claimed that the framers were engaged in a conspiracy to protect their immediate and personal economic interests. Those who controlled the convention and the ratification process after the convention, he suggested, were owners of public securities who were interested in a government that could pay its debts, merchants interested in protections of commerce, and land speculators interested in the protection of property rights.

Beard has had legions of defenders and detractors.[27] Historians today generally agree that Beard overemphasized the degree to which the framers were driven by the immediate need to "line their own pockets," failed to give credit to their more noble motivations, and even got many of his facts wrong. So a simple self-interest analysis is not supportable. But Beard was probably on the mark when he suggested that broad economic and social-class motives were at work in shaping the actions of the framers. This is not to suggest that they were not concerned about the national interest, economic stability, or the preservation of liberty. It does suggest, however, that the ways in which they understood these concepts were fully compatible with their own positions of economic and social eminence. In conclusion, it is fair to say that the Constitutional Convention was the work of American leaders who were authentically worried about the instability and economic chaos of the confederation as well as the rise of a democratic and equalitarian culture among the common people.

That being said, we must also acknowledge that the framers were launched on a novel and exciting adventure, trying to create a form of government that existed nowhere else during the late eighteenth century. The success of their efforts was not guaranteed. They were, in effect, sailing in uncharted waters, guided by their reading of history and of the republican philosophers, their understanding of the nature of the unwritten English constitution, and their experience with colonial governments before the Revolution and state governments after.

Consensus and Conflict at the Convention

The delegates to the convention were of one mind on many fundamental points. Most importantly, they agreed that the Articles of Confederation had to be scrapped and replaced with a new constitution.

Most of the delegates also agreed about the need for a substantially strengthened national government to protect American interests in the world, provide for social order, and regulate interstate commerce. Such a government would diminish the power and sovereignty of the states. Supporters of the idea of a strong, centralized national government, such as Alexander Hamilton, had long argued this position. By the time of the convention, even such traditional opponents of centralized governmental power as James Madison had changed their minds. As Madison put it, some way must be found "which will at once support a due supremacy of the national authority, and leave in force the local authorities so far as they can be subordinately useful."[28]

But the delegates also believed that a strong national government was potentially tyrannical and should not be allowed to fall into the hands of any particular interest or set of interests, particularly the majority of the people, referred to by Madison as the "majority faction." The delegates' most important task became that of finding a formula for creating a republican government based on popular consent but a government not unduly swayed by public opinion and popular democracy. As Benjamin Franklin put it, "We have been guarding against an evil that old states are most liable to, excess of power in the rulers, but our present danger seems to be a defect of obedience in the subjects."[29]

The Great Compromise

By far the most intense disagreements at the convention concerned the issue of representation in Congress, especially whether large or small states would wield the most power in the legislative branch. The **Virginia Plan**, drafted by James Madison, proposed the creation of a strong central government dominated by a powerful Congress controlled by the most populous states: Virginia, Massachusetts, and Pennsylvania. The Virginians proposed a government with a strong national legislature with seats apportioned to the states on the basis of population size and with the power to appoint the executive and the judiciary and to veto state laws. The smaller states countered with a set of proposals drafted by William Paterson of New Jersey (thereafter known as the **New Jersey Plan**), whose central feature was a unicameral national legislature whose seats were apportioned equally among the states with representatives selected by state legislatures. The New Jersey Plan envisioned a slightly more powerful national government than the one that existed under the Articles of Confederation, but one that was to be organized on representational lines not unlike those in the Articles, in which each of the states remained sovereign. The Virginia Plan, by contrast, with its strong national government run by a popularly elected legislature, represented a fundamentally different kind of national union, one in which national sovereignty was superior to state sovereignty.[30]

Debate over this issue was so intense that no decision could be reached on the floor of the convention. As a way out of this impasse,

Virginia Plan

Proposal by the large states at the Constitutional Convention to create a strong central government with power in the government apportioned to the states on the basis of population.

New Jersey Plan

Proposal of the smaller states at the Constitutional Convention to create a government based on the equal representation of the states in a unicameral legislature.

the convention appointed a committee to hammer out a compromise. The so-called Committee of Eleven met over the Fourth of July holiday while the convention was adjourned. It presented its report, sometimes called the Great Compromise and sometimes the **Connecticut Compromise** (because it was drafted by Roger Sherman of that state), on July 5, 1787. Its key feature was a bicameral (two-house) national legislature in which each state's representation in the House of Representatives was to be based on population (thus favoring the large states), while representation in the Senate was to be equal for each of the states (thus favoring the small states). The compromise, adopted on July 16, broke the deadlock at the convention and allowed the delegates to turn their attention to other matters.[31] (See the "Mapping American Politics" feature for more on the enduring effects of the compromise.)

> **Connecticut Compromise**
> Also called the *Great Compromise;* the compromise between the New Jersey and Virginia plans formulated by the Connecticut delegates at the Constitutional Convention; called for a lower legislative house based on population size and an upper house based on equal representation of the states.

Slavery Despite great distaste for the institution of slavery among many delegates—it is said that Benjamin Franklin wanted to insert a provision in the Constitution condemning slavery and the slave trade

> **?** How does the bicameral legislature created by the Great Compromise affect your own state's relative influence in Congress?

but was talked out of it for fear of splintering the convention[32]—slavery was ultimately condoned in the Constitution, although only indirectly; the word *slavery*, in fact, does not appear in the Constitution at all. But even without using the term, the legal standing of slaves is affirmed in three places. First, the delegates agreed, after much heated debate, to count three-fifths of a state's slave population (referred to as "three-fifths of all other Persons") in the calculation of how many representatives a state was entitled to in the House of Representatives (Article I, Section 2, paragraph 3). Much harm was done by this; counting noncitizen slaves for purposes of representation in the House increased the power of the slave states in Congress as well as the number of their electoral votes in presidential elections. This imbalance would continue until 1865, when the Civil War and the Thirteenth Amendment, ratified after the war, ended slavery in the United States. Second, it forbade enactments against the slave trade until the year 1808 (Article I, Section 9). Third, it required nonslave states to return runaway slaves to their owners in slave states (Article IV, Section 2, paragraph 3).

THE FRAMERS RETAIN SLAVERY One of the great shortcomings of the framers was their inability or unwillingness to abolish slavery in the Constitution. Here, slaves toil under the watchful eye of an overseer. What were some of the consequences for the nation of the framers not addressing slavery at the Convention?

Equal and Unequal Representation in the House and Senate

Introduction One of the fundamental decisions made by the framers at the Constitutional Convention in Philadelphia in 1787 was to create a two-chamber legislative branch with each branch based on a different principle of representation. Each state's representation in the House of Representatives is based on its relative population size, with the proviso that no state shall have fewer than one representative. Representation in the House, because it very nearly mirrors the distribution of the American population among the states, then, can fairly be called democratic, based on the principle of one person, one vote. The Senate, on the other hand, is based on equal representation of the states—each state has two senators regardless of its population size—giving disproportionate political power to low-population states. We can see this by comparing the two cartograms.

Different Maps; Different Stories The cartogram on the left shows states drawn in proportion to the number of representatives each has in the House of Representatives. Because representation in the House is based roughly on population size, the largest numbers of representatives come from more populous states, such as California, Texas, Florida, Ohio, Illinois, New York, and Pennsylvania, as one would expect in a democratic system. Equal representation of each state in the Senate, combined with vast

States in Proportion to Number of U.S. Representatives

Many Americans today are bothered by the fact that a significant number of the delegates to a convention whose goal was to build a nontyrannical republic were themselves slaveholders (although a few, including George Washington, had provisions in their wills freeing their slaves upon their death). To understand more fully why the delegates did not abolish slavery, see the "Using the Framework" feature.

It would finally take a terrible civil war to abolish slavery in the United States. At the convention, Virginia delegate George Mason had a foreboding of such an outcome when he observed about slavery that "providence punishes national sins by national calamities."[33]

The Presidency The Virginia Plan called for a single executive, while the New Jersey Plan called for a multiperson executive. In the spirit of cooperation that pervaded the convention after the Great Compromise, the delegates quickly settled on the idea of a single executive. They could not agree, however, on how this executive should be selected. Both sides rejected direct election by the people of the chief executive, of course, because this would be "too much upon the democratic order," but they locked horns over and could not agree to the Virginia Plan's method of selection: by the vote of state legislatures. The compromise that population differences among the states, however, leads to serious representational distortions from a democratic theory point of view. In 2009, for example, almost 37 million people lived in California while slightly more than a half-million people lived in Wyoming—yet each state had two senators. Thus, each California senator represented about 18.5 million people, while each Wyoming senator represented just over 270,000. In terms of representation, each person in Wyoming had 68 times the power in the Senate in 2009 as each person in California. The cartogram on the right reflects the representational power of the people in each state in the Senate, measured as the number of senators—always two—divided by state population size. The most populous states, such as California, New York, Texas, and Florida, almost disappear, while less populous states, such as Wyoming, Montana, Delaware, and the two Dakotas, loom large.

What Do You Think? For the most part, the framers of the Constitution were eighteenth-century republicans, distrustful of popular democracy. They created the Senate not only as a tactical maneuver to gain ratification of the Constitution by nine states, but to make the legislative branch more deliberative and less prone to follow the ebbs and flows of public opinion. Was it a wise decision by the framers to give equal representation to the states in the Senate? How might Congress make different kinds of policies if the Senate were organized to more closely reflect the size of state populations?

Sources: www.house.gov; http://www.census.gov/population/www/censusdata/apportionment.html; and www.senate.gov.

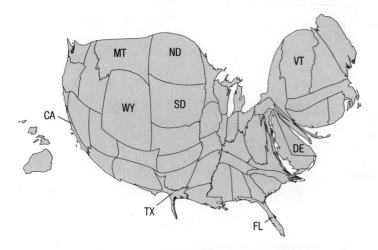

States in Proportion to Number of Residents per Senator

Standard US Map

was eventually struck involved a provision for an **Electoral College** that would select the president. In the Electoral College, each state would have a total of votes equal to its total number of representatives and senators in Congress. Selection of electors was left to state legislatures. (Electoral College votes are determined today by popular vote in each state.) Elected members of the Electoral College would then cast their votes for president. Should the Electoral College fail to give a majority to any person, which most framers assumed would usually happen, the House of Representatives would choose the president, with each state having one vote (Article II, Section 1, paragraphs 2 and 3). The Electoral College will be described in more detail in Chapter 10. For now, see the "By the Numbers" feature to better understand how the Electoral College and democracy are sometimes at odds.

What the Framers Created

The Constitution of the United States (which is reprinted in its entirety in the Appendix) deserves a careful reading. Each word or phrase tells something important about how American government works. If you

Electoral College

Elected representatives of the states, a majority of whose votes formally elect the President of the United States. The number of electors in each state is equal to the total number of its senators and representatives.

Why was slavery allowed in the Constitution of 1787?

Background: Slavery was allowed in the Constitution until passage, after the Civil War, of the Thirteenth Amendment, which ended involuntary servitude in the United States. Although the words "slave" or "involuntary servitude" never appear in the document, slavery is given constitutional standing in the original document in Article I, Section 2, paragraph 3; Article I, Section 9; and Article IV, Section 2, paragraph 3. For Americans today, it seems almost inconceivable that such a thing could have happened. Taking a broader and more historical view makes the story clearer, though hardly more acceptable.

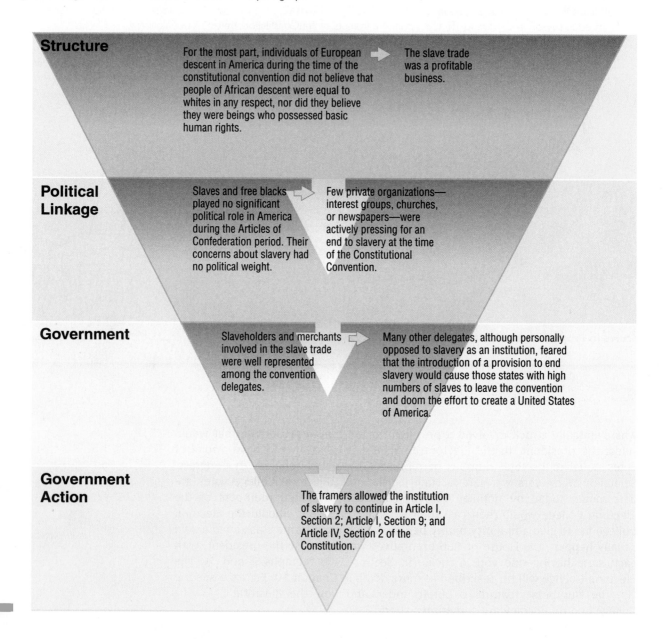

Structure

For the most part, individuals of European descent in America during the time of the constitutional convention did not believe that people of African descent were equal to whites in any respect, nor did they believe they were beings who possessed basic human rights. → The slave trade was a profitable business.

Political Linkage

Slaves and free blacks played no significant political role in America during the Articles of Confederation period. Their concerns about slavery had no political weight. → Few private organizations—interest groups, churches, or newspapers—were actively pressing for an end to slavery at the time of the Constitutional Convention.

Government

Slaveholders and merchants involved in the slave trade were well represented among the convention delegates. → Many other delegates, although personally opposed to slavery as an institution, feared that the introduction of a provision to end slavery would cause those states with high numbers of slaves to leave the convention and doom the effort to create a United States of America.

Government Action

The framers allowed the institution of slavery to continue in Article I, Section 2; Article I, Section 9; and Article IV, Section 2 of the Constitution.

keep in mind how the document is organized, it will help you understand the structure of the Constitution, locate specific provisions, and understand what kind of government the framers created. (A brief outline of provisions is provided in Table 2.2.) Let us examine the fundamental design for government laid out in the Constitution.

TABLE 2.2 Reading the Constitution

Article	What It's About	What It Does
Preamble	States the purpose of the Constitution	Declares that "we the people" (not just the separate states) establish the Constitution.
		Lists the purposes of the Constitution.
Article I	The Legislative Branch	Provides for a House of Representatives, elected by the people and apportioned according to population.
		Provides for a Senate, with equal representation for each state.
		Discusses various rules and procedures, including the presidential veto.
		Enumerates specific powers of the Congress, concluding with the necessary and proper clause.
		Limits Congress's powers.
		Limits the powers of the States.
Article II	The Executive Branch	Vests executive power in a single President of the United States.
		Describes the Electoral College scheme for electing presidents indirectly (changed, in effect, by the development of a party system).
		Describes the qualification, removal, compensation, and oath of office for the presidency.
		Describes presidential powers and duties.
		Provides for impeachment.
Article III	The Judicial Branch	Vests judicial power in a Supreme Court, letting Congress establish other courts if desired.
		Provides for a limited original jurisdiction and (subject to congressional regulation) for broader appellate jurisdiction (i.e., jurisdiction to review lower court decisions).
		Specifies a right to jury trials.
		Defines treason, ruling out certain punishments for it.
Article IV	Interstate Relations	Requires that full faith and credit be given other states.
		Requires that fugitives (slaves) be delivered up to the authorities.
		Provides for the admission of new states and the regulation of new territories.
		Guarantees a republican form of government to the states.
Article V	Amending the Constitution	Provides two ways of proposing amendments to the Constitution and two ways of ratifying them.
		Forbids amendments changing equal state suffrage in the Senate or (before 1808) prohibiting the slave trade or changing the apportionment of taxes.
Article VI	Miscellaneous	Assumes the debts of the Confederation.
		Makes the Constitution, laws, and treaties of the United States the supreme law of the land.
		Requires an oath by U.S. and state officials.
Article VII	Ratification of the Constitution	Provides that the Constitution will be established when ratified by nine state conventions.

Did George W. Bush really win the 2000 presidential vote in Florida?

George W. Bush was officially certified the winner of the presidential contest in Florida on December 12, 2000—35 days after the November election. Florida's 25 electoral votes brought his national total to 271, just barely enough to win the White House.

Interestingly, however, a comprehensive review of Florida ballots has come up with several other possible outcomes to the Florida vote, depending on different ways the ballots could have been counted. In fact, the possible outcomes vary from Bush winning by 537 votes to Gore winning by 200!

Why It Matters Elections must be fair if they are to play the role assigned to them in democratic theory. Part of a fair election is an accurate count of votes cast. Without an accurate count, voter wishes will not be conveyed to public officials, and the legitimacy of elected officials is at risk, making governance more difficult.

Behind the Vote Count
Numbers A consortium of eight leading news organizations—including *The Wall Street Journal*, *The New York Times*, *The Washington Post*, the Associated Press, and CNN—sponsored a 10-month study by the widely respected National Opinion Research Center at the University of Chicago. Center researchers examined every uncounted "under-vote" ballot

(where no vote for president was recorded by the voting machine), with an eye toward determining each voter's intent. Only ballots that showed evidence of clear voter intention were included in the consortium's recount. These included ballots with "hanging" and "pregnant" chads which the machines failed to record and optical scan ballots where voters indicated their vote with a check mark or an "X" rather than filling in the bubble as instructed.

Calculating the Winner's Margin
of Victory The official tally concluded that Bush won by 537 votes. However, Center investigators found that different counting methods would have yielded the results shown on page 45. There are some incredible ironies in these numbers.

- **Scenario 1** Had the Gore team gotten everything it asked for from election officials and the courts, Gore still would have lost to George W. Bush.
- **Scenario 2** The U.S. Supreme Court did not steal the election, as many Gore supporters claimed, for had it allowed the Florida Supreme Court's solution to stand, Bush would have won anyway.
- **Scenario 3** A majority of Florida voters went to the polls on November 8 to cast a vote for Al Gore for president. The method proposed by the

U.S. Supreme Court shows this; recounting all "under-count" disputed ballots on a statewide basis using consistent standards yields a Gore victory. The upshot: Gore was badly advised by his team of lawyers, who insisted on recounts in only certain counties.

Because of the enormous boost in George W. Bush's popularity following the terrorist attack on the United States and the widely supported attack on the Taliban regime in Afghanistan that followed, most Americans ignored the consortium's findings when it was published after 9/11. Most seemed perfectly content to have Bush as president, no matter what had happened in Florida.

Criticisms of the Florida
"Recount" Some have argued that the consortium's recount was flawed in two major ways:

- First, it did not include "over-votes" in its estimates—those ballots where more than one name for president was indicated or where the same name was entered more than once—which were also ruled invalid by election officials in Florida. For the most part, these involved ballots where voters made two punches on very confusing ballots (the infamous "butterfly ballots") or where voters wrote in the same name as the

A Republican Form of Government Recall that eighteenth-century republican doctrine advocated a form of government that, while based on popular consent and some popular participation, places obstacles in the path of majoritarian democracy and limits the purposes and powers of the government in order to prevent tyranny.

Elections and Representation Republican government is based on the principle of representation, meaning that public policies are made not by the people directly but by the people's elected representatives acting in their stead. Under the rules created by the Constitution, the president and members of Congress are elected by the people, although in the case of the presidency and the Senate, to be sure, they are elected only indirectly (through the Electoral College and the state

candidate they had punched or marked, presumably to make clear to election officials who they had voted for. A substantial majority of over-vote ballots had Gore as one of the choices.

- Second, there is the issue of absentee ballots from overseas armed forces personnel. Had they been counted in the same way other ballots were counted—that is, not counting ballots kicked out because of "under-vote" or "over-vote" problems—Bush would have lost hundreds of votes to Gore

and probably lost Florida and the White House.

What to Watch For When counting votes, as in all other counts, the rules for doing so matter. This is why the lawyers from the Gore and Bush teams fought so ferociously following the Florida election about how to do the recount. Whenever you run across a statistic that involves counting, in one form or another, you might want to look further into what counting rules were used.

What Do You Think? Can you think of any other way to decide the winner of an election when the race ends up in a dead heat? Some countries use a "run-off" system in which the two top people run against each other to determine who has won a majority of popular votes before a winner is declared. In the 2000 presidential elections, this would have meant a run-off election between Gore and Bush, without Ralph Nader or Pat Buchanan on the ballot. How might a run-off have changed the face of the election?

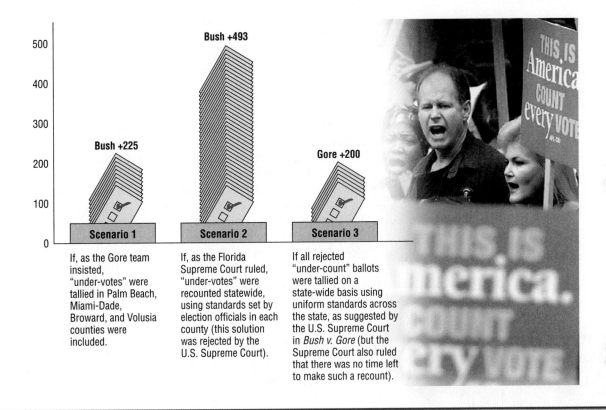

Scenario 1
If, as the Gore team insisted, "under-votes" were tallied in Palm Beach, Miami-Dade, Broward, and Volusia counties were included.

Scenario 2
If, as the Florida Supreme Court ruled, "under-votes" were recounted statewide, using standards set by election officials in each county (this solution was rejected by the U.S. Supreme Court).

Scenario 3
If all rejected "under-count" ballots were tallied on a state-wide basis using uniform standards across the state, as suggested by the U.S. Supreme Court in *Bush v. Gore* (but the Supreme Court also ruled that there was no time left to make such a recount).

legislatures, respectively). The upshot, then, is that government policies at the national level are mostly made by either directly or indirectly elected officials. (The Seventeenth Amendment, ratified in 1913, transferred election of senators from legislatures to the people.) This filters the voices of the people by encouraging the election to office of those "whose enlightened views and virtuous sentiments render them superior to local prejudices and to schemes of injustice."[34] This guarantees a degree of popular consent and some protection against the possibilities of tyrannical government arising from misrule by the *one* or by the *few*, given the electoral power of the *many*, but the many are still several steps removed from direct influence over officials.

? Can you think of any government policies today that seem to run counter to popular opinion, or to the desires of the national majority? Can you explain this disconnect?

federal

Describing a system in which significant governmental powers are divided between a central government and smaller territorial units, such as states.

supremacy clause

The provision in Article VI of the Constitution that states that the Constitution and the laws and treaties of the United States are the supreme law of the land, taking precedence over state laws and constitutions.

elastic clause

Article I, Section 8, of the Constitution, also called the *necessary and proper clause;* gives Congress the authority to make whatever laws are necessary and proper to carry out its enumerated responsibilities.

Federalism   The Articles of Confederation envisioned a nation structured as a loose union of politically independent states with little power in the hands of the central government. The Constitution fashioned a **federal** system in which some powers are left to the states, some powers are shared by the states and the central government, and some powers are granted to the central government alone.

The powers in the Constitution tilt toward the center, however.[35] This recasting of the union from a loose confederation to a more centralized federal system is boldly stated in Article VI, Section 2, commonly called the **supremacy clause**:

> This Constitution and the Laws of the United States which shall be made in Pursuance thereof; and all Treaties made, or which shall be made, under the Authority of the United States, shall be the supreme Law of the Land; and the Judges in every State shall be bound thereby, any Thing in the Constitution or Laws of any State to the Contrary notwithstanding.

The tilt toward national power is also enhanced by assigning important powers and responsibilities to the national government: to regulate commerce, to provide a uniform currency, to provide uniform laws on bankruptcy, to raise and support an army and a navy, to declare war, to collect taxes and customs duties, to provide for the common defense of the United States, and more. (See Article I, Section 8.) Especially important for later constitutional history is the last of the clauses in Section 8, which states that Congress has the power to "make all laws which shall be necessary and proper" to carry out its specific powers and responsibilities. We shall see later how this **elastic clause** became one of the foundations for the growth of the federal government in the twentieth century.

The Constitution left it up to each of the states, however, to determine qualifications for voting within their borders. This left rules in place in all the states that denied the right to vote to women, slaves, and Native Americans; it left rules untouched in many states that denied the vote to free blacks and to white males without property. Most states removed property qualifications by the 1830s, establishing universal white male suffrage in the United States. It would take many years and constitutional amendments to remove state restrictions on the voting rights of women and racial minorities.

Limited Government   The basic purpose of the U.S. Constitution, like any written constitution, is to define the purposes and powers of the government. Such a definition of purposes and powers

VENERATING THE CONSTITUTION   Americans generally believe that the Constitution fashioned by the framers in Philadelphia in 1788 is one of the main reasons the American system of government has proved to be so enduring. Here, young people look at the original document at the National Archives. What reasons might there be for our system enduring, other than the Constitution?

automatically places a boundary between what is permissible and what is impermissible. By listing the specific powers (as in Article I, Section 8) of the national government and specifically denying others to the national government (as in Article I, Section 9, and in the first 10 amendments to the Constitution, known as the **Bill of Rights**), the Constitution limited what government may legitimately do.

> **Bill of Rights**
> The first 10 amendments to the U.S. Constitution, concerned with the protection of basic liberties.

Checks on Majority Rule Afraid of unbridled democracy, the framers created a constitution by which the people rule only indirectly, barriers are placed in the path of majorities, and deliberation is prized over conformity to majority opinion. As political philosopher Robert Dahl puts it, "To achieve their goal of preserving a set of inalienable rights superior to the majority principle...the framers deliberately created a framework of government that was carefully designed to impede and even prevent the operation of majority rule."[36] Let us see what the framers did to try to dilute the power of the majority in the national government.

Of the three branches of government, they made only a part of one of them subject to election by the direct vote of the people: the House of Representatives (Article I, Section 2, paragraph 1). They left the election of the president to an electoral college whose members were selected by state legislatures and not by the direct vote of the people. They gave the responsibility of electing senators to state legislatures (since changed by the Seventeenth Amendment). They placed selection of federal judges in the hands of the president and the Senate. They arranged, as well, that representatives, senators, and presidents would serve for different terms (two years for representatives, four years for presidents, and six years for senators), and be beholden to different constituencies. These non-congruencies in terms of office, constituencies, and methods for selecting members of each of the branches were intended to ensure that popular majorities, at least in the short run, would be unlikely to overwhelm those who govern. Finally, the framers rejected the advice of radical democrats, such as Thomas Paine, Samuel Adams, and Thomas Jefferson, to allow the Constitution to be easily amended. Instead, they created an amending process that is exceedingly cumbersome and difficult (see Figure 2.2).

Thus, the framers designed a system in which majority opinion, although given some play (more than anywhere in the world at the time),[37] was largely deflected and slowed, allowing somewhat insulated political leaders to deliberate at their pleasure.

? How well does the republican form of government fashioned by the framers meet the demands set forth in the Preamble to the Constitution (provided in the Appendix to this book)? Would a more perfect democracy be better equipped to fulfill the Preamble's lofty goals?

Separation of Powers; Checks and Balances During the American Revolution, American leaders worried mainly about the misrule of executives (kings and governors) and judges. As an antidote, they substituted legislative supremacy in state constitutions and in the Articles of Confederation, thinking that placing power in an elected representative body would make government effective and nontyrannical. The men who drafted the Constitution, however, though still leery of executive and judicial power, were more concerned by 1787 about the danger of legislative tyranny. To deal with this problem, the framers turned to the ancient notion of balanced government, popularized by the French philosopher Montesquieu. The central idea of balanced government is that concentrated power of any kind is dangerous and that the way to prevent tyranny is first to fragment governmental power into its constituent parts—executive, legislative,

FIGURE 2.2 Amending the Constitution

With two ways of proposing a constitutional amendment and two ways of ratifying one, there are four routes to changing the Constitution. In all but one case (the Twenty-First Amendment, which repealed Prohibition), constitutional amendments have been proposed by Congress and then ratified by the state legislatures.

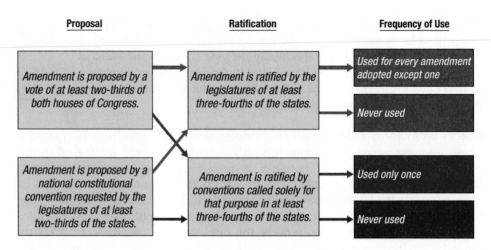

Proposal	Ratification	Frequency of Use
Amendment is proposed by a vote of at least two-thirds of both houses of Congress.	Amendment is ratified by the legislatures of at least three-fourths of the states.	Used for every amendment adopted except one
		Never used
Amendment is proposed by a national constitutional convention requested by the legislatures of at least two-thirds of the states.	Amendment is ratified by conventions called solely for that purpose in at least three-fourths of the states.	Used only once
		Never used

separation of powers

The distribution of government legislative, executive, and judicial powers to separate branches of government.

checks and balances

The constitutional principle that each of the separate branches of government has the power to hinder the actions of the other branches as a way to prevent tyranny.

and judicial—then place each into a separate and independent branch. In the U.S. Constitution, Article I (on the legislative power), Article II (on the executive power), and Article III (on the judicial power) designate separate spheres of responsibility and enumerate specific powers for each branch. We call this the **separation of powers**.

To further ensure that power would not be exercised tyrannically, the framers arranged for the legislative, executive, and judicial powers to check one another in such a way that "ambition . . . be made to counteract ambition."[38] They did this by ensuring that no branch of the national government would be able to act entirely on its own without the cooperation of the others. To put it another way, each branch has ways of blocking the actions of the others. For instance, Congress is given the chief lawmaking power under the Constitution, but a bill cannot become law if a president exercises his veto, unless Congress manages to override it with a two-thirds majority in both the House and Senate. The Supreme Court, moreover, has the power (although it is not specifically mentioned) to reject a law formulated by Congress and signed by the president if it is contrary to the Constitution. What is at work here was described nicely by Thomas Jefferson: "The powers of government should be so divided and balanced among several bodies of magistracy, as that no one could transcend their legal limits, without being effectually checked and constrained by the others."[39] We call the provisions that accomplish this objective **checks and balances**. Figure 2.3 shows in detail how each separate branch of the federal government can be checked by the other two. In this constitutional scheme, each branch has power, but none is able to exercise all of its powers on its own, without some concurrence and cooperation by the other branches.

The Foundations for a National Free Enterprise Economy The framers believed that the right to accumulate, use, and transfer private property was one of the fundamental and inalienable rights that governments were instituted to defend, so they looked for ways to protect it. They also believed that the obstacles to trade allowed under the Articles of Confederation were threatening to block the emergence of a vibrant national economy in which most of them were involved.

Property rights are protected in several places in the Constitution. Article I, Section 10, forbids the states to impair the obligation of contracts, to coin money, or

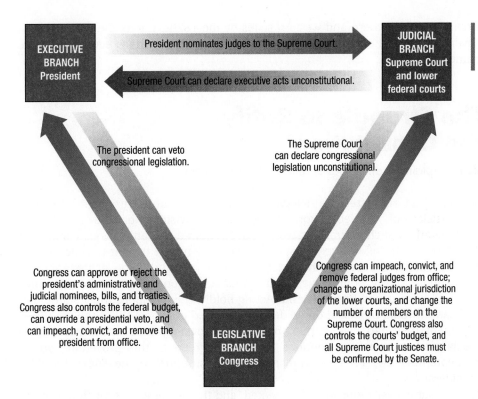

FIGURE 2.3 Separation of Powers and Checks and Balances

The framers of the Constitution believed that tyranny might be avoided if the power of government were fragmented into its executive, legislative, and judicial components and if each component were made the responsibility of a separate branch of government. To further protect against tyranny, they created mechanisms by which the actions of any single branch could be blocked by either or both of the other branches.

to make anything but gold and silver coin a tender in payment of debts. In other words, the states could no longer help debtors by printing inflated money, forgiving debts, or otherwise infringing on the property of creditors, as had happened in such places as Rhode Island and North Carolina under the Articles of Confederation. Article IV, Section 1, further guarantees contracts by establishing that the states must give "full faith and credit" to the public acts, records, and judicial proceedings of every other state, which means that one could no longer escape legal and financial obligations in one state by moving to another. In addition, the Constitution guaranteed that the U.S. government would pay all debts contracted under the Articles of Confederation (Article VI, Section 1). Article IV, Section 2, paragraph 3, even protected private property in slaves by requiring states to deliver escaped slaves back to their owners.

Besides protecting private property, the framers took additional steps to encourage the emergence of a national **free enterprise** economy. Article I, Section 8, grants Congress the power to regulate interstate commerce (thus ending the chaos of individual states' regulations), to coin money and regulate its value (thus establishing a uniform national currency), to establish uniform laws of bankruptcy, and to protect the financial fruits of invention by establishing patent and copyright laws. At the same time, Article I, Sections 9 and 10, broke down barriers to trade by forbidding the states to impose taxes or duties on other states' exports, to enter into foreign treaties, to coin money, or to lay any imposts or duties on imports or exports.

It took a little while for a national free enterprise system to emerge and flower in the United States because of the existence of an entirely different sort of economy in the slave south. Although free enterprise was

free enterprise

An economic system characterized by competitive markets and private ownership; similar to capitalism.

thriving in the northern and western states by the 1820s, it took the destruction of slavery during and after the Civil War to create a free enterprise economy for the country as a whole.

The Struggle to Ratify the Constitution

2.5 Explain the difficulties of ratifying the Constitution

Congress had instructed the delegates to the convention to propose changes to the Articles of Confederation. Under the provisions of the Articles of Confederation, such alterations would have required the unanimous consent of the 13 states. To follow such a course would have meant instant rejection of the new constitution, because Rhode Island, never friendly to the deliberations in Philadelphia, surely would have voted against it, and one or two additional states may well have joined Rhode Island. Acting boldly, the framers simply stated that ratification would be based on guidelines specified in Article VII of the unratified document they had just written, namely, approval by nine states meeting in special constitutional conventions. Congress agreed to this procedure, voting on September 28, 1787, to transmit the Constitution to the states for their consideration.

The battle over ratification was heated, and the outcome was far from certain. That the Constitution eventually carried the day may be partly attributed to the fact that the **Federalists** (those who supported the Constitution) did a better job of making their case than the **Anti-Federalists** (those who opposed the Constitution). Their intellectual advantages were nowhere more obvious than in the 85 articles written in defense of the Constitution for New York newspapers, under the name "Publius," by Alexander Hamilton (who wrote the most), James Madison, and John Jay (who wrote only three). Collected later and published as *The Federalist Papers* (which Thomas Jefferson judged to be "the best commentary on the principles of government which ever was written"[40]), these articles strongly influenced the debate over ratification and remain the most impressive commentaries ever written about the U.S. Constitution.

Anti-Federalist opposition to the Constitution was based on fear of centralized power and concern about the absence of a bill of rights.[41] Although the Federalists firmly believed that a bill of rights was unnecessary because of the protection of rights in the state constitutions and the many safeguards against tyranny in the federal Constitution, they promised to add one during the first session of Congress. Without this promise, ratification would probably not have happened. The Federalists kept their word. The 1st Congress passed a bill of rights in the form of 10 amendments to the Constitution (see Table 2.3 and the Appendix), and the amendments were eventually ratified by the required number of states by 1791.

Ratification of the Constitution was a close call. Most of the small states quickly approved, attracted by the formula of equal representation in the Senate. Federalists organized a victory in Pennsylvania before the Anti–Federalists realized what had happened. After that, ratification became a struggle. Rhode Island voted no. North Carolina abstained because of the absence of a bill of rights and did not vote its approval until 1790. In the largest and most important states, the vote was exceedingly close. Massachusetts approved by a vote of 187–168; Virginia, by 89–79; and New York, by 30–27. The struggle was especially intense in Virginia, where prominent, articulate, and influential men were involved on both

Federalists

Proponents of the Constitution during the ratification fight; also the political party of Hamilton, Washington, and Adams.

Anti-Federalists

Opponents of the Constitution during the fight over ratification.

TABLE 2.3   The Bill of Rights

Amendment I	Freedom of religion, speech, press, and assembly
Amendment II	The right to bear arms
Amendment III	Prohibition against quartering of troops in private homes
Amendment IV	Prohibition against unreasonable searches and seizures
Amendment V	Rights guaranteed to the accused: requirement for grand jury indictment; protections against double jeopardy and self-incrimination; guarantee of due process
Amendment VI	Right to a speedy and public trial before an impartial jury, to cross-examine witnesses, and to have counsel
Amendment VII	Right to a trial by jury in civil suits
Amendment VIII	Prohibition against excessive bail and fines and against cruel and unusual punishment
Amendment IX	Traditional rights not listed in the Constitution are retained by the people
Amendment X	Powers not denied to them by the Constitution or given solely to the national government are retained by the states

Note: See the Appendix for the full text.

sides. The Federalists could call on George Washington, James Madison, John Marshall, and Edmund Randolph. The Anti-Federalists countered with George Mason, Richard Henry Lee, and Patrick Henry. Patrick Henry was particularly passionate, saying that the Constitution "squints towards monarchy." Although New Hampshire technically put the Constitution over the top, being the ninth state to vote approval, the proponents did not rest easily until approval was narrowly voted by Virginia and New York.

The Changing Constitution, Democracy, and American Politics

2.6 Identify three processes by which the Constitution changes

The Constitution is the basic rule book for the game of American politics. Constitutional rules apportion power and responsibility among governmental branches, define the fundamental nature of the relationships among governmental institutions, specify how individuals are to be selected for office, and tell how the rules themselves may be changed. Every aspiring politician who wants to attain office, every citizen who wants to influence what government does, and every group that wants to advance its interests in the political arena must know the rules and how to use them to their best advantage. Because the Constitution has this character, we understand it to be a fundamental *structural* factor influencing all of American political life.

Like all rules, however, constitutional rules can and do change over time. Their tendency to change with the times is why we sometimes speak of the "living Constitution." Constitutional changes come about in three specific ways: formal amendment, judicial interpretation, and political practices.

The Constitution may be formally amended by use of the procedures outlined in Article V of the Constitution (again, refer to Figure 2.2). This method has resulted in the addition of 27 amendments since the founding, the first 10 of which (the Bill of Rights) were added within three years of ratification. That only 17 have been added in the roughly 200 years since suggests that this method of changing the Constitution is extremely difficult. Over the years, proponents of constitutional amendments that would guarantee equal rights for women, ban same-sex marriages, and ban the burning of the American flag have learned how difficult it is to formally amend the Constitution; none of these amendments were added, despite polls reporting majorities in favor of them. Nevertheless, several formal amendments have played an important role in expanding democracy in the United States by ending slavery; extending voting rights to African Americans, women, and young people ages 18–20; and making the selection of senators the business of voters, not state legislatures.

The Constitution is also changed by decisions and interpretations of the U.S. Supreme Court found in the written opinions of the justices. In *Marbury* v. *Madison* (1803), the Court claimed the power of **judicial review**—the right to declare the actions of the other branches of government null and void if they are contrary to the Constitution—even though such a power is not specifically mentioned in the Constitution (see Chapter 14 for a full discussion of judicial review). In *Griswold* v. *Connecticut* (1965), and later in *Roe* v. *Wade* (1973), to take another example, the Court supported a claim for the existence of a fundamental right to privacy even though such a right is not explicitly mentioned in the Constitution. Many conservatives believe that such actions by the Supreme Court are illegitimate because they go beyond the original intentions of the framers, or cannot be justified in the written provisions of the Constitution. Many others disagree, believing that the Court has and must interpret the Constitution in light of changing circumstances that the framers could not have envisioned.

judicial review

The power of the Supreme Court to declare actions of the other branches and levels of government unconstitutional.

VOICING CONCERNS AT THE COURT
The Constitution has evolved over the years in three ways: through the amendment process, through evolving political practices, and through the Supreme Court's changing interpretation of the Constitution's meaning. Here antiabortion protesters demonstrate in front of the Supreme Court building on the anniversary of the Court's *Roe* v. *Wade* decision to demand a reversal of that landmark decision. How does the Constitution protect both the Supreme Court's decision and these people's public protest of it? How likely is it that the present Supreme Court will listen to these and other voices and overturn *Roe*?

The meaning of the Constitution also changes through changing political practices, which end up serving as precedents for political actors. Political parties, party primaries, and presidential nominating conventions are not mentioned in the Constitution, for example, but it would be hard to think about American politics today without them. It is also fair to say that the framers would not recognize the modern presidency, which is now a far more important office than they envisioned, a change that has been brought about largely by the political and military involvement of the United States in world affairs, tied to vigorous assertion of the office's diplomatic and Commander-in-Chief powers by many presidents, and the widespread demand that the president do something during economic crises. The Constitution does not specify, for example, that the Treasury Secretary, acting for the president, can force the merger of failing financial firms as they did in the last months of the George W. Bush presidency in the depths of the recession. Nor would they have predicted the increasing use of **signing statements** (see the chapter-opening story) by which a president can alter the meaning of a bill even as he signs it into law.

Throughout this book you will see many examples of these three forms of constitutional change that have shaped our current understanding of the meaning of the Constitution and its many provisions. You also will learn that the third factor—changing political practices, itself a product of social and cultural change and pressure from the American people—is at least as important as amendments and judicial rulings in adjusting the Constitution to its times.[42]

> **signing statement**
> A document sometimes issued by the president in connection with the signing of a bill from Congress that sets out the president's understanding of the new law and how executive branch officials should carry it out.

Using the DEMOCRACY STANDARD

How democratic is the Constitution?

Scarred by the failings of the Articles of Confederation, the framers endeavored to create a republic that would offer representative democracy without the threat of majority tyranny. Consequently, they wrote a number of provisions into the Constitution to control the purported excesses of democracy. These include the separation of powers into executive, legislative, and judicial branches; checks and balances to prevent any of the branches from governing on its own; federalism to fragment government powers between a national government and the states; an appointed federal judiciary with life tenure charged with, among other things, protecting private property; selection of the president by the Electoral College; election of members of the Senate by state legislatures; and a process for changing the Constitution that makes it exceedingly easy for small numbers of people in Congress and a very few states to block amendments favored by national majorities.

Although the framers had every intention of creating a republic and holding democracy in check, the tide of democracy has gradually transformed the original constitutional design. For example, the Seventeenth Amendment created a Senate whose members are directly elected by the people. The Supreme Court, moreover, has extended civil rights protections to racial and ethnic minorities. And, the presidency has become both more powerful and more attentive to majority opinion. By formal amendment, through judicial interpretations, and through changing political practices, government has been fashioned into a more responsive set of institutions that, eventually, must heed the voice of the people.

Yet it can be argued that, despite these changes, the American system of government remains essentially "republican" in nature, with the majority finding it very difficult to prevail. Provisions of the Constitution, designed to keep the majority in check, effectively provide minorities with disproportionate power in government. For example, four times in our history, presidents have taken office without having won a majority of votes in the country (John Quincy Adams, 1825; Rutherford B. Hayes, 1877; Benjamin Harrison, 1889; George W. Bush, 2001). And while the Seventeenth Amendment did make the election of senators more democratic, the Senate itself—which provides equal representation to all states regardless of population—remains skewed toward smaller states, thus serving as a major barrier in the translation of what the American people want into what government does.[43]

SUMMARY

2.1 Assess the enduring legacies of the American Revolution and the Declaration of Independence

- The Revolutionary War and the Declaration of Independence helped establish the ideas of self-government and inalienable individual rights as the core of the American political ideology.

2.2 Describe the governmental system established by our first constitution

- The first constitution joining the American states was the Articles of Confederation. Under its terms, the states were organized into a loose confederation in which the states retained full sovereignty and the central government had little power.

2.3 Analyze the issues that led to the Constitutional Convention

- Defects in the Articles of Confederation, along with fears that democratic and egalitarian tendencies were beginning to spin out of control, prompted American leaders to gather in Philadelphia to amend the Articles. The delegates chose instead to formulate an entirely new constitution.

2.4 Evaluate the framework that emerged from the Constitutional Convention

- The framers created a constitutional framework for republican government including separation of powers and separation of powers, and federalism.
- The Connecticut Compromise settled the tensions between large and small states by giving states equal representation in the Senate and representation based on population in the House of Representatives.
- The framers legitimated slavery.
- The framers created the legal foundations for a thriving commercial republic.

2.5 Explain the difficulties of ratifying the Constitution

- The Constitution was ratified in an extremely close vote of the states after a hard-fought struggle between the Federalists, who wanted a more centralized republicanism, and the Anti-Federalists, who wanted small-scale republicanism.
- The promise by the Federalists to introduce amendments specifying the rights of Americans in the 1st Congress helped swing the vote in favor of ratification in a number of key states.
- Despite its "close shave," the Constitution became very popular among the American people within only a few years of the ratification fight.

2.6 Identify three processes by which the Constitution changes

- The Constitution changes by three processes: amendments to the document, judicial interpretations of the meaning of constitutional provisions, and the everyday political practices of Americans and their elected leaders.
- Because of the continuing struggle for democracy by the American people, the Constitution has become far more democratic over the years than was originally intended by the framers.

TEST YOURSELF

Answer key begins on page T-1.

2.1 Assess the enduring legacies of the American Revolution and the Declaration of Independence

1. The Declaration of Independence strongly condemns the practice of slavery in the colonies.
True / False

2. According to the Declaration of Independence, why do people create government?
   a. To protect fundamental rights, including "life, liberty, and the Pursuit of Happiness"
   b. To create prosperous economic communities
   c. To ensure that they retain dominion over natural resources
   d. To enhance electoral viability
   e. To turn chaos into order.

3. The Declaration of Independence states that citizens have the right to void their social contract if the government fails to protect the rights of citizens. Defend or criticize this assertion.

2.2 Describe the governmental system established by our first constitution

4. The Articles of Confederation created a strong central government that unified the new nation.
True / False

5. In which of the following areas was the Articles of Confederation most successful?
   a. Regulation of commerce between the states
   b. Preservation of state sovereignty
   c. Creation of a constitution that could be easily amended to remedy defects
   d. The ability to settle disputes between the states
   e. The collection of significant tax revenue

6. In your opinion, what was the biggest shortcoming of the Articles of Confederation? Why?

2.3 Analyze the issues that led to the Constitutional Convention

7. Which of the following strategies did the Founders employ in an effort to prevent tyranny?
   a. Government leaders would be appointed
   b. A concentration of powers in the federal government
   c. Facilitation of majority rule
   d. The election of representatives to lead the government
   e. Establishment of a popular democracy

8. What was the significance of Shays's Rebellion?
   a. It led to important amendments to the Articles of Confederation.
   b. It convinced Americans that a stronger national government was necessary to maintain public order.
   c. It damaged diplomatic relations between the young nation and various Indian tribes.
   d. It caused Britain to station additional soldiers in the United States in order to keep the peace.
   e. It illustrated the dangers of a powerful national government.

9. Evaluate the extent to which the Founders' distrust of common citizens was well founded.

2.4 Evaluate the framework that emerged from the Constitutional Convention

10. The Constitution strongly condemns both the practice of slavery and the slaveholders who propagate it.
True / False

11. Which of the following is not a central element of the Constitution?
    a. Compromise
    b. Limited government
    c. A fusion of powers
    d. Checks and balances
    e. A republican form of government

12. Evaluate historian Charles Beard's claim that the framers were primarily concerned about protecting their own economic interests.

2.5 Explain the difficulties of ratifying the Constitution

13. The Anti-Federalists were concerned that the proposed Constitution gave too much power to the central government and did not adequately protect against tyranny.
True / False

14. Changes to the Articles of Confederation required unanimous approval by all 13 states. Yet the proposed Constitution stated that the new government would take effect upon ratification by only 9 states. Given this situation, evaluate whether the adoption of the Constitution was legitimate.

2.6 Identify three processes by which the Constitution changes

15. Constitutional amendments are the most common way for the meaning of the Constitution to change.
True / False

16. Which of the following tools does the president use in an attempt to influence the meaning of the Constitution?
    a. Judicial review
    b. The supremacy clause
    c. Constitutional amendments
    d. Signing statements
    e. Discharge petitions

mypoliscilab EXERCISES

Apply what you learned in this chapter on MyPoliSciLab.

Read on **mypoliscilab.com**

eText: Chapter 2

Study and **Review** on **mypoliscilab.com**

Pre-Test
Post-Test
Chapter Exam
Flashcards

Watch on **mypoliscilab.com**

Video: Animal Sacrifice and Free Exercise
Video: Polygamy and the U.S. Constitution

Explore on **mypoliscilab.com**

Simulation: You Are James Madison
Simulation: You Are Proposing a Constitutional Amendment
Comparative: Comparing Constitutions
Timeline: The History of Constitutional Amendments
Visual Literacy: The American System of Checks and Balances

INTERNET SOURCES

Annotated Constitution
www.gpoaccess.gov/constitution/index.html
An annotation of the Constitution in which each clause is tied to Supreme Court decisions concerning its meaning; done by the Library of Congress.

Biographical Sketches of the Delegates to the Constitutional Convention
www.archives.gov/national-archives-experience/charters/ constitution_founding_fathers.html
Profiles of the delegates to the Constitutional Convention.

Constitutional Finder
http://confinder.richmond.edu
A site with links to constitutions for most nations of the world.

Cornell University Law School
www.law.cornell.edu/
Pathways to the full text of U.S. Supreme Court decisions and opinions, articles on constitutional issues, and much more.

Political Science Resources: Political Thought
www.psr.keele.ac.uk/
A vast collection of documents on democracy, liberty, and constitutionalism around the world.

The U.S. Constitution Online
www.usconstitution.net
A very rich site that presents material on every aspect of the history and development of the Constitution.

SUGGESTIONS FOR FURTHER READING

Ellis, Joseph J. *Founding Brothers: The Revolutionary Generation.* New York: Alfred Knopf, 2001.

    An entertaining and accessible look at the intertwined lives of the men who wrote the Declaration of Independence, fought the Revolutionary War, fashioned the Constitution, and launched the new American government.

Levinson, Sanford. *Our Undemocratic Constitution: Where the Constitution Goes Wrong.* New York: Oxford University Press, 2006.

    An argument by a leading constitutional scholar that the framers did their job of protecting against majority rule so well that it severely cripples American democracy today.

Rossiter, Clinton, ed. *The Federalist Papers.* New York: New American Library, 1961.

    Classic commentaries on the Constitution and its key provisions, written by Alexander Hamilton, John Jay, and James Madison.

Storing, Herbert J. *What the Anti-Federalists Were For.* Chicago: University of Chicago Press, 1981.

    The most complete collection available on the published views of the Anti-Federalists. Includes convincing commentary by Storing.

Sunstein, Cass R. *A Constitution of Many Minds: Why the Founding Document Doesn't Mean What It Meant Before.* Princeton, NJ: Princeton University Press, 2009.

    An analysis of why the meaning of the Constitution has changed over the course of American history and will do so in the future.

Wood, Gordon S. *The Creation of the American Republic.* New York: Norton, 1972.

    The most exhaustive and respected source on America's changing ideas during the period 1776–1787, or from the start of the American Revolution to the writing of the Constitution.

Wood, Gordon S. *The Radicalism of the American Revolution.* New York: Knopf, 1992.

    Examines and rejects the argument that the American Revolution was merely a political and not a social and economic revolution.

Federalism:
States and Nation

LEARNING OBJECTIVES

After reading this chapter, you will be able to:

3.1 Define federalism and explain why we have it

3.2 Establish the basis for federalism in the Constitution

3.3 Trace the evolution of American federalism

3.4 Analyze how federal grants structure national and state government relations

3.5 Evaluate the arguments for and against federalism

WHO'S IN CHARGE HERE?

It didn't take very long for the "blame game" to begin.[1] Even as scenes of utter chaos and destruction in New Orleans caused by Hurricane Katrina were broadcast around the world in late August 2005, federal, state, and local officials started pointing fingers at each other. Democratic Louisiana Governor Kathleen Blanco asked why the Federal Emergency Management Agency (FEMA) was so slow to respond to the disaster and why active-duty military forces were not sent to help provide shelter, food and water, and order. Democratic Mayor Ray Nagin complained about the slow federal response in radio and television interviews and estimated that at least 2,000 people died from the flooding, violence, loss of power, and toxic wastes. FEMA Director Michael Brown said he hadn't known thousands of people were in the Superdome with little food, water, or sanitation, although conditions there were widely reported even before Katrina struck. Brown and some White House officials laid the blame squarely on state and local officials for failing to plan properly for the emergency, botching the evacuation, and failing to enforce law and order.

It will take investigators and scholars a while longer to properly apportion the blame and begin to fix the problems Katrina revealed. One reason it will take so long is the complexity created by our federal system of government—the division of powers and responsibilities among the national and state governments (which, in turn, create and oversee local governments). In some matters, federal and state government powers and responsibilities are separate and clearly defined, but in others they are shared. Furthermore, the boundary lines for shared matters—including such crucial areas as law and order, disaster preparedness, and disaster relief—are not always clear and stable. The disaster resulted not just from the storm, but from the failure of all levels of government to fulfill their core responsibilities and to coordinate activities in areas of shared responsibilities. The failure to coordinate with other government jurisdictions may have been due to genuine confusion or political rivalries—Republican President Bush and Democratic Governor Blanco found it difficult to work with one another, and it became known that the administration was loath to loosen the federal purse strings for state and local governments known for unusually high levels of corruption—or both.

Even without political rivalries, figuring out who has core responsibility for various activities was not easy in this case. For example, the federal government is in charge of maintaining

the health and vitality of inland waterways used for transporting goods and people and for protecting river communities from floods. Over many years, the Army Corps of Engineers has built and maintained an elaborate system of levees on the lower Mississippi to straighten it and prevent flooding of low-lying cities, including New Orleans. Despite many warnings from scientists and engineers that the levee system was inadequate, Democratic and Republican presidents and Congresses failed to provide funds for a levee system that could adequately protect the city. For its part, FEMA failed to pre-position enough rescue teams and supplies and responded slowly when the levees broke. Finally, it took the president and his team a few days to realize that state and local officials were simply overwhelmed.

The Louisiana state government also failed to meet some of its core responsibilities. It did not come close to implementing its own disaster mitigation and relief plan. Furthermore, over the years it had adopted a series of tax, subsidy, and regulatory policies that encouraged construction along low-lying coastal areas, putting people at risk and helping destroy wetlands that once protected populated areas from hurricane storm surges. Nor did local New Orleans officials meet their core responsibilities. The mayor delayed in ordering a mandatory evacuation, failed to provide transportation for people without cars once the order was given, and failed to provide adequate policing during and after the emergency. In addition, city officials had for years avoided upgrading and protecting vital infrastructure (pumps, sewage treatment facilities, emergency medical services, and more) or improving building codes for residential and commercial structures.

Some of the problems surrounding Katrina arose from very real confusion about who was to do what when.[2] Traditionally, state and local governments have been the first responders to disasters, with the federal government providing backup, financial and logistical aid, and help with long-term recovery. The federal government will enter the picture earlier if state officials ask, or if federal officials determine that state and local officials cannot protect their citizens. But that didn't happen with Katrina; communication broke down. White House officials claim, for example, that Governor Blanco refused to ask the federal government to take control of the Louisiana National Guard and New Orleans police. They also said they wanted to send the 82nd Airborne to restore order and coordinate logistics, but hesitated because the governor had not made a specific request. The governor said she told President Bush, "I need everything you have got." She never specified what kinds of troops she needed because "nobody told me that I had to request that. I thought that I requested everything they had. . . . We were in a war zone by then."

Though the Gulf deep well blowout and subsequent environmental tragedy in 2010 was not the result of a natural event as in the case of Katrina—British Petroleum's negligence and lax regulatory oversight seem to have been the main culprits—the governmental response was eerily similar, with lack of cooperation and jurisdictional disputes central features of the aftermath. The Katrina and Gulf oil spill cases show that American federalism is a very complex system in which both cooperation and tension exist among the various levels of government. In this chapter, you will learn about the American system of federalism, where it came from, how it works, what strengths and weaknesses are associated with it, and how it contributes to or detracts from democracy.

THINKING CRITICALLY About This Chapter

This complex mixture of state and national government authority and responsibilities highlighted in the story of the response to Hurricane Katrina is an important characteristic of American federalism today and in the past.

Using the FRAMEWORK

In this chapter, you will learn how and why federalism is one of the most important structural factors that affect American politics and government and shape public policy. You will learn how federalism influences our entire system, from the kinds of political parties we have and the workings of Congress to how domestic programs are affected. You will also learn how federalism itself has changed over time.

Using the DEMOCRACY STANDARD

Using the evaluative tools you learned in Chapter 1, you will be able to judge for yourself whether federalism enriches or diminishes democracy in the United States.

Federalism as a System of Government

3.1 Define federalism and explain why we have it

The United States is full of governments. We have not only a federal government in Washington, D.C., but also governments in each of the 50 states and in each of thousands of smaller governmental units, such as counties (about 3,000 of them), cities, towns and townships, school districts, and special districts that deal with such matters as parks and sanitation.

All these governments are organized and related to each other in a particular way. The small governments—those of counties, cities, towns, and special districts—are legal creations of state governments. They can be created, changed, or abolished by state legislatures or by state constitutional revisions, at the convenience of the states or its voters. But state governments themselves have much more weight and permanence because of their prominent place in the Constitution. Together with the central government in Washington, D.C., they form what is known as a federal system. The *federal system* is part of the basic structure of U.S. government, deeply rooted in our Constitution and history. It is one of the most important features of American politics, since it affects practically everything else.

SECTARIAN VIOLENCE IN IRAQ   Deep divisions among Sunnis, Shias, and Kurds in Iraq made it inevitable that the nation's constitution would take the form of a federation in which no single group controls the central government. Widespread sectarian violence, as seen in this scene from a suicide bombing in Baghdad in 2007, underscored this point to constitution makers. Were there similar ethnic and religious divisions among America's framers?

The Nature of Federalism

Federalism is a system under which significant government powers are divided between the central government and smaller units, such as states or provinces. Neither one completely controls the other; each has some room for independent action. A federal system can be contrasted with two other types of government: a confederation and a unitary government. In a **confederation,** the constituent states get together for certain common purposes but retain ultimate individual authority and can veto major central governmental actions. The United Nations and the American government under the Articles of Confederation are examples. In a **unitary system,** the central government has all the power and can change its constituent units or tell them what to do. China, Japan, the United Kingdom, Iran, and France have this kind of government, as do a substantial majority of nations around the world. These three different types of governmental systems are contrasted in Figure 3.1.

Comparing American Federalism

Some of the elements of federalism go back in history at least as far as the Union of Utrecht in the Netherlands in 1579, but federalism as it exists today is largely an American invention,[3] although it has come to take on a variety of forms internationally. Including the United States, only 18 nations, accounting for more than one-third of the world's population and 40 percent of its land area, are federal in nature.[4]

Historical Origins of American Federalism   American federalism emerged from the way in which the states declared independence from Britain—becoming, in effect, separate countries—and then joined to form a confederation and then a single nation, as discussed in Chapter 2. Recall that the framers of the Constitution turned to federalism as a middle-ground solution between a confederation form of government—which was deemed a failed model based on the experience under the Articles of Confederation—and a unitary form of government—which a majority of states, jealous of their independence and prerogatives, found unacceptable. Federalism was also a form of government that was consistent with the eighteenth-century republicanism of the framers because it helps

federalism

A system in which governmental powers are divided between a central government and smaller units, such as states.

confederation

A loose association of states or territorial divisions in which very little power or no power at all is lodged in a central government.

unitary system

A system in which a central government has complete power over its constituent units or states.

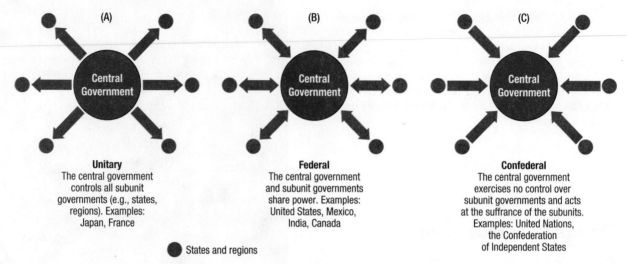

Unitary
The central government controls all subunit governments (e.g., states, regions). Examples: Japan, France

Federal
The central government and subunit governments share power. Examples: United States, Mexico, India, Canada

Confederal
The central government exercises no control over subunit governments and acts at the suffrance of the subunits. Examples: United Nations, the Confederation of Independent States

● States and regions

FIGURE 3.1 Types of Political Systems

A majority of countries have unitary systems (A), in which the central government controls the state and local governments, which in turn exert power over the citizens. The United States, however, has a federal system (B), in which the central government has power on some issues, the states have power on other issues, and the central and state governments share power on yet others. In a confederation (C), the central institutions have only a loose coordinating role, with real governing power residing in the constituent states or units.

fragment government power. But we can gain further insight into *why* the United States adopted and has continued as a federal system if we look at what other countries with similar systems have in common.

Role of Size and Diversity Federalism tends to be found in nations that are large in a territorial sense and in which the various geographical regions are fairly distinctive from one another in terms of religion, ethnicity, language, and forms of economic activity. In Canada, for example, the farmers of the central plains are not much like the fishers of Nova Scotia, and the French-speaking (and primarily Catholic) residents of Quebec differ markedly from the mostly English-speaking Protestants of the rest of the country. In Spain there are deep divisions along ethnic and language lines (as in the distinctive Basque and Catalan regions).[5] Other important federal systems include such large and richly diverse countries as India, Pakistan, Russia, and Brazil. In all these countries, federalism gives diverse and geographically concentrated groups the degree of local autonomy they seem to want, with no need to submit in all matters to a unified central government.

> Do you think that it would be possible to have a unitary system in a nation as large and diverse as the United States? Would it be possible for such a system to be democratic?

The United States, too, is large and diverse. From the early days of the republic, the slave-holding and agriculture-oriented South was quite distinct from the mercantile Northeast, and some important differences persist today. Illinois is not Louisiana; the farmers of Iowa differ from defense and electronics workers in California. States today also vary in their approaches to public policy, their racial and ethnic composition, and their political cultures.[6] In *The Federalist Papers*, the Founders argued that this size and diversity made federalism especially appropriate for the new United States.

While the American system of federalism was truly exceptional at the founding, other large and important countries have taken on federal forms in the years since, especially since the end of World War II. To this extent, the United States is no longer the single exception or one among a handful of exceptions to the unitary nature of the majority of the world's governments.

Federalism in the Constitution

3.2 Establish the basis for federalism in the Constitution

Federalism is embodied in the U.S. Constitution in two main ways: (1) power is expressly given to the states, as well as to the national government, and (2) the states have important roles in shaping, and choosing officials for, the national government itself, and in amending the Constitution.

Independent State Powers

Although the Constitution makes the central government supreme in certain matters, it also makes clear that the state governments have independent powers. The **supremacy clause** in Article VI states that the Constitution, laws, and treaties of the United States shall be the "supreme law of the land," but Article I, Section 8, enumerates what kinds of laws Congress has the power to pass, and the **Tenth Amendment** declares that the powers not delegated to the central government by the Constitution or prohibited by the Constitution to the states are "*reserved to the states* [emphasis added] respectively, or to the people." This provision is known as the **reservation clause.**

In other words, the U.S. Constitution specifically lists what the national government can do. Its powers include authority to levy taxes, regulate interstate commerce, establish post offices, and declare war, plus make laws "necessary and proper" for carrying out those powers. The Constitution then provides that all other legitimate government functions may be performed by the states, except for a few things, such as coining money or conducting foreign policy, that are forbidden by Article I, Section 10. This leaves a great deal in the hands of state governments, including licensing lawyers, doctors, and dentists; regulating businesses within their boundaries; chartering banks and corporations; providing a system of family law; providing a system of public education; and assuming the responsibility for building roads and highways, licensing drivers, and registering cars. Under terms of the reservation clause, states exercise what are called their police powers to protect the health, safety, and general well-being of people living in their states. The police powers have allowed states to make decisions independent of the federal government and other states on matters such as stem-cell research, minimum gas mileage standards for cars, the death penalty, emissions of greenhouse gases, and the regulation of abortion services.[7] The reservation clause is unique to the United States and shows how important states are in American federalism. Other federal systems, such as Canada's and Germany's, reserve to the national government all functions not explicitly given to the states.

Lest this sound too clear-cut, there also are broad areas of overlapping or shared powers—called **concurrent powers;** both levels of government, for example, can and do levy taxes, borrow

---

supremacy clause

The provision in Article VI of the Constitution that the Constitution itself and the laws and treaties of the United States are the supreme law of the land, taking precedence over state laws and constitutions when they are in conflict.

Tenth Amendment

Part of the Bill of Rights, the Amendment that says that those powers not given to the federal government and not prohibited for the states by the Constitution are reserved for the states and the people.

reservation clause

The Tenth Amendment to the Constitution, reserving powers to the states or the people.

concurrent powers

Powers under the Constitution that are shared by the federal government and the states.

? What issues do you think are best handled locally? Are there others that you think that the federal government is better equipped to handle? Is there any specific national policy that you would rather see in state hands, or vice versa?

money for public purposes, and spend money for the protection and well-being of their populations (e.g., public health programs and product safety regulation). With both independent national and state powers and responsibilities, as well as concurrent or overlapping powers and responsibilities, the Constitution is not crystal clear about the exact shape of federalism, leaving ample room for the meaning of federalism to change with the times, the preferences of the American people, and the calculations of political leaders. Figure 3.2 shows how powers and responsibilities are distributed.

The States' Roles in National Government

Moreover, the Constitution's provisions about the formation of the national government recognize a special position for the states. The Constitution declares in Article VII that it was "done in Convention by the unanimous consent of the *states* present" (emphasis added) and provides that the Constitution would go into effect not when a majority of all Americans voted for it but when the conventions of nine *states* ratified it. Article V provides that the Constitution can be amended only when conventions in or the legislatures of three-quarters of the states ratify an amendment. Article IV, Section 3, makes clear that no states can be combined or divided into new states without the consent of the state legislatures concerned. Thus, the state governments have charge of ratifying and amending the Constitution, and the states control their own boundaries.

The Constitution also provides special roles for the states in the selection of national government officials. The states decide who can vote for members of the U.S. House of Representatives (Article I, Section 2) and draw the boundaries of House districts. Each state is given two senators (Article V) who were, until 1913, to be chosen by the state legislatures rather than by the voters (Article I, Section 3; altered by the Seventeenth Amendment). And the states play a key part in the complicated Electoral College system of choosing a president in which each state has votes equal to the number of its senators and representatives combined, with the president elected by a majority of *electoral* votes, not a majority of popular votes (Article II, Section 1).

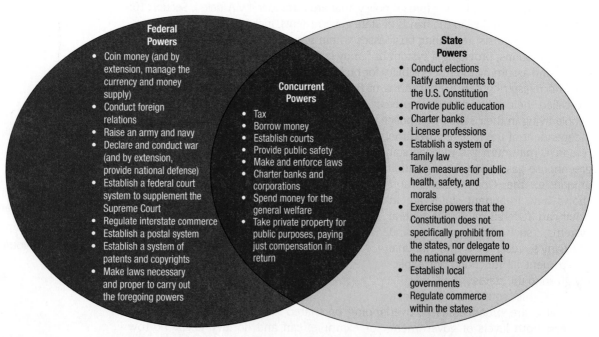

Federal Powers
- Coin money (and by extension, manage the currency and money supply)
- Conduct foreign relations
- Raise an army and navy
- Declare and conduct war (and by extension, provide national defense)
- Establish a federal court system to supplement the Supreme Court
- Regulate interstate commerce
- Establish a postal system
- Establish a system of patents and copyrights
- Make laws necessary and proper to carry out the foregoing powers

Concurrent Powers
- Tax
- Borrow money
- Establish courts
- Provide public safety
- Make and enforce laws
- Charter banks and corporations
- Spend money for the general welfare
- Take private property for public purposes, paying just compensation in return

State Powers
- Conduct elections
- Ratify amendments to the U.S. Constitution
- Provide public education
- Charter banks
- License professions
- Establish a system of family law
- Take measures for public health, safety, and morals
- Exercise powers that the Constitution does not specifically prohibit from the states, nor delegate to the national government
- Establish local governments
- Regulate commerce within the states

▌ FIGURE 3.2 How Responsibilities Are Distributed in the Federal System

THEN-GOVERNOR SCHWARZENEGGER "FILLS 'ER UP" With the federal government slow to respond to the rising price of gasoline and the problem of global warming, several states have taken it upon themselves to move ahead on the development of alternative energies. California, in particular, has been a leader in directly funding and offering tax breaks for research in alternative energies and requiring their use in everyday life as a way to reduce greenhouse gases. Do you think issues such as gas prices should be dealt with by the federal government? Why or why not?

Relations Among the States

The Constitution also regulates relations among the states (these state-to-state relations are sometimes called **horizontal federalism**). Article IV of the Constitution is particularly important in this regard (see Table 3.1). For example, each state is required to give "full faith and credit" to the public acts, records, and judicial proceedings of every other state. This means that private contractual or financial agreements among people or companies in one state are valid in all the other states and that civil judgments by the courts of one state must be recognized by the others. Because of this constitutional provision, people in one state cannot evade financial obligations—for example, credit card or department store debts, alimony and child-support payments—by moving to another state.

The "full faith and credit" provision is what worries some people about the legalization of same-sex marriage in a handful of states: Maine, Vermont, New Hampshire, Massachusetts, Connecticut, and Iowa, as of 2010. When people of the same sex are married in these states, do they remain legally married when they move elsewhere? Are they eligible for federal benefits that go to married heterosexual couples? Worried about the possibility that such things might happen, Congress passed the Defense of Marriage Act (DOMA), denying federal benefits (such as Medicaid and Medicare) to spouses in same-sex marriages and authorized states that wished to do so to enact legislation barring recognition of same-sex marriages from other states. As of 2010, 40 states had done so, either by statute or constitutional change. While the Supreme Court has yet to decide a case involving the "full faith and credit" obligations of the states on this issue, it has permitted Congress broad latitude in regulating interstate relations on other matters in the past, so it is unlikely that it will void DOMA on these grounds (though a federal district judge ruled in 2010 that the act violated the equal protection clause of the Fourteenth Amendment).[8]

Article IV also specifies that the citizens of each state are entitled to all the "privileges and immunities" of the citizens in the several states. That means that whatever citizenship rights a person has in one state

horizontal federalism

Term used to refer to relationships among the states.

TABLE 3.1 Constitutional Underpinnings of Federalism

Provisions	Where to Find Them in the Constitution	What It Means
Supremacy of the national government in its own sphere	Supremacy clause: Article VI	The supremacy clause establishes that federal laws and the Constitution take precedence over state laws and constitutions.
Limitations on national government powers and reservation of powers to the states	Enumerated national powers: Article I, Section 8	The powers of the federal government are laid out specifically in the Constitution, as are strict limitations on the power of the federal government. Powers not specifically spelled out are reserved to the states or to the people.
	Limits on national powers: Article I, Section 9; Article IV, Section 3; Eleventh Amendment	
	Bill of Rights: First through Tenth Amendments	
	Reservation clause: Tenth Amendment	
Limitations on state powers	Original restrictions: Article I, Section 10	The Constitution places strict limitations on the power of the states in particular areas of activity.
	Civil War Amendments: Thirteenth through Fifteenth Amendments	Compels the states to uphold the civil liberties and civil rights of people living there.
State role in national government	Ratification of Constitution: Article VII	The states' role in national affairs is clearly laid out. Rules for voting and electing representatives, senators, and the president are defined so that state governments play a part.
	Amendment of Constitution: Article V	
	Election of representatives: Article I, Section 2 and Section 4	
	Two senators from each state: Article I, Section 3	
	No deprivation of state suffrage in Senate: Article V Choice of senators: Article I, Section 3 (however, see Seventeenth Amendment)	
	Election of president: Article II, Section 1 (however, see Twelfth Amendment)	
Regulation of relations among states	Full faith and credit: Article IV, Section 1	Constitutional rules ensure that the states must respect each other's legal actions
	Privileges and immunities: Article IV, Section 2	

apply in the other states as well. For example, because of this provision, out-of-state residents have the same access to state courts as in-state residents, as well as an equal right to own property and to be protected by the police. However, the Supreme Court has never clearly defined the meaning of "privileges and immunities" nor have they been entirely consistent in applying them in practice. The Court has allowed states to charge students different tuition rates in their public universities, for example, depending on their in-state or out-of-state status (see the "Using the Framework" feature later in this chapter).

Agreements among a group of states to solve mutual problems, called **interstate compacts,** require the consent of Congress. The framers inserted this provision (Article I, Section 10) into the Constitution

interstate compacts
Agreements among states to cooperate on solving mutual problems; requires approval by Congress.

BORDER FENCE How to control illegal immigration across the U.S.–Mexican border, and what to do about those who make it across, have become contentious issues between several border states and the federal government. Why might this be an issue where some state majorities conflict with the wishes of the national majority?

as a way to prevent the emergence of coalitions of states that might threaten federal authority or the union itself. Interstate compacts in force today cover a wide range of cooperative state activities. For example, New York and New Jersey created and Congress approved a compact to create the Port of New York Authority. Other compacts among states include agreements to cooperate on matters such as pollution control, crime prevention, transportation, and disaster planning.

The Evolution of American Federalism

3.3 Trace the evolution of American federalism

It took a long time after the adoption of the Constitution for the present federal system to emerge. There were and continue to be ebbs and flows in the nature of the relationship between the states and national government and in the relative power of the states and the federal government as they interacted with one another.[9] Eventually, however, the national government gained ground.[10] There are many reasons for this:

- Economic crises and problems generated pressures on the government in Washington to do something to help fix the national economy. The Great Depression in the 1930s is the primary example, but even today, we expect the president, Congress, and the Federal Reserve to competently manage national economic affairs, something the states cannot do for themselves. Most Americans wanted the government in Washington to do something to get us out of the deep recession of 2008–2009, though many did not like what was done in the end (bailing out banks without limiting executive pay and bonuses in financial firms proved extremely unpopular).

- War and the preparation for war are also important spurs to national-level actions, rather than state-level ones, because it is only the government in Washington that can raise an army and a navy, generate sufficient revenues to pay for military campaigns, and coordinate the productive resources of the

nationalist position
The view of American federalism that holds that the Constitution created a system in which the national government is supreme, relative to the states, and that it granted that government a broad range of powers and responsibilities.

necessary and proper clause
Article I, Section 8, of the Constitution, also known as the *elastic clause;* gives Congress the authority to make whatever laws are necessary and proper to carry out its enumerated responsibilities.

states' rights position
The view of American federalism that holds that the Constitution created a system of dual sovereignty in which the national government and the state governments are sovereign in their own spheres.

nation to make sustained war possible. It is no accident, then, that each of our major wars has served to enhance the power of government in Washington.

- Finally, a number of problems emerged over the course of our history that most political leaders and the public believed could be solved most effectively by the national government rather than by 50 separate state governments: air and water pollution; unsafe food, drugs, and consumer products; the denial of civil rights for racial minorities; anticompetitive practices by some large corporations; poverty; and more.

The Perpetual Debate About the Nature of American Federalism

From the very beginnings of our nation, two political philosophies have contended with one another over the nature of American federalism and the role to be played by the central government. These are generally referred to as the nationalist position and the states' rights position.

The Nationalist Position
Nationalists believe that the Constitution was formed by a compact among the people to create a single national community, pointing to the powerful phrase that opens the preamble: "We the People of the United States" (not "We the States"). Nationalists also point to the clear expression in the preamble of the purposes for which "we the people" formed a new government, namely to "create a more perfect union…and to promote the General Welfare." Also important in the nationalist brief are provisions in the Constitution that point toward a strong central government with expansive responsibilities, including the "commerce clause," the "supremacy clause," and the "elastic" or **"necessary and proper" clause.** Not surprisingly, proponents of the nationalist position such as Alexander Hamilton, Chief Justice John Marshall, Abraham Lincoln, Woodrow Wilson, and the two Roosevelts (Theodore and Franklin) advocated an active national government with the capacity and the will to tackle whatever problems might emerge to threaten the peace and prosperity of the United States or the general welfare of its people. Liberal Democrats, including President Barack Obama, are the main proponents of this position today, believing that civil rights and environmental protection, for example, are safer in the hands of the federal government than the state governments.

The States' Rights Position
Proponents of the states' rights position argue that the Constitution was created as a compact among the states and that the framers meant for the states to be coequal with the national government. They base their argument on a number of things. They note, for instance, that the Constitution was written by representatives of the states; that it was ratified by the states and not by a vote of the public; and that the process for amending the Constitution requires the affirmative votes of three-fourths of the states, not three-fourths of the people. They also point to the Tenth Amendment's "reservation" clause, which says, as we pointed out earlier, that powers not given to the national government nor denied to the states reside in the states and the people.

Not surprisingly, proponents of the states' rights position have argued that the Constitution created a form

? Does a nationalist or states' rights position make the most sense in the United States today? Should the states have more power than they do now, or should the national government have more—or is it just about right?

of government in which the national government is strictly limited in size and responsibility and in which states retain broad autonomy in the conduct of their own affairs. Popular among states' rights proponents is the concept of **dual federalism,** which suggests that, much like in a layer cake, there are distinct, nonoverlapping areas of responsibility for the national government and the state governments and that each level of government is sovereign in its own sphere. Thomas Jefferson, John C. Calhoun, the New England and Southern secessionists, the southern resistors to the civil rights revolution, and many contemporary conservative Republican Tea Party activists are associated with this view of federalism.

> **dual federalism**
> An interpretation of federalism in which the states and the national government have separate jurisdictions and responsibilities.
>
> **nullification**
> An attempt by states to declare national laws or actions null and void.

We shall see in the pages ahead that the nationalist view has prevailed over the long haul of American history. However, the states' rights view has always been and remains today a vital position from which to oppose too much power and responsibility in the government in Washington. After the Health Reform bill was passed in 2010, for example, several states passed laws and referenda proclaiming that the mandatory health insurance provisions of the national law did not hold within their boundaries. Utah and Wyoming passed laws in the same year stating that the federal government could not regulate firearms manufactured and sold there. (See Figure 3.3 for an overview of this history.)

Federalism Before the Civil War

In the late 1790s, during the administration of John Adams, Thomas Jefferson's Democratic Republicans deeply resented the Alien and Sedition Acts, which the Federalists used to punish political dissent by followers of Jefferson. In response, Jefferson and Madison secretly authored the Virginia and Kentucky Resolutions, which declared that the states did not have to obey unconstitutional national laws and left it to the states to decide what was unconstitutional. In this case, the Democratic Republicans, representing the more agricultural South, were advocating states' rights and the principle of dual federalism against a national government run by the more merchant-oriented Federalists of the Northeast. About a decade later, however, the merchants of New England used the southerners' own arguments to oppose President Madison's War of 1812 against Britain, which they felt interfered with their trade. Neither of these efforts at **nullification** prevailed.

One crucial question about federalism in the early years of the United States concerned who, if anyone, would enforce the supremacy clause. Who would make sure that the U.S. laws and Constitution were actually the "supreme law of the land," controlling state laws? The answer turned out to be the U.S. Supreme Court, but this answer emerged only gradually and haltingly as the Court established its power within the federal system. Only after the strong-willed and subtle John Marshall became chief justice and, in 1803, established the Supreme Court's authority to declare national laws unconstitutional (called judicial review; discussed in detail in Chapter 14) did the Supreme Court turn to the question of national power relative to the states. In *Fletcher* v. *Peck* (1810), it established the power of judicial review over the states, holding a state law unconstitutional under the U.S. Constitution.[11] Chief Justice Marshall cleverly avoided explicit discussion of the Court's power of judicial review over state laws. He simply took it for granted and used it.

The Supreme Court also provided crucial legal justification for the expansion of federal government power in the historic case of *McCulloch* v. *Maryland* (1819). The case involved action by the state of Maryland to impose a tax on the Bank of the United States. The state of Maryland argued that the creation of the bank had been

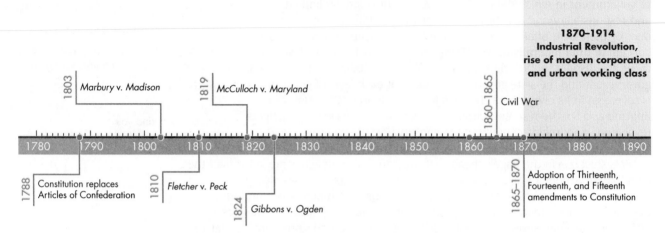

FIGURE 3.3 Timeline: Landmarks in the History of U.S. Federalism*

*Additional information provided only for items not discussed in the text.

unconstitutional, exceeding the powers of Congress, and that, in any case, states could tax whatever they wanted within their own borders.

But Chief Justice Marshall upheld the constitutionality of the bank's creation and its immunity from taxation and, in the process, made a major statement justifying extensive national authority.[12] In his opinion for the Court, Marshall declared that the Constitution emanated from the sovereign people who had made their national government supreme to all rivals within the sphere of its powers, and those powers must be construed generously if they were to be sufficient for the "various crises" of the age to come. Congress, declared Marshall, had the power to incorporate the bank under the clause of Article I, Section 8, authorizing Congress to make all laws "necessary and proper" for carrying into execution its named powers. Moreover, Maryland's tax was invalid because "the power to tax involves the power to destroy," which would defeat the national government's supremacy. Justice Marshall's broad reading of the *necessary and proper* clause laid the foundation for an expansion of what the national government could do in the years ahead. He made it clear that states would not be allowed to interfere.

In several later cases, the Supreme Court also ruled that provisions of the U.S. Constitution *excluded* the states from acting in certain areas where they might interfere with federal statutes or authority. According to this doctrine known as **preemption,** which remains in place today,[13] states cannot act in certain matters when the national government has done so.

The Civil War and the Expansion of National Power

The Civil War profoundly affected the relationship between the states and the national government. First, the unconditional southern surrender decisively established that the Union was indissoluble; states could not withdraw or secede. Hardly any American now questions the permanence of the Union.

Second, passage of what has become known as the **Civil War Amendments** resulted in constitutional changes that subordinated the states to certain new national standards, enforced by the central government. For example, the Thirteenth Amendment abolished slavery,

preemption

Exclusion of the states from actions that might interfere with federal authority or statutes.

Civil War Amendments

The Thirteenth, Fourteenth, and Fifteenth Amendments to the Constitution, adopted immediately after the Civil War.

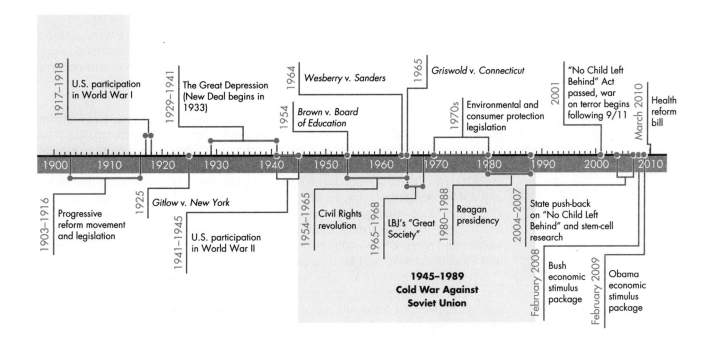

and the Fifteenth gave former male slaves and their descendants a constitutional right to vote. (This right was enforced by the national government for a short time after the Civil War; it was then widely ignored until passage of the 1965 Voting Rights Act.)

Moreover, the Fourteenth Amendment (1868) included broad language going well beyond the slave issue: it declared that *no state* shall "deprive any person of life, liberty, or property, without due process of law; nor deny to any person within its jurisdiction the equal protection of the laws." The **due process clause** eventually became the vehicle by which the Supreme Court ruled that many civil liberties in the Bill of Rights, which originally protected people only against the national government, also provided protections against the states. (See Chapter 15.) And the **equal protection clause** eventually became the foundation for protecting the rights of blacks, women, and other categories of people against discrimination by state or local governments. (See Chapter 16.)

Expanded National Activity Since the Civil War

Since the Civil War, and especially during the twentieth century, the activities of the national government expanded greatly, so that they now touch on almost every aspect of daily life and are thoroughly entangled with state government activities.

The Late Nineteenth Century to World War I During the late nineteenth century, the national government was increasingly active in administering western lands, subsidizing economic development (granting railroads enormous tracts of land along their transcontinental lines), helping farmers, and beginning to regulate business, particularly through the Interstate Commerce Act of 1887 and the Sherman Antitrust Act of 1890. Woodrow Wilson's New Freedom domestic legislation—including the Federal Reserve Act of 1913 and the Federal Trade Commission Act of

due process clause

The section of the Fourteenth Amendment that prohibits states from depriving anyone of life, liberty, or property "without due process of law," a guarantee against arbitrary or unfair government action.

equal protection clause

The section of the Fourteenth Amendment that provides equal protection of the laws to all persons.

1914—spurred even greater national government involvement in social and economic issues as did the great economic and military effort of World War I. During that war, for example, the War Industries Board engaged in a form of economic planning whose orders and regulations covered a substantial number of the nation's manufacturing firms.

The New Deal and World War II

Still more important, however, was Franklin Roosevelt's New Deal of the 1930s. In response to the Great Depression, the New Deal created many new national regulatory agencies to supervise various aspects of business, including communications (the Federal Communications Commission, or FCC), airlines (the Civil Aeronautics Board, or CAB), financial markets (the Securities and Exchange Commission, or SEC), utilities (the Federal Power Commission, or FPC), and labor–management relations (the National Labor Relations Board, or NLRB). The New Deal also brought national government spending to such areas as welfare and relief, which had previously been reserved almost entirely to the states, and established the Social Security pension system.

World War II involved a total economic and military mobilization to fight Germany and Japan. Not surprisingly, directing that mobilization, as well as collecting taxes to support it, planning for production of war materials, and bringing on board the employees to accomplish all of this, was centered in Washington, D.C., not in the states.

The Post-War Period

Ever since World War II, the federal government has spent nearly twice as much per year as all of the states and localities put together. Much of the money has gone in direct payments to individuals (including, most especially, Social Security benefits) and for national defense, particularly during the height of the Cold War with the Soviet Union, and during the Vietnam War.

OUR BLOODY CIVIL WAR One important principle of American federalism was settled by the Civil War: the nation is indissoluble; no state or group of states can decide on its own to withdraw from it. Establishing that principle required a bloody contest of arms. Here, Union dead litter the field at Gettysburg in 1863, a Union victory and a key turning point in the war. Why was this issue so crucial to the survival of the country?

PUTTING PEOPLE TO WORK   The Works Progress Administration (WPA), created by Franklin Roosevelt as part of the New Deal, put many unemployed Americans to work on federal building projects during the Great Depression. How does the legacy of the WPA survive today?

Two other trends in the last third of the twentieth century enhanced the role of the national government relative to the states. The first was the civil rights revolution (discussed in Chapters 8 and 16), and the second was the regulatory revolution, especially regulation re-

? Many increases in federal government activity have resulted from national and international events and trends, including wars, economic depression, and increases in the size and population of the country. What kinds of circumstances might lead to decreases in federal government activity?

lated to environmental protection (discussed in Chapter 17). With respect to both, national standards, often fashioned by bureaucrats under broad legislative mandates and watched over by federal courts, were imposed on both states and localities. The civil rights revolution also had a great deal to do with the creation of Lyndon Johnson's Great Society program designed both to alleviate poverty and politically empower the poor and racial minorities. The Great Society not only increased the level of domestic spending but also increased the federal role in the political lives of states and localities.

The Supreme Court's Support for the Nationalist Position   For several decades, beginning in the late nineteenth century, the U.S. Supreme Court resisted the growth in the federal government's power to regulate business. In 1895, for example, it said that the Sherman Antitrust Act could not forbid monopolies in manufacturing, since manufacturing affected interstate commerce only "indirectly." In 1918, the Court struck down as unconstitutional a national law regulating child labor. During the 1930s, the Supreme Court declared unconstitutional such important New Deal measures as the National Recovery Act and the Agricultural Adjustment Act.[14]

After 1937, perhaps chastened by President Roosevelt's attempt to enlarge the Supreme Court and appoint more friendly justices, the Court became a centralizing force, immediately upholding essential elements of the New Deal, including the Social Security Act and the National Labor Relations Act. Since that time, and until the Rehnquist Court began to rethink federalism questions in the 1990s, the Court upheld virtually every piece of national legislation that came before it even when this legislation preempted or limited powers of the states.

An important example is the Civil Rights Act of 1964, which rests on a very broad interpretation of the Constitution's commerce clause. In the 1964 act, the national government asserted a power to forbid discrimination at lunch counters and other public accommodations on the grounds that they are engaged in interstate commerce: they serve food imported from out of state. State economies are so closely tied to each other that by this standard, practically every economic transaction everywhere affects interstate commerce and is therefore subject to national legislative power.

Devolution

Devolution During the 1980s and 1990s, **devolution**—the idea that some of the powers and responsibilities of the national government ought to be distributed back to the states—became popular. President Ronald Reagan made this one of the hallmarks of his administration, as did George H. W. Bush, who followed him in office. President Bill Clinton, a former governor of the state of Arkansas, was also an enthusiastic devotee of devolution, freely granting waivers from federal regulations to the states for experimenting with new forms of welfare, boasting of cuts in federal government employment, and touting the benefits of state government. And the Republican majority in the 104th Congress, working with President Clinton (but few from his party), passed legislation restricting "unfunded mandates" (about which we will have more to say later) and transferring welfare responsibility to the states. The public seemed to be on board at the time. Polls showed, for example, that a substantial majority of Americans believed that state governments were more effective and more trustworthy than the government in Washington and more likely to be responsive to the people. And Americans said that they wanted state governments to do more and the federal government to do less.[15]

For a time during the height of devolution's popularity, the Rehnquist Court supported increasing the power of the states and decreasing that of the national government. It overruled a number of federal actions and laws on the ground that Congress had exceeded its constitutional powers, reversing more than half a century of decisions favoring an increased federal government role. In 1995, for example, the Court overturned federal legislation banning guns from the area around schools and legislation requiring background checks for gun buyers, arguing that both represented too broad a use of the commerce power in the Constitution. The Court used similar language in 2000 when it invalidated part of the Violence Against Women Act and in 2001 when it did the same to the Americans with Disabilities Act. However, in the last years of Rehnquist's leadership, the Court retreated a bit from this states' rights position, supporting federal law over that of the states on issues ranging from the use of medical marijuana to the juvenile death penalty, affirmative action, and gay rights.

National Power Reasserted

National Power Reasserted Talk of devolution ended with the Clinton presidency. George W. Bush, who followed Clinton in the Oval Office, signaled during the 2000 presidential campaign that he was willing to use the federal government to serve conservative ends. He termed his position "compassionate conservatism," suggesting that he would use the power of his office to try to, among other things, end abortion and protect the family, enhance educational performance, and do more to move people from welfare to jobs. While preserving his traditional Republican conservative credentials on a number of fronts on gaining the presidency—cutting taxes, for example, and pushing for looser environmental regulations on businesses—Bush gave a big boost to the power, cost, and scope of the federal government.[16] Most important was his sponsorship of the No Child Left Behind educational reform, which imposed testing mandates on the states, and a prescription drug benefit under Medicare, which substantially increased the cost of the program. Mandatory spending by the states on Medicaid also expanded rapidly during the Bush presidency.

devolution

The delegation of power by the central government to state or local bodies.

GUNS FOR SALE Many states and localities have tried to ban the importation of guns into their jurisdictions. Here, a gun dealer in Virginia in 2007 offers "Bloomberg gun give-away" tickets in honor of New York City Mayor Michael Bloomberg, who filed a federal lawsuit to keep out of his city guns bought in places with weak gun-control laws such as Virginia. The efforts of Mayor Bloomberg and others taking such actions were undermined in 2008 and again in 2010 when the Supreme Court ruled that gun ownership is an individual right under terms of the Second and Fourteenth Amendments. Why is the right to bear arms such an important issue to many Americans?

The terrorist attacks of September 11, 2001, the subsequent global "war on terrorism" (the president's phrase), and the wars in Iraq and Afghanistan further focused the nation's attention on national leaders in Washington, D.C. As in all wartime situations during our country's history, war and the mobilization for war require centralized coordination and planning. This tendency toward nationalism during war has been further exaggerated by the perceived need for enhancing homeland security, with the national government in Washington playing a larger role in areas such as law enforcement, intelligence gathering, bank oversight (to track terrorist money), public health (to protect against possible bioterrorism), and more. (These activities began during George W. Bush's presidency and continued during Barack Obama's.)

Perhaps inevitably, the flow of power to Washington during the Bush years triggered a reaction among the public and leaders in the states, disturbed by the increasing budget demands, regulatory burdens, and loss of state control tied to programs: the No Child Left Behind; the Real ID Act, aimed at standardizing driver's license issuance among the states; and changes in states' ability to write work rules in TANF (welfare program for the poor, discussed in Chapter 18). Combined with a sense among many at the state level that important national problems were being ignored and mishandled and the collapse in public support for President Bush and his policies after 2004, the ground was set for a rather extraordinary revitalization of state innovations.[17] Between 2004 and 2008, several states passed laws allowing, and sometimes subsidizing, stem-cell research. Others passed minimum wage legislation, while others legislated gas mileage requirements for cars and trucks. Many legislated incentives for companies and consumers to use energy more efficiently and find alternative fuel sources. California even passed legislation to reduce overall greenhouse gas emissions.

The economic crisis of 2008, 2009, and 2010, sometimes called the Great Recession (much like the Great Depression), generated an expanded role for the national government relative to the states in economic affairs. In the last months of

Federal dollars: Which states win and which ones lose?

Introduction Our system of federalism involves a complex set of relationships between the federal government and the states. These relationships are spelled out in the text of the Constitution; decisions of the Supreme Court, interpreting the meaning of constitutional provisions concerning federalism; and bills passed by Congress and signed by the president, creating federal programs and imposing taxes and regulations. One aspect of federalism that often draws attention is the flow of money between the federal government and the states. The flow goes in two directions. Money flows from people and firms in the states to the federal government in the form of taxes (income, corporate, excise, and

payroll). Money flows from the federal government to people and firms in the states in the form of grants-in-aid, block grants, and expenditures for specific programs (such as payments to defense contractors) and projects (such as payments for highways and bridges). Given the nature of the political process and differences in the needs and resources of people and firms in the states, some states will inevitably come out ahead in this process (get more money from Washington than they pay in taxes), and some will come out behind, paying more than they receive.

The Story in the Cartogram The cartogram shows winners and losers in the

federalism money story. The size of each state has been adjusted using a mathematical formula derived by Gastner and Newman that takes into account a simple ratio: federal funds received by each state on a per-capita basis divided by taxes paid by each state on a per-capita basis. If a state received and paid the same amount, the ratio would be 1, meaning that its size would not change in the cartogram. States that receive more from Washington than they pay in taxes have ratios higher than 1 and are expanded in the cartogram. States that receive less than they pay have ratios less than 1 and are reduced.

It is readily apparent that a number of states are winners, namely, those in the

the Bush presidency, Congress passed a $700 billion rescue package for financial institutions that gave the Treasury secretary broad powers to rescue and reorganize banks and investment firms even as the Federal Reserve (the Fed), under the leadership of Ben Bernanke, undertook its own rescue and reorganization efforts. These mandates greatly expanded the role of the federal government in managing the economy. When he became president, Barack Obama not only continued to support the efforts of the Treasury and the Fed to bolster the national economy, but insisted on the sale of Chrysler and the managed bankruptcy of General Motors as conditions of a rescue package. Within 30 days of his inauguration as president, moreover, Congress passed a $787 billion stimulus bill that did a great deal to backstop the states, almost all of whom were in deep budgetary crises. The stimulus package was a combination of tax cuts and new expenditures in programs that, among other things, extended unemployment benefits, funded new research and development in alternative energy sources, put monies into school construction and keeping teachers on the job, massively increased spending on infrastructure projects (i.e., roads, bridges, canals, and the like), and helped the states pay for some of their rising Medicaid outlays.

Perhaps most consequentially, in a long-term sense, President Obama and the Democratic Congress passed a health care bill that will transform America's health care system and a financial regulation bill they hope will prevent the type of financial collapse that happened in 2008 and brought on the Great Recession. President Obama also proposed a major effort to make the nation less dependent on fossil fuels, hoping that the tragic Gulf oil spill and the environmental disaster that followed would convince Americans that the time was ripe for such a change. Republicans and coal-state Democrats stopped the climate bill in the Senate, however, in July 2010.

southeast and the middle south, with Connecticut thrown in (their ratios are above 1, thus expanding their size in the cartogram), while a handful of large states are the biggest losers. Note how New York, Illinois, Texas, and California fare; each is dramatically diminished. They receive back from the federal government only a portion of what they pay in taxes.

What Do You Think? Why do monies flow between Washington and the states as they currently do? What would be the consequences if all states had similar money flow profiles? Do monies flow to where they are needed? Why do you think some states stand out from others on this issue? Where does your own state fit in the overall picture?

Sources: IRS Data Book for FY 2008 (Table 5); *Statistical Abstract of the United States, 2010* (Table 467); Michael T. Gastner and Mark E. J. Newman, "Diffusion-Based Method for Producing Density-Equalizing Maps," *Proceedings of the National Academy of Sciences* 101 (May 18, 2004), pp. 7499–7504.

State Sizes Adjusted to Reflect Ratio of Federal Taxes Paid and Federal Monies Received per Capita

Standard US Map

As suggested earlier in this chapter, there has been a great deal of push-back at this increase in national government power relative to the states. Several states, primarily Republican in their voting habits, have passed laws opposing the health care initiative, for example. The Tea Party movement, to take another example, complains vociferously about the size, cost, and intrusiveness of the federal government.

Changing American Federalism   Today's federalism is very different from what it was in the 1790s or early 1800s.[18] One major difference is that the national government is dominant in many policy areas; it calls many shots for the states. Another difference is that state and national government powers and activities have become deeply intertwined and entangled. The old, simple metaphor for federalism was a "layer cake": a system of dual federalism in which state and national powers were neatly divided into separate layers, with each level of government going its own way, unencumbered by the other. If we stay with bakery images, a much more accurate metaphor for today's federalism is a "marble cake," in which elements of national and state influence swirl around each other, without very clear boundaries.[19] The "marble cake" itself has taken on several forms. During the 1960s and 1970s, for example, the federal and state governments seemed to many to be working smoothly together to solve problems, leading scholars and politicians to use the term **cooperative federalism** to characterize the period. Today, no one talks any longer of cooperative federalism, although no single term has replaced it.

Whether cooperative or not, our federal system today is a "marble cake" in which the federal government and state governments are densely intertwined. Much of this intertwining is a product of the financial links

cooperative federalism

Federalism in which the powers and responsibilities of the states and the national government are intertwined and in which they work together to solve common problems; said to have characterized the 1960s and 1970s.

among the national and state governments, which we address in the next section, as well as in the "Mapping American Politics" feature.

Fiscal Federalism

3.4 Analyze how federal grants structure national and state government relations

One of the most important elements of modern American federalism is **fiscal federalism**—the transfer of money from the national government to state and local governments. These **grants-in-aid** have been used to increase national government influence over what the states and localities do. The grants have grown from small beginnings to form a substantial part of state government budgets. In the following sections, you will learn how and why this trend began, what kinds of grants have and are being made, and how they affect national–state relationships.

Origin and Growth of Grants

National government grants to the states began at least as early as the 1787 Northwest Ordinance. The U.S. government granted land for government buildings, schools, and colleges in the Northwest Territory and imposed various regulations, such as forbidding slavery there. During the early nineteenth century, the federal government provided some land grants to the states for roads, canals, and railroads, as well as a little cash for militias; after 1862, it helped establish agricultural colleges. Some small cash-grant programs were begun around 1900 for agriculture, vocational education, and highways.[20]

However, it was during the 1950s, 1960s, and 1970s, under both Republican and Democratic administrations, that federal grants to the states really took off. Such programs as President Dwight Eisenhower's interstate highway system and President Lyndon Johnson's Great Society poured money into the states.[21] After a pause during the Reagan presidency, grants began to increase again in the 1990s (see Figure 3.4). Federal grants to the states increased because presidents and Congress sought to deal with many nationwide problems—especially transportation, education, HIV/AIDS, poverty, crime, and air and water pollution—by setting policy at the national level and providing money from national tax revenues, while having state and local officials carry out the policies. The big jump in grant totals in 2008 and 2009 were tied to various efforts by the federal government to stimulate the economy during the Great Recession, including assistance to states for Medicaid, unemployment insurance, education, and infrastructure.

Types of Grants

Over the years, many of the new programs were established through **categorical grants**, which give the states money but clearly specify the category of activity for which the money has to be spent and often define rather precisely how the program should work. For example, Lyndon Johnson's antipoverty initiatives—in the areas of housing, job training, medical assistance, and more—funneled substantial federal

fiscal federalism
That aspect of federalism having to do with federal grants to the states.

grants-in-aid
Funds from the national government to state and local governments to help pay for programs created by the national government.

categorical grants
Federal aid to states and localities clearly specifying what the money can be used for.

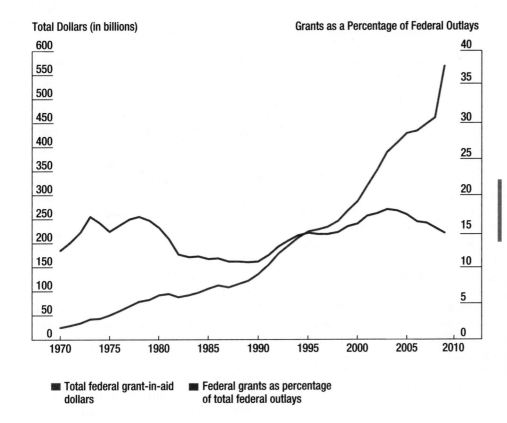

Total Dollars (in billions)

Grants as a Percentage of Federal Outlays

■ Total federal grant-in-aid dollars ■ Federal grants as percentage of total federal outlays

FIGURE 3.4 The Growth in Federal Grants-in-Aid to States and Localities

Federal grants-in-aid to state and local governments have grown steadily since 1970, the only exception being during the first half of the 1980s during the Reagan presidency. A big jump occurred in 2008 and 2009 as federal assistance to the states increased to address problems caused by the financial collapse and economic recession. *Source: Statistical Abstract of the United States*, 2010.

money to states and localities, but attached strict rules on how the money could be used.

Responding to complaints from the states, and seeking to reduce federal government power to better fit their ideas about the proper role of government, Republican presidents Nixon and Ford succeeded in convincing Congress to loosen centralized rules and oversight, first instituting **block grants** (which give money for more general purposes such as secondary education and with fewer rules than categorical grant programs), then, for a short time, **general revenue sharing**, which distributed money to the states with no federal controls at all. President Nixon spoke of a "New Federalism" and pushed to increase these kinds of grants with few strings attached. General revenue sharing ended in 1987 when even proponents of a smaller federal government realized that giving money to the states with "no strings attached" meant that elected officials in the federal government were losing influence over policies in which they wanted to have a say.

Categorical and block grants often provide federal money under an automatic formula related to the statistical characteristics of each state or locality (thus the term "formula grant"), such as the number of needy residents, the total size of the population, or the average income level. Disputes frequently arise when these formulas benefit one state or region rather than another. Because statistical counts by the census affect how much money the states and localities get, census counts themselves have become the subject of political conflict. Illinois, New York, and Chicago sued the Census Bureau for allegedly undercounting their populations, especially the urban poor, in the 1990 census. (See "By the Numbers" for more information about how population counts are done and why it matters.)

block grants
Federal grants to the states to be used for general activities.

general revenue sharing
Federal aid to the states without any conditions on how the money is to be spent.

conditional grants
Federal grants with provisions requiring that state and local governments follow certain policies in order to obtain funds.

mandate
A formal order from the national government that the states carry out certain policies.

Debates About Federal Money and Control

Most contemporary conflicts about federalism concern not just money but also control.

Conditions on Aid
As we have seen, categorical grant-in-aid programs require that the states spend federal money only in certain restricted ways. Even block grants—such as grants that support social welfare for the poor—have conditions attached, thus the term **conditional grants**. In theory, these conditions are "voluntary" because the states can refuse to accept the aid. But in practice, there is no clear line between incentives and coercion. Because the states cannot generally afford to give up federal money, they normally must accept the conditions attached to it.

Some of the most important provisions of the 1964 Civil Rights Act, for example, are those that declare that no federal aid of any kind can be used in ways that discriminate against people on grounds of race, gender, religion, or national origin. Thus, the enormous program of national aid for elementary and secondary education, which began in 1965, became a powerful lever for forcing schools to desegregate. To take another example, the federal government in 1984 used federal highway money to encourage states to adopt a minimum drinking age of 21.

Mandates
The national government often imposes a **mandate**, or demand, that the states carry out certain policies even when little or no national government aid is offered. (An "unfunded" mandate involves no aid at all or less aid than compliance will cost.) Mandates have been especially important in the areas of civil rights and the environment. Most civil rights policies flow from the equal protection clause of the Fourteenth Amendment to the U.S. Constitution or from national legislation that imposes uniform national standards. Most environmental regulations also come from the national government, since problems of dirty air, polluted water, and acid rain spill across state boundaries. Many civil rights and environmental regulations, therefore, are enforced by the federal courts.

Federal courts have, for example, mandated expensive reforms of overcrowded state prisons. National legislation and regulations have required state governments to provide costly special facilities for the disabled, to set up environmental protection agencies, and to limit the kinds and amounts of pollutants that can be discharged. The states often complain bitterly about federal mandates that require state spending without providing the money.

Cutting back on these "unfunded mandates" was one of the main promises in the Republicans' 1994 Contract with America.[22] The

SPEWING POLLUTION   Industrial pollution, such as these untreated emissions from this massive steel complex, often affects people of more than one state and requires the participation of the national government to clean up the mess and prevent recurrences. What role should the federal government take in environmental issues within states?

congressional Republicans delivered on their promise early in 1995 with a bill that had bipartisan support in Congress and that President Clinton signed into law. Because it did not apply to past mandates, however, and did not ban unfunded mandates but only regulated them (e.g., requiring cost-benefit analyses), unfunded mandates have continued to proliferate, as does the debate about their use. The main complaints coming from governors today concern the substantial costs imposed on the states by the No Child Left Behind testing program and by the rising costs to the states of required Medicaid support for certain categories of people. Pressures on state budgets became especially pronounced in from 2008 through 2010 when revenues from sales and other taxes plummeted because of the national economic downturn.

Preemption The doctrine of preemption, based on the supremacy clause in the Constitution and supported by a series of decisions by the Supreme Court, says that federal statutes and rules must prevail over state statutes and rules when the two are in conflict. Recently, for example, several states have attempted to tax Internet purchases by people residing in their jurisdictions, but Congress has forbidden them to do so. Research suggests that the number of preemption statutes passed by Congress has increased substantially over the past three decades and has been unaffected by which political party is in control.[23]

U.S. Federalism: Pro and Con

3.5 Evaluate the arguments for and against federalism

Over the years, from the framing of the U.S. Constitution to the present day, people have offered a number of strong arguments for and against federalism, in contrast to a more unitary system. Let us consider some of these arguments.

Pro: Diversity of Needs The oldest and most important argument in favor of decentralized government is that in a large and diverse country, needs and wants and conditions differ from one place to another. Why not let different states enact different policies to meet their own needs? California, New York, and New Jersey, for example, all densely populated, have tougher fuel mileage standards in place than those set by the federal government. (See the "Using the Framework" feature on tuition for out-of-state students.) The border state of Arizona, feeling overwhelmed by illegal immigrants, passed a law in 2010 allowing police to stop and interrogate people they think may be in the state illegally. A federal judge threw out most provisions of the law soon after. Arizona is appealing the decision.

Con: The Importance of National Standards However, the needs or desires that different states pursue may not be worthy ones. Political scientist William Riker has pointed out that, in the past, one of the main effects of federalism was to let white majorities in the southern states enslave and then discriminate against black people, without interference from the North.[24] Perhaps it is better, in some cases, to insist on national standards that apply everywhere.

How do we know how many people there are in each of the states?

Utah officials were angry. Convinced that the counting method used for the 2000 census had undercounted the number of people residing in the state, thereby "robbing" them of a congressional seat, they sued the U.S. Census Bureau.

How can something as simple as counting people become so controversial? And why are these census figures so important to states, anyway?

Why It Matters The Constitution specifies that every 10 years, a census will be taken of the population of the United States. One purpose of the census is to determine how the finite number of seats in the House of Representatives (435) will be divided among the states, based on the size of their populations. A state's population also determines how much federal money (e.g., highway money) it will get. Moreover, counts of certain categories of people, like the poor, determine how much aid (e.g., Medicaid) the state will receive.

The Story Behind the Number For most of our nation's history, the Census Bureau hired people to go door-to-door across the United States—from isolated farms to packed apartment buildings—to conduct a direct count of the population. Many people were missed in this process. Some were not home when the census takers came by; others lived in high-crime neighborhoods, where census takers did not want to venture; some had no home other than a crude shelter under a highway overpass. Recent immigrants had trouble communicating in English, and illegal aliens did not necessarily want to be found by census takers.

Indeed, the undercounted population in every recent census has been comprised mainly of racial minorities, recent immigrants, the homeless, and the undocumented. This pattern has generated complaints from a wide range of people and organizations: advocates of the poor who want more federal government monies directed to the problem of poverty in each state; civil rights organizations that believe that racial minorities are underrepresented in the House of Representatives; and Democratic Party politicians who believe that a more accurate count would benefit their party (the assumption being that lower income people, racial minorities, and recent immigrants tend to vote for Democrats).

In an attempt to remedy these undercount problems, the Census Bureau wanted to use "statistical sampling" of the population to fill in the gaps. However, the Supreme Court ruled in 1999 that the Bureau could not do so for purposes of reapportioning congressional seats, and President Bush announced that sampling could not be used to determine how much federal money the states would get. As an alternative, the Bureau has increasingly relied on a statistical procedure called "imputing."

Calculating Population Size and Characteristics Although Census Bureau statisticians have been using "imputing" in limited ways since the 1940s to fill in the gaps left by the inevitable undercounting, they relied much more on it for the 2000 and 2010 censuses. In imputing, estimates are made about the characteristics of people living in a household where the Bureau has been unable to collect information. The estimates are based on what their neighbors are like (whether they are poor or rich, white or African American, and so on).

In the 2000 census, using imputing, almost 6 million people who had not actually been counted were included in the nation's population total. In some states, most notably in those with large numbers of racial minorities and immigrants (including California, Arizona, New Mexico, and Texas), more than 3 percent of the state's total population was imputed. The Census Bureau reported roughly similar overall levels of imputing in the 2010 census.

This brings us back to the state of Utah. Utah's suit claimed that the Census Bureau had illegally imputed tens of thousands of additional people to the state of North Carolina, resulting in North Carolina receiving the congressional seat that properly should have gone to

Pro: Closeness to the People   It is sometimes claimed that state governments are closer to the ordinary citizens, who have a better chance to know their officials, to be aware of what they are doing, to contact them, and to hold them responsible for what they do.

Con: Low Visibility and Lack of Popular Control   However, others respond that geographic closeness may not be the real issue. More Americans are better informed about the federal government than they are about state governments, and more people participate in national than in state elections. When more people know what the government is doing and more people vote, they are better able to insist that the government do what they want. For that reason, responsiveness to ordinary citizens may actually be greater in national government.

Utah. Unfortunately for Utah, the Supreme Court approved imputing in 2002.

Imputing Criticized Although most statisticians believe that imputing is a reasonable way to solve the problem of undercounting, the technique has its critics:

- The Utah suit pointed out, and others agree, that imputing—much like more standard sampling—makes statistical inferences about parts of the population rather than counting people directly, as implied by the wording in the Constitution (Article I, Section 2).

- Imputing assumes that neighborhoods are homogenous; it is based on the assumption that a household's characteristics can be estimated from the characteristics of its neighbors. Members of several minority groups who tend to live in less segregated circumstances—Asians and Pacific Islanders, for example—may find themselves undercounted.

What to Watch For Official statistics are often published in both "adjusted" and "unadjusted" forms. "Adjusted" means that the raw information has been corrected in one way or another. Usually, the reasons for doing so are very reasonable and defensible. You might want to look at the documentation that is associated with all government statistical information to learn how the numbers have been "adjusted."

What Do You Think? In your view, does it make sense to depend solely on methods of counting the U.S. population that were in use at the time the Constitution was written? Are there good reasons to keep using traditional methods even if it can be shown that statistical methods such as imputing and sampling increase accuracy?

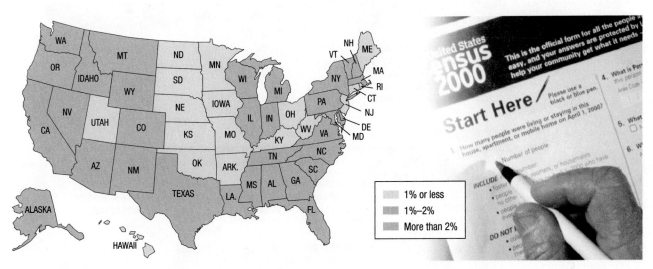

Percentage of People Imputed by the U.S. Census Bureau in Its Population Total, by State
Source: The Wall Street Journal, August 30, 2001.

Pro: Innovation and Experimentation When the states have independent power, they can try out new ideas. Individual states can be "laboratories." If the experiments work, other states or the nation as a whole can adopt their ideas, as has happened on such issues as allowing women and 18-year-olds to vote, fighting air pollution, reforming welfare, and dealing with water pollution. Massachusetts passed a law in 2006 mandating health insurance coverage for every person in the state, and a number of other states are currently looking into providing similar coverage, including Connecticut, California, Vermont, and Maine. Also in 2006, California passed a law committing itself to reducing greenhouse gas emissions to 1990 levels by 2020. New York passed a Green Jobs initiative in 2009 to encourage both employment and more energy-efficient buildings.

Likewise, when the national government is controlled by one political party, federalism allows the states with majorities favoring a different party to

I thought that attending a public university would save a lot of money, but it hasn't because I have to pay out-of-state tuition. Why do I have to pay so much money?

Background: All over the United States, students who choose to attend out-of-state public universities pay much higher tuition than state residents. For example, at the University of Colorado, Boulder, tuition in 2009–2010 for in-state students was $7,932; out-of-state students paid $28,186. Some educational reformers have suggested that the system be reformed so that students might attend public universities wherever they choose without financial penalty.

They have suggested that over the long haul and on average, such a reform would not have much impact on state budgets because students would randomly distribute themselves across state borders. Such proposals have never gotten very far. Taking a broad view of how structural, political linkage, and governmental factors affect this issue will help explain the situation.

Structure

The states are mainly responsible for education in our federal system; standardizing national tuition rates would require agreements among all the states, or federal legislation preempting the states.

Political Linkage

Voters in each state insist on access for their children and the children of their neighbors to low-cost public higher education. → There is little political pressure on elected leaders within the states to lower or eliminate out-of-state tuition, whether from
– Public opinion and voters.
– Parties.
– The mass media.
– Interest groups.
– Social movements. → Out-of-state students rarely vote in the states where they go to school; politicians have no incentive to think seriously about their tuition concerns.

Government

Elected leaders know that voters want access to low-cost higher education for state residents. → Elected leaders are not subject to political pressures to change tuition policy. → Elected leaders are concerned with short-term budget issues; high out-of-state tuition allows them to raise part of the higher education budget out of such revenues.

Government Action

State legislatures decline to pass uniform tuition legislation.

The Supreme Court rules that different tuition rates for in-state and out-of-state residents do not violate the "privileges and immunities" section of Article IV, Section 2, of the Constitution.

compensate by enacting different policies. This aspect of diversity in policymaking is related to the Founders' contention that tyranny is less likely when government's power is dispersed. Multiple governments reduce the risks of bad policy or the blockage of the popular will; if things go wrong at one governmental level, they may go right at another.

Con: Spillover Effects and Competition   Diversity and experimentation in policies, however, may not always be good. Divergent regulations can cause bad effects that spill over from one state to another. When factories in the Midwest spew out oxides of nitrogen and sulfur that fall as acid rain in the Northeast, the northeastern states can do nothing about it. Only nationwide rules can solve such problems. Similarly, it is very difficult for cities or local communities in the states to do much about poverty or other social problems. If a city raises taxes to pay for social programs, businesses and the wealthy may move out of town, and the poor may move in, impoverishing the city.[25]

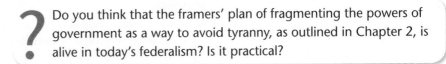
? Do you think that the framers' plan of fragmenting the powers of government as a way to avoid tyranny, as outlined in Chapter 2, is alive in today's federalism? Is it practical?

What Sort of Federalism?

As the pros and cons indicate, a lot is at stake in determining the nature of federalism. It is not likely, however, that Americans will ever have a chance to vote yes or no on the federal system as a whole or to choose a unitary government instead. What we can decide is exactly *what sort* of federalism we will have—how much power will go to the states and how much will remain with the federal government. Indeed, we may want a fluid system in which the balance of power varies from one kind of policy to another. Over the long term of American history, of course, the nationalist position on federalism has generally prevailed over the states' rights position, but the states remain important, and there are many reasons to expect that the American people will continue to want the states to play an important role in fashioning policies that affect them.

It is important to keep in mind that arguments about federalism do not concern just abstract theories; they affect who wins and who loses valuable benefits. People's opinions about federalism often depend on their interests, their ideologies, and the kinds of things they want government to do.

Using the **DEMOCRACY STANDARD**

American federalism: How democratic?

Federalism is one of the foundation stones of the Constitution of the United States. Along with the separation of powers and checks and balances, its purpose, from the framers' point of view, was to make it impossible for any person or group (and, most especially, the majority faction) to monopolize the power of government and use it for tyrannical purposes. By fragmenting government power among a national government and 50 state governments and by giving each of the states some say on what the national government does, federalism makes it difficult for any faction, minority or majority, to dominate government. On balance, federalism has served the intentions of the framers by toning down the influence of majoritarian democracy in determining what the national government does, even while maintaining the principle of popular consent.

Federalism successfully constrains democracy in at least five ways:

1. It adds complexity to policymaking and makes it difficult for citizens to know which elected leaders to hold responsible for government actions.

2. Many policy areas, including education and voting eligibility, are mainly the responsibility of the states, where policymakers are insulated from national majorities, although not from majorities in their own states.

3. Small-population states play a decisive role in the constitutional amending process, where each state counts equally, regardless of the size of its population.

4. Small and large states have equal representation in the Senate, meaning that senators representing a minority of the population can block actions favored by senators representing the majority.

5. State politics are much less visible to the public; citizens are much less informed about what goes on in state governments where many important policies are made, and thus, popular participation tends to be lower.

? If a majority of people in your state wish to create a policy that conflicts with the policy preferences of a majority of people in the nation (e.g., changing seat belt laws or legalizing a specific drug), should your state be able to do so? Which majority is more important, state or national?

All of this makes state-level politics especially vulnerable to the influence of special interests and those with extensive political resources. Because the well-organized and the affluent have extra influence, political equality and popular sovereignty have pretty tough challenges in many of the states.

In the end, the story of federalism is not entirely about the persistence of the framer's initial eighteenth-century republican constitutional design. The democratic aspirations of the American people have also shaped federalism and turned it into something that might not be entirely familiar to the framers. We noted in this chapter how the nature of federalism has changed over the course of American history, with the national government assuming an ever-larger role relative to the states. Much of this, we have suggested, has been brought about by the wishes of the American people as expressed in elections, public opinion polls, and social movements. Repeatedly, Americans have said they want a national government capable of addressing a broad range of problems, including economic difficulties (such as depressions, recessions, and inflation); persistent poverty; environmental degradation; unsafe food, drugs, and other consumer products; racial and ethnic discrimination; and foreign threats to the United States. Over the years, public officials and candidates have responded to these popular aspirations, altering federalism in the process.

SUMMARY

3.1 Define federalism and explain why we have it

- Federalism is a system under which political powers are divided and shared between the state and federal governments, and is a key structural aspect of American politics.

- Federalism in the United States was the product of both important compromises made at the Constitutional Convention and eighteenth-century republican doctrines about the nature of good government.

3.2 Establish the basis for federalism in the Constitution

- There is no section of the Constitution where federalism is described in its entirety. Rather, federalism is construction from scattered clauses throughout the document that describe what the federal government may do and not do, how relations among the states are structured, the role of the states in amending the Constitution and electing the president, and how the states are represented in the national government.

- The U.S. Constitution specifies the powers of the national government and reserves all others (except a few that are specifically forbidden) to the states. Overlapping, or concurrent, powers fall within the powers of both the national government and the states.

3.3 Trace the evolution of American federalism

- The story of American federalism is the story of the increasing power of the federal government relative to the states.

- The trend toward national power is lodged in the "supremacy" and "elastic" clauses in the Constitution and propelled by war and national security demands, economic troubles and crises, and a range of problems that no state could handle alone.

3.4 Analyze how federal grants structure national and state government relations

- Contemporary federalism involves complex "marble cake" relations among the national and state governments, in which federal grants-in-aid play an important part. Except for the Reagan years, grant totals have grown steadily; they took a big jump upward as the country battled the deep recession and high unemployment during the 2008–2010 period.

- The national government also influences or controls many state policies through mandates and through conditions placed on aid.

3.5 Evaluate the arguments for and against federalism

- Arguments in favor of federalism have to do with diversity of needs, closeness to the people, experimentation, and innovation.

- Arguments against federalism involve national standards, popular control, and needs for uniformity.

TEST YOURSELF

Answer key begins on page T-1.

3.1 Define federalism and explain why we have it

1. What is federalism?
   a. A system of government where the states are sovereign and have authority over the central government.
   b. A system of government where the central government has complete power and can tell lower levels of government what to do.
   c. A system of government where local representatives are elected directly by the voters. These representatives then select the members of the central government.
   d. A system of government where the representatives of the central government are elected directly by the voters. These representatives then select the members of the local government.
   e. A system of government where power is divided between the central government and smaller units, such as states.
2. Why did the authors of the U.S. Constitution create a federal system of government?
   a. Federalism is best suited for small, homogenous countries such as the United States at founding.
   b. The U. S. Constitution was modeled after European countries, most of which used a federal system.
   c. Federalism had worked well under the Articles of Confederation, and the framers wanted to build off this success.
   d. Federalism was a reasonable compromise between a confederation and a unitary system.
   e. The system would help ensure a concentration of powers between the federal government and the state governments.
3. Evaluate whether the United States under the Articles of Confederation would have been more successful if it had used a federal system of government. Why or why not?

3.2 Establish the basis for federalism in the Constitution

4. All powers that are not explicitly mentioned in the Constitution are given to the national government. True / False
5. Which part of the Constitution favors the authority of the national government over the state governments?
   a. Tenth Amendment
   b. Reservation clause
   c. Supremacy clause

d. Concurrent powers

e. Full faith and credit clause

6. Use the privileges and immunities clause to make an argument for why public universities should not be allowed to charge different rates for in-state and out-of-state tuition.

3.3 Trace the evolution of American federalism

7. Which of the following leaders was best known for advocating that the national government should give up significant authority to the states?

a. John Marshall

b. Franklin D. Roosevelt

c. Ronald Reagan

d. George W. Bush

e. Barack Obama

8. Which metaphor best explains how federalism operates today?

a. Federalism is like a layer cake.

b. Federalism is like a marble cake.

c. Federalism is like an upside-down cake.

d. Federalism is like Jell-O.

e. Federalism is like an ice cream cone on a hot summer day.

9. Which event most significantly changed the nature of American federalism? Justify your answer.

3.4 Analyze how federal grants structure national and state government relations

10. Recently, the national government has given grant money to states in an effort to help stimulate the economy.

True / False

11. Which kind of grants do states most like to receive?

a. Categorical grants

b. Block grants

c. General revenue sharing

d. Conditional grants

e. Mandates

3.5 Evaluate the arguments for and against federalism

12. An advantage of federalism is that individual states can experiment with different public policies. If the policies are successful, other states or the national government can adopt them.

True / False

13. Which of the following illustrates a disadvantage of federalism?

a. Air pollution produced in one state may drift into another state.

b. Local governments can craft public policies so that they meet their specific needs.

c. National standards ensure that all Americans understand how government works.

d. States can implement innovative public policies.

e. Local governments are well equipped to tackle pressing social problems such as poverty and drug abuse.

14. In your opinion, under what circumstances should the national government establish public policy, and under what circumstances should the states establish public policy?

PEARSON mypoliscilab EXERCISES

Apply what you learned in this chapter on MyPoliSciLab.

Read on **mypoliscilab.com**

eText: Chapter 3

Study and **Review** on **mypoliscilab.com**

Pre-Test
Post-Test
Chapter Exam
Flashcards

Watch on **mypoliscilab.com**

Video: Water Wars
Video: Proposition 8
Video: The Real ID

Explore on **mypoliscilab.com**

Simulation: You Are a Federal Judge
Simulation: You Are a Restaurant Owner
Comparative: Comparing State and Local Governments
Comparative: Comparing Federal and Unitary Systems
Timeline: Federalism and the Supreme Court
Visual Literacy: Federalism and Regulations

INTERNET SOURCES

Center for the Study of Federalism
www.csfederalismo.it
Scholarly studies of the theory and practice of federalism around the world.

National Center for State Courts
www.ncsconline.org
Links to the home pages of the court systems of each of the states.

National Conference of State Legislatures
www.ncsl.org
Information about state governments and federal relations, including the distribution of federal revenues and expenditures in the states. Links to the "Mandate Monitor" and the "Preemption Monitor."

Publius
www.oxfordjournals.org/our_journals/pubjof/index.html
Home page of the leading academic journal on federalism.

State Constitutions
www.findlaw.com/
A site where the constitutions of all the states may be found.

Stateline
www.stateline.org
A very comprehensive site covering politics and policies in the states.

SUGGESTIONS FOR FURTHER READING

Brinkley, Douglas G. *The Great Deluge: Hurricane Katrina, New Orleans, and the Mississippi Gulf Coast.* New York: Harper Collins, 2006.
Much more than a blow-by-blow telling of the Hurricane Katrina story, this text provides a detailed description of how the complex interactions of local, state, and federal politics and policies over the years contributed to the disaster.

Derthick, Martha. *Keeping the Compound Republic: Essays in American Federalism.* Washington, D.C.: Brookings, 2001.
An examination of the enduring features of federalism, as well as its most important changes, in light of the framers' original design, in Madison's words, of a compound republic.

Hero, Rodney E. *Faces of Inequality: Social Diversity in American Politics.* New York: Oxford University Press, 1998.
An impressive argument with strong empirical evidence that the racial and ethnic composition of states matters for patterns of state politics.

Nagel, Robert. *The Implosion of American Federalism.* New York: Oxford University Press, 2002.
Argues that American federalism has largely disappeared as power in the United States has flowed steadily to Washington, D.C.

Peterson, Paul E. *The Price of Federalism.* Washington, D.C.: Brookings Institution, 1995.
Describes modern federalism and argues that the national government is best at redistributive programs, while the states and localities are best at economic development.

Riker, William H. *The Development of American Federalism.* Boston: Kluwer Academic, 1987.
An influential discussion of what American federalism is and how it came about.

Zimmerman, Joseph F. *Contemporary American Federalism.* Albany: State University of New York Press, 2008.
A comprehensive examination of federalism in the United States with an emphasis on the growing centralization of power in Washington.

The Structural Foundations of American Government and Politics

LEARNING OBJECTIVES

After reading this chapter, you will be able to:

4.1 Determine how changes in the location and diversity of the population have affected American politics

4.2 Assess how the American economy shapes government and politics

4.3 Evaluate how America's power in the world has changed and why it matters

4.4 Analyze Americans' political culture and its implications for government and politics

BOEING GOES GLOBAL

The Boeing 747, the world's first "super-jumbo," is one of the most successful and iconic passenger airplanes ever built. First flown by Pan American Airlines in 1970, it is now in its eighth version. The 1970 airplane was designed in its entirety by Boeing engineers, mostly located near Seattle. The tens of thousands of engineering drawings required for the plane were done by hand. Parts manufacturing was mostly done in-house, although engines for the plane were provided by Pratt and Whitney. At the time, Boeing was the dominant airplane maker in the world, with its domestic competitors (Douglas, McConnell, and Lockheed) in decline and Airbus, the European company that would eventually challenge Boeing's supremacy in commercial aviation, just getting started.

The Boeing 787 Dreamliner, whose maiden flight took place in 2010 (more than two years behind schedule), is the fastest-selling new airplane in aviation history. Airlines have been attracted to the 787 by its ability to fly approximately 300 passengers very long distances on a point-to-point basis (with no need for passengers to endure the agony of jammed hub airports) cleanly and fuel-efficiently because of its extensive use of ultra-strong, light-weight carbon composites rather than aluminum. Boeing had

launched the 787 project as part of its strategy for regaining its lead over European Airbus in the global commercial airplane market, where Airbus had reached parity in sales by the early 2000s. Unlike the early versions of the 747 that were designed, manufactured, and assembled almost entirely by Boeing employees in the United States, however, around 70 percent of the 787 is sourced (i.e., manufactured by other American companies) and outsourced (i.e., manufactured by foreign companies). Although final assembly is being done in Everett, Washington, 30 miles north of Seattle, parts and sections for the Dreamliner are being produced at 135 sites in two dozen countries.[1]

More importantly for the passenger aircraft industry and American workers in the future is the business model that Boeing is using for the 787. Rather than a typical subcontractor arrangement—in which subcontracting companies typically do what the contracting company wants them to do, following precise directions for an agreed-upon fee—Boeing has moved to what it calls a "global partnering" model. In this model, the partner firms that come together under Boeing's leadership make sizable investments in the 787 project and share in the financial risks of failure and the rewards of success. Additionally, partner

firms are doing the design and engineering work for entire sections of the airplane, with the right to secure patents for whatever innovations they come up with. With most of the design, engineering, and manufacturing taking place in partner firms (some in the United States, more abroad), Boeing's main job on the 787 has become that of systems integrator, supply chain manager, and final assembler.

The worldwide collaborative effort on the 787 would not have been possible without incredible advances in the reach, scale, and ease-of-use of global financial markets (where money was raised for the launch of the new plane), telecommunications networks, and the Internet (which did not exist in 1970 when the first 747 flew). It could not have happened without the appearance of cheap, fast, and reliable freight service (including containerized ships, trucks, and trains) and airfreight services. And it could not have happened, most importantly, without the dramatic increases in computing power that have occurred in the past 10 years or so and the attendant breakthroughs in engineering, planning, and financial software. Engineers at Boeing and partner companies around the world, for example, collaborated on the design and production of every part and section of the 787 using a single, linked computer system with a common database. Impressed by what was happening, one Boeing engineer pointed out that "information technology and communications technology have enabled Boeing people to be in touch at all times from anywhere. Design anywhere, build anywhere is now possible. True globalization is now possible."[2]

The 787 project ran into tremendous problems in 2008 and 2009, however, that delayed deliveries of planes to the airlines and cost Boeing billions of dollars. For example, Boeing failed to adequately oversee and coordinate its supply chain and ended up with some sections that didn't "snap-and-fit" together as planned. The company also learned that manufacturing and working with carbon fiber was trickier than expected. Nevertheless—and despite the deep recession that hit the world economy, with airlines taking a particularly big blow—there is every reason to believe that the 787 will be a winner once Boeing works out its engineering and manufacturing bugs.[3] Should this turn out to be true, it will be good for Boeing, its partner firms, and its investors. But what about the future for Boeing employees or other Americans who might have become Boeing employees? The lessons learned from the 787 global collaborative effort are now being used at Boeing in the upgrading of the 777 and 747 (yes, it's still around) and the planning for the plane that will replace the venerable 737 in a few years. More and more design, engineering, and manufacturing work once lodged at Boeing near Seattle will be sourced and outsourced. Technological advances that increase productivity and global partnering are sure to continue. Inevitably, all this means that Boeing will need fewer of its own engineers, technicians, machinists, and assemblers; much of Boeing's engineering capabilities and a wide range of jobs in producing airplanes will migrate elsewhere.[4] And, even if some of this migration is to other places in the United States, it will almost certainly be to places where labor unions are not a factor and where labor costs (wages, salaries, and benefits) are lower than they are in the state of Washington. No one was much surprised when the company announced in November 2009 that it would build its second 787 final assembly line in South Carolina, a place decidedly unfriendly to unions like those found at Boeing plants in Washington, California, and Missouri.

What has been happening in recent years at Boeing has been happening in other American manufacturing companies as well, ranging from automobiles to steel and microchips.[5] Polls show that many Americans are worried about things like outsourcing, their ability to adapt to the many technological changes going on around them, and whether the United States can remain competitive in the global economy. Many are worried about whether the nation's high standard of living can be maintained and whether they can continue to provide for themselves and their families.

When they are worried about such matters, Americans tend to turn to their elected officials for solutions. Some want outsourcing to be stopped or regulated. Others want government to provide health insurance so that they will not be left in the lurch when companies downsize their workforces. Still others want more retraining and education assistance. And others want lower taxes and fewer regulations to help the competitiveness of American companies. Whatever the particulars might be, it is inevitably the case that big economic and technological changes find expression in the political arena and shape what government does. What to do about such things is part of the continuing debate between Democrats and Republicans and liberals and conservatives.

THINKING CRITICALLY About This Chapter

In addition to the changes described in the chapter-opening story, other important changes are going on in American society, culture, economy, and our place in the world that are shaping and reshaping American politics and government. Tracking these many changes in the structural level of our analytical model, and examining how they are influencing American politics and what government does, is the focus of this chapter.

Using the **FRAMEWORK**

In this chapter, you will learn about the most important demographic characteristics of the American population (race, ethnicity, geographical location, occupation, income, and the like), the U.S. economy and how it is evolving and changing, and the core beliefs of Americans—sometimes referred to as the American political culture. Together with the constitutional rules you learned about in previous chapters, you will see how these structural factors have a great deal to do with what issues dominate the political agenda, how political power is distributed in the population, and what ideas Americans bring to bear when grappling with complex public policy issues.

Using the **DEMOCRACY STANDARD**

Popular sovereignty, political equality, and liberty require a supportive economic and social environment. These include (but are not confined to) such things as a well-educated population; a sizable middle class with access to resources, allowing its members to participate in public affairs; conditions of nondiscrimination against racial and ethnic minorities; and a culture that values and protects liberty. In this chapter you will begin to learn whether or not such an environment exists.

America's People

4.1 Determine how changes in the location and diversity of the population have affected American politics

Where we live, how we work, our racial and ethnic composition, and our average age and standard of living have all changed substantially over the course of our history. Each change has influenced and continues to influence our political life.

Becoming More Diverse

Ours is an ethnically, religiously, and racially diverse society. The white European Protestants, black slaves, and Native Americans who made up the bulk of the U.S. population when the first census was taken in 1790 were joined by Catholic immigrants from Ireland and Germany in the 1840s and 1850s (see Figure 4.1). In the 1870s, Chinese migrated to America, drawn by jobs in railroad construction. Around the turn of the twentieth century, most emigration was from eastern, central, and southern Europe, with its many ethnic, linguistic, and religious groups. Today most emigration is from Asia and Latin America, with people from Mexico representing the largest single component. Starting in the 1990s and continuing today, according to the U.S. Census, there also has been a significant increase in the number of immigrants from the Middle East and other locations with Muslim populations.[6]

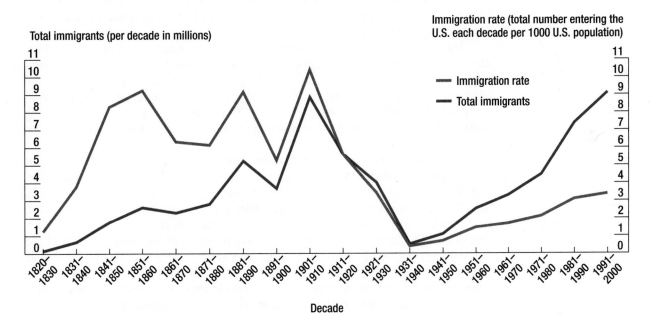

FIGURE 4.1 Immigration to the United States, by Decade

Measuring immigration to the United States in different ways gives rise to quite different interpretations of its scale. Measured in total numbers, the high points of immigration were the 1880s, the decade and a half after 1900, and the 1980s and 1990s. Measured in terms of the total U.S. population, however, immigration was an important factor in population change for much of the nineteenth century and the early part of the twentieth century, but fell after that as stringent immigration laws came into force. The rate of recent immigration, relative to the total U.S. population—even with the high numbers of immigrants who have come to the country over the past two decades—remains historically low, although it is has been increasing steadily since its low point in the 1930s. In what ways do we still see the effects of this immigration history? *Note:* The 2010 census provides new data on immigration. Check at www.census.gov. *Source:* U.S. Bureau of the Census.

Until recently, the rate of migration to the United States had been accelerating. During the 1990s, more immigrants arrived than in any decade in American history (9.1 million legal, 3.5 million illegal).[7] From 2000 through 2007, about 1 million immigrants arrived each year (78 percent from Latin America), although the flow slowed in 2008 and 2009 to about 600,000 a year because of fewer jobs in a depressed economy and tougher border enforcement.[8] As a result of this and other immigration streams, the percentage of foreign-born people resident in the United States has almost tripled since 1970, reaching almost 12.5 percent of the population in 2009. Although the foreign-born population is concentrated in a handful of states—mainly California, New York, New Jersey, Florida, Illinois, and Texas—and a handful of cities and localities—mainly Miami, New York, Los Angeles–Long Beach, Orange County, Oakland, and Houston—the presence of new immigrants is being felt almost everywhere in America, including the Midwest (Ohio, Michigan, and Wisconsin) and the Deep South (North Carolina and Georgia, especially). In California, more than 27 percent of the population is foreign-born.[9]

Although the total number of current immigrants is substantial, it is worth noting that the number of new immigrants as a proportion of the population (the red line in Figure 4.1) is lower than it was for much of our history. Furthermore, as a percentage of the total population, the foreign-born population of the United States today is lower than it was in the late nineteenth and early twentieth centuries, when it reached almost 15 percent. (We will reach the 15 percent level, according to one authoritative estimate, sometime between 2020 and 2025, unless the rate of increase is slowed by additional and more effective restrictions on illegal immigration or if economic conditions fail to improve significantly.)[10] For most people, of course, it is what has been happening recently that is most important to them, not historical comparisons.

The natural outcome of this history of immigration is substantial racial and ethnic diversity in the American population. Although the United States is still overwhelmingly non-Hispanic white, its diversity is growing with every passing year. The Hispanic population has been growing rapidly and is now the nation's largest minority group, with African Americans second. The Asian-origin population is growing faster in a proportional sense than any other group, but it is still relatively small. (See Figure 4.2.)

The most recent wave of immigration, like all previous ones, has added to our rich linguistic, cultural, and religious traditions; it has also helped revitalize formerly poverty-stricken neighborhoods in cities such as Los Angeles, New York, and Chicago. Immigrants from Asia and Europe especially have also made a mark in science and technology, earning a disproportionate share of PhDs in the sciences as well as technology patents, and are responsible for creating some of the hottest high-technology companies (e.g., one of the founders of Google, as well as the creators of Yahoo!, YouTube, and Hotmail).[11] Because immigrants tend to be younger and have more children than non-immigrants, moreover, they have slowed the rate at which the American population is aging, particularly when compared with the rapidly aging populations of Japan, Russia, China, and most of Europe.

But immigration also has generated political and social tensions at various times in our history. The arrival of immigrants who are different from the majority population in significant ways has often sparked anti-immigration agitation and demands that public officials stem the tide. **Nativist** (antiforeign) reactions to Irish Catholic migrants were common throughout the nineteenth century. Anti-Chinese agitation swept the western states in the 1870s and 1880s. Alarm at the arrival of waves of immigrants from eastern, southern, and central Europe in the early part of the last century led Congress virtually to close the doors of the United States in

nativist

Antiforeign; applied to political movements active in the nineteenth century in the United States.

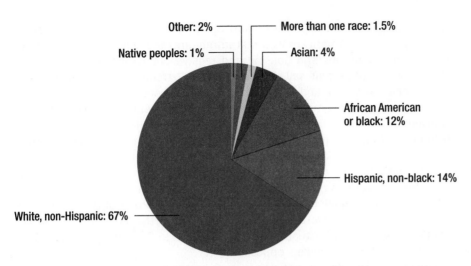

Other: 2%

More than one race: 1.5%

Native peoples: 1%

Asian: 4%

African American or black: 12%

Hispanic, non-black: 14%

White, non-Hispanic: 67%

FIGURE 4.2 Race and Hispanic Composition of the United States, 2005

The United States is a racially and ethnically diverse society and it is becoming more so every year, although non-Hispanic whites—who are themselves made up of many ethnic groups—are in the majority and will be for some time to come. It is important to note that Hispanics are defined by the Census Bureau as an ethnic group rather than a racial group, because Hispanics include people with different racial backgrounds. In this graph, we use data that combine Census Bureau figures on Hispanic ethnicity and U.S. racial composition. Native peoples include native Hawaiian and Pacific Islanders and American Indians and Alaska Natives. How do these immigrants shape contemporary American society and politics? *Note:* The 2010 census provides new data on race and ethnicity. Check at www.census.gov. *Source:* U.S. Bureau of the Census.

1921 and keep them closed until the 1950s. Wars have also triggered hostile actions against certain immigrant groups: German immigrants during World War I; Japanese Americans during World War II; and people from Middle Eastern and other Muslim countries after the September 11, 2001, terrorist attacks on the United States.

The current wave of Hispanic immigration, much of it illegal, has caused unease among many Americans. It is estimated that there are about 12 million people in the

VALUE-ADDED IMMIGRANTS Many immigrants to the United States have played important roles in science, technology, and business. Here, YouTube founders Chad Hurley, left, and Steven Chen, right, from Taiwan, pose with their laptops at company headquarters in San Mateo, California.

United States illegally, with Hispanics making up about 75 percent of that number.[12] In 2009, 40 percent of Americans said that immigrants today are a burden "primarily because they take jobs and housing and receive public benefits." (Though, it should be noted, 46 percent say that immigrants "strengthen the United States because of their hard work and talents.")[13] Concerns about illegal immigration are among the most often expressed discontents of people who are active in the Tea Party movement, for example.

Responding to the rising chorus of complaints about illegal immigration from Mexico, President George W. Bush sent National Guard units to help patrol the border. In 2007, he proposed a temporary-worker program, granting stays of up to six years for Mexican workers not otherwise allowed in the United States and a road to citizenship for several million already here illegally. The proposal drew angry fire from his party's conservative base and normally supportive talk-radio hosts. The president's immigration reform proposal was defeated in Congress in 2007 when a majority of Republican lawmakers opposed Bush.[14]

President Obama acted inconsistently on how or whether to address the problem of illegal immigration. In 2009, he made sweeping changes in the immigration detention system by executive order, thus reducing the number of people in prison awaiting determination of their cases. However, he found it prudent to avoid introducing a major new immigration bill in 2010 as he had promised to do during his campaign because Democrats in Congress were reluctant to take up such a controversial piece of legislation with elections on the horizon. Following the uproar over passage of a law in Arizona allowing police to interrogate people suspected of being in the country illegally—a federal judge later ruled the law unconstitutional—Obama dispatched troops to help guard Arizona's border, disappointing those proponents of immigration reform wanting a pathway to citizenship.

Where immigrants settle is very important for American politics. As is clear from the many news stories about the issue, states and localities with high concentrations of immigrants must find additional monies for social services, health care, and education in order to service a growing and changing population, though the taxes paid by immigrants, whether legal or illegal, help pay for these things. A less well-known impact of immigrant populations is the increase that destination states gain in Congress, where apportionment of seats in the House of Representatives is calculated on the basis of a state's entire adult population regardless of legal status. And, because each state's Electoral College vote is the sum of the number of its representatives in the House and its two senators, high-immigration states play a larger role in presidential elections than they might if only adult citizens and legal aliens were counted in population surveys.

Even while waves of immigration often trigger an initial negative response from the native population (among all races and ethnic groups, it is important to add) and opportunistic politicians, elected officials invariably begin to pay attention to immigrant groups as more become citizens and voters. Indeed, immigrants now represent the fastest-growing voting bloc in the American electorate.[15] The upshot of this change is that elected officials at all levels of government are likely to become more responsive to the needs and interests of recent immigrant groups, even as they try to balance demands from anti-immigration groups who want the border with Mexico sealed. The growing political importance of immigrants in the United States, especially Hispanics, reflects both sheer numbers and the geographic concentration of immigrants in states with very large or closely contested blocs of electoral votes in presidential elections. In 2008, Hispanic voters were especially important in determining the outcome of the presidential contest between John McCain and Barack Obama in the closely contested states of Colorado, New Mexico, and Nevada.

? What practical challenges does a diverse society present for democracy? How has the United States dealt with such challenges in the past? Would such solutions work today?

Changing Where We Live

Where the growing population of the United States is located also matters. Although we began as a country of rural farms and small towns, we rapidly became an urban people. By 1910, some 50 cities had populations of more than 100,000, and 3 (New York, Philadelphia, and Chicago) had more than 1 million. **Urbanization**, caused mainly by **industrialization**—the rise of large manufacturing firms required many industrial workers, while the mechanization of farming meant that fewer agricultural workers were needed—continued unabated until the mid-1940s. After World War II, a massive federal and state road-building program and government-guaranteed home loans for veterans started the process by which the United States became an overwhelmingly suburban nation (see Figure 4.3). In recent years, "exurbia"—the areas beyond the older, first-ring of suburbia—has become the fastest growing part of America's metropolitan areas, though high gas prices and the real estate collapse (and many foreclosures in the exurbs) during the Great Recession of 2008–2009 slowed the process down and even reversed it in some areas. Meanwhile, rural communities across the country, but especially in the northern Rockies and western Great Plains states, are losing population.[16]

This shift in the location of the American population has important political ramifications. The continued drain of population from rural areas, for instance, has diminished the power of the rural voice in state and national politics (with the exception of the Senate, where such rural, low-population states as Wyoming and Idaho have the same number of seats as large-population, highly urbanized states such as California and Florida). On the other hand, suburban voters have become more visible, persuading politicians to talk more about issues such as traffic congestion, urban sprawl, and the price of gasoline and less about inner-city problems.

The U.S. population has also moved steadily westward and southward over the years. The shift accelerated after World War II as people followed manufacturing jobs to these regions (many companies were attracted to the western and southern states because of their low taxes and anti-union policies). This population shift has led to changes in the relative political power of the states. Following each census from 1950 to 2000, states in the East and the upper Midwest lost congressional seats and presidential electoral votes. States in the West and the South—often referred to as the **Sun Belt** because of their generally pleasant weather—gained at their expense. After the 2010 census, Iowa, Missouri, Ohio, Pennsylvania, New York, and Massachusetts likely will lose House seats and electoral votes; Florida, Georgia, Texas, Arizona, Utah, and Nevada will pick them up.[17]

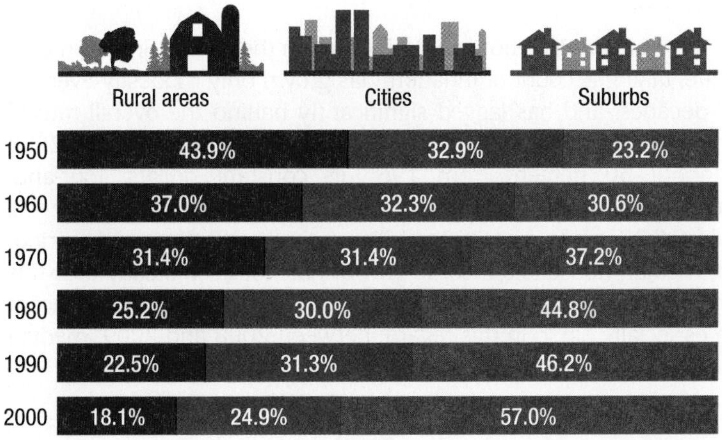

urbanization
The movement of people from rural areas to cities.

industrialization
The transformation of a society's economy from one dominated by agricultural pursuits to one dominated by manufacturing.

Sun Belt
States of the Lower South, Southwest, and West, where sunny weather and conservative politics have often prevailed.

	Rural areas	Cities	Suburbs
1950	43.9%	32.9%	23.2%
1960	37.0%	32.3%	30.6%
1970	31.4%	31.4%	37.2%
1980	25.2%	30.0%	44.8%
1990	22.5%	31.3%	46.2%
2000	18.1%	24.9%	57.0%

FIGURE 4.3 Where Americans Live

In a relatively short period of time, the United States has changed from a society in which the largest percentage of the population lived in rural areas to one in which the largest percentage lives in suburbs. This development has produced several important changes in American politics and in the fortunes of our political parties. What are the political implications of this shift? *Note:* The 2010 Census provides new data on where Americans live. See www.census.gov. *Source:* U.S. Bureau of the Census.

Growing Older

One of the most significant demographic trends in the United States and in other industrialized countries is the aging of the population. In 1800, the median age of the United States was just under 16; today it is 35. By 2030, it will be about 38. The proportion of the population over age 65 has been growing, while the proportion between the ages of 18 and 64 has been shrinking. Today 12.7 percent of Americans are elderly. Moreover, the number of the very old—over age 85—is the fastest-growing age segment of all. By 2030, this figure is likely to rise to about 20 percent. Meanwhile, the proportion of the population in the prime working years is likely to fall from 61.4 percent today to about 56.5 percent in 2030. Thus, an increasing proportion of Americans is likely to be dependent and in need of services, and a shrinking proportion is likely to be taxpaying wage or salary earners, though, to be sure, more Americans over 65 are staying employed, both for financial reasons and for reasons of staying active and engaged.[18] The United States is aging much less rapidly, however, than other countries and regions, primarily because so many young immigrants of child-bearing age are coming here. Aging is happening much more rapidly in Japan, Italy, Russia, and China, for example.[19]

Because the population is aging, how to finance Social Security and Medicare is likely to remain an important political question for the foreseeable future. The voting power of the elderly is likely to make it difficult for elected officials to substantially reduce social insurance programs for Americans over the age of 65. Meanwhile, the tax load on those still in the workforce may feel increasingly burdensome. Also, more and more middle-aged people are trying to figure out how to finance assisted-living and nursing home care for their elderly parents. How these issues will play out in the political arena in the near future will be interesting to follow.

Becoming More Unequal

The United States enjoys one of the highest standards of living in the world, consistently ranking first, second, third, or fourth in **gross domestic product (GDP)** per capita[20]—Luxembourg, Denmark, Switzerland, and Norway are the other countries always in the running for the top spot—and in the top group on the U.N.'s Human Development Index, which takes into account education and life expectancy as well as per-capita GDP (with Australia, Belgium, Canada, France, Ireland, Norway, Iceland, the Netherlands, Japan, and Sweden), with little apparent difference among the members of this group.[21] However, the high standard of living represented by these numbers is not shared by all Americans.

gross domestic product (GDP)

Monetary value of all goods and services produced in a nation each year, excluding income residents earn abroad.

median household income

The midpoint of all households ranked by income.

Income   Overall, **median household income** in the United States (in constant dollars, taking account of inflation) has grown only modestly over the past four decades, and has lagged significantly behind the overall rate of growth in the economy (see Figure 4.4). Median household income in 2008 was up about 30 percent from 1967 in constant dollars, four-and-a-half decades ago, when the federal government first began to collect this statistic, but GDP grew more than 300 percent over the same period. Moreover, median household income growth has not been steady over this period but has taken hard hits during recessions, with the most recent recession especially harsh in this regard; between 2008 and 2009, median

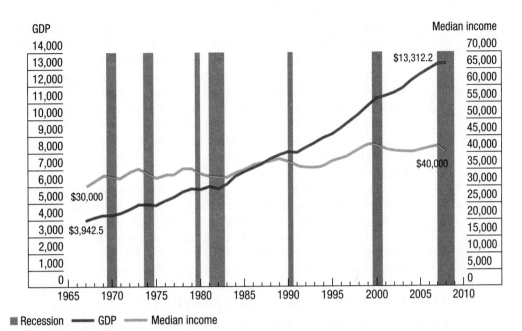

FIGURE 4.4 Median Household Income and GDP (in constant dollars), 1967–2008

While the size of the economy grew by more than 300 percent between 1967 and 2008, median household income increased by only 30 percent. It is worth noting that income distribution became more unequal over time, with more going to the top income earners, suggesting that household incomes for many Americans did not increase at all over this time period. How might the slow gains in household income for most Americans affect what people want from government? *Source:* U.S. Bureau of the Census, "Income, Poverty, and Health Insurance Coverage in the United States: 2008," September 2009.

household income fell $2,000. It is worth noting that median household income has not yet climbed back to late 1990s levels[22] and is unlikely to do so soon, given the "jobless recovery" from the Great Recession, the unemployment rate hovering around 10 percent in 2009 and 2010, and continuing wage stagnation.[23] It is important to point out, as well, that median household income varies across demographic groups. African American and Hispanic households have the lowest household incomes—and took the hardest hits in the economic collapse—while Asian Americans and non-Hispanic whites have the highest. In the recent recession, white non-college-educated men also were hit hard because they were the most directly affected by the decline in manufacturing.

> How might the growing disparity between rich and poor in the United States affect the distribution of political power? How might having wealth concentrated in a small minority affect the workings of a "majority rule" democracy?

Changes in household income can have important political effects. Not surprisingly, when household income is rising, Americans tend to express satisfaction with their situation and confidence in elected leaders. During periods of stagnation and decline, the opposite is evident. During the long 1973–1983 period of stagnation, for example, political observers talked about the rise of an "angry" middle class and the decline of the Democrats, capped in 1980 by the election of Ronald Reagan and a Republican Senate.[24] In 2008, with the United States mired in an economic recession, 81 percent of Americans said that "things have

poverty line

The federal government's calculation of the amount of income families of various sizes need to stay out of poverty. In 2008 it was $22,025 for a family of four.

pretty seriously gotten off on the wrong track" in the country—the highest percentage ever recorded on this standard survey question—while President Bush's approval dropped to only 28 percent.[25] What to do about the deeply troubled American economy became an important issue during the 2008 presidential election contest and had a great deal to do with Barack Obama's win over John McCain (see Chapter 10). Interestingly, Obama and the Democrats ran into trouble in the 2010 congressional elections when income and wages failed to rebound in the jobless recovery from the Great Recession.

Poverty In 1955, almost 25 percent of Americans fell below the federal government's official **poverty line** (discussed in detail in the "By the Numbers" feature in Chapter 18). Things improved a great deal after that, dropping to 11.1 percent in 1973. It then rose again to about 15 percent during and after the recessions of the early 1980s and early 1990s, then fell (i.e., poverty decreased) through the 1990s economic boom, dropping to 11 percent in 1999. It rose relentlessly after that, reaching 14.3 percent in 2009 in the midst of the Great Recession.[26]

Is poverty a problem? Here is why many people think so:

- A distressingly large number of Americans still live in poverty, almost 44 million in 2009 (more than 50 million using the poverty formula from the National Academy of Sciences, which is examined in Chapter 18).[27]

- The poverty rate is unlikely to fall much unless there is sustained job growth, especially in jobs that will be available to low-skill workers who make up the bulk of the poor. This seems unlikely in light of zero job growth in the economy from 1999 through 2010.

- There is every reason to believe that the poverty rate and the number of people in poverty will grow over the near term. Job growth has been very slow coming out of the Great Recession, with low-skilled jobs taking the worst hits. The poverty rate has increased every year during the decade, with especially big jumps from 2007 on.[28]

- The poverty rate in the United States remains substantially higher than in the other rich democracies, even though they have had troubles of their own.

The distribution of poverty is not random. It is concentrated among racial minorities and single-parent, female-headed households and their children.[29] In 2009, almost 26 percent of African Americans and 25 percent of Hispanic Americans lived in poverty, for example (although a sizable middle class has emerged in both communities), compared with a little more than 9 percent among non-Hispanic whites and 12 percent among Asians. Almost 21 percent of children under the age of 18 lived in poverty, as did almost 30 percent of people in single-parent, female-headed households.[30]

Obviously, the extent of poverty is politically consequential. While the poor have little voice in the American political system—a point that will be elaborated in several later chapters—poverty tends to be linked to a range of socially undesirable outcomes, including crime, drug use, and family disintegration,[31] which draws the attention of other citizens who want government to do something about these problems. The cause of poverty reduction has also drawn the attention of many Americans who are offended on moral and other grounds by the extent of the poverty that exists in what is still the world's largest economy. (See "Using the Framework" for insight into why it has been so difficult to further diminish poverty in the United States.)

Inequality The degree of income and wealth inequality has always been higher in the United States than in the other rich democracies.[32] Over the past three

It's easy to understand why the number of poor people increases during recessions, but why did poverty only barely decline during recent periods of strong economic growth?

Background: Despite strong economic growth in the United States from 1993 to 2000, and from 2003 to 2006, the rate of poverty during these years never dropped below 12 percent. (The poverty line for a family of four in 2008 was $22,025. See more on the poverty line in Chapter 18.) Surveys show that Americans would like government to do something to help the poor, although there is not much consensus on precisely what should be

done to solve the problem of persistent poverty, except for a general unwillingness to go back to the traditional system of welfare that ended in 1996 (again, see Chapter 18). So, why doesn't the federal government do more to try to end poverty? Taking a look at how structural, political linkage, and governmental factors interact on this issue will help explain this situation.

Structure

American core beliefs about individualism, initiative, and opportunity make it difficult for proposals to assist the poor to gain recognition. ➡ The economic boom of the 1990s and mid-2000s reinforced the belief that anyone who wants to work, can. ➡ The decrease in the number of high-wage, high-benefit jobs in manufacturing has diminished the economic prospects for unskilled, less-educated people.

Political Linkage

The poor are politically invisible; they represent a small minority of the electorate, have few organized groups to push their interests, and have not been able to build a social movement. ➡ Wealthier Americans and large corporations make large contributions to candidates who promise to keep taxes low and government small. ➡ Public opinion opposes big federal government programs to redistribute income. ➡ Until recently, the Democratic Party, historically the party championing the interests of the poor, has been afraid of being tagged with the "tax and spend" label.

Government

Proposals to eliminate poverty do not improve the electoral prospects of public officials at the present time. ➡ Until the Great Recession of 2008–2009 hit, elected leaders in both parties voiced support for balanced budgets, deregulation, and a friendly environment for investors rather than poverty reduction.

Government Action

While the national government provides small safety nets for the poor, it has not created major programs to eliminate poverty.

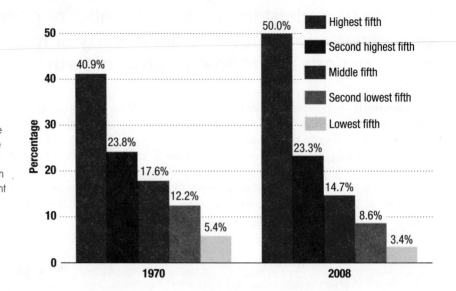

FIGURE 4.5 Household Income Distribution in the United States, by Quintiles, 1970 and 2008

Income inequality has been increasing in the United States, reaching levels not seen since the 1920s. A standard way to measure income inequality is to compare the proportion of national income going to each 20 percent (quintile) of households in the population. Especially striking is the shrinking share of the bottom 60 percent and the increasing share of the top 20 percent. *Source*: U.S. Bureau of the Census, Current Population Survey, 2009.

decades, income and wealth inequality has become even more pronounced; income and wealth inequality actually grew during the economic booms of the 1980s and 1990s. By 2008, the top quintile (the top 20 percent) of households took home more than 50 percent of national income (see Figure 4.5), the second highest ever recorded (the highest was in 2006, 50.6 percent). The top 1 percent took home almost 24 percent of national income, the highest share since pre–Great Depression 1928.[33] Partly this can be explained by the big jump in CEO salaries in large corporations: from 27 times as much as the average worker in 1973 to 262 times in 2005.[34] By 2006, the top five executives in *Fortune* 500 companies were earning eight times more than they had in the mid-1980s relative to the earnings of their companies. In sharp contrast, the share of total national income going to ordinary Americans in the form of wages, salaries, and benefits fell by 3.3 percentage points between 2000 and 2006 to its lowest number since the statistic was first collected in 1929.

More gains at the top have come from annual bonuses. In 2006, for example, three hedge fund managers each earned more than $1 billion in salary and bonuses. Big bonuses were handed out to top executives in 2008 and 2009 at several large commercial and investment banks receiving government bailout money, including Bank of America, JPMorgan Chase, and Goldman Sachs, prompting public outcry and congressional hearings. Despite these well-documented bonuses, the Great Recession ultimately took a small toll on the top people in the biggest companies. *The Wall Street Journal* reported in its annual compensation survey of the top 200 American companies that CEO total compensation declined 2 percent between 2007 and 2008, from $11.2 million to $10.9 million.[35]

Wealth (assets such as real estate, stocks and bonds, art, bank accounts, cash-value insurance policies, and so on) in the United States is even more unequally distributed than income and, until the recent recession when the stock and real estate portfolios of the wealthiest were hit hard, was becoming even more unequal. According to a study by economist Edward Wolff, the top 1 percent of households accounted for 34 percent of the total net worth of Americans in 2004.[36]

For more on how to conceptualize and measure inequality and on what inequality might mean for American politics, especially as it affects the distribution of power in political affairs, see the "By the Numbers" feature.

America's Economy

4.2 Assess how the American economy shapes government and politics

capitalism

An economic system characterized by private ownership of productive assets where decisions about how to use these assets are made by individuals and firms operating in a market rather than by government.

Virtually everything we have discussed so far in this chapter is shaped by the American economy. The growth, diversification, and geographic dispersion of the American population, for example, can be traced directly to changes in the economy. The way we earn our livings, our standard of living, and the distribution of income and wealth in the nation are closely connected to the operations of our economic institutions. Even important elements of the American political culture, as we shall soon see, are associated with our economy and how it works.

America's economy is a **capitalist** one, meaning that it is an economy where the productive assets of society (e.g., land, machinery, factories and offices, financial capital) are privately owned and where most decisions about how to use them are made not by the government but by individuals and firms. Buying and selling products and services in the pursuit of profits is the driving engine of such an economy. For the most part, prices for products and services are set by buyers and sellers in the market, as are incomes and profits to individuals and firms. Although the role of government today varies quite considerably among countries with capitalist economies, they all see protecting property rights, creating the legal framework for allowing markets to operate, and providing law and order as a minimum set of government responsibilities.

Capitalism has some important tendencies that have political consequences:

1. Capitalist economies are tremendously productive. It is no mystery that societies with the highest standards of living for their populations and the most wealth—usually measured by gross domestic product—are capitalist in one form or another. Capitalism, unlike, let us say, the Soviet-style command economies of the Soviet Union and its eastern European satellite nations for most of the post-WWII era and China and India until quite recently, rewards entrepreneurial risk-taking, innovation, and responsiveness to consumer preferences. Productivity gains and economic growth tend to follow, at least over the long run. The tremendous performance of China and India in the current period is related to their loosening of many state controls on individuals and firms, opening up to world markets, and doing more to protect property rights. They have become more capitalist, that is to say—though the Chinese state continues to exercise much more control over individuals and firms than is the norm in the United States.

2. Capitalist economies tend to produce substantial income and wealth inequalities. Capitalism is a system that rewards those who win in the competition in the marketplace. It is an economic system that tends to pay off for those with high skills, entrepreneurs and firms that successfully innovate, and those who satisfy consumers. Where there are winners, of course, there are also losers—that is, individuals and firms who do not do well in the competitive market. It is not surprising, then, that fast-growing capitalist economies such as Brazil, China, and India are all experiencing a rising tide of income and wealth inequality. Inequality is also characteristic of the United States, western Europe, Australia, and New Zealand. Where capitalist countries differ considerably, of course, is the degree to which government acts to alter this situation by redistributing income and wealth, by imposing high tax rates on high-income earners and delivering programs that provide generous educational, unemployment, retirement, and medical benefits for all. The United States does less redistributing than virtually any other rich capitalist country.[37]

Is America becoming more unequal?

Scholars and journalists have been claiming for some time now that economic inequality in the United States is not only the highest among all rich democracies, but is becoming steadily more pronounced. As the highly respected *Economist* put it, "Income inequality [in the United States] is growing to levels not seen since the Gilded Age, around the 1880s."[a]

Why It Matters Rising economic inequality, if it is, in fact, happening, has troubling implications for the practice of democracy in the United States. It is undeniably the case that such inequalities all too often spill over into inequalities in politics. Those with substantially more income and wealth tend to have a stronger voice in politics and better access to political decision makers than people with lower incomes. Those at the top are more likely to vote; can and do make more contributions to candidates, parties, and advocacy groups; and have more information available to them than those on the bottom. The fundamental democratic principle of political equality is at risk when economic inequality is substantial.[b]

Calculating the Numbers There are many ways to measure economic inequality. Each provides a slightly different angle for viewing the issue. We examine here two sets of numbers collected by international organizations that allow us to compare how the United States is doing on the distribution of earnings—money earned by working—with other rich countries. The first graph is based on data from the Organization of Economic Cooperation and Development (OECD) that reports ratios created by dividing the earnings among full-time employed individuals in the 90th percentile of the population by the earnings of working individuals in the 10th percentile. (These data, called P90/P10 ratios, were collected at two

points in time, mostly in the early 1980s and the mid- to late 1990s.) Higher ratios mean higher levels of inequality. Thus, a ratio score of 2 means that individuals in the 90th percentile earn twice as much as individuals in the 10th percentile. A ratio score of 8 means that those in the 90th percentile earn eight times as much. From the graph, several things are apparent. First, the more recent P90/P10 ratio is higher in the United States than in the other comparison countries, with the average individual in the 90th percentile earning about four-and-a-half times the average individual in the 10th percentile. Second, earnings inequality has increased in a majority of the rich countries (Japan, Finland, Norway, Switzerland, and Belgium are the exceptions). Third, the rise in earnings inequality over this time period has been most pronounced in the United States.

The second graph is based on the Luxembourg Income Study of household earnings over time and shows Gini coefficients of inequality. The Gini coefficient is a number between "0" and "1," where "0" is perfect equality (everyone has the same earnings) and "1" is perfect inequality (where one person or household takes all earnings, leaving nothing for anyone else). The higher the Gini coefficient, the higher the measured inequality. Several conclusions can be drawn from the graph. First, the United States does not have the highest level of inequality among the rich countries in the more recent observations—the United Kingdom (Great Britain) does—although we are very close. Second, the United States ranks third among these countries in how much inequality has increased, with Sweden, of all places, sneaking into the second spot. Third, and finally, with the exception of the Netherlands, earnings inequality among households is rising in all the rich countries shown.

What Do the Numbers Mean, Really? Calculations using alternative data sources yield roughly the same result: the United States ranks very high on measures of economic inequality—and has been growing more unequal. But, does high and rising inequality mean that those at the bottom of the distribution are worse off? Not necessarily. During the 1990s, for example, even as earnings inequality was increasing in the United States, poverty rates were falling (poverty has increased in the last several years, however). How can this be? The answer is that rising inequality can be the outcome of a number of income distribution processes, only one of which involves the worst off becoming even worse off. These processes include the following: (1) the people on top become better off while those on the bottom become worse off; (2) the people on both the top and the bottom become worse off, but those on the bottom decline faster; (3) everyone is better off, but incomes rise faster for those on the top than those on the bottom. Situation 1 is what many critics say has been going on and what many people tend to think is going on when they see inequality statistics. Situation 3 is what many defenders of the American economy say was going on during the Clinton and Bush years, although many acknowledge that improvements at the bottom of the income scale have been modest.[c] Inequality tends to decrease a little during deep recessions as the assets of the wealthy become less valuable, and this may have been the case during the Great Recession of recent years, though official figures are not yet available.

What Do You Think? Some people think that inequality is inherently unjust and that rising inequality, even in cases where people on the bottom are better off in an absolute sense, is something that

3. Capitalist economies invariably have business cycles, alternating periods of high and low (or even negative) economic growth. In the former, firms, investors, and those who have jobs all tend to gain, to one degree or another; in the latter down period, rewards to firms, investors, and workers grow only slowly, stagnate, or even decline. Historically, capitalism has experienced these fluctuations around a general upward trend of economic

society must rectify. How do you feel about this? Why might one argue that inequality is acceptable if people in all parts of the income structure are better off even if those on the bottom only improve a little? What do you think about the issue of inequality and democracy? If those on the top have relatively more income every year, what might be the effect of their continually increased political influence?

[a]"Ever Higher Society, Ever Harder to Ascend," *The Economist* (January 1, 2005), p. 22. Also see Kevin Phillips, *Wealth and Democracy: How Great Fortunes and Government Created America's Aristocracy* (New York: Broadway Books, 2002).

[b]"American Democracy in an Age of Rising Inequality," Report of the American Political Science Association's Taskforce on Inequality and American Democracy,

Perspectives on Politics, 2 (2004), pp. 651–666; Larry M. Bartells, "Is the Water Rising? Reflections on Inequality and American Democracy," *PS* (January, 2006), pp. 39–42.

[c]Gregg Easterbrook, *The Progress Paradox: How Life Gets Better While People Feel Worse* (New York: Random House, 2003).

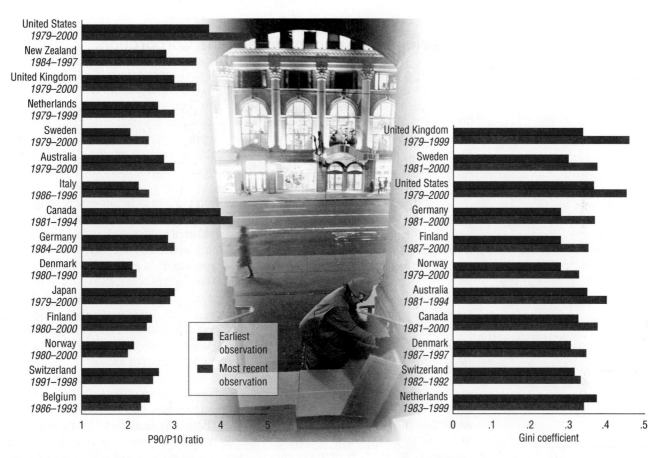

P90/P10 Ratios for Earnings Among Full-Time Employed Individuals, 1979–2000

Note: Countries are ordered by change in inequality (most recent observation minus earliest observation). Data for Norway include part-time employees.

Gini Coefficients for Market Income Among Working-Age Households, 1979–2000

Note: Countries are ordered by change in inequality (most recent observation minus earliest observation). *Source:* The 90/10 ratio graph and the Gini coefficient graph are from Lane Kenworthy and Jonas Pontusson, "Rising Inequality and the Politics of Redistribution in Affluent Countries," *Perspectives on Politics* 3, no. 3 (Washington, D.C.: The American Political Science Association, 2005), pp. 451–452.

growth. One reason for this overall growth, despite periods of negative growth, seems to be that in bad times, inefficient and ineffective firms fall by the wayside and innovative and nimble firms emerge better positioned for the next phase of growth.

At times, the up and down cycles can become quite extreme, a so-called boom-and-bust pattern. The biggest bust of the twentieth century in American capitalism was the Great Depression of the 1930s, when industrial production fell by half and unemployment at one point reached 31 percent. Our current economic troubles—a long and deep recession and a "jobless" recovery—followed the bursting of a gigantic real estate bubble (fueled by a flood of easy credit) and the collapse of the financial industry, and it was the deepest downturn since the Great Depression.

Though the United States has had a capitalist economy for a very long time, it has changed considerably over our history.

Industrialization and the Rise of the Corporation

At the time of the first census in 1790, almost three-quarters of all Americans worked in agriculture. Most of the remainder of the population worked in retail trade, transportation, and skilled trades closely connected to agriculture. About 80 percent of the working, male, nonslave population was self-employed, owning small farms, stores, wagons and horses, and workshops.[38] Until the Civil War, the American capitalist economy (with the notable exception of the slave-holding South) was highly competitive, with many small enterprises, first tied to agriculture and then increasingly to manufacturing.

After the Civil War, and partly as a result of it, the economy became increasingly industrialized and concentrated in giant enterprises.[39] By the turn of the twentieth century, the United States was the world's leading industrial nation, with many Americans working in manufacturing jobs in enterprises of unprecedented size. Partly, this change in scale was related to technology: the steam engine, electrical power, and the assembly line provided the means of bringing thousands of working people together for industrial production. Partly, this change in scale was tied to cost: most of the new industrial technologies required unheard-of levels of investment capital. Large enterprises were also encouraged by changes in the laws of incorporation, which allowed competing corporations to merge into single, giant enterprises. A wave of mergers between 1896 and 1904 fashioned the corporate-dominated economy familiar to us today.

The American economy and American corporations grew impressively during the first two-thirds of the twentieth century. Although thrown seriously off track for at least a decade by the Great Depression, the economy was pushed forward again by World War II and the Cold War that followed; both triggered rapid and substantial increases in government spending, research and development, and technological innovation. By 1975, 11 of the largest 15 corporations in the world were American; by

MASS PRODUCTION MANUFACTURING   The principles of assembly-line, mass production manufacturing were honed to near perfection by Henry Ford in the early twentieth century at his Highland Park complex in Michigan. Here, workers assemble a portion of a Model T, the first car to reach the mass public in the United States. How did Ford's innovation help change the face of the nation?

1981, 40 percent of the world's total foreign direct investment was still accounted for by the United States.[40]

American corporations were in the saddle in the years stretching from the end of World War II to the mid-1970s. Most major industries in the United States were dominated by three or four firms—such as GM, Ford, and Chrysler, or the "Big Three," in autos—that mass-produced commodities such as steel, cars, and refrigerators. Facing little domestic or foreign competition in the U.S. market and protected in their market dominance by federal regulators, major companies enjoyed substantial and stable profits over many years. Because they could easily pass on their costs in the prices they charged consumers, corporations were happy to enter into contracts with labor unions that provided good wages and benefits for their employees, as well as employment stability, and predictability for themselves. One result was an impressive expansion of the middle class and a general rise in the American standard of living.

Globalization and Hyper-Competition

The relatively protected and stable world of the post–World War II corporation is gone, replaced by a form of capitalism in the United States in which major companies face intense and unrelenting competition at home and abroad. Their changed situation was brought about by a set of near-simultaneous transformations across a broad front. There were, for example, revolutionary changes in technology, including rapid computerization and the development of the Internet, and dramatic improvements in the speed and costs of moving raw materials and commodities here and abroad (containerized trucking and shipping, bigger and faster jet planes, high-speed trains, improved highways). There was also a strong move in the United States, beginning in the 1970s and picking up steam after that, to deregulate a broad range of industries (including shipping, banking, securities, and telecommunications, among others) in hopes of fighting inflation and improving American competitiveness in the face of the galloping economies of Japan, the so-called Asian tigers, and the European Union. And, finally, a number of international agreements came into force that diminished barriers to trade and investment across national borders.

GLOBALIZATION The largest American corporations are also global corporations in the sense that they produce, market, and sell their products all over the world. Here, men take a break at a Starbucks in a shopping mall in Khobar, Saudi Arabia. How does American globalization create advantages or disadvantages for the countries affected?

Will the United States be the world's largest economy for long?

Introduction The relative size of one's economy is very consequential for countries. Domestically, a large economy allows governments, if they so choose, to provide generous safety nets, social services, and amenities for their people. Internationally, a large economy allows governments, again if they so choose, to exercise influence in world affairs, whether through the use of military power, the export of cultural products, or the extension of development assistance. It is extremely fortunate for Americans that our economy is so large; indeed, it remains the largest in the world today—even in the wake of the Great Recession—though that status is likely to change in favor of China before too long. Nevertheless, we remain extremely wealthy compared to other countries. What we choose to do with these bountiful resources depends on what the American people want from their government and how responsive political leaders are to what their citizens convey to them.

Mapping the Relative Size of the American Economy Here are two cartogram maps provided by Worldmapper.org, developed by researchers at the University of Sheffield and the University of Michigan. Each shows the countries of the world drawn in proportion to their share of world gross domestic product, based on what is called "purchasing power parity," that is, taking into account the purchasing power of each nation's currency. The one on the left shows the world in

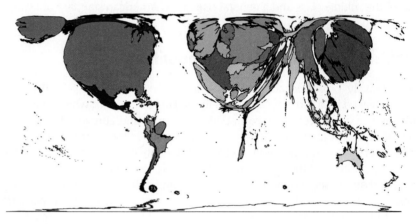

GDP 2002

© Copyright 2006 SASI Group (University of Sheffield) and Mark Newman (University of Michigan).

---

globalization

The increasing tendency of information, products, and financial capital to flow across national borders, with the effect of more tightly integrating the global economy.

Globalization[41] is the term that is often used to describe this new world where goods, services, and money flow easily across national borders. In this new world, companies can and must produce and sell almost anywhere and seek hard-working and talented employees where they can find them. They can also find subcontractors and partner companies in diverse geographical locations to supply them with parts, as Boeing does for the airplanes it assembles, or with finished products, as Walmart does to supply its many stores. With the infrastructure provided by global financial markets, investors can move money to those places and into those companies wherein they believe they can get the highest rate of return. Customers, having a wider range of choices, increasingly insist on the best possible products at the lowest prices possible, and will switch where they shop with breathtaking speed to make sure this happens.[42]

With many emerging markets, new industry-spawning technologies, fickle investors and customers, and ample investment capital for new companies— though finance froze for a period in 2008 and 2009 despite massive infusions of government money into the banking system—large companies everywhere face fierce competition. Growth and profitability,

? How does the rapid globalization of the economy present challenges or opportunities for leveling the playing field among rich and poor in the United States?

2002. Though rivaled by the countries of the European Union taken together, the American economy was by far the world's largest national economy, with Japan in second place. Continental South America and Africa hardly register at all. The map on the right is a cartogram that summarizes expert opinion on the likely size of national economies in 2015. The changes are rather startling. The United States remains extremely wealthy, though it is predicted to trail a surging China which has been growing at roughly three to four times the rate of the rich democracies. The forecast also shows the European Union countries and Japan accounting for smaller shares of the global economy, with India, Brazil, and Southeast Asia accounting for more.

What Do You Think? Americans have been accustomed to being the leading global economic power. As the leading power, the United States was able for a long time, especially in the half century after the Second World War, to dominate the deliberations and decisions of international economic organizations such as the World Bank and the International Monetary Fund, often to its advantage. The United States also has been able to finance its comfortable way of life with money borrowed from the rest of the world on relatively reasonable terms. Much of this may change as China becomes more important economically (and, inevitably, militarily). How will Americans and their leaders respond to our nation's changing status? Though we will remain an impressively wealthy country, what will it be like to share our former leading role with another country so different from our own? And, in the face of the economic surge of China, India, and Brazil, what will we choose to do as a nation to remain globally competitive? How wisely will we use our considerable human and economic assets in the years ahead? And what role will government play in all of this? Will it do more or less? Should it do more or less?

Source: Worldmapper, map numbers 164 and 169 (**www.worldmapper.org**). The SASI Group (University of Sheffield) and Mark Newman (University of Michigan), accessed February 2010.

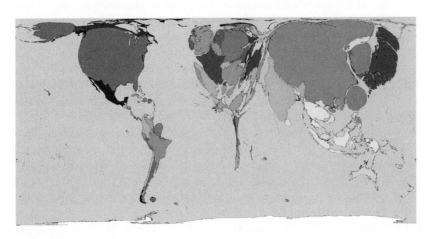

GDP 2015
© www.worldmap

Standard World Map

even survival, for many of them, are no longer routine as they were for much of the post-war period. Some formerly powerful companies, for example, simply disappeared (including TWA, Eastern, and Pan Am among American airlines), giving way to more innovative and nimble challengers (e.g., JetBlue and Southwest), while others were forced to dramatically change their business model (e.g., Kodak shifting from film to digital photography and IBM focusing on IT services after offloading its computer manufacturing division to the Chinese company Lenovo). With the possible exception of large oil companies, even the most powerful companies today dare not stand pat for fear of losing out to new competitors. Microsoft, for example, must figure out how to meet the challenge of Google and its Internet-based model of computing.

In some sense, all of this has been quite positive. In 2009, the American economy was still the largest in the world measured by GDP, about as large as the combined economies of Japan, Germany, Great Britain, France, and Brazil (but smaller than that of the European Union). To be sure, the rise of China, India, and Brazil, and the success of the European Union, mean that America's share of world GDP is shrinking, but it still remains impressive in size. (See the "Mapping American Politics" feature for more on America's changing share of global GDP.)

But globalization and hyper-competition, in association with productivity-producing innovation, can have negative consequences as well. In a global economy where companies are fighting for labor cost, technological, and price advantages over other firms, most companies feel compelled to become, in the popular phrase, "lean and mean," with many of them trimming or eliminating health care plans and shedding employees (because technological advances mean they can do more with less) as part of their competitive strategies. Some companies, moreover, believe they must outsource to lower-cost suppliers and shift some operations to other locations. In this highly competitive economy, unions are being forced to make wage and benefit concessions, the number of manufacturing jobs has stopped growing (although manufacturing output continues to grow because of technological innovations), and certain "creative class" skills are highly sought after and rewarded[43]—software engineers, portfolio managers, website creators, filmmakers, and business strategists, for example—while others are not—low-skill manual and service workers, for example. For the former, work tends to be both exciting and lucrative. For the latter, work is routine, not very well paid, and characterized by frequent layoffs and part-time status. This may be part of the reason why a booming economy in the 1990s and a growing economy in 2003–2006 did not diminish income inequality in the United States. Indeed, with most of the economic gains since the early 1990s going to highly prized talent, asset owners, and top executives of large companies, inequality has actually increased as we saw earlier in the "By the Numbers" feature.[44]

And, for many Americans, change is coming so fast that it is unsettling familiar ways of working and living and bringing unwelcome volatility and uncertainty to family incomes.[45] The new economy makes many Americans nervous. No wonder. The combination of innovative but risky new products from the mortgage industry, backed by real estate securities sold to American and foreign investors in the global financial market and customer desires to buy more expensive houses than they might be able to afford, for example, led to the sub-prime mortgage disaster in 2007, a real estate bust of historic proportions in 2008, and a credit freeze and stock market collapse that same year. Many Americans lost their homes and their retirement savings.

America in the World

4.3 Evaluate how America's power in the world has changed and why it matters

In addition to its prominent, although somewhat reduced, role in the global economy, America's powerful diplomatic, cultural, and military standing in the world is another important structural fact that has shaped our politics and government. We will discuss this in depth in Chapter 19. For now we will simply note that while the United States has economic, diplomatic, cultural, and military rivals in the world, no other country can lay claim to leadership in all areas as America can. While the United States has been so positioned since the end of World War II, matters crystallized in the 1990s, when startling changes happened in the world's military, political, and economic systems—all of which heightened, for a time, U.S. power in the world. Communism collapsed in eastern Europe. The Soviet Union ceased to exist. Communist China switched to a market economy. Most developing countries rejected the socialist development model, embraced "privatization," and welcomed foreign investment. Moreover, the United States took the lead in organizing the global economy. Many observers began to refer to the United States as the world's only superpower. The wars in Iraq and Afghanistan and the world recession of 2008 and 2009 (which many blamed on the reckless and under-regulated American financial industry), however, have depleted U.S. resources and capabilities, to some degree, and lessened the attractiveness of our economic model. So there is less talk today about the United States as the world's sole superpower, especially in light of the rise of the economic power of China and its rapid military modernization.

Even if it is reasonable to say that the United States remains the most powerful nation in the world in terms of military strength, and even if enthusiasm for President Obama abroad has brought approval ratings back to where they were before George W. Bush's presidency,[46] the United States has not had its way on many important matters, either with allies or adversaries, nor is it likely to do so in the future. With the threat of the Soviet Union no longer supplying the glue to hold them together, U.S. allies feel freer to go their own way on a wide range of international issues. The United States and the European Union nations have been deeply divided, for example, over trade issues and international treaties on the environment. Disagreements about NATO (the North Atlantic Treaty Organization) expansion and Iran have strained U.S. relations with Russia, while security issues, human rights violations, trade imbalances, currency issues, and protection of intellectual property have been an irritant in our relations with China. Turkey and Brazil in 2010 voted against the United States in the UN Security Council on imposing further sanctions on Iran for its nuclear program. Nor has the United States been able, in spite of all of its power, to bring the Palestinians and Israelis together. Nor, finally, has the threat of a terrorist attack gone away.

America's expansive role in world diplomatic, economic, and military affairs in the post–World War II era has had many implications for U.S. politics and government policies. For one thing, American leaders and the public have judged that our role requires a large military establishment and tilts a large portion of government spending priorities toward national security. For another thing, as we will see in later chapters, it has enhanced the role of the president in policymaking and diminished that of the Congress. Being the world's dominant military power is also very costly, and not simply in a budgetary sense (though that is the case as well). Americans have discovered that fighting insurgencies in Iraq and Afghanistan have seriously stretched the manpower resources of the military, leading to a greater-than-normal reliance on reserve and National Guard units as well as multiple deployments.

America's Political Culture

4.4 Analyze Americans' political culture and its implications for government and politics

Evidence strongly suggests that Americans share a core set of beliefs about human nature, society, and government that is very different from the core beliefs of people in

A TOUGH TIME IN AFGHANISTAN Even with its overwhelming military superiority, the United States cannot always meet its military and foreign policy objectives when force is applied. Insurgents in Afghanistan have proved resilient, and the counterinsurgency war there has stretched the United States's resources and tested the patience of the public. Why are we fighting in Afghanistan? What national security needs are being addressed by being there?

core beliefs

The most fundamental beliefs in a national population about human nature, the country, government, and the economy.

political culture

The set of core beliefs in a country that help shape how people behave politically and what they believe government should do.

political socialization

The process by which individuals come to have certain core beliefs and political attitudes.

other societies.[47] To be sure, we are a vast, polyglot mixture of races, religions, ethnicities, occupations, and lifestyles. Nevertheless, one of the things that has always struck foreign observers of the American scene, ranging from Alexis de Tocqueville (*Democracy in America*, 1835 and 1840), to James Bryce (*The American Commonwealth*, 1888), and John Micklethwait and Adrian Wooldridge (*The Right Nation*, 2004), is the degree to which a broad consensus seems to exist on many of the **core beliefs** that shape our attitudes and opinions, our ways of engaging in politics, and what we expect of our government, and how different the elements of this consensus are from political cultural elements elsewhere. To be sure, consensus on core beliefs does not mean that people always agree on what government should do in particular situations. Thus, people who agree that government's role should be limited might disagree on what specific things government should do (say, national defense or school lunch programs). To be sure, people in other societies share some of the core beliefs of Americans, but the package of core beliefs is truly exceptional.

Understanding our **political culture**—the set of core beliefs about human nature, society, and government—is important for understanding American politics and government. Why? Because the kinds of choices Americans make in meeting the challenges posed by a changing economy, society, and post–Cold War world depend a great deal on the core beliefs Americans hold about human nature, society, economic relations, and the role of government. In Chapter 5 we examine in some detail how Americans pass on these core beliefs to each new generation—a process called **political socialization**. In the remainder of this chapter, we look at the content of these core beliefs.

Individualism

Americans believe that individuals have, as the Declaration of Independence puts it, inalienable rights, meaning that individual rights take priority over rights that might be attributed to society or government. Indeed, the very purpose of government, following John Locke's ideas in *The Second Treatise on Government* (1690) and Jefferson's in the Declaration (1776), is to protect these rights. In formal, legal terms, this has meant that Americans have worked hard to protect the constitutional rights of speech, belief, and association (among others). In a more informal sense, this has meant an abiding belief among Americans in the importance of personal ambition and choosing one's own life goals and way of life.

American individualism is also expressed as a belief that one's fate is (and ought to be) in one's own hands, rather than the product of impersonal social and economic forces beyond one's own control. In particular, one's fortunes are tied to one's own efforts. Those with talent, grit, and the willingness to work hard, Americans believe, are more likely than not to end up on top; those without at least some of these qualities are more likely to wind up at the bottom of the heap. Americans tend to assume that people generally get what they deserve in the long run.

Americans are also more likely to believe that people are naturally competitive, always striving to better themselves in relation to others. Popular literature in America has always conveyed this theme, ranging from the Horatio Alger books of the late nineteenth century to the many contemporary self-help books with keys to "getting ahead," "making it," and "getting rich." The French have been known to refer to this celebration of the competitive individual over the community as the "Anglo-Saxon disease" (thus including the English) and profess to want no part of it in continental Europe.

This core belief about individualism affects American attitudes toward many issues, including inequality and what should be done about it.[48] Americans overwhelmingly endorse the idea of "equality of opportunity" (the idea that people ought to have an equal shot in the competitive game of life), for instance, yet they also overwhelmingly reject the idea that people should be guaranteed equal rewards, especially if this outcome comes from actions by government.[49]

> **?** How do the differing levels of support among the American people for the notions of "equality of opportunity" and "equality of condition" play out in the kinds of public policies we have in this country?

Not surprisingly, Americans tend to look favorably on government programs that try to equalize opportunity—Head Start, education programs of various kinds, school lunch programs, and the like—but are less favorable to welfare-style programs that seem to redistribute income from the hard-working middle class to individuals who are considered "undeserving."[50] Not surprisingly, given this core belief, Americans are less likely to support government efforts to equalize matters than are people in other rich democracies, especially if efforts to equalize outcomes in society involve imposing limits on individual striving and achievement[51] (see Figure 4.6).

Distrust of Government

From the beginning, Americans have distrusted government. Indeed, as you will recall from the discussion in Chapter 2, the framers created a republican constitutional system precisely because they distrusted government and were trying to create a set of constitutional rules that would deny government the means to act in mischievous or evil ways. Americans have long believed that when governments are imbued with too much power, they are tempted to interfere with private property, individual rights, and economic efficiency. Distrust of government still remains attractive to most Americans today, even though most Americans expect government to do far more than the framers ever imagined, such as Social Security, Medicare, environmental protection, and trying a variety of measures to get the country out of its recent deep recession. In this respect—distrusting government yet supporting a range of programs that seem essential to the public's well-being—Americans are conflicted, to some extent, being what some have called ideological conservatives and operational liberals. As Ben Page and

ALL FOR ONE, ONE FOR ALL In Japan, commitment to the work team and the company are more important cultural values than they are in the United States. These Japanese supermarket workers start their day as a team. What might be some advantages and disadvantages to the Japanese viewpoint?

Which is more important for government to do?

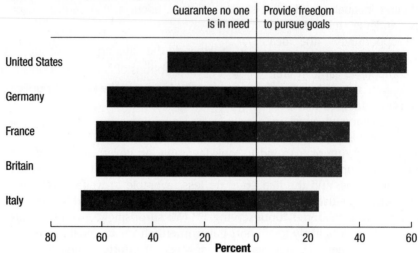

FIGURE 4.6 Freedom and Equality

American beliefs about the role of government are substantially different from those of people living in other rich democracies. Americans are much less likely to want government to do something about poverty and more likely to want to leave such an objective up to individuals. What are some pros and cons of this viewpoint? *Source:* Pew Research Center, reported in *The Economist* (November 8, 2003), p. 4.

Lawrence Jacobs put it: " … most Americans are philosophical conservatives but also pragmatic egalitarians. They look to government for help in ensuring that everyone has genuine equal opportunity plus a measure of economic security with which to exercise that opportunity."[52] But their distrust of government increases further when the help provided by government does not, in reality, seem to help or seems to help those who are already powerful and privileged as in the bank and auto company bailouts in the midst of the Great Recession.[53]

Distrust of government remains the "default" position of a majority of Americans. Even when they support particular government programs, they worry that government is getting too big, too expensive, and too involved in running things. During the health care debate in 2009, for example, the respected Pew survey discovered that a majority supported each major element of the Democrats health care package, but only 34 percent favored the package as a whole, with widespread concern that the bill created too much government control.[54] As one commentator put it, " … Americans are looking to the government for help, but they still don't like the government."[55] This core belief is not universally shared. In Germany, France, and Italy, for example, where governments have always played an important role in directing society and the economy, people are much more likely to trust the intentions and trustworthiness of government.

Democracy and Freedom

Certain beliefs about what kind of political order is most appropriate and what role citizens should play shape the actual daily behavior of citizens and political decision makers alike.

Democracy   At the time of the nation's founding, democracy was not highly regarded in the United States. During our history, however, the practice of democracy has been enriched and expanded, and the term *democracy* has become an honored one.[56] While regard for democracy is one of the bedrocks of the American belief system today, Americans have not necessarily always behaved democratically. After all, African Americans were denied the vote and other citizenship rights in many parts of the nation until the 1960s. It is fair to say, nevertheless, that most Americans believe in democracy as a general principle and take seriously any claim that their behavior is not consistent with it. For example, public opinion surveys done during the past 25 years consistently show that about 60 to 70 percent of Americans want to abolish the Electoral College in favor of a direct, popular vote for the president.

Freedom   Foreign visitors have always been fascinated by the American obsession with individual "rights," the belief that in the good society, government leaves people alone in their private pursuits. Studies show that freedom (also called *liberty*) is at the very top of the list of American beliefs and that it is more strongly honored here than elsewhere.[57] From the very beginning, what attracted most people to the United States was the promise of freedom in the New World. Many came for other reasons, to be sure: a great many came for strictly economic reasons, some came as convict labor, and some came in chains as slaves. But many who came to these shores seem to have done so to taste the freedom to speak and think as they chose, to worship as they pleased, to read what they might, and to assemble and petition the government if they had a mind to.

As in many cases, however, to believe in something is not necessarily to act consistently with that belief. There have been many intrusions on basic rights during our history. Later chapters address this issue in more detail.

Populism

The term **populism** refers to the hostility of the common person to concentrated power and the powerful. While public policy is not often driven by populist sentiments (for the powerful, by definition, exercise considerable political influence), populism has always been part of the American core belief system and has sometimes been expressed in visible ways in American politics.

One of the most common targets of populist sentiment has been concentrated economic power and the people who exercise it. The Populist movement of the 1890s aimed at taming the new corporations of the day, especially the banks and the railroads. Corporations were the target of popular hostility during the dark days of the Great Depression and also in the 1970s, when agitation by consumer and environmental groups made the lives of some corporate executives extremely uncomfortable. Populism is a staple of contemporary conservatism in the United States with its attacks on Hollywood, the media, and academic elitists.[58] Members of the modern Tea Party movement have directed their anger at bankers and bank bailouts, big government and taxes, and bicoastal elites who fail, they believe, to appreciate the values of ordinary Americans.

Populism celebrates the ordinary person. Given this widespread belief, it behooves political candidates in America to portray themselves as ordinary folks, with tastes and lifestyles very much like everyone else's. How else might one explain private-school-educated and aristocratically born-and-bred George H. W. Bush expressing his fondness for pork rinds and country and western music during the 1988 presidential campaign?

> **populism**
> The belief that the common person is every bit as good as those with wealth and power.

Percent saying they believe in God or a Supreme Being

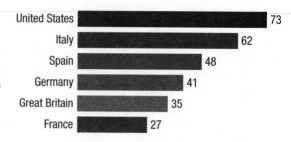

United States	73
Italy	62
Spain	48
Germany	41
Great Britain	35
France	27

FIGURE 4.7 Comparing Nations on Their Strength of Religious Belief

Compared with people in other rich democracies, a substantially higher proportion of Americans say they believe in God. In what ways might this shape what Americans want from government? *Source:* Harris Interactive, "Religious Views, and Belief Vary," press release (December 20, 2006).

Religious Beliefs

The United States is, by any measure, a strikingly religious society.[59] Polls conducted over the past three or four decades show that more Americans believe in God, regularly attend church, and say that religion is important in their lives, than people in any of the other rich democracies (see Figure 4.7). Levels of religiosity in the United States, in fact, approach those found in Muslim countries of the developing world.[60] This commitment to religion has existed from the beginning of the republic and is integrally related to the practice of politics in the United States—something that often baffles foreign observers.[61] Religious sentiments have been invoked by most important political leaders in the United States in their public pronouncements, and Americans have come to expect religious references when leaders talk about public matters. During the intense Democratic presidential nomination campaign in 2008, for example, Hillary Clinton and Barack Obama spoke often of their religious faith, something one is unlikely to hear in political campaigns in other rich democracies.

Religious faith affects politics in important ways. For one thing, it affects which issues become part of political debate and election campaigns. School prayer and the teaching of evolution have not been part of the political debate in many other democracies, for example. For another thing, religious belief has been important in drawing ideological lines. While churches and religious believers have often been on

? What developments and conditions in American society, economy, culture, and its position in the world might be democracy-enhancing? Which might be democracy-diminishing?

COURTING THE RELIGIOUS VOTE Religious believers are such an important component of the American electorate that office-seekers in both parties try to reach out to them with varying degrees of enthusiasm and success. Here, presidential candidates John McCain and Barack Obama greet one another before their appearance on Pastor Rick Warren's TV show from the Saddleback Church in Lake Forest, California, in August 2008. Why does religion figure so prominently in American politics, despite the separation of church and state?

the liberal side of the political divide to be sure—note the substantial involvement of religious leaders, organizations, and believers in the civil rights and anti–Vietnam War movements—strong religious beliefs are most associated with conservative tendencies in American politics. Public opinion polls show that the most religiously committed Americans (of all denominations) are also the most conservative Americans on issues ranging from abortion to prayer in the schools, social welfare, and military spending; church attendance, in the end, is a better predictor of party affiliation than income.

Using the DEMOCRACY STANDARD

Do structural factors in the United States support democracy?

Throughout this book, we have examined a number of structural factors that influence American politics. Chapters 2 and 3 examined the constitutional rules, and this chapter considered the main features of American society, economy, political culture, and America's place in the world and how each influences important aspects of politics and government in the United States. All of these structural factors are interrelated. The constitutional rules are substantially shaped by our beliefs about the nature of the individual, society, and government that make up our political culture. The political culture, in turn—with its celebration of the market, competitive individualism, and private property—is perfectly attuned to a capitalist economy. How the economy operates and develops has a lot to do with the life of the American people (where people live, what kind of work they do, and so on), as does the nation's place in the world. The characteristics of the American population trigger their own effects; the populace's level of education and skill has a lot to do with American economic performance, for instance.

The interplay of each of these factors—and the ways in which they are interpreted and played out through government policy and action—affects the quality and nature of democracy in the United States. But there is some disagreement on whether or not the American political structure, created by economics, culture, and social realities, fosters democracy.

On the one side, some argue that American society is open, diverse, and filled with opportunity for those who are ambitious and hard working. Economic growth is raising the living standards of the population (if modestly for most), which bodes well for democracy; note the evidence that high living standards and democracy seem to go together. Also, economic, technological, and social changes—including the Internet, ease of travel, medical advances, and more—are allowing more and more people to develop their unique abilities and capacities, to become informed, to link together with others who share their public concerns, to get involved in community and political affairs, and to have their voices heard by public officials. Most importantly, perhaps, these developments make it possible for Americans to shape their own lives, improving their situations and those of their families, without the need of government. In short, equality of opportunity and technological and social changes are making American society more hospitable to democracy.

Yet others counter that the American society fails to live up to the promise of equal opportunity and access to government, making it, in fact, far less democratic than other wealthy democracies. The economic system of the United States, while incredibly productive, distributes wealth and income in a highly unequal way, leaving the very few at the top with the lion's share. This leads to substantial inequalities in political power and influence among different income and wealth groups, as well as dividing Americans along ethnic, racial, religious, and regional lines. Such divisions undermine democracy because economic inequality always spills over into political inequality. To make matters worse, the American political culture celebrates an extreme form of individualism and antigovernment sentiments that makes it hard for Americans to cooperate in a way that makes it possible for the people to use government to serve public purposes.

SUMMARY

4.1 Determine how changes in the location and diversity of the population have affected American politics

- The most important changes in the American population are its diversification along ethnic, religious, and racial lines and its relocation from rural to urban and suburban areas and to the Sun Belt.

- These changes have enhanced the political influence of the southern and western states in Congress and presidential elections and of voters in suburban areas around the country. The influence of rural voters has diminished.

- Minority racial and ethnic groups have gained political influence as their numbers have grown.

4.2 Assess how the American economy shapes government and politics

- The American economy is a capitalist economy that has evolved from a highly competitive, small-enterprise form to a corporate-dominated one with a global reach.

- The American economy has shown itself to be productive and wealth producing, resulting in a high standard of living, yet it has also produced high levels of income and wealth inequality and periods of economic instability and financial difficulties.

- The political responses to difficult economic times like the Great Depression of the 1930s and the Great Recession of 2008–2009 and the jobless recovery

that followed have increased the role of government in society and the economy.

4.3 Evaluate how America's power in the world has changed and why it matters

- America's diplomatic, political, and military standing in the world has been largely unrivaled since the downfall of the Soviet Union. But the United States's power in world affairs is limited in important ways and becoming ever more limited, making it harder for the country to get its way in foreign affairs.

- The United States's status as a military superpower has changed the content of foreign policy, the balance of power between the president and Congress, the size of the federal government, and the priorities of the government's budget.

4.4 Analyze Americans' political culture and its implications for government and politics

- Americans believe strongly in individualism, limited government, and free enterprise. Beliefs about democracy, liberty, the primacy of the common people, and a strong religious orientation also help define the political culture.

- The political culture shapes American ideas about what the good society should look like, the appropriate role for government, and the possibilities for self-government.

TEST YOURSELF

Answer key begins on page T-1.

4.1 Determine how changes in the location and diversity of the population have affected American politics

1. Citizen dissatisfaction with immigration has recently resulted in which of the following government responses?
   a. President Obama's dispatch of troops to help guard Arizona's border with Mexico
   b. The closure of American borders to most immigrants
   c. A guest-worker program enacted under George W. Bush that provides illegal immigrants with a path to citizenship
   d. Reduced efforts to prevent illegal immigration of those fleeing economic hardship
   e. All of the above

2. Which of the following government policies encouraged Americans to move out of the cities and into the suburbs?
   a. Generous farm subsidies enacted during the Great Depression to prevent food shortages
   b. Government-sponsored land give-away programs in urban fringe areas
   c. Massive government road-building programs enacted after World War II
   d. Public transportation programs that linked small towns and urban areas with free train and bus service
   e. Direct government gasoline subsidies aimed at revitalizing domestic energy exploration
3. What political consequences are likely to result as the U.S. population ages?

4.2 Assess how the American economy shapes government and politics

4. Which of the following frequently occurs in a capitalist economy?
   a. Income inequality
   b. Productivity declines
   c. Economic stagnation
   d. Constant, monotonic economic growth
   e. Social upheaval
5. Which of the following is an advantage of globalization for typical American citizens?
   a. Increased depletion of natural resources
   b. Increased choices in consumer goods
   c. Increasingly generous health care plans and other employee benefits
   d. Increased outsourcing
   e. Increased career opportunities in the manufacturing sector
6. Evaluate whether the current economic environment is friendly or hostile to the interests of labor unions.

4.3 Evaluate how America's power in the world has changed and why it matters

7. Which of the following worked to diminish America's power in the world?
   a. The collapse of communism
   b. The world recession of 2008 and 2009
   c. The elimination of a market economy in China
   d. Enthusiasm for Barack Obama at home and abroad
   e. The peace accords reached between Israelis and Palestinians
8. America's position as the only superpower is being challenged by China, which has experienced rapid economic expansion and military modernization. True / False

4.4 Analyze Americans' political culture and its implications for government and politics

9. Which of the following core beliefs is engrained in American political culture?
   a. Collectivism
   b. Trust of government
   c. Agnosticism
   d. Populism
   e. Economic egalitarianism
10. Which of the following government policies is least consistent with the American belief in egalitarianism?
    a. Head Start
    b. School lunch programs
    c. Welfare-style programs
    d. Income tax
    e. Student loans
11. Explain why Americans are sometimes described as simultaneously being ideological conservatives and operational liberals.

myp⊕liscilab EXERCISES

Apply what you learned in this chapter on MyPoliSciLab.

Read on **mypoliscilab.com**

eText: Chapter 4

Study and Review on **mypoliscilab.com**

Pre-Test
Post-Test
Chapter Exam
Flashcards

Watch on **mypoliscilab.com**

Video: America's Aging Population
Video: Who Is in the Middle Class?
Video: Facebook Privacy Concerns
Video: The President Addresses School Children

Explore on **mypoliscilab.com**

Simulation: What Are American Civic Values?
Comparative: Comparing Political Landscapes
Timeline: Major Technological Innovations That Have Changed the Political Landscape
Visual Literacy: Using the Census to Understand Who Americans Are

INTERNET SOURCES

Fedstats
www.fedstats.gov/
Statistical information on the U.S. economy and society from more than 70 government agencies.

Pew Hispanic Center
http://pewhispanic.org
A rich site for data on Hispanic immigration to the United States and polling information on public opinion on immigration topics.

The International Monetary Fund on Globalization
http://www.imf.org/external/np/exr/key/global.htm
A site with a wealth of statistical information on the extent and impacts of globalization, as well as expert analyses of globalization trends and developments.

Pew Research Center
http://people-press.org
Notable not only for its U.S. and global public opinion surveys but a leader in presenting information on social and demographic trends in America.

Statistical Abstract of the United States
www.census.gov/statab/
A vast compendium of statistical information on the government, the economy, and society.

Worldmapper: The World as You've Never Seen It
www.worldmapper.org/index.html/
A collection of world statistical information presented in cartogram form; useful for comparing the United States with other countries.

SUGGESTIONS FOR FURTHER READING

Bartels, Larry M. *Unequal Democracy: The Political Economy of the New Gilded Age.* New York and Princeton, NJ: Russell Sage Foundation and Princeton University Press, 2008.
An examination of growing income and wealth inequality in America and how it is shaped by and shapes our politics.

Gosselin, Peter. *High Wire: The Precarious Financial Lives of American Families.* New York: Basic Books, 2008.
Suggests that more and more Americans are close to financial disaster because of cutbacks in public and private safety nets.

Hochschild, Jennifer L. *Facing Up to the American Dream.* Princeton, NJ: Princeton University Press, 1995.
A brilliant examination of the ideology of the American dream and how race and social class affect its interpretation and possibilities.

Page, Benjamin I., and Lawrence R. Jacobs. *Class War: What Americans Really Think About Economic Inequality.* Chicago: University of Chicago Press, 2009.
Based on their own national opinion survey, the authors suggest that Americans across the board recognize and are worried about rising inequality and support many specific government programs to improve the lot of those less well off.

Reich, Robert B. *Supercapitalism: The Transformation of Business, Democracy, and Everyday Life.* New York: Alfred A. Knopf, 2007.
A description of how the arrival of hyper-competitive capitalism has increased our power as consumers and investors but decreased our power as citizens.

Zolberg, Aristide R. *A Nation by Design: Immigration Policy in the Fashioning of America.* New York and Cambridge, MA: Russell Sage Foundation and Harvard University Press, 2006.
The definitive work on why the United States has the immigrant mix that it does.

In Part 2, we discussed a number of fundamental structural factors that affect how American politics works: the Constitution, our federal system, the nature of the American society and economy, the political culture, and the international system. In Part 3, we turn to what we call political linkage factors: public opinion, the mass media, organized interest groups, political parties, elections, and social movements. These people and institutions are affected in many ways by the structural factors already discussed. They, in turn, strongly affect the governmental institutions that are the subject of the next portion of the book. They are not a formal part of government, but they directly influence what sorts of people are chosen to be government officials—who is elected president and who goes to Congress, for example. They also affect what these officials do when they are in office and what sorts of public policies result.

5 | Public Opinion

LEARNING OBJECTIVES

After reading this chapter, you should be able to:

5.1 Characterize the ideal role of public opinion in a democracy

5.2 Describe methods used to measure public opinion

5.3 Analyze the process of political socialization

5.4 Relate political attitudes to race, gender, age, income, and other factors

5.5 Assess the American public's ability to rule

THE VIETNAM WAR AND THE PUBLIC

On August 2, 1964, the Pentagon announced that the U.S. destroyer *Maddox*, while on "routine patrol" in international waters in the Gulf of Tonkin near Vietnam, had undergone an "unprovoked attack" by three communist North Vietnamese PT boats. Two days later, the Pentagon reported a "second deliberate attack" on the *Maddox* and its companion destroyer, the *C. Turner Joy*. In a nationwide television broadcast, President Lyndon Johnson referred to "open aggression on the high seas" and declared that these hostile actions required that he retaliate with military force. Air attacks were launched against four North Vietnamese PT boat bases and an oil storage depot.[1]

Years later, the *Pentagon Papers*, a secret Defense Department study leaked to the news media by defense analyst Daniel Ellsberg, revealed that the American people had been deceived. The *Maddox* had not been on an innocent cruise; it had, in fact, been helping South Vietnamese gunboats make raids on the North Vietnamese coast. The second "attack" apparently never occurred. At the time, however, few skeptics raised questions. On August 7, 1964, by a vote of 88–2, the Senate passed the Tonkin Gulf Resolution, which

approved the president's taking "all necessary measures," including the use of armed force, to repel any armed attack and to assist any ally in the region. A legal basis for full U.S. involvement in the Vietnam War had been established.

For more than a decade, the United States had been giving large-scale military aid to the French colonialists, and then to the American-installed but authoritarian South Vietnamese government, to fight nationalists and communists in Vietnam. More than 23,000 U.S. military advisers were there by the end of 1964, occasionally engaging in combat. On the other side of the world, the American public knew and cared little about the guerrilla war. In fact, few knew exactly where Vietnam was. Nevertheless, people were willing to go along when their leaders told them that action was essential to resist communist aggression.

After the Tonkin incident, people paid more attention. Public support for the war increased. When asked in August what should be done next in Vietnam, 48 percent said to keep troops there, get tougher, or take definite military action while only 14 percent said to negotiate or get out.[2] Through the fall of 1964, more people wanted to step up

the war than wanted to pull out, and many endorsed the current policy.

But the number of U.S. troops in Vietnam rose rapidly, reaching 536,100 at the end of 1968, and casualties increased correspondingly. A total of 1,369 Americans were killed in 1965; 5,008 in 1966; 9,377 in 1967; and 14,589 in 1968.[3] Television news began to display weekly casualty counts in the hundreds, with pictures of dead American soldiers going home in body bags. The war became expensive, as politicians put it, in "American blood and treasure." Senate hearings aired antiwar testimony. Peace marches and demonstrations, though resented by much of the public, nonetheless increased pressure to end the war. By December 1967, about as many people (45 percent) agreed as disagreed with the proposition that it had been a "mistake" to send troops to fight in Vietnam.

Then catastrophe struck. In January 1968, during Vietnam's Tet holidays, the North Vietnamese army launched what became known as the *Tet Offensive:* massive attacks throughout South Vietnam, including an assault on the U.S. embassy in Saigon. The American public was shocked by televised scenes of urban destruction and bloody corpses, of U.S.

soldiers destroying Ben Tre village "in order to save it," of marines bogged down in the rubble of the ancient city of Hue, and of a 77-day siege of the American firebase at Khe Sanh. The chief lesson seemed to be that a U.S. victory in Vietnam, if feasible at all, was going to be very costly in terms of lives and dollars.

After Tet, criticism of the war—by politicians, newspaper editorials, and television commentators such as Walter Cronkite and others—mushroomed, and public support for the war diminished. President Johnson, staggered by a surprisingly strong vote for antiwar candidate Eugene McCarthy in the New Hampshire primary, announced that he would limit the bombing of North Vietnam, seek a negotiated settlement, and withdraw as a candidate for reelection. In March 1968, only 41 percent of Americans described themselves as hawks (supporters of the war), a sharp drop from the 61 percent of early February. Anger over Vietnam contributed to the election defeat of the Democrats the following November.

After taking office in January 1969, President Richard Nixon announced a plan to begin a slow withdrawal of troops from Vietnam, with the aim of turning the fighting over to South Vietnamese forces. A majority of the public supported the plan but soon supported calls for a more rapid withdrawal, telling pollsters they wanted to move in this direction even if it might lead to the collapse of the South Vietnamese government. The shift in mood was propelled, no doubt, by rising American casualties, numerous congressional hearings on the war, and massive anti-war demonstrations. After a slow start on withdrawals in 1969 (about 100,000), the pace picked up, and most American troops were gone by mid-1973. There can be little doubt that public opinion influenced U.S. disengagement from the war.

The Vietnam story shows how government officials can sometimes lead or manipulate opinion, especially when it concerns obscure matters in faraway lands, and how opinion is affected by events and their presentation in the mass media. The story also shows that public opinion, even on foreign policy matters, can sometimes have a strong effect on policymaking. This complex interaction between public opinion, the news media, elected officials, and foreign policy in Vietnam is not very different from what has been going on with respect to the war in Iraq where a substantial majority of the public, believing administration claims about the existence of weapons of mass destruction in Iraq (since proved untrue), supported the invasion of that country in 2003 to topple Saddam Hussein. By 2006, a majority of Americans were telling pollsters that the war was a mistake, a shift in mood propelled by mounting American casualties, a lack of progress in achieving either democracy or stability in Iraq, and news about the mistreatment of prisoners at the Abu Ghraib prison. The shift in public attitudes was a major factor in the Democratic Party's victory in the 2006 congressional elections and Barack Obama's win in 2008.

THINKING CRITICALLY About This Chapter

This chapter is about public opinion, how it is formed, and what effect it has on American politics and government.

Using the FRAMEWORK

You will learn in this chapter how the structural-level factors we learned about in Chapter 4—including historical events, the political culture, economic and social change—as well as family and community socialization, shape public opinion. You will also learn how public opinion influences the behavior of political leaders and shapes many of the policies of the federal government.

Using the DEMOCRACY STANDARD

Based on the standard of democracy described in Chapter 1, public opinion should be one of the decisive factors in determining what government does. You will see in this chapter, however, that while the influence of public opinion is important, public officials must pay attention to other political forces as well. They sometimes pay close attention to public opinion; at other times, they pay only slight attention to it.

Democracy and Public Opinion

5.1 Characterize the ideal role of public opinion in a democracy

core beliefs (political)
Individuals' views about the fundamental nature of human beings, society, the economy, and the role of government; taken together, they comprise the political culture.

Most Americans share certain **core beliefs** about the nature of human beings, society, and the political order. These core beliefs—including belief in individualism, limited government, and free enterprise, among others—make up the American political culture, as described in Chapter 4. In addition to their overarching core beliefs, most Americans also have

political attitudes about the specific political issues of the day, including attitudes about government policies, public officials, political parties, and candidates. **Public opinion** refers to these political attitudes expressed by ordinary people and considered as a whole—particularly as they are revealed by polling surveys.

Public opinion is particularly important in a democracy if we understand democracy to be fundamentally about the rule of the people. For the people to rule, they must have their voice heard by those in government. To know whether or not the people rule, we require evidence that those in government are responsive to the voice of the people. The best evidence that those in power are responsive to the voice of the people is a strong showing that what government does reflects the wishes of the people. The wishes of the people can be discerned in elections, to be sure, but a particularly powerful way to know what the people want is to ask them directly in a polling survey. In a real democracy, there must be a close match between public opinion and government policies and actions, at least in the long run.

Curiously, however, many leading political theorists, including some who say they believe in democracy, have expressed grave doubts about the wisdom of the public. James Madison, Alexander Hamilton, and other Founders of our national government worried that the public's "passions" would infringe on liberty and that public opinion would be susceptible to radical and frequent shifts.[4] Journalist and statesman Walter Lippmann declared that most people do not know what goes on in the world; they have only vague, media-provided pictures in their heads. Lippmann approvingly quoted Sir Robert Peel's reference to "that great compound of folly, weakness, prejudice, wrong feeling, right feeling, obstinacy and newspaper paragraphs which is called public opinion."[5]

Modern survey researchers have not been much kinder. The first voting studies, carried out during the 1940s and 1950s, turned up what scholars considered appalling evidence of public ignorance, lack of interest in politics, and reliance on group or party loyalties rather than judgments about the issues of the day. Repeated surveys of the same individuals found that their responses seemed to change randomly from one interview to another. Philip Converse, a leading student of political behavior, coined the term *nonattitudes:* on many issues of public policy, many or most Americans seemed to have no real views at all but simply offered "doorstep opinions" to satisfy interviewers.[6] Political scientist Larry Bartels recently

> **political attitudes**
> Individuals' views and preferences about public policies, political parties, candidates, government institutions, and public officials.
>
> **public opinion**
> Political attitudes and core beliefs expressed by ordinary citizens as revealed by surveys.

NOT ALL CAMPAIGNS ARE THE SAME   While many survey researchers and scholars lament America's general lack of interest in all matters political, some elections are so compelling that more people pay attention. The Obama–Clinton contest for the Democratic nomination and the Obama–McCain general election contest drew more attention, turnout, and volunteering than is usually the case, especially among young people like these students working the "get out the vote" phones for Obama. What factors might induce young people to stay politically attentive and involved?

demonstrated in a rigorous analysis of a multitude of surveys that middle class and lower income Americans know surprisingly little about the economy and tend to support government policies that make their economic positions worse than they might be.[7] Economist Bryan Caplan argues that public opinion is more influential than it should be, having shown that widespread public ignorance about how the economy works leads people to support harmful public policies.[8]

? When might it be acceptable for the government to act against the will of the majority of citizens?

What should we make of this? If ordinary citizens are poorly informed and their views are based on whim, or if they have no real opinions at all, or if these opinions are wrong-headed in a serious way, it hardly seems desirable—or even possible—that public opinion should determine what governments do. Both the feasibility and the attractiveness of democracy seem to be thrown into doubt. When we examine exactly what sorts of opinions ordinary Americans have, however, and how those opinions are formed and changed, we will see that such fears about public opinion have been exaggerated.

Measuring Public Opinion

5.2 Describe methods used to measure public opinion

Decades ago, people who wanted to find out anything about public opinion had to guess, based on what their barbers or taxi drivers said, on what appeared in letters to newspaper editors, or on what sorts of one-liners won cheers at political rallies. But the views of personal acquaintances, letter writers, or rally audiences are often quite different from those of the public as a whole. Similarly, the angry people who call in to radio talk shows may not hold views that are typical of most Americans. To figure out what the average American thinks, we cannot rely on unrepresentative groups or noisy minorities. Fortunately, social scientists have developed some fairly reliable tools for culling and studying the opinions of large groups of people.

Public Opinion Polls

A clever invention, the public opinion poll, or **sample survey**, now eliminates most of the guesswork in measuring public opinion. A survey consists of systematic interviews conducted by trained professional interviewers who ask a standardized set of questions of a rather small number of randomly chosen Americans—usually about 1,500 of them for a national survey. Such a survey, if done properly, can reveal with remarkable accuracy what the rest of us are thinking.

The secret of success is to make sure that the sample of people interviewed is representative of the whole population; that is, that the proportions of people in the sample who are young, old, female, college-educated, black, rural, Catholic, southern, western, religious, secular, liberal, conservative, Democrat, Republican, and so forth are all about the same as in the U.S. population as a whole. This representativeness is achieved best when the people being interviewed are chosen

sample survey

An interview study asking questions of a set of people who are chosen as representative of the whole population.

through **random sampling**, which ensures that each member of the population has an equal chance of being selected. Then survey researchers can add up all the responses to a given question and compute the percentages of people answering one way or another. If for some reason some element of the population is under-represented or over-represented in the sample—say young people or people living in rural areas—researchers can "weight" the relevant population group, giving it more or less importance in the total sample, so that the mix of elements in the final sample closely matches the general population. Statisticians can use probability theory to tell how close the survey's results are likely to be to what the whole population would say if asked the same questions. Findings from a random sample of 1,500 people have a 95 percent chance of accurately reflecting the views of the whole population within about 2 or 3 percentage points.[9]

> **random sampling**
> The selection of survey respondents by chance, with equal probability of being selected, to ensure their representativeness of the whole population.

For a number of reasons, perfectly random sampling of a national population is not feasible. Personal interviews have to be clustered geographically, for example, so that interviewers can easily get from one respondent to another. Telephone interviews—the cheapest and most common kind—are clustered within particular telephone exchanges. Still, the samples that survey organizations use are sufficiently representative so that survey results closely reflect how the whole population would have responded if everyone in the United States had been asked the same questions at the moment the survey was carried out. Recently, some commercial polling organizations have tried to do polling on the Internet. For the most part, these attempts fall prey to the problem of nonrandom sampling. Not all Americans own computers; not all computer owners regularly use the Internet. So, polling people by Internet is going to capture a sample that is very unrepresentative of the American population.

Challenges of Political Polling

Those who use poll results—including citizens encountering political polls in newspapers and on television—should be aware of the following problems with polls and what competent pollsters try to do about them. (See the "By the Numbers" feature for more on what to watch out for.)

Issues of Wording   The wording of questions is important; the way in which a question is worded often makes a big difference in the way it is answered.

- A question that asks "do you favor the death penalty?" is likely to get a higher proportion of people saying they are in favor than a question that asks "do you favor or oppose the death penalty?" because the former gives only one option.[10] Attaching the name of a popular president or an unpopular one to a survey question—as in "Do you support President X's proposal for Medicare reform?"—affects how people respond. Good survey questions try to avoid such "leading" wording.

- "Closed-ended" or "forced-choice" questions, which ask the respondents to choose among preformulated answers, do not always reveal what people are thinking on their own or what they would come up with after a few minutes of thought or discussion. So, in this sense, a survey may not always be capturing what people think is important or what choices they would make. Some scholars believe that such questions force people to express opinions about matters on which they really don't have an opinion or don't even know what the question means.[11] For these reasons, "open-ended"

Do Americans support stem-cell research? How do we know which surveys to believe?

Should the federal government encourage or discourage medical research that uses embryonic stem cells? President George W. Bush issued an executive order in 2001 severely restricting this kind of research for institutions and individuals funded by federal grants (most biomedical research). President Barack Obama in 2009 issued an executive order lifting most of these restrictions. Proponents say the use of such cells, often harvested from unused embryos from fertility clinics, is almost certain to lead to new medical treatments for a wide range of genetically linked diseases, such as Parkinson's and juvenile diabetes. Opponents say the expanded use of stem cells for research will encourage more abortions—aborted embryos being a potentially important source of stem cells—as well as the creation of cloned embryos, both of which, in their view, are morally unacceptable.

Why It Matters In the long run, government policies tend to follow public opinion on major issues. Whether the federal government will allow research in this emerging biomedical field, and whether it will help pay for basic research through grants, will depend a great deal on how strongly the public supports or rejects the idea.

Behind the Number When the issue first came to the attention of the American public, it certainly looked as if the public strongly supported stem-cell research. In early 2001, several leading survey organizations reported the public in favor of moving along this path: an NBC News/*Wall Street Journal* poll showed 69 percent in favor, Gallup reported 54 percent in favor, ABC News weighed in with 58 percent in favor, and the Juvenile Diabetes Foundation reported 70 percent in favor. On the other hand, a poll sponsored by the Conference of Catholic Bishops showed only 24 percent in favor of stem-cell research.

Calculating the Number In the surveys reported here from 2001, the various polling organizations did not simply ask respondents whether they were in favor of stem-cell research or against it, but offered alternative positions for respondents to consider, briefly spelling out the arguments being made for both sides in the debate. So it would seem, given the care with which questions were written and the opinion

numbers reported above, that proponents of stem-cell research had won the initial public opinion battle.

Criticisms of the Number But not so fast! Consider a number of problems raised by academic critics, all of which are related to a concern about whether Americans really had opinions at all about stem-cell research when they were first polled:

- High levels of "don't know" responses are a clue that the public has not formed well-grounded opinions about the survey issue. Unfortunately, among the surveys cited, only the Gallup organization offered such an option to respondents. The Gallup finding of high numbers of "don't know" responses suggests Americans may have been more uncertain about stem-cell research in 2001 than appears on the surface.
- When wide variations in opinion are reported—in this case, between those in the Catholic Bishops' survey and the others—the culprit may be the question wording. Well-established and strongly held opinions are not easily shaken or changed by question wording.

questions are sometimes asked in order to yield more spontaneous answers, and small discussion groups or "focus groups" are brought together to show what emerges when people talk among themselves about the topics a moderator introduces.

Issues of Intensity and Timing

Often, while the wording of a question may be perfectly acceptable, the question may not capture the relative intensity of respondents' feelings about some policy or political issue. Thus, for example, a substantial majority of Americans has, for a long time, supported increased government control of the sale and ownership of guns. But, for the most part, they do not feel very strongly about it and rarely base their vote on where a candidate stands on the issue. Pollsters try to get around this problem by trying to build in intensity measures into the responses that are offered to people participating in a survey. Most commonly pollsters will provide more than simple "yes–no" or "agree–disagree" answer options, including instead a set of five to seven options ranging from "strongly agree" to "strongly disagree." At other times, surveys will ask how respondents would rank the importance of certain problems or policies. Still, these remain fairly indirect ways of getting at intensity.

Consequently, when question wording leads to wide variations in expressed opinions, public opinion specialists suspect that the public has not yet formed opinions about the issues being addressed in the survey. There is some evidence of this in the Bishops' survey; examination of the survey shows that some fairly loaded language was used, including wording such as "the live

embryos would be destroyed in their first week of development." Their questionnaire, moreover, states that the embryos would be used "in experiments," leaving unmentioned possible medical advances arising from research.

What to Watch For Although respondents in a survey are generally willing to help out survey researchers by saying whether they are "for" or "against" one thing or another, they may not really have solid, well-formed opinions about the issue being addressed. Three very useful clues are

- A high number of "don't know" responses. Check the original source of the survey results reported in the newspaper or on television to find out the number of these responses.
- Wide variations in the results of opinion surveys on a particular issue. Do not depend on the results of one survey, but look at several on the same subject.
- The presence of highly detailed questions that explain the issue to the respondent. Go to the original source and see how the question or questions are worded.

It is worth pointing out that recent polling shows far fewer "don't know" responses than were evident at the beginning of the decade, suggesting that people's views are solidifying. In Gallup's poll on the subject in 2009, for example, only 7 percent had no opinion. And, it seems that public sentiment is solidifying on the side of stem-cell research's advocates, with 51 percent saying they favored easing existing restrictions on stem-cell research or having no restrictions at all. Also, those who say they believed stem-cell research to be morally objectionable fell from 39 percent in 2003 to 30 percent in 2009.

What Do You Think? Have you formed an opinion about the benefits and drawbacks of stem-cell research? How do newly announced breakthroughs in the development of stem cells from sources other than unused embryos affect how you feel about the issue, if at all? If you have an opinion, do you believe it is based on information you have encountered and thought about carefully? If you have formed a solid point of view on stem-cell research, you may want to contact various elected officials and let them know where you stand.

Sources: Adam Clymer, "The Unbearable Lightness of Public Opinion Polls," *The New York Times* (August 12, 2001), "Week in Review," p. 1; Richard Morin, "Who Knows?" *The Washington Post National Edition* (September 10–16, 2001), p. 34; the Gallup Poll, February 20–22, 2009.

The timing of a survey can be important. For elections, in particular, polling needs to happen as close to election day as possible in order not to miss last-minute switches and surges. Most famously, survey organizations in 1948 predicted a comfortable victory of Republican Thomas Dewey over Democratic president Harry Truman, feeling so confident of the outcome that they stopped polling several weeks before election day, missing changes in public sentiments late in the campaign. Similarly, every major polling organization missed Hillary Clinton's win over Barack Obama in the 2008 New Hampshire primary partly because they finished their polling before an important television debate between the candidates two days before the election.

Issues of Sampling

Scholars and survey professionals worry about a number of things that can undermine the validity of survey research by making it difficult to draw a sample that is random, meaning representative of the entire population. In some cases, the problems seem to be getting worse. Here are the principal things they are concerned about:

- Because they are inundated by phone calls from advertisers who sometimes try to disguise themselves as researchers, Americans have become less willing to answer pollsters' questions.

THE POLLSTERS GET IT WRONG Harry Truman ridicules an edition of the *Chicago Tribune* proclaiming his Republican challenger, Thomas Dewey, president. Opinion polls stopped asking questions too early in the 1948 election campaign, missing Truman's last-minute surge. Top pollsters today survey likely voters right to the end of the campaign. Is it ever safe to rely heavily on polls?

- Finding themselves bothered by telephone solicitations that interrupt their lives, Americans are increasingly using answering machines and "caller ID" to screen their calls. Pollsters are finding it increasingly difficult to get past the screening.

- More and more Americans are turning to cell phones and cutting their reliance on land lines. Because mobile phones are often turned off, survey researchers cannot always get through to people who are part of the prospective random sample. Also, because people don't want to use their minutes up when they are reached, many are unwilling to take part in lengthy surveys. And, pollsters cannot use autodialing technology to randomly call hundreds or thousands of potential respondents because the Federal Communications Commission requires that pollsters dial cell numbers directly.

The top academic and commercial polling firms claim they are taking steps to overcome these problems—using repeated call-backs and statistical methods to fill in for missing people, for example—but the problems are likely to get worse before they get better. For now, we will have to make do with polling results from quality researchers and firms. A good rule of thumb is to see which polls are most relied upon by public opinion scholars and other specialists on American politics.

Political Socialization: Learning Political Beliefs and Attitudes

5.3 Analyze the process of political socialization

The opinions and attitudes revealed by public opinion polls do not form in a vacuum. A number of important factors—among them families, schools, churches, the mass media, and social groups with which individuals are most closely associated—significantly influence both our core beliefs and our political attitudes. Political scientists refer to the process by which individuals acquire these beliefs and attitudes as **political socialization**. The instruments by which beliefs and attitudes are conveyed to individuals in society (such as our families, schools, and so on) are called **agents of socialization**.

Political socialization is a lifetime process in the sense that people engage in political learning throughout the life-course.[12] However, political learning in childhood and adolescence seems to be particularly important, as childhood is the period when people attain their core beliefs and general outlooks about the political world.[13]

The *family* plays a particularly important role in shaping the outlooks of children. It is in the family—whether in a traditional or nontraditional family—that children pick up their basic outlook on life and the world around them. It is mainly from their family, for example, that children learn to trust or distrust others, something that affects a wide range of political attitudes later in life. It is from the family, and the

political socialization

The process by which individuals come to have certain core beliefs and political attitudes.

agents of socialization

Those institutions and individuals that shape the core beliefs and attitudes of people.

LEARNING ABOUT DEMOCRACY
Children gain many of their initial ideas about how the American political system works in their school classrooms. In the early grades, children gain impressions about the nation, its most important symbols (such as the flag), and its most visible and well-known presidents. They also learn the rudiments of democracy. Here, elementary school students take part in a mock election. How could breeding an entire generation of active participants change the face of American politics?

neighborhood where the family lives, that children learn about which ethnic or racial group, social class or income group, and religion they belong to and begin to pick up attitudes that are typical of these groups. In dinner table conversations and other encounters with parents, children start to acquire ideas about the country—ideas about patriotism, for example—and their first vague ideological ideas: whether government is a good or bad thing, whether taxes are a good or bad thing, and whether certain people and groups in society are to be admired or not (welfare recipients, rich people, corporations, and the like). Most importantly, because it represents the filter through which a great deal of future political learning takes place, many children adopt the political party identifications of their parents, especially if the parents share the same party identification. Although the relationship between parent and child party identification is weaker now than it was in the 1940s and 1950s, a majority of adult Americans still identify with the same party as their parents.

Schools are also important as agents of political socialization. In the early grades, through explicit lessons and the celebration of national symbols—such as the flag in the classroom, recitation of the Pledge of Allegiance, pictures on the walls of famous presidents, patriotic pageants, and the like—schools convey lessons about American identity and patriotism. In the middle grades, schools teach children about the political process by sponsoring mock presidential elections and elections to student government. In the upper grades, most students in most school districts take courses in American history and American government and continue learning about participation through student government.

Popular culture—movies, music, and advertising—also shapes the budding political outlooks of young people.[14] To be sure, most of the messages coming from the popular culture have more to do with style, fashion, and attitude. But much in popular culture conveys political messages. Many rock performers such as U2, Bruce Springsteen, and Rise Against, for example, embed political messages in their songs. Many Hollywood movies come with a political message; for example, themes of sleazy politicians and untrustworthy or corrupt elected officials are quite common.

Political socialization does not stop when children become adults. Substantial evidence shows that a *college education* affects people's outlooks about public policies and the role of government. People with a college education, for example, are more likely to support government programs to protect the environment. We know, moreover, that people's political outlooks are shaped by *major events* or developments that affect the country during their young adult years. In the past, such events have included the Great Depression, World War II, the civil rights movement and the countercultural revolution of the 1960s, the Reagan Revolution of the 1980s, and the 9/11 terrorist attacks on the United States. The recent Great Recession may similarly shape long-term outlooks about government and large corporations, as may British Petroleum's Gulf oil spill. The effect of these events and developments seems most pronounced for young people who are just coming to a sense of political awareness. Political scientists identify this phenomenon as a *generational effect*. Thus, young people coming of age politically during the 1960s turned out to be much more liberal throughout their lives than young people coming of age during the 1950s or during the Reagan years.

Finally, a number of socializing agents affect people's attitudes and expressed political opinions throughout adulthood. *Jobs* and experiences at work can affect the confidence that people express about the future for themselves and their families. The *news media* affects people's attitudes by how they select and frame the issues they cover, as you will see in Chapter 6. Getting *married* and buying a home—because they bring with them new concerns with things such as the quality of local schools and neighborhoods, interest rates on home mortgages, and more—cause many people to alter their positions on political parties, candidates, and issues. So too does *retirement,* which often brings a new sense of urgency about government support for retirement and health care benefits.

How and Why People's Political Attitudes Differ

5.4   Relate political attitudes to race, gender, age, income, and other factors

We learned in Chapter 4's section on the political culture that Americans share a range of core beliefs. And, as we learned in the previous section, a broad range of socialization agents—from the news media and popular entertainment to government leaders and the schools—reinforce one another to shape our ideas about what it means to be an American and to live in the United States. However, Americans also grow up and live in a variety of distinctive environments that shape general political outlooks and specific attitudes in distinctive ways. In this section, we explore some of the most significant circumstances that define and often divide us in our political views.

? Which of the assorted factors discussed here have the strongest impact on political attitudes and beliefs? Is there one that trumps all the others on a range of issues—is wealth more important than race, ethnicity, or culture, for example? Does gender outweigh religion?

Race and Ethnicity

Polling reveals differences in political attitudes that divide significantly along racial and ethnic lines. Among the biggest differences are those between white and black Americans. Hispanics and Asian Americans also have some distinctive political opinions. Many white ethnic groups, however, are no longer much different from other members of the population.

African Americans On most core beliefs about the American system, few differences are discernible between black Americans and other Americans.[15] Similar percentages of each group believe, for example, that people can get ahead by working hard, that providing for equal opportunity is more important than ensuring equal outcomes, and that the federal government should balance its budget. Equal numbers say they are proud to be Americans and believe democracy to be the best form of government.[16] On a range of other political issues, however, the racial divide looms large,[17] though Barack Obama's election to the presidency has made African Americans more confident in the country and their place in it. Indeed, African Americans now believe more than white Americans that voting is a duty and that casting a ballot makes a difference.[18]

Partisanship is one important area where African Americans differ from whites. Blacks, who stayed loyal to the Republican party (the party of Lincoln and of Reconstruction) long after the Civil War, became Democrats in large proportions in the 1930s during the presidency of Franklin D. Roosevelt, whose New Deal greatly expanded the federal government's role in providing safety nets for the poor and unemployed. Most black Americans have remained Democrats, especially since the civil rights struggles of the 1960s. In 2008, African Americans were the most solidly Democratic of any group in the population: 69 percent called themselves Democrats, while only 3 percent called themselves Republicans (see Figure 5.1). In 2008, 95 percent of African Americans voted for African American Democrat Barack Obama; only 4 percent supported Republican John McCain.[19]

Black Americans also tend to be much more liberal than whites on economic issues, especially on those involving government programs to provide assistance to those who need help in the areas of jobs, housing, medical care, education, and so on. This liberalism reflects African Americans' economically disadvantaged position in American society and the still-real effects of slavery and discrimination. However, blacks tend to hold strong religious values and to be rather conservative on some social issues. More are opposed to abortion, for example, than are whites. In general, however, African Americans are very liberal (i.e., favor an activist government to help solve social ills). More blacks identify themselves as liberals than as conservatives or moderates, a pattern that is almost exactly reversed among whites.[20] African Americans also are more likely than Americans in general to favor government regulation of corporations to protect the environment and to favor labor unions.[21] Black and white divisions are most apparent on issues related to affirmative action. For example, 58 percent of African Americans but only 26 percent of whites agree with the statement that "the government should make every effort to improve the position of blacks and minorities, even if it means giving preferential treatment."[22]

Hispanics Hispanics—people of Spanish-speaking background—are the fastest-growing ethnic group in America and the largest minority group in the nation. As a whole, the Hispanic population identifies much more with the Democrats than the Republicans; among this group, Democrats enjoy a 47 percent to 13 percent

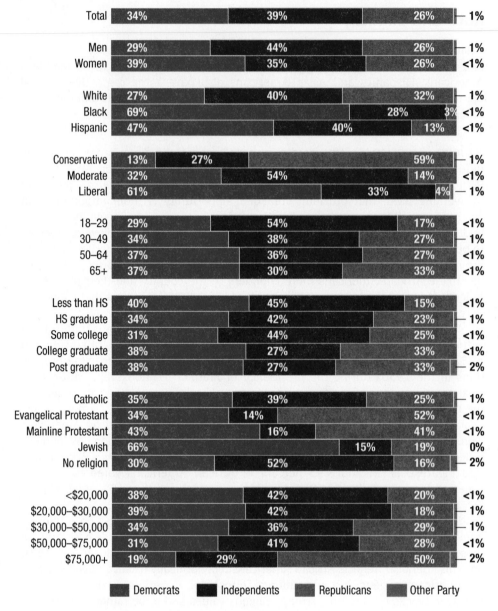

	Democrats	Independents	Republicans	Other Party
Total	34%	39%	26%	1%
Men	29%	44%	26%	1%
Women	39%	35%	26%	<1%
White	27%	40%	32%	1%
Black	69%	28%	3%	<1%
Hispanic	47%	40%	13%	<1%
Conservative	13%	27%	59%	1%
Moderate	32%	54%	14%	<1%
Liberal	61%	33%	4%	1%
18–29	29%	54%	17%	<1%
30–49	34%	38%	27%	1%
50–64	37%	36%	27%	<1%
65+	37%	30%	33%	<1%
Less than HS	40%	45%	15%	<1%
HS graduate	34%	42%	23%	1%
Some college	31%	44%	25%	<1%
College graduate	38%	27%	33%	<1%
Post graduate	38%	27%	33%	2%
Catholic	35%	39%	25%	1%
Evangelical Protestant	34%	14%	52%	<1%
Mainline Protestant	43%	16%	41%	<1%
Jewish	66%	15%	19%	0%
No religion	30%	52%	16%	2%
<$20,000	38%	42%	20%	<1%
$20,000–$30,000	39%	42%	18%	1%
$30,000–$50,000	34%	36%	29%	1%
$50,000–$75,000	31%	41%	28%	<1%
$75,000+	19%	29%	50%	2%

FIGURE 5.1 Party Loyalties Among Various Social Groups

African Americans, people who call themselves liberals, women, and Jews are the strongest Democratic identifiers. Evangelicals, people who call themselves conservatives, and high-income earners are the strongest Republican identifiers. *Source:* American National Election Studies. 2008; and the General Social Survey 2008.

advantage over Republicans (see Figure 5.1). However, the Hispanic population itself is quite diverse. Cuban Americans, many of them refugees from the Castro regime, tend to be conservative, Republican, strongly anticommunist, and skeptical of government programs. The much more numerous Americans of Mexican, Central American, or Puerto Rican ancestry, by contrast, are mostly Democrats and quite liberal on economic matters, although rather traditional on social questions—reflecting their predominant Roman Catholicism.[23] In 2008, 67 percent of the Hispanic vote went to Democrat Barack Obama. Republican support for the Arizona law giving police permission to stop and question people they suspect of being illegally in the country—most of those stopped are likely to be Hispanic—may make this group even more favorable toward the Democrats in the future (even though a federal district court ruled the law unconstitutional in 2010).

HISPANIC CHURCH-GOERS
Hispanic church-goers, like these at St. Francis Xavier Catholic Church, in Tulsa, Oklahoma, are likely to be economically liberal but socially conservative on issues such as same-sex marriage and abortion. How does culture affect political beliefs?

Asian Americans Asian Americans, a small but growing part of the U.S. population—a little more than 4 percent of the population in 2008—come from quite diverse backgrounds in the Philippines, India, Vietnam, Korea, Thailand, China, and elsewhere. As a group, Asian Americans are more educated and economically successful than the general population but are less likely to vote and express an interest in politics than people of equal educational and financial status. On social issues, Asian Americans support the death penalty and oppose same-sex marriage; on economic issues they are slightly more conservative than average. In recent elections, they have favored the Democrats; in 2008, 62 percent voted for Obama.

White Ethnics Other ethnic groups are not so distinctive in their political opinions. Irish Americans and people of Italian, Polish, and other southern or eastern European ancestry, for example, became strong Democrats as part of the New Deal coalition. But as they achieved success economically, their economic liberalism tended to fade, and their social conservatism became more prominent. By the 1980s, these groups were not much different from the majority of other white Americans in their attitudes about political and social issues.

Social Class

Compared with much of the world, the United States has had rather little political conflict among people of different income or occupational groupings; in fact, rather few Americans think of themselves as members of a social "class" at all. When forced to choose, about half say they are "working class" and about half say they are "middle class."[24] In Great Britain, on the other hand, where the occupational structure is similar to that of the United States, 72 percent of the population calls itself "working class."[25]

Still, since the time of the New Deal, low- and moderate-income people have identified much more strongly with Democrats than with Republicans. This still holds true today;[26] households in the lowest two income quintiles (the lowest 40 percent) are almost three times as likely to call themselves Democrats as Republicans. Upper-income people—whether high-salaried business executives, doctors, accountants, and lawyers or asset-rich people with no need to hold a job—have identified more strongly with the Republican Party for a long time, but this advantage for the GOP has narrowed, with many upper-income people increasingly identifying themselves as independents.[27]

People in union households have long favored the Democrats and continue to do so. About 6 in 10 people in union households say they favor the Democrats, roughly 11 percentage points higher than the party's support among all voters. In 2008, 59 percent of them voted for Barack Obama. This Democratic advantage has changed hardly at all since the mid-1970s, although it is important to be aware that the proportion of Americans who are members of labor unions is quite low compared with other rich countries and has been steadily declining, notwithstanding a small bounce-back in 2008 (see Chapter 7).

Lower-income people have some distinctive policy preferences. Not surprisingly, they tend to favor much more government help with jobs, education, housing, medical care, and the like, whereas the highest-income people, who would presumably pay more and benefit less from such programs, tend to oppose them.[28] To complicate matters, however, many lower-income people, primarily for religious and cultural reasons, favor Republican conservative positions on social issues such as abortion, law and order, religion, civil rights, education, and gay rights. Furthermore, many high-income people—especially those with postgraduate degrees—tend to be very liberal on lifestyle and social issues involving sexual behavior, abortion rights, free speech, and civil rights. They also tend to be

THE UAW ON BOARD   Barack Obama and other Democratic candidates can generally count on the support of union members, like these members of United Auto Workers Local 550 in Indianapolis. How might Republicans enhance their appeal to labor?

especially eager for government action to protect the environment. We can see this manifested in recent elections where more high-income, high-education congressional districts in places such as California and Connecticut have elected Democrats, while low-income districts in Kentucky, Tennessee, and West Virginia have sent Republicans to Congress.

Region

Region is an important factor in shaping public opinion in the United States. Each region is distinctive, with the South especially so. Although southern distinctiveness has been reduced somewhat because of years of migration by southern blacks to northern cities, the movement of industrial plants and northern whites to the Sun Belt, and economic growth catching up with that of the North, the legacy of slavery and segregation, a large black population, and late industrialization have made the South a unique region in American politics.[29]

Even now, white southerners tend to be somewhat less enthusiastic about civil rights than northerners; only people from the Mountain West (excluding Colorado and New Mexico) are as conservative on race. Southern whites also tend to be more conservative than people in other regions on social issues, such as school prayer, crime, and abortion, and supportive of military spending and a strong foreign policy (although they remain fairly liberal on economic issues, such as government health insurance, perhaps because incomes are lower in the South than elsewhere).[30]

These distinctive policy preferences have undercut southern whites' traditional identification with the Democrats, especially since the 1960s and 1970s, when Democrats became identified with liberal social policies. The white South's switch to the Republican party in the 1994 elections, in fact, is one of the major reasons Republicans were able to maintain control of Congress for a dozen years until the Democrats won back both houses in 2006. Though still in the majority among white southerners, there is some evidence that the Republican advantage is slipping in favor not of Democrats but of independents.[31] Moderate Democrats who appeal to independents have been making inroads in the region; Jim Webb won a Senate seat in Virginia in 2006 as did Kay Hagen in North Carolina in 2008. And Barack Obama won Virginia and North Carolina in the presidential race in 2008.

On many issues, northeasterners tend to be the most different from southerners, with midwesterners, appropriately, in the middle. Pacific Coast residents resemble northeasterners in many respects, but people from the Rocky Mountain states, with the exception of those in Colorado, tend to be quite conservative, with majorities opposed to a big government role in health insurance, for example.[32] The mountain states' traditions of game hunting in wide-open spaces have led them to cherish the right to bear firearms and to resist gun controls.

These regional differences should not be exaggerated, however. Long-term trends show a narrowing in regional differences on many core beliefs and political attitudes.[33] This is the outcome of years of migration of Americans from one region to another and the rise of a media and entertainment industry that is national in scale, beaming messages and information across regional lines.

Education

The level of formal education that people reach is closely related to their income level because education helps people earn more and also because the wealthy can pay for more and better schooling for their children. But education has some distinct political effects of its own.

As we will see in Chapter 10, education is generally considered the strongest single predictor of participation in politics. College-educated people are much more likely to say that they vote, talk about politics, go to meetings, sign petitions, and write letters to officials than people who have attained only an elementary or a high school education. The highly educated know more about politics. They know what they want and how to go about getting it—joining groups and writing letters, faxes, and e-mail messages to public officials. Within every income stratum of the population, moreover, college-educated people are somewhat more liberal than others, being more in favor of, for example, increased domestic spending to combat poverty and provide national health insurance. They also are more likely than other people in their same income stratum to favor multilateralism in international affairs, favoring the use of diplomacy, multination treaties, and the United Nations to solve global problems.[34]

People who have earned postgraduate degrees also have some distinctive policy preferences. They are especially protective of the civil rights, civil liberties, and individual freedom of atheists, homosexuals, protesters, and dissenters. Education may contribute to tolerance by exposing people to diverse ideas or by training them in elite-backed norms of tolerance.

Gender

A partisan "gender gap" first appeared in the 1980s and persists today, with the percentage of women who identify themselves as Democrats about 10 percentage points higher than men (see Figure 5.1). What seems to have been happening is a decline in the proportion of men and women who identify with the Republicans; a steady rise in the proportion of men who identify themselves as independents; and a sharp rise in women's identification as Democrats, particularly among unmarried women.[35] The differences show up in elections; in 2008, only 43 percent of women voted for Republican John McCain, compared with 48 percent of men. However, although the partisan gender gap is real and persistent—women identify more with the Democrats and are more likely to vote for Democratic candidates—the scale of the gap is not enormous, leading some scholars to suggest that the gender gap issue has been exaggerated.[36]

Women also differ somewhat from men in certain policy preferences. Women tend to be somewhat more supportive of protective policies for the poor, the elderly, and the disabled. Women tend to be more opposed to violence, whether by criminals or by the state. More women over the years have opposed capital punishment and the use of military force abroad and favored arms control and peace agreements.[37] Perhaps surprisingly, there is no gender gap on the issue of abortion.[38]

Age

Younger citizens are less likely to identify with a political party than older cohorts, although those who do are increasingly leaning toward the Democrats.[39] The young and the old also differ on certain matters that touch their particular interests: the draft in wartime, the drinking age, and, to some extent, Social Security and Medicare. But the chief difference between old and young has to do with the

SHOULDER TO SHOULDER Americans who came of age during the civil rights struggles of the 1960s are more likely than others to favor civil rights protections for African Americans. Here, white and black demonstrators march together in Selma, Alabama, in 1965 in support of voting rights for African Americans. Why do relatively short time periods, such as the Great Depression or the civil rights movement, have such a lasting influence on one's political outlook?

particular era in which they were raised. Those who were young during the 1960s were especially quick to favor civil rights for blacks, for example. In recent years, young people have been especially concerned about environmental issues, and they are much less supportive than other Americans of traditional or conservative social values on homosexuality and the role of women in society. More than any other age cohort, those between the ages of 18 and 29 support the idea of government-sponsored universal health insurance and legalization of same-sex marriage.[40] And, they were particularly attracted to the Democrats' youthful presidential candidate, Barack Obama, in 2008, with 66 percent voting for him. Often social change occurs by generational replacement in which old ideas, like the Depression-era notion that women should stay at home and "not take jobs away from men," die off with old people. But it is worth noting that older Americans are not necessarily entirely fixed in their views; like other Americans, those over the age of 60 have become, over the past decade or so, more tolerant of homosexuality and more supportive of the idea of women pursuing careers.[41]

? Does your generation have different views of politics from that of your parents? How did generational politics affect the 2008 presidential election? How about the 2010 congressional elections?

Religion

Although religious differences along denominational lines are and have always been important in the United States,[42] the differences between the religiously observant of all denominations and more secular Americans is becoming wider and more central to an understanding of contemporary American politics. We look first at denominational differences, then at what has come to be called the "culture wars."

Religious Denominations Roman Catholics, who constitute about 24 percent of the U.S. population, were heavily Democratic after the New Deal but now resemble the majority of Americans in their party affiliations—pretty evenly split between the Democrats and Republicans.[43] Catholics' economic liberalism has faded somewhat with rises in their income, although this liberalism remains substantial. Catholics have tended to be especially concerned with family issues and to espouse measures to promote morality (e.g., antipornography laws) and law and order. But American Catholics disagree with many church teachings; they support birth control and the right to have abortions in about the same proportions as other Americans, for example.

A majority of Americans (51 percent) are Protestant. Protestants come in many varieties—the relatively high-income (socially liberal, economically conservative) Episcopalians and Presbyterians; the generally liberal Unitarian-Universalists and middle-class northern Baptists; and the lower-income and quite conservative Southern Baptists and evangelicals of various denominations. The sharpest dividing line seems to be that between evangelical Protestants and mainstream Protestants. Evangelicals are much more likely to identify themselves as Republicans than as Democrats (52 percent compared to 34 percent) while those in mainstream churches favored the Democrats more (43 percent Democrat compared to 41 percent Republican). Evangelicals and mainstream Protestants also are sharply divided, with evangelicals taking decidedly more conservative positions on homosexuality and abortion.[44] In 2008, evangelicals cast an astounding 73 percent of their votes for John McCain.

A little under 2 percent of Americans are Mormons, members of the fast-growing Church of Jesus Christ of Latter-Day Saints. They are the most staunchly conservative and most solidly Republican of any major religious denomination in the country. Sixty percent claim to be conservative in their political orientation, with only 10 percent choosing liberal. They also favor Republicans over Democrats by a margin of 65 percent to 22 percent.

American Jews (like Mormons, just under 2 percent of the U.S. population and very much their mirror image politically) began to join the Democratic Party in the 1920s and did so overwhelmingly in the 1930s, in response to Franklin D. Roosevelt's New Deal social policies and his foreign policy of resisting Hitler. Most Jews have stayed with the party. Next to African Americans, they remain the most Democratic group in the United States: about 65 percent identify themselves as Democrats and only 23 percent as Republicans. In the 2008 presidential election, Jews cast 78 percent of their votes for Obama and only 21 percent for McCain. Jews are exceptionally liberal on social issues such as civil liberties and abortion. They also tend to be staunch supporters of civil rights. Although rising incomes have somewhat undercut Jews' economic liberalism, they remain substantially more supportive of social welfare policies than other groups.

People who say they are not affiliated with any religious institution or belief system at all are strongly Democratic in their party identification and relatively liberal on most social issues; 54 percent are Democrats and 23 percent are Republicans. Seventy percent of the unaffiliated say that abortion should always be legal or legal most of the time. Seventy-one percent of them agree with the statement that "homosexuality should be accepted by society."

Religiously Committed Versus the Less Committed and Secular

Among the factors that most differentiate Americans on political attitudes and partisanship is their degree of religious belief and practice.[45] The religiously committed, no matter the religious denomination, are the most likely Americans to vote Republican and to hold conservative views, particularly on social issues such as abortion, the death penalty, same-sex marriage, and stem-cell research. Committed and observant Catholics, Jews, and Protestants are not only much more Republican and socially conservative than people who practice no religion and/or claim to be totally secular, but they are also more Republican and socially conservative than their less committed and observant co-religionists. As an example, 55 percent of committed white evangelicals identify as Republican compared with only 38 percent of other Evangelicals (and a miniscule 15 percent among people who say they are secular). Among mainstream Protestant denominations, the committed are 38 percent Republican, compared with 31 percent among the less

LIBERAL BELIEVERS Although they are a distinct minority among believers, there is an increasing number of religiously committed people in all denominations who take liberal positions on matters such as global warming, poverty and its alleviation, and gay rights. Here, believers demonstrate in support of same-sex marriage in front of the state capitol in Olympia, Washington. How does this affect your view of religion as it relates to partisan politics?

committed. Taking all denominations together, to look at another example of how relative religious commitment matters, the "churched" are far more likely to vote Republican than those who are less "churched" or who don't go to church (or synagogue or mosque) at all (see Figure 5.2).

The gap between the religiously committed and other Americans—particularly those who say they never or almost never go to church—on matters of party identification, votes in elections, and attitudes about social issues has become so wide and the debates so fierce that many have come to talk about America's culture wars. On a range of issues—including Supreme Court appointments, abortion, the rights of gays and lesbians, prayer in the public schools, and the teaching of evolution—passions on both sides of the divide have reached what can only be called white-hot fever pitch. To be sure, much of the noise in the culture wars is being generated by leaders of and activists in religiously affiliated organizations and advocacy groups, exaggerating, perhaps, the degree to which most Americans disagree on most core beliefs and political attitudes.[46] But, the battle between the most and least religiously observant and committed has helped heat up the passions in American politics because each group has gravitated to one or the other political party—the former to the Republicans and the latter to the Democrats—and become among the strongest campaign activists and financial contributors within them.

FIGURE 5.2 Church Attendance and Vote in the 2008 Presidential Election

Source: National Election Pool (Washington, D.C.: Edison Media Research and Mitofsky International, November 4, 2008).
* Numbers in million

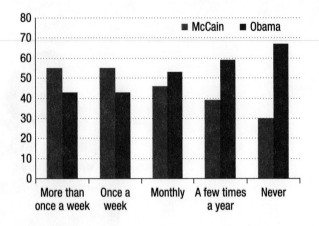

Party

People who say they are Democrats differ considerably in their political attitudes from those who say they are Republicans. Republicans are much more likely than Democrats to vote for Republican candidates and approve of Republican presidents; they tend to belong to different social and economic groups; and they are more likely to favor policies associated with the Republican Party. Republicans are much more likely than Democrats to support big business and an assertive national security policy, and to be against stem-cell research, same-sex marriage, and abortions, for example; Democrats are much more likely than Republicans to support government programs to help the poor and help racial minorities get ahead, to regulate business for consumer protection and greenhouse gas emissions, and to support gay rights and abortion on demand. Table 5.1 shows big differences on some of the major issues of the day between Republicans and Democrats. Figure 5.3 shows that the differences between them are growing ever wider. Republicans and Democrats, then, face each other today across a wide chasm.

TABLE 5.1 Partisanship and Issue Positions, 2009

Survey Statement	Percentage Agreeing with the Statement	
	Democrats	Republicans
Government should take care of people who can't take care of themselves.	77%	46%
Government should help more needy people even if the national debt increases.	65	29
Poor people have become too dependent on government programs.	62	83
The best way to ensure peace is through military strength.	43	75
We should restrict and control people coming into our country to live more than we do now.	64	83
The government is really run for the benefit of all the people.	60	41
[I am] in favor of same-sex marriage.	50	17
I am very patriotic (completely agree).	46	71

Source: Trends in Political Values and Core Attitudes, 1987–2009 (Washington, D.C.: Pew Research Center, 2009).

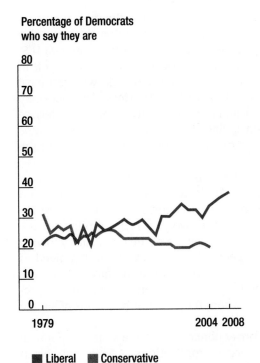

Percentage of Democrats who say they are

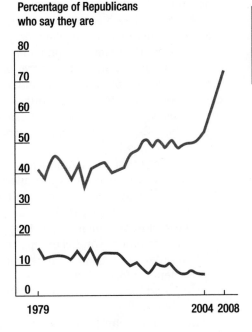

Percentage of Republicans who say they are

■ Liberal   ■ Conservative

FIGURE 5.3 The Growing Ideological Homogeneity of Party Identifiers

Party identification and political ideology are becoming more closely related. Republican identifiers, more conservative than Democratic Party identifiers anyway, are becoming even more conservative. At the same time, Democratic Party identifiers are becoming more liberal. The deep divide that reflects the confluence of parties and ideologies has become a key feature of modern American politics and contributes to much of the incivility and intensity of public affairs in recent years. *Source: New York Times/CBS News/Gallup Poll, 1979–2009.*

The Contours of American Public Opinion: Are the People Fit to Rule?

5.5   Assess the American public's ability to rule

Now that we know more about how public opinion is measured and why people hold certain core beliefs and political attitudes, we can return to the issue raised in the opening pages of this chapter concerning the place of public opinion in a society that aspires to be a democracy. Recall from the earlier discussion that many observers of American politics in the past and today have had little confidence in the abilities of the average person to understand vital public issues or to rationally engage in public affairs. If, as they have feared, ordinary citizens are uninformed, prone to rapid and irrational changes in their political attitudes, and easily led astray, there is not much reason to assume that public opinion can or ought to play a central role in deciding what government should do. However, as we will see in this section, further examination of the opinions of ordinary Americans and how they change in response to events and new information will demonstrate that such fears about an uninformed and irrational public may have been exaggerated.

?   To what extent are Americans equipped for self-government? Do they know or care enough about social issues and government policies to be trusted?

What People Know About Politics

Several decades of polling have shown that most ordinary Americans do not know or care a lot about politics.[47] Nearly everyone knows some basic facts, such as the name of the capital of the United States and the length of the president's term of office. But only about two-thirds of adults know which party has the most members in the House of Representatives. Only about 30 percent know that the term of a U.S. House member is two years; only about one-half know that there are two U.S. senators from their state.[48] And barely one in four Americans can explain what is in the First Amendment. Furthermore, people have particular trouble with technical terms, geography, abbreviations, and acronyms like NATO (the North Atlantic Treaty Organization) and NAFTA (the North American Free Trade Agreement). And, despite the explosion of information sources—including the Internet and 24-hour cable news—there has been no improvement in Americans' political knowledge over the past two decades.[49]

The things that most Americans don't know may not be vital to their role as citizens, however. If citizens are aware that trade restrictions with Canada and Mexico have been eased, does it matter that they recognize the acronym NAFTA? How important is it for people to know about the two-year term of office for the U.S. House of Representatives, as long as they are aware of the opportunity to vote each time it comes along? Perhaps most people know as much as they need to know in order to be good citizens, particularly if they can form opinions with the help of better-informed cue givers (experts, political leaders, media sources, informed friends, interest groups, and so on) whom they trust or by means of simple rules of thumb.[50]

We do not mean to minimize the consequences of people's lack of political knowledge. It has some extremely important implications. As we will see in Chapter 7, for example, when policy decisions are made in the dark, out of public view, interest groups may influence policies that an informed public would oppose. Nor do we mean to encourage complacency, fatalism, or ignorance. Individuals should take the personal responsibility to be good citizens, and organized efforts to alert and to educate the public are valuable. But low levels of information are a reality that must be taken into account. Perhaps it is unrealistic to expect everyone to have a detailed knowledge of a wide range of political matters.

IDEOLOGICAL DIFFERENCES The battle over health care reform often took place in the context of a broader ideological conflict about the role of government. Here, a demonstrator from the conservative Americans for Prosperity squares off against a Democratic Party activist in Lincoln, Nebraska, in 2009.

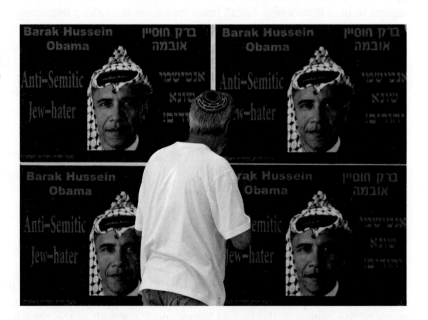

By the same token, we should not expect the average American to have an elaborately worked-out **political ideology**, a coherent system of interlocking attitudes and beliefs about politics, the economy, and the role of government. You yourself may be a consistent liberal or conservative (or populist, socialist, libertarian, or something else), with many opinions that hang together in a coherent pattern. But surveys show that most people's attitudes are only loosely connected to each other. Most people have opinions that vary from one issue to another: conservative on some issues, liberal on others. Surveys and in-depth interviews indicate that these are often linked by underlying themes and values, but not necessarily in the neat ways that the ideologies of leading political thinkers would dictate.[51]

For the same reasons, we should not be surprised that most individuals' expressed opinions on issues tend to be unstable. Many people give different answers when the same survey question is repeated four years or two years or even a few weeks after their first response. Scholars have disagreed about what these unstable responses mean, but uncertainty and lack of information very likely play a part.

None of this, however, means that the opinions of the public, taken as a whole, are unreal, unstable, or irrelevant. The *collective whole* is greater than its individual parts. Even if there is some randomness in the average individual's expressions of political opinions—even if people often say things off the top of their heads to survey interviewers—the responses of thousands or millions of people tend to average out this randomness and reveal a stable **collective public opinion**. Americans' collective policy preferences are actually very stable over time. That is, the percentage of Americans who favor a particular policy usually stays about the same, unless circumstances change in important ways, such as a major war or economic depression. Moreover, even if most people form many of their specific opinions by deferring to others whom they trust (party leaders, television commentators, and the like) rather than by compiling their own mass of political information, the resulting public opinion need not be ignorant or unwise because the trusted leaders may themselves take account of the best available information. Some research, moreover, indicates that Americans' collective policy preferences react rather sensibly to events, to changing circumstances, and to new information, so that we can speak of a **rational public**.[52]

> **political ideology**
>
> A system of interrelated and coherently organized political beliefs and attitudes.
>
> **collective public opinion**
>
> The political attitudes of the public as a whole, expressed as averages, percentages, or other summaries of many individuals' opinions.
>
> **rational public**
>
> The notion that collective public opinion is rational in the sense that it is generally stable and consistent and that when it changes it does so as an understandable response to events, to changing circumstances, and to new information.

Attitudes About the System in General

At the most general level, Americans are proud of their country and its political institutions. For example, about 7 in 10 Americans say they feel it is important to vote (but not that many do vote; see Chapter 10).[53] In 2008, about 90 percent of Americans said they were proud to be an American; in a survey a few years earlier, only 43 percent of British, 33 percent of French, and 23 percent of Germans said the same about their own countries.[54]

However, there are indications that Americans have become more pessimistic about the ability of the country to solve its problems, perhaps no surprise given the wars in Iraq and Afghanistan, recessions in 2001 and 2008–2009 and slow job and income growth during the decade, and the government's poor handling of the Hurricane Katrina and Gulf oil spill disasters. The Pew Research Center, reporting results from its own polls and other leading surveys, put the level of "trust in government"—those who say they trust

government to do the right thing "always" or "most of the time"—at around 20 percent, down from the 40 percent average for most of the 1980s, and the 70 percent trust in government levels during the 1960s[55] By the summer of 2010, with the Gulf oil spill in the news and the war in Afghanistan dragging on, only 37 percent of Americans said the country was moving in the right direction.[56]

One important aspect of happiness or unhappiness with government is a judgment about how well Congress is doing. For much of the past four decades or so, the proportion of Americans disapproving of the job Congress is doing has been twice as high as the proportion approving. Things became especially bad for Congress in the last year of the Bush administration when unpopular bailouts of financial institutions were approved. Things improved a little (into the high 20s) in the first year of the Obama administration, but fierce partisan conflict over a stimulus bill and health care continued to hammer the legislative branch's public reputation.[57] By spring, 2010, only about 20 percent approved of how Congress was handling the nation's business.[58]

Another indicator of government performance is how well Americans judge the president has been doing his job. The public's evaluations of presidents' handling of their jobs depend on how well things are actually going. The state of the economy is especially important: when the country is prosperous and ordinary Americans are doing well and feeling confident about the future, the president tends to be popular; when there is high inflation or unemployment or when general living standards remain stagnant, the president's popularity falls. Pollsters have been asking Americans for many decades whether they approve or disapprove of the way the president is doing his job. The percentage of people saying they approve—the **presidential approval rating**—is taken as a crucial indicator of a president's popularity. Job approval fluctuates up and down with particular events and trends—Lyndon Johnson's approval fluctuated with events in Vietnam, and he decided not to run for reelection when his ratings fell to historic lows after the Tet Offensive—but in the current era, most presidents have come on hard times. Richard Nixon, Gerald Ford, and Jimmy Carter all had low approval ratings by the end of their terms. George H. W. Bush reached a then-record 89 percent approval in March 1991 in the aftermath of the Gulf War but fell below 30 percent by the summer, an unprecedented collapse.

presidential approval rating

A president's standing with the public, indicated by the percentage of Americans who tell survey interviewers that they approve a president's "handling of his job."

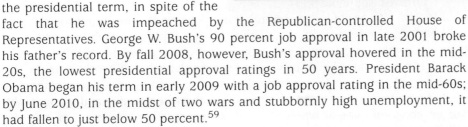

CLINTON GREETS THE PUBLIC Despite his tumultuous presidency and efforts by Republicans in Congress to remove him from office, Bill Clinton's approval rating among the American public at the end of his presidency was higher than that of any president since the end of World War II, with the exception of Eisenhower. Ronald Reagan came close, but still trailed Clinton. How can a president retain such popularity in the face of such conflict?

Oddly, Bill Clinton enjoyed the highest job approval ratings of any recent president for the final two years of the presidential term, in spite of the fact that he was impeached by the Republican-controlled House of Representatives. George W. Bush's 90 percent job approval in late 2001 broke his father's record. By fall 2008, however, Bush's approval hovered in the mid-20s, the lowest presidential approval ratings in 50 years. President Barack Obama began his term in early 2009 with a job approval rating in the mid-60s; by June 2010, in the midst of two wars and stubbornly high unemployment, it had fallen to just below 50 percent.[59]

There is growing evidence of an increase in "populist" anger directed against large corporations and banks, illegal immigrants, globalization, high levels of unemployment, bailouts and loan guarantees to financial institutions, and a growing national government involved in everything from owning financial institutions and auto companies to mandating health insurance coverage and doing more to control greenhouse gas emissions. Much like earlier manifestations of populist anger, cultural, media, and academic elites are handy targets for seemingly supporting most of these changes. Typically, populist movements both here and in other rich democracies have appealed to farmers and small businesspeople, those without college degrees, and many blue-collar and service workers barely hanging on to middle-class lifestyles. Today's "Tea Party" movement, encouraged and partially organized by conservative talk radio and cable television personalities such as Glenn Beck on FOX News, helped generate an enthusiasm gap between Republican and Democratic identifiers in the lead-up to the 2010 national elections and contributed to Democratic Party losses in congressional and state races.

Liberals and Conservatives

Although most Americans do not adhere to a rigid political ideology of the sort beloved by certain political philosophers or adhered to by many people around the world—for example, Marxism, communism, socialism, fascism, anarchism, radical political Islam, and the like—they do divide on the role they believe government should play. To complicate matters, Americans generally divide along two dimensions when it comes to government: one related to government's role in the economy, the other related to government's role in society. Some Americans—those we usually label **economic conservatives**—tend to put more emphasis on economic

> **economic conservatives**
> People who favor private enterprise and oppose government regulation of business.

economic liberals

People who favor government regulation of business and government spending for social programs.

social (lifestyle) liberals

People who favor civil liberties, abortion rights, and alternative lifestyles.

social (lifestyle) conservatives

People who favor traditional social values; they tend to support strong law-and-order measures and oppose abortion and gay rights.

policy preferences

Citizens' ideas about what policies they want government to pursue.

liberty and freedom from government interference; they believe that a free market offers the best road to economic efficiency and a decent society. Others—whom we usually label **economic liberals**—stress the necessary role of government in ensuring equality of opportunity, regulating potentially damaging business practices, and providing safety nets for individuals unable to compete in the job market. Government regulation of the economy and spending to help the disadvantaged are two of the main sources of political disputes in America; they make up a big part of the difference between the ideologies of liberalism and of conservatism. However, this accounts for only one of the two dimensions. It is also useful to distinguish between **social (or lifestyle) liberals** and **social (or lifestyle) conservatives**, who differ on such issues as abortion, prayer in the schools, homosexuality, pornography, crime, and political dissent. Those who favor free choices and the rights of the accused are often said to be liberals, while those preferring government enforcement of order and traditional values are called conservatives (see Table 5.2).

It should be apparent that opinions on economic and social issues do not necessarily go together. Many people are liberal in some ways but conservative in others. A gay activist, for example, would likely be a social liberal, but might also be an economic conservative when it comes to taxes and regulation of business. An evangelical minister preaching in a poor community might be a social conservative on issues such as homosexuality and pornography but an economic liberal when it comes to government programs to help the disadvantaged.

Policy Preferences

According to democratic theory, one of the chief determinants of what governments do should be what the citizens *want* them to do, that is, citizens' **policy preferences**. By and large, while more Americans say they are conservative or moderate than say they are liberal, they want government to do a great deal to address societal needs. One might say that a majority of Americans are philosophical conservatives and moderates but operational liberals.[60]

TABLE 5.2 Positioning Prominent Americans

	Economic Liberal	Economic Conservative
	(favors more government regulation of business to protect the environment and consumers, more progressive taxes, and more programs to help low-income Americans)	(favors less government involvement in economy and society, leaving more to the private sector)
Social Liberal (favors the right to abortion, more rights for gays and lesbians, more civil rights protections for minorities, and separation of church and state)	Bill and Hillary Clinton Barack Obama Nancy Pelosi	Milton Friedman Michael Bloomberg
Social Conservative (against abortion, supports traditional families and gender roles, favors more religious practices in public life)	Rev. Rick Warren Mike Huckabee	Ronald Reagan George W. Bush

Spending Programs   As Figure 5.4 shows, Americans have been consistent over the years in their positions on a range of things they want from government. We can see that large and rather stable majorities of Americans think we are spending "too little" on education, fighting crime, and providing health insurance. Many polls show that the public also gives consistently high support to Social Security, Medicare, and environmental protection programs. Substantial majorities, moreover, have said for many years that they want the government to pay for more research on diseases such as cancer and AIDS and to "see to it" that everyone who wants to work can find a job.[61]

By contrast, few people think too little is being spent on foreign aid; many more think too much is being spent. Except for disaster relief, such as for the 2005 tsunami in the Indian Ocean, foreign aid is generally unpopular. (The reason may be, in part, that few realize how little is spent on foreign aid—only about 1 percent of the annual federal budget is devoted to economic and humanitarian assistance; when this is made clear, support for economic aid rises sharply.[62]) Large majorities of the public oppose military aid or arms sales abroad. The space program wins only slightly greater support.

When public opinion changes, it usually does so for perfectly understandable reasons. Hard economic times, for example, often cause shifts in attitudes. It is perhaps not surprising then that economic troubles in 2001–2003 and 2008–2009 formed the backdrop for significant increases in public support for programs to "care for those who can't care for themselves" (increased from 57 percent in 1994 to 67 percent in 2007, but dropped to 63 percent in 2009).[63]

Social Issues   As Figure 5.5 shows, Americans make distinctions among different circumstances when deciding whether they favor permitting abortions. For much of the past three decades, about 55 percent of Americans have reported that they support the legality of abortion under certain circumstances. Thus, more are likely to find abortion acceptable if the life of the mother is in danger, but fewer support abortion when a woman says she simply does not want another child. About 25 percent say abortion should be legal under all circumstances; about 20 percent believe that abortion always should be illegal.[64] Views about abortion, then, have remained consistent over many years, even in the face of the furious cultural war that has swirled around this issue.[65]

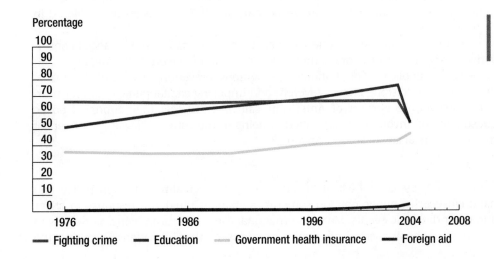

FIGURE 5.4   Public Support for Spending Programs

Large, fairly stable majorities of Americans have favored increased spending for fighting crime, aiding education, and government health insurance, but very few have favored increased foreign aid over the years (though support increased after 2000). *Note:* Year-to-year fluctuations have been averaged to create the trend line. *Source:* American National Election Study, 2008.

Military Spending Compared to Other Nations

Introduction While Americans generally do not call for more spending on the military and national defense, and while they tell pollsters they are hesitant to use troops abroad unless it is important in the defense of the nation, they have—since the end of the Second World War and at the urging of their leaders—supported a very large military establishment. Americans' firmly "isolationist" inclinations were transformed by the experiences of the Second World War, which the United States entered into largely unprepared; the perceived threat of the Soviet Union and communism; and the continuing problem of terrorism.

Mapping the World's Military Spending This cartogram map is provided by Worldmapper.org and was developed by researchers at the University of Sheffield and the University of Michigan. In the cartogram, each nation is drawn in proportion to its share of total world military spending. It includes monies spent by governments on military personnel and equipment as well as military assistance to other countries in 2002. The result is "eye-popping." The cartogram shows that the United States by this measure is the world's military superpower, dwarfing every other nation or group of nations. In that year, the United States was nine times larger than the second place military spender Japan, and much larger than all of the western European nations taken together. Russia and China lagged far behind. Indeed, in 2002, the United States accounted for fully 45 percent of all military spending in the world.

What Do You Think? Given the nature of the threats we face in the world today, do you think that the United States spends too much, too little, or just about the right amount on the military? If you think we spend too much, would you cut taxes and put back more money into the

As the nation has become more educated and its mass entertainment culture more open to diverse perspectives and ways of life, public opinion has become more supportive of civil liberties and civil rights for women and minorities. Beginning in the 1940s or 1950s, for example, more and more Americans have come to favor having black and white children go to the same schools and integrating work, housing, and public accommodations. In 2009, fully 83 percent of Americans said it was all right for blacks and whites to date one another, a big jump from 1987 when only 48 percent endorsed this view.[66] At the same time, however, there is considerable opposition among whites to affirmative action programs that involve the use of racial preferences. And, there has been a slow but steady increase in support of equal treatment for gays and lesbians, including rapidly increasing support for same-sex marriage.[67] These issues are explored in depth in Chapter 17.

On a number of issues, Americans support positions favored by social conservatives. Large majorities, for example, have consistently favored allowing organized prayer in the public schools, banning pornography, preventing flag burning, penalizing drug use, punishing crimes severely, and imposing capital punishment for murder. Moreover, 62 percent of Americans said in 2010 that they approved police questioning of anyone they suspected of being in the country illegally, the heart of the controversial law passed in Arizona.[68]

Foreign Policy and National Security In the realm of foreign policy and national security, public opinion sometimes changes rapidly in response to crises and other dramatic events. Major international events affect opinions, as we saw in the chapter-opening story on public reactions to the Tet Offensive during the

pockets of Americans, or would you want the government to spend the money on other things like environmental protection and health care? If you think we don't spend enough on the military, into what programs would you put extra monies? Military assistance to allies? More special forces? More high-tech warfare capabilities?

Source: Worldmapper, map number 279. The SASI Group (University of Sheffield) and Mark Newman (University of Michigan), 2006. (www.worldmapper.org)

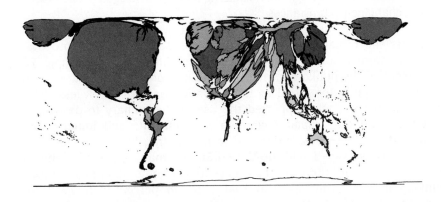

Standard World Map

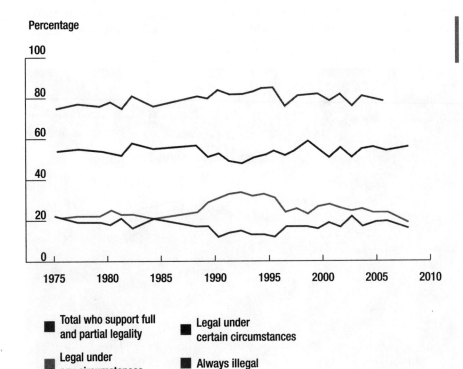

Percentage

1975 1980 1985 1990 1995 2000 2005 2010

■ Total who support full and partial legality

■ Legal under certain circumstances

■ Legal under any circumstances

■ Always illegal

FIGURE 5.5 Public Approval for Allowing Abortions

Only a minority of Americans supports or rejects abortion under any and all circumstances. For a long time now, a majority of Americans say they believe abortion should be legal, but only under certain circumstances. *Sources:* General Social Survey, 2006; Pew Research Center, "Trends in Political Views" 2009, for 2008 data.

isolationism

The policy of avoiding involvement in foreign affairs.

unilateralist

The stance toward foreign policy that suggests that the United States should "go it alone," pursuing its national interests without seeking the cooperation of other nations or multilateral institutions.

multilateralist

The stance toward foreign policy that suggests that the United States should seek the cooperation of other nations and multilateral institutions in pursuing its goals.

Vietnam War. The percentage of Americans saying we were wrong to invade Iraq steadily increased as the news from there got worse. Confidence in the effectiveness of American foreign and military policies declined sharply between 2005 and 2007.[69] This seems understandable given events on the ground. But often foreign policy opinions are quite stable. Since World War II, for example, two-thirds or more of those giving an opinion have usually said that the United States should take an "active part" in world affairs. The percentage supporting a U.S. role has remained relatively high, not fluctuating much with alleged public moods and changing circumstances.[70]

The public has been quite hesitant to use troops abroad, however, unless the threat to the United States is tangible. Just before U.S. troops were sent as peacekeepers to Bosnia in 1994, for example, 78 percent of the public opposed the idea and only 17 percent were in favor.[71] Opposition faded as the operation began to look less risky. The public strongly supported the use of the military to destroy Al Qaeda and the Taliban regime in Afghanistan[72] and initially supported President Bush's decision to invade Iraq in 2003, when only 23 percent of those surveyed said the United States "made a mistake sending troops to Iraq." By fall of 2005, with bad news from Iraq dominating the news, those thinking it was a mistake had soared to 58 percent.[73] Support for the armed conflict in Afghanistan, nine years after it began, was low by mid-2010; only 44 percent of Americans said it was "worth fighting."[74]

Although not many Americans embrace pure **isolationism**—the view that the United States should not be involved abroad and should only pay attention to its own affairs—the public (and political and economic leaders, as well) is divided over whether its involvement in the world should take a **unilateralist** or a **multilateralist** form. Unilateralists want to go it alone, taking action when it suits our purposes, and not necessarily seeking the approval or help of international organizations such as the United Nations or regional organizations such as NATO. Unilateralists are also uncomfortable with entering into too many international

SAYING "NO" TO THE WAR IN IRAQ Many Americans—including these demonstrators marching in New York City on March 23, 2003—opposed the decision to go to war in Iraq without the backing of the United Nations or the support of many traditional U.S. allies. Much to their disappointment, President Bush ignored their wishes and invaded Iraq in April. Why can the government continue with an action that so many citizens disagree with?

treaties. Multilateralists believe that the protection of American interests requires continuous engagement in the world, but do not think that the United States has the resources or ability to accomplish its ends without cooperating with other nations and with international and regional organizations. According to most surveys, roughly two out of three Americans are in the multilateralist camp, telling pollsters they oppose unilateral U.S. military intervention in most cases and support cooperation with the United Nations and NATO and international treaties on human rights, the environment, and arms control. In this regard, they are considerably more multilateralist than American legislative and executive branch officials.[75] Despite low public support for military interventions and strong support for multilateralism in foreign affairs, U.S. military spending is the highest in the world (see the "Mapping American Politics" feature on pages 150–151).

The People's "Fitness to Rule" Revisited

This examination of collective public opinion, its evident stability on a wide range of issues over time, and why it sometimes changes on some issues leads us to conclude that confidence in the role of the public in the American political system is warranted. The evidence demonstrates that collective public opinion is quite stable and sensible when it comes to core beliefs and attitudes about government, the parties, and policy preferences.[76] The evidence further shows that when collective public opinion does change, it does so for perfectly understandable reasons: dramatic events, new information, or changes in perspective among American leaders. The conclusion we draw is a simple yet powerful one: the American people are fit to rule. The next question to address is whether the people, in fact, do rule.

Using the **DEMOCRACY STANDARD**

Do the public's opinions determine what government does?

We have argued that a crucial test of how well democracy is working is how closely a government's policies match the expressed wishes of its citizens over time. Do the actions of the U.S. government match what collective public opinion says it wants government to do? Some scholars claim that yes, the government generally acts in ways that reflect public opinion. But others argue that public officials sometimes ignore public opinion; that public opinion is often heavily manipulated by government leaders so that it tends to reflect rather than influence government action; and that the public is inattentive and has no opinions on many important policy issues, leaving political leaders free to act on their own. In the remainder of this chapter, we'll take a look at just how much of an impact public opinion has on government action, and consider whether public opinion works in the United States to make our system more democratic.

As our opening story about the Vietnam War suggests, at least under some circumstances, public opinion does affect policymaking. We have encountered other examples that tell the same "government responsiveness" story in this book. President Bush's attempt to alter Social Security in 2005, for example, was blocked by congressional opponents backstopped by strong public support for the current system.

These stories about government responsiveness to public opinion have been buttressed by important assessments by scholars that indicate a strong statistical correlation between public opinion and government action.[77] Looking at many different policy issues—foreign and domestic—one scholar found, for example, that about two-thirds of the time, U.S. government policy coincides with what opinion surveys say the public wants. The same two-thirds correspondence has appeared when other scholars investigated how *changes* in public opinion relate to changes in federal, state, and local policies. Moreover, when public opinion changes by a substantial and enduring amount and the issue is prominent, government policy has moved in the same direction as the public 87 percent of the time within a year or so afterward.[78] Yet another influential study shows that substantial swings in the national political mood have occurred over the past half century or so and that public policy has followed accordingly. As the American people have moved first in a liberal direction, then a conservative direction, and back again over the years, elected leaders in Washington have shaped their policies to fit the public mood, being more activist in liberal periods and less activist in conservative periods.[79] Finally, one scholar concludes, after carefully reviewing the results of 30 studies, that public opinion almost always has some effect on what government does, and when an issue is visible and important to the people, public opinion is the decisive factor in determining the substance of government policy.[80] Although these studies seem to lend substantial support for the idea that public opinion is a powerful determinant of what government does in the United States, showing a strong statistical correlation between public opinion and government policy does not prove that public opinion *causes* government policies. There is any number of plausible reasons why a "causal relationship" may not really exist. Here is what the critics say:[81]

- It may be the case that public opinion and government policies move in the same direction because some third factor causes both of them to change. In this example, the true cause of government action is this third factor, not public opinion. There are many instances in the real world in which this has happened. For example, the news media often play up a particular incident or situation and persuade both public opinion and government policymakers that action is needed. This is clearly what happened when the Hearst newspaper chain whipped up fervor among both the public and elected leaders for war against Spain in the wake of the sinking of the battleship *Maine* in Havana harbor in 1898. Or an interest group or set of interest groups might sway public opinion and government officials in the same direction at the same time, as medical, insurance, and hospital associations did when they launched a successful campaign to sink Bill Clinton's health care initiative in 1994.
- Even if public opinion and government actions are highly correlated, it may be the case that it is government that shapes public opinion. In statistical language, we might say that the causal arrow is reversed, going not from the public to government, but the other way around: that officials act to gain popular support for policies and actions these officials want.[82] Such efforts can range from outright manipulation of the public—the Tonkin Gulf incident described in the opening story in this chapter is such a case; some would claim that the use of the "weapons of mass destruction" rhetoric to raise support for the invasion of Iraq in 2003 is another compelling case[83]—to the conventional public relations efforts carried out every day by government officials and agencies. This is why both the legislative and executive branches of the federal government are so well equipped with communications offices, press secretaries, and public liaison personnel.

So where does all of this leave us on the question of public opinion's influence on government? It is probably reasonable to say that public opinion often plays an important role in shaping what government does: political leaders seem to pay attention to public opinion when they are in the midst of deciding on alternative courses of action. Some would argue that they do entirely too much of this, in fact, pandering to the whims of the public rather than exercising leadership. This desire to find out what the public thinks and what it wants is why congressional incumbents, candidates for office, presidents, and government agencies spend so much time and money polling their relevant constituencies. And it is no mystery why elected officials do this, as do their challengers: public opinion is eventually translated into votes at election time. So, staying on the right side of public opinion—giving people what they want in terms of policies—is how people gain and keep elected offices.

But it is the case that the public does not always pay attention or have an opinion about important matters. This has led scholars to suggest that while public opinion plays an important role in shaping government policy under certain conditions, it plays a lesser role in others. In particular, public opinion seems to matter most when issues are highly visible to the public (usually because there has been lots of political conflict surrounding the issue), are about matters that affect the lives of Americans most directly, and concern issues for which people have access to reliable and understandable information. When economic times are tough—during a recession, for example—no amount of rhetoric from political leaders, the news media, or interest groups is likely to convince people "that they never had it so good." People have a reality check in such circumstances.

By the same token, many foreign policy questions are distant from people's lives and involve issues in which information is scarce or incomplete. In this circumstance, government officials act with wide latitude and play an important role in shaping what the public believes. After studying decades' worth of surveys of public and elite opinion on foreign policy issues collected by the Chicago Council on Foreign Relations, for example, researchers concluded that a deep disconnect exists between the public and elites, with the public much less eager than elites to use force in foreign affairs and more supportive of international cooperation—in the form of international treaties and the United Nations—to tackle global problems.[84] Additionally, some issues, such as the details of tax legislation or the deregulation of the telecommunications industry, are so obscure and complex that they become the province of interest groups and experts, with the public having but ill-formed and not very intense opinions.[85] Moreover, public opinion is only one factor in shaping what government does, something we will address in later chapters. A range of other political actors and institutions, including political parties, interest groups, the news media, and social movements, also influence government, and many scholars argue that their combined influence has far more of an effect than public opinion on what government does. It is probably reasonable to say, moreover, that the influence of public opinion on government is significantly less than the statistical studies suggest (e.g., the "two-thirds" rule) for the reasons given: the impact of third factors on both opinion and government and the significant amount of influence government officials have over popular opinion.[86] And it is hard to avoid noticing the many times government acts almost exactly contrary to public opinion—Congress's decision to go ahead with the impeachment and trial of Bill Clinton in late 1998 and early 1999 in the face of strong public opposition comes to mind, as does inaction on gun control (see the "Using the Framework" feature).

If a majority of Americans say they want gun control, why hasn't the federal government done much about it?

Background: Public opinion surveys have consistently indicated high public support for stricter federal gun control laws. At a general level, around two-thirds of Americans say they want stricter laws. Several specific proposals receive even higher levels of support. For example, about 80 percent of Americans say they want a nationwide ban on assault weapons, while 70 percent want the government to ban gun sales by mail-order and over the Internet. Although some laws, such as the Brady Bill—which requires background checks of gun buyers and a waiting period—have passed Congress, proposals for stricter control over the sale and distribution of weapons almost never get very far. Taking a broad look at how structural, political linkage, and governmental factors affect gun control legislation will help explain the situation.

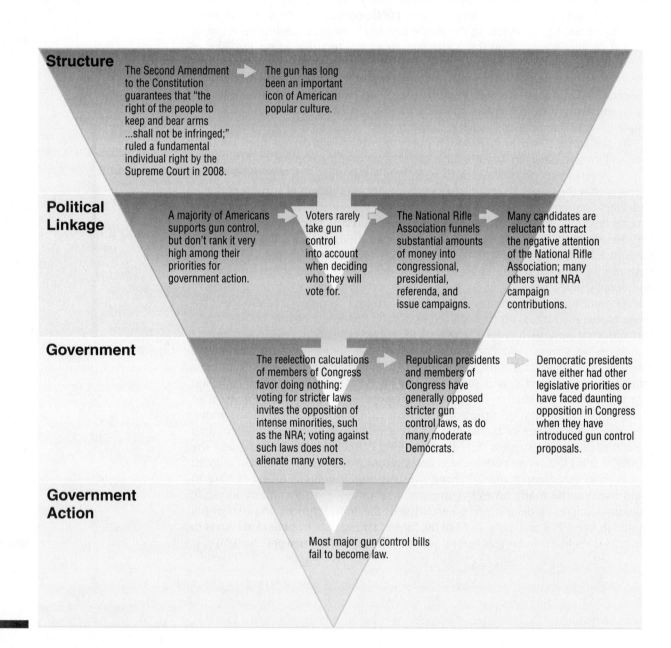

Structure

The Second Amendment to the Constitution guarantees that "the right of the people to keep and bear arms ...shall not be infringed;" ruled a fundamental individual right by the Supreme Court in 2008.

The gun has long been an important icon of American popular culture.

Political Linkage

A majority of Americans supports gun control, but don't rank it very high among their priorities for government action.

Voters rarely take gun control into account when deciding who they will vote for.

The National Rifle Association funnels substantial amounts of money into congressional, presidential, referenda, and issue campaigns.

Many candidates are reluctant to attract the negative attention of the National Rifle Association; many others want NRA campaign contributions.

Government

The reelection calculations of members of Congress favor doing nothing: voting for stricter laws invites the opposition of intense minorities, such as the NRA; voting against such laws does not alienate many voters.

Republican presidents and members of Congress have generally opposed stricter gun control laws, as do many moderate Democrats.

Democratic presidents have either had other legislative priorities or have faced daunting opposition in Congress when they have introduced gun control proposals.

Government Action

Most major gun control bills fail to become law.

SUMMARY

5.1 Characterize the ideal role of public opinion in a democracy

- Public opinion consists of the core political beliefs and political attitudes expressed by ordinary citizens; it can be measured rather accurately through polls and surveys.

- The democratic ideals of popular sovereignty and majority rule imply that government policy should respond to the wishes of the citizens, at least in the long run. An important test of how well democracy is working, then, is how closely government policy corresponds to public opinion.

5.2 Describe methods used to measure public opinion

- Today most polling is done by telephone.

- The foundation of a legitimate survey is that respondents in a sample are randomly selected.

- The increased use of answering machines on land lines and of mobile phones make it more difficult to develop a random sample.

5.3 Analyze the process of political socialization

- People learn their political attitudes and beliefs from their families, peers, schools, and workplaces, as well as through their experiences with political events and the mass media. This process is known as political socialization.

- Changes in society, the economy, and America's situation in the world affect political attitudes and public opinion.

5.4 Relate political attitudes to race, gender, age, income, and other factors

- Opinions and party loyalties differ according to race, religion, region, urban or rural residence, social class, education level, gender, and age. Blacks, Jews, city dwellers, women, and low-income people tend to be particularly liberal and Democratic; white Protestants, suburbanites, males, and the wealthy tend to be more conservative and Republican.

5.5 Assess the American public's ability to rule

- Political knowledge among the public is low, but cue-givers allow people to make fairly rational decisions about their policy preferences.

- Public opinion, considered in the aggregate as a collection of randomly selected respondents, tends to be stable, measured, and rational over the years. Some political scientists call this the "rational public."

TEST YOURSELF

Answer key begins on page T-1.

5.1 Characterize the ideal role of public opinion in a democracy

1. Political scientists have consistently found the American public to be well informed about politics. True / False

2. How are political attitudes different from public opinion?
   a. Political attitudes are individual preferences; public opinion describes the collective preferences of ordinary Americans.
   b. Political attitudes have positive connotations; public opinion has negative connotations.
   c. Political attitudes are the preferences of political elites; public opinion summarizes the attitudes of ordinary Americans.
   d. Political attitudes relate to elections; public opinion relates to public policy.
   e. Political attitudes are fairly stable; public opinion fluctuates considerably.

3. When Congress enacted legislation to reform the health care system in 2010, public opinion polls suggested that a majority of Americans opposed the plan being considered. Why do some consider this an indication that democracy may not be working well?

5.2 Describe methods used to measure public opinion

4. Why is random sampling used to select those who will participate in public opinion polls?
   a. Random sampling is easy to use and cheap to employ.
   b. Random sampling helps ensure that the sample will be representative of the population.
   c. Random sampling reduces that probability that Americans will be informed about the issues being addressed.
   d. Random sampling promotes high response rates.
   e. All of the above

5. Which of the following is a practical advantage of including an intensity measure on a public opinion survey?
   a. An intensity measure encourages people to give a response even if they do not have a well-developed attitude about an issue.
   b. An intensity measure increases participation rates in the public opinion survey.
   c. An intensity measure prevents citizens from changing their opinion after the survey has begun.
   d. An intensity measure can be used to counteract the influence of poor question wording.
   e. An intensity measure can be used to suggest whether citizen behavior is likely to be influenced by their attitudes on an issue.

6. How does the proliferation of cell phones among college students pose additional challenges for conducting public opinion polls?

5.3 Analyze the process of political socialization

7. Young voters typically rebel against their parents by registering with and voting for a different political party than their parents support.
   True / False

8. Which of the following is the least likely to play a prominent role as an agent of socialization?
   a. Families
   b. Schools
   c. Popular culture
   d. Gender
   e. The media

9. How would you expect the generational affect to influence the political beliefs of those who were just starting to become politically aware when the September 11, 2001, terrorist attacks occurred?

5.4 Relate political attitudes to race, gender, age, income, and other factors

10. Young people are less likely to identify with a political party than are older Americas, but those who do are more likely to identify as Democrats.
    True / False

11. Members of which of the following groups are most likely to support the Democratic Party?
    a. Blacks
    b. Cuban Americans
    c. Doctors
    d. Southerners
    e. Those who are religiously committed

5.5 Assess the American public's ability to rule

12. Access to increasing amounts of political information via the Internet helps explain why Americans are becoming increasingly informed about politics.
    True / False

13. Which of the following most accurately describes American public opinion?
    a. Public opinion is irrelevant.
    b. Public opinion is unstable.
    c. When public opinion shifts, it is generally for understandable reasons.
    d. Public opinion suggests that Americans support spending cuts for social programs, especially Social Security and Medicare.
    e. Public opinion suggests that most Americans prefer isolationist foreign policy.

14. Evaluate the authors' assessment that Americans are fit to rule.

PEARSON mypoliscilab EXERCISES

Apply what you learned in this chapter on MyPoliSciLab.

📖 **Read** on mypoliscilab.com
   eText: Chapter 5

✓ **Study** and **Review** on mypoliscilab.com
   Pre-Test
   Post-Test
   Chapter Exam
   Flashcards

👁 **Watch** on mypoliscilab.com
   Video: Opinion Poll on the U.S. Economy
   Video: Obama Approval Rating

✳ **Explore** on mypoliscilab.com
   Simulation: You Are a Polling Consultant
   Comparative: Comparing Governments and Public Opinion
   Timeline: War, Peace, and Public Opinion
   Visual Literacy: Who Are Liberals and Conservatives? What's the Difference?

INTERNET SOURCES

American Association for Public Opinion Research
http://www.aapor.org/Poll_andamp_Survey_FAQs.htm
An online guide for understanding and interpreting polls.

Doonesbury
http://cgi.doonesbury.com/cgi-bin/view_poll.cgi
A daily online poll on current issues; participate and see results as well.

Gallup Organization
http://www.gallup.com
Access to recent Gallup polls as well as to the Gallup archives. Requires a paid subscription.

American National Election Studies
http://www.electionstudies.org
Biennial survey of voters, focusing on electoral issues.

Pew Research Center for the People and the Press
http://pewresearch.org
Complex, in-depth polls on domestic and foreign issues.

Political Compass
www.politicalcompass.org
Determine where you stand in ideological terms by completing the online survey.

Polling Report
http://www.pollingreport.com
A compilation of surveys from a variety of sources on politics and public affairs.

Public Agenda Online
http://publicagenda.org/issues/issuehome.cfm
A comprehensive collection of opinion polls and background reports on public issues.

SUGGESTIONS FOR FURTHER READING

Asher, Herbert. *Polling and the Public: What Every Citizen Should Know.* Washington, D.C.: CQ Press, 2010.
How public opinion surveys are done and what they mean.

Caplan, Bryan. *The Myth of the Rational Voter: Why Democracies Choose Bad Policies.* Princeton, NJ: Princeton University Press, 2007.
Argues that the public is systematically—rather than randomly—misinformed about economic matters and that this leads to irrational government policies to the extent that government leaders follow public opinion.

Erikson, Robert S., and Kent L. Tedin. *American Public Opinion,* 8th ed. New York: Longman Publishers, 2010.
A comprehensive survey of what we know about American public opinion and how we know it.

Page, Benjamin I., with Marshall Bouton. *The Foreign Policy Disconnect: What Americans Want from our Leaders but Do Not Get.* Chicago: University of Chicago Press, 2006.
Based on surveys of the public and elites sponsored by the Chicago Council on Foreign Relations, the authors demonstrate the existence of a deep disconnect between the public and elites on what kind of foreign policy the United States should have.

Weissberg, Robert. *Polling, Policy, and Public Opinion: The Case Against Heeding the "Voice of the People."* New York: Palgrave, 2002.
A passionate argument on why government officials should not be too responsive to public opinion.

Wolfe, Alan. *Does American Democracy Still Work.* New Haven ,CT: Yale University Press, 2006.
Suggests that Americans are neither interested in nor informed about public affairs and the effects of these twin conditions undermine democracy in the nation.

6

The News Media

LEARNING OBJECTIVES

After reading this chapter, you should be able to:

6.1 Evaluate the various roles of the news media in a democracy

6.2 Assess the respective roles of traditional and other news media today

6.3 Analyze how the news is gathered and disseminated and evaluate the outcome of this process

6.4 Identify the ways in which the news media affect public opinion and policymaking

6.5 Compare and contrast government regulation of the different media

BIG STORIES WITHOUT LEGS

It had all the markings of a major news story that would rock Washington and trigger a major rethinking of war policies in Iraq.[1] All the pieces seemingly were in place. In an article published on April 30, 2005, the prestigious British newspaper, *The Times* of London, reported the minutes of a secret meeting between Prime Minister Tony Blair and his top military and intelligence officials that featured a report by a British intelligence operative that Washington officials had "cooked the books" to justify the invasion of Iraq in spring 2003. The operative had been at several pre-war meetings with White House and Pentagon officials where it was evident, he claimed, that the decision for war already had been made and that intelligence information about Saddam Hussein's purported "weapons of mass destruction" program and ties to the 9/11 terrorists was being organized and interpreted to build a case for going to war. In his words, the "facts were being fixed around the policy."[2]

As news stories go, the seeming blockbuster turned out to be a dud. The story failed to merit a lead on any of the network newscasts. While the story of the so-called Downing Street memo appeared on the front page of *The Washington Post*, it was there for only a single day. Other newspapers relegated it to the inside pages. For the most part, the story was " . . . treated as old news or a British politics story" rather than as story about Americans being mislead into war by the Bush administration, something that might call into question the entire enterprise.[3] The liberal blogosphere jumped on the issue, but the story failed to stir more mainstream media attention or action from congressional Democrats, who were in the minority in both the House and Senate and unsure about what position to take on the war in the upcoming 2006 elections. When Representative John Conyers (D–MI) sought to bring attention to the misuse of intelligence information to encourage the Iraq war by holding an "informational hearing" (being in

the minority, the Democrat Conyers could not schedule an official set of hearings), *The Washington Post* treated it as a joke; the headline read "Democrats Play House to Rally Against the War" and opened with the line, "In the Capitol basement yesterday, long suffering House Democrats took a trip to the land of make-believe."[4]

Similarly, in an article published in early 2006—roughly three years after the invasion of Iraq—*The New York Times* reported a British press story, based on a memo written by a Blair aide who had attended a meeting of Prime Minister Tony Blair and President George W. Bush at a January 2003 pre-war meeting at the White House, that the president had made it clear to the British leader that he was determined to go to war even without evidence that Iraq was building weapons of mass destruction or had links to Al Qaeda. (At the same time, the president was making numerous statements that he had not made up his mind about an invasion and was

making every effort to solve the issue diplomatically in cooperation with the United Nations and close allies.) While the revelation elicited a few comments from Democratic leaders and some blog activity, it didn't get a mention on CBS, NBC, or FOX News, and no follow-up stories appeared in the *Los Angeles Times*, *The Wall Street Journal*, *The Washington Post*, or *USA Today*. At around the same time this story about the Bush-Blair meeting came and went with hardly a murmur, a feeding frenzy was swirling around an unfortunate incident in which Vice President Richard Cheney accidentally shot a long-time friend in the face while hunting. For four or five days after the accidental shooting, every type of news media outlet—including the network and cable news networks, news magazines, local and national newspapers, news websites, and blogs—ran full coverage on the story, examining every nuance and speculating about why it happened, why an official press release about it was delayed for a few hours, and what it might all mean. Late-night comedy hosts had a field day with the story for months.

Many critics claim the news media are biased and cannot be relied upon to tell an objective story. Other critics claim that the mainstream news media in particular are becoming irrelevant in the face of the Internet, with its multiple information and opinion sources. We suggest that the principal problems of the news media concern their under-reporting of stories that might help American citizens better understand events and trends that are affecting their lives, including those involving government and political leaders, and over-attention to stories that involve sensation, entertainment, or scandals. This chapter is about the news media and why certain things become news we pay attention to while other things, many of them very important to public conversations about government policies and the direction of the country, do not.

THINKING CRITICALLY About This Chapter

In this chapter, we turn our attention to the diverse news media in the United States to learn how they are organized, how they work, and what effects they have on the quality of our political life.

Using the FRAMEWORK

In this chapter, you will learn about the role the news media play in influencing significant actors in the political system, including citizens and elected leaders. You also will learn how the news media can shape what government does. And you will learn how the news media are influenced by changes in technology and business organization and by government regulation and constitutional rules regarding freedom of the press.

Using the DEMOCRACY STANDARD

Using the tools presented in Chapter 1, you will be able to evaluate the degree to which the news media advance democracy in the United States or retard it. You will be able to judge whether the media promote popular sovereignty, political equality, and liberty. Finally, you will see how certain changes in the media may be cause for concern in terms of the health of democracy.

Roles of the News Media in Democracy

6.1 Evaluate the various roles of the news media in a democracy

The central idea of democracy is that ordinary citizens should control what their government does. However, citizens cannot hope to control officials, choose candidates wisely, speak intelligently with others about public affairs, or even make up their minds about what policies they favor unless they have good information about politics and policies. Most of that information must come through the news media, whether newspapers, radio, television, or, increasingly, the Internet. How well democracy works, then, depends partly on how good a job the news media are doing. The news media, ideally, should fulfill several roles in this democracy.

Watchdog Over Government

One role of the news media in a democracy is that of **watchdog** over government. The Founders, although not entirely enamored of democracy, as we have seen, nevertheless fully subscribed to the idea that a free press was essential for keeping an eye on government and checking its excesses. This is why protection of press freedom figured so prominently in the First Amendment. This role for the press is essential to the practice of democracy as well. The idea is that the press should dig up facts and warn the public when officials are doing something wrong. Citizens can hold officials accountable for setting things right only if they know about errors and wrong doing.

> **watchdog**
> The role of the media in scrutinizing the actions of government officials.

The First Amendment to the Constitution ("Congress shall make no law … abridging the freedom … of the press") helps ensure that the news media will be able to expose officials' misbehavior without fear of censorship or prosecution. This is a treasured American right that is not available in many other countries. Under dictatorships and other authoritarian regimes, the news media are usually tightly controlled, with government censorship of the press and intimidation of journalists all too common.[5] Even in a democratic country such as Great Britain, strict secrecy laws limit what the press can say about certain government activities. In many countries, including France, Israel, and Sweden, the government owns and operates major television channels and sometimes pressures news executives to tone down their criticism of political leaders.

As you will see, even without formal censorship or government ownership of the media, various factors, including the way in which the news media are organized as privately owned, profit-seeking enterprises, and their routines of news gathering, may limit how willing or able the news media are to be critical of government policies. In addition, the media may be too quick to blow scandals out of proportion and to destroy political leaders' careers.[6]

Clarifying Electoral Choices

A second role of the news media in a democracy is to make clear what electoral choices the public has: what the political parties stand for and how the candidates shape up in terms of personal character, knowledge, experience, and positions on the issues. Without such information, it is difficult for voters to make intelligent choices. Unfortunately, the news media tend to pay attention more to the "horse race" (who is ahead? who is behind?) aspect of campaigns, or go overboard in digging up dirt and reporting negative material, than to the policy positions of the candidates.

Providing Policy Information

A third role of the news media is to present a diverse, full, and enlightening set of facts and ideas about public policy. Citizens need to know about emerging problems that will need attention and how well current policies are working, as well as the pros and cons of alternative policies that might be tried. In a democracy, government should respond to public opinion, but that opinion should be reasonably well informed. You will see later in this chapter why many observers worry that the news media do not provide unbiased information and analysis.

PUBLIC WATCHDOG

Mainstream and Nonmainstream News Media

6.2 Assess the respective roles of traditional and other news media today

The Pew Research Center's Project for Excellence in Journalism (www.journalism.org) claims that the coming of the digital age in the news media represents "an epochal transformation, as momentous probably as the invention of the telegraph or television."[7] This new digital age in news is described as one in which there is virtually unlimited access to information, news, and analysis, untold opportunities for ordinary people to express their views on public issues, and a decline in the presence and importance of the mainstream or traditional media. Despite the unmistakable and dramatic growth of alternative news and information sources and outlets for people to express themselves, however, we suggest that the mainstream media and traditional forms of reporting remain at the center of the news operations that most affect American politics and government.

Alternatives to the Mainstream

The most important development in the collection, organization, and distribution of information of all kinds is, of course, the Internet, allowing instant access to a vast treasure trove of digitalized information in every field of human knowledge. (See Figure 6.1 for a timeline on the development of the Internet.) The growth in the reach, capabilities, and use of the Internet, through broadband connections in homes, schools, libraries, and the workplace, and increasingly over wireless networks to handheld devices such as netbooks, e-readers, smart phones, and other smart devices, has been stunning. By the end of 2009, according to the Pew Research Center, 63 percent of Americans reported having a broadband connection

BLOGGING THE REPUBLICAN NATIONAL CONVENTION Alternative media are becoming increasingly mainstream. Both the Republican and Democratic conventions in 2008 allocated space not only to the mainstream media but to bloggers as well. These bloggers are sharing ideas and interpretations on proceedings at the GOP convention that nominated John McCain and Sarah Palin for the national ticket. How did this development happen, and to what extent does it enhance the quality of political information that is available to the public?

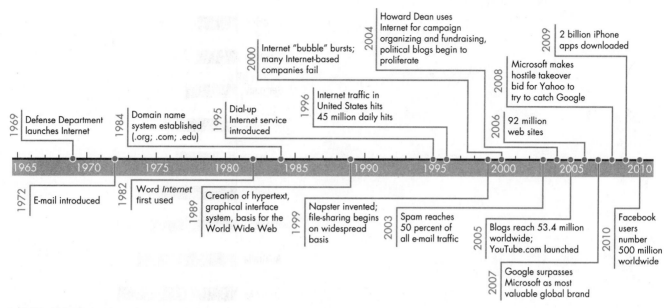

FIGURE 6.1 Timeline: The Internet

Sources: Infoplease, www.infoplease.com; "The New News Landscape: Rise of the Internet" (Washington, D.C.: Pew Research Center, March 1, 2010).

in their home, for example, up 15 percent from a year earlier. (While this may seem like a big number, it puts us only in 16th place among nations, down from 4th place in 2000; other countries are growing their broadband penetration much faster than the United States.)[8] Moreover, the ownership of handheld devices with access to the Internet—iPhones, iTouches, Kindle readers, BlackBerrys, Android-enabled phones, tablet computers such as the iPad with Wi-Fi and/or 3G connections, and more—is rapidly rising here and abroad, though the exact numbers are hard to pin down. In 2009, the United States led the world by a wide margin in the number of Internet hosts (sites ending with .com, .org, or .net), with more than 330,000 of them, almost eight times more than second-place Japan. On a per-capita basis, the U.S. lead was less pronounced but still impressive (see Figure 6.2).

To be sure, most people use the Internet for such nonpolitical activities as sending and receiving e-mail, sharing photos and videos, sending tweets about their lives, arranging travel and vacations, participating in online auctions, shopping for products, playing interactive games, and more. But many millions use it for explicitly political purposes, to both inform and express themselves. Here are a few examples:

? Do you rely on "alternative" news sources, like blogs or opinion magazines, for political information? Are your favorite sites truly independent of mainstream news sources, or do they frequently link to or comment on stories from the mainstream media?

- People visit political party and candidate websites, as well as interest and advocacy group websites, to get information, make contributions, learn how to organize, and leave comments. They also visit fact-check sites to test the claims of government officials, candidates, and parties.

- People visit government websites to access a vast trove of information ranging from statistics on demographic change and performance of the economy to the details of the U.S. budget and bills being considered by Congress.

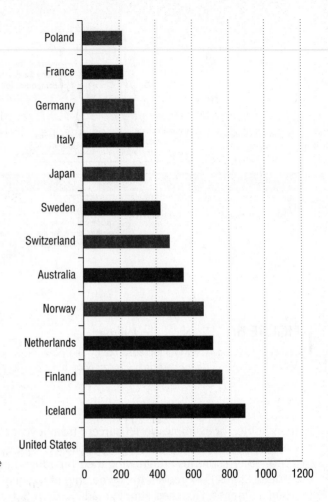

FIGURE 6.2 Number of Internet Hosts, per 1,000 People (2009)

Source: Pocketworld in Figures, 2010 (London: The Economist/Profile Books, 2010), p. 94.

- People read commentaries on thousands of political **blog** sites and respond with their own commentary, and they can easily set up their own blogs without much trouble.

- People visit specialized political news websites, some with their own reporters like Politico.com, for breaking news and background information on what is going on in Washington or state capitals.

- Millions of people go to the websites of traditional news organizations such as CNN, *The New York Times,* and *The Wall Street Journal* for their news. They also go to news aggregator sites such as Yahoo! News and Google News or to Digg, where users' votes determine which stories appear on the site's front page.

- People use the Internet to access public affairs information from online university and public libraries, as well as from online encyclopedia-type sites such as Wikipedia.

- People watch newscasts, political commentators, and breaking news on video sites like YouTube.

- People sometimes use social-networking sites like Twitter, Facebook, and MySpace to inform others about breaking stories—the Hurricane Katrina story in New Orleans, demonstrations in Teheran, or a sighting of financial swindler Harry Madoff walking near his condo in Manhattan—or passing on bits and pieces of news stories from other sources. They also sometimes use social-networking sites to organize demonstrations as Tea Party activists did several times in their effort to stop health care reform.

blog

The common term for a *weblog,* a website on which an individual or group posts text, photos, audio files, and more, on a regular basis for others to view and respond to.

- People use various devices to listen to political **podcasts,** though most listeners, to be sure, are more interested in music and entertainment podcasts.

During the 2007–2008 election cycle, about one-quarter of Americans reported that they depended on the Internet as their main source for news about the campaigns, candidates, and issues, double the proportion that had done so during the 2004 election cycle. This was especially true for those between the ages of 18 and 29; 42 percent of this group turned to the Internet for their news about the campaigns. Almost 100 million people have used government websites; almost as many have used the Internet to look for political news or for information about candidates and political campaigns.[9] For the first time ever in 2008, a majority of adults reported they had gone online for campaign information.[10]

At the same time that Internet use has expanded at an exponential rate, there has been a decline in the audience for traditional news outlets; both newspaper readership and the number of viewers who watch network television news have been declining (see Figure 6.3). People consistently report that television is their main source of news over newspapers and news magazines, with the Internet closing fast. The collapse in circulation for metropolitan newspapers has been stunning. In 2009, for example, the *Los Angeles Times* lost 11 percent of its readers, the *Boston Globe* lost 18 percent, and the *San Francisco Chronicle* bled 26 percent. The average daily circulation of almost 400 newspapers across the country fell by almost 11 percent.[11] Young people have almost entirely given up on newspaper reading; one survey reports that only 16 percent of 18- to 30-year-olds said they read a newspaper every day.[12] (More than a third of 18- to 24-year-olds reported they got no news at all on the previous day, from whatever source, new media or old.[13]) While network news on ABC, CBS, and NBC is still far ahead of cable TV in numbers of viewers, their viewership has been declining. Cable news operations, especially CNN and FOX News, claim a larger share than in the past, especially among younger adult viewers, but viewership even here has leveled off in recent years. Even with this, television remains the favorite source of political news for Americans.[14] A substantial fraction of younger news consumers report that they also rely on satirical television shows like *The Daily Show* or the *Colbert Report* on Comedy Central for their news.

podcast
Digital audio and video files made readily available to interested people via computers and portable devices.

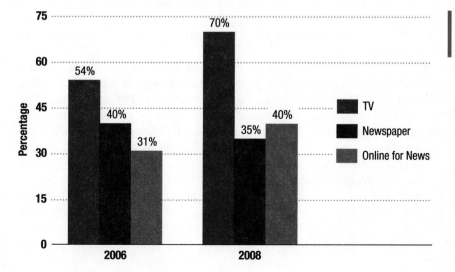

FIGURE 6.3 Where People Get Their News

In recent years, people have turned increasingly to the Internet as a source of news, while decreasing somewhat their reliance on television, newspapers, and radio. Although the Internet still trails the other forms of news sources, it is catching up quickly. *Source:* "Internet Overtakes Newspapers As News Outlet" (Washington, D.C.: Pew Research Center, press release, December 23, 2008).

NEWS WITH LAUGHS Increasingly, young people report that their most trusted news sources are to be found on Comedy Central on shows like *The Daily Show* and *The Colbert Report,* rather than from the major network or cable news offerings. Here, Stephen Colbert tapes a show at the University of Pennsylvania in 2008. What accounts for the switch?

The Continuing Importance of the Mainstream

Despite these developments, the mainstream news media retain their central role in the gathering and reporting of serious political and governmental news. The mainstream or traditional news media are the collection of nationally prominent newspapers (such as *The Wall Street Journal, The New York Times,* and *The Washington Post*), national news magazines (such as *Time* and *Newsweek*), TV network news organizations, local newspapers, and local TV news operations that gather, analyze, and report politically important events, developments, and trends, usually with the help of **wire services** such as the Associated Press (AP) and Reuters, the resources of newspaper chains, and syndication services, but sometimes on their own.[15] Research by media scholars shows that the mainstream news organizations, taken as a whole, remain the most important set of institutions for setting the agenda of American politics and shaping how we interpret what is going on in politics and government. Why do they make this claim?

There are a number of reasons the mainstream or traditional news organizations remain central to political news. For one thing, much of the rich and diverse information on the Internet, whether in the form of advocacy organization websites, political blogs, citizen journalism, or academic and government reports, only reach small and fragmented audiences and usually have an impact only when and to the extent they can attract the attention of the mainstream news media. Bloggers' unearthing of news anchor Dan Rather's sloppy reporting on President George W. Bush's National Guard service during the Vietnam War, for example, only mattered once the story began to run in the nation's leading newspapers and on network and cable news networks. Tens of thousands of bloggers voice their views every day, to take another example, but few gain an audience. One scholar, using a vast database to chronicle the number of daily hits on blogger sites, has determined that only 10 to 20 of them have a readership of any size. Of the 5,000 most-visited political blog sites, for example, the top 5 of them account for 28 percent of all blog visits, while the top 10 accounted for almost half. Also, fully half of the top 10 bloggers are or were at one time professional journalists.[16]

It turns out, moreover, that the most visited hard-news sites are those that are run by traditional media organizations. Among the most popular are those of CNN, Gannett Newspapers, Cox Newspapers, *The New York Times, The Washington Post,* and *USA Today.*[17]

Much more telling, most political and public policy–related news on the Internet at sites such as Yahoo! News, Google News, AOL, and Digg is simply content collected from the mainstream wire services and major newspaper and network news organizations. The same is true for the matters that most political bloggers talk about, and the bits of news that get passed around on social-networking sites: they come mainly from the material that has been collected by reporters in the traditional news sector. The grist for commentary at the most popular political sites, in-

wire service

Organizations such as the Associated Press and Reuters that gather and disseminate news to other news organizations.

cluding the liberal *Daily Kos* and the *Huffington Post* and the conservative *Free Republic* and Townhall.com comes mainly from traditional news organizations. Much of the airtime on cable news networks, moreover, is devoted to reporting or commenting on material gathered from the major wire services such as the AP or Reuters or prestigious newspapers. And, it is to the mainstream media that eager politicians and government officials generally look for clues about what the public and other leaders want and where they try to gain attention for their own views and achievements.

What seems on the surface, then, to be a fantastic expansion in the amount of political news in reality is an expansion in the number of ways in which the news is distributed. It is the same news being passed around and around on the Internet, and an exponential growth in commentary on that news, but it is not the same thing as an expansion in the size or quality of the core of political news. As far as scholars have been able to tell, the new digital age news operations have done very little by way of original, in-depth stories.[18]

So, while the news media have changed greatly over our history and continue to change ever more rapidly, and while people can get their news and commentary from many different places ranging from the Internet to cable television, talk radio, and television satire and comedy programs, mainstream news organizations remain the most important set of institutions in the American political news system. It is the reason we mostly focus on the mainstream news media in this chapter, asking how well they play the role assigned to them by democratic theorists.

PUTTING OUT THE DAY'S PAPER
Newspapers such as the Philadelphia *Evening Bulletin* tend to rely on wire services for source materials for their national and international news stories, although they will often have several of their own reporters in important cities such as Washington and New York. Much of their original journalistic efforts are aimed at local and regional issues. Why do local papers use this system for gathering information?

How the Mainstream News Media Work

6.3 Analyze how the news is gathered and disseminated and evaluate the outcome of this process

Whether citizens get from the news media the kinds of information they need for democracy to work properly depends on how the media are organized and function. In the remainder of this chapter, we focus on news media organizations and journalists with an eye toward better understanding the influences that affect the content of their news product and how the news shapes politics and government in the United States.

Organization of the News Media

News media in the United States are privately owned businesses. Most are either very large businesses in their own right or, more typically, part of very large corporate empires.

Corporate Ownership   Some television stations and newspapers—especially the smaller ones—are still owned locally by families or by groups of investors, although they account for a rapidly declining share of the total. Most of the biggest stations and newspapers, however, as well as the television and cable networks, are owned by large media corporations, some of which, in turn, are subsidiaries of enormous conglomerates.

? How might independent, alternative news sources provide a check on larger, corporate-owned ones? How about nonprofit news sources (such as NPR and PBS)? Does competition between large news organizations keep the news diverse?

Each media sector is dominated by a few firms.[19] Gannett (*USA Today* and almost 100 other dailies), Newhouse (Advanced Publications, Inc.), and the McClatchy company dominate the newspaper business, a media sector that has fallen on hard times because of declining readership, especially among young adults, and shrinking ad revenues as classified advertising migrates to online sites such as Craigslist. Time Warner dominates magazine publishing. General Electric, Disney, News Corp., and Viacom dominate network and cable television. Clear Channel, while suffering major setbacks, still owns about 600 stations across the country and dominates radio (although it is losing audience to alternatives to portable devices such as iPods and MP3 players). And five firms (Warner Communications, Vivendi Universal, Sony, Viacom, and Disney) receive most of the gross box office revenues from movies.[20]

Mergers across media lines have accelerated in recent years, leaving a handful of giant conglomerates. Disney, for example, owns not only its theme parks, movie production and distribution operations, and sports teams, but the ABC television network, local TV and radio stations in the nation's largest cities, cable television operations, and book publishers. Rupert Murdoch's News Corp. owns local TV stations in many of the nation's largest cities, cable and satellite operations (including FOX News and Direct TV), the 20th Century Fox film company, the *New York Post* and major newspapers in Great Britain and Australia, a stable of magazines and journals, Harper Collins and Harper Morrow book companies, and radio and TV operations in Europe and Asia. In 2007, he acquired one of the most influential news organizations in the world, *The Wall Street Journal.* (Journalists at the paper were dismayed, perhaps because Murdoch says "he finds long stories about complicated subjects to be rather trying."[21])

So, behind the apparent proliferation of news sources—new magazines, online news and opinion operations, cable television news and commentary, handheld devices with links to the Web, and the like—is substantial concentration of ownership and dense interconnections among the vast cornucopia of news and entertainment outlets. Some have used the term **media monopoly** to suggest how serious the situation is; although most scholars are loath to go that far, believing that some competition remains.[22]

Scholars disagree about the effect of corporate ownership and increased media concentration. A few see efficiency gains and an increase in the output and availability of information. But some critics maintain that the concentrated corporate control of our media

media monopoly
Term used to suggest that media corporations are so large, powerful, and interconnected that the less economically and politically powerful cannot have their views aired.

I WANT MORE   Rupert Murdoch has created a global entertainment and news operation that gives him influence with the public, opinion leaders, and government officials in a wide range of countries. Does this development diminish the number of viewpoints citizens get to consider, or is there sufficient alternative information from other outlets?

adds dangerously to the already strong business presence in American politics. Those who use the term *media monopoly* worry that media corporations are so large, powerful, and interconnected that alternative voices to the economically and politically powerful cannot have their views aired. Still others are concerned that the concentration of media ownership may lead to less diversity of news and opinion or a preference for entertainment values trumping news values as powerful profit-seeking enterprises focus on the bottom line. Still others worry that news organizations may pull their punches when reporting about the activities of their corporate parents or partners. Will ABC News go easy on problems at Disney, for example, which owns ABC?

Uniformity and Diversity Whoever owns them, most newspapers and television stations depend largely on the same sources for news. Political scientist Lance Bennett points out that while there is a growing diversity of news outlets in the United States—more specialized magazines, television channels, and newspaper home pages on the Web—news sources are contracting. That is to say, much of what comes to us over a multitude of media avenues originates in fewer and fewer centralized sources.[23] Local radio stations increasingly buy headlines for their brief on-the-hour updates from a handful of headline service providers. Television news increasingly buys raw video footage, for in-house editing and scripting, from a handful of providers, including Independent Television News (ITN), rather than having their own reporters and film crews on the ground. The AP supplies most of the main national and international news stories for newspapers and local news (although Reuters is increasingly important)—even those that are rewritten to carry a local reporter's byline. Most of what appears on network and cable television news, too, is inspired by the AP wire, although they often take their lead on the major stories of the day from the major national newspapers such as *The New York Times, The Wall Street Journal,* and *The Washington Post.*[24] National and local television news organizations depend on centralized news and video suppliers, with fewer of them using their own reporters. This is why viewers are likely to see the same news (and sports) footage on different stations as they switch channels, although each station adds its own "voiceover" from a reporter or news anchor. In most cases, the person doing the voiceover has no direct relationship to the story. (For more on the state of local news, see the "By the Numbers" feature.)

Profit Motives Media companies, like other companies, are in business to make a profit. This is entirely appropriate in general terms but has some important and unfortunate consequences for how media companies create and disseminate the news. For many newspapers and television news organizations, this often means closing down foreign bureaus and cutting the number of reporters focused on government affairs in Washington or the economy and financial system. For many traditional news organizations, there are market pressures to alter their news coverage to appeal to audiences who are more interested in entertainment than public affairs and want their news short, snappy, and sensational. This sort of **infotainment** is increasingly offered on network and cable television news and in *USA Today.* If consumers of the news do not want long and detailed investigative reports, and given that such stories are very expensive to do because of the cost of having many seasoned reporters on the payroll—according to one seasoned newsman, "a skilled investigative reporter can cost a news organization more than $250,000 a year in salary and expenses for only a handful of stories"[25]—then news media companies may be tempted to shift to infotainment or to use generic news created by others. These trends toward infotainment and generic news are especially

infotainment
The merging of hard news and entertainment in news presentations.

How much serious crime is there in the United States?

"If it bleeds, it leads" seems to be the mantra of television news. Indeed, we are in danger in this country of being overwhelmed by news stories about crime, and the problem seems to be getting worse. While coverage of public affairs and foreign affairs has been falling, news coverage of crime has flourished, especially on local news telecasts.

Why It Matters If television news broadcasts are accurately portraying real trends in crime, then they are doing a public service. If portrayals are inaccurate, then the public is being misled. This is problematic because public and official perceptions about the scale of particular social problems affect politics and government deeply. For example,

- When pressed by the public to address a perceived problem, government officials respond by redirecting resources at the problem and make budget and personnel decisions in light of it. If the problem is a false one, then government attention and resources get used ineffectively.
- Candidates campaign on issues that are most salient to the public. When the public misperceives the scale of a problem, it makes electoral choices based on irrelevant grounds.

- The more threatening the public finds a particular problem, the more it pushes aside other public priorities, such as education and health care.

The Story Behind the Crime Numbers How accurately are the news media portraying the true state of affairs? To put it bluntly, not very well. Crime in general, and violent crime in particular, declined substantially during the 1990s, at precisely the same time that concerns about crime were at the forefront of media, popular attention, and political saliency. How do we know this to be the case?

The two most widely used measures of the incidence of crime in the United States are the Uniform Crime Report (UCR) of the FBI and the National Crime Victimization Survey (NCVS) of the Department of Justice. Each counts the incidence of crime in a different way. The UCR is based on reports from law enforcement agencies and is meant to help state and local police departments track their own performance and plan their budgets. The NCVS is based on a survey of victims of crime and is used to assess how crime is experienced by Americans and how it affects them and their families.

Calculating the Crime Rate The FBI's UCR, based on reports submitted

voluntarily by state and local law enforcement agencies, counts the annual incidence of "violent crimes" (murder, forcible rape, robbery, and aggravated assault), "property crimes" (burglary, larceny-theft, motor vehicle theft, and arson), and "serious crimes" (all of the above). However, here is what is most important about the FBI's methodology: *it only counts crimes that come to the attention of police*

The Justice Department's NCVS is based on an annual survey of roughly 50,000 randomly selected U.S. households. One person over the age of 18 in each household is interviewed about any crimes that may have been committed against any member of the household during the previous year. The result is annual crime *victimization* information for more than 100,000 people, a very large number for a national survey. Because the NCVS includes crimes experienced by people that are never reported to the authorities, it tends to show higher rates of serious crime than the UCR.

Criticisms of Crime Rate Calculations The experts generally prefer the NCVS numbers to those of the UCR for understanding the dimensions of the crime problem. The principal problems with the UCR concern the accuracy

well developed in evening local news broadcasts, where coverage of politics, government, and policies that affect the public have been "crowded out by coverage of crime, sports, weather, lifestyles, and other audience-grabbing topics."[26]

Political Newsmaking

The kind of news that the media present is affected by the organization and technology of news gathering and news production. Much depends on where reporters are, what sources they talk to, and what sorts of video pictures are available.

The Limited Geography of Political News
Serious national news comes from a surprisingly few places. For the most part, the news comes from Washington, D.C., the seat of the federal government, and New York City, the center of publishing and finance in the United States. This is where most news media companies locate their

of recording and reporting crime. For example,

- Many serious crimes, especially rape, go unreported to police. The fact that the UCR came closer to the NCVS numbers starting in the 1990s may mean that more crimes are being reported than in the past.
- Ideas about what constitutes a serious crime may change as social mores change. Domestic violence was treated in the past by police as a family matter; now it tends to get recorded and reported by police.
- A small number of law enforcement agencies do not participate in the UCR reporting system or do not treat it with the seriousness that the FBI hopes for.

What to Watch For Each way of measuring crime is valid and has its purposes. Although the UCR measure has some problems, it does a fairly good job of telling us what is going on year to year with respect to police encounters with crime. This, in turn, is useful to national, state, and local governments in deciding on budget and staffing issues for law enforcement. The NCVS does a very good job of telling us what is going on year to year with respect to overall victimization trends, and gives us a handle on the size of the underlying crime problem. The lesson here is to use the statistic that conforms most closely to the purposes of your inquiry.

What Do You Think? How do television news programs underplay or overplay the incidence of violent crime? Monitor local and national news for the next week or so and try to keep a running count of stories about crime. How does your count match what the UCR and NCVS numbers are telling us about crime?

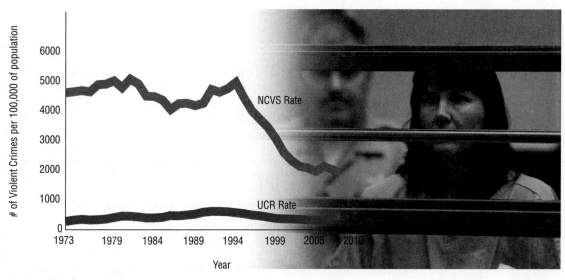

Serious Violent Crimes

Source: *Crime Victimization 2009* and *Uniform Crime Reports*, Bureau of Justice Statistics, 2009.

reporters, though a few other areas get coverage as well. We show how the news is geographically concentrated in the "Mapping American Politics" feature.

The major television networks and most newspapers cannot afford to station many reporters outside Washington or New York.[27] The networks usually add just Chicago, Los Angeles, Miami, and Houston or Dallas. When stories break in San Francisco or Seattle, news organizations can rush reporters to the area or turn to part-time "stringers" to do the reporting. Some significant stories from outside the main media centers simply do not make it into the national news. News-only channels, such as CNN, CNBC, and FOX News, have a big advantage on fast-breaking news, which they are ready to cover (through their own reporters or the purchase of local footage) and use immediately on their continuous newscasts.

While some newspapers have strong regional bureaus, the majority print mostly wire service reports of news from elsewhere around the country. The television networks' assignment editors also rely on the wire services to decide what stories to cover.

The Limited Geography of National News

Introduction Most national political reporters are located in and file their stories from two main locations: Washington, D.C., site of the federal government and most of the nation's most influential think tanks and interest group organizations, and New York City, the center of most media operations and key national and global financial institutions. For national news involving more than politics and governmental affairs or closely related economic issues, reporters tend to file stories from a broader range of geographical locations, although not equally from all areas around the United States. This is hardly surprising: maintaining reporters is expensive, so news organizations concentrate their news gathering where they will get the most bang for the buck—where the most important news occurs.

Mapping the News The cartogram depicts the states and the District of Columbia resized from normal in proportion to the number of headlines in wire-service stories originating from these locations in recent years. If news stories had originated in various states in proportion to their populations, the states' size would correspond to the relative sizes of their populations. In this cartogram, however, New York City, New York State, New Jersey, and California stand out as sites that generate a disproportionate share of news stories, as do Georgia, Florida, and, given its tiny geographic area (less than 10 miles square), Washington, D.C. New York City and its metropolitan area (which includes parts of New York State, New Jersey, and Connecticut) and Washington, D.C.,

generate so much news for the reasons cited earlier. Georgia's relatively large size may be due to the fact that both CNN and the federal government's Centers for Disease Control and Prevention are based there. Florida is in the news often because of tight and controversial political contests as well as more than its share of hurricanes. California generates many stories from the entertainment industry, much of which is centered there, as well as from Silicon Valley, the heart of the nation's high-tech industry. Some states virtually disappear, with very few news stories originating in the Mountain West, Southwest, Great Plains, and Midwest (other than Illinois), or the New England states of New Hampshire, Vermont, and Maine. News stories from Texas are less than one might expect, given

Because so much expensive, high-tech equipment is involved, and because a considerable amount of editing is required to turn raw video into coherent stories, most television news coverage is assigned to predictable events—news conferences and the like—long before they happen, usually in one of the cities with a permanent television crew. For such spontaneous news as riots, accidents, and natural disasters, special video camera crews can be rushed to the location, but they usually arrive after the main events occur and have to rely on "reaction" interviews or aftermath stories. This is not always true; occasionally television news organizations find themselves in the middle of an unfolding set of events and can convey its texture, explore its human meaning, and speculate about its political implications in particularly meaningful ways. This was certainly true of television coverage of the Hurricane Katrina disaster and its immediate aftermath in 2005.

Dependence on Official Sources
Most political news is based on what public officials say. This fact has important consequences for how well the media serve democracy.

? As watchdogs on government, is it more important for reporters to maintain an objective distance from their stories than it is for them to acquire intimate knowledge of their beats?

Beats and Routines A newspaper or television reporter's work is usually organized around a particular **beat,** which he or she checks every day for news stories. Most political beats center on some official government

beat
The assigned location where a reporter regularly gathers news stories.

institution that regularly produces news, such as a local police station or city council, the White House, Congress, the Pentagon, an American embassy abroad, or a country's foreign ministry.

the importance of the state in American politics, energy production, music, and the high-technology industry in Austin.

What Do You Think? Why might one argue that it is reasonable that news stories are concentrated in America's centers of governance, communications, finance, and entertainment? Can you think of some way that news might be gathered to avoid such concentrations? Some people say that the news media are out of touch with the American people. What is the basis of this argument? Does the pattern in the cartogram showing the origins of news stories help explain the situation?

Map note: Alaska is not shown (although information about Alaska is included in calculations where relevant), and Hawaii is moved closer to the mainland.

Source: Data from Michael Gastner and described in M. T. Gastner and M. E. J. Newman, "Diffusion-Based Method for Producing Density-Equalizing Maps," *Proceedings of the National Academy of Sciences,* 101 (May 18, 2004), pp. 7499–7504. Wire service news headlines from 1994 to 1998.

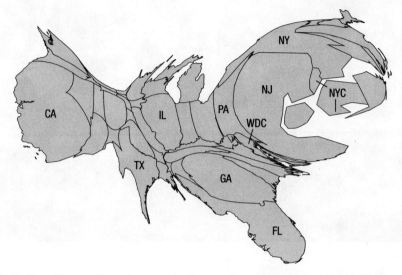

Headline News: Size of States in Proportion to Number of Headlines

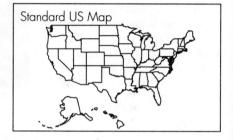

Standard US Map

In fact, many news reports are created or originated by officials, not by reporters. Investigative reporting of the sort that Carl Bernstein and Robert Woodward did to uncover the Watergate scandal, which led to the impeachment and resignation of President Richard Nixon in 1974, is rare because it is so time-consuming and expensive. Most reporters get most of their stories quickly and efficiently from press conferences and the press releases that officials write, along with comments solicited from other officials. One pioneering study by Leon Sigal found that government officials, domestic or foreign, were the sources of nearly three-quarters of all news in *The New York Times* and *The Washington Post.* Moreover, the vast majority, 70 to 90 percent of all news stories, were drawn from situations over which the newsmakers had substantial control: press conferences (24.5 percent), interviews (24.7 percent), press releases (17.5 percent), and official proceedings (13 percent).[28] Recent research suggests that the situation described by Sigal remains relatively unchanged.[29]

Beats and news-gathering routines encourage a situation of mutual dependence by reporters (and their news organizations) and government officials. Reporters want stories; they have to cultivate access to people who can provide stories with quotes or anonymous leaks. Officials want favorable publicity and want to avoid or counteract unfavorable publicity. Thus, a comfortable relationship tends to develop. Even when reporters put on a show of aggressive questioning at White House press conferences, they usually work hard to stay on good terms with officials and to avoid fundamental challenges of the officials' positions. Cozy relationships between the Washington press corps and top government officials are further encouraged by the fact that the participants know each other so well, often living in the same neighborhoods, attending the same social gatherings, and sending their children to the same private schools.[30]

REPORTING FROM THE WHITE HOUSE   David Gregory (NBC), Carl Cameron (FOX), Bill Plante (CBS), John King (CNN), and Terry Moran (ABC) signal their cameramen and news producers that President Bush is about to begin his news conference. Much national newsmaking appearing on television today is from Washington, D.C., and involves transmitting the views of government officials. Why is so much television news centered around Washington? Is this the news Americans are most interested in?

While often decried by officials hurt by a damaging revelation, the **leak** is an important part of news gathering that is useful both to journalists and officials, part of the normal currency of journalist–official working relationships. Indeed, Woodward and Bernstein's Watergate story got its start with leaks from the anonymous "Deep Throat," revealed in 2005 to be Mark Felt, deputy director of the FBI during the Nixon administration. Most commonly, leaking is a way for officials to float policy ideas, get themselves noticed and credited with good deeds, undercut rivals in other government agencies, or report real or imagined wrongdoing. Because the practice is so common and useful, it is likely to remain central to how news is made.

News Management   The news media's heavy reliance on official sources means that government officials are sometimes able to control what journalists report and how they report it.[31] This is commonly referred to as **spin.** Every president and high-ranking official wants to help reporters spin a story in a way that is most useful or favorable to the office holder. The Reagan administration was particularly successful at picking a "story of the day" and having many officials feed that story to reporters, with a unified interpretation.[32] The Clinton administration tried to do the same but was not disciplined enough to make it work. President George W. Bush's administration pushed the news management envelope the farthest, eventually acknowledging that it had paid three journalists to write favorable stories, encouraged executive agencies to create news videos for media outlets without revealing the source of the videos, and allowed a political operative to be planted among the accredited White House press corps to ask questions at presidential news conferences.[33] President Obama's team ran an impressive news management operation using many of the same Internet-based tools honed during his nomination and election campaigns to get his administration's story out, partially bypassing the

leak, news

Inside or secret information given to a journalist or media outlet by a government official.

news management

The attempt by those in political power to put the presentation of news about them and their policies in a favorable light.

spin

The attempt by public officials to have a story reported in terms that favor them and their policies; see news management.

traditional news media. But he also generated a great deal of criticism when his press aides announced in 2009 that the president and his administration would have nothing more to do with FOX News because the network, in their view, failed to separate its news reporting and editorial (strongly conservative) functions. Obama did this after FOX News allowed on-screen personalities like Glenn Beck and Sean Hannity to help mobilize the Tea Party movement to hold rallies across the country to protest the health reform bill, then sent its news cameras and correspondents to give the gatherings extensive coverage.

Managing images in press reports is also important. Every administration in the modern era has tried to manage public perceptions by staging events that convey strong symbolic messages. For example, George W. Bush announced that the invasion of Iraq had been successfully concluded not in a press release but from the deck of the aircraft carrier the *USS Lincoln* on May 2, 2003, in front of a massive sign "Mission Accomplished," after landing a jet on its runway. Barack Obama told Americans about his new strategy in Afghanistan not from his desk in the Oval Office but in a televised address in front of the cadets at West Point.

Of course, news management doesn't always work as planned. When the war in Iraq took a bad turn, Bush's "Mission Accomplished" came to seem false and hollow to many Americans, and the president's popularity took a dramatic plunge. If Obama's plans for Afghanistan are not successful, his effort to manage public perceptions about the war there likely will fail as well.

Military Actions   Dependence on official sources is especially evident in military actions abroad. Because it is wary of the release of information that might help an adversary or undermine public support for U.S. actions—as happened during the Vietnam conflict—the Defense Department tries to restrict access of reporters to military personnel and the battlefield and provide carefully screened information for use by the news media. Information management was especially evident during the 1991 Gulf War to expel Saddam Hussein from Kuwait, with its carefully stage-managed news briefings at U.S. military headquarters in Saudi Arabia featuring video of "smart" weapons, Defense Department organization of press pools to cover parts of the war, and tight restrictions on reporters' access to the battlefields in Kuwait and Iraq.

During the rapid advance to Baghdad to topple Hussein's regime in 2003, the Defense Department encouraged coverage of combat by journalists embedded in combat units, although administration officials continued to exercise control over information about the big picture during the initial stages of the war. In the end, however, the administration was unable to control news about military and civilian casualties during the long occupation, the difficulties of helping to create a new constitution and government for that country, and the abuse of Iraqi prisoners at Abu Ghraib and other prisons. There were simply too many journalists and news organizations from around the world reporting on events there—and too many American soldiers and Iraqi civilians posting what they were seeing and experiencing to blogs—for the administration and military officials to be able to control the news.

Newsworthiness   Decisions about what kinds of news to print or televise depend largely on professional judgments about what is **newsworthy**. Exactly what makes a story newsworthy is difficult to spell out, but experienced editors make quick and confident judgments of what their audiences (and their employers) want. If they were consistently wrong, they would probably not remain in their jobs very long.

newsworthy
Worth printing or broadcasting as news, according to editors' judgments.

NEWS FROM THE FIELD Increasingly, news from the battlefield is reaching the public from soldiers blogging about their experiences and observations. Tight control of the news by officials has become more difficult because of this. To what extent does this help or hinder the public's understanding of our engagement in armed conflict abroad?

In practice, newsworthiness seems to depend on such factors as novelty (man bites dog, not dog bites man), drama and human interest, relevance to the lives of Americans, high stakes (physical violence or conflict), and celebrity. Some trivial topics are judged newsworthy, such as the child-rearing practices of Britney Spears. As the term *news story* implies, news works best when it can be framed as a familiar kind of narrative: an exposé of greed, sex, or corruption; conflict between politicians; or a foreign affairs crisis. On television, of course, dramatic or startling film footage helps make a story gripping. Important stories without visuals are often pushed aside for less important stories for which visuals exist.

This can often lead to missing very big stories in the making. For example, though experts had been worried for many years about the safety of New Orleans, and had been publishing their research results in specialized journals for some time, the news media did not pay much attention until the levees broke when Hurricane Katrina struck in 2005. To take another example, no reporters were at an important meeting in 2004 of the Securities and Exchange Commission when the SEC decided to relax capital requirements—how much money firms had to have on hand to deal with crises—for big financial firms.[34] This decision played an important role in the collapse of the financial system in the late summer and early fall of 2008.

Templates On many important stories, a subtle "governing template" may prevail—a sense among both reporters and editors that news stories must take a generally agreed-upon slant to be taken seriously and to make it into the news broadcast or the newspaper. This is not because of censorship but because of the development of a general agreement among news reporters and editors that the public already knows what the big story looks like on a range of issues—filling in the details is what is important. Take reporting from China as an example. For many years, editors only wanted to hear about economic prosperity, emerging democratic freedoms, and happy peasants liberated from the economic and personal straightjacket of the Maoist collective farm system. After the pro-democracy demonstrations in Tiananmen Square were brutally repressed by the People's Liberation Army, however, reporters say that it became almost impossible to write anything positive about China, because the prevailing template about China had changed.[35] Now that China has become a very important trading partner, stories about the Chinese economic miracle have proliferated (as well as some worrying about China as a potential economic, diplomatic, and military rival and as a source of tainted goods). Coverage of the Beijing Olympics became almost euphoric, despite ill-treatment of dissidents during the Games.

Episodic Foreign Coverage

Very few newspapers other than *The New York Times* can afford to station reporters abroad. Even the *Times* and the networks and wire services cannot regularly cover most nations of the world. They keep reporters in the countries of greatest interest to Americans—those that have big effects on American interests or enjoy close economic or cultural ties with the United States, such as Great Britain, Germany, Japan, Israel, Russia, and China—and they have regional bureaus in Africa and Latin America. In many countries, however, they depend on "stringers" (local journalists who file occasional reports). During major crises or big events, the media send in temporary news teams, such as the armies of reporters that swarmed to Bosnia and Kosovo during the conflicts with the Serbs and to the countries surrounding Afghanistan during the war to unseat the Taliban and find Osama bin Laden. The result is that most media devote the majority of their attention to limited areas of the world, dropping in only occasionally on others.

Foreign news, therefore, tends to be episodic. An unfamiliar part of the world, such as the Darfur region of the Sudan, suddenly jumps into the headlines with a

WAITING FOR HELP These women refugees from the genocidal conflict in the Darfur region of Sudan wait for their daily food ration in the El Fasher camp. The conflict in this region has displaced almost 2 million people to date, with most living in dreadful conditions. News coverage of Darfur and the state of its people is spotty, however, gaining attention for a time when a celebrity or prominent politician visits a refugee camp, or when a demonstration takes place in a major city in Europe or the United States, then fading into the background. Why isn't media coverage of these kinds of international issues more consistent?

? How much international news are you regularly exposed to? What would make you more interested in international events?

spectacular story of ethnic cleansing, or elsewhere a coup, an invasion, or a famine comes as a surprise to most Americans because they have not been prepared by background reports. For a few days or weeks, the story dominates the news, with intensive coverage through pictures, interviews, and commentaries. Then, if nothing new and exciting happens, the story grows stale and disappears from the media. Most viewers are left with little more understanding of the country than they began with. Thus, they find it difficult to form judgments about U.S. foreign policy.[36]

Interpreting   Political news may not make much sense without an interpretation of what it means. Under the informal rules of **objective journalism**, taught in university journalism schools and practiced by the nation's leading newspapers and network news programs, however, explicit interpretations by journalists are avoided, except for commentary or editorials that are labeled as such (some cable news operations, however, and without apology, freely mix commentary and news). Thus, even if a reporter knows that an official is lying, he or she cannot say so directly but must find someone else who will say so for the record.[37] Staged events—such as a president holding a "town meeting" using carefully selected and screened audience members—are rarely identified by reporters as staged events. In news stories, most interpretations are left implicit (so that they are hard to detect and argue with) or are given by so-called experts who are interviewed for comments. Often, particular experts are selected by print, broadcast, and telecast journalists because the position the experts will take is entirely predictable.

Experts are selected partly for reasons of convenience and audience appeal: scholars and commentators who live close to New York City or Washington, D.C., who like to speak in public, who look good on camera, and who are skillful in coming up with colorful quotations on a variety of subjects, are contacted again and again. They often show up on television to comment on the news of the day, even on issues that are far from the area of their special expertise. In many cases, these **pundits** are simply well known for being on television often and are not experts on any subject at all. The experts and commentators featured in the media are often ex-officials. Their views are usually in harmony with the political currents of the day; that is, they tend to reflect a fairly narrow spectrum of opinion close to that of the party in power in Washington, D.C., or to the prevailing "conventional wisdom" inside the beltway.

objective journalism

News reported with no evaluative language and with opinions quoted or attributed to a specific source.

pundits

Somewhat derisive term for print, broadcast, and radio commentators on the political news.

bias

Deviation from ideal standards such as representativeness or objectivity.

Is the News Biased?

Few topics arouse more disagreement than the question of whether the mass media in the United States have a liberal or conservative **bias**—or any bias at all. Many liberal critics believe the news media favor Republicans and the business establishment,[38] while many conservative critics believe the news media are unfair to Republicans and favor liberal social causes.[39] A majority of Americans (60 percent in 2009) supported the proposition that the news media are biased; only 18 percent thought the news media were fair. Among this group, a majority of Republicans and independents say the news media are biased in a liberal direction.[40]

Liberal Reporters

Surveys of reporters' and journalists' opinions suggest that these individuals tend to be somewhat more liberal than the average American on certain matters, including the environment and such social issues as civil rights and liberties, affirmative action, abortion, and women's rights.[41] This is especially true of those employed by certain elite media organizations, including *The New York Times, The Washington Post,* and PBS. It is likely that reporters' liberalism has been reflected in the treatment of issues such as global warming, same-sex marriage, and abortion. In recent years, to be sure, more conservative reporters and newscasters have gained prominence, especially on cable news telecasts. Bill O'Reilly, Sean Hannity, and Glenn Beck at FOX News are some examples.

There is, however, little or no systematic evidence that reporters' personal values regularly affect what appears in the mainstream news media.[42] Journalists' commitment to the idea of objectivity helps them resist temptation, as do critical scrutiny and rewriting by editors. In any case, the liberalism of journalists may be offset by their need to rely on official sources, their reliance on experts who are either former officials or associated with centrist or conservative think tanks, and the need to get their stories past editors who are accountable to mostly conservative owners and publishers. So for every set of stories considered biased by conservatives—for example, reporting on the abuse of prisoners at Guantanamo Bay—there is a matching set of stories considered biased by liberals—for example, not carefully examining the Bush administration's claims about weapons of mass destruction in Iraq before we invaded.

Not-so-Liberal Owners and Corporations

The owners and top managers of most news media organizations tend to be conservative and Republican. This is hardly surprising. The shareholders and executives of multi-billion-dollar corporations are not very interested in undermining the free enterprise system, for example, or, for that matter, increasing their own taxes, raising labor costs, or losing income from offended advertisers. These owners and managers ultimately decide which reporters, newscasters, and editors to hire or fire, promote or discourage. Journalists who want to get ahead, therefore, may have to come to terms with the policies of the people who own and run media businesses.[43]

STUNNED BY KATRINA Many conservative commentators charged that the news media focused on poor African Americans in New Orleans as the main victims of Hurricane Katrina when, in fact, the range of victims was much more diverse and living across a broad swath of Gulf Coast states. Is this a fair assessment of the media coverage?

Biases that Matter The question of political bias in the mainstream news media—whether in a liberal or conservative sense, or in a Democratic or Republican sense—is not so easily answered. Both reporters and news media owners considered as individuals have such biases, but it is difficult to see that these views consistently move news reports in one direction or another. Other biases perhaps matter more. One such bias is reporters' dependence on official sources, a matter examined in a previous section. Another is the bias or set of biases generated by the marketplace. News media organizations are themselves business enterprises or part of larger corporate entities and are in business to make a profit for themselves or their corporate parents. This leads many of them to engage in certain practices in news gathering and presentation that may be harmful to their central role in a democratic society. We examine these practices in much of the remainder of this chapter.

Prevailing Themes in Political News

Even if we cannot be sure whether or how the news media are biased, it is easy to identify certain tendencies in news coverage, certain beliefs that are assumed, and certain values and points of view that are emphasized.

Nationalism Although perhaps not terribly surprising, most news about foreign affairs takes a definitely pro-American, patriotic point of view, usually putting the United States in a favorable light and its opponents in an unfavorable light. This tendency is especially pronounced in news about military conflicts involving U.S. troops, as in Iraq and Afghanistan, but it can be found as well in a wide range of foreign affairs news reports, including those concerning conflicts with other governments on trade, arms control, immigration, and intellectual property rights (patents and copyrights).

News organizations also focus on subjects that interest and concern ordinary Americans, regardless of their importance in the larger picture. For example, in the early 1990s, they exhaustively covered a U.S. pilot, Scott O'Grady, who had been shot down over Bosnia. But much less attention was paid to the slaughter of millions of people during the same time in Indonesia, Nigeria, East Timor, Cambodia, and Rwanda.

This nationalistic perspective, together with heavy reliance on U.S. government news sources, means that coverage of foreign news generally harmonizes well with official U.S. foreign policy. Thus, the media tend to go along with the U.S. government in assuming the best about our close allies and the worst about official "enemies." When the United States was assisting Iraq in its war against Iran during the 1980s, for example, Saddam Hussein was depicted in a positive light; during the 1991 Gulf War and the Iraq war that started 12 years later, media characterizations of him changed dramatically negative.

In foreign policy crisis situations, the reliance on official news sources means that the media sometimes propagate government statements that are false or misleading, as in the announcement of unprovoked attacks on U.S. destroyers in the Gulf of Tonkin at the beginning of the Vietnam War (recall the chapter-opening story in Chapter 5). Secret information can also be controlled by the government. And political leaders know that the news media will be cautious in its criticism when troops are deployed and put in harm's way.

It is important to point out that when the use of American armed forces abroad drags on beyond expectations and goals are not met (as in the conflicts in Vietnam and Iraq), the news media can and do become exceedingly negative in their coverage.

This may simply reflect the mood change among nonadministration leaders and the public, or it might be a reaction among journalists and news organizations to their initial uncritical coverage of administration policies.

Approval of the American Economic System   Another tendency of the news media is to run stories generally approving of the basics of the American free enterprise system—free markets, strong property rights, and minimal government—and critical of systems that take a different approach: European social democracies with comprehensive social welfare programs, for example, rarely win praise and are often chided for their economic inefficiencies. Countries such as France and Germany are commonly criticized for labor policies that make it difficult to fire employees and downsize companies, again on economic efficiency grounds. Meanwhile, countries whose economic policies mirror those of the U.S. economy, such as Poland and Chile, win praise. To be sure, individual U.S. corporations (e.g., Enron and Halliburton) and particular industries (e.g., the sub-prime mortgage sector) are criticized for errors and misdeeds, but the basics of the economic system itself are rarely challenged. When an economic disaster like the Great Recession happens, news consumers and news organizations are eager to focus on "who is to blame" rather than on issues like instability that may be inherent in market-driven financial systems.[44]

Negativity and Scandal   One sign that the news media are neither Republican nor Democratic, conservative nor liberal in their sympathies is the relish they take in covering and magnifying scandals involving political leaders and candidates of all stripes. Although the catalyst for these stories may be leaks from inside the government; negative ads aired by rival candidates, political parties, or advocacy groups; or postings to partisan and ideological blogs, they often are picked up by major news media outlets and developed further, occasionally with great relish.[45] These stories are especially compelling to the news media when even the appearance of wrongdoing in the personal lives of prominent people creates dramatic human interest stories. Sex scandals dogged Bill Clinton for most of his presidency and contributed to his eventual impeachment (see more about this in the "Using the Framework" feature).

CAUGHT   Governor Mark Sanford of South Carolina, a champion of family values, announces his resignation as head of the Republican Governors Association at this news conference in 2009. He had been having a long-term extra-marital affair with a woman in Argentina and had been away from his office and out of contact with other state officials while visiting her when the affair came to light. The media and blogosphere focused on these sordid events for weeks. Should these sorts of scandals dominate the news? What public purpose is served?

Why did the news media pay so much attention to the Monica Lewinsky story?

Background: President Clinton's sexual liaison with White House intern Monica Lewinsky and his affair with Paula Jones when he was governor of Arkansas dominated the nation's political news from the early summer of 1998 through the end of the Senate impeachment trial of the president in early 1999. It was almost as if nothing else of importance was happening in the nation or around the world. Why is that?

Taking a look at how structural, political linkage, and governmental factors affected news coverage will help explain the situation. While the story of Monica Lewinsky may seem like old news, it perfectly illustrates how structural, political, and government factors came together in a near "perfect storm" to create a media frenzy whose effects are still with us these many years later.

Structure

Technological innovations multiplied the number of television channels, all of which require content to fill the hours. ➡ As the Internet developed, it became (among other things) a medium for the distribution of information, opinion, and rumors.

Political Linkage

Media television executives used "attack journalism," "infotainment," and scandal as a way to attract viewers from a highly fragmented set of media consumers. ➡ The media fell into their "one big story at a time" syndrome. ➡ Web-based and scandal-sheet papers fed leads to major mainstream news media. ➡ The Republican Party used the Lewinsky scandal in advertising for the 1998 congressional elections. ➡ Conservative interest groups also saw advantages in a weakened President Clinton and ran ad campaigns highlighting the Lewinsky matter.

Government

President Clinton engaged in behavior that was offensive to most Americans. ➡ Many members of Congress believed that President Clinton had obstructed justice in the Paula Jones and Monica Lewinsky affairs. ➡ A bitter partisan atmosphere permeated the 105th Congress. ➡ The Republican Congress and Democratic President Bill Clinton were bitterly deadlocked on a wide range of issues; severe tensions existed between the two branches of government.

Government Action

Impeachment hearings and vote in the House provided dramatic news material.

Senate deliberations and vote to remove the president from office provided dramatic news material.

Sex or financial scandals also claimed, among others, Senator Gary Hart (D–CO), former House Speakers Jim Wright (D–TX) and Newt Gingrich (R–GA), Mark Foley (R–FL), Larry Craig (R–ID), and South Carolina Governor Mark Sanford, whose staff in 2009 reported him hiking the Appalachian Trail even as he was in Argentina visiting his mistress.

Infotainment The prominent place of scandal in the news media is but one example of a larger and troubling trend: the massive invasion of entertainment values into political reporting and news presentation. As little as 15 to 20 years ago, news was monopolized by the three major television networks and the big-city daily newspapers, and the audiences for the news were fairly stable. In the intervening years, we have seen the media revolutionized by the growth of cable television and the Internet and the multiplication of news outlets. In this new world, the networks and the big-city dailies have lost audience, leaving the fragments of the old and new media to fight for audience share. The best way to do this, media executives have discovered, is to make the news more entertaining, for the worst sin of this brave new media world is to be boring.[46] All too often, "more entertaining" means that sensation and scandal replace consideration of domestic politics, public policies, and international affairs. In June 2007, for example, Paris Hilton's incarceration was the fifth most frequent story in the news; on February 8 and 9 of the same year, Anna Nicole Smith's death took up 60 percent of the time of the morning news shows.[47] In 2009, Michael Jackson accounted for 60 percent of television news shows during the two days following his death, far more coverage than the mass, antigovernment demonstrations in Iran.[48] More entertaining also means short and snappy coverage rather than longer, more analytical coverage; dramatic visuals push aside stories that cannot be easily visualized; and stories that feature angry conflict displace stories in which political leaders are trying to make workable compromises.[49]

The current "culture wars" between liberals and conservatives over the various legacies of the 1960s—involving issues such as abortion, affirmative action, religious values, teaching evolution in schools, same-sex marriage, and more—are perfect grist for the infotainment mill.[50] Thus, a current staple of cable and broadcast television public affairs programming is the gathering of pundits from both sides of the cultural and political divide angrily shouting at one another for 30 or 60 minutes. And, because bringing together shouting pundits is far cheaper than sending reporters into the field to gather hard news, this form of news coverage is becoming more and more common, especially in the world of cable TV. It is highly unlikely that this emergent journalism of assertion and attack improves public understanding of the candidates, political leaders, or public policies.

Conflict and contest are also evident in coverage of campaigns, where the media concentrate on the "horse-race" aspects of election contests, focusing almost exclusively on who is winning and who is losing the race and what strategies candidates are using to gain ground or to maintain their lead. When candidates sometimes make a stab at talking seriously about issues, the media almost always treat such talk as a mere stratagem of the long campaign. The perpetual struggle between Congress and the president, built into our constitutional system, is also perfect for the infotainment news industry, especially if the struggle can be personalized, as it was in the years when House Speaker and Democrat Nancy Pelosi was doing battle with President George W. Bush.

Limited, Fragmented, and Incoherent Political Information Most communications scholars agree that the media coverage of political news has certain distinctive features that result from characteristics of the mass media themselves, including the prevailing technology and organization of news gathering, corporate ownership, and the profit-making drive to appeal to mass audiences. These characteristics of the media mean that news, especially on television, tends to be episodic and fragmented rather than sustained, analytical, or dispassionate. Information comes in bits and pieces, out of context, and without historical background. Its effect is to entertain more than to inform. This may or may not be what people want—some scholars suggest that the people, in fact, do not want hard news at all; others suggest that they want a strong dose of entertainment and diversion with their news[51]—but it is what they get.

Having said that, it is important to point out that the news media often do deep and thorough investigative reporting that matters. *The Wall Street Journal, The New York Times,* and *Bloomberg Businessweek*, for example, each did in-depth stories in late 2009 and early 2010 on lobbying and big campaign contributions by large financial firms who tried, with some success, to turn back regulatory reforms in Congress not to their liking. But the pressure to stick to infotainment is relentless, and all news organizations feel it in one way or another—even the best of them.

Effects of the News Media on Politics

6.4 Identify the ways in which the news media affect public opinion and policymaking

The old idea among social scientists that the news media have only "minimal effects" on politics is now discredited. The contents of the news media do make a difference; they affect public opinion and policymaking in a number of ways, including setting the agenda for public debate and framing how issues are understood.[52]

Agenda Setting

Several studies have demonstrated the effect known as **agenda setting**. The topics that get the most coverage in the news media at any point in time are the same ones that most people tell pollsters are the most important problems facing the country. This correlation does not result just from the news media's reporting what people are most interested in; it is a real effect of what appears in the news. In controlled experiments, people who are shown doctored television news broadcasts emphasizing a particular problem (e.g., national defense) mention that problem as being important more often than people who have seen broadcasts that have not been tampered with.[53]

Of course, media managers do not arbitrarily decide what news to emphasize; their decisions reflect what is happening in the world and what American audiences care about. If there is a war or an economic depression, the media report it. But some research has indicated that what the media cover sometimes diverges from actual trends in problems. Publicity about crime, for example, may reflect editors' fears or a few dramatic incidents rather than a rising crime rate. When the two diverge, it seems to be the media's emphasis rather than real trends that affects public opinion.[54]

When the media decide to highlight a human rights tragedy in "real time," such as "ethnic cleansing" in Kosovo, public officials often feel compelled to act, as Bill Clinton did when he was president. (This is sometimes called the CNN effect.) When the media ignore equally troubling

agenda setting
Influencing people's opinions about what is important.

THE TELEVISED WAR The Vietnam War was the first American war fully covered by television. Footage of American deaths and casualties, as well as visual reminders of the terrible consequences of the conflict on the Vietnamese civilian population, helped turn public opinion in the United States against the war. This still from television footage of children napalmed by an accidental American attack on a village of Trang Bang in 1972 is a particularly powerful example of the war coming home to American living rooms. How do the media continue to influence American public opinion about our role in foreign conflicts?

human tragedies, such as the more recent genocide in Darfur, public officials can attend to other matters. One scholarly study shows that in the foreign policy area, media choices about coverage shape what presidents pay attention to.[55] But influences go in both directions. News media scholar Lance Bennett suggests that journalists and the news organizations they work for are very attuned to the relative power balance in Washington between Democrats and Republicans, and between liberals and conservatives, and focus on matters that are of most concern to those in power at any particular time. Thus, Social Security reform becomes an important issue in the press when important political actors want to talk about it. The same is true for other issues, whether taxes or nuclear threats from countries such as Iran and North Korea.[56]

Framing and Effects on Policy Preferences

Experiments also indicate that the media's **framing**, or interpretation of stories, affects how people think about political problems and how they assign blame. Several commentators noticed during the Katrina disaster in New Orleans, for example, that TV news stories featuring whites talked of "foraging for food and supplies," while those featuring blacks talked of looting. There are reasons to believe that public impressions of what was going on in the city were affected by this coverage. To take another example, whether citizens ascribe poverty to the laziness of the poor or to the nature of the economy, for example, depends partly on whether the news media run stories about poor individuals (implying that they are responsible for their own plight) or stories about overall economic trends such as economic recessions and unemployment.[57]

What appears in the news media affects people's policy preferences as well. One study found, for example, that the public is more likely to favor government programs to help African Americans when the news media frame racial problems in terms of failures of society to live up to the tradition of equality in the United States. The public is less supportive of these programs when the news media frame the origins of racial problems in

framing
Providing a context for interpretation.

terms of individual failures to be self-reliant and responsible.[58] Another study found that changes in the percentages of the public that favored various policies could be predicted rather accurately by what sorts of stories appeared on network television news shows between one opinion survey and the next. News from experts, commentators, and popular presidents had especially strong effects.[59]

Fueling Cynicism

Americans are quite cynical about the political parties, politicians, and most incumbent political leaders. To some extent, this has been true since the founding of the nation. Nevertheless, scholars and political commentators have noted a considerable increase in negative feelings about the political system over the past two decades or so. Many students of the media believe that news media coverage of American politics has a great deal to do with this attitude change.[60] As the adversarial-attack journalism style and infotainment have taken over political reporting, serious consideration of the issues, careful examination of policy alternatives, and dispassionate examination of the actions of government institutions have taken a back seat to a steady diet of charges about personal misbehavior and political conflict. When President George H. W. Bush joined a world leader at a press conference in 1992 to describe the nature of the agreement they had reached, reporters asked him instead about rumors of an extramarital affair a few years earlier. With the message being delivered by the mass media that political issues are really about special-interest maneuvering, that political leaders and aspiring political leaders never say what they mean or mean what they say, that all of them have something in their personal lives they want to hide, and that even the most admired of the lot have feet of clay, is it any wonder that the American people are becoming increasingly disenchanted with the whole business?

Government Regulation of the Media

6.5 Compare and contrast government regulation of the different media

Our Constitution protects freedom of the press, and the U.S. government has less legal control over the media than the governments of most other countries do (see Chapter 16 for more on press freedoms). But our government has the authority to make various technical and substantive regulations on the electronic media, if it wishes.

Print Media

Because freedom of the press is enshrined in the First Amendment to the Constitution as one of our basic freedoms, the print media—newspapers and magazines—are exempt from most government regulations (these will be reviewed in detail in Chapter 16). Not that government leaders did not try from time to time, starting in the early years of the republic. Under the Alien and Sedition Acts of 1798, for example, several Anti-Federalist newspaper editors were jailed for criticizing John Adams's administration. In recent years, however, the Constitution has been interpreted as forbidding government from preventing the publication of most kinds of political information or from punishing its publication afterward.

Several U.S. Supreme Court decisions, beginning in the 1920s and 1930s, have ensured the press a great deal of constitutional protection. The First Amendment provision that Congress shall make no law "abridging freedom of speech, or of the press" has been held by the Supreme Court to prevent the federal censorship of newspapers or magazines. Only under the most pressing circumstances of danger to national security can the government engage in **prior restraint** and prevent the publication of material to which it objects.

> **prior restraint**
> The government's power to prevent publication of material to which it objects, as opposed to punishment afterward.

On June 30, 1971, for example, the Supreme Court denied a request by the Nixon administration to restrain *The New York Times* and *The Washington Post* from publishing excerpts from the *Pentagon Papers,* a secret Defense Department history of the United States' involvement in Vietnam. The Court declared that "the Government 'thus carries a heavy burden of showing justification for the enforcement of such a restraint.'...The Government had not met that burden." Justice Hugo Black's concurring opinion has become an important statement on freedom of the press that subsequent Courts have not overturned. The result is that the government can do very little to restrain newspapers from printing the stories their editors and publishers wish to print, even during times of military action. At most, it can try to manage the flow of information to journalists and journalists' access to military personnel and the civilian population in combat areas.

Electronic Media

Over-the-air electronic media—broadcast television and radio—are regulated by government, though more lightly than in the past. Cable and the Internet are mostly beyond the reach of government, though certain of the business practices of firms in these sectors can be and are regularly scrutinized.

Government Licensing of the Airwaves
The federal government has broad powers to regulate the use of the airwaves, which are limited in number (there are only so many frequencies available under existing technologies) and considered public property. Ever since the passage of the Radio Act of 1927 and the Communications Act of 1934, which established the Federal Communications Commission (FCC), the government has licensed radio and television stations and has required them to observe certain rules as a condition for obtaining licenses.

FCC rules specify the frequencies on which stations can broadcast and the amount of power they can use in order to prevent interference among broadcasters of the sort that had brought chaos to radio during the 1920s. Government regulations divide the VHF television band into 12 channels and allocate them in such a way that most major cities have three VHF stations—the main reason for the early emergence of only three major networks. The development of cable television, which does not require the use of airwaves for delivery of video content to customers, has greatly expanded variety and competition, as has the Internet.

For a long time, to prevent monopolies of scarce channels, federal rules prohibited networks or anyone else from owning more than five local VHF stations around the country.[61] Deregulation during the 1990s loosened these rules. The most important step was passage of the Telecommunications Act of 1996, which, in addition to removing most restrictions on competition among telephone, cable, and broadcast companies and providing new frequencies for high-definition TV, removed most restrictions on the number of radio and television stations that a company could own nationally and within a single media market. The act also reduced restrictions on ownership across media sectors, nationally and locally, meaning that single giant

fairness doctrine

The former requirement that television stations present contrasting points of view.

companies could increase their holdings of radio and television stations, cable operations, and newspapers. To the surprise of no one, the industry experienced a wave of mergers in the years following passage of the act.

The FCC is also required by law to regulate the airwaves for the "public interest, convenience, or necessity." This vague phrase has been interpreted as including "the development of an informed public opinion through the public dissemination of news and ideas concerning the vital public issues of the day," with ideas coming from "diverse and antagonistic sources," and with an emphasis on service to the local community. In practice, this requirement has mainly meant FCC pressure (backed up by the threat of not renewing stations' licenses) to provide a certain number of hours of news and "public service" broadcasting on licensed television channels. Thus, government regulation created an artificial demand for news programming, before it became profitable, and contributed to the rise and expansion of network news and to the development of documentaries and news specials. In that way, government regulation presumably contributed to informed public opinion and to democracy. Recently, however, this public service requirement has been eroded and the amount of this kind of programming has declined.

For many years, the **fairness doctrine** of 1949 required that licensees present contrasting viewpoints on any controversial issue of public importance that was discussed. This requirement led to efforts at balance—presenting two sides on any issue that was mentioned—and sometimes to the avoidance of controversial issues altogether. It was left mostly up to broadcasters, however, to decide what was important or controversial and what constituted a fair reply and a fair amount of time to give it. In 1985, citing the growing diversity of news outlets on broadcast and cable television for the airing of contending points of view, the FCC abolished the fairness doctrine. Congress has tried several times since then to restore the doctrine, but has not been able to do so.

EQUAL TIME   When actor and former senator Fred Thompson became a candidate for the Republican presidential nomination in 2008, NBC refused to telecast reruns of episodes of *Law and Order* in which he appeared as District Attorney Arthur Branch. The network was concerned that it would run afoul of the FCC's "equal time" provision and be forced to give other candidates for the nomination as much time on the air as Thompson. How else could the network have handled this unique situation?

Similarly, the **equal time provision** of the 1934 Communications Act required that except for news programs, stations that granted (or sold) air time to any one candidate for public office had to grant (or sell) other candidates equal time. This requirement threatened to cause the media great expense when minor party candidates insisted on their share of air time or when opponents wanted to reply to political speeches by incumbent presidents in election years. Contrary to its intent, therefore, this requirement led to some curtailment of political programming.

> **equal time provision**
> The former requirement that television stations give or sell the same amount of time to all competing candidates.

The equal time provision was suspended in 1960 to allow televised debates between candidates John F. Kennedy and Richard M. Nixon and it has been that for most of the time since then, with television broadcasters free to stage debates at all political levels among candidates of their own choosing. Broadcasters and the Commission on Presidential Debates (a nonpartisan corporation created to sponsor presidential debates) decided to allow Independent candidate Ross Perot to join the debates in 1992 (Bush versus Clinton) and 1996 (Clinton versus Dole), but chose not to include Green Party candidate Ralph Nader in 2000 (Bush versus Gore), much to the chagrin of Nader and his supporters. In 2004, the presidential debates included only John Kerry and George W. Bush, the major party candidates. Similarly, in 2008, the presidential debates included only the Democratic and Republican candidates, Barack Obama and John McCain.

Concerns among many Americans about the increased availability of sexually suggestive materials on network and cable television and on radio have triggered increased scrutiny of media decency practices and standards by the FCC. Public officials were especially sensitive to the public outcry over Janet Jackson's televised half-time performance at the Super Bowl in 2004. Worried by the FCC's new willingness to levy fines for on-air indecency, some media corporations moved quickly to try to stem the tide. The major broadcast TV networks beefed up their standards departments and began to delay many live broadcasts for a few seconds so that potentially offensive material might be deleted. In 2004, Clear Channel Communications, worried about potential fines from the FCC, dropped "shock-jock" Howard Stern from its radio stations. Stern then migrated to satellite radio, which is unregulated. (In 2010, a federal court threw out the FCC rules regarding indecency, saying they were arbitrary, unenforceable, and had a chilling effect on free speech.)

HOWARD STERN ON THE AIR Controversial talk show host Howard Stern, shown here doing his radio show in January 2006, has been able to escape the scrutiny of federal regulators worried about his use of indecent language by moving to Sirius Satellite Radio. Subscription-based satellite broadcasts fall outside the regular regulatory domain of the Federal Communications Commission. Why aren't these broadcasts FCC regulated?

Regulation of Cable For a time during the Bush administration, the FCC's chairman tried to assert tighter regulatory control over the cable television industry. Regulation of cable, which is now unregulated, is allowed under a 1984 law when and if cable reaches 70 percent of the national television market. The other FCC commissioners—political opponents of the chair—refused to accept an FCC staff report showing such a milestone had been reached early in 2008. Responding to mostly conservative critics of the cable industry and many parents, President George W. Bush's FCC chair had wanted to force the cable industry to allow people to choose individual programs for their cable service rather than packages of programs. The cable industry lobbied hard to stop the change and succeeded with the other commissioners and members of Congress. Thus, cable remains outside of the regulatory reach of the FCC.

The Internet When television and radio were introduced, the industries were regulated by the federal government almost immediately because the number of channels had to be limited in order to have interference-free broadcasts and telecasts, so licenses had to be applied for and granted (with strings attached, as noted earlier). No such technological limits hinder the Internet, and it has grown rapidly without government regulation. Although the Internet was initially a product of government encouragement and financial support—it was first created to link together university and government defense researchers—government has not interfered much in its operations, although there have been repeated calls for government to prevent certain content from appearing on it. The few attempts that have been made have not been successful. For example, Congress tried to ban obscenity on the Net, but the Supreme Court in 1997 declared the statute an unconstitutional restriction of free speech. When the Clinton administration tried to prevent people from posting encryption codes, a federal court declared the effort as unconstitutional on the same grounds. In the view of the federal courts, at this writing, the

SURFING THE NET As Internet usage has expanded in the United States, various and sundry individuals and groups have called for tighter federal regulation of the new medium, primarily to protect children like this young girl from material with sexual content and to prevent dissemination of hate material to young and old. So far, none of the bills passed by Congress to achieve these regulatory goals has passed constitutional muster with the Supreme Court. Why is the Internet so difficult to regulate?

Internet is an open medium through which people are free to express their views, no different from dissemination of ideas by voice from atop a soap-box or by a pamphlet. Statute and case law in this area are sure to grow, however, as the Internet comes to play an ever-larger role in our lives. The story of Internet regulation is not yet finished. For example, Congress revisited the issue of Internet pornography when it passed the Child Online Protection Act of 1998, designed to block access to material on the Web that might be harmful to children. In 2004, however, the Supreme Court upheld a lower court's ruling blocking the law from taking effect, with the majority suggesting that the new law was an unconstitutional restriction on free speech.

Using the **DEMOCRACY STANDARD**

Do the news media help or hinder democracy?

The framers favored a form of government based on the consent of the governed, but one in which most of the governed played only a limited and indirect role in political life. They believed that government was best run by talented, educated, and broad-minded individuals who attained office through indirect elections based on a limited franchise, and who governed at several removes from the people. According to such an understanding of the ideal form of government, there was no pressing need for news media to educate the general public and prepare it for active participation in politics. For the framers, the purpose of the news media—newspapers, in their day—was to serve as a mechanism allowing economic, social, and political leaders to communicate with each other and to help them deliberate on the issues of the day.

For democratic theorists, the people play a more central role in governance and the news media play an accordingly larger role in preparing the people to participate. As we pointed out earlier, accurate, probing, and vigorous news media are essential building blocks for democratic life to the extent that the broad general public cannot be rationally engaged in public affairs without them. In this respect, the spread of the news media in the United States, and the penetration of millions of homes by newspapers, radio, television, and the Internet, has undoubtedly enriched democracy. It has made it much easier for ordinary citizens to form policy preferences, to judge the actions of government, and to decide whom they want to govern them. News media thus tend to broaden the scope of conflict and contribute to political equality. When citizens as well as political leaders and special-interest groups know what is going on, they can have a voice in politics. Moreover, interactive media and media-published polls help politicians hear that voice.

Scholars and media critics who want the news media to be highly informative, analytical, and issue oriented, however, are often appalled by the personalized, episodic, dramatic, and fragmented character of most news stories, which do not provide sustained and coherent explanations of what is going on. Still other critics worry that constant media exposés of alleged official wrongdoing or government inefficiency, and the mocking tone aimed at virtually all political leaders by journalists and talk-radio hosts, have fueled the growing political cynicism of the public. To the extent that this is true, the news media are not serving democracy as well as they might.

It is undeniably the case that the news media have not performed their civic responsibilities very well. They do tend to trivialize, focus on scandal and entertainment, and offer fragmented and out-of-context political and governmental information. However, things may not be quite as bad as they appear. For one thing, for those who are truly interested in public affairs, there is now more readily accessible information than at any time in our history. For those willing to search for it, there is now little information that is relevant to public affairs that can be kept hidden, ranging from official government statistics to academic and other expert studies. Additionally, the American people have demonstrated an admirable ability on many occasions to sift the wheat from the chaff, to glean the information they need from the background noise, as it were.[62] On balance, then, the news media have probably helped advance the cause of democracy in the United States and helped transform the American republic into the American democratic republic. There is no doubt, however, that the news media could also do a considerably better job than they do at the present time.

SUMMARY

6.1 Evaluate the various roles of the news media in a democracy

- One role for the news media in a democracy is to serve as a watchdog over government, uncovering government corruption and keeping government officials accountable to the public.

- Other important roles are to help citizens evaluate candidates for public office and to think about what kinds of government policies might best serve the public interest.

6.2 Assess the respective roles of traditional and other news media today

- Traditional news media such as newspapers and televisions still gather and report the most news, even as more people get their information from the Internet.

- Internet news is rarely based on independent reporting. Most is from the traditional media, either taken directly, rewritten, or commented upon.

- Television is still the most trusted source of news.

6.3 Analyze how the news is gathered and disseminated and evaluate the outcome of this process

- The shape of the news media in the United States has been determined largely by structural factors: technological developments; the growth of the American population and economy; and the development of a privately owned, corporation-dominated media industry.

- New Internet-based media have not replaced traditional reporting and news organizations. For the most part, these new media use materials gathered by old media.

- News gathering is limited by logistics. Most news gathering is organized around New York City, Washington, D.C., and a handful of major cities in the United States and abroad. Most foreign countries are ignored unless there are crises or other big stories to communicate.

6.4 Identify the ways in which the news media affect public opinion and policymaking

- News media stories have substantial effects on the public's perceptions of problems, its interpretations of events, its evaluations of political candidates, and their policy preferences.

- The news media affects the public not only by providing information but also by agenda setting and framing.

6.5 Compare and contrast government regulation of the different media

- The First Amendment to the Constitution allows broad freedom to the print news media from many kinds of government interference. But censorship occurs during wars and crises, and officials have indirect ways of influencing the news.

- The government, mostly through the FCC, can regulate the airwaves, namely, broadcast radio and television. These have traditionally included the fairness doctrine and the equal time provision, but these have become less important.

- Cable is subject to some indirect regulation—those regulations that pertain to any and all business firms—but is outside the purview of the FCC. The Internet remains relatively free from government regulation.

TEST YOURSELF

Answer key begins on page T-1.

6.1 Evaluate the various roles of the news media in a democracy

1. The most prominent role of the media in a democracy is to shape public opinion.
   True / False
2. In which of the following ways do the media fail to fully play their role in clarifying electoral choices?
   a. The media not only tell Americans what to think about, they also tell them what to think.
   b. The media focus on the "horse race" of the campaign rather than on the issues.
   c. Media coverage of elections ignores important campaign information about who is ahead and who is behind.
   d. The media do not cover sensational political stories.
   e. There are too many media outlets for the media to adequately undertake their watchdog role.
3. Why is freedom of the press so important in a democracy?

6.2 Assess the respective roles of traditional and other news media today

4. Where do Americans get most of their political news?
   a. The Internet
   b. Radio
   c. News magazines
   d. Newspapers
   e. Television
5. What is the source of most of the political news found on the Internet?
   a. Academics
   b. Original research conducted by ordinary citizens
   c. Political parties and candidates
   d. Interest groups
   e. The mainstream media
6. Evaluate the extent to which the Internet has expanded the amount of political information available to ordinary citizens.

6.3 Analyze how the news is gathered and disseminated and evaluate the outcome of this process

7. Newsworthiness is primarily determined by the extent to which the story contains information that will help citizens make informed political decisions.
   True / False
8. Which of the following most accurately describes media bias?
   a. The media have a clear liberal bias.
   b. The media have a clear conservative bias.
   c. The media have a bias in favor of entertaining news.
   d. The media have a bias in favor of in-depth coverage of policy issues.
   e. The media have a bias against free enterprise economic systems.
9. Evaluate the extent to which the media should supplement objective reporting with an interpretation of what the story means.

6.4 Identify the ways in which the news media affect public opinion and policymaking

10. Americans are more likely to favor programs that help African Americans when the media frame racial problems as a societal failure to live up to our commitment to equality.
    True / False
11. How do the media influence the political agenda?
    a. The media tell the public how to interpret important political events.
    b. The public places greater importance on those issues that are covered by the media.
    c. The government is more likely to confide in the media than in the public.
    d. The media focus on those news stories that contain a strong public policy focus.
    e. The public tends to discount those stories that are covered through unflattering frames or that focus on negative information.
12. Why do some believe that the way the media cover politics fuels American cynicism about government?

6.5 Compare and contrast government regulation of the different media

13. The fairness doctrine requires that all current media programs include contrasting viewpoints on any controversial political topics that are discussed. True / False

14. Why does the government have greater authority to regulate broadcast television and radio than it has to regulate other types of media?
    a. Visual and audio information has a greater impact on political attitudes than does written information.
    b. Citizens are more likely to consume political information from the television and radio than from newspapers.
    c. Citizens have increased trust in television and radio news than in news from other media.
    d. The airwaves are limited in number and are considered public property.
    e. The First Amendment's freedom of press guarantee applies only to television and radio news; it does not apply to news from other media.

mypPEARSONoliscilab EXERCISES

Apply what you learned in this chapter on MyPoliSciLab.

Read on mypoliscilab.com

eText: Chapter 6

Study and Review on mypoliscilab.com

Pre-Test
Post-Test
Chapter Exam
Flashcards

Watch on mypoliscilab.com

Video: YouTube Politics
Video: The Pentagon's Media Message

Explore on mypoliscilab.com

Simulation: You Are the News Editor
Comparative: Comparing News Media
Timeline: Three Hundred Years of American Mass Media
Visual Literacy: Use of the Media by the American Public

INTERNET SOURCES

The Center for Media and Public Affairs
www.cmpa.com
Studies, commentaries, and forums on media and public affairs.

The Pew Project for Excellence in Journalism
www.stateofthenewsmedia.org
Annual scholarly review of the state of the news media, with attention to new developments.

The Berkman Center for the Internet and Society
http://cyber.law.harvard.edu
A research and information center at the Harvard Law School that follows the development of the Internet and its impact on law and society.

The Columbia Journalism Review
www.cjr.org
The website of the leading scholarly monitor of journalism and journalists; loaded with useful information about all aspects of newsmaking and dissemination.

The Pew Research Center for the People and the Press
www.people-press.org/
The most complete public opinion surveys on citizen evaluations of the quality of media coverage of public affairs.

SUGGESTIONS FOR FURTHER READING

Alterman, Eric. *What Liberal Media? The Truth About Bias and the News.* New York: Basic Books, 2003.

An impassioned yet well-documented answer to the charge that the news media are biased against conservatives.

Bennett, W. Lance. *News: Politics of Illusion,* 8th ed. New York: Longman, 2009.

A critique of the news as trivial and uninformative.

Bennett, W. Lance, Regina G. Lawrence, and Steven Livingston. *When the Press Fails: Political Power and the News from Iraq to Katrina.* Chicago: University of Chicago Press, 2007.

A devastating critique of the news media limited by the pressures of the marketplace and the balance of political power in Washington.

Goldberg, Bernard. *Bias: A CBS Insider Exposes How the Media Distort the News.* New York: Harper Paperbacks, 2003.

A conservative critique of CBS News in particular and the mainstream news media in general.

Hindman, Matthew. *The Myth of Digital Democracy.* Princeton, NJ: Princeton University Press, 2009.

Based on compelling empirical evidence, the author shows that many of the inequalities that characterize American society and politics are recreated on the Internet.

Graber, Doris. *Mass Media and American Politics,* 8th ed. Washington, D.C.: CQ Press, 2010.

A comprehensive examination of the news media's effect on American politics.

Interest Groups and Business Corporations

LEARNING OBJECTIVES

After reading this chapter, you should be able to:

7.1 Compare and contrast theories about the role of interest groups in a democracy

7.2 Distinguish the two kinds of interests at work in American politics

7.3 Explain why interest groups have proliferated

7.4 Distinguish the methods through which interest groups try to shape policy

7.5 Determine the biases in the interest group system

7.6 Assess the steps that have been taken to control factions

DISASTER IN THE GULF

In the Gulf of Mexico on April 20, 2010, the Deepwater Horizon drilling rig was ripped apart by a series of spectacular explosions just before midnight that killed 11 oil rig workers and unleashed an oil spill of near-historic proportions.[1] The Deepwater Horizon, owned by the Transocean Corporation and leased to oil giant BP, was finishing the final phases of drilling a well more than a mile beneath the platform when disaster struck. The temporary cement cap that topped off the well failed, releasing a potent and out-of-control flow of a natural gas and crude oil mixture to the platform where a spark set off the explosion. The shattered pipe in the middle of the drill hole poured natural gas and crude oil into the Gulf at the rate of 35,000 to 60,000 barrels a day (BP first reported 1,000 barrels per day), defying initial efforts to cut off the flow at the pipe. Efforts to funnel the crude to storage and transport vessels on the surface in the months after the blowout, even as relief wells were being drilled, did some good, but massive amounts of natural gas and crude oil continued to escape for months. The spill fouled the beaches and marshlands of Gulf Coast states and formed deep, underwater natural gas and oil plumes, whose long-term environmental effects are unknowable at this time.

How did it happen? Though it will probably be some time before the final evidence is in, it soon emerged that BP had insisted that the platform operator, Transocean, take a number of operational steps that were quite risky and would, in the end, prove disastrous to oil rig workers and the Gulf environment and economy. These steps were a series of shortcuts that put cost-saving before safety. These included using too few "centralizers" to stabilize the cement that held the drilling pipe in place in the ocean floor, skipping critical inspections and tests of emergency cut-off mechanisms, using one rather than the industry-standard two pipe "pinchers" (called "blind shear rams") to cut off oil flow in the main pipe in the event of a blowout, and using pipes of lower quality than BP's own experts advised. Though Transocean engineers and many workers aboard the Deepwater rig apparently expressed concerns about these decisions, operations never slowed as BP executives pushed everyone to finish on time and under budget so it could temporarily cap the well and move on to other drilling opportunities.

Though BP was at fault in this case, it emerged in congressional testimony during early summer, 2010 that other oil company operators doing deep well drilling in the Gulf and other places in the world had no better solutions than did BP to a blowout at these depths once a blowout occurred. Oil and drilling company executives testified that they would also first try using shear ram blowout preventers—massive four- to five-story-high devices weighing hundreds of thousands of pounds with many widely acknowledged vulnerabilities when working at very deep depths—then drill relief wells to cap the runaway reservoir, and install top-hat and other devices to funnel escaping oil to surface ships or platforms for processing and transporting. They agreed that more onsite testing of critical blowout preventers should be done given the Deepwater Horizon event, but they were somewhat at a loss for words when congressional committee members produced a report from the industry itself pointing out that most companies cut corners in their testing programs given the costs involved: about $700 a minute to suspend operations while testing.

We have a rough idea, then, of why the Deepwater Horizon happened from a technical point of view. But other

factors involving the oil industry's political influence are also important in this story. There is, first, the absence of a national energy policy that might encourage the development and use of renewable energy. Without this, for now and the foreseeable future, Americans must depend on fossil fuels, especially coal and oil, to provide the power they need to run a modern, industrial society. Inevitably, as easily recoverable oil reserves are depleted, and as global warming concerns put a damper on a greater reliance on coal, oil companies are forced to look in less hospitable places for oil, including the deep ocean floor. But the absence of a national energy policy that would encourage alternative fuels is itself partly the result of the long-term oil industry influence in American politics; the industry has been among the very largest contributors to the campaigns of presidential, congressional, and state-level candidates and among the industries that spend the most on direct lobbying to keep oil at the center of our energy economy.

The oil industry also has been a central player in the three-decade-long effort to deregulate the American economy, that is, leave more and more decisions to private firms operating in the marketplace, largely freed from federal and state government oversight. We shall have a great deal more to say about this in Chapter 17, but the overall story is one in which business leaders, the economics profession, conservative think tanks, and Republican and centrist Democrats came to believe that government is generally bad for economic efficiency and growth and ought to exit the game, as it were.[2] The oil industry contribution to the deregulation movement has been multifaceted, including campaign contributions and lobbying, but also the generous funding of anti–big government think tanks that have churned out reports on the evils of regulation for many years. Deregulation has had some good outcomes, to be sure, as in restraining air travel and freight shipping costs, but bad ones in a wide range of areas, including the collapse of the financial system as the most obvious recent case. But the deregulation spirit has infused the oil industry as well, with fewer personnel in agencies that are responsible for oversight and less willingness on the part of mid-level government bureaucrats, given the political environment, to ask too much of industry operators. One of the things congressional testimony revealed in summer 2010 was how few rules the Minerals Management Service (MMS) issued regarding deep ocean drilling and how often they failed to enforce the few rules that were in place.

Finally, there is what political scientists call "agency capture" in which a regulatory agency, designed to regulate an industry in the public interest, comes to act as a partner instead. This happens for a number of reasons, including possible future employment in the regulated industry for the regulator, dependence on the industry for the technical information that the agency needs to issue regulations and monitor performance, and long-term relationships among regulators and firms that encourage commonality in points of view. Sometimes, there is even gift-giving from the wealthy industry to those who work in the regulatory agency.

Each of these elements of "capture" can be seen in the MMS oil and drilling industry relationship. Congressional hearings and an Interior Department inspector general's report in 2010 revealed, for example, that companies paid for meals and hotel stays, elaborate vacations, and tickets to premium athletic events for agency employees and that several inspectors had examined operations at companies where they hoped to work. The hearings and report also uncovered the cozy relationship that developed between oil rig inspectors and drilling companies. For example, many instances were uncovered in which industry officials were allowed to fill out MMS inspection report forms in pencil, with the inspectors going over the pencil traces later in pen. Equally important, the MMS was entirely dependent on the technical information provided by regulated companies having neither the personnel nor agency resources to develop information or independent testing equipment and instruments "in-house." During the Coast Guard inquiry on the failure of the various safety devices to work at the Deepwater Horizon platform, Captain Hung Nguyen was astonished when he received a simple "yes" answer from the MMS's regional supervisor for field operations to the following question: "So my understanding is that [the shear ram tool] is designed to industry standard, manufactured by industry, installed by industry, with no government witnessing oversight of the construction or the installation. Is that correct?"

Much of what the federal government does in the United States is influenced by what the general public wants it to do. Elected and other public officials, you have seen, pay attention to things such as public opinion polls and news media characterizations of popular preferences. You will see in later chapters in this book, moreover, that political leaders must be responsive to the electorate if they want to gain and retain their elected offices. But it is also the case that a wide array of private interest and advocacy groups, with business leading the way, also play an enormously important, although less visible role, in determining what government does and influencing who wins and who loses from public policies.

THINKING CRITICALLY About This Chapter

This chapter is about the important role interest groups play in American government and politics, how they go about achieving their ends, and what effects they have in determining government policies in the United States.

Using the FRAMEWORK

You will see in this chapter how interest groups, in combination with other political linkage institutions, help convey the wishes and interests of people and groups to government decision makers. You will also learn how the kind of interest group system we have in the United States is, in large part, a product of structural factors, including our constitutional rules, political culture, social organization, and economy.

Using the **DEMOCRACY STANDARD**

Interest groups have long held an ambiguous place in American politics. To some, interest groups are "special" interests that act without regard to the public interest and are the instruments of the most privileged parts of American society. To others, interest groups are simply another way by which people and groups in a democratic society get their voices heard by government leaders. Using the democracy standard described in Chapter 1, you will be able to evaluate these two positions.

Interest Groups in a Democratic Society: Contrasting Views

7.1 Compare and contrast theories about the role of interest groups in a democracy

Interest groups are private organizations and voluntary associations that try to influence what government does. They are not part of government themselves. Nor are they political parties that try to place candidates carrying the party banner into government offices; though, as shown later in this chapter, interest groups play an important role in U.S. elections. Interest groups are firms, formal organizations, or voluntary groups that share an interest or cause they are trying to protect or advance with the help of government.[3] The interests and causes these organizations and associations press on government range from narrowly targeted material benefits (e.g., passage of a favorable tax break or the issuance of a helpful regulation) to more broadly targeted outcomes for society at large (e.g., new rules on auto emissions or abortion availability). To do this, interest groups try to influence the behavior of public officials, such as presidents, members of Congress, bureaucrats, and judges. The framers knew that interest groups were inevitable and appropriate in a free society but were potentially harmful as well, so they paid special attention to them in the design of the Constitution.

The Evils of Faction

The danger to good government and the public interest from interest groups is a familiar theme in American politics. They are usually regarded as narrowly self-interested, out for themselves, and without regard for the public good.

This theme is prominent in *The Federalist,* No. 10 (see the Appendix), in which James Madison defined **factions** (his term for interest groups and narrow political parties) in the following manner: "A number of citizens, whether amounting to a majority or a minority of the whole, who are united and actuated by some common impulse of passion, or of interest, adverse to the rights of other citizens or to the permanent and aggregate interests of the community."[4] The "evils of faction" theme recurs throughout our history, from the writings of the "muckrakers" at the turn of the twentieth century to news

interest group

A private organization or voluntary association that seeks to influence public policy as a way to protect or advance its interests.

faction

Madison's term for groups or parties that try to advance their own interests at the expense of the public good.

BOSSES OF THE SENATE   In the late nineteenth century, most Americans thought of the Senate as the captive of large corporate trusts and other special-interest groups, as depicted in this popular cartoon, "Bosses of the Senate." How has the public's view changed, if at all?

accounts and commentary on the misdeeds of the leaders of the financial industry in the 2008 financial collapse.

Interest Group Democracy: The Pluralist Argument

According to many political scientists, however, interest groups do not hurt democracy and the public interest but are an important instrument in attaining both. The argument of these **pluralist** political scientists is shown in Figure 7.1 and goes as follows:[5]

- Free elections, while essential to a democracy, do not adequately communicate the specific wants and interests of the people to political leaders on a continuous basis. These are more accurately, consistently, and frequently conveyed to political leaders by the many groups and organizations to which people belong.

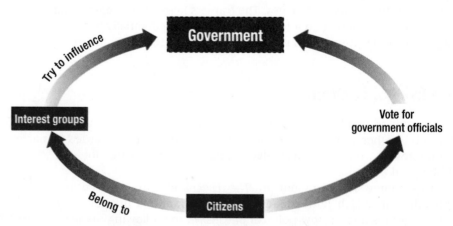

FIGURE 7.1   The Pluralist View of American Politics

In the pluralist understanding of the way American democracy works, citizens have more than one way to influence government leaders. In addition to voting, citizens also have the opportunity to participate in organizations that convey member views to public officials. Because of weak political parties, federalism, checks and balances, and the separation of powers, access to public officials is relatively easy.

- Interest groups are easy to create; people in the United States are free to join or to organize groups that reflect their interests.

- Because of federalism, checks and balances, and the separation of powers, government power in the United States is broadly dispersed, leaving governmental institutions remarkably porous and open to the entreaties of the many and diverse groups that exist in society.

- Because of the ease of group formation and the accessibility of government, all legitimate interests in society can have their views taken into account by some public official. Farmers and business owners can get heard; so too can consumers and workers. Because of this, the system is highly democratic.

Pluralists see interest groups, then, not as a problem but as an additional tool of democratic representation, similar to other democratic instruments such as public opinion and elections. We shall explore the degree to which this position is valid in this and other chapters.

The Universe of Interest Groups

7.2 Distinguish the two kinds of interests at work in American politics

What kinds of interests find a voice in American politics? A useful place to start is with political scientist E. E. Schattschneider's distinction between "private" and "public" interests. Although the boundaries between the two are sometimes fuzzy, the distinction remains important. **Private interests** are organizations and associations that try to gain protections or material advantages from government for their own members rather than for society at large.[6] For the most part, these represent economic interests of one kind or another. **Public interests** are organizations and associations that try to gain protections or benefits for people beyond their own members, often for society at large. Some are motivated by an ideology or by the desire to advance a general cause—animal rights, let us say, or environmental protection—or by the commitment to some public policy—gun control or an end to abortion. Some represent the nonprofit sector, and some even represent government entities such as state and local governments.

Private and public interest groups come in a wide range of forms. Some, including the AARP, are large membership organizations with sizable Washington and regional offices. Some large membership organizations have passionately committed members active in its affairs—such as the National Rifle Association—while others have relatively passive members who join for the benefits the organization provides—such as the American Automobile Association with its well-known trip assistance and car buying service. Other groups are trade associations whose members are business firms. Still others are rather small organizations, without members, run by professionals and sustained by foundations, wealthy donors, and a sizable mailing list for soliciting contributions—the Children's Defense Fund and the National Taxpayers Union come to mind. We examine these in more detail below (see also Table 7.1).

Private Interest Groups

Many different kinds of private interest groups are active in American politics.

private interest

An interest group that seeks to protect or advance the material interests of its members rather than society at large.

public interest

An interest group that works to gain protections or benefits for society at large.

TABLE 7.1   The Diverse World of Interest Associations

Interest	Interest Subtypes	Association Examples
Private Interests (focus on protections and gains for their members)		
Business	Corporations that lobby on their own behalf	Microsoft
		Boeing
	Trade associations	Chemical Manufacturers Association
		Health Insurance Association of America
	Peak business organizations	Business Roundtable
		Federation of Small Businesses
Professions	Doctors	American Medical Association
	Dentists	American Dental Association
	Accountants	National Society of Accountants
	Lawyers	American Bar Association
Labor	Union	International Association of Machinists
	Union federation	AFL-CIO
Public Interests (focus on protections and gains for a broader public or society in general)		
Ideological and cause	Environment	Environmental Defense
	Pro-choice	National Abortion Rights Action League
	Pro-life	National Right to Life Committee
	Anti-tax	Americans for Tax Reform
	Civil rights	National Association for the Advancement of Colored People
		Human Rights Campaign
Nonprofit sector	Medical	American Hospital Association
	Charitable	American Red Cross
Governmental entities	State	National Conference of State Legislatures
	Local	National Association of Counties

Business   Because of the vast resources at the disposal of business and because of their strategic role in the health of local, state, and national economies, groups and associations representing business wield enormous power in Washington. Large corporations such as Boeing, Microsoft, and Google are able to mount their own **lobbying** efforts and often join with others in influential associations such as the Business Roundtable. Medium-sized businesses are well represented by organizations such as the National Association of Manufacturers and the U.S. Chamber of Commerce. Even small businesses have proved to be quite influential when joined in associations such as the National Federation of Independent Business, which helped stop the Clinton health plan in 1994. Agriculture and agribusinesses (fertilizer, seed, machinery, biotechnology, and food-processing companies) have more than held their own over the years through organizations such as the American Farm Bureau Federation and the Farm Machinery Manufacturer's Association and through scores of commod-

lobbying
Effort by an interest or advocacy group to influence the behavior of a public official.

ity groups, including the American Dairy Association and the National Association of Wheat Growers.

The Professions Several associations represent the interests of professionals, such as doctors, lawyers, dentists, and accountants. Because of the prominent social position of professionals in local communities and their ability to make substantial campaign contributions, such associations are very influential in the policymaking process on matters related to their professional expertise and concerns. The American Medical Association (AMA) and the American Dental Association (ADA), for instance, lobbied strongly against the Clinton health care proposal and helped kill it in the 103rd Congress. (These associations changed their tune in 2009, however, when they backed Barack Obama's health care reform overhaul, perhaps because the new law promised to bring about 32 million more insured people into the existing system.) The Trial Lawyers Association has long been a major financial contributor to the Democratic Party and active in blocking legislation to limit the size of personal injury jury awards.

Labor Although labor unions are sometimes involved in what might be called public interest activities (such as supporting civil rights legislation), their main role in the United States has been to protect the jobs of their members and to secure maximum wages and benefits for them. Unlike labor unions in many parts of the world, which are as much political and ideological organizations as economic, American labor unions have traditionally focused on so-called bread-and-butter issues. As an important part of the New Deal coalition that dominated American politics well into the late 1960s, labor unions were influential at the federal level during the years when the Democratic Party controlled Congress and often won the presidency.

Although organized labor is still a force to be reckoned with in electoral politics—they played a big role in fund-raising and mobilizing voters for Barack Obama in the 2008 presidential contest—most observers believe that the political power of labor unions has eroded in dramatic ways over the past several decades.[7] Organized labor's main long-range problem in American politics and its declining power relative to business in the workplace is its small membership

TINA FEY ON THE PICKET LINE AT NBC HEADQUARTERS A long strike in 2007 by television and film writers to gain concessions from the networks and film studios on use of writers' materials on the Internet was successful, partly because of the strong support it received from leading actors and performers, including Tina Fey (herself a writer and a member of the Writers Guild of America). Despite successes such as this one, union membership has been steadily declining in the United States. What accounts for declining union membership?

> **advocacy group**
>
> An interest group organized to support a cause or ideology.

base; in 2008, only 12.4 percent of American wage and salary workers—and only 7.6 percent of private-sector workers—were members of labor unions compared with 35 percent in 1954.[8] The long but steady decline in union membership is strongly associated with the decline in the proportion of American workers in manufacturing, the economic sector in which unions have traditionally been the strongest, primarily because of productivity gains (more can be manufactured with fewer workers) and pressures on companies to cut operating costs in a hyper-competitive global economy.[9] The erosion in labor union membership continues despite substantial levels of unionization among public sector workers; about 37 percent of government workers such as teachers, firefighters, police, and civil servants belong to unions.

Public Interest Groups

Public interest groups or associations try to get government to act in ways that will serve interests that are broader and more encompassing than the direct economic or occupational interests of their own members. Such groups claim to be committed to protecting and advancing the public interest, at least as they see it.[10]

One type of public interest group is the **advocacy group.** People active in advocacy groups tend to be motivated by ideological concerns or a belief in some cause. Such advocacy groups have always been around, but a great upsurge in their number and influence has taken place since the late 1960s.[11] Many were spawned by social movements. In the wake of the civil rights and women's movements (see Chapter 8), it is hardly surprising that a number of associations have been formed to advance the interests of particular racial, ethnic, and gender groups in American society. The National Organization for Women advocates policies in Washington that advance the position of women in American society, for example; the League of Latin American Citizens has been concerned, among other things, with national and state policies that affect migrants from Mexico and other Latin American countries. Similarly, the NAACP and the Urban League are advocates for the interests of African Americans.

The environmental movement created organizations such as the Environmental Defense Fund, the Nature Conservancy, Clean Water Action, and

IT'S TIME FOR HEALTH CARE REFORM Liberal interest and advocacy groups let Democratic members of Congress know that they wanted a health care reform bill to pass. Here, members of nurses' and teachers' organizations demonstrate in favor of health care reform in Washington, D.C., in October 2009. To the surprise of many close political observers, a reform bill passed in March 2010. How could this happen when big insurance companies and many other business interests seemed united in opposition?

the Natural Resources Defense Council, for example. The evangelical Christian upsurge led to the creation of such organizations as the Moral Majority, the Christian Coalition, the National Right-to-Life Committee, Focus on the Family, and the Family Research Council. The gay and lesbian movement eventually led to the creation of organizations such as the Gay and Lesbian Alliance Against Defamation (GLAAD). Some have been around for many years, such as the American Civil Liberties Union, committed to the protection of First Amendment freedoms, and the Children's Defense Fund, an advocate for poor children.

> **?** Are advocacy groups a tool for democratic involvement, as described by pluralists? How might they, too, take on the trappings of factions, as described by Madison?

Most advocacy groups retain a professional, paid administrative staff and are supported by generous large donors (often foundations), membership dues, and/or donations generated by direct mail campaigns. While some depend on and encourage grassroots volunteers and some hold annual membership meetings through which members play some role in making association policies, most advocacy associations are organizations without active membership involvement (other than check writing) and are run by lobbying and public education professionals.[12]

Two other types of public interest groups play a role in American politics, although usually a quieter one. First, associations representing government entities at the state and local levels of our federal system attempt to influence policies made by lawmakers and bureaucrats in Washington. The National Association of Counties is one example, as is the National Governors Association. Second, nonprofit organizations and associations try to influence policies that advance their missions to serve the public interests. Examples include the American Red Cross and the National Council of Non-Profit Associations.

Why There Are So Many Interest Groups

7.3 Explain why interest groups have proliferated

Nobody knows exactly how many interest groups exist in the United States, but there is wide agreement that the number began to mushroom in the late 1960s and that it has grown steadily ever since. We can see this increase along several dimensions. The number of groups listed in the *Encyclopedia of Associations,* for example, has increased from about 10,000 in 1968 to about 22,000 today. Moreover, the number of paid **lobbyists,** that is, people who work for interest groups in Washington and try to affect government policies on their behalf, today totals about 35,000, double what it was then, and that number does not include thousands of others who work for law firms whose main business is lobbying. One estimate is that about 260,000 people in Washington and its surrounding areas work in the lobbying sector.[13] These associations and other lobbyists spent around $3.3 billion on lobbying efforts in Congress in 2008.[14] Because lobbying Congress is only a part of what interest groups do, as you will see in the next section, these statistics show only the tip of a very large iceberg.

> **lobbyist**
>
> A person who attempts to influence the behavior of public officials on behalf of an interest group.

There are a number of reasons so many interest groups exist in the United States.

The Constitution

The constitutional rules of the political game in the United States encourage the formation of interest groups. The First Amendment to the Constitution, for instance, guarantees citizens the right to speak freely, to assemble, and to petition the government, all of which are essential to citizens' ability to form organizations to advance their interests before government. Moreover, the government is organized in such a way that officials are relatively accessible to interest groups. Because of federalism, checks and balances, and the separation of powers, there is no dominant center of decision making, as there is in unitary states such as Great Britain and France. In unitary states (see Chapter 3), most important policy decisions are made in parliamentary bodies. In the United States, important decisions are made by many officials, on many matters, in many jurisdictions. Consequently, there are many more places where interest group pressure can be effective; there are more access points to public officials.

Diverse Interests

Being a very diverse society, there are simply myriad interests in the United States. Racial, religious, ethnic, and occupational diversity is pronounced. Also varied are the views about abortion, property rights, prayer in the schools, and environmental protection. Our economy is also strikingly complex and multifaceted, and becoming more so. In a free society, these diverse interests usually take organizational forms. Thus, the computer revolution spawned computer chip manufacturers, software companies, software engineers, computer magazines and blogs, Internet services, technical information providers, computer component jobbers, Web designers, and countless others. Each has particular interests to defend or advance before government, and each has formed an association to try to do so.[15] Thus, software engineers have an association to look after their interests, as do software and hardware companies, Internet access providers, digital content providers, industry writers, and so on. After it went public in 2004, Google opened its own Washington office to ensure that its interests were protected before Congress and important regulatory agencies against competing interests such as Microsoft and wireless phone carriers such as AT&T, Verizon, and Sprint.[16]

A More Active Government

Government does far more today than it did during the early years of the Republic. As government takes on more responsibilities, it quite naturally comes to have a greater effect on virtually all aspects of economic, social, and personal life. People, groups, and organizations are increasingly affected by the actions of government, so the decisions made by presidents, members of Congress, bureaucrats who write regulations, and judges are increasingly important. It would be surprising indeed if in response, people, groups, and organizations did not try harder to influence the public officials' decisions that affect them.[17] During the long, drawn-out deliberations in Congress in 2009 and 2010 that resulted in new rules for banks and the financial industry, bank and financial industry lobbyists flooded Capitol Hill to make sure that the most onerous provisions—for example, a limit on the size of banks so they would not be "too big to fail"—did not make it into the final bill.

Some part of the growth in lobbying by business firms and industry and trade groups may be tied to the emergence of hyper-competition in the global economy, where even giant enterprises like Microsoft must fight to protect their positions not only against competitors but against threatening actions by one or more government agencies. The Seattle-based company has been fighting antitrust actions initiated by the U.S. Justice Department and the European Union Commission for many years and has dramatically enhanced its lobbying presence in Washington (and Brussels) and increased its campaign contributions.[18]

Some groups form around government programs in order to take advantage of existing government programs and initiatives. The creation of the Department of Homeland Security (DHS), with its large budget for new homeland defense technologies, stimulated the formation of new companies to serve this market, as well as new trade associations—including the Homeland Security Industries Association—to represent them. Rising interest in alternative energy and its prominent place in President Obama's stimulus package (the proposal became law in February 2009) led to an explosion of lobbying for attractive tax breaks and government spending in the bill by firms and associations—including the American Wind Energy Association and Hawkeye Renewables—in the corn and ethanol, wind and solar, geothermal, and biomass industries, among others.

> **?** What kinds of changes in government activity are likely to lead to an increase in interest group activity in Washington? Are there changes that are likely to decrease it?

Disturbances

The existence of diverse interests, the rules of the game, and the importance of government decisions and policies enable and encourage the formation of interest groups, but formation seems to happen only when interests are threatened, usually by some change in the social and economic environment or in government policy.

LOBBYING FOR ETHANOL   Corn farmers and organizations that represent them have been very successful in convincing Americans and their elected officials to pass laws requiring that ethanol from corn be added to gasoline and to keep out—mainly by the imposition of high tariffs—more efficiently produced ethanol from other countries, especially Brazil, which uses sugar cane and switch grass. Billboards along major highways such as this one near Boone, Missouri, have been very effective tools of public persuasion in this campaign by corn and domestic ethanol producers, but they deploy many other tools as well. What are some other powerful lobbying tools?

RELIGION IN POLITICS   Evangelical Christian advocacy groups play a visible and important role in American politics. Here, a member of Focus on the Family makes a point about the unacceptability of homosexuality. In a religiously diverse country such as the United States, how can these groups influence policy-makers?

This is known as the **disturbance theory** of interest group formation.[19] To take one example, Focus on the Family, a conservative religious advocacy group, was formed when many evangelical Christians began to feel threatened by what they considered to be a rise in family breakdown, an increase in the number of abortions, the sexual revolution, and the growing visibility of gays and lesbians in American life.

What Interest Groups Do

7.4   Distinguish the methods through which interest groups try to shape policy

Interest groups, whether public or private in nature, are in the business of conveying the policy views of individuals and groups to public officials. There are two basic types of interest group activity: the inside game and the outside game.[20] The inside game—the older and more familiar of the two—involves direct, personal contact between interest group representatives and government officials. The outside game involves interest group mobilization of public opinion, voters, and important contributors in order to bring pressure to bear on elected officials.

The Inside Game

When lobbying and lobbyists are in the news, the news generally is not good. In early 2006, "super-lobbyist" Jack Abramoff pled guilty to three felony counts for fraud, tax evasion, and conspiracy to bribe public officials; he was then convicted and sentenced to 10 years in prison. Prosecutors had amassed evidence that he had funneled millions on behalf of his clients to a long list of representatives and senators, mostly on the Republican side of the aisle, for campaign war chests and elaborate gifts, including vacations. During the 2008 presidential campaign, Republican candidate John McCain made the very common practice of **earmarking**—setting aside money in appropriations bills for pet projects for constituents and private interests, usually at the behest of an army of lobbyists[21]—an important theme.

The inside game of lobbying—so named because of the practice of interest group representatives talking to legislators in the lobbies outside

disturbance theory

A theory positing that interest groups originate with changes in the economic, social, or political environment that threaten the well-being of some segment of the population.

earmarking

Practice of appropriating money for specific pet projects of members of Congress, usually done at the behest of lobbyists, and added to bills at the last minute with little opportunity for deliberation.

House and Senate committee rooms—does not customarily involve bribing legislators. Rather, it is more the politics of insiders and the "old boy" network (although, increasingly, women are also part of the network). It is the politics of one-on-one persuasion, in which the skilled lobbyist tries to get a decision maker to understand and sympathize with the interest group's point of view or to see that what the interest group wants is good for the politician's constituents. Access is critical if one is to be successful at this game.

Many of the most successful lobbyists are recruited from the ranks of retired members of the House and Senate, congressional staff, and high levels of the bureaucracy. About one-third of outgoing lawmakers, for example, are hired by lobbying firms or hang out their own lobbying shingle.[22] Former Democratic Senate leader Tom Daschle consults for the United Health Group, an association of health insurance giants deeply involved in the formulation of the health care reform bill, as does Steve Elmendorf, former chief of staff to Democratic House leader Dick Gephardt.[23] Between 1998 and 2009, 39 people associated with Senator Ted Kennedy (D–MA) became high-profile lobbyists, as did 32 people associated with Max Baucus (D–MT), 29 with Mitch McConnell (R–KY), and 21 with Nancy Pelosi (D–CA). The promise of lucrative employment based on their skills—and especially on their many contacts—is what keeps so many of them around Washington after they leave office or quit federal employment.

The inside game seems to work best when the issues are narrow and technical, do not command much media attention or public passion, and do not stir up counter-activity by other interest groups.[24] This is not to say that interest groups play a role only on unimportant matters. Great benefit can come to an interest group or a large corporation from a small change in a single provision of the Tax Code or in a slight change in the wording of a regulation on carbon emissions or what percentage of deposits banks must keep in reserve. Enron was very successful at getting Congress to remove federal oversight on many of its energy-trading and acquisitions activities. These stayed well out of public view until they came to light after Enron's spectacular collapse in 2001.

Lobbyists from citizens groups also play the inside game, often with great skill and effect. Many environmental regulations have been strengthened because of the efforts of skilled lobbyists from the Sierra Club, for example.

Political scientist E. E. Schattschneider has pointed out that the inside game—traditional lobbying—is pretty much outside the view of the public.[25] That is to say, the day-to-day details of this form of lobbying are not the stuff of the evening news, nor the fodder of open political campaigns or conflict; such lobbying largely takes place behind closed doors.

Lobbying Congress The essence of the inside game in Congress is the cultivation of personal relationships with people who matter—Senate and House leaders, other influential and well-placed legislators, chairpersons of important committees or subcommittees, a broad swath of rank-and-file members, and key staff members.[26] Because much of the action in Congress takes place in the committees and because senators and representatives are busy with a wide range of responsibilities, cultivating relationships with important legislative and committee staff members is especially important for successful lobbyists. As one lobbyist put it, "If you have a staff member on your side, it might be a hell of a lot better than talking to the member [of Congress]."[27]

Lobbyists are also expected to make substantial contributions to the campaign war chests of representatives and senators and to persuade their clients to do the same.[28] One influential lobbyist is reported to have said recently that "about one-third of my day is spent raising money from my clients to give to people I lobby."[29]

Lobbying the Executive Branch   Career civil servants and political appointees in the executive branch have a great deal of discretionary authority because Congress often legislates broad policies, leaving it to executive branch agencies to promulgate rules to fill in the details (see Chapter 13). Congress rarely passes legislation involving broadcasting, for example, leaving regulatory decisions to the Federal Communications Commission. Because of this, the National Association of Broadcasters focuses its time and energies on the FCC, trying to establish stable and friendly relationships with them. The payoffs can be quite high for lobbying executive branch agencies like the FCC. In 2003, for example, large media company and news organization leaders and lobbyists met with the top staff of the FCC in a successful effort to get the agency to loosen rules on ownership so that big companies could grow even bigger.

? Do negotiations between nonelected members of the executive branch and nonelected lobbyists pose a threat to democracy? Where do the American people fit into such negotiations?

The key to success in lobbying the executive branch is similar to that in lobbying Congress: personal contact and cooperative long-term relationships.[30] Interest group representatives can convey technical information, present the results of their research, help a public official deflect criticism, and show that what the group wants is compatible with good public policy and the political needs of the official.

Lobbying the Courts   Interest groups sometimes lobby the courts, although not in the same way as they lobby the other two branches. A group may find that neither Congress nor the White House is favorably disposed to its interests and will bring a test case to the courts. Realizing that the improvement of the lot of African Americans was very low on the agenda of presidents and members of Congress during the 1940s and 1950s, for example, the NAACP turned to the courts for satisfaction. The effort eventually paid off in 1954 in the landmark *Brown* v. *Board of Education* decision.

amicus curiae

Latin for "friend of the court"; describes a legal brief in which individuals not party to a suit may have their views heard in court.

Interest groups sometimes lobby the courts by filing **amicus curiae** ("friends of the court") briefs in cases involving other parties. In this kind of brief, a person or an organization that is not a party in the suit may

CELEBRATING A HISTORIC COURT DECISION   Dick Heller—here signing his autograph on the placards of gun rights advocates in front of the Supreme Court in June 2008—won his suit against the city government of Washington, D.C., in a case that established a constitutional right to own a firearm. The legal and financial resources that made his suit possible were provided by the NRA and other organizations against gun control. Why are gun lobbies such a powerful force in American politics?

file an argument in support of one side or the other in the hope of swaying the views of the judge or judges. Major controversies before the Supreme Court on such issues as abortion, free speech, or civil rights attract scores of *amicus curiae* briefs. Nineteen *amicus* briefs were filed by supporters and opponents of gun control, for example, in the recently decided case, *District of Columbia* v. *Heller* (2008), in which the Court ruled that Americans have an individual right under the Constitution to own a gun.

Interest groups also get involved in the appointment of federal judges. Particularly controversial appointments, such as the Supreme Court nominations of Robert Bork (whom many women's and civil rights interests considered too conservative) in 1987, Clarence Thomas (who was opposed by liberal and women's groups) in 1992, and Samuel Alito in 2005 (Democrats and liberals considered him much too conservative on a wide range of issues) drew interest group attention and strenuous efforts for and against the nominees. Though they ultimately failed, conservative groups mobilized in 2009 to block the appointment of Sonia Sotomayor to the Court.

The Outside Game

The outside game is being played when an interest group tries to mobilize local constituencies and shape public opinion to support the group's goals and to bring that pressure to bear on elected officials. Defenders of the status quo can mostly depend on the inside game; those who are trying to change existing policies or create new legislation are more likely to use the outside game.[31] By all indications, the outside game—sometimes called **grassroots lobbying**—has been growing steadily in importance in recent years.[32] This may be a good development for democracy, and here is why. Although groups involved in the outside game often try to hide their true identities—Americans for Fair Drug Prices, for example, may well be funded by the pharmaceutical industry—and while some groups involved in the outside game have more resources than others, it is still the case that this form of politics has the effect of expanding and heightening political conflict. This brings issues out into the open and subjects them to public scrutiny—what Schattschneider has called the "socialization of conflict."[33]

Mobilizing Membership
Those interest groups with a large membership base try to persuade their members to send letters and to make telephone calls to senators and representatives when an important issue is before Congress. They sound the alarm, using direct mail and, increasingly, e-mail. They define the threat to members; suggest a way to respond to the threat; and supply the addresses, phone numbers, and e-mail addresses of the people to contact in Washington. Members are grouped by congressional district and state and are given the addresses of their own representatives or senators. The National Rifle Association (NRA) is particularly effective in mobilizing its considerable membership whenever the threat of federal gun control rears its head. Environmental organizations such as Friends of the Earth sound the alarm to people on their mailing list whenever Congress threatens to loosen environmental protections.

Organizing the District
Members of Congress are especially attuned to the individuals and groups in their states or districts who can affect their reelection prospects. The smart interest group, therefore, not only will convince its own members in the state and district to put pressure on the senator or congressional representative, but will also make every effort to be in touch with the most important campaign contributors and opinion leaders there.

> **grassroots lobbying**
> The effort by interest groups to mobilize local constituencies, shape public opinion to support the group's goals, and bring that pressure to bear on elected officials.

Shaping Public Opinion

"Educating" the public on issues that are important to the interest group is one of the central features of new-style lobbying. The idea is to shape opinion in such a way that government officials will be favorably disposed to the views of the interest group. These attempts to shape public and elite opinion come in many forms. One strategy is to produce and distribute research reports that bolster the group's position. Citizen groups such as Environmental Defense and the Food Research and Action Center have been very adept and effective in this area.[34]

Another strategy is media advertising. Sometimes this takes the form of pressing a position on a particular issue, such as the Teamsters Union raising the alarm about open borders with Mexico, focusing on the purported unsafe nature of Mexican trucks roaming American highways. Sometimes it is "image" advertising, in which some company or industry portrays its positive contribution to American life.[35] Thus, large oil companies often feature their regard for the environment in their advertising, showing romantic forest scenes or a pristine beach, with nary a pipeline, or tanker, or refinery in sight.

In the effort to shape public opinion, the well-heeled interest group will also prepare materials that will be of use to radio and television broadcasters and to newspaper and magazine editors. Many produce opinion pieces, magazine articles, television spots and radio "sound bites," and even television documentaries. Others stage events to be covered as news. The environmentalist group Greenpeace puts the news media on full alert, for example, when it tries to disrupt a whaling operation.

Finally, interest groups, using the latest computer technology, identify target groups to receive information on particular issues. Groups pushing for cuts in the capital gains tax rate, for instance, direct their mail and telephone banks to holders of the American Express card or to addresses in zip code areas identified as upper-income neighborhoods. They are increasingly using the Internet, as well, in the effort to mobilize the public on issues of concern to them. For example, most have their own websites and publish position papers and other materials there. Many arrange postings to friendly blogs in hopes of further disseminating their message. Some will use their websites and e-mail to organize e-mails to lawmakers from their constituents.[36] Many interest and advocacy groups have made big commitments recently to the use of social media such as Facebook and Twitter to spread their message.

Getting Involved in Campaigns and Elections

Interest groups try to increase their influence by getting involved in political campaigns.[37] Many interest groups, for example, issue a report card indicating the degree to which members of the House and Senate supported the interest group's position on a selection of key votes. The report card ratings are distributed to the members of the interest group and other interested parties in the hope that the ratings will influence their voting behavior. We show how groups do this in the "By the Numbers" feature.

? Do you think interest group activity had an influence on the 2008 presidential election? Did interest group efforts have any impact on how you voted?

Interest groups also encourage their members to get involved in the electoral campaigns of candidates who are favorable to their interests. Groups often assist campaigns in more tangible ways—allowing the use of their telephone banks, mailing lists, fax and photocopy machines, computers, and the like. Some interest groups help with fund-raising events or ask members to make financial contributions to candidates.

Interest groups also endorse particular candidates for public office. The strategy may backfire and is somewhat risky, for to endorse a losing candidate is to risk losing access to the winner. Nevertheless, it is fairly common now for labor unions, environmental organizations, religious groups, and liberal and conservative ideological groups to make such endorsements.

Interest groups are also an increasingly important part of campaign fundraising. This topic will be explored briefly in the next section and in substantial detail in Chapter 10 on campaigns and elections.

Interest Groups and Inequality in American Politics

7.5 Determine the biases in the interest group system

Overall, between the inside game and the outside game, interest groups have a diverse set of tools for influencing elected officials, bureaucrats in the executive branch, judges, and the public. And the number of groups capable of deploying these tools is large and growing every year. On the surface, it might look like the proliferation of interest groups has enhanced the democratic flavor of our country, allowing more and more Americans to have their interests represented. But not all agree that this is so. Let's take a look at the various viewpoints.

Political scientist E. E. Schattschneider once observed that the flaw in the pluralist (or interest group) heaven is "that the heavenly chorus sings with a strong upper class accent." If his observation is accurate, then political equality is undermined by the interest group system, and democracy is less fully developed than it might be, even taking into account the new importance of the outside game (which, as we have said, tends to "socialize conflict"). In this section, we look at inequalities in the interest group system and evaluate their effects.

Representational Inequalities

Not all segments of society are equally represented in the interest group system. The interest group inside lobbying game in Washington, D.C., is dominated, in sheer numbers and weight of activity, by business corporations, industry trade associations, and associations of the professions, although liberal and conservative advocacy groups lobby as well. Organized labor, we have seen, although still a powerful player in Washington, has lost much of its lobbying clout in recent years, mainly because of declining membership. Passage in 2005 of several pro-business bills that it strongly opposed—namely, bills making it more difficult to declare bankruptcy and to bring class-action lawsuits in state courts—showcases labor's declining fortunes. For their part, the vast majority of advocacy groups, even those that perceive themselves as liberal and lean toward the Democrats, attract members and contributors who have much higher incomes, more elite occupations, and more education than the general public. Not surprisingly, given those whom these advocacy groups represent, they tend to focus less on issues of poverty and income inequality, the traditional purview of labor unions, let us say, and more on "quality of life" issues such as environmental protection, consumer protection, globalization, women's rights, racial and ethnic civil rights, gay and lesbian rights, and civil liberties.[38]

Is there a reliable way to evaluate the performance of your representative in Congress?

Imagine you are at the end of the semester and four different teachers give you a grade in your introductory political science course. One looks at your performance and gives you a grade of 100 percent. Your day is made! Teacher number 2 gives you an 83. OK, you might say, "I can live with that." Teachers 3 and 4 slam you with a 20 and a 10. Ouch! How to make sense of all of this? How come two teachers love you and two hate you? Surely they must be biased in some way.

This is exactly what happens to members of Congress when they are graded on their performance by interest groups. Unlike you, the confused student in the preceding example, congressional representatives expect the wide disparity in the grades they receive, understand what is going on, and are even proud of most of their grades, whether high or low. Note the wildly contrasting grades for Republican Senator Jim DeMint of South Carolina and Democratic Senator Barbara Boxer of California given by four organizations in 2009: the Americans for Democratic Action (ADA), the American Conservative Union (ACU), the League of Conservation Voters (LCV), and the National Taxpayers Union (NTU).

Why It Matters Having a consistent and reliable way to grade each member of Congress can help voters make more rational electoral choices. Without such grades, each citizen would have to investigate the record of his or her member of Congress, rely on news reports, or depend on information provided by the member.

Behind the Numbers How are members of Congress graded? The answer is pretty straightforward. Each interest group in this example is strongly ideological or committed to a certain set of concerns, and each grades members of Congress in terms of these standards. The ADA is very strongly liberal—interested in civil liberties, civil rights, and economic and social justice; while the ACU is strongly conservative—in favor of capitalism, traditional moral values, and a strong national defense. The LCV supports legislation to protect the environment, while the NTU wants lower taxes, less wasteful government spending, and a balanced budget. So, members of Congress who vote to increase spending on child welfare programs, let us say, are likely to get high grades from the ADA, but low grades from the ACU and the NTU. Members who vote to open the Alaska National Wildlife Reserve for oil exploration would surely receive a low grade from the folks at LCV.

Calculating Interest Group Scores: Although each group uses a slightly different method to do its grading, at base, each approaches grading in pretty much the same way. For each interest group, its professional staff, sometimes

Resource Inequalities

Business corporations and professionals are the most economically well-off parts of American society. It is hardly surprising that interest groups representing them can afford to spend far more than other groups to hire professional lobbying firms, form their own Washington liaison office, place advertising in the media, conduct targeted mailings on issues, mobilize their members to contact government officials, and pursue all of the other activities of old- and new-style lobbying. Lobbying in Washington is especially tilted toward business. Registered lobbyists for the various drug companies, for example, total more than the combined membership of the House and Senate.[39] (You can learn more about the influence of the drug industry, as well as the insurance industry, in the "Using the Framework" feature on passage of the Medicare drug prescription program.) Business lobbyists flooded Capitol Hill during the long and drawn-out deliberations on a bill to regulate the financial industry in the wake of the collapse of the financial sector in 2008 and the Great Recession that followed. Despite anger at Wall Street, the bill that passed in 2010 did not include a number of provisions that some analysts say are essential to prevent another financial collapse but were opposed by financial industry lobbyists: a cap on the size of institutions so that they cannot become "too big to fail, a tax on large bonuses, and a required separation of trading and commercial banking.[40] The situation is

in conjunction with outside experts, selects a set of key votes on which to assess members of Congress. The particular votes selected by each group will differ—a group interested solely in civil rights issues will not, for example, use a vote on the defense budget for its scorecard—but each identifies a set of votes it considers to be a good indicator of ideological or policy loyalty. On each vote, members of Congress are scored "with the group" or "against the group." The numbers are added up, then transformed to percentage terms, with 100 being the highest score and 0 the lowest.

What to Watch For Oddly enough, although not terribly sophisticated in either conceptual or computational terms, these are numbers you can trust. You can, as they say, "take them to the bank." Why? Because each interest group is clear about what it stands for, and each makes it clear that it is judging members of Congress from a particular perspective. When you are considering whether to vote for or against an incumbent member of Congress, a good method would be to check member scores from organizations whose ideology and/or policy views you support.

What Do You Think? How does your representative in Congress score with those groups whose values and policy position come closest to your own? You can investigate this at the Project Vote Smart website at www.votesmart.org, where you can find how your representative is evaluated by different interest groups.

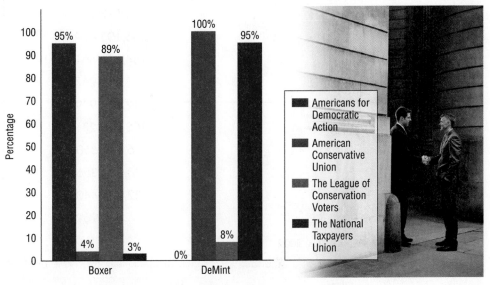

Interest Group Ratings of Senators Boxer and DeMint, 2008

Source: Project Vote Smart (**www.votesmart.org**)

highlighted by Table 7.2, which shows the amount of money spent by different sectors on lobbying activities. It is worth noting that nonbusiness groups and associations—listed in the table as other, ideological/single-issue, city/county, and organized labor—spent only a small fraction of what was spent by business in 2009.

Corporate, trade, and professional associations also are important in campaign finance, with an especially prominent role played by **political action committees (PACs),** which are entities created by interest groups—whether business firms, unions, membership organizations, or liberal and conservative advocacy groups—to collect money and make contributions to candidates in federal elections (i.e., to candidates for the presidency, the House of Representatives, and the Senate). Corporate, trade, and professional PACs lead other groups in both sheer numbers and levels of spending, although labor unions give a great deal, and large and committed advocacy organizations such as the NRA are also important. During the 2007–2008 election cycle, for example, political action committees representing business

> **?** Is there anything that can (or should) be done to reduce resource inequalities among interest groups? Are there ways that people and groups with few resources can gain a better spot at the table?

political action committee (PAC)

An entity created by an interest group whose purpose is to collect money and make contributions to candidates in federal elections.

TABLE 7.2 Major Spending on Federal Lobbying in 2009, by Industry Sector

Sector	Total
Health	$396,240,855
Miscellaneous business	362,259,396
Finance, insurance, and real estate	334,341,984
Energy and natural resources	300,512,509
Communications/electronics	266,103,829
Transportation	184,606,661
Other	182,632,267
Ideological/single-issue	112,914,979
Agribusiness	103,924,231
Defense	96,174,660
Construction	40,387,356
Labor	32,015,440
Lawyers and lobbyists	24,617,969

Source: Center for Responsive Politics, 2009.

and the professions accounted for 69 percent of the $585 million spent by all PACs on candidates for federal office, while labor unions accounted for only about 16 percent.[41] PACs representing the least-privileged sectors of American society are notable for their absence. As former Senator (R–KS) and presidential candidate Bob Dole once put it, "There aren't any poor PACs or food stamp PACs or nutrition PACs or Medicaid PACs."[42] (More details on our campaign finance system and the role of business and interest groups in it can be found in Chapter 10.)

Perhaps more important than PACs, in the long run, was the Supreme Court decision *Citizens United* v. *The Federal Election Commission* (2009), which decided that the provisions of the McCain-Feingold law prohibiting corporations (and by extension, unions and advocacy organizations) from spending whatever they would like on electioneering for and against particular candidates in the periods before primary and general elections was an unconstitutional violation of free speech. While this likely will increase union advocacy group spending and strategy in elections, most seasoned observers believe the big winners in political influence will be large corporations, given the big financial advantages corporations have over unions and other groups, and their keen interest in electing people who will be sympathetic to business interests.[43]

Access Inequality

iron triangle

An enduring alliance of common interest among an interest group, a congressional committee, and a bureaucratic agency.

sub-government

Another name for an iron triangle.

Inequalities of representation and resources are further exaggerated by the ability of some groups to play a central role in the formation and implementation of government policies, based on the membership of these groups in informal networks within the government itself that are involved in policy areas of interest to them. These networks, often called **iron triangles** or **sub-governments,** customarily include a private interest group (usually a corporation or business trade association), an

How did the long-awaited prescription drug benefit get added to Medicare in 2003, and why were drug and insurance companies so happy about it?

Background: Democratic presidents and members of Congress had tried—but failed—for more than 20 years to add a prescription drug benefit to the Medicare program. In 2003, with Republicans in control of both the House and Senate, President George W. Bush was able to deliver on his campaign promise to the elderly. Although many elderly Americans continue to pay a substantial amount of money for their prescription drugs and many are perplexed by the program's complexity, most are now paying less than they would have without the new program. But others gained as well: drug companies won provisions forbidding the importation of

cheaper drugs from abroad, and the negotiation of lower prices for drugs by the government; insurance companies were granted subsidies for providing drug benefit policies; and doctors won a provision in the bill loosening some of the restrictions on fees they receive under Medicare. Passage of the prescription drug benefit may even have paved the way for passage of Barack Obama's health reform bill in 2010 as provider resistance to reform began to weaken. So how did the 2003 drug benefit bill happen? Looking at how structural, political linkage, and governmental factors affected the political process will help us explain the outcome.

Structure

The number of Americans over the age of 65 has been growing, and their prescription drug costs have been rising much faster than the cost of living. → Scientific innovation has helped create increasingly powerful, effective, and expensive drugs. → The drug industry is dominated by a handful of very large and economically powerful firms. → Insurance in the United States, including health care and medical insurance, is provided by a handful of very large and economically powerful firms.

Political Linkage

During the 2000 presidential election campaign, both Al Gore and George W. Bush promised help to seniors with their rising drug costs. During the 2002 election campaign, many congressional candidates in both parties made similar promises. → Surprisingly, the most important interest group representing seniors, the usually Democratic-leaning American Association for Retired People (AARP), endorsed the plan fashioned by a Republican president and the Republican leaders of Congress.

Relative to other groups, the elderly vote in very high proportions in both presidential and congressional elections. These voters have said time and again that they want assistance with rising drug costs. → Drug and insurance companies, as well as the AMA, made very large campaign donations during the 2000 and 2002 election cycles. → Drug and insurance companies, as well as the AMA, mounted major lobbying efforts in the 108th Congress to ensure that the new program would take their interests into account.

Government

A Republican president, George W. Bush, was in the White House. His plan for a prescription drug benefit under Medicare was introduced in the House and the Senate. → Republicans controlled both houses of Congress; a slightly different version of the bill passed in each one.

The House easily passed the bill that emerged from the Republican-controlled conference committee. → Senate Republicans won a close vote for the bill, after defeating a Democratic filibuster on the conference report. → President Bush signed the bill in an elaborate ceremony in the White House.

Government Action

The drug benefit under Medicare becomes law.

issue networks

Broad coalitions of public and private interest groups, policy experts, and public officials that form around particular policy issues; said to be more visible to the public and more inclusive.

agency in the executive branch, and a committee or subcommittees in Congress, which act together to advance and protect certain government programs that work to the mutual benefit of their members. Most scholars believe that iron triangles have become less important in American government,[44] with more open and inclusive **issue networks**—coalitions that form around different policy areas that include a range of public and private interest groups and policy experts as well as business representatives, bureaucrats, and legislators—taking their place. Iron triangles suggest a closed system in which a small group of actors controls a policy area. Issue networks suggest a more fluid situation with more actors and visibility, where control of policymaking is less predictable. Be that as it may, corporations, trade associations, and associations of professionals not only play a prominent role in issue networks, but also participate in those iron triangles that are still evident. These are especially prominent in shaping and carrying out public policies in the areas of agriculture, defense procurement, public lands, highway construction, and water. Large-scale water projects—dams, irrigation, and levees, for example—are supported by farm, real estate developer, construction, and barge-shipping interest groups; members of key Senate and House committees responsible for these projects, who can claim credit for bringing jobs and federal money to their constituencies; and the Army Corps of Engineers, whose budget and responsibilities grow apace as it builds the projects. Another iron triangle is shown in Figure 7.2.

The Privileged Place of Business Corporations

Economist and political scientist Charles Lindblom has argued that corporations wield such disproportionate power in American politics that they undermine

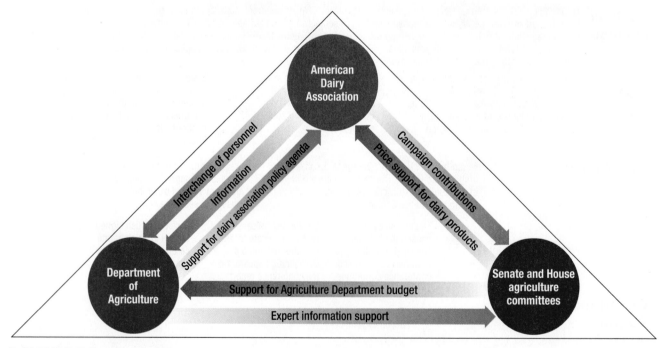

FIGURE 7.2 Iron Triangle

In an iron triangle, an alliance based on common interests is formed among a powerful corporation or interest group, an agency of the executive branch, and congressional committees or subcommittees. In this example from the dairy industry, an alliance is formed among parties that share an interest in the existence and expansion of dairy subsidies. Most scholars think iron triangles are less common today than in the past, though they are alive and well in a number of policy areas, including the one illustrated here.

democracy. He closes his classic 1977 book *Politics and Markets* with this observation: "The large private corporation fits oddly into democratic theory. Indeed, it does not fit."[45] Twenty years later, political scientist Neil Mitchell concluded his book *The Conspicuous Corporation,* which reported the results of careful empirical testing of Lindblom's ideas, with the conclusion that "business interests (in the United States) are not routinely countervailed in the policy process. Their political resources and incentives to participate are usually greater than other interests."[46] Let's see why these scholars reached their somber conclusion about business corporations in American politics.

We have already learned about many of the advantages that corporations and business trade associations representing groups of corporations enjoy over others in the political process. The largest corporations are far ahead of their competitors in the number of lobbyists they employ, the level of resources they can and do use for political purposes, their ability to shape public perceptions and opinions through such instruments as issue advertising and subsidization of business-oriented think tanks like the American Enterprise Institute, and the ease of access they often have to government officials. To take but one area, the vast increase in lobbying that has occurred in Washington is accounted for mostly by business corporations and trade groups.[47] Looking at total spending on lobbying from 1998 through 2009, 18 of the top 20 spenders were corporations or industry trade associations (insurance, pharmaceuticals, hospitals, and telecommunications), with the U.S. Chamber of Commerce at the top of the list with a cumulative total of $527 million spent. The AFL-CIO labor federation spent only $44 million on lobbying during the same period. No environmental, consumer protection, or human rights advocacy group made it into the top 100.[48]

An additional source of corporate power is the high regard in which business is held in American society and the central and honored place of business values in our culture. Faith in free enterprise gives special advantages to the central institution of free enterprise, the corporation. Any political leader contemplating hostile action against corporations must contend with business's special place of honor in the United States. To be sure, scandals involving large business enterprises such as Enron, Goldman Sachs, and BP can tarnish big business now and then, but in the long run, as President Coolidge once famously said, "the business of America is business."

Business corporations are also unusually influential because the health of the American economy—and thus the standard of living of the people—is tied closely to the economic well-being of large corporations. It is widely and not entirely unreasonably believed that what is good for business is good for America. Because of their vital role in the economy, government officials tend to interpret business corporations not as "special interests" but as the voice of the national interest and to listen more attentively to their demands than they do to those of other sectors of American society. Some companies are so important

? Is business so important to the health and well-being of American society that efforts to control lobbying by them are inappropriate or doomed to fail?

for the overall operation of the American and global economies that they are considered "too big to fail"—think AIG, Citigroup, Bank of America, and General Motors, among others in 2008 and 2009—and were bailed out even when their downfall was from self-inflicted wounds. In this sense, corporations enjoy an especially privileged position in American politics. (See the "Mapping American Politics" feature for an example of how the power of large auto and oil companies has had important negative impacts on the environment.)

Corporations are also powerful because their mobility is an important counterweight to any government effort (local, state, or national) to raise taxes or impose regulations that business deems especially onerous. Increasingly, large

Fueling the American Driving Habit

Introduction The United States uses enormous amounts of fuel to power its economy and enhance the quality of life of its citizens, with a great deal of it taking the form of gasoline for cars and trucks. Indeed, all rich countries use enormous amounts of fuel; it being essential for powering industrialization, people's homes and apartments, and modern transportation and shipping systems, including cars, trucks, trains, and planes. Recently, rapidly industrializing and modernizing countries such as India and China have joined the ranks of the high-fuel-consuming countries. With the many benefits that come with high fuel consumption, however, come some problems as well. There is, most importantly, perhaps, the massive amount of carbon that is released into the atmosphere when fuels are burned, contributing to the problem of global climate change. There is also the problem of dependency on foreign oil that worries many Americans. There is reason to worry. About two-thirds of all the fuel consumed in the United States is in the form of gasoline for cars and trucks. This requires massive imports of crude oil to be refined in the United States as well as rising imports of gasoline because refining capacity here has not kept up with demand.

Mapping Fuel Usage This cartogram shows the proportion of the world's fuel used by each country. Fuel includes oil, coal, nuclear, and wood. For the entire world in 2004, the fuel equivalent of about 11.6 trillion kilograms of oil was consumed. Examining the cartogram, it is evident that the United States accounts for an enormous proportion of the world's fuel consumption, with two-thirds of its annual fuel consumption in the form of gasoline for cars and trucks, as pointed out earlier. While European countries taken together account for a large proportion of the world's fuel consumption, Europe uses only about one-half as much gasoline per person to fuel vehicles as the United States.

There are many reasons Americans use so much vehicle-related gasoline, including the vast size of the country, space for cities to expand into suburban-dominated metropolitan areas, excellent road systems, and low investment in mass transportation. But also important is the low gas mileage efficiency of cars and trucks, much of this the product of the lobbying activities of oil companies and automobile manufacturers to block higher CAFE (corporate average fuel economy) requirements. Although rising

corporations are able to design, produce, and market their goods and services all over the world; they are not irrevocably tied to a single location. If government threatens their interests, large corporations can credibly counter with a threat to move all or part of their operations elsewhere. In this new global economic environment, political leaders are increasingly of a mind to maintain a friendly and supportive business climate.

Large corporations do not, of course, run the show entirely. Although they have the most resources, for instance, these resources do not translate automatically into real political influence. One interest group may have enormous resource advantages over other interest groups, for instance, but may use its resources ineffectively. Or an interest group with great resources may find itself opposed by other interest groups that together are able to mobilize impressive resources of their own. A powerful interest group may also find that an elected politician is not cooperative because the voters in the district are of a different mind from the interest group. So even with this immense set of resources, business power is not automatically and inevitably translated into political power.[49]

Nor does business always get its way in Washington. There are many issues of great importance on which business in general, or one corporation in particular, loses in the give-and-take of politics. There are times when business finds itself squared off against powerful coalitions of other interest groups (labor, consumer, and environmentalist groups, let us say). Corporations did not get their way in 2007 on loosening immigration controls, something that would have allowed them access to a larger pool of cheap labor. On many occasions, corporations also find themselves at odds with one another on public policy issues. Thus, Internet service providers, computer and handheld device makers, software developers, and the music and film industries are locked in a battle over file-sharing.

gasoline prices and troubles in oil-producing nations and regions such as Nigeria, Venezuela, and the Persian Gulf finally compelled lawmakers to increase CAFE requirements for cars and trucks in 2007, which the EPA increased even more in 2009 under a directive from President Obama, the tougher standards were a long time coming because of the resistance of these industries—and will take a long time to go into effect. Automakers must boost the average for their cars and small trucks (including SUVs) to 35.5 miles per gallon by 2020.

What Do You Think? How concerned are you about global climate change and America's dependence on imports of foreign oil? Is there a way to use less fuel in general and gasoline in particular without undermining the American standard of living and the well-being of its people? Does solving these problems require curtailing the lobbying power of the energy and automobile industries, or would this be an unacceptable limitation of free speech and the right to petition the government?

Source: Worldmapper, map number 119. The SASI Group (University of Sheffield) and Mark Newman (University of Michigan), 2006 (www.worldmapper.org) from data provided by United Nations Development Programme's Human Development Report 2004, Table 21.

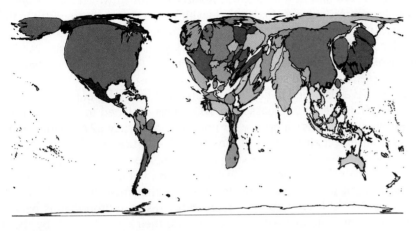

Fuel Use

Source: © Copyright 2006 SASI Group (University of Sheffield) and Mark Newman (University of Michigan). (www.worldmapper.org).

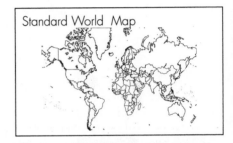

Standard World Map

Corporations are most powerful when they can build alliances among themselves. Most of the time, corporations are in competition with one another; they do not form a unified political bloc capable of moving government to action on their behalf. On those few occasions when corporations feel that their collective interests are at stake, however,—as on taxes, for example, or on protection of intellectual property—they are capable of coming together to form powerful and virtually unbeatable political coalitions.[50] As political scientist David Vogel put it, "When business is both mobilized and unified, its political power can be formidable."[51]

In our view, the best way to think about corporations in American politics is to see their power waxing and waning within their overall privileged position. Corporate power may be greater at certain times and weaker at other times, but always in a game in which, for most of the time, corporations enjoy advantages over other groups in society. If corporations feel that their collective interests are at stake—as when labor unions are particularly aggressive or when government's regulatory burden is perceived to be too heavy—and they are able to present a united front, they are simply unbeatable. This cannot be said about any other sector of American society.[52]

Curing the Mischief of Factions

7.6 Assess the steps that have been taken to control factions

Americans have worried about the "mischief of factions" ever since James Madison wrote about them in *The Federalist,* No. 10 (see the Appendix). Over the years, various things have been tried to control the purported negative effects of these special interests.[53] Disclosure has been the principal tool of regulation. In 1946, Congress

revolving door

The common practice in which former government officials become lobbyists for interests with whom they formerly dealt in their official capacity.

imposed a requirement (in the Federal Regulation of Lobbying Act) that all lobbyists working in Congress be registered. The Lobby Disclosure Act of 1995 requires a wider range of political actors to register as lobbyists and makes them report every six months on which policies they are trying to influence and how much they are spending to do it.

Reformers have also tried to regulate some of the most troublesome abuses of the politics of factions. Sections of the Ethics in Government Act (1978) aim at the so-called **revolving door** in which former government officials become lobbyists for interests with whom they formerly dealt in their official capacity. A 1995 measure specifies that former U.S. trade representatives and their deputies are banned for life from lobbying for foreign interests. The 2007 measure increases the one-year waiting period in the 1995 measure to two years and adds representatives and senators to those who must wait.

Reformers have also tried to control the effects of interest group money in politics. The McCain-Feingold bill, passed in 2002, was designed to limit the use of soft money, but it left a huge loophole for nonprofit, advocacy 527 organizations—so named because of their location in the Tax Code—to use unlimited amounts of money to support or oppose candidates and issues, the only restrictions being a ban on radio and television advertising for a period before elections. It also increased the amount people could give to PACs. Another measure passed in 2007 requires congressional leaders to identify all earmarks in appropriations bills and post them to the Internet at least 48 hours before their consideration by the full House and Senate, along with information about their sponsors and intended purposes. The same measures require lobbyists to certify that no one in their firm or organization has provided gifts to members of Congress or their staffs and post this to a site on the Internet. Moreover, the measures require lobbyists to file and also post to the Internet quarterly reports on their lobbying activities in Congress.

The 2007 lobbying reform measure was passed in the wake of the corruption conviction of super-lobbyist Jack Abramoff, revelations of widespread influence peddling by lobbyists who formerly worked in Congress or the executive branch agencies, and the explosion of special interest earmarks in appropriations bills. Most keen Washington observers remain unconvinced that the new rules will diminish in a major way the influence of privileged interest groups in shaping what government does. Like water seeking its own level, it may be that powerful and wealthy interests will find a way to have their needs and wishes attended to in one way or another.

THE MAN WHO BOUGHT WASHINGTON   Jack Abramoff, one of the most well-known and best-connected Republican lobbyists in Washington, was convicted on five felony counts for fraud and the corruption of public officials in 2006 and jailed. Official and media investigations of his operations uncovered evidence of widespread corrupt influence peddling in Washington and contributed to passage of a lobbying reform bill in 2007. Can this bill level the lobbying playing field?

Using the **DEMOCRACY STANDARD**

Do interest groups help or hinder American democracy?

There is no doubt that the interest group system plays an important role in shaping what government does in the United States; elected officials pay lots of attention to them, for all the reasons explored in this chapter. Whether the interest group system advances or retards democracy, however, can only be determined by knowing which sectors of the American population are represented by interest groups, and how well interest groups represent the people they claim to be representing. There is considerable disagreement regarding the role that interest groups play in American democracy.

There are many who believe that the interest group system enhances democracy because it gives individuals and groups in American society another tool to keep elected and appointed officials responsive and responsible to their needs, wants, and interests. Political parties are important for making popular sovereignty work, to be sure, but being broad and inclusive umbrella organizations, they often ignore the interests of particular groups. And, although elections are essential for keeping public officials on their toes, they happen only every two to four years. Proponents of this pluralist view argue that the day-to-day work of popular sovereignty is done by interest groups. Additionally, pluralists point to the rise of advocacy groups—supported by thousands of ordinary people with ordinary incomes—as an indication that the interest group system is being leveled, with a wider range of groups representing a broad swath of the population now playing a key role in the political game.

Having said that, there is more than ample evidence that narrow, special, and privileged interests dominate the interest group world and play the biggest role in determining what government does in the United States. The powerful interest groups that play the largest role in shaping public policies in the United States represent, by and large, wealthier and better-educated Americans, corporations, and other business interests and professionals such as doctors and lawyers. In this view, the proliferation of interest groups, mostly in the form of associations and firms that represent business, has made American politics less and less democratic. This inequality of access and influence violates the democratic principle of political equality, with less influence in the hands of ordinary Americans. Thus, some argue, the present interest group system poses a real threat to democratic ideals.

SUMMARY

7.1 Compare and contrast theories about the role of interest groups in a democracy

- Americans have long denigrated special interests as contrary to the public good. Many political scientists, however, see interest groups as an important addition to the representation process in a democracy, enhancing the contact of citizens with government officials in the periods between elections.

7.2 Distinguish the two kinds of interests at work in American politics

- Private interests are organizations and associations that try to gain protections or material advantages from government for their own members rather than for society at large. For the most part, these represent economic interests of one kind or another.

- Public interests are organizations and associations that try to gain protections or benefits for people beyond their own members, often for society at large. Public interests are motivated by ideological or issue concerns.

7.3 Explain why interest groups have proliferated

- There has been a significant expansion in the number of public interest or citizen groups since 1968.

- The United States provides a rich environment for interest groups because of our constitutional system, our political culture, and the broad responsibilities of our government.

- Interests tend to proliferate in a complex and changing society, which creates a diversity of interests.

- Government does more than it did in the past and affects the interests of various people, groups, and firms who organize to exert influence over laws and regulations.

7.4 Distinguish the methods through which interest groups try to shape policy

- One way that interest groups attempt to influence the shape of public policy is the inside game: interest group representatives are in direct contact with government officials and try to build influence on the basis of personal relationships.

- The outside game is being played when an interest group tries to mobilize local constituencies and shape public opinion to support the group's goals and to bring that pressure to bear on elected officials.

7.5 Determine the biases in the interest group system

- Some groups, especially corporations, trade associations, and high-income professionals, have more resources to put into lobbying officials and better access to them than other groups.

7.6 Assess the steps that have been taken to control factions

- Lobbying reform has focused on requiring interest and advocacy groups to report on their lobbying activities, trying to control the revolving door, and limiting what private and public interest groups are allowed to spend in elections.

TEST YOURSELF

Answer key begins on page T-1.

7.1 Compare and contrast theories about the role of interest groups in a democracy

1. James Madison was a strong advocate for interest groups, writing that "a healthy democratic government is unthinkable save in terms of factions."
   True / False

2. Which of the following is consistent with arguments advanced by pluralist theorists?
   a. Free elections adequately communicate the specific wants and interests of the people to political leaders.
   b. Governmental institutions are impenetrable to most societal interests.
   c. The American political system is highly democratic because all legitimate interests can have their views taken into account by public officials.
   d. Interest groups are difficult to create.
   e. Only political and economic elites can organize groups that reflect their interests. Other groups lack the resources necessary to organize and sufficient clout to have their concerns addressed.

7.2 Distinguish the two kinds of interests at work in American politics

3. Interest groups that represent the interests of professionals are very influential when it comes to issues that are related to areas of their professional expertise.
True / False

4. Which of the following is an example of a private interest group?
   a. The American Civil Liberties Union (ACLU)
   b. The National Rifle Association (NRA)
   c. The U.S. Chamber of Commerce
   d. The National Organization for Women (NOW)
   e. Focus on the Family

5. Why has the influence of labor unions waned?

7.3 Explain why interest groups have proliferated

6. America's unitary system of government has encouraged interest group to proliferate.
True / False

7. Which of the following helps to explain why interest groups have proliferated?
   a. The U.S. is a diverse society.
   b. The First Amendment prohibits factionalism.
   c. Federal regulations have decreased the number of lobbyists, forcing many would-be-lobbyists to form interest groups instead.
   d. Americans are more interested in (and informed about) politics than ever before.
   e. Congress recently repealed the prohibition on interest group efforts aimed at influencing government decisions.

8. Why does a more active government encourage interest group proliferation?

7.4 Distinguish the methods through which interest groups try to shape policy

9. Interest groups try to influence public policy outcomes; they refrain from efforts to influence election outcomes.
True / False

10. Which of the following strategies do interest groups use to influence the federal courts?
    a. Making campaign contributions to federal judges
    b. Paying for expensive junkets for sitting judges and justices
    c. Joining iron triangles or issue networks
    d. Filing *amicus curiae* briefs
    e. Holding national nominating conventions

11. What is the difference between the inside lobbying game and the outside game?

7.5 Determine the biases in the interest group system

12. A recent Supreme Court decision permits corporations and labor unions to spend an unlimited amount of money to influence election outcomes.
True / False

13. Which of the following does not contribute to the inordinate power held by corporations?
    a. Business values are important components of American political culture.
    b. Corporations have considerable financial resources to spend on lobbying.
    c. Economic health is closely tied to the fortunes of major American corporations.
    d. Corporations pay the bulk of all federal taxes, giving them greater input into how that money is spent.
    e. In a global economy, corporations can relocate to countries that offer a more favorable business environment if the government doesn't yield to their demands.

14. Assess the pluralist argument in light of existing inequalities in the interest group system.

7.6 Assess the steps that have been taken to control factions

15. Disclosure requirements have been the main mechanism that Congress has used to help control the "mischief of factions."
True / False

16. Which of the following has Congress recently enacted in an attempt to reform lobbying practices?
    a. Lobbyists are required to be part of the revolving door.
    b. Lobbyists are required to lobby on behalf of only one client in a given year.
    c. Lobbyists are prohibited from discussing legislation that is currently under consideration in Congress.
    d. Corporate interests are prohibited from trying to influence legislation that would have a direct impact on their business interests.
    e. Former government officials are restricted in their ability to lobby for interests with whom they formerly dealt in their official capacity.

myp⬤liscilab EXERCISES

Apply what you learned in this chapter on MyPoliSciLab.

📖 Read on mypoliscilab.com

eText: Chapter 7

✔ Study and Review on mypoliscilab.com

Pre-Test
Post-Test
Chapter Exam
Flashcards

👁 Watch on mypoliscilab.com

Video: American Cancer Society Recommendation
Video: California Teachers Stage Sit-Ins
Video: Chicago Gun Laws
Video: Murtha and the PMA Lobbyists

✳ Explore on mypoliscilab.com

Simulation: You Are a Lobbyist
Comparative: Comparing Interest Groups
Timeline: Interest Groups and Campaign Finance

INTERNET SOURCES

Center for Responsive Politics
www.opensecrets.org/
Follow the money trail—who gets it? who contributes?—in American politics.

National Taxpayers Union
www.ntu.org
Conservative group that advocates for lower taxes.

National Organization for Women
www.now.org
The women's organization that has long been a "player" in Washington politics.

National Rifle Association
www.nra.org/
Home page of one of America's most politically successful interest groups.

Project VoteSmart
www.votesmart.org/
Information on interest group campaign contributions to and ratings for all members of Congress.

Student Environmental Action Committee
www.seac.org/
A grassroots coalition of student environmental groups.

Townhall
www.townhall.com
A portal to scores of conservative organizations and citizen groups.

Yahoo/Organizations and Interest Groups
www.yahoo.com/Government/Politics/
Direct links to the home pages of scores of public and private interest groups as well as to Washington lobbying firms.

SUGGESTIONS FOR FURTHER READING

Andres, Gary J. *Lobbying Reconsidered: Under the Influence.* New York: Pearson Longman, 2009.
A fascinating tour of the world of lobbying by an author who not only knows the scholarly literature on the subject, but also has years of experience as a lobbyist.

Ainsworth, Scott H. *Analyzing Interest Groups: Group Influence on People and Policies.* New York: W. W. Norton, 2002.
Shows how economic forms of reasoning can be used to better understand how interest groups work and what effect they have on politics and government.

Berry, Jeffrey M., and Clyde Wilcox, *The Interest Group Society,* 5th ed. New York: Pearson Longman, 2009.
A leading textbook on interest groups, filled with up-to-date insights from scholars and political journalists.

Dahl, Robert A. *A Preface to Democratic Theory.* Chicago: University of Chicago Press, 1956.
The leading theoretical statement of the pluralist position and the democratic role of interest groups.

Davidson, Roger H., Walter J. Oleszek, and Frances E. Lee. *Congress and Its Members,* 12th ed. Washington, D.C.: CQ Press, 2010.

> *A comprehensive book on Congress that carefully examines the role of organized interests in the legislative process.*

Hacker, Jacob S., and Paul Pierson. *Winner-Take-All Politics: How Washington Made the Rich Ricer—and Turned Its Back on the Middle Class.* New York: Simon and Schuster, 2010.

> *Shows how interest groups representing business and the wealthy have dominated public policymaking in Washington and made the distribution of income and wealth much more unequal.*

Skocpol, Theda. *Diminished Democracy: From Membership to Management in American Civil Life.* Norman, OK: University of Oklahoma Press, 2003.

> *An analysis of the decline of mass membership associations and how it hurts American civic life.*

Smith, Mark A. *American Business and Political Power: Public Opinion, Elections, and Democracy.* Chicago: University of Chicago Press, 2000.

> *An argument, counter to that of Lindblom, that business corporations are not as powerful in American politics as often perceived.*

8 Social Movements

IN THIS CHAPTER

8.1 Analyze why social movements develop

8.2 Illustrate how important social movements have shaped American society

8.3 Evaluate how social movements make U.S. politics more democratic

8.4 Identify factors that give rise to social movements

8.5 Evaluate tactics used by social movements to influence what government does

8.6 Determine what makes a social movement successful

WOMEN WIN THE RIGHT TO VOTE

The struggle for women's suffrage (i.e., the right to vote) was long and difficult. The main instrument for winning the struggle to amend the Constitution to admit women to full citizenship was a powerful social movement that dared to challenge the status quo, used unconventional tactics to gain attention and sympathy, and demanded bravery and commitment from many women.[1] One of these women was Angelina Grimké.

Abolitionist Angelina Grimké addressed the Massachusetts legislature in February 1838, presenting a petition against slavery from an estimated 20,000 women of the state. In doing so, she became the first woman to speak before an American legislative body. Because women at this time were legally subordinate to men and shut out of civic life—the life of home and church were considered their proper domains—Grimké felt it necessary to defend women's involvement in the abolitionist movement to end slavery. She said the following to the legislators:

Are we aliens because we are women? Are we bereft of citizenship because we are mothers, wives and daughters of a mighty people? Have women no country—no interests staked in public weal—no partnership in a nation's guilt and shame?...I hold, Mr. Chairman, that American women have to do this subject [the abolition of slavery], not only because it is moral and religious, but because it is political, inasmuch as we are citizens of the Republic and as such our honor, happiness and well-being are bound up in its politics, government and laws.

Although this bold claim of citizenship for women did not fall on receptive ears—Grimké was derided as ridiculous and blasphemous by press and pulpit—it helped inspire other women who had entered political life by way of the abolitionist movement to press for women's rights as well. Meeting at Seneca Falls, New York, in 1848, a group of women issued a declaration written by Elizabeth Cady Stanton stating that "all men and women are created equal, endowed with the same inalienable rights." The declaration, much like the Declaration of Independence on which it was modeled, then presented a long list of violations of rights.

The Seneca Falls Declaration remains one of the most eloquent statements of women's equality ever written, but it failed to have an immediate effect because most politically active women (and men) in the abolitionist movement believed that their first order of business was to end slavery. Women's rights would have to wait.

After the Civil War destroyed the slave system, women's rights leaders such as Stanton, Susan B. Anthony, and Lucy Stone pressed for equal citizenship rights for all, white or black, male or female. They were bitterly disappointed when the Fourteenth Amendment, ratified after the war, declared full citizenship rights for all males born or naturalized in the United States, including those who had been slaves, but failed to include women. Women's rights activists realized that they would have to fight for rights on their own, with their own organizations.

Women's rights organizations were formed soon after the Civil War. For more than two decades, though, the National Woman Suffrage Association (NWSA) and the American Woman Suffrage Association (AWSA) feuded over how to pressure male politicians. Susan B. Anthony (with the NWSA) and Lucy Stone (with the AWSA) were divided by temperament

and ideology. Anthony favored pressing for a broad range of rights and organized dramatic actions to expose men's hypocrisy. At an 1876 centennial celebration of the United States in Philadelphia, Anthony and several other women marched onto the platform, where the emperor of Brazil and other dignitaries sat, and read the declaration aloud. Stone favored gaining the vote as the primary objective of the rights movement and used quieter methods of persuasion, such as petitions.

In 1890, the two main organizations joined to form the National American Woman Suffrage Association (NAWSA). They dropped such controversial NWSA demands as divorce reform and legalized prostitution in favor of one order of business: women's suffrage. The movement was now focused, united, and growing more powerful every year.

In 1912, the NAWSA organized a march to support a constitutional amendment for suffrage. More than 5,000 women paraded through the streets of Washington before Woodrow Wilson's inauguration. The police offered the marchers no protection from antagonistic spectators who pelted the marchers with rotten fruit and vegetables and an occasional rock, despite the legal parade permit they had obtained. This lack of protection outraged the public and attracted media attention to the suffrage movement.

Almost immediately after the United States entered World War I in April 1917, with the express purpose of "making the world safe for democracy," women began to picket the White House, demanding that full democracy be instituted in America. One demonstrator's sign quoted directly from President Wilson's war message—"we shall fight for the right of those who submit to authority to have a voice in their own government"—and asked why women were excluded from American democracy. As the picketing at the White House picked up in numbers and in intensity, the police began arresting large groups of women. Other women took their place. The cycle continued until local jails were filled to capacity. When suffragists began a hunger strike in jail, authorities responded with forced feedings and isolation cells. By November, public outrage forced local authorities to relent and

free the women. By this time, public opinion had shifted in favor of women's right to vote.

In the years surrounding U.S. entry into the war, other women's groups worked state by state, senator by senator, pressuring male politicians to support women's suffrage. After two prominent senators from New England were defeated in 1918 primarily because of the efforts of suffragists and prohibitionists, the political clout of the women's groups became apparent to most elected officials. In June 1919, Congress passed the Nineteenth Amendment, and the necessary 36 states ratified it the following year. By uniting around a common cause, women's organizations gained the right to vote for all women.

Although few social movements have been as effective as the women's suffrage movement in reaching their primary goal, other social movements have also played an important role in American political life. This chapter is about what social movements are, how and why they form, what tactics they use, and how they affect American political life and what government does.

THINKING CRITICALLY About This Chapter

This chapter is about the important role of social movements in American government and politics.

Using the FRAMEWORK

You will see in this chapter how social movements are a response to structural changes in the economy, culture, and society and how they affect other political linkage actors and institutions—parties, interest groups, and public opinion, for example—and government. You will learn, most importantly, under what conditions social movements most effectively shape the behavior of elected leaders and the content of government policies.

Using the DEMOCRACY STANDARD

At first glance, because social movements are most often the political instrument of numerical minorities, it may seem that they have little to do with democracy, which is rooted in majority rule. You will see in this chapter, however, that social movements play an especially important role in our democracy, principally by broadening public debate on important issues and bringing outsiders and nonparticipants into the political arena.

What Are Social Movements?

8.1 Analyze why social movements develop

> **social movement**
> A loosely organized group that uses unconventional and often disruptive tactics to have their grievances heard by the public, the news media, and government leaders.

Social movements are loosely organized collections of ordinary people, working outside established institutions, using unconventional and often disruptive methods, act to get their voices heard by the public at large, the news media and leaders of major institutions, and government officials, in order to promote, resist, or undo some social change. They are different than interest groups, which are longer lasting and more organized, with permanent employees and budgets, for example, and more committed to conventional and nondisruptive methods such as lobbying and issue advertising. They are different than political parties, whose main purpose is to win elective offices for candidates who campaign under the party banner and to control government and what it does across a broad range of policies. Social movements are more ephemeral in nature, coming and going as people feel they are needed, sometimes leaving their mark on public policies, sometimes not. What sets social movements apart from parties and interest groups is their focus on broad, societywide issues and their tendency to act outside the normal channels of government and politics, using unconventional and often disruptive tactics.[2] Some scholars call social movement politics "contentious politics."[3] When suffragists disrupted meetings, went on hunger strikes, and marched to demand the right to vote, they were engaged in contentious politics. The most important such social movement in recent times is the civil rights movement, which pressed demands for racial equality on the American public and elected officials, primarily during the 1960s.

This general definition of social movements requires further elaboration if we are to understand their role in American politics.[4] Here we highlight some important things to know about them:

- *Social movements are the political instrument of political outsiders.* Social movements often help people who are outside the political mainstream gain a hearing from the public and from political decision makers. The women's suffrage movement forced the issue of votes for women onto the public agenda. The civil rights movement did the same for the issue of equal citizenship for African Americans. Gays and lesbians forced the country to pay attention to issues that had long been left "in the closet." Insiders don't need social movements; they can rely instead on interest groups, political action committees (PACs), lobbyists, campaign contributions, and the like to make their voices heard.

  Christian conservatives, now a political force to reckon with, with many well-established interest groups such as the Family Research Council and remarkable influence within the Republican Party, were at one time largely ignored by the cultural and political establishment. Their grassroots movement to resist the general **secularization** of American life and to promote their vision of religious values in American life was built at first around local churches and Bible reading groups and often took the form of protests, whether at abortion clinics or at government locations where some religious symbol (like a manger scene at Christmas-time) was ordered removed by the courts because of the violation of the principle of separation of church and state (see Chapter 16).

- *Social movements are generally mass grassroots phenomena.* Because outsiders and excluded groups often lack the financial and political resources of insiders, they must take advantage of what they have: numbers, energy, and commitment. They depend on the participation of large numbers of ordinary people to act in ways that will move the general public and persuade public officials to address issues of concern to those in the movement.

- *Social movements are populated by individuals with a shared sense of grievance.* People would not take on the considerable risks involved in joining others in a social movement unless they felt a strong, shared sense of grievance against the status quo and a desire to bring about social change. Social movements tend to form when a significant number of people come to define their own

secularization
The spread of nonreligious values and outlooks.

TEA'D OFF   The Tea Party movement, deeply opposed to President Obama and his agenda for an energetic government to solve the economic crisis and longer-term problems like health care, became a force to be reckoned with in American politics only months after the president's inauguration. These people gathered in Freedom Plaza in Washington, D.C., in April 2009 to express their anger at passage of the "stimulus package."

troubles and problems not in personal terms but in more general social terms (the belief that there is a common cause for all of their troubles) and when they believe that the government can be moved to take action on their behalf. Because this is a rare combination, social movements are very difficult to organize and sustain.

• *Social movements often use unconventional and disruptive tactics.* Officials and citizens almost always complain that social movements are ill-mannered and disruptive. For social movements, that is precisely the point. Unconventional and disruptive tactics help gain attention for movement grievances. While successful movements are ones that eventually bring many other Americans and public officials over to their side, it is usually the case that other Americans and public officials are not paying attention to the issues that are of greatest concern to movement participants, so something dramatic needs to be done to change the situation.

• *Social movements often turn into interest groups.* Although particular social movements eventually fade from the political scene, for reasons we explore later, the more successful ones create organizations that carry on their work over a longer period of time. Thus, the women's movement spawned the National Organization for Women, while the environmental movement created organizations such as Environmental Defense and the Nature Conservancy. The movement of Christian evangelicals spurred the creation of groups such as the Family Research Council and the National Right to Life Committee.

? Have major social movements shaped your daily life? Do you see the goals of these movements as having been met—or as continually developing?

Major Social Movements in the United States

8.2   Illustrate how important social movements have shaped American society

Many social movements have left their mark on American political life and have shaped what government does in the United States. Here we describe some of the most important.

The Abolitionists

This movement's objective was to end slavery in the United States. The movement was most active in the northern states in the three decades before the outbreak of the Civil War. Their harsh condemnation of the slave system helped heighten the tensions between the North and the South, eventually bringing on the war that ended slavery. Their tactics included antislavery demonstrations and resistance (sometimes violent) to enforcement of the Fugitive Slave Act, which required all states to identify, capture, and return runaway slaves to their owners.

The Populists

The Populist movement was made up of disaffected farmers of the American South and West in the 1880s and 1890s who were angry with business practices and developments in the American economy that were adversely affecting them. Their main grievance was the concentration of economic power in the banking and railroad industries, both of which favored (with loans on better terms, cheaper shipping rates, and the like) their larger customers. The aim of the movement was to force public ownership or regulation of banks, grain storage companies, and the railroads. Small demonstrations at banks and at foreclosed farms were part of their repertoire, but they used the vote as well. For a short time, they were quite successful, winning control of several state legislatures, sending members to Congress, helping to nominate William Jennings Bryan as the Democratic candidate for president in 1896, and forcing the federal regulation of corporations (e.g., in the Interstate Commerce Commission Act).

Women's Suffrage

This movement, active in the late nineteenth and early twentieth centuries, aimed to win the right to vote for women. As we saw in the chapter-opening story, the movement won its objective when the Nineteenth Amendment to the Constitution was ratified in 1920. We also saw that the tactics of the movement were deliberately disruptive and unsettling to many.

The Labor Movement

The labor movement represented efforts by working people over the years to protect jobs, ensure decent wages and benefits, and guarantee safe workplaces. The periods of greatest militancy—when working people took to the streets and the factory floors to demand recognition of their unions—were in the 1880s, the 1890s, and the 1930s. The labor movement eventually forced the federal government to recognize the right of working people to form labor unions to represent them in negotiations with management. We saw in Chapter 7, however, that labor unions, the fruit of this successful movement, have been steadily losing members.

The Civil Rights Movement

The civil rights movement began in the mid-1950s, reached the peak of its activity in the mid-1960s, and gradually lost steam after that (see Figure 8.1). The movement, which was committed to nonviolent civil disobedience as one of its main tactics, remains one of the most influential on record, having pressed successfully for the end of formal segregation in the South and discriminatory practices across the nation (see Chapters 1 and 17). The main weapons of the movement were nonviolent civil disobedience and mass demonstrations. The outbreak of violence in urban centers after the assassination of Martin Luther King in 1968 and the rise

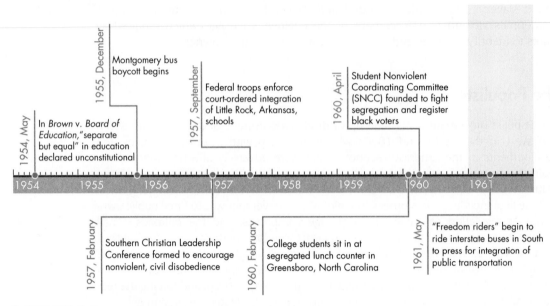

1954, May In *Brown* v. *Board of Education*, "separate but equal" in education declared unconstitutional

1955, December Montgomery bus boycott begins

1957, September Federal troops enforce court-ordered integration of Little Rock, Arkansas, schools

1960, April Student Nonviolent Coordinating Committee (SNCC) founded to fight segregation and register black voters

1957, February Southern Christian Leadership Conference formed to encourage nonviolent, civil disobedience

1960, February College students sit in at segregated lunch counter in Greensboro, North Carolina

1961, May "Freedom riders" begin to ride interstate buses in South to press for integration of public transportation

❚ FIGURE 8.1   Timeline: The Nonviolent Civil Rights Movement

in prominence at the same time of black power advocates like Stokely Carmichael and Malcolm X, who rejected nonviolence as a basic principle, marked for many people the end of the movement.

Contemporary Antiwar Movements

Antiwar movements have accompanied virtually every war the United States has waged. The most important ones that have affected American politics in contemporary times were associated with military conflicts in Southeast Asia and the Middle East. The *anti–Vietnam War* movement was active in the United States in the late 1960s and early 1970s. Its aim was to end the war in Vietnam. It used a wide variety of tactics in this effort, from mass demonstrations to voting registration and nonviolent civil disobedience. Fringe elements even turned to violence, exemplified by the Days of Rage vandalism along Chicago's Gold Coast mounted by a wing of Students for a Democratic Society and the bombing of a research lab at the University of Wisconsin in which a graduate student was killed.

BRAVING THE MOB   Nonviolent civil disobedience proved the most effective tool of the civil rights movement. By violating unjust laws quietly and nonviolently, protesters alerted outsiders to the injustice of their situation. A sit-in at a "whites only" lunch counter in Greensboro, North Carolina, in 1957 by black college students and white allies, and publicity about the ill treatment they received at the hands of locals, sparked a wave of sit-ins by black college students and a few white sympathizers across the South. The arrest of nonviolent demonstrators generated sympathetic interest among previously apathetic whites across the nation. How did such quiet protest start such a large and vehement movement?

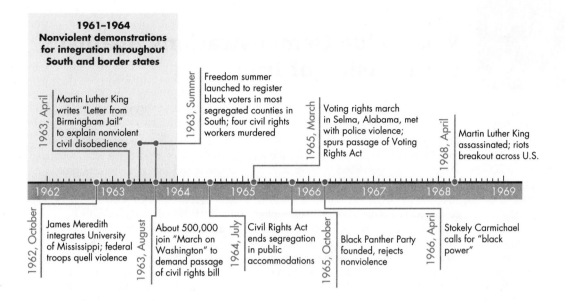

An *anti-Iraq war* movement quickly formed in the months leading up to the U.S. invasion of Iraq in 2003. The movement's most dramatic political act was the organization of massive demonstrations across the world on February 15, 2003. In the United States, demonstrations took place in 150 cities; in New York, the crowd converging on the U.N. headquarters building filled a space 20 blocks long, along First and Second Avenues (huge demonstrations occurred around the world as the "Mapping American Politics" feature shows).[5] The massive demonstrations did not convince President Bush to put off the Iraq invasion, however. The movement lost support after the invasion of Iraq in April 2003, as patriotic feelings rose as troops went into battle, but the subsequent insurgency, and the high cost to the United States of the insurgency in lives and money, rekindled the movement in late 2005. Changing public opinion on the war, some of it attributable to the antiwar demonstrations, perhaps, helped set the stage for the Republican's big losses in the 2006 congressional elections.

The Women's Movement

This movement has been important in American life since the late 1960s. Its aim has been to win civil rights protections for women and to broaden the participation of women in all aspects of American society, economy, and politics. Although it did not win one of its main objectives—passage of the **Equal Rights Amendment (ERA)** to the U.S. Constitution that guaranteed equal treatment for men and women by all levels of government—the broad advance of women on virtually all fronts in the United States attests to its overall effectiveness. The movement has been sufficiently successful, in fact, that it helped trigger a counter-movement among religious conservatives of all denominations worried about purported threats to traditional family values.

The Environmental Movement

The environmental movement has been active in the United States since the early 1970s. Its aim has been to encourage government regulation of damaging environmental practices and to raise the environmental sympathies of the public. While the vitality of the movement has waxed and waned over the years, the public's strong support for environmental

> **Equal Rights Amendment (ERA)**
> Proposed amendment to the U.S. Constitution stating that equality of rights shall not be abridged or denied on account of a person's gender; failed to win the approval of the necessary number of states.

Worldwide Demonstrations Against the Invasion of Iraq

Introduction The build-up to the invasion of Iraq was a long time coming. President Bush named Iraq one of the three members of his axis-of-evil countries in his State of the Union address in January 2002 because of their purported weapons of mass destruction (WMD) programs. U.S. diplomats pushed the U.N. Security Council to pass a resolution pushing for renewed inspections of possible violations of international restrictions on chemical, biological, and nuclear weapons programs in Iraq. U.N. inspectors found very little and reported skepticism that such programs still existed. The administration kept up the pressure, gaining congressional approval in October 2002 for the use of force against Iraq if there was evidence of WMD

programs and the U.N. failed to act. Other Security Council members were not convinced by Secretary of State Colin Powell's presentation of evidence for WMDs in early 2003, causing the United States to withdraw its resolution for the use of force in early March 2003. The United States then pulled together a group of 18 countries that President Bush called the "coalition of the willing" that agreed to use force if necessary and warned U.N. weapons inspectors to leave Iraq. The invasion of Iraq began on March 20, 2003.

Mapping World Demonstrations Rough estimates are that about 16 million people worldwide gathered over the weekend of

February 13–15, 2003, to protest against the coming invasion of Iraq. Researchers at Worldmapper found evidence of protest demonstrations in 96 of the world's mapped countries and territories. The cartogram map, showing the proportion of the world total accounted for by each country, reveals that the largest demonstrations took place in Europe, especially in Italy, Spain, and the United Kingdom, and also in the United States. The demonstrations in Rome drew 3 million; the ones in London, about 1.4 million. New York saw about 125,000 protestors, while the march in San Francisco drew about 65,000. It is worth noting, however, as you look at this map, that estimates of the size of demonstrations are just that—estimates—though whenever possible, the

regulation suggests that it has been unusually successful. Although disruptive and even violent tactics have sometimes been used, the movement has depended more on legal challenges to business practices and the creation of organizations to lobby in Washington. Rising concerns among Americans about fuel shortages and global warming have revitalized the movement and enhanced its influence.

The Gay and Lesbian Movements

These movements began in earnest in the late 1960s. Their aim was to gain the same civil rights protections under the law enjoyed by African Americans and other minority groups and to gain respect from the public. Ranging from patient lobbying and voting to mass demonstrations and deliberately shocking actions by groups such as ACT-UP, the movement's efforts have been only partially successful (see Chapter 16 for more details). They also have sparked strong counterattacks by groups such as the Christian Coalition and Focus on the Family that are opposed to their objectives.

Religious Conservatives

Religious conservative movements have occurred at several different moments in American history and have been very influential. These movements have brought together strongly religious people trying to infuse American society and public policies with their values. The contemporary movement of religious conservatives falls within this tradition and has become very important in American politics, especially on the issues of abortion, school prayer, educational curriculum, and same-sex marriage. The *pro-life (anti-abortion)* movement is part of this larger religious conservative movement. Its main objective is to end the legal availability of abortion in the United States.

researchers depended on more than a single source, leaning toward academic, press, and official estimates rather than those of the demonstration organizers. (See the "By the Numbers" feature in this chapter on how to count crowds.)

What Do You Think? Why might the president and his advisers make decisions or policies with which large portions of the public disagree? Given what occurred in Iraq after the invasion in March 2003, how could American officials have better taken into account what protesters around the world and in the United States were saying? Even if you believe that presidents must be free to act as they choose, within the constitutional boundaries of their office, how should global and American public opinion factor into their policymaking, if at all?

Source: Worldmapper, map number 361. The SASI Group (University of Sheffield) and Mark Newman (University of Michigan), 2006 **(www.worldmapper.org)**. See the technical notes on the worldmapper web site for this cartogram map for information on data collection.

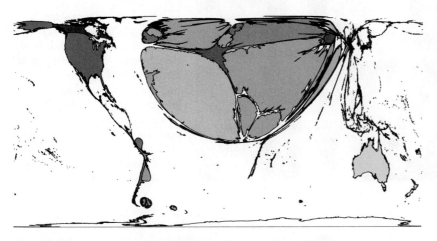

Worldwide Demonstrations Against the Invasion of Iraq
© Copyright 2006 SASI Group (University of Sheffield) and Mark Newman (University of Michigan).

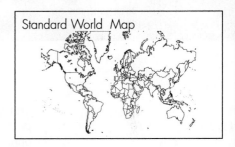

Standard World Map

The Antiglobalization Movement

An emergent antiglobalization movement announced itself to the public with demonstrations in Seattle in late 1999 targeted at the World Trade Organization (WTO), whose trade ministers were meeting in the city to fashion an agreement to further open national borders to trade and foreign investment.[6] The demonstrations were mostly peaceful, but some demonstrators turned violent. This movement is extremely diverse and includes people who are worried about the effects of globalization on the environment, income inequality in the United States and Third World countries, food safety, labor rights, sweat shops, unfair trade, and national sovereignty. The movement remains intermittently active, with protesters showing up at large WTO gatherings, as well as those put on by the World Bank, the International Monetary Fund, the World Economic Forum (which meets annually in Davos, Switzerland), and the G-8 summit meetings of the leaders of the major industrial democracies.

Undocumented Immigrants Movement

A series of massive demonstrations in the spring of 2006 in cities across the nation signaled the rise in the United States of a movement of and for illegal immigrants. Although the goals of movement leaders, activists, and joiners were quite diverse, they were joined by a wish to give legal status to those presently living and working in the United States illegally, to allow more legal immigration from Mexico, and to increase Americans' understanding of the positive role played by immigrants—legal and illegal—in the American economy. Demonstration participants included not only legal immigrants, American citizens of Mexican descent, and sympathizers from many other ethnic and racial groups but, remarkably, tens of thousands of undocumented people subject to deportation if they came to the attention of the authorities.[7] This and subsequent demonstrations failed to convince Republicans in Congress in 2007 to support an

SAYING NO TO CITIZENSHIP These sisters in Dallas in 2006 were having nothing to do with demands from demonstrators to provide a path to citizenship for illegal immigrants. Like many other social movements, the movement demanding rights for the undocumented triggered a backlash from some other people in the United States. How might social movements be affected by counter-movements?

immigration bill favored by President Bush that included a path toward citizenship for people living in the United States illegally. It also helped galvanize groups of Americans opposed to illegal immigration.

Tea Party Movement

This movement exploded onto the American political scene on tax deadline day (April 15) 2009, with demonstrations in scores of locations around the country denouncing bank bailouts, the Democrats' health care reform effort, rising government deficits, taxes and regulations, illegal immigration, and, for many among the participants, the legality of the Obama presidency. Urged on by conservative talk radio hosts and the intense coverage of their activities by FOX News, and funded by the Koch brothers' oil fortune, the Tea Party staged a series of demonstrations across the country and mobilized in August 2009 to flood and take over health care town hall meetings held by Democratic members of Congress. The movement seems to represent a modern-day angry populism directed against an activist federal government that, in the view of movement activists and followers, has been favoring the rich and powerful at the expense of ordinary people rocked by the country's economic troubles.

Social Movements in a Majoritarian Democracy

8.3 Evaluate how social movements make U.S. politics more democratic

At first glance, social movements do not seem to fit very well in a democracy. First, social movements usually start out with only a small minority of people, whereas democracy requires majority rule. Second, social movements often use disruptive tactics—though rarely overtly violent ones—when it seems that many channels already exist (e.g., voting, petitioning and writing to policymakers, and writing letters to newspapers) for people to express their grievances. In this section, we talk about how social movements can (and often do) help make American politics more democratic.

Encouraging Participation

Social movements may increase the level of popular involvement and interest in politics. In one sense, this is true simply by definition: social movements are the instruments of outsiders. Thus, the women's suffrage movement showed many middle-class women that their activities need not be confined exclusively to home, family, church, and charity work and encouraged them to venture into political life by gathering petitions or joining demonstrations demanding the vote for women. The civil rights movement in the 1960s encouraged southern African Americans, who had long been barred from the political life of their communities, to become active in their own emancipation. The religious fundamentalist movement spurred the involvement of previously politically apathetic evangelicals. The pro-immigration movement may yet spur increased political participation by Hispanic citizens.

Social movements also encourage popular participation by dramatizing and bringing to public attention a range of issues that have been ignored or have been dealt with behind closed doors. The reason is that their contentious actions make these movements' members highly visible. They offer irresistible fare for the television camera. This ability to make politics more visible—called broadening the **scope of conflict** by political scientist E. E. Schattschneider[8]—makes politics the province of the many rather than the few.

Overcoming Political Inequality

Social movements also sometimes allow individuals and groups without substantial resources to enter the game of politics. Many social movements are made up of people who do not have access to the money, time, contacts, or organizational resources that fuel normal politics.[9] The ability of those without resources to disrupt the status quo by mobilizing thousands to take to the streets to voice their demands—what sociologists call **mass mobilization**—is a powerful political tool for people on the outside looking in. In the right circumstances, the disruptive politics of social groups can become as politically useful as other resources such as money and votes. Seemingly politically powerless women were able to mobilize to win the vote in the early part of the twentieth century; seemingly politically powerless African Americans in the Deep South were able to secure full citizenship rights in the 1960s.

Creating New Majorities

Over time, social movements may also help create new majorities in society. Social movements are the province of numerical minorities in most cases, and in a majoritarian democracy, minorities should have their way only if they can convince enough of their fellow citizens that what they want is reasonable. Before the 1930s, for instance, only a minority of Americans may have been convinced that labor unions were

scope of conflict

Refers to the number of groups involved in a political conflict; a narrow scope of conflict involves a small number of groups, and a wide scope of conflict involves many.

mass mobilization

The process of involving large numbers of people in a social movement.

Great Depression

The period of economic crisis in the United States that lasted from the stock market crash of 1929 to America's entry into World War II.

a good idea. The **Great Depression** and a vigorous, militant labor movement changed the opinion climate in the nation and created the basis for federal laws protecting the right of working people to form labor unions. Such issues as gender-based job discrimination and pay inequity, to take another example, were not important to the general public until they were brought center stage by the women's movement.

Overcoming Constitutional Limitations on Change

Sometimes it takes the energy and disruption of a social movement to overcome the antimajoritarian aspects of our constitutional system (explored in Chapter 2) and get anything done at all.[10] As political scientist Theodore Lowi describes the issue:

> Our political system is almost perfectly designed to maintain an existing state of affairs. Our system is so designed that only a determined and undoubted majority could make it move. This is why our history is replete with social movements. It takes that kind of energy to get anything like a majority. . . .
> Change comes neither from the genius of the system nor from the liberality or wisdom of its supporters and of the organized groups. It comes from new groups or nascent groups—social movements—when the situation is most dramatic.[11]

? Does the First Amendment guarantee of the right to assemble and petition the government indicate that the Founders saw the necessity of social movements? Or were they more likely to see social movements as akin to factions?

It is important to note that many of the social reforms of which most Americans are most proud—women's right to vote, equal citizenship rights for African Americans, Social Security, collective bargaining, and environmental protection—have been less the result of "normal" politics than of social movements started by determined and often disruptive minorities.[12]

Factors That Encourage the Creation of Social Movements

8.4 Identify factors that give rise to social movements

A certain combination of factors seems necessary for a social movement to develop.[13] We review the most important ones here.

Real or Perceived Distress

People who are safe, prosperous, respected, and contented generally have no need of social movements. By contrast, those whose lives are difficult and unsafe, whose way of life or values is threatened, or whose way of life is disrespected often find social movements an attractive means of calling attention to their plight and of pressing for changes in the status quo.[14]

? Do you see some ongoing social, economic, or technological development that is likely to serve as a disturbance for some people and groups in American society that might trigger a social movement?

Social distress caused by economic, social, and technological change helped create the conditions for the rise of most of the major social movements in

American history. For example, the Populist movement occurred after western and southern farmers suffered great economic reverses during the latter part of the nineteenth century. The labor movement during the 1930s was spurred by the Great Depression—the virtual collapse of the industrial sector of the American economy, historically unprecedented levels of unemployment, and widespread destitution. The rise of the Christian conservative movement seems to be associated with the perception among conservatives that religious and family values had been declining in American life. For many women, distress caused by discriminatory hiring, blocked career advancement—in the form of the "glass ceiling" and the "mommy track"—and unequal pay at a time when they were entering the job market in increasing numbers during the 1960s and 1970s made participation in the women's movement attractive.[15] Discrimination, police harassment, and violence directed against them spurred gays and lesbians to turn to "contentious politics."[16] The AIDS epidemic added to their sense of distress and stimulated further political participation.[17] The rise of the Minute Men volunteers to help control the border with Mexico and legislation in several border states to deny certain benefits to illegal immigrants helped spur the mass demonstrations in 2006 and 2007 in favor of both legal and illegal immigrants.

Ironically, perhaps, as evident from the previous paragraph, the rise of one social movement demanding a change in how its people are regarded and treated often triggers the rise of a counter–social movement among people who come to feel distressed in turn. Thus, the women's and gay and lesbian movements were powerful stimulants for the rise of the Christian conservative movement, whose people worried that traditional family values were under assault.

Availability of Resources for Mobilization

Social strain and distress are almost always present in society. But social movements occur, it seems, only when aggrieved people have the resources sufficient to organize those who are suffering strain and distress.[18] A pool of potential leaders and a set of institutions that can provide infrastructure and money are particularly helpful. The grievances expressed by the labor movement had existed for a long time in the United States, but it was not until a few unions developed—generating talented leaders like John L. Lewis and Walter Reuther, a very active labor press, and widespread media attention—that the movement began to take off. Martin Luther King and the nonviolent civil rights movement found traction in the 1960s partly because network news telecasts had just increased from 15 minutes to half an hour and civil rights demonstrations and marches, and the sometimes violent response to them, provided dramatic footage to fill out the news programs. The women's movement's assets included a sizable population of educated and skilled women, a lively women's press, and a broad network of meetings to talk about common problems[19] (generally called **consciousness-raising groups**). The Christian conservative movement could build on a base of skilled clergy (for instance, Jerry Falwell and Pat Robertson), an expanding evangelical church membership, religious television and radio networks, and highly developed fund-raising technologies. The antiglobalization and anti-Iraq war movements, highly decentralized and organizationally amorphous, skillfully used social networking sites and cell phone messaging to spread information, raise money, and organize demonstrations here and abroad.[20] Spanish-language radio stations played a big role in mobilizing people to join pro-immigrant marches and rallies in spring 2006.

consciousness-raising groups
Meetings of small groups of women designed to raise awareness of discrimination against women and to encourage involvement in movement activities.

ANGRY TOWN HALL Though Fox News personalities helped mobilize their audience to attend and sometimes disrupt town hall meetings in the home districts of Democratic members of Congress, there is no getting away from the fact that a substantial number of Americans are upset about continuing economic troubles, mounting budget deficits, and immigration. Here, a very angry Randall Terry, founder of anti-abortion Operation Rescue, lets supporters of health care reform and the economic stimulus know how he feels at a town meeting. In what ways has the increase in anger and incivility in our society affected the democratic process?

A Supportive Environment

The rise of social movements requires more than the existence of resources for mobilization among aggrieved groups. The times must also be right, in the sense that a degree of support and tolerance must exist for the movement among the public and society's leaders.[21] The civil rights movement took place when overt racism among the public was declining (even in the then-segregated South) and national leaders were worried about the bad effects of segregation in the South on American foreign policy. Christian conservatives mobilized in an environment in which many other Americans were also worried about changes in social values and practices and when the Republican Party was looking for a way to detach traditional Democratic voters from their party. The labor movement's upsurge during the 1930s coincided with the electoral needs of the Democratic Party.[22] The women's movement surged at a time when public opinion was becoming much more favorable toward women's equality.[23] In 1972, for example, two out of three Americans reported to pollsters that they supported the proposal for an Equal Rights Amendment; the same proportion said they believed that the issues raised by the women's movement were important.[24] Gays and lesbians have benefited from the more tolerant attitudes toward alternative lifestyles, including homosexuality, that have developed in the United States since the late 1960s. Asked whether school boards should have the right to fire teachers who are homosexuals, only 28 percent of Americans agreed with the statement in 2009, compared with 51 percent as recently as 1987.[25]

Especially important for a social movement is acceptance among elites that the concerns and demands of a social movement are worth supporting. A group of corporate leaders in the 1930s, for example, believed that labor peace was crucial for ending the Great Depression and making long-term economic stability possible, and openly supported labor union efforts to organized industries and enter into labor-management contracts.[26] As noted earlier and in Chapter 1, in the 1950s and 1960s, American political leaders—concerned that widespread reports of violence and discrimination against African Americans was undermining U.S. credibility in the struggle against the Soviet Union for the loyalties of people of color in Asia, Africa, and Latin America—were ready for fundamental changes in race relations in the South and supported the civil rights movement. Leaders of the film, music, and television industries, whether for reasons of belief or economic gain, have increased the visibility of gay and lesbian performers and themes in their offerings.

> **political efficacy**
> The sense that an individual can affect what government does.

A Sense of Efficacy Among Participants

Some scholars believe that to develop an effective social movement, people who are on the outside looking in must come to believe that their actions can make a difference, that other citizens and political leaders will listen and respond to their grievances.[27] Political scientists call this "I can make a difference" attitude a sense of **political efficacy**. Without a sense of efficacy, grievances might explode into brief demonstrations or riots, but they would not support a long-term effort requiring time, commitment, and risk.

It may well be that the highly decentralized and fragmented nature of our political system helps sustain a sense of efficacy, because movements often find places in the system where they will be heard by officials. Christian conservatives have had little effect on school curricula in unitary political systems like that of Great Britain, for instance, where educational policy is made centrally, so few try to do anything about it. In the United States, however, they know they can gain the ear of local school boards and state officials in parts of the country in which conservative religious belief is strong. Gays and lesbians have been able to convince public officials and local voters to pass antidiscrimination ordinances in accepting communities— such as San Francisco, California, and Boulder, Colorado—and to win cases in several state courts.

Some scholars have suggested that a strong sense of common identity among protest groups contributes to efficacy. Knowing that one is not alone, that others see the world in common ways and have common concerns, is often the basis for people's willingness to commit the time and energy and to take the risks that social movements require. (Large demonstrations often help in this development; how the size of demonstrations is calculated is shown in the "By the Numbers" feature.) Growing gay and lesbian identity seems to be an important component of the rising political self-confidence of this movement.[28] The same can be said for Christian conservatives and Tea Party activists.

A Spark to Set Off the Flames

Social movements require, as we have seen, a set of grievances among a group of people, the resources to form and sustain organization, a supportive environment, and a sense of political efficacy among the potential participants in the movement. But they also seem to require something to set off the mix, some dramatic precipitating event (or series of events), sometimes called a *catalyst,* to set them in motion. Passage of the Fourteenth Amendment, protecting the citizenship rights of males, galvanized the early women's suffrage movement, as we saw in the chapter-opening story. The gay and lesbian movement seems to have been sparked by the 1969 "Stonewall rebellion"—three days of rioting set off by police harassment of the patrons of a popular gay bar in Greenwich Village in New York City. An important catalyst for the civil rights movement was Rosa Parks's simple

Just how many people were at that demonstration?

Calculating the size of demonstrations has always depended on estimates, although, as we will see, some estimates are more reliable than others. It was once standard practice for people to make educated guesses, with demonstration organizers always guessing on the very high side and officials in charge of controlling the crowd or sometimes unfriendly to the message of the demonstrators guessing on the very low side. For example, the organizers of the March 2003 antiwar rally in Washington, D.C., variously claimed, depending on which one was being quoted, a crowd of between 200,000 and 600,000, while D.C. police said it was more like 60,000. The same mismatch happened in 1996 when Louis Farrakhan claimed a crowd between 1.5 and 2 million at his Million Man March, a bit higher, to say the least, than the National Park Service's estimate of 400,000. Farrakhan threatened to sue over the disparity, arguing that the Park Service was out to discredit him and his movement.

Why It Matters Whether it makes sense or not, demonstration organizers, sympathetic supporters, and critics of any particular protest demonstration often use the size of the crowd to convey the reach and strength of a movement and make it the foundation for why the public and elected officials should pay attention to it or not. Organizers want a big number; critics want a small number. Journalists often simply average the high and low estimates and report that as the actual number. The rest of us would probably like a reliable number. But how to do that without lining everyone up and counting them or have them go through a turnstile on their way to a demonstration?

Calculating Crowd Sizes A fairly reliable method has emerged based on advances in aerial photography and digitalized remote sensing. What is now done regularly by news organizations and many governments is to take an aerial photograph, divide the area the crowd occupies into grids, then determine the density of

each area, namely, how many people are in the bounded area of the grid. Researchers do not take the time, of course, to count each person in each grid, but divide the grids into a range of density types—from very tightly packed to very thinly packed—count the actual number in a sample grid of each type, then multiply by the number of grids of each. As an example, say that one type of 10' x 10' grid packs in 25 people, another 10' x 10' type packs in 20 people, and yet another has only 10 people wandering around the space. If there are 100 grids of the first type (let's call it "very dense"), 100 grids of the second type (let's call it "dense"), and 100 grids of the third type (let's call it "not very dense"), then the total crowd is 5,500 based on the formula: (25 x 100) + (20 x 100) + (10 x 100). This is not a very big crowd, of course, not likely to make an impression, but you get the idea.

What to Watch For What to mainly watch out for and avoid are crowd estimates based on guesswork methods from

refusal to give up her seat on a Montgomery, Alabama, bus in 1957. Sending her to jail spurred the Montgomery bus boycott and associated demonstrations, led by a young minister named Martin Luther King. In 2006, Latinos were moved to action when the House passed a bill sponsored by James Sensenbrenner (R–WI) making illegal immigrants felons, subjecting long-time undocumented immigrants to deportation, and beefing up control of the U.S.–Mexican border.

? What events have you witnessed during your lifetime that have served as a "spark" to ignite a social movement?

Tactics of Social Movements

8.5 Evaluate tactics used by social movements to influence what government does

Because they often represent people and groups that lack political power, social movements tend to use unconventional tactics to make themselves heard. Such tactics depend on the dramatic gesture and are often disruptive.[29] As you saw in the chapter-opening story, the women's suffrage movement used mass demonstrations

"interested" parties, that is, from those who have an "axe to grind." Numbers from demonstration organizers should simply not be believed because they have an interest in reporting as high a number as they can. Numbers from critics of a demonstration—say, spokespersons from pro-life organizations estimating the size of a pro-choice rally—should be dismissed out of hand. Rely instead on reports from disinterested parties such as mainstream news organizations or academics, if possible, who use one form or another of counting using aerial photography. But note as well, even here, that the photograph/grid method is an estimate (just how dense is that grid, one might ask?), though it comes closer than any other method available for producing a hard and accurate number.

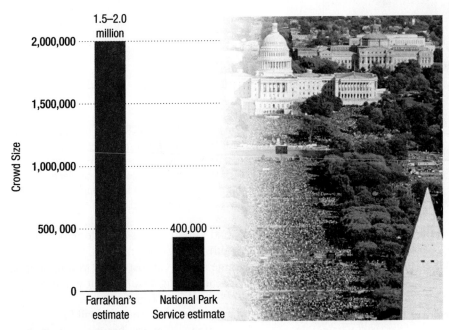

Variations in Crowd-Size Estimates at the Million Man March

What Do You Think? Do you think that the size of a demonstration or a series of demonstrations is a good indicator of the strength of a movement? If not, why not? Should movements that are able to mount large demonstrations have more attention paid to them by the public and elected officials than movements that can't do so? Why? Can you think of mass demonstrations that have had a big impact on what government does? Or, on the other hand, can you think of mass demonstrations that have had no impact at all?

Sources: Farouk El-baz, "Remote Sensing, Controversy, and the Million Man March," *Earth Observation Magazine* (February 1996), accessed at **www.eomonline. com/Common/ Archives/1996feb;** J. Patrick Coolican, "Crowd Count Adds Up to Infinite Interpretation," *Seattle Times* (February 17, 2003), p. 1; "Using Aerial Photography to Estimate the Size of Sunday's Peace March in San Francisco," *The San Francisco Chronicle* (February 21, 2003).

and hunger strikes to great effect. The labor movement invented **sit-down strikes** and plant takeovers as its most effective weapons in the 1930s. Pro-life activists added to the protest repertoire clinic blockades and the harassment of clinic patients, doctors, and employees.

The most effective tool of the civil rights movement was nonviolent **civil disobedience**, a conscious refusal to obey a law that a group considers unfair, unjust, or unconstitutional, courting arrest by the authorities and assault from others, without offering resistance, as a way to highlight injustice and gain broader public sympathy. Dr. Martin Luther King was the strongest advocate for and popularizer of this strategy, having borrowed it from Mahatma Gandhi, who used it as part of the campaign that ended British colonial rule in India after the Second World War.[30] A particularly dramatic and effective use of this tactic took place in Greensboro, North Carolina. Four black students from North Carolina Agricultural and Technical State University sat down at a "whites only" lunch counter in a Woolworth's store on February 1, 1960, and politely asked to be served. When requested to leave, they refused. They stayed put and remained calm even as a mob of young white men screamed at them, squirted them with ketchup and mustard, and threatened to lynch them. Each day, more students from the college joined them. By the end of

sit-down strike
A form of labor action in which workers stop production but do not leave their job site.

civil disobedience
Intentionally breaking a law and accepting the consequences as a way to publicize the unjustness of the law.

SIT-DOWN STRIKE AT GM The sit-down strike was invented by labor movement activists in the American auto industry in the 1930s. Here, union members strike but stay put on the job site, daring management to use violence to end the work stoppage at General Motors in 1937. Is this demonstration akin to the lunch counter sit-ins of the civil rights movement? How does it differ?

the week, more than 1,000 black students had joined the sit-in to demand an end to segregation. These actions ignited the South. Within two months, similar sit-ins had taken place in nearly 60 cities across nine states; almost 4,000 young people, including a number of white college students from outside the South, had tasted a night in jail for their actions. Their bravery galvanized blacks across the nation and generated sympathy among many whites. The student sit-in movement also spawned a new and more impatient civil rights organization, the Student Non-Violent Coordinating Committee (SNCC). (See the story of SNCC in Chapter 1.)

? Are civil disobedience and other disruptive tactics appropriate in a democracy?

For his part, Dr. King led a massive nonviolent civil disobedience campaign in Birmingham, Alabama, in 1963 demanding that the city abide by the Supreme Court's decision in *Brown* v. *Board of Education* (1954) to end the segregation of schools and demanding the more broadly based **integration** of public services, especially public transportation. Nonviolent demonstrators, many of them school-children, were assaulted by snarling police dogs, electric cattle prods, and high-pressure fire hoses that sent demonstrators sprawling. Police Commissioner Eugene "Bull" Connor filled his jails to overflowing with hundreds of young marchers, who resisted only passively, alternately praying and singing civil rights songs, including "We Shall Overcome." The quiet bravery of the demonstrators and the palpable sense among public officials and private sector leaders in the nation that matters were quickly spinning out of control convinced President John Kennedy on June 11, 1963, to introduce his historic civil rights bill for congressional consideration.

This is not to say that unconventional and disruptive tactics always work, something addressed in more detail in the next section. No matter how peaceful, some fail to strike a cord with the public or elites. And, there are times when fringe elements within movements do things that are so disruptive or violent that the movement itself is discredited. In the late 1960s, urban riots and the rise of African American leaders and groups committed to black power undermined the broad popularity of the civil rights movement. The antiglobalization movement has been similarly undermined by its anarchist wing, which, committed to violence against property and

integration

Policies encouraging the interaction between different races in schools or public facilities.

confrontations with police, usually draws the most attention from the television cameras at antiglobalization gatherings, whether in Seattle or Davos.

Why Some Social Movements Succeed and Others Do Not

8.6 Determine what makes a social movement successful

Social movements have had a significant effect on American politics and on what government does. Not all social movements are equally successful, however. What makes some more successful than others seems to be:

- *The proximity of the movement's goals to American values.* Movements that ask for fuller participation in things that other Americans consider right and proper—such as voting and holding office or opportunities for economic advancement—are more likely to strike a responsive cord than movements that, let us say, demand a redistribution of income from the rich to the poor or government ownership of large companies.

- *The movement's capacity to win public attention and support.* Potential movements that fail to gain public attention, either because the news media do not pay much attention, or because there is little sympathy for the cause the movement espouses, never get very far. Things become even more problematic when a social movement stimulates the formation of a counter-social movement.

- *The movement's ability to affect the political fortunes of elected leaders.* Politicians tend to pay attention to movements that can affect their electoral fortunes one way or another. If support for the aims of a movement will add to their vote totals among movement members and a broader sympathetic public, politicians likely will be more inclined to help. If opposition to the movement is a better electoral strategy for politicians, they are likely to act as roadblocks to the movement.

We can see how these factors play out in the life-histories of the social movements that have made their mark or tried with varying degrees of success to make their mark in American political life.

Low-Impact Social Movements

The poor people's movement, which tried to convince Americans to enact policies that would end poverty in the United States, failed to make much of a mark in the late 1960s. This social movement was never able to mobilize a large group of activists, had little support among the general public because of its fairly radical proposals for income redistribution, and was unable to disrupt everyday life significantly or to affect the electoral prospects of politicians. Not very many voters were telling public officials their vote depended on support for antipoverty policies.

The women's movement, while successful in a number of areas, was unable to win passage of a proposed Equal Rights Amendment to the Constitution banning discrimination on the grounds of gender. The ERA

? Does the failure of a social movement to achieve its primary goal make it a failure across the board? What determines the success of a social movement?

failed to receive the approval of the necessary three-fourths of the states by the amendment's 1979 deadline, mainly because the effort to ratify this new amendment stirred up a counter-movement among religious conservatives in every religious denomination.[31]

Repressed Social Movements

Social movements committed to a radical change in the society and the economy tend to threaten widely shared values and the interests of powerful individuals, groups, and institutions.[32] As a result, they rarely gain widespread popular support and almost always arouse the hostility of political leaders. Such movements very often face repression of one kind or another.[33] In the late nineteenth and early twentieth centuries, for instance, the labor movement was hindered by court injunctions forbidding strikes and boycotts, laws against the formation of labor unions, violence by employer-hired armed gangs, and strikebreaking by the National Guard and the U.S. armed forces. In 1877, 60,000 National Guardsmen were mobilized in 10 states to break the first national railroad strike. The strike against Carnegie Steel in 1892 in Homestead, Pennsylvania, brought the mobilization of 10,000 militiamen, the arrest of 16 strike leaders on conspiracy charges, and the indictment of 27 labor leaders for treason. The Pullman strike of 1894 was abruptly ended by the use of federal troops and by the arrest and indictment of union leaders.

? Does the repression of certain social movements uncover some limits on democracy? Do you think there are certain issues that will never find a voice in American politics?

Partially Successful Social Movements

Some social movements have enough power and public support to generate a favorable response from public officials but not enough to force them to go very far. In these situations, government may respond in a partial or halfhearted way. President Franklin D. Roosevelt responded to the social movements pressing for strong antipoverty measures during the Great Depression by proposing the passage of the Social Security Act, which fell far short of movement expectations.[34] The pro-life movement discovered that President Reagan was willing to use movement rhetoric to appoint sympathetic judges but was unwilling to submit anti-abortion legislation to Congress. Christian conservatives enjoyed some legislative successes during the height of their power in the 1990s and were important voices in the nominations of John Roberts and Samuel Alito to the Supreme Court by President Bush in 2005, but they failed to achieve some of their primary objectives: enact a law to ban late-term (in their words, "partial birth") abortions, pass a constitutional amendment banning same-sex marriages, and remove Bill Clinton from the presidency by impeachment and trial. Gays and lesbians enjoyed some important successes, but encountered setbacks as well. (For more on gay and lesbian advances and setbacks, see the "Using the Framework" feature, as well as Chapter 16.)

Successful Social Movements

Social movements that have many supporters, win wide public sympathy, do not challenge the basics of the economic and social orders, and wield some clout in the electoral arena are likely to achieve a substantial number of their goals. The women's suffrage movement, described in the chapter-opening story, is one of the

Why didn't Bill Clinton deliver on his promise to drop all restrictions on gays and lesbians in the military?

Background: Almost immediately after he was elected to office in 1992, Bill Clinton announced that, in his constitutional capacity as commander-in-chief, he intended to lift restrictions on gays and lesbians in the armed forces of the United States. In doing so, he was delivering on a campaign promise he had made to gay and lesbian organizations. After only a few weeks, however, he backed off from his promise and instituted a policy that came to be called "don't ask, don't tell, don't pursue." This policy of "turning a blind eye," yet allowing dismissal of gay and lesbian military personnel once

discovered, satisfied no one. (Barack Obama asked Congress to repeal "don't ask, don't tell" and ordered the Pentagon to plan for the transition on the condition that Congress would pass the necessary legislation. A federal judge ruled the policy unconstitutional in 2010 but an appeals court issued a stay to allow more time to consider the issue.) Taking a broad view at how structural, political linkage, and governmental factors affected Clinton's ultimate policy on gays and lesbians in the military will shed light on President Clinton's decision as well as President Obama's slow pace in changing the policy.

| **Structure** | Higher levels of education among the population increases toleration of alternative lifestyles. | → | Urbanization creates enclaves where gays and lesbians build communities, create social networks, and develop economic and political resources. | → | The individualistic component of American culture and the Fourteenth Amendment to the Constitution favor a nondiscriminatory environment. | → | However, the strongly religious component of American culture is also the foundation for widespread antihomosexual attitudes among religious conservatives. |

| **Political Linkage** | Gays and lesbians form and effectively use social protest groups beginning in the 1970s. | → | Gays and lesbians play an increasingly open role in political campaigns, as candidates, financial contributors, and party activists. | → | The Democratic Party increasingly welcomes gay and lesbian support and participation. | → | The mass media and entertainment industries become more sympathetic to gays and lesbians. |
| | | The gay and lesbian movement creates a backlash, particularly among religious conservatives in all denominations. | ⇨ | The Republican Party makes rolling back the so-called gay agenda a major part of its platform. | ⇨ | Public opinion is conflicted; Americans support nondiscrimination against gays and lesbians in principle, but oppose gays and lesbians on a wide range of specific proposals. |

| **Government** | | Members of Congress from both parties strongly oppose lifting restrictions on gays and lesbians in the military. | ⇨ | The Chiefs of each of the branches of the military vehemently and publicly oppose lifting restrictions. | ⇨ | The president, though committed to lifting restrictions on gays and lesbians, realizes that pushing the policy will lead to tension with Congress and the military services, and get his new administration off to a shaky start, so he retreats. |

| **Government Action** | | Bill Clinton announces that he will institute a "don't ask, don't tell" policy for gays and lesbians in the military. |

PATROLLING THE NEIGHBORHOOD
The massive increase in the size of the African American electorate in the South after passage of the 1965 Voting Rights Act resulted in the election of many African Americans to state and local offices and the integration of many government agencies, including police and sheriff's departments. Here, an officer patrols an urban neighborhood. What other social movements have helped change the face of the American workforce?

best examples. The civil rights movement is another, yielding, after years of struggle, the Civil Rights Act of 1964—which banned segregation in places of public accommodations such as hotels and restaurants—and the Voting Rights Act of 1965—which put the might of the federal government behind efforts to allow African Americans to vote and hold elected office. These enactments helped sound the death knell of the "separate but equal" doctrine enunciated in the infamous *Plessy* decision (1896), engineered the collapse of legal segregation in the South, and made the guarantee of full citizenship rights for African Americans a reality.

The Voting Rights Act was particularly important in transforming the politics of the South. Black registration and voting turnout increased dramatically all over the region during the late 1960s and the 1970s. Elected black officials filled legislative seats, city council seats, the mayors' offices in large and small cities, and sheriffs' offices. Between 1960 and 2001—the last year for which this statistic is available—the number of elected black officials in the United States increased from a mere 40 to more than 9,000.[35] Also, white politicians, tacking with the new winds of change, began to court the black vote in the years after passage of the Voting Rights Act. George Wallace, who first became famous by "standing in the schoolhouse door" to prevent the integration of the University of Alabama and who once kicked off a political campaign with the slogan "Segregation Today, Segregation Tomorrow, Segregation Forever," actively pursued the black vote in his last run for public office.

Movements can be successful even if no new laws are passed. Other measures of success include increased respect for members of the movement, changes in fundamental underlying values in society, and increased representation of the group in decision-making bodies. The women's movement has had this kind of success. Although the Equal Rights Amendment (the movement's main goal) failed, women's issues came to the forefront during these years, and, to a very substantial degree, the demands of the movement for equal treatment and respect made great headway in many areas of American life.[36] Issues such as pay equity, family leave, sexual harassment, and attention to women's health problems in medical research are now a part of the American political agenda. Women have made important gains economically and are becoming more numerous in the professions, corporate managerial offices (although there is some evidence that a glass ceiling remains in

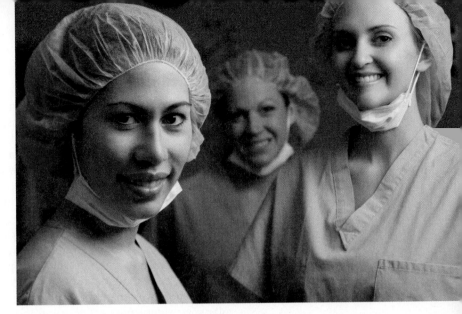

CLIMBING THE LADDER   These three women doctors smile for the camera during their hospital rounds. Women have made major advances toward equality in the professions, the result of changing social attitudes, expanded educational opportunities, and government actions to create a fairer playing field. Advances in the corporate world have been less pronounced. What are some explanations for this?

place), and political office. In 2008, Hillary Clinton came close to winning the Democratic presidential nomination, and Sarah Palin gained the GOP's vice presidential nomination.

Using the DEMOCRACY STANDARD

Do social movements make us more or less democratic?

The story of American democracy has been shaped by social movements—from the first stirrings of rebellion in the British colonies to the emancipation of African American slaves to the granting of the right to vote to women. But in a nation that is supposed to be governed by majority rule, expressed primarily through elections, are social movements that empower minorities truly democratic? Just what role do social movements play in a democracy?

In a perfect democratic society, of course, social movements would be unnecessary: change would happen through political linkages like elections and public opinion and through party and interest group activity. Indeed, a democracy that depended entirely on social movements to bring needed change would not be working very effectively at all. But in an imperfect and incomplete democracy like ours, social movements play a valuable and important role, creating an additional linkage between portions of the American public and their government.

Social movements affect our democracy in several ways. First of all, social movements represent a way—a difficult way, to be sure—by which political outsiders and the politically powerless can become players in the political game. Our constitutional system favors the status quo—federalism, separation of powers, and checks and balances make it extremely difficult to institute fundamentally new policies or to change existing social and economic conditions. The primacy of the status quo is further enhanced by the political power of economically and socially privileged groups and individuals who generally resist changes that might undermine their positions. Movements present a way for such groups and individuals to gain a hearing for their grievances, work to win over a majority of their fellow citizens, and persuade elected leaders to take action. Equal citizenship for women and for African Americans, for example, would not have happened at all, or would have been much longer in coming, if not for the existence of social movements demanding change. Thus, social movements are valuable tools for ensuring that popular sovereignty, political equality, and political liberty—the key ingredients in a democracy as we have defined it—are more fully realized.

To be sure, in some cases, at least theoretically, social movements can pose a threat to democracy. Small minorities who force elected officials to respond to their demands because of the tangible threat of social disruption might occasionally get their way, even though the majority does not favor such action. Some social movements, moreover, might push policies that run counter to democratic ideals of popular sovereignty, political equality, and political liberty, making them dangerous for democracy if they take hold. Anti-immigrant movements during several periods in the nineteenth century, for example, tried to deny citizenship rights to various groups, including people from China and southern and eastern Europe. But these threats to the fundamentals of democracy emanating from social movements seem minor compared to the persistent citizen inequalities that arise from other quarters, including the interest group system described in the previous chapter.

SUMMARY

8.1 Analyze why social movements develop

- Social movements emphasize rather dramatically the point that the struggle for democracy is a recurring feature of our political life.

- Social movements are mainly the instruments of political outsiders with grievances who want to gain a hearing in American politics.

8.2 Illustrate how important social movements have shaped American society

- Social movements, by using disruptive tactics and broadening the scope of conflict, can contribute to democracy by increasing the visibility of important issues, encouraging wider participation in public affairs, often creating new majorities, and sometimes providing the energy to overcome the many antimajoritarian features of our constitutional system.

8.3 Evaluate how social movements make U.S. politics more democratic

- Social movements often produce changes in government policies.

- Social movements try to bring about social change through collective action.

- Movements can also serve as a tension-release mechanism for aggrieved groups even when major policy shifts do not happen.

- Social movements have had an important effect on our political life and in determining what our government does. Some of our most important legislative landmarks can be attributed to them.

- Social movements do not always get what they want. They seem to be most successful when their goals are consistent with the central values of the society, have wide popular support, and fit the needs of political leaders.

8.4 Identify factors that give rise to social movements

- Social distress caused by economic, social, and technological change often creates the conditions for the rise of social movements in the United States.

- Social distress that encourages the formation of social movements comes from change that proves difficult and unsafe for people, threatens their way of life or basic values, and lessens the respect they feel from others.

- Social movements can be a means for calling attention to their plight and pressing for changes in the status quo.

8.5 Evaluate tactics used by social movements to influence what government does

- Social movements tend to be most successful when the political environment is supportive, in the sense that at least portions of the general population and some public officials are sympathetic to the movements' goals.
- Movement ideas often are taken up by one of the major political parties as it seeks to add voters.
- To the degree that parties attract new voters and change the views of some of its traditional voters

because of social movement activities, elected officials are more likely to be receptive to responding to grievances.

- Social movements sometimes spark counter–social movements, which, if strong enough, can make government leaders reluctant to address grievances.

8.6 Determine what makes a social movement successful

- Social movements that have many supporters, win wide public sympathy, do not challenge the basics of the economic and social orders, and wield some clout in the electoral arena are most likely to achieve their goals.

TEST YOURSELF

Answer key begins on page T-1.

8.1 Analyze why social movements develop

1. Interest groups often have their roots in social movements.
   True / False
2. Which of the following most accurately explains why social movements develop?
   a. They provide a mechanism for political outsiders to express shared grievances.
   b. They are effective platforms for conventional political participation.
   c. They enable elites to affect the policy agenda without disrupting their chances of electoral success.
   d. They are sponsored by interest groups as a means to attract media attention to the interest groups' causes.
   e. They facilitate political discussion between members of Congress from rival political parties or ideological orientations.

8.2 Illustrate how important social movements have shaped American society

3. The success of the antiglobalization social movement stems from the homogeneity of its membership and goals.
   True / False
4. Which of the following social movements was the most successful?
   a. The labor movement
   b. The anti-Iraq war movement
   c. The gay and lesbian movement
   d. The undocumented immigrants movement
   e. The civil rights movement

5. Compare the Tea Party movement with the populists.

8.3 Evaluate how social movements make U.S. politics more democratic

6. The essence of social movements is to protect the status quo and defend the interests of those who currently hold political power.
   True / False
7. Which of the following most accurately describes what social movements do?
   a. Suppress voter turnout and other forms of political participation
   b. Exaggerate political inequality
   c. Act as agents of change
   d. Reinforce the power of political elites
   e. Promote mass demobilization
8. Describe a policy position that a social movement has moved from minority to majority status.

8.4 Identify factors that give rise to social movements

9. Those who lack political efficacy are the most likely to form social movements.
   True / False
10. Which of the following factors is most likely to encourage the development of social movements?
    a. Prosperity
    b. Safety
    c. Contentment
    d. Distress
    e. Economic stability

11. Which of the following correctly pairs a social movement with its catalyst?
    a. The women's rights movement and the Great Depression
    b. The gay and lesbian movement and the passage of California's Proposition 9
    c. The civil rights movement and Rosa Parks's refusal to give up her seat on the bus
    d. The undocumented immigrants rights movement and the Chinese Exclusion Act
    e. The populist movement and the election of Ronald Reagan

8.5 Evaluate tactics used by social movements to influence what government does

12. Social movements tend to use unconventional tactics to make their voices heard.
    True / False
13. Which of the following best describes the tactics used by the civil rights movement?
    a. Voting
    b. International treaties
    c. Peer pressure and social isolation
    d. Violent acts of rebellion
    e. Nonviolent civil disobedience

14. Some fringe elements that may have been associated with the Tea Party movement engaged in some unsavory tactics aimed at members of Congress during the recent debates over health care reform. These tactics included spitting, the use of racial epitaphs, and threats. Evaluate whether such tactics are likely to be effective.

8.6 Determine what makes a social movement successful

15. A social movement cannot be successful unless it results in a change to society's underlying values.
    True / False
16. Under which of the following conditions is a social movement most likely to be successful?
    a. The political fortunes of elected officials are independent of the social movement.
    b. The social movement operates without attracting the attention of the public.
    c. The public is disgruntled with social movement.
    d. The goals of the social movement are similar to American values.
    e. The social movement is unpopular.

myp⬤liscilab EXERCISES

Apply what you learned in this chapter on MyPoliSciLab.

📖 **Read** on **mypolisilab.com**

   eText: Chapter 8

✔ **Study** and **Review** on **mypoliscilab.com**

   Pre-Test
   Post-Test
   Chapter Exam
   Flashcards

👁 **Watch** on **mypolisilab.com**

   Video: Chicago Worker Protest
   Video: L.A. Riots: 15 Years Later
   Video: Teen Sues for Equal Protection

✳ **Explore** on **mypoliscilab.com**

   Simulation: You Are the Leader of Concerned Citizens for World Justice

INTERNET SOURCES

African American News and Issues
www.aframnews.com/
  A website devoted to materials on African American political, social, economic, and cultural life.

Family Research Council
www.frc.org
  Information, news, and links from one of the nation's most influential Christian conservative organizations.

The Lesbian and Gay Alliance Against Defamation
www.glaad.org
  News, issues, and links related to the gay and lesbian movement.

Pew Hispanic Center
http://pewhispanic.org

A rich site for data on Hispanic immigration to the United States and polling information on public opinion on immigration topics.

The Smithsonian Exhibits: Disability Rights
http://americanhistory.si.edu/disabilityrights/welcome.html
  A Smithsonian online exhibit featuring the history of the disability rights movement.

Yahoo! Society and Culture
www.yahoo.com/Society_and_Culture/Issues_and_Causes/
  A gateway with links to a multitude of social movements, issues, and groups.

SUGGESTIONS FOR FURTHER READING

Branch, Taylor. *Parting the Waters: America in the King Years, 1954–1963.* New York: Simon & Schuster, 1988.
  A detailed and compelling description of the civil rights movement, with a particular focus on Martin Luther King Jr.; winner of the National Book Award and the Pulitzer Prize.

Chafe, William H. *The Unfinished Journey: America Since World War II.* New York: Oxford University Press, 2006.
  A justly celebrated history of America since 1945, with a particular focus on the civil rights and women's movements.

Dudziak, Mary L. *Cold War Civil Rights.* Princeton, NJ: Princeton University Press, 2002.
  A compelling history of how the Cold War struggle with the Soviet Union provided a supportive environment for the civil rights movement.

Horton, Carol A. *Race and the Making of American Liberalism.* New York: Oxford University Press, 2005.

Suggests that American liberalism has been useful in ending discrimination and expanding diversity, but much less useful in diminishing dramatic racial inequalities in status, power, and wealth.

McAdams, Doug, Sidney Tarrow, and Charles Tilly. *Dynamics of Contention.* Cambridge, UK: Cambridge University Press, 2001.
  A book that attempts to bridge the gap between the leading but competing theories of social movements by the field's three leading scholars.

Opp, Karl-Dieter. *Theories of Political Protest and Social Movements.* New York: Routledge, 2009.
  A comprehensive examination of the scholarly debates surrounding our understanding of social movements and the role they play not only in the United States but in other countries as well.

Rosen, Ruth. *The World Split Open: How the Modern Women's Movement Changed America.* New York: Penguin, 2006.
  A history of the modern women's movement, filled with detailed accounts of the origins, operations, and impacts of the movement.

9 | Political Parties

LEARNING OBJECTIVES

After reading this chapter, you should be able to:

9.1 Evaluate the importance of political parties in democracies

9.2 Distinguish American political parties from parties in other democra

9.3 Compare and contrast today's Republican and Democratic parties

THE REPUBLICAN ESTABLISHMENT UNDER SIEGE

In a special election in New York's 23rd congressional district in 2009, conservative activists showed they were less interested in electing a Republican than in keeping the GOP's feet to the ideological fire. Party leaders in the district had nominated a moderate, Dede Scozzafava, as its candidate. The problem for conservatives was that Scozzafava supported gay rights and abortion and expressed her belief that portions of the Obama economic stimulus package were acceptable. To take her and the Democratic candidate on, the activists threw their support to New York Conservative party candidate Douglas Hoffman. Though Scozzafava was the pick of the local party organization and endorsed by Republican congressional leaders and Newt Gingrich (former Republican Speaker of the House), Hoffman was supported by an all-star list of economic and social conservatives. *The Wall Street Journal* and the *Weekly Standard* told readers to reject the Republican nominee in favor of the more conservative candidate. Sarah Palin endorsed Hoffman and attacked Scozzafava, as did Rush Limbaugh, Glenn Beck, and Dick Armey, the former Republican House majority leader. Money poured in from a host of advocacy organizations such as the

Susan B. Anthony List and the National Organization for Marriage. Attack ads funded by the conservative group Club for Growth flooded the upstate New York district. Tea Party activists became a vocal and often disruptive presence at Scozzafava's town hall meetings.

Battered by the flood of conservative anger, money, and volunteers, Scozzafava quit the race just days before the election, endorsing her Democratic opponent. Not surprisingly, perhaps, Democrat Bill Owens won the election, the first time the district had not gone Republican since 1872. Though the special election in upstate New York added to the size of the Democratic majority in the House of Representatives, conservatives said they were satisfied because their efforts had sent a message to the Republican Party that its conservative base must be served and that moderates in the party were at risk. Here is how Sarah Palin put it on her Facebook page:

Political parties must stand for something. When Republicans were in the wilderness in the late 1970s, Ronald Reagan knew that the doctrine of "blurring the lines" between parties was not an appropriate way to win elections...Republicans

and conservatives around the country are sending an important message to the Republican establishment in their outstanding grassroots support for Doug Hoffman: no more politics as usual.

Ominously for Republican moderates and long-serving incumbents, conservative activists, campaign contributors, FOX News personalities, and the Tea Party, then turned their attention to the task of denying Republican Party nominations for the 2010 elections to a number of other Republicans who were not, in their view, conservative enough or who were incumbents seemingly tied to the mess in Washington. Governor Charlie Crist was forced to withdraw from the nomination contest for the GOP senatorial bid in Florida, for example—his fatal mistake being appearing with President Obama to support the economic stimulus bill.[1] Three-term Senator Bob Bennett of Utah, a member of the Republican leadership council and one of the most conservative members of the Republican Party, could not overcome the anti-incumbent mood among conservative and Republican activists and was rudely swept aside, failing to receive enough votes in local caucuses to even be considered in the Republican

Party's state nominating convention. Nikki Haley, a Tea Party favorite and one of the people honored by Sarah Palin as "mamma grizzlie," won the South Carolina GOP nomination for governor over the candidate backed by the state's Republican Party establishment. In Nevada, another Tea Party candidate—with a platform that included privatizing Social Security and eliminating the Department of Energy—won the Republican nomination over the candidate favored by party leaders and the right to square off against Senate majority leader Harry Reid in the general election.

American political parties often are described as "big tent" parties, comprised of broad and diverse coalitions of groups and viewpoints. This was generally true for most of our history. But starting in the 1980s, things began to change. Since then, the Democratic Party has become slightly more economically and socially liberal while the Republican Party has become much more economically and socially conservative (please refer again to Figure 5.2). The number of Democratic moderates in Congress has declined, though they remain significant—senators Ben Nelson (NE) and Max Baucus (MT), for example, were key architects of the health care reform bill. Moderates have almost disappeared from the Republican Party in Congress, however. Increasingly, Republicans in the House and Senate vote on important bills as relatively homogeneous blocks. The Obama stimulus bill in 2009, for example, drew no Republican votes in the House and only three in the Senate. The health care reform bill drew only a single Republican vote in the House of Representatives and none in the Senate.

Democrats and Republicans in Washington and across the country have become engaged in increasingly bitter disputes over many issues, including the wars in Iraq and Afghanistan, abortion, same-sex marriage, global warming, Social Security reform, judicial appointments, spending and taxes, disaster and homeland security preparedness, and changes in bankruptcy and tort law. Incivility has become the order of the day when party leaders and elected officials deal with one another. Opponents in Congress are accused of being scoundrels, liars, or cowards. Conference committees to iron out differences between Senate and House versions of important bills freeze out members of the minority party. Presidents are accused by their **partisan** opponents of plotting to undermine civil liberties, squash religious freedom, enrich their friends, or turn the country toward socialism. In this environment, it is hardly surprising that cooperation across party lines is increasingly rare, not only in Congress but in state legislatures and city councils as well. And those who try to do so are, more often than not, vilified by their co-partisans.

American politics is no stranger to partisan politics; to one extent or another, Democratic and Republican leaders and activists have always been in the business of making the other party look bad. It's good politics. However, things seem to be getting worse, at least according to most veteran observers of American politics.[2]

What accounts for the intense partisanship of American politics today? Scholars and journalists have lots of ideas on this. Many point to the explosion in the number and influence of liberal and conservative advocacy groups, and their blogosphere cousins, who demand unity on bedrock issues such as abortion, taxes, and global warming. Others point to the decline in the number of competitive districts in House races, meaning that most representatives can win and retain their seats without regard to voters in the other party. Others suggest that our presidential primary system (see Chapter 10) forces candidates for party presidential nominations to play to the most ideologically extreme elements within each of the parties. Still others suggest that the very closeness of presidential and congressional elections in the late 1990s and much of the 2000s convinced party strategists that the best way to win elections was to mobilize the party base and get them to the polls. And what better way to do this than to get partisans angry at the other party and worried about what it would do if it were to win?

Political parties are an important part of democratic political systems. How well they function and fulfill their responsibilities has a lot to do with determining the health and vitality of democratic polities. We examine political parties in this chapter and ask whether heightened levels of interparty conflict make our system more or less responsive to the people and our government more or less able to fashion coherent and workable public policies.

partisan

A committed supporter of a political party; also, seeing issues from the point of view of a single party.

THINKING CRITICALLY About This Chapter

This chapter is about American political parties, how they evolved, what they do, and how their actions affect the quality of democracy in the United States.

Using the FRAMEWORK

You will see in this chapter how parties work as political linkage institutions connecting the public with government leaders and institutions. You will see, as well, how structural changes in the American economy and society have affected how our political parties function.

Using the DEMOCRACY STANDARD

You will see in this chapter that political parties, at least in theory, are one of the most important instruments for making popular sovereignty and majority rule a reality in a representative democracy, particularly in a system of checks-and-balances and separated powers such as our own. Evaluating how well our parties carry out these democratic responsibilities is one of the main themes of this chapter.

The Role of Political Parties in a Democracy

9.1 Evaluate the importance of political parties in democracies

Although the framers worried about the possible pernicious effects of factions, a category that included interest groups and political parties in today's terminology, and designed a constitution to address these effects, most political thinkers today believe that political parties are essential to democracy. They agree with E. E. Schattschneider that "political parties created democracy and…modern democracy is unthinkable save in terms of the parties."[3] So, what are political parties and why are they essential to the practice of democracy?

Political parties are organizations that try to win control of government by electing people to office who carry the party label. In representative democracies, parties are the principal organizations that recruit candidates for public office, run their candidates against the candidates of other political parties in competitive elections, and try to organize and coordinate the activities of government officials under party banners and programs. In going about the business of electing people to office and running government, political parties make it possible for the people to rule,[4] for parties can only gain power and govern with the approval of the majority. As discussed in Chapter 1, majority rule is one of the things that makes popular sovereignty possible. As Schattschneider once put it: "The parties are the special form of political organization adapted to the mobilization of majorities. How else can the majority get organized? If democracy means anything at all it means that the majority has the right to organize for the purpose of taking over the government."[5]

In theory, political parties can do a number of things to make popular sovereignty and political equality possible:[6]

- *Keep elected officials responsive.* Competitive party elections help voters choose between alternative policy directions for the future. They also allow voters to make a judgment about the past performance of a governing party and decide whether to allow that party to continue in office. And, a party can adjust its **party platform**—the party's statement of its position on the issues—to reflect the preferences of the public as a way to win elections.

- *Stimulate political interest.* When they are working properly, moreover, political parties stimulate interest in politics and public affairs and increase participation. They do this as a natural by-product of their effort to win or retain power in government; they mobilize voters, bring issues to public attention, and educate on the issues that are of interest to the party.[7] Party competition, by "expanding the scope of conflict," attracts attention and gets people involved.[8]

- *Ensure accountability.* Parties can help make officeholders more accountable. When things go wrong or promises are not kept, it is important in a democracy for citizens to know who is responsible. Where there are many offices and branches of government, however, it is hard to pinpoint responsibility. Political parties can simplify this difficult task by allowing for collective responsibility. Citizens can pass judgment on the governing ability of a party as a whole and decide whether to retain the incumbent party or to throw it out of office in favor of the other party.

- *Help people make sense of complexity in politics.* Party labels and party positions on the issues help many people make sense of the political world. Few people have the time or resources to learn

political party

An organization that tries to win control of government by electing people to office who carry the party label.

party platform

A party's statement of its positions on the issues of the day passed at the quadrennial national convention.

THE GOVERNMENT IS CLOSED Struggles over the budget between the Republican-led Congress and President Clinton (a Democrat) led to temporary closures of all nonessential government departments and agencies in 1995. How is it possible that party disagreements can go this far?

about and reach decisions on every candidate on the ballot or the issues before the public at any period in time. Party labels and policy positions can act as useful shortcuts enabling people to cut through the complexities and reach decisions that are consistent with their own values and interests.

- *Make government work.* In a system like ours of separation of powers and checks and balances, designed to make it difficult for government to act decisively, political parties can encourage cooperation across the branches of government among public officials who are members of the same party. Parties can help overcome gridlock, an all too common feature of our constitutional system.

Political parties, then, can be tools of popular sovereignty. Whether our own political parties fulfill these responsibilities to democracy is the question we explore in the remainder of this chapter as well as in Chapter 10.

two-party system

A political system in which two parties vie on relatively equal terms to win national elections and in which each party governs at one time or another.

multiparty system

A political system in which three or more viable parties compete to lead the government; because a majority winner is not always possible, multiparty systems often have coalition governments where governing power is shared among two or more parties.

The American Two-Party System

9.2 Distinguish American political parties from parties in other democracies

The United States comes closer to having a "pure" **two-party system** than any other nation in the world. Most Western democracies have **multiparty systems.** In the United States, however, two parties have dominated the political scene since 1836, and the Democrats and the Republicans have controlled the presidency and Congress since 1860. As eminent political party scholar Marjorie Randon Hershey shows in Table 9.1, there have only been five major parties in the history of the United States, that is, parties that have led at least one of the branches of

---

TABLE 9.1 Major Political Parties in American History

1. **The Federalist Party, 1788–1816.** The champion of the new Constitution and strong national government, it was the first American political institution to resemble a political party, although it was not a full-fledged party. Its strength was rooted in the Northeast and the Atlantic Seaboard, where it attracted the support of shopkeepers, manufacturers, financiers, landowners, and other established families of wealth and status. Limited by its narrow, electoral base, it soon fell before the success of the Democratic-Republicans.

2. **The Democratic-Republican Party, 1800–1832.** Many of its leaders had been strong proponents of the Constitution but opposed the extreme nationalism of the Federalists. This was a party of the small farmers, workers and less privileged citizens, plus southern planters, who preferred the authority of the state governments and opposed centralizing power in the national government. Like its leader. Thomas Jefferson; it shared many of the ideals of the French Revolution, especially the extension of the right to vote and the notion of direct popular self-government.

3. **The Democratic Party, 1832–Present.** Growing out of the Jacksonian wing of the Democratic-Republicans, it was the first really broad-based, popular party in the United States. On behalf of a coalition of less-privileged voters it opposed such business-friendly policies as national banking and high tariffs. It also welcomed the new immigrants (and sought their votes) and opposed nativist (anti-immigrant) sentiment.

4. **The Whig Party, 1834–1856.** This party, too, had roots in the old Democratic-Republican Party, but in the Clay-Adams faction and in opposition to the Jacksonians. Its greatest leaders, Henry Clay and Daniel Webster, stood for legislative supremacy and protested the strong presidency of Andrew Jackson. For its short life, the Whig Party was an unstable coalition of many interests among them nativism, property, and business and commerce.

5. **The Republican Party, 1854–Present.** Born as the Civil War approached, this was the party of northern opposition to slavery and its spread to the new territories. Therefore it was also the party of the Union, the North, Lincoln, the freeing of slaves, victory in the Civil War, and the imposition of Reconstruction on the South. From the Whigs it also inherited a concern for business and industrial expansion.

Source: Marjorie Randon Hershey, *Party Politics in America,* 12th ed. (New York: Pearson Longman, 2007), p. 15.

---

the national government at one time or another. Minor or third parties have rarely polled a significant percentage of the popular vote in either presidential or congressional elections (more will be said later about third parties), although they are sometimes successful at the state and local levels. Jesse Ventura, for example, a former professional wrestler, was elected governor of Minnesota in 1998 as the nominee of the Reform Party.

> **?** What advantages might a multiparty system have in terms of representing minority views? Is including in government many different parties with different points of view more democratic, or does it ultimately undermine the voice of the majority?

Why a Two-Party System?

Why are we so different from other countries? Why do we have only two major parties? There are several reasons.

Electoral Rules The kinds of rules that organize elections help determine what kind of party system exists.[9] Which rules are chosen, then, have important consequences for a nation's politics.

Proportional Representation Most other democratic nations use some form of **proportional representation** (PR) to elect their representatives. In PR systems, each party is represented in the legislature in rough proportion to the percentage of the popular vote

> **proportional representation**
> The awarding of legislative seats to political parties to reflect the proportion of the popular vote each party receives.

it receives in an election. In a perfect PR system, a party winning 40 percent of the vote would get 40 seats in a 100-seat legislative body, a party winning 22 percent of the vote would get 22 seats, and so on. In such a system, even very small parties would have a reason to maintain their separate identities because no matter how narrow their appeal, they would win seats as long as they could win a proportion of the popular vote. Voters with strong views on an issue or with strong ideological outlooks could vote for a party that closely represented their views. A vote for a small party would not be wasted, because it would ultimately be translated into legislative seats and, perhaps, a place in the governing coalition.

Israel and The Netherlands come closest to having pure PR systems, organized on a national basis; most western European nations depart in various ways from the pure form. Most, for instance, vote for slates of party candidates within multimember electoral districts, apportioning seats in each district according to each party's percentage of the vote. In Germany, seats in the Bundestag (the lower house of the national parliament) are filled by a combination of elections from single-member districts and a party's share of the nationwide vote. Russia has a similar system for elections to the lower house of the state Duma. Most democracies that use proportional representation also have a minimum threshold (often 5 percent) below which no seats are awarded to a party. In the Russian parliamentary elections in 2007, so many parties were on the ballot that only a handful were able to cross the minimum-vote threshold for parliamentary seats.

Winner-Take-All, Plurality Election, Single-Member Districts Elections in the United States are organized on a winner-take-all, single-member-district basis. Each electoral district in the United States—whether it is an urban ward, a county, a congressional district, or a state—elects only one person to a given office and does so on the basis of whoever wins the *most* votes (not necessarily a majority). This is why our way of electing leaders is sometimes called a "first

VOTE FOR MY PARTY

In parliamentary systems, the leader of a political party becomes the prime minister when he or she has or can form a majority in the parliament. In such systems, whether they have proportional representation systems or not, people generally cast their votes for a party rather than an attractive candidate. Here, party activists hold up signs for their party in the 2010 parliamentary elections in the United Kingdom. Is this so different from how we vote in the United States?

IT'S ALL ABOUT THE ELECTORAL COLLEGE
The winner of the presidential election is the person who receives a majority of Electoral College votes, not the person who wins the most popular votes. Here, two young women get ready to tally up vote totals during the 2008 presidential contest. Why is the Electoral College method preferable to a majority popular vote? Or is it?

past the post" system, analogous to a horse race. This arrangement creates a powerful incentive for parties to coalesce and for voters to concentrate their attention on two big parties. The two-party outcome of plurality elections in single member district voting systems is often called Duverger's Law after the French political scientist who first discovered and systematically examined the relationship.[10] Here is how it works.

From the vantage point of party organizations, this type of election discourages minor-party efforts because failure to come in first in the voting leaves a party with no representation at all. Leaders of such parties are tempted to merge with a major party. Also, a disaffected faction within a party is unlikely to strike out on its own because the probability of gaining political office is very low. Thus, Tea Party candidates in 2010 ran as Republicans.

From the voter's point of view, a single-member, winner-take-all election means that a vote for a minor party is wasted. People who vote for a minor party may feel good, but most voters have few illusions that such votes will translate into representation and so are not inclined to cast them.

Note that the most important office in American government, the presidency, is elected in what is, in effect, a single-district (the nation), winner-take-all election. The candidate who wins a majority of the nation's votes in the Electoral College wins the presidency (see Chapter 10). A party cannot win a share of the presidency; it is all or nothing. In parliamentary systems, the executive power is lodged in a cabinet, however, where several parties may be represented.

Restrictions on Minor Parties Once a party system is in place, the dominant parties often establish rules that make it difficult for other parties to get on the ballot.[11] A number of formidable legal obstacles stand in the way of third parties and independent candidates in the United States. While many of these restrictions have been eased because of successful court challenges by recent minor-party and independent presidential candidates such as Ross Perot, the path to the ballot remains tortuous in many states, where a considerable number of signatures are required to get on the ballot. Moreover, the requirements for ballot access are different in every state. While the two main parties, with party organizations in place in each of the states and well-heeled national party committees, are able to navigate this legal patchwork, new and small parties find it quite difficult.

The federal government's partial funding of presidential campaigns has made the situation of third parties even more difficult. Major-party candidates automatically qualify for federal funding once they are nominated. Minor-party candidates must attract a minimum of 5 percent of the votes cast in the general election to be eligible for public funding, and they are not reimbursed until after the election. In recent decades, only the Reform Party among the legion of minor parties has managed to cross the threshold to qualify for federal funding. Because the Green Party's candidate, Ralph Nader, won only 2.7 percent of the national vote in the 2000 election, it was not eligible for federal funding for the 2004 election, something that hobbled its candidate. David Cobb, the Green Party's presidential candidate in 2004, hardly registered at the polls, winning about 0.1 percent of the vote.

The Role of Minor Parties in the Two-Party System

Minor parties have played a less important role in the United States than in virtually any other democratic nation, and have become even less important.[12] In our entire history, only a single minor party (the Republicans) has managed to replace one of the major parties. Only six (not including the Republicans) have been able to win even 10 percent of the popular vote in a presidential election, and only seven have managed to win a single state in a presidential election.

Minor parties have come in a number of forms:

- *Protest parties* sometimes arise as part of a social movement. The Populist Party, for instance, grew out of the western and southern farm protest movements in the late nineteenth century. The Green Party was an offshoot of the environmental and antiglobalization movements.

- *Ideological parties* are organized around coherent sets of ideas. The several Socialist parties have been of this sort, as has the Libertarian Party. The Green Party ran in the 2000 elections on an anticorporate, antiglobalization platform.

- *Single-issue parties* are barely distinguishable from advocacy groups. What makes them different is their decision to run candidates for office. The Prohibition Party and the Free-Soil Party fall into this category, as did Perot's "balanced budget" Reform Party in 1996.

- *Splinter parties* form when a faction in one of the two major parties bolts to run its own candidate or candidates. An example is the Bull Moose Progressive Party of Teddy Roosevelt, formed after Roosevelt split with Republican party regulars in 1912.

Minor parties do a number of things in American politics. Sometimes they articulate new ideas that are eventually taken over by one or both major parties. Ross Perot's popular crusade for a balanced budget during his 1992 campaign helped nudge the major parties toward a budget agreement that, for a while, eliminated annual deficits in the federal budget. The Tea Party revolt against the Republican Party establishment in 2010 made the already strongly conservative GOP even more conservative, the result being even less cooperation with President Obama and congressional Democrats in 2011 than before.

ROSS WINNING VOTES BUT NO STATES Ross Perot, here campaigning in 1996, ran for the presidency twice, first as an independent, then as the nominee of the Reform Party. In 1992, he received 19 percent of the national popular vote; in 1996, his vote total fell to 8 percent. These are big numbers for an independent and third-party candidate, but he failed to win a single vote in the Electoral College in either election. How democratic is this voting arrangement, and what other purposes, in addition to advancing democracy, does the Electoral College system serve?

It is also the case that third parties can sometimes change the outcome of presidential contests by changing the outcome of the electoral vote contest in the various states: in 1992, a substantial portion of the Perot vote was comprised of people who otherwise would have voted Republican, allowing Bill Clinton to win enough states to beat George H. W. Bush; in 2000, a substantial portion of the Nader vote in Florida was composed of people who otherwise would have voted Democratic, allowing George W. Bush to win Florida's electoral votes and the presidency over Al Gore.

Shifts in the American Two-Party System

While the United States has had a two-party system for most of its history, it is important to point out that the system has not been static. Scholars have identified a number of party eras in the United States, each different in one or more important ways from the others. Some scholars have developed a fairly elaborate theory of party **realignment** in which a party dominates American politics for periods lasting between 30 and 40 years, then gives way to the other major party during a short realigning period as voting coalitions in the country change around.[13] There are good reasons to be skeptical of a theory of realignment that posits decades of stability interspersed by sudden changes; recent history, for example shows an entirely different pattern of change.[14] Nevertheless, there seem to have been identifiable party eras over the course of our history. We show seven such periods in American history in Figure 9.1, though we only examine the last three in this book.

The New Deal Party Era The Great Depression, the **New Deal,** and the leadership of President Franklin D. Roosevelt ushered in a long

realignment

The process by which one party supplants another as the dominant party in a political system.

New Deal

The programs of the administration of President Franklin D. Roosevelt.

FIGURE 9.1 Timeline: Party Systems in the United States

American politics has been characterized by a series of relatively stable political party eras punctuated by periods of transition—some sudden, others much more drawn out—from one party era to another.

period of Democratic Party dominance. From 1932 through 1964, the Democrats won seven of nine presidential elections, controlled the Senate and the House of Representatives for all but four years, and prevailed in a substantial majority of governorships and state legislatures across the nation. Democratic dominance was built on an alliance of workers, Catholics, Jews, unionists, small- and medium-sized farmers, urban dwellers, white ethnics, southerners, and blacks that came to be known as the **New Deal coalition.** The New Deal coalition supported an expansion of federal government powers and responsibilities, particularly in the areas of old age assistance, aid for the poor, encouragement of unionization, subsidies for agriculture, and regulation of business. Much of this was described in Chapter 3 on federalism.

The Dealignment Era

The New Deal coalition began to slowly disintegrate in the 1968 election (won by Republican Richard Nixon) and finally collapsed in 1980 with the Republican capture of the presidency and the Senate.[15] The change in the party system was triggered by three major developments. First, strong support by the Democratic party for the civil rights revolution—which brought new antidiscrimination laws, busing to achieve school integration, and, eventually, minority set-asides for government jobs and contracts and affirmative action programs in higher education—caused many white southerners and blue-collar workers to switch their loyalties from the Democrats to the Republicans, even while African Americans became more loyal to the Democrats.[16] Second, the tendency of the Democrats to openly welcome feminists, gay men, and lesbians and support their bid for equal rights, as well as the growing identification of Democrats with the doctrine of strict separation of church and state, caused religious conservatives to abandon the party. Third, perceived Democratic Party opposition to the Vietnam War, especially during the Nixon years 1969 through 1973, caused many Americans who favored a strong national defense and an aggressive foreign policy to drift away as well.

New Deal coalition

The informal electoral alliance of working-class ethnic groups, Catholics, Jews, urban dwellers, racial minorities, and the South, that was the basis of the Democratic party dominance of American politics from the New Deal to the early 1970s.

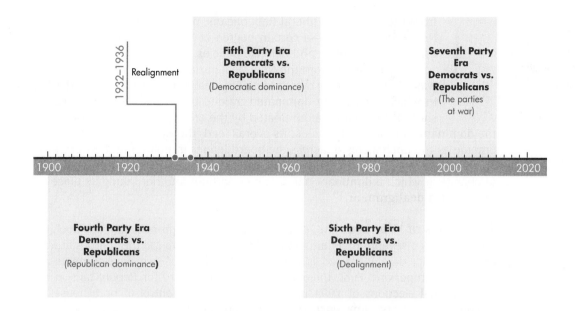

After 1980, the pace of Democratic decline began to pick up, with Democrats losing their big advantage in control of governorships and state legislatures, as well as in party identification among the electorate (see Figure 9.4 toward the end of this chapter). They also began to lose control in Congress, first in the Senate and then the House after the 1994 elections. The period was characterized by growing parity between the parties and the existence of **divided government**—one party in control of the presidency and the other with a majority in at least the House or Senate (sometimes both). Divided government was also typical in the states where Democrats and Republicans divided the governor's office and one or two chambers of state legislatures. Because each party contained a small wing within it open to cooperation with the other party—conservative Democrats, mainly

> **divided government**
> Control of the executive and legislative branches by different political parties.

FDR ADDS TO HIS COALITION The wealthy and patrician Franklin D. Roosevelt attracted a wide range of common people to his Democratic Party, including industrial workers, poor farmers, and farm laborers. Here he talks with Georgia farmers during his campaign for the presidency in 1932. How did a man of wealth and privilege become so popular among America's working class?

dealignment

A gradual reduction in the dominance of one political party without another party supplanting it.

from the South, and liberal Republicans, mainly from the Atlantic and New England states—a certain degree of bipartisanship was possible, especially on foreign and defense policies.[17]

The transition from the New Deal party era to the dealignment era was not the same as the classic party realignments of 1896 and 1932 in which a party era dominated by one party was replaced in rather short order by an era dominated by the other party. In this case, while the dominant Democratic Party lost its overall lead, the Republican Party did not emerge as the unchallenged, across-the-board leader in politics and governance. Nor did very many additional Americans call themselves Republicans. This form of change in which a dominant part declines without another taking its place often is called **dealignment**.[18]

The Parties at War Era We have taken the liberty of proposing in this book the emergence of a seventh party era in the mid-1990s that we call the "parties at war" era. The exact date it started is hard to pin down. But two developments are particularly important. First, there was the historic victory for Republicans in the congressional elections of 1994 in which they gained control of both houses of Congress for the first time since 1946, with much of the credit going to a unified conservative surge led by Republican House leader Newt Gingrich (R–GA) and supported by an array of conservative think tanks, media, and advocacy groups. Second, there was the successful effort by House Republicans to impeach Democratic president Bill Clinton in 1998 and a close vote along party lines in the Senate in early 1999 that fell just short of removing him from office—despite Democratic gains in the 1998 congressional elections and large majorities among the public saying they opposed these actions.

So, here is the potent mix that is the seventh party era, perhaps best exemplified by the disputed Bush–Gore presidential election of 2000. The public during most of this period was evenly divided—a little less than one-third said they were Republicans, a little more than one-third said they were Democrats, and a little more than one-third said they were independent. Elections were fought during this period by two well-funded and ideologically unified parties and allied advocacy groups whose supporters and activists were so committed to certain policy outcomes and ideological positions that emotions ran high, as each tried to turn out its base. Adding fuel to the fire, election outcomes in state and national races were extremely close, with Democratic and Republican votes on a national basis closely divided, and control of the House, the Senate, and the presidency seemingly hanging in the balance at every election.[19] In the governing process, bipartisanship was largely absent; consultations across the aisles in Congress and between the president and Congress during periods of divided government were rare. Underlying it all was a fundamental settling in of a new electoral geography defined by the shift of the South to the Republicans and the Northeast and coastal West to the Democrats (see the "Mapping American Politics" feature on this shift).

? Is the present close division between Democrats and Republicans likely to exist for a long time to come? Or will it tip in favor of one party or the other? What factors are likely to bring such a tip about?

Many confident Democrats claimed that their party's big wins in the 2006 and 2008 elections, as well as the sharp decline in Republican identifiers in the electorate (to the mid-20s by 2008), signaled another era shift in our two-party system in their favor. Unfortunately for Democrats, continuing economic troubles in 2009 and 2010 (the first two years of the Obama administration), the bruising and divisive battles over the economic stimulus package and the health care reform bill, and the devastating BP oil disaster in the Gulf of Mexico fed a strong anti-incumbent, anti-Washington mood in the country that advantaged the Republicans in the 2010 elections during which Republicans made big gains. Though Republicans increased their share of party identifiers in the electorate only a little by 2010, Democrats lost their lead, with independent identifiers making the biggest advances. Given all of this, it goes without saying, perhaps, that a new Democratic Party–dominated party system did not emerge during the Obama years. The parties, it seems, will remain evenly divided and at war for the time being, even taking into account the GOP's big 2010 win.

The Democratic and Republican Parties Today

9.3 Compare and contrast today's Republican and Democratic parties

The Democratic and Republican parties don't look much like parties in other rich democratic countries. In most of them, the political parties are hierarchically structured organizations led by full-time party professionals and are traditionally committed to a set of ideological principles. They also tend to have clearly defined membership requirements, centralized control over party nominations and electoral financing, and disciplinary authority over elected party members in the national parliament and cabinet ministries. The major American parties have almost none of these qualities, although the Republicans have become much more ideologically cohesive than has traditionally been the case in American politics.

The Parties as Organizations

The Republican and Democratic parties are not organizations in the usual sense of the term, but rather loose collections of local and state parties, campaign committees, candidates and officeholders, and associated interest and advocacy groups that get together every four years to nominate a presidential candidate. Unlike a corporation, a bureaucratic agency, a military organization, or even a political party in most other countries, the official leaders of the major American parties cannot issue orders that get passed down a chain of command. Even popular, charismatic, and skillful presidents, including George Washington, Abraham Lincoln, Woodrow Wilson, Franklin Roosevelt, Harry Truman, John Kennedy, and Ronald Reagan, have had nearly as much trouble controlling the many diverse and independent groups and individuals within their own parties as they have had dealing with the opposition. George W. Bush discovered this in his second term when a significant number of Republican members of the House and Senate, loyal followers throughout his first term, abandoned him on his plans for a pathway to citizenship for many undocumented immigrants.

Party Membership   The ill-defined nature of Republican and Democratic party membership is another indicator of how different American political parties are from political parties in other countries, as well as from private organizations. What does it mean, in fact, to be a Republican or a Democrat in the United States? Americans do not join parties in the sense of paying dues and receiving a membership card. To Americans, being a member of a party may mean voting most of the time for the candidate of a party or choosing to become a candidate of one of them. Or it may mean voting in a party primary. Or it may mean contributing money to, or otherwise helping in, a local, state, or national campaign of one of the party candidates. Or it may just mean generally preferring one party

The Shifting Geography of the Parties

Introduction The centers of strength of each of the major political parties changed during the last half century. In 1960 the Democrats tended to dominate in the southern states and in the industrial states of the Middle Atlantic and upper Midwest, while Republicans were particularly strong in parts of New England, the Great Plains, the Mountain West, and the Pacific Coast. Until 2004, the Plains and Mountain West states (other than Colorado) had become more reliably Republican, and the South moved solidly into the Republican column. At the same time, the Pacific Coast and New England became more reliably Democratic. In the 2008 election, Barack

Obama's big victory can be attributed to his success in former Republican or battleground states, including Colorado, New Mexico, Iowa, Indiana, Ohio, Virginia, North Carolina, and Florida. Because of population shifts, moreover, the distribution of electoral votes has shifted among the states over time, changing the calculations of those who plan and wage presidential campaigns.

Mapping Party Electoral Votes The states in the three cartograms are sized in proportion to their electoral votes in presidential elections and colored by whether they cast their electoral votes

for Democrats (blue) or Republicans (red) in 1960 (the cartogram on the left), 2004 (the cartogram on the upper right), and 2008 (the cartogram on the lower right). Because each state's electoral votes are the total of their representatives and senators in Congress, they are roughly proportional to the size of their populations. We can see at least three important things in the cartograms. First, between 1960 and 2004, electoral votes of the Middle Atlantic states, New England, and the upper Midwest decreased while they increased in California, the Southwest, and the South, reflecting the shift in the populations of the states over this time period. Second, both the 1960 and 2004 elections were extremely close, but the states that came together to elect Democrat John F. Kennedy in 1960 and those that combined to elect George W. Bush in 2004 were quite different, although there is some overlap. These changes have changed the strategies of the parties. The Democrats could pretty much count on winning California, Washington, Illinois, the New England states, New York, and New Jersey; Republicans could count on the South outside of Florida and the Southwest, Mountain West, and Plains states. The remaining states— often called battleground states— are where presidential campaigns recently have been waged today and where presidential elections have been won and lost. Third, comparing the 2004 and 2008 cartograms, you can see how the Democrats constructed their victory in the presidential election. Interestingly,

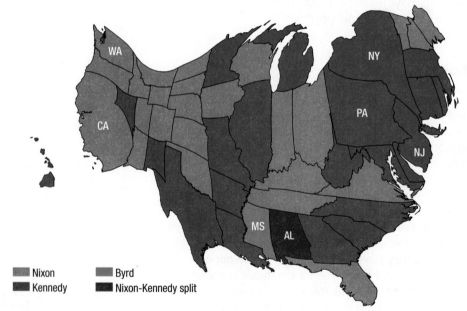

Nixon
Kennedy
Byrd
Nixon-Kennedy split

States by Number of Presidential Electoral Votes in the 1960 Election

over another most of the time. These are loose criteria for membership, to say the least—looser than for virtually any other organization that might be imagined.

However, membership in the sense of feeling closer to and identifying with one party or another—what political scientists call **party identification**—has proved to be a very powerful thing indeed. As

party identification
The sense of belonging to one or another political party.

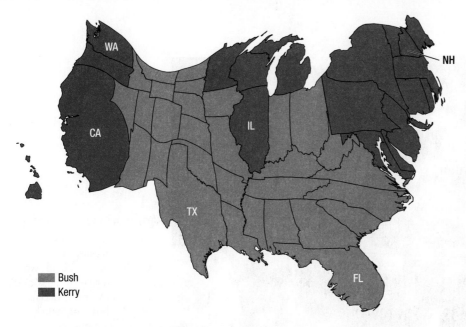

States by Number of Presidential Electoral Votes in the 2004 Election

Bush
Kerry

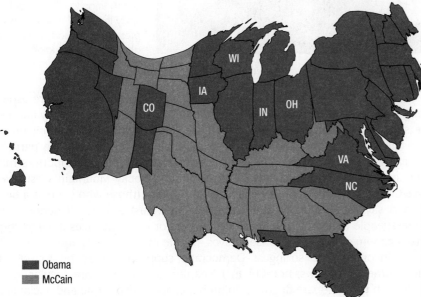

Obama
McCain

States by Number of Presidential Electoral Votes in the 2008 Election

Standard US Map

the Republican strategist and presidential advisor Karl Rove believed the 2004 electoral map ensured Republican dominance for the near future; Democratic strategists Howard Dean and Rahm Emmanuel thought the 2008 map portended the same for the Democrats.

What Do You Think? Why does it make sense to elect presidents by electoral votes rather than direct popular vote when so many states are safe for one party or the other? Some critics argue that having so many noncompetitive states in the Electoral College, with the bulk of the electioneering going on in the handful of states where the outcome is in doubt, deprives the majority of Americans of being fully engaged in the process of electing the president. How would you support this argument? How would you dispute it?

Map note: In 1960, Mississippi electoral votes were cast for Harry Byrd, an independent candidate. Alabama split its 11 electoral votes: 6 for Kennedy and 5 for Nixon.

Source: Election data are from historical tables, U.S. Bureau of the Census, *Statistical Abstract of the United States,* 2010.

suggested in Chapter 5, a majority of Americans say they identify with one of the two major parties. Party identification is important on a number of accounts. Most importantly, what party one identifies with and how strongly one holds that identification shapes how a person feels about a wide range of public issues, how likely that person is to vote, and which candidates the person votes for (see Chapter 10). (Party identification is addressed in greater depth later in this chapter.)

TOUCHING BASE WITH THE BASE Sarah Palin, the Republican party's nominee for vice president in 2008, was used most of the time by the McCain campaign to excite and mobilize the GOP base, especially religious conservatives. Here, she signs autographs at a rally at Capital University, a Christian college in Columbus, Ohio. Why is it so important for candidates to "rally the base" when the base is presumably already enthusiastic about their candidate?

Among party identifiers one can identify groups of people who are especially strong supporters of the party and its candidates at all levels. Each party has a set of core supporters—often called the party base—upon which it can count for votes, campaign contributions, and activists to advance the fortunes of the parties and their candidates for elected office.[20] The strongest Republican supporters may be found among whites (particularly in the South and Rocky Mountain West), conservative Christians and the most religiously committed (those who express a belief in God and say they regularly attend religious services) among all denominations, businesspeople (whether small business owners or top executives in large corporations), economic and social conservatives, people in rural areas, and those with the highest incomes. The strongest Democratic supporters may be found among African Americans, Jews, non-Cuban Hispanics, people who are secular in belief, people with postgraduate degrees, union households, economic and social liberals, people living on the West Coast and the Northeast, and lower-income people. Democrats find strong support, as well, among teachers and other government employees at the local, state, and national levels,[21] and people living in university towns and science and technology research centers such as the Silicon Valley (stretching from San Jose to San Francisco), Austin, Seattle, Boulder, the Research Triangle area in North Carolina, and the Route 128 economic corridor around Boston and Cambridge.[22]

Increasingly in recent years, Republicans and Democrats have tried to win elections by first mobilizing these core supporters—in a process often called "rallying the base"—by focusing on issues and symbolic gestures that will bring them to the polls, then trying to win a majority among those voters not automatically predisposed to one party or the other

? Are there ways to break the mold of election campaigns in which each party tries to mobilize its base as its first order of business, causing our politics to be so partisan and uncivil?

(Catholics are a good example, as are self-identified independents). In a situation where Republican and Democratic core supporters are about equal in strength—which was especially true between 1994 and 2004—winning even a small majority among these less partisan groups while mobilizing one's own partisans is the key to winning elections. Issue and ideological appeals are important in these efforts.

Party Organizations as Candidate-Centered   Unlike a traditional organization and unlike political parties in other democracies, the various elements of the Democratic and Republican parties are relatively independent from one another and act in concert not on the basis of orders, but on the basis of shared interests, sentiment, ideology, and the desire to win elections,[23] which can be quite powerful coordinators of party activities, to be sure. (See Figure 9.2 for a graphical representation of these ideas.) Most important, perhaps, the official party organizations do not control the nomination of candidates running under the party label—their most vital political role—or the flow of money that funds electoral campaigns or the behavior of its officeholders once elected. This was apparent in 2010 when Tea Party candidates enjoyed great success in wresting the Republican nominations for congressional and gubernatorial seats away from candidates favored by party leaders. In the past, party candidates were usually nominated in district, state, and national conventions, where party regulars played a major role. They are now almost exclusively nominated in primaries or grassroots caucuses in the states, where the party organizations help but do not run the show. Nomination comes to those who are best able to raise money, gain access to the media, form their own campaign organizations, and win the support of powerful interest and advocacy groups (such as the National Rifle Association in the GOP and the National

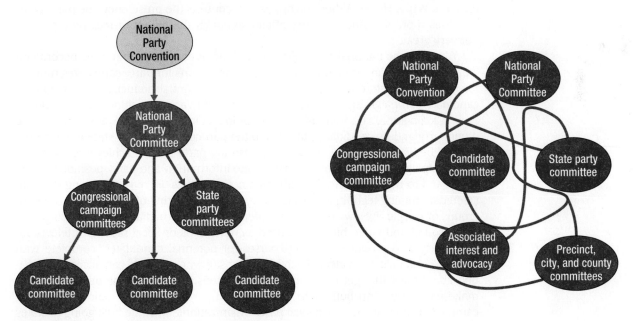

FIGURE 9.2   Political Party Organization in the United States

The graphic on the left shows a hypothetical organizational chart of the Republican and Democratic parties as if they were structured hierarchically like many other organizations you are familiar with. It would be a mistake, however, to think of our national parties this way. The drawing on the right, which depicts our national parties as network or weblike organizations, where there is neither central authority nor a chain of command, is closer to reality. The ties between elements of the parties include money, ideology, sentiment, and common interests.

Education Association in the Democratic Party). To a very large extent, Democratic and Republican party organizations are there to help candidates in these efforts, not order them about.[24] They have become, in effect, campaign machines in the service of candidates running for elected office.[25] It is because of this that many commentators have come to describe American political parties as being "candidate-centered."[26]

The Party Conventions

The national party conventions are the governing bodies of the parties. Convention delegates meet every four years not only to nominate presidential and vice presidential candidates but also to write a party platform and revise party rules. (See Chapter 10 for more detail on the role of party conventions.)

Although the national convention is the formal governing body of each of the parties, it cannot dictate to party candidates or party organizations at other levels of jurisdiction. The presidential nominee need not adhere to either the letter or the spirit of the party platform, for instance, although most nominees stay fairly close to the platform most of the time (usually because the winning candidate's supporters control the platform-writing committee). State and local party organizations may nominate whomever they choose to run for public office and may or may not support key planks in the national party's platform.

National Party Committees

The Democratic and Republican national committees conduct the business of the parties during the four years between national conventions. The national committees are made up of elected committeemen and committeewomen from each of the states, a sizable staff, and a chairperson, but they rarely meet. The real business of the committee is run by the party chair, assisted by the committee staff. The chair exercises little power when a president from the party is in office because the party chair is compelled to take direction from the White House. When the opposition controls the presidency, the party chair exercises more influence in party affairs, although the extent of that power is still not very great.

Although the national committees have little direct power, they have become increasingly important as campaign service organizations for party candidates running for national and state offices.[27] In addition to substantial financial contributions to candidate campaign organizations, they do a wide variety of things to help. Out of their Washington, D.C., in-house TV and radio studios come attack ads aimed at the other party and its candidates, tailored to the particular district or state in which the ads will be used. Other ads extol the sponsoring party and its achievements. Direct mail campaigns are mounted to disseminate information and party positions on the issues and to make appeals for campaign contributions, increasingly using sophisticated data-mining techniques to allow very narrow targeting of messages to different groups of people.[28] News releases are prepared for the media, as are campaign-oriented sound and video bites to be used as news clips on local radio and television. Each party also produces training courses for potential candidates, complete with "how-to" manuals and videos. Each has a website where people can access information about the party, get news about the nefarious behavior of the opposition, and make monetary contributions to the party and party candidates. And, they funnel campaign money to state and local party organizations, with the bulk going to states where competition between the parties is closest.[29]

To carry out these activities, both the Republican and Democratic national committees have steadily increased the number of employees in their national offices, especially in the areas of finance, advertising, information technology, campaign planning, and video specialist and support personnel, and they have expanded their budgets to carry out an ever-broader range of campaign activities for party candidates. Each of the national committees has become a highly professionalized campaign

MOVING JOE OUT   Some advocacy groups with close ties to political parties demand that party candidates adhere closely to some ideological standard as the price for their support. Here, the executive director of MoveOn.org, a very liberal organization, speaks in support of challenger Ned Lamont in his battle for the Democratic nomination for the Senate in Connecticut in 2008 against the fairly conservative incumbent, Joe Lieberman. Lamont won the Democratic nomination but ran as an independent and won the Senate seat in the general election. How important is it for parties to have advocacy groups to keep them in line ideologically—as the Tea Party is doing today in ensuring that Republicans stay conservative—or do parties need more ideological diversity to win in November?

organization, filled with highly skilled people able to provide party candidates with what they need to wage first-rate electoral campaigns.

Congressional Campaign Committees   Almost as old as the national party committees, but entirely independent of them, are the four congressional campaign committees—Republican and Democratic, for the House and for the Senate—that aid members of Congress in their campaigns for reelection. They help raise money, provide media services (e.g., making short videotapes of the members of Congress for local television news shows), conduct research, and do whatever else the party members in Congress deem appropriate. Increasingly, these committees have turned their attention to identifying and encouraging quality party candidates in districts and states where competition between the parties is close. Rahm Emanuel (D–IL), later President Obama's chief of staff, did this particularly well during the 2005–2006 elections cycle when he was head of the Democratic House Campaign Committee; many gave him the main credit for the Democrats' retaking the House in the 2006 elections.[30] These committees are controlled by the party members in Congress, not the party chair, the national committees, or even the president. Much as with the national committees, the congressional campaign committees have become highly professionalized and well funded.[31]

State Party Organizations   As expected in a federal system, separate political party organizations exist in each of the states. Although tied together by bonds of

ideology, sentiment, and campaign money and constrained in what they can do by rules set by the national party committees and conventions—rules on how and when to choose delegates to the national convention, for example—the state party organizations are relatively independent of one another and of the national party.

Associated Interest and Advocacy Groups Although not technically part of the formal party organizations, some groups are so closely involved in the affairs of the parties that it is hard to draw a line between them and the political parties.[32] The American Conservative Union, for example, is barely distinguishable from the Republican Party; it contributes campaign money almost exclusively to GOP candidates, encourages people it trusts on the issues to run in the Republican primaries, and plays an important role in the selection of delegates to the Republican National Convention. Organized labor has had a similar relationship with the Democratic Party since the Great Depression and the New Deal.

The main effect of the rise of advocacy groups in recent years has been to push the parties and their candidates into more ideological and partisan directions. MoveOn.org, for example, and liberal blogs such as the Daily Kos, push Democrats to be more assertive in opposing Republicans, offering a more liberal policy agenda, and pushing the candidacy of people they favor—such as Ned Lamont over long-time Democratic senator Joseph Lieberman in the 2006 Connecticut senate primary race. Republican advocacy groups, talk radio hosts such as Glenn Beck, and conservative blogs push the party and its candidates to oppose abortion and more open borders for immigrants and to favor tax cuts and fewer government regulations. We look at the issue of ideology in the parties in more detail in the next section.

Party Ideologies

Ideology may be understood as a coherently organized set of beliefs about the fundamental nature of a good society and the role government ought to play in achieving it. Because the Republican and Democratic parties have traditionally organized themselves as fairly broad coalitions, seeking to attract as many voters as possible in order to prevail in winner-take-all, single-member-district elections, there always have been strong pressures on them to tone down matters of ideology.[33] However, each party also has a core of loyal supporters and party activists, such as delegates to the party convention and caucus attendees, contributors to election campaigns, and closely allied advocacy groups, who are more ideologically oriented than the general public (nearly 40 percent of whom call themselves independents). Each party, moreover, has a stable core set of voters from groups concerned about particular issues and problems and committed to particular government policies. The result is a party system composed of parties with significant and growing ideological and policy unity within them and differences between them.[34] One veteran observer even claims that today "political leaders on both sides now feel a relentless pressure for party discipline and intellectual conformity more common in parliamentary systems than through most of American history."[35]

While Americans of all political stripes hold a range of core beliefs about free enterprise, individualism, the Constitution, and the Bill of Rights, the differences between Democrats and Republicans are becoming clearer every day. The Republican Party tends to endorse positions held by social and economic conservatives; for example, opposing abortion and same-sex marriage and regulating business, higher taxes, and generous social safety nets. The Democratic Party tends to endorse positions held by social and economic liberals; for example, supporting a strong government role in guiding the economy, protecting the environment, and providing civil rights protections for minority groups and gays and lesbians. Ideological and policy differences between the Democrats and Republicans are becoming so marked, and the tendency of the Republicans to become a more internally cohesive conservative party is so pronounced, that a number of observers now talk about the "Europeanization" of the American party system.[36] Pressure from Tea Party activists on candidates for nominations in the Republican Party in 2010 helped make the GOP even more conservative than it had been.

Let's see how ideological and policies differences manifest themselves in our political parties.

Ideology and Party in Public Perceptions For one thing, the Democratic and Republican parties differ in the electorate's perceptions of them; 79 percent of Americans, for example, report that they see the parties as different on a whole range of issues, up from 64 percent in 2004.[37] Most accurately see the Democrats as the more **liberal** party (in the sense of favoring an active federal government; helping citizens with jobs, education, and medical care; supporting a woman's right to choose; and protecting civil rights) and the Republicans as the more **conservative** party (opposing such government activism, supporting business, and opposing abortion and same-sex marriage).[38] (See Figure 9.3.) Democrats, moreover, are much more likely to say they are liberals; Republicans are much more likely than others to say they are conservative.[39] Additionally, those Americans who classify themselves as liberals overwhelmingly support Democratic candidates; self-described conservatives overwhelmingly support Republicans. In 2008, for example, 90 percent of self-identified Republicans voted for John McCain for president, while 89 percent of Democrats voted for Barack Obama. This

liberal

The political position, combining both economic and social dimensions, that holds that the federal government has a substantial role to play in economic regulation, social welfare, and overcoming racial inequality, and that abortion and stem-cell research should be legal and the civil rights of gays and racial minorities protected.

conservative

The political position, combining both economic and social dimensions, that holds that the federal government ought to play a very small role in economic regulation, social welfare, and overcoming racial inequality, that abortion should be illegal, and that family values and law and order should guide public policies.

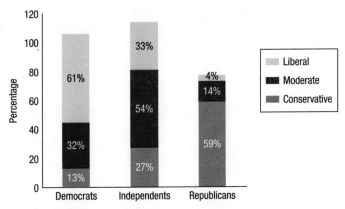

FIGURE 9.3 Party Identification and Ideology, 2008

Party identification and political ideology go hand-in-hand, something that has not always been the case in the United States. In 2008, at a time when Democrats enjoyed a big lead over Republicans in the proportion of Americans who identified with them, their supporters were overwhelmingly liberal. Among the minority Republicans, only a tiny percentage of their identifiers called themselves liberal. Not surprisingly, perhaps, a majority of independents—the largest group among Americans—defined its ideology as moderate. *Source:* Pew Research Center, "Trends in Political Values and Core Attitudes: 1987–2009" (Washington, D.C.: Pew Research Center for the People and the Press, report released May 21, 2009).

association of liberalism with the Democrats and conservatism with the Republicans is growing stronger all the time, with the gap in outlooks between the two parties growing ever larger.[40]

Ideology and Policies in Party Platforms Our parties also tend to write political platforms at their conventions that differ significantly from one another. Scholars have discovered persistent differences in the platforms of the two parties in terms of rhetoric (Republicans tend to talk more about opportunity and freedom), issues (Democrats worry more about poverty and social welfare), and the public policies advocated.[41]

The Ideologies of Party Activists The activists of one party are quite different in their views from activists and voters in the other party, as well as the general public. Republican delegates to the 2008 Republican National Convention, for example, as in all recent conventions, were more conservative than Republican voters and much more conservative than the average registered voter (see Table 9.2). They were also much more hostile to affirmative action, same-sex marriage, social spending programs, and

TABLE 9.2 Comparing Delegates to the 2008 National Party Conventions with Other Americans

	Delegates to Democratic National Convention	Democratic Voters	All Voters	Republican Voters	Delegates to This Republican National Convention
Is it more important to provide **health care** coverage for all Americans or hold down taxes? (percent saying "health care")	94	90	67	40	7
Looking back, do you think the United States did the right thing in taking military action against **Iraq**, or should the U.S. have stayed out? (percent saying "right thing")	2	14	37	70	80
Should protecting the environment or developing new sources of **energy** be a higher priority for the government? (percent saying "environment")	25	30	21	9	3
Should **abortion** be generally available to those who want it, be available but under stricter limits than it is now, or should it not be permitted? (percent saying "should not be permitted")	3	16	24	37	43
Should **gay couples** be allowed to legally marry, be allowed to form civil unions but not legally marry, or should there be no legal recognition? (percent choosing "same-sex marriage")	55	49	34	11	6

Source: New York Times/CBS News poll, September 1, 2008.

gun control than Republican voters and registered voters in general. Analogously, delegates to the Democratic National Convention were more liberal than Democratic voters and registered voters and much more favorable to gun control, affirmative action, gay rights, and a woman's right to an abortion than the other two groups.[42]

Divisions Within the Parties While differences between Democrats and Republicans have become more pronounced, and while ideological and policy cohesion within the parties has been increasing, especially in the GOP, there are still important disagreements within each of the parties.[43] There is not perfect unity, as one might have found in the past within communist and socialist parties, let us say, or as exists today in Islamist parties such as the Muslim Brotherhood in Egypt. The division in the Democratic Party is between a very liberal wing—found among Democratic activists and advocacy groups and among most officeholders in the West Coast and northeastern states—and a more "centrist" wing—typified by moderates elected in traditionally Republican areas such as senators Ben Nelson (D-NB), Max Baucus (D-MT), and Jim Webb (D-VA). The liberal wing supports traditional Democratic Party programs in which government plays a central role in societal improvement, leveling the playing field for minorities and women, supporting gay rights, protecting union jobs, providing substantial social safety nets, protecting civil liberties, and trying to avoid the use of military power in foreign affairs. The smaller centrist wing of the party tends to opposes racial preferences and supports lower taxes, free trade, deregulation, a crackdown on crime, and a strong military supported by a large defense budget.

? Does the fact that party activists tend to be more extreme in their ideology than most party supporters and voters damage the democratic process? How well does party activity represent the majority of voters who support the party?

Fissures have existed for a long time in the Republican Party, with the main fault line running between conservatives (including social and economic conservatives) and moderates (including social and economic moderates). The fissure widened during the Republican Bush administration, when seemingly intrusive and expensive programs such as No Child Left Behind and the Medicare prescription drug benefit were sponsored and supported by a Republican president. The fissure became a canyon in

? Does division within the political parties translate to healthy and productive debate that can help set party priorities? Or are such disagreements among the party faithful threatening to the power of the party?

2010 as party functionaries, supporters, and activists tried to explain the GOP's big electoral defeats in the 2006 and 2008 national elections and argued about how to revive the party's fortunes. The small moderate wing believed these elections were lost because the party had become too narrowly conservative, losing its appeal to independent voters. It wanted the GOP to play down the party's opposition to immigration and stem-cell research and to acknowledge an important role for government in keeping the economy on a steady course and helping out those hurt by the Great Recession (though without too much regulation or additional taxes, to be sure). The much larger conservative wing, represented by congressional leaders like House minority leader John Boehner (R–OH), Senate minority leader Mitch McConnell (R–KY), talk show hosts Rush Limbaugh and Glenn Beck, Sarah Palin, and Tea Party activists, among others, believed that past electoral defeats could be traced to Republicans not being conservative enough. In their view, the party should get back to emphasizing conservative economic and social principles, including law and order, small government, minimally regulated business, and

GLENN FIRES UP THE CROWD
TV personality Glenn Beck is shown here addressing attendees at the annual gathering in Washington in 2010 of the Conservative Political Action Committee. Beck and CPAC are major forces in the most conservative wing of the Republican Party that is now in the ascendency in the GOP. Why have moderates in the Republican Party had such a hard time recently?

support for traditional families. The small moderate wing believed there were times when cooperation with Democrats is acceptable; the conservative wing believed that defeating the Democrats and stopping President Obama's programs are both right and politically rational. In the run-up to the 2010 elections, it became clear that the conservative wing had won the day within the party, with moderates pushed out at the nomination stage or forced to take on more conservative positions as the price for electoral survival.

The Parties in Government and in the Electorate

The Republican and Democratic parties exist not only as network-like organizations of candidates, activists, contributors, and interest and advocacy groups, but as a presence in government and in the electorate.

Government   Fearful of the tyrannical possibilities of a vigorous government, the framers designed a system of government in which power is so fragmented and competitive that effectiveness is unlikely. One of the roles that political parties can play in a democracy such as ours is to overcome this deadlock by persuading officials of the same party in the different branches of government to cooperate with one another on the basis of party loyalty.[44] The constitutionally designed conflict between the president and Congress can be bridged, it has been argued, when there is **unified government**—when a single party controls both houses of Congress and the presidency—as the Democrats did during much of the 1960s and during Barack Obama's presidency in 2009 and 2010, and the Republicans did between 2001 and 2006 when George W. Bush was in office. When the parties are strong and unified, this bridging can occur even when a party controls the legislative branch with the tiniest of margins. (See "Using the Framework.") On the other hand, the existence of strong parties during periods of divided government, when Republicans and Democrats each control a branch of the federal government—as in 1995–2000 when Democrat Bill Clinton was president and the Republicans controlled both houses of Congress—often leads to **gridlock,** when very little gets done.[45]

It matters a great deal whether Democrats or Republicans control the House, the Senate, and the presidency because the two parties differ in what they do when they win control of government. Republican members of Congress tend to vote differently from Democrats; for example, the former are considerably more economically and socially

unified government

Control of the executive and legislative branches by the same political party.

gridlock

A situation in which things cannot get done in Washington, usually because of divided government.

282

How did Republicans manage to pass so many laws with such small majorities after they came to power in 2001?

Background: In the 1990s, official Washington seemed to grind to a screeching halt. Divided government was the rule. Not only was major legislation tough to come by, but partisan warfare between a Republican-dominated Congress and a Democratic president (Clinton) led to a budget crisis that twice closed the federal government (except for essential services) and to the impeachment of Bill Clinton on a straight party-line vote in the House. After the election of George W. Bush in 2000, however, new bills were passed with a fair degree of regularity despite very slim majorities

for Republicans in Congress: three different tax cuts, No Child Left Behind, a new prescription drug benefit under Medicare, creation of the Department of Homeland Security, the USA Patriot Act, restrictions on class-action lawsuits, the Energy Policy Act of 2005, the Bankruptcy Act of 2005, and the Sarbanes-Oxley Act regulating corporate accounting practices. Taking a look at how structural, political linkage, and governmental factors affect policymaking in Washington will help explain the changed situation from 2001 through 2005.

Structure	Separation of powers and checks and balances in the Constitution make gridlock the "default" condition in Washington. ➡	The end of the Cold War ended the semi-crisis atmosphere that encouraged the political parties in Congress, and the Congress and the president, to cooperate with one another on a wide range of issues. ➡	The sense of patriotism and shared threat arising from the 9/11 attacks created a brief period of Democratic-Republican and presidential-congressional cooperation in late 2001/ early 2002.

Political Linkage

The political parties became more ideological, with the virtual disappearance of conservative Democrats in the South and Mountain West and liberal Republicans in New England. ➡

Partisan warfare and scandals became standard fare in the mass media, making cooperation and civility in public affairs, in general, and between the parties, in particular, less likely.

Neither party enjoyed a commanding lead in party identification nationally during the 1990s or 2000s. ➡

Congressional elections became very close and hotly contested, with control of Congress hanging in the balance every two years, so partisanship increased.

Government

Because of their extremely high levels of party unity and discipline in both houses of Congress, but especially in the House of Representatives, Republicans were able to control the legislative agenda without much need of help from the Democrats, even though they held very slim majorities in the House and Senate.

From 1995 through 2000, divided government was the rule, with Republican majorities in the House and Senate and a Democratic president, Bill Clinton. ➡

The elections of 2000, 2002, and 2004 resulted in unified government, with Republicans in control of Congress and the presidency.

Government Action

Major bills are passed by Congress and signed into law by President Bush.

conservative on domestic issues. This difference translates into public policy. Republicans and Democrats produce different policies on taxes, corporate regulation, abortion and stem-cell research, and social welfare when they are in power.[46] It also matters whether a single party controls Congress and the presidency or whether control is divided between two parties not only for what bills become law but also for the composition of the federal judiciary and for what policies are implemented and what actions are taken by executive branch agencies. Consideration of the many complex issues associated with how political parties act in office and why it matters will be left to chapters later in this book that look in depth at the branches of the federal government. We will learn more about what parties do in government and what happens when government is unified or divided in the chapters on Congress (Chapter 11), the president (Chapter 12), the executive branch (Chapter 13), and the courts (Chapter 14).

The Electorate Parties are not only political organizations and sets of officeholders in government, but also images in the minds of voters and potential voters—that is, mental cues that affect the behavior of the electorate. This aspect of the parties is called party identification, as we discussed in Chapter 5. The distribution of party identification among the American people is important on a number of grounds. First, party identification helps determine people's political attitudes on a wide range of issues[47]; for a majority of Americans, party identity is a stable and powerful shaper of one's overall political identity. People use the party label to help organize their thinking about politics: to guide them in voting, judging new policy proposals, and evaluating the government's performance.[48] Second, how the parties stand relative to one another in the affections of the American people has a lot to do with which party controls the presidency, Congress, and, eventually, the federal courts. That distribution has changed over time and has affected what government does. (How party identification is measured by political scientists is shown in the "By the Numbers" feature.)

Beginning at the time of Roosevelt's highly popular New Deal in the 1930s and continuing to the late 1980s, the Democratic lead over Republicans among party identifiers was substantial, making them the majority party. At times their advantage was on the order of 35 percentage points. From the 1980s until quite recently, the Democrats lost their big lead but still enjoyed a consistent advantage, though the parties were pretty much even in popular sentiment in 1991, 1995, and 2003. Between 2004 and 2008, the Democratic advantage over Republicans increased. This happened because more Americans became Democratic identifiers during these years and fewer favored the Republicans—though the biggest change was the increase in the proportion of Americans who call themselves independents (see Figure 9.4). (Democrats lost their lead in 2010, however—a product, most likely, of the economic recession and the jobless recovery.) In general, however, because the parties have been relatively close to one another in terms of party identification among the American public since the late 1980s, even very small swings from election to election in Democratic and Republican voting turnout have had big effects on who wins and loses in presidential and congressional contests. Barack Obama's strong "get out the vote" effort among Democrats and independents helped him win big in the 2008 presidential election.

While Democratic and Republican identifiers are moving farther apart, the distances are even

? Do you think that political parties will one day cease to exist, their function of linking the public and government replaced by more direct means such as interactive television or other media? Would citizens' direct involvement in government support democratic goals, or is mediation by party organizations an essential element of democratic deliberation?

Percent

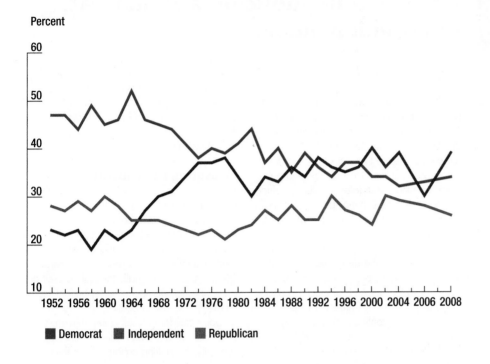

■ Democrat   ■ Independent   ■ Republican

FIGURE 9.4 Trends in Party Identification

The decades-long gap between the percentages of those who call themselves Democrats and those who call themselves Republicans had been getting smaller. This was happening because fewer Americans than in the 1950s were identifying as Democrats and more were identifying as independents. From 2006, the gap between Democrats and Republicans widened once again, primarily because of a significant drop in Republican identifiers, with independents accounting for most of the gain. After that, Democratic fortunes sank in the face of the lingering ill effects of the Great Recession—this is not shown in the graph—while Democratic President Obama occupied the White House. If these trends continue, how might the landscape of American politics change? *Source:* American National Election Studies, 2008.

greater between Democratic and Republican **active partisans,** those Republican and Democratic identifiers who not only vote but are engaged in other party, candidate, and party-support activities, such as making campaign contributions, attending candidate meetings, putting bumper stickers on their cars, and the like. Democratic active partisans are strongly liberal, with, for example, 78 percent supporting abortion, 70 percent supporting the use of diplomacy over force in international relations, and 70 percent favoring environmental protection over job protection. For their part, Republican active partisans are a near mirror image, reporting only 41 percent, 11 percent, and 24 percent approval, respectively, for these things.[49]

The proportion of people who say they are independents—including **leaners,** or those who say they are independents but lean slightly to one party or another—has steadily increased, from the low 20s in the 1960s to the high 30s today (the remainder are respondents who choose "no preference" or "don't know"). Although some scholars maintain that these figures exaggerate the rise of independents because many leaners behave the same way as people who say they consider themselves Republicans or Democrats[50]—in 2009, 17 percent of independents said they leaned Democratic, while 12 percent leaned Republican[51]—there has clearly been a decline in the proportion of Americans who identify with either of the two major parties. Oddly, then, while a growing proportion of the American population is calling itself independent, views about public policies in the United States are becoming increasingly polarized along party lines, primarily because partisans vote more than independents and participate more in campaigns, electing more liberal Democrats and conservative Republicans and fewer moderates in either party. Independents tell journalists, pollsters, and scholars that they are fed up with the general nastiness in politics and government ineffectiveness that seems to be associated with the intensification of partisanship in the political life of the country.[52]

active partisan

People who identify with a party, vote in elections, and participate in additional party and party-candidate activities.

leaners

People who claim to be independents but consistently favor one party over another.

Are you a Republican, a Democrat, or an independent?

One often hears people refer to themselves as a Republican or a Democrat or an independent. But what does that mean? Do people formally join a party organization? Do they fill out a paper or online form, pay annual membership dues, receive membership cards to slip into their wallets, and attend meetings with other members? Is it like joining, let us say, a labor union like the United Automobile Workers or the Screenwriters Guild? Is it like joining a service organization like the Rotary or a religious organization like the Knights of Columbus? Or is it like joining the Social Democratic Party in Germany where people do, in fact, join the party organization? And where do independents go in the United States? Who do they join? These questions are, of course, rhetorical. To be a Republican or a Democrat or an independent for most people in the United States—except for people who are, let us say, employed by or do volunteer work for the Democratic or Republican National Committees—is really a matter of sentiment, about which party one identifies with most of the time.

Why It Matters As you have learned in this chapter and in Chapter 5 on public opinion, one's party identification is very important in how one thinks about issues and decides who to vote for. Notice the directionality in this statement. There is growing evidence that people do not take on a party identification after assessing the issues and the candidates for elective office but the other way around: party identification does most of the shaping. Party identification matters not only because it influences the choices people make in politics but also because the distribution of party identifiers in the population is decisive in determining the outcome of elections and who controls the government. This is because party identifiers almost always vote for candidates with their preferred party's label. During times when Democratic identifiers enjoy strong pluralities—that is, when there are substantially more Democratic identifiers than Republican ones or people who say they are independents—they dominate elective office. When self-declared independents lead the other categories and

the proportions identifying with the two major parties are very close, elections are close and likely to go in unpredictable directions or switch from one election to the next given the "unanchored" status of independent voters.

Measuring Party Identification
Every major polling organization—whether commercial like Gallup, or nonprofit like Pew, or academic/scholarly like the American National Election Study at the University of Michigan—asks people one form or another of the question: "Generally speaking, do you usually think of yourself as a Republican, Democrat, independent, or what?" (Pew); or "In politics, as of today, do you consider yourself a Republican, a Democrat, or an independent?" (Gallup). Typically, the polling organizations then ask people who have answered Republican or Democrat whether they consider themselves to be strong or weak Republicans and Democrats. Independents are asked if they generally lean toward one of the two major parties, or whether they tend to vote for

Using the DEMOCRACY STANDARD

How do our major political parties affect democracy?

Democratic theorists, you will recall, believe that vigorous and healthy political parties are essential for democracy. They are essential because, in theory at least, they are among the principal political institutions that can make popular sovereignty and political equality a reality. They are able to do so—again in theory—because they can help keep elected officials responsive and responsible to the broad public, stimulate interest and participation among ordinary Americans, include a broad range of groups from all economic and social levels of the population, simplify voter choices, and make government work for the people by overcoming the problems of democratic government created by the separation of powers and checks and balances. For all these reasons, of course, the framers looked askance at political parties and worried about their effects on republican government. They were not inclined to include all groups in the population in political life, they were certainly not interested in stimulating widespread interest and participation by ordinary Americans, and they most certainly were not in favor of an institution that might overcome the constraints on the national government they had created.

The framers might have rested a bit easier had they known that our political parties were never quite able to fulfill their democratic promise primarily because the constitutional system they created makes it hard for even unified parties, swept into power by electoral majorities, to get their way. In the Senate, for example, a unified

candidates of one party or the other. These so-called leaners, according to some researchers, tend to vote for the candidates of a particular party almost as frequently as people who pick a party identification. Other researchers are not convinced.

Party Identification in the United States, 2009 by the Pew Research Center

Source: The Pew Research Center

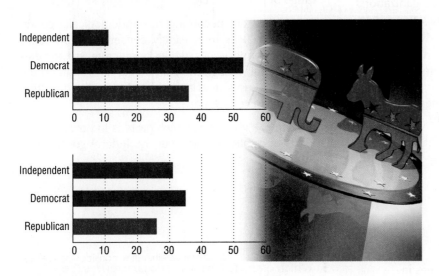

Party Identification in the United States, 2009 by the Harris Poll

Source: Harris Poll, 2009

minority party representing a minority of Americans (because each state gets two senators no matter the size of its population) can block important bills favored by the majority party. Still, our parties are the only mechanism we have for allowing voters to decide on a program for the government and to hold elected officials responsible in a collective sense, even if imperfectly. Interest groups and social movements are much too narrow in their outlooks and policy objectives, and voters have no control over what they do. Our parties are becoming better organized and more ideologically distinctive and clearer on the policy alternatives offered to the public, so voters increasingly know what they are getting when they put a party into office. However, the rise in the ideological coherence of the parties, potentially a boon to responsiveness and responsibility in government when a single party controls the presidency and Congress, adds to the possibilities of gridlock in periods of divided government.

SUMMARY

9.1 Evaluate the importance of political parties in democracies

- Theoretically, the electoral activities of political parties enable citizens to determine what the government does and to hold elected leaders accountable for achieving or failing to achieve what they promise.

- Theoretically, some of the gridlock built into our constitutional system can be overcome when the same party controls more than one branch of government.

9.2 Distinguish American political parties from parties in other democracies

- The American party system is unique among the Western democracies in that it is a relatively pure two-party system and has been so since the 1830s.

- The American parties are candidate-centered, having very little power in their national party organizations to affect the behavior of individual candidates, office-holders, or state and local party organizations.

- American parties traditionally have been less unified internally and less ideologically coherent than parties in many other democracies, although partisanship between the parties and ideological coherence within the parties are becoming much more pronounced and politically important.

9.3 Compare and contrast today's Republican and Democratic parties

- The Republican and Democratic parties differ from one another in the demographic groups that make up their electoral coalitions, the interest and advocacy groups that support them, and their stance on a wide range of public policies.

- The parties are becoming more ideologically coherent; the GOP is increasingly conservative on social and economic issues while Democrats are increasingly liberal, though the Democrats have many more moderate supporters and elected officials than their Republican counterparts.

- It matters a great deal which party is in power for the kinds of public policies that the federal government produces.

TEST YOURSELF

Answer key begins on page T-1.

9.1 Evaluate the importance of political parties in democracies

1. The party platform is the list of candidates who have the official endorsement of the political party.
   True / False

2. Which of the following illustrates the role that political parties play in keeping officeholders accountable?
   a. Parties can mobilize voters and bring important issues to their attention.
   b. Voters can rely on the political parties to inform them about how recently passed legislation is likely to affect them.
   c. Parties can help overcome legislative gridlock.
   d. Competition between the political parties heightens public interest and increases citizen involvement in politics.
   e. Citizens can determine whether government is working and use this information to decide whether to vote for or against the incumbent party.

3. How do political parties help citizens better understand complex political issues?

9.2 Distinguish American political parties from parties in other democracies

4. America's reliance on proportional representation helps explain why a two-party system has developed.
   True / False

5. Which of the following best characterizes the dealignment era?
   a. Single-issue parties
   b. The New Deal coalition
   c. Divided government
   d. Strong public commitment to well-funded and ideologically unified parties
   e. Splinter and protest parties

6. The authors argue that the U.S. is currently in the "parties at war" era. Others disagree, claiming that the U.S. is still in the "dealignment" era. Evaluate which theory best describes the current party era.

9.3 Compare and contrast today's Republican and Democratic parties

7. The criteria for party membership in the United States are looser than in most other democracies.
   True / False

8. The Republican Party is most likely to support which of the following positions?
   a. A strong government role in guiding the economy
   b. Expanding environmental protections
   c. Expanding civil rights protections granted to minority groups
   d. Elimination of affirmation action programs
   e. Enhanced gun control

9. Evaluate whether divided government or unified government is preferable.

mypoliscilab EXERCISES

Apply what you learned in this chapter on MyPoliSciLab.

Read on **mypoliscilab.com**

eText: Chapter 9

Study and **Review** on **mypoliscilab.com**

Pre-Test
Post-Test
Chapter Exam
Flashcards

Watch on **mypoliscilab.com**

Video: Green Party Candidates Stay on Ballot
Video: New Ballots Bring New Complications in New York
Video: Republicans and Democrats Divide on Tax Cut
Video: Senator Specter Switches Parties
Video: Tea Party Victories Concern for GOP

Explore on **mypoliscilab.com**

Simulation: You Are a Campaign Manager: Help McCain Win Swing States and Swing Voters
Comparative: Comparing Political Parties
Timeline: Third Parties in American History
Timeline: The Evolution of Political Parties in the United States
Visual Literacy: State Control and National Platforms

INTERNET SOURCES

Democratic National Committee
www.democrats.org
Information about Democratic Party candidates, party history, convention and national committees, state parties, stands on the issues, affiliated groups, upcoming events, and more.

National Political Index
www.politicalindex.com
Links to state and local parties and affiliated organizations and interest groups, as well as news and information about the parties.

Real Clear Politics
www.realclearpolitics.com
News and commentary on American politics from a wide and diverse range of sources.

Project Vote Smart
www.votesmart.org
A comprehensive collection of information on national and state party candidates and public officials, including biographies, voting records, and campaign finances.

Republican National Committee
www.rnc.org/
Information about Republican Party candidates, party history, convention and national committees, state parties, stands on the issues, affiliated groups, upcoming events, and more.

SUGGESTIONS FOR FURTHER READING

Black, Earle, and Merle Black. *Divided: The Ferocious Power Struggle in American Politics.* New York: Simon and Schuster, 2007.
 The authors demonstrate the extent to which the regional bases of the two major parties have changed and why it happened.

Brownstein, Ronald. *The Second Civil War: How Extreme Partisanship Has Paralyzed Washington and Polarized America.* New York: the Penguin Press, 2007.
 A passionate chronicle of the growth of partisanship, the coarsening of public life, and our consequent inability, in the author's view, to tackle the nation's problems.

Gould, Lewis. *Grand Old Party: A History of the Republicans.* New York: Random House, 2003.

 A comprehensive history of the Republican Party in the United States.

Hershey, Marjory. *Party Politics in America,* 13th ed. New York: Pearson Longman Publishers, 2009.
 A new edition of the leading political parties textbook in the United States; comprehensive, detailed, yet engaging.

Maisel, L. Sandy. *American Political Parties and Elections: A Very Short Introduction.* New York: Oxford University Press, 2007.
 The best short guide to American parties and elections.

Witcover, Jules. *Party of the People: A History of the Democrats.* New York: Random House, 2003.
 A comprehensive history of the Democratic Party in the United States.

10 Voting, Campaigns, and Elections

IN THIS CHAPTER

10.1 Evaluate three models of how elections can lead to popular control

10.2 Distinguish American elections from those in other countries

10.3 Analyze the importance of political participation in elections

10.4 Identify demographic factors that increase the likelihood of voting

10.5 Outline the process of campaigns for the presidency and Congress

10.6 Assess how voters make their decisions

HOW BARACK OBAMA WON THE 2008 PRESIDENTIAL ELECTION

Democrat Barack Obama won a sweeping victory in an historic presidential election in 2008. Early data indicated that Obama beat his Republican opponent John McCain by about 8.5 million votes, and won the all-important Electoral College by a comfortable margin of 365 to 173. With about 53 percent of the ballots cast, Obama garnered the highest winning percentage for a Democrat since Lyndon Johnson in 1964 and the highest for any presidential winner since George H. W. Bush in 1988. Compared with John Kerry in 2004, Obama improved the Democratic vote among nearly all social groups in the nation. For example, he gained 13 points among Hispanics; 12 percentage points among voters 18 to 29 years of age; 7 points among college graduates, higher-income people, and those living in the West; 6 points among self-defined moderates; and 5 points among both men and women.[1]

The election was historic on a number of grounds. Most obviously and importantly, Barack Obama became the first African American to be elected president of the United States. That such a thing could happen in a country where slavery once existed, where a brutal civil war over slavery was waged, where formal and informal segregation existed for decades after that war, and where racial tensions have never entirely disappeared proved astonishing for many Americans and for people watching our elections from abroad. John McCain acknowledged as much in his gracious concession speech, in which he said: "This is an historic election. I recognize the special significance it has for African Americans, for the special pride that must be theirs tonight. I've always believed that America offers opportunities to all who have the industry and will to seize it. Senator Obama believes that, too."

The election was historic, as well, in the geographical reach of the Obama campaign and the transformation, at least temporarily, of the normal map of American politics. With an unprecedented amount of money in his campaign chest, and a strong national organization built during the course of his long nomination struggle with Senator Hillary Clinton, Obama waged his presidential campaign well beyond the handful of battleground states that have been the focus of activity in recent elections. He carried the fight deep

into traditional Republican states such as Georgia, Mississippi, North Dakota, Kentucky, and Utah, for example, forcing John McCain to play defense on his home turf. In the end, Barack Obama won in all the states carried by Democrat John Kerry in 2004 and added nine more—many traditionally Republican states—that had gone for George W. Bush on the last go-around: Florida, North Carolina, Virginia, Ohio, Indiana, Iowa, Colorado, Nevada, and New Mexico.

It seemed to many seasoned observers that the 2008 election might also prove to be historic in triggering a realignment in American politics (see Chapter 9 on realignments). Not only did the Democrats win the presidency and both houses of Congress, but the victories coincided with strong Democratic gains in party identification, a growing advantage over the Republicans in registering voters, and a widening lead among the fastest-growing groups in the country, including Hispanics, young people, and suburban professionals. They also strengthened their hold on state legislatures and governorships across the country. (However, the big Republican win in the 2010 national elections, coupled with the accompanying drop in Democratic Party identification and image preceding them,[2] suggests that no such alignment took place.)

Other aspects of the 2008 presidential election were noteworthy. For one thing, turnout was high: about 131 million Americans cast ballots, an increase of 5 million over 2004. This represented roughly a one percentage point increase in turnout measured either as a percentage of the voting age population (about 57 percent) or as a percentage of the voting eligible population (a little more than 62 percent). Turnout was especially high among African Americans and younger people compared to recent elections. Many observers expected an even bigger turnout and had the impression from long lines at many polling places that this was happening. What actually occurred was that voting in Democratic areas increased, while voting in many Republican areas dropped.

The 2008 election also saw the coming-of-age of the Internet as an indispensable campaign tool for organizing campaign activities and as a place for operatives, activists, and ordinary citizens to go for political news. The Obama campaign proved particularly adept at using the Internet and social media for mobilizing volunteers and identifying potential supporters, fund-raising, viral political advertising, and more. It was also the most expensive campaign in American history, roughly double what was spent in 2004. Finally, Obama's decision to forgo public financing and his ability to gather record amounts of money for his campaign—much of it in small donations through the Internet—may effectively kill the public financing system. It is hard to imagine that any future presidential candidate would hamstring his or her campaign by limiting spending to levels required for participants in that system.

There are many reasons John McCain and the Republicans fared so poorly in 2008. In many respects, given the bad hand they were dealt, McCain and the GOP probably did better than anyone had any right to expect. They were saddled with the legacy of George W. Bush, whose public approval numbers were the lowest in the history of modern polling, two unpopular wars entered into and run by a Republican administration, and a financial collapse and a deep economic recession. Such conditions virtually guaranteed defeat for the incumbent party—and its presidential candidate.

But other factors may have contributed to the McCain loss as well. Many commentators, with Republicans and conservatives prominent among them, suggested that McCain ran a poor campaign, changing messages, themes, and strategies constantly and failing to build respectable ground operations in many hotly contested areas. Others said that McCain's selection of Alaska governor Sarah Palin, while popular with the Republican base and momentarily attention-grabbing, was disastrous in the end. Her selection undercut McCain's main campaign theme—Obama's lack of experience—and her evident lack of knowledge about important issues and her "hard

right" message drove away many independents. Still others pointed to McCain's principled but ultimately self-defeating decision to accept public financing and its associated limits on campaign spending. While John McCain's campaign was allotted $85 million for the entire post-convention campaign season, Barack Obama raised more than $250 million.

With all these disadvantages, and faced with an attractive and engaging candidate in Barack Obama, John McCain also had to contend with an Obama campaign organization that most seasoned political observers consider to be among the best in the history of American politics.[3] The Obama for President organization made its presence felt in nearly every nook and cranny in the American political landscape. The organization blanketed the nation with campaign offices, dominated the airwaves with advertising, constructed impressive voter registration and get-out-the-vote operations, encouraged early voting, and built a website that not only facilitated organizing and gathering contributions, but used social-networking tools to encourage grassroots participation. In the end, the Obama campaign was better able than the McCain campaign to identify potential supporters, convey its candidate's message to them, and encourage them to cast their ballots on November 4, 2008.

Nothing is forever, however, in American politics. Although Obama's big win helped him pass much of his legislative program after the election, continuing economic troubles led to declines in his job approval rating and big Democratic losses in the House and Senate in the 2010 elections.

THINKING CRITICALLY About This Chapter

The story of the 2008 presidential election focuses our attention on the issue of democratic control of the national government through the electoral process and on the degree to which the public participates in this key activity of the representative democratic process.

Using the FRAMEWORK

You will see in this chapter that elections are affected by the different rates of participation of groups in American society and how structural factors such as constitutional rules, unequal access to resources, and cultural ideas help determine why some groups participate more than others. You will also learn how elections affect the behavior of public officials.

Using the DEMOCRACY STANDARD

We suggest in this chapter that elections are the lynchpin of any discussion about the democratic quality of any system of government because they are, in theory, what makes popular sovereignty possible. You will see in this chapter that while elections in the United States do much to make our system democratic, they fall short of their democratic promise.

Elections and Democracy

10.1 Evaluate three models of how elections can lead to popular control

Elections are fundamental to democratic politics, the chief means by which citizens control what their government does. Many important struggles for democracy in the United States have involved conflicts over the right to vote. But can elections actually ensure that governments will do what their people want?

Democratic theorists have suggested several ways that elections in a two-party system like that found in the United States can bring about popular control of government. We will briefly discuss three of these ways, indicating how they might work in theory.[4] The remainder of this chapter is concerned with what actually happens in American national elections and with the question of whether these elections really bring about popular control of government.

> **responsible party**
> The notion that a political party will take clear and distinct stands on the issues and enact them as policy when in office.
>
> **prospective voting model**
> A theory of democratic elections in which voters decide what government will do in the near future by choosing one or another responsible party.

The Prospective (or Responsible Party) Voting Model

The idea of **responsible party** elections is based on the old commonsense notion that elections should present a "real choice": political parties should stand for different policies, the voters should choose between them, and the winning party should carry out its mandate. Political scientists call this the **prospective voting model**, meaning that voters are interested in and capable of deciding what government will do in the future.

Theory   For this system to work perfectly, each of the two parties must be cohesive and unified; each must take clear policy positions that differ significantly from the other party's positions; citizens must accurately perceive these positions and vote on the basis of them; and the winning party, when it takes office, must do exactly what it said it would do. It is in this sense—that parties stand for something and have the wherewithal and willingness to follow through once in power—that the model also is called the responsible party model. If all these conditions are met, then the party with the more popular policy positions will win and enact its program. In such an electoral system, government will do what the majority of the voters want.[5]

Potential Problems   One potential problem of elections fought by responsible parties is that it might increase the frequency and intensity of political conflicts in the country. If each party in such a system stands for ideologies and policies different from the other party, feels duty-bound to put promises into effect on attaining power, and has the means to do so, there would be no need for the victorious party to reach compromises with the losing party, even if it won by a razor-thin margin. The party in power can make the policies it wants, disregarding the objections of the losing party. The high stakes involved in winning and losing elections in such a system would make campaigns and elections very heated.

Others have pointed out that while responsible parties might make choices at the ballot box easier for voters, in a system of separation of powers and federalism, it is likely to lead to gridlock—a situation in which government cannot function very well because the different branches of government are controlled by different parties that are not prone to compromise with one another. It is quite common, for example, for Congress to be controlled by one party and the presidency by another

electoral competition model

A form of election in which parties seeking votes move toward the median voter or the center of the political spectrum.

median voter

The voter at the exact middle of the political issue spectrum.

(something that cannot happen in a parliamentary system) and, if the parties controlling them disagree clearly and fundamentally, then it's hard to get things done.[6] This is what happened several times in the late 1990s when a Republican-controlled Congress and Democratic President Bill Clinton could not agree on the budget, forcing parts of the government to shut down. The frequency of these types of events is likely to increase if our parties become more responsible, as seems to be happening (see Chapter 9).[7]

The Electoral Competition Voting Model

A very different, and less obvious, sort of democratic control can be found in what political scientists call the **electoral competition**, or **median voter**, **model** of democratic elections. In this sort of electoral model, unified parties compete for votes by taking the *most popular* positions they can. They do so by trying to take positions that will appeal to the voter at the exact midpoint of the political spectrum. Both parties are therefore likely to end up standing for the *same* policies: those favored by the most voters.

Theory   Scholars have proved mathematically that if citizens' preferences are organized along a single dimension (such as the liberal–conservative continuum shown in Figure 10.1), and if parties purely seek votes, both parties will take positions exactly at the *median* of public opinion, that is, at the point where exactly one-half the voters are more liberal and one-half are more conservative. If either party took a position even a bit away from the median, the other party could easily win more votes by taking a position closer to the median.[8]

If electoral competition drives parties together in this way, and if they keep their promises, then, in theory, it should not matter which party wins; the winner enacts the policies that the most voters want. Democracy is ensured by the hidden hand of competition, much as efficiency is ensured by competitive markets, according to standard economic theory.

Potential Problems   Again, however, the conditions for this electoral model to work perfectly are not likely to be met in the real world. Electoral competition ensures democratic control only if the parties are unified and take stands on the issues for pure and direct vote-seeking reasons; it can break down if the parties are

FIGURE 10.1   Electoral Competition Model

This model suggests that in the interest of winning the election, parties will move toward the median voter (where most votes are to be found) as the campaign progresses.

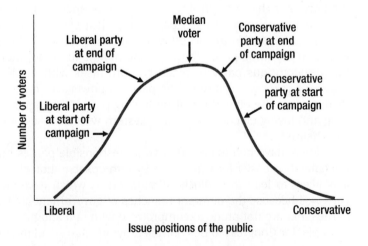

fragmented or ambiguous, if they care about policies for ideological reasons rather than for reasons of securing the most votes, or if they seek contributors' dollars rather than citizens' votes. Moreover, in this model, the voters must consider nothing but the issues (e.g., not being distracted by candidates' personalities or images) and must know exactly where the parties stand. And the parties have to keep their promises. There are reasons to doubt that any of these things will happen flawlessly.[9]

Still, we will see that these conditions are close enough to the truth so that electoral competition does work, to a significant extent, in real elections. Indeed, electoral competition is probably one of the main ways that elected officials are influenced by public opinion.

The Retrospective (or Reward and Punishment) Voting Model

A third process by which elections might bring about democratic control of government is **electoral reward and punishment**, a form of election in which voters judge how well a group in power has governed and decide if they want this group to continue in office.

Theory   Here the idea is that the voters simply make **retrospective**, backward-looking judgments about how well incumbent officials have done in the past, rewarding success with reelection and punishing failure by throwing the incumbents out. The result, in theory, is that politicians who want to stay in office have strong incentives to bring about peace and prosperity and to solve problems that the American people want solved. Politicians' ambitions force them to anticipate what the public wants and to accomplish it.[10] The reward-and-punishment process of democratic control has the advantage of simplicity. It requires very little of voters: no elaborate policy preferences, no study of campaign platforms, just judgments of how well or how badly things have been going. Voters seem to have punished Republicans in 2008 in such a way, expressing their displeasure with George W. Bush over the wars in Iraq and Afghanistan and a collapsed economy.[11]

> **electoral reward and punishment**
> The tendency to vote for the incumbents when times are good and against them when times are bad; same as retrospective voting.
>
> **retrospective voting**
> A form of election in which voters look back at the performance of a party in power and cast ballots on the basis of how well it did in office.

ACCEPTING DEFEAT   Some presidential elections are retrospective in nature, meaning that the electorate makes its decision based on an incumbent's performance in office. The electorate's concern about the poor performance of the American economy was a major factor in George H. W. Bush's defeat at the hands of challenger Bill Clinton in 1992. Here, the Republican president concedes the election to his Democratic rival. Who are some other presidents to have fallen prey to retrospective voting?

Potential Problems However, reward and punishment may be a rather blunt instrument. It gets rid of bad political leaders only after (not before) disasters happen, without guaranteeing that the next leaders will be any better. It relies on politicians *anticipating* the effects of future policies, which they cannot always do successfully. Moreover, the reward-and-punishment process focuses only on the most prominent issues and may leave room for unpopular policies on matters that are less visible. It may also encourage politicians to produce deceptively happy but temporary results that arrive just in time for election day and then fade away.

Imperfect Electoral Democracy

We will see that each of the three processes of democratic control we have discussed exists, to some extent, in American elections. On occasion, even, the three processes converge and help produce an election that is enormously consequential for the direction of the nation. The 1932 election was one of these occasions and is described in the "Using the Framework" feature.

But none of the three processes works well enough to guarantee perfectly democratic outcomes most of the time. In certain respects, they conflict: responsible parties and electoral competition, for example, tend to push in opposite directions. In other respects, all three processes require similar conditions that are not met in reality.

For example, none of the three can ensure government responsiveness to all citizens unless *all* citizens have the right to vote and exercise that right. Unfortunately, millions of Americans cannot or do not go to the polls. Their voices are not heard; political equality is not achieved.

Another problem with our system of elections was brought to public attention by the chaos and uncertainty of the disputed 2000 presidential election in Florida: not all ballots cast by voters are actually counted. For a variety of reasons, ranging from lack of voter education to confusing ballot layouts and malfunctioning voting machines, a number of ballots in every election in the United States are disqualified and not included in the final vote tally. A study commissioned by Congress on the 2000 election estimated that from 4 to 6 million votes of the roughly 100 million cast nationally were not counted, with the votes of poor people and members of racial minorities three times more likely than those of other Americans to be uncounted in the 2000 election.[12]

The Unique Nature of American Elections

10.2 Distinguish American elections from those in other countries

American elections differ quite dramatically from those of most other democratic countries. The differences are the result of rules—mainly found in the Constitution but also in federal statutes and judicial decisions—that define offices and tell how elections are to be conducted. Here are the distinguishing features of elections in the United States:

Elections Are Numerous and Frequent In some sense, we are "election happy" in the United States. We not only elect the president and members of Congress (senators and representatives), but also, being a federal system, we elect governors, state legislators, and (in most states) judges. In addition, state constitutions allow autonomy

Have elections ever changed the course of American government? Do elections ever really change what government does?

Background: Occasionally in American history, a national election is so consequential that it alters the overall direction of government policy and the role of government in the United States. The election of Franklin Delano Roosevelt and an overwhelmingly Democratic Congress in the 1932 elections was just such a moment. In the first 100 days of his administration, Roosevelt launched his New Deal, convincing Congress to pass bills to regulate the banking and securities industries, to bail out failing banks and protect the deposits of the public, to launch public works and relief efforts, and to provide price supports for farmers. This revolution in the role of the federal government was made possible by the 1932 elections, but to fully understand what happened, structural, political linkage, and governmental factors have to be taken into account.

Structure

The 1932 election was held in the midst of the Great Depression, with unemployment reaching 33 percent, bank failures at an all-time high, and industrial and farm production at 50 percent of their levels in the mid-1920s. ⮕ The preamble to the Constitution says that the Constitution was intended to create a government that would "…insure Domestic tranquility…[and]…promote the general Welfare."

Political Linkage

Public opinion strongly supported a greater role for the federal government in fighting the depression. ⮕ Social disorder was widespread, leading to concerns that the country was near the point of collapse. ⮕ Social movements that demanded government action were growing and making their presence felt. ⮕ Democrats won big majorities in the House (313 out of 435 total seats) and the Senate (59 of 96 seats) in 1932. ⮕ Roosevelt won an overwhelming victory in the 1932 presidential election, tallying 472 electoral votes to Hoover's 59.

Government

Franklin Roosevelt interpreted the 1932 election as a mandate for immediate and far-reaching actions by the federal government to meet the crisis of the Great Depression. ⮕ Roosevelt mobilized business and labor leaders, as well as the public, behind his emergency program. ⮕ The Democratic-controlled Congress, aware of Roosevelt's enormous popularity, and concerned about the national crisis, passed all the president's emergency measures.

Government Action

The New Deal is launched.

for counties, cities, and towns, and all of their top officials are elected by the people. All in all, we fill about 500,000 offices through elections.[13] We also elect school boards in most places, and the top positions in special districts (e.g., water or conservation districts). And then there are the many state and local ballot initiatives that add to the length and complexity of the ballot at election time. No other country holds so many elections, covering so many offices and public policy issues.

> **?** Does the frequency of American elections contribute to voter apathy? Do you think more Americans would vote if elections came up less often?

Elections Are Separate and Independent from One Another

Not only do we have a multitude of elections, but the election to fill each particular office is separate and independent from the others. In parliamentary systems, one votes for a party, and the party that wins a majority gets to appoint a whole range of other officials. The majority party in the British parliament (the legislative branch), for example, chooses the prime minister and cabinet ministers (the executive branch), who run the government. The government, in turn, appoints officials to many posts that are filled by elections here. In the United States, the president and members of Congress are elected independently from one another, as are governors, state legislators, mayors of cities, city council members, and school boards.

Inconsistent Election Procedures and Vote-Counting

With very few exceptions—such as the 1965 Voting Rights Act to protect the rights of African American voters and the 2002 law allowing the use of **provisional ballots** when voter registration issues arise on election day—the federal government plays no role in regulating and overseeing elections. This mainly is the role of states that, in most cases, further decentralize the process by lodging the management of elections in the hands of county officials. The result is wide variation across the country in voter registration rules, how absentee and early ballots are done and counted, what types of election devices are used (paper ballots, either counted by hand or scanned, computerized touch screen systems, and more), when and how recounts are done, and how election disputes are resolved.[14]

Elected Positions Have Fixed Terms of Office

The office of president of the United States is fixed at four years, representatives serve for two years, and senators for six. At the state level, terms of office for all important elected positions are fixed, whether for governors or legislators. The same holds true for county, city, and town elected offices. In parliamentary systems, the government can call an election at any time within a certain number of years (in Britain, it is five years), timing the election to maximize chances for reelection. One implication of fixed elections in the United States is that presidents cannot call for new elections in hopes of changing the party mix in Congress to their advantage. It also means that an unpopular president can stay in office until the next election, because there is no method to remove him other than by impeachment and trial. In parliamentary systems, elections customarily are held when the majority party or majority coalition in parliament loses support among its members, shown in a defeat on a major bill proposed by the government (the prime minister and cabinet) or on a "vote of confidence" called by the opposition.

provisional ballot
A vote that is cast but not counted until determination is made that the voter is properly registered.

Elections Are Held on a Fixed Date

In 1845, Congress determined that elections for president and members of Congress will occur on the Tuesday after the first Monday in November (the Constitution only requires that national elections be held on the same day throughout the country). States have generally followed suit for election of governors and members of the legislature. One implication, related to the fixed terms of offices described earlier, is that neither presidents nor governors can time elections to their political advantage as we have seen can happen in parliamentary systems. Another implication is that Tuesday elections may cut down on participation. In other democracies, elections are held either on the weekend or on days that are declared a national holiday.

> ? How might standardizing the elections process across the country make elections more democratic? In what ways is it more democratic to leave oversight of elections to the states?

"First Past the Post" Wins   Winners in most elections in the United States are those who win the most votes—not necessarily a majority—in a particular electoral district. This type of election is often called "first past the post," as in a horse race where the winner is the first past the finish line. This includes congressional elections and presidential contests for electoral votes in each of the states. We do not have proportional representation in national level races, nor do we have "run-off" elections between the top two vote-getters in presidential or congressional elections to ensure a majority victor. In 2004, as a matter of fact, George W. Bush became the first president since the election of his father in 1988 to win a majority of the national popular vote (all elected presidents come to office based on winning a majority in the electoral college), a feat repeated by Barack Obama in 2008. In France and Finland, by way of contrast, a second election is held if no candidate wins a majority in the first round of voting for the president. This type of election ensures that the person who is elected comes to office with majority support.

Voting in the United States

10.3   Analyze the importance of political participation in elections

In this section, we turn our attention to political participation. For elections to be democratic—whether in the prospective, electoral competition, or retrospective voting models—participation in elections must not only be at high levels, but also must not vary substantially across social groups in the population (e.g., by race, gender, income, occupation, religion, ethnicity, region, and so on), or else the principle of political equality would be violated.

Expansion of the Franchise

Until passage of the Fourteenth and Fifteenth Amendments after the Civil War, it was up to each state to determine who within its borders was eligible to vote. In the early years of the United States, many of the states limited the legal right to vote—called the **franchise**—quite severely. In fact, a majority of people could not vote at all. Slaves, Native Americans, and women were excluded altogether. In most states, white men without property or who had not paid some set level of taxes were not allowed to vote. In some states early on, white men with certain religious beliefs were excluded.

One of the most important developments in the political history of the United States, an essential part of the struggle for democracy, has been the expansion of the right to vote. The extension of the franchise has been a lengthy and uneven process, spanning 200 years.

> **franchise**
> The legal right to vote; see suffrage.

AT THE POLLS Early U.S. elections were poorly organized and hard to get to. In addition, only a small proportion of the population was eligible to vote. Here a group of white men, the only people with the right to vote in most places in the United States at the time, wait to vote in the presidential election of 1824 at a polling station near Boston. How did the voter profile of the time shape government policies?

suffrage

The legal right to vote; see franchise.

White Male Suffrage The first barriers to fall were those concerning property and religion. So strong were the democratic currents during Thomas Jefferson's presidency (1801–1809) and in the years leading up to the election of Andrew Jackson in 1828 that by 1829, property, tax-paying, and religious requirements had been dropped in all states except North Carolina and Virginia. That left universal **suffrage**, or the ability to vote, firmly in place for most adult white males in the United States.[15] Most of Europe, including Britain, did not achieve this degree of democracy until after World War I.

Blacks, Women, and Young People Despite this head start for the United States compared with the rest of the world, the struggle to expand the suffrage to include African Americans, women, and young people proved difficult and painful. Ironically, universal white male suffrage was often accompanied by the withdrawal of voting rights from black freedmen, even in states that did not permit slavery.[16] It took the bloody Civil War to free the slaves and the Fifteenth Amendment to the U.S. Constitution (1870) to extend the right to vote to all black males, in both North and South. Even so, most blacks were effectively disfranchised in the South by the end of the nineteenth century and remained so until the 1960s civil rights movement and the Voting Rights Act of 1965 (see Chapter 1).

Women won the right to vote in 1920 in all the states with the Nineteenth Amendment to the Constitution, after a long political battle. (See the chapter-opening story in Chapter 8 for details of this struggle.) Residents of the District of Columbia were allowed to vote in presidential—but not congressional—elections after 1961, and 18- to 20-year-olds gained the franchise in 1971.

The result of these changes at the state and national levels was an enormous increase in the proportion of Americans who were legally eligible to vote: from about 23 percent of the adult population in 1788–1789 to nearly 98 percent by the beginning of the 1970s—practically all citizens except people who have recently moved to another state, people in mental institutions, and incarcerated felons. However, the proportion of the voting-age population that is eligible to vote has dropped a bit in recent years, primarily because of the large influx of immigrants into the United States over the past two decades who cannot vote unless and until they become citizens.

Direct Partisan Elections A related trend has involved the more direct election of government officials, replacing the old indirect methods that insulated officials from the public. At the same time, the development of a two-party system has clarified choices by focusing citizens' attention on just two alternatives for each office.

The election of the president, even with the existence of the **Electoral College**, has become more directly democratic. By the time of the Jefferson–Adams presidential campaign of 1800, which pitted the new Republican and Federalist parties against each other, most state legislatures had stopped picking the presidential electors themselves (as the Constitution permits). Instead, the legislatures allowed a popular vote for electors, most of whom were pledged to support the presidential candidate of one party or the other.

This is the same system we use today: in practically every state, there is a winner-take-all popular vote for a slate of electors—positions usually awarded by each of the political parties to loyal party workers and contributors—who are pledged to a particular presidential candidate. In fact, only the name of the candidate and the party to whom the electors are pledged, not the names of the electors we are actually voting for, appear on the ballot. Thus, when the winning electors meet as the Electoral College in their respective states and cast ballots to elect the president, their actions are generally controlled by the popular vote that chose them. This system, odd and cumbersome as it is, almost always ensures that American citizens choose their president more or less directly. One recent exception is the 2000 election, when Gore won the popular vote by more than 500,000, but Bush captured a majority of the electoral votes.

By 1840, the parties had started nominating presidential candidates in national **party conventions** instead of in congressional party caucuses. Later still, the parties began letting voters select many convention delegates directly in state **primary elections** instead of having party activists choose them in political party conventions in each of the states. Today, most delegates to the Republican and Democratic national conventions are selected in primary elections or in state **party caucuses** in which party supporters and activists hold neighborhood and area wide meetings to select delegates. The important role of primaries and caucuses in nominating party candidates for elected office enhances democratic control of government, although we will see that each of them has antidemocratic features, too.

Until 1913, when the Seventeenth Amendment to the Constitution was ratified, U.S. senators were selected by state legislatures rather than directly by the people. Since then, all members of the Senate have been subject to direct choice by the voters.

Taken together, the expansion of the franchise and the development of direct, two-party elections have represented major successes in the struggle for democracy. But problems remain on the voting participation front.

Low Voting Turnout

During the first 100 years or so of the United States's existence, not only did more and more people gain the right to vote, but also higher and higher proportions of voters actually turned out on election day and voted. Because of data inaccuracies and voter fraud, it is difficult to determine voter **turnout** accurately in early American elections. But the percentage of American voters appears to have increased rapidly, from roughly 11 percent of eligible voters in 1788–1789, to about 31 percent in 1800 (when Thomas Jefferson was first elected), and to about 57 percent in 1828 (Andrew Jackson's first victory). By 1840, the figure had reached 80 percent, and it stayed at about that level until 1896.[17]

The disturbing fact is that today, despite higher turnout in recent presidential elections—as well as historically high turnout in the Democratic primaries and caucuses during the intense nomination battle between Hillary Clinton and Barack Obama

---

Electoral College

Representatives selected in each of the states, their numbers based on each state's total number of its senators and representatives; a majority of Electoral College votes elects the president.

convention, party

A gathering of delegates who nominate a party's presidential candidate.

primary election

Statewide elections in which voters choose delegates to the national party conventions.

caucus nominating system

The process for selecting delegates to the national party conventions characterized by neighborhood and area-wide meetings of party supporters and activists.

turnout

The proportion of eligible or voting age Americans who actually vote in a given election; the two ways of counting turnout yield different results.

Percentage of Americans voting

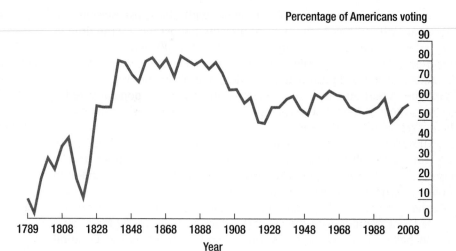

FIGURE 10.2 The Rise and Fall of Turnout in Presidential Elections, 1789–2008

Turnout in presidential elections rose sharply during the nineteenth century—except during the "era of good feelings" when there was no party competition and little interest in politics among the public—but declined in the twentieth century. In 2004, turnout increased dramatically, but only to a level typical of the 1950s and 1960s. *Note:* From 1920, the Census Bureau has calculated voting turnout as the percentage of the voting age population voting, not as a percentage of the total voting eligible population. *Source:* U.S. Bureau of the Census, 2009.

in 2008—proportionally fewer people vote today than during most of the nineteenth century. Since 1912, only about 50 to 65 percent of Americans have voted in presidential elections (see Figure 10.2) and still fewer in other elections: 40 to 50 percent in off-year (non-presidential-year) congressional elections and as few as 10 to 20 percent in primaries and minor local elections, although the exact number depends on how turnout is measured (see the "By the Numbers" feature). In addition, turnout in presidential elections remains well below turnout in other democratic countries; in western Europe, turnout rates regularly top 75 percent. When 60 percent of Israeli's voting age population voted in that nation's 2006 Israeli parliamentary elections, it was a historically low voter turnout and generated a flurry of news and academic commentary about what might be amiss with Israel's democracy.[18]

VOTING DAY IN FRANCE Voting day is a national holiday in many democratic countries, such as France. Here, voters cast their ballots in a voting center in Marseille in the first round of the 2002 presidential election. Would a day off work encourage more American voters to visit the polls?

Why do so few Americans vote compared to people in other democracies? Scholars have identified several possible factors.[19]

Barriers to Voting In the United States, only citizens who take the initiative to register in advance are permitted to vote in an election. Many people do not make the extra effort to register, or circumstances make it difficult. For example, people who move, either within a state or to another state, must find out where and when to register in their new location. Many procrastinate and do not register in time, lowering turnout, according to one study, by 9 percentage points.[20]

In most European countries with high turnout rates, the government, rather than individual citizens, is responsible for deciding who is listed as eligible to vote and registers them automatically. In some countries, such as Belgium and Italy, moreover, citizens are *required* to vote and may be fined if they don't. Also, in most countries, election days are holidays on which people don't have to go to work.

The United States might increase political equality and popular sovereignty by making voting easier. One way to do so would be to ease registration requirements,[21] perhaps allowing registration by postcard or same-day registration at polling places. It is worth noting that voting turnout in the United States among those who have registered to vote hovers at about 85 percent and that voting participation in the seven states that allow same-day registration is significantly higher than in other states.[22] In Minnesota and Wisconsin in 2008, where same-day registration is in effect, turnout was 78 percent and 73 percent, respectively, similar to turnout in other rich democracies. These findings suggest that the registration requirement for voting is probably a significant barrier to participation, because participation rates go up when such barriers are lowered.

Another way to increase participation would be to ease the voting act itself. Suggestions include making every election day a legal holiday, as is done in most western European countries; allowing an extended voting period—usually called early voting—which many states have instituted in recent elections; or expanding the use of mail balloting over a period of several weeks, which a growing number of states allow. Twenty-five states now require some form of identification at the polls as a way, its proponents claim, to diminish voter fraud. Many critics believe this will adversely affect the poor, the less educated, and the elderly who may not have the necessary documents close at hand.

Too Much Complexity As we suggested earlier, when voters go to the polls in the United States, they must make voting choices for a multitude of federal, state, and local offices and often decide on constitutional and policy measures put on the ballot by state legislatures (called **referenda**) or the public (called **initiatives**), especially in states such as California and Colorado where these are common. Research demonstrates that many potential voters are simply overwhelmed by the complexity of the issues and the number of choices they must make in the voting booth; some choose to stay home.[23]

Weak Voter Mobilization by the Parties Another reason voting turnout is low may be tied to the failure of the political parties to rouse people broadly and get them to the polls to vote. The parties mostly are in the business of getting their own supporters to the polls, to rally the base, as it were, not in the business of increasing the voter turnout in general as a sort of civic duty. The problem is that aiming at your own voters with highly partisan appeals delivered by mail, telephone, and, increasingly, by e-mail, by highly professionalized but distant party organizations and advocacy groups, does not increase turnout among the noncommitted public and may even persuade many of them to stay

referenda
Procedures available in some states by which state laws or constitutional amendments proposed by the legislature are submitted to the voters for approval or rejection.

initiatives
Procedures available in some states for citizens to put proposed laws and constitutional amendments on the ballot for voter approval or rejection.

Is voting turnout declining in the United States?

Commentators have been decrying the declining rate of voting in the United States for many years now. All sorts of explanations have been advanced to explain the decline; all sorts of remedies for the problem have been proposed. But what if there really hasn't been a decline in voting at all?

Why It Matters We have argued in this chapter that widespread participation in voting and other civic activities is one measure of the health of democracy in any society. If the way we measure participation is inaccurate, we cannot do a good job of assessing the quality of democracy in the United States, or identify what problems and shortcomings in our political system need to be addressed to make it more democratic.

Behind the Traditional Voting Turnout Measure Voter turnout in American elections *normally* is determined by a very simple calculation: the number of people who vote in a national

election divided by the number of people in the United States who are of voting age, that is, 18 years of age and older. The denominator for this equation—voting age population, or VAP—is provided by the Census Bureau. But there is a problem: the denominator may be misleading, because it includes millions of people who are not eligible to vote at all—residents who are not citizens, felons (some states), people with past felonies (some states), and the mentally incompetent. If we calculated voting turnout as the number of voters divided by the number of people in the United States who *actually* are eligible to vote—the voting eligible population, or VEP—turnout would always be higher than is now reported because the denominator would be smaller.

Calculating a VEP-based Measure of Turnout Two political scientists, Michael McDonald and Samuel Popkin, have done us the great service of transforming the Census Bureau's VAP number to a VEP number for every

national election from 1948 to 2008, pulling out noncitizens and ineligible felons and former felons in states where they cannot vote. Using the voting eligible population rather than the resident population over the age of 18 as the denominator in the voting turnout equation, McDonald and Popkin's figures show the following:

- Voting turnout is actually four or five percentage points higher in recent elections than usually reported.
- Voting turnout declined between 1960 and 1972 regardless of which method was used. However, voting turnout appears to decline further after 1972 only when using the traditional VAP method; the VEP method shows no decline in voting turnout over the past 30 years.
- Voting turnout jumped substantially in 2004 and 2008 for the hotly contested races between John Kerry and George W. Bush, and Barack Obama and John McCain, whether using the VEP numbers or the VAP

---

home.[24] As well, old-style, door-to-door canvassing in neighborhoods seems to have been far more effective in raising turnout than modern methods. Both parties have renewed their efforts in this area,[25] however, with the Obama campaign in 2008 particularly effective in increasing voter turnout by knocking on the doors of potential voters.

A Decline in Competitive Elections   It may seem exceedingly odd to suggest, given the rise of intense partisanship reviewed in Chapter 9, an increase in the shrillness and incivility in recent election campaigns, and the frequency of close elections in recent electoral rounds for the presidency and control of Congress, that very few Americans experience competitive elections where they live.[26] In most recent congressional elections, for example, no more than 30 or so of the 435 seats in the House really have been up for grabs (in 2008, it rose to about 60; in 2010, it jumped to about 100[27]). The remainder have resided safely in the hands of incumbents who won with at least 55 percent of the vote. In presidential elections, most states find themselves in the Democratic or Republican columns, and little campaigning takes place in them. California is safely Democratic in presidential elections, for example, so Republican presidential candidates don't spend much time or money there. Democratic candidates tend

numbers, although the former were significantly higher.

The main reason voting turnout has declined in recent elections using the traditional VAP method is that the number of people who are residents of the United States but who are not eligible to vote in American elections has increased at every election, mostly due to the number of noncitizens living here.

Criticism of the VEP-based Measure of Turnout Some critics suggest that the old way of calculating voting turnout serves a very useful purpose, namely, pointing out how far short we fall in our claim to being a democratic society. The low turnout number reported by VAP, it is argued, helps focus attention on the issue of nonvoting in the United States and encourages efforts to reform voting rules to increase turnout.

What to Watch For When you come across voter turnout numbers, pay attention to whether the figure has been calculated based on the voting age population or on the voting eligible population. The latter will always be higher than the former. It is important to be aware that both methods of calculating turnout make sense in their own way; each has a slightly different story to tell.

What Do You Think? How could the U.S. increase the rate of voting turnout, which, regardless of the calculation method, is low in comparison to other democratic countries? Should we have compulsory voting in the United States like several other democratic countries? What are the pros and cons of making noncitizens—who pay taxes and are subject to U.S. laws—eligible to vote? How about former felons who have paid their debt to society?

Sources: Michael P. McDonald and Samuel L. Popkin, "The Myth of the Vanishing Voter," *The American Political Science Review*, 95, no. 4 (December 2001), pp. 963–974; Michael McDonald, "Voting-Age and Voting-Eligible Population Turnout Rates," *ElectioNexus*, http://elections.gmu.edu/Turnout_2008G.html.

Voting Turnout in Presidential Elections, by Year

to skirt places that are reliably Republican, such as Utah, Wyoming, and Mississippi. In 2004 (see the "Mapping American Politics" feature later in this chapter), 88 percent of media ad buys in the last month of the presidential campaign were concentrated in only 10 states. If competition drives up voter turnout, as political scientists suggest, then an important reason for low turnout in the United States may be that most Americans do not live in an environment where elections are strongly contested.

Who Votes?

10.4 Identify demographic factors that increase the likelihood of voting

Voting in the United States varies a great deal according to people's income, education, age, and ethnicity. This means that some kinds of people have more representation and influence with elected officials than others, and, other things being equal, they are more likely to have their preferences and interests reflected in what government does.

Young people played an important role during the 2008 presidential election. They voted at higher levels than before and were a significant part of the ground operations of both parties, particularly for the Democrats. Here, high school and college students voice their support for Republican nominee John McCain at a rally in Bexley, Ohio. Youth involvement was much lower for the 2010 elections. How did this affect the outcomes of these elections?

Income and Education

For the most part, politically active people tend to be those with higher-than-average incomes and more formal education.[28] These people are also more likely to vote. In 2008, 78 percent of those with incomes of $75,000 or above said they had voted, but only 59 percent of those with incomes under $35,000 said they had done so (see Figure 10.3); 79 percent of college graduates or those earning post-graduate degrees reported that they had voted, but only 55 percent of high school graduates and 40 percent of those who had not graduated from high school had done so. Some statistical analyses have indicated that the most important factor determining whether people vote is their level of formal education. When other factors are controlled—including race, income, and gender—college-educated people are much more likely to tell interviewers that they have voted than are the less educated. There are several possible reasons: people with more education learn more about politics, are less troubled by registration requirements, and are more confident in their ability to affect political life.

Looking at political participation more broadly, citizens with lower incomes are also less likely to work in campaigns, give money, contact officials, and the like. Wealthier Americans, who have more time, more money, and more knowledge of how to get things done, tend to be much more active politically. As a result, they may have more political clout than their fellow citizens.

Race and Ethnicity

In the past, fewer black people than whites voted, but now the proportions are more nearly equal. Both non-Hispanic whites and blacks turned out at about 65 percent in 2008, with the black vote up five points from 2004, mostly because Barack Obama, the nation's first African American candidate for the presidency, was in the race. In 2010, a nonpresidential year, the differences between white and black turnout more closely resembled the pattern in 2004. In 2010, though African Americans voted for Democrats at even higher rates than they had in 2010, their proportion of the total electorate fell from 13 percent to 10 percent. Racial differences remain, then, but they are small. The gap can be attributed to African Americans' lower average levels of income and education. African Americans are at least equally likely to vote, and sometimes more likely, than non-Hispanic whites of similar educational and income backgrounds.

Hispanics have historically had very low participation rates; many are discouraged from participating by low incomes, language problems, or suspicion of government

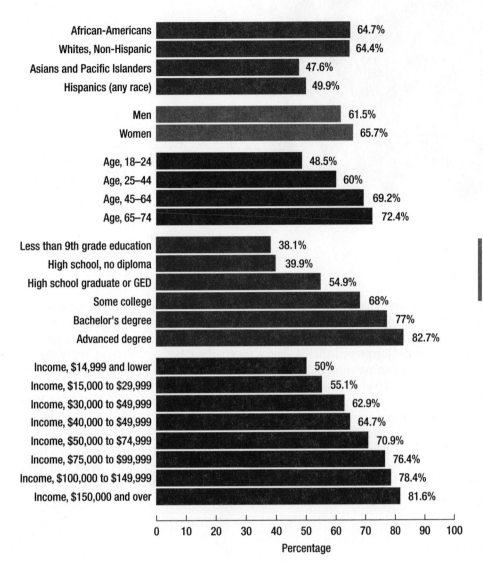

African-Americans — 64.7%
Whites, Non-Hispanic — 64.4%
Asians and Pacific Islanders — 47.6%
Hispanics (any race) — 49.9%

Men — 61.5%
Women — 65.7%

Age, 18–24 — 48.5%
Age, 25–44 — 60%
Age, 45–64 — 69.2%
Age, 65–74 — 72.4%

Less than 9th grade education — 38.1%
High school, no diploma — 39.9%
High school graduate or GED — 54.9%
Some college — 68%
Bachelor's degree — 77%
Advanced degree — 82.7%

Income, $14,999 and lower — 50%
Income, $15,000 to $29,999 — 55.1%
Income, $30,000 to $49,999 — 62.9%
Income, $40,000 to $49,999 — 64.7%
Income, $50,000 to $74,999 — 70.9%
Income, $75,000 to $99,999 — 76.4%
Income, $100,000 to $149,999 — 78.4%
Income, $150,000 and over — 81.6%

Percentage

FIGURE 10.3 Presidential Election Turnout by Social Group, 2008

Age, education, race, ethnicity, income, and gender all affect voting behavior. Members of certain social groups are more likely to vote in elections than others. The Census Bureau warns that these numbers may be inflated because of people's tendency to want to report positive citizen behavior to interviewers. What is important here, however, is not necessarily the accuracy of the turnout totals but the comparison between groups of people. The relative turnout comparisons between groups fit the general picture available from other academic research and government sources. *Source:* U.S. Bureau of the Census, Current Population Reports, 2009.

authorities. Although Hispanics continue to vote at lower rates than other Americans with a similar income and educational profile, the number appearing at the polls has been increasing. For example, while close to 50 percent voted in the 2008 presidential contest, this was a significant jump from 1996 when only 27 percent reported voting. In the congressional elections in 2002 and 2006, the percentage of Hispanics casting ballots increased by almost 18 percent.[29] This recent jump in the turnout rate for Hispanics has made a difference in states where Hispanic voters are concentrated. In 2008, Barack Obama and John McCain made special efforts to win over this group, especially in closely contested states such as Florida, Nevada, Colorado, and New Mexico—all won by Obama—demonstrating its rising importance. It may be that the Arizona law allowing police to stop people it considers to be in the country illegally—which by all accounts will mostly affect people of Hispanic descent—has caused anger and concern to rise among Hispanics in Arizona and other states and may increase voting turnout, as these things generally do.

Voting has also been relatively low among Asian Americans; only 47 percent reported voting in 2008. However, Asian American individuals and organizations have become more active in local politics and have increased campaign contributions to candidates and parties.

EXPANDING THE NUMBER OF HISPANIC VOTERS   Both major political parties are trying to attract new voters among the rapidly growing Hispanic population. Here, two Hispanic men add their names to the voter rolls at a Democratic party registration drive in Texas. What methods do parties use to court new groups of voters during a campaign?

Age

Age is one of the most important variables when explaining why some people vote and others do not. The youngest groups of eligible voters go to the polls much less often than older voters. This was true even in the exciting 2008 presidential election when young people played such a visible role in the Obama campaign in organizing state and local campaign organizations and get-out-the-vote efforts. Though 2 million more 18- to 29-year-olds voted than in 2004, their voting turnout was still only 51 percent (up 2 percent from the previous presidential election, to be sure).[30] In comparison, turnout among older voters age 65 to 74 was 72 percent. The reasons for low turnout among young people may be that they tend to be less rooted in communities, less familiar with registration and voting procedures, less in the habit of voting, and less clear about what stake they have in elections.[31] With that said, the youth vote has been growing steadily. Turnout among them was only 36 percent in 2000.

Gender

Women were prevented from participating in politics for a large part of our history; they got the vote, by constitutional amendment, only in 1920. Not all women immediately took advantage of this new opportunity. For many years, women voted and participated in politics at lower rates than men—about 10 or 15 percent lower in the elections of the 1950s, for example. The gender gap in voting and other forms of political participation disappeared in the United States by the end of the 1980s.[32] In fact, by 2008, women voted at a significantly higher rate than men, around 66 percent compared to 62 percent in that year's presidential election (again, see Figure 10.3). This marks a dramatic change over the past two or three decades and can probably be traced to the improvement in the educational attainments of women, the entrance of more women than ever into the paid workforce, and the increased importance of issues such as pay equity and abortion on the American political agenda.

Does It Matter Who Votes?

Some observers have argued that it doesn't matter if many people don't vote because their preferences aren't much different from those who do; the results would be about the same if everyone voted. In some elections, nonvoters have shown support for the same candidate who won, so their votes would apparently have changed nothing,[33] and some surveys have indicated that nonvoters' policy preferences differ little from those of voters.

? How does the fact that more educated, wealthy Americans vote than do less-educated, poor Americans fit in with the Founders' vision for the United States?

However, we should not be too quick to accept these arguments, just as few now accept the nineteenth-century view that there was no need for women to vote because their husbands could protect their interests. Even when the expressed preferences of nonvoters or nonparticipators do not look very distinctive, their objective circumstances, and therefore their needs for government services, may differ markedly.[34] Hispanics, the young, and those with low incomes might benefit from government programs that are of less interest to other citizens. A political system that included and mobilized these people vigorously might produce quite different government policies. There is a growing body of evidence, in fact, that high- and low-income people in the United States have very different preferences about what government should do and that elected officials are more likely to attend to the views of higher-income groups than others.[35] It is also known that government efforts to compensate people with low incomes in the rich democracies is associated with the degree to which low-income people vote, with the United States, where low-income people participate at far lower rates than others, doing the least in this area of government activity.[36]

Campaigning for Office

10.5 Outline the process of campaigns for the presidency and Congress

The ideas we discussed about how elections might ensure democratic policymaking all depend in various ways on what sorts of choices are presented to the voters. It makes a difference what kind of people run for office, whether they take clear policy stands, whether those stands differ from each other, and whether they stand for what the average voter wants. In evaluating how democratic our elections are, therefore, we need to examine what kinds of alternatives are put before the voters in campaigns.

Gaining the Nomination

We look here at campaigns for federal offices, namely, those for the presidency and Congress. The first step in these long election campaigns is winning the nomination of one's own party. For Senate and House incumbents—those who already hold office—as well as for sitting presidents seeking a second term, this is normally not a serious problem. They are the presumptive nominees. Thus, Bill Clinton did not face a serious threat to his renomination in 1996, nor did George W. Bush in 2004.

In a formal sense, the Republican and Democratic presidential nominees are selected at their national conventions in the summer before the presidential election. In both parties, the nomination goes to the winner of a majority of delegates to the national party convention mostly chosen in state primaries and caucuses (to be described later). The Republicans select their delegates on a "winner-take-all" basis, meaning that the candidate in a primary or caucus who wins the most

superdelegates

Elected officials from all levels of government who are appointed by party committees to be delegates to the national convention of the Democratic party; not selected in primary elections or caucuses.

votes wins all the delegates from that state. The Democrats select their delegates on a proportional basis, with the delegates to the convention distributed in rough proportion to the vote received by each candidate in primary and caucus elections. The Democrats' popularly elected primary and caucus delegates are supplemented by **superdelegates**, usually party luminaries and elected officials, including members of Congress, and state and local officials. In 2008, almost one in five delegates to the Democratic convention fell into this category.

Senate and House nominees are selected in different ways in the various states, with most using a combination of conventions and primaries where party activists and supporters predominate.[37] Senate incumbents and House incumbents rarely face renomination challenges, especially if they are on good terms with the people who are part of the party's base. In the House during the 2000–2008 election cycles, for example, as we show in Chapter 11, 70 percent of incumbents were generally renominated unopposed, with only 5 percent of them, on average, denied renomination. (In 2010, some of this changed as Tea Party candidates successfully challenged a number of House incumbent Republicans for renomination; see Chapter 11 for more on this.)

Who Has a Chance

In any given presidential election, only a handful of candidates are serious possibilities. So far in American history, these have virtually always been middle-aged or elderly white men with extensive formal educations, fairly high incomes,[38] and substantial experience as public figures—usually as government officials (especially vice presidents, governors, or senators) or military heroes. The Democrats broke the white male mold in 2008 when Hillary Clinton and Barack Obama contended for the nomination. Movie stars, media commentators, business executives, and others who would be president almost always have to perform important government service before they are seriously considered for the presidency. Ronald Reagan, for example, most of whose career was spent acting in motion pictures and on television, served as governor of California before being elected president.

Since the mid-1960s and until 2008, serious candidates for the presidency primarily have come from the ranks of former governors such as Bill Clinton and George W. Bush (who presumably had demonstrated executive ability) and vice presidents (who have a great deal of public visibility and name recognition). Indeed, the single best stepping-stone to becoming president has been the vice presidency,

COLD BUT WORTH IT John McCain's win in the New Hampshire primary gave him a leg up on his rivals in the race for the Republican presidential nomination in 2008. Here, he makes a campaign stop in Hanover with his wife, Cindy. Do primaries like New Hampshire's serve useful purposes in helping Americans choose their presidential nominees? If so, what are they?

which is usually filled by former senators or governors. Since 1900, 5 of the 18 presidents have succeeded from the vice presidency after the president's death or resignation, and two others, Nixon and Bush (the elder), were former vice presidents elected in their own right. In 2008, things changed dramatically. The Republican nominee John McCain and the two Democratic contenders who fought so closely and ferociously for the nomination, Hillary Clinton and Barack Obama, were sitting senators. Even in 2008, however, several governors were in the thick of things for awhile—Mike Huckabee, Mitt Romney, and Bill Richardson—although other sitting or former senators were in the mix as well—John Edwards, Christopher Dodd, and Fred Thompson. The outlier in the field was Rudolph Giuliani, a former and very prominent mayor of New York.

Serious candidates for president almost invariably represent mainstream American values and policy preferences. Seldom does an "extreme" candidate get very far. Serious candidates are also generally acceptable to the business community and have enthusiastic support from at least some sectors of industry or finance. They also must be considered "presidential" by the news media. And they must be attractive to those individuals and groups that fund campaigns.

In a number of respects, House and Senate candidates for their party nominations come from a similar mold. They are, on average, better educated and have higher incomes than most Americans; they are more likely to have business or professional backgrounds; and the vast majority are white men. Women and minorities have been making some inroads recently, however (see Chapter 11). In homogeneous and safe House districts, more extreme candidates can gain the party nomination because the only people they need appeal to are the party base, quite liberal in the Democratic Party and quite conservative in the Republican Party.

Getting Started   A person who wants to run for the presidency usually begins at least two or three years before the election by testing the waters, asking friends and financial backers if they will support a run, and observing how people react to the mythical "Great Mentioner." A friendly journalist may write that Senator Blathers "has been mentioned" as a smart, attractive, strong candidate; Blathers waits to see whether anyone agrees. The would-be candidate may commission a national survey to check for name recognition and a positive image. He or she may put together an exploratory committee to round up private endorsements, commitments, and financial contributions, perhaps setting up private political action committees to gather money.

? The media play a big role in a candidate's initial test of the waters for an electoral run, but Internet buzz, including social-network sites, is becoming increasingly useful, too. Assuming that electronic networking will grow more important in future campaigns, what new or unexplored innovations may be used in the future?

If all goes well in the early stages, the presidential aspirant becomes more serious, assembling a group of close advisers, formulating strategy, officially announcing his or her candidacy, forming a fund-raising operation, setting up campaign and personal websites, and putting together organizations in key states. Early money is crucial to finance organization and advertising.[39] Raising serious money from donors big and small—the latter, primarily through the Internet—is a clear sign to party bigwigs, associated interest and advocacy groups, and the news media that a candidate ought to be taken seriously. The relationship between money-raising and consideration as a serious candidate is now so important that it is commonly called the "invisible primary."

It is a vicious cycle of sorts. If a candidate can't raise money, she or he is not taken seriously. If a candidate is not taken seriously, then raising money becomes even more difficult. And with little money in the bank and not much coming in, failure in the first primaries and caucuses is inevitable. Candidates who can't raise money drop out early. In 2008, Bill Richardson, John Edwards, and Christopher Dodd were gone early from the Democratic nomination race, facing the awesome campaign finance machines of Hillary Clinton and Barack Obama, each of whom had raised about $100 million by the end of 2007 and each of whom was spending money almost as fast as it was coming in. When John McCain nearly ran out of money in mid-2007, he was largely written off by commentators in the news media and by many political professionals, with attention shifting to the deep-pocketed Mitt Romney, who in the end spent $42 million of his own money. To the surprise of nearly everyone, however, and contrary to what usually happens in this scenario, McCain rescued his campaign—borrowing money at first to do so—and started to raise money in earnest after his victory in the New Hampshire primary on January 8, 2008.

At one time, an important early decision was whether to be a part of the public campaign finance system—in which the federal government matches the first $250 from each individual donor on condition that candidates in the 2007–2008 election cycle limit preconvention campaign spending to around $50 million—or to go it alone, raise hard money contributions from individuals (limited to $2,300 in 2008) and PACs (limited to $5,000), and spend what they wish. But things began to change in 2000 when George W. Bush became the first serious candidate to eschew public financing since it was first established in 1976. Democrats John Kerry and John Dean, as well as Republican President Bush, skipped public funding in 2004. In the 2007–2008 election cycle, none of the leading contenders for the presidential nomination in either party, with the exception of John Edwards, chose public funding with its attendant spending limits. (McCain did for a time, then changed his mind.)

Public financing of presidential nomination campaigns seems to be going by the board for two reasons. First, the costs of running a credible campaign for the party presidential nomination have gone up much faster than the amount that candidates who choose the public funding route are allowed to spend. Most candidates do not want to handcuff themselves in this way. Second, it is easier now to raise money outside the public financing system. The campaign reform act in 2002 substantially increased the amount of money individuals can give to candidates. And the Internet has proved to be an incredibly efficient and cost-effective device for raising lots of money from individual contributors, something Barack Obama did particularly well in 2007 and 2008.

Another important early decision involves which state primaries and caucus contests to enter. Each entry takes a lot of money, energy, and organization, and any loss is damaging; many candidates drop out after just a few early defeats, as John Edwards, Fred Thompson, and Mitt Romney did in 2008. Rudy Giuliani gambled that he could skip all the early Republican primaries and caucuses and focus on the January 29 Florida primary where he thought he had a big advantage, but his campaign had lost momentum by then, and he lost badly in the state. Soon after, he withdrew from the race. To win the nomination, it is generally necessary to put together a string of primary and caucus victories, something John McCain was able to do in 2008, starting with New Hampshire. By the end of the day on March 4, after winning the big primaries in Ohio and Texas, he had secured the nomination with a majority of Republican convention delegates pledged to him, an outcome made possible by the winner-take-all rules of the Republican party. With no reason to go on, Mike Huckabee withdrew, throwing his support to McCain.

Presidential Primaries and Caucuses

Since 1952, no national party convention has taken more than one ballot to nominate its candidate for the presidency, and the pre-convention front-runner has always been the nominee.[40] Since the 1970s, a majority of the delegates to the conventions in each party have been chosen in state primary elections, with direct voting by citizens. A small majority of these primaries are closed, meaning they are open only to voters who have registered Republican or Democrat before the date of the primary; the others are open to all voters who can decide on the day of the election which party's ballot they wish to take into the voting booth. The type of primary can affect how one campaigns. Because closed primaries mean that the bulk of the voters likely will be party loyalists, candidates tend to pitch their appeal to the party base. In open primaries with more diverse voters, candidates tend to make broader appeals. Many states—most famously Iowa, but also Nevada, Washington, Wyoming, and Colorado, among others—use caucuses, where active party members and officials gather in meetings to select the delegates to the national convention. To confuse matters even further, some states select convention delegates in primaries and caucuses—most notably, Texas in 2008.

It is especially important for a candidate to establish momentum by winning early primaries and caucuses. Early winners get press attention, financial contributions, and better standings in the polls as voters and contributors decide they are viable candidates and must have some merit if people in other states have supported them. All these factors—attention from the media, money, and increased popular support—help the candidates who win early contests go on to win more and more contests.[41]

Because the states and the parties—not Congress or the president—control this nominating process, the system is a disorganized, even chaotic one, and it changes from one election to the next. Some states have primaries for both parties on the same day (including the all-important New Hampshire primaries); others hold primaries for the parties on separate dates. States are particularly anxious that they are not ignored, so an increasing number of them have moved their primary and caucus dates forward in the calendar. States with late primaries, even very large ones such as California, discovered in recent elections that the winners of early primaries had, for all intents and purposes, sewed up the party nominations, discounting the importance of their own primaries and caucuses. As a result, the primary and caucus season started to get "front-loaded" in 2004, with the bulk of delegates selected for both parties between the Iowa caucuses and the New Hampshire primaries in late January and the Kansas primaries in mid-March. In 2008, this became a stampede, with states leap-frogging over the others to position themselves earlier in the calendar. The result in 2008 was that 20 states—including big ones such as New York, New Jersey, Illinois, Missouri, and California—held their primaries on February 5, only a little more than a month after the first caucus in Iowa on January 3 (always the first caucus by state law) and a little less than a month after the first-in-the-nation primary in New Hampshire (always the first primary by state law) on January 8.

EVER SO CLOSE Hillary Clinton came very close to besting Barack Obama in the contest for the 2008 race for the Democratic nomination and becoming the first major-party female candidate for the presidency. She did well against Obama in primary contests but lost badly to him in the caucus states. She had about the same number of popular votes nationally as Obama. How might a Clinton–McCain contest have played out?

The large states of Florida and Michigan held their Democratic primaries in mid and late January, respectively, against the rules of the Democratic National Committee, and were penalized for doing so. Perhaps ironically, the Clinton–Obama race was so close that states with late primaries, such as North Carolina and Indiana, became very important in 2008.

Congressional Nomination Machinery

Primaries are held in every state—sometimes in conjunction with caucuses and conventions—to select party nominees for House and Senate seats. These are done separately from the presidential primaries and caucuses and take place later in the election calendar. Because these congressional nominating primaries are not tied to the more visible presidential nomination process, public interest and news media attention are lower, with extremely low turnout the inevitable result.[42] Turnout increased some in 2010 when Tea Party activists challenged several Republican incumbents who they considered not conservative enough, including Senator Bob Bennett in Utah and Governor Charlie Crist (an aspirant for the Republican Senate nomination) of Florida.

The Presidential Nominating Conventions

Because the front-runner now comes to the national convention with enough delegates to win on the first ballot, the gathering has become a coronation ceremony in which pre-pledged delegates ratify the selection of the leading candidate, accept that candidate's choice for the vice presidency, and put on a colorful show for the media and the country. Enthusiasm and unity are staged for the national television audience. Barack Obama's acceptance speech before 80,000 wildly cheering supporters at Invesco Field in Denver drew a national television audience of more than 38 million. John McCain's "town hall–style" acceptance speech at the Republican National Convention in Minneapolis, before an equally enthusiastic crowd, drew a slightly larger national television audience.

It is a disaster for a political party if serious conflicts break out or the timing of the elaborate nomination process goes wrong. The Democrats were in turmoil over the Vietnam War at their 1968 gathering, for example, with the conflict played out on the convention floor and in the streets of Chicago, carried live on television. By all accounts, the conflict and disunity played a role in Hubert Humphrey's loss in the general election to Republican Richard Nixon. In 1972, conflict between the eventual nominee George McGovern and Ted Kennedy, as well as procedural snafus, meant that McGovern didn't deliver his televised acceptance speech until early morning, well after most people on the East Coast and the Midwest had gone to bed.

In 2008, disappointed supporters of Hillary Clinton—whom Barack Obama barely beat for the Democratic nomination—threatened to carry their campaign to the floor of the convention in Denver. Fortunately for the Democrats, both Hillary and Bill Clinton gave eloquent speeches in support of Obama, nipping the rebellion in the bud.

Nominating Incumbent Presidents

We have been focusing on how outsiders and political challengers try to win party presidential nominations. Things are very different for incumbent presidents seeking reelection, like Bill Clinton in 1996 or George W. Bush in 2004. These candidates must also enter and win primaries and caucuses, but they have the machinery of government working for them and, if times are reasonably good, a unified party behind them. They also have an easier time getting campaign contributions, especially for the primaries when incumbent presidents only occasionally meet serious competition. They campaign on the job, taking credit for policy successes while discounting or blaming others, such as Congress, for failures. Winning renomination as president is usually easy, except in cases of disaster such as the 1968 Vietnam War debacle for Lyndon Johnson.

THE PUBLIC FACE OF PARTY CONVENTIONS   The impression conveyed by political conventions can have an important impact on elections. The apparent unhappiness of many anti–Vietnam War delegates with their party's selection at the 1968 Democratic convention in Chicago severely damaged the campaign of nominee Hubert Humphrey. In contrast, the 1984 Republican convention that selected Ronald Reagan as its nominee more nearly resembled a coronation and gave Reagan and the GOP a fast start in the fall campaign. Are party conventions still necessary? Might there be an easier way to certify each party's nominee? Do they still exist because of their pep-rally appeal?

Nomination Politics and Democracy   What does all this have to do with democratic control of government? Several things. On the one hand, as we have indicated, the presidential nomination process has some success in coming up with candidates who take stands with wide popular appeal, much as electoral competition theories dictate. On the other hand, as the sharp differences between Republican and Democratic convention delegates suggest (see Table 9.2), Republican and Democratic nominees tend to differ in certain systematic ways, in responsible party fashion. Party platforms—the parties' official statements of their stand on issues—tend to include appeals to average voters but also distinctive appeals to each party's base constituencies.

? How closely did you follow the 2008 presidential primaries and caucuses? Did the long presidential nomination campaign season change your opinion of any of the candidates? Did it make you more—or less—inclined to vote?

Both these tendencies might be considered good for democracy. However, the crucial role of party activists and money givers in selecting candidates means that nominees and their policy stands are chosen partly to appeal to party elites, financial contributors, and strong partisans rather than to ordinary voters. Thus, neither party's nominee may stand for what ordinary citizens want, the result being voter dissatisfaction and no ideal democratic outcome.

These problems are even more evident with regard to House and Senate nomination processes. Even more than candidates for the party presidential nominations, House and Senate candidates in the states are tightly bound to the wishes of local and state party activists and party officials, and beholden to the financial and other assistance provided by advocacy and interest groups, in the context of low visibility, low turnout elections. The general public is almost entirely shut out.

The General Election Campaign

The general election campaign pitting the candidates of the two major parties against one another, with an occasional third party thrown into the mix, is a very different sort of contest than the run for party nomination. It requires different things from the candidates, campaign organizations, and associated interest and advocacy groups, and has an entirely different tone and set of rules, both formal and informal. The general election campaign season, much like the nomination campaign season, has gotten much longer as well.

Getting the Campaign Up and Running In the not-too-distant past, the general election campaign generally began on or about Labor Day, some weeks after the Republican and Democratic conventions were done with their business. That's why it was referred to as the "autumn campaign" and the "fall campaign." Today, however, as we have suggested, the presidential nominees for both parties are known months before the conventions even convene and they begin to campaign for the presidency months before their formal nomination. Flush with campaign money and unworried about their no-longer-relevant challengers within their own party, each of the presumptive nominees—George W. Bush and Al Gore in 2000, Bush and John Kerry in 2004, and McCain in 2008—repositioned their campaigns by mid-spring to take on their general election foe: setting up a campaign organization in each state, sending aides to coordinate backers and local party leaders, and continuing the money-raising effort. Barack Obama swung into general election mode by early June in 2008 once he had bested Hillary Clinton for the nomination.

Once the post-convention autumn campaign begins in September, the candidates' staffs have the nominees making speeches in six or seven media markets each week, with the pace intensifying as the November election draws closer, concentrating on so-called battleground states, where the contest between the presidential candidates is deemed to be very close and could go either way (see the "Mapping American Politics" feature on campaign ad buys). In all of this, hired pollsters and campaign consultants are deeply involved, playing a role in virtually all tactical and strategic decision making.[43]

A new media blitz begins, with many brief spot commercials on television, including "attack" ads such as Democrat Bill Clinton's in 1992 mocking George H. W. Bush's "read my lips, no new taxes" pledge (which he did not keep). Political consultants use voter focus groups to identify hot-button emotional appeals. Negative advertising has been heavily criticized as simplistic and misleading, but it has often proved effective and is difficult to control or counteract. (Some scholars even argue that such ads increase voter interest and provide needed information.[44]) In 2004 and 2008, much of this advertising, as well as fund-raising, took place on the Internet. In 2008, Barack Obama's campaign took things a step further, becoming very adept in using social media such as Facebook, MySpace, and Twitter not only to spread positive and negative campaign messages, but also to organize events and mobilize volunteers.

Each campaign also uses micro-targeting techniques to identify and communicate with base supporters and persuadable voters who might be convinced to vote for the candidate. Sophisticated software allows campaign organizations to combine surveys, census track data, and materials from marketing research firms to identify base and persuadable voters and to tailor messages to particular groups and people and deliver the message by mail, door-to-door canvassing, e-mail, and social-network tools. Republican messages are directed, for example, not only to well-off people but more specifically to those who subscribe to *Golf Weekly* and shop at Nordstrom. Democratic messages, using the same micro-targeting, might be directed to members of teachers unions and contributors to the American Civil Liberties Union.[45]

In all of these activities, presidential candidates, with lots of help to be sure, run their own campaigns. They and not the political parties decide on campaign themes, schedules, and strategies. The national party organizations are there to help, running parallel advertising campaigns supporting their candidate and attacking the opponent, channeling money to state and local party organizations, and getting potential supporters registered and to the polls. Meanwhile, interest groups and advocacy organizations run their own ad campaigns and get-out-the-vote efforts. Organized labor and advocacy organizations such as MoveOn.org, for example, run ads in support of the Democratic presidential candidate (and House and Senate Democratic candidates), raise money, and work on turning out Democrats, while conservative Christian groups and business-oriented organizations work to help the Republican side.

Informing Voters What kinds of information do voters get in presidential campaigns? Among other things, voters get information on the candidates' stands on the issues, their past performances, and their personal characteristics.

Issues Some of the information voters get concerns issues. In accord with electoral competition theories, both the Republican and the Democratic candidates typically have tried to appeal to the average voter by taking similar, popular stands on a range of policies; whether it be support for federal student loan programs, Head Start, or environmental regulation. In recent elections, however, intensification of partisanship has moved American presidential and congressional electoral campaigns in a more responsible party direction, with clear stands on the issues, differentiated from the other party. In 2004, Kerry and Bush, and Democratic and Republican congressional candidates, differed on private accounts under Social Security, a prescription drug program, tax cuts, faith-based initiatives,

GETTING "SWIFT BOATED" In the 2004 presidential campaign, 527 advocacy organizations became very important, mostly by running attack ads. One of the most effective was the Swift Boat group, which attacked Democratic candidate John Kerry's war record, calling his wartime awards and citations "dishonest and dishonorable." Is it truly possible or even reasonable for an organization to promote certain issues while not endorsing a candidate?

MAPPING AMERICAN POLITICS

Ad Buys and Battleground States

Introduction As you have seen, presidents are selected not by the people directly, but by votes in the Electoral College. The winner is that candidate who wins a majority of electoral votes. Campaigns are conducted on a state-by-state basis in a bid to put together a majority of electoral votes. With the exception of Nebraska and Maine, states use winner-take-all systems in which the candidate with the most votes (not necessarily a majority) wins all the state's electoral votes. Knowing this, campaign managers and their candidates focus on a relative handful of states where the contest is too close to call and where winning might affect the outcome of the presidential contest. They virtually ignore states that are not "in play," where the outcome is a foregone conclusion. In the 2008 election, for example, Democrats were in such a commanding position in California, New York, and Massachusetts that neither Democrats nor Republicans thought it wise

to use scarce funds to campaign there. Republicans were so far ahead in Texas, Utah, and Indiana that neither party thought it worthwhile to campaign there.

Mapping Ad Buys The cartogram below, with the size of the states reflecting the number of electoral votes, highlights the states where the parties and campaign

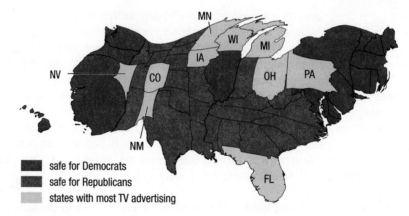

States Sized by Electoral Vote Totals, Colored by Party Leanings and Ad Buys

©2006 M. D. Ward

abortion, and Iraq, among other things. In 2008, as related in the chapter-opening story, Barack Obama and John McCain took decidedly different stands on major issues, especially on the wars in Iraq and Afghanistan, global warming, and health care reform. On these issues, the Democratic candidate tends to take a more liberal (on both economic and social dimensions) stand than the Republican, just as Democratic party identifiers, activists, money givers, and convention delegates tend to be more liberal than their Republican counterparts.

Past Performance Often candidates focus on past performance in their campaigns. The "outs" blame the "ins" for wars, recessions, and other calamities. The "ins" brag about how they have brought peace and prosperity and paint a warm picture of a glorious future, without saying exactly how it will come about. When these issues become the overriding theme in a campaign, the result is a "retrospective," "reward–punish" type of election. Democrat Franklin Roosevelt won a landslide victory in 1932, for example, because of popular discontent with government performance under Herbert Hoover in the face of the Great Depression; Republican Ronald Reagan capitalized on economic and foreign policy troubles under Jimmy Carter to win in 1980.

Incumbent presidents, of course, can do things that accurately or inaccurately suggest successful performance. They can try to schedule recessions for off years, pumping up the economy in time for reelection. Or they can make dramatic foreign policy moves just before election day, like Nixon's 1972 trips to the Soviet Union and China.

organizations bought the greatest number of television ads urging votes for their candidate in the month or so before the 2004 election. You can see that significant television ad buys occurred in only 10 states, but those 10 accounted for 88 percent of all such ads bought across the entire country. The focus of the campaign on battleground states is very evident. Note that several of the very largest Electoral College states were not among those 10, including California, Illinois, New Jersey, and New York (reliably Democratic) and Texas (reliably Republican). Ad buys occurred overwhelmingly in states where party and campaign professionals believed either party's presidential candidate had a chance to win. The cartogram below shows the final electoral vote outcome.

What Do You Think? Taking a look at how the vote turned out in the battleground states, whose campaign seems to have done a better job of using ad buys effectively? If you lived in a nonbattleground state, did it seem that there was very little campaign advertising on television? If you lived in a battleground state, did it seem that there was too much advertising? Is there any way to convince parties and presidential campaigns to wage the presidential battle on a nationwide basis so long as we use the Electoral College system for selecting presidents?

Note: In cartograms, Alaska is not shown (although information is included in calculations), and Hawaii is moved closer to the mainland.

Source for top left cartogram: "Presidential TV Advertising Battle Narrows to Just Ten Battleground States," Nielsen Monitor-Plus and the University of Wisconsin Advertising Project (press release, October 12, 2004).

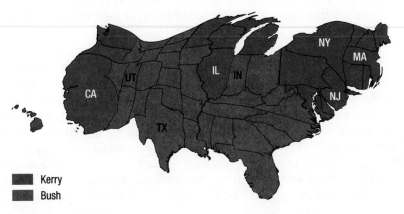

■ Kerry
■ Bush

States Sized by Electoral Vote Totals, Colored by Election Outcomes, 2004
©2006 M. D. Ward

Standard US Map

Personal Characteristics Most of all, however, voters get a chance during the general election campaign to learn about the real or alleged personal characteristics of the candidates. Even when the candidates are talking about something else, they give an impression of either competence or incompetence. Jimmy Carter, for example, emphasized his expertise as a "nuclear engineer," whereas Gerald Ford was haunted by films of him stumbling on airplane ramps.

Candidates also come across as interpersonally warm or cold. Dwight D. Eisenhower's radiant grin appeared everywhere in 1952 and 1956, as Reagan's did in 1984, but Richard Nixon was perceived as cold and aloof in 1968, despite clever efforts at selling his personality.

Still another dimension of candidates' personalities is a candidate's presumed strength or weakness. George H. W. Bush overcame the so-called wimp factor in 1988 with his tough talk about crime and the flag. Merely by surviving many personal attacks in 1992 and 1996, Clinton appeared strong and resilient.

The sparse and ambiguous treatment of policy issues in campaigns, as well as the emphasis on past performance and personal competence, fits better with ideas about electoral reward and punishment than with responsible parties or issue-oriented electoral competition models of democratic elections. Candidate personalities are not irrelevant to the democratic control of government. Obviously, it is useful for voters to pick presidents who possess competence, warmth, and strength. And citizens may be more skillful in judging people than in figuring out complicated policy issues.

Voters can be fooled, however, by dirty tricks or slick advertising that sells presidential candidates' personalities and tears down the opponent. Moreover, the focus on personal imagery may distract attention from policy stands. If candidates who favor unpopular policies are elected on the basis of attractive personal images, democratic control of policymaking is weakened. By the purchase of advertising and the hiring of smart consultants, money may, in effect, overcome the popular will.

Money in General Elections

Money plays a crucial role in American general election campaigns and elections. Not surprisingly, parties and candidates spend much of their time and effort raising money for campaigns.

The Scale of Campaign Money and Where It Comes From   Presidential and congressional campaigns cost a great deal of money, although the system is so complex that even seasoned observers can make only educated guesses about the total. We have good data on money coming from certain sources but not from others. For example, we know that federal candidates during the 2007–2008 election cycle spent around $5.3 billion,[46] but we are less sure about a wide range of other expenditures on their behalf by advocacy groups. What we do know is that more money is raised and spent from one presidential election cycle to the next (see Figure 10.4) and the same is true of congressional election cycles.

Hard Money   Hard money refers to contributions and spending that fall under the jurisdiction of the Federal Election Commission. The rules followed by the FEC are the result of two major reform bills—the Federal Election Campaign Act and its later amendments passed during the 1970s and the McCain-Feingold Campaign Reform Act of 2002—interpretations of this legislation by the Supreme Court, and administrative rulings by the Commission itself. Importantly, in the case of *Citizens United* v. *Federal Election Commission* (2010), the Court ruled that corporations and

FIGURE 10.4   The Growth in Spending in Presidential Elections*

*Spending by candidates, party, and independent committees. All numbers are based on summary reports filed with the Federal Election Commission, January 31, 2009. *Source*: The Center for Responsive Politics.

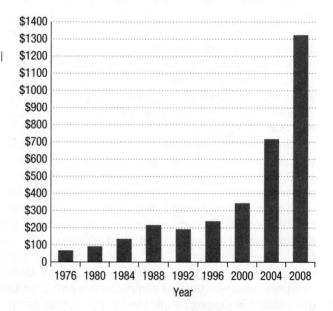

unions may not be limited on what they spend on advertising in support of or opposition to a candidate, nor can any pre-election advertising-free time period be imposed on them so long as they do not work in close collaboration with party or candidate committees. This means that corporations and unions likely will play a much bigger role than in the past in financing campaigns, from federal elections to local races.

Individuals   The largest single source of funding for presidential and congressional campaigns is from individual contributors, ranging from those who make small contributions to the candidates in response to an e-mail or letter solicitation or a call from a party worker, to wealthier individuals who give the maximum amount allowed in 2008 of $2,400 to a single candidate (or a total of $42,700 to several candidates) and $28,500 to a national party committee per year. (See Table 10.1 for FEC rules on contributions limits for the 2009–2010 election cycle.) Before passage of the Federal Election Campaign Act (FECA), individuals could make contributions of unlimited size, and candidates and the parties depended on a handful of very rich individuals to fund their operations. After limits were placed on the size of allowable contributions, both parties invented a variety of ways to attract small contributions from hundreds of thousands of people, beginning with targeted mail and telephone solicitations, then adding Internet fundraising, a development that fueled much of the funding for the Obama campaign. Indeed, roughly 55 percent of Obama's funds came from individuals giving $200 or less.[47]

Candidates   Senate and House candidates often contribute and lend money to their own campaigns, usually on the order of 15 percent for the former and 9 percent for the latter.[48] Sometimes Senate candidates will spend spectacular amounts of their own money; Democrat John Corzine set the record in 2000 with contributions of $62 million to his winning campaign (in 2007, he spent about $100 million of his own money in an unsuccessful attempt to stay on as New Jersey's governor). On the presidential side, candidates seeking the party nomination will often contribute or lend money to their campaigns; both John McCain and Hillary Clinton did this in 2007 and 2008. But once each party chooses its nominee for the presidency, presidential candidates have no need to use their personal resources. There are sufficient campaign monies coming from other sources to finance a full campaign.

Political Action Committees (PACs)   You will recall from Chapter 7 that PACs are entities created by interest groups—whether business firms, unions, membership organizations, or liberal and conservative advocacy groups—to collect money and make contributions to candidates in federal elections (i.e., to candidates for the presidency, the House of Representatives, and the Senate). In 2008, PACs raised about $1.2 billion to contribute to presidential and congressional candidates, party committees, and their own electioneering campaigning (television, radio, and Internet advertising on the issues or candidates).[49]

Oddly enough, passage of the Bipartisan Campaign Reform Act (McCain-Feingold) in 2002, which was aimed at banning soft money in federal elections—contributions with no limits on amounts to national party committees by groups and individuals for so-called party-building activities like get-out-the-vote efforts—gave an added boost to PACs by allowing corporate and labor PACs to accept larger donations from individual contributors than in the past, contribute more to candidates and parties than under the old law, and run issue campaigns (that did not ask voters to vote for or against specific candidates) on television and radio right up to the day of primary

TABLE 10.1 Contribution Limits 2009–2010

	To Each Candidate or Candidate Committee per Election	To National Party Committee per Calendar Year	To State, District, and Local Party Committee per Calendar Year	To Any Other Political Committee per Calendar Year	Special Limits
Individual	$2,400	$30,400	$10,000 (combined limit)	$5,000	$115,500 overall biennial limit: $45,600 to all candidates $69,900 to all PACs and parties
National Party Committee	$5,000	No limit	No limit	$5,000	$42,600 to Senate candidate per campaign
State, District, and Local Party Committee	$5,000 (combined limit)	No limit	No limit	$5,000 (combined limit)	No limit
PAC (multicandidate)	$5,000	$15,000	$5,000 (combined limit)	$5,000	No limit
PAC (not multicandidate)	$2,400	$30,400	$10,000 (combined limit)	$5,000	No limit
Authorized Campaign Committee	$2,000	No limit	No limit	$5,000	No limit

Source: Federal Election Commission.

and general elections, with no limitations on their aggregate or total expenditures. Business PACs were best able to take advantage of the loosened rules.

Political Parties The political parties also play an important role in helping out party candidates in congressional and presidential elections. Campaign finance laws limit the amount of money that can be contributed by parties to the candidates' official committees in House, Senate, and presidential elections, as well as the amounts they can spend on what are called "coordinated" campaigns, run in close cooperation with their candidates. (See Table 10.1.) This form of spending goes for services like polling and advertising. More importantly, as described later, parties can also run very large and mostly unregulated "independent" campaigns on behalf of candidates. For these various campaign activities, the Republican National Committee raised almost $1 billion in 2008, while the Democratic National Committee raised a little more than $900 million.[50]

Public Funding Since 1971—excepting 2008—most of the money spent in the fall presidential campaign by the two presidential candidates' official campaign committees has come from the federal treasury, paid by taxpayers. Taxpayers can check off a box on their tax returns to authorize a $3 contribution from public funds. The government uses these taxpayer contributions to provide matches for money contributors give to candidates during the primary and general election campaigns of those candidates who agree to spending limits. In 2004, the Kerry and Bush campaigns each received $74.4 million in public funds for the general election in the fall. Although Kerry and Bush refused public money for their nomination campaigns, both accepted it for the general election contest. Republican John McCain accepted public funding of roughly $84 million in 2008. But why would they do such a thing, given the fact that accepting public funding for their campaigns limits what they can spend?

- Because publicly provided funds are not inconsiderable.
- Because the two party presidential candidates get a great deal of free publicity simply by being the standard bearer of one of the two major parties.
- Because various state, local, and national party committees spend generously on the campaigns.
- Because interest groups and advocacy organizations spend lavishly on independent parallel campaigns (see Chapter 7).

Dramatically breaking with tradition, Democratic nominee Barack Obama chose in 2008 to reject public funding with its accompanying spending limits, primarily because of his remarkably successful fund-raising operation with monies coming to his campaign committee both from millions of small and medium-sized donations raised primarily online and from large donors. In doing so, he went back on a promise to use public funding and limit his spending, saying he needed to do so because of expected attacks from independent conservative advocacy groups and 527 and 501 organizations (explained later).

House and Senate candidate campaigns do not receive public funding and, by virtue of that fact, face no limits on what they can spend in the general election. They rely on contributions from individuals, PACs, and political party committees to their official campaigns; more than a few rich individuals self-fund a portion of their campaign expenses. And, of course, parties, interest groups, corporations, and advocacy organizations spend lavishly on issue ad campaigns and get-out-the-vote efforts that are extremely helpful to congressional candidates.

Other Money   After soft money was banned, 527 and 501 organizations gained favor, even as independent campaigns grew in importance.

527s   So named because of where they are defined in the Tax Code, 527s are entities that can use unregulated money to talk about issues, mobilize voters, and praise or criticize candidates and officeholders—the only restriction being the use of television and radio in the period immediately preceding primary and general elections. There are no limits on contributions to them, nor are 527s limited in what they can spend. Many of these groups devoted to liberal or conservative causes and candidates sprouted up after passage of McCain-Feingold and played a very large role in the 2004 presidential election—Swift Boat Veterans for Truth (anti-Kerry) and MoveOn.org (anti-Bush) were the most prominent—and the 2006 congressional elections. Many of these groups depend on very large contributions from a handful of rich individuals; George Soros contributed more than $15 million to anti-Bush 527s in 2004, while Texas oilman T. Boone Pickens gave $4.6 million to anti-Kerry groups.

501s   Although 527s are still around, they have lost favor. For one thing, both John McCain and Barack Obama condemned them in 2008 and informed 527 groups that they did not want their help. Perhaps more importantly, a better entity was discovered. 527s are required to report their total receipts and expenditures to the Internal Revenue Service (IRS) and report the identity of their contributors and how much they gave. *501* tax-exempt organizations—entities whose main purpose is to encourage "civic engagement"—must also report receipts and expenditures to the

IRS, but less frequently than 527s, and they are not obligated to report the identities of their contributors. And, like 527s, there are no limits on how much money they can collect or spend. Not surprisingly, 501s have come to play a bigger role in the campaign finance system.

Independent Campaign Spending The Supreme Court ruled in *Buckley* v. *Valeo* (1976) that individuals and interest groups, under the constitutional doctrine of free speech, can spend whatever amount they want on issue and candidate advertising so long as such efforts are not coordinated with the candidates' official campaign organizations. Because such spending is not regulated and has no reporting requirements, it is quite difficult to get a handle on how much money is involved.

Even the political parties can run independent campaigns, again with the proviso that they not coordinate with candidates' official candidate organizations. The Republican and Democratic parties accomplish this by having different sets of staff members working on the official campaign and the independent campaign. Party operatives like this mechanism because ads financed in this way cannot be attributed to or easily traced to the candidate. It is why so much independent campaign money is devoted to so-called attack ads.[51]

Does Money Talk?

Money matters a great deal in the presidential nomination process—aspirants for party nominations who cannot raise sizable funds always drop out of the race—but not so much during the post-convention run for the White House.[52] As we pointed out earlier, once a presidential campaign is under way, each of the major party candidates has at his or her disposal all of the organizational resources of the party organization and money from traditional party contributors and allied interest groups, as well as matching funds from the government (with the exception of Barack Obama in 2008, who chose to eschew public funding); each candidate has enough money to run a credible campaign.

Money may talk at a later stage, however. It is widely believed, although difficult to prove, that contributors of money often get something back.[53] The point is not that presidential, House, and Senate candidates take outright bribes in exchange for policy favors. Indeed, exchanges between politicians and money-givers are complex and varied, sometimes yielding little benefit to contributors. Undeniably, however, cozy relationships do tend to develop between politicians and major money-givers. Contributors gain access to, and a friendly hearing from, those whom they help to win office.

It is clear that money-givers are different from average citizens. They have special interests of their own. As we have indicated, a large amount of campaign money comes from large corporations, investment banking firms, wealthy families, labor unions, professional associations (e.g., doctors, lawyers, or realtors), and issue-oriented groups such as the National Rifle Association, Focus on the Family, and the National Abortion Rights Action League. The big contributors generally do not represent ordinary workers, consumers, or taxpayers, let alone minorities or the poor. Surveys show that the individuals who give money tend to have much higher incomes and more conservative views on economic issues than the average American.[54] This is true as well for those who contribute by way of the Internet.[55]

The result is political inequality. Those who are well organized or have a lot of money to spend on politics have a better chance of influencing policy than ordinary citizens do, and they tend to influence it in directions different from those the general public would want. The role of money in presidential and congressional nomination and election campaigns is a major problem for the working of democracy in the United States.

Election Outcomes

10.6 Assess how voters make their decisions

After the parties and candidates have presented their campaigns, the voters decide. Exactly how people make their voting decisions affects how well or how poorly elections contribute to the democratic control of government.

How Voters Decide

Years of scholarly research have made it clear that feelings about the parties, the candidates, and the issues, as well as their own social characteristics, have substantial effects on how people vote.[56]

> **?** Can a candidate win without appealing to at least some members of the opposite party, as well as to independents? What role did crossover appeal play in the 2008 election?

Social Characteristics People's socioeconomic status, place of residence, religion, ethnic backgrounds, gender, and age are related to how they vote (see Figure 10.5). African Americans, Jews, and lower-income citizens for many years have tended to vote for Democrats, while white Protestants and upper-income Americans have voted for Republicans. Much of this stayed the same in 2008, but some things changed as well. In 2008, traditional Democratic voters increased their support for the Democratic candidate: 95 percent of African Americans, 78 percent of Jews, 67 percent of Hispanics, and 78 percent of those making less than $30,000 voted for Obama. Many traditional Republican groups stayed with the party in 2008; 54 percent of Protestants voted for McCain, as did 55 percent of people who regularly attend church and 53 percent of rural people. But Obama won the suburbs, increased the Democratic advantage in cities, and won the vote in all educational groups. The gender gap narrowed a bit in 2008, not because of a fall-off in the women's vote for the Democrats but because more men voted for Obama than they had for Kerry, Gore, or Clinton. A big change in 2008 was the 2:1 Democratic advantage among younger voters. Similar patterns held for congressional voting in 2008.

Party Loyalties To some extent, these social patterns work through long-term attachments to, or identification with, political parties. As indicated earlier, a majority of Americans still say they consider themselves Republicans or Democrats. Party loyalties vary among different groups of the population, often because of past or present differences between the parties on policy issues, especially economic and social issues.[57] For this reason, when people use their party identification as a shortcut for choosing a candidate, they are likely choosing a candidate who is close to them on the issues. The ability of party identification to serve as a useful tool for people to choose candidates that are close to them on the issues is further enhanced by the close linkages between the parties and ideologies, with Democrats generally more liberal (including party identifiers, activists, and candidates) and Republicans generally more conservative.[58]

Party loyalties are very good predictors of how people will vote.[59] Those who say they consider themselves Republicans tend to vote for Republican candidates in one election after another, and those who consider themselves Democrats vote for Democratic candidates. This is especially true in congressional elections and in state and local races, where most voters know little more about the candidates than

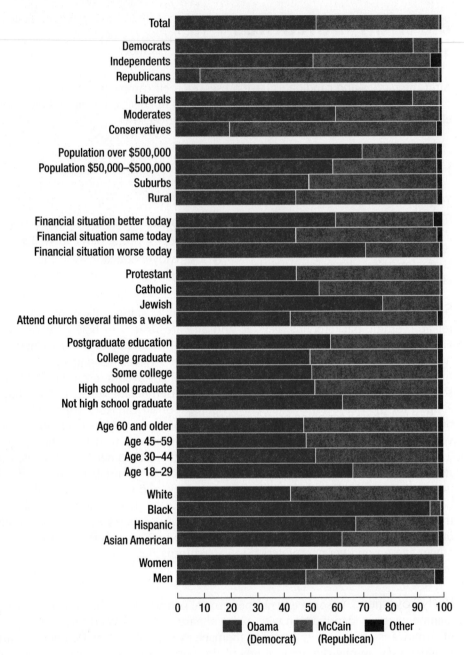

FIGURE 10.5 Presidential Vote in 2008, by Social Group

Minorities, urbanites, young people, liberals, and women voted strongly for Democrat Barack Obama in the 2008 election, while Protestants, regular church-goers, rural people, conservatives, and men favored Republican John McCain.
Source: "Edison/Mitofsky Exit Poll, 2008 Presidential Election," *CNN.com*, www.cnn.com/ELECTION/2008, November 5, 2008.

their party labels, but the party loyalty factor is extremely important in presidential elections as well. Thus, in 2008, 89 percent of Democratic identifiers voted for Obama, and 90 percent of Republican identifiers voted for McCain.

Candidates Presidential election outcomes have not simply reflected the party balance in the country; if that were true, Democrats would have won most presidential elections during the post–World War II period. Voters also pay a lot of attention to their perceptions of the personal characteristics of candidates. They vote heavily for candidates who have experience, appear strong and decisive, and convey personal warmth. The Republican candidate in 1952 and 1956, Dwight D. Eisenhower, had a tremendous advantage in these respects over his Democratic opponent, Adlai Stevenson[60]; so did Ronald Reagan over Walter Mondale in 1984, George H. W. Bush over Michael Dukakis in 1988, and George W. Bush over John

Kerry in 2004. In elections between 1952 and 1972, the contrast between Republican and Democratic candidates typically gained the Republicans four or five percentage points—just enough to overcome the Democrats' advantage in what political scientists call the *normal vote*: how votes would be cast if only party identification determined voters' choices for president. Democrats have won when they have managed to add attractive candidates to augment their lead in party identification; Bill Clinton in 1996 and Barack Obama in 2008 are examples.

Issues Voters also pay attention to issues. Sometimes this means choosing between different policy proposals for the future (as in the responsible party voting model), such as Reagan's 1980 promises to cut back federal government activity or Clinton's 1992 pledges of jobs and a middle-class tax cut. More often, however, issue voting has meant retrospective voting (the electoral reward and punishment model), making judgments about the past, especially on major questions about the state of the economy and war or peace.

The voters tend to reward the incumbent party for what they see as good times and to punish it for what they see as bad times. In especially bad economic times, for example, Americans tend to vote the incumbent party out of office, as they did the Republicans during the Great Depression in 1932. In 1992 the electorate punished Republican George H. W. Bush for the poor state of the economy and punished the Republicans in the midst of the Great Recession in 2008 when Obama handily beat McCain and the Democrats won big majorities in Congress. When Obama and the Democrats failed to bring the country out of bad economic times when they were in control, the voters punished them in the 2010 congressional elections, and gave big gains to the Republicans. In 1996, on the other hand, it rewarded Bill Clinton for being president during good economic times.

Foreign policy can be important as well, especially when war and peace are at issue. Bitter disillusionment over the Korean War hurt the Democrats in 1952, just as the Vietnam War cost them in 1968, and unhappiness about American hostages in Iran and the Soviet intervention in Afghanistan hurt Jimmy Carter in 1980. During nearly all of the past half-century, in fact, Republican candidates have been seen as

AN UNFORTUNATE TANK RIDE   News photos and video of Democratic presidential candidate Michael Dukakis taking a ride in a new M1-A-1 battle tank during the 1988 campaign did not convince very many people that he was strong on national defense, which was his apparent objective. Much to the chagrin of his campaign team, the ride became the butt of jokes by late-night comedians and editorial cartoonists. Can seemingly innocent gaffes kill a campaign? Can you think of any examples?

electors

Representatives who are elected in the states to formally choose the U.S. president.

plurality

More votes than any other candidate but less than a majority of all votes cast.

better at providing foreign policy strength and at keeping us out of war. The bloody, expensive, and drawn-out war in Iraq undermined traditional GOP advantages in this area in 2008, however. In most elections, though, foreign policy concerns take a back seat to domestic ones for most voters. Even in 2008, in the midst of war, economic troubles triggered by the sub-prime mortgage and credit crunch disasters trumped foreign policy issues for a majority of voters.

The Electoral College

Determining the winner of House and Senate elections is straightforward: the candidate with the most votes in a statewide contest for the Senate and the candidate with the most votes in a House district is elected. It's different for presidential elections. In contrast, the outcome of presidential elections is determined not by the number of popular votes cast for each candidate but by candidate who wins a majority in the Electoral College.

When Americans vote for a presidential candidate whose name appears on the ballot, they are actually voting for a slate of **electors** in their state—equal to the number of the state's U.S. senators and representatives—who have promised to support a party's presidential candidate. (Very rarely have electors reneged on their promises and cast ballots for someone else; there was one so-called faithless elector in 2000.) Nearly all states now have winner-take-all systems in which the winner of the popular vote wins the state's entire allotment of electoral votes; Maine and Nebraska, in slight variations, choose electors on a winner-take-all basis for each congressional district.

The "college" of electors from the different states never actually meets; instead, the electors meet in their respective states and send lists of how they have voted to Washington, D.C. (see the Twelfth Amendment to the Constitution). The candidate who receives a majority of all the electoral votes in the country is elected president. Not since 1824 has it been necessary to resort to the odd constitutional provisions that apply when no one gets a majority of electoral votes: the House of Representatives chooses among the top three candidates, by majority vote of state delegations. Each state in this procedure has one vote.

Most of the time, this peculiar Electoral College system works about the same way as if Americans chose their presidents by direct popular vote, although this was not true in 2000 when Bush won the electoral vote while losing the popular vote. The old idea that electors would exercise their independent judgments is long gone. But the system does have certain consequences:

- *It magnifies the popular support of winners.* A candidate who wins in many states, by a narrow margin in each, can win a "landslide" in the Electoral College. In 1996, for example, Bill Clinton's 49 percent of the popular vote translated into 379 electoral votes, or 70 percent of the total. Ordinarily, this magnification just adds legitimacy to the democratic choice, especially when the winner has only a **plurality** of the popular vote, that is, more than anybody else but less than a majority of all votes. Many of our presidents have been elected by a plurality, that is, with less than 50 percent of the popular vote—most recently, Clinton (1992 and 1996), Richard Nixon (1968), John Kennedy (1960), and Harry Truman (1948). (See Table 10.2.)

- *It may let the less popular candidate win.* A president can be elected who had *fewer* votes than an opponent, if those votes happened to produce narrow margins in many states. Such a result has occurred three times: in 1876, when Rutherford Hayes defeated Samuel Tilden; in 1888, when Benjamin Harrison beat the more popular Grover Cleveland; and in 2000, when George W. Bush defeated Al Gore. (Gore beat Bush by more than a half million votes nationally.)

TABLE 10.2 Election Results, 1980–2008

Year	Candidate	Party	Percentage of Popular Votes	Percentage of Electoral Votes
1980	Ronald Reagan	Republican	51%	91%
	Jimmy Carter	Democratic	41%	9%
	John Anderson	Independent	7%	0%
1984	Ronald Reagan	Republican	59%	98%
	Walter Mondale	Democratic	41%	2%
1988	George H. W. Bush	Republican	53%	79%
	Michael Dukakis	Democratic	46%	21%
1992	William Clinton	Republican	43%	69%
	George H. W. Bush	Democratic	37%	31%
	H. Ross Perot	Independent	19%	0%
1996	William Clinton	Democratic	49%	70%
	Robert Dole	Republican	41%	30%
	H. Ross Perot	Reform Party	8%	0%
2000	George W. Bush	Republican	48%	60.5%
	Albert Gore	Democratic	48%	49.5%
	Ralph Nader	Green Party	3%	0%
2004	George W. Bush	Republican	51%	53%
	John Kerry	Democratic	48%	47%
2008	Barack Obama	Democratic	53%	68%
	John McCain	Republican	46%	32%

Source: Data from the Federal Election Commission and Vital Statistics in American Politics, electronically accessed at http://www.fec.gov/pubrec/electionresults.html, June 15, 2009; two-party vote calculated from data.

Several early-nineteenth-century presidents were probably chosen with only small fractions of the popular vote, although we cannot be sure because some of the statistics are unreliable. Most notably, in 1824, John Quincy Adams defeated the very popular Andrew Jackson in the House of Representatives.

- *It discourages third parties.* Our constitutional arrangements for a single president and single-member congressional districts (rather than proportional representation) already discourage third parties; if candidates cannot win a plurality, they get nothing. The Electoral College adds significantly to this disadvantage: a third party with substantial support may get no electoral votes at all if its support is scattered among many states. In 1992, for example, Ross Perot's impressive 19 percent of the popular vote translated into zero electoral votes because he failed to win a plurality in any single state.

There have been many calls over the years to change the Electoral College system of electing the president.[61] Majorities of Americans have told pollsters repeatedly that they want a system based on direct popular vote. Simply count up the votes nationally, and the candidate with the most votes wins the presidency. Simple.

But perhaps it's not so simple. What if three, four, or five candidates run and the plurality winner only receives, let us say, 30 percent of the vote? Would Americans be comfortable with a president elected by so few people? One way to solve this, as they do in France, among other places, is to have a second-round run-off election between the top two candidates so that the person elected comes to office with majority support.

Another idea that has been floated around is to retain the Electoral College but to remove the "winner-take-all" feature whereby the winner of a state receives all of the state's Electoral College votes even if the win is by the slimmest of margins. Various methods for apportioning a state's electoral votes in a way that approximates the division in the popular vote in the state have been suggested.

One way to get to such a system would be for each of the states to act on its own. The Constitution leaves it up to the states to determine how they determine the distribution of their Electoral College votes. The problem here, of course, is that unless all states acted at the same time, the first movers would be disadvantaged. If a state were to divide up its electoral votes to approximate the popular vote division, it would no longer be such a prize for the candidates compared to those states that were still operating on a "winner-take-all" basis. First-movers would lose influence in national elections, and there would be no assurance that other states would live up to their reform promises down the road. So, a change in the Electoral College along these lines would require national action, perhaps even a constitutional amendment.

Additionally, some benefit from the current system and do not want to change it. Small states, for example, have more influence than they would have in a direct popular election system because the number of electoral votes a state has is determined by adding up its number of representatives (based on population) and senators (two for each state). Thus, small states have more weight in presidential elections than they would have if electoral votes were tied to the number of its seats in the House. Politicians and activists in battleground states also tend to like the Electoral College system because they gain attention—including visits, ad campaigns, and the like—from candidates and parties in close elections where a bloc of electoral votes might make the difference in the outcome of a national election. And, because a constitutional amendment requires ratification by three-fourths of the states, it would be very hard to make a change that small states and battleground states such as Ohio, Missouri, Florida, and Colorado, among others, are likely to oppose.

Using the DEMOCRACY STANDARD

Do voting and elections make government leaders listen to the people?

Elections and citizen political participation in the United States have been substantially democratized over the years, altering some of the constitutional rules introduced by the framers. For example, the Seventeenth Amendment, adopted in 1913, transformed the Senate into an institution whose members are elected directly by voters rather than by state legislatures. The manner of electing the president is completely different from what the framers thought they had created: an independent body for presidential selection. By custom or by law, virtually all electors today are pledged to a particular candidate before the presidential election, so that, for all intents and purposes, the president is directly elected by the people (although disparities between the electoral and popular vote occasionally happen, as in 2000). Equally important, the franchise has been so broadened—to include previously excluded racial minorities and women—that today almost all Americans 18 years and older are eligible to vote, something that few of the framers envisioned or would have found conducive to good government.

In addition to these institutional transformations, democratizing changes in the prevailing political culture have also been important. The spread of the ideas that political leaders ought to be responsible and responsive to the people, and that political leaders ought to pay attention to what the mass public wanted from them, represents a fundamental change from the prevailing view among the framers.

Elections are the most important means by which citizens can exert democratic control over their government. Although a variety of instruments help convey the people's wishes to officials—public opinion polls, interest groups, and social movements—it is ultimately the fact that officials must face the voters that keeps them in line. In terms of the responsible party idea, the fact that the Republican Party tends to be more conservative than the Democratic Party on a number of economic and social issues provides voters with a measure of democratic control by enabling them to detect differences and make choices about the future. Alternatively, through electoral punishment, voters can exercise control by reelecting successful incumbents and throwing failures out of office, thus making incumbents think ahead. Finally, electoral competition forces the parties to compete by nominating centrist candidates and by taking similar issue stands close to what most Americans want. This last force, in fact, may be the chief way in which citizens' policy preferences affect what their government does.

Clearly, then, U.S. elections help make the public's voice heard, but they do not bring about perfect democracy. Far from it. Elections do not lead to a greater degree of democracy for a number of reasons: the low turnouts that characterize American elections at all levels, the educational and income biases in participation rates, and the role of interest groups and well-off contributors in campaign finance. Uneven participation and the influence of money on campaigns undermine political equality by giving some people more political clout than others. So, notwithstanding the spread of democracy beyond the imaginings of the framers, those who support the democratic idea think we have some distance yet to travel.

SUMMARY

10.1 Evaluate three models of how elections can lead to popular control

- In theory, at least, elections are the most important means by which citizens can exert democratic control over their government by forcing elected officials to pay attention to the wishes of voters.

- Three theoretical models of voting are at play in making elections a potentially democratic instrument of the people: responsible parties/prospective voting; reward and punishment/retrospective voting; and the electoral competition/median voter model. Elections matter not only when there is a clear choice but also when electoral reward or punishment occurs or when electoral competition forces both parties to take similar popular stands.

10.2 Distinguish American elections from those in other countries

- There are more elections here than in other democratic countries. They are on a fixed date and the offices voted upon have a fixed term. Elections almost always are of the winner-take-all, first-past-the-post

variety, encouraging a two-party system. And, elections are administered by state and local governments rather than the national government.

10.3 Analyze the importance of political participation in elections

- The right to vote, originally quite limited, was expanded in various historical surges to include nearly all adults and to apply to most major offices. The changes came about because of changes in American society and the struggle for democracy waged by various groups of Americans.

10.4 Identify demographic factors that increase the likelihood of voting

- The higher the income and the higher the education a person has, the more likely that person is to vote. When education and income are accounted for, the long-time differentiation between white and black turnout disappears.

- Women now vote at a slightly higher rate than men.

10.5 Outline the process of campaigns for the presidency and Congress

- Candidates for president start by testing the waters, raising money, and forming campaign organizations; in a series of state primaries and caucuses, they seek delegates to the national nominating conventions, which generally choose a clear front-runner or the incumbent president.

- House and Senate candidates also must win party nominations in their districts or states, though incumbents generally have an easy time being renominated. House and Senate party nominees must create campaign organizations and raise money to contest for their offices, though again, incumbents are generally reelected.

- Candidates who cannot raise money or have money raised for them by others do not become serious contenders in the party nomination contests. Money

differences between the candidates in the presidential contest in the general election are less important in determining the outcome because of public financing, party spending, interest and advocacy group spending, and intense and costless press coverage of the election.

- The goal of presidential candidates in the fall campaign is to rally the party base and win over a substantial proportion of independent and moderate voters. Campaign activity and spending focus on battleground states.

10.6 Assess how voters make their decisions

- Voters' decisions depend heavily on party loyalties, the personal characteristics of the candidates, and the issues, especially the state of the economy.

- The president is selected not by direct popular vote but by a majority in the Electoral College vote.

TEST YOURSELF

Answer key begins on page T-1.

10.1 Evaluate three models of how elections can lead to popular control

1. One problem of the responsible party elections model is the increased potential for gridlock, especially during divided government.
   True/ False

2. Which of the following is consistent with the retrospective voting model?
   a. Voters reward incumbents with reelection.
   b. Political parties appeal to the media voter.
   c. Responsible parties implement those policies that make up the party platform.
   d. Voters select candidates based on what they say they will do in office.
   e. Both candidates offer moderate policy positions.

3. Assess which voting model (prospective, electoral competition, or retrospective) best describes the behavior of the American electorate in the 2008 presidential election.

10.2 Distinguish American elections from those in other countries

4. The United States holds more elections than any other country.
   True / False

5. How do American elections differ from parliamentary elections?
   a. American elections are separate and independent from each other.

   b. American elections use consistent election procedures throughout the country.
   c. American elections use consistent vote-counting procedures throughout the country.
   d. American elections are held at irregular intervals.
   e. The results of American elections are typically determined according to proportional representation.

6. Which element of parliamentary elections would you be most in favor of incorporating in the United States? Provide a rationale for your answer.

10.3 Analyze the importance of political participation in elections

7. The Constitution guaranteed the right of women to vote sooner than it guaranteed the right of African Americans to vote.
   True / False

8. Which of the following is a barrier to voting in U.S. elections?
   a. Citizen-initiated voter registration
   b. Legal requirements that Americans vote
   c. Overly simplistic electoral choices
   d. Strong voter mobilization efforts that intimidate would-be voters
   e. Increasingly competitive elections

10.4 Identify demographic factors that increase the likelihood of voting

9. Women are less likely than men to vote.
   True / False

10. Which of the following best explains differences in turnout between whites and African Americans?
    a. African Americans vote more than whites because they have more to gain from favorable election outcomes.
    b. African Americans vote more than whites because they have greater community pride and higher levels of civic duty.
    c. Ever since the civil rights movement, whites and African Americans have voted at an equal rate.
    d. Whites vote more than African Americans because they have higher mean education and income.
    e. Whites vote more than African Americans because they have less political efficacy and more political cynicism.

11. Does it matter that American voters have different characteristics than the population as a whole? Provide a rationale for your answer.

10.5 Outline the process of campaigns for the presidency and Congress

12. Federal elections for Congress and the president are financed entirely through public funding.
    True / False

13. Which of the following generally comes earliest in the presidential campaign process?
    a. Primary election
    b. Caucuses
    c. Exploratory committees
    d. Nominating conventions
    e. General elections

14. Evaluate why the nominating process for presidential candidates is chaotic.

10.6 Assess how voters make their decisions

15. In presidential elections, the winner of the popular vote is usually also the winner of the Electoral College vote.
    True / False

16. Members of which of the following groups were the least likely to vote for Barack Obama in 2008?
    a. Jews
    b. Women
    c. Hispanics
    d. Those with regular church attendance
    e. Suburbanites

17. How does the Electoral College affect third-party candidates?

mypoliscilab EXERCISES

Apply what you learned in this chapter on MyPoliSciLab.

Read on mypoliscilab.com

eText: Chapter 10

Study and Review on mypoliscilab.com

Pre-Test
Post-Test
Chapter Exam
Flashcards

Watch on mypoliscilab.com

Video: Candidates Court College Students
Video: Dissecting Party Primaries
Video: Oprah Fires Up Obama Campaign
Video: Money in the 2008 Presidential Race
Video: State Primary Race
Video: Who Are the Superdelegates?

Explore on mypoliscilab.com

Simulation: You Are a Campaign Manager: Countdown to 270!
Simulation: You Are a Campaign Manager: Lead Obama to Battleground State Victory
Simulation: You Are a Campaign Manager: McCain Navigates Campaign Financing
Simulation: You Are a Media Consultant to a Political Candidate
Simulation: You Are an Informed Voter Helping Your Classmates
Comparative: Comparing Voting and Elections
Comparative: Comparing Political Campaigns
Timeline: Initiatives and Referendums
Timeline: Close Calls in Presidential Elections
Timeline: Nominating Process
Timeline: Television and Presidential Campaigns
Visual Literacy: Voting Turnout: Who Votes in the United States?
Visual Literacy: Iowa Caucuses
Visual Literacy: The Electoral College: Campaign Consequences and Mapping the Results

INTERNET SOURCES

Open Secrets at the Center for Responsive Politics
www.opensecrets.org
An especially good site for following the money trail—how campaign money is gathered and spent.

Democratic National Committee
www.democrats.org/
Official site of the Democratic Party, with information on party positions and candidates, how to work as a volunteer or contribute money, and more.

The Federal Election Commission
www.fec.gov
Rules and data on campaign fund-raising and spending in federal elections.

The National Archives Electoral College Site
www.archives.gov/federal_register/electoral_college/index.html

Everything there is to know about the law and practices of the Electoral College and the process by which it elects the president.

Project Votesmart
www.vote-smart.org/
A political portal loaded with links to information about candidates, parties, election rules, and issues.

Republican National Committee Intrade
www.intrade.com
A futures market focusing on elections and public opinion about issues; extraordinarily accurate in predicting outcomes.
www.rnc.org/
Official site of the Republican Party with information on party positions and candidates, how to work as a volunteer or contribute money, and more.

SUGGESTIONS FOR FURTHER READING

Kamarck, Elaine C. *Primary Politics: How Presidential Candidates Have Shaped the Modern Nominating System.* Washington, D.C.: Brookings Institution Press, 2009.
A history of the changing presidential nominating process and how candidates take advantage of existing primary and caucus rules and try to change rules to their advantage.

Maisel, Sandy L. *American Political Parties: A Very Short Introduction.* New York: Oxford University Press, 2007.
The best brief book on American voting and elections; surprisingly insightful for such a short book.

Polsby, Nelson W., and Aaron Wildavsky. *Presidential Elections,* 12th ed. Lanham, MD: Rowman & Littlefield, 2007.

A comprehensive textbook on the presidential nominating process, the general election, and voting.

Verba, Sidney, Kay Lehman Schlozman, and Henry E. Brady. *Voice and Equality: Civic Volunteerism in American Politics.* Cambridge, MA: Harvard University Press, 1995.
A comprehensive analysis of inequalities in political participation and their meaning for the quality of democracy in the United States.

Wattenberg, Martin P., *Where Have All the Voters Gone?* (Cambridge, MA: Harvard University Press, 2002).
A clear-headed and accessible look at this perennial and complex question.

The chapters in Part 4 examine how federal government institutions operate and how and why public officials, both elected and appointed, behave as they do in office. Part 4 includes chapters on Congress, the presidency, the executive branch, and the Supreme Court.

The chapters in this part assume that government institutions and public officials can be understood only in their structural and political contexts. What government does is influenced strongly by structural factors such as the constitutional rules, the economy, the political culture, society, and the nation's place in the world. What government does is also shaped by political linkage institutions such as elections, parties, interest groups, public opinion, and social movements that transmit the preferences of individuals and groups to public officials.

Democracy is the evaluative thread that runs through each chapter. We ask about the degree to which federal government institutions and public officials advance or retard the practice of democracy in the United States.

11 Congress

IN THIS CHAPTER

11.1 Identify the ways in which the Constitution shapes Congress

11.2 Assess how and to what extent the members of Congress represent their constituents

11.3 Describe what leaders, political parties, and committees do in Co

11.4 Outline the process by which a bill becomes a law

11.5 Explain why oversight is an important congressional responsibili

THE REPUBLICAN ELECTORAL LANDSLIDE

The Republican Party won an historic, across-the-board victory in the 2010 national elections, akin to the elections of 1948 or 1994—each, in its time, among the most decisive election victories by an opposition party in an off-year election in the twentieth century. In the words of pundits, newscasters, and politicians, 2010 was an earthquake, a landslide, a tsunami.[1]

In elections for the House of Representatives, Republicans gained votes in virtually every congressional district in the country, took away more than 60 seats from the Democrats, and won a decisive majority. The elections left Democrats with fewer than 200 seats in the 435-seat body for the first time in more than six decades. In the Senate, the Republican Party took six seats from the Democrats, leaving the latter with 53 seats, still a majority but well short of the filibuster-proof majority they enjoyed after the 2008 election. The Republican Party also took away 11 governorships from the Democrats, giving them a 29–20 advantage (Lincoln Chafee of Rhode Island won as an independent). Of the 87 legislative chambers for which elections were held in 2010, moreover, Republicans gained seats in 73 of them. When

the smoke cleared, Republicans had taken control of 19 legislative chambers, leaving them in control of the legislatures in 25 states compared to 16 for the Democrats, with the remainder divided between the parties or still undecided in mid-November.

How did this sweeping victory happen just two years after Democrats celebrated their own big win chronicled in Chapter 12's opening story? To some extent, substantial GOP gains and Democratic losses were entirely predictable given the political and economic situation at the time of the elections.[2] For example, it is fairly typical for the president's party to lose seats in the off-year election following his own victory; since 1914, the average has been 30 seats lost in mid-term elections for the president's party. Moreover, it is well established that a party is likely to lose seats when it finds itself defending seats in districts where the other party has traditionally held sway. Across two elections in 2006 and 2008, Democrats gained 55 seats, 47 of them in House districts carried by Republicans George W. Bush in 2004 and John McCain in 2008—an unenviable position to be in for the Democratic Party and its candidates in these districts in 2010. And, it is a truism among political scientists and

pollsters that the party in power during hard economic times, as was the case in 2010, usually loses.

Having said that, GOP gains and Democratic losses in races across the country at every level of government cannot be explained entirely by these factors. After all, surveys showed that the public thought even less of the Republicans than of the Democrats going into the elections, and that regard for the Republican Party among the public actually declined during the election season. So something else must have been going on. One explanation for the size of Democratic losses holds that Barack Obama's need to placate moderate "blue dog" Democrats in order to pass big programs, such as the economic stimulus, financial regulatory reform, and health care reform, led to watered-down bills that disappointed the liberal base of the party, sapping fund-raising efforts and turnout among African Americans; youth; educated, unmarried women; and people with advanced degrees, all of whom had enthusiastically embraced Obama and his change message in 2008. At the opposite extreme of this "Obama was too timid" are explanations that propose that Obama's and the Democrat's big reform bills were so radical in nature that they served to mobilize a fairly conservative public, with alarmed independents swinging decisively over to the GOP.

The president and his confidantes leaned toward a narrative in which the public simply did not understand the good things that had been accomplished by the Democrats; unappreciated, in this view, was the extent to which the stimulus and bailouts had saved the United States from falling into a deep depression, how health care reform would eventually broaden health care coverage even as it saved money, or how financial regulation would make financial meltdowns like the one that occurred in September 2008 less likely. The administration should have done a better job explaining what they were doing, the president believed. Contrary to this viewpoint, many analysts believed that Democrats missed the boat by concentrating on these mostly longer-term fixes, failing to focus on jobs, the overwhelming concern of voters expressed in pre-election surveys and exit polls (issues of deficits and taxes were quite low on the list of public concerns in these polls). Given that the economic crisis was the worst in the United States since the Great Depression, it is hardly surprising that people wanted their leaders to pay attention to this dire situation as a first order of business.

Two other factors may have advantaged the Republicans and contributed to their big win. The first is the Tea Party movement. Though the movement did not convert significant numbers of Americans to the GOP—surveys show that adherents of this movement were already Republicans or were independents leaning toward the Republicans—the movement energized a large number of people to get involved in GOP campaigns at all levels, especially after Tea Party candidates won a number of nominations on the Republican ticket. Coupled with a disillusioned and discouraged Democratic base, which turned out in much lower numbers than in 2008, the Tea Party mattered.

The second factor that cannot be ignored is the huge advantage that Republicans enjoyed in campaign finance. To be sure, Democratic campaign committees at all levels raised and spent at least as much on electoral campaigns as Republican committees did. Both parties' committees spent at historically high levels for a mid-term election. But Republicans were the big winners in independent spending on issue advertising where, freed by the Supreme Court in *Citizens United* v. *the Federal Election Commission* (2010) and guaranteed anonymity by Congress's failure to pass a disclosure bill, corporations and their trade associations spent unprecedented sums attacking President Obama, Nancy Pelosi, Harry Reid, and the Democratic Congress and directing people's anger and despair at targets far away from their own doors. Though scholars disagree about the degree to which money influences election outcomes, it is hard to avoid the conclusion that the drumbeat of anti-incumbent messages fueled by this money had a substantial anti-Democratic Party impact.

The elections changed the political landscape across the nation. The elections put Republicans in control of the House, with John Boehner (R–OH) in the Speaker's position and strong conservatives at the head of the chamber's major committees. House Republicans have announced they will try to roll back the most prominent legislative achievements of the Democrats, especially health care reform and financial regulation. Though passing bills reversing legislation will only be symbolic in nature—the Democratic Senate will undoubtedly not pass such bills, and the presidential veto serves as backup—House Republicans most certainly will use committee hearings to investigate the Obama administration and its programs and will exercise the House's traditional central role in the budget process to undermine many existing programs. In the Senate, the Democrat's reduced majority means that Republicans will be in a position, with the help of a handful of conservative Democrats, to more easily block President Obama's judicial and executive branch nominees, as well as his budget and other legislative initiatives. In the states, Republican advantages in governorships and state legislatures mean that the GOP is in position to exercise outsized influence in the next round of House redistricting, drawing lines to favor its own candidates (as any party would do), locking in important electoral advantages for itself for years to come.

In the remainder of this chapter, we will examine Congress with an eye toward understanding how its operations and organization are affected by our constitutional rules, the partisan divide in the nation and the electoral fortunes of the parties, the economic environment, and the expectations of the American people.

THINKING CRITICALLY About This Chapter

In this chapter, we turn our attention to the Congress of the United States, examining how Congress works as both a representative and governing institution.

Using the FRAMEWORK

In this chapter you will learn how the way in which Congress works is affected by other government actors and institutions; political linkage level factors such as interest groups, public opinion, the media, and elections; and structural factors, such as constitutional rules and economic and social change.

Using the DEMOCRACY STANDARD

Using the concept of democracy developed in Chapter 1, you will be able to evaluate how well Congress acts as a democratic institution. You will see that the story of Congress and democracy is a mixed one: Congress is, at times and under certain circumstances, highly responsive to the American public; at other times and under other circumstances, it is most responsive to special interest groups and large contributors.

Constitutional Foundations of the Modern Congress

11.1 Identify the ways in which the Constitution shapes Congress

As we saw in Chapter 2, the framers of the Constitution were concerned about the possibility of government tyranny. Yet they also wanted an energetic government capable of accomplishing its assigned tasks. These multiple objectives and concerns are reflected in the constitutional design of Congress.

Empowering Congress

The framers began by empowering Congress, making the legislative branch the center of lawmaking in the federal government. In Article I, Section 1, of the Constitution, they gave Congress the power to make the laws: "All legislative power herein granted shall be vested in a Congress of the United States." For the framers, Congress was the main bearer of federal governmental powers. In listing its powers and responsibilities in Article I, Section 8—the **enumerated powers**—they were largely defining the powers and responsibilities of the national government itself.[3] The framers enhanced the enumerated powers by adding the **elastic clause**, granting broad power to Congress to pass whatever legislation was necessary to carry out its enumerated powers.

Constraining Congress

Worried that too strong a legislative branch would lead to tyranny, the framers also limited congressional power. As we learned in Chapter 2, they made Congress a **bicameral** body—divided into two chambers—so that legislation could occur only after patient deliberation. Single-house legislative bodies, they believed, would be prone to rash action. They then added provisions—Article I, Section 9—specifically to prohibit certain kinds of actions: bills of attainder, ex post facto laws, the granting of titles of nobility, and the suspension of the right of habeas corpus (see Chapter 2 on these prohibitions and what they mean). In the 1st Congress, additional constraints on congressional action were added in the form of the Bill of Rights. Note that the First Amendment, perhaps the most important constitutional provision protecting political liberty, begins with the words "Congress shall make no law . . ."

We also learned in Chapter 2 that the national government was organized on the basis of a "separation of powers" and "checks and balances" so that "ambition might check ambition" and protect the country from tyranny. This means that although the framers envisioned the legislative branch as the vital center of a vigorous national government, they wanted to make sure that Congress would be surrounded by competing centers of government power. We will see that this fragmentation of governmental power in the United States affects how Congress works and often makes it difficult for it to fashion coherent and effective public policies. In this regard, we will see in this chapter and the next how separation of powers invites a situation of conflict between the president and Congress, especially when divided party government exists.

enumerated powers

Powers of the federal government specifically mentioned in the Constitution.

elastic clause

Article I, Section 8, of the Constitution, also called *the necessary and proper clause*; gives Congress the authority to make whatever laws are necessary and proper to carry out its enumerated powers.

bicameral

As applied to a legislative body, consisting of two houses or chambers.

Bicameralism and Representation

Congress is organized into two legislative chambers, each with its own principles of representation and constitutional responsibilities. While we often use the word "Congress" and think of it as a single institution, it is worth remembering that the House and Senate are very different from one another and are "virtually autonomous chambers."[4] Here are the most important things in the constitutional design of Congress that make the two chambers different from one another.

In what came to be known as the Great Compromise, the framers decided to apportion the House of Representatives on the basis of population and the Senate on the basis of equal representation of the states (see Chapter 2 for details). Equal representation in the Senate of states that are highly unequal in terms of population, we will see, has important negative impacts on democracy in the United States.[5] The terms of office of the members of the House of Representatives were set at two years. The terms of the members of the Senate were set at six years, with only one-third of the seats up for election in each two-year election cycle. We learn in this chapter how these differences affect the legislative process.

The Constitution called for the election of senators by state legislatures, not by the people. The objective was to insulate one house of Congress from popular pressures and to make it a seat of deliberation and reflection. As James Madison put it, "The use of the Senate is to consist in its proceeding with more coolness...and with more wisdom than the popular branch."[6] The election of senators by the state legislatures could not survive the democratizing tendencies in the country, however. The Seventeenth Amendment, passed in 1913 after years of agitation for reform pressed by labor and farm groups and progressive reformers, gave the people the power to elect senators directly.

In addition to its general grants of power to Congress, the Constitution assigns particular responsibilities to each of the legislative chambers (see Table 11.1). For example, the House of Representatives has the power to impeach the president for "high crimes and misdemeanors," which it did in the case of Bill Clinton arising out of the Monica Lewinsky affair; the Senate has the power to conduct the trial of the president and remove him from office, if the impeachment charges are proved to its satisfaction (which they were not for Clinton).

TABLE 11.1 Constitutional Differences Between the House and the Senate

	Senate	**House of Representatives**
Term	6 years	2 years
Elections	One-third elected in November of even-numbered years	Entire membership elected in November of even-numbered years
Number per state	2	Varies by size of state's population (minimum of 1 per state)
Total membership	100	435 (determined by Congress; at present size since 1910)
Minimum age for membership	30 years	25 years
Unique powers	Advice and consent for judicial and upper-level executive branch appointments	Origination of revenue bills
	Trial of impeachment cases	Bringing of impeachment charges
	Advice and consent for treaties	

Federalism

Congress is also greatly affected by the federal design of the Constitution. As we learned in Chapter 3, in our federal system, some powers and responsibilities are granted to the national government, some are shared between the national government and the states, and some are reserved for the states. It is inevitable in such a system that conflicts will occur between state governments and the national government and its legislative branch. Such conflicts sometimes reach the Supreme Court for resolution. In *United States* v. *Lopez* (1995), for instance, the Court ruled that Congress had gone too far in the use of its commerce clause powers when it passed a law banning firearms in and around public schools. Although the goal of the law might be worthy, such a matter, in the opinion of the Court, was the business of the states, not Congress.

? Has Congress gone too far in its use of the elastic clause and the interstate commerce clause? Has Congress's use of these provisions made the national government too powerful in our federal system?

Federalism also infuses "localism" into congressional affairs.[7] Although Congress is charged with making national policies, we should remember that the members of the Senate and the House come to Washington as the representatives of states and districts. They are elected by and are beholden ultimately to the voters at home and have voters' interests and opinions in mind even as they struggle with weighty issues of national importance. This remains true even as rising partisanship and the increasing influence of ideologically oriented advocacy groups have forced representatives and senators to be more sensitive to issues beyond their electoral districts and states.

Representation and Democracy

11.2 Assess how and to what extent the members of Congress represent their constituents

Members of Congress serve as our legislative representatives. But do they carry out this representative responsibility in a way that can be considered democratic?[8] To answer this question, we need to look at several aspects of representation: styles of representation, how closely the demographics of members of Congress match the demographics of the population in general, and the electoral process.

Styles of Representation

In a letter to his constituents written in 1774, English politician and philosopher Edmund Burke described two principal styles of representation. As a **delegate**, the representative tries to mirror perfectly the views of his or her constituents. As a **trustee**, the representative acts independently, trusting to his or her own judgment of how to best serve the public interest. Burke preferred the trustee approach: "Your representative owes you, not his industry only, but his judgment; and he betrays you, instead of serving you, if he sacrifices it to your opinion."[9]

Campaigning for Congress in Illinois several decades later, Abraham Lincoln argued otherwise: "While acting as [your] representative, I shall be governed by [your] will, on all subjects upon which I have the means of knowing what [your] will is."[10] (If only he had access to public opinion polls!)

Every member of the House and Senate chooses between these two styles of representation. Their choice usually has less to do with their

delegate

According to the doctrine articulated by Edmund Burke, an elected representative who acts in perfect accord with the wishes of his or her constituents.

trustee

An elected representative who believes that his or her own best judgment, rather than instructions from constituents, should be used in making legislative decisions.

personal tastes than it has to do with the relative safety of their seats and how often they must face the electorate. Senators with six-year terms face the electorate less often than members of the House, so they are generally freer than representatives to assume the trustee style. As they get closer to the end of their term and the prospect of facing the voters, however, senators edge toward the delegate style. Because members of the House must run for reelection every two years, and tend to be in campaign mode at all times, they are pushed almost inexorably toward the delegate style.[11]

Race, Gender, and Occupation in Congress

Representation also implies that elected officials are like us in important ways—that they represent us because they are similar to us. Which raises the question: is the makeup of Congress in a demographic sense similar to that of the nation as a whole? This is often called **descriptive representation**. From the point of view of descriptive representation, the views of significant groups—let us say, women and African Americans—will only be taken into account in policymaking if members of these groups hold seats in a legislative body in rough proportion to their size in the population. From this perspective, a perfectly representative legislative body would be similar to the general population in terms of race, sex, ethnicity, occupation, religion, age, and the like. In this sense, the U.S. Congress is highly *unrepresentative.*[12]

Gender and Race   Both women and racial minorities are significantly underrepresented in Congress, particularly in the Senate, despite important recent gains. We can see this in Figure 11.1, which compares the distribution of women and minorities in the 111th Congress (2009–2010) with their distribution in the country as a whole.

Black representation reached its peak during the post–Civil War Reconstruction period, when blacks played an important political role in several southern states. African Americans disappeared from Congress for many years after the reimposition of white supremacy and the creation of Jim Crow laws in the South at the end

FIGURE 11.1   Women and Minorities in the 111th Congress, 2009–2010

Although their numbers in Congress have increased in recent years, women and racial minorities are still substantially underrepresented compared with their proportion in the American population. This graph compares the percentage of women and racial minorities in each house of the 111th Congress with their percentages in the population in 2006. *Sources:* U.S. Bureau of the Census; the website of the U.S. Senate at www.senate.gov; the website of the House of Representatives at www.house.gov.

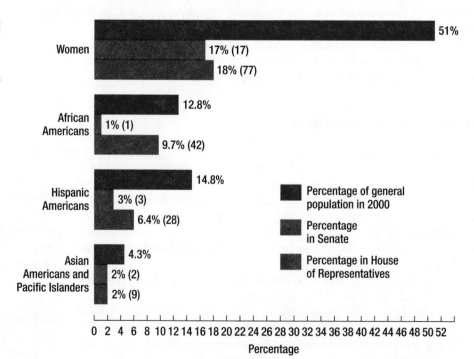

of the nineteenth century. Although a handful of black representatives from northern cities served during the first half of the twentieth century—Oscar De Priest from Chicago's predominantly black South Side and Adam Clayton Powell from New York City's Harlem, for example—very few African Americans were elected to Congress until the late 1960s. While there has been some improvement in representation of African Americans in the House of Representatives—from 26 to 42 between the 102nd (1991–1992) and 111th Congresses—their numbers are still well below what might be expected, given the proportion of African Americans in the population. All but four twentieth-century African American representatives were Democrats. There were no Republican African American representatives between the retirement of J. C. Watts in 2003 and the election of Allan West (R–FL) and Tim Scott (R–SC) in the 2010 Republican landslide. Barack Obama (D–IL) was the lone African American in the Senate during the 110th Congress before he was elected president in 2008. He was replaced by another African American, Roland Burris, who chose not to run for reelection in 2010. Hispanics are even more poorly represented than African Americans relative to their proportion of the population, but the increase in their number in recent years has given the Hispanic caucus a greater voice in legislative affairs than in the past. Interestingly, while Hispanics have now replaced African Americans as the largest minority group in the population, they are less well represented than African Americans in Congress. Twenty-eight served in the House and three in the Senate in the 111th Congress; Ken Salazar (D–CO) and Mel Martinez (R–FL) were elected to the Senate in 2004; Robert Martinez (D–NJ) was elected in 2006. Salazar left the Senate in 2009 to become Interior Secretary, and Mel Martinez did not run for reelection in 2010. Marco Rubio (R–FL) was elected in 2010. Other minority groups are represented in small numbers among members of the House. There were three Arab Americans in the House in the 111th Congress, for example. There are no Native American senators—Ben Nighthorse Campbell (R–CO) retired in 2004—and only a single Native American member of the House.

The first woman to sit in Congress was Jeannette Rankin of Montana, a suffragist and pacifist, elected in 1916. The number of women in Congress increased during the 1990s, with a big gain coming in the 1992 elections (often called the "year of the woman"), which sent 48 women to the House and 7 to the Senate in the 103rd Congress (compared with only 29 and 2, respectively, in the 102nd Congress). There were a record number of women in Congress in the 111th, with 17 in the Senate and 77 in the House. Proportionally, however, female representation in Congress is quite low, compared either to the percentage of women in the American population (slightly more than one-half) or to the percentage of women in national legislative bodies in countries globally. On the latter point, as of late 2009, the United States ranked only 73rd on the world list.[13] Leadership posts in Congress are overwhelmingly held by men, but a few women have gained important

LEADER OF THE HOUSE Nancy Pelosi, the first woman Speaker of the House in American history, was a key player in every major piece of legislation approved by Congress during the first two years of the Obama presidency. That and the fact that she is a liberal Democrat representing San Francisco in the House, made her a prime target for conservative activists and candidates during the 2010 campaign and helped to motivate Republicans to go to the polls. What factors contributed to making the Speaker the most visible legislator in the House of Representatives?

constituency

The district of a legislator.

constituent

A citizen who lives in the district of an elected official.

party and institutional leadership posts. Most notable is Nancy Pelosi (D–CA), who became the first female Speaker of the House in American history after the Democrats won the House in 2006. There were also six female committee chairs in the House and Senate in the 111th Congress. Women also held important party posts in the 111th, including Patty Murray (D–WA), secretary of the Senate Democratic Conference, and Debbie Stabenow (D-MI), chair of the Democratic Steering Committee.

Occupation Members of Congress are far better educated than the rest of the population. They also tend to come from high-income families, have personal incomes that are substantially above average, and lean heavily toward legal or business occupations. In 2008, for example, about three-fourths of the members of the House had legal or business backgrounds, while only 15 percent came from the ranks of the working class, whether of the blue-collar or white-collar service variety, and there was no one who had been a farm laborer.[14]

Most members of Congress, however, did not step into their current posts directly from a profession or occupation. Before putting themselves up for election, representatives and senators, for the most part, had been career politicians or in some other form of public service. Strikingly, 112 members of the House in 2010 had been staffers in Congress.[15] More than a few representatives and senators came from the military, while senators included former governors and cabinet secretaries in previous administrations.

Does it matter that descriptive representation is so low in Congress, that its members are so demographically unrepresentative of the American people? Some political scientists and close observers of Congress think not. They suggest that the need to face the electorate forces lawmakers to be attentive to all significant groups in their **constituencies.** A representative from a farm district tends to listen to farm **constituents,** for example, even if that representative is not a farmer.[16]

Nevertheless, many who feel they are not well represented—women, African Americans, Asian Americans, Hispanics, blue-collar workers, gays and lesbians, those with disabilities, and the poor—often believe that their interests would get a much better hearing if their numbers were substantially increased in Congress. There is significant evidence supporting this view: women members of the House introduce more bills related to women's and children's issues than do their male colleagues.[17] The same has been found to be true for African American legislators and issues considered to be important to African Americans in the country.[18] The demographic disparity between the American population and the makeup of Congress, then, suggests a violation of the norm of political equality, an important element of democracy.

? Does democratic representation require that each group in society have roughly the same proportion of representatives and senators in Congress as each group has in the population? Would such a thing be possible given the number of groups that exist?

The Electoral Connection

Members of the House of Representatives and Senate have particular constituencies they represent in Congress. They get to represent these constituencies by virtue of election to office. We have suggested that elections are the principal instrument in a democracy for keeping representatives responsive and responsible to citizens. Let's see how congressional elections affect the quality of representation in the United States. Recall that additional information on congressional electoral campaigns can be found in Chapter 10.

The State as the Senate's Electoral Unit

Each state elects two senators for six-year terms (though not at the same time). This has important implications for politics in the United States, as well as the quality of democratic representation here. Equal representation gives extraordinary power in the Senate to states with small populations. Wyoming, our least populous state, for example, has exactly the same number of senators as California, but it has less than one-seventieth of California's population; two senators in Wyoming in 2009, for example, represented only about 544,000 people, while the two senators from California represented almost 37 million. This means that a coalition of 51 senators from the 26 smallest population states, representing a mere 18 percent of the American population, can pass a bill in the Senate. (Recall the "Mapping American Politics" feature in Chapter 2, which graphically shows the disproportionate share of power in the Senate held by the nation's smallest states.) You will see later in this chapter that the Senate's rules and procedures give even more power in the body to a small minority of the population, magnifying the antimajoritarian qualities produced by the Constitution.

The District as the House's Electoral Unit

Each member of the House of Representatives is elected from a single-member geographical district (a 1967 law prohibits multimember districts). The number of representatives each state is entitled to in the House is determined by a state's population, with the proviso that each state must have at least one congressional district; the low-population states Alaska, Delaware, Montana, North Dakota, South Dakota, Vermont, and Wyoming fall into this category. The House of Representatives decided that, beginning in 1910, its upper limit would be 435 members (the House can change this number at any time, although it is highly unlikely).

Reapportionment Because the American population is constantly growing in size and changing where it lives, the 435 House representatives must be periodically redistributed among the states. **Reapportionment**, the technical name for this redistribution, occurs every 10 years, after the national census (see Figure 11.2 for the most recent changes). Based on the official census, some states keep the same number of seats; others gain or lose them depending on their relative population gains or losses.

Redistricting Except for states with only a single representative whose House district is the entire state, those states gaining or losing seats must redraw the boundary lines of their congressional districts so that they are of roughly equal population size.[19] Redrawing district lines within a state is known as **redistricting** and is done primarily by state legislatures, although the courts have been playing a more active role lately in cases in which legislatures are unable to decide (redistricting is the job of a nonpartisan commission in five states). Very often in the past, because it was then legal to do so, legislatures created congressional districts of vastly different population sizes—in New York in the 1930s, some congressional districts had 10 times the population of others—and significantly overrepresented rural populations. The Supreme Court ruled in *Wesberry* v. *Sanders* (1964), however, that the principle of one person, one vote applies to congressional districts, meaning that congressional districts within a state must be of roughly equal population size. Because the distribution of the population changes in many states over the course of 10 years—some people moving from the cities to the suburbs; some people moving from rural areas to cities—many congressional district boundaries must be redrawn even in those states that have neither gained nor lost congressional seats because of reapportionment because of the Supreme Court's ruling that districts within states must be roughly equal in population size.

reapportionment
The reallocation of House seats among the states, done after each national census, to ensure that seats are held by the states in proportion to the size of their populations.

redistricting
The redrawing of congressional district lines within a state to ensure roughly equal populations within each district.

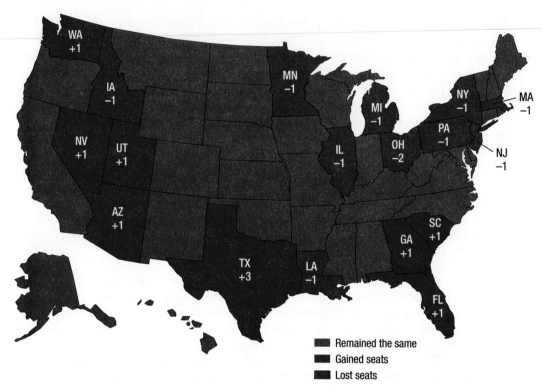

FIGURE 11.2 States Gaining and Losing Congressional Seats Following the 2010 Census

The number of representatives for each state in the House of Representatives is based on the size of its population. Because the relative sizes of the states' populations change over time while the number of representatives is fixed, the number of representatives from each state is recalculated after each census. This process is called reapportionment. This map shows which states will likely gain or lose seats after the 2010 census. *Sources:* "U.S. Population Estimates for 2010," press release, U.S. Bureau of the Census, December 23, 2009; Damien Cave, "Recession Slows Population Rise Across Sun Belt," *The New York Times* (December 26, 2009), p. A.1. House seat gains and loses calculated by Andrew A. Beveridge, Queens College.

Although congressional districts must hold approximately equal numbers of citizens, state legislatures are relatively free to draw district lines where they choose. The party that controls the state legislature and governorship usually tries to draw the lines in a way that will help its candidates win elections.[20] The results are often strange indeed. Rather than creating compact and coherent districts, neighborhoods, towns, and counties can be strung together in odd-looking ways in order to take full **partisan** advantage of the redistricting process. Taken to an extreme, the process is known as **gerrymandering,** after Governor Elbridge Gerry of Massachusetts, who signed a bill in 1811 that created a district that looked like a salamander. It made wonderful raw material for editorial cartoonists.

The Supreme Court has tried to prevent the most flagrant abuses, especially when some identifiable group of voters—for example, a racial or ethnic group—is disadvantaged, but it has turned a blind eye to partisan redistricting in which parties try to draw district lines to their own advantage. The Court, along with most politicians, seems to accept the notion that "to the victor belongs the spoils." Partisan redistricting happens when the same party controls both houses of the state legislature and the governor's office, although even here there are sometimes conflicts if one or another of the party's incumbent House members feels that he or she

partisan

A committed member of a party; seeing issues from the point of view of the interests of a single party.

gerrymandering

Redrawing electoral district lines to give an advantage to a particular party or candidate.

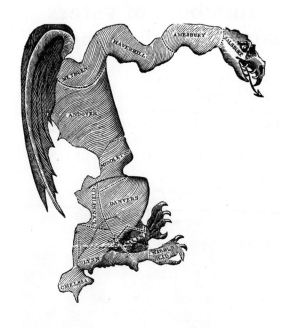

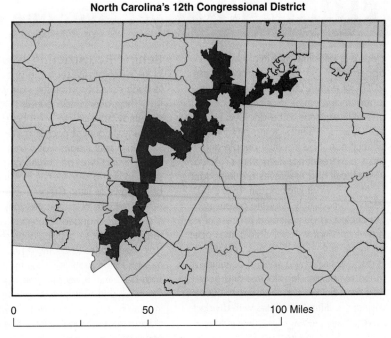

North Carolina's 12th Congressional District

0   50   100 Miles

THE DREADED GERRYMANDER   The term *gerrymander* is derived from the 1812 Elkanah Tinsdale cartoon that lampoons a Massachusetts district drawn to ensure the election of a Republican candidate. The "Gerrymander" was named after Massachusetts Governor Elbridge Gerry, who signed the bill that created the salamander-shaped district. The drawing of North Carolina's 12th Congressional District, designed to increase African American representation, shows that gerrymandering is alive and well. How is it possible that gerrymandering still happens today?

has been hurt by the redrawn district lines. But this situation of unified party control existed in only 15 states when the states began to redistrict after the 2000 census.

One of these unified states was Texas, where Republicans gained control of the governorship and the state legislature in the 2002 elections. In an unprecedented action in 2003—unprecedented in the sense that states always redistrict once every 10 years—the Texas legislature overturned a redistricting plan put in place after the 2000 census by a federal judicial panel and imposed a new redistricting plan favorable to the GOP. Tom DeLay, at the time the powerful majority leader of the U.S. House of Representatives and a member of Congress from Texas, was widely considered to have been the key player in this process. The redistricting carved out an additional five safe congressional seats for his party. The Supreme Court later ruled in *United Latin American Citizens* v. *Perry* (2006) that, with the exception of one redrawn district with a large Hispanic population, the Texas partisan-based, second-time-in-a-decade, redistricting was constitutionally acceptable. What Tom DeLay and Republicans in Texas did in 2003 is referred to as *cracking* a district. The idea is that a party does not want to have a district where it enjoys too large a majority—this wastes votes in a district where the party would win anyway—but chooses to draw district lines so that it spreads its strength across two or more districts in hopes of winning additional seats in a state's congressional delegation. The Republican Party's big victories in the states in the 2010 elections mean that it will control the post-2010 census redistricting process in virtually every state adding or losing seats and that it can use devices like *cracking* to increase its numbers.

Divided party control was common during the post-2000 census period, but much less so in the post-2010 census period, as we have seen, given big Republican gains in the 2010 elections. Needless to say, intense partisan conflict and deadlock are often the result, with resolution coming in many states only after the matter was

BY THE NUMBERS

Can congressional districts be drawn to include equal numbers of voters yet favor one party over the other?

Here is a headline that might have appeared in any city newspaper in late 2001 or early 2002: "Legislature fails to reach agreement on congressional district lines; Issue to be decided by the state courts." What's going on? How difficult can it be to count people and draw congressional district lines? Actually, it is difficult and the issues are important.

Here is what is going on. Every 10 years, immediately after the census is conducted, a complicated process of redrawing congressional district lines goes on in the states. In 12 states, redistricting is done entirely by a special commission; in the remainder, legislatures and governors must do the job. Agreement becomes especially difficult in states with divided government—those with a legislature controlled by one party and the governorship held by the other party, or those where the two houses of the legislature are controlled by different parties. Often, the courts are called upon to break the deadlock.

Why It Matters How congressional district lines are drawn has a lot to do with which political party will control the House of Representatives, at least until the next census.

Behind Redistricting In the House of Representatives, seats are apportioned to each state based on the state's population. Thus, after a new census is taken, a state may gain or lose seats based on the current count of people residing there. To gain a seat means that a new congressional district must be carved out of the state; to lose a seat means that lines must be redrawn to fill in the gap. Even in states where the size of its congressional delegation has not changed, lines must always be redrawn because of population shifts within state boundaries (e.g., more people moving to the suburbs). They must make such adjustments because the Supreme Court ruled in *Wesberry v. Sanders* (1964) that each congressional district within a state must be of roughly the same population size.

How District Lines Are Drawn In theory, as long as district lines create congressional districts of roughly equal size, and as long as district lines do not unduly disadvantage racial and ethnic groups, congressional district lines can be drawn in any way that politicians choose. The politicians can be very imaginative in doing so, as they try to ensure that their own party and

favored members of Congress are advantaged by the outcome.

Where the district lines are drawn is extremely important in determining the composition of the congressional delegation from each state. Note the following hypothetical

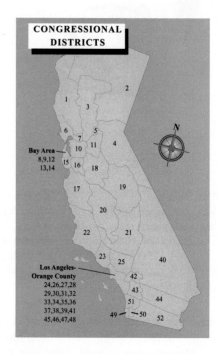

turned over to the courts. In states with divided party control, where neither party has sufficient strength to get its way, the two parties have increasingly made tacit bipartisan redistricting arrangements that protect their own incumbents, presumably on the grounds that the best each party can do is to protect hard-won gains. In large states such as California, Illinois, Michigan, New York, and Ohio, there is hardly a district anymore where the incumbent faces serious competition from the other party in the general election. Across the nation, incumbent-protection redistricting has become so extensive that only about 75 out of 435 seats in the 2008 elections to the House of Representatives, and about 100 in the 2010 elections, were actually competitive, where winners and losers were separated by five percentage points or less.[21]

The outcome of the decline in the number of competitive districts in House elections is that the vast majority of districts in the United States are safely Republican or safely Democratic where candidates need not appeal to the constituency in general but only to their partisan base to ensure that they show up at the polls. This has contributed to the ever-deepening partisan divide in Congress.

Majority-Minority Districts Amendments to the 1965 Voting Rights Act passed in 1982 encouraged the states to create House districts in which racial minorities would

example, which shows how easily district lines can be used to effect different outcomes. Let "D" stand for 100,000 Democratic voters; let "R" stand for 100,000 Republican voters; and let "A" stand for 100,000 African Americans, most of whom vote for Democrats. Taking the same number and locations of voters, district lines can be drawn to yield three Democratic seats and no Republican seats (map on left)

or to yield two Republican seats and one Democratic seat (map on right).

Comment on the Process for Drawing District Lines These alternative outcomes are somewhat exaggerated in order to make a point about how politicians strive for maximum flexibility in the redistricting process. In real life, the Court has also demanded that district lines not deviate too much from their historical patterns and that they be relatively compact, putting people who live near each other in the same district. The map on the right shows a majority-minority district sought at first by African American organizations and leaders as a way to increase their representation in Congress. The formation of such districts, especially in the South, was supported by Republicans because GOP leaders believed that draining traditional Democratic districts of supporters into new majority-minority districts would enhance their party's fortunes. The process of concentrating voters for the other party into fewer districts

in order to weaken them elsewhere is called **packing**. This is how things actually worked out in the end; majority-minority districts increased the number of African Americans in Congress, but concentrating black voters in these districts made the other districts in these states more homogeneously white and Republican, increasing the GOP advantage.

What to Watch For Redistricting is one of the most important things that goes on in our political system, yet it is virtually invisible to the general public. Pay attention to the debates over redistricting in your state and determine what political alliances appear and what political bargains are being struck.

What Do You Think? What might be a nonpartisan, scientific method to draw district lines that would avoid the sometimes unseemly process of reshaping congressional districts to suit political parties and interested groups? If there was such a method, do you think it would be better than our current system? Why or why not?

Result: districts equal in size (1.4 million each); three Democratic seats, zero Republican seats.

Result: districts equal in size (1.4 million each); one Democratic seat carved out to create a position for an African American and two Republican seats.

D = 100,000 white Democrats   R = 100,000 white Republicans
A = 100,000 African Americans, mostly Democrats

Different Congressional District Lines, Different Party Outcomes

be in the majority. Sponsors of the legislation hoped that this would lead to an increase in the number of members of racial minority groups elected to the House. The result was the formation of 24 new **majority-minority districts**, 15 with African American majorities and 9 with Hispanic American majorities.[22] The creation of some of these districts has taken great imagination. North Carolina's Twelfth District, for instance, created after the 1990 census, linked a narrow strip of predominantly African American communities along 160 miles of Interstate 85 connecting Durham and Charlotte. After going back and forth on the issue, the Court accepted a slightly redrawn North Carolina Twelfth District map in *Hunt* v. *Cromartie* (2001), ruling that race can be a significant factor in drawing district lines "so long as it is not the dominant and controlling one." This ruling suggests that most of the other majority-minority districts will probably survive legal challenges. (For more insight into how district lines are drawn, see the "By the Numbers" feature).

The creation of these special majority-minority districts has contributed to the increase in the number of racial minority representatives in Congress; each of the districts has consistently elected a member of a racial minority group to the House. Ironically, however, the creation of such districts has undermined Democratic Party strength in other districts by taking traditionally

open-seat election

An election in which there is no incumbent officeholder.

Democratic-oriented minority group voters away from previously Democratic-dominated districts in order to form majority-minority ones. (One political scientist reports that after 1991 Republicans won and held every congressional seat in which redistricting had reduced the African American population by 10 percentage points or more.[23]) Naturally, Republicans have been eager to support minority group efforts to form their own districts. Concentrating black voters in homogeneous districts has tipped the balance to Republicans in many congressional districts in the South. One result was that policies favored by African Americans were less likely to be enacted when Republicans were in the majority because of the decreased strength of Democrats in the House, this despite an increase in the number of African American representatives.[24]

Money and Congressional Elections We saw in Chapter 10 and the chapter-opening story in this chapter on the 2010 elections that running for the House or the Senate is a very expensive proposition, and it keeps getting more expensive. Money for the campaign committees of those running for House and Senate seats come from four main sources: individuals, political action committees (PACs), political parties, and the candidates themselves. Individuals contribute the largest amount, accounting for 54 percent of contributions to House candidates and 62 percent to Senate candidates in the 2007–2010 election cycle. PACs, heavily dominated by business corporations and trade groups, are the next largest, accounting for 31 percent of campaign contributions in the House contributions and 18 percent in the Senate.[25] Many especially wealthy candidates support their election campaigns out of their own pockets. In the record to date, Jon Corzine (D–NJ)—later governor of New Jersey—spent $62 million in his bid for a Senate seat in 2000. He only barely won.

Congressional candidates also receive campaign money from national, congressional, and state party committees. Party committees are allowed to make a $5,000 contribution per campaign ($10,000 total) to each House candidate. National and senatorial party committees are allowed to give $19,950 to each candidate for each stage of the two stages electoral process. Many congressional candidates also receive campaign contributions from PACs associated with congressional party leaders such as House Minority Leader John Boehner (R–OH) and Senate Majority Leader Harry Reid (D–NV) in the 111th Congress.

Incumbents, especially in the House, have an easier time raising money than their challengers and spend more (see Figure 11.3). **Open-seat election** races, in

FIGURE 11.3 Campaign Money Raised by Incumbents, Challengers, and Open-Seat Candidates, 2007–2008 Election Cycle

Because campaign contributors want access to important decision makers in Congress, contributors tend to give a disproportionate share of campaign contributions to incumbents and to those open-seat candidates who have a good chance to win their elections. *Source*: Federal Election Commission, 2009.

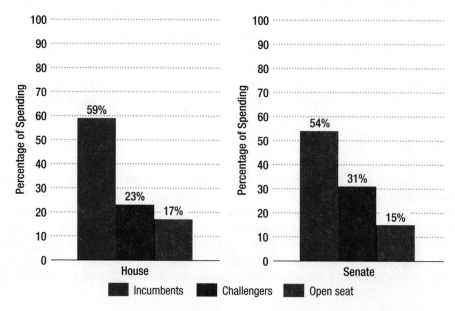

which no incumbent is involved, also attract and use lots of money, especially in the Senate, because the stakes are so high for each of the parties and allied interest and advocacy groups with control of Congress hanging in the balance at nearly every election. For example, in the 2007–2008 cycle, the average open-seat candidate in House and Senate races raised 46 percent more than challengers to incumbents.[26] Moreover, being a member of the majority party in Congress serves as a magnet for money because contributors generally want to be able to have access to those in power.[27] These money sources are for what is called "hard" or "regulated" money (see Chapter10 on this) that goes into the treasuries of the official campaign committees of House and Senate candidates. It is but the tip of a very large iceberg. Much more money is spent independently on issue ads and get-out-the vote campaigns by interest and advocacy groups and by 501 and 527 organizations that indirectly pump up the resources that support congressional candidate campaigns.

The Incumbency Factor   As we have seen, incumbents in Congress—current office-holders—win at very high rates, especially in the House (see Figure 11.4), meaning that the overwhelming majority of electoral contests for Congress are not really competitive; for the most part, seats in the House today are considered "safe," with the incumbent facing little serious challenge from the opposition party candidate. Since the end of World War II, in fact, on average, 93 percent of House incumbents have been re-elected and 80 percent of Senate incumbents have done the same. Incumbents won at very high rates even in big party swing elections as in 1994 and 2006.[28] In 1994, when Republicans took over control of Congress, incumbent losses were concentrated in Democratic districts and states; in 2006, when the Democrats took control, most incumbent losses were among Republicans. To be sure, there is still turnover in the House

> **?** Are high levels of incumbency reelection a problem for the quality of democratic representation? If so, what should be done about it? Would some form of term limits help, or would term limits create additional problems?

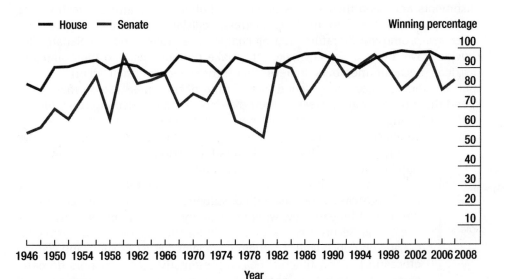

FIGURE 11.4   Rates of Incumbent Reelection in Congress
The probability that incumbents will be reelected remains at historic highs. This does not mean, however, that the membership of Congress is stagnant. Turnover in membership is substantial because of retirements and the defeat of incumbents in primary elections.
Sources: Congressional Quarterly Weekly Reports (November and December 2008); "Norm Colman Concedes," *Associated Press* (June 30, 2009).

IN THE HOME DISTRICT Members of Congress must spend a considerable amount of their time staying in touch with their constituents. Here, Representative Rosa DeLauro (D–CT) visits a computer class in a public school during one of her many trips back to her home district in Connecticut. How can members of Congress best balance their work in Washington with keeping in step with their constituents?

and Senate—some members retire, especially when prospects in the next election are not encouraging, others lose to challengers in their party's primary, and few die—but those who choose to stay and run usually win. In 2010, for example, the Tea Party wrested the Republican nominations away from sitting party stalwarts such as Bob Bennett in Utah.

There are several reasons incumbents almost always win when they seek reelection. The most important, of course, is that the redistricting process in many states in recent years—reviewed earlier in this chapter—has been fashioned to protect incumbents in each of the parties. On the face of it, this process has been very effective.

Incumbents also have the advantage of attracting and spending much more campaign money than their rivals. Many contributors look at campaign contributions as an "investment" in access to key members of Congress.[29] To contribute to a challenger is to jeopardize access if the challenger loses, which is most often the case.

Incumbents also use the congressional machinery to help their reelection chances.[30] Already well known to voters because they garner so much free media coverage, members of Congress have many ways to advertise their accomplishments and keep their names before the public. For example, the **franking privilege** allows them to mail newsletters, legislative updates, surveys, and other self-promoting literature free of charge. The House and the Senate also provide travel budgets for lawmakers to make periodic visits to their states or districts. Because members believe that time spent in their districts helps their electoral chances, they spend lots of time back home.[31] Some manage to spend three or four days a week in their districts or states, meeting constituents, giving speeches, raising money, and keeping in the public eye. The congressional leadership helps by scheduling important legislative business for the Tuesday-to-Thursday period and cutting down the number of hours Congress is in session.

Incumbents also use their offices to "service the district." One way is through **casework**, helping constituents cut through the red tape of the federal bureaucracy, whether it be by speeding up the arrival of a late Social Security check or expediting the issuance of a permit for grazing on public land.[32] Generous budgets for establishing and staffing offices in the constituency help representatives and senators do casework. Another way to service the district is to provide **pork**—federal dollars for various projects in the district or state. In 2005, for example, Congress passed a massive $286 billion highway and mass transit bill that, in addition to whatever improvements it might bring for the safety and convenience of Americans, poured lots of federal construction

franking privilege
Public subsidization of mail from the members of Congress to their constituents.

casework
Services performed by members of Congress for constituents.

pork
Also called *pork barrel;* federally funded projects designed to bring to the constituency jobs and public money for which the members of Congress can claim credit.

money into the constituencies of senators and representatives for highway and bridge projects, rail and bus improvements, urban bike paths, and more. (See the "Using the Framework" feature.)

How Representative?

There are several respects in which Congress may not be broadly representative of the American people. For one thing, as we have seen, women and members of minority racial and ethnic groups are vastly under represented in the ranks of House and Senate members compared with their proportions in the population. For another thing, we have seen that people in very small states have much more voice than people in large states in the U.S. Senate because of the constitutional provision mandating two senators for each state. This feature of the Constitution means that the 12 smallest states, with only about 5 percent of the American population, elect almost one-fourth of all senators.[33] Elections and attentiveness to public opinion on the part of lawmakers help rectify some of this, but imperfectly.

But representatives and senators pay a great deal of attention to the interests and the preferences of the people in their districts and states. Because they are worried about being reelected—even incumbents tend to run scared, perhaps afraid of being the exception that proves the rule—they try to see as many people as they can during their frequent visits home, and they pay attention to their mail and the public opinion polls. Moreover, they vote on and pass laws in rough approximation to public opinion. As we saw in Chapter 5, members of Congress vote in a manner that is consistent with public opinion in their districts and states about two-thirds of the time, and Congress produces laws that are consistent with national public opinion at about the same rate. Having said that, however, it is also the case, as we saw in Chapter 5, that members of Congress are very skilled at shaping public opinion in their districts[34] and at shaping legislation in ways that seem to address public concerns without actually doing so.[35] For example, responding to the widespread public concern about the state of private pension plans, Congress set about reforming the system in 2006. In the end, it gave companies more leeway in escaping pension obligations and lowered the amount of money companies had to contribute to the federal pension bailout program. This may reflect the very large amounts of money spent by business and trade groups on lobbying (see Chapter 7) and making contributions to congressional campaigns, and the tendency for Senators and representatives to listen to the wealthiest people in their constituencies.[36]

In a substantial number of cases, moreover, Congress does *not* follow public opinion, even on highly visible issues. If members of Congress follow public opinion two-thirds of the time on important bills, that still leaves one-third of the time that they go their own way. Moreover, on many issues of high complexity or low visibility, such as securities and telecommunications regulation, the public may have no well-formed opinions at all. It is in these areas that we can most fully see the influence of money and interest groups at work.

One of the reasons members of Congress have some latitude in representing public opinion in their districts—indeed, in the nation—is that, as we have shown, most come to Congress from relatively "safe" districts where being turned out by the voters is not common. Consequently, House elections do not adequately fulfill the role assigned to elections in democratic theory: as the principle instrument for keeping elected leaders responsive and responsible.[37]

If Republicans favor small government, why did they push through an expensive highway bill when they were in control of Congress?

Background: The Republican-controlled Congress passed a massive highway and transportation bill amounting to almost $300 billion in the late summer of 2005, despite warnings of a veto from President George W. Bush, who said he was worried about adding to the growing federal government deficit. A little over a week after Congress sent the bill to him, however, he signed it at a ceremony at a large Caterpillar manufacturing plant in Illinois, saying that with this new legislation, "there's going to be more demand for the machines you make." Scores of editorial writers heaped scorn on Republicans for passing this "pork"-laden legislation—literally thousands of projects requested by individuals members of

Congress for their states and districts were included—and small-government proponents such as the conservative Cato Institute expressed keen disappointment. As if this were not enough for critics, the Republican-controlled Congress and a Republican president legislated other expensive, government-expanding legislation, including a Medicare prescription drug benefit and a subsidy-filled energy bill. So how could such a thing have happened? We can see how by taking a broader view of the emergence of the Republicans as the party of government, despite small majorities in the House and Senate, and considering how structural, political linkage, and governmental factors shaped this outcome.

Structure	Separation of powers and checks and balances make it difficult for any party to be in effective control of the federal government; usually requires unified government and very large partisan majorities in both houses of Congress.	Long-term trends in society—decline of labor unions, the economic and social transformation of the South, a surge in religious commitment, and more—contribute to a decline in the fortunes of the Democratic Party beginning in the 1970s.		
Political Linkage	Party system dealigns during the 1970s, 1980s, and 1990s, leading to parity in support for the two parties among voters.	Republicans win control of Congress from the Democrats in 1994 and retain control for most of the period through 2006.	President George W. Bush wins the presidency in close and bitterly fought campaigns in 2000 and 2004.	Republicans enjoy unified government in Washington from 2003 to 2006, and seek to govern in a highly charged partisan environment.
Government		Republicans reach historically high levels of unity and cohesion in Congress, especially in the House but also in the Senate, allowing them to control the congressional agenda despite having only very small majorities.	Like any governing party wishing to remain in power, Republicans try to reward friends, enhance the reelection prospects of their members of Congress, and firm up support among potential campaign contributors.	
Government Action		Congress passes and president signs massive highway and transportation bill in 2005 and subsidy-laden energy bill in same year.		

How Congress Works

11.3 Describe what leaders, political parties, and committees do in Congress

Congress is a vital center of decision making and policymaking in our national government. It is not a place where the executive's bills are simply rubber-stamped, as it is in legislative bodies in many parliamentary systems. By all accounts, Congress is the most influential and independent legislative body among the Western democratic nations. In this section, we turn our attention to how Congress is organized and how it functions as a working legislative body.[38]

There are a number of very important things to keep in mind as we examine how Congress is organized and operates. First, while they are alike in many ways, the House and Senate are very different institutions. The bodies differ in size, the kinds of constituencies House members and senators represent, the terms of office of their members, and their constitutional responsibilities; together, these differences give each chamber a distinctive character.

Second, both the House and Senate have had a tendency over the years to succumb to centrifugal forces, always seemingly on the verge of flying apart, with each representative and senator tempted to go his or her own way. The task of running each body has been likened to "herding cats." The reasons are fairly obvious: representatives and senators in some sense are like independent contractors. Congressional leaders lack the normal tools of organizational leadership to force compliance with their wishes; they cannot order members about, they cannot hire or fire them (this is the role of voters), nor can they control the size of their paychecks or benefits. Moreover, in our candidate-centered form of politics, congressional leaders traditionally have had little control over the reelection of representatives and senators who run their own campaigns.

Between 1995 and 2006, however, Republicans used party resources and leadership positions to gain a great deal of control over legislative affairs, especially in the House of Representatives (see the "Using the Framework" feature). Republicans not only granted more formal powers to the office of the Speaker but learned to channel campaign money from their own PACs, party campaign committees, and conservative groups and individuals to maintain discipline among members who might be tempted to stray too far from where legislative party leaders want them to be on important matters. The process of centralization of leadership in the Senate did not advance as far as in the House but, given leadership influence over the flow of campaign money from diverse sources, some centralization occurred there as well.[39] When they regained control of Congress after the 2006 elections, Democrats tried with some success to become more centralized and coordinated as well, using the political party and congressional leadership positions as its main tools. But the game remains one of "herding cats," typified by majority leader Harry Reid's months-long effort to put together the 60 votes he needed to break a Republican filibuster and pass a health insurance reform bill on the morning of Christmas eve, 2009. Gaining the votes of Ben Nelson (D–NE) and Joe Lieberman (I–CT) didn't happen until a few days before the final vote.

Political Parties in Congress

Political parties have a very strong presence in Congress. Its members come to Washington, D.C., as elected candidates of a political party. At the start of each session, they organize their legislative business along political party lines. At the

party conference

An organization of the members of a political party in the House or Senate.

caucus

A regional, ethnic, racial or economic subgroup within the House or Senate. Also used to describe the party in the House and Senate, as in Republican caucus.

start of each new Congress, each **party conference**—all the members of a political party in the House or the Senate (although House Democrats use the term **caucus** rather than conference)—meets to select its leaders; approve committee assignments, including committee and subcommittee chairs; and reach agreement on legislative objectives for the session. The majority party in the House selects the Speaker of the House, while the majority party in the Senate selects the president pro tempore (usually its most senior member) and the majority leader. The minority party in each chamber also selects its leaders. Political parties, as we shall see, also are influential in what policies representatives and senators support and how they cast their votes on important bills. So, political parties are at the very core of legislative business in the United States and are becoming ever more important as the partisan divide between Democratic and Republican voters, activists, advocacy groups, and elected officials gets steadily wider.[40]

The Party Composition of Congress   From the 1932 elections in the midst of the Great Depression until the 1994 elections, with brief interludes of Republican control along the way, Congress was dominated by the Democratic Party. Democratic domination of House elections during this period is especially notable, even surviving GOP landslide wins in the presidential elections of 1980 (Reagan), 1984 (Reagan), and 1988 (G. H. W. Bush). In the Senate, Republicans were in the majority for only 10 years during this same period. Democratic Party domination ended with the 1994 elections, however, when Republicans won control of both houses of Congress for the first time in 40 years. Because Republicans were unusually unified from 1995 through 2006, especially in the House, they were very successful in controlling the congressional agenda. The Democrats regained control of both houses of Congress in 2006 and extended their advantage in both the House and the Senate in 2008. In 2010, as described in the chapter-opening story, Republicans made big gains, winning control of the House and coming within three seats of reaching parity in the Senate, where Democrats retained control.

PARTY DIVISION   Democratic administrative and congressional leaders applaud the president during his State of the Union address to the nation in January 2010, while Republicans "sit on their hands." This graphically illustrates how Congress operated in the first years of the Obama administration: Democrats largely supported major legislation while Republicans were nearly unanimous in saying no. In spite of this, President Obama and the Democrats produced a historic legislative record: an economic stimulus, health care reform, and financial industry regulation, among other things. Is this development of party government a good thing or something to be worried about? Why?

Party Voting in Congress   The political parties provide important glue for the decentralized fragments of Congress and the legislative process. Party labels are important cues for members of Congress as they decide how to vote on issues before the
committees and on the floor of the House and the Senate. Indeed, it has been shown
that party affiliation is the best predictor of the voting behavior of members of the
Congress and that it is becoming
ever more important. In the words of
several leader congressional scholars,
following what party leaders and
other party legislators want is the default position of most senators and
representatives.[41]

? Is rising partisanship in Congress a good or bad thing? Does it
help get things done that the public wants, or does it get in the
way?

One way to track partisanship is a statistic showing how often the average
Democrat and Republican voted with his or her party in partisan votes in Congress
(see Figure 11.5). You can see that partisanship has been rising steadily since the
early 1970s and is evident today in about 9 out of 10 votes. In 2009, for example,
Democratic leaders were only able to muster three Republican votes in the Senate
for President Obama's emergency economic stimulus package and none at all for
the final health care bill in 2010.

One result is that reaching bipartisan agreements is becoming more difficult. As
Maine Republican Senator Olympia Snowe has observed, "The whole Congress has

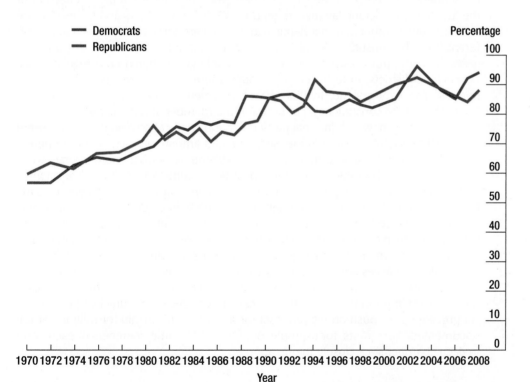

FIGURE 11.5   Party Voting in Congress

Partisanship has been growing in Congress. One indicator is the increase in the percentage
of times the average Democrat and Republican in the House and Senate sided with his/her
party on partisan votes—those votes when a majority of Democrats voted against a majority
of Republicans. *Source:* Roger H. Davidson, Walter J. Oleszek, and Francis E. Lee, *Congress
and Its Members,* 12th ed. (Washington, D.C.: CQ Press, 2010), p. 284.

become far more polarized and partisan so it makes it difficult to reach bipartisan agreements. The more significant the issue, the more partisan it becomes."[42]

There are a number of reasons partisanship is increasing.[43] One factor is the changing regional bases of the parties, particularly the historic transformation of the Deep South from a solidly Democratic region at the congressional level to a solidly Republican one.[44] The resulting transformation in party regional representation has been stunning; in the 109th Congress, only four Democrats were left in the Senate from the 11 states of the former Confederacy. However, the Republican momentum was reversed some in the 2006 and 2008 national elections. Democrat Jim Webb won a Senate seat in Virginia in 2006. In 2008, Democrats held on to Senate seats in Louisiana and Arkansas and won Senate seats from the Republicans in North Carolina and Virginia. In 2010, however, the traditional pattern reasserted itself in the South, where Republicans won every contested Senate seat and virtually all competitive House seats..

Another reason that partisanship is on the rise in Congress is that partisan conflict has been on the rise nationally, especially among party activists and party-associated advocacy groups as discussed in Chapters 5, 9, and 10. The inevitable result is that members of Congress have been facing an ever-more partisan-divided electorate and interest group environment.

It is not entirely clear whether party voting differences are caused directly by party affiliation or indirectly by the character of constituencies or by the preexisting ideological commitments of members of Congress. Some scholars have found strong independent party effects regardless of constituency or ideology. Others argue that the tendency of people in the same party to vote together is simply a reflection of the fact that Democratic lawmakers tend to come from districts and states that are similar to one another and that Republican lawmakers come from places that are different from the constituencies of Democrats. Compared to Democrats, Republicans generally come from districts where more people go to church on a regular basis. Democratic districts, in turn, tend to contain more union members and racial minorities. The strongest tie, in this line of argument, is between the member of Congress and the constituency, not between the member and the party.

Increasingly, however, internal party unity and conflict between the parties seem attributable to ideology. Both in the electorate and among the members of Congress and other political elites, Democrats have become somewhat more liberal, while Republicans have become much more consistently conservative.[45] Political scientist and former Democratic representative from Oklahoma Mickey Edwards observes the following about the ideological tendencies of members of Congress: "Most people who run for office have...[strong] feelings not only about specific issues but about general philosophical concepts, such as the proper role of government, the impact of taxation on investment and savings, and the reasons for crime and poverty."[46]

While our parties are more ideological and unified in Congress than at any time in recent memory, senators and representatives can and do stray from the party turf, even on important matters. Republicans in Congress were unwilling in 2007 to support President Bush on his proposal for a road to citizenship for millions of undocumented immigrants, for example. But most of the time, members of each party in each chamber stick closely to one another.

Congressional Leadership

The political parties work through the leadership structure of Congress because the leaders of the majority political party are, at the same time, the leaders of the House and the Senate.[47] As Congress becomes more partisan, party becomes ever more important in shaping the actions of House and Senate leaders.[48]

Leadership in the House The leader in the House of Representatives is the Speaker of the House. This position is recognized in the Constitution and stands second in the line of succession to the presidency, immediately after the vice president.

> **?** In the House, has too much power gravitated to the Speaker, or is this a good development that helps Congress function better?

Until 1910, the Speaker exercised great power over the House legislative process. The bases of his power were his right to appoint committees and their chairs and his position as chair of the powerful Rules Committee, which controls the flow of legislation in the House. The revolt of the rank-and-file against Speaker "Uncle Joe" Cannon in 1910 resulted in the Speaker's removal from the Rules Committee and the elimination of the Speaker's power to appoint committees and their chairs.

From 1910 until the early 1970s, the weakened Speaker competed with a handful of powerful committee chairs for leadership of the House. A few Speakers, such as Sam Rayburn of Texas, were able to lead by sheer dint of their personalities and legislative skills, but power tilted toward the committee chairs most of the time.

The Democratic Caucus staged a revolt against the committee system after 1974 and restored some of the powers of the Speaker, especially in making committee assignments. The Democratic Conference also gave the Speaker more power to refer bills to committee, control the House agenda, appoint members to select committees, and direct floor debate. This change gave Speakers Tip O'Neill, Jim Wright, and Tom Foley considerable leadership resources.

In 1995, the Republican Caucus gave even more power to control the House legislative process to their first Speaker since 1954, Newt Gingrich. Some scholars suggest that Gingrich's speakership was the most powerful one since Cannon's.[49] Unexpected losses of Republican House seats in the 1998 elections, after a campaign featuring a Gingrich-designed advertising blitz to impeach the president, led to his resignation of the speakership and from the House.

Democrat Nancy Pelosi (D–CA) exercised a strong hand as Speaker of the House from 2007 through 2010, when the Republicans took over. She believed and was adept at top-down, energetic leadership. She largely controlled the Democratic message in the House, leaned on committee chairs to push her agenda, and used the levers of campaign finance—the Democratic Congressional Campaign Committee and her own leadership PAC, which reportedly gave $40 million to Democratic House candidates in 2007–2008 election cycle—to influence representatives in her then-majority party. To push the Democratic agenda in the 111th Congress, she pushed through several important rules in 2009, one to make it harder for representatives—in practice, aimed at Republican members of the House—to bring a motion to send a bill back to committee from the floor.[50] She is generally credited with convincing the president, several of his advisers, and other Democratic congressional leaders to make a final push for health care reform when they were wavering—and eventually prevailed.[51]

Today's Speaker, now John Boehner (R–OH), has more power and influence in the legislative branch than any other representative or senator. This power and influence has come about because of House rules and political party rules that have evolved since the 1970s that give the Speaker important powers and prerogatives in determining the flow of legislative business. The Speaker can replace conference committee members, appoints members to the powerful Rules Committee, and exercises strong influence over the appointment of the chairs of other committees and referral of bills to committees for hearings and review. The Speaker appoints the leaders of the majority party's organizations, including the campaign finance committee and the party caucus. The Speaker also has the power to recognize (or not recognize) people to speak during floor debates and is in charge of the House's schedule, which can be used to encourage favored bills and stop others.[52]

whip

A political party member in Congress charged with keeping members informed of the plans of the party leadership, counting votes before action on important issues, and rounding up party members for votes on bills.

The majority party in the House also selects a majority leader to help the Speaker plan strategy and manage the legislative business of the House, and a majority **whip**. Neither House nor party rules spell out their precise responsibilities. The nature of these jobs depends very much on what the Speaker wants, on the majority leader's talents and energy, and on what the Speaker and majority leader want the whip to do. In general, however, the Speaker may be likened to the chairman of the board in a business corporation, while the majority leader may be likened to the chief executive officer, responsible for the day-to-day operations of the enterprise.[53] The whip is the majority leader's deputy, carrying out many of the tasks of getting bills passed, including counting votes and twisting arms.

The minority party elects a minority leader, who acts as the chief spokesperson and legislative strategist for the opposition. The minority leader not only tries to keep the forces together but also seeks out members of the majority party who might be willing to vote against the House leadership on key issues, although this is getting more difficult to do because of rising partisanship. The House minority leader in the 111th Congress (and Speaker in the 112th) was John Boehner (R–OH), a strong conservative who used his position to harshly criticize the Democrats and rally the Republican base in the electorate. Like the majority party, the minority party elects a whip to help the minority leader count and mobilize votes.

Leadership in the Senate Leadership in the Senate is less visible. Senators with formal leadership titles, such as the president pro tempore, exercise little influence. The Senate majority leader is as close as one comes to a leader in this body, but the powers of the office pale before those of the Speaker of the House. The Senate majority leader has some influence in committee assignments, office space designation, and control of access to the floor of the Senate. The majority leader is also important in the scheduling of the business of the Senate. The degree of actual influence is based less on formal powers, however, than on skills of personal persuasion, the respect of colleagues, visibility in the media as majority party spokesperson, and a role at the center of many of the various communication networks. In addition, campaign contributors

LEADING THE MINORITY IN THE SENATE Minority leader, Mitch McConnell (R–KY), worked effectively to keep his Republican colleagues united against legislation being pushed by the majority Democrats in the 111th Congress. Here, with the help of Senator John McCain (R–AZ), he signals the Republican view of the Democrats' health care reform proposal in December 2009. Did Republican resistance to nearly every aspect of President Obama's legislative agenda help explain their big gains in the 2010 elections? Why?

A SENATE LEGEND IN ACTION Later president of the United States, Lyndon B. Johnson of Texas was one of the most effective majority leaders in the history of the United States Senate. Here, he urges Senators Kennedy, Smathers, Humphrey, and Proxmire to vote for an important civil rights bill in 1957. Why is the position of majority leader such a difficult one?

often take the advice of the majority leader in how they allocate money for incumbents seeking reelection, giving the majority leader additional influence.

The power of the position is personal and not institutional; it cannot be passed on to the next leader. The Senate remains a body of independent, relatively equal members loosely tied together by threads of party loyalty, ideology, and mutual concern about the next election. It is not an environment conducive to decisive leadership, although a few, such as Lyndon Johnson, managed to transcend the limits of the office. And, with partisanship on the rise in the Senate, it is increasingly difficult for any majority leader to push the majority party's agenda because important bills now require 60 votes to pass because of the increasing use of the filibuster by the minority party. Remarkably, however, the majority leader in the 111th Congress, Harry Reid (D–NV), was able to keep together the 60 votes on his side of the aisle that he needed to pass health insurance reform legislation in 2009 and 2010, and the bill to regulate the financial industry in 2010, something few observers thought possible.

Congressional Committees

Much of the work of Congress takes place in its many committees and subcommittees. Committees are where many of the details of legislation are hammered out and where much of the oversight of the executive branch takes place. As recently as the 1960s and 1970s, committees and their chairs were relatively autonomous, exercising great power over the course of legislation, because parties were not unified and House and Senate leaders had little power. As partisanship rose in the country and Congress, however, Republicans and Democrats decided, as we have seen, to give much more power to the Speaker and some additional powers to the majority leader in the Senate, especially over committee appointments and most especially to appointments to the most important committees. The result is a dramatic decline in the power of committees and of committee chairs in the legislative process and an increase in the influence of the parties and their leaders.[54] Sometimes, and most especially in the House, leaders will completely bypass the committee process, creating special party task forces to consider important bills or bringing bills to the floor directly by the leadership team. This direct leadership-to-floor consideration of legislation happened with the pay equity bill passed early in 2009, for example.

Why Congress Has Committees Committees serve several useful purposes. For one thing, they allow Congress to process the huge flow of business that comes before it. The committees serve as screening devices, allowing only a small percentage of the bills put forward to take up the time of the House and the Senate.

Committees are also islands of specialization, where members and staff develop the expertise to handle complex issues and to meet executive branch experts on equal terms. The Ways and Means Committee of the House can go toe-to-toe with the Treasury Department, for instance, on issues related to taxation. Committee expertise is one of the reasons Congress remains a vital lawmaking body.

Members of Congress also use their committee positions to enhance their chances for reelection. Rational lawmakers usually try to secure committee assignments that will allow them to channel benefits to their constituents or to advance an ideological agenda popular in their district or state.

Types of Committees in Congress There are several kinds of committees, each of which serves a special function in the legislative process.

Standing committees are set up permanently, as specified in the House and Senate rules. These committees are the first stop for potential new laws. The ratio of Democrats to Republicans on each committee is set for each house through a process of negotiation between the majority and minority party leaders. The majority party naturally enjoys a majority on each of the committees and controls the chair, as well as a substantial majority on the most important committees, such as the Budget and Finance Committee in the Senate and the Rules Committee and the Ways and Means Committee in the House. Not surprisingly, the ratio of Democrats and Republicans on committees is a point of considerable contention between the two parties, especially when they are evenly divided.

The avalanche of legislative business cannot be managed and given the necessary specialized attention in the full House and Senate standing committees. For most bills, **hearings**, negotiations, and **markup** take place in subcommittees. It is in the subcommittees, moreover, that most oversight of the executive branch takes place.

Select committees are usually temporary committees created by congressional leaders to conduct studies or investigations. Their distinguishing feature is that they have no power to send bills to the House or Senate floor. They exist to resolve matters that standing committees cannot or do not wish to handle. Often the issues before select committees are highly visible and gain a great deal of public attention for their members. Select committees investigated the Watergate scandal, the Iran-Contra affair, and intelligence failures regarding the 9/11 attacks and the run-up to the war in Iraq.

Joint committees, with members from both houses, are organized to facilitate the flow of legislation. The Joint Budget Committee, for instance, helps speed up the normally slow legislative process of considering the annual federal budget.

Before a bill can go to the president for signature, it must pass in identical form in each chamber. The committee that irons out the differences between House and Senate versions is called a **conference committee**, and one is created as needed for each piece of major legislation.

---

standing committees

Relatively permanent congressional committees that address specific areas of legislation.

hearings

The taking of testimony by a congressional committee or subcommittee.

markup

The process of revising a bill in committee.

select committees

Temporary committees in Congress created to conduct studies or investigations; they have no power to report bills.

joint committees

Congressional committees with members from both the House and the Senate.

conference committees

Ad hoc committees, made up of members of both the Senate and the House of Representatives, set up to reconcile differences in the provisions of bills.

Members are selected by the Speaker of the House and the Senate majority leader in consultation with the chairs of the committees that originally considered the bills in each chamber and sometimes with the leaders of the minority party. While it is probably an exaggeration to call conference committees the "third house of Congress," as some political observers do, there is no denying their central role in the march of bills through the legislative labyrinth. Although they are supposed to reconcile versions of bills coming out of the House and the Senate, conference committees sometimes add, subtract, or amend provisions that are of great consequence. Much of the power of conference committees comes from the fact that bills reported by them to the House and Senate must be voted up or down; no new amendments are allowed. During the early and mid-2000s, Republican leaders often excluded their Democratic counterparts from conference committees considering important bills, making conference a place to work out differences among House and Senate Republicans. Given the unanimous opposition of Senate Republicans to the health reform bill, and the near unanimous opposition to it by House Republicans, Democrats did not include GOP members on the conference committee for this legislation in 2010.

How Members of Congress Get on Committees

Because committees are so central to the legislative process, getting on the right one is important for reelection and for achieving policy and ideological goals. Committee assignments are determined by party leaders in each house, assisted by party steering committees, and guided (but not determined) by the members' **seniority** and preferences. Lawmakers have traditionally tried to land positions on committees that will help them serve their constituents and better their prospects for reelection. Thus, they will try to join a committee that directly serves their constituency—Agriculture if the member is from a farm district or state, or Interior if the member is from a mining or oil district—or one of the elite committees, such as Rules, Ways and Means, Finance, or Appropriations. Appointment to an elite committee gives a lawmaker not only high visibility and a central role in policymaking, but also a strategic vantage point from which to help the constituency, advance personal and party policy and ideological goals, and attract campaign contributions—all of which help his or her reelection prospects. There is a long waiting list for assignments to the most powerful committees, so new members are unlikely to be appointed to them. Lawmakers are more likely to gain a position on one of the elite committees if they make significant contributions to the national party committees or to other party congressional candidates from their own campaign funds.[55] For assignments to nonelite standing committees, congressional leaders try to accommodate the wishes of their members, within the constraints of the seniority system and the needs of the party.[55]

Committee Chairs and Ranking Members

For most of the twentieth century before the 1970s, appointment by seniority was an unbreakable rule. The most senior committee member of the majority party automatically became chair of the committee; the most senior member of the minority party automatically became the **ranking minority member**. After 1974, however, both Republicans and Democrats in the House instituted the secret ballot among party members for the election of chairs, and seniority was occasionally ignored. Seniority became even less important in the 1990s when Speaker Newt Gingrich began to bypass the most senior committee members in favor of members who would support his conservative legislative program. Appointment of committee chairs in the House remains firmly in the hands of majority party leaders today. In the 111th Congress, Speaker Pelosi selected committee chairs, paying attention to seniority but more

seniority
The principle that one attains a position on the basis of length of service.

ranking minority member
The highest ranking member of the minority party on a congressional committee.

to the needs of the Democratic legislative agenda, though the Democratic Steering Committee (whose members the Speaker selects) had to approve her actions. In the Senate, however, seniority continues to be an important criterion for appointment to a chairmanship position although, even there, party leaders and members increasingly are demanding more ideological and policy conformity as a condition of appointment.

Not long ago, chairs of committees were the absolute masters of all they surveyed. From the early twentieth century to the early 1970s, the heads of congressional committees went virtually unchallenged. They hired and assigned staff, controlled the budget, created or abolished subcommittees at will, controlled the agenda, scheduled meetings, and reported (or refused to report) bills to the floor. Things are different today. As we have shown, much of the power of committee chairs over legislation has migrated to the party leadership in each house. The upshot is that decisions that were entirely the province of the chair in the past have now been greatly diminished and are shared with others.[57] Committee chairs and ranking minority members—who were, oftentimes in the past, mavericks opposed to their own parties protected by seniority—now must be attentive to the party caucus and party leaders or risk losing their positions.[58] Still, committee chairs remain the most influential and active members within their committees, being at the center of all of the lines of communication, retaining the power to schedule meetings and organize the staff, having an important say on the committee's agenda and appointments to conference committees, and often winning deference as the most experienced members of their committees.

Rules and Norms in the House and Senate

Like all organizations, Congress is guided by both formal rules and informal norms of behavior.[59] Rules specify precisely how things should be done and what is not allowed. Norms are generally accepted expectations about how people ought to behave and how business ought to proceed.

Traditionally, members of the House have been expected to become specialists in some area or areas of policy and to defer to the judgment of other specialists on most bills. This mutual deference is known as **reciprocity**. While reciprocity is still common, deference to specialists—usually chairs or ranking members of committees—is declining in favor of deference to the wishes of party leaders. In the Senate, the norm of reciprocity was always less prevalent than it was in the House. Because there are fewer members in the Senate, because senators are elected on a statewide basis, and because the Senate has been the breeding ground for many presidential candidacies, a senator has more prestige, visibility, and power than a member of the House. As a result, senators are generally unwilling to sit quietly for a term or two, waiting their turn. It is not unusual for a first-term senator to introduce major bills and make important speeches. In the House, such a thing was very unusual in the past. There the old rule held sway: "To get along, go along."

Legislative life is much more rule-bound in the House of Representatives, because of its large size, than in the Senate; it tends to be more organized and hierarchical (see Table 11.2). Leaders in the House have more power, the majority party exercises more control over legislative affairs, the procedures are more structured, and the individual members have a harder time making their mark. It is geared toward majority rule, with the minority playing a lesser role. The Senate tends to be a more open and fluid place, and it lodges less power in its leaders than the House does. Each senator is more of an independent operator than his or her House colleagues. The Senate is a much more relaxed place, one that accommodates mavericks (though less so than in

reciprocity

Deferral by members of Congress to the judgment of subject-matter specialists, mainly on minor technical bills.

TABLE 11.2 Differences Between House and Senate Rules and Norms

Senate	House
Informal, open, nonhierarchical	Rule-bound, hierarchical
Leaders have only a few formal powers	Leaders have many formal powers
Members may serve on two or more major committees	Members restricted to one major committee
Less specialized	More specialized
Unrestricted floor debate	Restricted floor debate
Unlimited amendments possible	Limited amendments possible
Amendments need not be germane	Amendments must be germane
Unlimited time for debate unless shortened by unanimous consent or halted by invocation of cloture	Limited time for debate
More prestige	Less prestige
More reliance on staff	Less reliance on staff
Minority party plays a larger role; hard to put majority rule into effect	Minority party plays a smaller role; majority rule drives legislative process

the past), tolerates the foibles of its members, and pays more attention to members of the minority party. It is a place where the minority and individual senators play important roles in the legislative process.

Differences between the House and the Senate are especially apparent in floor debate. Bills are scheduled for floor debate in the Senate, for instance, not by a powerful committee but by **unanimous consent**, meaning that business can be blocked by a single dissenter. Outgoing Senator Jim Bunning (R–KY) blocked Senate consideration of an unemployment insurance extension for a whole week in early 2010 by responding "no" to the majority leader Harry Reid's request for unanimous consent to bring the bill to the floor. In the Senate, moreover, each senator has the power to place a **hold** on a bill or nomination to delay consideration by the whole body. While holds cannot be found in the formal rules of the Senate, they have become part of the many informal customs of the body. Their use is regulated only by the majority leader, who may decide on whether to grant holds and how long they can be in effect, but only by using complex and time-consuming procedural mechanisms. In 2009, Senator Jim DeMint (R–SC) held up President Obama's nominee to head the Transportation Safety Administration (TSA) for months in an effort to block TSA employees from joining a union. Later that same year, Senator Richard Shelby of Alabama blocked consideration of 70 presidential nominees, using the hold as a tool to force the Obama administration to put a new FBI lab in his state and to award a military tanker contract to a firm in Alabama. (As part of the 2007 lobbying reforms, the identity of senators asking for holds and an explanation for the action must now appear in the *Congressional Record*). Unlike the House, moreover, where debate on a bill is strictly regulated as to the number and kinds of amendments, as well as time limits for debate (determined by the Rules Committee with the agreement of the Speaker), the Senate's tradition allows for unlimited numbers of amendments—that need not be germane to the bill under consideration—and unlimited debate.

unanimous consent

Legislative action taken "without objection" as a way to expedite business; used to conduct much of the business of the Senate.

hold

A tactic by which a single senator can prevent action on a bill or nomination; based on an implied threat of refusing to agree to unanimous consent on other Senate matters or willingness to filibuster the bill or nomination.

Majorities, Minorities, and Senate Filibusters

Introduction Unlimited debate is a tradition in the U.S. Senate. Senate rules make it very difficult to end debate on a proposed bill and bring it to a vote if a number of senators wish to continue deliberations. Increasingly, senators try to kill a bill by "filibustering"—talking it to death, if you will—by not allowing other business to be taken up on the floor of the Senate. Filibusters can only be ended by passage of a cloture motion, which requires 60 votes, so the votes of only 41 senators can keep a filibuster going. The filibuster is often defended as an important instrument of deliberative democracy, because it allows the minority in the Senate to have an important say in legislative matters and not be steamrolled by the majority. Critics of the filibuster, whether Democrats or Republicans, liberals or conservatives, usually claim that filibusters are contrary to the principle of majority rule. Who is right?

Different Maps; Different Stories Both are right and wrong. The filibuster can be considered to serve the minority or the majority, depending on who we think the senators represent. Sustaining a filibuster, while requiring the votes of only 41 of 100 senators, may involve senators representing a large majority of the American population, a small minority, or anything in between. A filibuster sustained by a coalition of 41 senators from the most populous states would represent about 75 percent of Americans (red states on the cartogram), but a filibuster sustained by a coalition of 41 senators from the least populous states would represent only about 11 percent of Americans (green states). The cartogram, with states drawn to reflect the sizes of their populations, shows this very clearly. *

Today, of course, the filibuster usually is the tool of the minority party. In the first year of the 111th Congress, for example, 40 GOP senators forced cloture votes on nearly every major piece of legislation. These 40 senators represented about 36 percent of the American population.

Senators in the minority have increasingly used this tolerance of unlimited amendments and debate to good effect. Because limiting debate is so difficult in the Senate, the opponents of a bill can tie up legislative business by refusing to stop debating its merits. This practice is known as the **filibuster**. In the past, senators engaged in a filibuster had to be on the floor of the Senate addressing the body. Senators trying to hold up a bill often talked for hours through night and day, working together in shifts. Under Senate rules, filibustering senators did not even have to talk about the bill itself; some read from novels or quoted verse, others told stories about their children, and still others quoted long lists of sports statistics. The purpose was serious, however: to force the majority to give up the fight and move on to other business. This tactic was highly successful but used only occasionally because it was so hard to pull off; filibustering senators had to hold the floor for hours and days, fending off challenges to end debate. And, it held up all other business in the Senate.

Today, it is much easier to filibuster because a group of senators can simply announce a filibuster—not actually engage in the act of filibustering, that is to say—and a bill is stopped in its tracks unless 60 votes to end the filibuster can be mustered (Senate Rule XXII). Needless to say, the motion to end debate, known as **cloture**, is very hard to pass in an evenly divided Senate, where a party with a small majority must attract several members of the minority party to reach the 60-vote threshold. Or, in the rare case when the majority party has 60 or more votes—which the Democrats had in 2009 and 2010—cloture is possible only if the leadership can prevent defections from its side. This gives enormous power to a handful of senators who can threaten defection. On the health care reform bill, for example, Harry Reid, the majority leader, was forced to drop the so-called public option to meet the demands of Senator Lieberman (I–CT), and make it harder to use public monies to fund abortions to satisfy Senator Nelson (D–NE).

Not surprisingly, given the power that the filibuster gives to the minority party and to a handful of senators in the majority party, the number

filibuster

A parliamentary device used in the Senate to prevent a bill from coming to a vote by "talking it to death," made possible by the norm of unlimited debate.

cloture

A vote to end a filibuster; requires the votes of three-fifths of the membership of the Senate.

What Do You Think? When they were a majority in the Senate, Republicans wanted to change the filibuster rule, especially on votes that involve judicial appointments on which the Senate has constitutional "advise and consent" responsibilities. Their argument was that a minority should not be able to block this important constitutional role. But what if the minority in the Senate actually represents states with a majority of the population? Some have suggested that a filibuster should be sustained only when the 41 senators supporting it represent a majority of Americans. What do you think about this idea?

*41 senators represent 20½ states, but there is no way reasonably to draw one-half of a state. In this cartogram, the large-state bloc and the small-state block each is composed of 21 states.

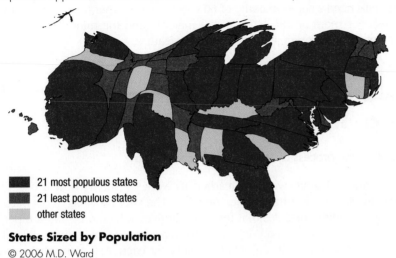

■ 21 most populous states
■ 21 least populous states
□ other states

States Sized by Population
© 2006 M.D. Ward

Standard US Map

of filibusters and the number of cloture votes to end them have multiplied dramatically. Political scientist Barbara Sinclair has shown that "extended debate" tactics—filibusters threatened or used—affected 8 percent of important bills during the 1960s, 27 percent during the 1980s, and a staggering 70 percent after the Democrats took control of the Senate in 2007.[60]

Senators' positions on the filibuster depend somewhat on whether one's party is in the majority or the minority. When Republicans were in the majority in 2005 and Democrats were holding up President Bush's judicial nominations, Republicans threatened passage of a rule that came to be called the "nuclear option" that would end the use of the filibuster entirely on matters of judicial appointments. When they were in the minority from 2007 through 2010, however, Republicans used the filibuster repeatedly to slow or stop majority Democrats from passing

I SAID "NO PUBLIC OPTION" Because Democrats in the 111th Congress needed 60 votes on every piece of their ambitious agenda, concessions had to be made to those who caucused with the party but who threatened not to vote for final approval on bills unless they were satisfied with particular provisions. Joe Lieberman (I–CT) said "no" to a public option in the health reform bill, for example, so Democratic leaders were forced to take it out. Are there methods of voting in legislative bodies that might better accommodate the majority and decrease the power of one or two swing voters? Would that be a good outcome?

bills to change Iraq war policy, provide stimulus spending and tax relief, reform the health care system, regulate the financial industry, and slow emissions of greenhouse gases. Whatever one thinks of the filibuster—some condemn it as a device that undermines majority rule; others praise it as a device that guarantees that the voice of the minority is heard—it is inescapably the case today, given the deep partisan divisions between the parties and the difficulty of acting in a bipartisan fashion, that most major bills need a super-majority of 60 votes to pass rather than a simple majority (51 votes). For more on the status of the majority and the minority in filibusters and cloture, see the "Mapping American Politics" feature.

Legislative Responsibilities: How a Bill Becomes a Law

11.4 Outline the process by which a bill becomes a law

We can put much of what we have learned to work by seeing how a bill moves through the legislative labyrinth to become a law. The path by which a bill becomes a law is so strewn with obstacles that few bills survive; in fact, only about 6 percent of all bills that are introduced are enacted. To make law is exceedingly difficult; to block bills from becoming laws is relatively easy. At each step along the way (see Figure 11.6), a "no" decision can stop the passage of a bill in its tracks. As one account points out, members of the House or the Senate have "two principal functions: to make laws and to keep laws from being made. The first of these [they] perform only with sweat, patience, and a remarkable skill in the handling of creaking machinery; but the second they perform daily, with ease and infinite variety."[61]

What follows describes how major bills become law most of the time. Minor bills are often considered in each house under special rules that allow shortcuts. Thus, in the House, the "suspension calendar" and the "corrections calendar" set aside certain times for consideration of minor matters. It is also worth noting that bills involving the federal budget—authorization and appropriations bills—have several unique aspects to them, which need not concern us here. And, more importantly, on some major bills, House and Senate leaders have made changes in bills coming out of committee on their way to floor action, or made important changes to bills in conference committees. Some observers claim that these "unorthodox" routes for lawmaking are becoming more and more common.[62]

Introducing a Bill

A bill can be introduced only by a member of Congress. In reality, bills are often written in the executive branch. The initial draft of the bill that became the Tax Reform Act of 1986, for instance, was fashioned in the Treasury Department by a committee headed by the department's secretary, James Baker. Bills are also often written by interest groups. Industry trade groups, for example, wrote substantial parts of bills designed to roll back timber and mining regulations in 1995, while pharmaceutical industry trade group representatives wrote key portions of the Medicare drug benefit bill that went into effect in 2006.

With the exception of tax bills (which must originate in the House), a bill may be introduced in either the House or the Senate. In the House, a member introduces a bill by putting it into the **hopper** (a box watched over by one of the House clerks). In the Senate, a member must announce a bill to the body after being recognized by the presiding officer. The bill is then assigned a number, with the prefix *H.R.* in the House or *S.* in the Senate.

hopper
The box in the House of Representatives in which proposed bills are placed.

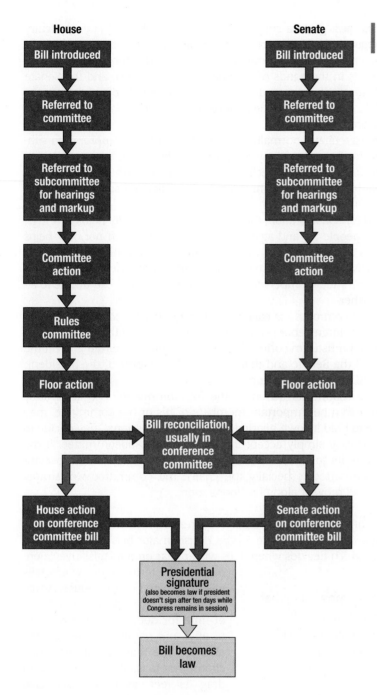

House

- Bill introduced
- Referred to committee
- Referred to subcommittee for hearings and markup
- Committee action
- Rules committee
- Floor action

Senate

- Bill introduced
- Referred to committee
- Referred to subcommittee for hearings and markup
- Committee action
- Floor action

Bill reconciliation, usually in conference committee

House action on conference committee bill

Senate action on conference committee bill

Presidential signature
(also becomes law if president doesn't sign after ten days while Congress remains in session)

Bill becomes law

FIGURE 11.6 How a Bill Becomes a Law

This diagram shows the path by which major bills introduced in Congress become law. As explained in the text, the road that bills must travel is complex and difficult, and few bills survive it. A bill can be derailed at any stop in its passage. A subcommittee can refuse to report a bill; a bill may be defeated on the floor of each chamber; a conference committee may fail to reach an agreement on a compromise; the conference bill may be defeated in either chamber; or the president may veto the bill.

Committee Action on a Bill

The presiding officer in the Senate or the Speaker in the House refers the bill to the appropriate standing committee. In the majority of cases, referral to committee is routine; the subject matter of the bill clearly indicates the appropriate committee. Revenue bills go automatically to the Ways and Means Committee in the House and to the Finance Committee in the Senate, for instance. In a small but still significant number of cases, however, the relevant committee is not so obvious because of overlapping committee jurisdictions. For example, the House Committee on International Relations is in charge of "international policy," whereas the Commerce Committee is in charge of "foreign commerce generally." In such cases, the Speaker can make multiple referrals, that is, send a bill to more than one committee for consideration. In the

discharge petition

A petition signed by 218 House members to force a bill that has been before a committee for at least 30 days while the House is in session out of the committee and onto the floor for consideration.

Senate, bills must go to a single committee, regardless of any ambiguity that may exist about its exact content. Needless to say, the more bills there are without an obvious committee destination, the more discretionary power there is in the hands of the Speaker of the House and the Senate majority leader. Where they decide to send such bills often determines whether bills will survive the legislative process and what form they will take in the end.

Committee chairs normally pass the bill on to the appropriate subcommittee for hearings. Many a bill dies at this stage, when either the subcommittee or the full committee declines to consider it further. A bill quietly killed in committee can reach the floor only by a device called a **discharge petition**, which is rarely successful.

If a bill is accepted for consideration, the subcommittee generally holds hearings, taking testimony from people for and against it. Subcommittee staff not only helps prepare representatives and senators for the questioning but also often take part in the questioning themselves. The subcommittee may then forward the bill as rewritten by the staff and subcommittee members to the full committee, or it can decide to allow the bill to go no further.

Rewriting the bill in committee is called the *markup* (discussed earlier), which usually occurs amid very intense bargaining and deal making, with an eye toward fashioning a bill that will muster majority support in the full committee and on the floors of the House and the Senate and that will gain the support of the president. The staff plays a central role in the markup.

The subcommittee reports its action to the full committee. The committee chair, in consultation with other important members of his or her committee, may opt for the committee to hold its own hearings and markup sessions, may decide to kill the bill outright, or may simply accept the action of the subcommittee. If the subcommittee has done its job well and has consulted with the most important players on the full committee (especially the chair), the committee will simply rubber-stamp the bill and move it along for floor action.

Floor Action on a Bill If a bill is favorably reported from committee, congressional leaders schedule it for floor debate. In the House, major bills must first go to the Rules Committee, which decides where bills will appear on the legislative calendar and the terms under which bills will be debated by the House. A rule specifies such things as the amount of time for debate and the number (if any) and nature of amendments allowed. The Rules Committee may choose not to issue a rule at all or to drag its feet, as it did with civil rights bills until the mid-1960s. This has happened less often in recent years because both Democratic and Republican Speakers have had more power over Rules Committee appointments. The committee can also grant a "closed rule," allowing only a yes or no vote without amendments, as it generally does with tax bills.

Floor debate in the Senate, where rules do not limit debate as in the House, is much more freewheeling. Floor debate is also more important in the Senate in determining the final form a bill will take because Senate committees are less influential than House committees. Senators are also less likely to defer to committee judgments. Also, the threat of a hold or a filibuster means that the minority in the Senate plays an important role in determining the final shape of legislation.

After floor debate, the entire membership of the chamber votes on the bill, either as reported by the committee or (more often) after amendments have been

? Is the process of passing a law so complex and time consuming that it undermines the ability of the national government to meet the needs of the American people? Or, are the American people well served by the deliberation that is required for a bill to become a law?

added. If the bill receives a favorable vote, it then goes through the same obstacle course in the other chamber or awaits action by the other house if the bill was introduced there at the same time.

Conference Committee   Even if the bill makes it through both houses, its journey is not yet over. Bills passed by the House and the Senate almost always differ from one another, sometimes in minor ways and sometimes in quite substantial ways. Before the bill goes to the president, its conflicting versions must be rewritten so that a single bill gains the approval of both chambers of Congress. This compromise bill usually is fashioned in a conference committee made up of members from both the House and the Senate appointed by the Speaker and the Senate majority leader, customarily from the relevant committees but not always. Increasingly, House and Senate leaders appoint people who will write a final bill that will be acceptable to them and to their party. Sometimes a conference committee is not used; separate House and Senate versions of a bill can be reconciled by the two trading amendments until they are similar, for example, or one chamber can simply defer to the other and accept its version of a bill.

A bill from a conference committee must be voted up or down on the floors of the House and the Senate; no amendments or further changes are allowed. If, and only if, both houses approve it, the bill is forwarded to the president for consideration.

Presidential Action   Because the president plays an important constitutional role in turning a bill into a law, he or his assistants and advisers are usually consulted throughout the legislative process, especially if the president is of the same party that controls Congress. If the president approves the bill, he signs it and it becomes law. If he is not particularly favorable but does not want to block the bill, it becomes law after 10 days if he takes no action. He can also **veto** the bill and return it to Congress. A bill can still become law by a two-thirds vote of each house, which will override the president's veto. A president can also kill a bill at the end of a congressional session if he takes no action and Congress adjourns before 10 days pass. This is known as a **pocket veto**. We will have more to say about the presidential veto in Chapter 12.

> **veto**
> Presidential disapproval of a bill that has been passed by both houses of Congress. The president's veto can be overridden by a two-thirds vote in each house.
>
> **pocket veto**
> Rejection of a bill if the president takes no action on it for 10 days and Congress has adjourned during that period.
>
> **oversight**
> Congressional responsibility for monitoring the actions of executive branch agencies and personnel to ensure conformity to federal statutes and congressional intent.

Legislative Oversight of the Executive Branch

11.5   Explain why oversight is an important congressional responsibility

Oversight is another important responsibility of Congress. Oversight involves keeping an eye on how the executive branch carries out the provisions of the laws that Congress has passed and on possible abuses of power by executive branch officials, including the president.

Oversight is primarily the province of the committees and subcommittees of Congress, and it is among Congress's most visible and dramatic roles, guided by the wishes of House and Senate leaders and the majority party caucus in each. High-profile examples of legislative probes of alleged administrative malfeasance or incompetence include Watergate, the Iran-Contra affair, the savings-and-loan collapse and bailout, corporate accounting scandals, intelligence failures, the federal response to the Hurricane Katrina disaster in New Orleans, and the sub-prime mortgage meltdown.

In these highly partisan times, whether oversight hearings take place and the relative vigor with which they are carried out depend increasingly on which party

PUBLIC WHIPPING   John Mack, chairman of Morgan Stanley, tries to explain to members of the Senate Finance Committee in January 2010 why the financial collapse happened, why industry profits were soaring, and why bonuses were being paid, even as loan money for small businesses and homeowners was scarce. The chief executives of other leading financial firms wait their turns to testify. What role in our political system do congressional hearings play? Do they lead to substantive changes in regulations and laws, or are they more often opportunities to play to the anger or frustration of the public?

controls which branch of government. In the years 2003 through 2006, when Republicans controlled both houses of Congress and Republican George W. Bush was president, Congress did not probe very deeply into a number of troublesome areas, including failed prewar intelligence on weapons of mass destruction in Iraq or warrantless searches and eavesdropping on American citizens. Asked why not much oversight took place during these years representative Chris Shays (R–CT) remarked that fellow Republicans asked him, "Why do we want to embarrass the administration?"[63] After the 2006 elections, when Democrats won majorities in both chambers, oversight hearings ratcheted up on a wide range of issues, including the alleged use of harsh interrogation methods like water-boarding on detainees and access to the courts for terrorism detainees being held at Guantanamo Bay. Democrats, apparently, were not as concerned as Republicans about embarrassing a Republican administration. After Barack Obama came to office, Democrats in Congress were less aggressive in their use of the oversight tools, though they held hearings in 2009 on bank bailouts and approval of lucrative bonuses to many of their executives, in 2010 on the TSA's and the Department of Homeland Security's failure to detect a suicide bomber (whose bomb failed to detonate) on a flight from Europe to the United States, and on BP's oil blowout in the Gulf of Mexico.

Hearings are an important part of the oversight process. Testimony is taken from agency officials, outside experts, and congressional investigatory institutions such as the Government Accounting Office and the Office of Technology Assessment. The hearings are not simply information-gathering exercises, however. As often as not, they are designed to send signals from committee members to the relevant part of the bureaucracy. Hearings that focus on the overly aggressive efforts of Internal Revenue Service agents to collect taxes, for example, are a clear signal to IRS officials that they had better rein in their agents before the next round of hearings on the budget.

Congress's most powerful instrument of oversight of the Executive Branch is **impeachment** (responsibility of the House) and trial and removal from office (responsibility of the Senate) of high executive officials, including the president. This is a blunt tool, rarely used, except in the most

impeachment

House action bringing formal charges against a member of the executive branch or the federal judiciary that may or may not lead to removal from office by the Senate.

partisan atmosphere or in cases involving truly egregious executive behavior. Over the course of American history, only seven executives have been removed from office by the Senate. No president has ever been convicted and removed from office, but the impeachment processes in the House of presidents Andrew Johnson, Nixon, and Clinton were deeply divisive, so Congress treads very cautiously in this area.

Using the **DEMOCRACY STANDARD**

Is Congress out of touch with the American people?

Although Congress was significantly democratized by passage of the Seventeenth Amendment in 1913, which transferred the election of senators from state legislatures to voters, the institution is still significantly shaped by the antimajoritarian constitutional design of the framers. Most important in this regard is its bicameral nature, the equal representation of the states in the Senate, and its immersion in a system of checks and balances.

The framers settled on bicameralism for two reasons. First, it was the only way to break the deadlock between large and small states at the constitutional convention. Had the Connecticut Compromise not been agreed to, the convention would most likely have adjourned without completing its historic task. Second, bicameralism conformed to the framers' belief that the legislative branch—the center of policymaking for government—ought to be a place where the public's business is deliberated carefully and slowly, free from the pressure of fickle public opinion. As any observer of our national legislature can report, this part of the vision was fulfilled: Congress is a place where the legislative process grinds slowly, with only a few pieces of major legislation produced in each Congress and most bills never seeing the light of day. The need for legislation to pass through two powerful chambers—one upper and one lower, each organized in different ways and each tuned to different election cycles and constituencies—is the central reason for the slow pace of this process.

As noted earlier, equal representation of the states in the Senate violates the democratic principle of political equality. Small-population states such as Wyoming, Nevada, and North Dakota have the same number of senators as large-population states such as California, New York, Texas, and Florida, meaning that the people in each of the states are unequally represented. This characteristic affects much of what the Senate does and does not do. For example, a coalition of 41 senators from the smallest population states, representing a mere 11 percent of the American population, can block any bill in the Senate (because 60 votes are needed to override a filibuster). To say that the Senate enshrines unequal representation is no exaggeration.

We must not forget, moreover, the antimajoritarian effects of the system of checks and balances within which Congress operates. Designed by the framers as the most "popular" branch—and not very "popular" at that in its original design—Congress finds itself continually hemmed in by the other two branches. Even on those rare occasions when it acts vigorously in response to public opinion, it may not always have the support it needs from the president and the courts. Further, the balance against democracy in Congress is even more disproportionate once one takes into account the important role played by interest groups and campaign contributors in its affairs.

It appears, then, that Congress has not drifted very far from what the framers had envisioned. To be sure, senators are now elected directly by the people. Also, senators and members of the House are more prone than in the past to pay attention to public opinion. Nevertheless, it remains an institution that the framers would recognize as their own creation.

SUMMARY

11.1 Identify the ways in which the Constitution shapes Congress

- The framers of the Constitution granted Congress legislative power, gave it an existence independent of the executive branch, enumerated an impressive range of powers, and gave it elastic powers sufficient to carry out its enumerated ones. However, they also gave the other branches powers to check legislative excesses, created a bicameral body, and strictly denied certain powers to Congress.

11.2 Assess how and to what extent the members of Congress represent their constituents

- Congress is a representative institution but not necessarily fully democratic; its members are constantly balancing the preferences of the people in their constituencies and important interest groups and contributors as well as their own conceptions of the public interest.

- Because elections are the most important mechanism for representation, and because they are the way in which members attain office, elections dominate the time and energy of lawmakers and shape how Congress organizes itself and goes about its business.

11.3 Describe what leaders, political parties, and committees do in Congress

- Nearly every aspect of congressional organization and operations are defined by political parties. Leadership in each of the chambers, committee leadership and membership, and the agenda are determined by the majority party.

- The House invest great powers in its leaders, with the Speaker of the House acting very much like a leader in a parliamentary system. Leadership in the Senate is much more illusive; each senator has a great deal of independent power and must be persuaded to side with party leaders.

- Most of the business of the House and Senate takes place in committees and their subcommittees. Here hearings are held on bills, negotiations on bills take place, and members of Congress can bring their subject matter expertise to bear. Over the past several decades, however, each of the political parties has given its leaders more powers, reducing that of committees and their chairs.

- To conduct its business, Congress depends on an elaborate set of norms and rules and a web of committees and subcommittees, political parties, legislative leaders, and an extensive staff.

11.4 Outline the process by which a bill becomes a law

- After they are introduced, bills are referred to committee. Only a few make it out of committee for consideration by the entire membership of the House or Senate. In the House, the Rules Committee must issue a rule for a bill to reach the floor for debate.

- If related bills pass each chamber, but in different forms, differences must be resolved in a conference committee. The report of the conference committee cannot be amended and must be voted up or down in the House and the Senate. If a bill makes it this far, it goes to the president for his signature or veto.

- A bill becomes law if the president signs it, or absent his signature, if 10 days pass while Congress is in session, or if both the House and the Senate vote by a two-thirds majority to override a veto.

11.5 Explain why oversight is an important congressional responsibility

- Oversight is a way for members of Congress to bring attention to issues and to turn the spotlight on the performance of executive branch agencies. Oversight is done through committee or subcommittee hearings.

TEST YOURSELF

Answer key begins on page T-1.

11.1 Identify the ways in which the Constitution shapes Congress

1. The principles of federalism ensure that members of Congress look out for national interests, even when doing so conflicts with the preferences of local districts and states.
True / False

2. Which of the following statements about the Senate is correct?
   a. The Senate is apportioned on the basis of population.
   b. Senators serve an unlimited number of 10-year terms.

c. Approximately one-third of the Senate seats are up for election every two years.

d. Senators are currently selected by state legislatures.

e. The Senate conducts impeachment trials.

3. How does the Constitution limit congressional power?

11.2 Assess how and to what extent the members of Congress represent their constituents

4. Representatives who act like trustees make political decisions based on what their constituents want.
True / False

5. Which of the following has been used to improve descriptive representation?
a. Casework
b. Open-seat election races
c. Reapportionment
d. Majority-minority districts
e. The franking privilege

6. Elections are said to be the main mechanism by which politicians hold public officials accountable. Evaluate whether congressional elections do a good job in serving this function.

11.3 Describe what leaders, political parties, and committees do in Congress

7. Party affiliation is the best predictor of how a member will vote in Congress.
True / False

8. Who has the most power in the House of Representatives?
a. The majority leader
b. The Speaker

c. The whip
d. The member with the most seniority
e. The member who can raise the most money

9. What is the most significant role played by congressional committees? Provide a rationale for your answer.

11.4 Outline the process by which a bill becomes a law

10. A discharge petition is used to move a proposed bill from the executive branch to the legislative branch.
True / False

11. What is the role of the conference committee?
a. To establish the legislative agenda
b. To determine what bills will be placed in the hopper
c. To reach a compromise between House and Senate versions of a bill
d. To hold hearings and take testimony from those with an interest in the bill
e. To determine the rules under which a bill will be debated on the House floor

11.5 Explain why oversight is an important congressional responsibility

12. Which of the following is the most common means by which Congress exercises oversight?
a. Impeachment
b. Administrative adjudication
c. Hearings
d. Legislative vetoes
e. Cloture

13. Why does Congress take oversight more seriously during divided government?

PEARSON
myp⬤liscilab EXERCISES

Apply what you learned in this chapter on
MyPoliSciLab.

📖—[Read on **mypoliscilab.com**

eText: Chapter 11

✓—[Study and **Review** on **mypoliscilab.com**

Pre-Test
Post-Test
Chapter Exam
Flashcards

👁—[Watch on **mypoliscilab.com**

Video: Unknown Wins South Carolina Senate
Primary
Video: Kagan Hearing

✳—[Explore on **mypoliscilab.com**

Simulation: You Are a Member of Congress
Simulation: You Are Redrawing the Districts in Your
State
Simulation: How a Bill Becomes a Law
Comparative: Comparing Legislatures
Timeline: The Power of the Speaker of the House
Visual Literacy: Congressional Redistricting
Visual Literacy: Why Is It So Hard to Defeat an
Incumbent?

INTERNET SOURCES

CongressLink at the Dirksen Center
www.congresslink.org
*Designed for teachers of American government, history, and civics,
this is a very rich information site on Congress. Features include
access to information on pending legislation, legislative schedules,
caucuses, committees, rules, histories of the House and Senate,
ways to contact members of Congress, and much more.*

National Atlas
http://nationalatlas.gov/printable/congress.html
Maps of all House districts.

Congress.org by Capitol Advantage
www.congress.org
*Congressional news, legislation, issues, personalities, and more,
as well as information on how to have your voice heard on Capitol
Hill.*

CQ Moneyline/Federal Election Commission
http://moneyline.cq.com/pml/home.do

*Information on campaign finance for presidential and congres-
sional elections.*

Thomas
http://thomas.loc.gov/
*Expansive repository of information on the House of
Representatives, including the full text and progress of bills, the
Congressional Record, legislative procedures and rules, committee
actions, and more.*

U.S. House of Representatives Home Page
www.house.gov
*House schedule, House organization and procedures, links to House
committees, information on contacting representatives, and historical documents on the House of Representatives.*

U.S. Senate Home Page
www.senate.gov
*Similar to the House of Representatives home page, focused on the
Senate. One exciting new feature is a virtual tour of the Capitol.*

SUGGESTIONS FOR FURTHER READING

Adler, E. Scott, and John S. Lapinski, eds. *The Macropolitics of Congress.* Princeton, NJ: Princeton University Press, 2006.
  A collection of recent research by leading scholars on the impact of congressional lawmaking on American society.

Caro, Robert. *The Years of Lyndon Johnson.* New York: Knopf, 1982.
  This classic and award-winning biography of Lyndon Baines Johnson of Texas reveals more about how Congress worked in the "old days" than virtually any academic treatise.

Davidson, Roger H., Walter J. Oleszek, and Frances E. Lee. *Congress and Its Members,* 12th ed. Washington, D.C.: CQ Press, 2010.
  The classic textbook on Congress, now in its 12th edition.

Oleszek, Walter J. *Congressional Procedures and the Policy Process,* 8th ed. Washington, D.C.: CQ Press, 2010.
  The most comprehensive compilation yet published of the rules and operations of the legislative process in Congress, written by a scholar who served as the policy director of the Joint Committee on the Organization of Congress.

Quirk, Paul J., and Sarah A. Binder. *The Legislative Branch.* New York: Oxford University Press and the Annenberg Foundation Trust, 2005.
  A very accessible compendium of essays by leading scholars on every aspect of Congress and the legislative process.

Sinclair, Barbara. *Unorthodox Lawmaking: New Legislative Processes in the U.S. Congress,* 3rd ed. Washington, D.C.: CQ Press, 2007.
  Argues that the traditional textbook rendition of "how a bill becomes a law" has dramatically changed over the past two decades.

Specialized newspapers and journals: *The Hill, Roll Call, Congressional Quarterly, National Journal.*
  Valuable sources for up-to-the-minute, in-depth coverage of what is happening in Congress.

12 | The Presidency

CHAPTER

IN THIS CHAPTER

12.1 Trace the expansion of presidential responsibilities and power

12.2 Identify the many roles presidents play

12.3 Outline the functions filled by the president's many advisers and helpers

12.4 Analyze the conflict between presidents and Congress

12.5 Assess how democratic the presidency is and whether presidents respond to the public

PRESIDENT OBAMA'S UNITARY POWERS

Barack Obama inherited a range of national problems that were almost unprecedented in their depth and complexity when he became president of the United States. When he took the oath of office on January 20, 2009, the nation was involved in two armed conflicts abroad, engaged in a prolonged conflict in many places (Pakistan, Yemen, and Somalia, among others) against Al Qaeda and related jihadist groups, worried about the possibility of a nuclear-armed Iran and North Korea, stuck in the deepest and most prolonged economic recession since the Great Depression, devastated by the collapse of the financial system that froze credit and wiped out the savings of many ordinary Americans, hit hard by the bursting of a massive real estate bubble and rising foreclosures, and uncertain about its future global economic role in the face of a rising China and a falling dollar. Barack Obama promised in his campaign and in his inaugural address to boldly take on these problems, to bring "change we can believe in," using an energized and activist government to make the promised changes happen.

Working with a Democratic-controlled Congress, and initially making overtures to moderate Republicans in the House and Senate, Obama pressed for a number of major legislative initiatives. He succeeded on several very important ones.

Congress passed his massive $787 billion economic stimulus bill within one month of his swearing in (no House Republicans and only three Senate Republicans supported the measure); about one-half of the cost of the bill was in tax cuts, with the other half in new spending for school construction, student loans, scientific research, transportation infrastructure, alternative energy development, and extended unemployment insurance payments. Two months later, the president signed the $3.4 trillion fiscal year 2010 budget, which included monies not only for ongoing domestic and military and national security programs, but also for a massive new national health insurance program, a cap-and-trade system to reduce carbon consumption, aid to financially stressed states, and increased spending on research and development and education. The budget also provided for an extension of middle-class tax cuts.

But passing bills in Congress to establish new programs on which to spend these new monies proved to be a more difficult task. Passage of the health care reform bill took a full year to pass Congress and be signed into law by President Obama. His proposal to impose new regulations on the financial and mortgage industries to prevent another crisis met stiff resistance from Republicans and a few senators from his own party, and took a

378

year-and-a-half to make its way through Congress. His cap-and-trade carbon emissions initiative was unsuccessful; the battles over the stimulus, health care, and financial regulation were so partisan, brutal, and drawn out that the cap-and-trade proposal never got off the ground as the 2010 elections loomed.

Passing multiple bills that transform major elements of American public policy is a very difficult thing to do at any time, given our constitutional system of separated powers and checks and balances. Our system, as you have learned, is better geared to stopping big policy changes than to encouraging them. Making big policy changes in a bitterly partisan environment, especially in the Senate where major bills now must garner a super-majority of 60 votes to pass, is even more difficult. Is it any wonder, then, that Barack Obama, like all modern presidents, has made liberal use of the unitary powers of the presidency to move public policies in a direction he wants? As commander-in-chief, for example, he was able to carry out his promise to shift the attention of the military from Iraq to Afghanistan and the Pakistan border area without the need to ask Congress. He not only increased troop levels there, but dramatically increased the number of drone attacks on Al Qaeda sites in this region and authorized special forces actions against

radical jihadist groups in Somalia and Yemen. In his capacity as chief executive—that is, the administrative head of the executive branch of government (see Chapter 13)—he issued a string of executive orders to various bureaucratic agencies reversing Bush administration policies on stem-cell research, climate change, and the use of torture in the interrogation of enemy combatants; ordered the Department of Transportation to allow states to impose emissions requirements that exceed those of the federal government; and overturned the ban on government contributions to international organizations that offer family planning services that include abortion. He also ordered the Department of Homeland Security to allow people seeking asylum from torture or persecution in their home countries to stay in the United States and live freely until they receive a hearing before an immigration judge, reversing a Bush-era policy that placed most of them in detention. He issued orders, as well, to stop raids on companies to find and deport illegal immigrants and to shift attention to audits of companies who hire significant numbers of illegal immigrants, with stiff fines for violating firms.

President Obama, like all presidents, must gain the cooperation of Congress on many matters if he is to achieve the major elements of his policy agenda and fulfill the promises made during his campaign for office, in his inauguration speech to the nation, and his several State of the Union addresses. What many people fail to appreciate, however, is the degree to which presidents can act first and on their own, without Congress, on many important matters. This is usually referred to as the unitary power of the president and encompasses a broad range of tools, including executive orders, executive agreements, signing statements, presidential proclamations, and regulatory review, as well as his authority over the armed forces and American foreign policy. In this chapter we will examine the key features of the modern presidency, including the broad range of the office's unitary powers, the rise of the office to a position of preeminence in American government, and why it happened.

THINKING CRITICALLY About This Chapter

This chapter is about the American presidency: how it has evolved and what role it plays in American politics and government.

Using the FRAMEWORK

You will see in this chapter how the presidential office has changed substantially from how the framers envisioned it, primarily because of changes in America's international situation, the nature of its economy, and popular expectations. You will also see how presidents interact with other governmental institutions (such as Congress and the Court) and with political linkage–level actors (such as political parties, public opinion, the mass media, and interest groups), and how these interactions influence what government does.

Using the DEMOCRACY STANDARD

You will see in this chapter how the presidential office, although not envisioned by the framers to be a democratic one, has become more directly connected to and responsive to the American people. On the other hand, you will be asked to think about whether presidents' growing ability to influence the thinking of the public and shape their perceptions of public events undermines democracy.

The Expanding Presidency

12.1 Trace the expansion of presidential responsibilities and power

The American presidency has grown considerably since our nation's beginning. The increase has occurred in presidential responsibilities, burdens, power, and impact.

When George Washington took office as the first president, he had a total budget (for 1789–1792) of just over $4 million. Washington had only a handful of federal employees. Even by 1801, there were only about 300 federal officeholders in the capital. Washington's cabinet consisted of only five officials: the secretaries of state, war, and the treasury; a postmaster general; and an attorney general (who acted as the president's personal attorney, rather than as head of a full-fledged Justice Department). The entire Department of State consisted of one secretary, one chief clerk, six minor clerks, and one messenger. In 1790, only about 700 Americans were in uniform, and they had no way to project force around the world. Federal government functions were few. The entire United States consisted of the 13 original eastern and southeastern states, with only 864,746 square miles of land area; the population was only about 4 million persons, most living on small farms.[1]

When Barack Obama was first sworn into office 220 years later, he presided over a federal budget with more than $2.7 trillion in annual expenditures and a federal

WASHINGTON REVIEWS THE TROOPS   The presidency has grown in scale and responsibility. As commander-in-chief of the armed forces, President George Washington, here reviewing his troops during his first year as president, commanded an army of just over 700 soldiers and had little to do with affairs outside the United States. Today, the president commands a force of about 1.5 million active duty personnel stationed all over the world. How has this change in the role of the president affected the relative balance of power among the three branches of government? *Source*: Washington Reviewing the Western Army at Fort Cumberland, Maryland by Frederick Kemmelmeyer. The Metropolitan Museum of Art, Gift of Edgar William and Bernice Chrysler Garbish 1963. (63.201.2) Photograph © 1983 The Metropolitan Museum of Art.

bureaucracy with approximately 2.7 million civilian employees (postal workers accounted for 656,000 employees). He was commander-in-chief of the armed forces, with about 1.5 million men and women in active-duty service; hundreds of military bases at home and scattered throughout the world; and about 10,000 nuclear warheads, 2,600 of which are operational, enough to obliterate every medium-sized or large city in the world many times over.[2] The United States in early 2009 had a population of almost 307 million diverse people; a gross domestic product of more than $14 trillion; and a land area of some 3.8 million square miles, stretching from Alaska to Florida and from Hawaii to Maine.[3]

The Founders' Conception of the Presidency

The Founders certainly had in mind a presidency more like Washington's than Obama's. As discussed in Chapter 2, Article II of the Constitution provided for a single executive who would be strong, compared with his role under the Congress-dominated Articles of Confederation, but the Constitution's sparse language declaring that "The executive power shall be vested in a President of the United States," barely hinted at the range of things twentieth- and twenty-first-century presidents would do.[4]

The Constitution made the president "commander-in-chief" of the armed forces, for example, without any suggestion that there would be a vast standing army that presidents could send abroad to fight without a declaration of war. It empowered presidents to appoint and to "require the opinion in writing" of executive department heads without indicating that a huge federal bureaucracy would evolve. The Constitution provided that presidents could from time to time "recommend … measures" to Congress without specifying that these proposals would very often come to dominate Congress's agenda. Still, the vague language of the Constitution proved flexible enough to encompass the great expansion of the presidency.

The Dormant Presidency

From the time of George Washington's inauguration at Federal Hall in New York City to the end of the nineteenth century, the presidency, for the most part, conformed to the designs of the Founders. The presidency did not, by and large, dominate the political life of the nation. Presidents saw their responsibility as primarily involving the execution of policies decided by Congress. Congress was a fully equal branch of government, or perhaps more than equal. But the office changed after that.

Structural Factors   Why does the early presidency seem so weak in comparison with the contemporary presidency? Surely it is not because early presidents were less intelligent, vigorous, or ambitious; indeed, this era produced some of our greatest presidents—as well as some who are largely forgotten. A more reasonable answer is that the nation did not often require a very strong presidency before the twentieth century, particularly in the key areas of foreign policy and military leadership. Only in the twentieth century did the United States become a world power, involved in military, diplomatic, and economic activities around the globe. With that *structural* development came a simultaneous increase in the power and responsibility of the president.

It was not until the late nineteenth century, moreover, that the economy of the United States was transformed from a simple free market economy of farmers and small firms to a corporate-dominated economy, with units so large and interconnected that their every action had social consequences. This transformation eventually led to demands for more government supervision of the American economic system. As this role of government grew, so did the president's role as chief executive of the federal government.

? Does it strike you as odd that an era that produced some of our most respected presidents—Washington, Jefferson, and Lincoln, for example—was in fact a time of congressional dominance? In what ways did constraints on the executive branch factor into these men's legacies?

Although the presidency was largely dormant until the end of the nineteenth century, events and the actions of several presidents during the early period anticipated what was to happen to the office in our own time. Presidential actions created precedents for their successors; expectations among the public and political elites about what they expected of presidents changed; and new laws were passed that gradually enhanced presidential responsibilities and powers.

Important Early Presidents   The war hero George Washington solidified the prestige of the presidency at a time when executive leadership was mistrusted.[5] Washington also affirmed the primacy of the president in foreign affairs and set a precedent for fashioning a domestic legislative program. Thomas Jefferson, although initially hostile to the idea of a vigorous central government, boldly concluded the Louisiana Purchase with France, which roughly doubled the size of the United States and opened the continent for American settlement. Andrew Jackson, elected with broader popular participation than ever before, helped transform the presidency into a popular institution, as symbolized by his vigorous opposition to the Bank of the United States (which was seen by many ordinary Americans as a tool of the wealthy).

> **habeas corpus**
> The legal doctrine that a person who is arrested must have a timely hearing before a judge.

James Polk energetically exercised his powers as commander-in-chief of the armed forces, provoking a war with Mexico and acquiring most of what is now the southwestern United States and California. Abraham Lincoln, in order to win the Civil War, invoked emergency powers based on his broad reading of the Constitution: he raised and spent money and deployed troops on his own initiative, with Congress acquiescing only afterward; he temporarily suspended the right of **habeas corpus** and allowed civilians to be tried in military courts; and he unilaterally freed the slaves in the Confederate states by issuing the Emancipation Proclamation.

The Twentieth-Century Transformation

More enduring changes in the presidency came only in the twentieth century, when new structural conditions made an expanded presidency both possible and necessary. Theodore Roosevelt vigorously pushed the prerogatives and enhanced the powers of the office as no president had done since Lincoln. Roosevelt was happiest when he was deploying the troops as commander-in-chief or serving as the nation's chief diplomat to protect American economic and political interests. On the domestic front, Roosevelt pushed for regulation of the new and powerful business corporations, especially by breaking up trusts, and he established many national parks. In Teddy Roosevelt, we see the coming together of an energetic and ambitious political leader and a new set of structural factors in the United States, particularly the nation's emergence as a world power and an industrialized economy. The interplay of these three factors expanded the power and responsibilities of the presidency.

Woodrow Wilson's presidency marked further important steps in the expansion of the federal government and the presidency. Wilson's "New Freedom" domestic program built on the Progressive Era measures of Teddy Roosevelt, including further regulation of the economy by establishment of the Federal Reserve Board (1913) and the Federal Trade Commission (1914). Under Wilson, World War I brought an enormous increase in activity: a huge mobilization of military personnel and a large, new civilian bureaucracy to oversee the production and distribution of food, fuel, and armaments by the American "arsenal of democracy."

TR MAKES HIS POINT Popular presidents can use the office, in Teddy Roosevelt's words, as a "bully pulpit" to move the nation to action on a broad range of fronts, even in noncrisis times. Roosevelt was very effective in using the bully pulpit to establish the national park system, build a more powerful navy, and move vigorously against the powerful "trusts" that dominated the American economy in the early years of the twentieth century. How did Roosevelt set the stage for the transformation of the presidency?

It was Franklin D. Roosevelt, however, who presided over the most significant expansion of presidential functions and activities in American history and changed American expectations about the office. In response to the Great Depression, Roosevelt and the Democratic majority in Congress pushed into law a series of measures for economic relief that grew into vast programs of conservation and public works, farm credit, business loans, and relief payments to the destitute. Roosevelt's New Deal also established a number of independent commissions to regulate aspects of business (the stock market, telephones, utilities, airlines) and enacted programs such as Social Security, which provided income support for retired Americans, and the Wagner Act, which helped workers join unions and bargain collectively with their employers. As Congress created these and many other new agencies in the executive branch, the role of the presidency grew because of his constitutional powers as chief executive.

Even bigger changes, however, resulted from World War II, when the government mobilized the entire population and the whole economy for the war effort. With the end of World War II, the United States was established as a military superpower. Since the time of Franklin Roosevelt, all U.S. presidents have administered a huge national security state with large standing armed forces, nuclear weapons, and bases all around the world.

Although he accomplished little on the legislative front during his brief time in office—he did introduce the 1964 Civil Rights Act, passed after his death—John F. Kennedy was the first president to appreciate the importance of television as both a campaign tool and as an instrument for influencing the public and political actors in Washington, the states, and other countries. His televised speeches and press conferences, where his charm, intelligence, and sense of humor were clearly evident, became one of his most effective governing tools. Presidents after him tried to follow his lead, but only Ronald Reagan, Bill Clinton, and Barack Obama matched Kennedy's mastery of the medium.

In the 1980s, Ronald Reagan managed to bring many of the main items of the conservative agenda to fruition: a massive tax cut to stimulate the economy, cutbacks in the number of regulations that affect business, cuts in a wide range of domestic social programs, and a substantial buildup of U.S. armed forces. Perhaps more importantly, he showed the American people and others around the world that a vigorous and popular presidency was still possible after the failed presidency of Richard Nixon, and the relatively weak presidencies of Gerald Ford and Jimmy Carter.

After the 9/11 terrorist attacks on the United States, George W. Bush pushed what many consider to be among the most expansive readings of presidential power in American history. In order to protect the United States against future terrorist attacks, President Bush felt it both necessary and constitutionally permissible, for example, to advise the armed forces and the CIA

REAGAN AND GORBACHEV IN RED SQUARE Whether rightly or wrongly, Ronald Reagan—whose foreign policies included a dramatic arms buildup followed by proposals to refashion the basic relationship between the two superpowers—is often given credit for ending the Cold War and nurturing the collapse of the Soviet Union. Here, President Reagan and Soviet leader Mikhail Gorbachev enjoy the sun and meet people in Red Square. How do world events shape the president's popularity in the United States?

to ignore the Geneva Convention on the treatment of detainees captured in the war on terrorism, even to the point of allowing torture. He claimed the right, moreover, to keep detainees indefinitely without trial or hearings, even if they were American citizens. More than any president in American history, he used signing statements to announce which parts of new laws would be carried out by his administration and which would not. He authorized warrantless surveillance of American citizens by the National Security Agency, which the agency is forbidden to do without the permission of a special court set up under the Foreign Intelligence Surveillance Act. And, under a doctrine known as the Unitary Executive—which will be explored later in this chapter—the president forbade a number of civil servants to testify at congressional hearings on matters the president opposed, including the findings of scientists at NASA on global warming. President Bush backed off from some of these claims to power by the end of his second term in response to changing public opinion, congressional criticism after the Democrats came to power in 2007, and a series of adverse judicial decisions. It remains to be seen whether President Obama and presidents after him will return to the Bush model if a major terrorist attack should occur again on American soil.[6]

How Important Are Individual Presidents?

We cannot be sure to what extent presidents themselves caused this great expansion of the scope of their office. Clearly, they played a part. Lincoln, Wilson, and Franklin Roosevelt, for example, not only reacted vigorously to events but also helped create events; each had something to do with the coming of the wars that were so crucial in adding to their activities and powers. Yet these great presidents were also the product of great times; they stepped into situations that had deep historical roots and dynamics of their own.

Lincoln found a nation in bitter conflict over the relative economic and political power of North and South and focused on the question of slavery in the western territories; war was a likely, if not inevitable, outcome. Wilson and Franklin Roosevelt each faced a world in which German expansion threatened the perceived economic and cultural interests of the United States and in which U.S. industrial power permitted a strong response. The Great Depression fairly cried out for a new kind of presidential activism. Kennedy faced an international system in which the Soviet Union had become especially strident and menacing. George W. Bush was president when the 9/11 terrorist attacks on the United States occurred, allowing him to make the broadest claims possible concerning the president's powers to defend the nation. Barack Obama came to office, as we saw in the chapter-opening story, in the midst of war and economic crisis. Thus, the great upsurges in presidential power and activity were, at least in part, a result of forces at the *structural* level, stimulated by events and developments in the economy, American society, and the international system.

We see, then, that it is this mixture of a president's personal qualities (personality and character) and deeper structural factors (such as the existence of military, foreign policy, or economic crises) that determines which presidents transform the office. Most of these big presidential transformations become part of the presidency as an institution. Presidents want and need the powers accumulated by their predecessors, and use the precedents set by them. The American people have tended to support—and in crisis situations, demand—strong presidential leadership. Congress has passed laws over the years in response to new challenges that directly or indirectly increase presidential responsibilities and power. And the courts, with some notable exceptions to be mentioned elsewhere in this book, generally have accepted the development path the presidency has taken as it became the preeminent office in American government.

The Powers and Roles of the President

12.2 Identify the many roles presidents play

The American presidency has assumed powers and taken on roles unimaginable to the Founders. Each touches on the daily lives of everyone in the United States and affects tens of millions of people around the world as well. In this section, we examine the many roles of the president and see how each role has a set of responsibilities associated with it as well as a set of powers that have become more expansive over the years.

Chief of State

The president is both the chief executive of the United States—responsible for the executive branch of the federal government—and the chief of state, a symbol of national authority and unity. In contrast to European parliamentary democracies such as Britain or Norway, where a monarch acts as chief of state while a prime minister serves as head of the government, in the United States the two functions are combined. It is the president who performs many ceremonial duties (attending funerals of important people, proclaiming official days, lighting the national Christmas tree, honoring heroes, celebrating national holidays) that are carried out by members of royal families in other nations. As one journalist once put it, "The office of President is such a bastardized thing, half royalty and half democracy, that nobody knows whether to genuflect or spit."[7] Because it adds to their prestige and standing with other government officials and the public, presidents have always found the chief of state role to be a useful tool in their political arsenal, enabling them to get their way on many important issues. Especially in times of armed conflict, criticism of the president seems to many Americans to amount to criticism of the country itself and the troops who are in harm's way, something skilled presidents can and do use to maximize support for their policies.

Domestic Policy Leader

The president has taken on important responsibilities on the domestic front that were probably not anticipated by the

CHEERLEADER-IN-CHIEF As chief of state, the president presides over many ceremonial events such as honoring the winners of the Super Bowl to the White House. Here, President Obama shows off a jersey with his name on it from the New Orleans Saints, winners of Super Bowl XLIV. Successful presidents can often translate their role as ceremonial leader of the nation into political influence in other areas of governing. Why are ceremonial duties an important part of the president's job as well as a source of power?

framers. These include his role as the nation's legislative leader and manager of the economy.[8]

Legislative Leader

While the Constitution seems to give primary responsibility for the legislative agenda of the United States to Congress, over time, the initiative for proposing big policy changes and new programs has shifted significantly to the president and the executive branch. The bases of this change may be found in the Constitution, statutes passed by Congress, and the changing expectations of the American people. The Constitution, for example, specifies that the president must, " … from time to time give the Congress information on the state of the union, and recommend to their consideration such measures as he shall judge necessary and expedient." Until Woodrow Wilson's presidency, the "**State of the Union**" took the form of a written report sent every year or every two years to Congress for its consideration. These reports often gathered dust in the House and Senate clerks' offices. Wilson, a strong believer in the role of the president as chief legislative leader similar to the prime minister in a parliamentary system, began the practice of delivering the State of the Union to Congress in an address to a joint session of the House and Senate, in which the president sets out his agenda for congressional legislation. Wilson correctly sensed that the American people were in the mood for vigorous legislative leadership from the president, given the enormous technological, economic, and social changes that were happening in the United States and the problems that were being generated by these changes.

In modern times, the State of the Union address has become one of the most important tools by which presidents gain the attention of the public and other public officials for what they want to accomplish. The state of the nation is now a very dramatic and visible event, delivered before a joint session of Congress, with members of the Supreme Court, the president's cabinet, and the military joint chiefs in attendance, and a national television audience. In the State of the Union, presidents, much as Wilson did, set out what issues they hope Congress will address, with a promise that detailed proposals for legislation will be forthcoming. In doing so, presidents now have the biggest say in defining the political agenda for the nation.

The president's legislative role also was enhanced by the Budget Act of 1921, which requires the president to submit an annual federal government budget to

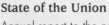

> **State of the Union**
>
> Annual report to the nation by the president, now delivered before a joint session of Congress, on the state of the nation and his legislative proposals for addressing national problems.

THE PRESIDENT AS LEGISLATIVE LEADER Despite the separation of powers design in the Constitution, presidents have become the nation's legislative leader, responsible time and time again for taking the initiative on landmark bills. Here Lyndon Johnson addresses Congress, urging members of the House and Senate to pass the 1965 Voting Rights Act. How does the president's backing give more weight to proposed bills? Or does it?

Congress for its consideration, accompanied by a budget message setting out the president's rationale and justifications. Prior to the Act, the budget of the United States was prepared initially in Congress. This change in the location of where initial decisions were to be made about proposed spending for government programs and agencies from the legislative to the executive branch represented a formidable enhancement in both the responsibilities and power of the president. We will have more to say about the federal budget in Chapter 17.

Although the House and Senate often take action on their own with regard to the nation's legislative agenda, what is striking is the degree to which Congress waits for and acts in response to presidential State of the Union addresses, budgets, and legislative proposals to meet various national problems. Indeed, the twentieth century is dotted with presidential labels on broad legislative programs: Wilson's New Freedom, Roosevelt's New Deal, Truman's Fair Deal, Kennedy's New Frontier, and Johnson's Great Society.

Manager of the Economy We now expect presidents to "do something" about the economy when things are going badly. The Great Depression taught most Americans that the federal government has a role to play in fighting economic downturns, and the example of Franklin Roosevelt convinced many that the main actor in this drama ought to be the president. Congress recognized this in 1946 when it passed the Employment Act, requiring the president to produce an annual report on the state of the economy, assisted by a new Council of Economic Advisers, with a set of recommendations for congressional action to maintain the health of the American economy. The role is now so well established that even conservative presidents like Ronald Reagan and George W. Bush felt compelled to involve the federal government in the prevention of bank failures, the stimulation of economic growth, and the promotion of exports abroad. George W. Bush, for example, supported an economic stimulus package in 2008 to fight a growing recession and the collapse of the real estate market, and the reorganization of investment banks, the bailout of big commercial banks, and the takeover of failing mortgage giants Freddie Mac and Fannie Mae by the Treasury Department in order to avert a financial collapse. Though he came to office in the midst of recession, a credit freeze, mounting foreclosures, and rising unemployment, President Obama's popularity was damaged badly as his actions failed to visibly change the situation for average Americans by the end of his first two years in office.

In the rapidly expanding global economy, moreover, presidents have become increasingly engaged in the effort to open world markets on equitable terms to American goods and services. The first President Bush helped push through an agreement with Japan on semiconductors. President Clinton was especially active as a spokesperson for the benefits of the American way of doing business and pushed hard to expand a global free trade regime, negotiating and gaining congressional approval for the North American Free Trade Agreement (NAFTA) treaty and the creation of the World Trade Organization.

Chief Executive

Although he shares influence over the executive branch of the federal government with Congress and the courts, the president is the chief executive of the United States, charged by the Constitution and expected by the American people to ensure that the nation's laws are efficiently and effectively carried out by bureaucratic agencies such as the Justice, Interior, and Commerce Departments; the National Aeronautics and Space Administration (NASA); and the National Weather Service. When an agency fails, as the Federal Emergency Management Agency (FEMA) did spectacularly in the aftermath of the Katrina disaster, and the Department of the Interior and the Minerals Management Service did in the face of the BP oil blowout in the Gulf of Mexico, the president invariably takes the heat. The problem is that presidents have something less than full control over the federal bureaucracy—for reasons that will be explored in Chapter 13—so they cannot be certain that agency leaders and personnel will do what presidents want them to do.[9] Nevertheless, presidents exercise more influence over executive branch agencies than any other government actor or set of actors.

Presidents have various tools to shape the behavior of executive branch agencies. Sometimes presidents try to get federal bureaucrats to act by issuing **executive orders**—formal directives to executive branch departments and agencies that have the force of law. They take many forms, including presidential proclamations, decision memoranda, and national security directives. The legitimacy of such orders is based sometimes on the constitutional positions of the president as chief executive and commander-in-chief, sometimes on discretionary authority granted to the president by Congress in statutes, and often on precedents set by past presidents. Executive orders are not only about minor administrative matters; many have been issued by presidents to institute important federal policies and programs.[10] Thomas Jefferson executed the Louisiana Purchase by proclamation (though he needed money appropriated by Congress to complete the agreement with France), and Abraham Lincoln did the same when he ordered the emancipation of slaves held in states that were in revolt against the United States during the Civil War. Franklin Roosevelt ordered the internment of Japanese Americans during World War II. His successor Harry Truman ordered the end of racial segregation in the armed forces. Bill Clinton issued orders to set aside millions of acres of land as national monuments off-limits to logging and roads. President George W. Bush issued executive orders to, among other things, establish the White House Office of Faith-Based and Community Initiatives and restrict stem-cell research supported by federal funds. President Obama issue scores of executive orders in his first two months in office rescinding many of Bush's orders, but adding many of his own (increasing fuel mileage requirements on cars and trucks, for example). Some scholars worry that the use of executive orders has become so important in fashioning government policies that it amounts to unilateral presidential rule, legislating, as it were, without need of Congress or public support.[11]

Believing that the presidency had been crippled by too much congressional and judicial interference in recent decades, members of George W. Bush's administration and many conservatives revived and gave a very expansive reading to a long-dormant constitutional theory known as the **unitary executive** in an attempt to "unstymy" the office. The concept is based on Article II's "vesting" ("The executive Power shall be vested in a President of the United States of America.") and "take care" clauses ("The President shall take care that the laws be faithfully executed ... ") to suggest that the office is free to exercise command and authority over the executive branch in all respects. Presidential adviser and Justice Department official John Yoo proposed early in the Bush administration that the Constitution created a unified and hierarchical executive branch under the direct control of the president, who has all authority necessary to control the actions of federal bureaucracy personnel and units without interference from the other federal branches.[12]

Under this doctrine, the president has the sole authority, for example, to direct the actions of agencies such as the Central Intelligence Agency (CIA) and the National Security Agency (NSA) and the armed forces in the defense of the nation. He alone can interpret, in his signing statements, the meaning of laws passed by Congress for executive branch personnel and units (see the opening story in

executive order

A rule or regulation issued by the president that has the force of law, based either on the constitutional powers of the presidency as chief executive or commander in chief or on congressional statutes.

unitary executive

Constitutional doctrine that proposes that the executive branch is under the direct control of the president, who has all authority necessary to control the actions of federal bureaucracy personnel and units without interference from the other federal branches.

? Are there adequate checks in place to reign in the power of the president when it comes to issuing executive orders? In what ways do the other two branches oversee—or fail to oversee—the issuing and implementation of executive orders?

Chapter 2). He alone can determine the degree to which departmental and agency personnel cooperate with Congress, in terms of the release of documents or testimony before congressional committees, for example. And, he can order the review of all regulations issued by regular and independent regulatory agencies for their consistency with the law as interpreted by the president. The doctrine of the unitary executive is, to say the least, controversial, and it is not broadly accepted among constitutional scholars or by the courts. More importantly, the reality of politics on the ground is that the president cannot entirely control what the executive branch does.

In the day-to-day operations of the federal bureaucracy, direct command is seldom feasible. Too much is going on in hundreds of agencies. Presidents cannot keep track personally of each one of the millions of government officials and employees. Most of the time, the president can only issue general guidelines and pass them down the chain of subordinates, hoping that his wishes will be followed faithfully. But lower-level officials, protected by civil service status from being fired, may have their own interests, their own institutional norms and practices, that lead them to do something different. President Kennedy was painfully reminded of this during the Cuban Missile Crisis of 1962, when Soviet Premier Khrushchev demanded that U.S. missiles be removed from Turkey in return for the removal of Soviet missiles from Cuba: Kennedy was surprised to learn that the missiles had not already been taken out of Turkey, because he had ordered them removed a year earlier. The people responsible for carrying out this directive had not followed through.[13] In 2009, President Obama was frustrated by the amount of time it took federal agencies to arrange for the production and distribution of the H1N1 flu vaccine, despite his demand for swift action.

To a significant extent, a president cannot simply order things to be done to accomplish his goals but must also *persuade* other executive branch officials to do things. He must bargain, compromise, and convince others that what he wants is in the country's best interest and in their own interest as well. One prominent presidential scholar has said, "Presidential power is the power to persuade."[14] Of course, presidents can do many things besides persuade: appoint top officials who share the president's goals; put White House observers in second-level department positions; reshuffle, reorganize, or even—with the consent of Congress—abolish agencies that are not responsive; influence agency budgets and programs through Office of Management and Budget review; and generate pressure on agencies by Congress and the public.[15]

Foreign Policy and Military Leader

Although the framers gave a role to Congress in fashioning foreign and military policies—note congressional control of the federal purse strings, its role in declaring war, and the Senate's "advice and consent" responsibilities with respect to treaties and appointment of ambassadors—they wanted the president to be the major player in these areas. What they could not have anticipated was that the United States would develop into the world's superpower, with global responsibilities and commitments, a development that enormously expanded the power of the presidency in the federal government.

Foreign Policy Leader
In a case decided in 1936, the Supreme Court confirmed the president's position as the nation's preeminent foreign policy maker, saying: " ... the president is the sole organ of the federal government in the field of international relations."[16] The president's role as foreign policy leader is rooted in the diplomatic and treaty powers sections of Article II of the Constitution, as well as in his role as commander-in-chief of the armed forces.[17]

OUTREACH TO THE MUSLIM WORLD President Obama made reaching out to the world's 1.5 billion Muslims one of the main priorities of his foreign policy agenda. Here, he is greeted in Cairo by Egyptian Foreign Minister Ahmed Abul Gheit in June 2009. The president later gave an historic and widely-televised speech before Egypt's parliament to say the U.S. and Muslims were not enemies. What effects might the ongoing wars in Iraq and Afghanistan have had on the effectiveness of the president's message?

The Constitution specifies that the president shall have the power to appoint and receive ambassadors and to make **treaties**. Although these formal constitutional powers may seem minor at first glance, they confer on the president the main responsibility for fashioning American foreign policy. Take the power to appoint and receive ambassadors. From the very beginning of the American republic, presidents have used this provision as a tool for recognizing or refusing to recognize foreign governments. In 1793, for example, George Washington refused to accept the credentials of the French ambassador, Citizen Edmond Genet, signaling that the United States did not recognize the legitimacy of the French revolutionary government. In the twentieth century, presidents Wilson, Harding, Coolidge, and Hoover refused to recognize the revolutionary communist government of the Soviet Union, a policy that was reversed by Franklin D. Roosevelt in 1933. The Chinese communist government went unrecognized by the United States for 23 years after it came to power, a policy that was eventually reversed by Richard Nixon. The president's sole power to proclaim U.S. policy in this area is suggested by the following: neither Franklin D. Roosevelt nor Richard Nixon required the permission of any other government institution or public official—whether Congress or the courts or state legislatures, for example—to change American policy with respect to the Soviet Union or Communist China. The decision was the president's alone to make.

The power to initiate the treaty-making process is also a powerful tool of presidential diplomacy and foreign policymaking. By virtue of this power, the president and the foreign policy officials in the State, Treasury, Commerce, and Defense departments that report to him consult, negotiate, and reach agreements with other countries. Sometimes the agreements with other countries take the form of treaties—the Paris Treaty ending the Revolutionary War is an example, as are the various arms control, human rights, trade, and environmental treaties to which the United States is a party (see the "Mapping America Politics" feature). More often, however, international agreements take the form of **executive agreements** entered into by the president and one or more foreign governments. Originally understood to be agreements about minor or technical details associated with a treaty, executive agreements eventually began to be used for very important matters. In 2002, for example, President Bush entered into an executive agreement with Russia that committed the two countries to reducing the size of their nuclear stockpiles.[18]

Commander-in-Chief
Article II, Section 2, of the Constitution specifies that the president is the commander-in-chief—without saying anything at all about what this actually means. On the other hand, Article I, Section 8, specifies that Congress has the power to declare war. What the framers seemed to have had in mind was a distinction between defensive war and

treaty
A formal international agreement between two or more countries; in the United States, requires the "advice and consent" of the Senate.

executive agreement
An agreement with another country signed by the president that has the force of law, like a treaty; does not require Senate approval; originally used for minor technical matters, now an important tool of presidential power in foreign affairs.

MAPPING AMERICAN POLITICS

Kyoto, Copenhagen, and Greenhouse Gas Emissions

Introduction It is by now generally accepted that global warming is occurring and that human activities, particularly the production of heat-trapping greenhouse gases, is an important factor in this process. Most countries in the world have signed the Kyoto Treaty, which went into effect when Russia ratified it in 2004. When the newly elected government in Australia joined the Treaty in 2007, the United States remained the only rich industrialized democracy outside of the agreement.

Many Americans, political observers, and people abroad blame President George W. Bush for this situation. He had, after all, withdrawn as a signatory to the treaty in 2001 in one of the most controversial acts in the first year of his presidency. In so doing, it appeared as if the Bush administration was reneging on a solemn international agreement signed by then–Vice President Al Gore on behalf of the United States in 1998 and executing a major reversal in its global warming policies. In fact, the United States had never been a party to the treaty because it had never been ratified by the U.S. Senate as the Constitution requires. Indeed, in 1997, before the treaty

was finalized, the Senate voted 95–0 in favor of a resolution saying that the United States should not sign the treaty unless it required greenhouse gas emission reductions for developing as well as developed countries. Senators from both parties were signaling that they would consider ratifying a treaty if and only if rapidly industrializing and polluting countries such as China and India were included. In the end, developing countries were not included in the mandatory reductions section of the treaty.

No doubt, Democratic and Republican senators were also concerned about possible negative effects on the economy and the health of particular industries, including the auto and oil industries, if serious steps were taken to cut back emissions, especially after hearing from a range of industry lobbyists and trade groups and labor unions. Recognizing that the treaty was "dead on arrival," President Bill Clinton never submitted the Kyoto Treaty to the Senate. Al Gore's signature was strictly symbolic. So, too, was George W. Bush's withdrawal from it since it had never become part of American law. And Barack Obama did not do much more, though he

tried. At the December 2009 Climate Summit meeting in Copenhagen, President Obama helped draft, then signed, an agreement pledging that the world's nations would do what was necessary to keep global warming in the future to less than 2 degrees Centigrade since the beginning of the Industrial Revolution. The agreement is not binding, however, on any nation and includes no mandatory steps to reach the goal.

Mapping Greenhouse Gas Emissions The cartogram shows the contribution that each nation makes to total greenhouse gas emissions. Data for the cartogram, drawn by the Worldmapper project of the University of Sheffield and the University of Michigan, is from the United Nations' Statistical Division, which gathers information from the statistical or environmental agencies of member governments. In the cartogram, the territorial size of each country is drawn according to its proportional share of the world's annual emissions (in this case, 2005) of carbon dioxide,

offensive war, with the president the primary decision maker with respect to the former and Congress preeminent with respect to the latter. Thus, the president was given the power to deploy and use the armed forces in order to protect the United States against external invasions and internal insurrections; Congress was given the power to declare war against another country.[19] Over the years, this distinction between offensive and defensive war disappeared; American forces are now sent into hostilities abroad, deployed by presidents without a formal declaration of war by Congress, in the name of defending the United States. In fact, there have been only five war declarations in American history—the last came in December 1941 after the Japanese attack on Pearl Harbor. Here is what seems to have been going on: as the United States became a global power, presidents, other American leaders, and the public came to believe that defending the United States required more than simply defending against cross-border invasions from other countries. Other threats seemed to many to be equally dangerous, including communism, nationalist threats to American economic interests, drug trafficking, and, most recently, terrorism.

Here is a sampling of how presidents have used American military power abroad since the Second World War. In the early 1950s, Harry Truman fought a bitter war in Korea against North Korean and Chinese forces, without a declaration of war from Congress, in the name of halting communist aggression. Presidents Eisenhower,

methane, and nitrous oxide. As is apparent in the cartogram, the United States was the largest producer of greenhouse gases in 2005, although China, the European Union, Japan, South Korea, and the Russian federation follow closely. In 2006, China became the world's top emitter of carbon dioxide and will soon pass the United States for total emissions of greenhouse gases. It is also apparent that big oil producers in the Middle East such as Saudi Arabia, Qatar, and the United Arab Emirates produce a lot—mostly from the flaring of natural gas at wellheads. On the flip side, the African continent and Latin America (with the notable exceptions of Venezuela, Chile, and Brazil) produce relatively little in the way of greenhouse gases.

What Do You Think?

President Bush was harshly criticized for his withdrawal as a signatory from the Kyoto Treaty, yet it was clear, despite President Clinton's support for it before him and Obama's scant gains in Copenhagen after Bush's term, that the Senate is unlikely to ratify a meaningful international emissions treaty even though polls show that public opinion more strongly supports such agreements than in the past. Americans are much more aware of global warming and its main causes. More and more Americans tell pollsters that the country needs to cooperate with others to get the problem under control. Do you think the United States should reconsider its position? What would it take for the United States to join a binding international agreement on greenhouse gas emissions? If such a step were to occur, how might complying with such an agreement significantly change your lifestyle and the lifestyles of other Americans?

Source: Worldmapper, map number 299, (**www.Worldmapper.org**). The SASI Group (University of Sheffield) and Mark Newman (University of Michigan), 2006.

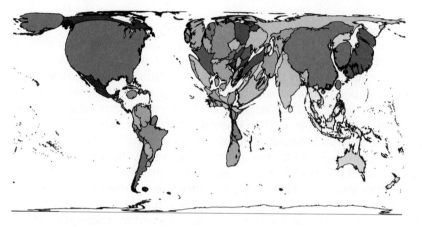

Greenhouse Gases

Source: © Copyright 2006 SASI Group (University of Sheffield) and Mark Newman (University of Michigan).

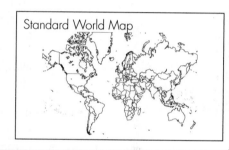

Standard World Map

Kennedy, Johnson, and Nixon did the same in Vietnam. Ronald Reagan used American forces in Grenada and Nicaragua to fight communism and launched an air attack against Libya to punish it for its involvement in terrorism. George H. W. Bush launched an invasion of Panama to capture its president and drug lord Manuel Noriega, and in 1991 used more than 500,000 U.S. troops in Operation Desert Storm to push Iraq out of Kuwait. President Bill Clinton sent several thousand American troops as peacekeepers to Bosnia in 1995, Haiti in 1996, and Kosovo in 1999 and waged an air war against Serbia to try to prevent "ethnic cleansing" in its province of Kosovo. After the September 11, 2001, attacks on the United States, George W. Bush launched a military campaign against the Taliban regime and the Al Qaeda terrorist network in Afghanistan, then invaded and occupied Iraq in 2003 to protect the country against the Iraqi regime's purported weapons of mass destruction program and ties to the 9/11 terrorists (both claims proved, in the end, to be untrue). President Barack Obama, as we have seen, increased the number of troops in Afghanistan, upped the number of drone attacks on terrorist targets along the Pakistan border, and used special forces in operations in Somalia and Yemen. In none of these or related cases was Congress called upon to pass a formal declaration of war.

To be sure, when presidents choose to use American military power, they ordinarily consult widely with members of Congress and other government and opinion

leaders. They do everything they can, moreover, to enlist the support of the public. They may even at times ask that Congress pass a resolution of support authorizing presidential use of the armed forces to defend the national security of the United States, although they are not legally bound to do so. Thus, President George H. W. Bush asked Congress to pass a resolution supporting Desert Storm in 1991, which it did. Likewise, in 2002, his son, President George W. Bush, asked Congress for a resolution supporting military action against Saddam Hussein's Iraq, which it did. Tellingly, each of the Bush presidents let it be known that military action would be forthcoming no matter the outcome of congressional deliberations. (See the "By the Numbers" feature to learn how Americans felt about how the United States was doing in the world.)

Some presidents also have claimed that the office's commander-in-chief powers allow them to take extraordinary actions on the home front that seemingly violate civil liberties of some Americans if such actions are required to defend the nation. Thus, Abraham Lincoln used military tribunals to try a number of southern sympathizers during the Civil War, Woodrow Wilson censored the press during World War I, Franklin Roosevelt ordered placement of Japanese Americans into internment camps during World War II, and George W. Bush detained without trial American citizens he defined as "enemy combatants" and authorized domestic eavesdropping by the National Security Agency to find terrorists.

President Bush's actions after 9/11 at home and abroad to defend the United States, several of which seemed contrary to laws passed by Congress and to rulings of the Supreme Court on the protected status of rights and liberties (see Chapter 15), have been vigorously defended by a number of conservative scholars who believe that the president has emergency powers based on his oath of office (" . . . I will faithfully execute the Office of President of the United States, and will to the best of my ability, preserve, protect, and defend the Constitution of the United States . . . "), that transcend the Constitution itself. They have suggested that some provisions of the Constitution might for a time need to be set aside or ignored in order to defend the nation and its constitutional order.[20] As Abraham Lincoln once asked regarding his own use of emergency powers, "Was it possible to lose the nation, and yet preserve the constitution?" Needless to say, other scholars and political observers worry that the use of such emergency powers over time might well lead to tyranny.[21] John Yoo, then an attorney with the Justice Department, was a particularly influential and vocal advocate of the broadest reading of the president's commander-in-chief powers. In 2009, the Justice Department's Office of Professional Responsibility concluded that Yoo's advice to the president on circumventing American and international law on torture was so egregious that it amounted to ethical misconduct, leaving Yoo subject to disbarment. Though the Justice Department ultimately declined to bring ethics charges, its report in 2010 concluded that " . . . John Yoo's loyalty to his own ideology and convictions clouded his view of his obligations to his client and led him to author opinions that reflected his own extreme, albeit sincerely held, view of executive power."[22]

Head of His Political Party

One of the great difficulties all presidents face is the seeming contradiction between their role as president of all the people—as commander-in-chief, chief diplomat, and chief executive, for example—and their role as the leader of their political party seeking partisan advantage as well as the public good.[23] Much of the apparent contradiction has been eased by the fact that presidents, like all political leaders, generally see the public good and commitment to party principles and programs as one and the same. Thus, Ronald Reagan, as leader of the Republican party and as president, believed that the public good and his own party's prospects in upcoming elections were well served by his successful efforts to increase defense spending, deregulate the economy, and decrease domestic spending. For his part, Lyndon Johnson, as the leader of the Democratic party and as president, believed that the public and his party would benefit from programs to end racial discrimination and reduce poverty. Sometimes, however, the public reacts negatively when a president plays his party leader role too vigorously, seeing it as perhaps unpresidential. In 1936, in an oft-cited example, Franklin Roosevelt's effort to campaign for Democratic congressional candidates was not well received and his party won fewer seats than expected. George W. Bush's campaign involvement in the 2006 congressional elections did not prevent Democrats from winning control of both houses of Congress, nor did Obama's do much for the Democrats in 2010.

> **?** Do you think that the current president has taken a less partisan or more partisan approach to governing than has marked recent years?

The President's Staff and Cabinet

12.3 Outline the functions filled by the president's many advisers and helpers

Each of the president's functions is demanding; together, they are overwhelming. Of course, presidents do not face their burdens alone; they have gradually acquired many advisers and helpers. The number and responsibilities of these advisers and helpers have become so extensive, and the functions they perform so essential, that they have come to form what some call the **institutional presidency**.[24]

The White House Staff

The White House staff, for example, which is specially shaped to fit the particular needs of each president, includes a number of close advisers.

One top adviser, usually designated **chief of staff**, tends to serve as the president's right hand, supervising other staff members and organizing much of what the president does. Presidents use their chiefs of staff

> **institutional presidency**
> The permanent bureaucracy associated with the presidency, designed to help the incumbent of the office carry out his responsibilities.
>
> **chief of staff**
> A top adviser to the president who also manages the White House staff.

Are Americans worried about U.S. foreign policy?

According to one measure, Americans are anxious about how the United States is doing in the world. This is hardly surprising; in 2008 when the public was questioned for the measure reported here, the United States was mired in military conflict in Iraq and Afghanistan, anti-Americanism was on the rise in many countries, and many Americans were feeling threatened by globalization and terrorism.

Why It Matters If and when the American people lose confidence in the direction of U.S foreign policy, it indirectly signals a loss of confidence in those who fashion it, especially the president. It is the president, after all, who is the chief decision maker in foreign policy matters—being constitutionally the nation's chief diplomat and its commander-in-chief—as well as the face of the American people in the eyes of the rest of the world. Loss of public confidence suggests that people may be anxious for a new direction and perhaps new leadership. It also tends to weaken the hand of the president in his deal-

ings with both allies and enemies, and it lessens his support among other decision makers in the United States, such as members of Congress, the news media, and business leaders, making it harder to get things accomplished. Given the levels of anxiety among the public in 2008, it is hardly surprising that George W. Bush faced tough sledding in the last years of his administration and saw his popularity fall.

The Measure As part of its annual survey of American opinion on U.S. foreign policy, *Public Agenda Online* (www.publicagenda.org) and the journal *Foreign Affairs* created a set of questions in 2006 that it uses in its surveys every year to serve as the basis for a new indicator of Foreign Policy Anxiety. Their aim, stated in their online report, was to create a simple, straightforward indicator—somewhat akin to the Consumer Confidence Index—that would be reported each year. The indicator is an additive index, meaning that answers to a set of questions are simply added up, then placed on a scale that has a bottom score and a top score. A certain number of points is given for answers to questions

that have two possible answers, such as "yes" or "no," and "agree" or "disagree"; similarly, a certain number of points is given for responses that range from "strongly agree" to "strongly disagree." (The details of the scoring system are described at http://www.publicagenda. com/foreignpolicy/foreignpolicy_ method.htm.)

The Foreign Policy Anxiety indicator is based on responses to the following five questions:

- Are U.S. relations with the rest of the world on the right or wrong track?
- Is the world becoming safer or more dangerous for Americans?
- Does the public believe the rest of the world sees the United States in a positive or negative light?
- How successful is the United States as a leader working toward a more peaceful and prosperous world?
- To what degree do Americans say they worry about the way things are going for the United States in world affairs?

The indicator, designed by Daniel Yankelovich, chairman of *Public Agenda* and one of the nation's leading pollsters,

? How might the president's working style affect his policies and effectiveness? Should the way the president manages his staff matter to the American people?

in different ways. Franklin Roosevelt kept a tight rein on things himself, granting equal but limited power and access to several close advisers in a *competitive* system. Dwight Eisenhower, on the other hand, used to the *hierarchical* army staff system, gave overall responsibility to his chief of staff, Sherman Adams.

Another important staff member in most presidencies is the **national security adviser**, who is also head of the president's National Security Council, operating out of the White House. The national security adviser generally meets with the president every day to brief him on the latest events that might affect the nation's security and offer advice on what to do. Several national security advisers, including Henry Kissinger (under Nixon) and Zbigniew Brzezinski (under Carter), have been strong foreign policy managers and active, world-hopping diplomats who sometimes clashed with the secretaries of state and defense. Most recent presidents, however, have appointed team players who have closely reflected the president's wishes and quietly coordinated policy among the various executive departments. This is true

national security adviser
A top foreign policy and defense adviser to the president who heads the National Security Council.

is scaled from 0 to 200, with 100 being the neutral point—where the public is neither anxious nor confident. A score higher than 100 means that more Americans are anxious rather than confident about U.S. foreign policy; a score lower than 100 means that more Americans are confident than anxious. The indicator score was 132 in 2008, significantly above the neutral point of 100, suggesting that Americans were very anxious about U.S. foreign policy. We show it here in graphic form.

200	Totally anxious
175	
150	
132	2008 Score
125	
100	Neither confident nor anxious
75	
50	
25	
0	Totally confident

What to Watch For Let us simply assume, given the experience of those conducting the national survey, that the highest standards for drawing a random sample were used here. Having said that, there are a number of things you might want to pay attention to as you evaluate this measure. First, we might ask whether the five questions used to create the indicator are the best possible ones to gain a general sense of how Americans feel about the course of U.S. foreign policy. On their face, they seem reasonable, especially because they do not refer to specific events or developments that might change year to year but to an overall sense of how things are going. But, we might always come up with alternative questions. More importantly, perhaps, we might ask if the questions should have equal weight in the indicator or whether some might be more important than others, suggesting that they should carry more wallop in the final indicator. So, for example, should feeling more or less safe carry the same weight in the indicator as feeling that the country is moving in the right or wrong direction? Or should one count more than the other? This is always a judgment call in building an additive indicator, to be sure, but you should be aware of it.

What Do You Think? How is it useful to have a single indicator akin to the Consumer Confidence Index for American confidence in U.S. foreign policy? What do you think about the particular indicator created by *Public Agenda* and *Foreign Affairs*? Can you think of a way to improve it, particularly different questions from the ones they use? How anxious or confident are you about U.S. foreign policy? Where would you put yourself on the scale?

Source: Public Agenda and Foreign Affairs, "Confidence in U.S. Foreign Policy Index," http://www.publicagenda.com/foreignpolicy/index.htm.

of President Obama's national security advisor, former Marine Corps commandant James Jones.

Most presidents also have a top domestic policy adviser who coordinates plans for new domestic laws, regulations, and spending, although this role is often subordinate to that of the chief of staff and is not usually very visible. Close political advisers, often old comrades of the president from past campaigns, may be found in a number of White House or other government posts (e.g., James Baker served as George H. W. Bush's secretary of state, while Karen Hughes served as White House counselor to the younger Bush during his first term) or may have no official position at all (such as consultant Dick Morris, who crafted Clinton's 1996 reelection strategy). Prominent in every administration is the press secretary, who holds press conferences, briefs the media, and serves as the voice of the administration. All have a legal counsel. There are also one or more special assistants who act as a liaison with Congress, deal with interest groups, handle political matters, and consult on intergovernmental relations. Facing a deep recession and continuing financial crisis when he came to office, President Obama appointed a team of economic advisers, led by Larry Summers, to try to keep him abreast of daily developments.

However, the exact shape of the White House staff changes greatly from one presidency to another, depending on the preferences and style of the president.

GOING OVER THE DAY'S BUSINESS Rahm Emmanuel, President Obama's first chief of staff, played a central role in helping the president fashion and implement his most important policy priorities, including health care reform, the economic stimulus, and regulation of the financial industry. Should close advisers and presidential staff be required to gain Senate approval, or do presidents, in order to carry out their many responsibilities, need people close to them who serve only one master?

What was particularly striking about President George W. Bush's management style was his penchant for setting overall goals and policies but giving his staffers a great deal of freedom and latitude in getting the job done.[25] President Obama seems to be more closely involved in the day-to-day work of his staff.

The Executive Office of the President

One step removed from the presidential staff, and mostly housed in the Executive Office Building next door to the White House, is a set of organizations with more than 1,800 employees that forms the **Executive Office of the President (EOP)**.

Most important of these organizations is the **Office of Management and Budget (OMB)**. The OMB advises the president on how much the administration should propose to spend for each government program and where the money will come from. The OMB also exercises legislative clearance; that is, it examines the budgetary implications of any proposed bills that will be sent to Congress and sometimes kills proposals it deems too expensive or inconsistent with the president's philosophy or goals.

The **Council of Economic Advisers (CEA)** advises the president on economic policy. Occasionally, the head of the council exercises great influence, as Walter Heller did during the Kennedy administration. More often, the head of the CEA is inconspicuous.

The Executive Office of the President also includes the **National Security Council (NSC)**, a body of leading officials from the Departments of State and Defense, the Central Intelligence Agency (CIA), the military, and elsewhere who advise the president on foreign affairs. The NSC has been particularly active in crisis situations and covert operations. The NSC staff, charged with various analytical and coordinating tasks, is headed by the president's national security adviser.

Executive Office of the President (EOP)

A group of organizations that advise the president on a wide range of issues; includes, among others, the Office of Management and Budget, the National Security Council, and the Council of Economic Advisers.

Office of Management and Budget (OMB)

An organization within the Executive Office of the President that advises on the federal budget, domestic legislation, and regulations.

Council of Economic Advisers (CEA)

An organization in the Executive Office of the President made up of a small group of economists who advise on economic policy.

National Security Council (NSC)

An organization in the Executive Office of the President made up of officials from the State and Defense Departments, the CIA, and the military, who advise on foreign and security affairs.

Increasingly important in the effort to protect the United States against terrorist attacks is the **Intelligence Advisory Board**, which provides information and assessments to the president's director of national intelligence and to the president directly. This agency was criticized for failing to "connect the dots" that allowed Nigerian national Umar Farouk Abdulmutallab to carry explosives onto a Delta airlines flight from London to Detroit on Christmas Day 2009.

> **Intelligence Advisory Board**
>
> An organization in the Executive Office of the President that provides information and assessments to the president's director of national intelligence and to the president directly.

The Vice Presidency

Until quite recently, the vice presidency has not been a highly regarded office. John Nance Garner, Franklin Roosevelt's first vice president, has been quoted as saying in his earthy Texan way that the office was "not worth a pitcher of warm piss."[26] Within administrations, vice presidents were considered to be fifth wheels, not fully trusted (because they could not be fired) and not personally or politically close to the president. Vice presidents used to spend much of their time running minor errands of state, attending funerals of foreign leaders not important enough to demand presidential attention, or carrying out limited diplomatic missions. Some vice presidents were virtually frozen out of the policymaking process. For example, while vice president, Harry Truman was never informed of the existence of the Manhattan Project, which built the atomic bomb. He learned of the bomb only months before he was obligated to make a decision on using it to end the war against Japan, soon after he became president on the death of Franklin D. Roosevelt.

Recent presidents, however, have involved their vice presidents more.[27] Bill Clinton gave Al Gore important responsibilities, including the formulation of environmental policy, coping with Ross Perot's opposition to NAFTA, and the ambitious effort to "reinvent government." Barack Obama promised his vice president Joe Biden that he would be at every meeting when important policies are decided and gave him a number of delicate foreign policy missions in the first years of his administration. More than any other vice president in American history, however, Dick Cheney was at the center of the policymaking process in the White House,

A UNIQUELY POWERFUL VICE PRESIDENT Richard Cheney is generally acknowledged to be the most engaged and influential vice president in American history, playing especially prominent roles in the development of doctrines and policies ranging from the use of American military power, to the treatment of prisoners detained in the "war on terrorism" and the particulars of national energy policy. Is it important to the nation and presidents that vice presidents play a central role in fashioning administration policies or should they stay more in the background?

serving (by all accounts) as President George W. Bush's principal adviser on both domestic and foreign policy, the key player within the administration on long-range policy planning and selection of Supreme Court justices, the main liaison to Republicans in Congress,[28] an important consumer of information from the intelligence community,[29] the chief advocate for a war against Iraq, and the leading advocate of a muscular interpretation of presidential war powers.[30]

In 1804, the Twelfth Amendment fixed the flaw in the original Constitution in which the person with the second most electoral votes became the vice president. Under the old rules, Aaron Burr, Thomas Jefferson's running mate in 1800, had tied Jefferson in electoral votes and tried, in the House of Representatives, to grab the presidency for himself. Since then, vice presidents have been elected specifically to that office on a party ticket with their presidents. But now there is also another way to become vice president. The Twenty-Fifth Amendment (ratified in 1967) provides for succession in case of the temporary or permanent inability of a president to discharge his office. It also states that if the vice presidency becomes vacant, the president can nominate a new vice president, who takes office on confirmation by both houses of Congress. This is how Gerald Ford became vice president in 1973 when Spiro Agnew was forced to resign because of a scandal, and how Nelson Rockefeller became vice president in 1974, when Ford replaced Richard Nixon as president.

The Cabinet

The president's cabinet is not mentioned in the Constitution. No legislation designates the composition of the cabinet, its duties, or its rules of operation. Nevertheless, all presidents since George Washington have had one. It was Washington who established the practice of meeting with his top executive officials as a group to discuss policy matters. Later presidents continued the practice, some meeting with the cabinet as often as twice a week, and others paying it less attention or none at all. Today, the cabinet usually consists of the heads of the major executive departments, plus the vice president, and whichever other officials the president deems appropriate. In the Obama administration, the cabinet also included White House Chief of Staff Rahm Emmanuel; Budget Director Peter Orszag; UN representative Susan Rice; and the heads of the EPA, CIA, Office of the U.S. Trade Representative, and Council on Economic Advisers.

Presidents do not rely on the cabinet as a decision-making body. Not only is there no constitutional warrant for such a body to make policies, presidents know that they alone will be held responsible for decisions, and they alone keep the power to make them. According to legend, when Abraham Lincoln once disagreed with the entire cabinet, he declared, "Eight votes for and one against; the nays have it!"

Most recent presidents have convened the cabinet infrequently and have done serious business with it only rarely. Ronald Reagan held only a few cabinet meetings each year, and those were so dull and unimportant that Reagan was said to doze off from time to time. Bill Clinton, with his "policy wonk" mastery of details, thoroughly dominated cabinet discussions. Barack Obama hardly ever met with his full cabinet, preferring instead to consult with advisers and department secretaries only when he needed their specific expertise.

One reason for the weakness of the cabinet, especially in recent years, is simply that government has grown large and specialized. Most department heads are experts in their own areas, with little to contribute elsewhere. It could be a waste of everyone's time to engage the secretary of housing and urban development in discussions of military strategy. Another reason is that cabinet members occupy an ambiguous position: they are advisers to the president but also represent their own constituencies, including the permanent civil servants in their departments and the

PRESSING AMERICAN INTERESTS   Secretary of State Hillary Clinton meets with her Saudi counterpart in February 2010 to gain the cooperation of Saudi Arabia on imposing new UN sanctions on Iran for the development of its nuclear weapons program. Clinton's considerable impact as secretary of state comes not only because she is an appointee of the president, but because of the considerable stature she brought to the office as a former senator and contender for the Democratic Party's presidential nomination. How might foreign leaders be affected by dealing with secretaries of state who have their own independent standing in politics?

organized interests that their departments serve. They may have substantial political stature of their own—consider Hillary Clinton, Obama's secretary of state—somewhat independent of the president's.

The President and Congress: Perpetual Tug-of-War

12.4   Analyze the conflict between presidents and Congress

The president and Congress are often at odds. This is a *structural* fact of American politics, deliberately intended by the authors of the Constitution.[31]

Conflict by Constitutional Design

The Founders created a system of separation of powers and checks and balances between Congress and the president, setting "ambition to counter ambition" in order to prevent tyranny. Because virtually all constitutional powers are shared, there is a potential for conflict over virtually all aspects of government policy. We saw in Chapter 2 that our system is quite exceptional in this regard. In parliamentary systems such as Great Britain, Germany, Sweden, and Japan, there is no separation of powers between the executive and legislative branches. Recall that in such systems the prime minister and cabinet—who together make up the government, what we would call the executive branch—are themselves parliamentarians selected by the majority party or a majority coalition of parties in parliament. The executive and legislative functions thus are fused in such systems, not separated. The government—the prime minister and the cabinet—serves at the behest and will of parliament and can be dissolved by it. So checks and balances between the executive and legislative powers do not exist because the executive and the legislative are one and the same. Not so in the United States; separated powers and mutual checks are real and consequential for what government does; even though presidents have, as we have seen, dramatically expanded their powers by increasing their use of signing statements, executive orders, and executive agreements, and interpreting their war powers quite expansively.

Shared Powers   Under the Constitution, presidents may propose legislation and can sign or veto bills passed by Congress, but both houses of Congress must pass any laws and can (and sometimes do) override presidential vetoes. Presidents can appoint ambassadors and high officials and make treaties with foreign countries, but the Senate must approve them. Presidents nominate federal judges, including U.S. Supreme Court justices, but the Senate must approve the nominations. Presidents administer the executive branch, but Congress appropriates funds for it to operate, writes the legislation that defines what it is to do, and oversees its activities.

divided government

Control of the executive and the legislative branches by different political parties.

Presidents cannot always count on the members of Congress to agree with them. The potential conflict written into the Constitution becomes real because the president and Congress often disagree about national goals, especially when there is **divided government**, that is, when the president and the majority in the House and/or the Senate belong to different parties. Bill Clinton was impeached by the Republican-controlled House of Representatives in late 1998, for example, while George W. Bush's Iraq war policies were bitterly opposed by a Democratic-dominated Congress in the last two years of his presidency. It is not uncommon, however, for presidents to clash with members of Congress even if they are of the same party. George W. Bush ran into trouble with co-partisans on a number of issues during his second term, especially on the issue of immigration.

Separate Elections   In other countries' parliamentary systems, the national legislatures choose the chief executives so that unified party control is ensured. But in the United States, there are separate elections for the president and the members of Congress. Moreover, our elections do not all come at the same time. In presidential election years, two-thirds of the senators do not have to run and are insulated from new political forces that may affect the choice of a president. In nonpresidential, "off" years, all members of the House and one-third of the senators face the voters, who sometimes elect a Congress with views quite different from those of the president chosen two years earlier. In 1986, for example, halfway through Reagan's second term, the Democrats recaptured control of the Senate and caused Reagan great difficulty with Supreme Court appointments and other matters. The Republicans did the same thing to Clinton in 1994 after they gained control of Congress. Obama ran into trouble with his programs in Congress after the 2010 election, when Republicans made gains in both the House and Senate.

Outcomes   In all these ways, our constitutional structure ensures that what the president can do is limited and influenced by Congress, which in turn reflects various political forces that may differ from those that affect the president. At its most extreme, Congress may even be controlled by the opposing party. This divided government situation always constrains what presidents can do and may sometimes lead to a condition called "gridlock," in which a president and Congress are locked in battle, neither able to make much headway. This is hardly surprising; a president is not only the chief executive and commander in chief of the United States but the leader of his party, so members of the opposition are not inclined to give him what he wants on the chance that it will benefit his election prospects or those of his party in Congress.

? Does the separate election of the executive and legislative branches help ensure deliberation in government, or does it promote gridlock?

What Makes a President Successful with Congress?

A number of political scientists have studied presidents' successes and failures in getting measures that they favor enacted into law by Congress and have suggested reasons some presidents on some issues do much better than others.[32]

Party and Ideology   The most important factor is a simple one: when the president's party controls both houses of Congress, he is much more likely than at other times to find that he gets his way in terms of legislation, approval of his appointments, and more gentle handling of executive branch problems by congressional oversight committees.[33] The president's success under this condition of unified control does not come from the president ordering party members around. Rather, the president and the members of his party in Congress tend to be like-minded on a wide range of issues, sharing values and policy preferences and a common interest in reelection. For these reasons, members of Congress tend to go along most of the time with a president of their own party.[34]

Because the parties have become so ideologically cohesive since the mid-1990s (see Chapter 9), presidents can get their way with Congress even when they have only a very slim party majority in the House and a small but somewhat larger majority in the Senate—where 60 votes are needed, as you learned in Chapter 11, to get past the filibuster barrier. Between 2001 and 2006, for example, George W. Bush enjoyed many legislative successes though Republican majorities in the House and Senate were paper thin. He was able to do this because the highly cohesive and disciplined Republican Party in the Senate was joined by a handful of moderate Democrats on many bills, making Democratic filibusters rare events. (The "Using the Framework" feature shows, however, that President Bush did not always get his way, even with a GOP-controlled Congress.) Because he enjoyed bigger party majorities in Congress than did George W. Bush during his first two years in office—with a 60–40 margin in the Senate (counting two independents who caucused with the Democrats)—and because the party stayed cohesive when it came to decisive votes partly because of the impressive legislative skills of House Speaker Nancy Pelosi and Senate majority leader Harry Reid, Barack Obama was able to put together a very substantial legislative record. According to the *Congressional Quarterly (CQ)*, Obama forged the highest presidential success score with Congress since *CQ* began keeping score in 1953.[35] The result was victory for the president on a wide range of matters, including a massive economic stimulus bill, an historic overhaul of health insurance in the United States, and wide-ranging regulation of the financial services industry.

Foreign Policy and National Security Issues Presidents tend to do better with Congress on foreign policy issues than on domestic ones, mainly because Americans want to appear united when dealing with other countries and because members' constituents pay less attention to events abroad than to what is going on in the United States. Political scientist Aaron Wildavsky went so far as to refer to "two presidencies," domestic and foreign, with the latter presidency much more dominant.[36]

This difference between domestic and foreign policy success by the president has decreased since the Vietnam War, but it remains significant. Although there was significant dissent, Congress voted in January 1991, despite many misgivings, to authorize President George H. W. Bush to use force against Iraq, once again illustrating presidential primacy in foreign affairs. Congress eventually supported Clinton's decision to send U.S. forces to Haiti, Bosnia, and Kosovo as part of multinational peacekeeping operations, despite considerable initial grumbling.

The generalization about presidents having an easier time with Congress on foreign policy issues than on domestic ones does not hold, however, when foreign policy concerns trade and other global economic issues that directly affect constituents. Nor does it hold when foreign policy and military action go wrong. In 2005 and 2006, as news of prisoner abuse and secret prisons for suspected terrorism detainees held by the United States began to trouble increasing numbers of Americans and to prompt criticism from friendly governments, Congress passed laws outlawing harsh and inhumane treatment and requiring periodic reports from the administration on such prisons and prisoners.

Vetoes When the issue is a presidential veto of legislation, the president is again very likely to prevail.[37] Vetoes have not been used often, except by certain "veto-happy"

Why did President Bush fail to change Social Security despite Republican control of Congress and his win in the 2004 presidential election?

Background: President George W. Bush tried hard to convince Congress to add voluntary private accounts to the Social Security system. The idea was that a portion of the payroll tax paid into Social Security would be turned over to individuals to invest on their own. He claimed that such private accounts would bring bigger returns for seniors and ease long-term fiscal problems in the federal retirement system. Though he featured private accounts in his State of the Union address on February 2, 2005, and launched a 60-day 60-stop campaign-style national tour to push his idea, it went nowhere in Congress, though Republicans controlled both the House and Senate. How could a president with such a good track record on many important pieces of legislation, coming off an impressive electoral win, fail to achieve one of his most cherished legislative objectives? We can understand what happened—or in this case, what failed to happen—by looking at how structural, political linkage, and governmental factors affected congressional behavior.

Structure

| The number of Americans reaching retirement age has been steadily increasing. | → | Most Americans have come to depend on Social Security for all or a substantial portion of their retirement income. | → | Social Security benefits, in conjunction with Medicare, have reduced the frequency of poverty among older Americans. | → | But Americans are living longer and receiving Social Security benefits over a longer time, putting strains on the long-term financial viability of the system. |

Political Linkage

Public support for private accounts diminishes further, even among many Republicans, after President Bush reveals in April that private accounts will require Social Security benefit cuts. → Opinion among the elderly about proposed changes becomes particularly negative. → Mainstream media and academic experts skeptical about accounts' solving fiscal problems in the system.

Polls in February 2005 show few Americans believe that Social Security is in crisis; many believe it has problems that should be fixed. → Advocacy groups fight over private accounts; AARP and organized labor lead the fight against; the Club for Growth leads the fight in favor. → The Democratic Party and affiliated groups mount campaign against private accounts.

Government

Several prominent Republicans express disappointment that president didn't concentrate on the more important issue of tax reform. → Swing Democrats in Senate announce they are opposed to private accounts; several moderate Republicans announce opposition as well. → Congressional Republicans drop consideration of private accounts amid rising concern about mounting budget deficits exacerbated by spending for the Iraq War and recovery from Hurricane Katrina.

President Bush presses Republicans in Congress to pass legislation. → House Democrats are united in opposition; say will bankrupt Social Security and lead to deep cuts in benefits. → Many Republicans in House and Senate worry about lack of public support for private accounts.

Government Action

Congress does not legislate private accounts for Social Security; President Bush acknowledges in October 2005 that the issue is dead.

presidents, such as Franklin Roosevelt, Truman, and Ford. But when vetoes have been used, they have seldom been overridden—only 5 percent of the time for Truman and only 1.5 percent for Roosevelt. Bill Clinton did not use the veto at all during his first two years in office, when he had a Democratic majority in Congress, but then used it 11 times in 1995 alone during his budget battles with the Republican-controlled 104th Congress. Because Republicans committed to the president's agenda controlled the House from 2001 through 2006 and the Senate between 2003 and 2006, George W. Bush did not resort to the veto at all during this period. However, he used the veto several times in 2007 and 2008, most especially on bills from the Democratic-controlled Congress setting a timetable for withdrawal of American forces from Iraq and for expanding the number of children covered by the Children's Health Insurance Program (CHIP). With his party in control of Congress, Barack Obama did not use the veto in 2009 and vetoed a single bill—a minor one, fixing a technical matter on a stop-gap defense appropriations bill—in 2010.

Popularity   Most scholars and observers of Washington politics, as well as elected officials and political operatives, agree that presidential effectiveness with Congress is significantly affected by how popular a president is with the American people.[38] The reasons are not hard to fathom. Voting against proposals from a very popular president may encourage quality challengers in the next election, for example, or slow the flow of campaign funds to one's war chest, whether the president is of one's party or not. Voting with a popular president, on the other hand, can offer protective cover for a member of Congress who favors the proposal but whose constituents may not ("This is a vote for the president.").[39] When a president's popular approval collapses—as George W. Bush's did after 2004—even members of his own party are loath to follow executive leadership. Bush was unable to win his own party's approval in Congress, for example, for policies he favored on immigration, Social Security reform (see, again, the "Using the Framework" feature), and the bank bailout bill. Barack Obama may have been the proverbial "exception that proves the rule." Because the Democrats stayed disciplined in the House and Senate, President Obama enjoyed several of his most important legislative victories in 2010—the final health care reform bill and financial regulation, for example—even as his job approval numbers were trending downward, with more disapproving his job performance than approving by the summer of that year.

The President and the People: An Evolving Relationship

12.5   Assess how democratic the presidency is and whether presidents respond to the public

The special relationship between the president and the general public has evolved over many years to make the presidency a more democratic and powerful office. Let's look at several aspects of this relationship.

Getting Closer to the People

The Founders thought of the president as an elite leader, relatively distant from the people, interacting with Congress often but with the people only rarely. Most nineteenth-century presidents and presidential candidates thought the same. They seldom made speeches directly to the public, for example, generally averaging no more than 10 such speeches per year.[40] In the earliest years of the American Republic, presidents were not even chosen directly by the voters but by electors chosen by state legislators or, in case no one got an electoral college majority, by the House of Representatives. The Constitution thus envisioned very indirect democratic control of the presidency.

As we have also seen, however, this system quickly evolved into one in which the people played a more direct part. The two-party system developed, with parties nominating candidates and running pledged electors and the state legislators allowing ordinary citizens to vote on the electors. Presidential candidates began to win clear-cut victories in the Electoral College, taking the House of Representatives out of the process. Voting rights were broadened as well. Property and religious qualifications were dropped early in the nineteenth century. Later, slaves were freed and former male slaves were granted the right to vote; still later, women, Native Americans, and 18-year-olds won the franchise.

By the beginning of the twentieth century, presidents began to speak directly to the public. Theodore Roosevelt embarked on a series of speech-making tours in order to win passage of legislation to regulate the railroads. Woodrow Wilson made appeals to the public a central part of his presidency, articulating a new theory of the office that highlighted the close connections between the president and the public. Wilson saw the desires of the public as the wellspring of democratic government: "As is the majority, so ought the government to be."[41] He argued that presidents are unique because only they are chosen by the entire nation. Presidents, he said, should help educate the citizens about government, interpret their true will, and faithfully respond to it.

Wilson's theory of the presidency has been followed more and more fully in twentieth-century thought and practice. All presidents, especially since Franklin Roosevelt, have attempted to both shape and respond to public opinion; all, to one degree or another, have attempted to speak directly to the people about policy.[42]

More and more frequently, presidents go public, using television and the Internet to bypass the print media and speak to the public directly about policy. They have held fewer news conferences with White House correspondents (where awkward questions cannot be excluded).[43] Richard Nixon pioneered prime-time television addresses, at which Ronald Reagan later excelled. Bill Clinton was more interactive with citizens, appearing on radio and TV talk shows and holding informal but televised "town hall meetings." George W. Bush liked to appear before carefully screened audiences of supporters. Barack Obama was most comfortable doing speeches and town hall–style meetings, but he also depended upon the same Internet-based technologies he used so successfully in his 2008 campaign to get his message to the public, unfiltered by the news media.

Leading Public Opinion

Especially since the rise of television, modern presidents have enhanced their power to shape public opinion. Some studies have indicated that when a popular president takes a stand in favor of a particular policy, the public's support for that policy tends to rise.[44] But there are many cases where presidents have tried but failed to move public opinion in a favorable direction, despite strong efforts to build public support for favored programs. Barack Obama gave a televised address from the Oval Office to build support for his approach to the BP oil crisis in the Gulf in June 2010, but he was unable to improve his own flagging job ratings or build much enthusiasm or political support for his program of alternative energy development or a proposed "cap-and-trade" system to fight global warming.

The power to lead the public, though not as likely to happen as often believed, also implies a power to *manipulate* public opinion if a president is so inclined—that is, to deceive or mislead the public so that it will approve policies that it might oppose if it were fully informed.[45] It is useful to remember that every modern White House has had communications specialists adept at getting out the administration's views, whether through formal channels—such as press releases, the daily briefing for reporters, and materials posted on the White House website—or informal ones, including leaks to favored journalists and in-house-written but anonymous news stories and commentaries for use in newspapers, television news broadcasts, and weblogs.[46] Especially in foreign affairs, presidents can sometimes control what information the public gets, at least in the short run.

Responding to the Public

Besides trying to lead the people, presidents definitely tend to respond to public opinion. Electoral competition (see Chapter 10) produces presidents who tend to share the public's policy preferences. Moreover, most presidents want to be reelected or to win a favorable place in history, and they know that they are unlikely to do so if they defy public opinion on many major issues. Usually, they try to anticipate what the public will want in order to win electoral reward and avoid electoral punishment.

There is plenty of evidence that presidents pay attention to what the public is thinking. At least since the Kennedy administration, presidents and their staffs have carefully read the available public opinion surveys and now have full-blown polling operations of their own.[47] Although such polling is often deplored, it helps presidents choose policies that the American public favors and change or discard those that are unpopular. It is worth considering another view about the role of presidential polling, however: that its purpose is to uncover not what the public wants but what words and symbols can be used by a president to sell his program.[48]

> **?** Why should (or should not) the president be concerned with polling numbers? Does it help the president make more effective policies? Or simply more popular ones?

Presidential Popularity

Presidential popularity or unpopularity affects how influential a president is with Congress, the judicial branch, and elected officials at the state and local level. Since the 1930s, Gallup and other poll takers have regularly asked Americans whether they approve or disapprove of "the president's handling of the job." The percentage of people who approve varies from month to month and year to year, and as time passes, these varying percentages can be graphed in a sort of fever chart of how the public has thought the president was doing (see Figure 12.1). A number of factors seem to be especially important in determining presidential popularity, including the stage in the president's term of office, the state of the economy, and foreign policy crises.[49]

Historically, most presidents have begun their terms of office with a majority of Americans—usually 60 percent or more—approving of how they are handling their job. Most presidents have tended to lose popularity as time passes. But this loss of popularity does not represent an inexorable working of time: Eisenhower, Reagan, and Clinton actually gained popularity during their second terms. Those who lose popularity do so in response to bad news. Good news generally makes presidents more popular.[50]

One of the most serious kinds of bad news involves economic recession. When the economy goes sour, fewer Americans approve of the job the president is doing. This happened to George H. W. Bush in mid-1991, as the economy faltered. Barack Obama, too, felt the sting of the public's disapproval when unemployment stayed high and disposable income stagnated throughout 2009 and 2010, even though he had inherited a deep recession and financial crisis when he became president.

> **presidential popularity**
> The percentage of Americans who approve a president's handling of his job.

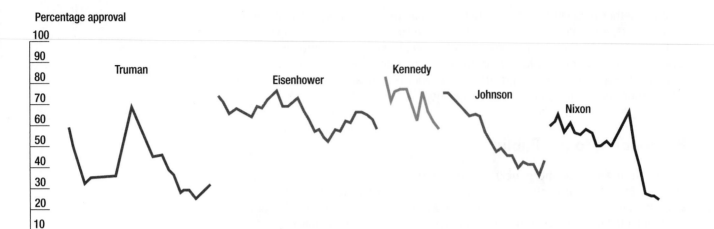

Percentage approval

FIGURE 12.1 Trends in Presidential Popularity, 1946–2010

Popularity ratings of presidents rise and fall in response to political, social, and economic events. *Source:* Gallup surveys (graph based on average job approval for each year through 2008; 2009 based on January, June, and December surveys; and 2010 is based on March and June numbers.).

Successful military actions tend to add to presidential popularity, as Ronald Reagan happily discovered after the U.S. invasion of Grenada in 1982. The senior Bush's approval rating soared during the 1991 Gulf War, while the junior Bush's initial success in Afghanistan sustained his popularity. Conversely, an unsuccessful war is bad news for a president, as president Harry Truman learned regarding the Korean War. Bad news from Iraq—perhaps in combination with the administration's apparent failures in the Katrina disaster—steadily eroded George W. Bush's public approval after 2003. Bad news on the war and economic fronts at the same time can be especially lethal to a president's approval, as George W. Bush learned in 2008 when his rating reached an historic low in presidential polling, and Barack Obama did in 2010 as economic troubles and a stuttering war in Afghanistan combined to undermine his standing with the American public.

BAD ECONOMY, POOR PRESIDENTIAL APPROVAL   Here, a woman in New York City in late 2009 shops for bargains before yet another retail store closed in this section of the city. The scene could have been repeated in cities and towns across the country as the nation suffered through a deep recession and jobless recovery from late 2007 through 2010. As is almost always the case, a bad economy, especially joblessness and declining disposable income, led to blows to public approval of the president and his party. Is this fair? Should we judge presidents mainly on the state of the economy, or are there other matters that are equally as important?

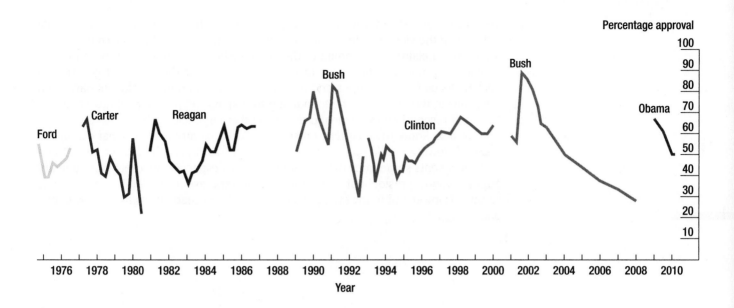

DEMOCRACY STANDARD

Presidents and the American People

When considering the role of the chief executive, the framers never intended that it be a democratic office. In creating the Electoral College, for example, they imagined an independent body whose members (or electors) would be chosen in a manner decided by state legislatures. For the most part, they understood that state legislatures would leave the responsibility of selecting electors to themselves rather than the people. The electors from the states would then meet to elect the president from among the nation's leading citizens, free from the pressures of public opinion. As Alexander Hamilton put it in *The Federalist Papers,* No. 68, "The immediate election [of the president] should be made by men most capable of analyzing the qualities adapted to the station, and acting under circumstances favorable to deliberation, and to a judicious combination of all the reasons and inducements which were proper to govern their best choice." Because a president chosen in such a manner would not be beholden to the people for his election or reelection, he would not be overly concerned with or unduly influenced by the views of the mass public.

In addition, when designating the powers and responsibilities of the president in Article II of the Constitution, the framers evidently envisioned an office somewhat detached from national policymaking, something like a constitutional monarchy, in which the officeholder would symbolize the nation but not do much in the way of running it. Although they gave the president important powers for conducting foreign affairs and defending the nation against civil unrest and invasion by foreign powers, they placed most national policymaking powers in Congress.

More than any other of the three branches of government in the Constitution created by the framers, the presidency has been democratized, with the changes so dramatic that the office would be hardly recognizable to them. As we have described this situation at various places in this chapter, the presidency has become a popular office, tied to the American people in a variety of important ways. Although the Electoral College remains in place—and can still have anti-majoritarian democratic outcomes, as in the 2000 election—for all intents and purposes, presidents are elected directly by the American people as a whole, the only national office (other than the vice president) carrying this distinction. As such, modern presidents are prone to claim the mandate of the people when governing, and the American people are prone, for their part, to see the president as the center of governance and the locus for their hopes and aspirations for the nation. Presidents have used these ties to the people as the foundation for expanding presidential powers in the course of responding to national problems and emergencies.

We also know that modern presidents pay close attention to what the public wants, following public opinion polls closely and commissioning their own. To be sure, presidents sometimes manipulate the public, especially in foreign and military affairs, where presidential constitutional powers are considerable and public scrutiny is lower, but in the end, presidents cannot succeed unless they enjoy strong public support.

SUMMARY

12.1 Trace the expansion of presidential responsibilities and power

- The American presidency began small; only a few nineteenth-century presidents (among them Jefferson, Jackson, Polk, and Lincoln) made much of a mark.

- In the twentieth century, however, as a result of the problems of industrialization, two world wars and the Cold War, and the Great Depression, presidential powers and resources expanded greatly. The presidency attained much of its modern shape during Franklin Roosevelt's presidency.

- The constitutional bases of the expansion of presidential responsibilities and power lie in his roles as chief executive, commander-in-chief, and chief diplomat.

- Additional sources of presidential expansion come from public expectations, legislative grants of power, and the office's role as de facto legislative leader of the nation.

12.2 Identify the many roles presidents play

- Presidents play many roles, including that of chief of state, chief executive, domestic policymaking leader, foreign policy and military leader, and head of his political party.

- Some of the president's roles are formally inscribed in the Constitution, but others have evolved through precedent, public expectations, and congressional actions.

12.3 Outline the functions filled by the president's many advisers and helpers

- The job of the president has become so complex and the range of the office's responsibilities so broad that the occupant needs a great deal of help carrying out his duties. The staff and agencies in the White House and the Executive Office Building that help him carry out his duties have grown to such an extent that they have come to be called the institutional presidency.

- White House staff members are numerous and do such things as advise the president on domestic and national security policies, maintain relationships with Congress, convey the president's views to the media and the public, and help fashion legislation.

- The main agencies in the Executive Office of the President advise and help the president carry out policies regarding the economy, the federal budget, and national security.

12.4 Analyze the conflict between presidents and Congress

- The tug of war between the president and Congress is an inherent part of the constitutional design of our government as embodied in the separation of powers and checks and balances.

- Presidents also have different constituencies than members of the House and Senate, the president being the only nationally elected office.

- Representatives and senators often are elected at times when the president is not a candidate so they may come to office propelled by a different public mood than that which prevailed when the president was elected.

12.5 Assess how democratic the presidency is and whether presidents respond to the public

- The presidency has become a far more democratic office than the framers envisioned: the people play a more important role in the election of the president, and research shows that presidents listen to public opinion and respond to it most of the time (though they sometimes do not).

TEST YOURSELF

Answer key begins on page T-1.

12.1 Trace the expansion of presidential responsibilities and power

1. When drafting the Constitution, the Founders envisioned a presidency that would have expansive powers similar to those of recent presidents.
   True / False

2. Which of the following best explains the Franklin D. Roosevelt presidency?
   a. He cut regulations on business and increased the size of the military.
   b. He cut social programs and cut taxes to stimulate the economy.
   c. He used signing statements more frequently than any other president.
   d. He presided over the largest expansion of presidential functions and activities.
   e. He epitomized the dormant presidency.

3. Evaluate whether George W. Bush's response to the terrorist attacks is best explained by Bush's personal qualities (such as his personality and character) or by deeper structural factors (such as the existence of military, foreign policy, or economic crises).

12.2 Identify the many roles presidents play

4. Presidents tend to believe that the public good is best served by advancing the principles and programs preferred by their political party.
   True / False

5. Which role are presidents fulfilling when they influence how the bureaucracy carries out laws passed by Congress?
   a. Chief of state
   b. Legislative leader
   c. Manager of the economy
   d. Chief executive
   e. Commander-in-chief

6. Compare executive orders with executive agreements.

12.3 Outline the functions filled by the president's many advisers and helpers

7. As mandated by the Constitution, presidents rely on their cabinets to make important decisions on their behalf.
   True / False

8. Which of the following best describes the vice presidency of Dick Cheney?
   a. Cheney was mostly dispatched to conduct minor diplomatic missions.
   b. Cheney was virtually shut out of the presidential decision-making process.
   c. Cheney was the principle policy adviser to President George W. Bush.
   d. Cheney was relegated to a mostly ceremonial role.
   e. Cheney was participant in the day-to-day business conducted by the Senate.

12.4 Analyze the conflict between presidents and Congress

9. Presidents frequently veto legislation passed by Congress, especially during periods of unified party control.
   True / False

10. Under which of the following scenarios is a president *least* likely to be successful when dealing with Congress?
    a. When there is divided government
    b. When dealing with foreign policy issues
    c. When the president is popular with the public
    d. When Congress contemplates overriding a presidential veto
    e. When the president's party controls both houses of Congress

11. Compare the relationship between the president and Congress in the United States with the relationship between the executive and legislative bodies in parliamentary systems.

12.5 Assess how democratic the presidency is and whether presidents respond to the public

12. Presidents tend to make political decisions without considering public opinion.
True / False

13. Which of the following tends to improve presidential popularity?

a. The passage of time
b. An economic recession
c. A military success
d. A war that has become a quagmire
e. A pending reelection bid

mypoliscilab EXERCISES

Apply what you learned in this chapter on MyPoliSciLab.

📖 **Read** on **mypoliscilab.com**

eText: Chapter 12

✔ **Study** and **Review** on **mypoliscilab.com**

Pre-Test
Post-Test
Chapter Exam
Flashcards

👁 **Watch** on **mypoliscilab.com**

Video: Bush and Congress
Video: The Government Bails Out Automakers

✳ **Explore** on **mypoliscilab.com**

Simulation: Presidential Leadership: Which Hat Do You Wear?
Simulation: You Are a President During a Nuclear Meltdown
Comparative: Comparing Chief Executives
Timeline: The Executive Order Over Time
Visual Literacy: Presidential Success in Polls and Congress

INTERNET SOURCES

Executive Orders
http://www.archives.gov/federal-register/executive-orders/index.html
A complete list with full text of presidential executive orders from the National Archives, from Herbert Hoover through Barack Obama.

Miller Center of Public Affair's "American Presidency" website
www.millercenter.virginia.edu/academic/americanpresident
A site full of historical documents, current developments, and descriptions of how the role of the president has changed.

Potus
www.potus.com
Biographies and other information about every American president.

National Archives Presidents Site
www.archives.gov/presidential_libraries/addresses/addresses.html
Access to presidential addresses, libraries, and other information about the office.

Pollingreport.com
www.pollingreport.com
Collection of all major presidential job performance and popularity polls.

White House Home Page
www.whitehouse.gov/
Information on the first family, recent presidential addresses and orders, text from news conferences, official presidential documents, and ways to contact the White House.

SUGGESTIONS FOR FURTHER READING

Crenson, Matthew, and Benjamin Ginsberg. *Presidential Power, Unchecked and Unbalanced.* New York: Norton, 2007.

> The authors submit that the American system has been sliding toward "presidentialism," a system in which presidents are no longer checked by the other branches of government, the press, or the public.

Edwards III, George C., and Stephen J. Wayne. *Presidential Leadership: Politics and Policy Making.* Belmont, CA: Cengage Wadsworth, 2009.

> A comprehensive textbook on the American presidency by two of the leading scholars of the office.

Howell, William G. *Power Without Persuasion: The Politics of Direct Presidential Action.* Princeton, NJ: Princeton University Press, 2003.

> Rejecting the common view among political scientists that presidential power is based primarily on the president's ability to persuade, Howell suggests instead that presidents have many tools for taking unilateral action to get their way.

Pfiffner, James, and Roger H. Davidson, eds. *Understanding the Presidency,* 5th ed. New York: Pearson Longman Publishers, 2009.

> A comprehensive anthology of recent scholarship on all aspects of the presidency and its place in the American political system.

Wills, Gary. *Bomb Power: The Modern Presidency and the National Security State.* New York: Penguin Press, 2010.

> Traces the rise in presidential powers to the rise of the national security state associated with nuclear weapons and the secrecy surrounding them, suggesting that these developments are dangerous to democracy and liberty, and unconstitutional.

Yoo, John. *The Powers of War and Peace: The Constitution and Foreign Affairs After 9/11.* Chicago: University of Chicago Press, 2005.

> An argument for expansive and unitary presidential powers in the post–9/11 world by one of the architects of Bush administration policies on the treatment of detainees during war.

13 | The Executive Branch

IN THIS CHAPTER

13.1 Compare and contrast our executive branch bureaucracy with those in other countries

13.2 Outline the structure of the executive branch

13.3 Identify the kinds of activities bureaucrats perform

13.4 Determine how demographically representative bureaucrats are

13.5 Isolate various influences on executive branch decision making

13.6 Assess what's wrong and what's right with the federal bureaucracy

CUTTING FAT OR CUTTING BONE?

Bending to harsh criticism from the news media, consumer groups, and members of Congress for its lax oversight, and to specific regulatory requests from companies like Mattel and Walmart, the Consumer Product Safety Commission (CPSC) in June 2007 issued recalls for "...68,000 folding chairs, 2,300 toy barbecue grills, 12,000 space heaters, 5,300 earrings, 1.5 million 'Thomas the Tank Engine' toy trains and 19,000 children's necklaces" imported from China because of defects in manufacturing or the use of dangerous materials such as lead paint that might harm the American public.[1] American companies had been losing sales because scared consumers were refusing to buy goods made in China even when they carried American brand names, and they wanted action. So, too, did consumer groups. The Consumer Product Safety Commission had been slow to do its own research on the safety of many of these products and had not been thorough in its efforts. Agency leaders were reluctant to take regulatory action until public, business, and political pressure mounted. But, it's hard to blame CPSC's career employees

for all of this, given the size of the agency, their limited resources, and the antiregulatory atmosphere in Washington during the Bush years, all coupled with the explosion of imports from China.

Between 1997 and 2007, the value of consumer product imports from China had surged from $62 billion to $246 billion, roughly 20 percent of all consumer goods sold in the United States. To ensure the safety of the public of some 15,000 consumer products sold in the United States, the CPSC had only about 400 employees in 2007, down from about 1,000 in 1980; its budget for inspections and compliance had shrunk in real terms over the same period. In 2007, the agency had one person—yes, one person—assigned to test all domestic- and foreign-produced toys. Another person was assigned to test the flammability of consumer products using techniques and technologies that are at least three decades old. In that year, the agency had only 81 field investigators, all working out of their homes, rather than the 133 who had worked out of a national network of field offices as recently as 2002. In the Los Angeles–Long Beach port area,

which transfers 15 million truck-sized shipping containers a year and where most Chinese imports enter the country, the agency had assigned a lone inspector, working two or three days a week. In the gigantic harbor of New York, goods-laden shipping containers were mostly inspected by customs agents looking for counterfeit goods, with an inspector or two from CPSC occasionally showing up. When asked in September 2007 when he had last seen a CPSC inspector, one customs inspector supervisor reported, "It was around December."[2]

Oddly enough, in the midst of the recalls and news about dangerous imported consumer products, the acting head of the agency, Bush-appointee Nancy Nord, wrote two letters to Congress (in October 2007) in which she voiced her opposition to new legislation that would have doubled the agency budget, allowed for a 20 percent increase in the number of staff, and given it more enforcement powers. The letters suggested that her agency was already doing a top-flight job and that, more importantly, voluntary compliance and cooperation from industry and reliance on the free market was the best strategy for protecting consumers and helping companies stay profitable. This was hardly surprising coming from a person who once had been an official with the U.S. Chamber of Commerce, an interest group representing American businesses. Under heavy criticism for the performance of her agency and her lobbying against measures to improve it, she announced in early 2008 that she would add inspectors at the nation's busiest ports and cooperate more closely with U.S. Customs.

Anti–big government and deregulatory rhetoric has been part of the standard stump speech of virtually every aspiring politician in the country for many years. Although pushed especially hard by Republicans—most of the big changes in budgets and staffs in regulatory agencies came during the Ronald Reagan (who during his 1980 campaign repeatedly said that "government is not the solution to our problem. Government is the problem.") and George H. W. Bush presidencies—Democrats have played a role as well, especially Jimmy Carter, who helped deregulate the transportation and shipping industries, and Bill Clinton, who famously said that "the era of big government is over."

The result is that various executive branch departments and agencies, responsible for seeing that laws are carried out and regulations complied with, have less capacity and capability than in the past, with resources perhaps below what is minimally acceptable, according to many observers. We saw the Federal Emergency Management Agency (FEMA) fail miserably in the aftermath of Hurricane Katrina, for example. Also, tainted meat, produce, and peanut butter have recently made their way through the thinning inspection net at the Department of Agriculture. Lax regulation by distracted and under-staffed agencies such as the Securities and Exchange Commission and the Federal Deposit Insurance Corporation was a big part of the story in the collapse of the financial industry in 2008 (see Chapter 17 for more on this) that plunged the country into the deepest recession since the Great Depression. As well, loose oversight of deep ocean oil drilling by Minerals Management Service contributed to the BP well blowout that befouled much of the Gulf of Mexico in 2010.

Have we managed over the past two decades or so to not only cut out the fat from the federal government, but also cut into the bone of very important agencies, making them less effective than they might be in serving the public interest? President Obama pushed hard during the first two years of his presidency for increased regulatory capacities of federal agencies and for additional rules for the financial industry, but Congress was slow to respond—issues we address in Chapter 17. The question of whether to increase or decrease the responsibilities of federal bureaucratic agencies is an enduring one in American politics and will remain an important one in our politics for many years to come, because it is a matter that fires partisan passions.

THINKING CRITICALLY About This Chapter

This chapter is about the executive branch of the federal government—often called the federal bureaucracy—responsible for carrying out programs and policies fashioned by Congress, the federal courts, and the president. We focus on how the executive branch is organized, what it does, and what effects its actions have on public policies and American democracy.

Using the FRAMEWORK

You will see in this chapter how the federal bureaucracy has grown over the years, primarily as a result of structural transformations in the economy and international position of the United States, but also because of the influence of political linkage level actors and institutions, including voters, public opinion, and interest groups. Primary responsibility for many of the enduring features of the federal bureaucracy will be shown to be associated with our political culture and the Constitution.

Using the DEMOCRACY STANDARD

You will see in this chapter that the federal bureaucracy in general, despite much speculation to the contrary, is fairly responsive to the American people, reacting in the long run to pressures brought to bear on it by the elected branches, the president, and Congress. On the other hand, bureaucrats in specific agencies, in specific circumstances, can be relatively immune from public opinion, at least in the short and medium run. You will be asked to think about what this means in terms of our democratic evaluative standard.

The American Bureaucracy: How Exceptional?

13.1 Compare and contrast our executive branch bureaucracy with those in other countries

The **federal bureaucracy** in America—that is, the executive branch of the national government—is different from government bureaucracies in other democratic nations. Structural influences such as the American political culture and the constitutional rules of the game have a great deal to do with these differences. Before looking at how we are different, however, it is important that we are clear about the term **bureaucracy**.

Bureaucracy has always been a dirty word in American politics, implying red tape, inefficiency, and non-responsiveness. To social scientists, however, *bureaucracy* and *bureaucrat* are neutral terms describing a type of social organization and the people who work in them. Bureaucracies are large organizations in which many people with specialized knowledge are organized into a clearly defined hierarchy of bureaus or offices, each of which has a specified mission. There is a clear chain of command and a set of formal rules to guide behavior. Appointment and advancement, moreover, are based on merit rather than inheritance, power, or election. This is, of course, a model or "ideal type" traceable back to the German sociologist Max Weber;[3] in the real world, there are many variations.

Bureaucracy exists in a wide range of sectors including government, private business (as in most large corporations), and the nonprofit sector, including big organizations like the Red Cross and the Girl Scouts of America. The fact that it is so common suggests that bureaucracy serves important purposes even if the popular mantra in business circles these days is to flatten hierarchies and to be more nimble. One advantage of bureaucracy is its ability to organize large tasks like delivering Social Security checks, churning out automobiles from factories, delivering overnight packages, or fighting wars. Hierarchical organizations with clear chains of command are able to mobilize and coordinate the activities of thousands of people. Another advantage of bureaucracies is the concentration of specialized talent that is found in them. When Apple wants to bring a new product to market, it has thousands of software engineers, product design specialists, and marketing experts on hand to do the necessary work, though it may, at times, subcontract work to other firms, many of which are themselves bureaucratic organizations. When a pandemic threatens, the federal government is able to mobilize an impressively talented group of doctors and scientists at the National Institutes of Health and at the Centers for Disease Control and Prevention to find a solution and put it into effect.

Despite the complaints and jokes about federal bureaucrats, then, bureaucracies have certain advantages as a form of organization both in the private sector and the public sector. This is not to say, of course, that bureaucracy is unproblematic; it is to say that the American rhetorical distaste for bureaucracy tends to hide some of its benefits. In this chapter, we look at the large and complex bureaucracy that is the executive branch of the federal government. In this section, we focus how our government bureaucracy is different from those in other rich democratic countries.

Hostile Political Culture

Americans generally do not trust their government and government leaders (see Chapter 4's section on political culture), nor do they have much confidence that government can accomplish most of the tasks assigned to it. They believe, on the whole, that the private sector can usually do a better job and, most of the time,

> **federal bureaucracy**
> The totality of the departments and agencies of the executive branch of the national government.
>
> **bureaucracy**
> A large, complex organization characterized by a hierarchical set of offices, each with a specific task, controlled through a clear chain of command, and where appointment and advancement of personnel is based on merit.

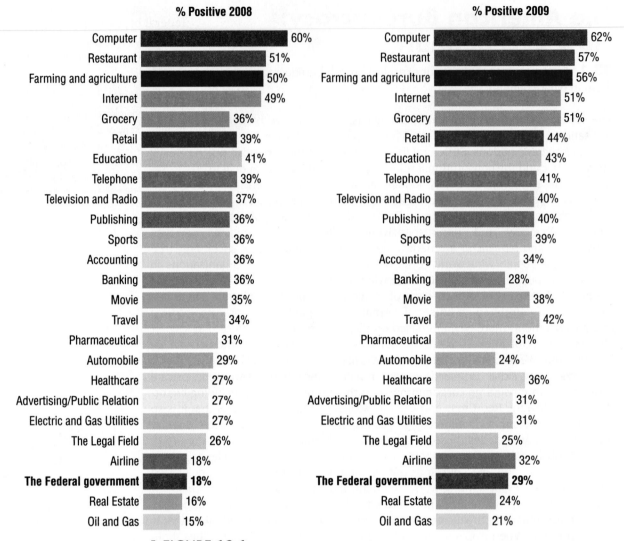

% Positive 2008		% Positive 2009	
Computer	60%	Computer	62%
Restaurant	51%	Restaurant	57%
Farming and agriculture	50%	Farming and agriculture	56%
Internet	49%	Internet	51%
Grocery	36%	Grocery	51%
Retail	39%	Retail	44%
Education	41%	Education	43%
Telephone	39%	Telephone	41%
Television and Radio	37%	Television and Radio	40%
Publishing	36%	Publishing	40%
Sports	36%	Sports	39%
Accounting	36%	Accounting	34%
Banking	36%	Banking	28%
Movie	35%	Movie	38%
Travel	34%	Travel	42%
Pharmaceutical	31%	Pharmaceutical	31%
Automobile	29%	Automobile	24%
Healthcare	27%	Healthcare	36%
Advertising/Public Relation	27%	Advertising/Public Relation	31%
Electric and Gas Utilities	27%	Electric and Gas Utilities	31%
The Legal Field	26%	The Legal Field	25%
Airline	18%	Airline	32%
The Federal government	**18%**	**The Federal government**	**29%**
Real Estate	16%	Real Estate	24%
Oil and Gas	15%	Oil and Gas	21%

FIGURE 13.1

Americans do not think much of the federal government. Though its favorability ratings improved between 2007 and 2009 as the government responded to the financial and economic collapse in the country, less than 30 percent of Americans viewed the government in a favorable light. Not surprisingly, given their role in the economic collapse, the regard for the banking and real estate industries fell sharply, bailouts for GM and Chrysler didn't help the auto industry's standing, and oil and gas failed to rally from its last place position. *Source:* http://www.gallup.com/poll/122342/Automobile-Banking-Industry-Images-Slide-Further.aspx.

want responsibilities lodged there rather than with government. Figure 13.1 shows how low the federal government was regarded by the American public in 2009 compared to various private-sector industries. At the same time, when difficulties or emergencies occur—whether economic depression, natural disasters, or terrorist attacks—they want the federal government to be ready and able to respond.

This generally hostile environment influences the American bureaucracy in several important ways that, paradoxically, make it more difficult for it to respond when needed. For one thing, our public bureaucracy is surrounded by more legal restrictions and is subject to more intense legislative oversight than bureaucracies in other countries. Because **civil servants** have so little prestige, moreover, many of the most talented people in our society do not aspire to work in government. In many other democratic countries, by way of contrast, civil service is highly respected and

civil servants

Government workers employed under the merit system; not political appointees.

ELITES IN TRAINING In some democratic societies such as Japan, Great Britain, and France, the upper reaches of the civil service are staffed by people from upper-class backgrounds, schooled in the nation's most prestigious academic institutions, side-by-side with people who will run their nation's top business corporations. This photo shows students at one of these institutions, France's L'Ecole Nationale D'Administration in Strasbourg. If such a system were introduced in the United States, how might it change the nature of the federal bureaucracy?

attracts talented people. In France, Britain, and Germany, for example, the higher **civil service** positions are filled by the top graduates of the countries' elite universities on the basis of rigorous examinations and are accorded enormous prestige. Not surprisingly, given the elite educations that are required for these posts and the prestige accorded to civil servants, people of decidedly upper-class and aristocratic back-grounds fill the top civil service posts in France, Great Britain, and Germany; in the United States, the civil service looks much more like the general American population in terms of family background, race, gender, and the like.[4] Finally, the highest policymaking positions in the U.S. executive branch are closed to civil servants; they are reserved for presidential political appointees. This is not true in other democracies.

> **civil service**
> Federal government jobs held by civilian employees, excluding political appointees.

Incoherent Organization

Our bureaucracy is an organizational hodgepodge. It does not take the standard pyramidal form, as bureaucracies elsewhere do. There are few clear lines of control, responsibility, or accountability. Some executive branch units have no relationship at all to other agencies and departments. As one of the leading students of the federal bureaucracy once put it, other societies have "a more orderly and symmetrical, a more prudent, a more cohesive and more powerful bureaucracy," whereas we have "a more internally competitive, a more experimental, a noisier and less coherent, a less powerful bureaucracy."[5] Our bureaucracy was built piece by piece over the years in a political system without a strong central government. Bureaucracies in other democratic nations were often created at a single point in time by powerful political leaders, such as Frederick the Great in Prussia and Napoleon in France.[6]

Divided Control

Adding to the organizational incoherence of our federal bureaucracy is the fact that it has two bosses—the president and Congress—who are constantly vying with one another for control. In addition, the federal courts keep an eye on it. This situation is created by the separation of powers and checks and balances in our Constitution, which give each branch a role in the principal activities and responsibilities of the other branches.[7] To be sure, the president is the chief executive and has significant influence over agencies in the executive branch, but Congress plays a very large

? Would the executive branch work better if the president had more direct control over what it does? Or does congressional and judicial oversight help keep the bureaucracy in check?

role in the creation of executive branch units, determining their annual budgets and exercising oversight of its many activities, and the courts make their presence felt as well. No other democratic nation has opted for this arrangement. Civil servants in parliamentary democracies are accountable to a single boss, a cabinet minister appointed by the prime minister.

How the Executive Branch Is Organized

13.2 Outline the structure of the executive branch

The Constitution neither specifies the number and kinds of departments to be established nor describes other bureaucratic agencies. The framers apparently wanted to leave these questions to the wisdom of Congress and the president. Over the years, a large and complex bureaucracy was created to meet a wide range of needs. The most immediate reasons behind the transformation of the federal government's role and the growth of the bureaucracy have been political sector pressures—from public opinion, voters, parties, interest groups, and social movements—on government decision makers. The more fundamental reasons have been changes in such structural factors as the U.S. economy, the nation's population, and the role of the United States in the world, including involvement in war. In Chapter 3, we examined how these things transformed the role and responsibilities of the federal government over the course of American history. The general picture has been one of growth in the government's size and responsibilities.

The executive branch is made up of several kinds of administrative units, which make the federal bureaucracy a very complicated entity (see Figure 13.2):[8]

- The most familiar are **departments**, which are headed by cabinet-level secretaries, appointed by the president and approved by the Senate. Departments are meant to carry out the most essential government functions, as suggested by the first three to be established—War, State, and Treasury. Departments vary greatly in size and internal organization. The Department of Agriculture, for example, has almost 50 offices and bureaus, whereas the Department of Housing and Urban Development has only a few operating agencies. And they range in size from the Department of Defense, with almost 700,000 employees (civilian) in 2009, to the Department of Education, with about 4,200 employees. Over the years, departments (and employees) were added as the need arose, as powerful groups demanded them, or as presidents and members of Congress wished to signal a new national need or to cement political alliances with important constituencies (see Chapter 3 for a discussion of the expansion of the federal government). The timeline in Figure 13.3 shows when each department was established. The newest department, Homeland Security, was created in the wake of the 9/11 terrorist attacks on the United States.

- Subdivisions within cabinet departments are **bureaus** and **agencies**. Departmental bureaus and agencies are not only numerous but varied in their relative autonomy. In some departments, such as the Department of Defense, bureaus and agencies are closely controlled by the department leadership, and the entire department works very much like a textbook hierarchical model. In other cases, where the bureaus or

departments
Generally the largest units in the executive branch, each headed by a cabinet secretary.

bureau
Generally, a subunit of a cabinet department.

agency
A general name used for a subunit of a cabinet department.

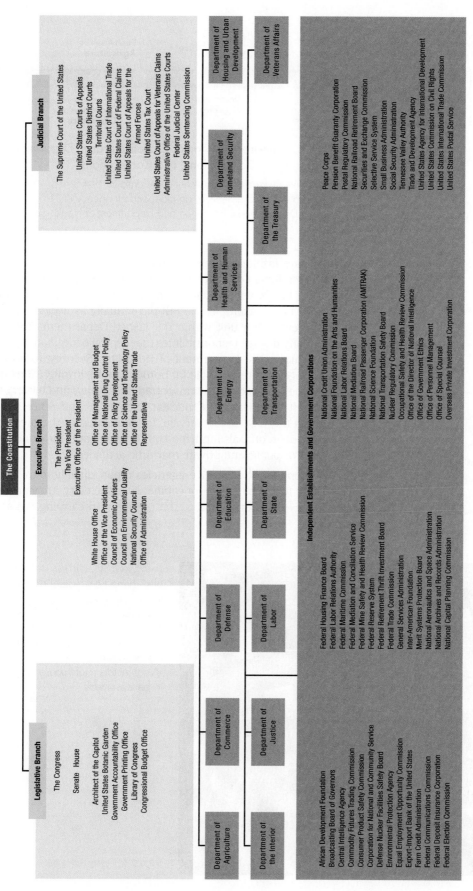

FIGURE 13.2 The Executive Branch of Government

Source: U.S. Government Organization Manual.

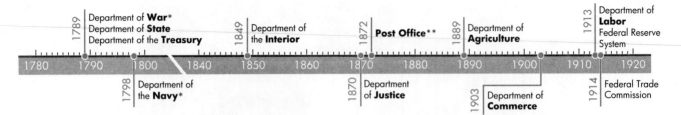

FIGURE 13.3 Timeline: Creation of Executive Branch Departments and Selected Agencies, Independent Commissions, and Corporations

*Became part of newly formed Department of Defense in 1947.
**Transformed into U.S. Postal Service, an independent agency in 1970.
***Later split into Department of Education and Department of Health and Human Services.

agencies have fashioned their own relationships with interest groups and powerful congressional committees, the departments are little more than holding companies for powerful bureaucratic subunits.[9] During the long reign of J. Edgar Hoover, for example, the FBI did virtually as it pleased, even though it was (and remains) a unit within the Justice Department. Some departments have so many diverse responsibilities that central coordination is almost impossible to achieve. The Department of Homeland Security, for example, has bureaus and agencies responsible for border control; immigration and citizenship; disaster relief and recovery; transportation security; and emergency preparedness against terrorist use of nuclear, biological, and other weapons. It also houses the U.S. Secret Service, for protection of the president and other high public officials, and the U.S. Coast Guard, for protection and assistance for public and private maritime activities.[10]

independent agency

A unit of the executive branch outside the control of executive departments.

- **Independent executive agencies** report directly to the president rather than to a department- or cabinet-level secretary. They are usually created to give greater control to the president in carrying out some executive

AIRPORT SECURITY   New national problems often bring new federal agencies to address them. The Transportation Security Agency (TSA) was created in the wake of the 9/11 terrorist attacks on the United States (in which airplanes were used to attack the World Trade Center and the Pentagon) to screen airline passengers. What factors might cause federal agencies to be dissolved?

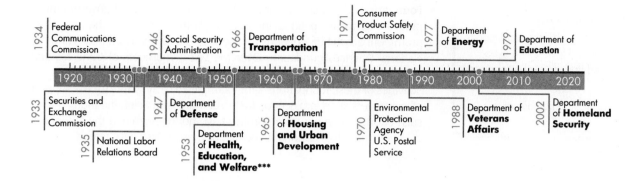

function or to highlight some particular public problem or issue that policymakers wish to address. The Environmental Protection Agency, for example, was given independent status to focus government and public attention on environmental issues and to give the federal government more flexibility in solving environmental problems.

- **Government corporations** are agencies that operate very much like private companies. They can sell stock, retain and reinvest earnings, and borrow money, for instance. They are usually created to perform some crucial economic activity that private investors are unwilling or unable to perform. The Tennessee Valley Authority, for example, was created during the Great Depression to bring electricity to most of the upper South; today it provides about 6 percent of all U.S. electrical power.[11] The U.S. Postal Service was transformed from an executive department to a government corporation in 1970 in the hope of increasing efficiency.

- **Quasi-governmental organizations** are hybrids of public and private organizations. They allow the federal government to be involved in a particular area of activity without directly controlling it. They are distinguished from government corporations by the fact that a portion of the boards of directors are appointed by the private sector. The Federal Reserve Board, responsible for setting the nation's monetary policy, and increasingly a key player in restructuring the financial system and saving it from collapse, is owned by 12 regional banks but run by a Board of Governors and a Chairman (all of whom serve overlapping, staggered terms) appointed by the president. (See Chapter 17 for more on the Fed and what it does.) The Corporation for Public Broadcasting fits into this category, as do the mortgage institutions Fannie Mae (The Federal National Mortgage Association) and Freddie Mac (the Federal Home Mortgage Corporation), so much in the news because of the real estate crisis.

- **Independent regulatory commissions**, such as the Securities and Exchange Commission and the Consumer Product Safety Commission, are responsible for regulating sectors of the economy in which it is judged that the free market does not work properly to protect the public interest. The commissions are "independent" in the sense that they stand outside the departmental structure and are protected against direct presidential or congressional control. A commission is run by commissioners with long, staggered, and overlapping terms, and many require a balance between Republicans and Democrats.

government corporation

A unit in the executive branch that operates like a private business but provides some public service.

quasi-governmental organization

An organization that has governmental powers and responsibilities but has substantial private-sector control over its activities.

independent regulatory commission

An entity in the executive branch that is outside the immediate control of the president and Congress that issues rules and regulations to protect the public.

government foundation

An entity of the executive branch that supports the arts or sciences and is designed to be somewhat insulated from political interference.

bureaucrat

A person who works in a bureaucratic organization.

- **Foundations** are units that are separated from the rest of government to protect them from political interference with science and the arts. Most prominent are the foundations for the Arts and for the Humanities and the National Science Foundation. Over the years, members of Congress and presidential administrations have tried on various occasions to redirect the activities of these foundations—for example, to deny grants for the support of controversial art projects or for certain areas of scientific inquiry—but such efforts, while not unimportant, have not undermined the autonomy of government foundations to the extent many critics have feared.

What Do Bureaucrats Do?

13.3 Identify the kinds of activities bureaucrats perform

Bureaucrats engage in a wide range of activities that are relevant to the quality of democracy in the United States and affect how laws and regulations work. Let's look at the more prominent and significant of these activities.

Executing Programs and Policies

The term *executive branch* suggests the branch of the federal government that executes or carries out the law. This is sometimes called implementation. The framers of the Constitution assumed that Congress would be the principal national policymaker and stipulated that the president and his appointees to administrative positions in the executive branch "shall take care that the laws be faithfully executed" (Article II, Section 2). For the most part, this responsibility is carried out routinely; mail is delivered, troops are trained, Social Security checks are mailed on time, and foreign intelligence is collected.

Sometimes, executing the law is not so easy, however, because it is not always clear what the law means. Often, Congress passes laws that are vague about goals and short on procedural guidelines. It may do so because its members believe that something should be done about a particular social problem but are unclear on specifics about how to solve it or disagree among themselves. This, perhaps, is why Congress gave so much

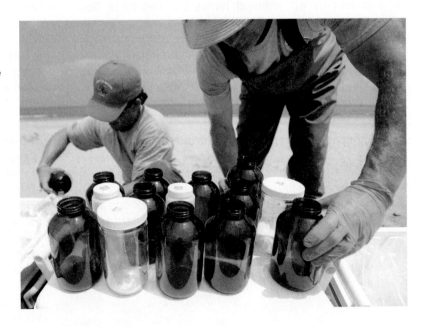

ANALYZING THE DAMAGE   Here, scientists from the EPA collect water samples at a beach near Grand Isle, Louisiana, in June 2010 in an effort to understand the possible environmental impacts of the massive BP oil spill in the Gulf. Should we continue to have a robust capacity in the federal government to monitor and issue rules to protect the environment, or are these best left to the states or to private firms such as BP? Why?

How can unelected bureaucrats make important rulings that affect people's lives?

Background: One of the emerging conflicts that will be playing itself out over the next few years, both in the United States and in the global economy, concerns the safety of genetically engineered food and the rules that will apply for protecting the public from its possible harmful effects. In the United States, unless Congress chooses to act in its own right, the rules will be made by the Food and Drug Administration. We can better understand why the FDA can make rules on genetically engineered foods by using a broad perspective that takes into account structural, political linkage, and governmental level factors.

| Structure | The Constitution says little about the organization and operations of the Executive Branch and leaves the details to be filled in by Congress. | → Scientific researchers have made dramatic breakthroughs in plant and animal genetics, causing some segments of society to call for regulations. | → Global agribusiness corporations are always looking for the most efficient forms of production, and genetically engineered products help them do this. |

| Political Linkage | Public opinion polls show that some Americans are beginning to worry about genetically engineered food and want some action. | → Interest groups, for and against genetically engineered food, have pressed their positions on public officials, using both "inside" and "outside" forms of lobbying. |

Government

The Court has allowed bureaucratic agencies to make rules within the boundaries set by Congress. → Congress created the Food and Drug Administration, defined its overall mission, but left room for the FDA to make rules in its areas of responsibility.

The FDA scientific staff has pressed the FDA's leadership to become more active in rulemaking for genetically engineered food. ⇨ The FDA leadership, attentive to the growing interest in rules to regulate in the area of genetically engineered food, held a series of hearings on the subject in 1999. ⇨ No laws specifically addressing genetically engineered food have been enacted, leaving rulemaking in this area to the FDA.

Governmental Action

The FDA issued rules in 2000 specifying how genetically engineered food is to be tested for safety and wholesomeness and requiring packaging to carry a warning label for consumers.

discretionary power to Treasury Secretary Henry Paulson to respond to the credit freeze and stock market collapse in fall 2008. Vaguely written statutes and directives, then, leave a great deal of discretion to bureaucrats (see the "Mapping American Politics" feature later in this chapter on discretionary leeway at Homeland Security).

Regulating

Congress often gives bureaucratic agencies the power to write specific rules. Because of the complexity of the problems that government must face, Congress tends to create agencies and to specify the job or mission that it wants done and then charges the agency with using its expertise to do the job. Congress created the Environmental Protection Agency (EPA), for instance, and gave it a mission—to help coordinate the cleanup of the nation's air and water—but it left to the EPA the power to set the specific standards that communities and businesses must meet. The standards set by the EPA have the force of law unless they are rescinded by Congress or overruled by the courts. The Food and Drug Administration (FDA) writes rules about the introduction of new drugs that researchers and pharmaceutical companies are obliged to follow. (See the "Using the Framework" feature for more on the FDA.)

? Does the congressional grant of broad authority to nonelected executive branch officials to interpret the meaning of laws make our system less democratic than it might be? How can bureaucrats entrusted with policy decisions be held more accountable to the public?

Some critics believe that Congress delegates entirely too much lawmaking to the executive branch,[12] but it is difficult to see what alternative Congress has. It cannot micromanage every issue; Congress lacks the time, resources, and expertise. And in the end, Congress retains control; it can change the rules written by bureaucrats if they drift too far from congressional intent or constituent desires.

Other critics believe there simply are too many rules and regulations. When candidates promise to "get government off our backs," they usually are referring to regulatory burdens, though taxes are a target as well. Several attempts have been made to roll back executive branch rule-making. Under Ronald Reagan, **cost-benefit analysis** was introduced as a way to slow the rule-making process, for example, and the result was a decline in the number of rules issued. After a period of growth in federal regulations during the presidencies of George H. W. Bush and Bill Clinton, the second President Bush managed to cap further growth, consistent with his conservative philosophy (see Figure 13.4). Bush issued an executive order in 2007 mandating that prior to issuing a new rule, agencies must first determine and report why market forces are unable to address a problem the new rule is designed to solve. He then ordered that each agency appoint a presidentially approved regulatory policy officer to review all proposed rules to see if they fit the administrations priorities. Clearly this was an effort to slow the pace of rule-making by federal agencies by a president who opposed a too active government in domestic affairs. Barack Obama, more supportive of an active government, rescinded both rules within the first 10 days of his new administration.[13] Many blame regulatory cutbacks for the rising incidence of safety problems in our food supply and imported consumer goods as well as the financial collapse in 2008, matters explored in the chapter-opening story.

cost-benefit analysis
A method of evaluating rules and regulations by weighing their potential costs against their potential benefits to society.

Adjudicating

Congress has given some executive branch agencies the power to conduct quasi-judicial proceedings in which disputes are resolved.

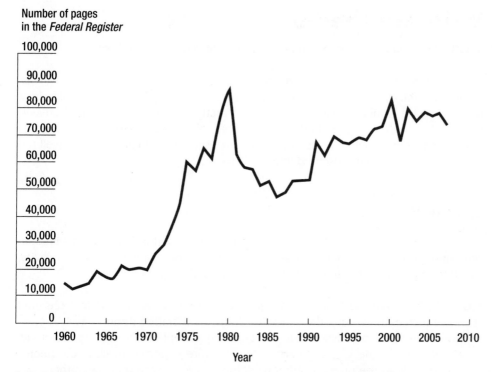

Number of pages
in the *Federal Register*

FIGURE 13.4 Growth in Federal Agency Rules and Regulations

This graph shows the annual number of pages in the *Federal Register*, which is published daily and contains all new rules and changes to existing rules proposed by each and every executive branch agency. While not perfect, tracking its growth is an interesting way, widely used by scholars and journalists, to chart the course and scale of bureaucratic regulation in the United States. The graph shows the dramatic rise in regulations during the 1970s, the decline during the Reagan years, the slow increase in rule writing during the first Bush and Clinton presidencies, and a leveling out during George W. Bush's tenure in office. In his first year, Barack Obama issued executive orders at a pace that was similar to that of George W. Bush.

Much as in a court of law, the decisions of an administrative law judge have the force of law, unless appealed to a higher panel. The National Labor Relations Board, for instance, adjudicates disputes between labor and management on matters concerning federal labor laws. Disputes may involve claims of unfair labor practices, for example—firing a labor organizer falls into this category— or disagreements about whether proper procedures were followed in filing for a union certification election.

Discretion and Democracy

It is quite clear, then, that bureaucrats exercise a great deal of discretion. They do not simply follow a set of orders from Congress or the president, but find many opportunities to exercise their own judgment. Because bureaucrats make important decisions that have consequences for many other people, groups, and organizations, we can say that they are policymakers. And, because they make the overwhelming majority of public policy decisions in the United States,[14] we can say they are important policymakers. They are *unelected* policymakers, however, and this fact should immediately alert us to some potential problems with regard to the practice of democracy.

Who Are the Bureaucrats?

13.4 Determine how demographically representative bureaucrats are

Because bureaucrats exercise substantial discretion as policymakers, we want to know who they are. How representative are they of the American people? In a democracy, we would probably want to see a pretty close correspondence between the people and bureaucrats. In the sections that follow, we'll take a look at each of the different personnel systems in the executive branch and consider how well the American people are represented in their ranks.

The Merit Services

Merit services choose employees on the basis of examinations, educational credentials, and demonstrable skills. These services have evolved in size and complexity, in tandem with the federal bureaucracy, and are of three general types.

Competitive Civil Service From the election of Andrew Jackson in 1828 until the late nineteenth century, the executive branch was staffed through what is commonly called the **spoils system**. It was generally accepted that the "spoils of victory" belonged to the winning party. Winners were expected to clear out people who were loyal to the previous administration and to replace them with their own people. Also known as **patronage**, this system of appointment caused no great alarm in the beginning because of the small and relatively unimportant role of the federal government in American society. The shortcomings of the War Department and other bureaucratic agencies during the Civil War, however, convinced many people that reform of the federal personnel system was required. Rampant corruption and favoritism in the government service during the years after the Civil War gave an additional boost to the reform effort, as did the realization that the growing role of the federal government required more skilled and less partisan personnel. The final catalyst for change was the assassination in 1881 of President James Garfield by a person who, it is said, badly wanted a government job but could not get one.

The Civil Service Act of 1883, also known as the Pendleton Act, created a bipartisan Civil Service Commission to oversee a system of appointments to certain executive branch posts on the basis of merit. Competitive examinations were to be used to determine merit. In the beginning, the competitive civil service system included only about 10 percent of federal positions. Congress gradually extended the reach of the career civil service; today, it covers about 60 percent of the roughly 2.7 million federal civilian employees. In 1978, Congress abolished the Civil Service Commission and replaced it with two separate agencies, the Office of Personnel Management (OPM) and the Merit Systems Protection Board. The former administers the civil service laws, advertises positions, writes examinations, and acts as a clearinghouse for agencies that are looking for workers. The latter settles disputes concerning employee rights and obligations, hears employee grievances, and orders corrective action when needed.

spoils system

The practice of distributing government offices and contracts to the supporters of the winning party; also called *patronage*.

patronage

The practice of distributing government offices and contracts to the supporters of the winning party; also called the *spoils system*.

Agency Merit Services Many federal agencies require personnel with particular kinds of training and experience appropriate to their special missions. For such agencies, Congress has established separate merit systems administered by each agency itself. The Public Health Service, for instance, recruits its own doctors. The Department of State has its own examinations and procedures for recruiting foreign service officers. The National Aeronautics and Space Administration (NASA) recruits scientists and engineers without the help of the Office of Personnel Management. About 35 percent of all federal civilian employees fall under these agency-specific merit systems.

Excepted Services There are other variations on how civil servants are hired.[15] Positions in the federal government are classified by a schedule system that determines specific requirements for filling each job. Schedule A allows various departments and agencies to hire attorneys and accountants who are tested and certified by professional associations. Schedule B appointments are used to hire people with skills that are needed and in short supply, as determined by the agencies themselves, in consultation with the OPM. Schedule C is used to hire people in what are called "policy-sensitive" positions, such as personal assistants and drivers. Other excepted authorities allow hiring for short assignments in areas of special service to the country, such as the Peace Corps.

Senior Executive Service Created in 1978, these 9,000 or so positions were meant to be a sort of super–civil service, somewhat akin to the top civil service posts in France filled by *grandes ecoles* graduates, requiring high levels of education and skills. Individuals in these positions are granted broad responsibilities and autonomy, with promotions, salary increases, and termination determined by rigorous performance reviews. The original idea was that they would serve as a corps of highly skilled people who could be deployed to various agencies as need appeared for their services, serving as a bridge between political appointees at the tops of the agencies and the career civil service. Things have not worked out that way, however; members of the senior executive service have not been entirely trusted by political appointees, and most have stayed put within their agencies throughout their careers.[16]

How Different Are Civil Servants? Civil servants are similar to other Americans.[17] Their educational levels and regional origins are close to those of other Americans, for example, although they tend to be a little bit older (37 percent are over the age of 50)[18] and a little better paid (higher-level civil servants still seriously lag behind their counterparts in the private sector), and they have better job security, retirement plans, and health insurance than most. Civil servants' political beliefs and opinions also are pretty close to those of the general American public, although they tend to favor the Democrats a bit more than the general public and are slightly more liberal on social issues than the national average.[19] Women and minorities are very well represented (the latter are actually over-represented), with women holding 44 percent of all nonpostal jobs and racial and ethnic minorities 31 percent.[20] It is worth noting, however, that women and minorities are over-represented in the very lowest civil service grades and are under-represented in the highest. They also are far less evident in the special-agency merit systems (such as the Foreign Service and the FBI) and in the professional categories (scientists at the National Institutes of Health; doctors in the Public Health Service).[21]

Political Appointees

The highest policymaking positions in the federal bureaucracy (e.g., department secretaries, assistants to the president, leading officials in the agencies), about 3,000 in number, enter government service not by way of competitive merit examinations but by presidential appointment. About 600 of them—designated Executive Schedule appointees—require Senate confirmation. These patronage positions, in theory at least, allow the president to translate his electoral mandate into public policy by permitting him to put his people in place in key policymaking jobs. Top appointees who have the confidence of the president tend to become important policymakers and public figures in their own right. Treasury Secretary Timothy Geithner and Budget Director Peter Orszag, because of the central roles they played in the administration's economic recovery plans, achieved this status during Barack Obama's first term.

Most presidents use patronage not only to build support for their programs but also to firm up their political coalition by being sensitive to the needs of important party factions and interest groups. Ronald Reagan used his appointments to advance a conservative agenda for America and made conservative beliefs a prerequisite for high bureaucratic appointments.[22] President Clinton, by contrast, promised to make government "look more like America" and did so by appointing many women and minorities to top posts in his administration.

Presidents also reserve important appointments for people they trust and who bring expertise and experience. John F. Kennedy appointed his brother and political confidant Bobby to the post of attorney general. George W. Bush was particularly eager to fill cabinet posts and his inner circle with people with a great deal of experience in the upper reaches of the federal government, including several who had served in his father's administration; namely, Donald Rumsfeld (secretary of defense), Colin Powell (secretary of state in his first administration), and Condoleezza Rice, his first national security adviser and second secretary of state.

Presidents also want to find places for appointments for people who played important roles in their election, whether or not they possess the requisite skills for the job.[23] The idea is to give them less skilled positions where they will be out of harm's way, in places not critical to advancing the president's agenda. In Republican administrations, political cronies are likely to end up in Housing and Urban Development, although the inexperienced Michael Brown was made head of FEMA for no apparent reason—his only executive experience was as the director of the Arabian Horse Association—with disastrous results for New Orleans and the Gulf Coast following Katrina. Democratic administrations tend to use the Department of Commerce and the Small Business Administration to reward their campaign workers and contributors.

WHAT TO DO ABOUT THE ECONOMY?   The president and his economic team walk to the microphone for a press conference after a meeting on what to do about the stalled economy. Treasury Secretary Tim Geithner is behind President Obama, followed by Budget Director Peter Orszag and Lawrence Summers, then-director of the president's National Economic Council. Geithner headed one of the oldest departments in the executive branch and was subject to the Senate's advise and consent, while Summers ran an institution within the White House created by a Clinton executive order in 1993 to coordinate economic policymaking and was not subject to Senate approval. Do presidents need this kind of flexibility in meeting new needs and responsibilities, or should the Senate play a role in all appointments to important executive branch offices? Why?

Top political appointees do not last very long on the job. On average, they stay in office only 22 months; political scientist Hugh Heclo called them "birds of passage."[24] They leave for many reasons. Most are accomplished people from the private sector who see government service as only a short-term commitment. Most make financial sacrifices to become top bureaucratic officials. Many don't find the public notoriety appealing. Some find themselves the target of partisan campaigns that later prove groundless but leave them with damaged reputations. Finally, many become frustrated by how difficult it is to change and implement public policy.

Political and Governmental Influences on Bureaucratic Behavior

13.5 Isolate various influences on executive branch decision making

Rather than there being a single chain of command with clear lines of authority, the bureaucracy in general (and bureaucrats in particular) must heed several important voices. The president is the most important, but Congress, the courts, the public (including interest groups), and the press play a significant role in influencing what agencies do. Figure 13.5 gives an overview of these several influences on bureaucratic behavior.

The President and the Bureaucracy

Being the nation's chief executive, the president is the formal head of the executive branch. But, as we saw in Chapter 12, the president's ability to control the executive branch is not unlimited. In fact, virtually every modern president has been perplexed by the discovery that he cannot assume that bureaucrats will do what he wants them to do.[25] Richard Nixon was so frustrated by his inability to move

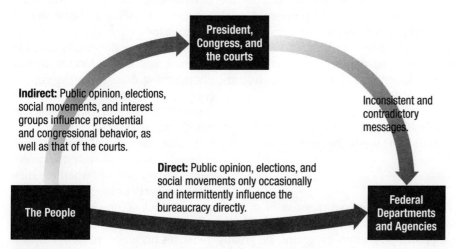

FIGURE 13.5 Popular Control of the Bureaucracy: Imperfect Popular Sovereignty
Popular control of the federal bureaucracy is complex, indirect, and only partially effective. The public does not elect government bureaucrats, and public opinion has little direct effect on their behavior. However, members of Congress and the president, all of whom are answerable to the electorate and attentive to public opinion, exercise an important influence on bureaucratic behavior. So, too, do federal judges. Because elected officials and judges often send mixed signals, however, some of the effectiveness of such controls is diminished.

the federal bureaucracy that he came to think of it as an alien institution filled with Democratic Party enemies. His strategy was to intimidate bureaucrats or bypass them. He created the notorious "plumbers" unit in the White House to act as his personal domestic surveillance and espionage unit. Revelation of its activities was one of the factors leading the House Judiciary Committee to recommend approval of three articles of impeachment in the Watergate scandal.

Why Presidents Often Feel Stymied by the Bureaucracy

The sheer size and complexity of the executive branch is one reason presidents are frustrated by it. There is so much going on, in so many agencies, involving the activity of tens of thousands of people, that simply keeping abreast of it all is no easy task even with a large White House staff to help. Moreover, because of civil service regulations, presidents have no say about the tenure or salary of most federal bureaucrats beyond those they have appointed. When presidents want something to happen, they are unlikely to get instantaneous acquiescence from bureaucrats, who do not fear their nominal boss as they would fear a private employer. Bureaucratic agencies also are heavily insulated against presidential efforts to control them because of agency alliances with powerful interest groups and various House and Senate committees. Above all, presidents find that they are not the only ones with the authority to influence how officials and civil servants in the executive branch behave; they find that they share this authority with Congress and often with the courts.

Tools of Presidential Leadership

Presidents hardly are helpless, of course; they have a number of ways to encourage bureaucratic compliance.[26] Occasionally, because of a crisis or a widely shared national commitment, decisive bureaucratic action is possible, as during Roosevelt's New Deal era, Lyndon Johnson's first years as president, Ronald Reagan's first administration, and George W. Bush's war on terrorism.

Even during ordinary times, however, the president has important management tools. First, although it is difficult to measure precisely, the president's prestige as our only nationally elected political leader makes his wishes hard to ignore. When Teddy Roosevelt called the presidency a "bully pulpit," he meant that only the president can speak for the nation, set the tone for the government, and call the American people to some great national purpose. A popular president, willing and able to play this role, is hard to resist. Bureaucrats are citizens and respond like other Americans to presidential leadership. When a president chooses to become directly involved in some bureaucratic matter—for example, with a phone call to a reluctant agency head or a comment about some bureaucratic shortcoming during a press conference—most bureaucrats respond. Research done over many years in many agencies demonstrates, in fact, that career civil servants will generally go along with the president, regardless of whether they share his party or ideology.[27]

? Should members of the federal bureaucracy defer to the president, regardless of whether they agree with him? What dangers might this tendency present?

The power of appointment is also an important tool of presidential leadership.[28] If a president is very careful to fill the top administrative posts with people who support him and his programs, he greatly increases his ability to have his way. The Senate must advise on and consent to most of his top choices, and the process of approving the president's appointees has become much more contentious and drawn out than in the past. It is not unusual for important posts to be empty for a long time. For example, Republican resistance meant that the position of Head of the Transportation Security Administration (TSA) was not filled for more than a full year after Barack Obama's swearing in as president.

The president's power as chief budget officer of the federal government is also a formidable tool of the administration. No agency of the federal bureaucracy, for instance, can make its own budget request directly to Congress; its budget must be submitted to Congress as part of the president's overall budget for the U.S. government formulated by the Office of Management and Budget (OMB), whose director reports directly to the president. The OMB also has the statutory authority to block proposed legislation coming from any executive branch agency if it deems it contrary to the president's budget or program.

And finally, as we saw in Chapter 12, presidents have broad unitary powers to help in controlling executive branch agencies, including regulatory review and executive orders. To repeat a point we made in that chapter:

> [...George W. Bush and Vice President Dick Cheney...] revived and gave a very expansive reading to a long-dormant constitutional theory known as the **unitary executive** in an attempt to "unstymy" the office. The concept is based on Article II's "vesting" ("The executive Power shall be vested in a President of the United States of America.") and "take care" clauses ("The President shall take care that the laws be faithfully executed...") to suggest that the [president] is free to exercise command and authority over the executive branch in all respects. Presidential adviser and Justice Department official John Yoo proposed early in the Bush administration that the Constitution created a unified and hierarchical executive branch under the direct control of the president who has all authority necessary to control the actions of federal bureaucracy personnel and units without interference from the other federal branches.[29]

What this meant in practice was the aggressive use by President Bush of powers all presidents have used, including signing statements, executive orders, and regulatory review.[30] Though President Bush tried to exercise this form of tight control over executive agencies and personnel, in the end it proved too difficult to achieve. For example, though his staffers and agency appointees tried to edit and change the conclusion of several reports from government scientists on global warming, the information still found its way to the public through leaks to the news media and the appropriate people in Congress.

> **unitary executive**
>
> Constitutional doctrine that proposes that the executive branch is under the direct control of the president, who has all authority necessary to control the actions of federal bureaucracy personnel and units without interference from the other federal branches.

Congress and the Bureaucracy

Congress exercises considerable influence over the federal bureaucracy by legislating agency organization and mission, confirming or refusing to confirm presidential appointments, controlling the agency budget, holding oversight hearings, and using inspectors general.

Legislating Agency Organization and Mission

The president and Congress share control over the executive branch. The congressional tools of control, in fact, are at least as formidable as those of the president.[31] Congress legislates the mission of bureaucratic agencies and the details of their organization and can change either one, and alter agency policy as well. In 1999, for example, Congress passed a bill requiring the Census Bureau to do the 2000 census by direct count, disallowing the use of statistical sampling, which the technical staff at the Bureau wanted to use. Congress also can and does create new departments, such as the Department of Homeland Security. The new department was created by Congress in 2002 after members of both parties in the House and Senate determined that the president's approach—an

Tracking Where Homeland Security Dollars First Ended Up

Introduction The Department of Homeland Security (DHS) was established in 2002 to coordinate federal, state, and local efforts to defend the nation against terrorist attacks and deal with their aftermath and recovery. The establishment of the new executive branch department was triggered, of course, by the 9/11 terrorist attacks on the World Trade Center in New York City and on the Pentagon near Washington, D.C. The terrorists selected targets that were not only of great symbolic importance—the plane that crashed in Pennsylvania seems to have been headed toward a major target in the nation's capital as well—but also critical to the operations of American government and economy. One would assume, then, that the Department of Homeland Security would have distributed its funds to states and communities in some rough proportion to their vulnerability to attack and their centrality to the health and survival of the nation. In fact, as with other executive agencies, the distribution depended not just on assessments by professionals and leaders at

Homeland Security, but also on the wishes of representatives and senators ever anxious to bring federal dollars to their districts and states. But just how far did the initial spending by the DHS deviate from the nation's security and recovery needs when DHS first got started?

Mapping Importance and Spending There is no commonly agreed upon metric to say how important different targets might be for potential terrorists, no sure way to gauge symbolic importance and economic impact. As a rough measure, we use the total size of

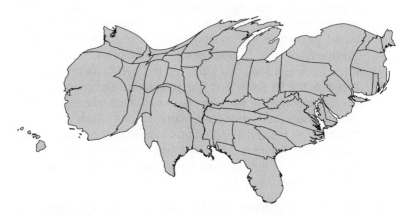

Gross State Products: States Drawn to Size of Their Economy
©2006 M. D. Ward

Office of Homeland Security in the White House Office—would not have the necessary authority and resources to coordinate the government's antiterrorism activities. After initial resistance, the president agreed and signed legislation creating the new cabinet-level department.

Confirming Presidential Appointments Top-level executive branch posts are filled through presidential nomination and Senate confirmation. Although the Senate almost always approves presidential nominations to these posts, it will sometimes use the "advice and consent" process to shape policies in bureaucratic departments and agencies. It occasionally turns down presidential nominations, as it did in the case of George H. W. Bush's nominee for the post of defense secretary, John Tower. At other times, it can simply draw out and delay the process in a bid to gain concessions from the president and the nominee on future policies. Former Senate Foreign Relations Committee Chairman Jesse Helms was a master at this, for example, by gaining concessions on policies concerning Cuba, foreign aid, and funding for international population control agencies. Defeat of nominees and long delays are most likely to happen during periods of divided government.[32] Democrats managed to hold up several presidential nominations in late 2005 and early 2006 for top positions at FEMA, for example, questioning the backgrounds and qualifications in disaster relief and recovery of several of the president's nominees, given the nation's unfortunate experience with FEMA's then-director Michael Brown during the Hurricane Katrina disaster.

each state's economy, shown in the cartogram on the left. This assumes that the size of a state's economy indicates its importance in the overall economic life of the nation and that serious damage to targets in the most economically important states would have the most negative effects on the entire country. The cartogram on the right shows states drawn in terms of per-capita DHS spending. If spending were going to where it was needed, and if the size of a state's economy is a reasonable indicator of its importance as a possible terrorist attack, the two cartograms should look very similar. It is clear that they do not. Note how much money from the DHS's first distribution of funds in 2004 went to less economically important states, including Idaho, Wyoming, the Dakotas, New Hampshire, Vermont, Rhode Island, and Maine. Note, as well, how little went to California, Texas, New York, and Florida.

What Do You Think? How do you assess DHS initial spending in terms of national needs? What might be a better measure of a state or city's symbolic and economic importance than we used here, the total size of a state's economy? Finally, if you believe there is a serious and troubling mismatch between needs and spending, how do you think we might improve matters? Should the influence of individual members of Congress influence how executive departments and agencies spend their appropriated budget or should the advice of professionals carry more weight?

Map note: Alaska is not shown, although information about Alaska is included in calculations where relevant, and Hawaii is moved closer to the mainland.

Sources: (gross state product for 2004): Bureau of Economic Analysis (**www.bea.gov/bea/regional/data.htm**); the U.S. Bureau of the Census, *Statistical Abstract of the United States, 2006,* Table 17.

Source: (for HSD spending in 2004): V. de Rugy, "What Does Homeland Security Spending Buy?" (Washington, D.C.: The American Enterprise Institute, 2005).

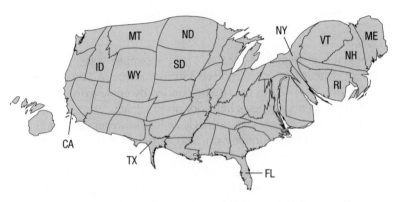

Homeland Security Department: Spending per Capita by State
©2006 M. D. Ward

Standard US Map

Controlling the Agency Budget

Congress can also use its control over agency budgets to influence agency behavior. (One common result is the seemingly irrational distribution of agency funds as you can see in the "Mapping American Politics" feature.) In theory, Congress uses the budget process to assess the performance of each agency each year, closely scrutinizing its activities before determining its next **appropriation**, the legal authority for the agency to spend money. Congress has neither the time nor the resources actually to do such a thing and usually gives each agency some small increment over what it had in the previous year.[33] Of course, if a particular agency displeases Congress, its budget may be cut; if a new set of responsibilities is given to an agency, its budget is usually increased. Sometimes these agency budget actions are taken with the full concurrence of the president; often they are not. Congress sometimes lends a sympathetic ear and increases the budgets of agencies that are not favored by the president. In the 1980s, Congress consistently gave more money than President Reagan wanted given to the EPA, the National Institutes of Health, and the National Science Foundation.

> **appropriation**
> Legal authority for a federal agency to spend money from the U.S. Treasury.

Holding Oversight Hearings

Oversight hearings are an important instrument for gathering information about the policies and performance of executive branch departments and agencies and a handy forum for conveying the views of the members of Congress to bureaucrats. There is a great deal of evidence that agency heads

SIGNS OF THE TIMES   The bursting of the "housing bubble" and the subsequent wave of foreclosures led many Americans to wonder if Congress could do something to help. In a series of oversight committee hearings, prominent representatives and senators pressed Fed and Treasury officials to give direct assistance to troubled homeowners from the previously passed rescue package, which they did on a limited basis. In what other circumstances might it make sense for the government to intervene in private markets?

listen when the message is delivered clearly.[34] For example, after the Senate Finance Committee held hearings on purported Internal Revenue Service harassment of taxpayers in 1999, the head of the IRS responded by apologizing to taxpayers and promising changes in his agency's behavior and policies.

Congress does not always speak with a single voice, however. Congress is a highly fragmented and decentralized institution, and its power is dispersed among scores of subcommittees. Often the activities of a particular bureaucratic agency are the province of more than a single committee or subcommittee, and the probability of receiving mixed signals from them is very high. A skilled administrator can often play these competing forces off of each other and gain a degree of autonomy for his or her agency.

Using Inspectors General   Starting in 1978, Congress has established the office of inspector general in nearly every executive branch department and agency. These inspectors general report directly to Congress and are charged with keeping an eye out for waste, fraud, and bureaucratic abuses of power. The inspectors general in the Department of Education, for example, recently reported widespread fraud in several department grant and loan programs. Inspectors general issue periodic formal reports to the relevant congressional committees, and many meet with congressional staffers on a regular basis, giving Congress a good handle on what is going on in the bureaucracy.

? All in all, who do you think holds more power over the bureaucracy, Congress or the president? Is each one an effective check on the other?

The Courts and the Bureaucracy

In our system of separation of powers and checks and balances, the federal judiciary also has a say in what bureaucratic agencies do. It does so in a less direct manner than the president and Congress, to be sure, because the judiciary must wait for cases to reach it and cannot initiate action on its own (see Chapter 14 for more details). Nevertheless, the courts affect federal agencies on a wide range of issues. For example, executive branch agencies cannot violate the constitutional protections afforded to citizens by the Bill of Rights, so citizens who feel their rights have been violated have turned to the courts for relief on a variety of issues, including illegal searches, detentions without trials, denial of access to an attorney, and harsh treatment by federal authorities. Executive branch agencies are also obligated to treat citizens equally, that is, on a nondiscriminatory basis, and turn to the courts for relief when they feel that discriminatory practices have occurred. The Small Business Administration cannot deny loans to women or racial minorities, for example, nor can federal highway funds be denied to minority contractors. The role of the courts in constraining and monitoring federal authorities on issues related to individual rights and equal protection is covered in detail in Chapters 15 and 16.

The Administrative Procedure Act of 1946, amended several times since, sets out a set of procedures on how executive branch agencies must make their decisions.[35] Basically, the Act attempts to make sure that agencies are bound by the due process guarantees in the Fifth and Fourteenth Amendments; which means, in the end, that they cannot act capriciously or arbitrarily when carrying out their missions, whether distributing benefits, overseeing federal programs, enforcing regulations, or formulating new regulatory rules. The amended Act requires, among other things, that agencies give adequate notice of their actions, solicit comments from all interested parties, and act without bias or favoritism. Citizens, advocacy groups, and interest groups pay attention to decisions and rules from agencies that directly affect them, and it is quite common for them to turn to the courts when they feel that agencies have acted improperly.

The Public and the Press

Most Americans pay little attention to bureaucratic agencies as such. The public focuses mainly on the *content* of public policies rather than on the bureaucratic agencies or the bureaucrats who carry them out. Americans have opinions about Social Security—level of benefits, eligibility, taxes, and so on—but do not concern themselves much with the Social Security Administration per se. In general, then, the public does not directly know or think much about bureaucratic agencies.

There are exceptions to this generalization, however. Some agencies are constantly in the public eye and occasion the development of opinions. Because taxes are a constant irritant for most people, Americans tend to have opinions about the Internal Revenue Service. Foul-ups can often focus public attention on an agency, as well. The FBI and the CIA came under fire in 2005, for example, for intelligence failures relating to 9/11 and Iraq's purported weapons of mass destruction. Later in

NOT HAPPY WITH THE MEDIA   For the most part, regulatory agencies go about their business without much public attention. Occasionally, however, people become sufficiently concerned about regulatory agency actions or lack of action that they find ways to express their views. Here, a demonstrator concerned about (in her view) the unsuitability of programming on network television shows her displeasure outside a meeting of the Federal Communications Commission. Should regulatory agencies take notice of such public protests?

the same year, the Army Corps of Engineers and FEMA were strongly criticized during and after the Hurricane Katrina disaster, the first for its failed levee system in and around New Orleans, the second for its painfully slow and incomplete rescue and recovery operations. The Fed and Treasury were the brunt of widespread discontent in 2009 and 2010 because of a public perception that they were more interested in bailing out and helping financial firms than in helping consumers. The Department of the Interior and its head, Ken Salazar, were heavily criticized in 2010 for its late and uncoordinated response to the BP oil spill in the Gulf.

Needless to say, bureaucratic failures are pointed out to the public by the various news media and information sources described in Chapter 6. Scandals and disasters, we learned, are particularly attractive to the news media, so information about them gets to the public in short order through a variety of outlets, from television news broadcasts to blogs. The news media are also more likely to report goings-on in bureaucratic agencies when there is controversy—for example, the debate over the FBI's use of the USA Patriot Act to conduct surveillance on American citizens. The news media are less likely, perhaps, to report on the routine activities of reasonably effective agencies, whether the Agriculture Extension Service or the National Archives.

Interest Groups

Because bureaucratic agencies make important decisions that affect many people, interest and advocacy groups pay lots of attention to what they do and use a variety of lobbying tools (see Chapter 7) to influence these decisions. Groups lobby Congress, for example, to shape the missions of executive branch departments and agencies, as environmental organizations did to give the EPA authority over development in wetland areas. Groups also lobby bureaucratic agencies directly, as when they appear before them to offer testimony on proposed rules. (Public comment is required in many agencies before binding rules can be issued.) Although various environmental, labor, and consumer advocacy associations regularly offer formal comment on rules, this process is dominated by associations that represent business and the professions who often get their way,[36] as we found to be the case in Chapter 7. It is hardly surprising, then, to learn that livestock producers for years have been able to prevent the imposition by the Department of Agriculture of stringent rules for tracking cattle products despite several outbreaks of "mad cow" disease in recent years.

? How is interest groups' lobbying of federal agencies different from lobbying Congress or the president directly? In what ways does this kind of lobbying support or veer from the democratic model?

Reforming the Federal Bureaucracy

13.6 Assess what's wrong and what's right with the federal bureaucracy

How can we improve the federal bureaucracy? The answer depends on what a person thinks is wrong with it and what needs improving. Let's look at some possibilities.

Scaling Back Its Size

If the problem with the federal bureaucracy is perceived to be its size, there are two ways to trim government activities: slimming them down and transferring activities to others, usually states and private-sector contractors. Each solution has its own set of problems.

Cutting the Fat   For observers who worry that the federal bureaucracy is simply too big and costly, mainly due to bloat and waste, the preferred strategy is what might be called the "meat ax" approach. Virtually every candidate seeking office promises to "cut the fat" if elected. Bill Clinton made such a promise during the 1992 presidential campaign, and he carried through after his election. In the early weeks of his administration, he ordered that 100,000 federal jobs be eliminated within four years, that freezes be placed on the salaries of government workers, that cost-of-living pay adjustments be reduced, and that the use of government vehicles and planes be sharply restricted. Needless to say, this approach probably doesn't do much to enhance the morale of federal government employees who receive the clear message in these sorts of actions that they are held in low regard by political leaders and the public.

To some extent this effort to cut the size and cost of the bureaucracy has worked; the number of federal employees has diminished steadily since the early 1990s. The cuts have taken place even as the government has initiated new programs. (See the "By the Numbers" feature for data on the change and information on how to count the number of employees.) One way this has been done is to offload many activities and their costs to the states; the No Child Left Behind testing requirement, for example, has forced them to hire more people in order to comply with federal law without providing enough federal money to fully compensate the states. Some of the opposition to President Obama's health care reform proposal was that it substantially increased the cost of Medicaid to the states at a time during the Great Recession and the years that followed when the states were in terrible fiscal shape.

As we saw in the chapter-opening story, furthermore, "cutting the fat" sometimes goes too far and cuts into the bone of programs. This often results in decreases in important services and protections for the public. Fewer campgrounds may be available in national parks, for example, the Food and Drug Administration may take longer to examine and approve new drugs, and the Army Corps of Engineers may slow the pace of repairing levees along important waterways.

Privatizing   A much-discussed strategy for scaling back the federal bureaucracy is to contract out some of its functions and responsibilities to the private sector.[37] This **privatization** approach is based on two beliefs:

- Private business can almost always do things better than government.
- Competitive pressure from the private sector will force government agencies to be more efficient.

Privatization has actually been happening for many years. For example, the Defense Department does not produce its own weapons systems but uses an elaborate contracting system to design, build, and purchase fighter planes, submarines, and missiles from private corporations. In Iraq, moreover, the Defense Department depended on private contractors, including companies such as Halliburton and its subsidiary Kellogg Brown and Root, to feed and house soldiers, fight oil field fires and

? What government departments or agencies do you think would work better if they were privatized? Are there any private-sector activities that you think could be managed more effectively or efficiently by the government?

PRIVATE CONTRACTORS AT WAR In recent years, private contractors are increasingly taking on responsibilities once done by government employees. In Iraq and Afghanistan, they have even taken on military roles. Here, contractors help defend American and Spanish troops against Iraqi insurgents in the city of Najaf. How much control does the government have over private contractors?

rebuild oil pipelines, build telephone networks, maintain the military's high-tech weapons, make gasoline deliveries to Iraqi consumers, train local police, protect dignitaries, and interrogate detainees. The Corps of Engineers uses private contractors to build and maintain levees and clear waterways. NASA uses private contractors to build and maintain the space shuttle. Some agencies use private companies to manage their payroll systems and run their food services. Homeland Security has contracted out its effort to build a high-tech security system along the U.S.–Mexican border to Boeing. By the end of President Obama's first year in office, the number of private contractors employed by the U.S. military in Iraq and Afghanistan exceeded the total number of American troops engaged in these two conflicts.[38]

While it is evident to all observers that the contracting out has been expanding dramatically, the exact number of people working on a contract basis for the federal government is hard to determine.[39] But expand it has; money in the federal budget for private contracts roughly doubled between 2000 and 2007. According to Paul Light, the leading expert in this area, the number of private contractor jobs done for departments and agencies of the executive branch stood at about 7.5 million in 2007, about four times more than the total of federal civilian employees.[40]

Advocates of privatizing simply want to expand the process, turning over to private companies functions such as the postal system, the federal prisons, and air traffic control. Critics worry that privatizing government carries significant costs.[41]

- Some matters seem so central to the national security and well-being that citizens and officials are unwilling to risk that the private sector will necessarily do the job well or at all. A good example is the transfer after 9/11 of the responsibility for screening airline passengers and baggage from the airlines to a new government agency, the Transportation Security Administration.

- Private business firms might not be willing to provide services that are unprofitable. Delivering mail to remote locations is a service the Postal Service provides, for instance, but that a private company might determine is too costly, and eliminate.

- A private business under government contract is several steps removed from political control, and the normal instruments of democratic accountability, however imperfect, might not be as effective in controlling private business as they are in controlling government agencies. The voice of the public, expressed in public opinion polls or elections, might not be heard with much clarity by private companies, particularly if they are the only supplier of some essential service.

- Private contractors may not be bound by many of the regulations and statutes that apply to other executive branch employees. For example, the military apparently has depended a great deal on private contractors to interrogate detainees in Afghanistan, Iraq, and Guantanamo Bay, believing, perhaps, that contractors could use methods not sanctioned for use by active service military personnel. After abuses were uncovered involving security personnel working in Iraq for Blackwell International, the Pentagon said it was tightening the rules under which its contractors worked.

- Citizens are not customers, and privatization tends to serve the latter. A citizen in a democracy usually requires not only satisfaction with a product or service like a customer; but also equity, transparency, and accountability as required by our constitutional rules.

- Many public services and the agencies that provide them were created because of what are called "market failures," activities that are necessary but that private firms either cannot provide or cannot be trusted to provide. One of the things that led to the collapse of the financial industry, for example, was that the private rating agencies like Moody's and Standard and Poors, hired by investment banks to rate their securities, gave AAA and AA ratings to mortgage-backed securities built on a weak foundation of subprime loans.[42]

Some common criticisms of privatizing are that government exists in some areas precisely because of market failure; and government in a democracy emphasizes accountability and equity, often at the expense of efficiency and effectiveness, because of our constitution.

Becoming More Businesslike

If the problem with the federal bureaucracy is perceived to be the inefficiencies of its operations and excessive **red tape**, then the key to reform might be to reinvent governmental bureaucracy along businesslike lines. President Clinton turned over the responsibility for "reinventing government" to Vice President Al Gore at the beginning of his administration. The term "reinventing government" comes from a popular and influential book by that name written by David Osborne and Ted Gaebler,[43] although the ideas for these reforms come from advocates of what is called "the new public management."[44] "Reinventing" advocates propose transforming the federal bureaucracy not only by cutting the fat and privatizing (as discussed in the preceding section), but also by introducing business principles into the executive branch. They believe that government agencies will provide better public services if they are run like private businesses: using pay-for-performance to determine salaries, for example, or focusing more on customer needs. Most observers have not been impressed by either the scale or effectiveness of efforts to make government more "businesslike."[45]

Protecting Against Bureaucratic Abuses of Power

Many people believe that the problem with a bureaucracy of the size, shape, and power of our present one is that it is potentially unresponsive to the public and a

How big is the federal government?

When Bill Clinton proclaimed in 1996 that "the era of big government is over," he was sharing a vision of government espoused by his two conservative predecessors: Ronald Reagan and George H. W. Bush. The notion that the government in Washington is too big and ought to be cut down to size is a recurring theme in American political discourse. Recently, the call to "downsize" or "right size" government has taken an especially strong turn, with recent presidents committed to this vision of a "leaner" and theoretically more efficient government. But just how big is government really?

Why It Matters A significant number of Americans want a smaller government that does less; a significant number of Americans want a bigger government that does more. Whichever camp you fall into, it makes sense that we have accurate measures of what is actually going on.

Calculating the Size of the Federal Government In addition to using the size of the federal budget as a measure of the size of government—we do this in Chapter 17—it is fairly common among academics, journalists, and politicians to use the number of federal employees as a simple, straightforward measure. Using this metric, the size of the federal government (not including the armed services or the U.S. Postal Service) is not only relatively small at roughly 1.8 million employees out of a total of 154 million civilian employees in 2007, but shrinking.

Criticism of the Measure of Government Size Critics point out that the number of federal civilian employees measures only a portion of the total number of employees who produce goods and services for the federal government. Paul Light, the leading student of this issue, suggests that the following employees should be added to the total:

- Employees who work in government contract–created jobs, such as employees working for defense contractors on federal projects.
- Employees who work in government grant–created jobs, such as employees working on federally funded road construction grants or on federally funded university research projects.
- Employees hired by state and local governments to meet federal mandates in areas such as child health and nutrition, safe schools, and pollution control.
- U.S. Postal Service workers, who are not counted as federal civilian employees because they work for a government corporation.
- Uniformed military personnel.

Adding these categories for 2002, the last year for which we have reasonable reliable data in all categories, gives a total of direct and indirect federal government employment of almost 17 million people, about as many as worked in the American manufacturing sector that year.

So, is the federal government growing or shrinking in terms of the number of its employees? The following graph shows what is happening. (Unfortunately, there is no information available for "mandate-created jobs" prior to 1996, so it cannot be included in the graph.)

The picture is pretty clear: although the overall size of government is considerably larger than it first appears using only the numbers of federal civilian employees, the size of government diminished a bit between 1990 and 2002. While the number of federal civilian employees decreased, as did the

---

whistle-blowers

People who bring official misconduct in their agencies to public attention.

dangerous threat to individual liberty. The preferred solution has been closer control over the bureaucracy by elected political bodies and by clear legislative constraints. Accordingly, many legislative enactments have tried to keep bureaucratic activity within narrow boundaries. The Freedom of Information Act of 1966 was designed to enhance the ability of the press and private citizens to obtain information about bureaucratic policies and activities. The Ethics in Government Act of 1978 strengthened requirements of financial disclosure by officials and prohibitions against conflicts of interest. Some reformers would like to see greater protection provided for **whistle-blowers**—bureaucrats who report corruption, financial mismanagement, abuses of power, or other official malfeasance.

A potentially important innovation has been the rapid growth in what has been called e-government (and sometimes, "Google your government"), a reform based on a statute passed in 2006, that requires the OMB to make more information available online in a user-friendly database for public inspection of bureaucratic activities and expenditures. People can go, for example, to stimulus.gov to track where their economic stimulus dollars are being spent.

number of uniformed military personnel before 9/11, these were almost offset by increases in the numbers of employees covered by grants and contracts. It is worth noting that after 2002 (not shown in this graph), the number of jobs accounted for by federal contractors—mainly associated with the wars in Iraq and Afghanistan, defense-related procurement and research, the post-Katrina rebuilding, and border control—soared to 7.5 million in 2007, up from a little more than 5 million in 2002.

What to Watch For Numbers that are reported by government, journalists, and academics about government may often be correct, yet incomplete. Always try to expand your search to include multiple measures of the phenomenon or institution you are trying to understand.

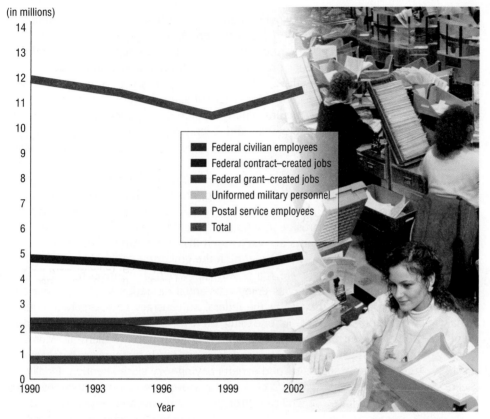

Legend:
- Federal civilian employees
- Federal contract–created jobs
- Federal grant–created jobs
- Uniformed military personnel
- Postal service employees
- Total

Federal Government Jobs

What Do You Think? In formulating an opinion about the appropriate size for government, consider what responsibilities and tasks should be the responsibility of the federal government. Are these responsibilities and tasks being accomplished to your satisfaction? Are there too many people working either directly or indirectly for the federal government in terms of the responsibilities and tasks? If so, where should staff be cut? Too few? Where should people be added?

Sources: Paul C. Light, *The True Size of Government* (Washington, D.C.: The Brookings Institution, 1999); Paul Light, *Fact Sheet on the True Size of Government* (Washington, D.C.: Brookings Center for Public Service, 2004); Bernard Wysocki Jr., "Is U.S. Government Outsourcing Its Brain," *The Wall Street Journal,* March 30, 2007, p. 1.

Increasing Presidential Control

One suggestion for reform of the federal bureaucracy is to have it more closely controlled by elected representatives of the people. This suggestion follows directly from the principle of popular sovereignty, which requires that the elected representatives of the people closely control the bureaucracy. Popular sovereignty implies that administrative discretion should be narrowed as much as possible and that elected officials should communicate clear directions and unambiguous policies to bureaucratic agencies. (Note that this goal is very different from the one envisioned by the advocates of privatization and reinventing government.) Some advocates of popular sovereignty have argued that the president is the only public official who has an interest in seeing that the bureaucracy *as a whole* is well run and coherently organized. Accordingly, one suggestion for reform is to increase the powers of the president so that he can be the chief executive, in fact and not just in name.[46] This is the view of the president and the bureaucracy shared by many liberals who admire the leadership of Franklin Roosevelt during the Great Depression and the Second World War and many conservatives who advocated so strongly for the concept of the unitary executive during George W. Bush's two terms.

Does the bureaucracy advance or retard democracy?

The framers of the Constitution would no doubt be surprised by the great expansion in the responsibilities of the national government and the growth in the size of the bureaucracy required to carry out these responsibilities. Although they believed they had put in place constitutional provisions to restrain the size and reach of the national government—federalism, separation of powers, and checks and balances—they failed to account for the substantial democratization of the American republic or for structural changes demanding increased government involvement: urbanization, scientific and technological innovations, economic crises, the emergence of the United States as a superpower, and the need to provide national security in an interconnected world.

But as it has grown in size and reach, the federal bureaucracy has also grown more democratic in many ways. For one thing, most of what government bureaucrats do is carry out the missions defined for them by elected public officials, namely, Congress and the president, who are quite attentive to public opinion. And for the most part, civil servants are very much like other Americans, both in their demographic makeup and in what they think the government should be doing.

On the other hand, there are many ways in which the bureaucracy falls short in terms of democracy. Bureaucrats enjoy substantial discretion in carrying out their missions—much of what they do in the federal bureaucracy goes largely unnoticed, making popular control difficult. For one thing, there are so many decisions being made and rules being issued that no one could possibly keep track of them all. Moreover, many of the rules issued by bureaucrats and decisions made by them are highly technical in nature, with only specialists and experts paying very close attention. Finally, the elite and big business backgrounds of most high-level presidential appointees must cause some concern for those who care strongly about democratic responsiveness.

While democratic theorists may not be comfortable with every aspect of bureaucratic growth, the expansion of the role of government in American life, and the creation of the bureaucratic machinery associated with this expansion, is testament to the impact of democratic forces in American politics. Government has taken on new responsibilities in large part because of the demands of the people over many years that it do so. That the bureaucracy that emerged to carry out these new government responsibilities has sometimes seemed inefficient and at cross purposes is probably best explained by the separation of powers and checks and balances designed by the framers.

SUMMARY

13.1 Compare and contrast our executive branch bureaucracy with those in other countries

- Compared to public bureaucracies in the other rich democracies, ours in the United States operates in a more hostile political culture environment where anti–big government attitudes are widespread, it is less coherently organized, and it has several masters in addition to the chief executive (the president).

13.2 Outline the structure of the executive branch

- The federal bureaucracy is comprised of cabinet departments, agencies and bureaus within departments, independent agencies, government corporations and foundations, independent regulatory commissions, and quasi-governmental organizations such as the Federal Reserve Board.

- The executive branch has grown in size and responsibility over the course of our history. This growth is a consequence of a transformation in the conception of the proper role of government because of structural changes in the economy and society.

13.3 Identify the kinds of activities bureaucrats perform

- Bureaucrats are involved in three major kinds of activities: executing the law, regulating, and adjudicating disputes. In each of these, they exercise a great deal of discretion.

- Although *bureaucracy* is not a popular concept in the American political tradition, we have created a sizable one. The reason is partly that bureaucratic organizations have certain strengths that make them attractive for accomplishing large-scale tasks like preparing for war and delivering retirement checks.

13.4 Determine how demographically representative bureaucrats are

- Bureaucrats in the merit services are very much like other Americans in terms of demographic characteristics and attitudes. Political appointees (the most important bureaucratic decision makers) are very different from their fellow citizens, coming from more elite backgrounds.
- Because they are unelected policymakers, democratic theory demands that we be concerned about who the bureaucrats are.

13.5 Isolate various influences on executive branch decision making

- Though bureaucrats are technically independent of influences beyond the bureaucratic chain of command

and the rules and regulations that define their agency missions and operations, bureaucrats are in fact influenced by other political and governmental actors and institutions, including the president, Congress, and the courts, as well as public opinion and interest groups.

13.6 Assess what's wrong and what's right with the federal bureaucracy

- Proposals to reform the executive branch are related to what reformers believe is wrong with the federal bureaucracy. Those who worry most about size and inefficiency propose budget and personnel cuts, privatization, and the introduction of business principles into government. Those who want to make democracy more of a reality propose giving more control over the bureaucracy to the president and diminishing the role of interest groups.
- Problems with the bureaucracy, while real, are either exaggerated or the result of forces outside the bureaucracy itself: the constitutional rules and the struggle between the president and Congress.

TEST YOURSELF

Answer key begins on page T-1.

13.1 Compare and contrast our executive branch bureaucracy with those in other countries

1. The United States has a large bureaucracy because Americans have tremendous confidence in the ability of government to tackle our nation's problems.
True / False
2. Which of the following does *not* accurately describe the U.S. bureaucracy?
a. The U.S. bureaucracy is accountable to Congress.
b. The U.S. bureaucracy is accountable to the president.
c. The U.S. bureaucracy was designed in a piecemeal fashion.
d. The U.S. bureaucracy is an organizational hodgepodge.
e. The U.S. bureaucracy has clear lines of control, responsibility, and accountability.
3. Evaluate whether the European civil service model or the U.S. civil service model is superior.

13.2 Outline the structure of the executive branch

4. The size of government and the scope of its responsibilities have increased since the founding.
True / False

5. Which of the following are headed by cabinet-level secretaries?
a. Bureaus
b. Agencies
c. Government corporations
d. Independent regulatory commissions
e. Departments

13.3 Identify the kinds of activities bureaucrats perform

6. Policies established by regulatory agencies carry the force and effect of law only after they have been formally approved by Congress.
True / False
7. Which of the following bureaucratic functions was the Transportation Department engaged in when it levied a $1.4 million fine on Toyota in 2010 for its slow response to safety problems with some of its vehicles?
a. Regulating
b. Adjudicating
c. Implementing
d. Executing programs
e. Executing policies

8. Evaluate whether bureaucratic discretion helps or hinders democracy.

13.4 Determine how demographically representative bureaucrats are

9. The president is constitutionally prohibited from appointing anyone who played an active role in the president's election campaign to serve as a high-level member of the executive branch.
   True / False
10. Most bureaucrats are selected using what primary criterion?
    a. Merit
    b. Partisanship
    c. Patronage
    d. Spoils
    e. Nepotism
11. Evaluate whether you are more interested in a career with the civil service or with the private sector.

13.5 Isolate various influences on executive branch decision making

12. The federal courts may determine whether bureaucratic actions violate the Constitution.
    True / False
13. Which of the following is *not* a way for Congress to influence the bureaucracy?
    a. Congress passes laws that establish the mission of bureaucratic agencies.
    b. The House confirms presidential appointments to the executive branch.
    c. Congress controls the budgets of the various bureaucratic agencies.

d. The Senate can hold oversight hearings to gather information about the performance of the bureaucracy.
   e. Congress uses inspectors general to watch for waste, fraud, and bureaucratic abuse of power.
14. What is the most powerful tool that the president has to influence the decisions made by bureaucracies? Provide a rationale for your answer.

13.6 Assess what's wrong and what's right with the federal bureaucracy

15. Due to recurring problems with the shoddy workmanship and other abuses of authority, the executive branch has dramatically reduced the number of federal contractors.
    True / False
16. Which of the following arguments is most likely to be made by someone in favor of privatizing government functions?
    a. Some governmental functions are so vital to America's well-being that they should be turned over to the private sector.
    b. Private firms may be unwilling to perform services that are unprofitable.
    c. Private firms are less likely to respond to electoral pressures to do a good job.
    d. Private firms are best able to address "market failures."
    e. Private-sector competition promotes government efficiency.
17. Would becoming more businesslike improve the federal bureaucracy?

PEARSON mypoliscilab EXERCISES

Apply what you learned in this chapter on MyPoliSciLab.

Read on **mypoliscilab.com**

eText: Chapter 13

Study and Review on **mypoliscilab.com**

Pre-Test
Post-Test
Chapter Exam
Flashcards

Watch on **mypoliscilab.com**

Video: The CDC and the Swine Flu
Video: Internal Problems at the FDA

Explore on **mypoliscilab.com**

Simulation: You Are a Deputy Director of the Census Bureau
Simulation: You Are a Federal Administrator
Simulation: You Are the Head of FEMA
Simulation: You Are the President of MEDICORP
Comparative: Comparing Bureaucracies
Timeline: The Evolution of the Federal Bureaucracy
Visual Literacy: The Changing Face of the Federal Bureaucracy

INTERNET SOURCES

The Federal Register
www.archives.gov/federal_register
All rules issued by federal agencies can be found here.

Fedworld
www.fedworld.gov/
The gateway to the federal government's numerous websites; connections to virtually every federal department, bureau, commission, and foundation, as well as access to government statistics and reports.

Government Is Good
www.governmentisgood.com
A site replete with information about what government does well.

The President's Cabinet
www.whitehouse.gov/government/cabinet.html

A site listing all cabinet members, as well as links to each department's website.

Office of Personnel Management
www.opm.gov/
The best site to find statistics and other information about federal government employees.

The Cato Institute
www.cato.org
The conservative institute's home page, featuring defenses of small government and proposals to solve social and economic problems without creating a bigger government.

SUGGESTIONS FOR FURTHER READING

Aberbach, Joel D., and Mark A. Peterson, eds., *The Executive Branch* (New York: Oxford University Press, 2005).
A highly accessible collection of essays on diverse aspects of the federal executive branch by leading scholars and practitioners.

Goodsell, Charles T. *The Case for Bureaucracy,* 4th ed. Washington, D.C.: CQ Press, 2003.
A well-written polemic that suggests that most criticisms of bureaucracy are not well founded.

Gormley, William T., and Steven J. Balla. *Bureaucracy and Democracy: Accountability and Performance.* Washington, DC: CQ Press, 2007.
Examination of how well government bureaucracies perform and how accountable they are to the public.

Kerwin, Cornelius M. *Rulemaking: How Government Agencies Write Law and Make Policy.* Washington, D.C.: CQ Press, 2003.
A comprehensive treatment of rule-making by executive branch agencies.

Light, Paul C. *A Government Ill Executed: The Decline of the Federal Service and How to Reverse It.* Cambridge, MA: Harvard University Press, 2009.
A thorough examination of what has gone wrong with the executive branch's ability to execute the law and serious proposals on what to do about it by America's leading scholar on the federal bureaucracy.

The 9/11 Commission Report: Final Report of the National Commission on Terrorist Attacks Upon the United States. New York: W. W. Norton, 2004.
An exhaustive study of how 9/11 happened and a set of recommendations—including reorganization of the executive branch—for better homeland defense and security.

Washington Monthly.
Washington's leading journal of "bureaucracy bashing"; filled with outrageous and (sometimes) illuminating stories.

14 | The Courts

IN THIS CHAPTER

14.1 Trace the evolution of judicial power in the United States

14.2 Outline the organization of the U.S. court system

14.3 Describe the background of appointees to the federal bench and the process by which they are appointed

14.4 Outline how the Supreme Court decides on cases

14.5 Evaluate the Supreme Court as a national policymaker

14.6 Assess the factors and players that influence Supreme Court decisions

THE BATTLE FOR THE COURTS

Tension filled the hearing room as Samuel Alito, President Bush's nominee for a position on the U.S. Supreme Court, began testifying before the Senate Judiciary Committee on January 9, 2006. Knowing that federal courts were deciding cases having to do with the most contentious issues of the day—including presidential powers in times of war, affirmative action, gay rights, the relationship between church and state, the role of the federal government in relationship to the states, and more—Republican and Democratic partisans and conservative and liberal advocacy groups were mobilized to contest Alito's nomination. Lurking in the background was the issue of the judicial filibuster. Republicans believed the filibuster (see Chapter 11 for more on the filibuster and cloture) could not be properly used when the Senate was exercising its constitutional duty to "advise and consent" on judicial nominations. Most Democrats believed it was the only way to prevent the accession of judges to the federal bench who would threaten hard-won rights and protections, particularly a woman's right to terminate her pregnancy. Would the Democrats use it to block Alito? If they did, would Republicans ban the practice,

using their majority in the Senate to redefine the chamber's rules?

Partisan tensions over the judicial filibuster had been festering for years. Things first came to a head on November 14, 2003, when, after 40 hours of continuous debate, Republicans fell 7 votes short of the 60 votes needed to end Democratic filibusters blocking Senate votes on several very conservative Bush federal judicial nominees, including Priscilla Owen for the Fifth Circuit. Republicans were furious. Senate Judiciary Chairman Orrin Hatch (R–UT) fumed, "This is petty politics ... cheap politics ... and can lead to more partisan division in the Senate."[1]

Democrats were not impressed, pointing out that Republicans had blocked many Clinton nominees during the 1990s but had not needed the filibuster because, as the majority, they could stop nominations in committee, never allowing them to reach the floor of the Senate. As chair of the Judiciary Committee during the Clinton years, the very same Orrin Hatch, who insisted in 2003 that every nominee was entitled to an "up or down" vote, refused to hold hearings for several

TO GO ON HER SEAT
SOME INTERES

Clinton nominees and delayed hearings for others for up to 18 months.

The issue was revived when President Bush renominated Priscilla Owen in early 2005. When Democrats announced they would again use the filibuster to block the nomination, Majority Leader Frist warned that he would ask the presiding officer of the Senate—Vice President Richard Cheney—to disallow it. If Democrats appealed, Republicans would approve the ruling by a simple majority vote—a filibuster cannot be used on issues related to rulings by the presiding officer—which they could easily muster. Democrats warned that if this so-called nuclear option was imposed by Republicans, they would tie up the business of the Senate for the foreseeable future, something they could easily do, given that much of the Senate's business is done through unanimous consent. Partisans on both sides in the Senate and the country were itching for a fight on this issue because they believed the stakes had never been higher. A train wreck loomed.

Into the fray stepped the so-called gang of 14, a group of Republican and Democratic moderates who worked out a compromise in May 2005. Wielding enormous power because their 14 votes would be decisive on any vote related to this issue, whether on a cloture vote to end a filibuster or a vote on rulings from the presiding officer, they agreed that the judicial filibuster could be used only in undefined "extraordinary circumstances." Under the agreement, the Senate confirmed the long-delayed nominations of Priscilla Owen and two other nominees, but took no action on two other nominees who presumably fit the "extraordinary circumstances" requirement that would allow Democrats to use the filibuster.

Most observers believed that the agreement was just a temporary truce that might break down at any time, especially when it came to nominations to the Supreme Court. The agreement held, however, when John Roberts was nominated for the post of Chief Justice after the death of Chief Justice William Rehnquist in late 2005, perhaps because he was a conservative jurist replacing the conservative Rehnquist. Conservative judge Samuel Alito was another matter entirely, because President Bush nominated him to replace the retiring Sandra Day O'Connor, a relatively moderate voice and swing vote on the Court who played an important role in protecting abortion rights and affirming the use, under certain circumstances, of affirmative action in higher education admissions. In the end, however, the Democrats were unable to mount much of a challenge to Alito, and calls for a filibuster by a few Democratic senators failed to gain traction. His nomination was confirmed on January 31, 2006. As predicted by almost everyone, Alito's ascension to the Court swung it sharply in a conservative direction on issues ranging from civil rights to environmental protection and the role of corporations in campaign finance,[2] matters to be examined in greater detail later in this chapter. The fundamental balance on the Court was not affected much when Obama nominee Sonia Sotomayor joined the Court in 2009 because she was a liberal replacing a liberal, David Souter, who retired. The same thing was true regarding the appointment of Elena Kagan in 2010; she was a liberal replacing a liberal stalwart, John Paul Stevens, so the balance on the Court was unaffected. The key appointment remained that of Alito replacing O'Connor in 2006, which created a solid conservative 5–4 majority under the able leadership of Chief Justice Roberts.

In the system of separated powers and federalism created by the framers, the judicial branch, most especially the Supreme Court, assesses, in cases that come before it, the legitimacy of actions taken by the other two branches and by the states in light of the Constitution. Although the Supreme Court does not legislate or regulate on its own, its decisions strongly influence the overall shape of federal and state policies in a number of important areas. As such, the Supreme Court is a key national policymaker, every bit as much of the governing process as the president and Congress.

THINKING CRITICALLY About This Chapter

Using the FRAMEWORK

You will see in this chapter that the Court is embedded in a rich governmental, political linkage, and structural environment that shapes its behavior. The other branches of government impinge on and influence its composition, deliberations, and rulings; political linkage institutions such as elections, interest groups, and social movements matter; and structural factors such as economic and social change influence its agenda and decisions.

Using the DEMOCRACY STANDARD

You will see in this chapter that an unelected Court makes important decisions about public policies, raising questions about the degree to which popular sovereignty and majority rule prevail in our system. You will also see that the Court often turns its attention to cases that involve issues of political equality and liberty, so essential to the existence of a healthy representative democracy.

The Foundations of Judicial Power

14.1 Trace the evolution of judicial power in the United States

The judicial Power of the United States shall be vested in one supreme Court, and in such inferior Courts as the Congress may from time to time ordain and establish.
—U.S. CONSTITUTION, ARTICLE III, SECTION 1

We are under a Constitution, but the Constitution is what the judges say it is, and the judiciary is the safeguard of our liberty and our property under the Constitution.
—CHIEF JUSTICE CHARLES EVANS HUGHES (1907)

Constitutional Powers

The Constitution speaks only briefly about the judicial branch and doesn't provide much guidance about what it is supposed to do or how it is supposed to go about its job. The document says little about the powers of the judicial branch in relationship to the other two federal branches or about its responsibilities in the area of constitutional interpretation. Article III is considerably shorter than Articles I and II, which focus on Congress and the president. It creates a federal judicial branch, it creates the office of "chief justice of the United States," it states that judges shall serve life terms, it specifies the categories of cases the Court may or must hear (to be explained later), and it grants Congress the power to create additional federal courts as needed. Article III of the Constitution is virtually devoid of detail.[3]

> **judicial review**
> The power of the Supreme Court to declare actions of the other branches and levels of government unconstitutional.

Judicial Review

Extremely interesting is the Constitution's silence about **judicial review**, the power of the Supreme Court to declare state and federal laws and actions null and void when they conflict with the Constitution. Debate has raged for many years over the question of whether the framers intended that the Court should have this power.[4]

The Framers surely believed that the Constitution ought to prevail when other laws were in conflict with it. But did they expect the Supreme Court to make the decisions in this matter? Jefferson and Madison thought that Congress and the president were capable of rendering their own judgments about the constitutionality of their actions. Alexander Hamilton, however, believed that the power of judicial review was inherent in the notion of the separation of powers and was essential to balanced government. As he put it in *The Federalist,* No. 78 (see the Appendix), the very purpose of constitutions is to place limitations on the powers of government, and it is only the Court that can ensure such limits in the United States. The legislative branch, in particular, is unlikely to restrain itself without the helping hand of the judiciary.

There is reason to believe that Hamilton's view was the prevailing one for a majority of the framers.[5] They were firm believers, for instance, in the idea that there was a "higher law" to which governments and nations must conform. Their enthusiasm for written constitutions was based on their belief that governments

ADVOCATES OF JUDICIAL REVIEW
Although the Constitution is silent on the issue of judicial review, many of the Founders probably agreed with Alexander Hamilton (left), who argued that the Supreme Court's power to interpret the Constitution and declare state and federal laws and actions unconstitutional is inherent in the notion of the separation of powers. However, it was not until the Supreme Court's 1803 *Marbury* v. *Madison* decision that Chief Justice John Marshall (right) affirmed the Court's power of judicial review. How might a lack of the power of judicial review hinder the classic American system of checks and balances?

must be limited in what they could do in the service of some higher or more fundamental law, such as that pertaining to individual rights. The attitudes of the time, then, strongly supported the idea that judges, conversant with the legal tradition and free from popular pressures, were best able to decide when statutory and administrative laws were in conflict with fundamental law.[6]

Marbury v. *Madison*

Chief Justice John Marshall boldly claimed the power of judicial review for the U.S. Supreme Court in the case of *Marbury* v. *Madison* in 1803.[7] The case began with a flurry of judicial appointments by President John Adams in the final days of his presidency, after his Federalist Party had suffered a resounding defeat in the election of 1800. The apparent aim of these so-called midnight appointments was to establish the federal courts as an outpost of Federalist Party power (federal judges are appointed for life) in the midst of Jeffersonian control of the presidency and the Congress.

William Marbury was one of the midnight appointments, but he was less lucky than most. His commission was signed and sealed, but it had not been delivered to him before the new administration took office. Jefferson, knowing what Adams and the Federalists were up to, ordered Secretary of State James Madison not to deliver the commission. Marbury sued Madison, claiming that the secretary of state was obligated to deliver the commission and asked the Supreme Court to issue a *writ of mandamus* to force Madison to do so.

Marshall faced a quandary. If the Court decided in favor of Marbury, Madison would almost surely refuse to obey, opening the Court to ridicule for its weakness. The fact that Marshall was a prominent Federalist political figure might even provoke the Jeffersonians to take more extreme measures against the Court. But if the Court ruled in favor of Madison, it would suggest that an executive official could defy without penalty the clear provisions of the law.

Marshall's solution was worthy of Solomon. The Court ruled that William Marbury was entitled to his commission and that James Madison had broken the law in failing to deliver it. By this ruling, the Court rebuked Madison. However, the Court said it could not compel Madison to comply with the law because the section of the Judiciary Act of 1789 that granted the Court the power to issue writs of mandamus was unconstitutional. It was unconstitutional, he said, because it expanded the **original jurisdiction** of the Supreme Court as defined in Article III, which could not be done except by constitutional amendment.

On the surface, the decision was an act of great modesty. It suggested that the Court could not force the action of an executive branch official. It suggested that Congress had erred in the Judiciary Act of 1789 by trying to give the Supreme Court too much power. Beneath the surface, however, was a less modest act: the claim that judicial review was the province of the judicial branch alone. In Marshall's words in his written opinion, "It is emphatically the province and duty of the judicial department to say what the law is." In making this claim, he was following closely Hamilton's argument in *The Federalist*, No. 78.

Until quite recently, the Supreme Court used the power of judicial review with great restraint, perhaps recognizing that its regular use would invite retaliation by the other branches. Judicial review of a congressional act was not exercised again until 54 years after *Marbury* and was used to declare acts of Congress unconstitutional only about 230 times from then until 2007. However, the Court has been much less constrained about overruling the laws of the states and localities; it did so more than 1,100 times during this same period.[8] During the 1990s and early 2000s, the Rehnquist Court was much more inclined to review and overturn congressional actions, especially in cases involving federalism and the powers of Congress under the commerce clause (see Chapter 3), trimming back the power of the federal government relative

original jurisdiction

The authority of a court to be the first to hear a particular kind of case.

to the states. Indeed, it invalidated congressional actions at a rate double that of the Warren Court of the 1960s, considered by many to be the most "activist" Court since the early 1930s.[9]

The Court has been less inclined to exercise judicial review on presidential actions, though some important ones have occurred during our history.[10] Between 2004 and 2008, however, the Court four times invalidated presidential actions pertaining to the treatment of detainees designated as enemy combatants (see Chapter 15).

Judicial Review and Democracy

Judicial review involves the right of a body shielded from direct accountability to the people—federal judges are appointed, not elected, and serve for life (barring impeachment for unseemly, unethical, or illegal behavior)—to set aside the actions of government bodies whose members are elected. Many believe that judicial review has no place in a democratic society. One prominent democratic theorist has described the issue this way:

> But the authority of a high court to declare unconstitutional legislation that has been properly enacted by the coordinate constitutional bodies— ... in our system, the Congress and the president—is far more controversial ... The contradiction remains between imbuing an unelected body—or in the American case, five out of nine justices on the Supreme Court—with the power to make policy decisions that affect the lives and welfare of millions of Americans. How, if at all, can judicial review be justified in a democratic order?[11]

Political scientists and legal scholars use the phrase the "counter-majoritarian difficulty," coined by Alexander Bickel in 1962, to describe this enduring problem in the American political system; Bickel described judicial review as a "deviant institution in American democracy."[12] On the other hand, some observers believe that judicial review is the only way to protect the rights of political and racial minorities, to check the potential excesses of the other two government branches and the states, and to preserve the rules of the democratic process.

Many political scientists believe that the problem of democratic accountability of a nonelected judiciary with life tenure is less dire than it seems on the surface because the Supreme Court and other federal courts are influenced directly and indirectly by elected officials, public opinion, and other important actors in American society.[13] We come back to this issue later in this chapter.

? Do you think that judicial review would be supported by the framers, even if it was not specifically detailed in the Constitution? Is support for the power of judicial review in the *Federalist Papers* enough to validate its use?

The U.S. Court System: Organization and Jurisdiction

14.2 Outline the organization of the U.S. court system

Our country has one judicial system for the national government (the federal courts) and another in each of the states. In each state, courts adjudicate cases on the basis of the state's own constitution, statutes, and administrative rules.[14] In total, the great bulk of laws, legal disputes, and court decisions (roughly 99 percent) are located in the states. Most important political and constitutional issues, however, eventually reach the federal courts. In this chapter, our focus is on these federal courts. In the following sections, we'll look at the source of the federal court's power and the organization of its system.

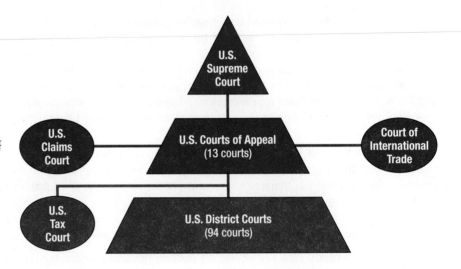

FIGURE 14.1 The U.S. Federal
Court System

The federal court system is a three-tiered
pyramidal system, with the Supreme Court
at the top. Below it are 13 federal courts of
appeal and 94 district courts, with at least
one district in each state. Additional courts
exist to hear cases in highly specialized
areas, such as taxes, international trade,
and financial claims against the U.S.
government. *Source:* Administrative Office
of the U.S. Courts.

constitutional courts

Federal courts created by Congress under
the authority of Article III of the Constitution.

legislative courts

Highly specialized federal courts created by
Congress under the authority of Article I of
the Constitution.

Constitutional Provisions

The only court specifically mentioned in the Constitution's Article III is the
U.S. Supreme Court. The framers left to Congress the tasks of designing
the details of the Supreme Court and establishing "such inferior courts as
the Congress may from time to time ordain and establish." Beginning
with the Judiciary Act of 1789, Congress has periodically reorganized the
federal court system. The end result is a three-tiered pyramidal system
(see Figure 14.1), with a handful of off-shoots. At the bottom are 94 U.S.
federal district courts, with at least one district in each state. In the middle
are 13 courts of appeal. At the top of the pyramid is the Supreme Court. These courts
are called **constitutional courts** because they were created by Congress under Article
III, which discusses the judicial branch. Congress has also created a number of courts
to adjudicate cases in highly specialized areas of concern, such as taxes, patents, and
maritime law. These were established under Article I, which specifies the duties and
powers of Congress, and are called **legislative courts**.

Article III does not offer many guidelines for the federal court system, but the
few requirements that are stated are very important. The Constitution requires, for
instance, that federal judges serve "during good behavior," which means, in practice, until they retire or die in office, as Chief Justice William Rehnquist did in 2005
at the age of 81. Because impeachment by Congress is the only way to remove
federal judges, the decision about who will be a judge is an important one. Article III
also states that Congress cannot reduce the salaries of judges once they are in
office. This provision was designed to maintain the independence of the judiciary
by protecting it from legislative intimidation.

Article III also specifies the subject matter of cases that are solely the province
of the federal courts:

- The Constitution (e.g., disputes involving the First Amendment or the commerce clause).

- Federal statutes and treaties (including disputes involving ambassadors and
other diplomats).

- Admiralty and maritime issues (disputes involving shipping and commerce
on the high seas).

- Controversies in which the U.S. government is a party.

- Disputes between the states.

- Disputes between a state and a citizen of another state.
- Disputes between a state (or citizen of a state) and foreign states or citizens.

Federal District Courts

Most cases in the federal court system are first heard in one of the 94 district courts. District courts are courts of original jurisdiction, that is, courts where cases are first heard; they do not hear appeals from other courts. They are also trial courts; some use juries—either **grand juries**, which bring indictments, or **petit (trial) juries**, which decide cases—and in some, cases are heard only by a judge.

Most of the business of the federal courts takes place at this level. In 2008, about 350,000 cases were filed; roughly 76 percent of them were civil cases, and 24 percent were criminal cases.[15] Civil cases include everything from antitrust cases brought by the federal government (as in the Justice Department's successful action against Microsoft in 2000) to commercial and contract disputes between citizens (or businesses) of two or more states. Criminal cases include violations of federal criminal laws, such as bank robbery, interstate drug trafficking, and kidnapping.

Most civil and criminal cases are concluded at this level. In a relatively small number of disputes, however, one of the parties to the case may feel that a mistake has been made in trial procedure or in the law that was brought to bear in the trial, or one of the parties may feel that a legal or constitutional issue is at stake that was not taken into account at the trial stage or was wrongly interpreted. In such cases, one of the parties may appeal to a higher court—a Court of Appeals.

grand juries
Groups of citizens who decide whether there is sufficient evidence to bring an indictment against accused persons.

petit (trial) juries
Juries that hear evidence and sit in judgment on charges brought in civil or criminal cases.

circuit courts
The 12 geographical jurisdictions and one special court that hear appeals from the federal district courts.

appellate courts
Courts that hear cases on appeal from other courts.

briefs
Documents setting out the arguments in legal cases, prepared by attorneys and presented to courts.

opinion
The explanation of the majority's and the minority's reasoning that accompany a court decision.

precedents
Rulings by courts that guide judicial reasoning in subsequent cases.

U.S. Courts of Appeal

The United States is divided into 12 geographic **circuit courts** (see the map in Figure 14.2) that hear appeals from federal district courts. The one for Washington, D.C., not only hears appeals from the federal district court there but also is charged with hearing cases arising from rule-making by federal agencies. There is also a 13th circuit court, called the U.S. Court of Appeals for the Federal Circuit, located in Washington, D.C., that hears cases from all over the nation on patents and government contracts. In 2008, about 61,000 cases were filed in the federal appeals courts, although only about 8,000 reached the formal hearing stage (most of these end in negotiated settlements without going to trial).[16] Cases cannot originate in these courts but must come to them from district courts. Because they exist only to hear appeals, they are referred to as **appellate courts**. New factual evidence cannot be introduced before such courts; no witnesses are called or cross-examined. At the appellate level, lawyers do not examine witnesses or introduce new evidence; instead, they submit **briefs**, which set out the legal issues at stake. Judges usually convene as panels of three (on important cases, there are more—sometimes seven members) to hear oral arguments from the lawyers on each side of the case and to cross-examine them on points of law. Weeks or even months later, after considerable study, writing, and discussion among the judges, the panel issues a ruling. In important cases, the ruling is usually accompanied by an **opinion** that sets forth the majority side's reasoning for the decision.

Once appellate decisions are published, they become **precedents** that guide the decisions of other judges in the same circuit. Although judges do not slavishly follow precedents, they tend to move away from them only when necessary and only in

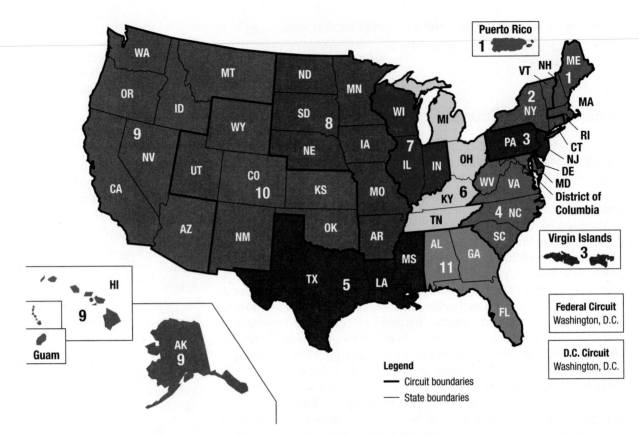

Legend
— Circuit boundaries
— State boundaries

FIGURE 14.2 U.S. Federal Circuit Courts

The United States is divided into 12 geographic regions (including the D.C. Circuit Court), each housing a federal circuit court of appeals. One additional circuit court of appeal, the Federal Circuit Court, is located in Washington, D.C. *Source:* Administrative Office of the U.S. Courts.

stare decisis

The legal doctrine that says precedent should guide judicial decision making.

very small steps. This doctrine of closely following precedents as the basis for legal reasoning is known as **stare decisis**.

It is important to know that the decisions of the 12 geographic circuit courts determine the meaning of laws for the people who live in the states covered by each circuit. They have become more important as they have ruled on more cases, without review by the Supreme Court, which decides fewer than 80 cases each year.

Sometimes particular circuits play a more important role than others in changing constitutional interpretation. For example, the Fourth Circuit Court, based in Richmond, Virginia, has been a leader in the trend toward reasserting the power of the states in the federal system.[17] The Ninth Circuit Court, which sits in San Francisco, on the other hand, is known to be especially liberal on civil rights and civil liberties cases. Because the Supreme Court considers only a relative handful of cases from the appeals courts each term, the rulings of the Fourth Circuit are binding for almost 29 million people in the southeastern United States, while the rulings of the Ninth Circuit Court of Appeal hold for 61 million people in the western United States, including California. Although it has had several of its rulings reversed in recent years by the more conservative U.S. Supreme Court, the Ninth Circuit's rulings, nevertheless, cover more than 61 million people, about 20 percent of the American population.

The Supreme Court

Congress decides how many judges sit on the Supreme Court. The first Court had six members. The Federalists, however, reduced the number to five in 1801 to prevent newly elected president Thomas Jefferson from filling a vacancy. In 1869, Congress set the number at its present nine members (eight associate justices and the chief justice). It has remained this way ever since, weathering the failed effort by President Franklin Roosevelt to "pack" the Court with more politically congenial justices by expanding its size to 15.

The Supreme Court is both a court of original jurisdiction and an appellate court. That is, some cases must first be heard in the Supreme Court. Disputes involving ambassadors and other diplomatic personnel, as well as disputes between two or more states, must start in the Supreme Court rather than in some other court, though the Court is not obliged to hear such cases.[18]

The Supreme Court also, in its most important role, serves as an appellate court for the federal appeals courts and for the highest courts of each of the states. Cases in which a state or federal law has been declared unconstitutional can be heard by the Supreme Court, as can cases in which the highest state court has denied a claim that a state law violates federal law or the Constitution (see Figure 14.3).

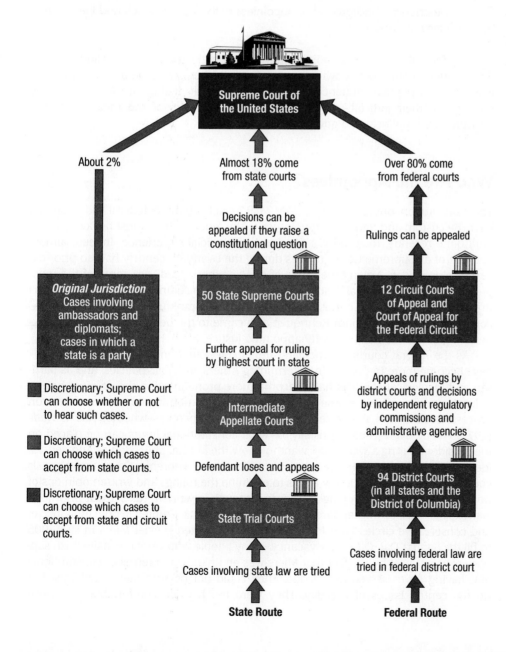

FIGURE 14.3 How Cases Get to the Supreme Court

The vast majority of cases that reach the Supreme Court come to it from the federal court system. Most of the others come on appeal from the highest state courts. A handful originate in the Supreme Court itself. *Source:* Adapted from David O'Brien, *Storm Center: The Supreme Court in American Politics,* 7th ed. (New York: Norton, 2005); percentages of cases are for 2008–2009, calculated by the authors.

Congress determines much of the appellate jurisdiction of the Court. In 1869, following the Civil War, a Congress controlled by radical Republicans removed the Court's power to review cases falling under the Reconstruction program for the South. In 1995, responding to a plea from Chief Justice Rehnquist to lighten the Court's caseload, Congress dropped the requirement that the Supreme Court *must* hear cases in which a state court declares a federal statute unconstitutional. It can choose, but is not obligated, to do so.

Because it is the highest appellate court in the federal court system, the decisions and opinions of the Supreme Court become the main precedents on federal and constitutional questions for courts at all other levels of jurisdiction. It is for this reason that Supreme Court decisions receive so much attention from other political actors, the media, and the public.

Appointment to the Federal Bench

14.3 Describe the background of appointees to the federal bench and the process by which they are appointed

Because federal judges are appointed for life and make important decisions, it matters in a democratic society who they are and how they get to the bench. If they are isolated from popular influence, democracy is at risk. If they are too responsive, they ignore their judicial role to act as neutral arbiters of the meaning of the Constitution in political and government affairs.

Who Are the Appointees?

The Constitution offers no advice on what qualifications a federal judge should have. By custom and tradition, appointees to the federal bench must be lawyers, but until quite recently, they did not have to have judicial experience. Indeed, almost one-half of all Supreme Court justices during the twentieth century had no prior experience as judges. Among the ranks of the "inexperienced" are some of the most prominent and influential justices in our history, including John Marshall, Louis Brandeis, Harlan Stone, Charles Evans Hughes, Felix Frankfurter, and Earl Warren.[19] Former Chief Justice William Rehnquist also came to the bench without judicial experience, as did the most recently appointed justice, Elena Kagan.

As the federal courts—particularly the circuit courts and the Supreme Court—have become more important in determining American public policies, and as partisan and ideological conflicts have become more pronounced in the country, having judicial experience has become more important in the nomination and confirmation process. Because the stakes seem so high to many people—whether *Roe* v. *Wade* (1973) will be overturned, let us say, or what constitutional limits can be placed on the president during a war—they want to know the judicial philosophies and general ideological outlooks of the people who will become Supreme Court and appeals court judges. One way to know this is to examine the rulings and written opinions of nominees who have been judges. The new, though unwritten, rules about prior judicial experience became apparent in the firestorm that erupted within Republican and conservative circles after President Bush nominated Harriet Miers in late 2005 to fill the Sandra Day O'Connor vacancy. Many people who were normally Bush supporters were upset by the fact that Miers was an unknown in terms of constitutional law, having never served as a judge. They could not be sure they could trust her on the central issues of the day. They were much more comfortable with Bush nominees John Roberts and Samuel Alito, who had established extensive conservative records on the federal bench.[20]

Like most lawyers, federal judges tend to come from privileged backgrounds. Moreover, federal judges, and particularly Supreme Court justices, come from the most elite parts of the legal profession. For most of our history, they have been white male Protestants from upper-income or upper-middle-class backgrounds, who attended the most selective and expensive undergraduate and graduate institutions.[21] The current Supreme Court has moved entirely away from the almost exclusive Protestant membership that marked its history—indeed three current members, Ginsburg, Breyer, and Kagan, are Jewish and six, Scalia, Thomas, Kennedy, Roberts, Alito, and Sotomayor, are Catholic—and is more diverse in terms of race and gender than has been true for most of its history as well. On the current Supreme Court, there is one African American (Clarence Thomas), one Hispanic (Sotomayor), and three women (Ginsburg, Sotomayor, and Kagan). The racial and gender representativeness of judicial appointees at the circuit and district court levels is better, and improving rapidly, but it is still a long way from reflecting the composition of the legal profession, much less the American people as a whole.

? Should there be a process for identifying a wider pool of potential candidates for the judiciary that would better reflect the demographic makeup of the American population? Or do you think the existing process has brought good results?

The Appointment Process

Federal judges assume office after they have been nominated by the president and confirmed by the Senate in a process that has become ever more contentious as national politicians have become more partisan.[22] Presidents pay special attention to judicial appointments, because they are a way for presidents to affect public policy long after they leave office.

Presidents take many things into consideration besides merit.[23] No president wants a nomination rejected by the Senate, for example, so he and his advisers consult with key senators, especially those on the Judiciary Committee, before nominations are forwarded. Nominations for district court judgeships are subject to what is called **senatorial courtesy**, the right of the senators in the state where the district court is located to approve the nominee. Senatorial courtesy does not operate, however, in appointments to the circuit courts, whose jurisdictions span more than a

senatorial courtesy
The tradition that a judicial nomination for a federal district court seat be approved by senators from the state where a district court is located before the Senate Judiciary Committee will consider the nomination.

JUDGE SOTOMAYOR MAKES THE ROUNDS Like most recent nominees for the Supreme Court, Sonia Sotomayor had extensive federal judicial experience before her elevation to the high court in 2009. Here, Sotomayor is greeted by Senator Olympia Snowe (R–ME), a member of the Judiciary Committee whose approval is the first step in Senate confirmation. Despite the friendly greeting in the photo, confirmation hearings and votes have become quite contentious. Are there ways to make the process more civil and bipartisan, or are we well served by the current process?

single state, or to the Supreme Court, whose jurisdiction is the entire nation. Nevertheless, presidents must be extremely attentive to the views of key senators.

On occasion, despite presidential efforts to placate it, the Senate has refused to give its consent. Of the 143 nominees for the Supreme Court since the founding of the Republic, the Senate has refused to approve 28 of them, although only five of these refusals have occurred since 1900. Rejection of nominees has usually happened when the president was weak or when the other party was in control of the Senate. The defeat of Ronald Reagan's nominee, Robert Bork, was the product of deep ideological differences between a Republican president and a Democratic-controlled Senate. There have also been several near defeats. G. H. W. Bush's nominee, Clarence Thomas, was confirmed by a margin of only four votes after questions were raised about his legal qualifications and about sexual harassment charges brought by law professor Anita Hill.

As the chapter-opening story shows, Senate confirmations of judicial nominees, especially for the federal appeals court and the Supreme Court, have become very contentious. Battles over presidential judicial nominees raged during the Clinton presidency and during the Bush presidency, culminating in the Democrats' use of the filibuster on several judicial nominations, Republican threats to use the nuclear option to end judicial filibusters, and the fight in the Senate and among advocacy groups over the nomination of Samuel Alito in early 2006.

Although presidents must be concerned about the merit of their candidates and their acceptability to the Senate, they also try by their appointments to make their mark on the future. Presidents go about this in different ways.

For the most part, presidents are interested in nominating judges who share their ideological and program commitments. John Adams nominated John Marshall and a number of other judges to protect Federalist principles during the ascendancy of the Jeffersonians. Franklin Roosevelt tried to fill the courts with judges who favored the New Deal. Ronald Reagan favored conservatives who were committed to rolling back affirmative action and other civil rights claims, abortion rights, protections for criminal defendants, and broad claims of **standing** in environmental cases. Both George H. W. Bush and his son George W. Bush carried on the Reagan tradition of nominating conservative judges to the federal courts.

Bill Clinton, eager to avoid a bitter ideological fight in the Senate, where he was trying to forge a bipartisan coalition to support the North American Free Trade Agreement and a national crime bill, nominated two judges with reputations as moderates for the High Court—Ruth Bader Ginsburg and Stephen Breyer—in the first years of his administration. The Ginsburg nomination was also indicative of Clinton's apparent commitment to diversifying the federal court system. (More than one-half of federal court nominees during his presidency were women and minorities.) Diversity was also important to President Barack Obama. During his first year in office, he nominated 12 people for federal circuit court positions. Of these 12, nine were women and/or minorities. He also was anxious to appoint the first Hispanic to the Supreme Court, and did so in 2009, choosing Sonia Sotomayor.[24] He added another woman to the Court when he nominated Elena Kagan in 2010.

Presidents are often disappointed in how their nominees behave once they reach the Court. Dwight Eisenhower was dumbfounded when his friend and nominee, Earl Warren, led the Court in a liberal direction by transforming constitutional law regarding civil rights and criminal procedure. Richard Nixon was stunned when Chief Justice Warren Burger voted with a unanimous Court to override the president's claim of **executive privilege** and forced him to give up the documents that would seal his fate in the Watergate affair. He and other Court observers were also surprised by the odyssey of his nominee Harry Blackmun, who, despite a conservative judicial record before joining the Court, had become

standing

Authority to bring legal action because one is directly affected by the issues at hand.

executive privilege

A presidential claim that certain communications with subordinates may be withheld from Congress and the courts.

one of its most liberal justices by the time of his retirement in 1994 (he wrote the majority opinion in *Roe* v. *Wade* [1973]). The elder George Bush no doubt was surprised when his nominee, David Souter, refused to vote for the overturn of *Roe* in *Planned Parenthood* v. *Casey* (1992). Despite these dramatic examples, the past political and ideological positions of federal court nominees are a fairly reliable guide to their later behavior on the bench.[25] No one was surprised that the Court moved in a very conservative direction after Bush nominees Roberts and Alito joined the Court, given the record of their past political activities and judicial opinions.

The Supreme Court in Action

14.4 Outline how the Supreme Court decides on cases

The Supreme Court meets from the first Monday in October until late June or early July, depending on the press of business. Let's see how it goes about deciding cases.[26]

Norms of Operation

A set of unwritten but clearly understood rules of behavior—called *norms*—shapes how the Court does things. One norm is *secrecy,* which keeps the conflicts between justices out of the public eye and elevates the stature of the Court as an institution. Justices do not grant interviews very often, though several recently have authored books. Reporters are not allowed to stalk the corridors for a story. Law clerks are expected to keep all memos, draft opinions, and conversations with the justices they work for confidential. Justices are not commonly seen on the frantic Washington, D.C., cocktail party circuit. When meeting in conference to argue and decide cases, the justices meet alone, without secretaries or clerks. Breaches of secrecy have occurred only occasionally. As a result, we know less about the inner workings of the Court than about any other branch of government.

Seniority is another important norm. Seniority determines the assignment of office space, the seating arrangements in open court (the most junior are at the ends), and the order of speaking in conference (the chief justice, then the most senior, and so on down the line). Speaking first allows the senior members to set the tone for discussion.

? Why should courts be guided by precedent? Can't cases be decided by comparing the merits of a case against the Constitution itself?

Finally, the justices are expected to stick closely to *precedent* when they decide cases. When the Court departs from a precedent, it is essentially overruling its own past actions, in effect, exercising judicial review of itself. In most cases, departures from precedent come in only very small steps over many years. For example, several decisions chipped away at the **separate but equal doctrine** of *Plessy* v. *Ferguson* (1896) before it was decisively reversed in *Brown* v. *Board of Education of Topeka* (1954) to end state and local laws requiring racial segregation.

Some legal theorists, both conservative and liberal, have begun to talk of **superprecedents** or super–*stare decisis* landmark rulings, that have been reaffirmed by the Court over the course of many years and whose reasoning has become part of the fabric of American law, making them especially difficult to reverse. Senator Arlen Specter, chair of the Senate Judicial Committee at the time, asked Chief Justice nominee John

separate but equal doctrine

The principle articulated in *Plessy* v. *Ferguson* (1896) that laws prescribing *separate* public facilities and services for nonwhite Americans are permissible if the facilities and services are *equal* to those provided for whites.

superprecedent

Landmark rulings that have been reaffirmed by the Court over the course of many years and whose reasoning has become part of the fabric of American law.

plaintiff

One who brings suit in a court.

in forma pauperis

Describing a process by which indigents may file a suit with the Supreme Court free of charge.

writ of certiorari

An announcement that the Supreme Court will hear a case on appeal from a lower court; its issuance requires the vote of four of the nine justices.

rule of four

An *unwritten* practice that requires at least four justices of the Supreme Court to agree that a case warrants review by the Court before it will hear the case.

Roberts during his confirmation hearings in 2005 where he stood on this issue. While Roberts agreed that such fundamental rulings exist, he was unwilling to say whether *Roe* v. *Wade* (1973) was one of them, leaving observers unsure how he would eventually stand on the abortion issue. Other legal thinkers and jurists, however, are not impressed with this idea of superprecedents; cases that are wrongly decided, they say, should not be protected against reversal, no matter how many times they have been affirmed in the past by the Court.[27]

Controlling the Agenda

The Court has a number of screening mechanisms to control what cases it will hear so that it can focus on cases that involve important federal or constitutional questions.[28]

Several technical rules help keep the numbers down. Cases must be *real* and *adverse;* that is, they must involve a real dispute between two parties. The disputants in a case must have *standing;* that is, they must have a real and direct interest in the issues that are raised. The Court sometimes changes the definition of *standing* to make access for **plaintiffs** easier or more difficult. The Warren Court (1956–1969) favored an expansive definition; the Rehnquist Court (1986–2005), a restricted one. Cases must also be *ripe;* that is, all other avenues of appeal must have been exhausted, and the injury must already have taken place (the Court will not accept hypothetical cases). Appeals must also be filed within a specified time limit, the paperwork must be correct and complete, and a filing fee of $300 must be paid. The fee may be waived if a petitioner is poor and files an affidavit *in forma pauperis* ("in the manner of a pauper"). One of the most famous cases in American history, *Gideon* v. *Wainwright* (1963), which established the right of all defendants to have lawyers in criminal cases, was submitted *in forma pauperis* on a few pieces of lined paper by a Florida State Penitentiary inmate named Clarence Earl Gideon. The Rehnquist Court was less friendly to indigent petitions than previous Courts and took several steps to cut down what the Chief Justice called "frivolous" suits by "jailhouse lawyers."

The most powerful tool that the Court has for controlling its own agenda is the power to grant or not to grant a **writ of certiorari**. A grant of "cert" is a decision of the Court that an appellate case raises an important federal or constitutional issue that it is prepared to consider.[29] Under the **rule of four**, petitions are granted cert if at least four justices vote in favor. There are several reasons a petition may not command four votes, even if the case involves important constitutional issues: it may involve a particularly controversial issue that the Court would like to avoid, or the Court may not yet have developed a solid majority and may wish to avoid a split decision. Few petitions survive all of these hurdles. Of the 10,000 or so cases that are filed in each session, the Court today grants cert for fewer than 80 (this number varies a bit year to year), down from the 150 that was typical in the 1970s and 1980s. In cases denied cert, the decision of the federal appeals court or the highest state court stands.

Deciding how freely to grant cert is a tricky business for the Court. Granted too often, it threatens to inundate the Court with cases. Granted too sparingly, it leaves in place the decisions of 13 different federal appeals courts on substantial federal and constitutional questions, as well as the decisions of state supreme courts, which often leads to inconsistent constitutional interpretations across the country. Because the Court now takes so few cases, more influence than ever is being exercised by the 13 federal circuit courts. For many important cases, the federal circuit courts have become the judicial forum of last resort.

CLERKING FOR JUSTICE THOMAS Law clerks play an extremely important role at the Supreme Court, with each justice selecting his or her own from among graduates of the nation's leading law schools. Here, Justice Clarence Thomas relaxes with three of his clerks after a long day. What is the importance of clerks to the effectiveness of the justices?

Deciding Cases

Almost all cases granted cert are scheduled for oral argument (about 10 to 15 are decided without oral argument, depending on the session). Lawyers on each side are alerted to the key issues that the justices wish to consider, and new briefs are invited. Briefs are also submitted on most important cases by other parties who may be interested in the disputes. These "friend of the court," or **amicus curiae**, briefs may be submitted by individuals, interest groups, or some agency of the federal government, including the Justice Department or even the president.

Each case is argued for one hour, with 30 minutes given to each side in the dispute. Oral argument is not so much a presentation of arguments, however, as it is a give-and-take between the lawyers and the justices and among the justices themselves. When the federal government is a party to the case, the solicitor general or one of his or her deputies presents the oral arguments. Some justices—Antonin Scalia and Chief Justice John Roberts, for example —are famous for their relentless grilling of lawyers. Ruth Bader Ginsburg often asks that lawyers skip abstract legal fine points and put the issues in terms of their effect on ordinary people.

After hearing oral arguments and reading the briefs in the case, the justices meet in conference to reach a decision. The custom is for each justice to state his or her position, starting with the chief justice and moving through the ranks in order of seniority. Chief justices of great stature and intellect, such as John Marshall and Charles Evans Hughes, used the opportunity to speak first as a way of structuring the case and of swaying votes. Those who did not command much respect from the other justices (e.g., Warren Burger) were less able to shape the decision process.

Political scientists have tried to determine what factors are most important in predicting how the justices will vote.[30] One approach looks at the ideological predilections of the justices and manages to explain a great deal about their voting behavior that way.[31] Another approach looks at the strategic behavior of judges, using the diaries and personal papers of retired justices to show that a great deal of negotiating and "horse trading" goes on, with justices trading votes on different cases and joining opinions they do not like so that they can have a hand in modifying them.[32] Another approach tries to link voting behavior to social background, types of previous judicial experience, and the political environment of family

ORAL ARGUMENT Each side in a case before the Supreme Court is generally granted 30 minutes to argue its position. Most of the 30 minutes is taken up, however, by questions the justices pose to the lead attorneys. Photography is not allowed in the Supreme Court building, so the media depend on artists' renderings of oral argument before the Court, as in this session in 2008 concerning the right of gun ownership under the Second Amendment in the case *DC* v. *Heller.* Is 30 minutes enough time to argue a case so big as to come in front of the Supreme Court? How would changing the time frame affect the Court's caseload and its process for accepting cases?

opinion of the Court

The majority opinion that accompanies a Supreme Court decision.

concurring opinion

The opinion of one or more judges who vote with the majority on a case but wish to set out different reasons for their decision.

dissenting opinion

The opinion of the judge or judges who are in the minority on a particular case before the Supreme Court.

upbringing.[33] Still another believes that justices vote strategically, departing from their own policy preferences when they believe a particular decision will enhance the influence of the Court in the federal government and American society.[34] Finally, others believe that justices often vote out of a sense of duty, committed to preserving the standing of the Court and their sense of professional responsibility. None of these approaches has been totally successful because much of what the Court does in conference is secret and can be only imperfectly reconstructed.

About all that one can say is that the justices tend to form relatively stable voting blocs over time.[35] For example, during the 1990s and early 2000s, the Rehnquist Court, on many cases involving federalism and the rights of criminal defendants, divided into two blocs, a five-member conservative one (Justices Scalia, Thomas, Rehnquist, Kennedy, and O'Connor) and a four-member liberal one (Justices Stevens, Breyer, Ginsburg, and Souter). The Roberts Court is dominated by a solid conservative majority, as has been shown.

The vote in conference is not final, however. As Justice John Harlan once explained, "The books on voting are never closed until the decision finally comes down."[36] The justices have an opportunity to change their votes in response to the opinion supporting the majority decision. An opinion is a statement of the legal reasoning that supports the decision of the Court. There are three kinds of opinions. The **opinion of the Court** is the written opinion of the majority. A **concurring opinion** is the opinion of a justice who supports the majority decision but has different legal reasons for doing so. A **dissenting opinion** presents the reasoning of the minority. Dissenting opinions sometimes become the basis for future Court majorities.

If he votes with the majority in conference, the chief justice assigns the writing of the opinion. He can assign it to any justice in the majority, often to himself. Some jurists and scholars believe that this power to assign is the most important role of the chief justice, and it is guarded jealously. Warren Burger was so eager to play a role in opinion assignments that, much to the distress of his colleagues, he would often delay announcing his vote so that he could place himself with the majority. Justice William Douglas angrily charged that Burger voted with the majority in *Roe* only so that he could assign the case to a justice who was closer to the minority view.[37] If the chief justice's opinion is with the minority, the opinion is assigned by the most senior member of the majority.

The justice assigned to write the opinion does not work in isolation. He or she is assisted not only by law clerks but also by other justices, who helpfully provide memoranda suggesting wording and reasoning. Justices also consider the legal reasoning presented to the Court in *amicus curiae* briefs.[38] Most opinions go through numerous revisions and are subject to a considerable amount of bargaining among the justices.

Only when an opinion is completed is a final vote taken in conference. The justices are free to change their earlier votes: they may join the majority if they are now persuaded by its reasoning, or a concurring opinion may be so compelling that the majority may decide to replace the original majority opinion with it.

The Supreme Court as a National Policymaker

14.5 Evaluate the Supreme Court as a national policymaker

People often say that the Court should settle disputes and not make policy. But because the disputes it settles involve contentious public issues (such as abortion rights and affirmative action) and fundamental questions about the meaning of our constitutional rules (such as the extent of presidential powers in wartime), the Court cannot help but make public policy.

It seems likely that the Court recognizes and cultivates its policymaking role. In the main, the Court does not see itself as a court of last resort, simply righting routine errors in the lower courts or settling minor private disputes. It sees itself, instead, as the "highest judicial tribunal for settling policy conflicts" and constitutional issues and chooses its cases accordingly.[39] The fact that decisions are not simply handed down but come with an opinion attached for the purpose of guiding the actions of other courts, litigants, and public officials is another demonstration that the Court recognizes its policymaking role. Let's look at judicial policymaking—which takes the form of the Court's constitutional interpretations as revealed in its decisions—and see how it has evolved over time.

Structural Change and Constitutional Interpretation

Scholars generally identify three periods in the history of constitutional interpretation by the Supreme Court in the United States, one stretching from the early 1800s to the Civil War, the next from the end of the Civil War to the Great Depression, and the last from World War II to the mid-1980s.[40] We would add a fourth, covering the years from 1991 to the present (see Figure 14.4). We will see how changes in constitutional law have been influenced by structural factors, particularly economic change.

Period 1: National Power and Property Rights We saw in Chapter 4 that the United States experienced significant growth and change during the first 75 years of its existence. This growth was accompanied by changes in constitutional law. Chief Justice John Marshall, who presided over the Supreme Court from 1801 to 1835, was the key judicial figure during this important period in our history.[41] Marshall was a follower of the doctrines of Alexander Hamilton, who believed that American greatness depended on a strong national government, a partnership between government and business in which industry and commerce were encouraged, and a national market economy free of the regulatory restraints of state and local governments. In a string of opinions that have shaped the fundamentals of American constitutional law—especially important are *Fletcher* v. *Peck* (1810), *Dartmouth College* v. *Woodward* (1819), *McCulloch* v. *Maryland* (1819), and *Gibbons* v. *Ogden* (1824), discussed elsewhere in this text—Marshall interpreted the Constitution to mean "maximum protection to property rights and maximum support for the idea of nationalism over states' rights."[42]

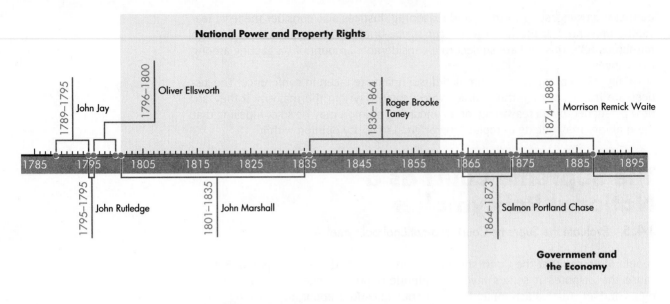

I FIGURE 14.4 Timeline: Chief Justices of the Supreme Court, 1789–2010

Period 2: Government and the Economy The Civil War and the Industrial Revolution triggered the development of a mass-production industrial economy dominated by the business corporation. Determining the role to be played by government in such an economy was a central theme of American political life in the late nineteenth and early twentieth centuries. The courts were involved deeply in this rethinking. At the beginning of this period, the Supreme Court took the position that the corporation was to be protected against regulation by both the state and federal governments; by the end, it was more sympathetic to the desire of the people and the political branches for the expansion of government regulation and management of the economy during the crisis of the Great Depression.

The main protection for the corporation against regulation came from the Fourteenth Amendment. This amendment was passed in the wake of the Civil War to guarantee the citizenship rights of freed slaves. The operative phrase was from Section 1: "nor shall any state deprive any person of life, liberty, or property without due process of law"—on its face, hardly relevant to the world of the corporation. But in one of the great ironies of American history, the Court took up this expanded federal power over the states to protect rights and translated it to mean that corporations (considered "persons" under the law) and other forms of business should have increased protection from state regulation.

This reading of **laissez-faire** economic theory into constitutional law made the Supreme Court the principal ally of business in the late nineteenth and early twentieth centuries.[43] Keeping the government out of the economy in general, the Court overturned efforts by both the state and federal governments to provide welfare for the poor; to regulate manufacturing monopolies; to initiate an income tax; to regulate interstate railroad rates; to provide scholarships to students; to regulate wages, hours, and working conditions; and to protect consumers against unsafe or unhealthy products. The Court also supported the use of judicial injunctions to halt strikes by labor unions.

The business–Supreme Court alliance lasted until the Great Depression. Roosevelt's New Deal reflected a new national consensus on the need for a greatly expanded federal government with a new set of

laissez-faire

The political-economic doctrine that holds that government ought not interfere with the operations of the free market.

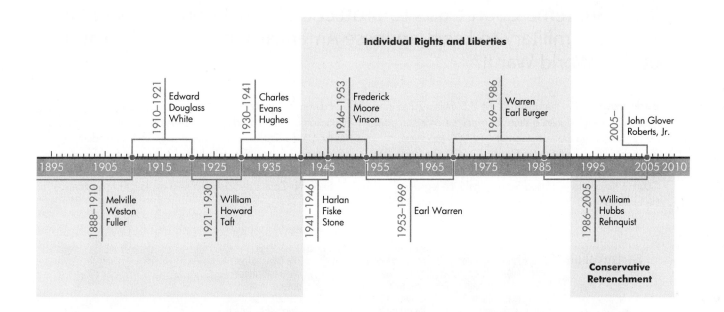

responsibilities: to manage the economy; to provide a safety net for the poor, the unemployed, and the elderly; to protect workers' rights to form labor unions; and to regulate business in the public interest. The Supreme Court, however, filled with justices born in the nineteenth century and committed to the unshakable link between the Constitution and laissez-faire economic doctrine, was opposed to the national consensus and in 1935 and 1936 declared unconstitutional several laws that were part of the foundation of the New Deal. In an extraordinary turn of events, however, the Supreme Court reversed itself in 1937, finding the Social Security Act, the Labor Relations Act, and state minimum wage laws acceptable. It is not entirely clear why the so-called switch-in-time-that-saved-nine occurred, but surely Roosevelt's landslide reelection in 1936, the heightening of public hostility toward the Court, and Roosevelt's threat to expand and "pack the Court" all played a role. Whatever the reason, the Court abandoned its effort to prevent the government from playing a central role in the management of the economy and the regulation of business, and it came to defer to the political linkage branches of government on such issues by the end of the 1930s. In doing so, it brought another constitutional era to a close.

Period 3: Individual Rights and Liberties

Three fundamental issues of American constitutional law—the relationship of the states to the nation, the nature and extent of private property rights, and the role of government in the management of the economy—were essentially settled by the time World War II broke out. From then until the mid- to late 1980s, the Court turned its main attention to the relationship between the individual and government.[44]

Most of this story is told in Chapters 15 and 16 on civil liberties and civil rights. For now, it is sufficient to point out that the Court, especially during the tenure of Chief Justice Earl Warren, decided cases that expanded protections for free expression and association, religious expression, fair trials, and civil rights for minorities. In another series of cases dealing with the apportionment of electoral districts, the Court declared for political equality, based on the principle of "one person, one vote." In many of its landmark decisions, the Court applied the Bill of Rights to the states. Although the Court's record was not without blemishes during and after World War II—see the "Using the Framework" feature on *Korematsu* v. *United States* (1944)—it made significant strides in expanding the realm of individual freedom.

If the Supreme Court exists to protect individual rights, why did it allow the military to keep Japanese Americans in internment camps during World War II?

Background: On the advice of the U.S. military, President Franklin Roosevelt signed a series of executive orders in early 1942 authorizing the relocation of 112,000 Japanese Americans living on the West Coast, 70,000 of whom were citizens, into internment camps. In 1944, the Supreme Court in *Korematsu* v. *United States* upheld the legality of the exclusion and confinement orders. Constitutional scholar

Edward Corwin described the internment and the Court's action as "the most drastic invasion of the rights of citizens of the United States by their own government" in modern American history. Taking a broad overview of structural, political linkage, and governmental factors that influenced the Supreme Court's decision will help explain this situation.

Structure

Japanese immigrants to the United States in the late nineteenth and early twentieth centuries settled mainly in the West Coast states. ➡ The Japanese attack on Pearl Harbor on December 7, 1941, plunged the United States into World War II and helped inflame negative attitudes toward Americans of Japanese descent. ➡ The Constitution vests enormous powers in the president as commander-in-chief during wartime.

Political Linkage

Anti-Japanese attitudes were widespread among the public, particularly in the West Coast states, who feared a Japanese invasion. ➡ Public opinion strongly supported the war against Japan and whatever military policies were necessary to win it. ➡ The media whipped up hysteria about a possible Japanese invasion.

Government

Military authorities believed that Japanese Americans living on the West Coast posed a national security threat to the United States; asked the president to authorize curfews, relocation, and confinement. ➡ Congress passed supporting legislation making relocation and internment possible.

President Franklin Roosevelt, troubled by the action, but fully aware of the feelings of the public and the wishes of military leaders in wartime, signed the necessary executive orders. ➡ The Supreme Court, unwilling to act against opinion of military leaders that Japanese Americans living on the West Coast posed a national security threat, supported the exclusion order in a case brought by Fred Korematsu.

Governmental Action

The Supreme Court announces its decision allowing the internment of Japanese Americans in *Korematsu* v. *United States* (1944).

Period 4: Conservative Retrenchment

A new conservative majority emerged on the Supreme Court in the early 1990s, fashioned by the judicial nominations of Presidents Ronald Reagan and George H. W. Bush, and the patient efforts of conservative Chief Justice William Rehnquist. This new majority—with O'Connor and Kennedy usually, but not always, joining the three most consistently conservative justices, Scalia, Thomas, and Rehnquist—moved the Court to reconsider many of its long-established doctrines in the areas of rights and liberties (to be discussed further in Chapters 15 and 16) and the relationship between the national and state governments. Its reconsideration of federalism in favor of "states' rights" was particularly noteworthy (see Chapter 3).

In a string of landmark cases, the Court curtailed national authority in favor of the states, overturning several federal statutes that were based, in its view, on an overly expansive reading by Congress of its powers under the interstate commerce clause. In 1995, for example, the Court overturned a federal statute that banned guns from the area immediately around public schools, saying that the statute was unrelated to interstate commerce. Using the same reasoning, it overturned legislation requiring background checks for gun buyers. In 2000, the Court used such reasoning to strike down parts of the Violence Against Women Act and the federal law barring age discrimination in employment.

For a brief time spanning the years 2002 through 2005, the Supreme Court became more moderate in a significant number of areas—especially on affirmative action, gay rights, the right of individuals to sue states for violations of federal civil rights laws, and the rights of terrorism detainees (see the discussion of these issues in Chapters 15 and 16)—with the now-retired Sandra Day O'Connor casting the decisive swing vote in many cases. Although O'Connor most often voted with the conservatives during her years on the Court—note especially her vote with the majority in 2000 in *Bush* v. *Gore* that settled the disputed vote in Florida in favor of Bush and determined the outcome of the presidential election—she surprised many people in 2003 when she joined the majority in the Michigan Law School case that upheld the use of race in law school admissions, the Texas case that banned states from forbidding private gay sexual behavior, and the challenge to the constitutionality of the McCain-Feingold Campaign Finance Reform law, which was rejected. In 2004 she wrote the majority opinion in the decision on the rights of citizens held as enemy combatants, pointing out that "a state of war is not a blank check for the president when it comes to the rights of the nation's citizens."[45]

After O'Connor retired and Samuel Alito joined the Court, and with the strong leadership of Chief Justice John Roberts, the conservative majority reemerged, but in a much more cohesive form. In 2006, for example, the Court approved state measures giving police greater power to execute a search warrant without "knocking and announcing" and approved Arizona's strict insanity tests under which a schizophrenic teen was convicted of shooting a police officer. In 2007, the Court ruled that school districts could not use racial criteria to promote school integration. And, it upheld federal restrictions on very late term abortions (called "partial birth abortions" by abortion opponents). In the first two terms of the Roberts Court, seven antitrust cases were considered by the Court, and all seven were decided in favor of business. In 2008, the Court for the first time ruled that Americans have a constitutional right to own guns for their personal use under terms of the Second Amendment; the Court later ruled in 2010 that state and local regulations that effectively banned guns were unconstitutional. In 2009, it ruled in favor of a group of New Haven firefighters (19 white and one Hispanic) in a reverse discrimination case that bodes ill for the constitutional acceptability of local, state, and national affirmative action programs (see Chapter 16).

The Roberts Court has been especially friendly to business interests and large corporations. In a stunningly broad ruling in 2010, the Court said that Congress could not restrict the campaign activities of corporations as specified by the McCain-Feingold reforms of 2002, in the process overturning two of its own past rulings (precedents) on the same issue in which it had upheld restrictions on corporations and statutes in 21 states. It ruled in another case that Exxon was not fully financially liable to communities damaged by the *Exxon Valdez* oil spill. In another case it said a women paid less than her male colleagues for many years could not sue because she had failed to file a suit within 180 days of the first violation, though she didn't learn about it for years. Consumers, it decided, could not sue a company that knowingly sold defective medical devices if the devices had been approved by federal regulators. All in all, according to one study, large corporations won 22 of 30 cases before the Roberts Court during the 2006–2007 term,[46] and the Court has become more conservative on economic matters since. Supporters of the new health care reform bill and new regulations to control some of the most risky activities of banks and financial institutions are deeply worried that the Roberts Court, hostile to an activist federal government and solidly aligned with the business community, may reverse congressional and presidential actions in these areas.

? If President Obama has the opportunity to make additional nominations to the Supreme Court, how will this affect the direction of the Court's rulings?

The Debate Over Judicial Activism

Has the Court become too involved in national policymaking? Many people think so; others think not. Let us examine several of the ways in which what is called **judicial activism** is expressed.

Judicial Review

We have already seen how the Court under John Marshall's leadership claimed the right of judicial review in the case of *Marbury* v. *Madison* (1803). Still, the power was not exercised by the Court to any great extent until the late nineteenth century. The use of judicial review increased during the twentieth century, however, with most of the Court's adverse attention being paid to the states. As described earlier, however, the Rehnquist Court was fairly aggressive in overturning federal statutes, averaging almost six per term in the years from 1994 to 2005, compared with one every two years from the end of the Civil War to the early 1990s.[47] Oddly, given the tendency of conservative activists and organizations to be the most vociferously concerned about an overly activist judiciary, it was the most conservative members of the Court who most frequently voted to overturn congressional statutes during these years.[48] The Roberts Court seems to be even more aggressively moving in this direction. These trends in the use of judicial review suggest that the Court over time has become more willing to monitor the activities of other governmental entities.

The aggressive use of judicial review in recent years, as well as the fairly broad claims in several of its opinions that it and it alone has the final say on the meaning of the Constitution, has prompted talk among many legal scholars about "judicial imperialism" and "judicial supremacy."[49] Ironically, perhaps, it is now mainly liberal scholars who worry that the Court, dominated by a solid conservative majority, is too frequently reversing the actions of popularly elected bodies—Congress and state legislatures—a position once held mostly by conservatives.[50]

judicial activism

Actions by the courts that purportedly go beyond the role of the judiciary as interpreter of the law and adjudicator of disputes.

Liberals worry that the Court will exercise judicial review on matters such as federal, state, and local governments' affirmative action programs as a violation of the "equal protection" clause of the Fourteenth Amendment.

Reversing the Decisions of Past Supreme Courts Despite the norm of precedent (stare decisis) that guides judicial decision making, the Warren, Burger, Rehnquist, and Roberts Courts overturned a number of previous Court decisions. The most dramatic instance was the reversal by the Warren Court of *Plessy* v. *Ferguson* (1896), which had endorsed legal segregation in the South, by *Brown* v. *Board of Education* (1954), which removed segregation's legal underpinnings. The Rehnquist Court overturned a number of previous Court decisions that had expanded the rights of criminal defendants and that had supported the extension of federal government power, reviewed earlier. When the Roberts Court upheld the federal Partial-Birth Abortion Ban Act, it reversed its own position on an identical Nebraska law it had declared unconstitutional in 2000. In *Citizens United* v. *Federal Election Commission* (2010), the Court overturned three of its own precedents, including cases from 1990, 2003, and 2007. In his dissent in this case, read from the bench as a sign of his deep displeasure with the majority, Justice John Paul Stevens lamented what he took to be the overly broad and ambitious reach of the majority, saying "essentially, five justices were unhappy with the limited nature of the case before us, so they changed the case to give themselves an opportunity to change the law." To be sure, the Court so far has been reluctant to overturn so-called superprecedents, but it can do so if it so chooses.

Deciding "Political" Issues Critics claim that the Court is taking on too many matters that are best left to the elected branches of government. An oft-cited example is the Court's willingness to become increasingly involved in the process of drawing congressional electoral district boundaries in the states. Defenders of the Court argue that when such basic constitutional rights as equality of citizenship are at peril, the Court is obligated to protect these rights, no matter what other government bodies may choose to do. The Court's intervention in the 2000 presidential election generated widespread criticism for its meddling in politics, although its many defenders insist that the Court's decision in *Bush* v. *Gore* saved the nation from a constitutional crisis.

Remedies The most criticized aspect of judicial activism is the tendency for federal judges to impose broad remedies on states

DECIDING THE 2000 PRESIDENTIAL ELECTION The outcome of the closely fought 2000 presidential election was not finally decided until the Supreme Court stopped the recount in Florida, giving the state's electoral votes to George W. Bush. Here, passionate supporters of Bush and Al Gore demonstrate in front of the Supreme Court building while awaiting its decision. Do you think the Court's intervention was in the nation's best interests?

TIGHT QUARTERS Federal courts often require states to "remedy" a situation found to be in violation of federal standards or constitutional protections. A good example is prison overcrowding, shown here in a California state prison in Los Angeles in 2010. For many years, the courts have insisted that the states do something to end the problem, even if it means spending additional state monies. What developments in our constitutional tradition allow federal courts to impose such mandates on states?

remedy

An action that a court determines must be taken to rectify a wrong done by government.

original intent

The doctrine that the courts must interpret the Constitution in ways consistent with the intentions of the Framers rather than in light of contemporary conditions and needs.

strict construction

The doctrine that the provisions of the Constitution have a clear meaning and that judges must stick closely to this meaning when rendering decisions.

and localities. A **remedy** is what a court determines must be done to rectify a wrong. Since the 1960s, the Court has been more willing than in the past to impose remedies that require other governmental bodies to take action. Some of the most controversial of these remedies include court orders requiring states to build more prison space and mandating that school districts bus students to achieve racial balance. Such remedies often require that governments spend public funds for things they do not necessarily want to do. Critics claim that the federal judiciary's legitimate role is to prevent government actions that threaten rights and liberties, not to compel government to take action to meet some policy goal.

Original Intent Much of the debate about the role of the Court centers on the issue of the original intent of the framers.[51] Advocates of **original intent** believe that the Court must be guided by the original intent of the framers and the exact words found in the Constitution, using **strict construction** as a way to stay close to its true meaning. Originalists believe that the expansion of rights that has occurred since the mid-1960s—such as the new right to privacy that formed the basis of the *Roe* v. *Wade* decision and rights for criminal defendants—is illegitimate, having no foundation in the framers' intentions or the text of the Constitution. Justices Antonin Scalia and Clarence Thomas are the strongest originalists on today's Court.

Opponents of original intent and strict construction believe that the intentions of the framers are not only impossible to determine but also unduly constricting. In this view, jurists must try to reconcile the fundamental principles of the Constitution with changing conditions in the United States and the democratic aspirations of the American people.

Clearly, the modern Supreme Court is more activist than it was in the past; most justices today hold a more expansive view of the role of the Court in forging national policy than did their predecessors. And because the Court is likely to remain activist under Chief Justice John Roberts, the debate about judicial activism is likely to remain important in American politics.

? Is it possible today to understand and adhere to the framers' original intent? Is it democratic?

Outside Influences on the Court

14.6 Assess the factors and players that influence Supreme Court decisions

The courts make public policy and will continue to do so, but they do not do so in splendid isolation; many other governmental and political linkage actors and institutions influence what they do. Indeed, many scholars suggest that what the federal courts do reflects the prevailing politics and opinion of the day. Judges, after all, are nominated by presidents and confirmed by senators whose views are known to the public and who are elected by them. As new coalitions come to power in American politics, they make appointments to the federal courts that are in tune with the electoral coalition supporting the president and a majority of the Senate. A highly politicized judiciary, whose decisions become entangled in and engaged with the prevailing issues of the day and whose decisions reflect the views of the winners, in this view, is not to be lamented but celebrated as a reflection of democratic politics. Aggressive use of judicial review by the Supreme Court, in the view of several leading scholars, is simply a way for the new majority in the country to clear the way for its own policies.[52] Critics of this view would point out, however, that the courts might be out of touch with the mood of the country for long periods of time because federal judges serve life terms and are slow to be replaced (see Table 14.1).

Government and political influences on the Court come not only during times of partisan realignment and the appearance of new electoral coalitions but on an everyday basis. Here are important ways this happens.

Governmental Influences

The Supreme Court must coexist with other governmental bodies that have their own powers, interests, constituencies, and visions of the public good. Recognizing this, the Court usually tries to stay somewhere near the boundaries of what is acceptable to other political actors. Being without "purse or sword," as Hamilton put it in *The Federalist,* No. 78, the Court cannot force others to obey its decisions. It can only hope that respect for the law and the Court will cause government officials to do what it has mandated in a decision. If the Court fails to gain voluntary compliance, it risks a serious erosion of its influence, for it then appears weak and ineffectual.

TABLE 14.1   Supreme Court Justices, 2010

Justice	Born	Sworn In	Appointed By
Chief Justice John Roberts	1955	2005	George W. Bush
Antonin Scalia	1936	1986	Ronald Reagan
Anthony M. Kennedy	1936	1988	Ronald Reagan
Clarence Thomas	1948	1991	George H. W. Bush
Ruth Bader Ginsburg	1933	1993	Bill Clinton
Stephen G. Breyer	1938	1994	Bill Clinton
Samuel A. Alito Jr.	1950	2006	George W. Bush
Sonia Sotomayor	1954	2009	Barack Obama
Elena Kagan	1960	2010	Barack Obama

The President   The president, as chief executive, is supposed to carry out the Court's decrees. However, presidents who have opposed particular decisions or been lukewarm to them have dragged their feet, as President Eisenhower did on school desegregation after the Court's *Brown* decision.

The president has constitutional powers that give him some degree of influence over the Court. In addition to the Court's dependence on the president to carry out its decisions (when the parties to a dispute do not do it voluntarily), for example, the president influences the direction of the Court by his power to nominate judges when there are vacancies. He can also file suits through the Justice Department or introduce legislation to alter the Court's organization or jurisdiction (as Franklin Roosevelt did with his Court-packing proposal).

Congress   Although Congress can alter the size, organization, and appellate jurisdiction of the federal courts, it rarely does so.[53] The size of the Court, for example, has not changed since 1860. Nor, since that time, has Congress changed its jurisdiction as a reaction to its decisions, despite the introduction of many bills over the years to do so. In 2003, for example, a bill was introduced by Republicans in the House to take away the Court's jurisdiction to hear cases challenging the inclusion of the phrase "under God" in the Pledge of Allegiance. In 2004 a resolution was introduced in the House decrying the citation of the opinions of foreign and international courts and international law in U.S. judicial pronouncements—something Justice Kennedy had done in his majority opinion in a case overturning the state of Texas's antisodomy statute in *Lawrence* v. *Texas* (2003)—and threatening impeachment for any federal judge doing so. (Neither bill passed.) Congress is more likely to bring pressure to bear on the courts by being unsympathetic to pleas from the justices for pay increases or for a suitable budget for clerks or office space. The Senate also plays a role in the appointment process, as we have learned, and can convey its views to the Court during the course of confirmation hearings. Finally, Congress can change statutes or pass new laws that specifically challenge Supreme Court decisions, as it did when it legislated the Civil Rights Act of 1991 to make it easier for people to file employment discrimination suits.[54] All of this matters. There is evidence that throughout American history, the Supreme Court exercises a great deal of restraint in its judicial review of congressional actions when Congress is clearly hostile to the Court.[55]

Political Linkage Influences

The Supreme Court is influenced not only by other government officials and institutions, but also by what we have termed political linkage factors.

Groups and Movements   Interest groups, social movements, and the public not only influence the Court indirectly through the president and Congress but often do so directly. An important political tactic of interest groups and social movements is the **test case**. A test case is an action brought by a group that is designed to challenge the constitutionality of a law or an action by government. Groups wishing to force a court determination on an issue that is important to them will try to find a plaintiff on whose behalf they can bring a suit. When Thurgood Marshall was chief counsel for the NAACP in the 1950s, he spent a long time searching for the right plaintiff to bring a suit that would drive the last nail into the coffin of the *Plessy* separate-but-equal doctrine that was the legal basis for southern segregation. He settled on a fifth-grade girl named Linda Brown who was attending a segregated school in Topeka, Kansas. Several years later, he won the landmark case *Brown* v. *Board of Education of Topeka* (1954).

test case

A case brought to force a ruling on the constitutionality of some law or executive action.

CIVIL RIGHTS CHAMPION   Social movements often use test cases to challenge the constitutionality of laws and government actions. After a long search, NAACP attorney Thurgood Marshall—shown here in front of the Supreme Court, where he would later sit as a justice—selected Linda Brown, a fifth-grader from Topeka, Kansas, who was not permitted to attend the school closest to her house because it was reserved for whites, as the principal plaintiff in *Brown* v. *Board of Education of Topeka,* the historic case that successfully challenged school segregation. How else has the Court been a vehicle for social action?

Many test cases take the form of **class-action suits**. These are suits brought by an individual on behalf of a class of people who are in a similar situation. A suit to prevent the dumping of toxic wastes in public waterways, for example, may be brought by an individual in the name of all the people living in the area who are adversely affected by the resulting pollution. Class-action suits were invited by the Warren Court's expansion of the definition of *standing* in the 1960s. The Rehnquist Court later narrowed the definition of *standing,* making it harder to bring class-action suits.

Interest groups often get involved in suits brought by others by filing *amicus curiae* briefs.[56] Pro-abortion and anti-abortion groups submitted 78 such briefs in *Webster* v. *Reproductive Health Services* (1989), a decision that allowed states to regulate and limit abortion availability.[57] These briefs set out the group's position on the constitutional issues or talk about some of the most important consequences of deciding the case one way or the other. In a sense, this activity is a form of lobbying. Some scholars believe that the Court finds such briefs to be a way to keep track of public and group opinion on the issues before it, which is helpful to its work.[58]

Leaders
The Supreme Court does not usually stray very far from the opinions of public and private sector leaders when a consensus exists among them.[59] Social and economic leaders use their influence in a number of ways. As we learned in earlier chapters, their influence is substantial in the media, the interest group system, party politics, and elections at all levels. It follows, then, that elites play a substantial role in the thinking of presidents and the members of Congress as they, in turn, deal with the Court. In addition to this powerful but indirect influence, the Court is also shaped by developments on issues and doctrine within the legal profession as these are expressed by bar associations, law journals, and law schools. To take but one example, Justice O'Connor, in her opinion in the 2004 Michigan Law School affirmative action case, justified her vote by pointing out that the use of race as one criterion among many in law school admission decisions was now widely accepted in the university and legal communities, as was the legitimacy of the goal of "diversity" in higher education.

Public Opinion
We might think that the Supreme Court is immune from public opinion, because the justices are appointed for life and do not need to face the electorate. There is reason to believe, however, that what the Court does and what the public wants—at least as expressed in public opinion polls—are highly correlated; a substantial body of research shows that Court rulings and public opinion are consistent with one another about two-thirds of the time, about the same as level of consistency with the public as the president and Congress.[60] There does not seem to be a yawning gap, then, between the public and the Supreme Court. We cannot say for

> **class-action suit**
> A suit brought on behalf of a group of people who are in a situation similar to that of the plaintiffs.

sure, however, that public opinion causes the Court to act in particular ways when making decisions.[61] Indeed, it is just as likely that third factors—such as major events, political developments, and cultural changes conveyed in the media—shape the perceptions of judges and citizens alike. Nevertheless, the close association between Court decisions and public opinion is good news in a society that aspires to be democratic.

Having said that, it also is important to point out that there have been times during our history when the Court was so influenced by other political actors that it set aside, if only for a short while, its responsibility to protect the rights and liberties of all citizens. Although the Court has played an important role in advancing rights and liberties in the United States (see Chapters 15 and 16), it has not been entirely immune from pressure brought to bear by the public, other government officials, and private-sector leaders to punish suspect groups. For example, the Court went along with local, state, and federal actions to punish dissident voices during the McCarthy era's anti-Communist hysteria of the 1950s. It also approved the forced relocation and internment of Japanese Americans during World War II, as discussed earlier in the "Using the Framework" feature.

Using the DEMOCRACY STANDARD

Does the Supreme Court enhance American democracy?

The framers designed the Supreme Court as an institution that would serve as a check on the other branches, most especially on Congress, the only semi-democratic institution of the lot in their original design. They also structured the Court to be the least democratic of the branches in the new federal government, with justices appointed rather than elected and serving for life rather than for a fixed term of office. The framers wanted the judiciary to function as a referee who stands above the fray, preserving the rules, overseeing the orderly changing of some rules when the situation demands it, protecting minorities against the potentially tyrannical behavior of the majority, and protecting individuals in the exercise of their constitutionally guaranteed rights. From the perspective of democratic theory, however, it is unacceptable that one of the three main branches of the federal government in the United States—with the power to override the decisions of presidents, Congress, and state legislatures and to make binding decisions for the nation as a whole—is staffed with members who never face the judgment of the voters.

Although designed as an anti-majoritarian institution, the Supreme Court is much more responsive to majoritarian political actors and to the public than the framers ever imagined would be the case. For example, we have seen that the Supreme Court does not often stray very far from what is acceptable to the president and Congress or to private elites; we have seen, also, that the Court acts consistently with public opinion about as often as Congress and the president do. Moreover, the chapters on civil rights and civil liberties show that the Court plays an important and positive role in the protection of minority rights and liberties in the United States, although it has often been inconsistent and slow in doing so.

The overall view suggests that, whatever the intention of the framers, the Court has not acted consistently as an anti-majoritarian institution, though it has sometimes done so. In fact, it has often protected popular democracy.

SUMMARY

14.1 Trace the evolution of judicial power in the United States

- Despite the fact that Article III of the Constitution is quite vague about the powers and responsibilities of the U.S. Supreme Court, the Court has fashioned a powerful position for itself in American politics, coequal with the executive and legislative branches.

- Under Justice John Marshall in the early nineteenth century, the Court first claimed its right to rule on the constitutionality of state and federal legislation. The Court exercised its power of judicial review in the nineteenth century primarily over state actions, with particular regard to preventing regulation of business.

- The Court became much more aggressive in overturning federal legislation during the New Deal and vigorously used the Fourteenth Amendment's due process and equal protection clauses starting in the 1960s to overrule state practices that restricted civil liberties and civil rights.

- The Rehnquist and Roberts Courts regularly overruled Congress and the president in the 1990s and 2000s.

14.2 Outline the organization of the U.S. court system

- The federal court system is made up of three parts. At the bottom are 94 federal district courts, in which most cases originate. In the middle are 13 appeals courts. At the top is the Supreme Court, with both original and appellate jurisdiction. Only a relative handful of the thousands of cases filed in the federal district courts make it to the Supreme Court.

14.3 Describe the background of appointees to the federal bench and the process by which they are appointed

- Until quite recently, the federal judiciary was dominated by white Protestant men from top law firms and law schools or government service.

- Today, many more women and racial and ethnic minorities serve in the federal judiciary, with two women, one African American, and one Hispanic woman on the Supreme Court. A majority on today's high court is Catholic.

- The appointment process is highly political and increasingly contentious, with presidents trying to leave their mark in the Courts, the political parties bringing ideological views to the process, and interest and advocacy groups fully engaged.

14.4 Outline how the Supreme Court decides on cases

- The Supreme Court operates on the basis of several widely shared norms: secrecy, seniority, and adherence to precedent. The Court controls its agenda by granting or not granting a writ of certiorari to cases filed with it.

- Cases before the Court wend their way through the process in the following way: submission of briefs, oral argument, initial consideration in conference, opinion writing, and final conference consideration by the justices.

- Published opinions serve as precedents for other federal courts and future Supreme Court decisions.

14.5 Evaluate the Supreme Court as a national policymaker

- The Supreme Court is a national policymaker of considerable importance. Its rulings settle disputes between political actors on critical matters and help define the meaning of the Constitution for others in the political system.

- Its unelected, life-tenured justices cannot, however, do anything they please, because the Court is significantly influenced by other political actors and government institutions. As a result, Court decisions rarely drift very far from public and elite opinion.

- The Court often serves as the referee of the democratic process and the rights of minorities, although it has sometimes failed to do this.

14.6 Assess the factors and players that influence Supreme Court decisions

- The decisions of the Court are influenced not only by the judicial philosophies of the justices themselves, but also by the actions and preferences of other political actors such as the president and Congress, as well as by interest groups and public and elite opinion.

- Increasingly the ideological predispositions of the justices are determinative. The Supreme Court is now dominated by a conservative majority.

TEST YOURSELF

Answer key begins on page T-1.

14.1 Trace the evolution of judicial power in the United States

1. The Constitution explicitly grants the power of judicial review to the Supreme Court.
   True / False

2. Which of the following accurately describes the Supreme Court's decision in *Marbury* v. *Madison*?
   a. The Judiciary Act of 1789 unconstitutionally expanded the Supreme Court's authority.
   b. The Supreme Court cannot use its power of judicial review to determine the constitutionality of state laws.
   c. The president has the authority to ignore laws passed by Congress.
   d. Congress lacked the authority to change the structure of the federal court system.
   e. James Madison was entitled to his executive branch commission.

3. Why do some believe that judicial review is inconsistent with democratic government?

14.2 Outline the organization of the U.S. court system

4. Which of the following is specifically mentioned in the Constitution?
   a. Courts of appeal
   b. Federal district courts
   c. Legislative courts
   d. Supreme Court
   e. All of the above

5. Which of the following has only original jurisdiction?
   a. Federal district courts
   b. Circuit courts
   c. Courts of appeal
   d. Ninth Circuit Court
   e. Supreme Court

6. How and when does Congress influence the structure of the Supreme Court and the cases that it hears?

14.3 Describe the background of appointees to the federal bench and the process by which they are appointed

7. Presidents make Supreme Court nominations on the basis of merit; they do not take the ideological views of the nominees into account.
   True / False

8. In recent years, the process used in the Senate for confirming judicial nominees has become more
   a. mundane.
   b. complaisant.
   c. contentious.
   d. bipartisan.
   e. traditional.

9. Compare Bill Clinton's Supreme Court nominees with George W. Bush's nominees.

14.4 Outline how the Supreme Court decides on cases

10. The rule of four states that only four Supreme Court justices are needed to overturn a lower court decision.
    True / False

11. Who is most likely to issue a concurring opinion?
    a. An interest group
    b. The chief justice
    c. A justice who does not support the majority decision
    d. A justice who supports the majority decision but has different legal reasons for doing so
    e. A justice who supports the majority decision and legal reasoning behind it

12. Evaluate whether *Roe* v. *Wade* is or should be a "superprecedent."

14.5 Evaluate the Supreme Court as a national policymaker

13. "Maximum protection to property rights and maximum support for the idea of nationalism over states' rights" is most closely associated with which of the following periods of constitutional interpretation?
    a. Period 1: National power and property rights
    b. Period 2: Government and the economy
    c. Period 3: Individual rights and liberties
    d. Period 4: Conservative retrenchment
    e. Period 5: Nationalism and judicial restraint

14. According to those who support original intent, how should the Supreme Court decide a particular case?
    a. In a way that promotes moral behavior
    b. In a way that is consistent with the framers' intentions
    c. In a way that promotes equality and social justice
    d. In a way that takes into account changing societal circumstances
    e. In a way that is consistent with public opinion

15. Evaluate whether the Supreme Court has become too involved in national policymaking.

14.6 Assess the factors and players that influence Supreme Court decisions

16. Federal law bans interest groups from attempting to influence the Supreme Court.
    True / False

17. Immediately after the passage of health care reform in 2010, several state attorneys general filed a lawsuit challenging the constitutionality of the bill. Which of the following tactics does this illustrate?
    a. Initiating a test case
    b. McCarthyism
    c. Filing a class-action lawsuit
    d. Filing an *amicus curiae* briefs
    e. Filing an affidavit *in forma pauperis*

mypoliscilab EXERCISES

Apply what you learned in this chapter on MyPoliSciLab.

Read on **mypoliscilab.com**

   eText: Chapter 14

Study and **Review** on **mypoliscilab.com**

   Pre-Test
   Post-Test
   Chapter Exam
   Flashcards

Watch on **mypoliscilab.com**

   Video: Court Rules on Hazelton's Immigration Laws
   Video: Prosecuting Corruption
   Video: Most Significant Abortion Ruling in 30 Years
   Video: Prosecuting Cyber Crime

Explore on **mypoliscilab.com**

   Simulation: You Are a Young Lawyer
   Simulation: You Are a Clerk to Supreme Court Justice Judith Gray
   Comparative: Comparing Judiciaries
   Timeline: Chief Justices of the Supreme Court
   Visual Literacy: Case Overload

INTERNET SOURCES

Federal Courts Home Page
www.uscourts.gov
   Information and statistics about the activities of U.S. District Courts, Circuit Courts of Appeal, and the Supreme Court.

Legal Information Institute, Cornell University Law School
www.law.cornell.edu
   The gateway to a world of information and links to associated law and court sites on the Web. Among its sections you will find the following: the Supreme Court Calendar; Biographies and Opinions of the Justices; Directories of law firms, law schools, and legal associations; Constitutions and Codes, including U.S. statutes, regulations, and judicial rules of procedure; and Court opinions, including those of state supreme courts.

The Oyez Project
www.oyez.org/oyez/frontpage
   A website that archives multimedia material concerning the United States Supreme Court (including recordings of oral arguments).

Certiorari Grants at Duke Law
www.law.duke.edu/publiclaw/supremecourtonline/certgrants/
   A website describing all recent cases that were granted a writ of certiorari and links to opinions for those cases that have been decided.

C-SPAN Judicial and Legal Resources
www.c-span.org/resources/judiciary.asp
   A treasure trove of links to sites having to do with the law and the courts.

Senate Judiciary Committee
http://judiciary.senate.gov/nominations/judicial.cfm
   Track the status of federal judicial nominations and confirmations.

Scotus Blog
www.scotusblog.com
   A blog on the inner workings of the Supreme Court administered by one of the nation's most experienced Supreme Court attorneys.

The Supreme Court
www.supremecourtus.gov/
   The official website of the Supreme Court with a wealth of information about the Court's docket and decisions.

SUGGESTIONS FOR FURTHER READING

Barnett, Randy E. *Restoring the Lost Constitution: The Presumption of Liberty.* Princeton, NJ: Princeton University Press, 2003.

A conservative case for understanding the Constitution as a legal framework for the protection of individual rights.

Breyer, Stephen. *Active Liberty: Interpreting Our Democratic Constitution.* New York: Knopf, 2005.

The Justice's attempt to define a coherent doctrine of a "Living Constitution."

Greenburg, Jan Crawford. *Supreme Conflict: The Inside Story of the Struggle for Control of the United States Supreme Court.* New York: Penguin, 2007.

A fascinating account of the politics behind the conservative transformation of the Supreme Court.

McCloskey, Robert G. *The American Supreme Court,* 5th ed. Chicago: University of Chicago Press, 2010.

First published 45 years ago, and revised for the 2005 and 2010 editions by noted legal scholar Sanford Levinson, this remains the classic interpretation of the Supreme Court's role in shaping the meaning of the Constitution.

Schwartz, Bernard. *Decision: How the Supreme Court Decides Cases.* New York: Oxford University Press, 2005.

A revealing behind-the-scenes look at how the Supreme Court considers and decides the cases before it.

Wittington, Keith E. *Political Foundations of Judicial Supremacy: the Presidency, the Supreme Court, and Constitutional Leadership in U.S. History.* Princeton, NJ: Princeton University Press, 2007.

A provocative book that suggests that the Supreme Court has not so much taken power over the course of U.S. history but has had power thrust upon it by presidents and senators as a way to advance their own political interests and agendas.

Parts 2 and 3 of this book examined the structural and political linkage influences on government institutions and public officials. Part 4 examined government institutions and public officials. This part examines what government does and how effective it is in tackling the most important problems facing the United States.

As such, this part represents a kind of summing up; it examines how effectively our political and governmental institutions operate to fulfill the needs and expectations of the American people. These chapters also address the democracy theme, asking whether public policies are the outcome of a democratic process and whether policies improve the health and vitality of democracy in the United States.

Chapters 15 and 16 look at the status of civil liberties and civil rights in the United States, with special attention paid to the decisions of the Supreme Court concerning our most cherished rights and liberties. We treat civil liberties and civil rights as "outcomes" or public policies because the status of liberties and equal rights in the United States are not simply specified in the original Constitution but are the product of complex political processes—social movements, news media attention, political parties and elections, and interest group pressures—and the actions of government officials and institutions. Chapter 17 examines the budget and economic policies. Chapter 18 looks at a range of social safety net policies that help protect against poverty and hunger and prop up the incomes of the elderly. Chapter 19 looks at American foreign and national defense policies.

A clarification about coverage is in order. We cannot cover everything that government does. This is especially true of domestic policies. In Chapter 17, we address a broad range of economic and budgetary issues. In Chapter 18, we look at a broad array of social safety net programs. We do not address education or public safety issues because these are mostly the responsibility of state and local governments. (Note, however, that No Child Left Behind is in Chapter 3 and that the status of rights for those accused of a crime is covered extensively in Chapter 15). Nor do we talk much about agricultural or transportation policies, although we have said something about each in the chapters on interest groups and Congress.

15 | Civil Liberties: The Struggle for Freedom

IN THIS CHAPTER

15.1 Identify civil liberties protections in the Constitution

15.2 Trace the evolution of civil liberties in the nineteenth century

15.3 Outline the liberties guaranteed by the Bill of Rights and their gradual application to the states by the Supreme Court

15.4 Analyze how concerns about terrorism may affect civil liberties

CAMPUS SPEECH CODES AND FREE SPEECH

- Campus newspapers across the nation in 2001 refused to accept a paid advertisement from conservative activist David Horowitz in which he opposed reparations for slavery. Many of the handful of newspapers that ran the ad "Ten Reasons Why Reparations for Slavery Is a Bad Idea—and Racist Too" faced angry demonstrations, vandalism of their offices, and theft of the papers containing the offending ads.

- During a class at the University of Michigan, a student argued that homosexuality could be treated with psychotherapy. He was accused of violating a campus rule against victimizing people on the basis of their sexual orientation.

- At Southern Methodist University, a student was sentenced to work for 30 hours with minority organizations because, among other things, he sang "We Shall Overcome" in a sarcastic manner.[1]

- At San Diego State University a student was admonished by school administrators and warned that he might be expelled for getting into a heated argument with four Arab students he encountered in the school's library who had been quietly celebrating the September 11 attacks on the World Trade Center.

- At Washington State University in 2005, a group of student protestors disrupted the performance of a play that poked fun at "political correctness" and that purposely offended gays, Jews, Christians, Muslims, and others. Responding to critics, the university's president suggested that the disruptive students had been simply expressing their First Amendment rights and were doing so in a responsible fashion.

- At Brandeis University in 2007, a professor was formally admonished for racial harassment for analyzing for his students the origin of the derogatory term "wetback."

- Stanford University enacted a speech code in 1990 that prohibits "personal vilification of students on the basis of their sex, race, color, handicap, religion, sexual orientation, or national and ethnic origin." The code was strongly opposed by Stanford's eminent constitutional scholar Gerald Gunther, who claimed that hate speech should not be banned but vigorously rejected "with more speech, with better speech, with repudiation and contempt." In 1995, the California Supreme Court agreed with Gunther's position, saying that the Stanford code unconstitutionally restricts free speech rights under the First Amendment to the Constitution.[2]

The college campus has become one of the most visible battlegrounds in the continuing struggle over the meaning of free speech in the United States, as traditional notions of liberty come into conflict with newer notions of equal citizenship (or civil rights, to be discussed in the next chapter). Campus speech codes have been instituted at many colleges and universities across the country in an effort to rid campuses of speech that may offend women and members of various minority groups. Many civil libertarians, like Gerald Gunther, although protective of the rights of minority students to have a supportive learning environment, have fought hard against such codes in the service of free speech and a free society. While state and lower federal courts generally have sided with the civil libertarians, as in the Stanford case, colleges and universities have continued to revise and issue rules to reduce gender, sexual orientation, and minority harassment on campus and to provide a supportive environment for these students. The Supreme Court has not as yet taken a case that would clarify the constitutional validity of such codes and rules.

THINKING CRITICALLY About This Chapter

Using the **FRAMEWORK**

You will see in this chapter how structural, political linkage, and governmental factors influence the meaning and practice of civic freedoms. Although the decisions of the Supreme Court are particularly important in determining the status of civil liberties at any particular moment in American history, you will learn how they are also the product of influences from a wide range of actors, institutions, and social processes.

Using the **DEMOCRACY STANDARD**

You will see in this chapter how the expansion of the enjoyment of civil liberties in the United States has been a product of the struggle for democracy and how civil liberties are fundamental to the democratic process itself.

Civil Liberties in the Constitution

15.1 Identify civil liberties protections in the Constitution

We saw in Chapter 2 that the framers were particularly concerned about establishing a society in which liberty might flourish. While government was necessary to protect liberty from the threat of anarchy, the framers believed that government might threaten liberty if it became too powerful. **Civil liberties** are freedoms protected by constitutional provisions, laws, and practices from certain types of government interference. As embodied in the Bill of Rights, civil liberties are protected by prohibitions against government actions that threaten the enjoyment of freedom. These liberties fall into two major groups: first, those associated with freedoms of expression, belief, and association; and second, those involving protections for people accused of committing a crime.

In the Preamble to the Constitution, the framers wrote that they aimed to "secure the Blessings of Liberty to ourselves and our Posterity." But in the original Constitution, they protected few liberties from the national government they were creating and almost none from state governments. To safeguard against tyranny, the framers preferred to give the national government little power with which to attack individual liberties. Rather than listing specific prohibitions against certain kinds of actions, then, they believed that a republican constitutional design that fragmented government power and that included separation of powers, checks and balances, and federalism would best protect liberty. Still, the framers singled out certain freedoms as too crucial to be left unmentioned. For example, the Constitution prohibits Congress and the states from suspending the writ of **habeas corpus**, except when public safety demands it because of rebellion or invasion, and from passing **bills of attainder** or **ex post facto laws** (see Table 15.1 for an enumeration).

As we saw in Chapter 2, many citizens found the proposed Constitution too stingy in its listing of liberties, so that the Federalists were led to promise a "bill of rights" as a condition for passing the Constitution. The Bill of Rights was passed by the 1st Congress in 1789 and was ratified by the required number of states by 1791. Passage of

civil liberties

Freedoms found primarily in the Bill of Rights, the enjoyment of which are protected from government interference.

habeas corpus

The legal doctrine that a person who is arrested must have a timely hearing before a judge.

bill of attainder

A governmental decree that a person is guilty of a crime that carries the death penalty, rendered without benefit of a trial.

ex post facto law

A law that retroactively declares some action illegal.

TABLE 15.1 Civil Liberties in the U.S. Constitution

The exact meaning and extent of civil liberties in the Constitution are matters of debate, but here are some freedoms spelled out in the text of the Constitution and its amendments or clarified by early court decisions.

Constitution

Article I, Section 9
Congress may not suspend habeas corpus.
Congress may not pass bills of attainder or ex post facto laws.

Article I, Section 10
States may not pass bills of attainder or ex post facto laws.
States may not impair obligation of contracts.

Article III, Section 2
Criminal trials in national courts must be jury trials in the state in which the defendant is alleged to have committed the crime.

Article III, Section 3
No one may be convicted of treason unless there is a confession in open court or testimony of two witnesses to the same overt act.

Article IV, Section 2
Citizens of each state are entitled to all privileges and immunities of citizens in the several states.

The Bill of Rights

First Amendment
Congress may not make any law with respect to the establishment of religion.
Congress may not abridge the free exercise of religion.
Congress may not abridge freedom of speech or of the press.
Congress may not abridge the right to assemble or to petition the government.

Second Amendment
Congress may not infringe the right to keep and bear arms.

Third Amendment
Congress may not station soldiers in houses against the owner's will, except in times of war.

Fourth Amendment
Citizens are to be free from unreasonable searches and seizures.
Federal courts may issue search warrants based only on probable cause and specifically describing the objects of search.

Fifth Amendment
Citizens are protected against double jeopardy (being prosecuted more than once for the same crime) and self-incrimination.
Citizens are guaranteed against deprivation of life, liberty, or property without due process of law.
Citizens are guaranteed just compensation for public use of their private property.

Sixth Amendment
Citizens have the right to a speedy and public trial before an impartial jury.
Citizens have the right to face their accuser and to cross-examine witnesses.

Eighth Amendment
Excessive bail and fines are prohibited.
Cruel and unusual punishments are prohibited.

the Bill of Rights made the Constitution more democratic by specifying protections of political liberty and by guaranteeing a context of free political expression that makes popular sovereignty possible.

Reading the Constitution and its amendments, however, reveals how few of our most cherished liberties are to be found in this document. Decisions by government officials and changes brought about by political leaders, interest groups, social movements, and individuals remade the Constitution in the long run; hence many of the freedoms we expect today are not specifically mentioned there. Some extensions of protected liberties were introduced by judges and other officials. Others have evolved as the culture has grown to accept novel and even once-threatening ideas. Still other liberties have secured a place in the Republic through partisan and ideological combat. The key to understanding civil liberties in the United States, then, is to follow their evolution over the course of our nation's history.

> **?** If the framers were so concerned about preventing tyranny, why did they guarantee so few liberties in the Constitution? Why might they have considered these specific protections more pressing than other liberties?

Rights and Liberties in the Nineteenth Century

15.2 Trace the evolution of civil liberties in the nineteenth century

During the nineteenth century, the range of protected civil liberties in the United States was somewhat different from their range today. Especially noteworthy were the special place of **economic liberty** and the understanding that the Bill of Rights did not apply to state governments.

Economic Liberty in the Early Republic

Liberty may be understood as protection against government interference in certain kinds of private activities. Among the few such protections mentioned in the original Constitution was one that concerned the use and enjoyment of private property. This is hardly surprising; recall from Chapter 2 that the constitutional convention was convened, in part, because many of the new nation's leading citizens by the mid-1780s were growing ever more alarmed by threats to their holdings represented by passage of stay laws and the production of cheap paper money in several states, and insurrections like Shays's Rebellion. Property rights protections are stated most directly in the Constitution in the language of contracts (i.e., the freedom to enter into binding private agreements about many things, including the use of one's property): "No State shall...pass any...Law impairing the Obligation of Contracts" (Article I, Section 10).[3] The framers protected private property in a number of other constitutional provisions as well, including provisions that created a system for recognizing intellectual property (patents and copyrights) and for safeguarding property in the form of slaves by requiring Americans to return runaway slaves to their owners (see Chapter 2). The **full faith and credit** clause (Article IV, Section 1), moreover, obligated each state to recognize contracts and other legal obligations entered into by its citizens with citizens or

economic liberty

The right to own and use property free from unreasonable government interference.

full faith and credit

The provision in Article IV, Section 1 of the Constitution which provides that states must respect the public acts, laws, and judicial rulings of other states.

legal bodies in other states. The so-called takings clause of the Fifth Amendment—ratified in 1791 with other amendments that constitute the Bill of Rights—declares that "private property [shall not] be taken for public use, without just compensation." The importance of property rights as a fundamental liberty in the body of the Constitution and its Amendments was reinforced by more than a century of judicial interpretation.[4]

> **contract clause**
>
> The portion of Article I, Section 10, of the Constitution that prohibits states from passing any law "impairing the obligations of contracts."

The Marshall Court (1801–1835) Although the Supreme Court ruled (in *Barron v. Baltimore,* 1833) that the Bill of Rights did not apply to the states, it ruled on several occasions that the **contract clause** in the Constitution directly applied against unwarranted state action. In the hands of Chief Justice John Marshall, the clause became an important defense of property rights against interference by the states. In *Fletcher v. Peck* (1810), for example, the Marshall Court upheld a sale of public land, even though almost all of the legislators who had voted for the land sale had been bribed by the prospective purchasers. Chief Justice Marshall wrote in his majority opinion that even a fraudulent sale created a contract among private individuals that the state could not void. In *Dartmouth College v. Woodward* (1819), Marshall argued in his majority opinion that New Hampshire could not modify the charter of Dartmouth College because the original charter constituted a binding contract, the terms of which could not be changed without impairing the obligations in the original contract. The framers' attempt to protect the contractual agreements of private parties ballooned in the hands of the Marshall Court to bar virtually any and all changes by the states of established property relations.[5] This expansion of property rights protections under the contract clause made it very difficult for states to regulate business activities because any such regulation could be interpreted as interfering with those binding contracts by which businesses were established and operated.

The Taney Court (1836–1864) Under the leadership of Chief Justice Roger Taney, the Court began to make a distinction between private property used in ways that encouraged economic growth and private property used for simple enjoyment. In landmark cases, the Taney Court issued rulings favoring the former when the two concepts of property conflicted.[6] In *Charles River Bridge v. Warren Bridge* (1837), investors who had secured a contract from the Massachusetts legislature for the construction of the Charles River Bridge charged that the state had violated its contract by chartering the construction of a competing bridge less than a decade later. In the majority opinion, Chief Justice Taney argued that the original charter for the Charles River Bridge did not imply a monopoly that closed off competitors. He ruled that Massachusetts could charter the rival Warren River Bridge because the states should encourage economic competition and technological advances. It did not matter that the second bridge would result in financial losses for stockholders in the Charles River Bridge. Taney argued that the "creative destruction" of established but idle property in a dynamic market economy is the price of economic and social progress.

The Court's defense of property rights was especially and tragically strong when it came to slavery. Until the Civil War, courts in the North and the South consistently upheld the right of slaveholders to recapture fugitive slaves. In his opinion in *Dred Scott v. Sandford* (1857)—a case that helped bring on the Civil War because it declared that Congress could not regulate slavery in any way, voiding the "Missouri Compromise" that had balanced the interests of free states and slave states as the country expanded westward—Chief Justice Taney declared that slaves

SLAVES BRINGING IN THE COTTON CROP   Prior to passage of the Thirteenth and Fourteenth Amendments after the Civil War, African American slaves were considered to be nothing more or less than the private property of their owners. How did the framers make the Constitution amenable to the practice of slavery?

who traveled to free states (nonslave) with their masters could not sue for their freedom because that would mean depriving slave owners of their property. Slaves, in this view, like land and tools, were nothing more nor less than private property belonging to their owners. not people in a legal sense.

Economic Liberty After the Civil War

The Fourteenth Amendment, passed after the Civil War, was designed to guarantee the citizenship rights of the newly freed slaves. It included a clause—the **due process clause**—stating that no state "may deprive a person of life, liberty, or property, without due process of law." Strangely, the Supreme Court in the late nineteenth century began to interpret this clause as a protection for businesses against the regulatory efforts of the states. In the view of the Court in *Santa Clara County* v. *Southern Pacific Railroad* (1886), corporations were "persons" in the eyes of the law and were subject to the same protections provided by the Fourteenth Amendment for any other "persons" in the United States.

The Court's most famous decision in this regard was *Lochner* v. *New York* (1905). Lochner ran a bakery in Utica, New York. He was convicted of requiring an employee to work more than 60 hours per week, contrary to a New York State maximum-hours statute. But Justice Rufus Peckham wrote for a 5–4 Supreme Court majority that the right of employer and employee to negotiate hours of work was part of the "liberty" of which, under the Fourteenth Amendment, no person could be deprived without due process of law. In other words, New York State had no right to regulate the hours of labor.

The nineteenth century was an era in which the rights of property were expanded, refined, and altered to become consistent with an emerging, dynamic industrial economy. The twentieth century would bring new approaches to property rights and to political liberties in general. These new approaches would be triggered by structural transformations in the economy and culture, the efforts of new political groups and movements, and the actions of government officials, all of which we will examine in greater detail.

Nationalization of the Bill of Rights

15.3 Outline the liberties guaranteed by the Bill of Rights and their gradual application to the states by the Supreme Court

Americans rightly understand the Bill of Rights to be a foundation of American freedom. Until the twentieth century, however, the protections of the Bill of Rights did not apply to the states, only to the

due process clause
The section of the Fourteenth Amendment that prohibits states from depriving anyone of life, liberty, or property "without due process of law," a guarantee against arbitrary or unfair government action.

national government. The Supreme Court only gradually applied the Bill of Rights to the states through a process known as **selective incorporation**.[7]

The framers were worried more about national government intrusions on individual freedom than about state government intrusions. Most of the states, after all, had bills of rights in their own constitutions, and, being closer to the people, state governments would be less likely to intrude on the people's freedom, or so the framers believed. This reading of the Bill of Rights as a prohibition of certain actions by the national government seems explicit in the language of many of the first 10 amendments. The first, for instance, starts with the words *"Congress shall make no law. . . ."* This understanding of the Bill of Rights as a set of prohibitions against certain actions by the national government and not the states was confirmed by John Marshall in *Barron* v. *Baltimore* (1833). It is apparent that the majority in Congress wanted to change the reach of the Bill of Rights, extending it to the states, however, when it approved the Fourteenth Amendment after the Civil War. Three clauses in this amendment specify that the states cannot violate the rights and liberties of the people living in them:

- The first specifies that all persons born or naturalized in the United States are citizens of both the United States and the states in which they reside.

- The **privileges and immunities clause** specifies that no *state* "shall make or enforce any law which shall abridge the privileges or immunities of citizens of the United States."

- The due process clause specifies that no *state* shall "deprive any person of life, liberty, or property, without due process of law."

Although Congress wrote the Fourteenth Amendment to guarantee that states would protect all of U.S. citizens' rights and liberties, including those found in the Bill of Rights, the Supreme Court was very slow in **nationalizing** or **incorporating** the Bill of Rights, making it binding on the state governments. Indeed, the Supreme Court has not yet fully incorporated or nationalized the Bill of Rights. Rather, it has practiced selective incorporation, only slowly adding, step by step, even traditional civil liberties to the constitutional obligations of the states. Several Amendments have not been incorporated, including the Third on quartering troops, the Fifth on a right to a grand jury hearing, the Seventh on a right to a jury trial in civil suits, and the Eighth's prohibition against excessive bail and fines.

The Second Amendment's right of gun ownership was declared a fundamental individual right by the Court in 2008 in *District of Columbia* v. *Heller* and was incorporated—that is, made incumbent upon the states to not unreasonably restrict the enjoyment of this right—soon after in *McDonald* v. *Chicago* (2010). The prevailing view in the courts until then had been that the wording of the Second Amendment protects a collective right to form militias rather than an individual right to have guns. Gun advocates such as the National Rifle Association and libertarian organizations like the Cato Institute, on the other hand, had long held that the Amendment is not a collective right but a fundamental individual right, which the Court affirmed in *Heller.* Strangely perhaps, a handful of influential liberal constitutional

---

selective incorporation

The gradual and piecemeal spread of the protections of the Bill of Rights to the states by the U.S. Supreme Court.

privileges and immunities clause

The portion of Article IV, Section 2, of the Constitution that says that citizens from out of state have the same legal rights as local citizens in any state.

nationalizing

The process by which provisions of the Bill of Rights become incorporated. See *incorporation.*

incorporation

The process by which the Supreme Court has made most of the provisions of the Bill of Rights binding on the states. See *nationalizing.*

? Was the Court's decision in *DC* v. *Heller* affirming a personal right to own a gun an expansion of individual rights, or does it restrict them? Do you think that the justices in the majority adhered to a strict constructionist view of the Constitution, or did they take a more activist approach?

IT'S A BIG DEER I'M AFTER
A man prepares to buy a rifle at a gun shop in Los Angeles. His right to do so was declared a fundamental right by the Supreme Court in 2008 and again in 2010. Those states and localities that wish to regulate the sale and ownership of guns will find it more difficult to do so after this decision.

scholars such as Sanford Levinson, Akhil Reed Amar, and Lawrence Tribe had come around to this "individual rights" understanding of the Second Amendment as well.[8] The issue of gun rights is not entirely settled, however; just how much state and local regulation of gun ownership the Court will allow remains an open question.

How does the Supreme Court decide whether to incorporate some portion of the Bill of Rights? That is, what standard does the Court use to protect a liberty specified in the Bill of Rights from violation by a state government? The answer is quite simple and is spelled out, strange as it may seem, in footnote 4 of the opinion of the Court in *United States* v. *Carolene Products Company* (1938), written by Justice Harlan Fiske Stone, where he set out the legal standards the Court had been using

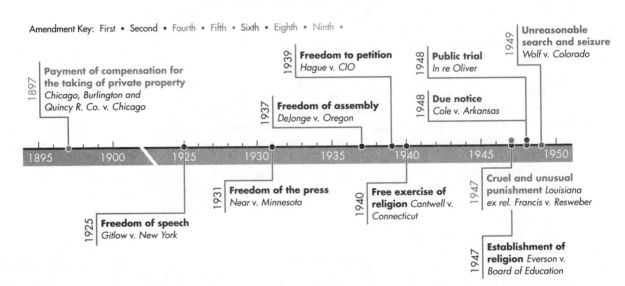

Amendment Key: First • Second • Fourth • Fifth • Sixth • Eighth • Ninth •

1897 **Payment of compensation for the taking of private property** *Chicago, Burlington and Quincy R. Co.* v. *Chicago*

1939 **Freedom to petition** *Hague* v. *CIO*

1948 **Public trial** *In re Oliver*

1949 **Unreasonable search and seizure** *Wolf* v. *Colorado*

1937 **Freedom of assembly** *DeJonge* v. *Oregon*

1948 **Due notice** *Cole* v. *Arkansas*

1895 1900 1925 1930 1935 1940 1945 1950

1931 **Freedom of the press** *Near* v. *Minnesota*

1940 **Free exercise of religion** *Cantwell* v. *Connecticut*

1947 **Cruel and unusual punishment** *Louisiana ex rel. Francis* v. *Resweber*

1925 **Freedom of speech** *Gitlow* v. *New York*

1947 **Establishment of religion** *Everson* v. *Board of Education*

FIGURE 15.1 Timeline: Milestones in Incorporation of the Bill of Rights
a"Privacy" does not appear in the Ninth Amendment, only reference to "other rights retained by the people."

in this area of constitutional interpretation, which he hoped and expected future justices would follow. Stone suggested in his footnote that most legislative enactments by states would fall under what he called **ordinary scrutiny**, meaning that the Court would assume, unless convinced otherwise, that its actions were constitutional. However, the footnote declares, three types of state actions would automatically be presumed unconstitutional, the burden being on the states to prove otherwise. When state actions are presumed to be unconstitutional, the Court is said to be exercising **strict scrutiny**. The three types of suspect state actions that bring strict scrutiny are the following:

> **ordinary scrutiny**
>
> The assumption that the actions of elected bodies and officials are legal under the Constitution.
>
> **strict scrutiny**
>
> The assumption that actions by elected bodies or officials violate constitutional rights.

- Those that seem to contradict specific prohibitions in the Constitution, including those in the Bill of Rights.
- Those that seem to restrict the democratic process.
- Those that seem to discriminate against racial, ethnic, or religious minorities.

The first of these is the subject matter of this chapter. The second has been addressed at several points in the text; for example in the cases establishing "one person, one vote." The third is the subject of Chapter 16 on civil rights. In the remainder of this chapter, we focus on specific civil liberties, clarifying their present status in both constitutional law and political practice.

Freedom of Speech

> *Congress shall make no Law ... abridging the freedom of speech.*
> —First Amendment to the U.S. Constitution

Speech can take many forms. The Court has had to consider which forms of speech are protected under the Constitution. (See Figure 15.1 for a timeline on milestones in free expression, of which speech is a key component.)

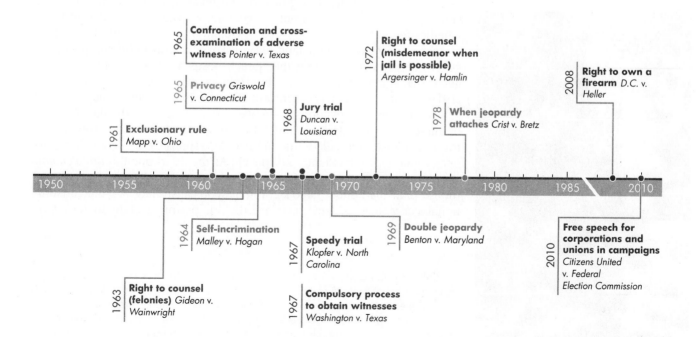

Political Speech For many people, the right to speak one's mind is the first principle of a free and democratic society. Democratic theorists have argued, by and large, that a democratic society is based not only on popular sovereignty, but on the existence of a range of freedoms that allow free and open conversations among the people about the kind of government that is best for them and the sorts of public policies they consider most appropriate. Central among these freedoms, as we discussed in Chapter 1, is speech, the idea being that public conversations about government and politics depend on the ability and willingness of people to express their views, even if it means saying unpopular, even inflammatory things. Justice Oliver Wendell Holmes described the centrality of this "marketplace of ideas" in a free society in his famous and influential dissenting opinion in *Abrams* v. *United States* (1919).

Given the centrality of free speech to democracy, it is perhaps odd that free speech was not incorporated (made applicable to state governments) by the Supreme Court until 1925 in *Gitlow* v. *New York* (1925). Benjamin Gitlow had published *The Left Wing Manifesto,* which embraced a militant, revolutionary socialism to mobilize the proletariat to destroy the existing order in favor of communism. Gitlow did not advocate specific action to break the law, but he was nonetheless convicted of a felony under the New York Criminal Anarchy Law (1902).

The Supreme Court majority held that New York State was bound by the First Amendment—thus incorporating the First Amendment, making it binding on all states—but then argued that even the First Amendment did not prohibit New York from incarcerating Gitlow for his publishing and distributing his pamphlet because it represented a danger to peace and order for which, said Justice Edward Sanford, "A single revolutionary spark may kindle a fire that, smoldering for a time, may burst into a sweeping and destructive conflagration. It cannot be said that the State is acting...unreasonably when...it seeks to extinguish the spark without waiting until it has enkindled the flame or blazed into the conflagration." In his famous dissent, Justice Oliver Wendell Holmes said, "Every idea is an incitement...Eloquence may set fire to reason. But whatever may be thought of the redundant discourse before us, it had no chance of starting a present conflagration."

Freedom of speech has grown in the ensuing years so that far more speech is protected than is not. In general, no U.S. government today—whether federal, state, or local—can regulate or interfere with the content of speech without a compelling reason. For a reason to be compelling, a government must show that the speech poses a "clear and present danger"—the standard formulated by Holmes in *Schenck* v. *United States* (1919)—that it has a duty to prevent. The danger, moreover, must be very substantial, and the relationship between the speech and the danger must be direct, such as falsely yelling "Fire!" in a crowded theater. The danger must also be so immediate that the people responsible for maintaining order cannot afford to tolerate the speech. As the Court put it in *Brandenburg* v. *Ohio* (1969), in a case involving an appeal of the conviction of a leader of the Ku Klux Klan under Ohio's criminal syndicalism law, "...the constitutional guarantees of free speech...do not permit a State to forbid or

BURNING THE FLAG Can state legislatures or Congress pass laws prohibiting flag burning? Although many Americans are infuriated by flag burning and want the practice banned, the Supreme Court has ruled that such laws violate freedom of expression. The only alternative for people who feel strongly about this issue is to amend the Constitution to protect the flag, but proposed amendments so far have not gained sufficient support in Congress.

proscribe advocacy of the use of force or of law violation except where such advocacy is directed to incitement or producing imminent lawless action and is likely to incite or produce such action." Abstract advocacy of ideas, even ideas considered dangerous by police, politicians, or popular majorities, is protected unless it meets both conditions.

In the name of free speech, the Court has been gradually taking apart legislative efforts to restrict campaign spending in federal elections. In *Buckley* v. *Valeo* (1976) it invalidated parts of the Federal Election Campaign Act, most significantly, a restriction on how much money a candidate for federal office might put into his or her own campaign. In *Federal Election Commission* v. *Wisconsin Right to Life* (2007), the Court ruled that restrictions on media advertising by corporations and labor unions in the period immediately before an election in the Bipartisan Campaign Reform Act of 2002 (McCain-Feingold) is an unconstitutional restriction on free speech. In *Citizens United* v. *Federal Election Commission* (2010), a bitterly divided Court ruled in the name of free speech that government could not restrict in any way what corporations and unions spend during campaigns, excepting direct contributions to candidate committees.

Not all political speech is protected against government restriction. The Supreme Court has allowed governments to restrain and punish speakers whose words can be shown to lead or to have led directly to acts of violence or vandalism, interfered with the constitutional rights of others (e.g., blocking access to an abortion clinic), disrupted a legitimate government function (e.g., a sit-in demonstration in the House chambers), talked to others of information contained in classified documents, or trespassed on private or public property, whether people's businesses and homes or a secured defense installation. The Court has also allowed some restrictions on speech during time of war. But over the years, the Court has been careful to keep the leash tight on government officials who have tried to quiet the voice of citizens. Any attempt to restrict political speech must be content neutral (i.e., it cannot favor some views over others), serve a legitimate government purpose, be narrowly tailored to address a specific problem (i.e., it cannot be vague), and not have a chilling effect on other people's willingness to exercise their free speech rights. All in all, then, freedom of speech has gained powerful legal foundations over the years and is an important component of democracy in the United States.[9]

Actions and Symbolic Speech

Difficult questions about free expression persist, of course. Speech mixed with *conduct* may be restricted if the restrictions are narrowly and carefully tailored to curb the conduct while leaving the speech unmolested. Symbolic expressions (such as wearing armbands or picketing) may also receive less protection from the Court. The use of profanity or words that are likely to cause violence ("fighting words") may be regulated in some cases, as may symbolic actions that prevent others from carrying out legitimate activities. Still, freedom of speech throughout the United States has grown to the point at which contenders wrestle with relatively peripheral issues, leaving a large sphere of expressive freedom. *Texas* v. *Johnson* (1989) shows just how far the protection of free speech has expanded. In this case, Gregory Johnson challenged a Texas state law against flag desecration under which he had been convicted for burning an American flag as part of a demonstration at the 1984 Republican convention. Although dominated by a conservative majority, the Rehnquist Court overturned the Texas law, saying that flag burning falls under the free expression protections of the Constitution unless imminent incitement or violence is likely. In response, some members of Congress have tried on several occasions, without success, to pass an anti-flag desecration constitutional amendment for consideration by the states.

Suppression of Free Expression   A major exception to the expansion of freedom of expression has been the periodic concern among the authorities about internal security and national defense.[10] Fearing a rise of radicalism inflamed by the French Revolution, Congress passed the Sedition Act of 1798 to forbid criticism of the government and its leaders. The Civil War saw some restrictions on speech by the states, although the national government remained surprisingly lenient on this score (the Lincoln administration did, however, jail some rebel sympathizers without trial and used military tribunals to try civilians accused of actively helping the southern cause). Censorship of dissent and protests occurred during and after World War I; 32 states enacted laws to suppress dangerous ideas and talk, and local, state, and national officials led raids on the offices of "radicals." Hoping to become president, Attorney General A. Mitchell Palmer conducted raids on the headquarters of suspect organizations in 1919 and 1920, sending the young J. Edgar Hoover out to collect information on suspected anarchists and communists.

A similar period of hysteria followed World War II. Its foundations were laid when the Democrat-controlled House of Representatives created the House Committee on Un-American Affairs (generally referred to as the HUAC). When the Republicans won control of the Congress in 1952, they professed to see security risks in the Truman administration, labor unions, and Hollywood. Soon Democrats and Republicans alike were exploiting the "Red scare" for political gain. The greatest gain (and, subsequently, the hardest fall) was for Senator Joseph McCarthy (R–WI). McCarthy brandished lists of purported communists and denounced all who opposed him as traitors.[11]

Many civil libertarians also worry about the possible chilling effect on free speech and privacy violations of new laws passed to fight what George W. Bush called the war on terrorism. Most important is the USA Patriot Act—passed in 2001 and renewed in 2006 with a few small changes to allow for a little more judicial oversight—granting the federal government access to Americans' private and business records. Revelations that the FBI and the NSA had been conducting secret and warrantless searches of phone conversations (land lines and cell phones), financial transactions, and Internet communications ever since 9/11 led to intense press scrutiny, public condemnation, and congressional probes in early 2006, but the opposition was unable to block renewal of the Patriot Act. In 2007, in a revelation that came too late to affect congressional deliberations on renewal, FBI director Robert Mueller reported to Congress that, since 2001, his agents had improperly and sometimes illegally obtained personal information on thousands of American citizens by overzealously using tools provided by the Act.[12]

Freedom of the Press

Congress shall make no law…abridging the freedom…of the press.
—First Amendment to the U.S. Constitution

In an aside in the opinion of the Court in *Gitlow* v. *New York* (1925), the Supreme Court included freedom of the press as a freedom guaranteed against state interference by the Fourteenth Amendment. Incorporation of this aspect of the Bill of Rights seems reasonable in light of the importance of the free flow of information in a society that aspires to freedom and democracy.

Prior Restraint   In *Near* v. *Minnesota* (1931), the Court made good on the promise of *Gitlow* by invalidating the Minnesota Public Nuisance Law as a violation of freedom of the press.[13] Jay Near published the *Saturday Press*, a scandal sheet that attacked local crime, public officials, and a few other groups that he disliked: Jews, Catholics, blacks, and unions, for example. Near and his associates were ordered by a state court not to publish, sell, or possess the *Saturday Press*. This sort of state action is called **prior restraint** because it prevents publication before it has occurred. Freedom of the press is not necessarily infringed if publishers are sued or punished for harming others after they have published, but Minnesota was trying to keep Near and his associates from publishing in the future.

> **prior restraint**
> The government's power to prevent publication, as opposed to punishment afterward.
>
> **obscenity**
> As defined by the Supreme Court, the representation of sexually explicit material in a manner that violates community standards and is without redeeming social importance or value.

The prohibition of prior restraint on publication remains the core of freedom of the press.[14] Freedom of the press and freedom of speech tend to be considered together as freedom of expression, so the general principles applicable to free speech apply to freedom of the press as well. Thus, the Court will allow the repression of publication only if the state can show some "clear and present danger" that publication poses, similar to its position on free speech. In *New York Times* v. *United States* (1971), the Court ruled that the U.S. government could not prevent newspapers from publishing portions of the Pentagon Papers, secret government documents revealing the sordid story of how the United States had become involved in the Vietnam War. A major expansion of freedom of the press in *New York Times* v. *Sullivan* (1964) protects newspapers against punishment for trivial or incidental errors when they are reporting on public persons. This limits the use or threat of libel prosecutions by officials because officials can recover damages only by showing that the medium has purposely reported untruths or has made no effort to find out if what is being reported is true.

> **?** In this age of instant, online publication, is prior restraint even an issue? Is there any way the government could prevent a story from being published today?

Protecting Sources Many reporters and executives in news organizations believe that reporters must be able to protect their sources if they are to have access to insider information that the public needs to know. Without protection of sources, newspeople suggest, the stream of information that the public requires in a democracy will flow more slowly. This is the argument that *New York Times* reporter Judith Miller made when she went to jail for 85 days in 2005 for refusing to testify about her source in the administration who had revealed the identity of CIA operative Valerie Plame, who happened to be the wife of a vocal critic of President Bush's reasons for going to war in Iraq. Although most states have shield laws allowing reporters to protect their sources, there is no such federal law, and the Supreme Court has rejected the argument that constitutional doctrines on freedom of the press give reporters immunity from testifying when they have been issued a subpoena by a court (see *Branzburg* v. *Hayes*, 1972).

Offensive Media *Pornography* is a nonlegal term for offensive sexual materials; the legal term is **obscenity**. Although the courts have held that *obscenity* is unprotected by the First Amendment, the definition of obscenity has provoked constitutional struggles for half a century. Early disputes concerned the importation and mailing of works that we regard today as classics: James Joyce's *Ulysses* and D. H. Lawrence's *Lady Chatterley's Lover*, for example.[15] Although the justices admitted that principled distinctions sometimes eluded them (Justice Potter Stewart once famously said that he did not know how to define hard-core pornography but that he knew it when he saw it), a reasonably

CONTROVERSIAL ART   The distinction between art and obscenity can be very difficult to establish, and battles over the banning of controversial works, such as Robert Mapplethorpe's homoerotic photographs, are quite common in American communities. How does the Court decide what constitutes obscenity?

clear three-part test emerged from *Miller* v. *California* (1973):

1. The average person, applying contemporary community standards, must find that the work as a whole appeals to the prurient interest (lust).

2. The state law must specifically define what depictions of sexual conduct are obscene.

3. The work as a whole must lack serious literary, artistic, political, or scientific value.

If the work survives even one part of this test, it is not legally obscene and is protected by the First Amendment. Community standards, applied by juries, are used to judge whether the work appeals to lust and whether the work is clearly offensive. However, literary, artistic, political, and scientific value (called the *LAPS test,* after the first letter of each of the four values) is *not* judged by community standards but by the jury's assessment of the testimony of expert witnesses. If, and only if, all three standards are met, the Supreme Court will allow local committees to regulate the sale of obscene materials. Because these tests are not easily met in practice, the *Miller* ruling has done little to stem the tide of sexually explicit material in American popular culture.[16] The Court has ruled, however, in *New York* v. *Ferber* (1982) that states can prohibit the production, distribution, and sale of child pornography.

Recently, many Americans have begun to worry about the availability to minors of sexually offensive material on the Internet. Responding to this concern, Congress and President Clinton cooperated in 1996 to pass the Communications Decency Act, which made it a crime to transmit over the Internet or to allow the transmission of indecent materials to which minors might have access. The Supreme Court, in *Reno, Attorney General of the United States* v. *American Civil Liberties Union* (1997), ruled unanimously that the legislation was an unconstitutional violation of the First Amendment, being overly broad and vague and violative of the free speech rights of adults to receive and send information (the Court reaffirmed this ruling in 2004). The strong and unambiguous words of the opinion of the Court make it clear that government efforts to regulate the content of the Internet will not get very far. It may well be the case, however, that Internet-filtering software that allows parents to keep objectionable material from their children will accomplish the same end as government regulation without danger of violating the Constitution.

Religious Freedom

For much of our history, Congress did not impede the exercise of religion because it did not legislate much on the subject. Because the states were not covered by the First Amendment, the free exercise of religion was protected by state constitutions or not at all. The Supreme Court was content to defer to the states on issues of religious freedom.

As late as 1940, in *Minersville School District* v. *Gobitis,* the Supreme Court upheld the expulsion of two schoolchildren who refused to salute the flag because it violated their faith as Jehovah's Witnesses. Justice Harlan Stone wrote a stinging dissent:

> The Constitution expresses more than the conviction of the people that democratic processes must be preserved at all costs. It is also an expression of faith and a command that freedom of mind and spirit must be preserved, which government must obey, if it is to adhere to that justice and moderation without which no free government can exist.

Stone's dissent, as well as a series of decisions deferring to state restrictions on Jehovah's Witnesses in 1941 and 1942, eventually moved other justices to Stone's side. In *West Virginia* v. *Barnette* (1943), the Court reversed *Gobitis* and firmly established free exercise of religion as protected against infringement by the states.

Free Exercise of Religion

Congress shall make no law … prohibiting the free exercise [of religion].
—First Amendment to the U.S. Constitution

The core of the **free exercise clause** today is that neither the federal government nor state governments may interfere with religious *beliefs*. This is one of the few absolutes in U.S. constitutional law. Religious *actions,* however, are not absolutely protected. Here the issue involves whether people with sincere religious beliefs are exempt from laws and regulations that hold for others in course of practicing their religion. The Court has upheld state laws, for instance, outlawing the use of peyote (an illegal hallucinogen) in Native American religious ceremonies (*Employment Division* v. *Smith,* 1990). Congress and President Clinton tried to overturn this decision with the Religious Freedom Restoration Act in 1993, but the Act was declared unconstitutional in *City of Boerne* v. *Flores* (1997) because the act, in view of the Court majority, unduly extended national government power over the states. By and large, then, people are free in the United States to believe what they want to believe religiously, and to worship as they wish unless worship practices violate general statutes that serve some compelling public purpose, such as state and federal drug laws or local public health ordinances (which in most locales do not permit such religious practices as animal sacrifice).

Establishment of Religion

Congress shall make no law respecting an establishment of religion.
—First Amendment to the U.S. Constitution

Many countries in the world have an official state religion. Sometimes this means that religious law trumps secular law in almost every instance, as in Saudi Arabia and Iran. Sometimes this means that religious law takes precedence in a narrow range of matters, usually involving family matters like marriage and divorce, as in Israel. Often, a state church will exist but not affect everyday life in many ways, playing more of a symbolic role. In most western European democracies that have monarchies, for example, the king or queen must be a member in good standing of the state church. Monarchs in Great Britain must be members of the Church of England.

There is no state church in the United States but many churches (and mosques and synagogues) and many religious people (see Chapter 4).

free exercise clause
That portion of the First Amendment to the Constitution that prohibits Congress from impeding religious observance or impinging upon religious beliefs.

establishment clause

The part of the First Amendment to the Constitution that prohibits Congress from establishing an official religion; the basis for the doctrine of the separation of church and state.

What allows them to peacefully coexist, in the view of many, is not only the broad freedom to worship or not worship as one pleases under terms of the "free exercise" clause of the First Amendment, but keeping religion and government at arms length from one another. Freedom of conscience, it is often argued, requires that government not favor one religion over another by granting it special favors, privileges, or status, or interfering in the affairs of religious institutions. It requires, in Jefferson's famous terms, "a wall of separation between church and state." Nevertheless, incorporation of the **establishment clause** proved to be a particularly messy matter. In *Everson* v. *Board of Education* (1947), Justice Hugo Black for the Supreme Court determined that no state could use revenues to support an institution that taught religion, thus incorporating the First Amendment ban into the Fourteenth Amendment. But the majority in that case upheld the New Jersey program that reimbursed parents for bus transportation to parochial schools. A year later, Justice Black wrote another opinion incorporating the establishment clause in *McCollum* v. *Board of Education* (1948). This time, a program for teaching religion in public schools was found unconstitutional. In *Zorach* v. *Clauson* (1952), however, the Court upheld a similar program in New York State that let students leave school premises early for religious instruction. The establishment clause had been incorporated, but the justices long have had a difficult time determining what "separation of church and state" means in practice.

? If a majority of Americans wish to have less of a wall between church and state—for example, by allowing prayer in public schools—is it democratic for the courts to stand in the way of the majority? What place do individual liberties have in a majoritarian democracy?

The *Lemon* Test   The Warren Court (1953–1969) brought together a solid church–state separationist contingent whose decisions the early Burger Court (1969–1973) distilled into the major doctrine of the establishment clause: the "*Lemon* test." In *Lemon* v. *Kurtzman* (1971), Chief Justice Warren Burger specified three conditions that every law must meet to avoid "establishing" religion:

1. The law must have a secular *purpose*. That secular purpose need not be the only or primary purpose behind the law. The Court requires merely some plausible nonreligious reason for the law.

2. The *primary effect* of the law must be neither to advance nor to retard religion. The Court will assess the probable effect of a governmental action for religious neutrality.

3. Government must never foster *excessive entanglements* between the state and religion.

While the *Lemon* test would seem to have erected substantial walls that bar mixing church and state, the Court has not been entirely consistent over time in applying it to real cases.[17] For example, while the Rehnquist Court took some bricks out of the walls, it was not altogether predictable in its rulings. In *Rosenberger* v. *University of Virginia* (1995), it ruled that the university (a state-supported institution) must provide the same financial subsidy to a student religious publication that it provides to other student publications. In 2002, in *Zelman* v. *Simmons-Harris,* decided by a 5–4 vote, the Court approved Cleveland's program of school vouchers that provides public money to parents who want to send their children to private schools, whether secular or religious. The Court majority based its ruling on the fact that public monies do not go directly to religious schools in the Cleveland program but rather to parents who are free to choose their children's school(s). In other cases, the Rehnquist Court ruled that public monies can go to parochial schools if they are for programs that are similar to ones in public schools and not used to advance religious instruction. This would include things such as funds to purchase science books or support drug education programs.[18] However, the Rehnquist Court was unwilling to depart too far from the principle of separation of church and state; in 2004, for example, the Court ruled that the state of Washington had done no constitutional harm when it denied a state-funded scholarship to a student studying for the ministry.

With regard to religious displays in courthouses and other public buildings, the Rehnquist Court seemingly adopted Justice Sandra Day O'Connor's somewhat vague proposition that the establishment clause does not forbid religious displays in courthouses and other public buildings unless a "reasonable observer would view them as endorsing religious beliefs or practices."[19] The Court seems to have decided that it will need to look at such things as religious displays—lights, manger scenes, and the like—at public buildings on a case-by-case basis. In 2005, it ruled in one instance that hanging framed copies of the Ten Commandments in a courthouse in Kentucky went too far in promoting a particular set of religious beliefs (*McCreary County, Kentucky, et al.* v. *ACLU*). As Justice David Souter put it in his majority opinion, "The reasonable observer could only think that the counties meant to emphasize and celebrate the religious message...The display's unstinting focus was on religious passages [posted with the Commandments], showed that the counties posted the Commandments precisely because of their sectarian content." In another ruling handed down the same day (*Van Orden* v. *Perry*), the Court allowed a display of a six-foot-high monument of the Ten Commandments in front of the state capitol in Austin because it was one of 40 monuments and historical markers that, in the words of Justice Stephen Breyer, "...served a mixed but primarily nonreligious purpose."

Waiting in the wings are a range of issues involving the separation of church and state that the Court will eventually consider, given the number of cases that are working their way up from state courts and federal district courts. These include the legitimacy of the words "one nation under God" in the Pledge of Allegiance, the acceptability of the nondenominational prayers that open the daily sessions in Congress, and the legitimacy of "faith-based" programs that deliver public services through religious organizations. The point here is fairly straightforward: the debate over where to draw the line that separates church and state is a continuing one in America and is unlikely to ever be resolved once and for all.

Religion in Public Schools

One of the most controversial aspects of constitutional law regarding the establishment of religion concerns school prayer. Although a majority of Americans support allowing a nondenominational prayer or a period of silent prayer in the schools, the Court has consistently ruled against such practices since the early 1960s, perhaps believing that children in school settings, as opposed to adults in other areas of life, are more likely to feel pressure from those conveying religious messages. In *Engel* v. *Vitale* (1962), the Court ordered the state of New York to suspend its requirement that all students in public schools recite a nondenominational prayer at the start of each school day. In *Stone* v. *Graham* (1980), the Court ruled against posting the Ten Commandments in public school classrooms. In *Lee* v. *Weisman* (1992), it ruled against allowing school-sponsored prayer at graduation ceremonies. In *Santa Fe Independent School District* v. *Doe* (2000), the Court ruled that student-led prayers at school-sponsored events such as football games are not constitutionally permissible because they have the "improper effect of coercing those present to participate in an act of religious worship." In these and other cases the Court has consistently ruled against officially sponsored prayer in public schools as a violation of the separation of church and state.

Returning prayer to the public schools and making schools less secular are very high on the agenda of religious conservatives. Bills supporting voluntary classroom prayer (such as a moment of silent contemplation) are constantly being introduced into Congress and state legislatures, with little success so far. Christian conservatives have also tried without success to pass a school prayer constitutional amendment. In several very religious communities, school officials have simply ignored the Supreme Court and continue to allow prayer in public classrooms.

An important battle about religion in the schools concerns attempts by some committed believers to either exclude Darwinian evolutionary biology from the school curriculum or to balance it with alternative interpretations such as "creationism" (the idea that God created the earth as described in the Bible) or "intelligent design" (the idea that the natural world is so complex that it could not have evolved as scientists propose, advocated by the Discovery Institute in Seattle). Because courts at all levels have rejected the teaching of "creationism" in the science curriculum as an improper intrusion of religion into public education, many religious activists have pushed "intelligent design" as an alternative approach that might pass

PRAY AND PLAY Here, a high school coach leads his team in prayer before a game. This practice, quite common across America, raises important questions about the "establishment" clause, especially the degree to which local school authorities in many communities are willing to comply with the doctrine of "separation of church and state." Should the federal government take a harder line against such practices, or should they be left alone as long as no one complains?

court muster. The Dover, Pennsylvania, school board tried this strategy but lost in federal court. As Judge John Jones put it in his opinion in *Kitzmiller* v. *Dover Area School District* (2005), "...we conclude that the religious nature of ID [intelligent design] would be readily apparent to an objective observer, adult, or child.... The overwhelming evidence at trial established that ID is a religious view, a mere relabeling of creationism, and not a scientific theory."

With no sign that the tide of religious feeling is about to recede in the United States, debates over school prayer, religious displays in school, and the teaching of evolution will continue for the foreseeable future. The main reason these issues will linger is that neither the courts nor the American people are entirely certain where the line between church and state should be drawn.

Privacy

The freedoms addressed so far—speech, press, and religion—are listed in the First Amendment. The freedom to be left alone in our private lives—what is usually referred to as the *right to privacy*—is nowhere mentioned in the First Amendment or any of the other amendments that make up the Bill of Rights. Nevertheless, most Americans consider the right to privacy to be one of our most precious freedoms; most believe we ought to be spared wiretapping, e-mail snooping, and the regulation of consensual sexual activities in our own homes, for instance. Many (though not all) constitutional scholars believe, moreover, that a right to privacy is inherent in the Bill of Rights, even if it is not explicitly stated; note the prohibitions against illegal searches and seizures and against quartering of troops in our homes, as well as the right to free expression and conscience. Such scholars also point to the Ninth Amendment as evidence that the framers believed in the existence of liberties not specifically mentioned in the Bill of Rights: "The enumeration in the Constitution of certain rights, shall not be construed to deny or disparage others retained by the people." The Supreme Court agreed with this position in *Griswold* v. *Connecticut* (1965), in which it ruled that a constitutional right to privacy exists when it struck down laws making birth control illegal.

? Is it reasonable to call privacy a right when it is not specifically spelled out as such in the Constitution? If most Americans believe they have a right to privacy, should the Constitution be amended to guarantee it?

Most jurists and legal scholars have come to accept that a fundamental right to privacy exists, though a group of "original intent" conservatives like Justice Clarence Thomas do not agree. Even among those who accept the fundamental right to privacy disagree on its specific applicability in the areas of abortion, gay and lesbian rights, the right to die, and the security of interpersonal communications during wartime.

Abortion *Griswold*'s right to privacy doctrine became the basis for Justice Harry Blackmun's majority opinion in the landmark case *Roe* v. *Wade* (1973), in which the Court ruled in favor of a woman's right to terminate her pregnancy. Blackmun's opinion in *Roe* prohibited the states from interfering with a woman's decision to have an abortion in the first two trimesters of her pregnancy and prohibited any state actions in the third trimester that might threaten the life or health of the mother. The ruling transformed abortion from a legislative issue into a constitutional issue, from a matter of policy into a matter of rights. It remains one of the most contentious issues in American politics.

The background to the ruling was a changing attitude towards abortion in many parts of the United States. By the time *Roe* was decided, 11 states already had reformed their statutes to allow women to have abortions when the woman's health, fetal abnormalities, or rape or incest were involved. Four more states (Alaska, Hawaii, Washington, and New York) had already gone further and repealed all prohibitions of abortion. In most state legislatures, however, progress was slow or nonexistent.

The litigation over abortion reflected changes in public opinion, pressure by interest groups, and persisting inequities against women. Disapproval of abortion decreased and discussion of abortion increased during the 1960s, even among Roman Catholics.[20] Numerous groups worked to reform or to eliminate abortion laws before *Roe* was decided.[21] The pro-choice team benefited from 42 amicus curiae briefs. The medical profession, which had been instrumental in making abortion a crime in the nineteenth century,[22] supported reform in the 1960s.

The Court's decision hardly resolved matters. Anti-abortion groups, energized by the repeal of abortion laws, struck back after *Roe*. Single-issue, anti-abortion politics surfaced in the 1976 and subsequent elections and became an important factor in the emergence of a conservative movement in American politics and the rising political power of the Republican Party. In this environment, and with the appointment of several Supreme Court justices concerned about the sweeping character of the *Roe* ruling, many states began to place restrictions on abortion, ranging from parental notification to waiting periods, counseling about alternatives to abortion, and prohibitions on the use of public money for the procedure. In *Webster* v. *Reproductive Health Services* (1989), the Court seemed to invite these restrictions. A few years later, however, in *Planned Parenthood* v. *Casey* (1992), the Court ruled that these restrictions cannot go so far as to make abortion impossible to obtain. In the words of Justice Sandra Day O'Connor, while some restrictions are acceptable, none could "place an undue burden" on a woman's fundamental right to terminate a pregnancy. Furthermore, the Court has ruled in a number of cases since *Casey,* most recently in 2006, that state and federal laws and regulations restricting abortions must always contain exceptions for situations in which the life or health of the mother is at risk.

Many abortion opponents, however, now believe that a direct challenge to *Roe* might be successful given the addition of two more conservatives to the Court (Roberts in 2005 and Alito in 2006). Friends of *Roe* were alarmed and its foes were encouraged by the Court's 5–4 ruling in 2007 upholding the federal Partial-Birth Abortion Act, the first time a specific abortion method had been banned. A similar ban by the state of Nebraska had been rejected by the Court in 2000 when Justice Sandra Day O'Connor was a member.

THE UNENDING ARGUMENT A Supreme Court decision on a controversial matter like abortion generally does settle things once and for all in American politics. The decision often is challenged in other venues by other political actors, enabling the Court to refine its initial decision over time or change it entirely. These anti-abortion protesters in Washington in 2010 were demanding that the Court overturn its decision in *Roe* v. *Wade* (1973) in which it ruled that a woman's right to terminate her pregnancy is a fundamental right. Is this lack of permanency in legal interpretation a bad thing, or is it an important part of how American democracy works?

Private Sexual Activity   The Supreme Court had ruled as recently as 1986 in *Bowers v. Hardwick* that private sexual activity between consenting adults was not a protected right under the constitution. States could, in its view, continue to outlaw certain sexual acts, particularly those involving homosexuals, as the state of Georgia continued to do after winning *Bowers*. Things changed after privacy was recognized as a fundamental right in *Griswold*. In *Lawrence* v. *Texas* (2003) the Court ruled that state anti-sodomy laws prohibiting consensual gay and lesbian sexual relations are unconstitutional. "Private lives in matters pertaining to sex," declared Justice Anthony Kennedy in his majority opinion, "are a protected liberty." This reversal of its own ruling in so short a period of time is unusual in the history of the Court; though, as we saw in this chapter's section on free speech, it did so recently in the campaign finance case, *Citizens United* v. *Federal Election Commission* (2010).

The Right to Die   It is relatively unclear yet whether the courts will support a privacy-based "right to die." So far the Supreme Court has refused to endorse or reject the existence of such a right. The status of this potential right was at the heart of the case of Terri Schiavo, a comatose heart attack victim with extensive brain damage, who was dependent on a feeding tube to keep her alive, albeit in a "persistent vegetative state." The Florida courts had ruled on several occasions that the feeding tube could be removed, per her husband's wishes; her parents were fighting that decision. A law passed in record time by Congress and signed by President Bush in 2005 insisted that the federal courts take up jurisdiction in the case. But both federal district and circuit courts supported the position of the Florida Supreme Court.

In 2004, the Ninth Circuit Court of Appeals upheld Oregon's assisted suicide law (called the Death with Dignity Act) passed by voters in 1994. In its opinion the justices strongly criticized Attorney General John Ashcroft's announcement that any doctor prescribing drugs that are used by patients to end their lives would be subject to prosecution under the federal Controlled Substances Act, saying that his action "far exceeds the scope of his authority under federal law." The Supreme Court upheld the ruling of the Ninth Circuit in 2006 in *Gonzales* v. *Oregon*. Interestingly, the ruling was based on very narrow grounds—whether the Attorney General could prosecute doctors for prescribing end-of-life drugs—but did not consider whether doctor-assisted suicide was a protected privacy-based right. The Court's ruling leaves the matter, at least for the time being, in the hands of the states, unless Congress chooses to legislate on the issue.

Private Communications   Finally, there are issues relating to government intrusion on private communications. News in late 2005 about the government's extensive surveillance operations targeting American citizens in the name of the war on terrorism—whether in a fashion authorized by the USA Patriot Act or in secret, warrantless phone and Internet searches by the NSA—created a firestorm of criticism about possible violation of fundamental American liberties. We will look at this in more detail later in this chapter.

So, a right to privacy is well established in principle. Disagreements continue to exist, however, on what this means in practice.

Rights of Those Accused of a Crime

The framers were so concerned about protections for individuals suspected, accused, or convicted of a crime that they included important protections in the main body of the Constitution. Article I, as you have learned, prohibits Congress, and by implication, the federal government, from issuing bills of attainder, passing ex post facto laws, or suspending the right of habeas corpus (this last is much in the news because of the types of hearings used for terrorism detainees, something we will look at later in the chapter). Further indication of their concern for the rights of those accused of a crime is the fact that five of the 10 amendments that make up the Bill of Rights are about providing such protections. Most Americans today treasure the constitutional rights and liberties that protect innocent individuals—what are generally termed *due process* protections—from wrongful prosecution and imprisonment. But most Americans also want to control crime as much as possible. The latter concern seems to be winning out; although the United States accounts for a little less than 5 percent of the world's population, it has almost one-fourth of the world's total prison population.[23]

When reading about the status of protections for those accused of a crime, it is well to keep in mind the discussion of constitutional eras from Chapter 14 on the Supreme Court.[24] The general pattern on constitutional protections in this area of the law follows the pattern on many other rights issues. Warren Court (1953–1969) rulings greatly expended protections, Burger Court (1969–1986) rulings trimmed protections for defendants, and the Rehnquist Court (1987–2004) quickened the pace of favoring prosecutors. It remains too early to predict the direction of the Roberts Court, though the strongly unified conservative majority and the addition to the Court of Obama nominee and former prosecutor Sonia Sotomayor suggests further movement away from the Warren Court on protections for those accused of a crime.

Unreasonable Searches and Seizures

The Fourth Amendment secures the right of all persons against unreasonable searches and seizures and allows the granting of search warrants only if the police can specify evidence of serious law-breaking that they reasonably expect to find. Until the Warren Court compelled the states to abide by the Fourth Amendment in 1961, they had frequently used searches and seizures that the federal courts would consider "unreasonable" in an effort to control crime. In *Mapp* v. *Ohio* (1961), the Supreme Court enunciated that the **exclusionary rule** to prevent the police and prosecutors from using evidence that had been gained through warrantless and unreasonable searches to convict people must be followed by the states. A majority of the justices believed that the threat of perpetrators' being freed in cases where unreasonable searches had been conducted eventually would force the police to play by the constitutional rules while conducting their investigations.

The Warren Court (1953–1969) demanded that the police get warrants whenever the person to be subjected to a search had a "reasonable expectation of privacy."[25] The Burger Court (1969–1986) limited the places in which privacy could be reasonably expected, allowing searches of moving cars stopped even for routine traffic infractions and of garbage cans set out for collection. The Burger Court authorized a "good-faith" exception to the exclusionary rule, under which prosecutors may introduce evidence obtained illegally if they can show that the police had relied on a warrant that appeared valid but later proved to be invalid.[26] The Court allowed another exception for illegally gathered evidence that would have been discovered eventually without the illegal search.[27] The Rehnquist Court went well beyond these exceptions. In *Murray* v. *United States* (1988), it allowed prosecutors to use products of illegal searches if other evidence unrelated to the illegal evidence would have justified a search warrant. The combination of "good faith," "inevitable discovery," and "retroactive probable cause" considerably narrowed the exclusionary rule. The Rehnquist Court (1986–2005) further narrowed the exclusionary rule when it held in *Wyoming* v. *Houghton* (1999) that police who have **probable cause** to search an automobile

exclusionary rule

A standard promulgated by the Supreme Court that prevents police and prosecutors from using evidence against a defendant that was obtained in an illegal search.

probable cause

Legal doctrine that refers to a reasonable belief that a crime has been committed.

CAR STOP Even the conservative Roberts Court has ruled that police cannot routinely search a car when it is stopped for a routine traffic violation; probable cause that a more serious crime has been committed or is being committed is the only ground to do so. What is the best course to take to protect both the rights of Americans and the need for public safety?

for illegal substances may also search personal possessions (in this case, a purse) of passengers in the car. In *Hudson* v. *Michigan* (2005), the Roberts Court ruled that police need not knock or announce their presence when entering a house with a search warrant.

However, the Court has stopped short of taking the exclusionary rule back to pre-Warren Court days. It ruled, for example, that police could not search every driver or car involved in petty traffic offenses. Thus, a bag of marijuana discovered in a search incident to a speeding ticket in *Knowles* v. *Iowa* (1998) was excluded as the product of an illegal search. Moreover, the Court ruled in *Kyllo* v. *United States* (2001) that police could not use high-technology thermal devices to search through the walls of a house to check for the presence of high-intensity lights used for growing marijuana. Justice Scalia was especially incensed, saying in his opinion that to allow such searches "would leave the homeowner at the mercy of advancing technology..." And, in 2009, the Court ruled that the police needed to demonstrate a threat to public safety or a need to preserve evidence to search a compartment in someone's car.

Self-Incrimination The Warren Court was instrumental in incorporating Fifth Amendment protections against self-incrimination. It determined, for example, that the privilege not to be forced to incriminate oneself was useless at trial if the police coerced confessions long before the trial took place. To forestall "third-degree" tactics in the station house, the Court detailed a stringent set of procedural guarantees: the famous rights established in *Miranda* v. *Arizona* (1966). Once detained by authorities, all persons had to be informed of their rights to remain silent and to consult with an attorney. Although the Burger Court upheld *Miranda,* it allowed exceptions: it allowed the use of information obtained without "Mirandizing" suspects if the suspects took the stand in their own defense. It also allowed the use of information obtained without *Miranda* warnings if some immediate threat to public safety had justified immediate questioning and postponing warnings.[28] The Rehnquist Court went beyond these exceptions when it held that a coerced confession may be "harmless error" that does not constitute self-incrimination.[29] The main principle of the Miranda decision was upheld by the Rehnquist Court, however, in *Dickerson* v. *United States* (2000) and reaffirmed in three 2004 decisions.

The Right to Counsel The Sixth Amendment's right to counsel was incorporated in two landmark cases. In *Powell* v. *Alabama* (1932)—the famed Scottsboro Boys prosecution—the Court ruled that legal counsel must be supplied to all indigent defendants accused of a **capital crime** (any crime in which the death penalty can be imposed). Before this decision, many poor people in the southern states, especially African Americans, had been tried for and convicted of capital crimes without the benefit of an attorney. Thirty-one years later, in *Gideon* v. *Wainwright* (1963), the Court ruled that defendants accused of any felony in state jurisdictions are entitled to a lawyer and that the states must supply a lawyer when a defendant cannot afford to do so. Justice Black wrote the following for a unanimous Court:

capital crime
Any crime for which death is a possible penalty.

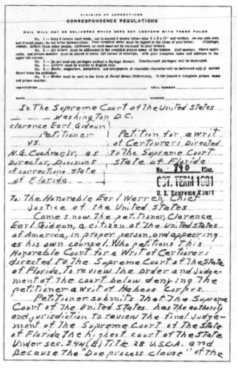

GIDEON'S PETITION Before Clarence Gideon won his case before the Supreme Court in 1963, states did not have to provide attorneys for people accused of a felony. Gideon wrote his appeal letter—shown here—from his prison cell in Florida. The Court agreed with Gideon, incorporating this part of the Sixth Amendment. How did the Court support its decision?

Above, Clarence Earl Gideon.

Left, Clarence Earl Gideon's handwritten petition to the Supreme Court.

Not only…precedents but also reason and reflection require us to recognize that in our adversary system of criminal justice, any person hauled into court, who is too poor to hire a lawyer, cannot be assured of a fair trial unless counsel is provided for him. This seems to be an obvious truth.

By incorporating the Sixth Amendment's guarantee of legal counsel, the Court has ensured that every criminal defendant in the United States can, at least in theory, mount a defense regardless of socioeconomic status.

Capital Punishment The Burger Court examined capital punishment in the states under the Eighth Amendment's prohibition of "cruel and unusual punishment." In *Furman* v. *Georgia* (1972), a split Court found that the death penalty, as used in the states, constituted "cruel and unusual punishment" because the procedures by which states were sentencing people to death sentence were, in its words, "capricious and arbitrary." Responding to the Court's criticisms, Congress and 35 states passed new authorizations of the death penalty aimed at rectifying procedural problems identified by the Court. The Burger Court held in *Gregg* v. *Georgia* (1976), after states had changed their sentencing procedures, that capital punishment was not inherently cruel or unusual so long as procedures were nonarbitrary and nondiscriminatory. However, the Court tended to create an "obstacle course" of standards that the states had to meet if they wanted to use the death penalty. Basically, the Court insisted that defendants be given every opportunity to show mitigating circumstances so that as few convicts as possible would be killed.

The Rehnquist Court at first expedited the use of the death penalty. (Some of the reasons are examined in the "Using the Framework" feature.) In *McCleskey* v. *Kemp* (1987), the Court said that statistical evidence that blacks who kill whites are four times more likely to be sentenced to death than whites who kill blacks is not sufficient to prove racism in death penalty cases; individual defendants, it ruled, must show that racism played a role in their specific cases. In *Penry* v. *Lynaugh* (1989), the Court allowed the execution of a convicted murderer who had the intelligence of a seven-year-old. In *Stanford* v. *Kentucky* (1989), it allowed the execution of a minor who had been convicted of murder. The Rehnquist Court also limited avenues of appeal and delay in death penalty cases. In *McCleskey* v. *Zant* (1991), it made delays much less likely by eliminating many means of challenging capital convictions. In *Keeney* v. *Tamayo-Reyes* (1992), the Court limited the right of "death row" inmates convicted in state courts to appeal to the Supreme Court.

From the middle of the 1960s to the late 1990s, political leaders and public opinion strongly supported the use of the death penalty. In this environment, the Court removed most of the obstacles to its use. It is hardly surprising, then, that the number of people executed in the United States in 1999 reached its highest level (98) since 1976, when the Court reinstated the death penalty, with Texas accounting for more than one-third of the total (see Figure 15.2).[30]

? Why is it that the United States remains virtually alone among the rich democracies in using the death penalty? Are there cultural, historical, and political reasons the United States is so different?

Much to the surprise of seasoned observers, the Rehnquist Court began in 2002 to pull back from its unstinting support for the death penalty. In *Atkins* v. *Virginia* (2002), the Court followed the lead of 18 states in banning the use of the death penalty for mentally retarded defendants, saying, in Justice John Paul Stevens's majority opinion, that "a national consensus now rejects such executions as excessive and inappropriate" and that "society views mentally retarded offenders as categorically less culpable than the average criminal." In *Ring* v. *Arizona* (2002), the Court overruled the death sentences of more than 160 convicted killers, declaring that only juries, and not judges, can decide on the use of the death penalty for those convicted of capital crimes. In 2005, the Supreme Court struck down death penalty convictions in cases in which it was convinced that a defendant had inadequate legal defense, another in which a defendant was brought to a death penalty sentencing hearing in shackles (terming it "inherently prejudicial"), and yet another in which the defendant was under the age of 18.

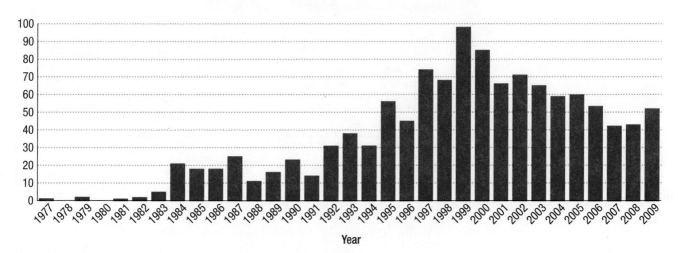

Year

FIGURE 15.2 Executions in the United States, 1977–2009

Fueled by fear of violent crime, executions in the United States increased dramatically from the early 1980s to the late 1990s but declined significantly after that as public concerns rose about how fairly the death penalty is used. *Source:* Bureau of Justice Statistics, "Capital Punishment 2010."

Why did executions in the United States peak in the 1990s, then decline?

Background: Between the reinstatement of the death penalty by the Supreme Court in 1976 and the end of 2001, 737 inmates were executed in the United States. Of the total, 619 (84 percent) took place in the 1990s. In 1999, 98 executions were carried out, the highest total since 1951, with Texas, Virginia, and Florida leading the way. During the first decade of the twenty-first century, however, the number of executions declined. In 2007, 43 people were executed, dropping to 37 in 2008, then jumping to 52 in 2009. We can understand better why this is so by looking broadly at how structural, political linkage, and governmental factors have influenced the death penalty issue.

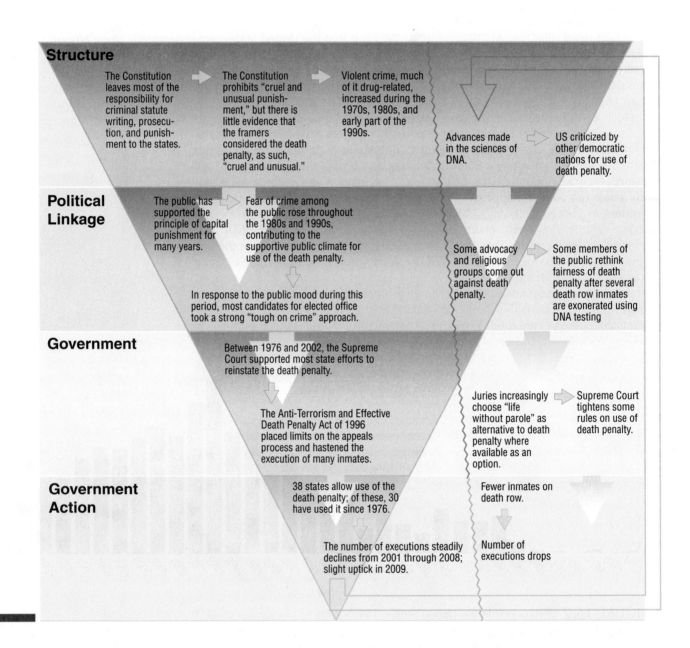

Structure

The Constitution leaves most of the responsibility for criminal statute writing, prosecution, and punishment to the states.

The Constitution prohibits "cruel and unusual punishment," but there is little evidence that the framers considered the death penalty, as such, "cruel and unusual."

Violent crime, much of it drug-related, increased during the 1970s, 1980s, and early part of the 1990s.

Advances made in the sciences of DNA.

US criticized by other democratic nations for use of death penalty.

Political Linkage

The public has supported the principle of capital punishment for many years.

Fear of crime among the public rose throughout the 1980s and 1990s, contributing to the supportive public climate for use of the death penalty.

In response to the public mood during this period, most candidates for elected office took a strong "tough on crime" approach.

Some advocacy and religious groups come out against death penalty.

Some members of the public rethink fairness of death penalty after several death row inmates are exonerated using DNA testing

Government

Between 1976 and 2002, the Supreme Court supported most state efforts to reinstate the death penalty.

The Anti-Terrorism and Effective Death Penalty Act of 1996 placed limits on the appeals process and hastened the execution of many inmates.

Juries increasingly choose "life without parole" as alternative to death penalty where available as an option.

Supreme Court tightens some rules on use of death penalty.

Government Action

38 states allow use of the death penalty; of these, 30 have used it since 1976.

Fewer inmates on death row.

The number of executions steadily declines from 2001 through 2008; slight uptick in 2009.

Number of executions drops

The Roberts Court has sent mixed signals about the nature of the hurdles it will accept in death sentencing and executions. In 2006, the Court ruled unanimously that states cannot deny the introduction of evidence in capital cases that suggests a person other than the defendant had committed the crime. In 2007, however, it made it easier than it had been for prosecutors to exclude from juries people who were unsure about the appropriateness and morality of the death penalty. In 2008, the Roberts Court ruled in a case involving the state of Kentucky that the most widely used method of execution by lethal injection was constitutionally permissible, rejecting the argument that it caused unacceptable pain. Chief Justice John Roberts wrote in his opinion that states using lethal injection protocols "substantially similar" to Kentucky's would be immune from challenge, leading many to assume that the pace of executions will again pick up. Indeed, the number jumped from 43 in 2008 to 52 in 2009.

Although still strongly in favor of capital punishment in principle, the public and many elected officials and judges seem to be having second thoughts about how fairly it is used in practice. Most of the rethinking about the death penalty is based on concerns about the quality of legal defense for those accused of murder, the fairness of the system toward racial minorities, and the desire to see a wider use of DNA evidence where relevant. The exoneration of several death row inmates by the use of DNA evidence in the early 2000s, as well as a long-term drop in the violent crime rate in the United States, have also had an effect on public opinion. A large majority of Americans still favors the death penalty—65 percent in 2009—but about one-half of those who are not opposed in principle to the death penalty say they support life sentences without the possibility of parole as an alternative to the death penalty.[31] President George W. Bush asked Congress to look at this alternative to the death penalty in federal cases in his 2005 State of the Union message. By 2005, 28 of 37 death penalty states, including Texas, had legislated life without parole as a sentence that juries might consider in capital cases. Even with that, however, Texas leads the states in executions; about one-half of all executions in the nation in 2009 occurred there. (See the "Mapping American Politics" feature for a consideration of how death penalty sentencing is related to the incidence of violent crime.)

Of course, the main evidence supporting the proposition that beliefs about the death penalty are changing among the public (whose members make up juries), lawyers (whether prosecutors or defense attorneys), and judges is that the number of executions each year in the United States has been falling from its high point in 1999 (see Figure 15.2). And the numbers will decline further, because fewer death penalty sentences are being imposed; in 2008 there were only 106 such sentences handed out in state and federal jurisdictions across the country, down dramatically from 296 in 1999.[32] It is not yet clear, however, what impact the recent Court ruling on lethal injections may have. In the short run, more executions may happen now that states with a large population on death row are free to move ahead; in the long run, the decline in the number of death sentences coming out of federal and state criminal trials may slow the rate down again.

Civil Liberties and Terrorism

15.4 Analyze how concerns about terrorism may affect civil liberties

Because involvement in war raises public and governmental concerns about public safety and national security and tends to encourage patriotic sentiments and feelings of national unity, wars have almost always led to some restrictions on civil liberties in

Violent Crime and the Death Penalty

Introduction It is well known that the United States has more prisoners on death row and executes more prisoners annually than any other rich democratic country. (The death penalty has been abolished in virtually all of them, in fact; abolition is a condition of membership in the European Union and the Council of Europe.) However, the use of the death penalty is not distributed uniformly across the United States. State-by-state variations are extraordinarily high. Why this is the case is not entirely obvious. One reason could be that the frequency of violent crime—including murder—varies substantially among the states. Or it could be that violent crime does not vary very much, but that the responses to it by the public, prosecutors, and juries vary a great deal. Some states, that is to say, may be more inclined than others to use the ultimate penalty in response to crime. We examine the two explanations in these cartograms.

Crime and Punishment Maps

The cartogram on the left shows the rate of violent crime for each state per 100,000 people. States are expanded or diminished from their normal size by incidence of violent crime. If the violent crime rates were relatively uniform across the country, the cartogram would appear undistorted, similar to a standard map. We can see that the cartogram is only slightly distorted. To be sure, Oklahoma, Louisiana, Florida, South Carolina, Tennessee, Maryland, and Delaware are enlarged a bit because they suffer from more violent crime than other states, and California, Texas, and New York are smaller because their crime rates are

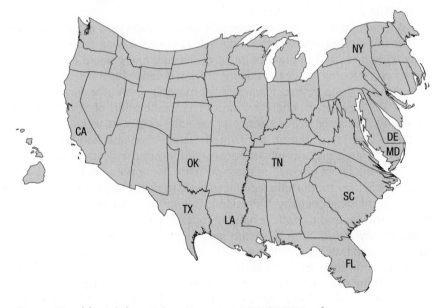

States Sized by Violent Crime Rate per 100,000 People
©2006 M. D. Ward

democratic countries, including the United States, particularly for those who vocally dissent from the war effort and those who seem to be associated with the enemy in one way or another.[33] Note, for example, the Sedition Act of 1798, which made criticism of government officials and their policies off limits, the use of military tribunals for civilians during the Civil War, the Red Scare following World War I, the forced internment of Japanese Americans during World War II, and the McCarthy anticommunist hysteria in the early years of the Cold War with the Soviet Union.[34]

Actions by President Bush to fight what he called the war on terrorism at home and abroad produced significant restrictions on civil liberties in the United States. Many Americans believed and continue to believe that what has been done is a reasonable price to pay in perilous times.[35] Others worry that these restrictions represent a serious long-term danger for American freedom. Here are some of the actions that were taken.

- The USA Patriot Act, passed soon after the 9/11 attacks on the United States, gave the federal government expanded powers to use wiretapping

lower than those of other states. Nevertheless, the variation among the states is not great. In the cartogram on the right, in contrast, each state is expanded or diminished by how many prisoners it has on death row per 100,000 people (the number of annual executions in the United States is not high enough to allow for statistical analysis of the sort being used here). This cartogram suggests that the imposition of capital sentences has little to do with levels of violent crime and much more to do with state-by-state differences in political cultures, legal codes, prosecutorial practices, and jury behaviors. States that are especially prone to impose death penalty sentences include many states of the Deep South (Texas, Mississippi, Arkansas, Alabama, North Carolina, South Carolina, and Georgia), as well as Nevada, Missouri, Oregon, Rhode Island, Connecticut, Maryland, and Delaware. Relative to their violent crime rates, Minnesota, Wisconsin, Maine, and Vermont have few people on death row, and Washington and California are quite low as well.

What Do You Think? Why is it acceptable, or unacceptable, that the penalty for a crime in one state might be different from that in another state? What kinds of federal statutes or guidelines would ensure national uniformity in sentencing for felony crimes, including the imposition of the death penalty? Or should the people in each state be free, as they are now, to treat crime in a way that seems most appropriate to them? How about your state? Does it have a relatively high death row population or a low one? Why do you think that might be the case?

Sources: U.S. Bureau of the Census, *Statistical Abstract of the United States, 2010,* Table 297 (violent crime); and Bureau of Justice Statistics, "Prisoners under Sentence of Death, by Region, Jurisdiction, and Race, 2007 and 2008."

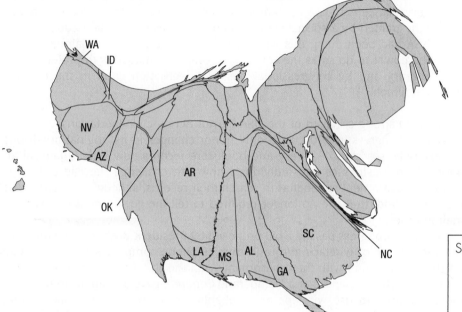

States Sized by Prisoners on Death Row per 100,000 People
©2006 M. D. Ward

Standard US Map

and electronic surveillance, impose stricter penalties for harboring or financing terrorists, monitor the bank accounts and e-mail of suspect individuals and organizations, turn away from our borders anyone who endorses terrorism, and detain any noncitizens living in the United States whom the attorney general deemed to be a threat to national security.

- By executive order, the president expanded the use of a little-known and little-used law created in the 1970s to give the FBI secret access to customer, telephone, and financial records of U.S. citizens. Between 2002 and 2005, almost 150,000 such "national security letters" were issued.[36] Under terms of the law, people were given no notice of the request, firms were obligated to comply, and no one was permitted to make public the fact that such requests had been made. Issuance of these letters required approval by the Office of Intelligence Policy and Review in the Justice Department; there was no judicial oversight.[37]

- The president authorized the indefinite detention without hearings of American citizens discovered to have been fighting against U.S. troops in Afghanistan or aiding Al Qaeda, designating them "enemy combatants."

- The administration instituted secret deportation hearings for detainees held on immigration violations and indefinite detention for people designated "material witnesses" in terrorism cases.

- The president authorized a vast eavesdropping and data-mining operation by the National Security Agency on the electronic and wire communications of American citizens. Under terms of the Foreign Intelligence Surveillance Act, NSA eavesdropping on American citizens requires a warrant granted by a special court. When it was revealed in late 2005 that the NSA had been doing this without warrants, the president claimed he had the power to do so as the commander-in-chief charged with protecting the country and by congressional post-9/11 legislation cited in the previous paragraph.

Despite strong criticism of the USA Patriot Act by civil libertarians, it was renewed by Congress in 2006, with only minor changes in its original provisions. For example, searches of library and bookstore records now require judicial approval. Also, businesses and individuals now can challenge the gag order surrounding government subpoenas to search their records, although only after waiting a year. And, they are no longer required to tell the government the name of their attorney.

In 2008, Congress passed a bill proposed by President Bush to allow more latitude in the use of wiretaps and to immunize phone companies against lawsuits for their cooperation with the government. That the USA Patriot Act was renewed with so few changes and that a Democratic Congress gave a Republican president more authority to use wiretaps are probably testament to the public's strong support for government actions that prevent terrorist attacks. By a 40–36 margin, Americans say they are more concerned that the government has not gone far enough in protecting the country as compared with not going far enough to protect civil liberties.[38]

Though Barack Obama campaigned against many of these Bush-era policies and made some stabs at improving the civil liberties climate—he released some documents related to the treatment of detainees, dropped the designation "enemy combatants" for people held without trial, drastically cut back the use of national security letters to gather information, and ended the use of most harsh interrogation techniques—he ended up continuing many of the policies bequeathed to him

SECRET SURVEILLANCE After the 9/11 attacks on the United States, President George W. Bush authorized the National Security Agency to conduct a secret surveillance program, targeting the electronic communications of U.S. citizens as a way to track terrorists. While the NSA's program worried many Americans and triggered congressional investigations, in the end, the president had his way. How can the U.S. government strike a proper balance between national security, an issue of great importance in our current society, and the civil liberties on which we pride ourselves?

by the Bush administration. He found it more difficult than he had planned to close the prison at Guantanamo, for example, changed his original plan to try 9/11 conspirators in civilian courts, fought efforts to reveal information about secret NSA wiretapping, and asked Congress to reauthorize the Patriot Act. His administration also successfully pressed the courts to prevent terrorism suspects at U.S. bases abroad from having access to American federal courts to review their confinement. In 2010, Obama's Attorney General Eric Holder asked Congress to consider new legislation allowing authorities to question terrorism suspects in the United States without reading them their Miranda rights.

Naturally, the courts have been wrestling with the issue of the proper balance between national security and civil liberties at a time when people feel legitimately threatened by terrorism. For the most part, they have rejected overly broad claims of presidential war powers. In a stunning blow to the Bush administration's claim of extraordinary executive power in wartime, for example, the Supreme Court ruled in 2004 (*Hamdi* v. *Rumsfeld*) that both foreigners and American citizens detained as "enemy combatants" have a right to have a hearing to contest the basis of their detentions. In her opinion in the case, Justice Sandra Day O'Connor reminded everyone, "We have long since made clear that a state of war is not a blank check for the president when it comes to the rights of the nation's citizens." In 2007, the Ninth Circuit Court ruled that enemy combatants could not be held indefinitely in military detention in the United States.

The Roberts Court has also been troubled by the legal treatment of foreign detainees. In 2006, the Court ruled that all detainees held at Guantanamo Bay and elsewhere are entitled to protections guaranteed under the Geneva Convention. It also ruled that the military tribunal-style hearings used at Guantanamo were unacceptable because they had not been authorized by Congress. In response, Congress passed the Military Commissions Act of 2006 which set up a system of tribunals but, almost provocatively, added language to the effect that no court would be allowed to consider habeas corpus petitions from foreigners held as enemy combatants. Perhaps seeing this "habeus" provision as a direct challenge by the legislative branch to the independent powers of the judicial branch, the Court rejected this in 2008 when it ruled that foreign detainees held at Guantanamo have a constitutional right to take their cases to the federal courts to challenge their detention.

With the exception of those instances when the executive branch seems to be challenging the authority and legitimacy of the judicial branch, the Court has granted broad leeway to the government in fighting terrorism. In the first test of the constitutionality of the Patriot Act's "material support" provision, for example, the Court ruled in 2010 that the government has very broad authority and can prosecute people for seemingly benign activities—for example, providing legal services and expert advice to government-designated terrorist organizations seeking to overturn their designation.

The direction that civil liberties will take as a result of the effort to protect the United States against terrorism is hard to predict. All we can say with any degree of certainty at this point is that some restrictions will exist for the duration of the campaign to contain terrorism, and that the severity of these restrictions will be directly related to the degree to which the American people feel afraid that further attacks will occur and their judgment about how much freedom they are willing to trade for security. In the aftermath of a failed attempt to blow up an airliner approaching Detroit on Christmas Day 2009, Americans seemed willing to allow more intensive screening by the TSA and the use of full-body scanners.

Using the DEMOCRACY STANDARD

Has the state of American freedom improved?

The protection of individual freedom—civil liberty—is a foundational principle of both the eighteenth-century republican philosophy of the framers and of democratic theory. For the framers, protection of individual freedom was not only an essential feature of good government and the good society, but also the very reason republican government was formed in the first place. Political liberty is also an essential feature of democratic theory, because it is necessary for both popular sovereignty and political equality. Popular sovereignty cannot be guaranteed if people are prevented from participating in politics or if opposition to the government is crushed by the authorities. Popular sovereignty cannot prevail if the voice of the people is silenced and if citizens are not free to argue and debate, based on their own ideas, values, and personal beliefs, and to form and express their political opinions. Political equality is violated if some people can speak out but others cannot.

Both the framers and more recent democratic theorists are committed to civil liberties, but each has taken a somewhat different approach concerning how civil liberties might be enjoyed by Americans. Recall that the framers focused their attention on the potential for violations of liberty by the national government and paid little attention to the states, believing that freedom in the states was well protected. Note as well that many of the framers and most political leaders who followed during the long course of the nineteenth century seemed most concerned about protecting property rights, or economic liberty. Civil liberties, broadly understood, became widely available to Americans only in the twentieth century in response to the spread of democratic aspirations in politics and of democratic ideas in the culture, the efforts of individuals and groups to struggle for liberty, and a federal judiciary that finally agreed to nationalize most of the protections of the Bill of Rights.

There has been an enormous expansion of freedom in the United States; the freedoms of speech, association, press, conscience, and religion, as well as the rights of those accused of a crime, are far more extensively developed and protected in the United States today than they were in the past. However, we must also recognize a serious flaw in the current status of civil liberties. While civil liberties today are fairly well protected against intrusions by government, not all people have the capacities and resources to use their liberties effectively. Substantial income and wealth inequality often creates political inequality. Thus, only a privileged few can make substantial campaign contributions; form political lobbying organizations; and run ads for their favorite candidates, parties, and issues.

We cannot say with total confidence, moreover, that freedom cannot and will not be violated by government at some point in the future. In the past, waves of hysteria among political leaders and the public have led to the violation of civil liberties. Given the right conditions—say, war, civil unrest, economic depression—the same might happen again. Many worry, with some justification, that the war on terrorism may represent just such a setting for the suppression of civil liberties. What makes the possibility especially troubling is the indeterminate time period of such a war. One can imagine it stretching on into the indefinite future. We can only hope that such a suppression of civil liberties will not happen and that people will struggle for democracy if it does.

SUMMARY

15.1 Identify civil liberties protections in the Constitution

- The formal foundation of American liberties is found in the Constitution and its amendments, particularly the Bill of Rights and the Fourteenth Amendment, but the degree to which civil liberties have been enjoyed in practice during our history has depended upon the actions of courts, the behavior of government officials, and the struggle for democracy by the American people.

15.2 Trace the evolution of civil liberties in the nineteenth century

- During the nineteenth century, the Supreme Court concerned itself mainly with protecting property rights. Somewhat belatedly, it used the Fourteenth Amendment to make the protections in the Constitution and the Bill of Rights apply to state and local governments. This considerably expanded Americans' enjoyment of the familiar liberties of expression, association, press, and religion.

- The Court's changing interpretation of the meaning of liberty was influenced by changing attitudes among the public and elected officials, as well as by the nation's leading law journals.

15.3 Outline the liberties guaranteed by the Bill of Rights and their gradual application to the states by the Supreme Court

- American history has witnessed an expansion of the boundaries of liberties, with the Supreme Court

gradually incorporating the Bill of Rights based on the Fourteenth Amendment under terms described in a footnote in the *Carolene* case. This footnote suggested that the Court would apply "strict scrutiny" to government actions that seemed to violate democracy, failed to offer equal protection to minorities, or prevented the enjoyment of liberties spelled out in the Bill of Rights.

- The broadest expansion of due process protections and equal protection came during the Warren and Berger Court years.

- The expansion of the rights of the accused was always a hotly disputed political issue, and the conservative orientation of the Rehnquist and Roberts Courts resulted in the reversal of many of the due process innovations of the Warren and Burger Courts. The Roberts Court also ruled against a number of government efforts to expand civil rights protections to racial minorities.

15.4 Analyze how concerns about terrorism may affect civil liberties

- The fight against terrorism has resulted in the widespread surveillance of American citizens and restrictions of the civil liberties of noncitizens living legally in the United States. How long these restrictions remain in place will depend on the severity of terrorist threats and public perceptions about these threats.

TEST YOURSELF

Answer key begins on page T-1.

15.1 Identify civil liberties protections in the Constitution

1. The only mechanism by which civil liberties protections can be expanded is through constitutional amendment.
   True / False
2. Which part of the Constitution and its amendments contains the greatest civil liberties protections?
   a. The Preamble
   b. Article I
   c. Article II
   d. Article III
   e. The Bill of Rights

15.2 Trace the evolution of civil liberties in the nineteenth century

3. During the nineteenth century, the Supreme Court repeatedly asserted that the constitution protected economic liberties.
   True / False
4. Which of the following is required by the full faith and credit clause?
   a. The federal government must protect the privacy rights of prisoners.
   b. The federal government cannot limit the ability of citizens to engage in interstate commerce.

c. States must recognize contracts entered into in other states.

d. States cannot tax private property that is used for simple enjoyment.

e. Citizens cannot discriminate in the provision of public accommodations.

5. How did the Marshall Court interpret property rights?

15.3 Outline the liberties guaranteed by the Bill of Rights and their gradual application to the states by the Supreme Court

6. According to the Supreme Court, freedom of the press includes the right of reporters who have been issued a subpoena to protect their sources without fear of prosecution.
True / False

7. Which of the following can government generally prohibit?
a. Fighting words
b. Flag burning
c. The publication of embarrassing documents
d. Campaign spending for political advertisements
e. Unpopular or un-American speech

8. Should the rights of the accused be narrowed, expanded, or kept the way they are?

15.4 Analyze how concerns about terrorism may affect civil liberties

9. The Supreme Court has ruled that only American citizens can challenge their detention in court.
True / False

10. Which of the following best describes how Barack Obama has dealt with the various policies enacted under George W. Bush related to civil liberties during wartime?
a. Obama closed the military prison at Guantanamo.
b. Obama urged Congress to overturn the Patriot Act.
c. Obama expanded the harsh interrogation tactics that are available to the military
d. Obama overturned most civil liberties restrictions enacted under George W. Bush.
e. Obama changed some Bush-era policies but has kept many others.

11. Are the restrictions on civil liberties enacted under George W. Bush reasonable, given the threat that America faces from terrorism?

mypoliscilab EXERCISES

Apply what you learned in this chapter on MyPoliSciLab.

Read on mypoliscilab.com

eText: Chapter 15

Study and Review on mypoliscilab.com

Pre-Test
Post-Test
Chapter Exam
Flashcards

Watch on mypoliscilab.com

Video: D.C.'s Right to Bear Arms
Video: Funeral Protestors Push the Limits of Free Speech

Explore on mypoliscilab.com

Simulation: You Are a Police Officer
Simulation: You Are a Supreme Court Justice Deciding a Free Speech Case
Simulation: Balancing Liberty and Security in a Time of War
Comparative: Comparing Civil Liberties
Timeline: Civil Liberties and National Security

INTERNET SOURCES

The American Civil Liberties Union
www.aclu.org
   Website of the long-time defender of civil liberties in the United States.

Oyez.com
www.oyez.com
   The most user-friendly site for Supreme Court actions on civil liberties and civil rights matters.

Bureau of Justice Statistics
www.ojp.usdoj.gov/bjs/
   Official statistics on crimes, trials, incarceration rates, and executions are available at this site.

The Cato Institute
www.cato.org
   A comprehensive site covering civil liberties issues from the conservative libertarian point of view.

The Death Penalty Information Center
www.deathpenaltyinfo.org
   Up-to-date information on the status of the death penalty in the United States and other nations around the world.

Findlaw Supreme Court Opinions
www.findlaw.com/casecode/supreme.html
   Find historical and contemporary Supreme Court decisions and opinions on civil liberties at this site.

First Amendment Center
www.firstamendmentcenter.org
   Rich source of history and recent developments related to First Amendment freedoms.

SUGGESTIONS FOR FURTHER READING

Abraham, Henry J., and Barbara A. Perry. *Freedom and the Court,* 8th ed. Lawrence, KS: University of Kansas Press, 2003.
   A trusted introduction to the study of civil rights and liberties for more than 30 years.

Epstein, Lee, and Thomas G. Walker. *Constitutional Law for a Changing America.* Washington, D.C.: CQ Press, 2005.
   Shows what aspects of constitutional law have changed over the years, and why.

Epstein, Lee, and Thomas G. Walker. *Rights, Liberties, and Justice.* Washington, D.C.: CQ Press, 2010.
   An exhaustive and compelling examination of the rulings that have shaped the status of civil liberties in the United States.

Fallon, Richard. *The Dynamic Constitution: An Introduction to American Constitutional Law.* New York: Cambridge University Press, 2005.
   An accessible introduction to all aspects of American constitutional law.

Lewis, Anthony. *Freedom for the Thought We Hate: A Biography of the First Amendment.* New York: Basic Books, 2007.
   A celebration of the expansion of First Amendment freedoms and the story of how it happened.

Stone, Geoffrey R. *Perilous Times: Free Speech in Wartime.* New York: W.W. Norton, 2004.
   A history of the tension between free speech and national security during American conflicts.

Zimring, Franklin. *The Contradictions of American Capital Punishment.* New York: Oxford University Press, 2003.
   Examines the question of why Americans so strongly support the death penalty compared with people in other rich democracies.

16
Civil Rights: The Struggle for Political Equality

IN THIS CHAPTER

16.1 Trace the evolution of civil rights protections for women and racial minorities to the twentieth century

16.2 Assess the present status of civil rights protections for racial minorities

16.3 Assess the present status of civil rights protections for women

16.4 Analyze the expansion of civil rights protections to the elderly, the disabled, and gays and lesbians

THE RETURN OF SEGREGATED SCHOOLS

"I don't know why they left," said one fourth-grader at Reid Park Elementary School in Charlotte, North Carolina. "Maybe they didn't like it here."[1] She was referring to the virtual disappearance of white children at her school where, only one year earlier, about one-third of her schoolmates had been white. What was happening at Reid Park Elementary was happening all over the South at the turn of the new century. Fifty years after the Supreme Court had ruled in *Brown* v. *Board of Education* (1954) that "separate but equal" was unconstitutional, schools were becoming more segregated. By 2003, only 29 percent of black children in the South were in schools that were majority white, a decrease from 44 percent as recently as 1988. By 2007, matters had grown worse.[2]

For those Americans committed to a racially integrated society, there was much to be proud of in the record of desegregation of public education in the United States after the *Brown* decision, especially in the South where school segregation was official policy from the early twentieth century until the Court's 1954 decision. After a slow start for a few years following *Brown*, school integration took off in the mid-1960s and gained steadily until it reached its peak in the late 1980s. By 1988, only one in four black children were in schools that were 90 to 100 percent black, a far cry from the

pre-*Brown* years when virtually all black children were in such schools. During the 1990s, however, the trend reversed all over the South, with more black children going to school where there were few whites or none at all and where white children had less contact with African American children than in many years.[3]

As troubling as the picture might be, the South is still doing better on the school integration front than other parts of the country. In the Northeast, for example, more than one-half of all African American children are in schools that are 90 to 100 percent black, closely followed by the states in the Midwest. In addition, black children are least exposed to white children in public schools in New York, Illinois, Michigan, California, Maryland, and New Jersey and are most exposed to their white counterparts in the South and the border states. And, as in the South, school segregation in every region of the nation has become more pronounced.[4]

So why did the trend in the South toward a more integrated public school system first level off, then recede during the 1990s and 2000s? The answer is fairly straightforward: The federal courts, following the lead of the Supreme Court in *Dowell* v. *Oklahoma City* (1991)—which ruled that school districts that had made lengthy good-faith

efforts to end the effects of previously legal school segregation in their jurisdictions had fulfilled their constitutional obligations for equal protection of the races in education—began to lift court-ordered desegregation plans that required busing and other methods to integrate schools across local jurisdictions. About 40 school districts over the past 10 years have been relieved of such orders, and it is precisely in these districts where the reversals in school integration trends are most evident.

But that still leaves the question of why lifting federal court orders would lead to such a development. Again, the answer is fairly straightforward: when most whites and most blacks live in racially homogeneous neighborhoods—as they do because of white flight to the suburbs and the existence of informally segregated housing markets—local neighborhood schools, absent busing or other student assignment strategies designed to foster integration, will also be racially homogeneous.

It remains to be seen what the outcomes of these changes will be. Many whites and African Americans believe that integrated schooling, whether achieved voluntarily or under court order, is important for children's educational achievement and for teaching tolerance in a racially diverse society. However, other whites and African Americans believe that integration by itself does little to increase academic achievement, and that court-ordered busing mainly leads to intergroup tensions and wasted tax money. Many African Americans who think this way are becoming attracted to the idea of school vouchers that allow children to use public funds to go to either a public or private school as a way to improve schools in predominantly black neighborhoods. Many others are being attracted to charter schools as an alternative within public schools. The thinking here is that competition for students between public and private schools, as well as competition between different kinds of public schools, will force schools to offer a better educational product.

Civil rights are government guarantees of equality for people in the United States regarding judicial proceedings, the exercise of political rights, treatment by public officials, and access to and enjoyment of the benefits of government programs. (The terms *equal citizenship* and *civil rights* often are used interchangeably.) The expansion of civil rights protections for African Americans as well as for other racial, ethnic, and religious minorities and for women is one of the great achievements of American history. Gays and lesbians have not gained "equal protection" status in the courts as of this writing and have suffered many recent political setbacks, but they have attained a level of rights protections never before achieved in our history, though fewer than gay and lesbian advocates have hoped for. These changes on the civil rights front have not come easily or quickly; it took the struggle of millions of Americans to force change from political leaders and government institutions. The result has been a significant democratization of the republican constitutional system of the Framers. As this opening story suggests, however, the expansion of civil rights protection in the United States is neither complete nor free of problems and controversy. And, there continue to be setbacks.

THINKING CRITICALLY About This Chapter

Using the FRAMEWORK

In this chapter, you will see that the meaning of civil rights has changed over the course of American history, and you will learn how structural, political linkage, and governmental factors, taken together, explain that change.

Using the DEMOCRACY STANDARD

In this chapter, you will learn how civil rights is at the very center of our understanding of democracy in the United States. You will see how the struggle for democracy helped expand civil rights protections. You also will see how the expansion of civil rights has enhanced formal political equality in the United States, one of the basic foundations of a democratic political order.

Civil Rights Before the Twentieth Century

16.1 Trace the evolution of civil rights protections for women and racial minorities to the twentieth century

Civil rights for women and racial minorities was a comparatively late development in the United States, and most major advances were not evident until well into the twentieth century. In this section, we look at the period before the expansion of civil rights.

An Initial Absence of Civil Rights

Neither the original Constitution nor the Bill of Rights said anything about equality beyond insisting that all Americans are equally entitled to due process in the courts.[5] Indeed, the word *equality* does not appear in the Constitution at all. Nor did state constitutions offer much in the way of guaranteeing equality other than equality before the law. Americans in the late eighteenth and early nineteenth centuries seemed more interested in protecting individuals against government (see Chapter 15) than in guaranteeing certain political rights through government.[6] For most racial or ethnic minorities and women, equality eluded

> **civil rights**
> Guarantees of equal treatment by government officials regarding political rights, the judicial system, and public programs.

constitutional protection until the twentieth century, although the groundwork was laid earlier.

The inequality of African Americans and women before the Civil War is quite striking. In the South, African Americans lived in slavery, with no rights at all. Outside the South, although a few states allowed African Americans to vote, the number of states doing so actually declined as the Civil War approached, even as universal white male suffrage was spreading. In many places outside the slave South, African Americans were denied entry into certain occupations, required to post bonds guaranteeing their good behavior, denied the right to sit on juries, and occasionally threatened and harassed by mobs when they tried to vote or to petition the government. Chief Justice Roger Taney, in *Dred Scott* v. *Sandford* (1857), went so far as to claim that the Founders believed that blacks had no rights that whites or government were bound to honor or respect. As for women, no state allowed them to vote, few allowed them to sit on juries, and a handful even denied them the right to own property or enter into contracts.

> **?** Did the absence of guarantees of political equality for African Americans and women in the original Constitution mean that the Framers failed in their task of protecting against tyranny?

Many African Americans and women refused to play a passive political role, however, even though the pre–Civil War period was not conducive to their participation in politics. African Americans, for instance, voted in elections where they were allowed, helped organize the Underground Railroad to smuggle slaves out of the South, and were prominent in the abolitionist movement against slavery. Both black and white women played an important role in the abolitionist movement— the antislavery speaking tours of Angelina and Sarah Grimké caused something of a scandal in the 1840s when women's participation in public affairs was considered improper—and a few began to write extensively on the need for women's emancipation and legal and political equality. In 1848, Elizabeth Cady Stanton issued her call for a convention on women's rights to be held at the village of Seneca Falls, New York. The Declaration of Sentiments and Resolutions issued by the delegates to the convention stands as one of the landmarks in women's struggle for political equality in the United States:

> *All men and women are created equal ... but the history of mankind is a history of repeated injuries and usurpations on the part of man toward woman, having in direct object the establishment of a direct tyranny over her ... [We demand] that women have immediate admission to all the rights and privileges which belong to them as citizens of the United States.*

ADVOCATING FOR WOMEN'S RIGHTS In 1848, Elizabeth Cady Stanton helped organize the Seneca Falls Convention on women's rights. The resulting Declaration of Sentiments and Resolutions was patterned after the Declaration of Independence, stating that "all men and women are created equal," and included a list of the injustices of men against women. Stanton remained an activist for many years, helping to found the National Women's Suffrage Association in 1896 to press for the vote for women, and became the first president of the National American Woman Suffrage Association in 1890. Why did it take so many years of such outspoken activism for women to finally be granted the right to vote?

The Civil War Amendments

In the years following the Civil War, Congress passed a number of constitutional amendments that essentially created the foundations for civil rights as we understand them today.

- The Thirteenth Amendment to the Constitution, passed in 1865, outlawed slavery throughout the United States, settling the most divisive issue of our early history as a nation.

- The Fourteenth Amendment (1868) reversed *Dred Scott* by making all people who are born or naturalized in the United States, black or white, citizens both of the United States and of the states in which they reside. To secure the rights and liberties of recently freed slaves, Article I of the amendment further provided that "no State shall make or enforce any law which shall abridge the privileges or immunities of citizens of the United States" (the **privileges and immunities clause**); "nor shall any State deprive any person of life, liberty, or property, without due process of law" (the **due process clause**); "nor deny to any person within its jurisdiction the equal protection of the laws" (the **equal protection clause**).

- The Fifteenth Amendment (1870) said states could not prevent people from voting on the grounds of "race, color, or previous condition of servitude" (former slaves). As imposing as this constitutional language sounds, the Supreme Court would soon transform it into a protection for property rights, but not for African American men.

Undermining the Civil War Amendments   In the two decades following their passage, the Supreme Court blocked the promise of equal citizenship for African Americans found in the Civil War amendments. During this time, when many Americans in the northern states had grown weary of efforts to reconstruct the South and uplift and protect former slaves, white supremacists were regaining control in many areas of the South, and racist attitudes were widespread across the nation, the Supreme Court struck against key provisions of the amendments. For example, the *Slaughterhouse Cases* (1873) rendered the privileges and immunities clause virtually meaningless. Writing for the Court, Justice Samuel Miller found that the clause did not guarantee citizenship rights against violations by state governments, only against violations by the federal government. The Court ruled that it was powerless to protect African Americans against abuses by state governments, including barriers to voting and office-holding. Within five years of its passage, then, this section of the Fourteenth Amendment was seriously compromised by the Court, foiling the attempt by the post–Civil War radical Republican Congress to amend the Constitution in favor of equality.

Though the equal protection clause of the Fourteenth Amendment survived the *Slaughterhouse Cases,* it soon lost all practical meaning as a guarantor of equality for African Americans. First, the Court ruled in the *Civil Rights Cases* (1883) that the Fourteenth Amendment gave Congress no power to prohibit discrimination unless it was practiced by state government. "Equal protection of the laws" did not, therefore, preclude race discrimination by private owners or managers of restaurants, theaters, hotels, and other public accommodations. Then the Court made even government-sponsored discrimination constitutional in *Plessy* v. *Ferguson* (1896). The Court said that the states could separate the races in intrastate railways if they provided "equal" facilities for the races. This ruling gave the doctrine of "separate but equal" full

privileges and immunities clause

The portion of Article IV, Section 2, of the Constitution that states that citizens from out of state have the same legal rights as local citizens in any state.

due process clause

The section of the Fourteenth Amendment that prohibits states from depriving anyone of life, liberty, or property "without due process of law," a guarantee against arbitrary or unfair government action.

equal protection clause

The section of the Fourteenth Amendment requiring states to provide equal treatment to all people within its boundaries.

JIM CROW   For more than half a century, until the Court's 1954 *Brown* decision, the civil rights movement, and the 1964 Civil Rights Act ended it, the Jim Crow system of racial segregation of public facilities was virtually universal in the southern states. Should states have been left alone to address how to change this system or was federal intervention essential?

constitutional status and legitimacy, and provided the legal underpinnings for the segregation of the races in nearly every area of life throughout the South. This system of racial segregation—usually referred to as **Jim Crow**—would remain in force until *Plessy was* overturned in *Brown* v. *Board of Education of Topeka* (1954) more than half a century later.

The Fifteenth Amendment's voting guarantees were also rendered ineffectual—this time by a variety of devices invented to prevent African Americans from voting in the former states of the Confederacy. The **poll tax** was a tax required of all voters in many states, and it kept many African Americans away from the polls, given their desperate economic situation in the South in the late nineteenth and early twentieth centuries. Several states required voters to pass a **literacy test** devised and administered by local officials (see Table 16.1). The evaluation of test results was entirely up to local officials, who rarely passed blacks, even those with a college education or a Ph.D. degree. If white voters failed the literacy test, many states allowed them to vote anyway under the **grandfather clause**, which provided that anyone whose ancestors had voted prior to 1867 could vote as well. Because the ancestors of African Americans in the South had been slaves, the grandfather clause was no help to them at all.

Several states instituted **white primaries** that excluded African Americans from the process of nominating candidates for local, state, and national offices. The states argued that excluding blacks from primaries was acceptable because political parties were private associations that could define their own membership requirements, including skin color. In the one-party (Democratic) South at the time, the actual election of public officials happened in the state Democratic primaries, leaving those few African Americans who voted in the November general elections without any voice at all. And, for those African Americans who might try to vote anyway in the face of the poll tax, the literacy test, and the white primary, there was always the use of terror as a deterrent: night riding, bombings, and lynchings were used with regularity, especially during times when blacks showed signs of assertiveness.

Jim Crow

Popular term for the system of state-sanctioned racial segregation that existed in the American South until the middle of the twentieth century.

poll tax

A tax to be paid as a condition of voting; used in the South to keep African Americans away from the polls.

literacy test

A device used by the southern states to prevent African Americans from voting before the passage of the Voting Rights Act of 1965, which banned its use; usually involved interpretation of a section of a state's constitution.

grandfather clause

A device that allowed whites who had failed the literacy test to vote anyway by extending the franchise to anyone whose ancestors had voted prior to 1867.

white primaries

Primary elections open only to whites in the one-party South where the only elections that mattered were the Democratic Party's primaries; this effectively disenfranchised blacks.

TABLE 16.1   Selected Items from the Alabama Literacy Test

These 10 questions are part of the 68-question Alabama Literacy Test used to decide on the eligibility of voters in that state. The test and others like it were declared illegal by the 1965 Voting Rights Act. Most white voters who were unable to pass this or similar tests in the states of the Deep South were protected by a "grandfather clause" allowing people to vote whose grandfathers had done so.

1. A person appointed to the U.S. Supreme Court is appointed for a term of _____.

2. If a person is indicted for a crime, name two rights which he has.

3. Cases tried before a court of law are of what two types: civil and _____.

4. If no candidate for president receives a majority of the electoral vote, who decides who will become president?

5. If no person receives a majority of the electoral vote, the vice president is chosen by the Senate. True or False?

6. If an effort to impeach the President of the United States is made, who presides at the trial?

7. If the two houses of Congress do not agree to adjournment, who sets the time?

8. A president elected in November takes office the following year on what date?

9. Of the original 13 states, the one with the largest representation in the first Congress was _____.

10. The Constitution limits the size of the District of Columbia _____.

Answers: (1) good behavior; life; (2) jury trial, protection against self incrimination, right to counsel, speedy trial, protection against excessive bail; (3) criminal; (4) the House of Representatives; (5) true; (6) although not stipulated in the Constitution, the House has always turned to its Judiciary Committee to manage the impeachment process; (7) the president; (8) January 20; (9) Virginia; (10) not to exceed 10 miles square.

The statutory devices for keeping African Americans away from the polls were consistently supported by state and federal courts until well into the twentieth century. Terror as a means of preventing voting remained a factor until the 1960s, when the civil rights movement and federal intervention finally put an end to it.

Women and the Fifteenth and Nineteenth Amendments   Politically active women were stung by their exclusion from the Fifteenth Amendment's extension of the right to vote, as the amendment said only that no state could exclude people on the grounds of "race, color, or previous condition of servitude." Thus, they quickly turned their attention to winning the vote for women. Once the Supreme Court had decided, in *Minor v. Happersett* (1874), that women's suffrage was not a right inherent in the national citizenship guarantees of the Fourteenth Amendment, many women abandoned legal challenges and turned to more direct forms of political agitation: petitions, marches, and protests. After years of struggle, the efforts of the women's suffrage movement bore fruit in the Nineteenth Amendment, ratified in 1920: "The right of citizens of the United States to vote shall not be denied or abridged by the United States or by any State on account of sex." This story of the women's suffrage movement was told in the opening pages of Chapter 8 and is worth re-reading.

The Contemporary Status of Civil Rights for Racial Minorities

16.2 Assess the present status of civil rights protections for racial minorities

We saw in Chapter 15 how the Supreme Court, using the guidelines written by Justice Harlan Fiske Stone in *United States* v. *Carolene Products Company* (1938), gradually extended the protections of the Bill of Rights to the states, based on the Fourteenth Amendment. Recall that among the actions by the states that would trigger **strict scrutiny** under the *Carolene* guidelines were those that either "restricted the democratic process" or "discriminated against racial, ethnic, or religious minorities." This reading of the Fourteenth Amendment, particularly the equal protection clause, lent judicial support to the gradual advance of civil rights guarantees for African Americans and other minorities and eventually (although less so) for women. In the following sections, we look at the extension of the civil rights of racial minorities, women, and other groups, including gays and lesbians. Here we concentrate mainly (although not exclusively) on Supreme Court decisions,[7] the actions of other branches of government regarding civil rights, and the standing of these groups in American politics. As you consider these materials, recall the important role that protest and social movements played in improving the civil rights of a broad range of Americans. Without these movements and the pressures they brought to bear on public opinion, elected officials, and the courts, many of the changes we now take for granted would surely not have happened. (See Chapter 8 on social movements for more on how a range of excluded and marginalized groups gained a foothold in American politics and pushed equal protection issues onto the nation's political agenda.)

Two basic issues have dominated the story of the extension of civil rights for African Americans since the mid-1960s:

- The ending of legally sanctioned discrimination, separation, and exclusion from citizenship.
- The debate over what actions to take to remedy the past wrongs done to African Americans.

We examine both in this section.

Ending Government-Sponsored Separation and Discrimination

We reviewed earlier how the Constitution was long interpreted to condone slavery and segregation. In the twentieth century, however, the legal and political battles waged by the civil rights movement eventually pushed the Supreme Court, the president, and Congress to take seriously the equal protection clause of the Fourteenth Amendment.

In 1944, amid World War II (a war aimed in great part at bringing down the racist regime of Adolf Hitler) and the NAACP's campaign to rid the nation of segregation, the Supreme Court finally declared that race was a **suspect classification** that demanded strict judicial scrutiny. This meant that any local ordinance, or state or national statute, using racial criteria was presumed to be unconstitutional unless it could

strict scrutiny

The assumption that actions by elected bodies or officials violate the Constitution.

suspect classification

The invidious, arbitrary, or irrational designation of a group for special treatment by government, whether positive or negative; historically, a discriminated against, visible minority without power to protect itself.

be shown that such an ordinance or statute was both necessary and compelling. Pressed by the legal efforts of the NAACP, the Court gradually chipped away at the *Plessy* "separate but equal" doctrine and the edifice of segregation it helped create. In *Smith* v. *Allwright* (1944), the Court declared that the practice of excluding nonwhites from political-party primary elections was unconstitutional. Then the Court ruled that the states' practice of providing separate all-white and all-black law schools was unacceptable. Many of the key cases before the Supreme Court that eroded the official structure of segregation were argued by Thurgood Marshall—later a justice of the Supreme Court—for the NAACP.[8]

The great legal breakthrough for racial equality came in *Brown* v. *Board of Education of Topeka* (1954), also argued on the plaintiffs' side by Thurgood Marshall. The Court declared that "separate but equal" was inherently contradictory and that segregation imposed by state and local laws was constitutionally unacceptable in public schools because it violated guarantees of equal protection. Chief Justice Earl Warren, speaking for a unanimous Court, said that education was "perhaps the most important function of state and local governments" and that segregation in education communicated the message that blacks were inferior and deserving of unequal treatment. "In the field of education [in Warren's words] the doctrine of 'separate but equal' has no place."[9] *Brown* was a constitutional revolution, destined to transform racial relations law and practices in the United States, because it struck down the foundations of segregation and discrimination.[10]

The white South did not react violently at first, but it did not desegregate either. Once recognition spread that the Court was going to enforce civil rights, however, massive resistance to racial integration gripped the South. Citizens Councils (white) committed to imposing economic sanctions and boycotts on anybody who supported desegregation had over 250,000 members by 1956. Membership in the KKK increased dramatically, along with beatings, cross-burnings, and killing of blacks and their white supporters.[11] This resistance was what Dr. Martin Luther King, Jr. and others had to work (and die) to overcome. The Court—even with many follow-up cases—was able to accomplish little before the president and Congress backed up the justices with the 1964 Civil Rights Act and the 1965 Voting Rights Act. (See Chapters 1 and 8 for details on these two groundbreaking bills.) The civil rights movement and supportive changes in American public opinion in favor of protections for blacks helped spur these legislative and judicial actions.

The drive to protect the rights of racial minorities has occupied the nation ever since. The main legal doctrine on racial discrimination is straightforward: Any use of race in law or government regulations to discriminate—sometimes called **de jure discrimination**—will trigger strict scrutiny (a presumption of

THE MARCH ON WASHINGTON Dr. Martin Luther King Jr. waves to a crowd of an estimated half-million people at the March on Washington at the Lincoln Memorial after delivering his "I Have a Dream" speech on August 28, 1963. This event, one of the high points of the civil rights movement, helped convince Congress to pass the Civil Rights Act of 1964.

unconstitutionality) by the courts. Recall from our earlier discussion that a state or the federal government can defend its acts under strict scrutiny only if it can produce a *compelling* government interest for which the act in question is a *necessary* means. Almost no law survives this challenge; laws that discriminate on the basis of race are dead from the moment of passage. In *Loving* v. *Virginia* (1967), for example, the Court ruled that Virginia's law against interracial marriage served no compelling government purpose that would justify unequal treatment of the races. Needless to say, other racial minority groups in addition to African Americans—Hispanics, Asian Americans, and Native Americans—have benefited from the constitutional revolution that has occurred.[12]

To say that racial discrimination in the law is no longer constitutionally acceptable does not mean that discrimination against racial minorities has disappeared from the United States. **De facto discrimination**—unequal treatment by private individuals, groups, and organizations—remains a fact of life, although its exact extent is hard to measure accurately. For example, 68 percent of African Americans and 52 percent of Hispanics tell pollsters they have experienced a specific instance in which they felt discriminated against, while 51 percent of blacks claim that there is job discrimination in their community.[13] Overwhelming majorities of African Americans, Latinos, and Asians say they have been subject to poor service in stores and restaurants because of their race and have had disparaging remarks directed at them.[14] All minorities report bad experiences with racial profiling by police. Fifty-two percent of black men and 25 percent of Latino and Asian men claim to have been stopped by police for no apparent reason. Although various police departments have taken steps to stop these practices, the courts have never defined racial profiling as suspect, especially if some important law enforcement need is being met by it.[15]

? Is it the government's responsibility to protect minorities from the discriminatory practices of private individuals? Or is it only responsible for protecting citizens from federal or state government-sponsored discrimination?

de jure discrimination
Unequal treatment based on government laws and regulations.

de facto discrimination
Unequal treatment by private individuals, groups, and organizations.

affirmative action

Programs of private and public institutions favoring minorities and women in hiring and contracting, and in admissions to colleges and universities, in an attempt to compensate for past discrimination or to create more diversity.

Affirmative Action

It is now widely accepted that the Constitution protects racial minorities against any discrimination or disadvantage that is sanctioned or protected by law or government action. The issues are not as clear-cut, however, in the area of government actions that *favor* racial minorities (and women) in **affirmative action** programs designed to rectify past wrongs.[16]

Origins of Affirmative Action

The main goal of the civil rights movement of the 1950s and 1960s was to remove barriers to equal citizenship for black Americans. This goal was largely accomplished in the federal courts by passage of the 1964 Civil Rights Act and the Voting Rights Act of 1965 and by broad changes in public attitudes about race. But even with these important changes, the economic and social situations of African Americans did not seem to be improving much. It seemed to an increasing number of people that ending discrimination was a start, but that more proactive government actions would be required if African Americans were to escape the conditions that years of discrimination had put them in. President Lyndon Johnson, Robert Kennedy, and Martin Luther King Jr., among others, eventually came to believe that the advancement of black Americans could happen only if there was a broad societal effort to eradicate poverty by equipping the poor, black and white, with the tools for success. This led to the founding of the Johnson administration's Great Society and War on Poverty and programs such as Head Start.

After Martin Luther King's assassination, however, and the urban riots that followed, many people in government, the media, higher education, and the major foundations began to support the notion that progress for African Americans would happen only if government encouraged proactive efforts to increase the levels of black representation in private and public sector jobs and contracting, and in colleges and universities.[17] Somewhat surprisingly, it was Richard Nixon, not generally thought of as a booster of civil rights, who took the most important step, requiring in his 1969 Philadelphia Plan that construction companies with federal contracts and the associated construction trade unions hire enough blacks and other minorities to achieve "racial balance" (a proportion roughly equal to the racial balance in the community).

Although initially skeptical of racial preferences, Justices William Brennan, Byron White, Thurgood Marshall, and Harry Blackmun supported temporary programs to remedy the effects of past discrimination. Joined by Justice Lewis Powell, they formed the majority in *Regents v. Bakke* (1978), in which the Court authorized a compromise on affirmative action programs. The Constitution and federal law prohibited employers and admissions committees from using strictly racial quotas, the Court said, but it saw no problem with the use of race as one factor among several in hiring or college admissions.

Since *Bakke,* government and higher education racial outreach, then preference, programs have become relatively permanent rather than temporary, and their aim has shifted from providing remedies for past discrimination to enhancing diversity. The proliferation of diversity programs, diversity training, and diversity offices has become commonplace in colleges and universities, in government, and in the corporate world.

Why Affirmative Action?

For the most part, according to proponents, affirmative action programs that promote diversity are needed for the following reasons:

- The effects of past discrimination disadvantage, to one degree or another, all members of discriminated-against groups, so simply removing barriers to advancement is insufficient. When government policies themselves have had profound and lasting effects—slavery being the most obvious, but also state-sanctioned segregation, and racial discrimination in major benefit programs such as the post–World War II GI Bill[18]—the proper remedy is to prefer members of such groups in hiring, contracts, and education until such time as they reach parity with the majority.

- In a diverse society such as the United States, tolerance and a sense of community can develop only if we work together in educational, workplace, and government institutions that are diverse.

- People from disadvantaged and discriminated-against groups will improve themselves only if they have experience with successful role models in important institutions.

Critics of affirmative action are not convinced by these arguments. They believe the following to be true:

- Affirmative action violates one of the most basic American principles: that people be judged, rewarded, and punished as individuals, not because they are members of one group or another.

- Affirmative action benefits those within each preferred group who are already advantaged and need little help. Thus, the main beneficiaries of affirmative action in higher education have been middle-class African Americans, not the poor.

- Affirmative action seeks to remedy the effects of past discrimination by discriminating against others today—most notably, white males—simply because they belong to nonpreferred groups.

- Affirmative action increases intergroup and interracial tension by heightening the saliency of group membership. That is, social friction is increased by encouraging people to think of themselves and others as members of groups and to seek group advantages in a zero-sum game in which one group's gain is another group's loss.

Public Opinion on Affirmative Action

In survey after survey, a vast majority of Americans say they approve of the diversity goals of affirmative action—special programs to help those who have been discriminated against get ahead; outreach

SHARING THE DANGER For many years, fire departments in all parts of the country were strictly segregated, with most firefighter spots going to white males as a matter of policy. In such situations, the Court has allowed the use of affirmative action to redress past discriminatory practices. These firefighters have just finished putting out a fire in Chapel Oaks, Maryland. What might have perpetuated the legacy of discrimination among this profession?

programs to hire minority workers and find minority students—but disapprove of racial preferences in hiring, awarding of government contracts, and admission to colleges.[19] Most polling organizations show the following pattern: when asked whether they generally support affirmative action, about 65 percent of Americans say they approve; when the survey asks whether they favor affirmative action programs that involve preferential treatment or "set-asides" for racial minorities and women, support erodes dramatically, to less than half among all Americans. Not surprisingly, perhaps, racial differences on the issue of preferential treatment are wide; in 2009, 58 percent of African Americans and 53 percent of Hispanics supported affirmative action programs that involved preferential treatment, whereas only 22 percent of whites did, a drop from 27 percent in 2007.[20]

? How do Americans' mixed feelings about affirmative action reflect contradictions in their core beliefs outlined in Chapter 4?

American discomfort with affirmative action programs can perhaps be best seen in actions in several of the states. For example, referenda banning affirmative action in any state and local government activity were passed in California (1996), Washington (1997), and Michigan (2006)—three very liberal states—and other states have severely restricted affirmative action by executive order of their governors.[21] In 2008, Nebraska voters approved a measure that bans government use of affirmative action; Colorado voters narrowly rejected a ban, the first time affirmative action bans at the state level had failed at the polls.

The Supreme Court on Affirmative Action

The Supreme Court has been grappling for years with the issue of which forms of affirmative action, if any, are constitutionally permissible. Recall that the prevailing constitutional doctrine on matters of race holds that any mention of race in a government statute, ordinance, or rule is subject to strict scrutiny—that is, unconstitutional—unless the government can show some compelling and necessary reason for it. Historically, of course, there is good reason for the Court to take this position, given the fact that laws mentioning race were usually designed to deny equal protection to African Americans and other racial and religious minorities. But what about government actions meant to compensate African Americans and others for past discriminatory actions? Or initiatives to increase diversity in a broad range of institutions such as police departments and universities?

Since the mid-1980s, the Supreme Court has been moving gradually toward the position that laws and other government actions that are not colorblind should be subject to strict scrutiny. In *Wygant* v. *Jackson Board of Education* (1986) and *Richmond* v. *Croson Co.* (1989), the Supreme Court said that programs that narrowly redress specific violations will be upheld as constitutional but that broader affirmative action programs that address society's racism will be struck down. In *Adarand Constructors* v. *Peña* (1995), the Court ruled by a 5–4 majority that the federal government must abide by the strict standards for affirmative action programs imposed on the states in the *Richmond* case and could not award contracts using race as the main criterion. In *Miller* v. *Johnson* (1995), the Court ruled, again by a 5–4 majority, that race could not be used as the basis for drawing House district lines in an effort to increase the number of racial minority members in Congress.[22] In 1997, the Court refused to overturn a ruling of the Ninth Circuit Court that California's anti–affirmative action Proposition 209 was constitutionally permissible. In 2001, the Court let stand a decision by the

Eleventh U.S. Circuit Court of Appeals that disallowed a Fulton County, Georgia, program setting annual goals for awarding county contracts to blacks, Hispanics, Asians, Native Americans, and women.

Given these rulings by the Rehnquist Court, civil rights organizations were braced for a decision by the Supreme Court that would render affirmative action admissions policies unconstitutional once and for all. When the Court agreed to hear two admissions cases involving the University of Michigan—one involving its undergraduate program, the other its law school—liberals dreaded the outcome, while conservatives could hardly wait for the ruling. The Court stunned virtually every political observer when it ruled by a 5–4 vote in late June 2003 that universities could take race into consideration when considering applications for admission, so long as the consideration of race was not done in a mechanically quantitative manner or used as part of a racial and ethnic quota system, reaffirming, as it were, its position in the 1978 *Bakke* decision. (See the "Using the Framework" feature for more on why this happened.) In its twin decisions, the Court rejected the University of Michigan's undergraduate admissions affirmative action program—because it automatically assigned extra points to each minority applicant—but accepted the law school's—whose admissions process uses race as but one among several factors in a holistic examination of each applicant's file. What surprised observers the most, perhaps, was not the decision itself, but the broad language that Justice Sandra Day O'Connor used in her majority opinion, in which she stressed that achieving diversity in universities, and especially in its elite law schools, was indeed a compelling reason for not applying strict scrutiny by the Court:

> In order to cultivate a set of leaders with legitimacy in the eyes of the citizenry, it is necessary that the path to leadership be visibly open to the talented and qualified individuals of every race and ethnicity ... Access to legal education (and thus the legal profession) must be inclusive of talented and qualified individuals of every race and ethnicity so that all members of our heterogeneous society may participate in the educational institutions that provide the training and education necessary to succeed in America ... Cross-racial understanding helps to break down racial stereotypes and better prepares graduates for the working world ... The law school's educational judgment that such diversity is essential to its educational mission is one to which we defer.[23]

After the University of Michigan cases, here is where affirmative action stands under federal constitutional law at the present time:

- Any program by a government entity that uses race to define who receives or does not receive benefits is subject to strict scrutiny—that is, considered unconstitutional unless compelling and necessary reasons for the program are proved. This holds whether or not such programs are designed to discriminate against or favor racial minorities.

- With respect to the award of government contracts and government hiring—whether federal, state, or local—affirmative action programs are acceptable only if they are narrowly tailored to rectify past discriminatory actions by that particular government agency. In the view of the Court, rectifying past racist actions by a particular government agency is a compelling reason. Such programs, however, must be temporary efforts to transcend past practices and not a permanent feature of hiring and contracting. Affirmative action in hiring and contracting is not valid if it is designed simply to increase diversity or to decrease racism in society.

- With respect to admission to educational institutions—into undergraduate and graduate programs, law schools, and medical schools—actions to rectify past discriminatory admissions policies by a particular higher education institution are compelling and necessary, and are permitted.

- With respect to higher education admissions, the goal of achieving a diverse student body is a compelling reason to have affirmative action programs. However, race can only be used if it is one among several factors in a holistic consideration of each applicant's file; formulas in which students of a particular race or ethnicity automatically receive a set number of points are not permissible.

With Justice O'Connor now retired and replaced by Samuel Alito, a strong conservative, and with the Supreme Court now led by Chief Justice John Roberts, on record as opposing the use of affirmative action for increasing diversity or fixing societal wrongs, many civil rights advocates worry that even the narrow opening provided by the Michigan decisions will not hold. They worry that any use of race in government programs will trigger strict scrutiny, even if they are designed to rectify a long history of exclusion. This almost happened in 2007; by a 5–4 margin, the Roberts Court ruled in two paired cases that race-based systems for making primary and secondary school assignments in Seattle and Louisville were unconstitutional.[24] Although the Chief Justice and three of his colleagues wanted to exercise strict scrutiny in both—as Roberts put it, "The way to stop discrimination on the basis of race is to stop discriminating on the basis of race"—Justice Anthony Kennedy, who cast the deciding votes on these cases, refused to go this far. He simply stated in his majority opinions that the Seattle and Louisville systems were not sufficiently tailored to remedy past discrimination in these particular school districts.

The Roberts Court edged even closer to ending the use of race in *Ricci* v. *DeStefano* (2009). The case was brought by 18 New Haven firefighters (1 Hispanic, 17 white) who claimed they were denied the opportunity for promotion when the city threw out promotion examination results because no African American was in the top group. The city decided not to promote anyone. The Supreme Court agreed with the firefighters that the city of New Haven had practiced reverse discrimination in throwing out the examination results, overturning New Haven's victories at the district and appeals court levels. Significantly, the Court based its ruling on narrow grounds, rather than on broad constitutional ones, saying that New Haven was guilty of "disparate treatment based on race," which was contrary to the Civil Rights Act. Justice Antonin Scalia was not happy, saying in his concurring opinion that the Court was simply postponing the inevitable day when race-based laws and programs would be deemed unconstitutional under the "equal protection" clause of the Fourteenth Amendment.[25] We are very close, then, to the day when the Court will rule that race cannot be used by government at all, except when it is in response to a clear act of discrimination or exclusion.

Affirmative action programs in the United States have been designed to help not only African Americans, of course, but other racial and ethnic minorities as well, including Hispanics, Asian Americans, and Native Americans. Most of the programs also include women as beneficiaries. The present Supreme Court guidelines on affirmative action described here apply to all of these groups, not only African Americans. What is clear from recent developments is that affirmative action programs have been narrowed considerably in their reach.

Why has the Supreme Court narrowed the scope of affirmative action programs?

Background: During the 1990s, the Supreme Court rendered a number of decisions that narrowed the use of racial preferences in the areas of government hiring and contracting, congressional redistricting, and university admissions. It therefore came as a great surprise to both proponents and critics of affirmative action when the Supreme Court ruled by a 5–4 vote in a pair of cases involving the University of Michigan in 2003 that

affirmative action of a certain kind—one that uses race as only one among several factors in a holistic consideration of each individual's file—is permissible in university admissions. The ruling was made possible by the emergence in the late 1990s of a new Court majority on certain issues led by Sandra Day O'Connor. After she was replaced by Samuel Alito in 2006, the Court veered again against affirmative action.

| Structure | The Fourteenth Amendment's promise of "equal protection of the laws" bars government discrimination against groups of citizens but is unclear about the need for remedies for past discrimination. | The political culture honors individual rather than group rights and responsibilities. | The white middle and working classes suffered economic reverses during the 1980s and early 1990s, creating a climate that was generally hostile to affirmative action programs. |

| Political Linkage | The political influence of civil rights organizations declined in the 1980s and 1990s. | The majority white population reported in polls that it believed the goals of the civil rights movement have been met. | A substantial majority of Americans reported support for nondiscrimination laws but distaste for laws that give minorities and women special advantages in college admissions, jobs, and government contracts. |

The Christian conservative movement and other conservative organizations—who are against affirmative action—gained political influence in the 1980s.

Republicans, whose platform rejects affirmative action, reached parity with Democrats in national elections.

Republicans won control of the Senate from 1981–1986 and from 1995 to 2000.

| Government | Republican presidents Reagan and Bush nominated conservatives to the Court. | The Senate approved the nominees. | A narrow but firm conservative majority under the leadership of Chief Justice William Rehnquist controlled the Court on many issues during the early 1990s. |

A new majority led by Sandra Day O'Connor appeared on a number of issues in the late 1990s. Briefs from elite universities, major corporations, and former top military officials convinced her that affirmative action to increase diversity is sometimes a compelling goal in important institutions.

| Government Action | The Supreme Court rejects diversity as a compelling state interest in programs involving government jobs and contracting, and in congressional districting. | The Court rules in 2003 that the use of race in university admissions is permissible if it is not used as part of a mechanical, quantitative formula. |

The Court rules that race cannot be used in school assignments in primary and secondary schools.

The Court rules that "reverse discrimination" is illegal under the Civil Rights Act.

Comparing Women's Progress

Introduction There are many ways to evaluate how well women are doing in the United States at the beginning of the twenty-first century. One way is to look at various over-time measures comparing women and men in the United States. On a number of these measures, cited at various points in this book, we have noted many signs of progress as well as areas where the news is not so good. On the plus side of the ledger, women have improved their relative position with men on measures such as median income; median income within occupations and professions; representation among the ranks of the professions, especially medicine, law, higher education, and journalism; and

improved legal protections. Not as much progress has been made, however, in breaking the "glass ceiling" in the corporate and financial worlds or in reaching parity in the holding of elective offices. To be sure, there are several women in politically powerful positions, including Speaker of the House Nancy Pelosi and Secretary of State and leading contender for the 2008 Democratic nomination Hillary Clinton. And Sarah Palin was the GOP nominee for vice president in 2008.

Another way to look at women's relative standing is to compare the situation in the United States to the situation in the rest of the world. Taking that approach, using the particular measure reflected in this

cartogram, women in the United States are doing very well indeed.

Mapping Women Managers and Professionals This cartogram shows each country's share of the world's 130 million female managers and professionals. Managers and professionals are defined in the data set used to draw the cartogram—from the United Nation's 2004 Human Development Report—as people working as technical workers, senior officials in the public and private sectors, managers, or legislators and making more than $30,000 a year. What the cartogram shows is that virtually all the world's female managers and

The Contemporary Status of Civil Rights for Women

16.3 Assess the present status of civil rights protections for women

As the civil rights movement helped put the issue of equality for African Americans on the nation's political agenda, so did several women's rights movements advance civil rights protections for women. The struggle for women's suffrage, for example, was long and hard, finally succeeding in 1920. Fifty years later, the women's movement of the 1970s and 1980s helped win civil rights protections for women and broaden the participation of women in all aspects of American society, economy, and politics. Although the movement did not win one of its main objectives—passage of the Equal Rights Amendment (ERA) to the U.S. Constitution—the broad advance of women in gaining equal treatment and respect on virtually all fronts in the United States attests to its overall effectiveness.[26] Issues such as pay equity, family leave, sexual harassment, and attention to women's health problems in medical research are now a part of the American political agenda. Women have made important gains economically and are becoming more numerous in the professions, corporate managerial offices (although there is evidence that a glass ceiling remains blocking many women from the most senior posts in corporations; in 2009, only 12 CEOs of *Fortune* 500 companies were women), and political office. (See the "Mapping American Politics" feature to see how women's standing in the private sector in the United States compares with their standing in other countries.) Having said that, it remains the case that a wage gap still exists between men and women, and that the poverty rate for women is considerably higher than it is for men.

In terms of constitutional law, however, the expansion of civil rights protections for women has taken a path that differs decidedly from that for African Americans.[27]

professionals are located in the United States and western Europe. Indeed, according to the data from the Human Development Report, almost one-half of all women managers and professionals in the world live and work in the United States. Doing particularly poorly on this measure are such emerging economic powers as China, India, and Russia and the oil-producing states of the Middle East.

What Do You Think? How have women's situation and standing in the United States been improving? Where do they still need improving? Does it matter how women are doing relative to women elsewhere, or do you think we should concentrate on how well women are doing in our own country relative to men over time? In what areas of American life are women doing better, and in what ar-

eas are they doing worse? If you see room for improvement, what role do you think government should play in helping out? Or, do you think matters such as this are best left to the private sector?

Source: Worldmapper, map number 133. The SASI Group (University of Sheffield) and Mark Newman (University of Michigan), 2006. (**www.worldmapper.org**).

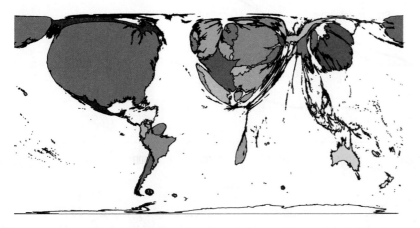

Source: www.worldmapper.org © Copyright 2006 SASI Group (University of Sheffield) and Mark Newman (University of Michigan).

Standard World Map

Intermediate Scrutiny

By 1976 the proposed Equal Rights Amendment (ERA) to the Constitution to guarantee full legal equality for women had stalled, falling short of the required three-fourths of the states. Moreover, the Supreme Court did not have the necessary votes for a strict scrutiny interpretation of gender classification. There was support, however, for the new doctrine that came to be called **intermediate scrutiny.** In *Craig* v. *Boren* (1976), six justices supported Justice William Brennan's compromise, which created a more rigorous scrutiny of gender as a *somewhat* suspect classification. In the view of the justices, the use of strict scrutiny would endanger traditional sex roles, while the use of ordinary scrutiny would allow blatant sex discrimination to survive. The Burger Court defined a test that it believed to be "just right." Under intermediate scrutiny, government enactments that relied on gender would be constitutional if the use of gender were *substantially related* to an *important objective.*[28] The test in *Craig* was refined in *United States* v. *Virginia* (1996), when the Court ruled that a male-only admissions policy at the state-supported Virginia Military Institute was unacceptable in that it discriminated against women. In this case, the standard to be met when men and women are treated differently in statutes and state government practices became "an exceedingly persuasive justification." Intermediate scrutiny defines a legal test, then, somewhere between strict and lax. Thus, for example, certain laws protecting pregnant women from dangerous chemicals in the workplace have passed this test. The improvement of women's rights under the doctrine of intermediate scrutiny is less than what many in the women's movement wanted.

Thus, women's rights have not followed the path of other rights and liberties. The nation has not restructured civil rights for women based on an expansive reading of the equal protection clause of the Fourteenth Amendment by the courts. Rather, advances have come by virtue of changing societal attitudes about the role of women in society, increased involvement of women in politics (see Figure 16.1), and new statutes

intermediate scrutiny

A legal test falling between ordinary and strict scrutiny relevant to issues of gender; under this test, the Supreme Court will allow gender classifications in laws if they are *substantially* related to an *important* government objective.

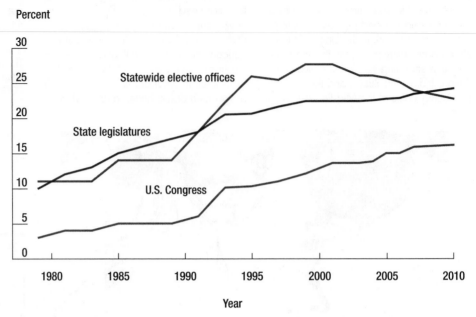

Percent

FIGURE 16.1 Percentage of Elective Offices Held by Women, 1979–2010

Although accounting for more than one-half the American population, women hold a much smaller proportion of elected federal, state, and local offices across the nation than men. However, the percentage of offices held by women has been increasing steadily since the 1970s. Given rising education and incomes among women, as well as changing social attitudes toward women's role in society, the proportion of elected offices held by women is likely to continue to increase. *Source:* Center for American Women and Politics (January 2010).

designed to equalize women's opportunities. In the private sector, women have made important advances in the corporate world and in the professions. Women now outnumber men among law school and medical school students, and more women than men go to college and graduate. While wage disparities still exist between men and women, the gap is narrowing, especially among college graduates between the ages of 25 and 34.[29] (In some cities— including New York, Chicago, Boston, and Minneapolis—young women under 30 actually earn more than their male counterparts.[30])

In the public sector, more and more women hold important elected and appointed positions in all levels of government and serve in all branches of the armed services. And, they hold increasingly influential positions. Nancy Pelosi is the Speaker of the House. Hillary Clinton, now Secretary of State, came very close to winning the Democratic Party's presidential nomination in 2008, and Sarah Palin was on the GOP national ticket as the vice presidential candidate.

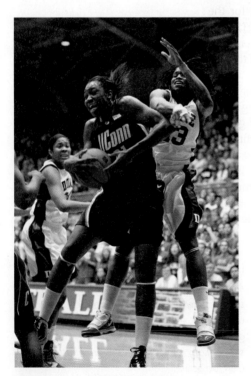

HOOPS CHAMPIONS Title IX had the effect of increasing funding for women's sports in American colleges and universities and encouraging more women to participate in sports. One result was dramatic improvement in the quality of women's sports teams across the board. Here, Connecticut's Tina Charles grabs a rebound on the way to her team's decisive win in the 2010 national championship game against Duke. What other landmark legislation or Court decisions advanced women's rights to the degree that Title IX did?

EVER SO CLOSE Hillary Clinton fell barely short of winning enough primary and caucus votes to capture the Democratic Party nomination for president in 2008, losing to Barack Obama. She would have been the first woman nominated by one of the major parties. Here, she signs the hands of a young supporter after her primary wins over Obama in West Virginia. Who in American politics today is likely to become that first woman presidential nominee?

Women have also successfully pushed for laws that compensate for past injustices. One example of such a law is Title IX of the Civil Rights Act of 1964, which prohibits discrimination against women at federally funded institutions, including universities. Title IX is generally credited with enhancing funding for women's sports programs in colleges and dramatically improving the quality of women's athletics in the United States. Another example is the Lilly Ledbetter Fair Pay Restoration Act, signed into law by President Barack Obama in January 2009 only days after his inauguration, which makes it easier for women and others to sue their companies over pay discrimination and may serve to narrow the pay gap between men and women. The new law was designed to over-ride the Supreme Court's ruling in *Ledbetter* v. *Goodyear Tire & Rubber Co.* (2007), which made pay discrimination lawsuits exceedingly difficult to mount.

? Do you think the improving position of young professional women in relation to men will be reflected in the corporate world in the years ahead? Will it change the gender makeup of the government?

Abortion Rights

For many women (and men), the right of women to abort an unwanted pregnancy is a central element of the civil rights agenda. (To be sure, many others are against abortion on religious grounds.) That may well be, but the Supreme Court, in a number of important cases beginning with *Roe* v. *Wade* (1973), has based a woman's right to terminate a pregnancy on privacy grounds rather than equal protection grounds. It is for this reason that we have addressed the abortion issue, with its contentious politics and string of Court rulings revising and refining *Roe,* in Chapter 15 on civil liberties. Please refer to that section of the previous chapter to see more on the politics and law of the struggle over abortion in the United States.

Sexual Harassment and Hostile Environment

Another issue of concern to many women (and many men) is sexual harassment in the workplace. One poll reported that 20 percent of women say they have experienced sexual harassment of one kind or another at work.[31] Many have filed

How much sexual harassment is there on the New York subways?

Newspaper, television, radio, and Internet news outlets reported in headlines and lead stories the shocking findings of a 2007 study: 63 percent of New York women said they had been sexually harassed on the subway; 10 percent said they had been sexually assaulted.

Why It Matters Sexual harassment and sexual assault are serious problems in American society. Any number of studies have shown this, including those conducted by academic researchers, the Equal Employment Opportunity Commission, and the U.S. Civil Rights Commission. Virtually all Americans agree that every effort should be made by government and by private-sector companies to eradicate it where it

exists. To go about this effort effectively, however, requires that information about the incidence and location of sexual harassment and sexual assault be accurate and informative, not just alarmist.

The Story Behind the Numbers
The numbers for the news media story came from the office of Manhattan borough president Scott Stringer. The survey was done online. The list of people to be surveyed came from two sources. One was an e-mail list kept by Stringer's office that included constituents, reporters, contributors, and members of various nonprofit groups. The other e-mail lists were from two advocacy groups active on the issue of sexual harassment and assault. "Holla Back New York" asks people

who visit its site to post reports of harassment and assault. "Right Rides for Women's Safety Inc." provides rides for people, mostly women, who want to avoid riding public transportation late at night.

Getting the Numbers Right Holla Back and Right Rides are doing important work. There is no doubt that they have helped focus public attention on a serious problem and have offered many women both solace and protection. But the people who are members of or in contact with each of them cannot be said to be a representative sample of female New York subway riders. It is unlikely, moreover, that the e-mail list of contacts kept in borough president Stringer's office is representative of such riders or of any-

complaints with the Equal Employment Opportunity Commission (EEOC), which reported that more than 12,000 complaints for sexual harassment (16 percent of them from men) were filed with the agency in fiscal year 2009.

People disagree, of course, about what kinds of behavior constitute sexual harassment, although the courts, regulatory agencies, and legislative bodies are gradually defining the law in this area. (See the "By the Numbers" feature on good and bad ways to figure this out.) In 1980, the EEOC ruled that making sexual activity a condition of employment or promotion violates the 1964 Civil Rights Act, a ruling upheld by the Supreme Court. The EEOC also ruled that creating "an intimidating, hostile, or offensive working environment" is contrary to the law. The U.S. Supreme Court took a major step in defining sexual harassment when it ruled unanimously, in *Harris* v. *Forklift Systems Inc.* (1993), that workers do not have to prove that offensive actions make them unable to do their jobs or cause them psychological harm, only that the work environment is hostile or abusive. In a pair of rulings in June 1998, the Court broadened the definition of sexual harassment by saying that companies were liable for the behavior of supervisors even if top managers were unaware of harassing behavior. However, companies were offered a measure of protection by the Court when it ruled that companies with solid and well-communicated harassment policies could not be held liable if victims failed to report harassment in a reasonable period of time.

An increase in public awareness about sexual harassment has triggered an increase in lawmaking by state legislatures to erase sexual harassment in the workplace. Moreover, most major corporations and state and local government entities (including public colleges and universities) have sexual harassment and hostile environment prohibitions in place and require their employees to participate in training programs to lessen their incidence.

thing else for that matter. In issuing his report, Stringer violated the first rule of survey research: randomness. That is to say, any survey on the incidence of sexual harassment and sexual assault experienced by women riding on New York subways would need to start with a random sample of all women who ride them. That is the only way to ensure that the survey respondents are not simply a self-selected group of people whose experiences are not typical of others.

What to Watch For Surveys come in every shape and form and are done and reported by all sorts of organizations. As suggested in Chapter 5, it is important to read the fine print in the reports to see how the polling was done. There are lots of things to watch for, but randomness is critically important. Unless everyone has an equal chance of being asked to participate in a survey—in this case, all women in New York who ride subways—then the results are meaningless. In the reports of the subway harassment story,

the news media outlets did not help much. In the *Associated Press* story, problems with the survey's methods did not appear until the fourth paragraph, while the *New York Daily News* offered no caveats at all. So you may have to do a little bit of digging on your own on surveys that are reported by organizations other than those with strong reputations for methodological rigor such as Gallup, Harris, and the Pew Research Center.

What Do You Think? How serious a problem is sexual harassment and sexual assault in your community? What kinds of information are available that track these things in your community? What do you think can and should be done about reducing their incidence? Would you more likely favor solutions from the private sector or government? What might these solutions be?

Source: The Numbers Guy, *The Wall Street Journal Online,* August 1, 2007, http://blogs.wsj.com/numbersguy.

Broadening the Civil Rights Umbrella

16.4 Analyze the expansion of civil rights protections to the elderly, the disabled, and gays and lesbians

The expansion of civil rights protections for women and racial minorities encouraged other groups to press for expanded rights protections.

The Elderly and the Disabled

Interest groups for the elderly have pressed for laws barring age discrimination and have enjoyed some success in recent years. Several federal and state laws, for instance, now bar mandatory retirement. And, the Age Discrimination in Employment Act passed in 1967 prohibits employers from discriminating against employees over the age of 40 in pay, benefits, promotions, and working conditions. The courts also have begun to strike down hiring practices based on age unless a compelling reason for such age requirements can be demonstrated. But problems persist; downsizing companies often lay off older workers first because the pay and benefits of older workers are almost always higher than those of younger workers. And, because people are living longer and worried about the size of their pensions and the rising costs of medical care (even with Medicare), many more Americans say they want to work, at least part time, beyond the normal retirement age.

Disabled Americans have also pushed for civil rights and other protections and have won some notable victories, including passage of the Americans with Disabilities Act (ADA) of 1990. The act prohibits employment discrimination

BETTER ACCESS Since passage of the Americans with Disabilities Act in 1990, increasing numbers of public and private buildings have become more accessible to people in wheelchairs. In spite of the act, accessibility for the disabled to public and private buildings remains less than many of its proponents had hoped when it was first signed into law. Why, even with the passage of the ADA, are so many public places not fully accessible to people with disabilities?

against the disabled and requires that reasonable efforts be made to make places of employment and public facilities (such as concert halls, restaurants, retail shops, schools, and government offices) accessible to them. The proliferation of wheelchair ramps and wheelchair-accessible toilet facilities is a sign that the legislation is having an important effect. Several advocates for the disabled, however, claim that the act depends too much on voluntary compliance.

In 2001, the Supreme Court dramatically narrowed the reach of the ADA, saying that state employees could not sue states for damages arising from violations of the act, as provided for in the legislation. Advocates for the rights of the disabled worried that this judicial ruling expanding the scope of state immunity from congressional actions means that other sections of the ADA act are doomed, including the requirement that state governments make their services and offices accessible to people with disabilities. Others worried that a wide range of civil rights laws that require nondiscriminatory behavior by state agencies—schools and hospitals, for example—may be at risk, as well, because the basis of the Court's decision was that Congress had gone beyond its authority in telling the states what to do under the interstate commerce clause.[32] If the states are immune from the requirements of the Americans with Disabilities Act, the reasoning goes, why should it not be immune from the provisions of other civil rights laws passed by Congress? In *Tennessee* v. *Lane* (2004), the Court ruled that the disabled could sue a state for money damages in federal court if the state fails to make its courts fully accessible. The Supreme Court was silent, however, on whether this right to sue extends to other areas in which states have not fully complied with other federal civil rights requirements, so the issue still remains unsettled.

? What practical considerations impact states' abilities to offer equal treatment to Americans with disabilities? Should costs and availability of resources come into play in enforcing these protections?

Gays and Lesbians

The gay and lesbian civil rights movement began in earnest following the 1969 "Stonewall rebellion"—three days of rioting set off by police harassment of the patrons of a popular gay bar in Greenwich Village in New York. The movement picked up steam as the gay community reacted to the powerful inroads of AIDS and in response to the Supreme Court's decision in *Bowers* v. *Hardwick* (1986) upholding Georgia's ban against homosexual sexual relations. The movement was also inspired by and borrowed many of the tactics of the civil rights and women's movements. The goal was to gain the same civil rights protections under the law enjoyed by African Americans and other minority groups and to gain respect from the public. The tactics have ranged from patient lobbying and voting to mass demonstrations and deliberately shocking actions by groups such as ACT-UP. While some important gains have been made by the gay and lesbian movement, its open advocacy for civil rights for homosexuals has triggered strong counterattacks over the years by groups strongly opposed to its objectives, such as the American Family Association, Concerned Women for America, and Focus on the Family.

Gays and lesbians have moved toward equal treatment in a variety of settings in the private sector. Gains in the areas of high culture and mass entertainment have been important. Sympathetic gay and lesbian characters appear regularly on network (*Ugly Betty, The Office, Glee, Modern Family*) and cable (*The L Word, South Park, Nip/Tuck, Project Runway*), as well as in movies and plays (*Brokeback Mountain, Angels in America, Rent*).[33] Not surprisingly, given the advances made in the arts and mass entertainment, public attitudes about gays and lesbians are growing steadily more tolerant. Fewer Americans today than in the past think that gay and lesbian relationships are wrong. Substantial majorities, moreover, favor ending discrimination against gays and lesbians in jobs, housing, and education and favor passing hate-crime legislation. Fully 57 percent of the public—and 68 percent of those between the ages of 18 and 29—favor **civil unions.** While a majority of Americans still oppose the idea of same-sex marriage, the number holding these views has been declining. In 2004, 63 percent were against it; in 2009 the percentage had dropped to 53. Again, younger Americans are the most open to equal rights for gays and lesbians with a clear majority supporting same-sex marriage.[34]

The gay and lesbian movement's political efforts have had mixed success. In presidential politics, partial advances have been the order of the day. When Bill Clinton was a presidential candidate, for example, he promised to lift the ban on gay people in the military, but as president he was forced in 1993 to reverse course in light of the hostile reaction from Congress and the armed services. The resulting "don't ask, don't tell, don't pursue" policy satisfied very few people, though it remained in place under his successor George W. Bush. President Barack Obama asked Congress in 2010 to pass new legislation allowing gays and lesbians to serve openly in the armed services. The House passed a bill, but it got nowhere in the Senate. Obama also directed the military to assess the possible impact of the change on morale and combat effectiveness. A federal judge ruled in fall 2010, however, that the "don't ask, don't tell" policy was unconstitutional because it violated the rights of gays and lesbians. A federal appeals court stayed the action, however, so it would have more time to consider the policy and its implications.

Civil rights for gays and lesbians have not been treated sympathetically by Congress. In 1993—responding to decisions by several major universities to bar military recruiters from campus because the military would not allow openly practicing homosexuals to serve—Congress passed the so-called Solomon Amendment, which bars federal money to colleges and universities that deny military recruiters the same campus access as other private and public employers. In 1996, Congress passed the Defense of Marriage Act, defining marriage as a union of a man and a woman and declaring that states are under no legal obligation to recognize same-sex marriages performed in other states. (A federal judge ruled this unconstitutional in 2010, suggesting that the Act was an inappropriate federal intrusion on states' traditional prerogatives regarding marriage; the issue is sure to reach the Supreme Court at some point.)

The most important civil rights gains for gays and lesbians have occurred in the courts. At the state level, Vermont's high court ruled in 2003 that same-sex couples must have the same legal rights, protections, and benefits as heterosexual married couples, including matters such as

civil union

A status in which same-sex couples have the same legal rights, benefits, and protections as married couples.

joint tax returns, property ownership, insurance benefits, and medical decisions involving a spouse. In 2004, the Massachusetts high court ruled that same-sex couples have the same right to marry as heterosexual couples, citing the state constitution's provision for equal rights for all citizens. In 2008, the Supreme Courts of California and Connecticut ruled that bans on same-sex marriages in their states were unconstitutional. (California voters reversed their Court in the November elections.)

Gays and lesbians also have won important Supreme Court cases. The Court ruled in *Romer* v. *Evans* (1996), for example, that state laws designed to deny basic civil rights to gays and lesbians are unconstitutional. In this case, the Court looked at Colorado's provision (known as Amendment 2) prohibiting local communities from passing gay antidiscrimination ordinances. The Court ruled that the law was constitutionally unacceptable because not only was there was no rational basis for the law but, as Justice Anthony Kennedy declared in his opinion, "a state cannot so deem a class of persons [gays and lesbians] a stranger to its laws." And, in a stunning and highly unexpected decision in 2003, the Supreme Court overturned its own *Bowers* decision from 1986 and ruled in *Lawrence* v. *Texas* that state anti-sodomy laws designed to make homosexual sexual relations illegal were unconstitutional. Justice Kennedy again gave the ruling a very expansive reading in his majority opinion, declaring that gay people "were entitled to freedom, dignity, and respect for their private lives." Interestingly, neither of these major cases was based on the equal protection clause of the Fourteenth Amendment, which is the foundation for equal treatment of racial and religious minorities.

Although gays and lesbians have won significant civil rights protections in a handful of states—Massachusetts, Vermont, New Hampshire, Connecticut, and Iowa permit same-sex marriage as does Washington, D.C; New Jersey and Nevada allow civil unions and mandate that people in such unions receive the same state rights and benefits as people in heterosexual marriages; Oregon and Washington permit same-sex civil partnerships but with fewer rights and benefits as those of married couples; and Illinois bars discrimination based on sexual orientation—13 states in 2004, 8 in 2006, and 3 more in 2008 passed initiatives banning same-sex marriage. As of 2010, 39 states had laws or constitutional provisions defining marriage as between one man and one woman.[35]

The same-sex marriage movement is very short on victories among voters. The only state to reject an initiative banning same-sex marriage is Colorado. Even voters in states considered to be liberal on social issues have surprised same-sex marriage advocates. In California, for example, voters passed Proposition 8 in 2008 overturning the California Supreme Court's decision allowing such marriages. When voters in Maine repealed a law passed by its state legislature legalizing same-sex marriage in 2009, it became the 31st state to reject such marriages at the ballot box.

ANGRY WITH THE CALIFORNIA HIGH COURT California voters supported a statewide ban on same-sex marriages in 2008, an action the California Supreme Court found to be acceptable under the state's constitution. Here, a crowd of supporters rally in Los Angeles in 2009 to protest their state high court's decision. How likely is it that the issue eventually will reach the U.S. Supreme Court? What judicial route will the issue take if it goes to the Court?

It is evident that the struggle over gay and lesbian civil rights will remain an important part of the American political agenda for a long time to come. The eventual outcome remains very much in doubt, however. While gays and lesbians have made important advances, to be sure, many religious conservatives have been politically mobilized by the possibility that state courts and the U.S. Supreme Court might eventually sanction same-sex marriage as a basic civil right, though that seems like a remote possibility today given the political leanings of the Roberts Court.

Using the DEMOCRACY STANDARD

Is equal citizenship a reality in the United States?

It is with respect to civil rights—guarantees of equality for people in the United States with regard to judicial proceedings, the exercise of political rights, treatment by public officials, and access to and enjoyment of the benefits of government programs—that the differences between the ideas of the framers and the demands of democracy theory are most evident. It is with respect to civil rights, moreover, that democratic aspirations and the struggle for democracy have most altered the original Constitution of the United States. Recall that the framers not only paid scant attention to guarantees of equality, but they also included a number of provisions in the Constitution that accepted and sustained the institution of slavery as well as the noncitizen status of Native Americans. Further, in leaving voting and office-holding requirements largely to the states, the framers implicitly accepted prevailing practices in the states, including the exclusion of women from political life, but also property qualifications and religious tests for voting and office holding. For the framers, civil rights guarantees—other than equality in the courts—were not among the first principles of good government. In fact, as shown in Chapter 2, the framers worried a great deal about "leveling tendencies" in society that might lead to too much equality and a system of governance in which people of virtue, character, and education would not be in control. In democratic theory, on the other hand, equal citizenship—another way of saying civil rights—is the very essence of good government, one of the three essential pillars of democracy, joining popular sovereignty and liberty. Absent equal citizenship, as explained in Chapter 1, democracy cannot be said to exist.

The glaring absence of a strong constitutional foundation for the principle of equal citizenship—buttressed for much of U.S. history by a popular culture that favored broad political inclusion for white males but not for other groups—meant that the spread of civil rights protections has been slow and uneven. Thus, women were denied the vote well into the twentieth century. Most African Americans were slaves until passage of the Thirteenth Amendment after the Civil War and were not admitted into full citizenship across the nation until at least 1965, after passage of the Civil Rights and Voting Rights Acts. Even today, women, racial and ethnic minorities, and gays and lesbians fail to play a role in the political process commensurate with their numbers in the population.

Having said that, it is undeniably true that civil rights dramatically increased in the United States during the second half of the twentieth century as guarantees of equal citizenship were extended—unevenly to be sure—to women, African

Americans, other racial and ethnic minorities, and partially to gays and lesbians. These developments were a product of the struggle for democracy by previously excluded groups who insisted on their right to full citizenship, the emergence of a more egalitarian society and culture in the United States, the rational behavior of elected public officials responding legislatively to a public increasingly supportive of civil rights, and changes in the judicial interpretation of equal citizenship in a country turned more favorable to claims of equality.

This advance of civil rights protections since the end of World War II has enriched American democracy because it has made political equality more of a reality in the United States. This is not to say that racial minorities and women have attained full social or material equality; many areas of American life, from wealth holding to representation in the professions and in Congress, remain unequal and unrepresentative. Nor is this to say that all civil rights issues are settled; note the continuing disagreements over same-sex marriages and affirmative action. Nevertheless, the attainment of formal political equality is real and something about which many Americans take a great deal of pride.

SUMMARY

16.1 Trace the evolution of civil rights protections for women and racial minorities to the twentieth century

- The original Constitution and the Bill of Rights were relatively silent on equality other than providing for equality before the law.

- The Fourteenth Amendment that was adopted after the Civil War was a foundation for later civil rights advances.

- Although the Court paid little attention to civil rights during the nineteenth century, structural changes in society, the transformation of attitudes about race and gender, and the political efforts of racial and ethnic minority group members and women of all races finally prompted the Court to begin to pay attention by the middle of the twentieth century. These contributed to important civil rights gains for racial and religious minorities and women.

16.2 Assess the present status of civil rights protections for racial minorities

- It is now settled law that discrimination of any kind against racial minorities in the statutes and administrative practices of federal, state, or local government

is unconstitutional. It is also settled law that governments may use affirmative action to rectify the past discriminatory practices of a particular public entity such as a fire department in its hiring practices or county government in letting road building contracts. The status of affirmative action programs meant to achieve general societal progress for minorities (or women) or to enhance diversity, however, remains unsettled, though the Court is leaning strongly against such efforts.

16.3 Assess the present status of civil rights protections for women

- The Court has taken the position that laws that mention gender fall under the doctrine of "intermediate scrutiny," signaling that it will allow more latitude than it does to race to federal, state, and local governments that wish to give gender special attention.

- Recent political, social, and economic gains by women are the result of changes in social attitudes, the political efforts of women, and the changing occupational needs of the American economy, rather than the product of a series of favorable Court rulings about gender equality.

16.4 Analyze the expansion of civil rights protections to the elderly, the disabled, and gays and lesbians

- The civil rights movement gave impetus not only to the women's movement but also to a range of other groups of Americans who felt they were discriminated against, including the elderly, the disabled, and gays and lesbians. Statutes have been passed at all levels of government addressed to the equal protection needs of the elderly and the disabled, though compliance has been very uneven.

- The question of whether lesbians and gay men can be discriminated against in housing, employment, and education has been largely settled in law and increasingly in social practice. However, the issues of gays and lesbians in the military and same-sex marriage remain the subject of considerable political debate and legal disputation.

TEST YOURSELF

Answer key begins on page T-1.

16.1 Trace the evolution of civil rights protections for women and racial minorities to the twentieth century

1. The principles of equality are the cornerstone of the Preamble to the Constitution.
   True / False
2. Which of the following did *not* undermine the Civil War amendments?
   a. Jim Crow
   b. Poll taxes
   c. Literacy tests
   d. Grandfather clauses
   e. *Brown* v. *Board of Education of Topeka*
3. Compare the protections afforded women in the Fifteenth and Nineteenth Amendments.

16.2 Assess the present status of civil rights protections for racial minorities

4. In a long list of decisions, the Supreme Court gradually eliminated all vestiges of de facto discrimination.
   True / False
5. Which of the following best describes the white South's response to *Brown* v. *Board of Education*?
   a. Immediate compliance with the Court's decision
   b. Immediate integration of all public facilities
   c. Massive resistance to Court-ordered integration
   d. Mass migration of white Southerners to the North
   e. Gradual compliance with Court-ordered segregation
6. What does Chief Justice John Roberts mean when he says, "the way to stop discrimination on the basis of race is to stop discriminating on the basis of race"?

16.3 Assess the present status of civil rights protections for women

7. Title IX of the Civil Rights Act of 1964 is often credited with expanding funding for women's collegiate athletics and for improving the overall quality of women's collegiate athletic programs.
   True / False
8. What sort of scrutiny do the courts generally give to laws that treat men and women differently?
   a. Ordinary scrutiny
   b. Scrutiny awarded to suspect classifications
   c. Strict scrutiny
   d. Intermediate scrutiny
   e. Lax scrutiny
9. How satisfied do you think the leaders of the women's movement are with the status of women's rights in the United States?

16.4 Analyze the expansion of civil rights protections to the elderly, the disabled, and gays and lesbians

10. The Americans with Disabilities Act has considerably expanded access to public facilities for those with disabilities.
    True / False
11. According to judicial interpretations of the Fourteenth Amendment, which of the following groups is afforded the weakest civil rights protections by the Constitution?
    a. Hispanics
    b. African Americans
    c. Women
    d. Jews
    e. Gays and lesbians
12. Evaluate the prospects that the United States will institute same-sex civil marriage within the next 50 years.

PEARSON
mypoliscilab EXERCISES

Apply what you learned in this chapter on MyPoliSciLab.

Read on mypoliscilab.com

eText: Chapter 16

Study and **Review** on **mypoliscilab.com**

Pre-Test
Post-Test
Chapter Exam
Flashcards

Watch on **mypoliscilab.com**

Video: Supreme Court: No Race-Based Admissions
Video: Should Don't Ask Don't Tell Go Away?

Explore on **mypoliscilab.com**

Simulation: You Are the Mayor and Need to Make Civil Rights Decisions
Comparative: Comparing Civil Rights
Timeline: The Mexican-American Civil Rights Movement
Timeline: The Civil Rights Movement
Timeline: Women's Struggle for Equality
Timeline: The Struggle for Equal Protection
Visual Literacy: Race and the Death Penalty

INTERNET SOURCES

Civil Rights Project
www.civilrightsproject.ucla.edu
Cutting-edge research on race in America.

Infoplease Civil Rights Timeline: Milestones in the Modern Civil Rights Movement
www.infoplease.com/spot/civilrightstimeline1.html
A richly detailed timeline of the African American civil rights movement.

Cornell Law Library/Civil Rights
www.law.cornell.edu/wex/index.php/Civil_rights
Links to the Constitution, landmark and recent Supreme Court civil rights decisions, international treaties on human rights, the Civil Rights Division of the Justice Department, and more.

Equal Opportunity Employment Commission
www.eeoc.gov
Statistics and reports about and rulings on employment discrimination.

Issues: Gay Rights
www.politics1.com/issues-gay.htm
Links to organizations in favor of and opposed to advancing gay and lesbian civil rights.

Martin Luther King Jr., Home Page
http://seattletimes.nwsource.com/mlk/
Created by the Seattle Times, the site includes study guides on King and the civil rights movement, interactive exercises, audios of King speeches, and links to other King and civil rights websites.

Yahoo/Civil Rights
www.yahoo.com/Society_and_Culture/Issues_and_Causes/Civil_Rights/
Links to a vast compendium of information on civil rights and to organizations devoted to the protection and expansion of domestic and international rights.

SUGGESTIONS FOR FURTHER READING

Baer, A. Judith, and Leslie Friedman Goldstein. *The Constitutional and Legal Rights of Women.* Belmont, CA: Roxbury Publishing, 2006.

A rich blend of judicial politics, the women's movement, and constitutional interpretation.

Barry, Brian. *Culture and Equality.* Cambridge, MA: Harvard University Press, 2001.

An assault on multiculturalism in the name of liberal egalitarianism by a distinguished political philosopher.

Bowen, William G., and Derek C. Bok. *The Shape of the River: Long-Term Consequences of Considering Race in College and University Admissions.* Princeton, NJ: Princeton University Press, 1998.

Based on surveys of more than 60,000 white and African American students at highly selective colleges and universities, Bowen and Bok argue that affirmative action in college and university admissions has had substantial and widespread positive effects on American society.

Branch, Taylor. *At Canaan's Edge: America in the King Years, 1965–1968.* New York: Simon and Schuster, 2006.

The third volume in Taylor Branch's brilliant and award-winning biographies of Martin Luther King; focuses not only on King in this volume but on the transformation of race relations and American politics during this decisive period.

Gates, Henry Louis, Jr. *America Behind the Color Line.* New York: Warner Books, 2004.

An examination of the legacy of the civil rights movement for African Americans.

Katznelson, Ira. *When Affirmative Action Was White: An Untold History of Racial Inequality in Twentieth-Century America.* New York: W.W. Norton, 2005.

An eye-opening look at how a long list of federal government programs, beginning in the New Deal, favored whites over blacks.

Koppelman, Andrew. *Same Sex, Different States: When Same Sex Marriage Crosses State Lines.* New Haven, CT: Yale University Press, 2006.

A careful examination of the constitutional issues at the root of this contemporary controversy, especially those having to do with what states owe to one another in a federal system.

17 | The Budget and Economic Policies

LEARNING OBJECTIVES

After reading this chapter, you should be able to:

17.1 Identify three types of public policies and assess how policies are formed

17.2 Analyze economic policymaking in terms of goals, players, and tools

17.3 Identify the components of the federal budget and analyze the problem of the national debt

17.4 Explain the reasons for government regulation and predict the future of regulation

ECONOMIC CRISIS AND THE EXPANSION OF THE FEDERAL GOVERNMENT

The economic collapse in the United States in 2008 and 2009 was, by all accounts, the worst since the Great Depression. The sluggish jobless recovery that followed, with unemployment around the 10 percent mark through much of 2010, continued the misery. Though it didn't match the depth or duration of the Great Depression, our recent economic troubles are the worst that most living Americans have ever experienced.[1]

Though the recession officially began in the fourth quarter of 2007, matters came to a head in the fall of 2008. Fannie Mae and Freddie Mac, the gigantic firms backing most mortgages in the United States, faced imminent collapse. The American International Group (AIG), the nation's largest insurance company, found itself owing tens of billions of dollars it could not pay to investment banks, commercial banks, hedge funds, and the sovereign wealth funds of other nations, because it had insured against the collapse of now nearly worthless mortgage-backed securities. The nation's best known and respected investment banks seemed to disappear

overnight, most notably Bear Stearns and Lehman Brothers. The contagion spread to seemingly safe commercial banks such as Washington Mutual, while Bank of America and Wells Fargo, among others, went right to the brink of failure. The collapse of the financial system led to a credit squeeze in which financial institutions, burned by bad loans and burdened by their own troubled mortgage-backed securities assets, cut back on lending. Without access to credit, many consumers cut back on their purchases, devastating many companies, big and small, as their sales plummeted. With revenues down and access to credit severely limited, many companies put off plans to expand, cut orders to their suppliers, and laid off employees. Investors withdrew from the stock market seeking safe-haven in government bonds, Treasury notes, and money market accounts.

The effects of these difficulties were reflected in all the major economic indicators. Overall economic activity contracted, with the gross domestic product (GDP) down 5.4 percent in the fourth quarter of 2008 compared to a year earlier and down

an additional 6.4 percent in the first quarter of 2009. The stock market lost more than half of its value as the Dow Jones Industrial Index fell from its record high of 14,165 on October 9, 2007, to a low of 6,440 in March 2009, recovering to only about 10,000 by early 2010, taking a toll on pension funds and many people's 401(k) retirement funds. Millions of people lost their homes to foreclosure as the housing market collapsed across the country, with Sunbelt states such as Florida, Arizona, and California especially hard hit. Between November 2008 and April 2009, about 645,000 Americans lost their jobs every month.[2] Unemployment broke 10 percent in October 2009, with more than one in three of those without jobs unemployed for more than 27 weeks, a post-war record.[3] Though the economy began to grow a little in early 2010, job creation lagged. By the spring of 2010, in fact, about 8.4 million jobs had been lost in the downturn.[4]

The economic crisis dramatically increased the role of the federal government. Though a Republican and a self-described conservative, George W. Bush's administration responded in a surprisingly vigorous manner. Bush and the Democratic Congress passed a $152 billion economic stimulus package in February 2008 to fight the recession. The Federal Reserve (the Fed), headed by Bush-appointee Ben Bernanke, aggressively cut short-term interest rates throughout the spring, summer, and fall to stimulate economic activity and stepped up its lending to banks in an attempt to head off troubles in the financial system. The Fed took the surprising step of arranging and partially paying for J.P. Morgan's purchase of the failing investment bank Bear Stearns, as well as for Bank of America's absorption of troubled Merrill Lynch. The Treasury Department, led by Secretary Hank Paulson, and the Federal Reserve together bailed out Fannie Mae and Freddie Mac to the tune of $25 billion (it had reached $85 billion by the end of summer 2009), then pumped more than $100 billion into AIG. The FDIC arranged and helped subsidize J.P. Morgan's purchase of Washington Mutual.

Worried that these steps were not enough to prevent a financial collapse, Bernanke and Paulson convinced President Bush and Congress to pass a massive $700 billion rescue package directed primarily at the nation's largest financial institutions (the Troubled Asset Relief Program, or TARP). The idea was to buy up the nearly worthless assets of the nation's major financial institutions and infuse massive amounts of new money into them, freeing them up to begin lending again to individuals and companies. Despite these actions, the economy was in terrible straits by the end of 2008, with the stock market in free fall (the Dow lost 18 percent of its value during the first week of October); economic growth going backward; banks refusing or unable to lend money, even to each other; and consumer confidence falling to one of its lowest points ever. In a remarkable step, Bernanke and Paulson decided to use a portion of TARP to inject money into the financial system by buying up ownership shares in banks and other financial institutions—in effect, partially nationalizing them. In doing this, these two Bush appointees had moved a considerable distance from the free market philosophy that had dominated Washington policies since the beginning of the Reagan administration in 1981.

After their big victories in the 2008 election, President Barack Obama and Democratic congressional leaders proposed further expansions in the size and reach of the national government, both to address the immediate crisis and to tackle a range of chronic problems. They did a number of things to deal with the recession and credit squeeze. Congress passed a $787 billion stimulus bill, which the president signed on February 17, 2009, less than 30 days from the date of his inauguration. The stimulus package was a combination of tax cuts and new expenditures in programs that, among other things, extended unemployment benefits, funded new research and development in alternative energy sources, put monies into school construction, helped first-time homeowners buy houses, and increased spending for infrastructure (roads, bridges, canals, and the like). Other changes were tied to fixing some of the problems that caused the financial meltdown, particularly mortgage securitization and subprime mortgage loans, and were regulatory in nature. One, for example, limited executive compensation at firms rescued with the public's money. To stave off the collapse of the American auto industry, the Obama administration arranged for the sale of Chrysler to Fiat, took a big ownership stake in General Motors, and created a "cash for clunkers" program to encourage people to buy new cars.

Obama and the Democratic-led Congress also passed a far-reaching reform of the financial industry in hopes of preventing another financial crisis in the future of the magnitude of that in 2008.

The reform of the American financial system passed Congress despite the Democrat's loss of their 60-vote filibuster-proof majority after Republican Scott Brown won a special election in January 2010 in Massachusetts to fill the seat of recently deceased liberal stalwart Ted Kennedy. Influenced perhaps by rising public anger over bailouts, seemingly excessive executive bonuses at financial firms such as Goldman Sachs, and continuing joblessness and economic distress, just enough Republican senators joined the majority to allow reform legislation to pass.

President Obama and the Democrats also used the crisis—"never let a good crisis go to waste," in the words of Rahm Emmanuel, the president's first chief of staff—and their big majorities in the House and Senate to address problems that had been on the liberal agenda for decades, namely health care reform and shifting energy (if ever-so-slightly) away from fossil fuels to cleaner energy sources. Most of this was accomplished through the legislative process despite strong Republican opposition—we will address health care reform in Chapter 18—but some was done unilaterally by the president, for example, when he issued executive orders increasing fuel efficiency requirements for cars and trucks. President Obama also proposed stiff regulation of off-shore drilling and a decreased dependence on fossil fuels after the BP disaster in the Gulf of Mexico, but Congress was unable to pass a bill before it adjourned for the November 2010 elections.

Despite these accomplishments, or perhaps because of them, Barack Obama's job approval rating plummeted throughout 2009 and 2010. The rise of the Tea Party movement, though it mostly threatened and affected Republican incumbents seeking renomination for the 2010 elections, was the tip of an apparent iceberg of public discontent. Many Americans worried about continued stagnation in the job market, others were angry at the attention and resources lavished on Wall Street, more than a few were disquieted by the rising federal budget deficits caused by addressing the economic crisis and chronic needs, and many were simply concerned that government was getting too big and intrusive. (In February 2010, 56 percent of Americans agreed with the statement that "the federal government has become so large and powerful that it poses an immediate threat to the rights and freedoms of ordinary citizens."[5])

It is no wonder that a substantial number of Americans were disquieted by all of this. After all, between the late summer and early fall of 2008 and the November 2010 national elections (see Chapter 10 for more on the elections), the size, range of responsibilities, and cost of the national government grew dramatically—and in the process, changed the role of government in American life in ways that were perhaps as significant as occurred during Lyndon Johnson's Great Society in the 1960s and the Reagan Revolution of the

1980s. The present expansion of the government's role, it should be noted, has occurred when Republican presidents were in charge as well as when Democratic were. This is what tends to happen in the wake of economic crises in the United States, despite the protestations of media conservatives like Glenn Beck and Tea Party activists.

THINKING CRITICALLY About This Chapter

This chapter explains the government's role in setting economic policies and managing the country's economy.

Using the FRAMEWORK

You will see in this chapter how the framework can be used to explain why government does what it does in the area of economic policy. You will use what you learned in previous chapters about structural, political linkage, and government factors to better understand what government does in terms of spending, taxing, regulating, and subsidizing.

Using the DEMOCRACY STANDARD

In previous chapters, you used the democracy standard to examine the extent to which American political and government institutions enhanced popular sovereignty, political equality, and liberty. You will use the democracy standard in this chapter to ask whether the American people get the sorts of economic policies they want from government.

Public Policy

17.1 Identify three types of public policies and assess how policies are formed

Public policies are decisions made by government that create laws, programs, and regulations that are binding on all people living within a defined jurisdiction—whether a county, a state, or the nation as a whole. Public policies usually address problems or concerns raised by individuals, groups, or firms. One problem might be, for example, that many people lack access to health insurance. One response to this problem was the creation of the Medicare program in 1965 to provide medical insurance for those over the age of 65; another was the establishment in 1997 of the Children's Health Insurance Program (CHIP), which provides funds to help pay for medical care for millions of poor children in the United States.

There are many ways to classify public policies. One way is to classify them according to the functions they serve, much as they are classified in government budget documents: national defense, social insurance, social welfare, transportation, and the like. Another commonly used classification scheme is that of political scientist Theodore Lowi, who proposed three basic types of domestic policies.[6] **Distributive policies** are those that target benefits to very narrowly defined groups or individuals, say, a bridge for a member of Congress's constituency or a tax break for a particular firm or industry. **Redistributive policies** transfer resources from one group

public policy

What government does, usually in the form of new laws and regulations or in the interpretation and implementation of existing laws and regulations.

distributive policies

Government policies targeted at narrowly defined groups or individuals.

redistributive policies

Government policies that transfer resources from one group or class to another.

or class to another. The Food Stamp program, which uses general tax revenues to help poor people eat better, is an example. **Regulatory policies** are targeted at a group or class of groups—say, drug companies or auto companies—that add to their costs of operations in the interests of serving some public purpose. Rules to make drugs safer or to increase gas mileage for cars fall into this category.

In this and the next chapter we will look at a wide range of economic and social policies. Each falls into one of these three categories. Foreign and national defense policies, which we examine in Chapter 19, fall into yet another category, often called **public goods,** which refers to programs that provide benefits for everyone. The federal government, for example, provides national defense for all, not particular groups or classes of people.

Why do we have particular public policies and not others? For example, why do we have the particular tax code that we do, and why did we bail out failing financial firms during our recent economic crisis rather than offering significant help to home-owners having trouble making mortgage payments? Marxists are prone to see public policies as the outcome of the power and wishes of a dominant capitalist class.[7] Elite theorists believe that public policies are made by the leaders of powerful institutions, including corporations, unions, think tanks, foundations and cultural organizations, and government, often related to one another through families, schooling, clubs, and other social networks. Other political scientists believe that a powerful and massive bureaucratic apparatus, with its own interests and standard operating procedures, is responsible for what government does.[8] Group theorists or pluralists—as we described in Chapter 7—believe that public policy is the product of the interaction of a vast multitude of interest and advocacy groups vying for power and influence, none of whom are dominant.[9] Still others think that ours, being a democratic system, produces government policies that match what the people want.[10]

We take the position in this book that no single overarching theory of what government does in the United States is persuasive. We have, instead, proposed an analytical framework, introduced in Chapter 1, for making sense of the question of why government does what it does. We have used this analytical framework throughout this book, including in each chapter a feature we have called "Using the Framework," to show why certain public policies happen and not others. We have also organized the sections of the book in a manner that reflects where actors, institutions, and developments fit into this analytical model. In a sense, the entire book up to this point, including Chapters 2 through 16, is an integrated road map for understanding the public policies that are produced by American government.

regulatory policies

Government policies that require a group or class of groups to change its behavior to serve some public purpose.

public goods

Government policies that provide benefits for everyone.

A CHIP IN TIME The Children's Health Insurance Program helps ensure that poor children not covered by Medicaid receive medical services. The program, reauthorized in 2009 and expanded as part of the Obama stimulus package, is funded by the states and the federal government. Here, a doctor treats a child in a local clinic. Why do we have these kinds of programs rather than relying on the private sector to provide medical services?

We have suggested that structural, political linkage, and government factors involved in creating public policies work in a holistic way and in a particular order (again see Figure 1.1). We have suggested throughout this book that action by public officials is, in the end, the product not simply of their personal desires (although these are important), but also of the influences and pressures brought to bear by other governmental institutions and by individuals, groups, and classes at work in the political linkage level of the model. Political linkage institutions and processes, in turn, can often be understood only when we see how they are shaped by the larger structural context, including such things as the national and global economies and the political culture.

There is much in the complex process by which public policies are made that is not democratic. We suggested in earlier chapters that the constitutional rules themselves, for example, are in many fundamental ways anti-majoritarian, especially the Electoral College, the process of amending the Constitution, and the way the Senate overrepresents people living in small population states. We pointed out, as well, that powerful interest groups representing business and advocacy groups representing those who are financially better-off play an important role in what presidents, executive branch agencies, Congress, and even the courts, do. We noted the very high degree of income and wealth distribution in the United States and how these inequalities play out in matters related to who plays a role in our politics and government and whose voices are heard in the political process. And, finally, we described how public opinion, which is supposed to play a decisive role in what government does in a democracy, is sometimes shaped by powerful interests and government leaders. These are important things to keep in mind as you read about public policies in this and the following two chapters.

> **?** Is there opportunity for democratic participation at every stage in the economic policymaking process? At which stage of the process do citizens have the most impact? The least impact?

Economic Policies

17.2 Analyze economic policymaking in terms of goals, players, and tools

It may seem odd at first glance that in a country long committed to the idea of limited government, the federal government plays such a large role in managing and steering the economy, regulating the activities of business firms, and subsidizing and encouraging a range of business activities. In this section we look at why government does these things and who makes the key decisions.

Why Government Is Involved in Economic Policymaking

No government today would dare leave problems such as stagnant economic growth, unemployment, the collapse of the financial sector, or inflation to work themselves out "naturally." Citizens and political leaders in all the rich democracies have learned from history that free enterprise, capitalist economies (described in Chapter 4), left to themselves, are subject to periodic bouts of trouble. One problem often faced is **inflation;** when prices rise, the value of money declines, and people can buy less with what they have. Another recurring problem is the speculative bubble that eventually bursts, bringing economic ruin to many, something Americans have seen up close with the dot-com and housing bubbles. Yet another problem is **recession,** defined by economists as a period of economic contraction

inflation
A condition of rising prices and reduced purchasing power.

recession
Two quarters or more of declining gross domestic product.

depression

A severe and persistent drop in economic activity.

(i.e., declining GDP) lasting at least two quarters (six months). There are occasional collapses into economic **depression** as well, a longer-lasting and deeper recession with high levels of unemployment, low or nonexistent business profits and investment, and low tax revenues for the government. (In talking about the economic troubles of 2007–2010, few commentators have used the term "depression"; the term "Great Recession" has usually been used, as we do in this book, tied to the term "jobless recovery" to cover the year 2010.) The worldwide trauma of the Great Depression in the 1930s, which was especially severe in the United States, was the event that etched the lesson that markets are not necessarily self-correcting into the minds of virtually everyone—until the lesson was largely forgotten in the market-oriented euphoria of the 1990s and 2000s[11]—and fundamentally changed the role of government in economic affairs. In light of these natural problems of the business cycle and the hardships they create for nearly everyone, voters, interest groups, business firms, and elected officials have come to accept, to one degree or another, that the government must be continuously and deeply involved in keeping the economy on the right path. Recent public demands that political leaders do something about the housing, jobs, and credit crises, as well as the steep downturn in the stock market, are the most recent examples of this fact. Disputes exist, of course, concerning precisely which policies government ought to pursue.

Government responsibility for the state of the national economy is now so widely accepted in practical politics, in fact, that national elections are often decided by the voters' judgment of how well the party in power is carrying out this responsibility. When times are good, the party or president in power is very likely to be reelected; when times are bad, those in power have an uphill battle staying in office. Concerns about lingering unemployment, stagnant incomes, and slow job growth had a great deal to do with the decline in the public's support for President Obama and his programs in late 2009 and 2010.

ELECTED IN TOUGH TIMES
Tough economic times have political consequences. Both Bill Clinton and Barack Obama were elected, in part, because the parties they were running against in their first presidential election campaigns were in power when the nation's economy turned sour. President Obama's Democrats suffered big election losses in the 2010 congressional elections because of the jobless and slow recovery from the Great Recession. Are voters acting rationally when they focus on the state of the economy, or should other factors play an equally important role?

The Goals of Economic Policy

Although economic policy goals sometimes conflict and involve important trade-offs,[12] they are consistently driven by six key concerns, which we will explore next.

Encourage Economic Growth The quintessential goal of economic policy-makers is sustained economic growth—defined here as an annual increase in the **gross domestic product (GDP).**[13] (GDP is a measure of the total value of goods and services produced in a nation on an annual basis.) A growing economy means more jobs, more products, and higher incomes, so most Americans support this goal. Economic growth is also the basis for increased profits, so business tends to support it as well. For political leaders, economic growth, accompanied by rising standards of living, brings public popularity and heightened prospects for reelection, as well as more revenues for government programs. (How to assess whether the economy is growing or not is examined in the "By the Numbers" feature.)

Control Inflation In addition to economic growth, most people want to avoid inflation, a condition in which the purchasing power of money declines. With serious inflation, people's wages, salaries, savings accounts, and retirement pensions diminish in value. So, too, do the holdings of banks and the value of their loans. To nobody's surprise, political leaders seek policies that dampen inflation and provide stable prices, usually by central bank management of interest rates.

Government leaders face a classic trade-off problem, however, in trying to have both economic growth and low rates of inflation. The problem is that addressing one goal often gets in the way of achieving the other goal. For example, one way to combat inflation is to slow down the economy by having the Fed raise interest rates. This slows down the economy because higher interest rates make it harder and more expensive for consumers to borrow for the purchase of a car or a house and for businesses to raise money to fund expansion. Conversely, when the economy is stagnant or declining, one strategy is to pump more money into the hands of consumers and businesses by either lowering interest rates or increasing government spending (or both, as the government did in 2008 and 2009, as described in the chapter-opening story). A little too much stimulus, however, can generate inflation as too many dollars chase too few goods and services.

gross domestic product (GDP)
Monetary value of all goods and services produced in a nation each year.

CHINA RISING One of the most important developments in the global economy is the emergence of China as a major player in the global economy—something that is reflected in this scene of Shanghai's rapidly rising skyline. China is the destination for many U.S. exports, while the United States is the destination for many Chinese exports. Unfortunately, the trade is heavily unbalanced in favor of China. Addressing this trade imbalance is a continuing concern of American policymakers, though little progress has been made to date. To what extent are policymakers correct in worrying about trade imbalances?

How well is the American economy performing?

Is the economy getting better or worse, and by how much? These seem like easy questions to answer, but consider the two examples graphed here from official U.S. government reports for the fourth quarter of 2009, when an important topic of debate in this country was whether the economy finally was turning around after two years of terrible economic times.

Why It Matters Government reports on the state of the American economy are very important. Such reports affect the mood of the public and their sense of confidence in the direction the country is moving and how much they support and trust elected leaders. These reports also influence investors' confidence in the American economy and their willingness to invest, thus shaping the future direction of the economy. They also are important pieces of information for government leaders—including the Federal Reserve Board, Congress, and the president—as they fashion policies to keep the economy on course. Finally, the reports trigger automatic changes in a wide range of government benefits and financial instruments, including Social Security checks

and inflation-adjusted bonds. So it is important to get the numbers right and correctly interpret the numbers the government reports.

The Story Behind the Numbers Let's look at the jobs numbers first. The Bureau of Labor Statistics (BLS)—which reported a drop in nonfarm payrolls of 36,000 in February 2010—bases its payroll numbers on reports by businesses and governments that are compared with unemployment insurance records in the states, which are fairly comprehensive and current. Total employment—which decreased by 26,000 according to the BLS—is based on a sampling of households that is compared with household employment figures from the census taken every 10 years. Most economists suggest nonfarm payroll is the better of the two measures of short-term job gains and losses because of the total employment number's dependence on census numbers as the base for calculations in a society whose household numbers are changing year to year.

The second type of number—quarterly economic growth—is reported in three ways because the data to make firmer

calculations come only in bits and pieces. Thus, the Bureau of Economic Analysis in the Commerce Department reports an advance number, a preliminary number, and a final number. The advance and preliminary numbers are particularly troublesome because they depend a great deal on incomplete information—businesses don't always get their quarterly government reports done on time, and reports in some areas of the economy (most notably the service sector) are not made on a quarterly basis. Thus, government statistical agencies have to do a substantial amount of statistical guesswork, inferring some numbers from more solid ones. As an example, the total amount of money paid in commissions for financial transactions—a component in the calculation of overall economic activity—is inferred from the total volume of stock market activity.

What to Watch For It is important to understand how important government statistics are collected and reported. This may seem like a pretty hard thing to do, but each statistical reporting agency in the federal government

---

balance of payments

The annual difference between payments and receipts between a country and its trading partners.

Avoid Balance of Payments Problems All nations, including the United States, strive to keep their **balance of payments** in positive territory, that is, to export more goods and services—things such as insurance, banking, accounting, and advertising, for example—than they import. They do so because sustained negative trade balances lead to a decline in the value of a nation's currency in international markets, as more money leaves the country than is brought in as people and firms buy more abroad than they sell. In this situation, businesses and consumers find that their dollars buy less, and they must either do without or borrow to make up the difference. The United States has run substantial balance-of-payments deficits for most of the past two decades. This narrowed in 2008 and 2009 as Americans bought fewer things manufactured abroad during the recession, but widened again in 2010 as consumer and business spending rose.

Maintain Budgetary Discipline All nations try—or at least claim they try—to keep their government budgets in rough balance between revenues (taxes and fees)

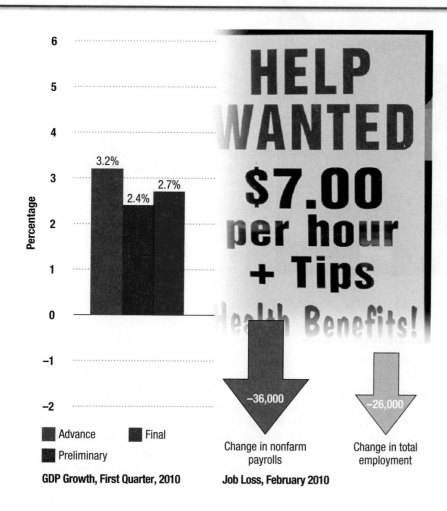

GDP Growth, First Quarter, 2010

Percentage

- ■ Advance
- ■ Preliminary
- ■ Final

Job Loss, February 2010

−36,000 Change in nonfarm payrolls

−26,000 Change in total employment

includes this information in its reports, although you may sometimes have to dig for it. The average person, of course, doesn't necessarily have the time or inclination to perform such investigations. It is probably reasonable to pay attention to professional economists and financial analysts as they discuss the meanings of competing numbers, especially to the ones who have been the most consistently on the mark over the years. It is also worth remembering that many government statistical agencies report preliminary and final numbers, and that the final numbers—taking advantage of the fact that they are based on more complete information—are worth waiting for.

What Do You Think? In your view, can we depend on government statistical reports to accurately reflect what they purport to measure? Why might it be OK to depend on statistics that are based on incomplete information and that depend on a great deal of statistical inference? Whose statistical reports might we depend on to be more accurate? Industry trade groups? Economic consulting firms? Do we have any other choice but to depend on government trend data, perhaps insisting that they gather the best information available and on a timely basis?

and expenditures on things like national defense and pensions for retirees. Most of the time since the end of World War II, budgets in the rich democracies have tilted slightly toward the deficit side of things, with spending outpacing revenues by a few percentage points. A small deficit helps spur economic growth if it is spent on things that improve long-range economic prospects: infrastructure, like roads and harbors, and human capital, like education, training, and research and development (R&D). A big deficit is trouble, however, because it can only be funded by borrowing from people here and abroad and from foreign governments through their purchase of U.S. government bonds and Treasury notes. (Deficits grew dramatically in 2009 and 2010 in the United States and in the European Union when spending increased for stimulus purposes and tax revenues plummeted because of the recession.) As more and more debt is purchased, it begins to pile up; at the beginning of 2010, the Chinese government held almost $800 billion in U.S. bonds and notes, while the Japanese held another $750 billion. And, if the value of the dollar declines, as it did between 2002 and 2009, the value of the dollar stockpiles held by foreign governments and investors erodes, raising questions about how much longer they might be willing to fund America's deficits.[14]

SURROUNDED BY OIL   The devastation wrought by BP's deep well disaster in the Gulf of Mexico is a classic case of a negative externality, a problem that is created by the market and private firms that is left to others to clean up. Governments in the rich democracies, under pressure from their citizens, have generally taken on the task of regulating dangerous activities of private firms and helping their citizens cope with the results when regulation is not enough and harmful things happen. Whether the federal, state, and local governments did a good job of regulating the oil industry in the Gulf or responding adequately to the spill remain open questions.

externalities

The positive and negative effects of economic activities on third parties.

Avoid Externalities   Most people also want to avoid negative **externalities,** the bad side-effects that often accompany normal economic activity. A growing manufacturing economy, for example, often produces things such as air and water pollution, toxic wastes, and workplace injuries and health hazards. High demand for oil and the decline of easily drilled areas on and near-shore have driven companies such as British Petroleum to drill in very deep waters, increasing the risk of blowouts and environmental catastrophes. In response to these negative externalities, the public over the years has pressed the government to take compensatory action.

Provide Firm Economic Foundations   Finally, there is a range of economic activities that is essential for the health of the national economy but that is unlikely to be provided by private firms. For example, the United States and all European countries subsidize farmers, who are vital to the nation's food supply. Also, the federal government encourages business activity in America's inner cities by using enterprise zone tax incentives; supports the defense industry by directly purchasing weapons systems and subsidizing research; and pays for essential infrastructure such as airports, harbors, and highways. Economic growth requires good roads, airports, and harbors, something the private sector normally does not provide on its own. Governments in the rich democracies have stepped into the breach and provided support for such vital activities and services, either by direct subsidy and tax incentives or by public ownership. A central element of the financial sector rescue plan of the Treasury Department started in late 2008, as described in the chapter-opening story, for example, involved the government taking a temporary ownership share in big banks.

? If the goals of economic policy are sometimes in conflict, which ones should take precedence? Are some more important than others?

The Main Players and Influences on Economic Policy

Many influences shape American economic policies. Here are the major ones, organized according to our analytical model of how American government and politics work.

Structural Factors   The state of the economy—whether it is growing or not, whether there is price inflation or not, and the like—is what influences individuals, groups, firms, and political leaders to seek government action on the economic front. The state of the economy is itself the product of developments in the United States and around the world. These include the pace of innovation in the economy, the relative balance of imports and exports, the strength of the dollar in the world markets, stock and bond market valuations, the price and availability of essential commodities like oil, and global economic growth or decline. Each of these things affects the fortunes of Americans and U.S.-based firms. In all of this, it is apparent that the increasing pace of globalization and our involvement in it (described in Chapter 4) are profoundly affecting the American economy. The reverse is also true; the global recession of 2007–2009 was closely tied to the real estate collapse in the United States and the nearly worthless mortgage-backed securities and other derivatives tied to the housing sector that were bought and held by foreign governments, investors, and companies.

Political Linkage Factors   Interest groups—particularly those representing business, but also labor, consumer, and environmental groups—take a keen interest in economic policy, and their permanent representatives in Washington are a constant presence in the halls of Congress and at regulatory agencies. Large firms, such as General Electric and Google, are also on the ground in Washington. Financial firms and their lobbyists helped prevent serious changes in the regulation of derivatives and securitization after the Great Recession. Voters and public opinion are important. The public is attuned to overall economic conditions and pays attention to what its elected leaders are doing to curb inflation, avoid high levels of unemployment, and stimulate growth. The public becomes especially vocal and politically visible during economic crises like the recent one. Chapter 10 showed that the general state of the economy is one of the most important factors in the outcome of national elections. Knowing this, elected leaders do what they can to protect the health of the economy. Political parties also play a role in economic policymaking. Because each has its own electoral and financial constituencies made up of groups with identifiable economic interests, the two parties tend to support different economic policies, as we saw in Chapter 9. For example, Democrats in Congress were eager in the wake of the economic collapse to regulate the practices of the financial industry that contributed to the nation and world's economic problems. Republicans were less eager to do so and slowed down but ultimately failed to block passage of financial industry regulatory reform in 2010.

Governmental Factors   The president, Congress, and the **Federal Reserve Board** (or **Fed**) are particularly important in fashioning economic policies.

The President   When things go wrong in the economy, it is the president to whom we usually turn for action. The role is recognized formally in the Employment Act of 1946, which requires that the president report on the state of the economy and recommend action to ensure maximum employment and economic stability. At the center of every modern president's legislative program are proposals for spending, taxing, and regulation that usually have broad macroeconomic effects, meaning effects on the performance of the economy as a whole. President George W. Bush, for example, favored deregulation, tax cuts, and decreases in the size of the

Federal Reserve Board (Fed)
The body responsible for deciding the monetary policies of the United States.

federal budget in virtually all areas not associated with national defense and homeland security. What he delivered, in the end, however, were unprecedented budget deficits, a massively subsidized and regulated financial industry, and vast new powers for the Secretary of the Treasury to bail out failing companies. President Obama continued many of the Bush administration's emergency policies, but also convinced Congress to pass a series of bills to stimulate the economy, reform the health care system, impose regulations on the financial industry, and encourage the production of clean energy. He also set up a commission to offer proposals after the 2010 elections to settle the long-term budget deficit.

The secretary of the Treasury, a presidential appointee, has become an increasingly visible and important figure in economic affairs. Robert Rubin served in the post during much of the Clinton administration and helped convince the president, Congress, and the public that the financial industry ought to be deregulated. Henry Paulson, George W. Bush's Treasury secretary, and Timothy Geithner, Barack Obama's, played very visible roles in trying to clean up the mess left in the wake of 2008's financial collapse, in some degree an outcome of deregulation.

Congress Nearly everything that Congress does has macroeconomic consequences, especially when it makes decisions about the annual federal budget. The decisions it makes about the overall balance of government spending and taxes is a powerful fiscal policy instrument—which we examine in the next section—either quickening or slowing down overall economic activity. Taxes levied by Congress shape the incentives for individuals and company economic decision making. Laws that regulate, grant subsidies, or supply loan guarantees influence private-sector economic behavior, and trade bills and treaties affect the fortunes of American consumers and companies.

Federal Reserve Board Traditionally, the Federal Reserve Board (commonly known as the Fed) has been responsible for monetary policy (to be discussed later). It is made up of seven members (called governors), who serve overlapping 14-year terms, and a chair, who serves a renewable 4-year term. Each is appointed by the president. Alan Greenspan was chair of the Federal Reserve from 1987 to 2006—spanning the presidencies of Ronald Reagan, George H. W. Bush, Bill Clinton, and George W. Bush—and was once credited with helping to encourage the economic good times of the 1990s and the 2003–2006 periods. His policies of loose oversight of the financial industry and low interest rates generally are understood to have been important factors in the dot-com and financial sector collapses. Benjamin Bernanke succeeded Greenspan and continued his policies until the American financial system reached the brink of disaster in late summer 2008. One of the leading scholars of the causes of the Great Depression, Bernanke reversed course and acted boldly to prevent a crash, moving the Fed into new areas: buying troubled assets of banks, subsidizing the merger of commercial and investment banks, imposing new rules to enhance transparency in the hitherto unregulated derivatives market, and more. Traditionally, the Fed has been closely connected with, and very solicitous of, the needs of commercial and investment bankers and generally prefers to control inflation as a first order of business to protect the value of financial assets. But, the Fed also worries about instability and volatility on Wall Street and contractions in the credit markets, and it can act aggressively

? Is it reasonable and fair that the Fed is so closely attuned to the financial community? Does this show bias, or is it in the general interest of American society and economy that the Fed focuses on financial stability?

WORRIED ABOUT THE ECONOMY
Federal Reserve Chairman Benjamin Bernanke, here meeting in his office with Treasury secretary Tim Geithner in 2010, acted quite aggressively to prop up a financial system poised on the brink of collapse in September 2008. Some of his actions, such as arranging for mergers between institutions and adding capital to floundering banks, were quite controversial. Should an unelected public official have such power in a democracy? Why do we have a federal reserve system in the first place?

to stimulate the economy, as we have seen. The Fed is relatively independent; aggressive actions by Congress or the president to pressure the Fed would surely trigger adverse reactions on Wall Street and in the financial community at home and abroad—reactions that neither the president nor Congress is eager to confront.

The Government's Macroeconomic Policy Tools

Government actions affect (but do not solely determine) the rate of inflation, the level of unemployment, and the growth of income and output in the national economy. This always has been so. What is new since the end of World War II is that government leaders, economists, business leaders, and citizens know this to be true and insist that government use whatever means it has available to ensure good economic outcomes.

Government efforts to encourage economic growth, low unemployment, and stable prices, and to rescue the economy after a disastrous collapse like our recent one, fall under the heading of **macroeconomic policy,** or policy that affects the performance of the economy as a whole. The main tools of macroeconomic policy are fiscal policy and monetary policy.

Fiscal Policy **Fiscal policy,** all government actions having to do with spending and taxes, is in theory a flexible tool for stimulating the economy when it is underperforming and for slowing down the economy when it is getting too hot—that is, growing so fast that it triggers inflation. The president and Congress can increase government spending or decrease taxes when economic stimulation is required, thus getting more money into circulation; they can cut spending or increase taxes when the economy needs a cooling-off period.

Fiscal tools are not easy to use. Decisions about how much government should spend or what level and kinds of taxes ought to be levied

macroeconomic policy

Policy that has to do with the performance of the economy as a whole.

fiscal policy

Government efforts to affect overall output and incomes in the economy through spending and taxing policies.

are not made simply on the basis of their potential effects on economic stability and growth. The elderly want Social Security and Medicare benefits to keep pace with inflation, for example, regardless of their effect on the overall economy. Similarly, auto companies want subsidies when faced with collapse, no matter the more general consequences. Timing also is a problem. When the country needs massive deficit spending to stimulate an economy in deep recession, as was the case in 2008 and 2009, it is easy enough to do, but knowing when to put on the brakes is difficult. Too soon, and economic recovery can stall; too late, and public debt mounts rapidly.

Monetary Policy **Monetary policy** refers to Fed policies that affect how much money is available to businesses and individuals from banks and how much it costs. The more money that is available and the lower the interest rates at which money can be borrowed, the higher overall consumer and business spending are likely to be. For example, if the Fed wants to increase total spending in the economy, it increases the money supply by buying government securities from the private sector. When it does this, paying from its reserve funds, it puts more money into circulation. It can also lower the discount rate, which lowers the cost member banks pay to borrow money from the Fed—which it can then lend at lower rates to consumers and firms.

During the 2008 financial collapse, the Fed moved into new territory in a big way, as shown earlier. Among other things, it organized the sale of the Bear Stearns and Merrill Lynch investment banks, lent unprecedented amounts of money to banks and other businesses, arranged insurance guarantees for money market funds and for interbank loans, and pitched in with the Treasury Department in the bailout of insurance giant AIG. The goal was to increase both confidence and money in the economy so that banks would begin lending again.

The Fed's influence on interest rates and the availability of credit is not unlimited. Interest rates, for example, are also affected by such things as the value of the dollar and the willingness of foreign investors to put their money into American firms, properties, and government bonds. Also, the Fed has very little impact on many factors that affect long-term economic performance, such as productivity growth or commodities prices.[15]

monetary policy
Government efforts to affect the supply of money and the level of interest rates in the economy.

Debates About the Best Use of the Government's Economic Tools People may agree that government has a role to play in the management of the economy, but they disagree about how

STIMULATING SOLAR POWER
President Obama's massive stimulus package, passed in early 2009, included generous tax credits for people who chose to improve the insulation of their homes, buy energy-saving appliances, and install alternative energy devices such as solar power. Here, a construction worker installs solar panels on a roof of a home in San Ramon, California. Are tax credits the best way to encourage energy savings? If not, what other strategies might work better?

it should be done. **Keynesians**—who trace their roots to English economist John Maynard Keynes's classic work, *The General Theory of Employment, Interest, and Money*—have one view. They believe that in an economy where the tools of production (labor, tools, factories, and the like) are not being used to full capacity, which they believe is the case most of the time, government must stimulate economic activity by increasing government spending or by cutting taxes (or both). Most Keynesians would prefer to see increased spending rather than lower taxes, and they are associated with an activist conception of the role of government most favored by liberal Democrats. Keynesians went out of fashion with the election of Ronald Reagan in 1980 and the ascendancy of the Chicago School of free market economics associated with Milton Friedman. In the midst of the Great Recession, the governments of virtually every capitalist country, ranging from those in the European Union to China and Japan, massively stimulated their economies, running big short-term deficits. Keynes once again became fashionable among policy experts and economists.[16]

Monetarists, such as Nobel Prize-winning economist Milton Friedman, believe that government (e.g., the Federal Reserve in the United States or the European Central Bank in the case of the European Union) should confine its activity to managing the growth in the supply of money and credit so that it closely tracks the growth in productivity in the economy as a whole. In the monetarist view, this will stimulate private investment, which in turn will allow slow but steady economic growth without inflation. Balanced federal budgets are essential in the monetarist position because unbalanced budgets, in their view, make it difficult for central banks to control the money supply properly. Monetarism is the economic policy, then, of those who believe in a minimal federal government and the virtues of the free market most associated with conservatives and Republicans.

Monetarists are closely associated with "efficient markets" economists who believe that markets tend toward efficiency and the rational allocation of resources if left alone, reducing the need for regulation by government.[17] These economists have dominated their discipline for several decades now and have influenced public policies on regulation, including the financial and oil industries.

> **Keynesians**
> Advocates of government programs to stimulate economic activity through tax cuts and government spending.
>
> **monetarists**
> Advocates of a minimal government role in the economy, limited to managing the growth of the money supply.

Taxing, Spending, and the Federal Budget

17.3 Identify the components of the federal budget and analyze the problem of the national debt

Decisions by the president and Congress on spending and taxes constitute America's fiscal policy. These matters are settled in the budget and in separate tax and spending bills.

The federal budget has a number of interesting characteristics.[18] First, it is an executive budget, meaning that it is prepared by the president and his staff (and the **Office of Management and Budget,** or the **OMB**); considered, amended, and passed by Congress; then put into effect by the president and the executive branch. Before 1921, the budget was prepared in Congress. Second, the budget is an annual one—that is, a new one is prepared and legislated each year—although many budget experts would prefer to see biennial budgets, as is the practice in many states. Third, the budget takes the form of line items,

> **Office of Management and Budget (OMB)**
> Part of the Executive Office of the President charged with helping the president prepare the annual budget request to Congress; also performs oversight of rule-making by executive branch agencies.

with funds allocated for specific activities of federal programs such as salaries, supplies, travel, and the like, rather than a lump sum given to an agency or department that might be used more flexibly.

Fashioning the Federal Budget

From start to finish, preparation of the annual budget takes longer than a year.[19] It is a complex and often harrowing process. (See Table 17.1 for a timeline of the budget process.)

The President and the OMB   In the spring, the president and his staff prepare a broad budget outline that is sent to all federal departments and agencies through the Office of Management and Budget, proposing total government spending, the revenues that will be available to fund this spending, and the spending limits that will apply to each department and agency. A process of negotiation then begins among executive branch departments and agencies, the OMB, and presidential staffers about these proposals. Because economic conditions and the business climate will affect how the budget works out in practice—for example, the level of government receipts that flow into government coffers from taxes will depend on how fast the economy is growing or contracting—the Council on Economic Advisors and the Treasury Department are active participants in the discussions surrounding these guidelines and the more formal budget that later gets put together.

The Executive Branch   Like most organizations, executive branch agencies try to gain more money and personnel to fulfill their missions, although they generally try not to be too unreasonable, given the competing demands of other agencies and the concern of the president to stay under the planned budget ceiling for the federal government. These requests are filtered through the OMB, whose job it is to examine department and agency requests (usually holding hearings in October and November as part of this process), negotiate changes, and package the requests into a final budget proposal that fits the priorities of the president. The director of the OMB then reviews the budgets for each department and agency and passes them on to the White House for its consideration. After some adjustments are made to accommodate new needs, changing economic forecasts, pleas from some departments and agencies, and the political agenda of the president, a final budget is prepared in the White House for presentation to Congress within 15 days from when it first convenes in January.

Congress   After receiving the budget request from the president, both the House and the Senate pass concurrent resolutions specifying the broad boundaries of the budget—how much total spending will be allowed—and what the deficit or surplus is likely to be. In drawing up these resolutions, technical advice is provided by the Congressional Budget Office, a counterpart to the OMB in the executive branch. Decisions about the budget for particular departments and agencies are then parceled out to the House and Senate **appropriations committees,** with subcommittees generally focusing on individual departments, such as the Department of Defense or the Commerce Department. Subcommittees hold hearings, taking testimony from department and agency officials as well as friends and (sometimes) critics of the programs in question, then mark up an appropriations bill for the appropriations committee for each chamber. The 13 or 14 appropriations bills that make their way to the floor of each house must be acted upon by September 15. Appropriations cannot be made, however, until standing committees pass funding

appropriations committees
The committees in the House and Senate that set specific spending levels in the budget for federal programs and agencies.

TABLE 17.1 Timeline: Fashioning the Federal Budget	
February–March	After consulting with staff, the OMB, and key congressional and executive branch officials, the president formulates general budget and fiscal guidelines.
Late spring	OMB issues specific budget guidelines for federal departments and agencies.
August–October	Executive branch departments and agencies submit budget proposals to OMB; OMB reviews requests and asks departments and agencies, in most cases, to refashion and resubmit to keep in line with presidential guidelines.
October–December	Consulting with presidential staff, as well as with the Council on Economic Advisors and Treasury officials, OMB staff and leaders formulate department and agency budgets for presidential review.
Late December	With presidential feedback, OMB prepares data and final budget documents for submission to Congress.
First Monday in February	President submits budget request to Congress.
February 15	Deadline for Congressional Budget Office to make recommendations to House and Senate Budget Committees on the overall shape of the budget.
March	Standing committees send their budget estimates to Budget Committees in each chamber.
April 1	Deadline for House and Senate Budget Committees to issue budget resolution on overall spending ceilings, revenues, and fiscal outlook.
April 15	House and Senate complete action on concurrent resolutions on budget; resolutions used as guidelines for committee and subcommittee actions.
Mid-April–end of June	Standing committees in House and Senate consider authorizing legislation for programs where needed (appropriations cannot be made unless authorizing legislation has been adopted, sometimes annually, sometimes every few years).
	Beginning in House, appropriations committees and subcommittees consider 13 or 14 appropriations bills and mark up final bills for floor action; bills are passed on to Senate after receiving House approval.
June 30	Deadline for House appropriations bills.
July–September 15	Senate completes action on appropriations bills; House–Senate conference committees meet to iron out differences in bills; conference reports on appropriations bills voted on in House and Senate.
September 25	Deadline for second concurrent resolution on overall budget, specifying total spending in all bills, revenues, and fiscal consequences of appropriations.
July–September	President signs appropriations bills after they are passed by House and Senate.
October 1	Fiscal year begins; departments and agencies operate under auspices of new budget authorities and appropriations.

A STAFFER GRABS THE BUDGET The federal government's budget process begins when the president submits his budget request to Congress. With hundreds of tables and budget justifications, as well as a discussion of the president's priorities, the budget ends up being a massive document. Here, staffers hurry to get copies for members of Congress, congressional leaders, and the relevant committees. How well does the federal government adhere to its budget?

deficit hawks

People committed to reducing budget deficits.

authority bills; some programs must do this annually, others every few years. The House and Senate must also pass a second concurrent resolution addressing the issue of how total appropriations affect previously agreed-upon spending ceilings and fit revenue projections for the coming period. They must agree on these numbers by September 25. The executive branch begins operation on the basis of the new budget on October 1, the beginning of the new fiscal year.

Congress has not done very well in living up to its own guidelines for keeping spending and revenues in line. The 1986 Gramm, Rudman, and Hollings legislation called for across-the-board spending reductions if an agreed-upon target for deficit reduction was not met. Unfortunately for **deficit hawks**—those committed to reducing budget deficits—too many programs were exempt from the cuts and those that were not suffered deep cuts. The pain was so severe that the law's provisions were generally evaded. In 1990, the Budget Enforcement Act came into effect requiring that increases in discretionary programs (such as federal grants-in-aid or agricultural subsidies) be offset by cuts or offsets in entitlement spending (things like Medicare and Social Security). These provisions were largely ignored as well, and the act was not renewed when it lapsed in 2002.[20]

The congressional portion of budget making is never easy, even in the best of times, when revenues are plentiful, economic prospects are good, and Republicans and Democrats are willing to settle their differences through compromise. Absent these conditions, the processes by which 13 or 14 separate annual appropriations bills work their way through Congress and by which new tax legislation is considered can become a torturous, conflict-laden, blame-apportioning business, filled with anger and vituperation. In recent years, as partisanship has increased, the budget process has become particularly

? Does the bitterness and partisanship involved in fashioning the budget reflect the wishes of the people? Does it serve their interests?

slow, with appropriations bills not passed by the dates specified in the rules of each house, leading either to the shutdown of the government—as happened twice during the Clinton administration—or the use of continuing resolutions to allow various government agencies to function temporarily. Needless to say, these outcomes make it exceedingly difficult for agencies to plan and execute policy on a rational and consistent basis.

Federal Spending

The federal government spent almost $3.7 trillion in 2010, about 25 percent of GDP, a big jump from only a few years earlier.[21] Figure 17.1 shows the change over time in federal outlays as a percentage of GDP. Several things are immediately apparent.

First, the most dramatic increases in federal government spending are associated with involvement in major wars; note the big spikes in the graph for the years associated with World War I and World War II. Second, the relative spending level of the federal government increased steadily from the early 1930s to the early 1980s, then leveled off and declined after that. This decrease was caused, in large part, by a substantial decrease in the relative size of the national defense budget after the end of the Cold War. Third, the wars in Afghanistan and Iraq, and the Medicare prescription drug program, pushed up federal spending relative to GDP once more after 2003. Then, the combination of massive stimulus spending, contraction of GDP, and falling tax receipts during the Great Recession dramatically increased federal government spending as a percentage of the economy in 2009 and 2010.

The largest portion of the federal budget—52 percent in 2010—is for mandatory spending, over which Congress and the president exercise little real control; changes in spending can occur only if Congress and the president agree to change the underlying program legislation or budget authorization bills, which is very hard to do. Mandatory expenditures are automatic, unless the program legislation is changed or language is changed in the budget authority bills, for programs such as Social Security retirement benefits or Medicare spending, which distribute benefits by formula. Medicare benefits go automatically to Americans over age 65, for example. Medicaid is distributed to the states according to a formula based on the number of poor people in each state. Expenditures on these programs happen outside the

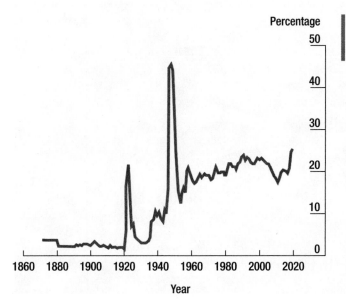

Percentage

FIGURE 17.1 Federal Government Spending as a Percentage of GDP, 1869–2010

This graph shows the scale of federal government spending relative to the size of the U.S. economy. We see that the increase in the relative size of the federal government is a twentieth-century phenomenon. We also see that involvement in major wars has been an important factor in the growth in federal spending, with the major spikes coming during World Wars I and II. The permanent change in the role of the federal government in American society is also seen in the steady rise in spending triggered by the Great Depression during the 1930s. Also noteworthy was the decline of relative federal spending through the 1980s and 1990s and the recent upsurge, a product of fighting two foreign wars, stimulus measures to grow the economy during the Great Recession, and a sharp decline in tax receipts tied to an economy in recession. *Source:* Office of Management and Budget, *Budget of the United States, Fiscal 2011*, Historical Table 2.1.

discretionary spending

That part of the federal budget that is not tied to a formula that automatically provides money to some program or purpose.

annual appropriations process and are triggered by changes in, for example, the number of elderly or poor people. Another 5 percent of the federal budget for 2010 was for payment of interest on the national debt; such payments are mandatory, as well. The upshot is that only 43 percent of the 2010 budget was discretionary, open to changes in funding through the annual appropriations process. And because the costs of mandatory programs are increasing rapidly—particularly Social Security and Medicare—elected leaders have less and less discretion over spending decisions.

Moreover, much of the **discretionary spending** budget—almost 61 percent, in fact—was taken up by national defense in 2010, which totaled $719 billion, representing about 19 percent of the total federal budget. Another $42 billion went to homeland security. Taking defense, homeland security, interest on the national debt, and mandatory programs together, only about 18 percent was left in the budget in 2010 for all other federal programs and activities. Only $666 billion of the total budget of $3.7 trillion was left for education, scientific and medical research, transportation, energy, agriculture, housing, national parks, the administration of justice, environmental protection, international affairs, the space program, public works projects, the arts and humanities, and everything else.

Another category of spending is off-budget supplemental appropriations, special one-time expenditures to cover emergencies. In 2008, for example, President Bush asked Congress for supplementary appropriations for the wars in Iraq and Afghanistan ($145 billion) and for the Hurricane Katrina disaster relief and recovery effort ($51.8 billion).[22] These appropriations are "off the books," as it were, meaning that the official deficits are more serious than officially reported.

Federal Taxes

Government can spend money, of course, only if it has a stream of revenues coming in. Such revenues are raised by various kinds of taxes.[23] Although the American system of taxation shares some features with those of other countries, it is unique in a number of ways.

MILITARY MIGHT ON DISPLAY Maintaining American military superiority is a very expensive proposition indeed, though expenditures for social programs such as Social Security, Medicare, and Medicaid now account for a larger share of the federal budget. How has the changing balance of national defense and social spending affected America's ability to both defend itself and project power?

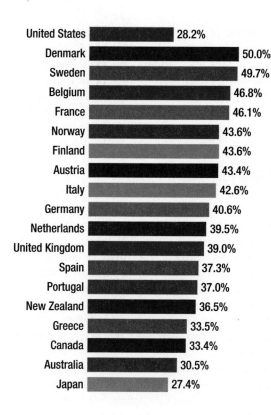

United States	28.2%
Denmark	50.0%
Sweden	49.7%
Belgium	46.8%
France	46.1%
Norway	43.6%
Finland	43.6%
Austria	43.4%
Italy	42.6%
Germany	40.6%
Netherlands	39.5%
United Kingdom	39.0%
Spain	37.3%
Portugal	37.0%
New Zealand	36.5%
Greece	33.5%
Canada	33.4%
Australia	30.5%
Japan	27.4%

FIGURE 17.2 Total Tax Burden as a Percentage of GDP in the United States and Other Rich Democracies, 2008

The total tax burden of the United States is lighter than that of most other rich democracies. *Source:* The Organization for Economic Cooperation and Development, 2010.

First, although Americans from all walks of life report feeling squeezed by taxes, the total of all taxes levied by all government jurisdictions in the United States as a proportion of GDP is relatively low when compared with the tax bite in the other rich democracies (see Figure 17.2). And, on average, what Americans pay in taxes as a percentage of their incomes has stayed about the same for the past 30 years.[24] Second, reflecting the fact that ours is a federal system, states and localities levy their own taxes. The national government depends primarily on individual income taxes (personal and corporate) and **payroll taxes** to fund its activities. Other rich democracies depend more on national sales and consumption taxes. In the United States, the states get most of their revenues from sales taxes, although many have income taxes as well. Local governments depend most heavily on property taxes.

Also, the American tax system is uniquely complex. The U.S. Tax Code is a voluminous document, filled with endless exceptions to the rules and special treatment for individuals, companies, and communities, usually the product of political influence of one kind or another. Few people besides accountants and tax attorneys fully understand the Code, and their services are available mainly to those who can afford them.

Perhaps most interesting of all, although the federal income tax looks to be quite **progressive**—a system in which tax rates increase as income and wealth increase—in actuality it is only mildly progressive; high-income individuals pay only a slightly higher percentage of their income than others, after all deductions, exclusions, credits, and tax shelters are taken into account. Other federal taxes, such as Social Security and Medicare payroll taxes, and excise taxes on alcohol and cigarettes, are **regressive**—that is, they take a higher proportion of income in taxes from those lower in the income scale. The result is an overall federal tax system that is relatively flat, meaning that most people in the

payroll tax
Tax levied on salaries and wages for Social Security and Medicare.

progressive taxation
A tax system in which higher-income individuals are taxed at a higher rate than those below them.

regressive taxation
A tax system in which lower-income individuals are taxed at a higher rate than those above them.

United States pay about the same percentage of their income in taxes, leaving the highly unequal income distribution of Americans relatively untouched.[25] The 2001 and 2003 tax cuts, which favored high-income earners and repealed the estate tax, made the effective tax rate on the wealthy lower than that for other groups for a number of years. The struggle between Republicans and Democrats on whether and how to extend these cuts went on in the post-2010 election session of Congress and on into 2011.

Annual Budget Deficits and the National Debt

In early 2001, federal officials and private economists issued confident predictions that the government's budget would be in the black by more than $230 billion in 2002 and that total cumulative surpluses through 2012 would be about $5.6 trillion. This changed dramatically in 2002. The Bush White House announced that the federal budget was going to be at least $106 billion in the red for 2002 and would remain in deficit for years. The **Congressional Budget Office (CBO)** estimated that the 10-year accumulated deficit would be $1.6 trillion. The change from an estimated surplus of $5.6 trillion to a deficit of $1.6 trillion represented the most dramatic reversal of the fiscal health of the nation in more than 50 years.

That proved to be an optimistic forecast, however. When President Bush submitted his last budget to Congress (fiscal year 2009), the CBO had increased its estimate for cumulative deficits for the years 2002–2012 to $2.75 trillion, all of which would be added to the national

Congressional Budget Office (CBO)

An agency of the U.S. Congress that provides technical support and research services on budget issues for its members and committees.

BUDGET SURPLUS OR DEFICIT? The federal budget, after years of deficits, produced surpluses in 1999, 2000, and 2001. Here President Bill Clinton and Vice President Al Gore celebrate this milestone. Deep deficit returned after 2001—the result of tax cuts, wars in Iraq and Afghanistan, the Medicare prescription drug program, and desperate economic times in 2001–2003 and in 2008–2010. When should Americans be concerned about the national debt?

debt. In his fiscal 2011 budget, President Obama reported deficits of $1.4 and $1.6 trillion in 2009 and 2010, respectively. These are stunning numbers, to say the least.

> ? Do you think the national debt is a serious enough problem that you and other Americans would be willing to cut popular programs and/or raise taxes? If not, what should we do about the national debt, if anything?

Why the turnaround in the deficit picture? One factor was economic trouble during the first Bush administration, which reduced federal government receipts: the 2001 recession, the 2002 stock market collapse (the market lost almost 20 percent of its value), and 2003's jobless recovery when job growth lagged GDP growth. During his second administration, the economy fell into recession in the last quarter of 2007 and stayed mired there in 2008, primarily because of the spreading sub-prime mortgage crisis, with stock markets taking a hit, credit becoming more expensive and less available, and incomes stagnating. Taken together, these developments put a serious dent in government receipts; with individuals and companies earning less and capital gains falling, fewer taxes were flowing into the federal treasury. On the expenditure side, a $700 million stimulus package was passed in early 2008 during the last year of the Bush administration, followed a year later by Obama's $787 billion stimulus bill.

Also adding to the long-term shift from surplus to deficit was the very expensive Medicare prescription drug benefit program that was legislated in 2003 and went into effect in 2006, something government budget officials had no way of predicting when they had painted their rosy budget portrait in 2001. The CBO estimated at the time of its passage that the new program would add $534 billion in accumulated deficits over the first 10 years of its existence.

Like any other person, organization, or institution that spends more than it makes—when it runs an annual **budget deficit**—the federal

budget deficit

The amount by which annual government expenditures exceed revenues.

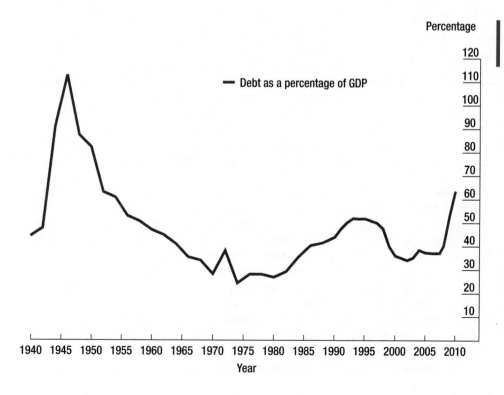

— Debt as a percentage of GDP

Percentage

120
110
100
90
80
70
60
50
40
30
20
10

1940 1945 1950 1955 1960 1965 1970 1975 1980 1985 1990 1995 2000 2005 2010

Year

FIGURE 17.3 The National Debt as a Percentage of GDP

After a long period of decline, the relative national debt—that is, the size of the debt compared with the total size of the American economy (GDP)—grew dramatically during the 1980s and early 1990s, but fell after 1993. The relative size of the debt is again increasing, quite dramatically from 2008 forward because of the increase in the size of annual deficits and the decline of GDP during the Great Recession. Even at its worst, however, the size of the relative national debt in recent decades was nowhere near the historic high point it reached during World War II. *Source:* Office of Management and Budget, *Budget of the United States, Fiscal 2011,* Historical Table 7.1.

The Flow of Stimulus Dollars

Introduction Within a month of taking his oath of office as president, in the middle of the most severe economic crisis since the Great Depression, Barack Obama signed the $787 billion American Recovery and Reinvestment Act of 2009. The stated purpose of the act was not only to get the economy growing again and get people back to work, but also to add to the long-term competitiveness of the American economy by encouraging green technologies; expanding broadband access; and increasing the energy efficiency of a wide range of products, including buildings. Of the total stimulus package, $228 billion was targeted at tax cuts for middle- and low-income families and small businesses. Another $224 billion was directed at education and health care, extending unemployment benefits, and helping the states pay for expanded Medicaid coverage; $275 billion was for federal contracts, grants, and loans

covering everything from infrastructure projects (roads, bridges, port facilities, and the like) to school construction, university-based research, and digitizing medical records.

We have learned that governments today have no choice but to respond to economic collapse. We know, as well, that the toolkit governments turn to contain the usual suspects for stimulating their economies: tax cuts, deficit spending, loans and loan guarantees (fiscal policies), and trying to lower the cost and increase the availability of credit (monetary policy). Where countries differ is in the way they mix these elements and whether their initiatives are aimed at the short run (e.g., immediate job creation) or the long run (e.g., encouraging new industries). In the United States and most of the other rich democracies, by the end of 2008, monetary policy eventually pushed the cost of money about as low as it could go, leaving no more

room for more interest rate cuts. So here and elsewhere, the focus turned to fiscal policy; hence the stimulus bill.

Mapping the Flow of Stimulus Dollars The cartogram shows how stimulus monies were allocated. In the cartogram, the normal geographical size of each state is expanded or diminished in terms of the proportion of stimulus dollars flowing to it on a per-capita basis. The map also uses colors to show the unemployment rate in the fall of 2009. Several things are immediately apparent. First, stimulus dollars did not go equally to the states. Had each state been awarded the same amount of money on a per-capita basis, the cartogram would look very much like a standard map of the United States. Instead we see that there are big winners—the Plains states and Mountain West, the southern states, and New England. The big losers were California, Texas, and New York. We

---

national debt

The total outstanding debt of the federal government; the sum total of all annual budget deficits and surpluses.

government must borrow from others to cover the shortfall and must pay interest to those from whom it borrows. The **national debt** is the total of what the government owes in the form of Treasury bonds, bills, and notes to American citizens and institutions (financial institutions, insurance companies, corporations, etc.), foreign individuals and institutions (including foreign governments and banks), and even to itself (i.e., to units such as the Social Security Trust Fund).

Are annual deficits necessarily bad? Is having a national debt a bad thing? It depends. Economists generally agree that running a budget deficit in a slow economy is a good thing because it helps stimulate economic activity. They also agree that a national debt that grows larger to meet emergencies—such as waging a war or fighting a recession—is unavoidable and that borrowing to make investments that will have positive long-term effects on society and the economy—such as building schools and roads, modernizing ports and airports, and funding research and development—is a good thing. However, borrowing to pay current operating costs is dangerous, something akin to living on one's credit card to buy groceries and pay the mortgage. Most economists believe that running annual deficits of this sort weakens the dollar and hurts purchasing power.

Before the 1980s, the national debt grew mainly because of deficit spending to wage war and declined afterward.[26] This pattern changed dramatically during the 1980s, however, when the size of annual federal budget deficits escalated—mainly because of a rapid build-up in the defense budget and big tax cuts (see Figure 17.3). The national debt as a percentage of GDP began to decline in the 1990s, however, as annual budget deficits turned into annual surpluses caused

also see that stimulus dollars were not distributed on the basis of how much unemployment there was in a state. Some high-unemployment states did well—note South Carolina and Rhode Island—but some did quite poorly, especially California.

There are a number of reasonable explanations for the patterns revealed in this cartogram. First, because each state has equal representation in the Senate, small-population states exercise disproportionate influence on what comes out of that body. This may explain why the Plains, Mountain West, and New England fared so well. Second, because it is the poorest area of the United States, southern states may have gained from expanded Medicaid spending and other elements in the stimulus bill aimed at helping the very poor. Most importantly, perhaps, the absence of a relationship between the unemployment rate and stimulus dollars received suggests that the stimulus bill was not targeted at short-term economic recovery alone but had other objectives in mind, including longer-term economic competitiveness.

What Do You Think? Are there other ways to measure the degree to which stimulus dollars were directed primarily to economic recovery and job creation? Are there better ways than the unemployment rate to assess economic distress in the states? The number of foreclosures, for example, or the rate of business and personal bankruptcies? How do you feel about the government playing such a large role in economic recovery and long-term economic development? Is it doing too much? Should we leave more to the market and private initiatives to deal with economic crises and planning for the future? Or has the recent emergency shown that market-only solutions are no longer credible?

Sources: The Bureau of the Census, 2010, for state populations; recovery.gov, for stimulus dollars awarded in 2009. (http://www.recovery.gov/Transparency/Recipient ReportedData/Pages/RecipientAward SummarybyState.aspx).

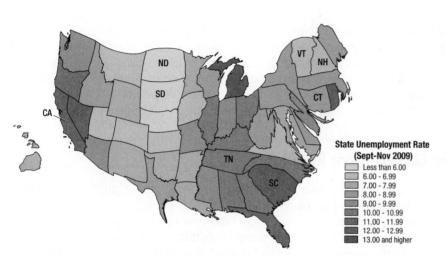

State Unemployment Rate
(Sept-Nov 2009)
- Less than 6.00
- 6.00 - 6.99
- 7.00 - 7.99
- 8.00 - 8.99
- 9.00 - 9.99
- 10.00 - 10.99
- 11.00 - 11.99
- 12.00 - 12.99
- 13.00 and higher

Standard US Map

Size of States Adjusted to Reflect Stimulus Dollars Awarded per Capita

by the tax windfalls from a booming economy. As suggested earlier, deficits returned with a vengeance in 2003 and jumped dramatically in 2008, 2009, and 2010. The budget will be in deficit territory for years to come, so the national debt will continue to grow, though perhaps more slowly as the economy recovers and grows.

One of the central obstacles to solving the long-term debt problem is the extreme partisanship that exists in Washington and across the country. Pushed by their base, including the Tea Party movement, Republicans now stand firmly against tax increases of any sort, even while refusing to cut spending on national defense or entitlements such as Social Security and Medicare. For their part, President Obama and the Democrats, while willing to raise taxes, also have pushed for increased government spending on a range of existing and new programs, including new entitlements, and strongly support stimulus spending during recessions to try to generate economic growth (see the "Mapping American Politics" feature). When President Obama asked Congress to create a bipartisan commission to make recommendations on how to tackle the debt problem, Republicans blocked the measure. Seven Republican senators who had originally co-sponsored the bill eventually voted against it. President Obama then issued an executive order in February 2010 creating a commission and appointed moderate Republican Alan Simpson and moderate Democrat Erskine Bowles to head it.[27]

It is not clear at this writing whether American political leaders of either political party will be willing and able to do what must be done to solve the long-term debt problem after the commission issues its report: raise taxes and cut expenditures and improve targeting of taxes and expenditures to encourage competitiveness and economic growth. Not only is partisanship a roadblock, but so is the mixed message coming from the American people: Americans are "in favor of Medicare, Social Security, good schools, wide highways, a strong military—and low taxes."[28]

Regulation

17.4 Explain the reasons for government regulation and predict the future of regulation

Regulation is one of the most visible and important activities of the federal government. For example, federal agencies issue rules that private businesses must follow. These rules may involve how a company treats its toxic wastes, what hiring procedures it practices, how much reporting it must do to inform its investors, what it must do with its toxic wastes, or how it reports its profits and losses. Much of what these agencies do was discussed at more length in Chapter 13.

Why Government Regulates

A free market economy, even when it is working optimally, produces a range of negative externalities—bad outcomes from normal market activities—that cannot be or are unlikely to be solved by private businesses on their own. These problems include, among others, air and water pollution, inadequate information for investors, unsafe products, unsafe and unwholesome workplaces, toxic wastes, and reckless financial practices. The American people have demonstrated on a number of occasions and consistently in public opinion surveys that they want government to do something about these problems. At various times, elected leaders have responded positively to these demands and increased regulation. As odd as it may seem, however, business leaders have also advocated government regulation to meet one problem or another. The *economic theory of regulation* holds that most regulation is caused by the political efforts of powerful businesses that turn to government for protection against competitors. This theory argues that regulation allows firms to restrict overall output, to deny entry to business competitors, and to maintain above-market prices.[29]

A History of American Regulation

A brief review of the history of regulation illustrates how the interaction of democratic and nondemocratic factors has produced today's regulatory agencies and policies.[30]

Between 1900 and World War I, laws were passed to regulate activities of powerful new corporations. These progressive era reforms were pushed by labor unions, the Populists, and middle-class Americans anxious about the conditions reported by muckraking journalists. Landmark regulatory measures included the Federal Trade Commission Act, the Meat Inspection Act, the Pure Food and Drug Act, and the Federal Reserve Act. These measures dealt with problems such as monopolies, unstable financial institutions, unwholesome products, and unsafe working conditions.

Some scholars believe, however, that large corporations were major players in the conception, formulation, and enactment of regulatory legislation.[31] Seen in this light, the Federal Reserve Act, which created the Federal Reserve System of banks and the Federal Reserve Board that is

regulation

The issuing of rules by government agencies with the aim of reducing the scale of negative externalities produced by private firms.

responsible for U.S. monetary policy, was primarily a government response to the entreaties of the American Bankers Association, which worried that financial panics would destroy its business.

Roosevelt's New Deal in the 1930s focused on speculative and unsafe practices in the banking and securities industries that had contributed to the onset of the Great Depression. The goal was to restore stability to financial markets and important industries. Legislation focused on such issues as federal bank inspection, federal deposit insurance, the prohibition of speculative investments by banks, and the creation of the Securities and Exchange Commission to regulate stock market operations. Again, the political sources of New Deal regulation were mixed. Some came from popular pressures,[32] but some also came from the business community, seeking stability in its various industries.[33]

The successes of the consumer, environmental, and civil rights movements from the late 1960s to the late 1970s resulted in a substantial increase in the federal government's regulation of business. The aim of these regulatory efforts was to protect against health and environmental hazards, to provide equal opportunity, and to allow more public access to regulatory rule-making. Under the authority of new laws, agencies such as the Environmental Protection Agency, the Equal Opportunity Employment Agency, and the Federal Drug Administration issued numerous rules that affected business operations and decisions. It was one of the only times in our history when business was almost entirely on the defensive, unable to halt the imposition of laws and regulations to which it was strongly opposed.[34]

By the end of the 1970s, the mood of opinion leaders had turned against regulation in the name of economic efficiency. Many blamed excessive regulation for forcing inefficient practices on American companies, contributing to sluggish economic growth, low productivity, and disappointing competitiveness in the global economy. And many found fault with the government for imposing uniform national standards, strict deadlines for compliance with regulations, and detailed instructions.[35] The deregulatory mood was spurred by a business political offensive that funded think tanks, foundations favorable to the business point of view, and electoral campaigns of sympathetic candidates.[36] From then until 2008, when the housing

FINANCIAL COLLAPSE
Investment banks disappeared during the financial collapse in September 2008. Here, former employees of Lehman Brothers carry away boxes of their belongings from their now-closed offices. How does the fall of investment banks affect the American economy?

and credit crises caused political and business leaders and the public to rethink the issue, the watchword was **deregulation,** the attempt to loosen the hand of government in a variety of economic sectors including banking and finance, transportation, and telecommunications.

The rollback in the regulation of the financial industry was a bipartisan affair. In 1999, Bill Clinton signed the Gramm-Leach-Bliley Act, which repealed the last remnants of the Glass-Steagall Act of 1933, which had long served as a stabilizing instrument for the industry. The bill Clinton signed allowed commercial banks, insurance companies, and investment banks to compete in the same markets and innovate new products (such as highly risky mortgage-backed securities and credit default swaps, among other things) relatively free from government oversight. During George W. Bush's administration, the SEC allowed Wall Street investment banks to regulate themselves and to dramatically lower the amount of money they had to keep on hand to back up the new securities they were inventing and marketing (called the "net capital rule"), with predictable results. In a speech in early 2010, Fed Chairman Ben Bernanke placed responsibility for the financial collapse in the United States on weak government regulation of the industry's underwriting and risk management practices, as well as on the lax ratings standards on the quality and safety of mortgage-backed securities and derivatives done by private agencies like Standard and Poor's, Moody's, and Fitch.[37]

The Future of Regulation

While the wave of deregulation of the past three decades eliminated especially egregious and inefficient regulations in transportation and telecommunications, the regulatory role of government is likely to grow once again as our much deregulated market economy generates more toxic negative externalities such as the collapse of the financial system in 2008, the BP deep well blowout in the Gulf of Mexico in 2010, and the explosion that killed 29 miners in the Upper Branch Mine in Montcoal, West Virginia, that same year. Given that the rollback of regulatory rules, budget starvation of regulatory agencies, and lax regulatory oversight by these agencies were implicated in each of these disasters, it is clear that expanded regulation by government is likely.

deregulation

The process of diminishing regulatory requirements for business.

VANISHING WETLANDS Development on former wetlands, such as this one in Kenner, Louisiana, became more common as local, state, and federal regulations limiting development were weakened or eliminated. Ever-more devastating damage from hurricanes in recent years in the Gulf of Mexico region, however—tied directly by scientists to the decline in the extent and health of wetlands—has led to a renewed demand for regulations restricting development in such sensitive areas. Is federal regulation the answer to such problems?

This is part of a more general pattern. Polling data have shown a consistent pattern on these issues: while supporting smaller and less expensive government in general, Americans want government to protect them against the bad practices of firms and other externalities. As economic activity and technological change generate new problems, and when firms take advantage of their market power, people demand that government intervene. Thus, when people become ill from tainted beef, the public demands higher standards of meat inspection and tracking. When companies such as Enron collapse, taking with them the retirement savings of their employees, or when accounting firms allow companies such as WorldCom to mislead investors, Americans demand that government protect them against similar behavior by other companies. When American companies import dangerous products from abroad—children's toys, for example—people demand closer scrutiny of manufacturing practices abroad and testing of imported products.

Growing concern about the environment is sure to increase regulation.[38] To be sure, some important advances have been made since the late 1960s on the environment because of federal regulatory efforts,

? In what sectors do you think regulation will become more common in the future?

most particularly in the areas of air and water pollution, endangered species protection, and toxic and solid waste disposal. But what is propelling the current concern and certain to force additional regulatory efforts now and in the coming years is the mounting evidence of global warming and potential shortfalls in nonrenewable energy resources, especially oil. At the end of 2007, a new law was passed mandating higher gas mileage standards for cars and encouraging the development and use of alternative fuels (see the "Using the Framework" feature). President Obama imposed more stringent mileage requirements by executive order in 2009. Although it is hard to predict the path that future regulation might take, it is possible that such regulation will include even further increases in fuel mileage standards for autos and trucks, more encouragement for the development and use of renewable energy sources, limitations on greenhouse gas emissions, and establishment of a "cap and trade" system for power producers. The 2010 BP deep water oil blowout in the Gulf will undoubtedly lead to stricter enforcement of existing regulations on deep water drilling and passage of additional provisions to protect against a recurrence of what some see as the worst environmental disaster of our time.

Importantly, American firms are affected not only by the regulatory activities of the U.S. government but by those of other governments and international agencies. For example, the European Union has fined Microsoft for violating its anticompetition rules. Increasingly, American firms are voluntarily conforming to tougher European standards on food additives, possible carcinogens in cosmetics, and mercury in electronic devices. They are doing so not only because they wish to sell in the huge European Union market but because they want access, as well, to the markets of fast-developing countries such as India, Brazil, and China that are slowly adopting the European regulatory standards on a wide range of products.[39]

Predictably, the collapse of the largely unregulated financial industry in 2008 and the Great Recession it helped trigger increased calls for government to better protect the public. In the immediate aftermath of the crisis, the Treasury and the Fed imposed higher capital requirements on banks (what they have to keep on reserve in case loans or securities go bad) and limited executive compensation in firms that had taken bailout money. But this still left in place an unregulated shadow banking system that had done great harm and might well do so again; hedge funds, investment banks, structured investment vehicles, and other institutions were free to issue and trade highly risky and undercapitalized over-the-counter derivatives, credit default swaps, collateralized debt obligations, and

How did Republican President George W. Bush and a Democratic-controlled Congress manage to get a deal done to make cars more fuel efficient?

Background: At the end of 2007, Congress passed and the president signed an energy bill whose major provision was a requirement that automakers boost the average fuel mileage of their fleets to 35 miles per gallon by 2020, up considerably from 2007's requirement for 27.5 for cars and 22.5 for light trucks and SUVs. This will require an annual improvement of 3.3 percent in fuel efficiency, well above the current rate of about 1.5 percent a year in the United States and 2.0 percent in Europe and Japan. Although many environmentalists wanted higher mileage targets and a shorter time period for implementation, most observers were pleasantly surprised by the outcome. So how did it happen? Taking a look at how structural, political linkage, and governmental factors affect policymaking in Washington will help explain the outcome.

Structure

Evidence mounts that the planet is warming and the climate is changing. ⇒ Easily and cheaply extractable petroleum reserves becoming less available. ⇒ Most of the world's oil reserves are located in politically unstable parts of the world. ⇒ The Constitution's interstate commerce clause allows the federal government to regulate businesses in the public interest.

Political Linkage

Public opinion shows growing concerns about global warming, foreign energy dependency, and gasoline prices. ⇒ Advocacy groups press the public and elected leaders to increase fuel efficiency standards, particularly in autos and light trucks. ⇒ Industry trade groups outside the energy and auto sectors say that increasing volatility in energy markets is damaging their competitiveness.

Big Three auto firms, as well as foreign firms such as Toyota, express willingness to consider greater efficiency, but fight against standards they believe would be too hard and expensive to meet. ⇒ Energy companies, at first opposed to any changes in the current mileage standards, come to see that the tide is turning against them, and try to limit the damage in the new bill. ⇒ Democrats gain control of the House and Senate in the 2006 elections.

Government

President Bush says he will support a bill that doesn't go too far. ⇒ Senate and House Democratic leaders convince automakers and state legislators that a bill is inevitable; make concessions to them on level and timing for new standards. ⇒ Not enough Democrats in Senate to defeat GOP filibusters, so must reach compromises with Republicans if any bill is to pass.

Energy companies mollified by defeat of Democratic provision to tax them to gain monies for sustainable energy programs. ⇒ Farmers and the farm lobby support the bill because of provision in it supporting increased biofuels production.

Government Action

The 2007 Energy Bill is passed

mortgage-backed securities.[40] Though it took time for final passage, given the press of other legislative business (particularly the stimulus package and health care reform) and the ferocious lobbying efforts by the financial industry to stop it, Congress finally passed a financial regulation reform bill in the middle of 2010. Key provisions of the legislation include provisions for the orderly liquidation of giant nonbank financial institutions to avoid institutional collapse and financial panics, more transparency in the marketing and trading of financial derivatives like credit default swaps, forbidding banks from trading for their own accounts rather than for their customers, and limiting how much banks can invest in hedge funds. The reform bill also requires banks to keep more of their money in reserve to respond to crises, sets up a consumer agency to protect against shady mortgage and credit card practices, and requires hedge funds to provide more information about their activities. The bill also cleans up some of the most egregious practices of the private agencies such as Moody's that rate the relative safety of bonds and securities.

This dynamic of the appearance of new problems, public pressures to regulate firms and activities related to these new problems, and industry push-back, is typical of American politics. Some periods see a wave of new regulatory initiatives; some periods experience some rollback of government regulation. Yet the need for regulation over a wide range of activities is evident to the public, political leaders, and many business leaders, and new technologies and a dynamic and changing economy cannot help but generate new regulatory demands. Government's regulatory role is here to stay and will likely increase.

Using the DEMOCRACY STANDARD

Do Americans get the economic policies they want from government?

It is difficult to draw general conclusions about the relative weight democracy has in determining what sorts of economic policies exist in the United States, partly because the government does so many different things in this area of activity. Economic policies that encompass spending and taxing, control of the money supply, and regulation are more often than not the result of the combined influences of popular pressures on elected political leaders and business and interest group influence. Business regulation is a good example of a set of policies that resulted from this joint influence.

To some extent, the American public gets at least part of what it wants in terms of economic policies from government. For example, people tell pollsters that they distrust big government and don't want to pay high taxes—which they don't, compared with other rich democracies. They want the government, moreover, to pursue policies that encourage economic growth and keep inflation under control—which it has done fairly effectively until the recent recession. And, they want government to control and help clean up some of the bad effects of economic activity like air and water pollution—which it has done with varying degrees of enthusiasm and success over the years.

So, to some extent, the American people get the sorts of economic policies they want. But it is also the case that the hand of special interests can be found in abundance in the details of many of our economic policies. This is the case for spending, for example, where commitments to specific priorities and projects, from weapons systems procurement to direct business subsidies, are hammered out in a legislative process where special interests dominate. Second, this is the case for taxation, where the detailed provisions of the Tax Code come from the efforts of special interests—who are also the main beneficiaries.[41] Third, this is the case in regulatory policy, where far too many regulatory agencies remain "captured" or heavily influenced by those they are charged with regulating. And, finally, the influence of special interests is found in monetary policy, where the Federal Reserve Board is especially sensitive to the needs of large investors and financial institutions.

SUMMARY

17.1 Identify three types of public policies and assess how policies are formed

- Public policies are decisions made by government that create laws and regulations that are binding on everyone.

- Political scientists distinguish three main categories of public polices: distributive policies target benefits to very narrowly defined groups or individuals, redistributive policies transfer resources from one group or class to another, while regulatory policies compel firms to behave in certain ways to serve some public purpose when the market fails to encourage such behavior.

- Scholars from a number of schools of thought—marxist, group theorists or pluralists, elite theorists, and others—believe that a particular theory can explain how the American political system works. In this book, we subscribe to no single theory of the political process, offering instead a framework for understanding how actors and institutions interact in patterned ways. We do suggest, however, that power and influence in the American system is biased toward firms, groups, and individuals that are financially advantaged over others. We further suggest that the constitutional system has important anti-majoritarian features that make our political process less democratic than it might be.

17.2 Analyze economic policymaking in terms of goals, players, and tools

- Policymakers try to achieve a number of objectives, including stimulating economic growth, preventing inflation and trade imbalances, providing infrastructure for economic activities, and compensating for or controlling negative externalities like air and water pollution.

- Fiscal policy refers to the overall spending and taxing impact of the federal government. Policymakers can use spending and taxing to stimulate economic activity—by increasing spending and/or cutting taxes—or slow it down—by cutting spending and/or increasing taxes. Fiscal policy is not very flexible because changes in program outlays and taxes are not easily legislated because people, groups, firms, and government agencies have a stake in the status quo.

- Monetary policy refers to Federal Reserve policies that influence the availability and cost of credit in the overall economy. The Fed uses these tools to expand credit when the economy is stalled or in decline and to shrink credit when inflation becomes a problem.

- Economic policies are fashioned by the president, Congress, and the Federal Reserve Board. But others are involved as well. Interest groups play a particularly central role. Political parties are also important: Democrats and Republicans take different approaches to economic questions and support different policies when in power.

17.3 Identify the components of the federal budget and analyze the problem of the national debt

- The federal budget is the detailed accounting of how government plans to spend taxpayer money, and the total and types of receipts (taxes of one kind or another) that have come in or will come in to pay for government programs.

- Federal government outlays cover a very broad range of programs, including national defense, social insurance such as Social Security and Medicare, safety nets for the poor such as Medicaid and food stamps, subsidies to various businesses such as agriculture and oil and natural gas, scientific research and higher education, food and drug safety regulation, and more. Government receipts mainly come from income, payroll, corporate, and excise taxes.

- The deficit is the difference each year between government outlays and government receipts. Annual deficits have grown dramatically in recent years.
- The national debt is the total of what the U.S. government owes to individuals, firms, and governments to pay for the sum total of annual deficits. The national debt has grown most dramatically during war and economic crises, including the recent Great Recession.

17.4 Explain the reasons for government regulation and predict the future of regulation

- The federal government subsidizes essential infrastructure and services that would otherwise not be made available by private enterprise, including airports, port facilities, energy grids, basic scientific research, and highways.
- It also plays an important regulatory role where markets do not operate to protect the public; these include things like food, drug, and product safety; the many unsafe and exploitative practices of financial institutions; air and water pollution; deep water oil drilling; and regulation of utility rates where companies have monopoly power.
- The deregulation fervor of the 1980s and 1990s has been doused by the reaction to the flood of unsafe products from abroad, the collapse of the financial system because of the unregulated practices of many of its leading firms, and the oil spill disaster in the Gulf of Mexico, and the demand that government do more to protect the public. The regulatory responsibilities of the federal government are likely to remain substantial, and even increase.

TEST YOURSELF

Answer key begins on page T-1.

17.1 Identify three types of public policies and assess how policies are formed

1. Only members of Congress participate in the policymaking process.
   True / False
2. Which of the following is most clearly a distributive policy?
   a. Fuel-efficiency standards for new cars
   b. Physician licensure requirements
   c. Social Security
   d. Crop subsidies
   e. Overtime rules
3. How democratic is the policymaking process?

17.2 Analyze economic policymaking in terms of goals, players, and tools

4. The most important role of the Federal Reserve is to regulate the stock market.
   True / False
5. In 2009, Congress passed the American Recovery and Reinvestment Act and, in the process, increased the deficit. The aim of this act was to pull the United States out of recession by stimulating economic activity through government spending. This strategy is most consistent with the views of
   a. monetarists.
   b. supply-siders.
   c. new growth theorists.
   d. Keynesians.
   e. Milton Friedman.
6. Evaluate the extent to which deficits are both beneficial and harmful.

17.3 Identify the components of the federal budget and analyze the problem of the national debt

7. The president determines the federal budget.
   True / False
8. Which of the following consumes the largest portion of the federal budget?
   a. Discretionary spending
   b. Mandatory spending
   c. Defense spending
   d. Social Security
   e. Interest on the national debt
9. How do taxes in the United States differ from taxes in other rich democracies?

17.4 Explain the reasons for government regulation and predict the future of regulation

10. Prior to the Great Recession, both Democrats and Republicans pushed to deregulate the financial industry.
    True / False
11. Why does the government regulate the economy?
    a. To minimize negative externalities
    b. To inhibit economic development
    c. To reduce the federal deficit
    d. To foster civic engagement
    e. To promote a negative balance of payments
12. How is the recent *Deepwater Horizon* oil spill in the Gulf of Mexico likely to affect future regulation of the oil and gas industry?

PEARSON
mypoliscilab EXERCISES

Apply what you learned in this chapter on MyPoliSciLab.

Read on mypoliscilab.com

eText: Chapter 17

Study and Review on mypoliscilab.com

Pre-Test
Post-Test
Chapter Exam
Flashcards

Watch on mypoliscilab.com

Video: Making Environmental Policy
Video: Recession Hits Indiana
Video: Economic Policy Debate at the G20
Video: Fed Approves Mortgage Crackdown
Video: The Stimulus Breakdown

Explore on mypoliscilab.com

Simulation: Making Economic Policy
Simulation: You Are the President and Need to Get a Tax Cut Passed
Simulation: You Are an Environmental Activist
Comparative: Comparing Economic Policy
Timeline: Growth of the Budget and Federal Spending
Visual Literacy: Evaluating Federal Spending and Economic Policy
Visual Literacy: Where the Money Goes

INTERNET SOURCES

American Enterprise Institute
www.aei.org
  A prominent conservative think tank with information about economic and social policies.

The Brookings Institution
www.brookings.org
  A left-of-center think tank with a wide-ranging agenda that includes many aspects of economic policy.

The Federal Reserve
www.federalreserve.gov
  The website of the Board of Governors of the Federal Reserve System; loads of statistical information and reports on the state of the economy and Fed policies on monetary policy.

Budget of the United States
www.whitehouse.gov/omb/budget/index.html
  The budget of the United States, with numbers, documentation, and analyses.

Fedstats
www.fedstats.gov
  Links to statistics and data from a broad range of federal government agencies, including those most relevant for economic policy in the United States. These include the Federal Reserve Board, the Bureau of Labor Statistics, the Bureau of the Census, and the Bureau of Economic Analysis.

Tracking Stimulus Spending
www.recovery.gov/Pages/home.aspx
  In an attempt to provide more transparency, this government website allows Americans to see where stimulus dollars are going.

The Peterson Institute for International Economics
www.iie.org
  A nonpartisan research center that focuses on international economic policies that affect the United States and other countries with a focus on trade, intellectual property rights, foreign investment, and currencies.

SUGGESTIONS FOR FURTHER READING

Baumol, William J., Robert E. Litan, and Carl J. Schramm, *Good Capitalism; Bad Capitalism.* New Haven, CT: Yale University Press, 2007.
  The authors argue that Americans must encourage an economy of entrepreneurship and innovation if the nation is to compete globally; they suggest a limited menu of tax and regulatory policies to accomplish this.

Cassidy, John. *How Markets Fail.* New York: Farrar, Straus and Giroux, 2009.
  The author discusses two things: first, he shows how and why market failures are inescapable and require government to fix them; second, he shows how the economics profession went off track and forgot this lesson and thus contributed to the current economic crisis.

Eisner, Marc Allen, Jeffrey Worsham, and Evan J. Ringquist. *Contemporary Regulatory Policy.* Boulder, CO: Lynn Reinner Publishers, 2006.
> *A broad overview of American regulatory policy; authors argue that regulatory policies are best understood in terms of the historical periods in which they were introduced.*

Peters, Guy B. *American Public Policy: Promise and Performance,* 8th ed. Washington, D.C.: CQ Press, 2010.
> *A comprehensive examination of the formation and content of American public policies.*

Reich, Robert B. *Supercapitalism: The Transformation of Business, Democracy, and Everyday Life.* New York: Knopf, 2007.
> *Suggests that corporations, being in a hypercompetitive environment, will not and cannot be expected to serve public purposes on a voluntary basis; serving broader public ends requires that government play a much larger role than it presently does.*

Posner, Richard A. *A Failure of Capitalism: The Crisis of '08 and the Descent into Depression.* Cambridge, MA: Harvard University Press, 2009.
> *A passionate but informed argument from one of the nation's most esteemed conservative thinkers that the free market by itself cannot solve deep recessions and depressions, making government intervention essential.*

Stiglitz, Joseph E. *Freefall: America, Free Markets and the Sinking of the World Economy.* New York: W.W. Norton, 2010.
> *A detailed and lively analysis by the Nobel Prize–winning economist on the causes of the financial collapse and the Great Recession and how it is affecting the long-term well-being of the country and its standing in the world.*

Wolf, Martin. *Fixing Global Finance.* Baltimore: Johns Hopkins University Press, 2008.
> *An accessible description of how global financial markets work, why the financial crisis hit in 2008, and what can be done to clean up the mess.*

18 | Social Safety Nets

IN THIS CHAPTER

18.1 Explain what safety nets are and why government provides them

18.2 Differentiate among types of safety net programs in the U.S.

18.3 Describe the main social insurance programs in the United States and assess their effectiveness

18.4 Describe the main means-tested programs in the United States and assess their effectiveness

18.5 Compare and contrast the American system of social safety nets with those in other rich democracies

PRESIDENT OBAMA WINS THE STRUGGLE TO REFORM AMERICAN HEALTH CARE

On March 23, 2010, President Barack Obama signed into law the most far-reaching reform of the nation's health care system since passage of Medicare in 1965. In doing so, he delivered on one of the main pledges of his 2008 presidential campaign. The bill he signed into law is long and complex, but it does a number of fairly straightforward things. First, the law extends health insurance coverage to roughly 32 million of the 46 million previously uninsured Americans. It does so by requiring states to expand the number of people who are covered by Medicaid, including poor adults without children; mandating that every American have health insurance either through their companies or on their own, with subsidies provided for those who can't afford to do so; and encouraging small businesses to offer coverage to their employees by enabling such businesses to shop for the best programs with the lowest rates in state insurance pools, if they wish to do so. Second, it sets a series of rules for insurance companies that keep people covered in a variety of circumstances where they would have lost

coverage in the past. For example, it forbids insurance companies from rejecting people for preexisting conditions or placing annual or lifetime limits on benefits and allows young people to stay on their parents' policies through age 26. Third, it fills in the Medicare prescription drug "donut hole" left over from the legislation passed under President George W. Bush (to be examined more later in the chapter) so that many of the elderly need no longer be faced with a choice of buying needed drugs or paying other expenses. Fourth, it provides money for research to discover the best medical practices to treat illness and disease and to make the results widely available to the public and medical practitioners in hopes of improving health outcomes and economic efficiencies.

Much to the chagrin of some health care reform advocates, the new law does not set up a "single-payer" system such as exists in Canada in which the government, as the "single payer," contracts with private firms to provide medical services, equipment, and drugs on behalf of the general public. Nor, to the disappointment of many Democrats, does the plan

include a "public option"—government insurance plans—to compete with private insurance companies within the state insurance pools. In the end, the new law, with its several mandates, subsidies, and changes in regulations, remains a system in which health care is provided by private practitioners, with insurance provided by private companies.

The program is expensive, to be sure, with the nonpartisan Congressional Budget Office (CBO) estimating the final bill for the program at $938 billion over 10 years. So how do Democrats and President Obama plan to pay for it? Perhaps most importantly, under the new law, Medicare taxes will now be collected on investment income and not only on wages and salaries as has been the case; this change will mostly affect the highest-income earners and wealth holders. Additional monies will come from a new tax on insurance policies for so-called Cadillac health care plans; this change will increase taxes for the wealthy but also for some labor union members. Third and finally, the bill mandates a $500 billion cut over 10 years in federal government reimbursements to

health care providers under the Medicare and Medicaid programs. When the dust settles, setting program costs against new taxes and savings, according to the CBO, federal budget balances will improve by about $138 billion over 10 years.

Such a comprehensive system of insurance coverage has long been a part of the Democrat's domestic policy agenda—with not much to show for it until 2010. Franklin Roosevelt and Harry Truman tried without success to pass similar legislation, for example; Lyndon Johnson, even with large majorities in the House and Senate during the years of the Great Society, could not convince Congress to provide universal coverage other than for those 65 years of age and older (Medicare); and President Bill Clinton's attempt to pass comprehensive reform crashed and burned in Congress in 1994. Obama's success came as something of a surprise because Democrats had lost their filibuster-proof 60-vote majority in the Senate when Republican Scott Brown won a special election on January 19 in Massachusetts to fill the seat of the late senator and health reform advocate Ted Kennedy, and Republicans were dead set against cooperating. Under the leadership of House Speaker Nancy Pelosi (D–CA) and Senate majority leader Harry Reid (D–NV), however, Democrats found a legislative workaround, avoiding the need for a conference committee to iron out differences in the health reform bills that the House and Senate had already passed (see Chapter 11 on conference committees). Republicans were furious, but there was nothing they could do to keep the legislation off the president's desk for his signature after the House voted to accept the Senate's version of health care reform, followed by passage of an additional bill to fix problems in the Senate's health care reform bill that bothered House Democrats, using the budget reconciliation process that forbids the use of the filibuster.

The politics of health care reform will play itself out over time. Democrats are hoping that the virtues of the new system will become evident as various provisions kick in over the next few years and will help them become the majority party in American politics. Republicans, who offered no alternative plans of their own, and who did not offer up a single vote for the bills in either the House or Senate, were gambling that their vigorous opposition to comprehensive reform requiring a substantial increase in the role of the federal government would play well with the American people and their own political base, paying off for them in the 2010 congressional elections and beyond. It is too early to tell who will turn out to have played the winning strategy. Nor will we know for some time the degree to which access to quality health care will improve for Americans and whether the new system will do anything to contain rising health care costs for the country.

The new health care reform legislation adds to the nation's safety net programs. In this chapter we look at federal government programs that provide safety nets for the American people. *Safety net* is the term used to describe programs that try to keep people from falling into poverty or poverty-like conditions, providing services in some cases and income support in others. Because such programs raise the most fundamental questions about the responsibilities of government and the individual, they have always been at the center of ideological and party conflict in the United States. In the remainder of this chapter, we look at the main safety net programs to see how they work and if they work, and think about why we have the kinds of programs that we do.

THINKING CRITICALLY About This Chapter

Using the FRAMEWORK

You will see in this chapter how the framework can be used to explain why government does what it does in the area of social safety net policies. You will use what you learned in previous chapters about structural, political linkage, and government factors to better understand what government does in terms of designing, paying for, and delivering programs that provide income and medical support for the elderly and the poor.

Using the DEMOCRACY STANDARD

In previous chapters, you used the democracy standard to examine the extent to which American political and government institutions enhanced popular sovereignty, political equality, and liberty. You will use the democracy standard in this chapter to ask whether the American people get the sorts of safety net policies they want from government.

Why Safety Net Programs?

18.1 Explain what safety nets are and why government provides them

safety nets
Government programs that protect the minimum standard of living of families and individuals against loss of income.

Why do we have such an extensive range of **safety net** programs in a country long committed to the idea of limited government and individualism where people are taught to stand on their own two feet? One might start, of course, with the Constitution itself, which gives the federal government a number of broad areas of responsibility, including the charges that it "establish Justice, insure Domestic tranquility … promote the general Welfare, and secure the blessings of Liberty. … " But it's clear that the framers had nothing like Social Security or food stamps in mind when they penned the Constitution.

The main clue to answering this puzzle is to note that providing safety net programs happens to one extent or another in all the rich democracies; it is one of the things rich democracies have in common. All have programs that protect the minimum standards of living of families and individuals against loss of income due to economic instability, old age, illness and disability, and family disintegration.[1] To be sure, there is a great deal of variation in the extent and forms these safety net programs take in these countries—with the United States being quite unique in many ways—but none simply leave their poor, disabled, unemployed, and elderly to fend for themselves.

Nations that provide such a range of safety net programs are often called **welfare states.** All rich democracies are also, to one degree or another, social welfare states. The term *welfare state,* of course, is often used pejoratively in the United States to refer to handouts to the "undeserving poor," but students of politics and government use the term to cover a range of income maintenance, health care, and other social welfare programs with a broad and diverse set of beneficiaries, not just the poor. We use the terms *social welfare* and *social safety nets* interchangeably in this chapter.

But noting that all rich democracies are welfare states with a rich collection of safety net programs still does not answer the question of why the United States and other countries have them. Why does the government in every one of these countries do these things? Why not simply leave the welfare of the people to the operations of the **market economy,** letting economic growth raise everyone out of need? One answer is that all rich, industrialized countries face a similar environment encouraging the establishment of social safety nets.[2]

Structural Factors

Industrialization has produced unprecedented levels of wealth and improved living standards in the Western countries over the past century, but it has also produced significant disruptions and hardships. Industrialized market societies are places of rapid economic growth and transformation. They are places where factories open and close, where some regions become prosperous while others languish, and where one technology supersedes another. We saw in Chapter 4, for example, that the American economy has been changing from one characterized by the factory and blue-collar work to one characterized by high technology offices with white-collar workers. Industrialized market societies are also places, as we saw in Chapter 17, where the business cycle, with its recurring periods of growth and recession, are part of life. Increasingly, our economy and that of the other rich democracies is becoming globalized, with cheaper products available, to be sure, but with many jobs migrating elsewhere. In such societies, including the United States, people may become unemployed or underemployed, or experience diminishing paychecks, through no fault of their own. Even highly skilled people may sometimes find themselves adrift when their companies leave or new technologies are introduced into their workplaces.

In rich industrialized countries, people also live longer because of advances in medical care and public health practices, including clean water and efficient solid waste disposal. But old age brings increased health care needs at the same time that people's separation from the workforce makes them less able to pay for those needs on their own. Work in the mines, factories, and transportation systems of industrial societies is not without risk, moreover, and occupational illness and disability are a problem.

welfare state

A government with a broad set of safety net programs.

market economy

Another term for capitalism.

LINING UP TO EAT   Here, people line up for food at a soup kitchen in Detroit. The one on the left is in 1932 during the Great Depression. The one on the right is in late 2008, where one in three people were below the poverty line. The troubles of the auto industry during the following year made matters even worse. As in other economic crises, the federal government took vigorous actions to try to reverse the decline, in this case extending unemployment benefits and temporarily taking over and restructuring GM and arranging the sale of Chrysler. Are such vigorous actions justified? Why or why not?

Rich, industrialized societies are not necessarily the most supportive environment for traditional extended families, which provided welfare and caring for the young, the elderly, the disabled, and the ill in pre-industrial societies. Rich, industrialized societies are mobile places: people often must move to follow jobs; others move to pursue their educations and new careers; and women have new and better opportunities for jobs and careers outside the family. In such circumstances, families are not only smaller than in the past but also less likely to stay intact—note the high divorce rate in the richest industrialized countries—or to form in the first place as more young adults choose to live alone and start families later, if at all. According to the U.S. Census, about 31 million Americans were living alone in 2009.

The upshot of all this is that rich, industrial societies, in addition to having high overall standards of living and lots of opportunity, also have, as a normal by-product of their dynamic market economies, a range of social problems that individuals and families did not create and that they cannot solve on their own. The expansion of safety net programs is deeply rooted in this reality, though countries have responded in decidedly different ways.

Political Linkage Factors

While structural factors provide the preconditions for the development of welfare states in the rich democracies, they do not entirely explain why political leaders created and expanded safety nets. One explanation is that the people wanted government's help in solving certain problems they couldn't solve by themselves—such as adequate income and health insurance in their old age—and they got that help because political leaders hold office only after facing the voters and winning elections. In a democracy, the argument goes, people get their way in the long run. Social safety net programs exist, in this view, because the people want them.[3]

?   Must a democratic government provide safety nets for its citizens? What would happen to elected officials if they failed to provide assistance that the public clearly wants?

There are a number of variations on this theme. One suggests that the main factor explaining the extent and generosity of social safety net programs across countries is the relative size and power of the industrial working class, especially the extent to which they are associated with strong and politically active labor unions. European welfare states are so developed compared to the United States, it is argued, because its labor unions were much more influential in government for long periods of time and pressed political leaders to expand the welfare state.[4] In support of this view, it is worth pointing out that it was the rising militancy and political influence of industrial workers and labor unions during the Great Depression of the 1930s that made Roosevelt's **New Deal** possible, including such landmark measures as Social Security and a great expansion in the federal government's role in providing public assistance. Labor unions also were major players within the Democratic Party during Lyndon Johnson's presidency in the 1960s, when Medicare was created and many poverty reduction programs were started.

Interest groups are another way that people are heard in the United States (see Chapter 7), and there is surely an interest group component to the story of the creation and expansion of social safety net programs in the United States. The elderly, for example, are well represented by organizations like the AARP—and they vote in high numbers and make campaign contributions as well—so elected officials are favorably disposed to programs that benefit them, such as Social Security and Medicare. Also, many middle-class Americans whose jobs and well-being are tied to a large government role in society—say, for example, teachers, welfare case workers, medical personnel working in hospitals and clinics, and the like—are strong voices for sustaining and expanding social safety nets whether spoken in the voting booth or through organizations like teachers' and nurses' unions.

Some scholars have argued that social safety nets were created at the behest of political and business leaders to help forestall popular discontent and to undermine radical movements for social change, especially during the Great Depression and during the years of the civil rights struggle in the 1960s.[5] Some point to the significant role played by corporate and banking leaders in the creation of the most important social safety net programs not only as a way to quell radicalism, but also to have the taxpayer pick up the tab for pension and health care programs they would otherwise have to pay for themselves.[6]

An Outline of American Safety Net Programs

18.2 Differentiate among types of safety net programs in the U.S.

We have suggested that social welfare or social safety nets refer to a broad range of programs that protect the minimum standards of living of families and individuals against some of life's unavoidable circumstances: unemployment, income loss and poverty, physical and mental illness and disability, family disintegration, and old age. Such programs come in a variety of forms and account for the largest share of the annual federal budget.

Types of Safety Net Programs

Social safety nets in the United States are made up of a fairly complex mix of programs, but we can distinguish two basic kinds. The first is **social insurance,** typified by Social Security and Medicare, in which individuals contribute to an insurance trust fund—in reality, a set of federal

New Deal

President Franklin Roosevelt's programs for economic recovery, income support, and business regulation during the Great Depression.

social insurance

Government programs that provide services or income support in proportion to the amount of mandatory contributions made by individuals to a government trust fund.

means-tested

Meeting the criterion of demonstrable need.

public assistance

Programs funded by general tax funds that provide money or services for the poor.

Temporary Assistance to Needy Families (TANF)

Program that provides income and services to many poor families; has benefit time limits and a work requirement.

Medicaid

Program administered by the states that pays for health care services for the poor; jointly funded by the federal government and the states.

entitlements

Government benefits that are distributed automatically to citizens who qualify on the basis of a set of guidelines set by law; for example, Americans over the age of 65 are entitled to Medicare coverage.

government bonds—by way of a payroll tax on their earnings and receive benefits based on their lifetime contributions. The second kind is **means-tested**, meaning that benefits are distributed on the basis of need to those who can prove that their income is low enough to qualify. These types of programs are often called **public assistance**. These programs are funded by general income tax revenues, rather than by payroll taxes. The food stamp program is an example, as are federal grants-in-aid to the states to help pay to support the very poor served by the **Temporary Assistance to Needy Families (TANF)** program.

Some safety net programs are administered directly from Washington, while others are jointly administered by federal and state governments. Social Security is an example of a program run from the nation's capital. Payroll taxes for Social Security are levied directly on wages and salaries by the federal government, and benefit checks are issued to the elderly and the disabled by the Social Security Administration. By contrast, **Medicaid** is jointly funded and administered by state and federal governments, as is the unemployment compensation system (funded by employers paying into a state-administered system). One result of such mixed programs is wide variation in benefit levels across the states.

Some social welfare programs are **entitlement** programs; that is, payments are made automatically to people who meet certain eligibility requirements. For example, citizens whose income is under a certain level are entitled to food stamps and Medicaid. People over the age of 65 are entitled to Medicare benefits. Because payments are made automatically, these expenditures are locked into the federal budget, and Congress can only tinker around the margins of the budget unless it changes the underlying statutes or passes revised program authorizations, which is hard to do, given the way the legislative process works.

The Costs of the Social Welfare State

We spend a substantial amount of money on what is designated in the annual federal budget as human resources (includes means-tested and social insurance programs, but also spending for student loan programs, job training, medical research, and military pensions). In 2010, total federal expenditure for this category was $3.8 trillion, amounting to more than two-thirds of total federal government outlays. This considerably outstrips spending in any other area of federal government responsibility, including national defense and homeland security.[7]

Social insurance represents the largest single portion of the federal budget. Social Security and Medicare, taken together, account for almost one-third of the federal budget. Moreover, Social Security and Medicare have been growing steadily as a share of federal expenditures. Means-tested programs (including Medicaid and TANF block grants to the states), on the other hand, are substantially smaller and have gotten smaller in relative terms (see Figure 18.1). This is hardly surprising in light of the fact that surveys show that a majority of Americans see social insurance recipients to be more deserving—because they have worked and paid payroll taxes—than those who receive one form or another of public assistance.

Several things are immediately evident from the pattern of expenditures shown in Figure 18.1. First, the nonpoor rather than the poor are the main beneficiaries of the American welfare state because social insurance programs are the largest programs and go mainly to those who have been employed the longest, had the highest incomes, and paid the maximum level of payroll taxes. Second, because

As percentage of federal government outlays

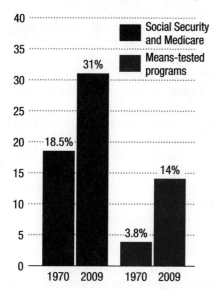

FIGURE 18.1 Comparing Social Insurance and Means-Tested Programs

The two social insurance programs, Social Security and Medicare, receive many more federal dollars than means-tested programs, such as public assistance, food stamps, and Medicaid. Social insurance now accounts for almost one-third of federal government spending. *Source:* Office of Management and Budget, *The Budget of the United States, 2011.*

Social Security and Medicare benefits go to those who are over 65, the elderly fare much better in the American welfare state than the young. One result has been a significant decline over the years in the poverty rate among the elderly and continuing high poverty among children: 20.7 percent of children lived below the poverty line in 2009; only 8.9 percent of those 65 years and older were in the same situation (see Figure 18.2).

In the next several sections, we examine the main safety net programs that make up the American welfare state. We start with social insurance programs.

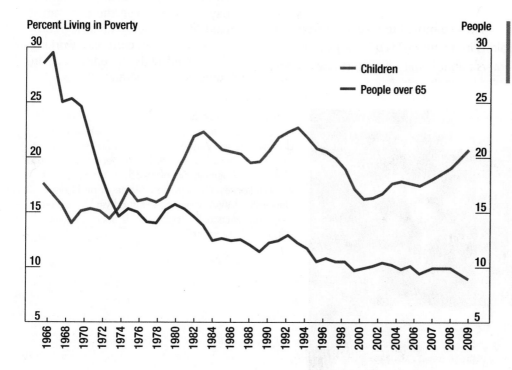

FIGURE 18.2 Poverty Among the Elderly and Among Children

Medicare and Social Security benefits, the largest social safety net programs in the United States, go mainly to people over age 65. Although large portions of the benefits from Medicaid and TANF go to poor children, and while CHIP benefits go to disadvantaged children not eligible for Medicaid, the totals come nowhere close to the totals for social insurance for the elderly. One result is that poverty has been reduced at a much more impressive clip for the elderly than for children. *Source:* U.S. Census Bureau, *Historical Poverty Tables.*

Social Security

Social insurance program that provides income support for the elderly, those with disabilities, and family survivors of working Americans.

Medicare

Federal health insurance program for the elderly and the disabled.

Great Depression

The period of economic crisis in the United States that lasted from the stock market crash of 1929 to America's entry into World War II.

Social Insurance

18.3 Describe the main social insurance programs in the United States and assess their effectiveness

The main social insurance programs in the United States are **Social Security** and **Medicare**. For the most part, benefits go to the elderly, although some are directed elsewhere. Social Security was created in 1935 in the midst of the **Great Depression** to provide income to the elderly. Within a year, however, benefits were added for survivors (popularly referred to as the "widows-and-orphans" program). Coverage for those with disabilities was added in 1956. Today, almost all employed Americans are covered by Social Security, the main exception being the employees of state and local governments that have Social Security–like programs of their own. Medicare was created in 1965 just after Lyndon Johnson's landslide election in 1964 and the Democrats' win of near-historic proportions in that year's congressional elections. In the following sections on social insurance, because of their importance for the federal budget and their broad impact on American society, we focus on the old age pensions in the Social Security program and Medicare. It is worth noting, however, that almost one-third of total benefits from the Social Security program go to survivors and those with disabilities.[8] We also look at unemployment insurance because of the political debates that surround it.

Social Security

Retirement income support for the elderly accounts for about two-thirds of Social Security expenditures; the other third goes to cover benefit payments for the disabled and survivors of deceased workers. The system is funded by a payroll tax on employees and employers under the Federal Insurance Contributions Act (the familiar FICA on your weekly or monthly pay stub). Because the program is paid for to a substantial degree by those who are currently working, the net effect is to redistribute income across generations.

? Will candidates for public office be tempted to play the intergenerational card in their campaigns in the future? Is there a possibility that younger and older voters might be pitted against one another?

ARCHITECTS OF SOCIAL SECURITY This telegram from Labor Secretary Francis Perkins, now displayed at the Wisconsin Historical Society, congratulates economics professor A. J. Altmeyer on the passage of the Social Security Act of 1935, a centerpiece of Franklin Roosevelt's New Deal. Altmeyer and fellow University of Wisconsin economist Edwin Witte were major architects of the legislation. Is Social Security still a viable program?

Social Security pensions were never meant to pay the full cost of retirement for Americans. Planners had always assumed that the program was part of a three-legged stool for income in old age that included private pensions from people's employers and individual savings. Unfortunately, most people do not make enough to save a substantial amount of money on their own, and company pensions, particularly of the "defined benefit" variety once common for employees of large companies, are less generous today and fewer in number. The latest surveys show that about one-third of Americans depend on Social Security for more than 90 percent of their retirement income, while another one-third say they depend on it for 50 percent of their retirement income.[9]

> **cost-of-living adjustment (COLA)**
> Automatic annual adjustment made to Social Security benefits.

Because inflation tends to undermine the purchasing power of benefits over time, Congress added automatic **cost-of-living adjustments (COLAs)** to Social Security in 1975. Alarm at the rising cost of COLAs during the Reagan years, however, led the National Commission on Social Security to recommend, and Congress to legislate, a provision for a cutback in the size of COLAs if the Social Security reserves fell to dangerously low levels. Bill Clinton asked Congress in 1993 to cut the size of COLAs as part of his deficit-reduction package, but a firestorm of protest from organizations representing the elderly forced him to withdraw the proposal. Because average wages and prices declined in the United States during the Great Recession—wages and prices are part of the formula for calculating annual increases—there was no COLA increase in 2010, the first time this had happened since the program was introduced in 1975.

Many Americans worry that Social Security funds will run out before they can begin collecting benefits. In large part, this is the result of years of commentary about the system's coming insolvency from conservative think tanks, political leaders, and radio and cable television talk-show hosts who have never been entirely friendly to the idea of government-mandated social insurance.[10] Alarm bells have also been raised by some economists about the long-term viability of the Social Security trust fund under current laws. Presently, with the exception of post–Great Recession 2010, Social Security takes in much more in payroll taxes than it pays out in benefits each year, so its trust fund shows a strong positive balance and is growing. However, because the population is aging—meaning there will be fewer working people paying taxes to pay the benefits for additional elderly recipients—a time will come when the fund will be paying out at a faster clip than it is being replenished. Especially troublesome to many is the sizable baby-boom generation, whose first members reached retirement age in 2010.

Here is what is going on in terms of Social Security solvency. The problems are serious but not alarming if Americans and their elected representatives decide to change certain features of the existing system. Even with no changes at all, the Social Security trust fund will not move into the red until the year 2037, according to the 2009 report of the trustees of the fund. (Using different assumptions, the Congressional Budget Office estimates that the tipping point will come later, in 2052.) The well will not run dry even then, of course; given a continued inflow of payroll taxes even after the fund goes into deficit, the current system will be able to pay 70 percent of full bene-

> **?** If solving the problem of Social Security financing is fairly straightforward—increasing payroll taxes, raising the retirement age, and reducing benefits—why have Americans and their elected leaders shied away from tackling it?

fits for a very long time after that, at least until 2081.[11] Some scholars have suggested that current projections are based on very conservative assumptions about future economic performance, the level of immigration, and the rate of aging in the American population; their more optimistic assumptions leave Social Security with another 80 years or so before deficits appear.[12] The system may also stay viable for a longer period of time if trends continue in which healthier and more active seniors choose not to retire.[13] Under this scenario, tax receipts will continue to roll in from people working past the full-benefits retirement age (66 in 2010) because they will continue to pay payroll taxes, even if they are drawing benefits, and their benefits are taxable as well.

Of course, well before then Americans could decide to solve the long-term trust fund problem. We could do it in any number of ways by, for example:

1. Raising the payroll tax rate.
2. Raising the ceiling on taxable income subject to the payroll tax ($106,800 in 2010).
3. Taxing all income rather than only income from wages and salaries, the current practice.
4. Cutting-back recipient benefits.
5. Taxing the benefits of the wealthy at higher rates.
6. Raising the retirement age.[14]

None of these changes would be politically popular or easy to achieve, to be sure—President Obama has said he is against raising the retirement age, for example, and Republicans in Congress have shown they will oppose tax increases of any kind—but adapting one or more would leave years more of Social Security surpluses. The problem, of course, is that older Americans approaching retirement would be unlikely to appreciate having to wait longer to retire. Because older Americans vote at high rates compared to others and support powerful groups like the AARP to represent their interests, elected leaders are likely to listen to them. And younger Americans are unlikely to be enthusiastic about the prospect of paying more payroll taxes or having to retire later.

The deep partisan divide also makes change difficult, though not impossible. Generally, Democrats think the system is in reasonably good health and requires only some tinkering to solve emerging problems. Many Republicans, on the other hand, believe the system is seriously flawed and that the only way to save it is with major overhauls, including using a portion of the payroll tax to set up individual investment accounts for retirement.[15] President Bush tried hard in 2005 to convince the public and members of Congress to adopt a system of private accounts, but the proposal never made it to the floor of either chamber. The problem with the Bush plan, as many who opposed it pointed out, was that diverting a portion of existing payroll taxes to private accounts—a system in which individuals would choose where to invest a portion of their payroll tax from a list of approved mutual funds, similar to a 401(k)—would have depleted the Social Security trust fund much faster than under the existing system. Democrats were willing to support private accounts as an add-on to the existing Social Security program—funded out of an additional payroll tax—but were unwilling to have private accounts take the place of all or part of the current system.

The question of "private accounts" in Social Security is probably off the table for now and the foreseeable future in the aftermath of the financial collapse and steep declines in stock markets during the Great Recession. Americans were sobered, no doubt, by the knowledge that an important backstop for their retirement years under this privatization model would be tied to a securities market that can decline as well as grow. None of the Republican or Democratic candidates for the party presidential nominations mentioned Social Security privatization during the 2008 campaign season. But the fiscal difficulties of Social Security will not go away. Action of some sort will have to happen at some point. But bitter partisan divisions, as well as an understandable aversion of elected officials to telling voters they will either have to pay more in taxes or get fewer benefits, may require copying an earlier strategy. In 1983, President Ronald Reagan managed to cut through partisanship and provide political cover for members of Congress when he used an executive order to create a bipartisan commission on Social Security to offer recommendations for reform, many of which were passed by Congress.

Medicare

Franklin Roosevelt wanted to include comprehensive health insurance for all Americans as part of Social Security when it was introduced to Congress in 1935. The proposal met fierce opposition from the American Medical Association (AMA), and the provision was dropped for fear of endangering prospects for passing Social Security. President Harry Truman tried to introduce a similar plan after the end of the Second World War, but the AMA and others were able to label the proposal "socialized medicine"—a very effective tool to block a new program during this time in American history when anticommunist sentiment was strong. Finally, with mounting evidence that health care costs were a leading cause of poverty, and buttressed with an electoral mandate and huge Democratic majorities in Congress after the 1964 elections, President Lyndon Johnson was able to create the Medicare insurance program for the elderly in 1965 and a means-tested Medicaid program for the poor in 1965. (We consider Medicaid later in this chapter.) These programs fell well short of a comprehensive plan that covered everyone, but they were highly significant nevertheless.

Medicare dramatically transformed access to health care for the elderly in the United States. Millions of people who at one time would have been priced out of the health care market now have quality care available to them. In 2010, it is estimated that almost 47 million people were enrolled in Medicare.[16] Everyone 65 and over is automatically enrolled in Medicare Part A, which pays for a portion of the bill for hospital stays and short-term skilled nursing after hospitalization. But people need to buy additional insurance (Medicare Part B) for coverage to help pay for doctors, durable medical equipment, tests, and X rays, if they choose to do so. And, because there are many gaps in coverage and significant co-pays under Parts A and B, many over the age of 65 choose as well to buy so-called *Medigap* insurance. As you might guess, all of this adds to the out-of-pocket costs for the elderly.

In a surprise to both Republicans and Democrats, President George W. Bush in 2003 successfully sponsored a big expansion of Medicare to include a drug coverage provision (Medicare Part D); before then, drugs were paid "out-of-pocket," with the total monthly bill for many of the elderly quite substantial. The program involves government subsidies to private insurance companies that offer policies covering prescription drugs. To keep down costs, the Bush bill included a so-called donut hole, where coverage was not provided. In 2009, the drug benefit covered only the first $2,830, for example, then covered nothing until out-of-pocket drug costs reached $6,440, then kicked in again after that. Enrollees paid 100 percent of drug costs in the donut hole between the two numbers. The 2010 health care reform bill described in the chapter opener gradually closes this donut hole.

There is no question that the Medicare program has been extremely successful. People over the age of 65 have more access to health care services today than at any time in American history and it shows; people are living longer and healthier lives.[17] But there are big problems as well. For one thing, people have to pay a substantial amount to achieve coverage that most Americans would consider reasonable. Medicare Part A requires patients to pay the first $1,068 costs of hospitalization and 20 percent of the bill after that. Medicare Part B costs about $1,200 annually and has significant co-pays and deductibles. Purchasing Medigap insurance to cover these deductibles and co-pays starts at $145 per month,[18] and will become more expensive when the new federal ban on insurance companies denying coverage to people with pre-existing conditions takes effect in 2014.

The problem of Medicare that is most in the news, however, concerns its costs and the growing threat of deficits in the government's Medicare accounts. Paying for Medicare over the long term is a problem. First, the American population is getting older, meaning that the number of people on Medicare is growing and those in the workforce paying payroll taxes supporting the program is shrinking in a relative sense. Second, health care costs—doctors, hospitals, tests, and prescription drugs—have been rising much faster than the payroll taxes that support Medicare Part A and general tax revenues that fund (in addition to premiums paid by beneficiaries) Parts B, C (Medicare Advantage plans), and D. The Medicare Part A Trust Fund is already paying out more than it receives from payroll taxes and will run out of money entirely by 2017. The shortfall will need to be paid out of general government revenues that are already paying for the large subsidies for Parts B (doctors and tests) and D (prescription drugs). The Medicare program is growing so fast that it will pass Social Security as the federal government's most expensive endeavor somewhere around the year 2030. One can see the scale of the problem in Figure 18.3, which shows the status of social insurance trust funds.

People disagree about what to do about this revenue-expenditure mismatch. Some combination of health industry cost-containment measures (e.g., limiting how much Medicare will reimburse doctors and hospitals for their services, or introducing more competition into the medical industry), limitations on covered services for patients, or increases in payroll taxes are probably what will happen in the long run, but liberals and conservatives, Democrats and Republicans cannot agree on what can and should be done. (The health care reform bill mandates $500 billion in Medicare cuts over 10 years, but it is not entirely clear how this will be accomplished.) Nevertheless, Medicare is here to stay. People use it, depend on it, and support it. Even at anti–big government rallies supported by

FIGURE 18.3 Medicare and Social Security Trust Fund Balances (in billions)

Though much of the political and public discussion of social insurance financing (OASI in the graph) tends to be on the long-term problems of funding retirement, a much bigger and more pressing problem concerns the financing of Medicare. Funding for the two main parts of Medicare, the hospital trust fund (HI) and the supplemental trust fund for paying for doctors and tests (DI), runs into the negative territory where outlays exceed receipts much earlier than is the case for Social Security. *Source: Annual Report, 2010,* The Social Security and Medicare Trustees.

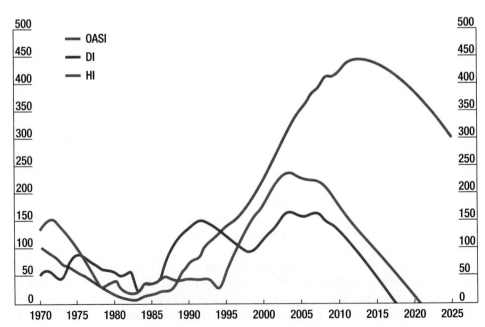

the Tea Party, it is not uncommon to see signs that read "keep government out of my Medicare."

Unemployment Insurance

> **unemployment insurance**
> Program funded by taxes on employers to provide short-term income support to laid-off workers; also called unemployment compensation.

Unemployment insurance, sometimes called unemployment compensation, was part of the original Social Security Act of 1935. Unlike Social Security and Medicare, the program is not funded by a payroll tax on the wages and salaries of employees but is levied entirely on employers. The program is administered by the states operating under federal guidelines. The states can and do add their own monies to the program and have broad discretion in determining eligibility and compensation levels. The result is that unemployment compensation checks vary widely across the states. In 2009, the average payment was about $300 a week,[19] with a wide range of variability among the states. Unemployment coverage was extended in 2008, 2009, and 2010 in the midst of the Great Recession to keep income flowing to unemployed people. The hope was that such payments would bolster consumer spending in the economy and help a significant number of people to keep their homes from being foreclosed.

The idea behind the program is to give people who have been laid off—not those who have been fired for cause, gone on strike, or who have quit—some support for a limited amount of time while they look for new jobs. At this writing, unemployment compensation is limited to 26 weeks, although extended benefits of an additional 13 weeks are possible and were done several times recently, as we saw earlier.

Small-business owners are especially unhappy with this program because they feel especially burdened by the employer tax that funds the program.

> **?** Should unemployment benefits be extended when economic times are tough? How might such an extension affect economic recovery?

Corporations and their trade associations are less hostile, perhaps because they recognize that unemployment compensation monies, when spent by recipients, help stimulate the economy when it has slowed down.

Liberal critics are unhappy about a number of things. Only a small percentage of low-income and part-time workers are covered by the program, for example, because many of these workers have not worked the minimum number of hours to be eligible. Moreover, only about a third of jobless workers receive benefits compared with 75 percent coverage in 1975. Many have exhausted the 26-week limit, others are not eligible, while still others never apply—some because they don't know how to go about it, and some because the reward may not seem worth the effort. And, the value of benefits for those who do receive benefits has declined substantially, worth only about one-third of lost wages today compared to a near 60 percent wage replacement rate in 1975.[20]

Do Social Insurance Programs Work?

In an era when it is fashionable to deride the ability of government to do anything well, it is important to recognize how successful America's social insurance programs have been. There is no doubt that Social Security and Medicare work beyond the wildest dreams of their founders. Although the benefits do not allow people to live luxuriously, they provide an income floor for the retired and pay for costly medical services that, before 1965, were as likely as not to impoverish those who had serious illnesses and long hospital stays.

The effectiveness of Social Security and Medicare was shown in a 1989 Census Bureau study on the effects of all federal government taxing and spending programs on income inequality and poverty. The principal finding was that Social Security (including Medicare) "is the Federal government's most effective weapon against poverty and reduces the inequality of Americans' income more than the tax system and more than recent social welfare [means-tested] programs."[21] This conclusion, in one form or another, has been reaffirmed repeatedly since then.[22] In fact, according to the Census Bureau, Social Security and Medicare have helped reduce the elderly poverty rate from about 48 percent in the mid-1950s to a little more than 9 percent today.[23] The Center for Budget Priorities reports almost one-half of all seniors would be below the poverty line without their Social Security payments. And it does so very efficiently; administrative costs for Social Security are about 0.6 percent of benefits distributed.[24]

Unemployment compensation is hard to evaluate. For those in the program, 26 or 39 weeks of benefits after being laid off is surely helpful to recipients who must pay for food and housing, among many other things. There is no gainsaying, moreover, the impact of unemployment compensation on economic growth, especially in periods when economic stimulus is needed because of hard times. Because people who are laid off are more likely than others to spend rather than save—because they must—benefits are circulated quickly into the economy. In a recent study, in fact, the Department of Labor estimated GDP grows by $2.15 for every dollar of unemployment compensation benefits.[25] On the other hand, the employer tax may have an effect on the ability and willingness to hire more people. Even taking this into account, on balance the program seems to be effective. Many liberal critics suggest that its main shortcoming is that so few are covered for so short a time.

Means-Tested Programs

18.4 Describe the main means-tested programs in the United States and assess their effectiveness

Means-tested programs, also called public assistance, are designed to provide income support and services for those with very low means who fall below certain income thresholds. One scholar suggests that these programs might more accurately be called "absence of means" programs.[26] Rather than being paid by payroll taxes, money for public assistance comes from government's general revenues. While accounting for a much smaller portion of the federal budget than social insurance programs (see Figure 18.1), means-tested programs have traditionally attracted more criticism than virtually anything else government does. While Social Security and Medicare enjoy widespread support, welfare (a common popular term for public assistance or means-tested programs) has long been the object of scorn.

Most Americans say they want government to help the poor,[27] but almost everyone disliked the longest lasting but now defunct public assistance program: **Aid to Families with Dependent Children (AFDC).** Not only conservatives, but liberals as well; not only average citizens, but also recipients; and not only voters and political leaders, but people who work for welfare agencies, disliked this program. A consensus long existed that something was wrong with AFDC.[28] For most Americans, AFDC and other means-tested programs seemed to contradict such cherished cultural values as independence, hard work, stable families, and responsibility for one's own actions. Public opinion polls consistently showed that Americans believed that welfare kept people dependent; didn't do a good job of helping people stand on their own two feet; and encouraged divorce, family disintegration, and out-of-wedlock births.[29] Although AFDC has now been replaced by the Temporary Assistance to Needy Families

Aid to Families with Dependent Children (AFDC)

The federal entitlement program that provided income support for poor families until it was replaced by TANF in 1996.

THE POOR ARE AMONG US   However poverty is measured, it is clear that the percentage of the population living in poverty in the United States is higher than in any other rich democracy. Although the United States arguably has the least generous set of safety nets among these countries, families like this one can usually depend on food stamps, some income support, and Medicaid to maintain a minimum standard of living. Why are so many people in the United States living at or below the poverty line?

program (TANF), much of the thinking about means-tested programs and public assistance recipients remains unchanged. (See the "By the Numbers" feature to learn more about how the number of poor people in the United States is calculated.)

The federal government has several means-tested programs to assist poor Americans. Let us look at the five most important ones.

Temporary Assistance to Needy Families

The Temporary Assistance to Needy Families (TANF) Act, passed in 1996, replaced AFDC with an entirely new system of public assistance, and "ended welfare as we know it," as President Bill Clinton put it. (See the "Using the Framework" feature on why the change happened.) Its major features were as follows:

- The status of welfare assistance as a federal entitlement was ended. The families of poor children are no longer guaranteed assistance by the federal government.

- The design and administration of welfare programs have been turned over to the states, meaning there are 50 different welfare programs in the United States.

- States receive block grants from the federal government to help them finance the welfare systems they devise. States add their own money in varying amounts, with some states, such as New York, much more generous than others.

WELFARE TO WORK   Like others covered by TANF, these aid recipients in Philadelphia are required to work or be in training for jobs as a condition for receiving assistance. These two young people are studying to be cooks. What are some advantages of the TANF program? Disadvantages?

How many Americans are poor?

Although the Bible says, "For you will have the poor with you always," it does not tell us how many of the poor will be with us at any given time.

Why It Matters Knowing how many poor there are, and being relatively confident in the validity and reliability of that number, is extremely important for a number of reasons:

- Comparing the number who are poor in the United States over time gives us an indication of how well we are doing as a society.
- Comparing the number who are poor in the United States over time lets us know the dimensions of a serious social problem that may require government action or the mobilization of private charities, or both.
- The number of people living in poverty helps determine the size (and thus the cost) of many government programs, including food stamps, Medicaid, rent supplements, and the Earned Income Tax Credit.

Interestingly, if the numbers are to be believed, we made good progress during the 1990s—the poverty rate fell to 11.3 in 2000, its lowest point in 21 years—but increased again as the United States went through a recession and a recovery that added jobs later than usual in such recoveries. By 2009, at the height of the Great Recession, 14.3 percent of Americans—almost 44 million people—were below the poverty line, according to the Census Bureau.

The Story Behind the Poverty Measure But what is poverty and how can we measure it? Most would probably agree that poverty involves living in dire circumstances; that is, being poorly housed, underfed, and without adequate medical care. But we might have a harder time agreeing on the exact dividing line between adequate and inadequate living standards. To get around this, government statisticians use *income* as a proxy for calculating poverty. Rather than collect information about how people live—what their homes and apartments are like, for example—the Census Bureau collects information about how much money they earn. The assumption, of course, is that in an economy such as ours, what one earns is directly related to how one lives and consumes.

Calculating the Poverty Line The poverty line was first calculated in 1964 by Census Bureau statisticians. They started with the Department of Agriculture's determination of what it would cost a family of four to buy enough food to survive (called the "emergency food budget"). Then, because it had been determined that the average American family in 1964 spent one-third of its after-tax income on food, the statisticians multiplied the Agricultural Department's emergency food budget figure by three to determine the official government poverty line. They then adjusted this income number for family size, creating poverty line numbers for single persons living alone, two-person families, and so on.

This 1964 baseline figure is used to the present day. Starting in 1965, and every year since then, the poverty line from the previous year is adjusted for inflation, taking into account different family sizes. The accompanying table shows the official poverty line thresholds for 2008. To be under the line is to be officially poor.

Criticisms of the Poverty Line Measure As with most official statistics, the poverty line calculation has its critics:

- Because the typical American household today spends a much lower proportion of its income on food than in 1964, the "emergency food budget" figure from the Agriculture Department should be multiplied not by three, as it has been since the beginning, but by five or six, to calculate the poverty threshold, say some critics. This would result in a substantial increase in the number of people officially designated as poor.

- States use these combined funds to give both direct cash assistance to families—usually, a monthly welfare check—and money for child care, education and training, and other services to encourage recipients to enter paid employment. Recently, the proportion going to cash benefits has fallen to a little more than one-third of program spending.[30]

- The head of every family receiving welfare is required to work within two years of receiving benefits and is limited to a total of five years of benefits. States are allowed to impose even more stringent time requirements. States are also allowed to use their own funds (not federal block grant money) to extend the two-year and five-year limits. Many are not willing to do so.

- Unmarried teenage parents can receive welfare benefits only if they stay in school and live with an adult.

- States must provide Medicaid and CHIP (to be described in a later section) health care benefits to all who qualify under current law.

- If poverty is really about lifestyles and consumption patterns, argue conservatives, then household income calculations should include the income equivalents of noncash government benefits such as public housing, rent supplements, Medicaid support, and food stamps. Doing this would reduce the number of people officially living in poverty.
- By calculating a single, national poverty threshold, the Census Bureau fails to take into account the substantial differences in the cost of living that exist across states and communities.

A family of four earning $17,000, for example, could no doubt stretch its dollars farther in rural Alabama than in San Francisco.

What to Watch For All government statistics are built on a set of assumptions, some of which are sensible and some of which defy common sense. Be aware of such assumptions when you use official statistics. Luckily, every government agency describes in detail how it collects and calculates statistics, so you can figure it out once you read the documentation.

What Do You Think? With all its problems, why do we continue to depend on the Census Bureau's poverty line calculation? Do the virtues of simplicity, consistency, and historical comparability of the present way of calculating poverty trump its several problems? How else could poverty rates be calculated? What do you think should be included and excluded from such a calculation?

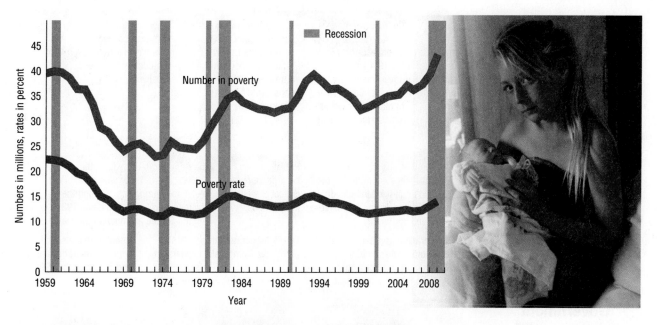

The Official Poverty Line in the United States in 2009

1 Person	2 People	3 People	4 People	5 People	6 People	7 People	8 People
$11,161	$14,366	$16,781	$22,128	$26,686	$30,693	$35,316	$39,498

Proponents of welfare reform believed the new welfare system would end welfare dependency, reestablish the primacy of the family in poor communities, improve the income situation of the poor as they enter the job market, and help balance the federal budget. Opponents of welfare reform believed the legislation would lead to more poverty, homelessness, and hunger—especially among children—once recipients reached their five-year time limit. Here is what the research shows to date about the effects of the reform. Welfare rolls across the country dramatically dropped after the new law was passed; many people trained for jobs and entered the paid workforce, and many raised their incomes, especially during the latter part of the 1990s and from 2004 until the financial collapse in 2008.[31] However, because pay levels for entry-level jobs are so low—about half take minimum-wage jobs—only a small percentage of former welfare recipients were able to cross the official **poverty-line** threshold in the first years of the

? Have the welfare rolls been pared down so much that people in need are being ignored? If poverty remains high, where did all the people go who were on welfare under AFDC?

poverty line
The federal government's calculation of the amount of income families of various sizes need to stay out of poverty.

Why did our welfare system change so drastically in 1996?

Background: America's traditional welfare system, created in 1935 almost as an afterthought to Social Security, had grown to the point that it provided cash payments to families of one in nine children in the United States by 1995. Although it did not pay very much to individual families and represented but a tiny portion of the federal government's budget, the program was never very popular with the public, grew even less popular in the 1980s and the 1990s, and was replaced by a radically new program in 1996. Examining structural, political linkage, and governmental factors that contributed to a dramatic change in welfare policy will make the story clearer.

Structure

The American political culture celebrates competitive individualism, small government, and self-reliance, and denigrates handouts to the "undeserving" poor. → Competitive pressures from the global economy in the 1990s pushed governments in all of the rich democracies to make their welfare states more efficient. → The fall of communism and the post–Cold War boom in the United States enhanced the attractiveness of conservative ideas in America. → Federalism allowed states to experiment with alternative modes of welfare delivery.

Political Linkage

Conservative intellectuals and think tanks attacked the AFDC welfare system during the 1980s on the grounds that it killed individual initiative and created dependency, destroyed families, and rewarded immorality. → Public opinion became more critical of welfare in the 1980s. → The Republican Party used the "welfare mess" issue with great effect in election campaigns, winning the presidency in 1980, 1984, and 1988 and the Senate for much of the 1980s.

The Democratic Party lost a substantial number of blue-collar, unionized workers, concerned about "wasteful spending" on welfare, from their electoral base. → Moderate Democrats of the Democratic Leadership Council (DLC) also embraced welfare reform. → Republican conservatives won control of the House and Senate in the 1994 elections.

Government

The Republican-controlled Congress delivered on its promise in the Republican Contract with America to pass a bill to radically transform welfare. → President Clinton, a believer in welfare reform (he had promised to "end welfare as we know it"), signed the bill into law near the beginning of the 1996 presidential campaign.

Government Action

The Temporary Assistance to Needy Families Act became law in 1996.

program. And, while the poverty rate decreased among former welfare recipients between 1996 and 2000, it slowly increased after that.[32] Even at its highest level of usage, moreover, only about one-quarter of families living below the poverty line receive TANF benefits, either because of the stigma of being on welfare, the complexities of signing up and determining eligibility, or reaching the program's time limits.[33] So the vast majority of poor families in the United States do not receive TANF benefits.

With states in dire economic straits today, moreover, many of them have been making it harder for people to get back on the welfare roles even when they are technically eligible for more benefits.[34]

Food Stamps

This program, funded from the budget of the Department of Agriculture and called the Supplemental Nutrition Assistance Program (SNAP) since 2008, helps poor Americans falling below a certain income to buy food for themselves and their families. Although other nutritional assistance programs exist to help the poor—the free or reduced-price school lunch program and the Women, Infants, and Children nutrition program are examples—the food stamp program does the most. (See the "Mapping American Politics" feature for more on child nutrition programs.) About 35 million people received food stamps in 2009. About 50 percent of food stamp recipients are children; about 80 percent of recipients are poor families with children. Food stamp benefit levels are set by the individual states under general federal guidelines, and states vary substantially in their generosity. Stamps can be used only for food; they cannot be used for alcohol, cigarettes, beauty care products, or gambling, despite rumors to the contrary. The program seems to have made a significant dent in the prevalence of malnutrition in the United States, even though the average benefit was only $1.05 per meal in 2007.[35]

Medicaid and Health Insurance for Poor Children

The federal government allocates money to the states to help them pay for medical services for many of their indigent adult citizens and children in two big and rapidly growing programs: Medicaid and **CHIP** (the **Children's Health Insurance Program**). Medicaid is now the nation's second largest public assistance program, with benefits going to 1 in 6 Americans.[36] When state expenditures for Medicaid are added to federal expenditures, Medicaid is almost as big as Medicare. The program is funded by both the states and the federal government; states receive from 50 to 83 percent of the cost of their state-designed and -administered Medicaid programs from Washington, with the poorest states receiving the highest percentage of reimbursements. Despite the federal assistance, funding Medicaid has become one of the most difficult fiscal problems for the states, especially during tough economic times such as in the years 2008–2011, when state tax revenues declined and the need for Medicaid assistance increased.

> **Child Health Insurance Program (CHIP)**
>
> Program that pays for health care services for children in households above the poverty line but below 133 percent to 400 percent of the poverty line, depending on the state.

GIVING PRESCHOOLERS A HEAD START
The Head Start program for preschool poor children is one of the few means-tested programs that enjoys widespread support across the ideological and partisan spectrums. Here, children take a snack break at a Head Start Center. Why has this program been popular with the public and elected leaders, even conservatives who usually oppose federal government social programs?

Childhood poverty and federal child nutrition programs

Introduction We saw in the Chapter 13 "Mapping American Politics" feature, where we considered spending by the Department of Homeland Security, that government spending often does not meet the purported purposes of federal programs. Many critics of government suggest that this mismatch between intentions and results is endemic, typical of an essentially ineffectual or feckless government. Are there programs that do what they set out to do? And if there are, what allows them to meet their goals? Here, we consider the child nutrition programs of the Department of Agriculture, which are intended to help poor children become more healthy and better able to take advantage of their schooling. The department administers four child nutrition programs: the National School Lunch Program, the School Breakfast Program, the Child and Adult Care Food Program, and the Summer Food Service

Program. If these programs are doing what they are supposed to be doing, they ought to be funneling a disproportionate share of funding to states with the most poor children.

Mapping Dollars Against Needs The states in the cartogram on the left are expanded or diminished according to their average poverty rates for children under 18. States with high child poverty

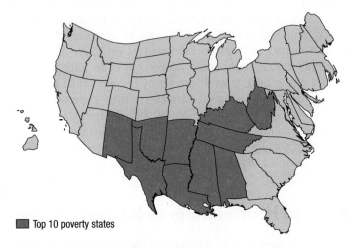

■ Top 10 poverty states

States Resized by Average Childhood Poverty Rates

Medicaid is quite complicated and varies a great deal by state; it is difficult to describe in simple terms. All one can say with assurance is that if a state chooses to participate in the program, it is required to provide a specific range of medical services for people who are defined as "medically indigent"—defined under the new health care reform legislation as anyone falling at or under 133 percent of the federal poverty line, including childless adults—or who receive food stamp and/or TANF benefits. Medicaid pays for hospital, physician, and nursing services; home health care; diagnostic screenings and tests; as well as nursing home costs—provided that recipients do not exceed the income ceilings for the program. Some states also provide prescription drug coverage. In addition to providing medical services for the very poor, Medicaid has become increasingly used to pay for nursing home care for those who have exhausted their savings, including many people who had been long-time members of the middle class. Indeed, about 70 percent of nursing home residents in the United States receive aid from the program to pay for their housing and care. States have some latitude in determining who receives benefits and who does not—federal statutes identify around 50 categories of people potentially eligible for Medicaid benefits—and how much service providers receive in compensation, so benefits vary widely across the states.[37]

Despite the size of the program and the seemingly broad eligibility, simply being poor does not necessarily mean that one receives benefits. In fact, less than one-half of the people who fall below the government's poverty line are covered by Medicaid in any given year.[38]

rates are larger than normal; states with low poverty rates are smaller than normal. The 10 states in green have the highest rates of poverty—more than 20 percent of the children under 18 living in each of these states were in poverty in 2007. The cartogram on the right highlights the 9 states that received the highest per-capita child nutrition program dollars (Alaska, not shown, is among the top 10) that same year. Comparing the two cartograms shows an almost exact match between needs and the flow of federal dollars. The states with the most poor children on a per-capita basis also, by and large, received the most help from the federal government to feed these children. So it seems at least one federal program is working as advertised. What seems to help make this program work is that federal dollars are distributed by a formula based on child poverty rates in school districts in states across the country. Programs based on formulas of one kind or another are probably more likely than programs supported by annual appropriations to meet program goals—if the formula is designed correctly in the first place, of course—because representatives and senators are less able to intervene to support pet projects for their districts and states.

What Do You Think? Why might it make sense for more federal programs to be based on formulas rather than annual appropriations? Do you believe they are more likely to meet program goals if taken out of the annual appropriations process? What are some drawbacks of formulas?

Source: U.S. Bureau of the Census, *Statistical Abstract of the United States, 2010* (tables on "child poverty rates in 2007" and "Federal nutrition program spending in 2007"). Alaska, one of the top 10 states receiving federal nutrition dollars, is not shown.

■ Top 9 recipient states for child nutrition spending

States Resized by Per-Capita Federal Child Nutrition Funds Received

Standard US Map

CHIP is a program that pays for medical care for poor children not covered by Medicaid. The program, first enacted in 1997, is funded jointly by the states and the federal government, with states having significant discretion in determining benefit levels and covered services. In terms of coverage, CHIP has been an unqualified success. Between 1997 and 2007, for example, the number of medically uninsured poor and near-poor children in the United States dropped by more than a third, down to 15 percent among poor children.[39] A congressionally mandated study demonstrates that virtually all children in CHIP would not have any health insurance at all if not for the program.[40] CHIP was much in the news in 2007 as Democrats in Congress tried on separate occasions to raise the income limits on eligibility to 400 percent of the poverty threshold so that many more children would be covered, even those not considered poor. President Bush vetoed several CHIP expansion bills in 2007, citing the rising expenses of the program. President Obama signed a bill in early 2009 expanding the program, bringing in an additional 4 million children.

There is no question that Medicaid and CHIP have been very successful in terms of allowing many poor and disadvantaged people to gain access to needed medical services. But many people are worried about the rising costs to the federal government and to the states of these programs. Others worry less about the costs than about the fact that people of limited means remain uninsured, eligible neither for Medicaid nor CHIP, and not old enough for Medicare.

The Earned Income Tax Credit

The working poor benefit greatly from a provision in the U.S. Tax Code that allows low-income individuals with at least one child to claim a credit against taxes owed or, for some, to receive a direct cash transfer from the IRS. The Earned Income Tax Credit (EITC) of the Tax Code benefits more than 56 million low-income Americans without much bureaucratic fuss,[41] with about three-fourths of the total going to households earning between $5,000 and $20,000 per year.[42]

Differences in the American System of Social Safety Nets

18.5 Compare and contrast the American system of social safety nets with those in other rich democracies

The American system of social welfare is quite exceptional compared with those found in most other rich democracies.[43]

How Exceptional?

Here are the main ways the United States is different:

- **The American system is much less costly.** Despite complaints about its overall cost, ours is among the least costly of the social welfare states.[44] Among the rich democracies, only Japan and Australia spend relatively less than we do on social welfare, and Japan is well known for the generosity of company benefits to workers. Sweden, Denmark, and Finland, on the other hand, devote fully a third of GDP to social welfare of one kind or another, compared with about 16 percent in the United States.[45] The Scandinavian countries spend only twice as much as the United States, however, if one takes into account the high taxes citizens there pay on the benefits they receive and the American tendency to fund social welfare indirectly by widespread use of tax subsidies: the EITC, tax deductions for home mortgage interest, child care tax credits, and more.[46] But that is still a big difference.

- **The American system covers fewer people than systems in other rich democracies.** Most of the western European nations blanket their entire populations with benefits. Family allowances in places such as Austria, the Netherlands, Norway, and Sweden, for instance, go to all citizens who have children. In the United States, in contrast, social welfare provision is a patchwork, and many citizens are not protected or covered at all. (To be sure, some programs work in the sense that they effectively address a given problem, as you can see in the "Mapping American Politics" feature).

- **The American system favors the elderly, while others distribute benefits more evenly across age groups.** Medicare and Social Security, aimed at people 65 and older, make up the largest parts of the federal government's social safety net spending, far larger than programs whose benefits go to the nonelderly poor, especially children. In most other systems, family allowances and universal health care coverage keep benefit distributions more balanced. One result is a significant long-term decrease in the poverty rate among the elderly in the United States and a slower rate of poverty decline among children, as we have seen at several points in this chapter and in

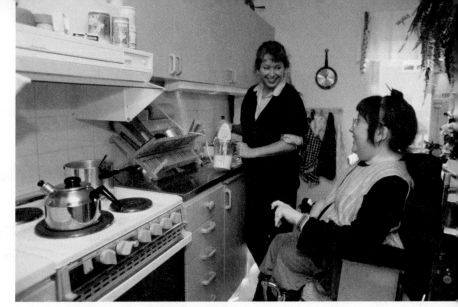

ENTITLED TO A HELPING HAND The Swedish universal health care system not only pays for almost all the costs of doctors, hospitals, and drugs, but it provides a wide range of services, including home helpers for those recovering from an illness or accident and for those with a permanent disability. Is such universal care a possibility for the United States? What difficulties might such a system pose?

Chapter 4. Recent expansions in the Medicaid and CHIP programs may reduce this disparity a little.

- **The American system is less redistributive.** The degree of income equality in the Organization for Economic Cooperation and Development (OECD) nations (with the exception of Japan) is a function of the amount of money they spend on social welfare programs and the degree to which program coverage is universal. The United States ranks very low on both, so our social welfare state does not make much of a dent in the degree of income and wealth inequality in comparison with those of other nations.[47] (See the "By the Numbers" feature in Chapter 4 for more on measuring cross-nation inequality.) Again, because the new health care system is funded to a substantial degree by increased taxes on upper-income groups in the United States, we may see a little more redistribution attributable to American safety net programs than has been the case so far in the years ahead.

- **The American system requires less of private employers.** All western European countries require that employers help employees with their parenting obligations. For example, all require employers to offer maternity and parenting leaves (now required for workers in firms with 50 or more employees in the United States under the Family and Medical Leave Act) with pay (not required here), and all require that work schedules be adjusted for parenting needs. German mothers receive six weeks' paid leave before giving birth and eight weeks' paid leave after. Further, all western European governments mandate four to six weeks of paid vacation.

- **The American system has not included universal health coverage until now, though it will get close to such coverage by the year 2020.** The OECD countries either provide health services directly to its populations (the National Health Service in Great Britain is an example), offer universal health insurance coverage (e.g., the Canadian system), or use some combination of the two. In the United States, the health care delivery and insurance systems have been extremely complex, with spotty and incomplete coverage for the population and with Medicare providing health insurance coverage for the elderly and a limited but important prescription drug benefit, Medicaid and CHIP providing coverage for many of the poor, and the Veterans Administration covering costs for veterans of the military and their dependents. Other Americans have depended on company-provided health insurance, bought their own private insurance, paid out-of-pocket for their health care needs, or did without. Until passage of the health reform act in 2010, more than 46 million people in the United States had no

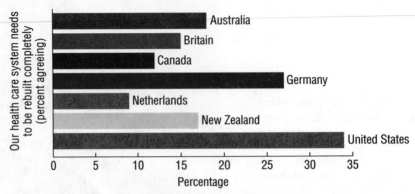

FIGURE 18.4 America's Health Care Compared

Americans told pollsters until quite recently that they were unhappy with their health care system, as this figure shows. Much more than in other rich democracies, they expressed a desire to see wholesale changes. Their dissatisfaction, until quite recently, is striking in light of the fact that Americans, through government and their own wallets, devoted much more of their national economic resources to health care than other rich countries. Will the recent health care reform change how Americans feel about their health care system and how much the system costs the nation? *Source:* Centers for Disease Control and Commonwealth Fund, as reported in "America's Angry Patients," *BusinessWeek*, November 12, 2007.

health insurance coverage at all. The system was very expensive compared to the systems in other rich democracies and people here were less satisfied with it than people elsewhere (see Figure 18.4). The new health care and insurance system that will gradually go into effect from now until 2020 will provide health care access to about three-quarters of the previously uninsured, fill many of the holes in coverage for the poor and the elderly, and keep insurance companies from denying coverage to people with preexisting conditions.

Factors That Influence the Shape of the American Welfare State

How to explain the special character of the American social welfare system? Here we identify structural and political linkage factors that influence the kind of social welfare state we have.

Constitutional Rules
Federalism is one reason social welfare programs were introduced here so late when compared to other rich democracies. Until the 1930s, it was not clear where the main responsibility for social welfare was constitutionally lodged. In fact, it was not generally accepted that the national government had any authority at all on social welfare matters until the U.S. Supreme Court belatedly relented and accepted the New Deal. Federalism is also responsible for the incredible administrative complexity of our system and for the great unevenness in program coverage. Because of federalism, that is, our system takes into account the needs and interests of each state. The result is great variation among the states in benefits, eligibility requirements, and rules. The only large-scale programs that are universal in the European sense (uniform,

comprehensive, and administered and funded by the national government) are Social Security and Medicare.

Racial Divisions

It is often argued that Europe's greater propensity toward welfare states with universal coverage is a result of the ethnic and racial homogeneity in their societies when they first created them. In homogeneous societies, the argument goes, voters are willing to support generous welfare programs because they believe recipients are very much like themselves—neighbors, down on their luck.[48]

Whether or not this argument is valid—the growing diversity within European countries, especially their large and growing Muslim populations, will eventually make it possible to test this idea—it is apparent that racial tensions influenced the shape of the American social welfare system. Some of the hostility toward AFDC, for instance, was probably related to the fact that African Americans made up a disproportionately large share of AFDC recipients (although less than a majority of all recipients) and that media stories about welfare recipients focused almost entirely on African Americans.[49]

Political Culture

Almost every aspect of the American political culture works against a generous and comprehensive social welfare system. The belief in competitive individualism is especially important. Voters who believe that people should stand on their own two feet and take responsibility for their lives are not likely to be sympathetic to appeals for helping able-bodied, working-age people.[50] Antigovernment themes in the political culture also play a role. Generous and comprehensive welfare states, such as those in Europe, are almost always large and centralized states supported by high taxes, and many Americans are deeply suspicious of politicians and centralized government, and resistant to high taxes. And, what one scholar calls the rise of the "cult of personal responsibility" is contributing to the privatization of social welfare with more pressure on people to take care of their own needs through devices like **health savings accounts (HSAs)** and 401(k) retirement plans.[51] Much of the Tea Party angry response to health care reform and the failure of the new program to rouse much enthusiasm so far among the public may have their roots in these strong cultural beliefs.

> **?** Will uncertainties about the availability of company-based pensions and medical coverage eventually convince people that government must do more in these areas, despite our "individualistic" political culture?

Business Power

Business plays a powerful role in American politics (see Chapter 7). Almost without exception, the business community has been a voice for low taxes and limited benefits and for voluntary efforts over government responsibility. This stance is most obvious in the area of medical care.[52] Ours is a patchwork quilt that combines social insurance for the elderly (Medicare), a means-tested program (Medicaid and CHIP) for *some* of the poor, private insurance (Blue Cross/Blue Shield, Prudential, etc.) for many Americans, and a multitude of for-profit hospitals and nursing homes. Doctors, hospital corporations, insurance companies, and nursing home owners are major players in the American system of interest group politics, and they continuously press politicians to maintain this system of mixed government–private enterprise medical care. Even when a massive health reform bill was passed in 2010, it happened in large part because most of the major business players in the system gained tangible benefits from it: more health insurance policies, many subsidized by government, for insurers to write; more paying patients for doctors and

health savings accounts (HSAs)
Tax-exempt savings accounts used for paying medical expenses.

hospitals; extension of Medicaid to help pay for nursing home beds; more Americans able to pay for prescription drugs from the large pharmaceutical firms; and few cost controls to slow the pace of national income going to the health care sector of the economy. A less costly single-payer system common in Canada and the OECD countries was a nonstarter in this environment, much to the chagrin of many liberal Democrats, as was a public option in state insurance pools.

Weak Labor Unions Countries where workers are organized and exercise significant political power have extensive and generous social welfare systems; countries where this is not the case have less extensive and generous social welfare systems.[53] American labor unions have never been as strong or influential as labor unions in most of the other rich democracies, partly because the proportion of American workers who belong to labor unions has always been and remains smaller than in comparable countries.

Using the **DEMOCRACY STANDARD**

Do Americans get the safety net policies they want from government?

It is extremely hard to determine if Americans get the kinds of safety net programs they want from government. On the one hand, we might easily argue that the size and types of programs fit what Americans say they want. For example, surveys show that strong majorities support Social Security and Medicare—achievements that were brought about by democratic struggles during the Great Depression (for the former) and the 1960s (for the latter), a fact confirmed on numerous occasions by voters' punishment of candidates who have dared to threaten either program. Although it took many years to achieve and the result is terribly complicated, Americans' desire for a prescription drug benefit was partially achieved. The public's desire for government to do something about lessening or eliminating poverty has borne some fruit, as programs such as the Earned Income Tax Credit, food stamps, CHIP, and Medicaid have helped to halve the poverty rate over the past five decades—although the poverty rate in the United States remains the highest among the rich democracies.

Until 2010, the most obvious hole in America's safety net was the absence of universal health insurance coverage. For many Americans, quality medical care had been out of reach because of high deductibles and denial of coverage by private insurance carriers for special-but-needed treatments and for numerous preexisting conditions; many were without health insurance coverage at all. Americans told pollsters for years that they wanted universal coverage—though there is a great deal of disagreement among people about what type of program would be best—and they had not gotten it, though it had been on the reform agenda of several Democratic and Republican presidents since the end of World War II. For the most part, these efforts were undermined by powerful interest groups—mainly doctors' and hospital associations, insurance companies, and pharmaceutical companies—that elected officials were loath to cross. To make health reform happen, these powerful interests had to be brought on board by accommodating their needs, perhaps undermining the objective of bringing overall health care costs under control. Whether a majority of the American public will eventually embrace the new health care system remains to be seen.

SUMMARY

18.1 Explain what safety nets are and why government provides them

- Safety nets are government protections for the minimum standards of living of its citizens.

- Safety nets typically are designed to compensate for some of the problems individuals face because of industrialization, urbanization, and technological change. In most of the rich democracies this includes income support for the poor and the elderly, direct provision of or insurance for health care services, nutrition support, and help during bouts of unemployment.

- Like all public policy, social welfare programs are largely a government response to structural and political linkage pressures; government is in the business of providing safety nets because voters and various interest groups have demanded them.

18.2 Differentiate among types of safety net programs in the U.S.

- The United States has a wide range of safety net programs that come in a variety of forms. The major distinction is between programs that are based on insurance principle such as Social Security and Medicare, and means-tested program such as food stamps and Medicaid.

- Programs can also be distinguished by whether they are funded and run out of Washington, joint programs of state and federal governments, or federal mandates on the states.

- Finally, programs may or may not be entitlements in which everyone who fits a particular description—age 65 or over for Medicare benefits, for example, or below a certain income level—is automatically covered.

18.3 Describe the main social insurance programs in the United States and assess their effectiveness

- Social insurance programs are programs like Social Security, Medicare, and unemployment compensation, in which individuals make contributions to an insurance trust fund by way of a payroll tax on their earnings and receive benefits based on their lifetime contributions.

- Social Security and Medicare have proven very successful and are highly popular. Both programs primarily benefit older Americans, as well as their dependents, survivors, and the disabled.

- The social welfare commitment of the federal government has grown substantially since the 1930s, with the most important recent growth occurring in the social insurance programs: Social Security and Medicare.

18.4 Describe the main means-tested programs in the United States and assess their effectiveness

- Means-tested benefits, also called public assistance, are benefits that are distributed on the basis of need to those who can prove that their income is low enough to qualify. These programs are funded by general income tax revenues, rather than by payroll taxes.

- The highly unpopular Aid to Families with Dependent Children (AFDC) was replaced in 1996 by Temporary Aid to Needy Families (TANF). TANF ended public assistance as an entitlement and handed much of the administrative duties for doling it out to the states in the form of block grants. TANF has been successful in shrinking the welfare rolls, but the degree to which it has helped lift former recipients out of poverty has not been impressive.

- Public assistance has grown more slowly than social insurance programs and accounts for a much smaller portion of the federal government's social welfare budget.

18.5 Compare and contrast the American system of social safety nets with those in other rich democracies

- The American welfare state is very different from others. Ours is smaller, less comprehensive, less redistributive, and more tilted toward the benefit of the elderly.

- Structural and political linkage factors explain most of the differences. Federalism and the decentralization of power in our constitutional system are important in this story, as is the prevailing political culture that celebrates individualism and is uncomfortable with big government. The power of business and the weakness of organized labor are important as well.

TEST YOURSELF

Answer key begins on page T-1.

18.1 Explain what safety nets are and why government provides them

1. The United States relies solely on a market economy to promote the welfare of its citizens.
   True / False
2. Why are industrialized democracies somewhat more difficult environments for traditional extended families than were pre-industrial societies?
   a. In industrialized democracies, citizens are less mobile.
   b. In industrialized democracies, women have fewer job prospects.
   c. In industrialized democracies, families are less likely to be intact.
   d. In industrialized democracies, citizens are more likely to get married and start families at a younger age.
   e. In industrialized democracies, government is less likely to look after the elderly and the infirm.

18.2 Differentiate among types of safety net programs in the U.S.

3. The poor are the main beneficiaries of American social welfare programs.
   True / False
4. Under the recently adopted health care reform legislation, nearly all citizens are required to have health insurance. Those who cannot afford insurance will receive government subsidies to enable them to purchase insurance. Which type of social safety net program does this most closely resemble?
   a. Medicare
   b. Medicaid
   c. Temporary Aid to Needy Families
   d. Social insurance programs
   e. Means-tested programs

18.3 Describe the main social insurance programs in the United States and assess their effectiveness

5. Many of those who are unemployed are not eligible for unemployment compensation.
   True / False
6. Which of the following would be the most effective in ensuring the long-term viability of Social Security?
   a. Cutting the payroll tax rate
   b. Lowering the ceiling of taxable income subject to the payroll tax

c. Lowering the retirement age
d. Reducing recipient benefits
e. Automatically adjusting benefits to account for the cost of living

7. Assess the effectiveness of Social Security and Medicare.

18.4 Describe the main means-tested programs in the United States and assess their effectiveness

8. While most Americans want to help the poor, they public remains deeply skeptical of means-tested programs.
   True / False
9. Which of the following means-tested programs has been eliminated?
   a. Temporary Aid to Needy Families
   b. Earned Income Tax Credit
   c. Food Stamps
   d. Children's Health Insurance Program
   e. Aid to Families with Dependent Children
10. Compare and contrast Temporary Aid to Needy Families and Aid to Families with Dependent Children.

18.5 Compare and contrast the American system of social safety nets with those in other rich democracies

11. The American social welfare system is much less expensive than those found in other rich democracies, in part because the American system covers fewer people.
    True / False
12. Which of the following tends to promote a more generous social welfare system?
    a. Strong labor unions
    b. A racially heterogeneous population
    c. Political culture that emphasizes individualism
    d. Political culture that stresses personal responsibility
    e. A federal system of government
13. If you were designing a social welfare system from scratch, would you follow the American model or the European model? Why?

myp⦿liscilab EXERCISES

Apply what you learned in this chapter on MyPoliSciLab.

📖—Read on **mypoliscilab.com**

    eText: Chapter 18

✓—**Study** and **Review** on **mypoliscilab.com**

    Pre-Test
    Post-Test
    Chapter Exam
    Flashcards

👁—Watch on **mypoliscilab.com**

    Video: Raising the Minimum Wage
    Video: Health Care Plan

✳—Explore on **mypoliscilab.com**

    Comparative: Comparing Health Systems
    Comparative: Comparing Social Welfare Systems
    Timeline: The Evolution of Social Welfare Policy

INTERNET SOURCES

American Enterprise Institute
www.aei.org
    A prominent conservative think tank with information about social policy.

The Center for Budget and Policy
http://www.cbpp.org/
    Descriptions of and studies on trends and outcomes for every federal social safety net program in the United States.

The Brookings Institution
www.brookings.org
    A center-left think tank with a wide-ranging agenda that includes many aspects of domestic policy.

Budget of the United States
www.whitehouse.gov/omb/budget/index.html
    The budget of the United States, with numbers, documentation, and analyses.

The Kaiser Family Foundation
www.kff.org
    A rich and unbiased source of information and analyses of virtually every aspect of America's health care system.

Fedstats
www.fedstats.gov
    Links to statistics and data from a broad range of federal government agencies, including those most relevant for economic and social welfare policy in the United States. These include the Federal Reserve Board, the Bureau of Labor Statistics, the Social Security Administration, the Bureau of the Census, the Bureau of Economic Analysis, and Administration for Children and Families.

Public Agenda Online
www.publicagenda.org/
    A nonpartisan site with comprehensive information about government policies, alternative proposals to solve societal problems, and what the public thinks about existing and alternative policies.

SUGGESTIONS FOR FURTHER READING

Hacker, Jacob S. *The Great Risk Shift.* New York: Oxford University Press, 2006.

Suggests that American social policies are moving away from public and shared provision of safety nets, leaving individuals increasingly to fend for themselves.

Handler, Joel F., and Yeheskel Hasenfeld. *Blame Welfare, Ignore Poverty and Inequality.* New York: Cambridge University Press, 2007.

A detailed history of American efforts to deal with the problems of poverty and inequality and why they mostly have failed.

Howard, Christopher. *The Hidden Welfare State.* Princeton, NJ: Princeton University Press, 2001.

Argues that the American welfare state is every bit as big and comprehensive as those of western Europe, but that they take a different form:

public–private partnerships, indirect subsidies and loan guarantees, and the like.

Page, Benjamin I., and James R. Simmons. *What Government Can Do: Dealing with Poverty and Inequality.* Chicago: University of Chicago Press, 2000.

A passionate, articulate, and empirically supported argument in favor of a larger role for government in alleviating poverty and making the United States a more equal society.

Peters, Guy B. *American Public Policy: Promise and Performance,* 8th ed. Washington, D.C.: CQ Press, 2010.

A comprehensive examination of the formation and content of American public policies.

IN THIS CHAPTER

19.1 Assess the extent to which foreign policymaking can be democratic

19.2 Explain why the United States is the world's superpower and analyze the policy choices it has in playing this role

19.3 Evaluate problems facing the post–Cold War world

19.4 Identify the main American foreign and national security policymakers

THE PRESIDENT MEETS WITH AMERICA'S BANKER

When President Barack Obama visited China for the first time in November 2009 for three days of talks with its president Hu Jintao, he brought along with him not only the usual officials responsible for military, diplomatic, and trade affairs, but also Peter Orszag, the director of the Office of Management and Budget. The budget director's job, as the title implies, is to help the president put together the annual budget of the United States, keep track of how executive branch agencies are sticking to budget targets, and plan with agency heads and top presidential aides on future budgets. So why was he in China? According to reports of the meetings, Chinese officials were concerned about the health care reform bill then being considered by Congress. They were not, of course, much concerned about whether the legislation, if it passed, would have a public option or ban the use of public monies for abortions. What they wanted to know was the likely long-term impact of the bill on American deficit spending. And the reason they wanted to know more about this is because China is the United States's biggest foreign lender, and it is likely to carry even more American loans on its books in the future.

The Chinese government, in the form of its sovereign wealth fund (a government-owned investment fund) and its treasury ministry, Chinese banks, and private Chinese citizens fund that debt mostly by buying U.S. Treasury securities. President Obama was in China, it soon became apparent, not only to talk with Chinese officials about nuclear proliferation in North Korea and Iran, the problems in U.S.–China relations tied to human rights, the status of Tibet, the future of Taiwan, and cyber attacks on American companies operating in China (Google in particular), but also to reassure one of its most important bankers that the United States would be able to pay its debts.[1]

This story is tied, of course, to China's remarkable rise as an economic power in the world since 1979, when market-oriented reforms were introduced by Deng Xiaoping and China opened itself to investment from abroad. Over the past quarter century, China's rate of GDP growth has been unprecedented, far higher than that of Great Britain, the United States, and Japan during their comparable periods of industrialization and "economic take-off." Over the past three decades, China grew by almost 10 percent a year, allowing

more people to leave the ranks of the poor over a shorter period of time than in any other place and in any other time in recorded history. By 2009, it had passed Germany as the world's biggest exporter and remains the destination of the largest pool of direct investment in the world. It was, at the time of President Obama's visit, the leading customer for the world's commodities as oil, iron ore, and phosphate ores poured into its ports to fuel its growth. The Chinese economy likely will surpass that of the United States by about 2027 if present trends continue. (China has almost five times as many people, however, so it will lag behind the United States for a very long time in terms of GDP per person; the standard of living of the average Chinese will not match that of the average American or European for some time to come.)[2]

Though it had been hit hard by the financial collapse in the United States and the world recession, China recovered fast and had begun to grow rapidly again in 2009, partly as a result of a massive stimulus funded by the country's huge financial reserves (it did not need to borrow money from others to stimulate its economy) even as the American and European economies languished and unemployment remained high. So, when President Obama paid his call, China had very strong cards to play on a wide range of issues. President Hu made no concessions to the U.S. president on the treatment of Tibet; offered no promises about doing anything concrete on North Korea or Iran (indeed, Chinese officials soon after announced that they did not consider more sanctions against Iran to be a useful strategy); and refused to consider revaluing its currency, the renminbi, which was contributing to America's enormous trade deficit with China. Nor did it offer to retreat from positions on greenhouse gas emissions that contributed to the failure of the Copenhagen meetings on climate to accomplish anything earlier that year. Nor did China release any political prisoners, a goodwill gesture that it had done routinely on past presidential visits.

The United States has gained a great deal from the rise of China, including a growing market for American manufacturers and farmers and a source of cheap consumer goods for American shoppers that contributes, for the most part, to higher standards of living here. And the willingness of the Chinese to buy up American debt and to accept very low rates of return on their investment has allowed us to expand public programs (including national defense) without fully taxing ourselves to pay for them. (Chapters 17 and 18 examine why this is not sustainable in the long run.) So in many ways, China and the United States are partners and allies. But our interests and those of China do not always coincide, and we continue to have deep disagreements on a wide range of issues. In the years ahead, China will have the means and perhaps the inclination to challenge the United States on a number of fronts internationally, because economic and political power in the world are usually closely associated. The same is true, over the long run, about the relationship of economic and military power. While the United States remains the world's unchallenged military superpower and continues to have the world's largest and most innovative economy, China is bound to have more say in the world's economic and diplomatic affairs in the years ahead, and its military capabilities are sure to improve. Figuring out how to deal with this rising power, how to make room for it, that is to say, is certain to be at the center of the concerns of American presidents and policymakers for a long time to come.

In this chapter, we examine American foreign and national security goals and policies, the nation's resources for achieving them, what constraints on America's freedom of action exist, and how policies in these areas are made. As always, we remain interested in whether the processes of making and carrying out these policies arise from democratic processes and whether Americans get the sorts of policies they want.

THINKING CRITICALLY About This Chapter

This chapter is about American foreign and military policies, how these policies are made, and how they affect Americans and others.

Using the FRAMEWORK

You will see in this chapter how foreign and military policies are the product of the interaction of structural factors (such as American economic and military power, and globalization), political linkage factors (such as the choices the media make about foreign news coverage, public opinion about what the U.S. role in the world ought to be, and what various interest groups want the government to do), and governmental factors (such as the objectives and actions of presidents, members of Congress, and important executive branch agencies such as the Central Intelligence Agency and the Joint Chiefs of Staff).

Using the DEMOCRACY STANDARD

Using the evaluative tools you learned in Chapter 1, you will see that foreign policy is not always made with the public as fully informed or as involved as they are in domestic affairs. You will see why this is so, ask whether policies would be better if they were made more democratically, and investigate how the public might play a larger role.

Foreign Policy and Democracy: A Contradiction in Terms?

19.1 Assess the extent to which foreign policymaking can be democratic

Making U.S. foreign and military policy has traditionally been different from making domestic policy. For one thing, presidents and the executive branch tend to play a much more important part than they do on domestic issues, primarily because the Constitution lodges most responsibilities and powers for foreign and military affairs there rather than in Congress. Most importantly, the Constitution makes the president commander-in-chief of the nation's armed forces as well as its chief diplomat, as described in Chapter 12 on the presidency. In the perpetual tug-of-war between presidents and Congress, presidents usually prevail in the midst of diplomatic or military crises. Also, the ordinary political factors, such as public opinion and interest groups, are sometimes set aside in favor of considerations of the **national interest,** as defined by a small number of national security advisers and other executive branch officials.

national interest
What is of benefit to the nation as a whole.

? How is the national interest determined? Do the people have a say in defining the country's goals? Should they have more of a say?

Other factors also explain why ordinary citizens play a smaller role in the formation of foreign and military policy than they do in the formation of domestic policy. Public opinion, for example, is sometimes reshaped or ignored by government leaders.[3] In crisis situations, moreover, the public often "rallies 'round the flag," accepting the president's actions, at least as long as the results seem good and there is little dissent among political leaders. When things go wrong or seem to be going wrong, however, domestic politics can return with a vengeance, as it did in the cases of both the Vietnam and Iraq wars, where public support eventually dwindled. Also, much of foreign policy is influenced by fundamental factors such as the power and resources of the United States and its economic interests abroad.

Involvement by ordinary citizens is also diminished by the sheer complexity of international matters, their remoteness from day-to-day life, and the unpredictability of other countries' actions; all of these tend to make the public's convictions about foreign policy less certain and more subject to revision in the light of events. In military matters, the need for speed, unity, and secrecy in decision making and the concentration of authority in the executive branch mandated by the Constitution mean that the public may be excluded and that government policy sometimes shapes public opinion rather than being shaped by it.

At the same time, however, the exclusion of the public is far from total. The American public has probably always played a bigger part in the making of foreign policy than some observers have imagined, and its role has become increasingly important in such foreign policy issues as trade, immigration, and global environmental protection. Note, for example, the very high involvement of the public in general, and interest groups in particular (labor unions, environmental organizations, corporations, business trade associations, and the like), in the struggle over ratification of the North American Free Trade Agreement (NAFTA) in 1993. Public involvement was high because most believed that the treaty would have important effects on jobs, wages, and environmental quality.

TINY COMPETITOR VW's Smart car will be a strong competitor in the global market for electric cars. To stay competitive, American companies also will need to produce appealing electric cars, either on their own or with direct or indirect assistance from government, something that governments do for all U.S. commercial rivals. What role should government play in this economic sector in the United States?

The World's Superpower (Still)

19.2 Explain why the United States is the world's superpower and analyze the policy choices it has in playing this role

superpower

A nation armed with nuclear weapons and able to project force anywhere on the globe.

In the autumn of 1990, the United States sent more than a half-million troops, 1,200 warplanes, and six aircraft carriers to the Persian Gulf region to roll back Iraq's invasion of Kuwait. In 1999, the United States supplied almost all the pilots, airplanes, ordinance, supplies, and intelligence for the NATO (the North Atlantic Treaty Organization) bombing campaign to force the Serb military out of Kosovo province. American armed forces overwhelmed the Taliban and Al Qaeda in Afghanistan in very short order following 9/11. In 2003, the United States invaded Iraq and in less than four weeks had routed Iraq's regular army and its Republican Guard; gained nominal control of all its major cities, including Baghdad; and removed the Saddam Hussein regime from power. These examples reflect the status of the United States as the world's **superpower**, the only nation strong enough militarily and economically to project its power into any area of the globe. (American forces have been used abroad for many years prior to the present period, of course, as the timeline in Figure 19.1 indicates.) In this section, we examine the foundations of this superpower status but also how these foundations are beginning to erode.

The American Superpower: Structural Foundations

A nation's place in the international system is largely determined by its *relative* economic, military, and cultural power. Since the end of the Second World War in 1945,

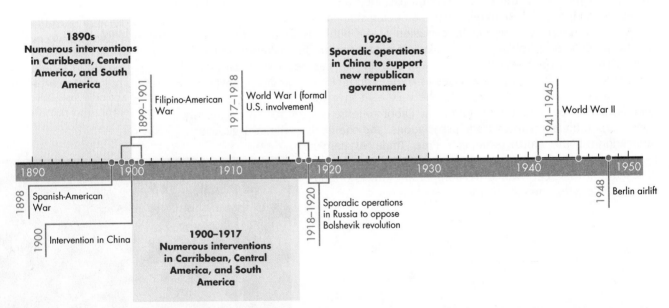

FIGURE 19.1 Timeline: Significant American Foreign Military Operations and Conflicts, Post–Civil War*

*Does not include foreign interventions by agencies, such as the CIA, that have not involved the armed services of the United States. *Source:* In part, from Pearson Education, publishing on Infoplease.com

the United States has enjoyed strong advantages over other countries in all three, although U.S. advantages have eroded to some degree. Still, the combination of economic, military, and cultural advantages the United States enjoys makes it the world's only superpower, although not as preeminent as some only recently had proposed. There was widespread talk in the United States and Europe in the late 1990s and early 2000s, some approving, some disapproving, of the emergence of a new American empire,[4] though the talk died out as the United States got bogged down in Iraq and Afghanistan, its financial system collapsed in 2008, and China began to play a more prominent role in world economic recovery.

Economic Power In 2009, the United States had a population of about 310 million people—considerably fewer than China's 1.3 billion or India's roughly 1.1 billion—but enough to support the world's largest economy, with an annual gross domestic product (GDP) of close to $14.3 trillion. This was about equal to the combined economies of the next four largest in the world, China, Japan, Germany, and France. The United States's GDP, moreover, was about three times larger than that of fast-rising China (but five times larger on a per-capita basis). The United States also ranked first in the world in total imports, though it trailed Germany and China in total exports.[5] (See the "Mapping American Politics" feature for more information on the United States's standing in world trade.)

Starting in the 1990s, U.S.-headquartered companies established preeminence in the economic sectors that count the most in the new global economy: telecommunications, mass entertainment, biotechnology, software, finance, e-commerce, business services, transportation, and computer chips (see Chapter 4). Despite the financial sector's 2008 disaster and the Great Recession associated with it, many U.S.-headquartered companies outside the automobile industry continued to prosper globally even as European-, Chinese-, Brazilian-, and Indian-based companies proved to be formidable competitors.

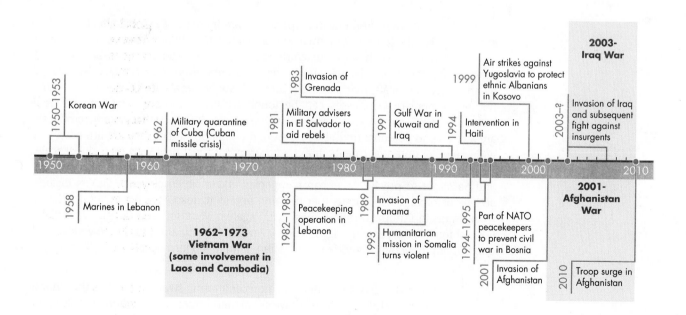

The United States in the World Trading System

Introduction What a government does is strongly influenced by the health and vitality of its economy. American political leaders recognize that their election or re-election to office depends a great deal on how well Americans are doing economically and strive to produce policies that contribute to economic growth and stability. Many of these policies have to do with the position of the United States in the world trading system. For the most part, government leaders, along with most economists, believe that participation in the global trading system benefits all countries that take part in it, a position that critics of globalization, including American trade unionists, dispute. Many political scientists and economists also believe that democracy and involvement in the global economy are strongly associated, primarily because countries that engage in the global

economy grow rich enough to generate a democracy-seeking middle class and cannot help but expose their people to a diverse set of ideas and cultural influences. So where does the United States stand in relationship to other countries in terms of its involvement in trade? And how democratic are trading nations?

Mapping Trade and Democracy The cartogram shows countries sized in relationship to their total trade, the sum of their exports and imports, in 2004. (China would be much larger if 2010 data were used but total trade numbers were unavailable for many countries at this writing.) The more trade a country

The fact that major American corporations are increasingly global affects U.S. foreign policy. For the largest of them, a substantial portion of their revenues comes from sales abroad, much of their manufacturing takes place in other countries, and many of the parts for items manufactured domestically are imported. And in industries such as oil and petrochemicals, many of the sources of raw materials are outside our borders. Because American businesses can be found almost anywhere, American national interests can be said to exist almost anywhere as well. It follows that American officials are attentive to potential trouble spots around the globe. Today, they are attentive to a wide range of potential threats that the government must deal with on a global scale. One is **terrorism** (whether the threat is to government installations, such as embassies and bases, or to private American companies and their employees). Others include actions of other governments that threaten access to resources (as in Venezuela) or markets (as in European Union fines levied against Microsoft and Google), and violations of intellectual property rights held by American companies (as in the widespread practice of producing counterfeit—and often, tainted—pharmaceuticals in China).

Military Power This enormous economic strength enables the United States to field the most powerful armed forces in the world. The scale of military American superiority, as well as the nation's ability to deploy and use these resources, is orders of magnitude beyond any existing or potential rival. Here are a few indicators of this disproportionality of U.S. military power:[6]

terrorism

The use of deadly violence against civilians to further some political goal.

engages in, the larger it is in the cartogram relative to its size on standard maps; the less trade a country engages in, the smaller it is relatively. The colors reflect levels of democracy based on Freedom House criteria that are similar to our definition of democracy in Chapter 1. Several things are immediately obvious. First, the United States is a major player in world trade, which most economists believe adds to its GDP and standard of living. Second, countries in western Europe are very big traders, as are Japan and South Korea. Third, some countries and regions play a relatively tiny role in world trade, including Central America, South America, and, most dramatically, sub-Sahara Africa (which, with the exception of South Africa, almost disappears from the cartogram). Russia also plays a surprisingly small role in the world trading system, although the emergence of its oil industry is changing this. Finally, the largest exporting countries tend to be democracies, although this is not true for China or Saudi Arabia, the former importing and exporting a wide range of products, the latter being the world's largest exporter of petroleum.

What Do You Think? Would it be a good thing if the United States further increased its level of trade? How would American workers and consumers be better off with more trade? With less? Does the cartogram suggest that freedom and trade are associated? What does the lack of freedom in China and Saudi Arabia suggest? If trade and democracy are linked, would you expect China and Saudi Arabia to become freer in the future?

Sources: Exports and imports in dollars taken from the World Bank: http://stat.wto.org/StatisticalProgram/WsdbExport.aspx? Language=E; democracy scoring from Freedom House online database at www.freedomhouse.org.

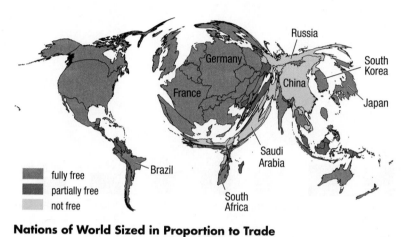

fully free
partially free
not free

Nations of World Sized in Proportion to Trade

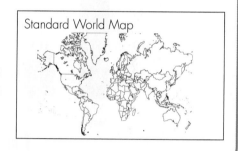

Standard World Map

- The United States's defense budget exceeded those of all other NATO countries (including the United Kingdom, France, Germany, Italy, and more), Russia, China, Japan, Saudi Arabia, and India combined (see Figure 19.2). Indeed, the defense budget of the United States was more than that of the next 25 nations combined.

- The United States's naval power is unrivaled. It has 11 super carrier battle groups in operation; no other country has even one super carrier vessel—ships that displace at least 70,000 tons—let alone full battle groups (though the U.K. is building two super carriers and France is building one). It has more modern submarines, moreover, than the rest of the world combined, including the stealthy Seawolf-class, nuclear-powered submarine.

- The United States's air power is unrivaled. It has more advanced fighter aircraft and bombers, many of the stealth variety, than the rest of the world combined. Its aerial tanker fleet allows these aircraft to reach any target in the world. These aircraft also have the advantage of carrying a varied arsenal of "smart" munitions.

- The United States's ground warfare capabilities are unrivaled. While China has a large standing army, it is not as well armed as U.S. ground forces and lacks many of the logistical and technological capabilities of American forces, though it is being rapidly modernized. In addition, no other nation comes close to matching America's armored forces, which include approximately 9,000 M1 Abrams tanks, firing smart munitions.

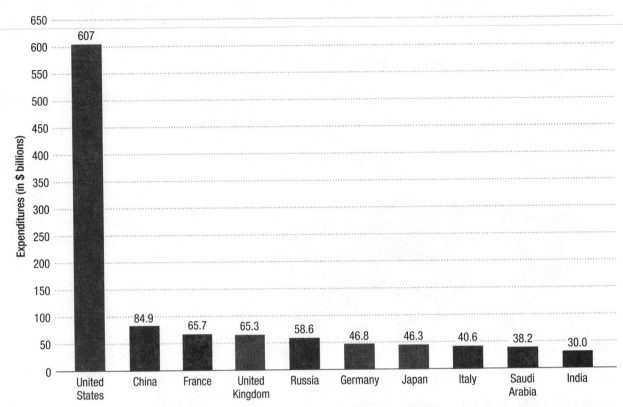

FIGURE 19.2 Expenditures for National Defense, 2008 (not including the cost of combat operations in Iraq or Afghanistan)

The national defense budget of the United States is orders of magnitude higher than those of friends and potential foes alike. There is no reason to suspect this will change, although China is rapidly modernizing its military forces. *Source:* Stockholm International Peace Research Institute.

- The United States's electronic warfare capabilities are unrivaled. These capabilities include, among other things, global positioning systems to guide smart weapons to their targets, self-guided anti-tank missiles that seek out enemy tanks, sophisticated jamming systems to confuse anti-aircraft guns and missiles, and underwater sensing systems to track submarines.

- The United States's strategic nuclear arsenal is unrivaled, with approximately 5,000 active and deployed nuclear warheads—to be cut to roughly 2,000 by 2012—that can be delivered to their targets by strategic bombers, land-based intercontinental ballistic missiles, and submarines.

- The United States is the only country in the world with permanent and often sizable military bases in every part of the world.[7]

- As demonstrated by its use of missiles coordinated by naval ships at sea to destroy an errant spy satellite in space in February 2008, the United States has formidable and growing capabilities in space warfare and, perhaps, missile defense.

Although potential rivals to American military dominance have a way to go, they remain formidable. Russia, after the breakup of the Soviet Union left its economy and once-proud military in disarray, for a time avoided foreign adventures and cut its nuclear and conventional arms under international treaties. In 2008, however, Russia invaded the small country of Georgia, serving notice that it could cause trouble if it or Ukraine were allowed to join NATO. It also reminded the West that it was eager to use its considerable reserves of oil and natural gas to wield diplomatic power in Europe and the world. Russia also announced a 25 percent increase in its military budget. China has a fast-growing economy and millions of military personnel and is rapidly upgrading its capabilities, but it remains far behind U.S. capabilities. A July 2005 Pentagon report concluded, in fact, that China's ability to project conventional military force beyond its borders remains limited for the time being,[8] although it did overtake Japan in 2007 in defense expenditures, has been growing its defense budget at 12 percent a year for a number of years (it announced that it would be reduced to 7.5 percent increase for 2010, however[9]), is dramatically improving its submarine force and anti-ship missile systems, is building its offensive and defensive cyber-war capacities, and has made great strides in developing anti-spy satellite missiles.[10] The richest countries of western Europe (United Kingdom, Germany, France, and Italy) together have relatively small military establishments and a relatively small number of nuclear weapons. They do, however, produce, deploy, and operate very sophisticated military technologies, usually under the umbrella of NATO, in which the United States plays the leading role.

As much as the United States spends on national defense, and as numerous and as sophisticated its weaponry, its military is clearly overstretched, according to most observers. This is partly a result of decreasing the size of the military, first, in the 1990s (after the collapse of the Soviet Union removed our main military threat at the time), and then during George W. Bush's first term when then Secretary of Defense Donald Rumsfeld pushed for a lighter, more mobile, and technologically advanced force. As a result of these changes, active-duty troop totals dropped from about 2 million in the early 1990s to about 1.4 million by 2006, then grew again to 1.6 million by 2009 as the United States was engaged in two wars. It is also partly the result of shifting procurement to high-tech weaponry at the expense of more mundane but vital equipment. The wars in Iraq and Afghanistan, added on top of the normal responsibilities of the military, exposed these problems for all to see: repeated and long tours of duty for active-duty troops and shorter rest periods between deployments, unprecedented

HARD DEPLOYMENT A Florida national guardsman hugs his wife before her unit is deployed to Iraq in early 2010. Fighting two wars at the same time, staffing military bases in scores of countries, searching out terrorists in many places, and patrolling most of the world's oceans has placed considerable stress on the American military services and the people who serve in them. Should we be playing such a large role in the world? With whom might we share the burden? Would that be in our national interest?

dependence on national guard and reserve forces, and shortages of equipment like body armor and armored Humvees. Outgoing Chairman of the Joint Chiefs of Staff General Peter Pace reported to Congress in late 2007 that the ability of the United States to respond to a major military crisis in another part of the world was eroding.[11]

Even with its considerable military power, the United States is not omnipotent. For example, conventional and strategic military power may not be terribly useful in rooting out terrorism. A terrorist enemy is not a country, but rather loosely organized shadow cells that may best be uprooted by police investigations and intelligence-gathering operations in cooperation with other countries. America's military might, moreover, has not enabled it to control events in important oil-producing nations—including Venezuela, Nigeria, Russia, and Iran—where direct intervention would adversely affect oil supplies and prices. It has not been of much use in leading Israel and the Palestinian Authority to a peace agreement. And, perhaps most importantly, we have seen that resourceful enemies, using what has been called **asymmetric warfare** tactics and weapons—roadside bombs, rocket-propelled grenades, sniper rifles, and AK-47 assault rifles—can inflict tremendous damage on U.S. conventional forces and on forces allied with us, as has happened in Iraq and Afghanistan. Worse yet, an overwhelming military response to these tactics against those who hide among the civilian population has proved extremely problematic in many cases.

? Is our military supremacy effective against those who use asymmetric tactics against us? How might we better counter such threats?

It seems as if the American military has gotten the message. Early in 2008, for example, the Army issued a new operations manual that not only emphasizes its traditional mission of defeating the adversary in the field, but gives equal footing to stabilizing war-torn nations and fighting counterinsurgencies against foes using asymmetric tactics from among vulnerable civilian populations.[12] (The Marines similarly changed their operations manual.) The idea is that the Army will emphasize these multiple missions in its training and operations, as well as in its procurement policies. The new manual was shaped by General David Petraeus's influential counterinsurgency manual written several years earlier (and ignored by then-Defense Secretary Donald Rumsfeld), parts of which were put into effect when he led the "surge" in Iraq in 2007 and 2008. Before he was removed from command and replaced by David Petraeus, General Stanley McChrystal employed similar counterinsurgency tactics in the Afghanistan surge in 2010, drastically reducing airstrikes in heavily populated areas, for example, unless U.S. forces were in imminent danger.

"Soft Power"   Although critics here and abroad often decry "Americanization"—by which they generally mean the spread of McDonald's, Kentucky Fried Chicken, Disney theme parks, and Hollywood movies and television sitcoms and dramas—we should not underestimate the influence of what some have called America's **soft power**: the attractiveness of its culture, ideology, and way of life for many people living in other countries. As political scientist Joseph Nye has pointed out, it is important for the U.S. position in the world that more than a half-million foreign students study in American colleges and universities; that people in other countries flock to American entertainment and cultural products; that English has become the language of the Internet, business, science, and technology; and that the openness and opportunity of American society are admired by many people around the world.[13] If this very openness and opportunity place the United States in the best position to prosper in the new global,

asymmetric warfare

Unconventional tactics used by a combatant against an enemy with superior conventional military capabilities.

soft power

Influence in world affairs that derives from the attractiveness to others of a nation's culture, products, and way of life.

information-based economy—which many believe to be the case—then the United States's soft power enhances its harder economic and military powers.[14]

? How important is soft power anyway? Is the need for it overrated? If you think it is important, how might President Obama begin repairing America's soft power?

The United States almost squandered its soft power advantage after the invasion of Iraq in the spring of 2003, when anti-Americanism rose dramatically. Although this was most pronounced in the Arab and Muslim worlds, it also intensified in western Europe, Latin America, and Russia.[15] The Pew Research Center reported the following grim news in 2005, based on its annual surveys in countries around the world: " ... anti-Americanism is deeper and broader now than at any time in modern history. It is most acute in the Muslim world, but it spans the globe—from Europe to Asia, from South America to Africa."[16] (See the drop in U.S. favorability between 1999 and 2007 in Figure 19.3.) The reasons for the drop were reasonably straightforward. First, the invasion was extremely unpopular outside the United States even in countries allied at the time with the United States, including the United Kingdom, Italy, and Spain.[17] Second, revelations of the use of torture of prisoners at Abu Ghraib in Iraq and at Guantanamo further undermined America's standing. Third and finally, both foreign publics and leaders expressed concern at the unilateralist tendencies of the United States under President George W. Bush, especially his renunciation of several international treaties and the proclamation of the right of the United States to take preemptive/preventive military action when the president considered it appropriate.

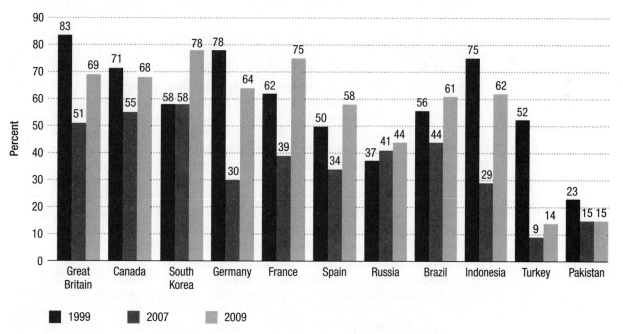

FIGURE 19.3 Favorable Views of the United States, 1999, 2007, and 2009
Based on its surveys in selected countries, the Pew Research Center reports that favorable views of the United States declined precipitously between 1999 and 2007 but rebounded a great deal in 2009 because of the popularity abroad of President Obama and his more multilateral approach to foreign affairs. *Source:* "Confidence in Obama Lifts U.S. Image Around the World" (Washington, D.C.: Pew Research Center Global Attitudes Survey, July 23, 2009).

President Barack Obama has made restoring America's image and standing in the world a top priority. Both his broad popularity[18] and changes in presidential language about America's place in the world—more negotiations with adversaries and increased collaboration with allies and international bodies—gave a big boost to the United States's favorability around the world (see the 2007–2009 differences in Figure 19.3). It is not clear, however, whether these effects will be long lasting, especially if the war in Afghanistan continues and civilian casualties increase. We do not know yet, moreover, whether the financial collapse and the Great Recession will negatively color how people and leaders around the world feel about the United States as a responsible and trusted leader of the world's trade and financial system.

The American Superpower: Strategic Alternatives

The United States must make a number of decisions about how to use its considerable power.

Goals   Like the leaders of any other country in the international system, foreign and military policymakers, most especially the president, take as one of their primary duties the defense of the nation against real or potential attacks. This goes almost without saying. Like the leaders of any other country in the international system, moreover, American leaders try to first define and then advance and protect the national interest. Components of the national interest are hard to clearly define, to be sure, and people disagree about what they might be, but at a minimum they include such things as protecting American citizens when they are living or traveling abroad and ensuring that American firms are treated fairly when operating in other countries, that vital raw materials (including oil) are available to consumers and firms, and that markets remain open to American goods and services.

But what about the goal of spreading American values? Whether rightly or wrongly, many Americans, including many political leaders, have believed that the United States has a special mission to improve the world by spreading liberty and representative democracy; many others have said that improving the world also involves spreading free enterprise and open markets. While President Bush perhaps more clearly articulated these goals as essential elements of American foreign policy than other recent presidents, his aspirations for American foreign policy would not have been unfamiliar to Thomas Jefferson (who referred to the United States as "the empire of liberty"), Woodrow Wilson ("the world must be made safe for democracy"), Franklin Roosevelt (the "four freedoms"), or John F. Kennedy (whose inaugural address pledged to "oppose any foe to assure the survival and success of liberty"). One scholar suggests, in fact, that while President Bush's rhetoric may have been different, "the U.S. quest for an international order based on freedom, self-determination, and open markets has changed astonishingly little."[19] President Barack Obama has expressed more modest goals.

Finally, it has long been argued by foreign policy experts and political leaders that the dominant global power—political scientists call such countries **hegemons**[20]— must provide a range of services to the international system if the world is to enjoy any degree of stability. These include using one's power to put down states that upset the global order, protecting the international trading system, and providing economic leadership. This role was played by the United Kingdom for much of the nineteenth century and by France and Spain before then in the European context. The Ottoman Empire played a similar role in the sixteenth century for large swatches of the known world. Until quite recently, many believed that it is the turn of the United States to play the role of hegemon.[21] It must not only protect itself from attack and

hegemon

Term used to refer to the dominant power during various historical periods that takes on responsibilities for maintaining and protecting a regional or global system.

pursue its own interests, but use its power to prevent the outbreak of regional wars (India and Pakistan, perhaps), stop the spread of **weapons of mass destruction,** coordinate the effort to prevent pandemics, provide protection for a wide range of countries important for the world economy (e.g., European countries and Japan), protect and maintain the international trading and financial systems (i.e., patrol key shipping lanes, provide the world's reserve currency, act as the world's banker—for the most part, through the World Bank and the International Monetary Fund), and help make and enforce trade rules.

Do Americans and their leaders believe that U.S. foreign policy goals should include more than national defense and a strict focus on defending national interests? It is not clear that either leaders or citizens support such goals, nor is it certain that they want to assume the responsibility for and shoulder the costs in lives and dollars of spreading American values and acting as the global hegemon. Nor is it clear that rising global powers such as China, Brazil, Russia, and India want the United States to fill the role of hegemon or believe it is capable of doing so. There is some talk in policy circles about a possible collaborative leadership by the United States and China, a group of 2 (G-2),[22] if you will, but that seems unlikely at the moment because neither U.S. nor Chinese leaders seem interested.

Approaches to Using America's Power

American leaders and citizens must decide not only what goals to pursue as a superpower, but how best to go about using its power. Debate about this has been organized around two poles:

- **Unilateralists** would have the United States pursue American national interests in the world on a "go it alone" basis, if necessary. While it might often act in concert with others, unilateralists would have the United States act on the international stage on its own terms, without asking the permission of others, binding itself to restrictive international agreements, or following the lead of international organizations such as the United Nations. The existence of this theme in American foreign policy may explain, for example, the United States's unwillingness to sign treaties to establish an international criminal court and ban land mines. Unilateralists are also interested in using American power unilaterally, if it comes to that, to spread American values such as liberty, free enterprise, and democracy, believing these values to be universally valid and appealing. Unilateralists do not see a contradiction between power and principle. Indeed, they believe that they are inextricable.[23]

weapons of mass destruction
Nuclear, biological, or chemical weapons with the potential to cause vast harm to human populations.

unilateralists
Those who believe the United States should vigorously use its military and diplomatic power to pursue American national interests in the world, but on a "go it alone" basis.

WAITING TO VOTE   Should the goal of American foreign policy be the extension of democracy, or is that a matter for people in other countries to decide for themselves? Here, women in Afghanistan wait to vote in a mosque in that country's presidential election in 2009 arranged with the help, encouragement, and pressure of the American government. Since then, widespread corruption and a Taliban revival have sapped some of the initial enthusiasm for democracy of the Afghan people.

multilateralists

Those who believe the United States should use its military and diplomatic power in the world in cooperation with other nations and international organizations.

global climate change

The upset of historical climate patterns, with rising temperatures and more extreme climate events, tied to the increase in atmospheric carbon whether caused by human activities or naturally occurring cycles.

Cold War

The period of tense relations between the United States and the Soviet Union from the late 1940s to the late 1980s.

For most of his presidency, George Bush was a strong advocate of unilateralism. By the end of the Bush years, the cost—in lives, treasure, and global favorability—of war and occupation in Iraq and the continuing struggle in Afghanistan had dampened much of the enthusiasm for unilateralism.

- **Multilateralists** believe that American interests are compatible with the interests of others in the world and that protecting these interests requires cooperation and collaboration with other nations and international organizations. Although the United States is undeniably the most powerful nation in the world, the thinking goes, it cannot solve all important problems on its own. Problems such as **global climate change**, pollution, the wider availability of the means to make weapons of mass destruction, the spread of AIDS and other infectious diseases, and terrorism threaten virtually every country in the world, and solving these problems, insist multilateralists, will require broad cooperation and collaboration by many countries and international organizations.[24] Barack Obama is a firm supporter of this view and articulates it often in his public addresses, though, to be sure, he intensified fighting in Afghanistan in 2010 despite unhappiness among and a drawdown of forces by some NATO allies.[25]

Problems of the Post–Cold War World

19.3 Evaluate problems facing the post–Cold War world

With the end of the **Cold War**, the main concerns of that era—the possibility of global thermonuclear war, a land war in Europe against the Soviet Union, and communist takeovers of Third World countries—have disappeared from the list of foreign policy problems that concern Americans and their leaders. But a host of problems remain and new ones have arisen. We review these in the next several sections, keeping in mind that the debate among unilateralists and multilateralists will help shape our response to each one.

Security Issues

Although the security threat represented by the Soviet Union has disappeared, many threats to American security remain.

Terrorism   The issue of terrorism moved front-and-center on the American political agenda after the September 11, 2001, attacks on the World Trade Center and the Pentagon. The retaliatory U.S. attacks on the Taliban regime and Al Qaeda in Afghanistan were the first among many steps that have been taken and will be taken in terms of a military response to terrorist attacks and threats. These include a wide range of overt and covert activities, some undertaken in cooperation with others, some undertaken unilaterally. At a minimum, American policymakers will try to improve intelligence gathering (sharply criticized by the 9/11 Commission in 2004), create rapid-strike armed forces to attack terrorist cells, and increase the use of drone aircraft surveillance and missile strikes as President Obama did in Yemen and the Afghanistan–Pakistan border area.

Despite all the attention and resources thrown at the problem of terrorism, a bleak 2007 National Intelligence Estimate concluded that the United States, on balance, was no safer from a terrorist attack than it had been prior to 9/11. This summary judgment by the nation's intelligence agencies reported that while important strides had been made in many areas to protect the homeland, these were counterbalanced by rising anger among many Muslims generated by the continuing conflict in Iraq, the proliferation of jihadist Internet sites, and the continuing presence of Al Qaeda and other radical jihadists in the frontier regions of Pakistan.[26]

Other nations are more skeptical of a military response to the threat of terrorism, believing that solid policing and intelligence operations offer better protection. Critics of this view would point to devastating terrorist attacks against civilians in London and Madrid, but European, Egyptian, and Pakistani officials also have exposed a number of terrorist plots and made widespread arrests using these methods. Military responses, moreover, are unlikely to improve America's security against large-scale cyber attacks on the nation's economic, military, energy, or communications infrastructure. And policing and intelligence gathering would seem to be the only way to address a possible increase in the number of homegrown terrorists. In the long run, then, it is likely that military, policing, and intelligence methods to counter terrorism will all be necessary, the choice of methods depending on circumstances.

> **axis of evil**
>
> Three countries—Iraq, Iran, and North Korea—named by President Bush in 2002 as significant threats to the security of the United States because of their purported ties to terrorism and/or weapons of mass destruction.

Weapons of Mass Destruction

In his 2002 State of the Union address, President Bush designated Iraq, Iran, and North Korea as the **axis of evil**, nations both capable of creating weapons of mass destruction—chemical, biological, and/or nuclear—and using them against neighbors, American allies, or the United States. We know now that Iraq did not have a credible nuclear weapons program—the original reason given for the invasion in 2003—but that North Korea has one and that Iran is well on its way to producing weapons-grade nuclear material. The problem of the spread and use of weapons of mass destruction, whether by so-called rogue nations—North Korea has given technical assistance to Iran—factions within disintegrating nations, terrorists, or nuclear scientists in places such as Pakistan seeking financial gain, is surely real, although how to go about addressing this danger is not entirely obvious.

With respect to North Korea and Iran, some mix of diplomatic pressure, multilateral organized sanctions, International Atomic Energy Agency inspections, and threats of force have all been used. North Korea eventually agreed in 2007 to stop its program but then restarted it and blocked weapons inspectors. Iran has rejected British, French, German, Russian, and U.N. diplomatic efforts to slow its nuclear development. President Obama in 2010 successfully pressed the U.N., and in particular Russia and China (each of whom has warm trade relations with Iran), to increase targeted sanctions against Iran's Revolutionary Guard who direct that nation's program while trying to hold off a military strike by Israel. Many commentators fear that

TERROR ATTACK ON MUMBAI Smoke pours from the Taj hotel after a coordinated attack on multiple locations in the city was carried out by Islamic extremists from Pakistan. How to keep the enduring conflict between India and Pakistan—both American allies with nuclear weapons—from getting out of hand remains a daunting puzzle for the people of the area and for U.S. foreign policymakers. How much influence does the United States have on the outcome of this conflict, and should it be an American foreign policy concern?

nuclear proliferation
The spread of nuclear weapons to additional countries or to terrorist groups.

development of a nuclear weapon by Shiite-led Iran might lead to a nuclear arms race that would include the Sunni-led regimes of Egypt, Saudi Arabia, and Syria.

The collapse of the centralized communist regime in the Soviet Union in the early 1990s and its breakup into several independent countries threw into question the fate of the vast Russian and former Soviet armed forces, with their millions of troops and many nuclear weapons—more than 10,000 of them. But the United States worked out agreements for drastic reductions in Russian, Ukrainian, and Kazakh nuclear weaponry while Ukraine and Kazakhstan renounced nuclear weapons altogether.

While a high-priority task for American foreign policy for decades has been to prevent **nuclear proliferation,** President Bush signed a nuclear cooperation treaty with India in 2006 that seemed to give India the go-ahead to speed up its weapons program. The new treaty allows India to import nuclear fuel and technology from abroad and keep its military facilities free from inspections, something that worries many advocates of nonproliferation in the United States and abroad. President Obama, on the other hand, says he wants to eliminate nuclear weapons entirely and has pressed hard with the Russians and Chinese in particular to reach further arms reduction agreements.

For many in the U.S. defense establishment, however, Pakistan represents the most significant proliferation threat, given its history and the turmoil that exists in the country. For one thing, Pakistan scientist A. Q. Khan, probably with help from parts of the state security services, was responsible for helping develop nuclear weapons programs in North Korea, Iran, and Libya. For another, Pakistan is itself a nuclear power, has regions under the control of jihadists, and has a state security service riddled with people with long-term ties to the Taliban and terrorists operating in Kashmir.

The Middle East Although some countries there have huge oil wealth, the Middle East is home to some of the least developed nations in the world in terms of economic development, democracy and freedom, women's rights, and education.[27] It is also a veritable tinderbox, with a number of conflicts festering. There is the one between Shiite and Sunni Muslims, intensified by the war in Iraq, to be sure, but tied in the long run to Shiite Iran's growing power and regional ambitions and discomfort with these developments on the part of the Sunni governments of Saudi Arabia, Egypt, Jordan, and Persian Gulf states. Ironically, perhaps, it was America's toppling of Saddam Hussein's regime, Iran's fiercest opponent in the region, that did the most to boost Iran's regional power.

There is, as well, the long conflict between Turkey and the Kurds, with Turkey conducting cross-border incursions into Iraq to battle anti-Turkish PKK guerillas and other elements yearning for an independent Kurdistan (which would include portions of Turkey). In this conflict, the United States is caught in the middle. Turkey is a NATO ally with a long-standing military alliance with the United States, while a vibrant Kurdistan of sorts has emerged in the north of Iraq, the product of American air protection against Saddam Hussein that had been in place since the First Gulf War.

Then there is the seemingly unending conflict between Israel and the Palestinians, which stirs passions in the Arab and Muslim worlds and feeds anti-Americanism. What to do about this conflict is a matter of intense debate. Although groups such as Hamas and Hezbollah are committed to the destruction of Israel, most of the Arab states in the region support some sort of two-state solution in which Israel and Palestine live side by side as independent countries. The United States and the European Union are committed to this outcome, as is the majority of the Israeli public. A majority of the Palestinian public was presumed to favor the same solution, but the election of Hamas as the majority party in the Palestinian parliament in early 2006 raised some doubts. The Israelis seem to have come to the conclusion that no negotiating partner exists on the Palestinian side and that the best policy is to simply disengage from the Palestinians unilaterally. Israel withdrew entirely from Gaza in 2005 under Ariel Sharon and started construction of a security wall to separate Israelis and Palestinians near the borders of Israel and the West Bank. Tensions in the area remain high, with the continuation of the harsh Israeli occupation of the West Bank and growing Israeli settlements in the occupied territories, and attacks by various militant Palestinian factions on Israeli targets. In 2006, Israel fought a war against the Iran-backed Hezbollah militia in the south of Lebanon, highlighted by fierce fighting, many civilian casualties, and missiles landing in northern Israel. In 2008, Israel invaded Gaza to root out Hamas and stop missiles fired from there; infrastructure destruction and civilian casualties in Gaza were substantial.

As if the Israeli-Palestinian and Israel-Hezbollah-Iran conflicts were not enough to render the Arab Middle East a tinderbox, it is also a place where people are saddled with unelected and corrupt governments, near-useless educational systems, stagnant economies, and mass unemployment. This inevitably feeds popular discontent and threatens instability in a region that is vital to the world's energy supply, although governments in the region have managed so far to channel most popular discontent into anger against the West, the Americans, the Jews, and Israel, using the government-controlled media to do so.

The Indian Subcontinent   U.S. policymakers must also be concerned about the possible outbreak of war between India and Pakistan, each armed with nuclear weapons. The issues between the two will not be easily resolved, given the history of enmity between them, past military conflicts, and the struggle over the fate of the future of Muslim-majority Kashmir. Indeed, the two countries mobilized for war in late 2001 and 2002, and each implied that it would use nuclear weapons if necessary. The situation is complicated for the United States by the fact that Pakistan is deemed crucial in the fight against the Taliban and Al Qaeda in Afghanistan and the frontier areas of Pakistan itself. At the same time, the United States is forming a stronger strategic alliance with India, partly as a counter to the rise of China, partly because of the increasing ties between the American and Indian economies, and partly because of sympathy with India as a target of terrorist attacks widely thought to be encouraged by Pakistan.

? Does trade trump security when it comes to international affairs? Or are they inextricably linked, with neither one taking precedence?

China   With its huge population, fast-growing economy, and modernizing military—it now is developing its first aircraft carrier—China someday may pose a security threat to the United States. Some Americans have warned of a great "clash of civilizations" between the West and "Confucian" China.[28] Disputes over trade, intellectual property rights protections (on software, movies, and so on), China-based cyber attacks on American firms, Taiwan, Tibet, and human rights periodically cloud U.S.–Chinese relations. In addition, China has been reluctant to help on reining in nuclear

CONTINUING STRUGGLE AND SUFFERING   The decades-long struggle between Israel and the Palestinians for statehood on the same piece of land in the Middle East shows few signs of ending. Here, a Palestinian woman mourns the loss of her home and family after the Israeli invasion of Hamas-controlled Gaza in late 2008 in response to rocket attacks on Israeli towns and settlements. Does the United States remain a so-called "honest broker" in potential negotiations between the two sides or has Washington become too closely identified with Israel to be able to play that role? Is there any other country or group of countries that might do better?

programs in Iran and North Korea, and has made strong diplomatic efforts to enhance its ties to oil- and other resource-rich countries in Africa and Latin America, joining with some of them (as in Sudan and Venezuela) to oppose U.S. policies in their regions. On the other hand, China and the United States have become strong trading partners and their financial systems are deeply entwined, making them economically dependent on one another. And, as we saw in the chapter-opening story, China is the most important purchaser of America's public and private debt.

Russia   For a period after the fall of the Soviet Union and during the years of Boris Yeltsin's presidency, relations between Russia and the United States were surprisingly cordial given the long Cold War that existed between them after the Second World War. Under Vladimir Putin, however, and quite naturally, Russia began to act again as a great power with its own national interests. At first relations were reasonably good—after all, President Bush once famously remarked about Putin that "he had looked into his eyes and seen his soul" and liked what he saw—with cooperation and sympathetic support the order of the day for awhile in the months following 9/11. But Putin did not like NATO expansion to the east and the incorporation into it of former republics of the Soviet Union. At home, Putin took control of the Russian media, parliament, and large portions of the economy, and he hand-picked his successor Dmitry Medvedev to be president, while he took the position of Prime Minister (he will become president again in 2012 if things go as he has planned). He opposed American efforts at the United Nations to gain final approval for the invasion of Iraq and was a harsh critic of the U.S. effort there. Putin was furious at the American proposal to put an antimissile defense system in Poland and the Czech Republic (which the U.S. said is meant to protect against Iranian missiles).

Emboldened, perhaps, by the vast oil and natural gas wealth pouring into Russia, Putin has used surprisingly harsh rhetoric in making it clear that he fundamentally opposes American policies across a broad front. In one speech in 2007, he likened America's use of its power to that of Nazi Germany. In that same year, he threatened to pull Russia out of a treaty limiting intermediate-range missiles in Europe and later proclaimed that the use of military force by anyone in the oil-rich Caspian Sea region (which includes Iran) was unacceptable. Putin also publicly and vocally opposed the United States, the United Nations, and the European Union on Kosovo independence (Russia is a traditional ally of Serbia), which happened in 2008. Later that year, he invaded Georgia on Russia's border and is intent on bringing Ukraine back into close association with Russia.

How to ease relations with this important continental power is an important long-range issue for American policymakers. A turn in relations may already be happening, with leaders in both countries perhaps coming to realize that a Russian–United States break would not be in the best interests of either country. In 2010, the United States and Russia signed a new nuclear arms control treaty, for example, and voted together at the United Nations for new sanctions against Iran and its nuclear program.

Economic and Social Issues

In addition to national security concerns, a number of other international issues have drawn the attention of American policymakers and the public.

globalization
The increasing worldwide integration of markets, production, and communications across national boundaries.

The Global Economy   **Globalization**, as described more fully in Chapter 4, is the integration of much of the world into a single market and production system in which the United States plays a leading role. It raises a number of new issues for American policymakers and citizens to address.

Trade Counting total imports and exports together, the United States is the world's largest trading nation—though second to the European Union (with 27 nations), with China closing fast—and a leading player in the design and management of the global trading system. Since the end of World War II, the United States has been the leading advocate of the freer and more open trading system that has evolved. In 1948, under American leadership, the most important trading nations adopted the **General Agreement on Tariffs and Trade (GATT)**, an agreement designed to lower, then eliminate, tariffs on most traded goods and to end nontariff trade restrictions as well. Periodically, members of GATT enter into talks (called rounds) and reach new agreements designed to refine and expand the system. The Uruguay Round in 1994 agreed to replace GATT with the **World Trade Organization (WTO)**, which came into being the following year. U.S. negotiators hoped that the new agreement eventually would open more markets to American agricultural products and services and halt the piracy of patented and copyrighted goods such as software and films. The failure of the Doha Round of negotiations in 2008 signals, perhaps, that the lowering of trade barriers has gone about as far as it's likely to go. Indeed, the financial collapse and recession in 2008–2009 pushed more than a few countries to raise trade barriers again—though not to previous levels—in an effort to protect jobs and keep stimulus spending within national boundaries.

Most economists believe that trade is generally good for all countries involved, whether rich or poor,[29] though not all agree.[30] Many Americans believe that the loss of manufacturing jobs can be traced to free trade and trade agreements such as the **North American Free Trade Agreement (NAFTA)** with Canada and Mexico, because goods manufactured abroad using cheap labor and by firms that have few labor protections or environmental requirements can enter the United States tariff-free. Most economists, however, believe the majority of manufacturing job loss can be linked to technological change and rising productivity. Organized labor passionately believes free trade costs American jobs. Others worry that a flood of cheap, yet high-quality, goods and services threatens firms that are important for the health of the American economy and point to the decline of the American auto, steel, and consumer electronics industries as examples. Still others believe that the threat of trade sanctions—a violation of free trade agreements—should be used to improve environmental standards, human rights practices, and religious toleration in other countries. Trade, then, is likely to remain an important political issue for a long time to come.

Intellectual Property Rights How strongly should our foreign policy attempt to protect the intellectual property rights—patents and copyrights—of American companies and citizens? The issue is fairly straightforward when it comes to the

> **General Agreement on Tariffs and Trade (GATT)**
>
> An international agreement that requires the lowering of tariffs and other barriers to free trade.
>
> **World Trade Organization (WTO)**
>
> An agency designed to enforce the provisions of the General Agreement on Tariffs and Trade and to resolve trade disputes between nations.
>
> **North American Free Trade Agreement (NAFTA)**
>
> An agreement among the United States, Canada, and Mexico to eliminate nearly all barriers to trade and investment among the three countries.

A SHORT BREAK IN THE INVASION   Showing that it would not tolerate military challenges to its interests in the outer areas of the old Soviet Union, Russia invaded Georgia and temporarily occupied parts of its territory in 2008 in retaliation for Georgia's bombardment of areas of South Ossetia, which wanted to rejoin North Ossetia, a Russian ally. Adding tension to the situation was the fact that Georgia is a close ally of the United States. How should the United States address the fact that Russia is a rising power with its own national interests?

"piracy" of movies, music tapes and CDs, and software in places such as China; Americans generally support policies that are aimed at ending these practices. Protection of patents for life-saving drugs is another matter—anti-malarial and anti-AIDS medications, for example. Many Americans believe companies ought to provide such drugs at low prices or allow poor countries to find or produce generic substitutes despite the patent protections of Western pharmaceutical companies. There has been some movement on this front. For example, the U.S. government signed an agreement in 2003 to suspend the normal trade rules of the WTO and allow the production and use of certain critical generic drugs. Global firms have lowered prices on a range of drugs—Bristol Myers Squibb announced in 2006, for example, that it would allow companies in India and South Africa to produce generic versions of its two most powerful AIDS drugs. In early 2008, GlaxoSmithKline announced its fifth cut in the prices of HIV/AIDS drugs. In 2010, the World Health Organization announced plans to form a public-private patent pool to lower the cost of the most expensive HIV treatments. Assistance with these drugs cannot come too soon; in 2009 almost 2 million people died of the disease, with more than 2.3 million more adults and children newly infected.[31]

Global Economic Instability The United States has been the leading player in the global economy since the end of World War II, and its leaders have been involved in trying to ensure the health and vitality of the overall global economy. In addition to encouraging trade, American leaders have been concerned with stabilizing global financial markets when necessary and in rescuing countries on the verge of economic collapse. They do so because our own economy is closely tied to the global economy. A strong American role is guaranteed by our leadership of and large financial contributions to the International Monetary Fund (IMF; charged with rectifying and preventing currency collapses) and the World Bank (charged with financing projects to assist economic development and poverty reduction). Aside from providing general leadership, the proper response to specific crises is not always clear. In 1982 and 1995, for example, the United States helped Mexico emerge from its financial collapse but refused to help Argentina in 2001. Ironically, perhaps, given its traditional financial leadership role, the United States's housing bubble, credit crunch, investment bank collapse, and stock market decline in 2008 imperiled the world's financial system.

The United States's role is also being undermined by the dramatic decline in the value of the dollar, fueled by huge federal budget deficits and a rising national debt and big imbalances in our terms of trade (we have been importing more than we have been exporting). To pay for all these imbalances, we borrow from others, increasingly foreign governments, who pump money into the American economy by buying U.S. Treasury securities. Although countries such as China and Japan have reason to continue to do this—it allows each to sell more goods to the United States—there have been hints from leading political figures in each country that their reserves ought to have fewer dollars and more euros, which increasingly are worth more. The dollar's decline gained momentum with the implosion of American financial markets and the huge infusion of money from the Fed and the Treasury to try to rescue the financial system beginning in late 2008. With things moving in this direction, the United States is being forced to share global financial and economic leadership with others.

Foreign Aid Rich nations, whether for humanitarian or security reasons, have given assistance to extremely poor countries for many years in an effort to improve living standards. There have been some successes—such as the conquest of

GLOBAL PRODUCTION AND SALES In a globalized economy, many products consumed by Americans are manufactured abroad. Here, a consumer evaluates a Japanese flat-screen television manufactured in China in a Costco store in California. How difficult is it to buy products that are made entirely in the United States? Does it matter where products are made that American consumers use?

riverblindness, a disease that once affected tens of millions of Africans. But dreadful poverty persists in places such as Bangladesh and sub-Saharan Africa. In the latter region, excepting South Africa, life expectancy has declined. Eighty-five percent of the world's roughly 1 million malaria deaths occurred there in 2009, as did 75 percent of the world's AIDS deaths.[32] Mean household income is lower there than it was in the 1960s, but GDP has been growing at a healthy pace over the past few years, especially in those countries enjoying large sales of commodities like oil, coal, and phosphate ores to China. Although the United States contributes to World Bank developmental loans for poor countries and has programs such as Food for Peace, the Peace Corps, and technical and educational assistance programs, U.S. government spending for foreign aid is very low. Spending for foreign aid in 2008 was about 0.6 percent of the federal budget and about 0.2 percent of U.S. GDP.[33] Although we spend more dollars on foreign assistance than any other country, relative to the size of our economy we spend the least (tied with Japan on this score) (see Figure 19.4). Moreover, only about two-thirds of U.S. foreign aid goes to economic development and humanitarian relief; the remainder is linked to promoting military and security objectives or encouraging the sale of American goods and services abroad. It is worth noting, however, that Americans give a great deal of aid through private philanthropy, with the Bill and Melinda Gates Foundation leading the way in assistance to poor countries. Between its founding in 2000 and the end of 2008, for example, the foundation gave about $8.6 billion to support global health initiatives, about the same as the WHO spent for its activities during the same period.

President Bush promised a big boost for development assistance and a new approach to foreign aid in his **Millennium Challenge Account**—a dramatically different form of aid in which across-the-board payments to countries have been replaced by a system in which money to poor countries is tied to a range of performance indicators for things like the rule of law, women's rights, protection of property rights, anticorruption measures, political rights, governmental effectiveness, and the like—but appropriated totals have fallen far short of promises because of deep cuts in the discretionary part of the federal budget in the last few years (see Chapter 17). The new approach was partly a product of a growing sense among many in the development community, scholars, and think tanks that not much development has occurred as a result of aid from rich governments and international organizations. Most of the

> **Millennium Challenge Account**
>
> A Bush administration initiative to distribute development aid on the basis of a country's degree of improvement in areas such as the rule of law, women's rights, protection of property rights, anticorruption measures, and political and civil rights.

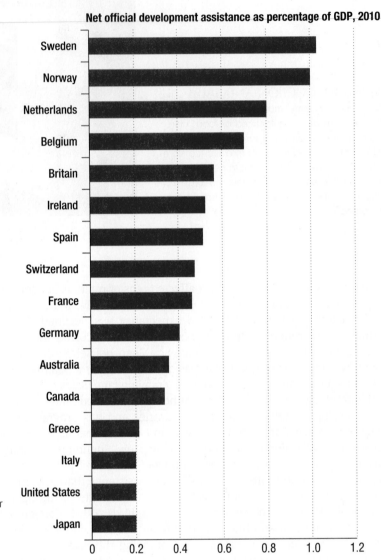

Net official development assistance as percentage of GDP, 2010

FIGURE 19.4 Foreign Aid as a Percentage of GDP

Although Americans often complain about how much aid we give to other countries, a comparison with other donor countries shows that we give very little as a percentage of GDP. *Source:* Organization for Economic Cooperation and Development, 2010.

aid, the argument goes, has gone to big projects that have had little development impact or has been siphoned off to government leaders and their followers and cronies.[34] Far better, critics of traditional foreign aid suggest, would be policies to encourage real economic development as in India, China, and Brazil. How to make economic development happen, of course, remains a much debated question. (See the "By the Numbers" feature for a better way to measure development assistance.)

The Global Environment Increasingly, Americans realize that environmental problems cross national borders. Thus, the United States and Canada have worked out a joint approach to reduce acid rain, and the United States has signed on to agreements on the prevention and cleanup of oil spills, the use of Antarctica, the protection of fish species, and the protection of the ozone layer. The United States is also a signatory to the biodiversity treaty. Global climate change is a different story, however. Although the Clinton administration was involved in hammering out the

CELEBRATING CHINA'S POWER   The Chinese leadership used the 2008 Beijing Olympic Games to announce the emergence of China as a power on the world stage. Although the government squelched domestic and foreign dissidents, many of whom were protesting Chinese actions in Tibet and Sudan, the games had the intended effect. The spectacular opening and closing ceremonies were held in the stunning "bird's nest" stadium pictured here. Did the grandeur of the opening and closing ceremonies and the excitement of the games work to make you forget the controversy and outcry leading up to them?

details of the Kyoto Protocol to limit greenhouse gases, Clinton, fearing rejection, never submitted the treaty to the Senate for its "advice and consent." In 2001, George W. Bush pulled out of the treaty entirely, citing his concern that strict controls on developed countries coupled with no controls on large, fast-growing economies in developing countries, such as China and India, would do irreparable harm to the American economy. President Obama professed a strong interest in bringing the United States into a new international agreement with mandatory targets for greenhouse gas reductions, with China, India, and Brazil included, but no agreement could be worked out at the Copenhagen climate summit in late 2009. China's reluctance to agree to mandatory measures and lack of confidence in Obama's ability to deliver a "cap and trade" climate bill in Congress were major issues in the Copenhagen failure.

Awareness of the threat of global climate change is high among Americans, although there is a deep divide, mostly along partisan lines, about how seriously to take the threat, whether human actions are responsible for warming, and what to do about it. Conservative Republicans are more inclined to see the trend as part of a natural cycle and oppose government policies to diminish carbon production; liberal Democrats are more likely to blame human activity for climate change and want governments to take action to diminish emissions.[35]

Who Makes Foreign Policy?

19.4   Identify the main American foreign and national security policymakers

We pointed out in Chapter 12, and at the outset of this chapter, that the president is the key player in making foreign and national security policies and is especially powerful during international crises and in times of war—recently in Afghanistan and Iraq and in the war on terrorism. (The "Using the Framework" feature examines the power of the presidency in waging war in threatening times.) But Congress has always been involved, especially in decisions about international trade, foreign aid, military spending, immigration, and other matters that clearly and directly touch constituents' local interests, but also when presidential policies and foreign and national security policies have not worked as promised (e.g., Iraq during the Bush administration). Public opinion, the mass media, the parties, and

How much do rich countries help poor countries develop?

There is a great deal of talk in the United States and other rich democracies about helping poor countries develop so they can provide a better standard of living for their people. Hollywood stars and other celebrities raise money for refugees, religious organizations of various denominations provide charity and education, and foundations address issues of clean water and public health. But what are rich-country governments doing to close the yawning gap between the rich and the poor in the world?

Why It Matters For many Americans and for many who live in the other rich democracies, the great inequalities in well-being and life prospects that exist between themselves and people in poor countries are morally wrong and must be rectified. For many others, particularly political and economic leaders, the existence of desperately poor countries represents a threat to global stability and security. Such places are more likely than others to become "failed states," where important resource supplies may be imperiled, terrorism may breed, and from which desperate refugees often stream to neighboring countries, destabilizing them as well.

What Governments Do People are most familiar with foreign aid in which rich-country governments give money to poor-country governments. But rich governments do many more things that affect poor-country development. They, for example, have a lot to say about whether farmers and firms in poor countries have access to rich-country markets to sell their products. They can encourage large companies to invest in countries that need it by, let us say, providing insurance for building new production facilities in poor countries where people want work. They can encourage or discourage migration to their own countries and make it more or less difficult for migrants to send remittances back home. Rich countries can help or hinder the security situation in poor countries—which affects whether investors are willing to be there—with some selling arms to one side or another in a civil war, and others providing peacekeepers. And rich countries will differ in their policies on intellectual property rights: some allowing substantial technology transfers to poor-country companies by their home-based companies, and others restricting transfers.

Measuring Commitment to Development The Center for Global Development and *Foreign Policy* magazine have created a measure they call the Commitment to Development Index (CDI) that seeks to capture the multidimensional nature of development assistance that rich countries can offer poor ones. In it, they use a panel of judges to rate the following things:

- The quantity of foreign aid relative to GDP and whether it is targeted to projects that encourage growth.
- The degree to which trade policies encourage poor-country imports.
- The degree to which investments in poor countries are encouraged.
- The relative contribution the country makes to peace and security in poor countries.
- The degree of openness to migrants from poor countries.
- The relative openness or restrictiveness of technology transfer to poor countries.
- The relative contribution to global climate change (based on the presumption that global climate change hurts people in poor countries more than in rich ones).

interest and advocacy groups (e.g., corporations, unions, nongovernmental organizations, and religious organizations) affect what both Congress and the executive branch do.

The President and the Executive Branch

As shown in many places in this book, presidents have broad discretion and sometimes exercise extraordinary powers in foreign and national security matters derived from the commander-in-chief and diplomatic powers in the Constitution and the deference to presidents over the years in the vigorous use of these powers by the public, Congress, and the courts.[36] In the end, for example, it was President Bush who made the decision to invade Iraq in 2003; it was President Obama who decided to increase troop levels in Afghanistan in 2009 and 2010 and to increase the use of drone attacks on the Taliban and Al Qaeda inside Pakistan. He also decided to increase military action against jihadists in Yemen and Somalia. Presidents

The graph shows the Commitment to Development Index for the year 2009. In the array of rich countries, the United States ranks 17th out of 22 developed countries. Examination of the individual components of the final score at the Center for Global Development's website (www.cgdev.org/doc/cdi/2009) shows that the United States would rank much higher were it not for two things: first, the United States scores very low on fighting global climate change compared with other rich democracies, according to the CGD; and second, its arms sales to the Third World are very high, giving it a low score on the peace and security component.

Should We Rely on This Index?

The index is very useful for alerting us to the fact that rich-country governments do lots of things in addition to providing foreign aid that might affect the prospects for economic development in poor countries. But critics could point to a number of problems with the CDI. First, it relies entirely on the evaluations of judges—academics, think tank scholars, and CGD staffers—giving quantitative form to what are highly qualitative judgments. How does one weigh, for example, the relative contribution to security and insecurity of arms sales as compared to a manpower contribution to a peacekeeping mission? Second, it includes components in the index that not everyone would agree are essential for the economic development of poor countries. The tie between global climate change and the economic development of such countries is not entirely self-evident, nor, for that matter, is openness to immigration. Third and finally, some critics might reject the entire premise, namely, that economic development in poor countries is primarily the product of the policies of rich-country governments. The examples of India and China would suggest that policies internal to poor countries may be much more important for economic development in the long run.

What Do You Think?

Do you think the United States can and should do more to help poor countries develop economically? If you think we should do more, would you like to see more put into foreign aid, or do you think there are other things we could do that might be more effective? What are some arguments for leaving countries alone to find their own paths to development? On the other hand, why might this tactic be detrimental to the United States?

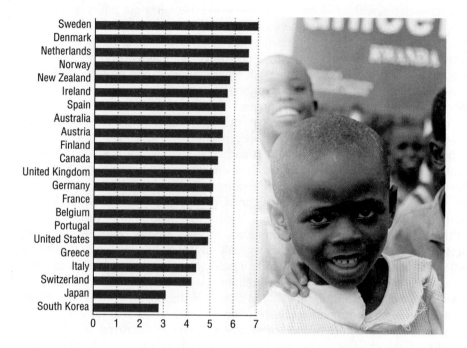

have the final word, to be sure, but they rely on many people and several government agencies to help them make military and foreign policy decisions. By most accounts, during George W. Bush's presidency and with his backing, Vice President Richard Cheney was the key architect of policies surrounding the invasion of Iraq, the treatment of enemy combatants and detainees captured in war zones and in antiterrorism efforts, and the secret and widespread surveillance program of American citizens and others. Secretary of Defense Donald Rumsfeld was influential until his failure to anticipate the insurgency in Iraq and his decision not to put "boots on the ground" to fight it led to his resignation after the public mood soured over Iraq and dealt the GOP a blow in the 2006 congressional elections. Robert Gates, who succeeded Rumsfeld—and who continued as defense secretary to President Obama—was instrumental in convincing President Bush to temporarily increase troop levels in Iraq (the so-called surge) in 2007 and support General David Petraeus's new counterinsurgency strategies there.

The national security adviser plays a prominent role in every administration, advising the president on a daily basis on foreign and national security matters. The

Department of State, headed by the secretary of state, is the president's chief arm for carrying out diplomatic affairs. Some secretaries of state have been extremely important in helping the president make foreign policy—Henry Kissinger in the Nixon and Ford administrations comes to mind, as does Hillary Clinton in the Obama administration—although others have not been among the key players in the inner circle around the president. It was widely reported, for example, that Colin Powell was less influential with President Bush, for example, than were Cheney and Rumsfeld. The department itself is organized along both functional lines—economic affairs, human rights, counterterrorism, and refugees—and geographic lines, with "country desks" devoted to each nation of the world. The State Department has 273 embassies, consulates, and missions around the world that carry out policy and advise the department on new developments. Attached to the State Department are the Arms Control and Disarmament Agency, the U.S. Information Agency, and the Agency for International Development, which oversees foreign economic aid. As issues of trade, U.S. corporate investment in other countries, and protection of intellectual property rights (patents and copyrights) become more important in the global economy, both the Department of Commerce, another cabinet department, and the Office of the U.S. Trade Representative, part of the Executive Office of the President, have become more important in foreign policymaking.

The Department of Defense (DOD) is particularly influential in shaping foreign and military policies. The DOD is headed by a civilian secretary of defense, who has authority over the entire department and reports directly to the president. Strong defense secretaries who enjoy the confidence of the president, such as Robert McNamara under President Kennedy and Donald Rumsfeld under President Bush, often impose policies about which the military services are not keen. Several Army leaders insisted that the light and technologically advanced fighting forces favored by Rumsfeld, for example, ignored the fact that holding and exploiting battlefield gains in places like Iraq and Afghanistan would require a larger military than Rumsfeld had planned for. Civilian secretaries are also in charge of the Departments of the Army, Navy, and Air Force and report to the secretary of defense. Each service also has a military command structure headed by people in uniform: the Army and Air Force chiefs of staff, the chief of naval operations, the commandant of the Marine Corps, and their subordinates. The uniformed chiefs of each branch serve together in the **Joint Chiefs of Staff (JCS)**, headed by the chairman of the Joint Chiefs, who reports not only to the secretary of defense but also directly to the president.

? Is there any way to address global climate change unilaterally? Or is the problem only solvable through multilateral efforts?

A large intelligence community is also involved in the fashioning and implementation of foreign and military policy. This community is made up of a number of specific agencies. The National Security Agency (NSA) is responsible for intercepting and monitoring electronic messages from around the world (including communications between people abroad and American citizens on U.S. soil, as we have learned), and the National Reconnaissance Office (NRO) is responsible for satellite reconnaissance. Each of the armed services also has a separate tactical intelligence unit. The Central Intelligence Agency (CIA) was established in 1947 to advise the National Security Council, to coordinate all U.S. intelligence agencies, to gather and evaluate intelligence information, and to carry out such additional functions as the NSC directs. Congress, the press, and the public subjected the CIA to intense scrutiny in 2004 because of its failure to alert the nation to the September 11, 2001, terrorist attacks, and its misreading of the existence of weapons of mass destruction in Iraq prior to the U.S. invasion. In 2005, a presidential commission excoriated the CIA for these failures. In response to these

Joint Chiefs of Staff (JCS)
The military officers in charge of each of the armed services.

Why did we invade Iraq in 2003?

Background: Operation "Iraqi Freedom" began on March 20, 2003, when American and British forces, supported by very small contingents from other countries in the so-called coalition of the willing, launched aerial bombardments across Iraq with initial strikes aimed at air defenses and command and control facilities and an ill-fated attempt to kill Saddam Hussein in a pre-dawn bomb attack. (The stated goal was to shut down Iraq's weapons of mass destruction program, which was later shown not to have existed at the time.) After the initial air strikes, American and British ground forces struck from the south—Turkey had turned down a request to allow American troops to attack Iraq from Turkish territory—while Kurdish militias attacked Iraq army units in the north. Baghdad fell on April 9. A Coalition Provisional Authority was put in place by the United States and the United Kingdom to govern Iraq until such time as the Iraqis could set up their own government. The rest, as they say, is history. Over the course of the next five years, a fierce insurgency and fierce conflicts between Sunni and Shiite militias raged, while member governments of the coalition of the willing gradually pulled out, with the British fielding only a token force by the end of 2008. So how did we get into this situation? Why did we invade in first place? Taking a look at how structural, political linkage, and governmental factors affect policymaking in Washington will help explain the outcome.

Structure

The United States is the world's only superpower in 2003, able and willing to project military power. → America's Constitution and the development of its constitutional rules over time give enormous powers to the president in the area of national security. → The know-how for making WMDs is broadly available in the world.

Political Linkage

Conservative and neo-conservative think tanks issue reports on the danger of Iraq's WMD and how democratizing Iraq will start democratizing the Middle East. → News media fail to examine WMD story line. → In the crisis atmosphere of post 9/11 period, the public is willing to give president broad latitude to protect the country. → Mass demonstrations in United States and around the world fail to stop the momentum toward war.

Democrats offer little resistance to the buildup for fear of being labeled weak on national defense. → Some critics are disarmed by Secretary of State Powell's presentation of WMD evidence before U.N. Security Council.

Government

Vice President Cheney and his aides push hard for invasion of Iraq, as does Defense Secretary Rumsfeld. → Intelligence agencies support WMD story; unclear whether they truly believe this or feel pressured to be "on board." → President Bush believes WMD program exists in Iraq; believes downfall of Iraq will be good for Middle East. → Mostly reluctant Democrats join Republicans in late 2002 to vote for joint congressional resolution authorizing use of force.

Government Action

President Bush orders the attack on Iraq.

failures, Congress and President Bush established a new cabinet-level post of Director of National Intelligence (DNI) to coordinate the intelligence-gathering and interpretation activities of 15 scattered agencies, thus taking over some important responsibilities from the CIA. It remains to be seen how effective this change will be, though the failure to "connect the dots" regarding a Nigerian terrorist planning to blow up a Delta flight from Amsterdam to Detroit in 2009 (the bomb failed to go off) did not fill Americans with confidence. One problem with coordinating intelligence is that the Defense Department, whose intelligence operations do not fall under the jurisdiction of the DNI, controls about 80 percent of the U.S. intelligence budget.

Congress

Congress has generally played a less active role in foreign and military policy than in domestic policy. Members of Congress not only recognize the strong constitutional foundations of the president's preeminence in these areas, but generally believe that their constituents care more about policies that are close to home than those that are far away. The exception, of course, is when wars go badly, not meeting public expectations, as in Vietnam and Iraq; then Congress becomes more assertive.

In national defense emergencies, Congress tends to take a back seat to the president. This was the case in the immediate aftermath of the terrorist attacks on the United States in 2001. No congressional leader or political party was about to take on George W. Bush's broad assertion of powers, given the crisis situation and the president's extraordinary popularity at the time. However, as reviewed earlier, as the occupation of Iraq dragged on and the president's popularity plummeted, and after Democrats gained control of the House and Senate after the 2006 elections, Congress reasserted itself, focusing most especially on the decision to invade Iraq and management by the president and his team of the aftermath. However, because Democrats did not have enough votes to break Republican filibusters in the Senate—see Chapter 11 for more on the filibuster—Congress failed on several occasions in 2007 and 2008 to pass legislation setting a date for withdrawal of troops from Iraq. It may not have mattered that much because President Bush had already announced plans for an end to combat missions in Iraq. President Obama moved the withdrawal of combat troops to an earlier date (the end of August 2010), though not early enough to satisfy the antiwar elements in the Democratic Party.

? Are checks and balances effective when it comes to foreign policy? Which branch has the upper hand in directing American foreign affairs?

The Constitution gives Congress the power to declare war—which it has not been asked to do since the beginning of World War II—and to decide about any spending of money. It also gives the Senate the power to approve or disapprove treaties and the appointment of ambassadors. At times, Congress has used its treaty or spending powers to challenge the president on important issues: trying to force an end to the Vietnam War, trying to gain some influence on the presidential use of American armed forces abroad (the War Powers Act of 1973 as described in Chapter 12), creating difficulties over the Panama Canal treaty and the SALT II arms control treaty, defeating the Nuclear Test Ban Treaty, resisting the Reagan administration's aid to the Nicaraguan Contras, and barely acquiescing to military and peacekeeping operations in Bosnia and Kosovo.

Congress has probably exerted its greatest foreign and military policy influence on issues that involve spending money, all of which must pass through the regular congressional appropriations process. It has tended to reduce foreign aid appropriations, for example. And military contracts are a special focus of attention because each has a great economic effect on many congressional districts and powerful interest groups.

Using the DEMOCRACY STANDARD

What role do the people play in foreign and defense policymaking?

Democracy is less evident in the process of making military and foreign policies than in making domestic policies. For one thing, Americans generally care more about what is going on in the United States and how it affects them directly than they do about issues and developments in distant places. They also know more about what is going on in the United States—whether it be health care, living standards, or the environment—than they do about what is happening elsewhere, particularly in the poor countries that get very little media news coverage. Additionally, to be effective, many foreign and military policies must be made in secret, so citizens often do not have the information necessary to be politically effective. And political leaders have sometimes misled or ignored the public.[37] Given this, Americans are clearly more competent as citizens when faced with domestic matters than with military and foreign affairs and are more interested in playing a role in shaping domestic policies. The result is that Americans give political, diplomatic, and military leaders a relatively free hand in making foreign and military policy. This is very much what the framers had in mind when they fashioned the Constitution.

Americans are not powerless in the foreign and military policy arenas, however. Although they give their leaders a great deal of latitude in this area, the leaders are ultimately answerable to the people, and they know it. Presidents and members of Congress pay very close attention to public opinion and worry about the next election, so they are careful to avoid actions that may eventually prove unpopular.

Furthermore, Americans seem to be becoming more informed about other places in the world—whether through the mass media or the Internet—and are coming to recognize the interconnectedness of our fate with the fates of others. For example, Americans are paying increased attention to and learning more about international trade and competitiveness, human rights violations abroad, terrorism threats, and global climate change and other environmental problems. Moreover, they are becoming more competent as citizens and seem to be paying closer attention to what our political leaders do in these policy areas and holding them accountable. This is all to the good if your interest is in seeing this country become more democratic, because democracy involves popular control of government leaders and the policies they make.

Nonetheless, it is still the case that the framers put the major responsibility for foreign and military affairs in the hands of the president and, by extension, the executive branch. Although Congress has control over the budget and the constitutional power to declare war against other nations, it is usually at a great disadvantage relative to the president in these areas, primarily because of the president's "war powers." As discussed in Chapter 12, the war powers represent a broad grant of constitutional power that presidents have used over the years to expand their responsibilities for national security, a concept that now involves a wide range of potential threats to the United States and its interests, ranging from direct military attacks on the nation (nuclear, conventional, terrorist), to attacks on U.S. citizens and business firms abroad. Moreover, in the president's treaty powers and in his responsibility for naming and receiving ambassadors, the Constitution gives the president working control over most other aspects of foreign policymaking. In crisis situations, such as existed after the 1941 attack on Pearl Harbor, and in 2001 after the attacks on the World Trade Center and the Pentagon, the president fashions foreign and military policies without much interference by Congress or the public. In such cases, the Constitution, historical precedents of strong leadership in crisis times by the chief executive, and public opinion all contribute to the broad powers and responsibilities of the president, with little scope, however, for conventional democratic processes.

SUMMARY

19.1 Assess the extent to which foreign policymaking can be democratic

- Democratic theorists tend not to make distinctions between domestic policy and foreign and national security policies, believing that democratic processes are relevant to each; the people can and should be sovereign in all areas, it is argued.

- In reality, however, democracy plays a less central role in foreign and national security policy making. The reasons are varied: the public, for the most part, knows and cares more about domestic policies; foreign and national security policy making often require secrecy and speed and are less amenable to full deliberation; and the constitutional powers of the president to act on his own are considerable.

19.2 Explain why the United States is the world's superpower and analyze the policy choices it has in playing this role

- The superpower status of the United States rests on three pillars: it has the world's largest and most innovative economy, it has the world's most powerful military, and it has enjoyed widespread admiration for its national culture and way of life.

- The United States is the world's only military superpower. The United States's advantages in high-tech and smart weapons, aerial reconnaissance, and the ability to deploy large forces to world trouble spots are particularly important.

- The United States also possesses a good deal of soft power, as American culture and ideology wield a fair amount of influence around the world. But Bush-era foreign policy decisions, especially the war in Iraq and treatment of detainees, put a dent in the goodwill other nations have for the United States, and the financial collapse increased skepticism about the American economic model. America's international favorability has increased under President Obama, however.

- The United States's policies during its superpower era have combined unilateralist and multilateralist tendencies. In certain periods, it has tilted toward unilateralism. At other periods, it has tilted toward a less "go it alone" stance, depending more on cooperation with allies, negotiations with antagonists, and collaboration with international institutions. Each administration faces the choice of what stance it will take toward the world in its foreign and national security policies.

- American policymakers also must decide on what goals to pursue. At the two extremes are policies to extend and protect a set of values or an ideology, and policies that are more pragmatic, such as providing for the material well-being and safety of the nation's people.

- The United States's superpower preeminence will likely be challenged at some point by the rise of China as an economic and military power.

19.3 Evaluate problems facing the post–Cold War world

- The collapse of the Soviet Union in the early 1990s changed the nature of American foreign and national security policy, which had been focused on fighting communism for more than 40 years.

- National security has expanded to include not only the threat of direct attack by large scale forces on American territory—the main concern during the Cold War years—but other threats including terrorism, global economic and financial instability, the rapid spread of infectious diseases, poverty in less developed countries, global climate change, and cyber attacks on the government and private firms.

- Traditional concerns like possible proliferation of weapons of mass destruction, and regional and interethnic conflicts that might lead to global instability, remain important elements on the agenda of policymakers.

- China is both an important economic partner of the United States and a potential rival whose interests are not always aligned with America's. Knowing how to balance these opposite tendencies will remain an important problem for American policymakers.

19.4 Identify the main American foreign and national security policymakers

- Foreign policy has traditionally been made mostly in the executive branch, where the president is assisted by a large national security bureaucracy, including the National Security Council, the Department of Defense, the Department of State, and various intelligence agencies.

- Congress has been little involved in crises or covert actions and has generally gone along with major decisions on defense policy; it has asserted itself chiefly on matters of foreign trade and aid, military bases, and procurement contracts.

- Public opinion affects policymakers, perhaps increasingly so, but this influence is limited by the executive branch's centralization of decision making, secrecy, and control of information. How large a part interest groups play is disputed, but is probably substantial in limited areas.

TEST YOURSELF

Answer key begins on page T-1.

19.1 Assess the extent to which foreign policymaking can be democratic

1. Public opinion has a smaller influence on foreign policy than it does on domestic policy.
   True / False

2. As it relates to foreign and military policy, who of the following has the biggest influence when shaping what is perceived to be in the national interest?
   a. The executive branch
   b. The states
   c. Interest groups
   d. The public
   e. The parliamentarian

19.2 Explain why the United States is the world's superpower and analyze the policy choices it has in playing this role

3. George W. Bush was primarily a unilateralist, while Barack Obama has primarily been a multilateralist.
   True / False

4. Which of the following is an example of America's soft power?
   a. The United States has a very powerful navy.
   b. The United States is a nuclear powerhouse.
   c. The United States has the world's largest economy.
   d. American corporations have a presence around the world.
   e. People throughout the world like to watch American movies.

5. Evaluate whether the United States will continue to be the world's only superpower for the foreseeable future.

19.3 Evaluate problems facing the post–Cold War world

6. The United States spends about 10 percent of the federal budget on foreign aid, which is a higher percentage of its GDP than is spent by any other country.
   True / False

7. Which of the following concerns are the most closely linked with both the Cold War and current security threats?
   a. Communism
   b. Nuclear weapons
   c. Terrorism
   d. Middle-East conflict
   e. War in Europe

8. Compare America's leadership in promoting free trade with its leadership in tackling the problems associated with global climate change.

19.4 Identify the main American foreign and national security policymakers

9. Congress is the most powerful player in foreign policy because it has the constitutionally granted powers to declare war and to command the armed forces.
   True / False

10. Which of the following is *not* a key player in the intelligence community?
    a. The National Security Agency
    b. The National Reconnaissance Office
    c. The Central Intelligence Agency
    d. The Director of National Intelligence
    e. The Secretary of State

11. Evaluate whether Congress or the president should take the leadership role in deciding how to respond to national defense emergencies.

mypoliscilab EXERCISES

PEARSON

Apply what you learned in this chapter on MyPoliSciLab.

Read on mypoliscilab.com

eText: Chapter 19

Study and Review on mypoliscilab.com

Pre-Test
Post-Test
Chapter Exam
Flashcards

Watch on mypoliscilab.com

Video: NYC's Subway Surveillance System
Video: Sanctions on Iran
Video: Three Vivid Years—But Progress?

Explore on mypoliscilab.com

Simulation: You Are President John F. Kennedy
Simulation: You Are the President of the United States
Comparative: Comparing Foreign and Security Policy
Timeline: The Evolution of Foreign Policy
Visual Literacy: Evaluating Defense Spending

INTERNET SOURCES

Amnesty International
www.amnesty.org
Reports and documents from the international human rights organization.

Center for Defense Information
www.cdi.org
Analyses of the defense budget, weapons systems, and national security threats.

Defense Link
www.defenselink.mil/
The home page of the Department of Defense.

World Bank
www.worldbank.org
The website for one of the most important actors in the distribution of aid to poor countries.

The State Department
www.state.gov
The website for the department responsible for U.S. diplomacy; the site contains a wealth of information relating to countries around the world and the United States's relations with them.

The U.N. Millennium Project
www.unmillenniumproject.org
The website for the United Nations' formal effort to reduce poverty in the Third World.

International Herald Tribune Online
www.iht.com/
Complete international news with a much broader perspective than that found in most U.S. newspapers and other media outlets.

National Security Website
www.nationalsecurity.org
Essays and news about foreign and military policy, sponsored by the Heritage Foundation, from a conservative point of view.

Organization for Economic Cooperation and Development
www.oecd.org
Its statistical section is loaded with information about the economic performance of its member states and how much each spends on programs, including national defense and foreign assistance and development aid.

Statistical Resources on the Web: Military and Defense
www.lib.umich.edu/govdocs/stats.html
A vast statistical and information compendium on military and national security issues; covers the United States and other countries.

United Nations
www.un.org
Home page of the United Nations; links to a wealth of statistics, documents and reports, U.N. departments and conferences, and information on reaching U.N. officials.

SUGGESTIONS FOR FURTHER READING

Ferguson, Niall. *Colossus: The Price of America's Empire.* New York: Penguin Books, 2004.
The author believes that an American empire would be good for the United States and for the world, but argues that it is unlikely that the United States will choose this course.

Jacques, Martin. *When China Rules the World: The End of the Western World and the Birth of a New Global Order.* New York: Penguin Group, 2009.
A somewhat breathless but still highly informative and detailed account of the rise of China and what it might mean for the United States and the world.

Nye, Joseph. *The Paradox of American Power: Why the World's Only Superpower Can't Go It Alone.* Oxford, U.K.: Oxford University Press, 2002.
A passionate argument for a multilateral rather than a unilateral foreign policy.

Sen, Amartya Kumar. *Development as Freedom.* New York: Knopf, 1999.
The Nobel Prize winner in economics argues that freedom is the basis for the development of poor countries, a fact that should inform the foreign policies of the rich countries.

Shapiro, Ian. *Containment: Rebuilding a Strategy Against Global Terror.* Princeton, NJ: Princeton University Press, 2008.
The author suggests that the classic containment policy used to counter the Soviet Union offers a model for how to counter global terrorism while maintaining American values and legitimacy.

U.S. Army/Marine Corps Counterinsurgency Field Manual. Chicago: University of Chicago Press, 2007.
Authored by a team assembled by General David Petraeus, the manual lays out a strategy for fighting counterinsurgencies involving not only rooting out the enemy but protecting the lives and well-being of the civilian population.

Zakaria, Fareed. *The Post-American World.* New York: W.W. Norton, 2008.
This provocative book suggests that America's relative power has declined in the world because of the rise of the "others," namely, China, India, Brazil, Russia, and the European Union.

APPENDIX

THE DECLARATION OF INDEPENDENCE

THE CONSTITUTION OF THE UNITED STATES

THE FEDERALIST PAPERS, NOS. 10, 51, AND 78

PRESIDENTS AND CONGRESSES, 1789–2013

THE **DECLARATION OF INDEPENDENCE**

When in the Course of human events, it becomes necessary for one people to dissolve the political bands which have connected them with another, and to assume among the Powers of the earth, the separate and equal station to which the Laws of Nature and of Nature's God entitle them, a decent respect to the opinions of mankind requires that they should declare the causes which impel them to the separation.

We hold these truths to be self-evident, that all men are created equal, that they are endowed by their Creator with certain unalienable Rights, that among these are Life, Liberty and the pursuit of Happiness. That to secure these rights, Governments are instituted among Men, deriving their just powers from the consent of the governed, That whenever any Form of Government becomes destructive of these ends, it is the Right of the People to alter or to abolish it, and to institute new Government, laying its foundation on such principles and organizing its powers in such form, as to them shall seem most likely to effect their Safety and Happiness. Prudence, indeed, will dictate that Governments long established should not be changed for light and transient causes; and accordingly all experience hath shown, that mankind are more disposed to suffer, while evils are sufferable, than to right themselves by abolishing the forms to which they are accustomed. But when a long train of abuses and usurpations, pursuing invariably the same Object evinces a design to reduce them under absolute Despotism, it is their right, it is their duty, to throw off such Government, and to provide new Guards for their future security.—Such has been the patient sufferance of these Colonies; and such is now the necessity which constrains them to alter their former Systems of Government. The history of the present King of Great Britain is a history of repeated injuries and usurpations, all having in direct object the establishment of an absolute Tyranny over these States. To prove this, let Facts be submitted to a candid world.

He has refused his Assent to Laws, the most whole-some and necessary for the public good.

He has forbidden his Governors to pass Laws of immediate and pressing importance, unless suspended in their operation till his Assent should be obtained; and when so suspended, he has utterly neglected to attend to them.

He has refused to pass other Laws for the accommodation of large districts of people, unless those people would relinquish the right of Representation in the Legislature, a right inestimable to them and formidable to tyrants only.

He has called together legislative bodies at places unusual, uncomfortable, and distant from the depository of their Public Records, for the sole purpose of fatiguing them into compliance with his measures.

He has dissolved Representative Houses repeatedly, for opposing with manly firmness his invasions on the rights of the people.

He has refused for a long time, after such dissolutions, to cause others to be elected; whereby the Legislative Powers, incapable of Annihilation, have returned to the People at large for their exercise; the State remaining in the mean time exposed to all the dangers of invasion from without, and convulsions within.

He has endeavoured to prevent the population of these States; for that purpose obstructing the Laws of Naturalization of Foreigners; refusing to pass others to encourage their migration hither, and raising the conditions of new Appropriations of Lands.

He has obstructed the Administration of Justice, by refusing his Assent to Laws for establishing Judiciary Powers.

He has made Judges dependent on his Will alone, for the tenure of their offices, and the amount and payment of their salaries.

He has erected a multitude of New Offices, and sent hither swarms of Officers to harass our People, and eat out their substance.

He has kept among us, in times of peace, Standing Armies without the Consent of our legislature.

He has affected to render the Military independent of and superior to the Civil Power.

He has combined with others to subject us to a jurisdiction foreign to our constitution, and unacknowledged by our laws; giving his Assent to their acts of pretended legislation:

For quartering large bodies of armed troops among us:

For protecting them, by a mock Trial, from Punishment for any Murders which they should commit on the Inhabitants of these States:

For cutting off our Trade with all parts of the world:

For imposing taxes on us without our Consent:

For depriving us in many cases, of the benefits of Trial by Jury:

For transporting us beyond Seas to be tried for pretended offences:

For abolishing the free System of English Laws in a neighbouring Province, establishing therein an Arbitrary government, and enlarging its Boundaries so as to render it at once an example and fit instrument for introducing the same absolute rule into these Colonies:

For taking away our Charters, abolishing our most valuable Laws, and altering fundamentally the Forms of our Governments:

For suspending our own Legislature, and declaring themselves invested with Power to legislate for us in all cases whatsoever.

He has abdicated Government here, by declaring us out of his Protection and waging War against us.

He has plundered our seas, ravaged our Coasts, burnt our towns, and destroyed the lives of our people.

He is at this time transporting large armies of foreign mercenaries to compleat the works of death, desolation and tyranny, already begun with circumstances of Cruelty & perfidy scarcely paralleled in the most barbarous ages, and totally unworthy the Head of a civilized nation.

He has constrained our fellow Citizens taken Captive on the high Seas to bear Arms against their Country, to become the executioners of their friends and Brethren, or to fall themselves by their Hands.

He has excited domestic insurrections amongst us, and has endeavoured to bring on the inhabitants of our frontiers, the merciless Indian Savages, whose known rule of warfare, is an undistinguished destruction of all ages, sexes and conditions.

In every stage of these Oppressions We have Petitioned for Redress in the most humble terms: Our repeated Petitions have been answered only by repeated injury. A Prince, whose character is thus marked by every act which may define a Tyrant, is unfit to be the ruler of a free People.

Nor have We been wanting in attention to our British brethren. We have warned them from time to time of attempts by their legislature to extend an unwarrantable jurisdiction over us. We have reminded them of the circumstances of our emigration and settlement here. We have appealed to their native justice and magnanimity, and we have conjured them by the ties of our common kindred to disavow these usurpations, which, would inevitably interrupt our connections and correspondence. They too have been deaf to the voice of justice and of consanguinity. We must, therefore, acquiesce in the necessity, which denounces our Separation, and hold them, as we hold the rest of mankind, Enemies in War, in Peace Friends.

We, therefore, the Representatives of the united States of America, in General Congress, Assembled, appealing to the Supreme Judge of the world for the rectitude of our intentions, do, in the Name, and by Authority of the good People of these Colonies, solemnly publish and declare, That these United Colonies are, and of Right ought to be Free and Independent States; that they are Absolved from all Allegiance to the British Crown, and that all political connection between them and the State of Great Britain, is and ought to be totally dissolved; and that as Free and Independent States, they have full Power to levy War, conclude Peace, contract Alliances, establish Commerce, and to do all other Acts and Things which Independent States may of right do. And for the support of this Declaration, with a firm reliance of the Protection of Divine Providence, we mutually pledge to each other our Lives, our Fortunes and our sacred Honor.

John Hancock,

Josiah Bartlett, Wm Whipple, Saml Adams, John Adams, Robt Treat Paine, Elbridge Gerry, Steph. Hopkins, William Ellery, Roger Sherman, Samel Huntington, Wm Williams, Oliver Wolcott, Matthew Thornton, Wm Floyd, Phil Livingston, Frans Lewis, Lewis Morris, Richd Stockton, Jno Witherspoon, Fras Hopkinson, John Hart, Abra Clark, Robt Morris, Benjamin Rush, Benja Franklin, John Morton, Geo Clymer, Jas Smith, Geo. Taylor, James Wilson, Geo. Ross, Caesar Rodney, Geo Read, Thos M:Kean, Samuel Chase, Wm Paca, Thos Stone, Charles Carroll of Carrollton, George Wythe, Richard Henry Lee, Th. Jefferson, Benja Harrison, Thos Nelson, Jr., Francis Lightfoot Lee, Carter Braxton, Wm Hooper, Joseph Hewes, John Penn, Edward Rutledge, Thos Heyward, Junr., Thomas Lynch, Junor., Arthur Middleton, Button Gwinnett, Lyman Hall, Geo Walton.

THE CONSTITUTION OF THE UNITED STATES

We the people of the United States, in Order to form a more perfect Union, establish Justice, insure domestic Tranquility, provide for the common defence, promote the general Welfare, and secure the Blessings of Liberty to ourselves and our Posterity, do ordain and establish this constitution for the United States of America.

Article I

Section 1 All legislative Powers herein granted shall be vested in a Congress of the United States, which shall consist of a Senate and House of Representatives.

Section 2 The House of Representatives shall be composed of Members chosen every second Year by the People of the several States, and the Electors in each State shall have the Qualifications requisite for Electors of the most numerous Branch of the State Legislature.

No person shall be a Representative who shall not have attained to the Age of twenty-five Years, and been seven Years a Citizen of the United States, and who shall not, when elected, be an Inhabitant of that State in which he shall be chosen.

Representatives and direct Taxes shall be apportioned among the several States which may be included within this Union, according to their respective Numbers, which shall be determined by adding to the whole Number of free Persons, including those bound to Service for a Term of Years, and excluding Indians not taxed, three fifths of all other Persons. The actual Enumeration shall be made within three Years after the first Meeting of the Congress of the United States, and within every subsequent Term of ten Years, in such Manner as they shall by Law direct. The Number of Representatives shall not exceed one for every thirty Thousand, but each State shall have at Least one Representative; and until such enumeration shall be made, the State of New Hampshire shall be entitled to chuse three, Massachusetts eight, Rhode-Island and Providence Plantations one, Connecticut five, New-York six, New Jersey four, Pennsylvania eight, Delaware one, Maryland six, Virginia ten, North Carolina five, South Carolina five, and Georgia three.

When vacancies happen in the Representation from any State, the Executive Authority thereof shall issue Writs of Election to fill such Vacancies.

The House of Representatives shall chuse their Speaker and other Officers; and shall have the sole Power of Impeachment.

Section 3 The Senate of the United States shall be composed of two Senators from each State, chosen by the Legislature thereof, for six Years; and each Senator shall have one Vote.

Immediately after they shall be assembled in Consequence of the first Election, they shall be divided as equally as may be into three Classes. The Seats of the Senators of the first Class shall be vacated at the Expiration of the second Year, of the second Class at the Expiration of the fourth Year, and of the third Class at the Expiration of the sixth Year, so that one-third may be chosen every second Year; and if Vacancies happen by Resignation, or otherwise, during the Recess of the Legislature of any State, the Executive thereof may make temporary Appointments until the next Meeting of the Legislature, which shall then fill such Vacancies.

No Person shall be a Senator who shall not have attained to the Age of thirty Years, and been nine Years a Citizen of the United States, and who shall not, when elected, be an Inhabitant of that State in which he shall be chosen.

The Vice President of the United States shall be President of the Senate, but shall have no vote, unless they be equally divided.

The Senate shall chuse their other Officers, and also a President pro tempore, in the absence of the Vice President, or when he shall exercise the Office of the President of the United States.

The Senate shall have the sole Power to try all Impeachments. When sitting for that purpose, they shall be on Oath or Affirmation. When the President of the United States is tried, the Chief Justice shall preside: And no person shall be convicted without the Concurrence of two thirds of the Members present.

Judgment in Cases of Impeachment shall not extend further than to removal from Office, and disqualification to hold and enjoy any Office of honor, Trust, or Profit under the United States: but the Party convicted shall nevertheless be liable and subject to Indictment, Trial, Judgment, and Punishment, according to Law.

Section 4 The Times, Places and Manner of holding Elections for Senators and Representatives, shall be prescribed in each state by the Legislature thereof; but the Congress may at any time by Law make or alter such Regulations, except as to the Places of Chusing Senators.

The Congress shall assemble at least once in every Year, and such Meeting shall be on the first Monday in December, unless they shall by Law appoint a different Day.

Section 5 Each House shall be the Judge of the Elections, Returns and Qualifications of its own Members, and a Majority of each shall constitute a Quorum to do Business; but a smaller number may adjourn from day to day, and may be authorized to compel the Attendance of absent Members, in such Manner, and under such Penalties, as each House may provide.

Each House may determine the Rules of its Proceedings, punish its Members for disorderly Behavior, and, with the Concurrence of two thirds, expel a Member.

Each House shall keep a Journal of its Proceedings, and from time to time publish the same, excepting such Parts as may in their Judgment require Secrecy; and the Yeas and Nays of the Members of either House on any question shall, at the Desire of one fifth of those Present, be entered on the Journal.

Neither House, during the Session of Congress, shall, without the Consent of the other, adjourn for more than three days, nor to any other Place than that in which the two Houses shall be sitting.

Section 6 The Senators and Representatives shall receive a Compensation for their Services, to be ascertained by Law, and paid out of the Treasury of the United States. They shall in all Cases, except Treason, Felony, and Breach of the Peace, be privileged from arrest during their Attendance at the Session of their respective Houses, and in going to and returning from the same; and for any Speech or Debate in either House, they shall not be questioned in any other Place.

No Senator or Representative shall, during the Time for which he was elected, be appointed to any civil Office under the Authority of the United States, which shall have been created, or the Emoluments whereof shall have been increased, during such time; and no Person holding any Office under the United States shall be a Member of either House during his continuance in Office.

Section 7 All Bills for raising Revenue shall originate in the House of Representatives; but the Senate may propose or concur with Amendments as on other bills.

Every Bill which shall have passed the House of Representatives and the Senate, shall, before it become a Law, be presented to the President of the United States; If he approve he shall sign it, but if not he shall return it, with his Objections, to that House in which it shall have originated, who shall enter the Objections at large on their Journal, and proceed to reconsider it. If after such Reconsideration two thirds of that House shall agree to pass the bill, it shall be sent, together with the objections, to the other House, by which it shall likewise be reconsidered, and if approved by two thirds of that House, it shall become a Law. But in all such Cases the Votes of both Houses shall be determined by Yeas and Nays, and the Names of the Persons voting for and against the Bill shall be entered on the Journal of each House respectively. If any Bill shall not be returned by the President within ten Days (Sundays excepted) after it shall have been presented to him, the Same shall be a Law, in like Manner as if he had signed it, unless the Congress by their Adjournment prevent its Return, in which Case it shall not be a Law.

Every Order, Resolution, or Vote to which the Concurrence of the Senate and House of Representatives may be necessary (except on a question of Adjournment) shall be presented to the President of the United States; and before the Same shall take Effect, shall be approved by him, or being disapproved by him, shall be repassed by two thirds of the Senate and House of Representatives, according to the Rules and Limitations prescribed in the Case of a Bill.

Section 8 The Congress shall have Power

To lay and collect Taxes, Duties, Imposts and

Excises, to pay the Debts and provide for the common Defence and general Welfare of the United States; but all Duties, Imposts and Excises shall be uniform throughout the United States;

To borrow money on the credit of the United States;

To regulate Commerce with foreign Nations, and among the several States, and with the Indian Tribes;

To establish a uniform Rule of Naturalization, and uniform Laws on the subject of Bankruptcies throughout the United States;

To coin Money, regulate the Value thereof, and of foreign Coin, and fix the Standard of Weights and Measures;

To provide for the Punishment of counterfeiting the Securities and current Coin of the United States;

To establish Post offices and post Roads;

To promote the Progress of Science and useful Arts, by securing for limited Times to Authors and Inventors the exclusive Right to their respective Writings and Discoveries;

To constitute Tribunals inferior to the Supreme Court;

To define and punish Piracies and Felonies committed on the high Seas, and Offences against the Law of Nations;

To declare War, grant Letters of Marque and Reprisal, and make Rules concerning Captures on Land and Water;

To raise and support Armies, but no Appropriation of Money to that Use shall be for a longer Term than two Years;

To provide and maintain a Navy;

To make Rules for the Government and Regulation of the land and naval forces;

To provide for calling forth the Militia to execute the Laws of the Union, suppress Insurrections and repel Invasions;

To provide for organizing, arming, and disciplining the Militia, and for governing such Part of them as may be employed in the Service of the United States, reserving to the States respectively, the Appointment of the Officers, and the Authority of training the Militia according to the discipline prescribed by Congress;

To exercise exclusive Legislation in all Cases whatsoever, over such District (not exceeding ten Miles square) as may, by Cession of particular States, and the acceptance of Congress, become the Seat of Government of the United States, and to exercise like Authority over all Places purchased by the Consent of the Legislature of the State in which the Same shall be, for the Erection of Forts, Magazines, Arsenals, dock-Yards, and other needful Buildings;—And

To make all Laws which shall be necessary and proper for carrying into Execution the foregoing Powers, and all other Powers vested by this Constitution in the government of the United States, or in any Department or Officer thereof.

Section 9 The Migration or Importation of such Persons as any of the States now existing shall think proper to admit, shall not be prohibited by the Congress prior to the Year one thousand eight hundred and eight, but a tax or duty may be imposed on such Importation, not exceeding ten dollars for each Person.

The privilege of the Writ of Habeas Corpus shall not be suspended, unless when in Cases of Rebellion or Invasion the public Safety may require it.

No Bill of Attainder or ex post facto Law shall be passed.

No capitation, or other direct, Tax shall be laid unless in Proportion to the Census or Enumeration herein before directed to be taken.

No Tax or Duty shall be laid on Articles exported from any State.

No Preference shall be given by any Regulation of Revenue to the Ports of one State over those of another: nor shall Vessels bound to, or from, one state, be obliged to enter, clear, or pay Duties in another.

No Money shall be drawn from the Treasury, but in Consequence of Appropriations made by Law; and a regular Statement and Account of the Receipts and Expenditures of all public Money shall be published from time to time.

No Title of Nobility shall be granted by the United States: And no Person holding any Office of Profit or Trust under them, shall, without the Consent of the Congress, accept of any present, Emolument, Office, or Title, of any kind whatever, from any King, Prince, or Foreign State.

Section 10 No state shall enter into any Treaty, Alliance, or Confederation; grant Letters of Marque and Reprisal; coin Money; emit Bills of Credit; make any Thing but gold and silver

Coin a Tender in Payment of Debts; pass any Bill of Attainder, ex post facto Law, or Law impairing the Obligation of Contracts, or grant any Title of Nobility.

No State shall, without the Consent of the Congress, lay any Imposts or Duties on Imports or Exports, except what may be absolutely necessary for executing its inspection Laws: and the net Produce of all Duties and Imposts, laid by any State on Imports or Exports, shall be for the Use of the Treasury of the United States; and all such Laws shall be subject to the Revision and Control of the Congress.

No State shall, without the Consent of Congress, lay any duty of Tonnage, keep Troops, or Ships of War in time of Peace, enter into any Agreement or Compact with another State, or with a foreign Power, or engage in War, unless actually invaded, or in such imminent Danger as will not admit of delay.

Article II

Section 1 The executive Power shall be vested in a President of the United States of America. He shall hold his Office during the Term of four years, and, together with the Vice President, chosen for the same Term, be elected, as follows:

Each State shall appoint, in such Manner as the Legislature thereof may direct, a Number of Electors, equal to the whole Number of Senators and Representatives to which the State may be entitled in the Congress; but no Senator or Representative, or Person holding an Office of Trust or Profit under the United States, shall be appointed an Elector.

The Electors shall meet in their respective States, and vote by Ballot for two persons, of whom one at least shall not be an Inhabitant of the same State with themselves. And they shall make a List of all the Persons voted for, and of the Number of Votes for each; which List they shall sign and certify, and transmit sealed to the Seat of the Government of the United States, directed to the President of the Senate. The President of the Senate shall, in the Presence of the Senate and House of Representatives, open all the Certificates, and the Votes shall then be counted. The Person having the greatest Number of Votes shall be the President, if such Number be a Majority of the whole Number of Electors appointed; and if there be more than one who have such Majority, and have an equal Number of Votes, then the House of Representatives shall immediately chuse by Ballot one of them for President; and if no Person have a Majority, then from the five highest on the List the said House shall in like Manner chuse the President. But in chusing the President, the votes shall be taken by States, the Representation from each State having one Vote; a quorum for this Purpose shall consist of a Member or Members from two-thirds of the States, and a Majority of all the States shall be necessary to a Choice. In every Case, after the Choice of the President, the Person having the greatest Number of Votes of the Electors shall be the Vice President. But if there should remain two or more who have equal votes, the Senate shall chuse from them by Ballot the Vice President.

The Congress may determine the time of chusing the Electors, and the Day on which they shall give their Votes; which Day shall be the same throughout the United States.

No person except a natural-born Citizen, or a Citizen of the United States, at the time of the Adoption of this Constitution, shall be eligible to the Office of President; neither shall any Person be eligible to that Office who shall not have attained to the Age of thirty-five years, and been fourteen Years a Resident within the United States.

In Case of the Removal of the President from Office, or of his Death, Resignation, or Inability to discharge the Powers and Duties of the said Office, the same shall devolve on the Vice President, and the Congress may by Law provide for the Case of Removal, Death, Resignation, or Inability, both of the President and Vice President, declaring what Officer shall then act as President, and such Officer shall act accordingly, until the disability be removed, or a President shall be elected.

The President shall, at stated Times, receive for his Services a Compensation, which shall neither be increased nor diminished during the Period for which he shall have been elected, and he shall not receive within that Period any other Emolument from the United States, or any of them.

Before he enter on the execution of his Office, he shall take the following Oath or Affirmation:—"I do solemnly swear (or affirm) that I will faithfully execute the Office of President of the United States, and will, to the best of my Ability, preserve, protect, and defend the Constitution of the United States."

Section 2 The President shall be Commander in Chief of the Army and Navy of the United States, and of the Militia of the several States, when called into the actual Service of the United States; he may require the Opinion, in writing, of the principal Officer in each of the executive Departments, upon any subject relating to the Duties of their respective Offices, and he shall have Power to Grant Reprieves and Pardons for Offences against the United States, except in Cases of Impeachment.

He shall have Power, by and with the Advice and Consent of the Senate, to make Treaties, provided two thirds of the Senators present concur; and he shall nominate, and by and with the Advice and Consent of the Senate, shall appoint Ambassadors, other public Ministers and Consuls, Judges of the supreme Court, and all other Officers of the United States, whose Appointments are not herein otherwise provided for, and which shall be established by Law: but the Congress may by Law vest the Appointment of such inferior Officers, as they think proper, in the President alone, in the Courts of Law, or in the Heads of Departments.

The President shall have Power to fill up all Vacancies that may happen during the Recess of the Senate, by granting Commissions which shall expire at the End of their next Session.

Section 3 He shall from time to time give to the Congress Information of the State of the Union, and recommend to their Consideration such Measures as he shall judge necessary and expedient; he may, on extraordinary occasions, convene both Houses, or either of them, and in Case of Disagreement between them, with respect to the Time of Adjournment, he may adjourn them to such Time as he shall think proper; he shall receive Ambassadors and other public Ministers; he shall take Care that the Laws be faithfully executed, and shall Commission all the Officers of the United States.

Section 4 The President, Vice President and all civil Officers of the United States, shall be removed from Office on Impeachment for, and Conviction of, Treason, Bribery, or other high Crimes and Misdemeanors.

Article III

Section 1 The judicial Power of the United States, shall be vested in one supreme Court, and in such inferior Courts as the Congress may from time to time ordain and establish. The Judges, both of the supreme and inferior Courts, shall hold their Offices during good Behaviour, and shall, at stated Times, receive for their Services, a Compensation, which shall not be diminished during their Continuance in Office.

Section 2 The judicial Power shall extend to all Cases, in Law and Equity, arising under this Constitution, the Laws of the United States, and treaties made, or which shall be made, under their Authority;—to all Cases affecting ambassadors, other public ministers and consuls;—to all cases of admiralty and maritime Jurisdiction;—to Controversies to which the United States shall be a Party;—to Controversies between two or more States;—between a State and Citizens of another State;—between Citizens of different States,—between Citizens of the same State claiming Lands under Grants of different States, and between a State, or the Citizens thereof, and foreign States, Citizens or Subjects.

In all Cases affecting Ambassadors, other public Ministers and Consuls, and those in which a State shall be Party, the supreme Court shall have original Jurisdiction. In all the other Cases before mentioned, the supreme Court shall have appellate Jurisdiction, both as to Law and Fact, with such Exceptions, and under such Regulations as the Congress shall make.

The trial of all Crimes, except in Cases of Impeachment, shall be by Jury; and such Trial shall be held in the State where the said Crimes shall have been committed; but when not committed within any State, the Trial shall be at such Place or Places as the Congress may by Law have directed.

Section 3 Treason against the United States, shall consist only in levying War against them, or in adhering to their Enemies, giving them Aid and Comfort. No Person shall be convicted of Treason unless on the testimony of two Witnesses to the same overt Act, or on Confession in open Court.

The Congress shall have power to declare the Punishment of Treason, but no Attainder of Treason shall work Corruption of Blood, or Forfeiture except during the Life of the Person attained.

Article IV

Section 1 Full Faith and Credit shall be given in each State to the public Acts, Records, and judicial Proceedings of every other State. And the Congress may by general Laws prescribe the Manner in which such Acts, Records and Proceedings shall be proved, and the Effect thereof.

Section 2 The Citizens of each State shall be entitled to all Privileges and Immunities of Citizens in the several States.

A Person charged in any State with Treason, Felony, or other Crime, who shall flee from Justice, and be found in another State, shall on demand of the executive Authority of the State from which he fled, be delivered up, to be removed to the State having Jurisdiction of the crime.

No Person held to Service or Labour in one State, under the Laws thereof, escaping into another, shall, in Consequence of any Law or Regulation therein, be discharged from such Service or Labour, but shall be delivered up on Claim of the Party to whom such Service or Labour may be due.

Section 3 New States may be admitted by the Congress into this Union; but no new State shall be formed or erected within the Jurisdiction of any other State; nor any State be formed by the Junction of two or more States, or parts of States, without the Consent of the Legislatures of the States concerned as well as of the Congress.

The Congress shall have Power to dispose of and make all needful Rules and Regulations respecting the Territory or other Property belonging to the United States; and nothing in this Constitution shall be so construed as to Prejudice any Claims of the United States, or of any particular State.

Section 4 The United States shall guarantee to every State in this Union a Republican Form of Government, and shall protect each of them against Invasion; and on Application of the Legislature, or the Executive (when the Legislature cannot be convened) against domestic Violence.

Article V

The Congress, whenever two-thirds of both Houses shall deem it necessary, shall propose Amendments to this Constitution, or, on the Application of the Legislatures of two-thirds of the several States, shall call a Convention for proposing Amendments, which, in either Case, shall be valid to all Intents and Purposes, as part of this Constitution, when ratified by the Legislatures of three-fourths of the several States, or by Conventions in three-fourths thereof, as the one or the other Mode of Ratification may be proposed by the Congress; Provided that no Amendment which may be made prior to the Year One thousand eight hundred and eight shall in any Manner affect the first and fourth Clauses in the Ninth Section of the first Article; and that no State, without its Consent, shall be deprived of its equal Suffrage in the Senate.

Article VI

All Debts contracted and Engagements entered into, before the Adoption of this Constitution, shall be as valid against the United States under this Constitution, as under the Confederation.

This Constitution, and the Laws of the United States which shall be made in Pursuance thereof; and all Treaties made, or which shall be made, under the Authority of the United States, shall be the supreme Law of the Land; and the Judges in every State shall be bound thereby, any Thing in the Constitution or Laws of any State to the Contrary notwithstanding.

The Senators and Representatives before mentioned, and the Members of the several State Legislatures and all executive and judicial Officers, both of the United States and of the several States, shall be bound by Oath or Affirmation to support this Constitution; but no religious Test shall ever be required as a qualification to any Office or public Trust under the United States.

Article VII

The Ratification of the Conventions of nine States shall be sufficient for the Establishment of this Constitution between the States so ratifying the same.

Done in Convention by the Unanimous Consent of the States present the Seventeenth Day of September in the Year of our Lord one thousand seven hundred and Eighty seven, and of the Independence of the United States of America the Twelfth. In Witness whereof We have here-unto subscribed our Names.

Go. Washington, President and deputy from Virginia; Attest William Jackson, Secretary; Delaware: Geo. Read,* Gunning Bedford, Jr., John Dickinson, Richard Basset, Jaco. Broom; Maryland: James McHenry, Daniel of St. Thomas' Jenifer, Danl. Carroll; Virginia: John Blair, James Madison, Jr.; North Carolina: Wm. Blount, Richd. Dobbs Spaight, Hu Williamson; South Carolina: J. Rutledge, Charles Cotesworth Pinckney, Charles Pinckney, Pierce Butler; Georgia: William Few, Abr. Baldwin; New Hampshire: John Langdon, Nicholas Gilman; Massachusetts: Nathaniel Gorham, Rufus King; Connecticut: Wm. Saml. Johnson, Roger Sherman,* New York: Alexander Hamilton; New Jersey: Wil. Livingston, David Brearley, Wm. Paterson, Jona. Dayton; Pennsylvania: B. Franklin,* Thomas Mifflin, Robt. Morris,* Geo. Clymer,* Thos. FitzSimons, Jared Ingersoll, James Wilson, Gouv. Morris.

Articles in Addition to, and Amendment of, the Constitution of the United States of America, Proposed by Congress, and Ratified by the Legislatures of the Several States, Pursuant to the Fifth Article of the Original Constitution.

Amendment I [1791]

Congress shall make no law respecting an establishment of religion, or prohibiting the free exercise thereof; or abridging the freedom of speech, or of the press; or the right of the people peaceably to assemble, and to petition the Government for a redress of grievances.

Amendment II [1791]

A well regulated Militia, being necessary to the security of a free State, the right of the people to keep and bear Arms shall not be infringed.

Amendment III [1791]

No Soldier shall, in time of peace, be quartered in any house, without the consent of the Owner, nor in time of war, but in a manner to be prescribed by law.

Amendment IV [1791]

The right of the people to be secure in their persons, houses, papers, and effects, against unreasonable searches and seizures, shall not be violated, and no Warrants shall issue, but upon probable cause, supported by Oath or affirmation, and particularly describing the place to be searched, and the persons or things to be seized.

Amendment V [1791]

No person shall be held to answer for a capital or otherwise infamous crime, unless on a presentment or indictment of a Grand Jury, except in cases arising in the land or naval forces, or in the Militia, when in actual service in time of War or public danger; nor shall any person be subject for the same offence to be twice put in jeopardy of life or limb; nor shall be compelled in any criminal case to be a witness against himself, nor be deprived of life, liberty, or property, without due process of law; nor shall private property be taken for public use, without just compensation.

Amendment VI [1791]

In all criminal prosecutions, the accused shall enjoy the right to a speedy and public trial, by an impartial jury of the State and district wherein the crime shall have been committed, which district shall have been previously ascertained by law, and to be informed of the nature and cause of the accusation; to be confronted with the witnesses against him; to have compulsory process for obtaining witnesses in his favor, and to have the Assistance of Counsel for his defence.

Amendment VII [1791]

In suits at common law, where the value in controversy shall exceed twenty dollars, the right of trial by jury shall be preserved, and no fact tried by a jury, shall be otherwise reexamined in any Court of the United States, than according to the rules of the common law.

Amendment VIII [1791]

Excessive bail shall not be required, nor excessive fines imposed, nor cruel and unusual punishments inflicted.

Amendment IX [1791]

The enumeration in the Constitution, of certain rights, shall not be construed to deny or disparage others retained by the people.

Amendment X [1791]

The powers not delegated to the United States by the Constitution, nor prohibited by it to the States, are reserved to the States respectively, or to the people.

Amendment XI [1798]

The Judicial power of the United States shall not be construed to extend to any suit in law or equity, commenced or prosecuted against one of the United States by Citizens of another State, or by Citizens or Subjects of any Foreign State.

Amendment XII [1804]

The Electors shall meet in their respective States and vote by ballot for President and Vice President, one of whom, at least, shall not be an inhabitant of the same State with themselves; they shall name in their ballots the person voted for as President, and in distinct ballots the person voted for as Vice President, and they shall make distinct lists of all persons voted for as President, and of all persons voted for as Vice President, and of the number of votes for each, which lists they shall sign and certify, and transmit sealed to the seat of the government of the United States, directed to the President of the Senate;— The President of the Senate shall, in the presence of the Senate and House of Representatives, open all the certificates and the votes shall then be counted;—The person having the greatest number of votes for President, shall be the President, if such number be a majority of the whole number of Electors appointed; and if no person have such majority, then from the persons having the highest numbers not exceeding three on the list of those voted for as President, the House of Representatives shall choose immediately, by ballot, the President. But in choosing the President, the votes shall be taken by states, the representation from each state having one vote; a quorum for this purpose shall consist of a member or members from two-thirds of the states, and a majority of all the states shall be necessary to a choice. And if the House of Representatives shall not choose a President whenever the right of choice shall devolve upon them, before the fourth day of March next following, then the Vice President shall act as President, as in the case of the death or other constitutional disability of the President.—The person having the greatest number of votes as Vice President, shall be the Vice President, if such number be a majority of the whole number of Electors appointed, and if no person have a majority, then from the two highest numbers on the list, the Senate shall choose the Vice President; a quorum for the purpose shall consist of two-thirds of the whole number of Senators, and a majority of the whole number shall be necessary to a choice. But no person constitutionally ineligible to the office of President shall be eligible to that of Vice President of the United States.

Amendment XIII [1865]

Section 1   Neither slavery nor involuntary servitude, except as a punishment for crime whereof the party shall have been duly convicted, shall exist within the United States, or any place subject to their jurisdiction.

Section 2   Congress shall have power to enforce this article by appropriate legislation.

Amendment XIV [1868]

Section 1   All persons born or naturalized in the United States, and subject to the jurisdiction thereof, are citizens of the United States and of the State wherein they reside. No State shall make or enforce any law which shall abridge the privileges or immunities of citizens of the United States; nor shall any State deprive any person of life, liberty, or property, without due process of law; nor deny to any person within its jurisdiction the equal protection of the laws.

Section 2   Representatives shall be apportioned among the several States according to their respective numbers, counting the whole number of persons in each State, excluding Indians not taxed. But when the right to vote at any election for the choice of electors for President and Vice President of the United States, Representatives in Congress, the Executive and Judicial officers of a State, or the members of the Legislature thereof, is denied to any of the male inhabitants of such State, being twenty-one years of age, and citizens of the United States or in any way abridged, except for participation in rebellion, or other crime, the basis of representation therein shall be reduced in the proportion which the number of such male citizens shall bear to the whole number of male citizens twenty-one years of age in such State.

Section 3   No person shall be a Senator or Representative in Congress, or elector of President and Vice President, or hold any office, civil or military, under the United States, or under any State, who, having previously taken an oath, as a member of Congress, or as an officer of the United States, or as a member of any State legislature, or as an executive or judicial officer of any State, to support the Constitution of the United States, shall have engaged in insurrection or rebellion against the same, or given aid or comfort to the enemies thereof. But Congress may by a vote of two-thirds of each House, remove such disability.

Section 4   The validity of the public debt of the United States, authorized by law, including debts incurred for payment of pensions and bounties for services in suppressing insurrection or rebellion, shall not be questioned. But neither the United States nor any State shall assume or pay any debt or obligation incurred in aid of insurrection or rebellion against the United States, or any claim for the loss or emancipation of any slave; but all such debts, obligations, and claims shall be held illegal and void.

Section 5   The Congress shall have the power to enforce, by appropriate legislation, the provisions of this article.

Amendment XV [1870]

Section 1   The right of citizens of the United States to vote shall not be denied or abridged by the United States or by any State on account of race, color, or previous condition of servitude—

Section 2   The Congress shall have power to enforce this article by appropriate legislation.

Amendment XVI [1913]

The Congress shall have power to lay and collect taxes on incomes, from whatever source derived, without apportionment among the several States, and without regard to any census or enumeration.

Amendment XVII [1913]

The Senate of the United States shall be composed of two Senators from each State, elected by the people thereof, for six years; and each Senator shall have one vote. The electors in each State shall have the qualifications requisite for electors of the most numerous branch of the State legislatures.

When vacancies happen in the representation of any State in the Senate, the executive authority of such State shall issue writs of election to fill such vacancies: Provided, That the legislature of any State may empower the executive thereof to make temporary appointments until the people fill the vacancies by election as the legislature may direct. This amendment shall not be so construed as to affect the election or term of any Senator chosen before it becomes valid as part of the Constitution.

Amendment XVIII [1919]

Section 1   After one year from the ratification of this article the manufacture, sale, or transportation of intoxicating liquors within, the importation thereof into, or the exportation thereof from the United States and all territory subject to the jurisdiction thereof for beverage purposes is hereby prohibited.

Section 2 The Congress and the several States shall have concurrent power to enforce this article by appropriate legislation.

Section 3 This article shall be inoperative unless it shall have been ratified as an amendment to the Constitution by the legislatures of the several States, as provided in the Constitution, within seven years from the date of the submission hereof to the States by the Congress.

Amendment XIX [1920]

The right of citizens of the United States to vote shall not be denied or abridged by the United States or by any State on account of sex.

Congress shall have power to enforce this article by appropriate legislation.

Amendment XX [1933]

Section 1 The terms of the President and Vice President shall end at noon on the 20th day of January, and the terms of Senators and Representatives at noon on the 3d day of January, of the years in which such terms would have ended if this article had not been ratified; and the terms of their successors shall then begin.

Section 2 The Congress shall assemble at least once in every year, and such meeting shall begin at noon on the 3d day of January, unless they shall by law appoint a different day.

Section 3 If, at the time fixed for the beginning of the term of the President, the President elect shall have died, the Vice President elect shall become President. If a President shall not have been chosen before the time fixed for the beginning of his term, or if the President elect shall have failed to qualify, then the Vice President elect shall act as President until a President shall have qualified; and the Congress may by law provide for the case wherein neither a President elect nor a Vice President elect shall have qualified, declaring who shall then act as President, or the manner in which one who is to act shall be selected, and such person shall act accordingly until a President or Vice President shall have qualified.

Section 4 The Congress may by law provide for the case of the death of any of the persons from whom the House of Representatives may choose a President whenever the right of choice shall have devolved upon them, and for the case of the death of any of the persons from whom the Senate may choose a Vice President whenever the right of choice shall have devolved upon them.

Section 5 Sections 1 and 2 shall take effect on the 15th day of October following the ratification of this article.

Section 6 This article shall be inoperative unless it shall have been ratified as an amendment to the Constitution by the legislatures of three-fourths of the several States within seven years from the date of its submission.

Amendment XXI [1933]

Section 1 The eighteenth article of amendment to the Constitution of the United States is hereby repealed.

Section 2 The transportation or importation into any State, Territory, or possession of the United States for delivery or use therein of intoxicating liquors, in violation of the laws thereof, is hereby prohibited.

Section 3 This article shall be inoperative unless it shall have been ratified as an amendment to the Constitution by conventions in the several States, as provided in the Constitution, within seven years from the date of the submission hereof to the States by the Congress.

Amendment XXII [1951]

No person shall be elected to the office of the President more than twice, and no person who has held the office of President, or acted as President, for more than two years of a term to which some other person was elected President shall be elected to the office of the President more than once.

But this Article shall not apply to any person holding the office of President when this Article was proposed by the Congress, and shall not prevent any person who may be holding the office of President or acting as President, during the term within which this Article becomes operative from holding the office of President or acting as President during the remainder of such term.

Amendment XXIII [1961]

Section 1 The District constituting the seat of Government of the United States shall appoint in such manner as the Congress may direct:

A number of electors of President and Vice President equal to the whole number of Senators and Representatives in Congress to which the District would be entitled if it were a State, but in no event more than the least populous State; they shall be in addition to those appointed by the States, but they shall be considered, for the purposes of the election of President and Vice President, to be electors appointed by a State; and they shall meet in the District and perform such duties as provided by the twelfth article of amendment.

Section 2 The Congress shall have power to enforce this article by appropriate legislation.

Amendment XXIV [1964]

Section 1 The right of citizens of the United States to vote in any primary or other election for President or Vice President, for electors for President or Vice President, or for Senator or Representative in Congress, shall not be denied or abridged by the United States or any State by reason of failure to pay any poll tax or other tax.

Section 2 The Congress shall have the power to enforce this article by appropriate legislation.

Amendment XXV [1967]

Section 1 In case of the removal of the President from office or his death or resignation, the Vice President shall become President.

Section 2 Whenever there is a vacancy in the office of the Vice President, the President shall nominate a Vice President who shall take the office upon confirmation by a majority vote of both houses of Congress.

Section 3 Whenever the President transmits to the President pro tempore of the Senate and the Speaker of the House of Representatives his written declaration that he is unable to discharge the powers and duties of his office, and until he transmits to them a written declaration to the contrary, such powers and duties shall be discharged by the Vice President as Acting President.

Section 4 Whenever the Vice President and a majority of either the principal officers of the executive departments, or of such other body as Congress may by law provide, transmit to the President pro tempore of the Senate and the Speaker of the House of Representatives their written declaration that the President is unable to discharge the powers and duties of his office, the Vice President shall immediately assume the powers and duties of the office as Acting President.

Thereafter, when the President transmits to the President pro tempore of the Senate and the Speaker of the House of Representatives his written declaration that no inability exists, he shall resume the powers and duties of his office unless the Vice President and a majority of either the principal officers of the executive departments, or of such other body as Congress may by law provide, transmit within four days to the President protempore of the Senate and the Speaker of the House of Representatives their written declaration that the President is unable to discharage the powers and duties of his office. Thereupon Congress shall decide the issue, assembling within 48 hours for that purpose if not in session. If the Congress, within 21 days after receipt of the latter written declaration, or, if Congress is not in session, within 21 days after Congress is required to assemble, determines by two-thirds vote of both houses that the President is unable to discharge the powers and duties of his office, the Vice President shall continue to discharge the same as Acting President; otherwise, the President shall resume the powers and duties of his office.

Amendment XXVI [1971]

Section 1 The right of citizens of the United States, who are 18 years of age or older, to vote shall not be denied or abridged by the United States or any state on account of age.

Section 2 The Congress shall have the power to enforce this article by appropriate legislation.

Amendment XXVII [1992]

No law varying the compensation for the service of Senators and Representatives shall take effect until an election of Representatives shall have intervened.

THE FEDERALIST PAPERS

The Federalist Papers is a collection of 85 essays written by Alexander Hamilton, John Jay, and James Madison under the pen name Publius. They were published in New York newspapers in 1787 and 1788 to support ratification of the Constitution. Federalist Nos. 10, 51, and 78 are reprinted here.

James Madison: Federalist No. 10

Among the numerous advantages promised by a well constructed Union, none deserves to be more accurately developed than its tendency to break and control the violence of faction. The friend of popular governments never finds himself so much alarmed for their character and fate as when he contemplates their propensity to this dangerous vice. He will not fail, therefore, to set a due value on any plan which, without violating the principles to which he is attached, provides a proper cure for it. The instability, injustice, and confusion, introduced into the public councils, have, in truth been the mortal diseases under which popular governments have everywhere perished; as they continue to be the favorite and fruitful topics from which the adversaries to liberty derive their most specious declamations. The valuable improvements made by the American constitutions on the popular models, both ancient and modern, cannot certainly be too much admired; but it would be an unwarrantable partiality, to contend that they have as effectually obviated the danger on this side, as was wished and expected. Complaints are everywhere heard from our most considerate and virtuous citizens, equally the friends of public and private faith, and of public and personal liberty, that our governments are too unstable; that the public good is disregarded in the conflicts of rival parties; and that measures are too often decided, not according to the rules of justice, and the rights of the minor party, but by the superior force of an interested and overbearing majority. However anxiously we may wish that these complaints had no foundation, the evidence of known facts will not permit us to deny that they are in some degree true. It will be found, indeed, on a candid review of our situation, that some of the distresses under which we labor, have been erroneously charged on the operation of our governments; but it will be found, at the same time, that other causes will not alone account for many of our heaviest misfortunes; and, particularly, for the prevailing and increasing distrust of public engagements, and alarm for private rights, which are echoed from one end of the continent to the other. These must be chiefly, if not wholly, effects of the unsteadiness and injustice, with which a factious spirit has tainted our public administrations.

By a faction, I understand a number of citizens, whether amounting to a majority or minority of the whole, who are united and actuated by some common impulse of passion, or of interest, adverse to the rights of other citizens, or to the permanent and aggregate interests of the community.

There are two methods of curing the mischiefs of faction: The one, by removing its causes; the other, by controlling its effects.

There are again two methods of removing the causes of faction: the one, by destroying the liberty which is essential to its existence; the other, by giving to every citizen the same opinions, the same passions, and the same interests.

It could never be more truly said, than of the first remedy, that it was worse than the disease. Liberty is to faction what air is to fire, an aliment, without which it instantly expires. But it could not be a less folly to abolish liberty, which is essential to political life because it nourishes faction, than it would be to wish the annihilation of air, which is essential to animal life, because it imparts to fire its destructive agency.

The second expedient is as impracticable, as the first would be unwise. As long as the reason of man continues fallible, and he is at liberty to exercise it, different opinions will be formed. As long as the connection subsists between his reason and his self-love, his opinions and his passions will have a reciprocal influence on each other; and the former will be objects to which the latter will attach themselves. The diversity in the faculties of men, from which the rights of property originate, is not less an insuperable obstacle to a uniformity of interests. The protection of those faculties is the first object of government. From the protection of different and unequal faculties of acquiring property, the possession of different degrees and kinds of property immediately results; and from the influence of these on the sentiments and views of the respective proprietors, ensues a division of the society into different interests and parties.

The latent causes of faction are thus sown in the nature of man; and we see them everywhere brought into different degrees of activity, according to the different circumstances of civil society. A zeal for different opinions concerning religion, concerning government, and many other points, as well of speculation as of practice; an attachment to different leaders, ambitiously contending for preeminence and power; or to persons of other descriptions, whose fortunes have been interesting to the human passions, have, in turn, divided mankind into parties, inflamed them with mutual animosity, and rendered them much more disposed to vex and oppress each other, than to cooperate for their common good. So strong is this propensity of mankind, to fall into mutual animosities, that where no substantial occasion presents itself, the most frivolous and fanciful distinctions have been sufficient to kindle their unfriendly passions, and excite their most violent conflicts. But the most common and durable source of factions has been the various and unequal distribution of property. Those who hold, and those who are without property, have ever formed distinct interests in society. Those who are creditors, and those who are debtors, fall under a like discrimination. A landed interest, a manufacturing interest, a mercantile interest, a moneyed interest, with many lesser interests, grow up of necessity in civilized nations, and divide them into different classes, actuated by different sentiments and views. The regulation of these various and interfering interests forms the principle task of modern legislation, and involves the spirit of party and faction in the necessary and ordinary operations of government.

No man is allowed to be a judge in his own cause; because his interest will certainly bias his judgment, and, not improbably, corrupt his integrity. With equal, nay, with greater reason, a body of men are unfit to be both judges and parties at the same time; yet what are many of the most important acts of legislation, but so many judicial determinations, not indeed concerning the rights of single persons, but concerning the rights of large bodies of citizens? And what are the different classes of legislators, but advocates and parties to the cause which they determine? Is a law proposed concerning private debts? It is a question to which the creditors are parties on one side, and the debtors on the other. Justice ought to hold the balance between them. Yet the parties are, and must be, themselves the judges; and the most numerous party, or, in other words, the most powerful faction, must be expected to prevail. Shall domestic manufactures be encouraged, and in what degree, by restrictions on foreign manufactures? are questions which would be differently decided by the landed and the manufacturing classes; and probably by neither with a sole regard to justice and the public good....

It is in vain to say, that enlightened statesmen will be able to adjust these clashing interests, and render them all subservient to the public good. Enlightened statesmen will not always be at the helm; nor, in many cases, can such an adjustment be made at all, without taking into view indirect and remote considerations, which will rarely prevail over the immediate interest which one party may find in disregarding the rights of another, or the good of the whole.

The inference to which we are brought is, that the causes of faction cannot be removed; and that relief is only to be sought in the means of controlling its effects.

If a faction consists of less than a majority, relief is supplied by the republican principle, which enables the majority to defeat its sinister views, by regular vote. It may clog the administration, it may convulse the society; but it will be unable to execute and mask its violence under the forms of the constitution. When a majority is included in a faction, the form of popular government, on the other hand, enables it to sacrifice to its ruling passion or interest, both the public good and the rights of other citizens. To secure the public good, and private rights, against the danger of such a faction, and at the same time to preserve the spirit and the form of popular government, is then the great object to which our inquiries are directed. Let me add, that it is the great desideratum, by which alone this form of government can be rescued from the opprobrium under which it has so long labored, and be recommended to the esteem and adoption of mankind.

By what means is this object attainable? Evidently by one of two only. Either the existence of the same passion or interest in a majority, at the same time must be prevented; or the majority, having such coexistent passion or interest, must be rendered, by their number and local situation, unable to concert and carry into effect schemes of oppression. If the impulse and the opportunity be suffered to coincide, we well know, that neither moral nor religious motives can be relied on as an adequate control. They are not found to be such on the injustice and violence of individuals, and lose their efficacy in proportion

to the number combined together; that is in proportion as their efficacy becomes needful.

From this view of the subject, it may be concluded, that a pure democracy, by which I mean a society consisting of a small number of citizens, who assemble and administer the government in person, can admit of no cure from the mischiefs of faction. A common passion or interest will, in almost every case, be felt by a majority of the whole; a communication and concert, results from the form of government itself; and there is nothing to check the inducements to sacrifice the weaker party, or an obnoxious individual. Hence it is, that such democracies have ever been spectacles of turbulence and contention; have ever been found incompatible with personal security, or the rights of property; and have, in general been as short in their lives, as they have been violent in their deaths. Theoretic politicians, who have patronized this species of government, have erroneously supposed that by reducing mankind to a perfect equality in their political rights, they would, at the same time, be perfectly equalized and assimilated in their possessions, their opinions, and their passions.

A republic, by which I mean a government in which the scheme of representation takes place, opens a different prospect, and promises the cure for which we are seeking. Let us examine the points in which it varies from pure democracy, and we shall comprehend both the nature of the cure and the efficacy which it must derive from the union.

The two great points of difference, between a democracy and a republic, are, first, the delegation of the government, in the latter, to a small number of citizens elected by the rest; secondly, the greater number of citizens, and greater sphere of country, over which the latter may be extended.

The effect of the first difference is on the one hand, to refine and enlarge the public views, by passing them through the medium of a chosen body of citizens, whose wisdom may best discern the true interest in their country, and whose patriotism and love of justice, will be least likely to sacrifice it to temporary or partial considerations. Under such a regulation, it may well happen, that the public voice, pronounced by the representatives of the people, will be more consonant to the public good, than if pronounced by the people themselves, convened for the purpose. On the other hand, the effect may be inverted. Men of factious tempers, of local prejudices, or of sinister designs, may by intrigue, by corruption, or by other means, first obtain the suffrages, and then betray the interests, of the people. The question resulting is, whether small or extensive republics are most favorable to the election of proper guardians of the public weal; and it is clearly decided in favor of the latter by two obvious considerations.

In the first place, it is to be remarked, that however small the republic may be, the representatives must be raised to a certain number, in order to guard against the cabals of a few; and that however large it may be, they must be limited to a certain number, in order to guard against the confusion of a multitude. Hence, the number of representatives in the two cases not being in proportion to that of the constituents, and being proportionally greatest in the small republic, it follows that if the proportion of fit characters be not less in the large than in the small republic, the former will present a greater option, and consequently a greater probability of a fit choice.

In the next place, as each representative will be chosen by a greater number of citizens in the large than in the small republic, it will be more difficult for unworthy candidates to practice with success the vicious arts, by which elections are too often carried; and the suffrages of the people being more free, will be more likely to center in men who possess the most attractive merit, and the most diffusive and established characters. . . .

The other point of difference is, the greater number of citizens, and extent of territory, which may be brought within the compass of republican, than of democratic government; and it is this circumstance principally which renders factious combinations less to be dreaded in the former, than in the latter. The smaller the society, the fewer probably will be the distinct parties and interests composing it; the fewer the distinct parties and interests, the more frequently will a majority be found of the same party; and the smaller the number of individuals composing a majority, and the smaller the compass within which they are placed, the more easily they will concert and execute their plans of oppression. Extend the sphere, and you take in a greater variety of parties and interests; you make it less probable that a majority of the whole will have a common motive to invade the rights of other citizens; or if such a common motive exists, it will be more difficult for all who feel it to discover their own strength, and to act in unison with each other. . . .

Hence, it clearly appears, that the same advantage, which a republic has over a democracy, in controlling the effects of faction, is enjoyed by a large over a small republic—is enjoyed by the union over the states composing it. Does this advantage consist in the substitution of representatives, whose enlightened views and virtuous sentiments render them superior to local prejudices, and to schemes of injustice? It will not be denied, that the representation of the union will be most likely to possess these requisite endowments. Does it consist in the greater security afforded by a greater variety of parties, against the event of any one party being able to outnumber and oppress the rest? In an equal degree does the increased variety of parties, comprised within the union, increase this security? Does it, in fine, consist in the greater obstacles opposed to the concert and accomplishment of the secret wishes of an unjust and interested majority? Here, again, the extent of the union gives it the most palpable advantage. The influence of factious leaders may kindle a flame within their particular states, but will be unable to spread a general conflagration through the other states; a religious sect may degenerate into a political faction in a part of the confederacy; but the variety of sects dispersed over the entire face of it, must secure the national councils against any danger from that source; a rage for paper money, for an abolition of debts, for an equal division of property, or for any other improper or wicked project, will be less apt to pervade the whole body of the union, than a particular member of it; in the same proportion as such a malady is more likely to taint a particular country or district, than an entire state.

In the extent and proper structure of the union, therefore, we behold a republican remedy for the diseases most incident to republican government. And according to the degree of pleasure and pride we feel in being republicans, ought to be our zeal in cherishing the spirit, and supporting the character of Federalists.

James Madison: Federalist No. 51

To what expedient then shall we finally resort, for maintaining in practice the necessary partition of power among the several departments, as laid down in the constitution? The only answer that can be given is, that as all these exterior provisions are found to be inadequate, the defect must be supplied, by so contriving the interior structure of the government, as that its several constituent parts may, by their mutual relations, be the means of keeping each other in their proper places. . . .

In order to lay a due foundation for that separate and distinct exercise of the different powers of government, which, to a certain extent, is admitted on all hands to be essential to the preservation of liberty, it is evident that each department should have a will of its own; and consequently should be so constituted, that the members of each should have as little agency as possible in the appointment of the members of the others. . . .

It is equally evident, that the members of each department should be as little dependent as possible on those of the others, for the emoluments annexed to their offices. Were the executive magistrate, or the judges, not independent of the legislature in this particular, their independence in every other would be merely nominal.

But the great security against a gradual concentration of the several powers in the same department, consists in giving to those who administer each department, the necessary constitutional means, and personal motives, to resist encroachments of the others. The provision for defense must in this, as in all other cases, be made commensurate to the danger of attack. Ambition must be made to counteract ambition. The interest of the man must be connected with the constitutional rights of the place. It may be a reflection on human nature, that such devices should be necessary to control the abuses of government. But what is government itself, but the greatest of all reflections on human nature? If men were angels, no government would be necessary. If angels were to govern men, neither external nor internal controls on government would be necessary. In framing a government, which is to be administered by men over men, the great difficulty lies in this: You must first enable the government to control the governed; and in the next place, oblige it to control itself. A dependence on the people is, no doubt, the primary control on the government; but experience has taught mankind the necessity of auxiliary precautions.

This policy of supplying by opposite and rival interests, the defect of better motives, might be traced through the whole system of human affairs, private as well as public. We see it particularly displayed in all the subordinate distributions of power; where the constant aim is, to divide and arrange the several offices in such a manner, as that each may be a check on the other; that the private interest of every individual, may be a sentinel over the public rights. These interventions of prudence cannot be less requisite to the distribution of the supreme powers of the state.

But it is not possible to give to each department an equal power of self-defense. In republican government, the legislative authority necessarily predominates. The remedy for this inconvenience is, to divide the legislature into different branches; and to render them by different modes of election, and different principles of action, as little connected with each other, as the nature of their common functions, and their common dependence on the society will admit. It may even be necessary to guard against dangerous encroachments, by still further precautions. As the weight of the legislative authority requires that it should be thus divided, the weakness of the executive may require, on the other hand, that it should be fortified. An absolute negative on the legislature, appears, at first view, to be the natural defense with which the executive magistrate should be armed. But perhaps it would be neither altogether safe, nor alone sufficient. On ordinary occasions, it might not be exerted with the requisite firmness; and on extraordinary occasions, it might be perfidiously abused. May not this defect of an absolute negative be supplied by some qualified connection between this weaker department, and the weaker branch of the stronger department, by which the latter may be led to support the constitutional rights of the former, without being too much detached from the rights of its own department?

There are, moreover, two considerations particularly applicable to the federal system of America, which place that system in a very interesting point of view.

First. In a single republic, all the power surrendered by the people is submitted to the administration of a single government, and the usurpations are guarded against by a division of the government into distinct and separate departments. In the compound republic of America, the power surrendered by the people is first divided between two distinct governments, and then the portion allotted to each subdivided among distinct and separate departments. Hence a double security arises to the rights of the people. The different governments will control each other, at the same time that each will be controlled by itself.

Second. It is of great importance in a republic not only to guard the society against the oppression of its rulers, but to guard one part of the society against the injustice of the other part. Different interests necessarily exist in different classes of citizens. If a majority be united by a common interest, the rights of the minority will be insecure. There are but two methods of providing against this evil: the one by creating a will in the community independent of the majority—that is, of the society itself; the other, by comprehending in the society so many separate descriptions of citizens as will render an unjust combination of a majority of the whole very probable, if not impracticable. The first method prevails in all governments possessing an hereditary or self-appointed authority. This, at best, is but a precarious security; because a power independent of the society may as well espouse the unjust views of the major, as the rightful interests of the minor party, and may possibly be turned against both parties. The second method will be exemplified in the federal republic of the United States. Whilst all authority in it will be derived from and dependent on the society, the society itself will be broken into so many parts, interests and classes of citizens, that the rights of individuals, or of the minority, will be in little danger from interested combinations of the majority. In a free government the security for civil rights must be the same as that for religious rights. It consists in the one case in the multiplicity of interests, and in the other in the multiplicity of sects. The degree of security in both cases will depend on the number of interests and sects; and this may be presumed to depend on the extent of country and number of people comprehended under the same government. This view of the subject must particularly recommend a proper federal system to all the sincere and considerate friends of republican government, since it shows that in exact proportion as the territory of the Union may be formed into more circumscribed Confederacies, or States, oppressive combinations of a majority will be facilitated; the best security, under the republican forms, for the rights of every class of citizens, will be diminished; and consequently the stability and independence of some member of the government, the only other security, must be proportionately increased. Justice is the end of the government. It is the end of civil society. It ever has been and ever will be pursued until it be obtained, or until liberty be lost in the pursuit. In a society under the forms of which the stronger faction can readily unite and oppress the weaker, anarchy may as truly be said to reign as in a state of nature, where the weaker individual is not secured against the violence of the stronger; and as, in the latter state, even the stronger individuals are prompted, by the uncertainty of their condition, to submit to a government which may protect the weak as well as themselves; so, in the former state, will the more powerful factions or parties be gradually induced, by a like motive, to wish for a government which will protect all parties, the weaker as well as the more powerful. It can be little doubted that if the State of Rhode Island was separated from the Confederacy and left to itself, the insecurity of rights under the popular form of government within such narrow limits would be displayed by such reiterated oppressions of factious majorities that some power altogether independent of the people would soon be called for by the voice of the very factions whose misrule had proved the necessity of it. In the extended republic of the United States, and among the great variety of interests, parties, and sects which it embraces, a coalition of a majority of the whole society could seldom take place on any other principles than those of justice and the general good; whilst there being thus less danger to a minor from the will of a major party, there must be less pretext, also, to provide for the security of the former, by introducing into the government a will not dependent on the latter, or, in other words, a will independent of the society itself. It is no less certain than it is important, notwithstanding the contrary opinions which have been entertained, that the larger the society, provided it lie within a practical sphere, the more duly capable it will be of self-government. And happily for the republican cause, the practicable sphere may be carried to a very great extent, by a judicious modification and mixture of the federal principle.

Alexander Hamilton: Federalist No. 78

We proceed now to an examination of the judiciary department of the proposed government.

In unfolding the defects of the existing confederation, the utility and necessity of a federal judicature have been clearly pointed out. It is the less necessary to recapitulate the considerations there urged; as the propriety of the institution in the abstract is not disputed; the only questions which have been raised being relative to the manner of constituting it, and to its extent. To these points, therefore, our observations shall be confined.

The manner of constituting it seems to embrace these several objects: 1st. The mode of appointing the judges; 2nd. The tenure by which they are to hold their places; 3rd. The partition of the judiciary authority between courts, and their relations to each other.

First. As to the mode of appointing the judges: This is the same with that of appointing the officers of the union in general, and has been so fully discussed . . . that nothing can be said here which would not be useless repetition.

Second. As to the tenure by which the judges are to hold their places: This chiefly concerns their duration in office; the provisions for their support; the precautions for their responsibility.

According to the plan of the convention, all the judges who may be appointed by the United States are to hold their offices during good behavior; which is conformable to the most approved of the state constitutions. . . . The standard of good behavior for the continuance in office of the judicial magistracy is certainly one of the most valuable of the modern improvements in the practice of government. In a monarchy, it is an excellent barrier to the despotism of the prince; in a republic, it is a no less excellent barrier to the encroachments and oppressions of the representative body. And it is the best expedient which can be devised in any government, to secure a steady, upright, and impartial administration of the laws.

Whoever attentively considers the different departments of power must perceive, that, in a government in which they are separated from each other, the judiciary, from the nature of its functions, will always be the least dangerous to the political rights of the constitution; because it will be at least in a capacity to annoy or injure them. The executive not only dispenses the honors, but holds the sword of the community. The legislature not only commands the purse, but prescribes the rules by which the duties and rights of every citizen are to be regulated. The judiciary, on the contrary, has no influence over either the sword or the purse; no direction either of the strength or of the wealth of the society; and can take no active resolution whatever. It may truly be said to have neither force nor will, but merely judgment; and must ultimately depend upon the aid of the executive arm for the efficacious exercise even of this faculty.

This simple view of the matter suggests several important consequences: It proves incontestably, that the judiciary is beyond comparison, the weakest of the three departments of power, that it can never attack with success either of the other two: and that all possible care is requisite to enable it to defend itself against their attacks. It equally proves, that, though individual oppression may now and then proceed from the courts of justice, the general liberty of the people can never be endangered from that quarter; I mean so long as the judiciary remains truly distinct from both the legislature and executive. For I agree, that "there is no liberty, if the power of judging be not separated from the legislative and executive powers." It proves, in the last place, that as liberty can have nothing to fear from the judiciary alone, but would have everything to fear from its union with either of the other

departments; that, as all the effects of such a union must ensue from a dependence of the former on the latter, notwithstanding a nominal and apparent separation; that as, from the natural feebleness of the judiciary, it is in continual jeopardy of being overpowered, awed or influenced by its coordinate branches; that, as nothing can contribute so much to its firmness and independence as permanency in office, this quality may therefore be justly regarded as an indispensable ingredient in its constitution; and, in a great measure, as the citadel of the public justice and the public security.

The complete independence of the courts of justice is peculiarly essential in a limited constitution. By a limited constitution, I understand one which contains certain specified exceptions to the legislative authority; such, for instance, as that it shall pass no bills of attainder, no ex post facto laws, and the like. Limitations of this kind can be preserved in practice no other way than through the medium of the courts of justice, whose duty it must be to declare all acts contrary to the manifest tenor of the constitution void. Without this, all the reservations of particular rights or privileges would amount to nothing.

Some perplexity respecting the right of the courts to pronounce legislative acts void, because contrary to the constitution, has arisen from an imagination that the doctrine would imply a superiority of the judiciary to the legislative power. It is urged that the authority which can declare the acts of another void, must necessarily be superior to the one whose acts may be declared void. As this doctrine is of great importance in all the American constitutions, a brief discussion of the grounds on which it rests cannot be unacceptable.

There is no position which depends on clearer principles than that every act of a delegated authority, contrary to the tenor of the commission under which it is exercised, is void. No legislative act, therefore, contrary to the constitution, can be valid. To deny this would be to affirm, that the deputy is greater then his principal; that the servant is above his master; that the representatives of the people are superior to the people themselves; that men, acting by virtue of powers, may do not only what their powers do not authorize, but what they forbid.

If it be said that the legislative body are themselves the constitutional judges of their own powers, and that the construction they put upon them is conclusive upon the other departments, it may be answered, that this cannot be the natural presumption, where it is not to be collected from any particular provisions in the constitution. It is not otherwise to be supposed that the constitution could intend to enable the representatives of the people to substitute their will to that of their constituents. It is far more rational to suppose that the courts were designed to be an intermediate body between the people and the legislature, in order, among other things, to keep the latter within the limits assigned to their authority. The interpretation of the laws is the proper and peculiar province of the courts. A constitution is, in fact, and must be, regarded by the judges as a fundamental law. It must therefore belong to them to ascertain its meaning, as well as the meaning of any particular act proceeding from the legislative body. If there should happen to be an irreconcilable variance between the two, that which has the superior obligation and validity ought, of course, to be preferred; in other words, the constitution ought to be preferred to the statute, the intention of the people to the intention of their agents.

Nor does this conclusion by any means suppose a superiority of the judicial to the legislative power. It only supposes that the power of the people is superior to both; and that where the will of the legislature declared in its statutes, stands in opposition to that of the people declared in the constitution, the judges ought to be governed by the latter, rather than the former. They ought to regulate their decisions by the fundamental laws, rather than by those which are not fundamental....

It can be of no weight to say, that the courts, on the pretense of a repugnancy, may substitute their own pleasure to the constitutional intentions of the legislature. This might as well happen in the case of two contradictory statutes; or it might as well happen in every adjudication upon any single statute. The courts must declare the sense of the law; and if they should be disposed to exercise will instead of judgment, the consequence would equally be the substitution of their pleasure to that of the legislative body. The observation, if it proved anything, would prove that there ought to be no judges distinct from the body.

If then the courts of justice are to be considered as the bulwarks of a limited constitution, against legislative encroachments, this consideration will afford a strong argument for the permanent tenure of judicial officers, since nothing will contribute so much as this to that independent spirit in the judges, which must be essential to the faithful performance of so arduous a duty.

This independence of the judges is equally requisite to guard the constitution and the rights of individuals, from the effects of those ill-humors which are the arts of designing men, or the influence of particular conjunctures, sometimes disseminate among the people themselves, and which, though they speedily give place to better information, and more deliberate reflection, have a tendency, in the meantime, to occasion dangerous innovations in the government, and serious oppressions of the minor party in the community .... Until the people have, by some solemn and authoritative act, annulled or changed the established form, it is binding upon themselves collectively, as well as individually; and no presumption, or even knowledge of their sentiments, can warrant their representatives in a departure from it, prior to such an act. But it is easy to see, that it would require an uncommon portion of fortitude in the judges to do their duty as faithful guardians of the constitution, where legislative invasions of it had been instigated by the major voice of the community.

But it is not with a view to infractions of the constitution only, that the independence of the judges may be an essential safeguard against the effects of occasional ill-humors in the society. These sometimes extend no farther than to the injury of the private rights of particular classes of citizens, by unjust and partial laws. Here also the firmness of the judicial magistracy is of vast importance in mitigating the severity, and confining the operation of such laws. It not only serves to moderate the immediate mischiefs of those which may have been passed, but it operates as a check upon the legislative body in passing them; who, perceiving that obstacles to the success of an iniquitous intention are to be expected from the scruples of the courts, are in a manner compelled by the very motives of the injustice they meditate, to qualify their attempts....

That inflexible and uniform adherence to the rights of the constitution, and of individuals, which we perceive to be indispensable in the courts of justice, can certainly not be expected from judges who hold their offices by a temporary commission. Periodical appointments, however regulated, or by whomsoever made, would, in some way or other, be fatal to their necessary independence. If the power of making them was committed either to the executive or legislature, there would be danger of an improper compliance to the branch which possessed it; if to both, there would be an unwillingness to hazard the displeasure of either; if to the people, or to persons chosen by them for the special purpose, there would be too great a disposition to consult popularity to justify a reliance that nothing would be consulted but the constitution and the laws.

There is yet a further and a weighty reason for the permanency of judicial offices, which is deducible from the nature of the qualifications they require. It has been frequently remarked, with great propriety, that a voluminous code of laws is one of the inconveniences necessarily connected with the advantages of a free government. To avoid an arbitrary discretion in the courts, it is indispensable that they should be bound down by strict rules and precedents, which serve to define and point out their duty in every particular case that comes before them; and it will readily be conceived, from the variety of controversies which grow out of the folly and wickedness of mankind, that the records of those precedents must unavoidably swell to a very considerable bulk, and must demand long and laborious study to acquire a competent knowledge of them. Hence it is, that there can be but few men in the society, who will have sufficient skill in the laws to qualify them for the stations of judges. And making the proper deductions for the ordinary depravity of human nature, the number must be still smaller, of those who unite the requisite integrity with the requisite knowledge...

Year	President and Vice President	Party of President	Congress	Majority Party	
				House	**Senate**
1789–1797	George Washington John Adams	None	1st 2nd 3rd 4th	Admin. Supporters Federalist Democratic-Republican Federalist	Admin. Supporters Federalist Federalist Federalist
1797–1801	John Adams Thomas Jefferson	Federalist	5th 6th	Federalist Federalist	Federalist Federalist
1801–1809	Thomas Jefferson Aaron Burr (to 1805) George Clinton (to 1809)		7th 8th 9th 10th	Democratic-Republican Democratic-Republican Democratic-Republican Democratic-Republican	Democratic-Republican Democratic-Republican Democratic-Republican Democratic-Republican
1809–1817	James Madison George Clinton (to 1813) Elbridge Gerry (to 1817)	Democratic-Republican	11th 12th 13th 14th	Democratic-Republican Democratic-Republican Democratic-Republican Democratic-Republican	Democratic-Republican Democratic-Republican Democratic-Republican Democratic-Republican
1817–1825	James Monroe Daniel D. Tompkins	Democratic-	15th 16th 17th 18th	Democratic-Republican Democratic-Republican Democratic-Republican Democratic-Republican	Democratic-Republican Democratic-Republican Democratic-Republican Democratic-Republican
1825–1829	John Quincy Adams John C. Calhoun	National-Republican	19th 20th	Admin. Supporters Jacksonian Democrats	Admin. Supporters Jacksonian Democrats
1829–1837	Andrew Jackson John C. Calhoun (to 1833) Martin Van Buren (to 1837)	Democratic	21st 22nd 23rd 24th	Democratic Democratic Democratic Democratic	Democratic Democratic Democratic Democratic
1837–1841	Martin Van Buren Richard M. Johnson	Democratic	25th 26th	Democratic Democratic	Democratic Democratic
1841	William H. Harrison (died a month after inauguration) John Tyler	Whig			
1841–1845	John Tyler (VP vacant)	Whig	27th 28th	Whig Democratic	Whig Whig
1845–1849	James K. Polk George M. Dallas	Democratic	29th 30th	Democratic Whig	Democratic Democratic
1849–1850	Zachary Taylor (died in office) Millard Fillmore	Whig	31st	Democratic	Democratic
1850–1853	Millard Fillmore (VP vacant)	Whig	32nd	Democratic	Democratic
1853–1857	Franklin Pierce William R. King	Democratic	33rd 34th	Democratic Republican	Democratic Democratic
1857–1861	James Buchanan John C. Breckinridge	Democratic	35th 36th	Democratic Republican	Democratic Democratic

Year	President and Vice President	Party of President	Congress	Majority Party	
				House	**Senate**
1861–1865	Abraham Lincoln (died in office) Hannibal Hamlin (to 1865) Andrew Johnson (1865)	Republican	37th 38th	Republican Republican	Republican Republican
1865–1869	Andrew Johnson (VP vacant)	Republican	39th 40th	Unionist Republican	Unionist Republican
1869–1877	Ulysses S. Grant Schuyler Colfax (to 1873) Henry Wilson (to 1877)	Republican	41st 42nd 43rd 44th	Republican Republican Republican Democratic	Republican Republican Republican Republican
1877–1881	Rutherford B. Hayes William A. Wheeler	Republican	45th 46th	Democratic Democratic	Republican Democratic
1881	James A. Garfield (died in office) Chester A. Arthur	Republican	47th	Republican	Republican
1881–1885	Chester A. Arthur (VP vacant)	Republican	48th	Democratic	Republican
1885–1889	Grover Cleveland Thomas A. Hendricks	Democratic	49th 50th	Democratic Democratic	Republican Republican
1889–1893	Benjamin Harrison Levi P. Morton	Republican	51st 52nd	Republican Democratic	Republican Republican
1893–1897	Grover Cleveland Adlai E. Stevenson	Democratic	53rd 54th	Democratic Republican	Democratic Republican
1897–1901	William McKinley (died in office) Garret A. Hobart (to 1901) Theodore Roosevelt (1901)	Republican	55th 56th	Republican Republican	Republican Republican
1901–1909	Theodore Roosevelt (VP vacant, 1901–1905) Charles W. Fairbanks (1905–1909)	Republican	57th 58th 59th 60th	Republican Republican Republican Republican	Republican Republican Republican Republican
1909–1913	William Howard Taft James S. Sherman	Republican	61st 62nd	Republican Democratic	Republican Republican
1913–1921	Woodrow Wilson Thomas R. Marshall	Democratic	63rd 64th 65th 66th	Democratic Democratic Democratic Republican	Democratic Democratic Democratic Republican
1921–1923	Warren G. Harding (died in office) Calvin Coolidge	Republican	67th	Republican	Republican
1923–1929	Calvin Coolidge (VP vacant, 1923–1925) Charles G. Dawes (1925–1929)	Republican	68th 69th 70th	Republican Republican Republican	Republican Republican Republican
1929–1933	Herbert Hoover Charles Curtis	Republican	71st 72nd	Republican Democratic	Republican Republican
1933–1945	Franklin D. Roosevelt (died in office) John N. Garner (1933–1941)	Democratic	73rd 74th 75th	Democratic Democratic Democratic	Democratic Democratic Democratic

Year	President and Vice President	Party of President	Congress	Majority Party	
				House	Senate
	Henry A. Wallace (1941–1945)		76th	Democratic	Democratic
	Harry S Truman (1945)		77th	Democratic	Democratic
			78th	Democratic	Democratic
1945–1953	Harry S Truman (VP vacant, 1945–1949) Alben W. Barkley (1949–1953)	Democratic	79th	Democratic	Democratic
			80th	Republican	Republican
			81st	Democratic	Democratic
			82nd	Democratic	Democratic
1953–1961	Dwight D. Eisenhower Richard M. Nixon	Republican	83rd	Republican	Republican
			84th	Democratic	Democratic
			85th	Democratic	Democratic
			86th	Democratic	Democratic
1961–1963	John F. Kennedy (died in office) Lyndon B. Johnson	Democratic	87th	Democratic	Democratic
1963–1969	Lyndon B. Johnson (VP vacant, 1963–1965) Hubert H. Humphrey (1965–1969)	Democratic	88th	Democratic	Democratic
			89th	Democratic	Democratic
			90th	Democratic	Democratic
1969–1974	Richard M. Nixon (resigned office) Spiro T. Agnew (resigned office) Gerald R. Ford (appointed vice president)	Republican	91st	Democratic	Democratic
			92nd	Democratic	Democratic
1974–1977	Gerald R. Ford Nelson A. Rockefeller (appointed vice president)	Republican	93rd	Democratic	Democratic
			94th	Democratic	Democratic
1977–1981	Jimmy Carter Walter Mondale	Democratic	95th	Democratic	Democratic
			96th	Democratic	Democratic
1981–1989	Ronald Reagan George H. W. Bush	Republican	97th	Democratic	Republican
			98th	Democratic	Republican
			99th	Democratic	Republican
			100th	Democratic	Democratic
1989–1993	George H. W. Bush J. Danforth Quayle	Republican	101st	Democratic	Democratic
			102nd	Democratic	Democratic
1993–2001	Bill Clinton Albert Gore Jr.	Democratic	103rd	Democratic	Democratic
			104th	Republican	Republican
			105th	Republican	Republican
			106th	Republican	Republican
2001–2009	George W. Bush Richard Cheney	Republican	107th	Republican	Democratic
			108th	Republican	Republican
			109th	Republican	Republican
			110th	Democratic	Democratic
2009–2013	Barack Obama Joseph Biden	Democratic	111th	Democratic	Democratic
			112th	Republican	Democratic

Notes

1. During the entire administration of George Washington and part of the administration of John Quincy Adams, Congress was not organized in terms of parties. This table shows that during these periods the supporters of the respective administrations maintained control of Congress.

2. This table shows only the two dominant parties in Congress. Independents, members of minor parties, and vacancies have been omitted.

Test Yourself Answers

CHAPTER 1

1. b; 2. c; 3. a; 4. b 5. Answers will vary. Sample answer: One recent government action is the health care reform law. Two governmental factors that influenced this legislation were Congress (which drafted and passed the bill) and the president (who advocated for it and signed it into law). This process was heavily influenced by two political linkages: public opinion (which was fairly skeptical of reform) and lobbying efforts (aimed at splintering the Democratic coalition). In addition, it was influenced by structural elements such as American political culture, which generally favors individualism and helps explain why the law avoids a single-payer, Canadian-style system.

CHAPTER 2

1. False 2. a 3. Answers will vary. Sample answer: Even though the Declaration of Independence was predicated on the notion that citizens could cast off a government that failed to live up to its social contract, such a notion can be particularly dangerous for democracy. The public as a whole will seldom agree when the social contract has been violated and whether the violation is severe enough to warrant dissolution of the government. This opens up the possibility for conflict within the population and for fringe elements to forcefully lead the county in a direction not favored by the majority. 4. False 5. b 6. Answers will vary. Sample answer: The biggest weakness of the Articles of Confederation was that it failed to unite the states as an economic union. Each state coined its own money and taxed goods that crossed state lines, severely hindering the American economy. 7. d; 8. b 9. Answers will vary. Sample answer: The framers' distrust of the American public was ungrounded. At its core, democracy is rule by the people. It is simply undemocratic to hinder the ability of the public to govern. The U.S. has slowly become more democratic over time, as evidenced by the expanding right to vote. This increase in democracy has made the U.S. a stronger country, suggesting that the framers' fears were misplaced. 10. False 11. c 12. Answers will vary. Sample answer: Beard claims that the framers were motivated by their own economic self-interest. This seems unlikely. The framers were mostly elites who had little to gain from rocking the boat (by declaring independence and drafting a new government) and much to lose if the new nation failed to be successful. At the same time, it seems likely that the framers intended that the new government would protect the interests of a broad category of citizens—including themselves. 13. True 14. Answers will vary. Sample answer: The Constitution was not adopted legitimately. The Articles of Confederation required unanimous consent to change and, quite simply, the ratification procedures established by the Constitution put the new government into effect without unanimous consent. However, Americans have considered the Constitution as legitimate for so long that its questionable origins are now irrelevant. 15. False 16. d

CHAPTER 3

1. e; 2. d 3. Answers will vary. Sample answer: Many of the failures of the Articles of Confederation can be traced to the fact that it was a confederation. For example, states had too much authority, and the national government was practically anemic. On the contrary, the Constitution has been so successful in part because it establishes a federal system of government, giving the national government real authority, but also ensuring that its power is checked by the states. 4. False 5. c 6. The privileges and immunities clause prevents governments from treating citizens from different states differently. Yet public universities, which are arms of state governments, regularly discriminate against out-of-state students by charging different tuition for the same education. This sort of discrimination is exactly what the privileges and immunities clause sought to prohibit. 7. c; 8. b 9. Answers will vary. Sample answer: The nature of American federalism changed most dramatically with the New Deal. Franklin D. Roosevelt succeeded in shifting significant power of government from the states to the national government. The public then began to view the national government as the institution responsible for addressing Americans' concerns. This also resulted in a tremendous expansion of national powers and laid the framework for modern American democracy. 10. True 11. c 12. True 13. a 14. Answers will vary. Sample answer: The national government should be responsible for establishing foreign and military policy and for regulating commerce between the states. The states should be responsible for establishing policies within their borders. This is essentially how the framers intended and is consistent with the language of the Tenth Amendment. In my opinion, the national government tries to do way too much and this ends up hurting our economy and weakening our federal system of government.

CHAPTER 4

1. a; 2. c 3. An aging population will put added pressures on social welfare programs such as Social Security and welfare. As more Americans become eligible for these programs, working Americans will have to pay additional taxes or seniors will have to receive fewer benefits (or some combination of both). 4. a; 5. b 6. The current economic environment is hostile to labor unions. In a global economy, industry has an incentive to reduce costs to be competitive with goods from other countries. Businesses have become "lean and mean," and labor unions have been forced to accept wage and benefit concessions to remain competitive. 7. b 8. True 9. d; 10. c 11. Americans have an inherent distrust of government, believing that government policy has a tendency to infringe on individual liberty. Thus, they seem to share the conservative belief in the value of a small government. At the same time, they want government to provide a range of services to the public, especially those services that are designed to promote equality of opportunity. The provision for a wide range of government services is an essentially liberal function of government.

CHAPTER 5

1. False 2. a

3. If democracy is best understood as "rule by the people," then the fact that Congress enacted a law that a majority of Americans opposes is troubling. Through public opinion polls, Americans showed considerable skepticism about the

proposed law, yet Congress did not appear to be responsive to the people's clearly stated preferences. **4.** b; **5.** e **6.** College students frequently lack a land line and rely solely on their cell phone. Yet it is harder for pollsters to reach people on their cell phones because of federal regulations that prevent automated dialing to cell phones, the reluctance to use cell minutes to talk to a pollster, and the fact that cell phones are often turned off. This means that college students are more likely to be excluded from public opinion surveys, decreasing the representativeness of the sample. **7.** False **8.** d **9.** Young people who were becoming politically aware when the terrorist attacks happened might be expected to have a deeper fear of terrorism and to be more accepting of government encroachment on civil liberties in the name of protecting the United States from future terrorist attacks. **10.** True **11.** a **12.** False **13.** c **14.** Answers will vary. Sample answer: I disagree with the authors' assertion that Americans are fit to rule. Most Americans are not very interested in or informed about politics. They do not know who represents them in Congress, where Iraq is located on a map, or what the First Amendment says. Most Americans do not use ideological reasoning to tie their opinions together in a coherent fashion. How can America be a vibrant democracy when its citizens are so ill-prepared to tackle the basic responsibilities of citizenship?

CHAPTER 6

1. False **2.** b **3.** Freedom of the press ensures that the media can act as a watchdog over the government without fear of reprisals. This watchdog function enables the public to hold politicians accountable for their actions. **4.** e; **5.** e **6.** The Internet has vastly expanded access to political information (at least among those Americans with Internet access). At the same time, most of the political information available on the Internet was originally reported by the mainstream media. While the Internet allows ordinary Americans to express their political opinions through blogs, most of these websites are rarely read by typical Americans. **7.** False **8.** c **9.** Answers will vary. Sample answer: In an effort to be objective, an unwritten media rule is that journalists should defer to experts to interpret political events. Thus, even though journalists might be able to provide useful information about what a story means, they typically refrain from doing so. This can leave the citizen in the dark about the true meaning and significance of political events. Some cable news programs, however, provide so much interpretation of events that their "newscasts" are little more than thinly disguised editorials. **10.** True **11.** b **12.** The media takes an adversarial and entertainment-based approach to covering politics. This comes at the expense of a serious discussion of the issues. When the media implies that politics is about backroom deals and dishonest politicians who cannot be trusted, it's no wonder that so many Americans are cynical. **13.** True **14.** d

CHAPTER 7

1. False **2.** c **3.** True **4.** c **5.** The influence of labor unions has waned as the percentage of the workforce that is unionized has plummeted. Fewer than 13 percent of American workers (and few than 8 percent of private-sector workers) are unionized. In the 1950s, more than one-third of American workers belonged to a labor union. One of the main reasons

for this decline is the decrease in the number of manufacturing jobs—an industry that has traditionally been heavily unionized. **6.** False **7.** a **8.** An active government takes on more responsibilities and makes policies that affect an increasing number of interests. Interest groups form to affect the policies that are created and to influence how they are implemented. Other groups might form to take advantage of various government programs and initiatives. **9.** False **10.** d **11.** In the inside game, the lobbyist works one-on-one with a policymaker in an effort to persuade him or her to pass favorable laws (or adopt favorable policies). The inside game is based on access to important decision makers. The outside game, however, involves working with constituents to shape public opinion through a process called grassroots lobbying. Once the public is on board, policymakers are more likely to follow suit. **12.** True **13.** d **14.** The pluralist argument is predicated on the belief that the American political system represents all interests. However, inequalities in the interest group system suggest that some groups have greater influence than others. For example, business interests are heavily represented in Washington, while organized labor has lost much of its clout. As political scientist E. E. Schattschneider noted, the flaw in the pluralist heaven is that the choir "sings with a strong upper class accent." **15.** True **16.** e

CHAPTER 8

1. True **2.** a **3.** False **4.** e **5.** Members of both the Tea Party movement and the populists were concerned about restoring power to ordinary citizens. In fact, the authors suggest that members of the Tea Party movement are "angry populists." However, the populists wanted increased government intervention in the economy to better regulate big business, while the Tea Party movement wants less government intervention in the economy. **6.** False **7.** c **8.** Answers will vary. Sample answer: Prior to the success of the women's movement, most Americans were content with the idea that men should earn higher income than women because men were responsible for providing for their families. Now, public opinion disapproves of gender-based job discrimination and supports pay equality. **9.** False **10.** d **11.** c **12.** True **13.** e **14.** These tactics run the risk of alienating voters and being ineffective (if not downright harmful to the movement). If the public believes that such tactics are condoned by the Tea Party movement, they threaten to discredit the entire movement. This is essentially what happened in the late 1960s when violent tactics attributed to the black power movement undermined public support for affirmative action. **15.** False **16.** d

CHAPTER 9

1. False **2.** e **3.** Citizens cannot possibly be expected to know and understand everything about politics. Party labels act as shortcuts that help voters make political decisions that are likely to be in their best interests. For example, if you know that you tend to prefer the policies advanced by the Republican Party, you can vote for the slate of Republican candidates without knowing the individual positions of each specific candidate. By taking this shortcut, you will likely select the candidate whose true positions are closest to your preferences. **4.** False **5.** c **6.** Answers will vary. Sample answer: Despite what the authors claim, I believe that the U.S. is still in the dealignment era. For starters, the number of independents continues to increase and divided government continues to remain fairly common, occurring as recently as 2008. Both of these indicators are consistent with the dealignment era. In addition, in the 2008 presidential election, the public did not appear to be evenly divided, which is counter to the authors' description of the parties at war era. For example, Barack Obama won a clear majority of the popular vote and Democrats controlled a clear majority of seats in Congress. **7.** True **8.** d **9.** Answers will vary. Sample answer: Unified government is preferable to divided government. Divided government has a tendency to lead to gridlock, which means that nothing gets accomplished. Unified government allows our elected officials to make decisions and address pressing national problems; it helps overcome obstacles to decision making that would otherwise result from our separation of powers system.

CHAPTER 10

1. True **2.** a **3.** Answers will vary. Sample answer: I believe that the retrospective voting model best explains what motivated voters in the 2008 presidential election. Because Republican George W. Bush was supremely unpopular—even among many Republicans—voters cast their ballots for the Democratic candidate, Barack Obama. The prospective model does not fit as well because, for example, the public was still deeply skeptical of Obama's proposals for healthcare reform. Likewise, the electoral competition model suggests that the two candidates (Obama and McCain) would both advocate for the policies favored by the media voter. Clearly, Obama and McCain argued for policies that were distinct from each other and from the media voter. **4.** True **5.** a **6.** Answers will vary. Sample answer: I believe that the U.S. should hold its elections on a Saturday or on a national holiday. Voting is a fundamental aspect of democracy and there is no reason to hold elections on a Tuesday—when most Americans are working. This depresses turnout and disadvantages those with less flexible work schedules. **7.** False **8.** a **9.** False **10.** d **11.** Answers will vary. Sample answer: No, it does not matter that some groups of people are more likely to vote than other groups. Surveys suggest that voters and nonvoters tend to prefer similar candidates and to have similar policy preferences anyway. In addition, because democracy works best when the public is informed, it is actually beneficial that those with more education are also more likely to vote. **12.** False **13.** c **14.** Each state decides whether they will hold primaries or caucuses, the dates they will occur, and the rules under which they will operate. States jockey with each other in an effort to have greater influence over which candidates will be selected. Thus, every year the rules and dates may change. All this contributes to a chaotic nomination season. **15.** True **16.** d **17.** The Electoral College hinders third-party candidates. Because states typically select electors using a winner-take-all system, third-party candidates may end up with an impressive showing in the popular vote, but without any electors. This is exactly what happened to Ross Perot.

CHAPTER 11

1. False **2.** e **3.** The Constitution establishes a bicameral legislature, a separation of powers system, and a system of checks and balances. Each of these fragments political power, ensuring that Congress (nor any other government institution) does not become too powerful. In addition, the bill of rights explicitly limits congressional power in order to protect individual liberty. **4.** False **5.** d **6.** Answers will vary. Sample answer: Elections are ineffective in holding members of Congress accountable. Our representatives have given themselves numerous advantages that help them win reelection. For example, the franking privilege and casework have contributed to incumbent reelection rates of more than 90 percent. Thus, congressional elections are not truly competitive; without true competition, there is no way to ensure that Congress remains responsive to the people. **7.** True **8.** b **9.** Answers will vary. Sample answer: The most significant role played by committees is that they allow members to specialize in a policy domain. This allows members to develop expertise, which allows for more-informed decision making. Without committees, Congress would be filled with generalists who would know a little bit about a lot of different things—but few would know about much with any depth. **10.** False **11.** c **12.** c **13.** During divided government, the president's party does not control both houses of Congress. When this happens, one chamber may wish to embarrass, weaken, or point out inconsistencies in the way the executive branch has operated. This opportunity to score political points at the cost of the opposition party is often irresistible and may help the opposition party recapture the presidency in the next election. Similarly, when the same party controls both houses of Congress and the presidency, why would it want to embarrass the executive branch?

CHAPTER 12

1. False **2.** d **3.** Answers will vary. Sample answer: Bush's response to the 9/11 terrorist attacks is best explained by his personal qualities. Bush ran the White House with a top-down decision-making structure, much as if he were a CEO. When it came to tackling terrorism, he also took a top-down approach by claiming vast executive authority that ignored established law and international treaties. In addition, his religious beliefs moved him to view events in straightforward, black-and-white fashion, and not in terms of shades of gray. **4.** True **5.** d **6.** Both executive orders and executive agreements are examples of how presidents can exercise expansive policymaking power. Executive orders are presidential directives to the bureaucracy about how to execute a law. They enable the president to shape public policies after they have been passed by Congress. Executive agreements are similar to treaties in that they are used to formalize agreements between the U.S. and a foreign country or countries. However, executive agreements do not need to be ratified by Congress, just as executive orders do not need congressional approval. **7.** False **8.** c **9.** False **10.** a **11.** The Founders designed the Constitution to create more conflict between the president and Congress than exists between the executive and legislative bodies in parliamentary systems. In fact, in parliamentary systems, the executive functions of government are performed by members of parliament. This ensures party unity and facilitates lawmaking. In contrast, the U.S. system separates the powers of government and selects members of each branch in separate elections, often pitting these two centers of power against each other in an "ambition to counter ambition" fashion. **12.** False **13.** c

CHAPTER 13

1. False **2.** e **3.** Answers will vary. Sample answer: The American civil service model is superior to that used in European democracies. American civil servants are broadly representative of the American people. European civil servants are economic and social elites who do not understand the people they are supposed to serve. The American civil service is

more democratic and better represents the interests of the general public.   **4.** True   **5.** e   **6.** False   **7.** b   **8.** Answers will vary. Sample answer: Discretion allows nonelected bureaucrats to craft public policy. This is undemocratic. The bureaucracy can effectively change the meaning of policies enacted by Congress in the implementation stage. It is the job of the bureaucracy to follow the laws as established by Congress; it is not appropriate for the bureaucracy to exercise its own judgment and thereby change the meaning of democratically enacted laws.   **9.** False   **10.** a   **11.** Answers will vary. Sample answer: While there are some advantages to working in the civil service (e.g., better job security, retirement plans, and health benefits), the disadvantages far outweigh the advantages. Most importantly, the salary ceiling for the civil service is considerably lower than for the private sector. While I might be able to do okay financially by working for the government, I will never become wealthy.   **12.** True   **13.** b   **14.** Answers will vary. Sample answer: The most powerful tool the president has for influencing the bureaucracy is his prestige. When the president speaks, people listen. Thus, the president has a "bully pulpit" that enables him or her to speak directly to the American people and to rally them to his or her causes. The president's easy access to media coverage ensures effective use of the president's prestige.   **15.** False   **16.** e
17. Answers will vary. Sample answer: Yes, the federal bureaucracy would be improved if it became more businesslike. Salaries should be determined in part by the quality of the job the bureaucrat is doing. For example, providing good "customer service" should be rewarded with a higher paycheck.

CHAPTER 14

1. False   **2.** a   **3.** Some people believe that judicial review allows a small group of unelected officials (i.e., the Supreme Court) to overturn policies enacted by democratically elected policymakers (i.e., Congress and the president). This undermines the most fundamental principle of a democratic government: that the people rule. Thus, judicial review is countermajoritarian and a "deviant" American political institution that should be scrapped.   **4.** d   **5.** a   **6.** Congress determines the number of justices who serve on the Supreme Court and much of its appellate jurisdiction. Theoretically, Congress can change either of these two elements for political purposes. In practice, the number of justices has been constant since 1869, and major changes in the Court's jurisdiction are also fairly rare.   **7.** False   **8.** c   **9.** Clinton nominated two reasonably moderate justices: Ruth Bader Ginsburg and Stephen Breyer. In contrast, Bush's nominees were decidedly conservative: John Roberts and Samuel Alito.   **10.** False   **11.** d   **12.** Answers will vary. Sample answer: "Superprecedents" are landmark Supreme Court cases that have been repeatedly reaffirmed by the Supreme Court and whose reasoning has been deeply engrained in American political culture. The decision in *Roe* v. *Wade*, which established a woman's right to an abortion, has certainly not become engrained in the fabric of American society. In fact, abortion rights remain a hotly debated issue, and public opinion on the issue does not even approach consensus. *Roe* v. *Wade* should not become a superprecedent; it is entitled to no more dignity than any other precedent established by the Supreme Court. If a future Court determines that the case was wrongly decided, they should feel free to overturn the decision and establish a new precedent.   **13.** a

14. b   **15.** Answers will vary. Sample answer: The Supreme Court has not become too involved in national policymaking. The Court only intervenes in policy matters if there is a constitutional principle at stake. This is exactly the role that the Supreme Court should play. The Supreme Court should not sit out important constitutional issues simply because the resolutions of those issues have political implications. In fact, it's hard to think of examples of Court decisions that do not shape policy or touch on political concerns.   **16.** False   **17.** a

CHAPTER 15

1. False   **2.** e   **3.** True   **4.** c   **5.** Using the contract clause, the Marshall Court greatly expanded private property rights. The Court severely limited the ability of states to pass laws that infringed on property rights. If government regulations infringed on binding contracts, they were likely to receive close scrutiny under the Marshall Court.   **6.** False   **7.** a
8. Answers will vary. Sample answer: The accused are given far too many rights, making it difficult for government to enforce law and order. Would-be criminals can often get off the hook on a "technicality." For example, if the cops fail to conduct a search in a specific manner, the exclusionary rule says that the evidence of a crime cannot be used in court. Or if the cops forget to read a suspect his or her *Miranda* warnings, it can be a get-out-of-jail-free card for the person being arrested. We would be better off focusing on protecting victims instead of coddling criminals.   **9.** False   **10.** e   **11.** Answers will vary. Sample answer: The Bush-era policies went too far in restricting our civil liberties in the name of fighting terror. Under certain circumstances, they permit the government to wiretap our phones, read our e-mail, look at our financial records, examine our reading habits at the public library, and detain us as a "material witness." The restrictions are even greater for noncitizens. Fighting terrorism is a noble goal, but it can and should be achieved without shredding the Constitution in the process.

CHAPTER 16

1. False   **2.** e   **3.** Much to the dismay of many women, the Fifteenth Amendment does not extend the right to vote to women. Guaranteed suffrage would not be extended to women for nearly 50 years, until the adoption of the Nineteenth Amendment. While the Fifteenth Amendment attempted to expand the right to vote regardless of race or ethnicity, the failure to include women's voting rights is palpable.   **4.** False   **5.** c   **6.** Roberts is expressing his dislike for affirmative action programs. Such programs treat people differently on account of their race. Conservatives sometimes call this "reverse discrimination." Roberts is expressing his desire to end the racial discrimination that has plagued the United States, but he believes that affirmative action programs are not the best way to accomplish this. Roberts clearly prefers color-blind means of overcoming racial discrimination.   **7.** True
8. d   **9.** While being thankful for the considerable progress that has been made, the leaders of the women's movement are likely disappointed that significant inequities still exist between men and women. For example, women make less money than men and are more likely to live in poverty. In addition, the courts are more tolerant of laws that treat men and women differently than they are of laws that treat people differently on account of race. That is, the courts use "intermediate scrutiny" for gender discrimination but "strict scrutiny" for racial discrimination.   **10.** True   **11.** e   **12.** Answers will

vary. Sample answer: The history of the United States shows a continual expansion of civil rights, first for African Americans and then for women. While the expansion of civil rights is often slow and intermittent, it is progress nonetheless. In a few states, gay couples have won some early victories—especially in the courts—and it seems likely that that the rest of the country will eventually follow suit. I think this will happen within the next 50 years, as the percentage of the population that is opposed to gay marriage dropped from 63 percent in 2004 to 53 percent in 2009. Younger Americans are most supportive of gay marriage, suggesting that generational replacement will continue to yield increasing support for gay rights.

CHAPTER 17

1. False **2.** d **3.** Several important aspects of the policymaking are inconsistent with democratic principles. The Constitution includes many anti-majoritarian elements, including the Electoral College, the process for amending the Constitution, and the underrepresentation of large states in the Senate. In addition, the policymaking process is heavily influenced by power interest groups. In sum, while the policymaking process is democratic in the sense that it responds to public opinion, it does so imprecisely—and even public opinion can be shaped by powerful and wealthy political interests. **4.** False **5.** d **6.** Deficits can be a good way to stimulate the economy and to provide the infrastructure for later economic success. Large deficits, however, can quickly pile up. If too much debt piles up, the United States may have a hard time finding buyers for U.S. bonds and Treasury notes. This could cripple the U.S. economy. **7.** False **8.** b **9.** Americans have a lower overall tax burden than do those in other industrialized democracies. In addition, the federal tax system relies more on income taxes while other countries rely more on consumption and sales taxes. In addition, the American tax system is uniquely complex, with innumerable loopholes, exemptions, and exceptions. **10.** True **11.** a **12.** The *Deepwater Horizon* oil spill is likely to lead to increased regulations affecting the oil and gas industry. Even before the spill, a large segment of the public was pushing for increased environmental protections, the development of alternative energy sources, and increased regulations to reduce global warming. The oil spill will likely further underscore public demand for increased regulations in these areas.

CHAPTER 18

1. False **2.** c **3.** False **4.** e **5.** True **6.** d **7.** Answers will vary. Sample answer: Social Security and Medicare have been very effective in lowering poverty among the elderly. In the past 50 years, the poverty rate among the elderly has dropped from nearly 5 percent to under 10 percent. At the same time, Social Security allows only a modest standard of living, and an increasing number of Americans are relying on Social Security as their only or primary source of retirement income. Furthermore, some point out that poverty remains a serious problem in the United States, especially among children.

8. True **9.** e **10.** One reason for AFDC's unpopularity was the perception that it created dependency. Thus, TANF is temporary by design (and name). In addition, TANF is designed to promote entrance into the workforce by providing money for job training and childcare. In short, TANF is not an entitlement program, while AFDC was. TANF also allows considerable discretion in how the states design and implement the program and bars unwed teenage mothers from receiving benefits unless they stay in school and live with an adult. **11.** True **12.** a **13.** Answers will vary. Sample answer: I would follow the European model. Americans are not satisfied with many aspects of their social welfare system, so it would be wise not to replicate them. I believe that as a society, we have an obligation to look after all citizens to ensure their general well being. There is no excuse for having the resources that the United States does, yet also have the large numbers of Americans who live in poverty or without adequate health care. Sure, a European-style system would be more expensive (resulting in higher taxes), but that is a price I am willing to pay.

CHAPTER 19

1. True **2.** a **3.** True **4.** e **5.** Answers will vary. Sample answer: The United States will continue to be the world's only superpower for some time to come. The United States's economic and military powers are unrivaled. Even though the Great Recession has hurt the American economy, the economies of other countries have taken an even harder hit. The only real competitor the United States has is China, but it is only challenging the United States in one area: the economy. China is not within striking range of American military power and lacks the soft powers that the United States has. Around the world, people yearn for an American lifestyle—something that is unlikely to change in the foreseeable future. **6.** False **7.** b **8.** The United States has been a strong leader for free trade, while its leadership in addressing climate change has been anemic. The United States led the effort to establish the General Agreement on Tariffs and Trade in 1948, which significantly lowered (and sometimes eliminated) many tariffs around the globe. In addition, the United States advocated for the North America Free Trade Agreement, which created a free trade zone that included the United States, Canada, and Mexico. In terms of climate change, however, the United States has been reluctant to follow, let alone lead. While President Clinton signed the Kyoto Protocol that limited greenhouse gas emissions, he refused to submit it to the Senate for ratification, and President George W. Bush withdrew from the treaty entirely. While President Obama expressed interest in a climate change agreement, his actions have not matched his words. **9.** False **10.** e **11.** Answers will vary. Sample answer: In national defense emergencies, the president should play a leadership role. The president commands the armed forces and can act decisively to respond to national security threats. Congressional decision making is slow and cumbersome—two traits that are completely undesirable when responding to a national defense crisis.

GLOSSARY

active partisan People who identify with a party, vote in elections, and participate in additional party and party-candidate activities.

advocacy group An interest group organized to support a cause or ideology.

affirmative action Programs of private and public institutions favoring minorities and women in hiring and contracting, and in admissions to colleges and universities, in an attempt to compensate for past discrimination or to create more diversity.

agency A general name used for a subunit of a cabinet department.

agenda setting Influencing people's opinions about what is important.

agents of socialization Those institutions and individuals that shape the core beliefs and attitudes of people.

Aid to Families with Dependent Children (AFDC) The federal entitlement program that provided income support for poor families until it was replaced by TANF in 1996.

amicus curiae Latin for "friend of the court"; describes a legal brief in which individuals not party to a suit may have their views heard in court.

Anti-Federalists Opponents of the Constitution during the fight over ratification.

appellate courts Courts that hear cases on appeal from other courts.

appropriation Legal authority for a federal agency to spend money from the U.S. Treasury.

appropriations committees The committees in the House and Senate that set specific spending levels in the budget for federal programs and agencies.

Articles of Confederation The first constitution of the United States, adopted during the last stages of the Revolutionary War, created a system of government with most power lodged in the states and little in the central government.

asymmetric warfare Unconventional tactics used by a combatant against an enemy with superior conventional military capabilities.

axis of evil Three countries—Iraq, Iran, and North Korea—named by President Bush in 2002 as significant threats to the security of the United States because of their purported ties to terrorism and/or weapons of mass destruction.

balance of payments The annual difference between payments and receipts between a country and its trading partners.

beat The assigned location where a reporter regularly gathers news stories.

bias Deviation from ideal standards such as representativeness or objectivity.

bicameral As applied to a legislative body, consisting of two houses or chambers.

bill of attainder A governmental decree that a person is guilty of a crime that carries the death penalty, rendered without benefit of a trial.

Bill of Rights The first 10 amendments to the U.S. Constitution, concerned with the protection of basic liberties.

block grants Federal grants to the states to be used for general activities.

blog The common term for a *weblog,* a website on which an individual or group posts text, photos, audio files, and more, on a regular basis for others to view and respond to.

briefs Documents setting out the arguments in legal cases, prepared by attorneys and presented to courts.

budget deficit The amount by which annual government expenditures exceed revenues.

bureau Generally, a subunit of a cabinet department.

bureaucracy A large, complex organization characterized by a hierarchical set of offices, each with a specific task, controlled through a clear chain of command, and where appointment and advancement of personnel is based on merit.

bureaucrat A person who works in a bureaucratic organization.

capital crime Any crime for which death is a possible penalty.

capitalism An economic system characterized by private ownership of productive assets where decisions about how to use these assets are made by individuals and firms operating in a market rather than by government.

casework Services performed by members of Congress for constituents.

categorical grants Federal aid to states and localities clearly specifying what the money can be used for.

caucus nominating system The process for selecting delegates to the national party conventions characterized by neighborhood and area-wide meetings of party supporters and activists.

caucus A regional, ethnic, racial or economic subgroup within the House or Senate. Also used to describe the party in the House and Senate, as in Republican caucus.

checks and balances The constitutional principle that each of the separate branches of government has the power to hinder the actions of the other branches as a way to prevent tyranny.

chief of staff A top adviser to the president who also manages the White House staff.

Child Health Insurance Program (CHIP) Program that pays for health care services for children in households above the poverty line but below 133 percent to 400 percent of the poverty line, depending on the state.

circuit courts The 12 geographical jurisdictions and one special court that hear appeals from the federal district courts.

civil disobedience Intentionally breaking a law and accepting the consequences as a way to publicize the unjustness of the law.

civil liberties Freedoms found primarily in the Bill of Rights, the enjoyment of which are protected from government interference.

civil rights Guarantees of equal treatment by government officials regarding political rights, the judicial system, and public programs.

civil servants Government workers employed under the merit system; not political appointees.

civil service Federal government jobs held by civilian employees, excluding political appointees.

civil union A status in which same-sex couples have the same legal rights, benefits, and protections as married couples.

Civil War Amendments The Thirteenth, Fourteenth, and Fifteenth Amendments to the Constitution adopted immediately after the Civil War.

class-action suit A suit brought on behalf of a group of people who are in a situation similar to that of the plaintiffs.

cloture A vote to end a filibuster; requires the votes of three-fifths of the membership of the Senate.

Cold War The period of tense relations between the United States and the Soviet Union from the late 1940s to the late 1980s.

collective public opinion The political attitudes of the public as a whole, expressed as averages, percentages, or other summaries of many individuals' opinions.

concurrent powers Powers under the Constitution that are shared by the federal government and the states.

concurring opinion The opinion of one or more judges who vote with the majority on a case but wish to set out different reasons for their decision.

conditional grants Federal grants with provisions requiring that state and local governments follow certain policies in order to obtain funds.

confederation A loose association of states or territorial divisions in which very little power or no power at all is lodged in a central government.

conference committees Ad hoc committees, made up of members of both the Senate and the House of Representatives, set up to reconcile differences in the provisions of bills.

Congressional Budget Office (CBO) An agency of the U.S. Congress that provides technical support and research services on budget issues for its members and committees.

Connecticut Compromise Also called the *Great Compromise;* the compromise between the New Jersey and Virginia plans formulated by the Connecticut delegates at the Constitutional Convention; called for a lower legislative house based on population size and an upper house based on equal representation of the states.

consciousness-raising groups Meetings of small groups of women designed to raise awareness of discrimination against women and to encourage involvement in movement activities.

conservative The political position, combining both economic and social dimensions, that holds that the federal government ought to play a very small role in economic regulation, social welfare, and overcoming racial inequality, that abortion should be illegal, and that family values and law and order should guide public policies.

constituency The district of a legislator.

constituent A citizen who lives in the district of an elected official.

constitution The basic framework of law that prescribes how government is to be organized, how decisions are to be made, and what powers and responsibilities it shall have.

constitutional courts Federal courts created by Congress under the authority of Article III of the Constitution.

contract clause The portion of Article I, Section 10, of the Constitution that prohibits states from passing any law "impairing the obligations of contracts."

convention, party A gathering of delegates who nominate a party's presidential candidate.

cooperative federalism Federalism in which the powers and responsibilities of the states and the national government are intertwined and in which they work together to solve common problems; said to have characterized the 1960s and 1970s.

core beliefs (political) Individuals' views about the fundamental nature of human beings, society, the economy, and the role of government; taken together, they comprise the political culture.

cost-benefit analysis A method of evaluating rules and regulations by weighing their potential costs against their potential benefits to society.

cost-of-living adjustment (COLA) Automatic annual adjustment made to Social Security benefits.

Council of Economic Advisers (CEA) An organization in the Executive Office of the President made up of a small group of economists who advise on economic policy.

de facto discrimination Unequal treatment by private individuals, groups, and organizations.

de jure discrimination Unequal treatment based on government laws and regulations.

dealignment A gradual reduction in the dominance of one political party without another party supplanting it.

deficit hawks People committed to reducing budget deficits.

delegate According to the doctrine articulated by Edmund Burke, an elected representative who acts in perfect accord with the wishes of his or her constituents.

democracy A system of government in which the people rule; rule by the many.

departments Generally the largest units in the executive branch, each headed by a cabinet secretary.

depression A severe and persistent drop in economic activity.

deregulation The process of diminishing regulatory requirements for business.

descriptive representation Sometimes called *statistical representation;* the degree to which the composition of a representative body reflects the demographic composition of the population as a whole.

devolution The delegation of power by the central government to state or local bodies.

direct democracy A form of political decision making in which the public business is decided by all citizens meeting in small assemblies.

discharge petition A petition signed by 218 House members to force a bill that has been before a committee for at least 30 days while the House is in session out of the committee and onto the floor for consideration.

discretionary spending That part of the federal budget that is not tied to a formula that automatically provides money to some program or purpose.

dissenting opinion The opinion of the judge or judges who are in the minority on a particular case before the Supreme Court.

distributive policies Government policies targeted at narrowly defined groups or individuals.

disturbance theory A theory positing that interest groups originate with changes in the economic, social, or political environment that threaten the well-being of some segment of the population.

divided government Control of the executive and legislative branches by different political parties.

dual federalism An interpretation of federalism in which the states and the national government have separate jurisdictions and responsibilities.

due process clause The section of the Fourteenth Amendment that prohibits states from depriving anyone of life, liberty, or property "without due process of law," a guarantee against arbitrary or unfair government action.

earmarking Practice of appropriating money for specific pet projects of members of Congress, usually done at the behest of lobbyists, and added to bills at the last minute with little opportunity for deliberation.

economic conservatives People who favor private enterprise and oppose government regulations of business.

economic liberals People who favor government regulation of business and government spending for social programs.

economic liberty The right to own and use property free from unreasonable government interference.

elastic clause Article I, Section 8, of the Constitution, also called the *necessary and proper clause;* gives Congress the authority to make whatever laws are necessary and proper to carry out its enumerated responsibilities.

Electoral College Elected representatives of the states a majority of whose votes formally elect the President of the United States. The number of electors in each state is equal to the total number of its senators and representatives.

electoral competition model A form of election in which parties seeking votes move toward the median voter or the center of the political spectrum.

electoral reward and punishment The tendency to vote for the incumbents when times are good and against them when times are bad; same as retrospective voting.

electors Representatives who are elected in the states to formally choose the U.S. president.

entitlements Government benefits that are distributed automatically to citizens who qualify on the basis of a set of guidelines set by law; for example, Americans over the age of 65 are entitled to Medicare coverage.

enumerated powers Powers of the federal government specifically mentioned in the Constitution.

equal protection clause The section of the Fourteenth Amendment that provides equal protection of the laws to all persons.

Equal Rights Amendment (ERA) Proposed amendment to the U.S. Constitution stating that equality of rights shall not be abridged or denied on account of a person's gender; failed to win the approval of the necessary number of states.

equal time provision The former requirement that television stations give or sell the same amount of time to all competing candidates.

establishment clause The part of the First Amendment to the Constitution that prohibits Congress from establishing an official religion; the basis for the doctrine of the separation of church and state.

ex post facto law A law that retroactively declares some action illegal.

exclusionary rule A standard promulgated by the Supreme Court that prevents police and prosecutors from using evidence against a defendant that was obtained in an illegal search.

executive agreement An agreement with another country signed by the president that has the force of law, like a treaty; does not require Senate approval; originally used for minor technical matters, now an important tool of presidential power in foreign affairs.

Executive Office of the President (EOP) A group of organizations that advise the president on a wide range of issues; includes, among others, the Office of Management and Budget, the National Security Council, and the Council of Economic Advisers.

executive order A rule or regulation issued by the president that has the force of law, based either on the constitutional powers of the presidency as chief executive or commander in chief or on congressional statutes.

executive privilege A presidential claim that certain communications with subordinates may be withheld from Congress and the courts.

externalities The positive and negative effects of economic activities on third parties.

faction Madison's term for groups or parties that try to advance their own interests at the expense of the public good.

fairness doctrine The former requirement that television stations present contrasting points of view.

federal bureaucracy The totality of the departments and agencies of the executive branch of the national government.

Federal Reserve Board (Fed) The body responsible for deciding the monetary policies of the United States.

federalism A system in which governmental powers are divided between a central government and smaller units, such as states.

Federalists Proponents of the Constitution during the ratification fight; also the political party of Hamilton, Washington, and Adams.

filibuster A parliamentary device used in the Senate to prevent a bill from coming to a vote by "talking it to death," made possible by the norm of unlimited debate.

fiscal federalism That aspect of federalism having to do with federal grants to the states.

fiscal policy Government efforts to affect overall output and incomes in the economy through spending and taxing policies.

framing Providing a context for interpretation.

franchise The legal right to vote; see *suffrage*.

franking privilege Public subsidization of mail from the members of Congress to their constituents.

free enterprise An economic system characterized by competitive markets and private ownership; similar to capitalism.

free exercise clause That portion of the First Amendment to the Constitution that prohibits Congress from impeding religious observance or impinging upon religious beliefs.

full faith and credit The provision in Article IV, Section 1 of the Constitution which provides that states must respect the public acts, laws, and judicial rulings of other states.

General Agreement on Tariffs and Trade (GATT) An international agreement that requires the lowering of tariffs and other barriers to free trade.

general revenue sharing Federal aid to the states without any conditions on how the money is to be spent.

gerrymandering Redrawing electoral district lines to give an advantage to a particular party or candidate.

global climate change The upset of historical climate patterns, with rising temperatures and more extreme climate events, tied to the increase in atmospheric carbon whether caused by human activities or naturally occurring cycles.

globalization The increasing tendency of information, products, and financial capital to flow across national borders, with the effect of more tightly integrating the global economy.

government corporation A unit in the executive branch that operates like a private business but provides some public service.

government foundation An entity of the executive branch that supports the arts or sciences and is designed to be somewhat insulated from political interference.

grand juries Groups of citizens who decide whether there is sufficient evidence to bring an indictment against accused persons.

grandfather clause A device that allowed whites who had failed the literacy test to vote anyway by extending the franchise to anyone whose ancestors had voted prior to 1867.

grants-in-aid Funds from the national government to state and local governments to help pay for programs created by the national government.

grassroots lobbying The effort by interest groups to mobilize local constituencies, shape public opinion to support the group's goals, and bring that pressure to bear on elected officials.

Great Depression The period of economic crisis in the United States that lasted from the stock market crash of 1929 to America's entry into World War II.

gridlock A situation in which things cannot get done in Washington, usually because of divided government.

gross domestic product (GDP) Monetary value of all goods and services produced in a nation each year, excluding income residents earn abroad.

habeas corpus The legal doctrine that a person who is arrested must have a timely hearing before a judge.

health savings accounts (HSAs) Tax-exempt savings accounts used for paying medical expenses.

hearings The taking of testimony by a congressional committee or subcommittee.

hegemon Term used to refer to the dominant power during various historical periods that takes on responsibilities for maintaining and protecting a regional or global system.

hold A tactic by which a single senator can prevent action on a bill or nomination; based on an implied threat of refusing to agree to unanimous consent on other Senate matters or willingness to filibuster the bill or nomination.

hopper The box in the House of Representatives in which proposed bills are placed.

horizontal federalism Term used to refer to relationships among the states.

impeachment House action bringing formal charges against a member of the executive branch or the federal judiciary that may or may not lead to removal from office by the Senate.

in forma pauperis Describing a process by which indigents may file a suit with the Supreme Court free of charge.

incorporation The process by which the Supreme Court has made most of the provisions of the Bill of Rights binding on the states. See *nationalizing*.

independent agency A unit of the executive branch outside the control of executive departments.

independent regulatory commission An entity in the executive branch that is outside the immediate control of the president and Congress that issues rules and regulations to protect the public.

industrialization The transformation of a society's economy from one dominated by agricultural pursuits to one dominated by manufacturing.

inflation A condition of rising prices and reduced purchasing power.

infotainment The merging of hard news and entertainment in news presentations.

initiatives Procedures available in some states for citizens to put proposed laws and constitutional amendments on the ballot for voter approval or rejection.

institutional presidency The permanent bureaucracy associated with the presidency, designed to help the incumbent of the office carry out his responsibilities.

integration Policies encouraging the interaction between different races in schools or public facilities.

Intelligence Advisory Board An organization in the Executive Office of the President that provides information and assessments to the president's director of national intelligence and to the president directly.

interest group A private organization or voluntary association that seeks to influence public policy as a way to protect or advance its interests.

intermediate scrutiny A legal test falling between ordinary and strict scrutiny relevant to issues of gender; under this test, the Supreme Court will allow gender classifications in laws if they are *substantially* related to an *important* government objective.

interstate compacts Agreements among states to cooperate on solving mutual problems; requires approval by Congress.

iron triangle An enduring alliance of common interest among an interest group, a congressional committee, and a bureaucratic agency.

isolationism The policy of avoiding involvement in foreign affairs.

issue networks Broad coalitions of public and private interest groups, policy experts, and public officials that form around particular policy issues; said to be more visible to the public and more inclusive.

Jim Crow Popular term for the system of legally sanctioned racial segregation that existed in the American South until the middle of the twentieth century.

Joint Chiefs of Staff (JCS) The military officers in charge of each of the armed services.

joint committees Congressional committees with members from both the House and the Senate.

judicial activism Actions by the courts that purportedly go beyond the role of the judiciary as interpreter of the law and adjudicator of disputes.

judicial review The power of the Supreme Court to declare actions of the other branches and levels of government unconstitutional.

Keynesians Advocates of government programs to stimulate economic activity through tax cuts and government spending.

laissez-faire The political-economic doctrine that holds that government ought not interfere with the operations of the free market.

leak, news Inside or secret information given to a journalist or media outlet by a government official.

leaners People who claim to be independents but consistently favor one party over another.

legislative courts Highly specialized federal courts created by Congress under the authority of Article I of the Constitution.

liberal democracy Representative democracy characterized by popular sovereignty, liberty, and political equality.

liberal The political position, combining both economic and social dimensions, that holds that the federal government has a substantial role to play in economic regulation, social welfare, and overcoming racial inequality, and that abortion and stem-cell research should be legal and the civil rights of gays and racial minorities protected.

literacy test A device used by the southern states to prevent African Americans from voting before the passage of the Voting Rights Act of 1965, which banned its use; usually involved interpretation of a section of a state's constitution.

lobbying Effort by an interest or advocacy group to influence the behavior of a public official.

lobbyist A person who attempts to influence the behavior of public officials on behalf of an interest group.

macroeconomic policy Policy that has to do with the performance of the economy as a whole.

majority rule The form of political decision making in which policies are decided on the basis of what a majority of the people want.

majority tyranny Suppression of the rights and liberties of a minority by the majority.

majority-minority districts Districts drawn to ensure that a racial minority makes up the majority of voters.

mandate A formal order from the national government that the states carry out certain policies.

market economy Another term for capitalism.

markup The process of revising a bill in committee.

mass mobilization The process of involving large numbers of people in a social movement.

means-tested Meeting the criterion of demonstrable need.

media monopoly Term used to suggest that media corporations are so large, powerful, and interconnected that the less economically and politically powerful cannot have their views aired.

median household income The midpoint of all households ranked by income.

median voter The voter at the exact middle of the political issue spectrum.

Medicaid Program administered by the states that pays for health care services for the poor; jointly funded by the federal government and the states.

Medicare Federal health insurance program for the elderly and the disabled.

Millennium Challenge Account A Bush administration initiative to distribute development aid on the basis of a country's degree of improvement in areas such as the rule of law, women's rights, protection of property rights, anticorruption measures, and political and civil rights.

monarchy Rule by the one, where power rests in the hands of a king or queen.

monetarists Advocates of a minimal government role in the economy, limited to managing the growth of the money supply.

monetary policy Government efforts to affect the supply of money and the level of interest rates in the economy.

multilateralists Those who believe the United States should use its military and diplomatic power in the world in cooperation with other nations and international organizations.

multiparty system A political system in which three or more viable parties compete to lead the government; because a majority winner is not always possible, multiparty systems often have coalition governments where governing power is shared among two or more parties.

national debt The total outstanding debt of the federal government; the sum total of all annual budget deficits and surpluses.

national interest What is of benefit to the nation as a whole.

national security adviser A top foreign policy and defense adviser to the president who heads the National Security Council.

National Security Council (NSC) An organization in the Executive Office of the President made up of officials from the State and Defense Departments, the CIA, and the military, who advise on foreign and security affairs.

nationalist position The view of American federalism that holds that the Constitution created a system in which the national government is supreme, relative to the states, and that it granted that government a broad range of powers and responsibilities.

nationalizing The process by which provisions of the Bill of Rights become incorporated. See *incorporation*.

nativist Antiforeign; applied to political movements active in the nineteenth century in the United States.

necessary and proper clause Article I, Section 8, of the Constitution, also known as the *elastic clause;* gives Congress the authority to make whatever laws are necessary and proper to carry out its enumerated responsibilities.

New Deal coalition The informal electoral alliance of working-class ethnic groups, Catholics, Jews, urban dwellers, racial minorities, and the South, that was the basis of the Democratic party dominance of American politics from the New Deal to the early 1970s.

New Deal President Franklin Roosevelt's programs for economic recovery, income support, and business regulation during the Great Depression.

New Jersey Plan Proposal of the smaller states at the Constitutional Convention to create a government based on the equal representation of the states in a unicameral legislature.

news management The attempt by those in political power to put the presentation of news about them and their policies in a favorable light.

newsworthy Worth printing or broadcasting as news, according to editors' judgments.

North American Free Trade Agreement (NAFTA) An agreement among the United States, Canada, and Mexico to eliminate nearly all barriers to trade and investment among the three countries.

nuclear proliferation The spread of nuclear weapons to additional countries or to terrorist groups.

nullification An attempt by states to declare national laws or actions null and void.

objective journalism News reported with no evaluative language and with opinions quoted or attributed to a specific source.

obscenity As defined by the Supreme Court, the representation of sexually explicit material in a manner that violates community standards and is without redeeming social importance or value.

Office of Management and Budget (OMB) An organization within the Executive Office of the President that advises on the federal budget, domestic legislation, and regulations.

oligarchy Rule by the few, where a minority group holds power over a majority, as in an aristocracy clerical establishment.

open-seat election An election in which there is no incumbent officeholder.

opinion of the Court The majority opinion that accompanies a Supreme Court decision.

opinion The explanation of the majority's and the minority's reasoning that accompany a court decision.

ordinary scrutiny The assumption that the actions of elected bodies and officials are legal under the Constitution.

original intent The doctrine that the courts must interpret the Constitution in ways consistent with the intentions of the Framers rather than in light of contemporary conditions and needs.

original jurisdiction The authority of a court to be the first to hear a particular kind of case.

oversight Congressional responsibility for monitoring the actions of executive branch agencies and personnel to ensure conformity to federal statutes and congressional intent.

packing The process of concentrating voters for the other party into fewer districts in order to weaken them elsewhere.

partisan A committed supporter of a political party; also, seeing issues from the point of view of a single party.

party conference An organization of the members of a political party in the House or Senate.

party identification The sense of belonging to one or another political party.

party platform A party's statement of its positions on the issues of the day passed at the quadrennial national convention.

patronage The practice of distributing government offices and contracts to the supporters of the winning party; also called the *spoils system.*

payroll tax Tax levied on salaries and wages for Social Security and Medicare.

petit (trial) juries Juries that hear evidence and sit in judgment on charges brought in civil or criminal cases.

plaintiff One who brings suit in a court.

pluralist A political scientist who views American democracy as best understood in terms of the interaction, conflict, and bargaining of groups.

plurality More votes than any other candidate but less than a majority of all votes cast.

pocket veto Rejection of a bill if the president takes no action on it for 10 days and Congress has adjourned during that period.

podcast Digital audio and video files made readily available to interested people via computers and portable devices.

policy preferences   Citizens' ideas about what policies they want government to pursue.

political action committee (PAC)   An entity created by an interest group whose purpose is to collect money and make contributions to candidates in federal elections.

political attitudes   Individuals' views and preferences about public policies, political parties, candidates, government institutions, and public officials.

political culture   The set of core beliefs in a country that help shape how people behave politically and what they believe government should do.

political efficacy   The sense that an individual can affect what government does.

political equality   The principle that says that each person carries equal weight in the conduct of the public business.

political ideology   A system of interrelated and coherently organized political beliefs and attitudes.

political liberty   The principle that citizens in a democracy are protected from government interference in the exercise of a range of basic freedoms, such as the freedoms of speech, association, and conscience.

political party   An organization that tries to win control of government by electing people to office who carry the party label.

political socialization   The process by which individuals come to have certain core beliefs and political attitudes.

poll tax   A tax to be paid as a condition of voting; used in the South to keep African Americans away from the polls.

popular sovereignty   The basic principle of democracy that the people are the ultimate source of government authority and of the policies that government leaders make.

populism   The belief that the common person is every bit as good as those with wealth and power.

pork   Also called *pork barrel;* federally funded projects designed to bring to the constituency jobs and public money for which the members of Congress can claim credit.

poverty line   The federal government's calculation of the amount of income families of various sizes need to stay out of poverty. In 2008 it was $22,025 for a family of four.

precedents   Rulings by courts that guide judicial reasoning in subsequent cases.

preemption   Exclusion of the states from actions that might interfere with federal authority or statutes.

presidential approval rating   A president's standing with the public, indicated by the percentage of Americans who tell survey interviewers that they approve a president's "handling of his job."

presidential popularity   The percentage of Americans who approve a president's handling of his job.

primary election   Statewide elections in which voters choose delegates to the national party conventions.

prior restraint   The government's power to prevent publication of material to which it objects, as opposed to punishment afterward.

private interest   An interest group that seeks to protect or advance the material interests of its members rather than society at large.

privatization   The process of turning over certain government functions to the private sector.

privileges and immunities clause   The portion of Article IV, Section 2, of the Constitution that says that citizens from out of state have the same legal rights as local citizens in any state.

probable cause   Legal doctrine that refers to a reasonable belief that a crime has been committed.

progressive taxation   A tax system in which higher-income individuals are taxed at a higher rate than those below them.

proportional representation   The awarding of legislative seats to political parties to reflect the proportion of the popular vote each party receives.

prospective voting model   A theory of democratic elections in which voters decide what government will do in the near future by choosing one or another responsible party.

provisional ballot   A vote that is cast but not counted until determination is made that the voter is properly registered.

public assistance   Programs funded by general tax funds that provide money or services for the poor.

public goods   Government policies that provide benefits for everyone.

public interest   An interest group that works to gain protections or benefits for society at large.

public opinion   Political attitudes and core beliefs expressed by ordinary citizens as revealed by surveys.

public policy   What government does, usually in the form of new laws and regulations or in the interpretation and implementation of existing laws and regulations.

pundits   Somewhat derisive term for print, broadcast, and radio commentators on the political news.

quasi-governmental organization   An organization that has governmental powers and responsibilities but has substantial private-sector control over its activities.

random sampling   The selection of survey respondents by chance, with equal probability of being selected, to ensure their representativeness of the whole population.

ranking minority member   The highest ranking member of the minority party on a congressional committee.

rational public   The notion that collective public opinion is rational in the sense that it is generally stable and consistent and that when it changes it does so as an understandable response to events, to changing circumstances, and to new information.

realignment   The process by which one party supplants another as the dominant party in a political system.

reapportionment   The reallocation of House seats among the states, done after each national census, to ensure that seats are held by the states in proportion to the size of their populations.

recession   Two quarters or more of declining gross domestic product.

reciprocity Deferral by members of Congress to the judgment of subject-matter specialists, mainly on minor technical bills.

red tape Overbearing bureaucratic rules and procedures.

redistributive policies Government policies that transfer resources from one group or class to another.

redistricting The redrawing of congressional district lines within a state to ensure roughly equal populations within each district.

referenda Procedures available in some states by which state laws or constitutional amendments proposed by the legislature are submitted to the voters for approval or rejection.

regressive taxation A tax system in which lower-income individuals are taxed at a higher rate than those above them.

regulation The issuing of rules by government agencies with the aim of reducing the scale of negative externalities produced by private firms.

regulatory policies Government policies that require a group or class of groups to change its behavior to serve some public purpose.

remedy An action that a court determines must be taken to rectify a wrong done by government.

representative democracy Indirect democracy, in which the people rule through elected representatives.

republicanism A political doctrine advocating limited government based on popular consent, protected against majority tyranny.

reservation clause The Tenth Amendment to the Constitution, reserving powers to the states or the people.

responsible party The notion that a political party will take clear and distinct stands on the issues and enact them as policy when in office.

retrospective voting A form of election in which voters look back at the performance of a party in power and cast ballots on the basis of how well it did in office.

revolving door The common practice in which former government officials become lobbyists for interests with whom they formerly dealt in their official capacity.

rule of four An *unwritten* practice that requires at least four justices of the Supreme Court to agree that a case warrants review by the Court before it will hear the case.

safety nets Government programs that protect the minimum standard of living of families and individuals against loss of income.

sample survey An interview study asking questions of a set of people who are chosen as representative of the whole population.

scope of conflict Refers to the number of groups involved in a political conflict; a narrow scope of conflict involves a small number of groups, and a wide scope of conflict involves many.

secularization The spread of nonreligious values and outlooks.

select committees Temporary committees in Congress created to conduct studies or investigations; they have no power to report bills.

selective incorporation The gradual and piecemeal spread of the protections of the Bill of Rights to the states by the U.S. Supreme Court.

senatorial courtesy The tradition that a judicial nomination for a federal district court seat be approved by senators from the state where a district court is located before the Senate Judiciary Committee will consider the nomination.

seniority The principle that one attains a position on the basis of length of service.

separate but equal doctrine The principle articulated in *Plessy* v. *Ferguson* (1896) that laws prescribing *separate* public facilities and services for nonwhite Americans are permissible if the facilities and services are *equal* to those provided for whites.

separation of powers The distribution of government legislative, executive, and judicial powers to separate branches of government.

signing statement A document sometimes issued by the president in connection with the signing of a bill from Congress that sets out the president's understanding of the new law and how executive branch officials should carry it out.

sit-down strike A form of labor action in which workers stop production but do not leave their job site.

social (lifestyle) conservatives People who favor traditional social values; they tend to support strong law-and-order measures and oppose abortion and gay rights.

social (lifestyle) liberals People who favor civil liberties, abortion rights, and alternative lifestyles.

social contract A philosophical device, used by Enlightenment thinkers, such as Locke, Rousseau, and Harrington, to suggest that governments are only legitimate if they are created by a voluntary compact among the people.

social insurance Government programs that provide services or income support in proportion to the amount of mandatory contributions made by individuals to a government trust fund.

social movement A loosely organized group that uses unconventional and often disruptive tactics to have their grievances heard by the public, the news media, and government leaders.

Social Security Social insurance program that provides income support for the elderly, those with disabilities, and family survivors of working Americans.

soft power Influence in world affairs that derives from the attractiveness to others of a nation's culture, products, and way of life.

spin The attempt by public officials to have a story reported in terms that favor them and their policies; see *news management*.

spoils system The practice of distributing government offices and contracts to the supporters of the winning party; also called *patronage*.

standing committees Relatively permanent congressional committees that address specific areas of legislation.

standing Authority to bring legal action because one is directly affected by the issues at hand.

stare decisis The legal doctrine that says precedent should guide judicial decision making.

State of the Union Annual report to the nation by the president, now delivered before a joint session of Congress, on the state of the nation and his legislative proposals for addressing national problems.

states' rights position The view of American federalism that holds that the Constitution created a system of dual sovereignty in which the national government and the state governments are sovereign in their own spheres.

stay acts Laws postponing the collection of taxes or mortgage payments.

strict construction The doctrine that the provisions of the Constitution have a clear meaning and that judges must stick closely to this meaning when rendering decisions.

strict scrutiny The assumption that actions by elected bodies or officials violate the Constitution.

sub-government Another name for an iron triangle.

suffrage The legal right to vote; see *franchise*.

Sun Belt States of the Lower South, Southwest, and West, where sunny weather and conservative politics often prevailed.

superdelegates Elected officials from all levels of government who are appointed by party committees to be delegates to the national convention of the Democratic party; not selected in primary elections or caucuses.

superpower A nation armed with nuclear weapons and able to project force anywhere on the globe.

superprecedent Landmark rulings that have been reaffirmed by the Court over the course of many years and whose reasoning has become part of the fabric of American law.

supremacy clause The provision in Article VI of the Constitution that states that the Constitution and the laws and treaties of the United States are the supreme law of the land, taking precedence over state laws and constitutions.

suspect classification The invidious, arbitrary, or irrational designation of a group for special treatment by government, whether positive or negative; historically, a discriminated against, visible minority without power to protect itself.

Temporary Assistance to Needy Families (TANF) Program that provides income and services to many poor families; has benefit time limits and a work requirement.

Tenth Amendment Part of the Bill of Rights, the Amendment that says that those powers not given to the federal government and not prohibited for the states by the Constitution are reserved for the states and the people.

terrorism The use of deadly violence against civilians to further some political goal.

test case A case brought to force a ruling on the constitutionality of some law or executive action.

treaty A formal international agreement between two or more countries; in the United States, requires the "advice and consent" of the Senate.

trustee An elected representative who believes that his or her own best judgment, rather than instructions from constituents, should be used in making legislative decisions.

turnout The proportion of eligible or voting age Americans who actually vote in a given election; the two ways of counting turnout yield different results.

two-party system A political system in which two parties vie on relatively equal terms to win national elections and in which each party governs at one time or another.

tyranny The abuse of the inalienable rights of citizens by government.

unanimous consent Legislative action taken "without objection" as a way to expedite business; used to conduct much of the business of the Senate.

unemployment insurance Program funded by taxes on employers to provide short-term income support to laid-off workers; also called unemployment compensation.

unicameral A legislative body with a single chamber.

unified government Control of the executive and legislative branches by the same political party.

unilateralist The stance toward foreign policy that suggests that the United States should "go it alone," pursuing its national interests without seeking the cooperation of other nations or multilateral institutions.

unilateralists Those who believe the United States should vigorously use its military and diplomatic power to pursue American national interests in the world, but on a "go it alone" basis.

unitary executive Constitutional doctrine that proposes that the executive branch is under the direct control of the president, who has all authority necessary to control the actions of federal bureaucracy personnel and units without interference from the other federal branches.

unitary system A system in which a central government has complete power over its constituent units or states.

urbanization The movement of people from rural areas to cities.

veto Presidential disapproval of a bill that has been passed by both houses of Congress. The president's veto can be overridden by a two-thirds vote in each house.

Virginia Plan Proposal by the large states at the Constitutional Convention to create a strong central government with power in the government apportioned to the states on the basis of population.

watchdog The role of the media in scrutinizing the actions of government officials.

weapons of mass destruction Nuclear, biological, or chemical weapons with the potential to cause vast harm to human populations.

welfare state A government with a broad set of safety net programs.

whip A political party member in Congress charged with keeping members informed of the plans of the party leadership, counting votes before action on important issues, and rounding up party members for votes on bills.

whistle-blowers   People who bring official misconduct in their agencies to public attention.

white primaries   Primary elections open only to whites in the one-party South where the only elections that mattered were the Democratic Party's primaries; this effectively disenfranchised blacks.

wire service   Organizations such as the Associated Press and Reuters that gather and disseminate news to other news organizations.

World Trade Organization (WTO)   An agency designed to enforce the provisions of the General Agreement on Tariffs and Trade and to resolve trade disputes between nations.

writ of certiorari   An announcement that the Supreme Court will hear a case on appeal from a lower court; its issuance requires the vote of four of the nine justices.

Endnotes

CHAPTER 1

1. William H. Chafe, *The Unfinished Journey: America Since World War II* (New York: Oxford University Press, 1986), p. 304; Howard Zinn, *SNCC: The New Abolitionists* (Boston: Beacon Press, 1964), p. 64.

2. Chafe, *Unfinished Journey*, p. 305.

3. Pei-te Lien, Dianne M. Pinderhughes, Carol Hardy-Fanta, and Christine M. Sierra, "The Voting Rights Act and the Election of Non-white Officials," *PS: Political Science and Politics* (July 2007), pp. 489–494.

4. See summary of polls at Latinobarometro at **www.latinobarometro.org,** Asiabarometer at **https://www.asiabarometer.org,** and the PEW Center for the People and the Press at **www.pewresearch.org**.

5. The number of fully or partly democratic countries has decreased somewhat in recent years, with democratic declines happening most evidently in Russia, Zimbabwe, Venezuela, and Iran. See *Freedom in the World, 2009* (Washington, D.C.: Freedom House, 2009).

6. James Surowiecki, *The Wisdom of Crowds* (New York: Doubleday, 2004).

7. For a fuller treatment of the claims in this paragraph, as well as supporting evidence for them, see Robert A. Dahl, *Democracy and Its Critics* (New Haven, CT: Yale University Press, 1989); Robert A. Dahl, *On Democracy* (New Haven, CT: Yale University Press, 1998). Also see Benjamin Radcliff, "Politics, Markets, and Life Satisfaction: The Political Economy of Human Happiness," *American Political Science Review,* 95 (December 2001), pp. 939–952.

8. Robert A. Dahl, "James Madison: Republican or Democrat?" *Perspectives on Politics,* 3, no. 3 (September 2005), pp. 439–448.

9. John Dewey, *The Public and Its Problems* (New York: Holt, 1927).

10. Charles Tilly, *Democracy* (Cambridge, UK: Cambridge University Press, 2007), p. 59.

11. Tilly, *Democracy,* pp. 26–28. Also see Josiah Ober, "What the Ancient Greeks Can Tell Us About Democracy," *The Annual Review of Political Science,* 11 (2008), pp. 67–91.

12. Dahl, *Democracy and Its Critics,* p. 13; Dahl, "James Madison: Republican or Democrat?"

13. See Robert A. Dahl, *After the Revolution: Authority in the Good Society* (New Haven, CT: Yale University Press, 1970); Dahl, *Democracy and Its Critics*; Jane Mansbridge, *Beyond Adversary Democracy* (New York: Basic Books, 1980). Also see Kevin O'Leary, *Saving Democracy* (Stanford, CA: Stanford University Press, 2006), ch. 1.

14. See Benjamin Barber, *Strong Democracy: Participatory Democracy for a New Age* (Berkeley, CA: University of California Press, 1984); Peter Bachrach, *The Theory of Democratic Elitism* (Boston: Little, Brown, 1967); Robert A. Dahl, *A Preface to Economic Democracy* (Berkeley, CA: University of California Press, 1985); Edward S. Greenberg, "Spillovers from Cooperative and Democratic Workplaces," in Brandon Sullivan and John Sullivan, eds., *Cooperation as the Basis of Individual and Group Functioning* (Minneapolis, MN: University of Minnesota Press, 2006); Edward S. Greenberg, *Workplace Democracy: The Political Effects of Participation* (Ithaca, NY: Cornell University Press,
1986); C. B. MacPherson, *Democratic Theory: Essays in Retrieval* (Oxford, UK: Clarendon Press, 1973); Carole Pateman, *Participation and Democratic Theory* (London: Cambridge University Press, 1970).

15. Esther Dyson, *Release 2.0* (New York: Broadway Books, 1997); Lawrence K. Grossman, *The Electronic Republic: Reshaping Democracy in the Information Age* (New York: Viking Press, 1995); Jerome Armstrong and Markos M. Zuniga, *Crashing the Gate: Netroots, Grassroots, and the Rule of People- Powered Politics* (White River Junction, VT: Chelsea Green Publishing Co., 2006).

16. Christian Welzel and Ronald Inglehart, "The Role of Ordinary People in Democratization," *Journal of Democracy,* 19, no. 1 (2008), p. 126.

17. On deliberation and democracy, see Jason Barabas, "How Deliberation Affects Policy Opinions," *American Political Science Review,* 98 (2004), pp. 687–701; Seyla Benhabib, "Toward a Deliberative Model of Democratic Legitimacy," in Seyla Benhabib, ed., *Democracy and Difference* (Princeton, NJ: Princeton University Press, 1996); John Dryzek, *Discursive Democracy* (Cambridge, UK: Cambridge University Press, 1990); Nancy Fraser, "Rethinking the Public Sphere," in Craig Calhoun, ed., *Habermas and the Public Sphere* (New Brunswick, NJ: Rutgers University Press, 1992), pp. 109–142; Amy Guttman and Dennis Thompson, *Democracy and Disagreement* (Cambridge, UK: Belknap Press, 1996); Jurgen Habermas, *The Structural Transformation of the Public Sphere* (Cambridge, MA: MIT Press, 1989).

18. Kenneth May, "A Set of Independent, Necessary, and Sufficient Conditions for Simple Majority Decision," *Econometrical,* 20 (1952), pp. 680–684, shows that only majority rule can guarantee popular sovereignty, political equality, and neutrality among policy alternatives. See also Douglas W. Rae, "Decision Rules and Individual Values in Constitutional Choice," *American Political Science Review,* 63 (1969), pp. 40–53; Phillip D. Straffin Jr., "Majority Rule and General Decision Rules," *Theory and Decision,* 8 (1977), pp. 351–360. On the other hand, Hans Gersbach argues in *Designing Democracy* (New York: Springer Publishers, 2005) that larger majorities ought to be required for more important decisions.

19. Mark Warren, "Democracy and the State," in John S. Dryzek, Bonnie Honig, and Ann Phillips, eds., *The Oxford Handbook of Political Theory* (Oxford, UK: Oxford University Press, 2006), pp. 385–386.

20. For a review of contemporary research on this issue, see Larry M. Bartels, *Unequal Democracy: The Political Economy of the New Gilded Age* (New York: Russell Sage Foundation, 2008); Seymour Martin Lipset and Jason M. Lakin, *The Democratic Century* (Norman, OK: University of Oklahoma Press, 2004); Tilly, *Democracy.*

21. Dahl, *A Preface to Economic Democracy,* p. 68.

22. Robert A. Dahl, "On Removing Certain Impediments to Democracy in the United States," *Political Science Quarterly,* 92, no. 1 (Spring 1977), p. 14; Elaine Spitz, *Majority Rule* (Chatham, NJ: Chatham House, 1984), p. 83; Dahl, *Democracy and Its Critics,* p. 170.

23. See Marc Plattner, "Liberalism and Democracy," *Foreign Affairs* (March–April 1998), pp. 171–180. On the inevitability of tension between and the necessity of balancing the

claims of liberty and majority rule see Adam Przeworski, "Self-Government in Our Times," *The Annual Review of Political Science,* 12 (2009), pp. 88–90.

24. David Caute, *The Great Fear* (New York: Simon & Schuster, 1978); Victor Navasky, *Naming Names* (New York: Viking, 1980); Michael Rogin, *The Intellectuals and McCarthy* (Cambridge, MA: MIT Press, 1967).

25. Fareed Zakaria, *The Future of Freedom: Illiberal Democracy at Home and Abroad* (New York: Norton, 2004).

26. See Bernard R. Berelson, Paul F. Lazarsfeld, and William N. McPhee, *Voting* (Chicago: University of Chicago Press, 1954); V. O. Key Jr., *Public Opinion and American Democracy* (New York: Knopf, 1961); Herbert McClosky and Alida Brill, *Dimensions of Tolerance* (New York: Russell Sage Foundation, 1983); Robert Weissberg, *Polling, Policy, and Public Opinion: The Case Against Heeding the Voice of the People* (New York: Palgrave Press, MacMillan, 2003); Robert Weissberg, "Politicized Pseudo-Science," *PS* (January 2006), pp. 39–42; Alan Wolfe, *Does American Democracy Still Work?* (New Haven, CT: Yale University Press, 2006). But see, in rebuttal, James L. Gibson, "Political Intolerance and Political Repression during the McCarthy Red Scare," *American Political Science Review,* 82 (1988), pp. 511–529; Benjamin I. Page and Robert Y. Shapiro, *The Rational Public: Fifty Years of Trends in Americans' Policy Preferences* (Chicago: University of Chicago Press, 1992).

27. Katherine Brandt, "Madisonian Majority Tyranny, Minority Rights, and American Democracy" (paper presented at the annual meetings of the Midwest Political Science Association, April 2004); Dahl, *A Preface to Democratic Theory.*

28. Dahl, *Democracy and Its Critics,* p. 161.

29. See Wolfe, *Does American Democracy Still Work?*

30. Thanks to Professor Larry Martinez of the California State University, Long Beach, for this insight.

31. Philip A. Klinkner with Rogers M. Smith, *The Unsteady March: The Rise and Decline of Racial Equality in America* (Chicago: The University of Chicago Press, 1999).

CHAPTER 2

1. The White House. Washington, D.C., January 14, 2005.

2. A bill also can become a law after 10 days if the president has not signed the bill and Congress is still in session.

3. **www.whitehouse.gov** (posted January 31, 2005).

4. January 4, 2006, p. 1.

5. Charlie Savage, "Obama Looks to Limit Impact of Tactic Bush Used to Sidestep New Laws," *The New York Times* (March 9, 2009), p. 1.

6. Charlie Savage, "Obama's Embrace of a Bush Tactic Riles Congress," *The New York Times* (August 9, 2009), p. 1.

7. Richard Bushman, "Revolution," in Eric Foner and John A. Garraty, eds., *The Reader's Companion to American History* (Boston: Houghton Mifflin, 1991), p. 936; Gordon S. Wood, *The Creation of the American Republic* (New York: Norton, 1972), p. 12.

8. Joseph J. Ellis, *Founding Brothers: The Revolutionary Generation* (New York: Alfred A. Knopf, 2001), pp. 212–213; Roger Wilkins, *Jacob's Pillow: The Founding Fathers and the Dilemma of Black Patriotism* (Boston: Beacon Press, 2002).

9. Sarah M. Evans, *Born for Liberty: A History of Women in America* (New York: Free Press, 1997); John Hope Franklin and Alfred A. Moss Jr., *From Slavery to Freedom* (New York: Knopf, 1967).

10. See Hannah Arendt, *On Revolution* (New York: Viking, 1965).

11. Page Smith, *A People's History of the Young Republic: Vol 3, The Shaping of America* (New York: McGraw-Hill, 1980).

12. Richard Hofstadter, *The American Political Tradition* (New York: Vintage Books, 1948), p. 4.

13. For a review of thinking about relevance of republicanism in our own time, see Frank Lovett and Philip Pettit, "Neorepublicanism: A Normative and Institutional Research Program," *Annual Review of Political Science,* 12 (2009), pp. 11–29.

14. Kevin O'Leary, *Saving Democracy* (Stanford, CA: Stanford University Press, 2006), ch. 3.

15. Alexander Hamilton, James Madison, and John Jay, *The Federalist Papers,* ed. Clinton Rossiter (New York: New American Library, 1961), No. 10. (Originally published 1787–1788.)

16. See Gordon S. Wood, *The Radicalism of the American Revolution* (New York: Knopf, 1992).

17. Wood, *Creation of the American Republic,* pp. 311–318.

18. Ibid., ch. 8.

19. Samuel Elliot Morison, *The Oxford History of the American People* (New York: Oxford University Press, 1965), p. 274.

20. See Wood, *Creation of the American Republic,* p. 400.

21. Smith, *The Shaping of America,* pp. 24–26.

22. Quoted in Jackson Turner Main, *The Anti-Federalists* (Chapel Hill: University of North Carolina Press, 1961), p. 62.

23. David Brian Robertson, "Madison's Opponents and Constitutional Design," *American Political Science Review,* 99 (May 2006), pp. 225–243.

24. Melvin I. Urofsky, *A March of Liberty* (New York: Knopf, 1988), p. 89.

25. Quoted in *The Washington Post* (May 7, 1987). Also see Lee Epstein and Thomas G. Walker, *Constitutional Law for a Changing America* (Washington, D.C.: CQ Press, 2000), p. 6.

26. Charles Beard, *An Economic Interpretation of the Constitution* (New York: Macmillan, 1913). For a more recent work broadly supporting Beard's interpretation, see Robert A. McGuire, *To Form a More Perfect Union: A New Economic Interpretation of the United States Constitution* (New York: Oxford University Press, 2003).

27. See Robert Brown, *Charles Beard and the Constitution* (Princeton, NJ: Princeton University Press, 1956); Hofstadter, *The American Political Tradition;* Leonard Levy, *Constitutional Opinions* (New York: Oxford University Press, 1986); Robert A. McGuire and Robert L. Ohsfeldt, "An Economic Model of Voting Behavior over Specific Issues at the Constitutional Convention of 1787," *Journal of Economic History,* 66 (March 1986), pp. 79–111; James A. Morone, *The Democratic Wish* (New York: Basic Books, 1990); Forrest McDonald, *We the People: The Economic Origins of the Constitution* (Chicago: University of Chicago Press, 1958); Gordon S. Wood, *The Convention and the Constitution* (New York: St. Martin's Press, 1965); Wood, *Creation of the American Republic.*

28. Quoted in Wood, *Creation of the American Republic,* p. 473.

29. Ibid., p. 432.

30. Charles Stewart, "Congress and the Constitutional System," in Paul J. Quirk and Sarah A. Binder, eds., *The Legislative Branch* (New York: Oxford University Press, Institutions of American Democracy Series, 2005).

31. See Robertson, "Madison's Opponents and Constitutional Design," for more information on how the Great Compromise shaped the Constitution as a whole.

32. Ellis, *Founding Brothers,* p. 110.

33. Max Farrand, *The Records of the Federal Convention of 1787* (New Haven, CT: Yale University Press, 1937).

34. Hamilton, Madison, and Jay, *The Federalist,* No. 10.

35. "The Invention of Centralized Federalism," in William H. Riker, ed., *The Development of Centralized Federalism* (Boston: Kluwer Academic, 1987).

36. Robert A. Dahl, "On Removing the Impediments to Democracy in the United States," *Political Science Quarterly,* 92 (Spring 1977), p. 5.

37. Akhil Reed Amar, *America's Constitution: A Biography* (New York: Random House, 2005), p. 14.

38. Hamilton, Madison, and Jay, *The Federalist Papers,* No. 51.

39. Thomas Jefferson, *Notes on the State of Virginia,* ed. Thomas Perkins Abernathy (New York: Harper & Row, 1964), p. 120.

40. In a letter to James Madison dated November 18, 1788, in Adrienne Koch and William Peden, eds., *The Life and Selected Writings of Thomas Jefferson* (New York: Random House/The Modern Library, 1944), p. 452.

41. See Main, *The Anti-Federalists;* Wood, *Creation of the American Republic;* Smith, *The Shaping of America,* p. 99; Herbert Storing, *What the Anti-Federalists Were For* (Chicago: University of Chicago Press, 1981), p. 71; Robertson, "Madison's Opponents and Constitutional Design."

42. See Cass R. Sunstein, *A Constitution of Many Minds: Why the Founding Document Doesn't Mean What It Meant Before* (Princeton, NJ: Princeton University Press, 2009) for a particularly compelling statement of this idea.

43. On the undemocratic Constitution see Sanford Levinson, *Our Undemocratic Constitution: Where the Constitution Goes Wrong* (New York: Oxford University Press, 2006).

CHAPTER 3

1. Material for this story is from "After the Flood," *The Economist* (September 3, 2005), pp. 27–31; "When Government Fails," *The Economist* (September 10, 2005), pp. 26–28; Bob Williams, "Blame Amid the Tragedy," *The Wall Street Journal* (September 6, 2005), p. A23; Eric Lipton, Christopher Drew, Scott Shane, and Dave Rohde, "Breakdowns Marked Path from Hurricane to Anarchy," *The New York Times* (September 11, 2005), p. A1. Also see Douglas G. Brinkley, *The Great Deluge: Hurricane Katrina, New Orleans, and the Mississippi Gulf Coast* (New York: Harper Collins, 2006), for the most complete description and analysis of the disaster and its causes.

2. On the possible impacts of federalism on disaster relief, see Thomas Birkland and Sarah Waterman, "Is Federalism the Reason for Policy Failure in Hurricane Katrina?" *Publius, The Journal of Federalism* 38, no. 4 (2008), pp. 692–714.

3. William H. Riker, *The Development of American Federalism* (Boston: Kluwer Academic, 1987), pp. 56–60.

4. Gabriel A. Almond, G. Bingham Powell Jr., Russell J. Dalton, and Kaare Strom, *Comparative Politics Today: A World View,* updated 9th ed. (New York: Pearson Longman, 2010), p. 108.

5. Mark Rush, "Voting Power in Federal Systems: Spain as a Case Study," *PS: Political Science and Politics* XL, no. 4 (October 2007), pp. 715–720.

6. Rodney Hero, *Faces of Inequality: Social Diversity in American Politics* (New York: Oxford University Press, 1998). Also see Regina P. Branton and Bradford S. Jones, "Reexamining Racial Attitudes: The Conditional Relationship Between Diversity and Socioeconomic Environment," *American Journal of Political Science* 49, no. 2 (April 2005), pp. 359–372.

7. Dale Krane, "The Middle Tier in American Federalism: State Government Policy Activism During the Bush Presidency," *Publius: The Journal of Federalism* 37, no. 3 (2007), pp. 453–477.

8. Gillian E. Metzger, "Congress, Article IV, and Interstate Relations," *Harvard Law Review,* 120 (2007), pp. 1468–1542.

9. The study of the complex constitutional, legal, fiscal, and political links between states and the national government is often called the study of *intergovernmental relations* (the ever-changing constitutional, legal, fiscal, and political linkages among the states and the national government). For more on this, see B. G. Peters and J. Pierre, "Developments in Intergovernmental Relations: Towards Multi-Level Governance," *Policy and Politics,* 29 (2001), pp. 131–141; R.B. Albritton, "American Federalism and Intergovernmental Relations," in Gillian Peele, Christopher J. Bailey, Bruce Cain, and B. Guy Peters, eds., *Developments in American Politics* (New York: Palgrave, 2008).

10. Thomas Gais and James Fossett, "Federalism and the Executive Branch," in Joel D. Aberbach and Mark A. Peterson, eds., *The Executive Branch* (New York: Oxford University Press, Institutions of American Democracy Series, 2005).

11. Hero, *Faces of Inequality,* pp. 31–34.

12. Robert G. McCloskey, *American Supreme Court,* 4th ed., ed. Sanford Levinsonn (Chicago: University of Chicago Press, 2004), pp. 49–51.

13. See the special "Symposium on Preemption" in *PS: Political Science and Politics* (Washington, D.C.: The American Political Science Association, July 2005), pp. 359–378.

14. McCloskey, *American Supreme Court,* pp. 104–107, 118–119.

15. "A Partisan Public Agenda: Opinion of Clinton and Congress Improves" (Washington, D.C.: Pew Research Center, 1997); "How Americans View Government: Deconstructing Distrust" (Washington, D.C.: Pew Research Center, 1998); "National Omnibus Survey" (Cambridge, MA: Cambridge Reports/Research International, 1982).

16. Tim Conlan and John Dinan, "Federalism, the Bush Administration, and the Transformation of American Conservatism," *Publius: The Journal of Federalism,* 37, no 3 (2007), pp. 279–303.

17. Krane, "The Middle Tier in American Federalism."

18. Ann O. M. Bowan and George A. Krause, "Power Shift: Measuring Policy Centralization in U.S. Intergovernmental Relations, 1947–1998," *American Politics Research* 31, no. 3 (May 2003), pp. 301–313; B. Guy Peters, *American Public Policy: Promise and Performance* (Washington, D.C.: CQ Press, 2004), pp. 22–27; Robert Nagel, *The Implosion of American Federalism* (New York: Oxford University Press, 2002).

19. Morton Grodzins, *The American System* (New Brunswick, NJ: Transaction Books, 1983).

20. Riker, *The Development of American Federalism;* David B. Walker, *Toward a Functioning Federalism* (Cambridge, MA: Winthrop, 1981), pp. 60–63.

21. Paul E. Peterson, Barry G. Rabe, and Kenneth Wong, *When Federalism Works* (Washington, D.C.: Brookings Institution, 1986), p. 2.

22. Ed Gillespie and Bob Schellhas, eds., *Contract with America: The Bold Plan by Rep. Newt Gingrich, Rep. Dick Armey and the House Republicans to Change the Nation* (New York: Random House, 1994), p. 125.

23. "Symposium on Preemption," *PS*. Also see the "Preemption Monitor" of the National Conference of State Legislatures at **http://www.ncsl.org/standcomm/sclaw/PreemptionMonitor_Index.htm**.

24. William H. Riker, *Federalism: Origin, Operation, Significance* (Boston: Little, Brown, 1964), ch. 6.

25. Paul E. Peterson, *City Limits* (Chicago: University of Chicago Press, 1981); Paul E. Peterson, *The Price of Federalism* (Washington, D.C.: Brookings Institution, 1995).

CHAPTER 4

1. Adam Cort, "Living the Dream," *Assembly Magazine on-line* (**www.assemblymag.com**, August 1, 2006).

2. Author interview, Seattle, WA, 2006.

3. John Newhouse, *Boeing versus Airbus: The Inside Story of the Greatest International Competition in Business* (New York: Knopf, 2007).

4. For a detailed examination of how these changes at Boeing affected the health and well-being of its employees, see Edward S. Greenberg, Leon Grunberg, Sarah Moore, and Pat Sikora, *Turbulence: Boeing and the Future of American Workers and Managers* (New Haven, CT: Yale University Press, 2010).

5. See James O'Toole and Edward E. Lawler III, *The New American Workplace* (New York: Palgrave, MacMillan, 2006).

6. Aristide R. Zolberg, *A Nation by Design: Immigration Policy in the Fashioning of America* (Cambridge, MA: Harvard University Press, 2006).

7. U.S. Department of Homeland Security, *Yearbook of Immigration Statistics* (Washington, D.C.: U.S. Government Printing Office, 2003).

8. Jeffrey S. Passel, "Recession Slows—but Does Not Reverse—Mexican Immigration," (Washington, D.C., Pew Hispanic Center, July 22, 2009), p. 1.

9. U.S. Bureau of the Census, "2006 American Community Survey" (Washington, D.C.: U.S. Government Printing Office, 2007).

10. "Population Projections, 2005–2025" (Washington, D.C.: The Pew Research Center, February 11, 2008).

11. Richard Florida, *The Flight of the Creative Class* (New York: HarperBusiness, 2005).

12. "Hispanics and Arizona's New Immigration Law" (Washington, D.C.: The Pew Hispanic Center, April 29, 2010).

13. Pew Research Center for the People and the Press, press release, October 15, 2009.

14. David Rogers, "Immigration Bill, President Suffer Significant Setback," *The Wall Street Journal* (January 28, 2007), p. 1.

15. Daniel J. Tichenor, *Dividing Lines: The Politics of Immigration Control in the United States* (Princeton, NJ: Princeton University Press, 2002), p. 284.

16. "Not Here, Surely," *The Economist* (December 10, 2005), p. 31.

17. National Governors Association, July 2007.

18. "Recession Turns a Graying Office Grayer" (Washington, D.C.: The Pew Research Center, September 3, 2009), p. 1.

19. U.S. Bureau of the Census, "Older Population in the United States," 2008.

20. Based on purchasing power.

21. *Human Development Report, 2009* (New York: The United Nations, 2009).

22. U.S. Bureau of the Census, "Current Population Survey, March, 2009 Supplement" press release, March 2009.

23. Ianthe Jeanne Dugan, "Returning Workers Face Steep Pay Cuts," *The Wall Street Journal* (November 12, 2009), p. 1.

24. Stanley B. Greenberg, *Middle-Class Dreams* (New York: Times Books, 1995); Susan J. Tolchin, *The Angry American* (Boulder, CO: Westview Press, 1999). On the more general relationship between income growth and political mood, see Benjamin M. Friedman, *The Moral Consequences of Economic Growth* (New York: Knopf, 2005).

25. David Leonhardt and Marjorie Connelly, "81 Percent in Poll Say Nation Is on the Wrong Track," *The New York Times* (April 4, 2008), p. A1. Also see Brian Blackstone, "Economy Sheds Jobs in March, Fueling Fears of Recession," *The Wall Street Journal* (April 4, 2008), p. 1.

26. U.S. Bureau of the Census, "Income, Poverty, and Health Insurance in the United States, 2009," September 2010.

27. Ibid.

28. Ibid.

29. Ibid.

30. Ibid.

31. William Julius Wilson, *When Work Disappears: The World of the New Urban Poor* (New York: Vintage, 1997).

32. Florence Jaumotte, Subir Lall, and Chris Papageorgiou, "Rising Income Inequality: Technology, or Trade and Financial Globalization," (Washington, D.C.: International Monetary Fund, July 2008).

33. Emmanuel Saez, "Striking It Richer," working paper, update with 2007 estimates (August 5, 2009); Thomas Piketty and Emmanuel Saez, "Income Inequality in the United States," *Quarterly Journal of Economics*, 118, no. 1 (2003), pp. 1–39.

34. Lawrence Mishel, Jared Bernstein, and Sylvia Allegretto, *The State of Working America, 2006* (Ithaca, NY: Economic Policy Institute and Cornell University Press, 2006).

35. "CEO Pay Sinks Along with Profits," *The Wall Street Journal* (April 3, 2009), p. A1.

36. Edward Wolff, "Recent Trends in Household Wealth in the United States," Bard College, Levy Economics Institute (June 2007). Also see Larry M. Bartels, *Unequal Democracy: The Political Economy of the New Guided Age* (New York and Princeton, NJ: The Russell Sage Foundation and Princeton University Press, 2008), ch. 1.

37. On the different forms of capitalism in the modern world, see William J. Baumol, Robert E. Litan, and Carl J. Schramm, *Good Capitalism, Bad Capitalism and the Economics of Growth and Prosperity* (New Haven, CT: Yale University Press, 2007); Gosta Esping-Andersen, "The Three Political Economies of the Welfare State," *Canadian Review of Sociology and Anthropology*, 26 (1989), pp. 10–36; Jonas Pontusson, "The American Welfare State in Comparative Perspective," *Perspectives on Politics* 4, no. 2 (June 2006); pp. 315–326. Harold L. Wilensky, *Rich Democracies: Political Economy, Public Policy, and Performance* (Berkeley, CA: University of California Press, 2002).

38. Michael Reich, "The Proletarianization of the Workforce," in Richard Edwards, Michael Reich, and Thomas A. Weisskopf, eds., *The Capitalist System* (Englewood Cliffs, NJ: Prentice Hall, 1966), p. 125.

39. See Edward S. Greenberg, *Capitalism and the American Political Ideal* (Armonk, NY: Sharpe, 1985), ch. 4.

40. U.S. Department of Commerce, *International Direct Investment* (Washington, D.C.: U.S. Government Printing Office, 1984), p. 1.

41. For entertaining yet highly informative critiques of extreme pro-globalization advocates and extreme anti-globalization advocates, see Michael Veseth, *Selling Globalization: The Myth of the Global Economy* (Boulder, CO: Lynne Rienner, 1998); Michael Veseth, *Globaloney: Unraveling the Myths of Globalization* (Lanham, MD: Rowman & Littlefield, 2005).

42. Robert B. Reich, *Supercapitalism: The Transformation of Business, Democracy, and Everyday Life* (New York: Alfred A. Knopf, 2007).

43. Richard Florida, *The Rise of the Creative Class* (New York: Basic Books, 2002).

44. Peter Cappelli, *The New Deal at Work: Managing the Market-Driven Workforce* (Boston: Harvard Business School Press, 2008); Peter Gosselin, *High Wire: The Precarious Financial Lives of American Families* (New York: Basic Books, 2008); Douglas S. Massey, "Globalization and Inequality," *European Sociological Review* 25, no. 1 (2009); Reich, *Supercapitalism*.

45. Jacob S. Hacker, *The Great Risk Shift: The Assault on American Jobs, Families, Health Care, and Retirement* (New York: Oxford University Press, 2006). For a contrary view on income volatility, see "Shifting Sands," *The Economist* (January 6, 2007), p. 63; David Leonhardt, "What's Really Squeezing the Middle Class?" *The New York Times* (April 25, 2007), p. A1.

46. "Confidence in Obama Lifts U.S. Image Around the World," (Washington, D.C.: Pew Global Attitudes Project, July 23, 2009); "Obama More Popular Abroad Than at Home, Global Image of U.S. Continues to Benefit" (Washington, D.C.: Pew Global Attitudes Project, June 17, 2010).

47. See Seymour Martin Lipset, *American Exceptionalism: A Double-Edged Sword* (New York: Norton, 1996); Jennifer L. Hochschild, *Facing Up to the American Dream* (Princeton, NJ: Princeton University Press, 1995), ch. 1; John Micklethwait and Adrian Wooldridge, *The Right Nation: Conservative Power in America* (New York: Penguin Press, 2004), part IV. For a contrary view—namely, that America is divided into distinct political cultural traditions—see Rogers M. Smith, *Civic Ideals: Conflicting Visions of Citizenship in American* (New Haven, CT: Yale University Press, 1997). For an answer to Smith that defends the idea that the American political culture is of a single large cloth, see Marc Stears, "The Liberal Tradition and the Politics of Exclusion," *Annual Review of Political Science,* 10 (2007), pp. 85–101.

48. For a contrary view of the place of individualism in American life, see Desmond King, *The Liberty of Strangers: Making the American Nation* (New York: Oxford University Press, 2004).

49. See Jennifer L. Hochschild, *What's Fair? American Beliefs about Distributive Justice* (Cambridge, MA: Harvard University Press, 1981); Herbert McClosky and John R. Zaller, *The American Ethos: Public Attitudes Toward Capitalism and Democracy* (Cambridge, MA: Harvard University Press, 1984); Sidney Verba and Gary R. Orren, *Equality in America* (Cambridge, MA: Harvard University Press, 1985). See Benjamin I. Page and Lawrence R. Jacobs, *Class War: What Americans Really Feel About Inequality* (Chicago: University of Chicago Press, 2009), however, which shows that public support exists for programs to lessen inequality.

50. See Joel F. Handler and Yeheskel Hasenfeld, *Blame Welfare, Ignore Poverty and Inequality* (Cambridge, UK: Cambridge University Press, 2007). For arguments suggesting that Americans are uncomfortable with income inequality and are willing to let government do something about making it less extreme, see Page and Jacobs, *Class War*.

51. Verba and Orren, *Equality in America,* p. 255.

52. Page and Jacobs, *Class War*, pp. 96–97.

53. The Gallup Poll, February 24, 2009.

54. "Support for Health Care Principles, Opposition to Package" (Washington, D.C.: Pew Research Center, October 8, 2009).

55. John Judis, "Anti-Statism in America," *The New Republic* (November 11, 2009), p. 2.

56. Russell Hanson, *The Democratic Imagination in America* (Princeton, NJ: Princeton University Press, 1985).

57. McClosky and Zaller, *The American Ethos,* p. 18; "Views of a Changing World 2003" (Washington, D.C.: Pew Research Center, 2003).

58. Alan Wolfe, *Does American Democracy Still Work?* (New Haven, CT: Yale University Press, 2006).

59. Gary Wills, *Under God: Religion and American Politics* (New York: Simon and Schuster, 1991); Micklethwait and Wooldridge, *The Right Nation;* Kevin Phillips, *American Theocracy: The Peril and Politics of Radical Religion, Oil, and Borrowed Money in the 21st Century* (New York: Viking, 2006).

60. "Views of a Changing World 2003."

61. Micklethwait and Wooldridge, *The Right Nation*.

CHAPTER 5

1. Joseph C. Goulden, *Truth Is the First Casualty: The Gulf of Tonkin Affair—Illusion and Reality* (Chicago: Rand McNally, 1969). Also see Scott Stane, "Vietnam War Intelligence Deliberately Skewed, Secret Study Says," *The New York Times* (December 2, 2005), p. A1.

2. All public opinion polls cited in this chapter-opening story are from John E. Mueller, *War, Presidents and Public Opinion* (New York: Wiley, 1973).

3. U.S. Department of Defense, OASD (Comptroller), *Selected Manpower Statistics* (Washington, D.C.: Government Publications, June 1976), pp. 59–60.

4. Alexander Hamilton, James Madison, and John Jay, *The Federalist Papers,* ed. Clinton Rossiter (New York: New American Library, 1961; originally published 1787–1788). See Benjamin I. Page and Robert Y. Shapiro, *The Rational Public: Fifty Years of Trends in Americans' Policy Preferences* (Chicago: University of Chicago Press, 1992), chs. 1 and 2.

5. Walter Lippmann, *Public Opinion* (New York: Macmillan, 1922), p. 127.

6. Philip E. Converse, "The Nature of Belief Systems in Mass Publics," in David Apter, ed., *Ideology and Discontent* (New York: Free Press, 1964), pp. 206–261; Philip E. Converse, "Attitudes and Non-Attitudes: Continuation of a Dialogue," in Edward R. Tufte, ed., *The Quantitative Analysis of Social Problems* (Reading, MA: Addison-Wesley, 1970), pp. 168–189. Also see Larry M. Bartels, *Unequal Democracy: The Political*

Economy of the Gilded Age (New York and Princeton, NJ: Russell Sage Foundation and Princeton University Press, 2008), for an argument that people find it hard to understand whether public policies are consistent with their values and wishes.

7. Bartels, *Unequal Democracy.*

8. Bryan Caplan, *The Myth of the Rational Voter: Why Democracies Choose Bad Policies* (Princeton, NJ: Princeton University Press, 2007).

9. Robert S. Erikson and Kent L. Tedin, *American Public Opinion: Its Origins, Content, and Impact,* 8th ed. (New York: Pearson Longman, 2009), table 2.1. This book offers an excellent introduction to how surveys are done.

10. Ibid., p. 38.

11. George F. Bishop, *The Illusion of Public Opinion: Fact and Artifact in American Public Opinion Polls* (Lanham, MD: Rowman & Littlefield Publishers, 2004).

12. For a review of the research literature on political socialization see Erikson and Tedin, *American Public Opinion,* ch. 5.

13. Austin Ranney and Thad Kousser, "Politics in the United States," in Gabriel A. Almond, G. Bingham Powell, Russell J. Dalton, and Kaare Strom, eds., *Comparative Politics Today* (New York: Pearson Longman, 2008), p. 724. Also see the discussion of the origin of "embedded preferences" in Clem Brooks and Jeff Manza, *Why Welfare States Persist: The Importance of Public Opinion in Democracies* (Chicago: University of Chicago Press, 2007), pp. 31–32.

14. Doris A. Graber, *Mass Media and American Politics,* 8th ed. (Washington, D.C.: CQ Press, 2010), pp. 161–166.

15. Paul Sniderman and Thomas Piazza, *Black Pride and Black Prejudice* (Princeton, NJ: Princeton University Press, 2002), pp. 175–179.

16. Erikson and Tedin, *American Public Opinion,* pp. 175–176.

17. "Trends in Political Values and Core Attitudes: 1987–2009" (Washington, D.C.: Pew Research Center for the People and the Press, report released May 21, 2009); Laura R. Olson and John C. Green, *Beyond Red State, Blue State: Electoral Gaps in the Twenty-First Century American Electorate* (New York: Pearson Prentice-Hall, 2009).

18. "Trends in Political Values and Core Attitudes: 1987–2009," pp. 78–79.

19. This and the votes of other groups reported in this section are from "The National Election Pool Exit Poll" (Washington, D.C.: Edison Media Research and Mitofsky International, November 4, 2008).

20. Pew Research Center, "Trends in Political Values and Core Attitudes: 1987–2009."

21. Ibid., section 9.

22. Ibid., p. 58.

23. Ibid., p. 87.

24. General Social Survey, 2006.

25. Bernadette C. Hayes, "The Impact of Class on Political Attitudes," *European Journal of Political Research,* 27 (1995), p. 76.

26. Nolan McCarty, Keith T. Poole, and Howard Rosenthal, *Polarized America: The Dance of Ideology and Unequal Riches* (Cambridge, MA: MIT Press, 2006), p. 107; Bartels, *Unequal Democracy.*

27. See "Trends in Political Values and Core Attitudes: 1987–2009," p. 24. For pre-2009 data see Erikson and Tedin, *American Public Opinion,* pp. 198–199, using over-time reports from the National Election Study surveys; McCarty, Poole, and Rosenthal, *Polarized America.*

28. "Trends in Political Values and Core Attitudes: 1987–2009," section 2.

29. Earl Black and Merle Black, *The Rise of Southern Republicans* (Cambridge, MA: Harvard University Press, 2002); Earl Black and Merle Black, *Divided America: The Ferocious Power Struggle in American Politics* (New York: Simon and Schuster, 2007).

30. General Social Survey, 2008.

31. Ibid.

32. Ibid.; Erikson and Tedin, *American Public Opinion,* pp. 216–221.

33. Morris P. Fiorina, *Culture War: The Myth of a Polarized American* (New York: Pearson Longman Publishers, 2005); Morris P. Fiorina and Samuel J. Abrams, "Political Polarization in the American Public," *The Annual Review of Political Science,* 11 (2008), pp. 563–588.

34. Erickson and Tedin, *American Public Opinion,* pp. 196–198.

35. "Trends in Political Values and Core Attitudes: 1987–2009," p. 21. The Pew Research Center had the gender gap at 16 percent in 2009.

36. Fiorina, *Culture War,* pp. 34–35, 66–76; Karen M. Kaufman, "The Gender Gap," *PS: Political Science and Politics,* 39, no. 3 (2006), pp. 447–453. For a contrary view see Janet M. Box-Steffensmeier, Suzanna De Boef, and Tse-Min Lin, "The Dynamics of the Partisan Gender Gap," *American Political Science Review,* 98, no. 3 (August 2004), pp. 515–528.

37. Mark Schlesinger and Caroline Heldman, "Gender Gap or Gender Gaps?" *The Journal of Politics,* 63, no. 1 (February 2001), pp. 59–92; Erikson and Tedin, *American Public Opinion,* pp. 222–225; General Social Survey, 2008.

38. Fiorina, *Culture War,* pp. 66–69.

39. Pew, "Trends in Political Values and Core Attitudes: 1987–2009."

40. *New York Times*/CBS News Poll, released June 26, 2007; General Social Survey, 2008.

41. Pew Research Center, "Trends in Political Values and Core Attitudes: 1987–2009," section 4; Nicholas L. Danigelis, Melissa Hardy, and Stephen J. Cutler, "Population Aging, Intracohort Aging, and Sociopolitical Attitudes," *American Sociological Review* 72 (2007), pp. 812–830.

42. For detailed information on the size, beliefs, and political attitudes of various religious denominations in the United States see "The U.S. Religious Landscape Survey" (Washington, D.C.: Pew Forum on Religion and Public Life, November 9, 2009). All of the survey data in this section, unless otherwise noted, comes from this source.

43. Black and Black, *Divided America.*

44. Pew, "The U.S. Religious Landscape Survey."

45. The data in this section is from *Trends, 2005* (Washington, D.C.: The Pew Research Center for the People and the Press, 2005).

46. Fiorina, *Culture War;* Fiorina and Abrams, "Political Polarization in the American Public."

47. Michael X Delli Carpini and Scott Keeter, *What Americans Know About Politics and Why It Matters* (New Haven, CT: Yale

University Press, 1996); Alan Wolfe, *Does American Democracy Still Work?* (New Haven, CT: Yale University Press, 2006).

48. See Erikson and Tedin, *American Public Opinion*, table 3.1, for full details. Also see Page and Shapiro, *The Rational Public,* pp. 9–14; Wolfe, *Does American Democracy Still Work?* pp. 24–30.

49. "Public Knowledge of Current Affairs Little Changed by News and Information Revolutions What Americans Know: 1989–2007" (Washington, D.C: Pew Research Center, April 15, 2007).

50. Paul M. Sniderman, Richard A. Brody, and Philip E. Tetlock, *Reasoning and Choice: Explorations in Political Psychology* (New York: Cambridge University Press, 1991). See also Carpini and Keeter, *What Americans Know About Politics;* Samuel Popkin, *The Reasoning Voter* (Chicago: University of Chicago Press, 1991). For the view that it matters a great deal that Americans don't know much of the details about what is going on in Washington see Caplan, *The Myth of the Rational Voter;* Wolfe, *Does American Democracy Still Work?*

51. Robert E. Lane, *Political Ideology: Why the American Common Man Believes What He Does* (New York: Free Press, 1962); Jennifer L. Hochschild, *What's Fair? American Beliefs about Distributive Justice* (Cambridge, MA: Harvard University Press, 1986); Curroll J. Glynn, Susan Herbst, Garrett O'Keefe, and Robert I. Shapiro, *Public Opinion* (Boulder, CO: Westview Press, 1999), ch. 8.

52. Page and Shapiro, *The Rational Public.* Also see Doris A. Graber, "Re-Measuring the Civic IQ: Decline, Stability, or Advance?" (paper prepared for presentation at the annual meeting of the American Political Science Association, Boston, August 28–31, 2008); Taeku Lee, *Mobilizing Public Opinion: Black Insurgency and Racial Attitudes in the Civil Rights Era* (Chicago: University of Chicago Press, 2002); Erikson and Tedin, *American Public Opinion,* pp. 93–94. This view is strongly rejected by Caplan, *The Myth of the Rational Voter,* who believes that, at least on issues related to economic policies, errors by the public are systematic rather than random so that they do not balance out.

53. Pew, "Trends in Political Values and Core Attitudes: 1987–2009," p. 78.

54. Harris Poll, June 2004.

55. "Trust in Government, 1958–2010," (Washington, D.C.: Pew Research Center for the People and the Press, March 2010).

56. An average of June 2010 surveys reported by Polling Report (**www.pollingreport.com**).

57. The Gallup Poll (November 5–9, 2009).

58. An average of March 2010 surveys reported by Polling Report (**www.pollingreport.com**).

59. An average of June 2010 surveys reported by Polling Report (**www.pollingreport.com**).

60. Benjamin I. Page and Lawrence R. Jacobs, *Class War? What Americans Really Think About Economic Inequality* (Chicago: University of Chicago Press, 2009).

61. American National Election Studies, 2008; Page and Jacobs, *Class War?*

62. Steven Kull, *Americans and Foreign Aid: A Study of American Public Attitudes* (Washington, D.C.: Program on International Policy Attitudes, 1995).

63. Pew, "Trends in Political Values and Core Attitudes: 1987–2009," p. 1.

64. Ibid., p. 59.

65. This may be changing; Gallup reported in May 2010 that 47 percent of Americans called themselves "pro-life" compared to 45 percent who called themselves "pro-choice." See the Gallup Report, May 6, 2010.

66. Pew, "Trends in Political Values and Core Attitudes: 1987–2009," p. 39.

67. Andrew Gelman, "Over Time, a Gay Marriage Groundswell," *The New York Times,* August 22, 2010, p. WK3.

68. "Broad Approval for New Arizona Immigration Law" (Washington, D.C.: Pew Research Center for the People and the Press, May 12, 2010).

69. "Confidence in U.S. Foreign Policy Index, 2007," *Public Agenda Online and Foreign Affairs Magazine* (**www.publicagenda.org/ foreignaffairs**).

70. William Caspary, "Then 'The Mood Theory': A Study of Public Opinion and Foreign Policy," *American Political Science Review,* 64 (1970), pp. 536–547; John E. Reilly, ed., *American Public Opinion and U.S. Foreign Policy, 1995* (Chicago: Chicago Council on Foreign Relations, 1995), p. 13; Princeton Survey Associates/ Pew Research Center, October 1999. Also see Pew, "Trends in Political Values and Core Attitudes: 1987–2009," section 6.

71. *Time*/CNN Survey, December 7, 1994.

72. Gallup Poll, conducted for CNN and *USA Today,* September 2001.

73. Gallup Poll, conducted for CNN and *USA Today,* September 2005.

74. ABC News/*Washington Post* Poll. June 3–6, 2010.

75. Summary of polls on American foreign policy reported at *The Public Agenda Online* at **www.publicagenda.org**; Benjamin I. Page with Marshall M. Bouton, *The Foreign Policy Disconnect: What Americans Want from Our Leaders But Don't Get* (Chicago: University of Chicago Press, 2006).

76. This seems to be the case in foreign and national defense issues as well. See John H. Aldrich, Christopher Gelpi, Peter Feaver, Jason Reifler, and Kristin Tompson Sharp, "Foreign Policy and the Electoral Connection," *Annual Review of Political Science,* 9 (2006), pp. 477–502.

77. For a summary of the evidence see Erikson and Tedin, *American Public Opinion,* pp. 302–308.

78. Alan D. Monroe, "Consistency Between Public Preferences and National Policy Decisions," *American Politics Quarterly,* 7 (January 1979), pp. 3–19; Benjamin I. Page and Robert Y. Shapiro, "Effects of Public Opinion on Policy," *American Political Science Review,* 77 (1983), pp. 175–190.

79. James A. Stimson, *Public Opinion in America: Moods, Cycles and Swings* (Boulder, CO: Westview Press, 1991).

80. Paul Burstein, "The Impact of Public Opinion on Public Policy: A Review and an Agenda," *Political Research Quarterly,* 56, no. 1 (March 2003). Also see Vincent L. Hutchings, *Public Opinion and Democratic Accountability: How Citizens Learn About Politics* (Princeton, NJ: Princeton University Press, 2003).

81. Summarized in Benjamin I. Page, "The Semi-Sovereign Public," in Jeff Manza, Fay Lomax Cook, and Benjamin I. Page, eds., *Navigating Public Opinion: Polls, Policy, and the Future of American Democracy* (New York: Oxford University Press, 2002).

82. Lawrence R. Jacobs and Robert Y. Shapiro, *Politicians Don't Pander: Political Manipulation and the Loss of Democratic Responsiveness* (Chicago: University of Chicago Press, 2000); John Zaller, *The Nature and Origins of Mass Opinion* (New York: Cambridge University Press, 1992); Wolfe, *Does American Democracy Still Work?*

83. W. Lance Bennett, Regina G. Lawrence, and Steven Livingston, *When the Press Fails: Political Power and the News Media From Iraq to Katrina* (Chicago: University of Chicago Press, 2007), ch. 5.

84. Page with Bouton, *The Foreign Policy Disconnect.* Also see Lawrence R. Jacobs and Benjamin I. Page, "Who Influences Foreign Policy," *American Political Science Review,* 99, no. 1 (February 2005), pp. 107–124. On the elite-mass public disconnect also see Daniel W. Drezner, "The Realist Tradition in American Public Opinion," *Perspectives on Politics* 6, no. 1 (March 2008), pp. 51–70.

85. Bartels, *Unequal Democracy.*

86. Public opinion scholar Larry Bartels suggests that the 2001 tax cut (the largest in two decades, with tax relief going overwhelmingly to upper-income people) was supported by the public out of sheer ignorance and confusion about the impact of changes in the Tax Code. See Larry M. Bartels, "Homer Gets a Tax Cut: Inequality and Public Policy in the American Mind," *Perspectives on Politics,* 3, no. 1 (March 2005), pp. 15–29. In the same issue (pp. 33–53), Jacob Hacker and Paul Pierson disagree; they suggest in their article "Abandoning the Middle: The Bush Tax Cuts and the Limits of Democratic Control," that manipulation and deception were prominent in the successful effort to raise public support for the 2001 tax cuts.

CHAPTER 6

1. Material for this chapter opener is from W. Lance Bennett, Regina G. Lawrence, and Steven Livingston, *When the Press Fails: Political Power and the News Media from Iraq to Katrina* (Chicago: University of Chicago Press, 2007), pp. 13–45.

2. Adam Schiffer, "Blogswarms and Press Norms: News Coverage of the Downing Street Memos" (Washington, D.C.: paper presented at annual meetings of the American Political Science Association, August 31–September 3, 2006).

3. Bennett, Lawrence, and Livingston, *When the Press Fails*, p. 27.

4. Dana Milbank, "Democrats Play House to Rally Against the War," *The Washington Post* (June 6, 2005), p. 17.

5. Doris Graber, *Mass Media and American Politics,* 8th ed. (Washington, D.C.: Congressional Quarterly Press, 2010), pp. 16–19.

6. Joseph Cappella and Kathleen Hall Jamieson, *Spiral of Cynicism: The Press and the Public Good* (New York: Oxford University Press, 1997); Larry J. Sabato, Mark Stencel, and S. Robert Lichter, *Peepshow: Media and Politics in an Age of Scandal* (Boulder, CO: Rowman & Littlefield Publishers, 2000).

7. *The State of the News Media, 2008* (Washington, D.C.: Pew Research Center, Project for Excellence in Journalism, 2008).

8. Statistical Division, Organization of Economic Cooperation and Development (2010).

9. Andrew Kohut, *Internet's Broader Role in Campaign 2008* (Washington, D.C.: Pew Research Center, 2008).

10. Pew Research Center, June 15, 2009.

11. "Big Is Best," *The Economist* (October 31, 2009), pp. 75–76; Shira Ovide, "U.S. Newspaper Circulation Falls," *The Wall Street Journal Online,* posted October 26, 2009 (**http://online. wsj.com**).

12. Alex S. Jones, *Losing the News: The Future of the News That Feeds Democracy* (New York: Oxford University Press, 2009), pp. 180–181.

13. *Audience Segments in a Changing News Environment* (Washington, D.C.: The Pew Research Center, press release, August 17, 2008).

14. *The State of the News Media, 2009* (Washington, D.C.: The Project for Excellence in Journalism, 2009), **www.stateofthe media.org/2009/index.htm.**

15. Bennett, Lawrence, and Livingston, *When the Press Fails,* pp. 57–59.

16. Matthew Hindman, *The Myth of Digital Democracy* (Princeton, NJ: Princeton University Press, 2009), ch. 6.

17. Nielsen Online Ratings, **www.netratings.com.**

18. Graber, *Mass Media and American Politics,* pp. 36–37.

19. "Who Owns What," *The Columbia Journalism Review online,* **www.cjr.org** (accessed March 31, 2010).

20. "Who Owns What," *Columbia Journalism Review Online,* the Media," **www.cjr.org/resources/** (updated and accessed, June 18, 2010).

21. "Read All About It," *The New Yorker* (August 13, 2007), p. 21.

22. W. Lance Bennett, *News: The Politics of Illusion* (New York: Pearson Longman, 2009), pp. 231–246, reviews the debate. The term *media monopoly* is from University of California–Berkeley journalism professor Ben Bagkikian's book, *Media Monopoly,* 5th ed. (Boston: Beacon Press, 1997).

23. Bennett, *News,* pp. 242–244.

24. Ibid., p. 241.

25. Jones, *Losing the News,* p. 7.

26. Doug Underwood, "Market Research and the Audience for Political News," in Doris Graber, Denis McQuail, and Pippa Norris, eds., *The Politics of News: The News of Politics* (Washington, D.C.: CQ Press, 1998), p. 171; also see Bennett, *News,* ch. 7.

27. Graber, *Mass Media and American Politics,* pp. 87–91.

28. Leon V. Sigal, *Reporters and Officials: The Organization and Politics of News Reporting* (Lexington, MA: Heath, 1973), p. 124.

29. Bennett, *News,* pp. 112–114; Steven Livingston and W. Lance Bennett, "Gatekeeping, Indexing, and Live Event News," *Political Communication,* 20, no. 4 (October–December 2003), pp. 363–380; Graber, *Mass Media and American Politics,* pp. 79–82.

30. Bennett, *News,* pp. 164–167.

31. Ibid., pp.127–134.

32. Mark Hertsgaard, *On Bended Knee* (New York: Farrar, Straus & Giroux, 1988), p. 5.

33. Anne E. Kornblut, "Administration Is Warned About Its News Videos," *The New York Times* (January 19, 2005), p. A9; Anne E. Kornblut, "Third Journalist Was Paid to Promote Bush Policies," *The New York Times* (January 29, 2005), p. A13; Charlie Savage and Alan Wirzbicki, "White House-Friendly Reporter Under Scrutiny," *The Boston Globe* (February 2, 2005), p. A1; "Source Watch," *Center for Media and Democracy* (**www.prwatch.org/cmd/index.html**), February 2005.

34. The Audit, "Learning Journalism Lessons of the Past," *Columbia Journalism Review* (posted June 5, 2009 at **www.cjr.org/the_ audit/learning_journalism_lessons_of.php**).

35. David Murray, Joel Schwartz, and S. Robert Lichter, *It Ain't Necessarily So: How Media Make and Unmake the Scientific Picture of Reality* (Lanham, MD: Rowan & Littlefield Publishers, 2001), pp. 29–30.

36. Graber, *Mass Media and American Politics,* ch. 11.

37. For the best analysis of how why and how this happens and its unfortunate impact on the democratic process, see Bennett, Lawrence, and Livingston, *When the Press Fails.*

38. Eric Alterman, *What Liberal Media?* (New York: Basic Books, 2003). Also see the online site FAIR (Fairness and Accuracy in Reporting) at **www.fair.org** for a liberal point of view about press bias, and AIM (Accuracy in Reporting) at **www.aim.org** for a conservative point of view.

39. Barnard Goldberg, *Bias in the News* (Washington, D.C.: Regnery, 2001).

40. "Press Accuracy Rating Hits Two Decade Low" (Washington, D.C.: Pew Research Center, September 13, 2009).

41. Neal Hickey, "Is Fox News Fair?" *Columbia Journalism Review,* 31 (March/April 1998), pp. 30–35; David Weaver and G. Cleveland Wilhoit, *The American Journalist* (Mahwah, NJ: Lawrence Erlbaum, 1996); Graber, *Mass Media and American Politics,* pp. 86–89.

42. Bennett, *News,* pp. 34–35; Graber, *Mass Media and American Politics,* pp. 76–77; Thomas E. Patterson and Wolfgang Donsbach, "News Decisions: Journalists as Partisan Actors," *Political Communications,* 13 (October–December 1996), pp. 455–468.

43. Robert S. Erikson and Kent L. Tedin, *American Public Opinion: Its Origins, Content, and Impact* (New York: Pearson Longman, 2007), pp. 238–239.

44. Carmen M. Reinhart and Kenneth Rogoff, *This Time Is Different: Eight Centuries of Financial Folly* (Princeton, NJ: Princeton University Press, 2009); John Cassidy, *How Markets Fail* (New York: Farrar, Straus, and Giroux, 2009).

45. John Zaller, *A Theory of Media Politics* (Chicago: University of Chicago Press, 2004).

46. Bennett, *News,* pp. 238–241. Graber, *Mass Media and American Politics,* pp. 97–100; Jones, *Losing the News,* p. 51.

47. News Index, *Project for Excellence in Journalism* (2007), at **www.journalism.org**.

48. "Coverage of Jackson's Death Seen as Excessive" (Washington, D.C.: Pew Research Center, July 1, 2009).

49. Bennett, *News,* pp. 238–240.

50. Alan Wolfe, *Does American Democracy Still Work?* (New Haven, CT: Yale University Press, 2006), pp. 108–110.

51. For a review of the literature on the subject, see Samuel L. Popkin, "Changing Media, Changing Politics," *Perspectives on Politics* (June 2006), pp. 327–341; Wolfe, *Does American Democracy Still Work?,* ch. 5.

52. David L. Paletz, "The Media and Public Policy," in Doris Graber, Denis McQuail, and Pippa Norris, eds., *The Politics of News: The News of Politics* (Washington, D.C.: CQ Press, 1998),

53. Shanto Iyengar and Donald R. Kinder, *News That Matters* (Chicago: University of Chicago Press, 1987); also see Erikson and Tedin, *American Public Opinion,* pp. 247–248, for a review of the research on news media agenda setting.

54. G. Ray Funkhauser, "The Issues of the Sixties: An Exploratory Study in the Dynamics of Public Opinion," *Public Opinion Quarterly,* 37 (Spring 1973), pp. 62–75.

55. George C. Edwards, "Who Influences Whom? The President, Congress and the Media," *The American Political Science Review,* 93 (June 1999), pp. 327–344.

56. Bennett, Lawrence, and Livingston, *When the Press Fails.*

57. Shanto Iyengar, *Is Anyone Responsible? How Television News Frames Political Issues* (Chicago: University of Chicago Press, 1991); Kathleen Hall Jamieson and Paul Waldman, *The Press Effect* (Washington, D.C.: CQ Press, 2002).

58. Paul M. Kellstedt, *The Mass Media and the Dynamics of American Racial Attitudes* (Cambridge, U.K.: Cambridge University Press, 2003).

59. Benjamin I. Page, Robert Y. Shapiro, and Glenn R. Dempsey, "What Moves Public Opinion?" *American Political Science Review,* 81 (1987), pp. 23–43.

60. Joseph Cappella and Kathleen Jamieson, *Spiral of Cynicism: The Press and the Public Good* (New York: Oxford University Press, 1997); Stephen C. Craig, ed., *Broken Contract: Changing Relations Between Americans and Their Government* (Boulder, CO: Westview Press, 1996); Mark J. Hetherington, "Declining Trust and Shrinking Policy Agenda," in Robert Hart and Daron R. Shaw, eds., *Communications in U.S. Elections* (Lanham, MD: Rowman & Littlefield, 2001); Bennett, *News;* Thomas E. Patterson, "Bad News, Period," *PS* (March 1996), pp. 17–20.

61. See Graber, *Mass Media and American Politics,* pp. 41–43, for the extent of and limits on FCC powers to regulate.

62. John A. Ferejohn and James H. Kuklinski, eds., *Information and Democratic Processes* (Urbana, IL: University of Illinois Press, 1990); Benjamin I. Page, *Who Deliberates? Mass Media in Modern Democracy* (Chicago: University of Chicago Press, 1996).

CHAPTER 7

1. Information for this story is from the following sources: David Barstow, Laura Dodd, James Glanz, Stephanie Sauo, and Ian Urbina, "Regulators Failed to Address Risks in Oil Rig Fail-Safe Device," *The New York Times* (June 20, 2010), p. 1; Ian Urbina, "Inspector General's Inquiry Faults Regulators," *The New York Times* (May 24, 2010), p. 1; "The Oil Well and the Damage Done," *The Economist Online* (June 17, 2010). **www.economist.com/node/16381032;** "How Did This Happen and Who Is to Blame," *Bloomberg Businessweek* (June 14–20, 2010), pp. 60–64.

2. On the most recent deregulation movement in American politics and the thinking behind it, see Richard Harris and Sidney Milkis, *The Politics of Regulatory Change* (New York: Oxford University Press, 1989); John Cassidy, *How Markets Fail* (New York: Farrar, Straus and Giroux, 2009). Also see Marver Bernstein, *Regulation by Independent Commission* (Princeton, NJ: Princeton University Press, 1955); Grant McConnell, *Private Power and American Democracy* (New York: Vintage Books, 1966); James Buchanan and Gordon Tullock, "Polluters, Profits and Political Responses: Direct Control versus Taxes," *American Economic Review,* 65 (1975), pp. 139–147; Murray Weidenbaum, *The Costs of Government Regulation of Business* (Washington, D.C.: Joint Economic Committee of Congress, 1978); Kevin P. Phillips, *The Politics of Rich and Poor: Wealth and the American Electorate in the Reagan Aftermath* (New York: Random House, 1990).

3. Jeffrey M. Berry and Clyde Wilcox, *The Interest Group Society,* 5th ed. (New York: Pearson Longman, 2009), pp. 4–6.

4. Alexander Hamilton, James Madison, and John Jay, *The Federalist Papers,* ed. Clinton Rossiter (New York: New American Library, 1961), No. 10. (Originally published 1787–1788.)

5. The classics of the pluralist tradition include Arthur F. Bentley, *The Process of Government* (Chicago: University of Chicago Press, 1908); David Truman, *The Governmental Process* (New York: Knopf, 1951); V. O. Key, Jr., *Politics, Parties, and Pressure Groups* (New York: A. Crowell, 1952); Robert A. Dahl, *A Preface to Democratic Theory* (Chicago: University of Chicago Press, 1956); Robert A. Dahl, *Who Governs?* (New Haven, CT: Yale University Press, 1961). For a summary treatment of the pluralist tradition and its thinking about interest groups see Berry and Wilcox, *The Interest Group Society*, ch. 1.

6. E. E. Schattschneider, *The Semi-Sovereign People* (New York: Holt, Rinehart & Winston, 1960).

7. Robert B. Reich, *Supercapitalism: The Transformation of Business, Democracy, and Everyday Life* (New York: Knopf, 2007), pp. 80–86; Jeffrey M. Berry, *The New Liberalism: The Rising Power of Citizen Groups* (Washington, D.C.: Brookings, 1999); Thomas Byrne Edsall, *The New Politics of Inequality* (New York: Norton, 1984); Michael Goldfield, *The Decline of Organized Labor in the United States* (Chicago: University of Chicago Press, 1987); Edward S. Greenberg, *Capitalism and the American Political Ideal* (Armonk, NY: Sharpe, 1985); David Vogel, *Fluctuating Fortunes: The Political Power of Business in America* (New York: Basic Books, 1989), ch. 8.

8. U.S. Bureau of Labor Statistics, press release, January 28, 2009.

9. Reich, *Supercapitalism*. A country's institutional and legal structure also matter. The proportion of workers in labor unions actually increased over the past several decades in the Scandinavian countries. See Lyle Scruggs and Peter Lange, "Where Have All the Workers Gone? Globalization, Institutions, and Union Density," *The Journal of Politics*, 64, no. 1 (February 2002), pp. 126–153.

10. Jeffrey M. Berry, *Lobbying for the People* (Princeton, NJ: Princeton University Press, 1977), p. 7; Berry and Wilcox, *The Interest Group Society*, pp. 24–26; Berry, *The New Liberalism*, p. 2.

11. Ronald Brownstein, *The Second Civil War: How Extreme Partisanship Has Paralyzed Washington and Polarized America* (New York: The Penguin Press, 2007), pp. 106–112; Berry, *Lobbying for the People*; David Broder, *Changing the Guard* (New York: Simon & Schuster, 1980); Hugh Heclo, "Issue Networks and the Executive Establishment," in Anthony King, ed., *The New American Political System* (Washington, D.C.: American Enterprise Institute, 1978); Kay Lehman Schlozman and John A. Tierney, *Organized Interests and American Democracy* (New York: Harper and Row, 1986); Jack L. Walker Jr., "The Origins and Maintenance of Interest Groups in America," *American Political Science Review*, 77 (1983), pp. 390–406; Theda Skocpol, *Diminished Democracy: From Membership to Management in American Civil Life* (Norman, OK: University of Oklahoma Press, 2003).

12. Skocpol, *Diminished Democracy*; Theda Skocpol, "Associations Without Members," *The American Prospect*, 10, no. 4 (July/August 1999), pp. 66–73; Theda Skocpol, "Voice and Inequality: The Transformation of American Civil Democracy," *Perspectives on Politics*, 2, no. 1 (March 2004), pp. 3–20.

13. The numbers above are from Roger H. Davidson, Walter J. Oleszek, and Francis E. Lee, *Congress and Its Members*, 12th ed. (Washington, D.C.: CQ Press, 2010), pp. 390–391.

14. The Center for Responsive Politics, based on required reports to the House and Senate, 2009.

15. Scott H. Ainsworth, *Analyzing Interest Groups* (New York: W. W. Norton and Co., 2002).

16. Reich, *Supercapitalism*, pp. 143–148; Ken Auletta, "The Search Party," *The New Yorker* (January 14, 2008), pp. 30–37.

17. Gary J. Andres, *Lobbying Reconsidered* (New York: Pearson Longman, 2009), ch. 4.

18. Reich, *Supercapitalism*, pp. 144–146.

19. Truman, *The Governmental Process*.

20. Jack L. Walker Jr., *Mobilizing Interest Groups in America* (Ann Arbor, MI: University of Michigan Press, 1991).

21. "Pork and Scandals," *The Economist* (January 28, 2006), p. 29.

22. From the watchdog group Public Citizen, reported in "The Lobbying Boom." Also see The Center for Public Integrity, "lobbying" press release, 2004, at **www.publicintegrity.org**.

23. Frank Rich, "The Rabbit Ragu Democrats," *The New York Times*, online (**www.nytimes.com**), October 4, 2009.

24. Mark A. Smith, *Business and Political Power: Public Opinion, Elections and Democracy* (Chicago: University of Chicago Press, 2000).

25. Schattschneider, *The Semi-Sovereign People*.

26. Frank R. Baumgartner, Jeffrey M. Berry, Marie Hojnacki, David C. Kimball, and Beth L. Leech, *Lobbying and Policy Change: Who Wins, Who Loses, and Why* (Chicago: University of Chicago Press, 2009), 150–155.

27. Berry and Wilcox, *The Interest Group Society*, p. 138.

28. Glen Justice, "New Rules on Fund-Raising Bring Lobbyists to the Fore," *The New York Times*, April 20, 2004, p. A1.

29. "The Lobbying Boom."

30. Berry and Wilcox, *The Interest Group Society*, p. 142–145.

31. Baumgartner et. al., *Lobbying and Policy Change*, pp. 155–157.

32. Berry and Wilcox, *The Interest Group Society*, pp. 118–120.

33. Schattschneider, *The Semi-Sovereign People*.

34. Berry, *The New Liberalism*.

35. Schlozman and Tierney, *Organized Interests and American Democracy*, p. 175.

36. Bruce Bimber, *Information and American Democracy* (New York: Cambridge University Press, 2003).

37. For a comprehensive and theoretically interesting examination of interest group involvement in campaigns see Michael M. Franz, *Choices and Changes: Interest Group in the Electoral Process* (Philadelphia: Temple University Press, 2008).

38. Berry, *Lobbying for the People*; Skocpol, "Voice and Inequality"; Dara Strolovitch, "Do Interest Groups Represent the Disadvantaged? Advocacy at the Intersections of Race, Class, and Gender," *Journal of Politics*, 68, no. 4 (November 2006), pp. 894–910.

39. Jim Drinkard, "Drugmakers Go Further to Sway Congress, *USA Today* (April 26, 2005), p. 2B; Leslie Wayne and Petersen Melody, "A Muscular Lobby Rolls Up Its Sleeves," *The New York Times* (November 4, 2001), p. 1.

40. Eric Dash and Nelson D. Schwartz, "As Reform Takes Shape, Some Relief on Wall St.," *The New York Times* (May 23, 2010), p. 1.

41. The Center for Responsive Politics, 2009.

42. "Money Talks, Congress Listens," *The Boston Globe* (December 12, 1982), p. A24.

43. Adam Liptak, "Justices, 5-4, Reject Corporate Spending Limit," *The New York Times* (January 21, 2010), p. 1; "Unbound: The

Supreme Court Undermines Convoluted Campaign Finance Rules," *The Economist* (January 30, 2010), p. 39.

44. The term "issue networks" is from Heclo, "Issue Networks." For a review and evaluation of the scholarly debate over sub-governments and issue networks see Baumgartner et. al., *Lobbying and Policy Change*, pp. 57–67. Also see Berry and Wilcox, *The Interest Group Society*, pp. 163–165; Berry, *The New Liberalism;* Ainsworth, *Analyzing Interest Groups;* Allan J. Cigler, "Interest Groups," in William Crotty, ed., *Political Science: Looking to the Future,* Vol. 4 (Evanston, IL: Northwestern University Press, 1991); Robert H. Salisbury, John P. Heinz, Edward O. Laumann, and Robert L. Nelson, "Triangles, Networks, and Hollow Cores," and Mark P. Petracca, "The Rediscovery of Interest Group Politics," both in Mark P. Petracca, ed., *The Politics of Interests: Interest Groups Transform* (Boulder, CO: Westview Press, 1992); Robert M. Stein and Kenneth Bickers, *Perpetuating the Pork Barrel: Policy Subsystems and American Democracy* (Cambridge, UK: Cambridge University Press, 1995).

45. Charles Lindblom, *Politics and Markets* (New York: Basic Books, 1977), p. 356.

46. Neil J. Mitchell, *The Conspicuous Corporation: Business, Public Policy and Representative Democracy* (Ann Arbor, MI: University of Michigan Press, 1997), p. 167.

47. For more empirical evidence on this and a discussion of why large business corporations must be deeply involved in government and politics, see Reich, *Supercapitalism.*

48. The Center for Responsive Politics, 2009.

49. Dan Clawson, Alan Neustadt, and Mark Weller, *Dollars and Votes* (Philadelphia: Temple University Press, 1998), pp. 26–28, 64–71, 97–99; Berry and Wilcox, *The Interest Group Society*, pp. 184–185.

50. Jeffrey A. Winters and Benjamin I. Page, "Oligarchy in the United States?" (Evanston, IL: Northwestern University, Working Paper, 2008).

51. Vogel, *Fluctuating Fortunes,* p. 291.

52. Jacob S. Hacker and Paul Pierson, *Winner-Take-All Politics* (New York: Simon and Schuster, 2010).

53. For a comparison of U.S. lobbying rules with other democracies see Raj Chari, Gary Murphy, and John Hogan, "Regulating Lobbyists: A Comparative Analysis of the United States, Canada, Germany, and the European Union," *Political Quarterly*, 78, no. 3 (July–September 2007), pp. 422–438.

CHAPTER 8

1. James MacGregor Burns and Stewart Burns, *A People's Charter: The Pursuit of Rights in America* (New York: Knopf, 1991), ch. 5; E. McGlen and Karen O'Connor, *Women's Rights* (New York: Praeger, 1983), ch. 3; Sarah M. Evans, *Born for Liberty: A History of Women in America* (New York: Free Press, 1997).

2. Sidney Tarrow, *Power in Movement* (New York: Cambridge University Press, 1998); David S. Meyer and Sidney Tarrow, eds., *The Social Movement Society* (Lanham, MD: Rowman & Littlefield Publishers, 1997); Doug McAdams, John D. McCarthy, and Mayer N. Zald, "Social Movements," in Neil J. Smelser, ed., *Handbook of Sociology* (Newbury Park, CA: Sage, 1994); Doug McAdams, *Political Process and the Development of Black Insurgency* (Chicago: University of Chicago Press, 1982); Doug McAdams, Sidney Tarrow, and Charles Tilly, *Dynamics of Contention* (Cambridge, UK: Cambridge University Press, 2001).

3. Sidney Tarrow, "Social Movements as Contentious Politics," *American Political Science Review,* 90 (1996), pp. 853–866; Ronald R. Aminzade, Jack A. Goldstone, Doug McAdam, Elizabeth J. Perry, William H. Sewell Jr., and Sidney Tarrow, eds., *Silence and Voice in the Study of Contentious Politics* (New York: Cambridge University Press, Cambridge Studies in Contentious Politics, 2001).

4. Our focus is on social movements in politics and their impact on public policies. For a review of the scholarly literature on social movements more broadly considered see Elizabeth A. Armstrong and Mary Bernstein, "Culture, Power, and Institutions: A Multi-Institutional Approach to Social Movements," *Sociological Theory,* 26, no. 1 (March, 2008), pp. 74–99.

5. CBS News telecast, February 16, 2003.

6. Jackie Smith, "Globalizing Resistance: The Battle of Seattle and the Future of Social Movements," *Mobilization: An International Journal,* 6, no. 1 (2000), pp. 1–19.

7. Mark Penn, *Microtrends: The Small Forces Behind Tomorrow's Big Changes* (New York: Twelve, Hachette Book Group, 2007), pp. 140–145.

8. E. E. Schattschneider, *The Semi-Sovereign People* (New York: Holt, Rinehart & Winston, 1960), p. 142.

9. Richard Polenberg, *One Nation Divisible* (New York: Penguin, 1980), p. 268; Craig A. Rimmerman, *From Identity to Politics: The Lesbian and Gay Movements in the United States* (Philadelphia, PA: Temple University Press, 2002), ch. 1.

10. Frances Fox Piven, *When Movements Matter: How Ordinary People Change America* (Lanham, MD: Rowman & Littlefield, 2006).

11. Theodore J. Lowi, *The Politics of Disorder* (New York: Basic Books, 1971), p. 54.

12. Piven, *When Movements Matter.*

13. Aminzade et. al., *Silence and Voice in the Study of Contentious Politics;* Meyer and Tarrow, *The Social Movement Society;* McAdams et al., "Social Movements"; Sidney Tarrow, *Social Movements, Collective Action, and Politics* (New York: Cambridge University Press, 1994).

14. Neil J. Smelser, *Theory of Collective Behavior* (New York: Free Press, 1962); Elaine Walker and Heather J. Smith, *Relative Deprivation: Specification, Development, and Integration* (Cambridge, UK: Cambridge University Press, 2001).

15. Barbara Sinclair Deckard, *The Women's Movement* (New York: Harper & Row, 1983); Ethel Klein, *Gender Politics: From Consciousness to Mass Politics* (Cambridge, MA: Harvard University Press, 1984), ch. 2.

16. Donald P. Haider-Markel, "Creating Change—Holding the Line," in Ellen D. B. Riggle and Barry L. Tadlock, eds., *Gays and Lesbians in the Political Process* (New York: Columbia University Press, 1999).

17. Rimmerman, *From Identity to Politics.*

18. William Gamson, *The Strategy of Social Protest* (Homewood, IL: Dorsey, 1975); John D. McCarthy and Mayer N. Zald, "Resource Mobilization and Social Movements: A Partial Theory," *American Journal of Sociology,* 82 (1977), pp. 1212–1241.

19. Jo Freeman, *The Politics of Women's Liberation* (New York: McKay, 1975); Nancy Burns, "Gender: Public Opinion and Political Action," in Ira Katznelson and Helen V. Milner, eds., *Political Science: The State of the Discipline* (New York: W. W. Norton, 2002), pp. 472–476.

20. Bruce Bimber, *Information and American Democracy: Technology and the Evolution of Political Power* (New York: Cambridge University Press, 2003), chs. 3 and 5.

21. McAdams, *Political Process;* Tarrow, *Social Movements, Collective Action, and Politics;* Peter K. Eisenger, "The Conditions of Protest Behavior in American Cities," *American Political Science Review,* 67 (1973), pp. 11–28.

22. Frances Fox Piven and Richard A. Cloward, *Poor People's Movements* (New York: Vintage, 1979), ch. 3.

23. Klein, *Gender Politics,* pp. 90–91.

24. National Opinion Research Center, General Social Survey, 1972.

25. *Trends in Political Values and Core Attitudes: 1987–2009* (Washington, D.C.: The Pew Research Center for the People and the Press, May 21, 2009).

26. G. William Domhoff, *The Higher Circles* (New York: Random House, 1970); Edward S. Greenberg, *Capitalism and the American Political Ideal* (Armonk, NY: Sharpe, 1985); Gabriel Kolko, *The Triumph of Conservatism* (Chicago: Quadrangle, 1967); James Weinstein, *The Corporate Ideal in the Liberal State* (Boston: Beacon Press, 1968).

27. Carol A. Horton, *Race and the Making of American Liberalism* (New York: Oxford University Press, 2005), pp. 140–141.

28. Rimmerman, *From Identity to Politics.*

29. Piven, *When Movements Matter.*

30. Taylor Branch, *Parting the Waters: America in the King Years* (New York: Simon and Schuster, 1986); William H. Chafe, *The Unfinished Journey: America Since World War II* (New York: Oxford University Press, 2003).

31. Jane Mansbridge, *Why We Lost the ERA* (Chicago: University of Chicago Press, 1986).

32. Christian Davenport, Hank Johnson, and Carol Mueller, eds., *Mobilization and Repression* (Minneapolis: University of Minnesota Press, 2005).

33. See David Caute, *The Great Fear* (New York: Simon & Schuster, 1978); Robert Justin Goldstein, *Political Repression in Modern America* (Cambridge, MA: Schenkman, 1978); Alan Wolfe, *The Seamy Side of Democracy* (New York: McKay, 1978).

34. Greenberg, *Capitalism and the American Political Ideal.*

35. Mart Martin, *The Almanac of Women and Minorities in American Politics* (Boulder, CO: Westview Press, 2002); Penn, *Microtrends,* pp. 43–52.

36. Chafe, *The Unfinished Journey: America Since World War II,* pp. 430–468; Deckard, *The Women's Movement;* Klein, *Gender Politics,* ch. 2; Freeman, *Politics of Women's Liberation.* Also see debates on the relative progress of women in the United States collected in Dorothy McBride Stetson, *Women's Rights in the United States: Policy Debates and Gender Roles* (London: Routledge, 2004).

CHAPTER 9

1. On the special election, see Perry Bacon Jr., "Democrat Wins Hard-Fought N.Y. House Special Election," *The Washington Post* (November 4, 2009), p. 1; Alex Isenstadt, "NY-23 Race First Test of Tea Party Power," *Politico* (**www.politico.com**; October 22, 2009); Jeremy W. Peters, "Conservative Loses Upstate House Race in Blow to the Right," *The New York Times,* November 3, 2009, p. 1; Anton Troianovski, "Democrat Wins New York House Race," *The Wall Street Journal,* November 3, 2009, p. 1.

2. Ronald Brownstein, *The Second Civil War: How Extreme Partisanship Has Paralyzed Washington and Polarized America* (New York: The Penguin Press, 2007); Nicol C. Rae, "Be Careful What You Wish For: The Rise of Responsible Parties in American National Politics," *Annual Reviews, Political Science,* 10 (2007), pp. 169–191.

3. E. E. Schattschneider, *Party Government* (New York: Holt, Rinehart & Winston, 1942), p. 208.

4. Robert A. Dahl, *On Democracy* (New Haven, CT: Yale University Press, 1998); Marjorie Randon Hershey, *Party Politics in America,* 13th ed. (New York: Pearson Longman, 2009), pp. 1–2.

5. Schattschneider, *Party Government,* p. 208.

6. See Hershey, *Party Politics in America,* ch. 1; A. James Reichley, *The Life of the Parties: A History of American Political Parties* (Lanham, MD: Rowman & Littlefield, 2002), ch. 1.

7. Steven J. Rosenstone and John Mark Hansen, *Mobilization, Participation, and Democracy in America* (New York: Macmillan, 1993).

8. E. E. Schattschneider, *The Semi-Sovereign People* (New York: Holt, Rinehart & Winston, 1960).

9. The classic statement on electoral rules is Maurice Duverger, *Political Parties* (New York: Wiley, 1954).

10. Ibid.

11. Marjorie Randon Hershey, "Like a Bee: Election Law and the Survival of Third Parties," in Matthew J. Streb, ed., *Election Law and Electoral Politics* (Boulder, CO: Lynn Rienner, 2004); Hershey, *Party Politics in America,* pp. 34–35.

12. Much of this discussion is drawn from Steven J. Rosenstone, Roy L. Behr, and Edward H. Lazarus, *Third Parties in America,* 2nd ed. (Princeton, NJ: Princeton University Press, 1996). Also see Paul S. Herrnson and John C. Green, *Multiparty Politics in America* (Lanham, MD: Rowman & Littlefield, 2002); Hershey, *Party Politics in America,* p. 37–41; John F. Bibby and Sandy Maisel, *Two Parties or More?* (Boulder, CO: Westview, 2003); Shigeo Hirano and James M. Snyder Jr., "The Decline of Third-Party Voting in the United States, *The Journal of Politics,* 69, no. 1 (February, 2007), pp. 1–16.

13. On realignment, see Walter Dean Burnham, *Critical Elections and the Mainsprings of American Politics* (New York: Norton, 1970); Jerome Clubb, William H. Flanigan, and Nancy H. Zingale, *Partisan Realignment* (Newbury Park, CA: Sage, 1980); V. O. Key Jr., "A Theory of Critical Elections," *The Journal of Politics,* 17 (1955), pp. 3–18; Hershey, *Party Politics in America,* ch. 7; James L. Sundquist, *Dynamics of the Party System* (Washington, D.C.: Brookings Institution, 1973); Samuel Merrill, Bernard Grofman, and Thomas L. Brunnell, "Cycles in American National Electoral Politics, 1854–2006," *The American Political Science Review,* 102, no. 1 (February 2008), pp. 1–17. For the special place that war has played in altering parties and party systems see David R. Mayhew, "Wars and American Politics," *Perspectives on Politics,* 3, no. 3 (September 2005), pp. 473–493.

14. See David R. Mayhew, *Electoral Realignments* (New Haven, CT: Yale University Press, 2004); Hershey, *Party Politics in America;* Peter F. Nardulli, "The Concept of a Critical Realignment, Electoral Behavior, and Political Change," *The American Political Science Review,* 89 (1995), pp. 10–22; Gary Miller and Norman Schofield, "The Transformation of the Republican and Democratic Party Coalitions in the U.S., *Perspectives on Politics,* 69, no. 3 (September, 2008), pp. 433–450; Matt Bai, "The Great Unalignment," *The New York Times, Sunday Magazine,* January 24, 2010, pp. 13–15.

15. John Aldrich and Richard Niemi, "The Sixth American Party System," in Stephen C. Craig, *Broken Contract: Changing Relationships Between Americans and Their Government* (Boulder, CO: Westview Press, 1996); Walter J. Stone and Ronald B. Rapoport, "It's Perot Stupid! The Legacy of the 1992 Perot Movement in the Major-Party System, 1994–2000," *PS: Political Science and Politics,* XXXIV, no. 1 (March 2001), pp. 49–56.

16. Larry M. Bartels, *Unequal Democracy: The Political Economy of the Guided Age* (New York and Princeton, NJ: Russell Sage Foundation and Princeton University Press, 2008); Thomas Byrne Edsall and Mary D. Edsall, *Chain Reaction: The Impact of Race, Rights and Taxes on American Politics* (New York: Norton, 1991); Stanley B. Greenberg, *Middle Class Dreams: The Politics and Power of the New American Majority* (New Haven, CT: Yale University Press, 1996).

17. Brownstein, *The Second Civil War,* pp. 93–136.

18. Larry Sabato, *The Party's Just Begun* (Glenview, IL: Scott, Foresman, 1988); Sundquist, *Dynamics of the Party System;* Martin P. Wattenberg, *The Decline of American Political Parties* (Cambridge, MA: Harvard University Press, 1994); Greenberg, *Middle Class Dreams;* Everett C. Ladd, "The 1994 Congressional Elections," *Political Science Quarterly,* 110 (1995), pp. 1–23.

19. Earl Black and Merle Black, *Divided America: The Ferocious Power Struggle in American Politics* (New York: Simon & Schuster, 2007); Stanley B. Greenberg, *The Two Americas: Our Current Political Deadlock and How to Break It* (New York: Thomas Dunn Books, 2004); Geoffrey C. Layman, Thomas M. Carsey, and Juliana Menaxce Horowitz, "Party Polarization in American Politics: Characteristics, Causes, and Consequences," *Annual Reviews: Political Science,* 9 (2006), pp. 83–110; Brownstein, *The Second Civil War,* pp. 137–174.

20. On the "great sorting out" of groups and regions along party lines in the United States, see Brownstein, *The Second Civil War,* ch. 6.

21. Hershey, *Party Politics in America,* ch. 6.

22. Richard Florida, *The Rise of the Creative Class: How It's Transforming Work, Leisure, Community, and Everyday Life* (New York: Basic Books, 2002); Richard Florida, *The Flight of the Creative Class* (New York: Harper Business, 2005).

23. Hershey, *Party Politics in America,* ch. 4.

24. J. A. Schlesinger, "The New American Political Party," *American Political Science Review,* 79 (1985), pp. 1152–1169; John Aldrich, *Why Parties?* (Chicago: University of Chicago Press, 1995).

25. L. Sandy Maisel, *American Political Parties and Elections: A Very Short Introduction* (New York: Oxford University Press, 2007), pp. 66–68.

26. Hershey, *Party Politics in America,* pp. 208–211.

27. David Menefee-Libey, *The Triumph of Campaign-Centered Politics* (New York: Chatham House Publishers, 2000); Hershey, *Party Politics in America,* pp. 75–78.

28. Stephen Doyle, "The Very, Very Personal Is the Political," *The New York Times Magazine,* February 15, 2004, pp. 42–47.

29. Maisel, *American Parties and Elections,* pp. 63–64.

30. Ibid., pp. 65–67.

31. Roger H. Davidson, Walter J. Oleszek, and Frances E. Lee, *Congress and Its Members,* 11th ed. (Washington, D.C.: CQ Press, 2008), pp. 73–74.

32. Norman Schofield and Gary Miller, "Elections and Activist Coalitions in the United States," *American Journal of Political Science,* 51, no. 3 (July 2007), pp. 518–531.

33. Hershey, *Party Politics in America,* pp. 284–285.

34. Greenberg, *The Two Americas;* Morris P. Fiorino, "Parties, Participation, and Representation in America," in Ira Katznelson and Helen V. Milner, eds., *Political Science: The State of the Discipline* (New York: W. W. Norton, 2002); Morris P. Fiorino, *Culture War? The Myth of a Polarized America* (New York: Pearson Longman, 2005), ch. 8; Hershey, *Party Politics in America,* ch. 15; Marc J. Hetherington, "Resurgent Mass Partisanship: The Role of Elite Polarization," *The American Political Science Review,* 95, no. 1 (September 2001), pp. 619–632; Gerald Pomper, "Parliamentary Government in the United States," in J. C. Green and D. M. Shea, eds., *The State of the Parties* (Lanham, MD: Rowman & Littlefield, 1999).

35. Brownstein, *The Second Civil War,* p. 12.

36. Lewis L. Gould, *Grand Old Party: A History of the Republicans* (New York: Random House, 2003); "When American Politics Turned European," *The Economist* (October 25, 2005), p. 74; Nils Gilman, "What the Rise of the Republicans as America's First Ideological Party Means for the Democrats," *The Forum,* 2, no. 1 (2004), pp. 1–4; Brownstein, *The Second Civil War;* Layman, Carsey, and Horowitz, "Party Polarization in American Politics."

37. *American National Election Studies,* 2008.

38. Ibid.

39. Ibid.

40. "Trends in Political Values and Core Attitudes: 1987–2009" (Washington, D.C.: Pew Research Center for the People and the Press, report released May 21, 2009).

41. Alan D. Monroe, "American Party Platforms and Public Opinion," *American Journal of Political Science,* 27 (February 1983), p. 35; Layman, Carsey, and Horowitz, "Party Polarization in American Politics"; Maisel, *American Political Parties and Elections,* pp. 73–76.

42. *New York Times*/CBS News, "Convention Delegate Polls," June 16–July 17, 2004, and August 3–23, 2004.

43. Hershey, *Party Politics in America,* pp. 288–289.

44. James MacGregor Burns, *Deadlock of Democracy* (Englewood Cliffs, NJ: Prentice Hall, 1967).

45. On the pernicious effects of divided government see Benjamin Ginsberg and Martin Shefter, *Politics by Other Means: The Declining Significance of Elections in America* (New York: Basic Books, 1990). For the contrary view see Morris P. Fiorina, *Divided Government* (New York: Macmillan, 1992); Gary Jacobson, *The Electoral Origins of Divided Government: Competition in U.S. House Elections* (Boulder, CO: Westview Press, 1990); David R. Mayhew, *Divided We Govern: Party Control, Lawmaking, and Investigations, 1946–1990* (New Haven, CT: Yale University Press, 1991); Layman, Carsey, and Horowitz, "Party Polarization in American Politics," pp. 88–101.

46. Jason M. Roberts and Steven S. Smith, "Procedural Contexts, Party Strategy, and Conditional Party Voting in the U.S. House of Representatives," *American Journal of Political Science,* 47 (2003), pp. 305–317; Douglas Hibbs, *The American Political Economy* (Cambridge, MA: Harvard University Press, 1987); Dennis P. Quinn and Robert Shapiro, "Business Political Power: The Case of Taxation," *American Political Science Review,* 85 (1991), pp. 851–874; Kenneth N. Bickers

and Robert M. Stein, "The Congressional Pork Barrel in a Republican Era," *The Journal of Politics*, 62, no. 4 (November 2000), pp. 1070–1086.

47. Donald Green, Bradley Palmquist, and Eric Schickler, *Partisan Hearts and Minds: Political Parties and the Social Identity of Voters* (New Haven, CT: Yale University Press, 2002); Robert S. Erikson and Kent L.Tedin, *American Public Opinion* (New York: Pearson Longman, 2007) pp. 77–83; Marjorie Randon Hershey, *Party Politics in America*, 13th ed. (New York: Longman Classics, 2009), pp. 107–111; "Trends in Political Values and Core Attitudes: 1987–2009," pp. 97–110.

48. Erikson and Tedin, *American Public Opinion*, p. 84.

49. Data are from 2004, reported in Alan Abramowitz and Kyle Saunders, "Culture War in America: Myth or Reality," *The Forum*, 3, no. 2 (2005), pp. 1–22.

50. Bruce E. Keith, David B. Magleby, Candice J. Nelson, Elizabeth Orr, Mark C. Westlye, and Raymond E. Wolfinger, *The Myth of the Independent Voter* (Berkeley, CA: University of California Press, 1992). Also see Marjorie Randon Hershey, *Party Politics in America*, 12th ed. (New York: Longman, 2006), pp. 113–115.

51. "Trends in Political Values and Core Attitudes: 1987–2009," p. 11.

52. Brownstein, *The Second Civil War;* Rae, "Be Careful What You Wish For;" Layman, Carsey, and Horowitz, "Party Polarization in American Politics."

CHAPTER 10

1. "General Election Exit Poll Pool for CNN, NBC, FOXNews, and CBS" (Somerville, NJ: Edison Media Research and Mitofsky International, November 4, 2008).

2. "Democratic Party Image Drops to Record Low," The Gallup Poll, April 9, 2010.

3. Information for this chapter-opening story is from the following sources: Gary C. Jacobson, "The 2008 Presidential and Congressional Elections: Anti-Bush Referendum and Prospects for the Democratic Majority," *Political Science Quarterly*, 124, no. 1 (2009), pp. 1–30; "Voting and Registration in the 2008 Elections," (Washington, D.C.: Pew Research Center, 2009); Demetrios James Caraley, "Three Trends Over Eight Presidential Elections, 1980–2008: Toward the Emergence of a Democratic Majority Realignment?" *Political Science Quarterly*, 124, no. 3 (2009); David B. Magleby, "How Barack Obama Changed Presidential Campaigns," in Tomas Dye et al., eds., *Obama: Year One* (New York: Pearson Longman, 2010); "The Ground Operation," *The Economist*, October 25, 2008, pp. 37–38; Michael McDonald, "Turnout," U.S. Election Project, **http://elections.gmu.edu/index.html**, posted November 9, 2008; Michael Luo, "Obama Recasts the Fund-Raising Landscape," *The New York Times*, October 20, 2008, p. A1; Laura Meckler, "In End, McCain Played to the GOP," *The Wall Street Journal*, November 7, 2008, p. 1; Adam Nagourney, Jim Rutenberg, and Jeff Zeleny, "Near-Flawless Run Is Credited in Victory," *The New York Times*, November 5, 2008, p. A1; and Jonathan Weisman and Laura Meckler, "Obama Sweeps to Historic Victory," *The Wall Street Journal*, November 5, 2008, p. 1.

4. For further discussion, see Benjamin I. Page, *Choices and Echoes in Presidential Elections: Rational Man and Electoral Democracy* (Chicago: University of Chicago Press, 1978), ch. 2; Robert A. Dahl, *Democracy and Its Critics* (New Haven, CT: Yale University Press, 1989); Robert A. Dahl, *On Democracy* (New Haven, CT: Yale University Press, 1998); Hans Gersbach, *Designing Democracy* (New York: Springer Publishers, 2005).

5. See Russell Muirhead, "A Defense of Party Spirit," *Perspectives on Politics*, 4, no. 4 (December, 2006), pp. 713–727; Austin Ranney, *The Doctrine of Responsible Party Government: Its Origins and Present State* (Urbana, IL: University of Illinois Press, 1962); E. E. Schattschneider, *Party Government* (New York: Holt, Rinehart & Winston, 1942).

6. Marjorie Randon Hershey, *Party Politics in America* (New York: Pearson Longman Publishers, 2009), pp. 269–270.

7. Nicol C. Rae, "Be Careful What You Wish For: The Rise of Responsible Parties in American National Politics," *Annual Reviews: Political Science* 10 (2007), pp. 169–191.

8. Anthony Downs, *An Economic Theory of Democracy* (New York: Harper & Row, 1957); Otto Davis, Melvin Hinich, and Peter Ordeshook, "An Expository Development of a Mathematical Model of the Electoral Process," *American Political Science Review*, 64 (1970), pp. 426–448. Also see Allen Brierly, "Downs Model of Political Party Competition," paper presented at the annual meeting of the Midwest Political Science Association, Palmer House Hilton, Chicago, IL (April 15, 2005).

9. Lawrence R. Jacobs and Robert Y. Shapiro, *Politicians Don't Pander: Political Manipulation and the Loss of Democratic Responsiveness* (Chicago: University of Chicago Press, 2000).

10. See V. O. Key Jr., *Public Opinion and American Democracy* (New York: Knopf, 1961); Morris P. Fiorina, *Retrospective Voting in American National Elections* (Cambridge, MA: Harvard University Press, 1981).

11. Jacobson, "The 2008 Presidential and Congressional Elections."

12. David Stout, "Study Finds Ballot Problems Are More Likely for Poor," *The New York Times* (July 9, 2001), p. A9; Katharine Q. Seelye, "Study Says 2000 Election Missed Millions of Votes," *The New York Times* (August, 10, 2001), p. A17.

13. L. Sandy Maisel, *American Political Parties and Elections: A Very Short Introduction* (New York: Oxford University Press, 2007), p. 5.

14. Mary Fitzgerald, "Greater Convenience but Not Greater Turnout: The Impact of Alternative Voting Methods on Electoral Participation in the United States," *American Politics Research*, 33, no. 6 (2005), pp. 842–867.

15. Chilton Williamson, *American Suffrage* (Princeton, NJ: Princeton University Press, 1960), pp. 223, 241, 260. Also see Hershey, *Party Politics in America*, pp. 139–144; Maisel, *American Political Parties and Elections*, pp. 47–51.

16. See John Hope Franklin, *From Slavery to Freedom* (New York: Knopf, 1967); Leon Litwack, *North of Slavery* (Chicago: University of Chicago Press, 1961); Alexander Keyssar, *The Right to Vote: The Contested History of Democracy in the United States* (New York: Basic Books, 2001).

17. Walter Dean Burnham, "The Turnout Problem," in A. James Reichley, ed., *Elections, American Style* (Washington, D.C.: Brookings Institution, 1987), pp. 113–114.

18. Maisel, *American Political Parties and Elections*, p. 135.

19. Kay Lehman Schlozman, "Citizen Participation in America: What Do We Know? Why Do We Care?" in Ira Katznelson and Helen V. Milner, eds., *Political Science: The State of the Discipline* (New York: W. W. Norton, 2002), pp. 439–443; Martin P. Wattenberg, *Where Have All the Voters Gone?* (Cambridge, MA: Harvard University Press, 2002); Andre Blais, "What Affects Voter Turnout?" *Annual Reviews, Political Science*, 9 (2006), pp. 111–125.

20. Peverill Squire, Raymond E. Wolfinger, and David P. Glass, "Residential Mobility and Voter Turnout," *American Political Science Review*, 81 (1987), pp. 45–65.

21. Nelson W. Polsby and Aaron Wildavsky, *Presidential Elections*, 12th ed. (Lanham, MD: Rowman & Littlefield, 2007), p. 17.

22. Ibid.; U.S. Bureau of the Census, 2007; Hershey, *Party Politics in America*, p. 141.

23. Wattenberg, *Where Have All the Voters Gone?*, ch. 6.

24. Steven J. Rosenstone and John Mark Hansen, *Mobilization, Participation, and Democracy in American* (New York: Macmillan, 1993).

25. Alan S. Gerber and Donald M. Green, "The Effects of Canvassing, Telephone Calls, and Direct Mail on Voter Turnout," *American Political Science Review*, 94 (2000), pp. 653–663.

26. Ronald Brownstein, *The Second Civil War: How Extreme Partisanship Has Paralyzed Washington and Polarized America* (New York: Penguin, 2007), ch. 6; Roger H. Davidson, Walter J. Oleszek, and Frances E. Lee, *Congress and Its Members*, 11th ed. (Washington, D.C.: CQ Press, 2008), pp. 62–65, 108–110; Maisel, *American Political Parties and Elections*, pp. 126–130; Steven S. Smith, Jason M. Roberts, and Ryan J. Vander Wielen, *The American Congress*, 5th ed. (New York: Cambridge University Press, 2007), pp. 68–78; Alan Wolfe, *Does Democracy Still Work?* (New Haven, CT: Yale University Press, 2006), pp. 50–56.

27. "House Members Who Won with 55 Percent or Less in 2008," The Cook Political Report, **http://www.cookpolitical.com/sites/default/files/55andunder_0.pdf**, November 10, 2008.

28. Sidney Verba, Kay Lehman Schlozman, and Henry E. Brady, *Voice and Equality: Civic Volunteerism in American Politics* (Cambridge, MA: Harvard University Press, 1995); Sidney Verba and Norman H. Nie, *Participation in America* (New York: Harper & Row, 1972); Hershey, *Party Politics in America*, pp. 146–149.

29. Pew Hispanic Center, "The Latino Electorate," survey report posted at **http://pewhispanic.org** on July 7, 2007.

30. Mark Hugo Lopez and Paul Taylor, "Dissecting the 2008 Electorate: Most Diverse in U.S. History" (Washington, D.C.: Pew Research Center, April 30, 2009), p. 6.

31. Susan A. MacManus, *Young v. Old* (Boulder, CO: Westview Press, 1996), ch. 2.

32. Margaret M. Conway, *Political Participation in the United States*, 3rd ed. (Washington, D.C.: CQ Press, 2000), p. 37.

33. E. J. Dionne, "If Nonvoters Had Voted: Same Winner, but Bigger," *The New York Times* (November 21, 1988), p. B16.

34. Sidney Verba, Kay Lehman Schlozman, Henry E. Brady, and Norman H. Nie, "Citizen Activity: Who Participates? What Do They Say?" *American Political Science Review*, 87 (1993), pp. 303–318; Robert S. Erikson and Kent L. Tedin, *American Public Opinion* (New York: Pearson Longman Publishers, 2007), ch. 7; Eric Shiraev and Richard Sobel, *People and Their Opinions* (New York: Pearson Longman Publishers, 2006), chs. 7–9.

35. Martin Gilens, "Preference Gaps and Inequality in Representation," *PS* (April, 2009), pp. 331–335; Lawrence R. Jacobs and Theda Skocpol, eds. *Inequality and American Democracy: What We Know and What We Need to Learn*, (New York: Russell Sage Foundation, 2005); Larry M. Bartels, Hugh Keclo, Rodney E. Hero, and Lawrence Jacobs, "Inequality and American Government" *Perspectives on Politics*, 2, no. 4 (20), pp. 651–668; and Larry M. Bartels, *Unequal Democracy: The Political Economy of the Gilded Age* (New York and Princeton, NJ: The Russell Sage Foundation and Princeton University Press, 2008); Bartels et al., "Inequality and American Government."

36. Jacob Hacker and Paul Pierson, *Off Center* (New Haven, CT: Yale University Press, 2005); Larry M. Bartels, "Is the Water Rising: Reflections on Inequality and American Democracy," *PS* (January 2006), pp. 39–42; Kay Lehman Schlozman, "On Inequality and Political Voice," *PS* (January 2006), pp. 55–57.

37. Davidson, Oleszek, and Lee, "Congress and Its Members," pp. 66–69; Hershey, *Party Politics in America*; pp. 158–161; Maisel, *American Political Parties and Elections*, pp. 118–125.

38. David D. Kirkpatrick, "Wealth Is a Common Factor Among 2008 Hopefuls," *The New York Times* (May 17, 2007), p. A1.

39. Polsby and Wildavsky, *Presidential Elections*, pp. 53–55, 57.

40. Stephen J. Wayne, *The Road to the White House* (Belmont, CA: Wadsworth, 2007).

41. Larry Bartels, *Presidential Primaries and the Dynamics of Public Choice* (Princeton, NJ: Princeton University Press, 1988); John H. Aldrich, *Before the Convention* (Chicago: University of Chicago Press, 1980); Wayne, *The Road to the White House*.

42. Smith, Roberts, and vander Wielen, *The American Congress*, pp. 64–65.

43. Polsby and Wildavsky, *Presidential Elections*, pp. 143–147.

44. John G. Geer, *In Defense of Negativity* (Chicago: University of Chicago Press, 2006); Ken Goldstein and Paul Freedman, "Campaign Advertising and Voter Turnout: New Evidence for a Stimulation Effect," *The Journal of Politics*, 64 (2002), pp. 721–740.

45. Anna Greenberg, "Targeting and Electoral Gaps," in Laura R. Olson and John C. Green, *Beyond Red State, Blue State: Electoral Gaps in the Twenty-First Century American Electorate* (Upper Saddle River, NJ: Pearson Prentice Hall, 2009); Magleby, "How Barack Obama Changed Presidential Campaigns." Also see D. Sunshine Hillygus and Todd G. Shields, *The Persuadable Voter: Wedge Issues in Presidential Campaigns* (Princeton, NJ: Princeton University Press, 2008).

46. Federal Election Commission, 2009.

47. The Center for Responsive Politics at **www.opensecrets.org/pres08/totals.php?cycle=2008**.

48. Hershey, *Party Politics in America*, pp. 224–225.

49. Federal Election Commission, 2009.

50. Federal Election Commission; the Center for Responsive Politics (both 2009).

51. Hershey, *Party Politics in America*, p. 228.

52. Polsby and Wildavsky, *Presidential Elections*, pp. 62–67.

53. On this research see Thomas E. Mann, "Linking Knowledge and Action: Political Science and Campaign Finance Reform," *Perspectives on Politics*, 1, no. 1 (2003), pp. 69–83.

54. See Verba, Schlozman, and Brady, *Voice and Equality*.

55. Matthew Hindman, *The Myth of Digital Democracy* (Princeton, NJ: Princeton University Press, 2009).

56. Efforts to sort out their relative contributions include Benjamin I. Page and Calvin Jones, "Reciprocal Effects of Policy Preferences, Party Loyalties, and the Vote," *American Political Science Review*, 73 (1979), pp. 1071–1089; Gregory B. Markus

and Philip E. Converse, "A Dynamic Simultaneous Equation Model of Public Choice," *American Political Science Review,* 73 (1979), pp. 1066–1070.

57. Gary Miller and Norman Schofield, "The Transformation of the Republican and Democratic Party Coalitions in the U.S.," *Perspectives on Politics,* 6, no. 3 (September 2008), pp. 433–450; Demetrios James Caraley, "Three Trends Over Eight Presidential Elections, 1980–2008: Toward the Emergence of a Democratic Majority Realignment," *Political Science Quarterly,* 124, no. 3 (2009), pp. 423–442.

58. Erikson and Tedin, *American Public Opinion,* pp. 83–91.

59. Larry M. Bartels, "Partisanship and Voting Behavior, 1952–1996," *American Journal of Political Science,* 44 (January 2000), pp. 35–50; Hershey, *Party Politics in America,* pp. 108–110; D. Sunshine Hillygus and Simon Jackman, "Voter Decision Making in Election 2000: Campaign Effects, Partisan Activation, and the Clinton Legacy," *American Journal of Political Science,* 47 (2003), pp. 583–596; Stephen A. Jessee, "Spatial Voting in the 2004 Presidential Election," *American Political Science Review,* 103, no. 1 (February 2009), pp. 59–81.

60. Donald E. Stokes, "Some Dynamic Elements of Contests for the Presidency," *American Political Science Review,* 60 (1966), pp. 19–28.

61. Maisel, *American Political Parties and Elections,* pp. 107–112.

CHAPTER 11

1. Sources for the story of the 2010 elections include the following: CNN Politics, Election Center (**www.cnn.com/ELECTION/2010**); Jonathan Haidt, "What the Tea Partiers Really Want," *The Wall Street Journal,* October 16, 2010, p. 1; Devin Leonard, "The U.S. Chamber of Commerce Takes on Obama," *Bloomberg Businessweek,* November 8, 2010, pp. 71–78; Mike McIntire, "Hidden Under Tax-Exempt Cloak, Political Dollars Flow," *The New York Times,* September 21, 2010, p. 1; David Leonhardt, "Job Losses Outweigh Obama's Successes," *The New York Times,* October 26, 2010, p. 1; National Conference of State Legislatures, *State Vote* (**www.ncsl.org/?tabid=21253**); Exit polls, *The New York Times* online (**http://elections.nytimes.com/2010/results/house/exit-polls**); and the Center for Public Responsibility, *Open Secrets* (**www.opensecrets.org/index.php**).

2. For an introduction to the political science literature on factors that affect the outcome of elections, see L. Sandy Maisel and Mark D. Brewster, *Parties and Elections in America: The Electoral Process,* 5th ed. (Lanham, MD: Rowman & Littlefield, 2009); and the special symposium on election 2010 forecasting edited by James E. Campbell in *PS,* October 2010, pp. 625–641.

3. Roger H. Davidson, Walter J. Oleszek, and Frances E. Lee, *Congress and Its Members,* 12th ed. (Washington, D.C.: CQ Press, 2010), pp. 15–23.

4. Ibid., pp. 23–24. Also see Oleszek, Walter J., *Congressional Procedures and the Policy Process,* 8th ed. (Washington, D.C.: CQ Press, 2010), pp. 23–28.

5. Sanford Levinson, *Our Undemocratic Constitution: Where the Constitution Goes Wrong* (New York: Oxford University Press, 2006); Robert A. Dahl, *How Democratic Is the American Constitution?* (New Haven, CT: Yale University Press, 2001).

6. Quoted in Charles Warren, *The Supreme Court in U.S. History* (Boston: Little, Brown, 1919), p. 195.

7. Oleszek, *Congressional Procedures and the Policy Process,* p. 5.

8. On this general question, see Jane Mansbridge, "Rethinking Representation," *American Political Science Review,* 97, no. 4 (2003), pp. 515–528; Nadia Urbinati and Mark E. Warrren, "The Concept of Representation in Contemporary Democratic Theory," *The Annual Review of Political Science,* 11 (2008), pp. 387–412. Also see Davidson, Oleszek, and Lee, *Congress and Its Members,* pp. 140–141.

9. Quoted in Charles Henning, *The Wit and Wisdom of Politics* (Golden, CO: Fulcrum, 1989), p. 235.

10. Abraham Lincoln, announcement in the *Sagamo Journal,* New Salem, Illinois (June 13, 1836).

11. Davidson, Oleszek, and Lee, *Congress and Its Members,* p. 141. For a dissenting view, one that suggests that senators, facing much more competitive elections than representatives, are just as likely as House members to lean toward the delegate style throughout their six-year term of office, see Charles Stewart III, "Congress and the Constitutional System," in Paul J. Quirk and Sarah A. Binder, eds., *The Legislative Branch* (New York: Oxford University Press, 2005).

12. Davidson, Oleszek, and Lee, *Congress and Its Members,* pp. 122–127.

13. The Inter-parliamentary Union, "Women in National Parliaments," **www.ipu.org/wnm-e/world.htm**.

14. Davidson, Oleszek, and Lee, p. 123; Steven S. Smith, Jason M. Roberts and Ryan J. Vander Wielen, *The American Congress* (New York: Cambridge University Press, 2007), pp. 17–18.

15. Davidson, Oleszek, and Lee, pp. 127–128.

16. The distinction between descriptive and substantive representation—the latter meaning that legislators act in the interests of their constituents irrespective of the demographic makeup of the constituency—is made by Hanna Pitkin in her classic work *The Concept of Representation* (Berkeley, CA: University of California Press, 1967).

17. Arturo Vega and Juanita Firestone, "The Effects of Gender on Congressional Behavior and the Substantive Representation of Women," *Legislative Studies Quarterly,* 20 (May 1995), pp. 213–222. Also see Michele L. Swers, *The Difference Women Make* (Chicago: University of Chicago Press, 2002); the collection of research on women's impact on the legislative process in Cindy Simon Rosenthal, ed., *Women Transforming Congress* (Norman, OK: University of Oklahoma Press, 2002).

18. Datina L. Gamble, "Black Political Representation," *Legislative Studies Quarterly,* 32 (2007), pp. 421–448.

19. For a review of research on the political impacts of redistricting, see Raymond La Raja, "Redistricting: Reading Between the Lines," *The Annual Review of Political Science* 12 (2009), pp. 202–223.

20. Gary W. Cox and Jonathan Katz, "The Reapportionment Revolution and Bias in U.S. Congressional Elections," *American Journal of Political Science,* 43 (1999), pp. 812–840; Davidson, Oleszek, and Lee, *Congress and Its Members,* pp. 46–51; Smith, Roberts and Vander Wielen, *The American Congress,* pp. 62–64.

21. CQ Voting and Elections Collection Online (**http://library.cqpress.com/elections**), 2007. Some have argued that districting is only one reason competitive elections have declined. Another may be that election districts are becoming more homogeneous as people increasingly move to areas where there are people like themselves. See the research of Bruce Oppenheimer and Alan Abramowitz, reported in Bill Bishop, "You Can't Compete With Voters' Feet," *Washington Post* (May 15, 2005), p. B2; Alan Abramowitz, Brad Alexander, and Matthew Gunning, "Drawing the Line on District Competition,"

PS (January 2006), pp. 95–97; Richard Florida, *The Flight of the Creative Class* (New York: Harper Business, 2005), pp. 217–222; Ronald Brownstein, *The Second Civil War: How Extreme Partisanship Has Paralyzed Washington and Polarized America* (New York: Penguin, 2007), ch. 6.

22. Davidson, Oleszek, and Lee, *Congress and Its Members,* pp. 53–58.

23. Charles S. Bulloch, "Affirmative Action Districts: In Whose Face Will They Blow Up?" *Campaigns and Elections,* April 1995, p. 22.

24. Charles Cameron, David Epstein, and Sharon O'Halloran, "Do Majority-Minority Districts Maximize Black Representation in Congress?" *American Political Science Review,* 90 (1996), pp. 794–812; David Epstein and Sharon O'Halloran, "A Social Science Approach to Race, Districting and Representation," *American Political Science Review,* 93 (1999), pp. 187–191; David Lublin, *The Paradox of Representation: Racial Gerrymandering and Minority Interests* (Princeton, NJ: Princeton University Press, 1997); David T. Canon, "Representing Racial and Ethnic Minorities," in Paul J. Quirk and Sarah A. Binder, eds., *The Legislative Branch* (New York: Oxford University Press, 2005), pp. 185–186.

25. Federal Election Commission, press release, December 29, 2009.

26. Ibid.

27. Gary W. Cox and Eric Magar, "How Much Is Majority Status in the U.S. Congress Worth?" *American Political Science Review,* 93 (1999), pp. 299–309.

28. Davidson, Oleszek, and Lee, *Congress and Its Members,* pp. 63–64.

29. Richard Hall and Frank W. Wayman, "Buying Time: Moneyed Interests and the Mobilization of Bias in Congressional Committees," *American Political Science Review,* 84 (1990), pp. 797–820.

30. See the classic work on this subject, David R. Mayhew, *Congress: The Electoral Connection* (New Haven, CT: Yale University Press, 1974). Also see Davidson, Oleszek, and Lee, *Congress and Its Members,* ch. 5; Smith, Roberts, and Vander Wielen, *The American Congress,* pp. 97–104.

31. Richard F. Fenno Jr., *Home Style: House Members and Their Districts* (New York: Pearson Longman, 2003); Richard F. Fenno Jr., *Senators on the Home Trail* (Norman, OK: University of Oklahoma Press, 1996).

32. Bruce Cain, John A. Ferejohn, and Morris P. Fiorina, *The Personal Vote: Constituency Service and Electoral Independence* (Cambridge, MA: Harvard University Press, 1987); Glenn Parker, *Homeward Bound: Explaining Change in Congressional Behavior* (Pittsburgh: University of Pittsburgh Press, 1986); Fenno, *Home Style.*

33. Levinson, *Our Undemocratic Constitution,* p. 51.

34. Lawrence Jacobs and Robert Shapiro, *Politicians Don't Pander* (Chicago: University of Chicago Press, 2000).

35. Jacob S. Hacker and Paul Pierson, *Off Center: The Republican Revolution and the Erosion of American Democracy* (New Haven, CT: Yale University Press, 2005).

36. Robert B. Reich, *Supercapitalism: The Transformation of Business, Democracy, and Everyday Life* (New York: Knopf, 2007), pp. 131–148; Larry M. Bartels, *Unequal Democracy: The Political Economy of the New Gilded Age* (New York and Princeton, NJ: Russell Sage Foundation and Princeton University Press, 2008), ch. 9.

37. Alan Wolfe, *Does American Democracy Still Work?* (New Haven, CT: Yale University Press, 2006), ch. 3.

38. Oleszek, *Congressional Procedures and the Policy Process,* ch. 1.

39. Hacker and Pierson, *Off Center.*

40. Hershey, *Party Politics in America,* pp. 243–244; Davidson, Oleszek, and Lee, *Congress and Its Members,* pp. 192–193; Garry W. Cox and Keith T. Poole, "On Measuring Partisanship in Roll-Call Voting," *American Journal of Political Science,* 46 (2002), pp. 477–489; Gerald D. Wright and Brian F. Schaffner, "The Influence of Party," *American Political Science Review,* 96 (2002), pp. 367–379; Smith, Roberts, and Vander Wielen, *The American Congress,* pp. 23–24.

41. Davidson, Oleszek, and Lee, *Congress and Its Members,* pp. 284–286.

42. Ibid., p. 193.

43. For the fullest review of the scholarly literature see Geoffrey C. Layman, Thomas M. Carsey, and Julianna Mnasce Horowitz, "Party Polarization in American Politics: Characteristics, Causes and Consequences." *Annual Reviews, Political Science,* 9 (2006), pp. 83–110.

44. On the transformation of the South in American politics and how it has affected Congress see Nelson W. Polsby, *How Congress Evolves: Social Bases of Institutional Change* (New York: New York University Press, 2004); Earl Black and Merle Black, *The Rise of Southern Republicans* (Cambridge, MA: Harvard University and Belknap Press, 2003); Earl Black and Merle Black, *Divided America: The Ferocious Power Struggle in American Politics* (New York: Simon and Schuster, 2007); Stanley B. Greenberg, *The Two Americas* (New York: St. Martins Griffin, 2005).

45. Alan I. Abramowitz and Kyle L. Saunders, "Ideological Realignment in the U.S. Electorate," *Journal of Politics,* 60 (1998), pp. 634–652; Nolan McCarty, Keith T. Poole, and Howard Rosenthal, *Polarized American: The Dance of Ideology and Unequal Riches* (Cambridge, MA: MIT Press, 2006); *Evenly Divided and Increasingly Polarized: The 2004 Political Landscape* (Washington, D.C.: Pew Research Center, 2003); "Trends in Political Values and Core Attitudes: 1987–2007" (Washington, D.C.: The Pew Research Center for the People and the Press, report released March 22, 2007); "Trends in Political Values and Core Attitudes: 1987–2009" (Washington, D.C.: The Pew Research Center for the People and the Press, report released May 21, 2009); Nils Gilman, "What the Rise of the Republicans as America's First Ideological Party Means for the Democrats," *The Forum,* 2, no. 1 (2004), pp. 1–4.

46. Mickey Edwards, "Political Science and Political Practice," *Perspectives on Politics,* 1, no. 2 (June 2003), p. 352.

47. See John J. Kornacki, ed., *Leading Congress: New Styles, New Strategies* (Washington, D.C.: Congressional Quarterly Press, 1990); David W. Rohde, *Parties and Leaders in the Postreform Congress* (Chicago: University of Chicago Press, 1991); Randall Strahan, *Leading Representatives: The Agency of Leaders in the Politics of the U.S. House* (Baltimore: The John Hopkins University Press, 2007); Hershey, *Party Politics in America,* pp. 244–249.

48. Alan A. Abramowitz, "'Mr. Mayhew, Meet Mr. DeLay,' or the Electoral Connection in the Post-Reform Congress," *PS,* 34, no. 2 (June 2001), pp. 257–258; Layman, Carsey, and Horowitz, "Party Polarization in American Politics," pp. 88–90.

49. Oleszek, *Congressional Procedures and the Policy Process,* pp. 160–161.

50. Davidson, Oleszek, and Lee, *Congress and Its Members,* pp. 157–159.

51. Sheryl Gay Stolberg, Jeff Zeleny, and Carl Hulse, "Health Vote Caps a Journey Back From the Brink," *The New York Times* (March 20, 2010), p. 1.

52. Smith, Roberts, and Vander Wielen, *The American Congress,* p. 137.

53. This analogy is that of Congressman Tom DeLay reported in Jonathan Kaplan, "Hastert, DeLay: Political Pros Get Along to Go Along," *The Hill,* July 22, 2003, p. 8.

54. Davidson, Oleszek, and Lee, *Congress and Its Members,* pp. 232–234; Smith, Roberts, and Vander Wielen, *The American Congress,* pp. 163–164; Brownstein, *The Second Civil War,* pp. 124–127.

55. Eric S. Heberlig, "Congressional Parties, Fundraising, and Committee Ambition," *Political Research Quarterly,* 56, no. 2 (June 2003), pp. 151–161.

56. Davidson, Oleszek, and Lee, *Congress and Its Members,* pp. 210–218; Smith, Roberts, and Vander Wielen, *The American Congress,* pp. 186–190.

57. Jonathon Allen, "The Legacy of the Class of '94," *CQ Weekly,* September 4, 2004.

58. Brownstein, *The Second Civil War,* p. 157.

59. Davidson and Oleszek, *Congress and Its Members,* ch. 8; Donald R. Matthews, *U.S. Senators and Their World* (Chapel Hill, NC: University of North Carolina Press, 1960).

60. Interview with Ezra Klein, *The Washington Post Online,* accessed December 28, 2009 at **http://voices.washingtonpost.com/ ezra-klein/2009/12/the_right_of_the_filibuster_an. html**.

61. Robert Bendiner, *Obstacle Course on Capitol Hill* (New York: McGraw-Hill, 1964), p. 15.

62. Barbara Sinclair, *Unorthodox Lawmaking: New Legislative Processes in the U.S. Congress* (Washington, D.C.: CQ Press, 2007).

63. Brownstein, *The Second Civil War,* p. 277.

CHAPTER 12

1. U.S. Department of Commerce, *Historical Statistics of the United States, Colonial Times to 1970* (Washington, D.C.: U.S. Government Printing Office, 1971), pp. 8, 1143.

2. Federation of American Scientists, 2009 (**http://www.fas.org/ programs/ssp/nukes/nuclearweapons/nukestatus.html**)

3. U.S. Bureau of the Census.

4. George C. Edwards III and Stephen J. Wayne, *Presidential Leadership: Politics and Policy Making* (Belmont, CA: Cengage Wadsworth, 2009), pp. 2–9.

5. On the contributions of particular presidents in shaping today's presidency, see Scott C. James, "The Evolution of the Presidency," in Joel D. Aberbach and Mark A. Peterson, eds., *The Executive Branch* (New York: Oxford University Press, 2005).

6. James P. Pfiffner, "Constraining Executive Power: George W. Bush and the Constitution," and Andrew Rudalevige, "A New Imperial Presidency?" both in James P. Pfiffner and Roger H. Davidson, eds., *Understanding the Presidency* (New York: Pearson Longman, 2009).

7. Jimmie Breslin, quoted in Laurence J. Peter, *Peter's Quotations* (New York: Morrow, 1977), p. 405.

8. See Edwards and Wayne, *Presidential Leadership,* ch. 12.

9. Richard E. Neustadt, *Presidential Power and the Modern Presidents: The Politics of Leadership from Roosevelt to Reagan* (New York: Free Press, 1990); David E. Lewis and Terry M. Moe, "The Presidency and the Bureaucracy: The Levers of Presidential Control," in Michael Nelson, ed., *The Presidency and the Political System* (Washington, D.C.: CQ Press, 2010).

10. William G. Howell, *Power Without Persuasion: The Politics of Direct Presidential Action* (Princeton, NJ: Princeton University Press, 2003); Phillip J. Cooper, *By Order of the President: The Use and Abuse of Executive Direct Action* (Lawrence, KS: University of Kansas Press, 2002); Adam L. Warber, *Executive Orders and the Modern Presidency* (Boulder, CO: Lynne Rienner Publishers, 2006); Andrew Rudalevige, "The Presidency and Unilateral Power: A Taxonomy," in Nelson, *The Presidency and the Political System.*

11. Matthew Crenson and Benjamin Ginsberg, *Presidential Power, Unchecked and Unbalanced* (New York: Norton, 2007); Pfiffner, "Constraining Executive Power: George W. Bush and the Constitution"; Rudalevige, "A New Imperial Presidency?"; Richard Pious, "Prerogative Power and the War on Terrorism," in Pfiffner and Davidson, eds., *Understanding the Presidency.*

12. See John Yoo, *The Powers of War and Peace: The Constitution and Foreign Affairs After 9/11* (Chicago: University of Chicago Press, 2005). In contrast see Matthew Crenson and Benjamin Ginsberg, *Presidential Power, Unchecked and Unbalanced* (New York: Norton, 2007).

13. Graham T. Allison, *Essence of Decision: Explaining the Cuban Missile Crisis* (Boston: Little, Brown, 1971), pp. 141–142.

14. Neustadt, *Presidential Power and the Modern Presidents,* ch. 2.

15. Michael Nelson, "Neustadt's *Presidential Power* at 50," *The Chronicle of Higher Education,* March 28, 2010, pp. 1–7.

16. *United States* v. *Curtiss-Wright* (1936). For more on judicial interpretations of presidential powers in foreign policy and war, see R. Shep Melnick, "The Courts, Jurisprudence, and the Executive Branch," in Joel D. Aberbach and Mark A. Peterson, eds., *The Executive Branch* (New York: Oxford University Press, 2005); Richard A. Brisbin Jr., "The Judiciary and the Separation of Powers," in Kermit L. Hall and Kevin T. McGuire, eds., *The Judicial Branch* (New York: Oxford University Press, 2005).

17. Melnick, "The Courts, Jurisprudence, and the Executive Branch."

18. Edwards and Wayne, *Presidential Leadership,* p. 480.

19. Arthur Schlesinger Jr., *The Imperial Presidency* (New York: Popular Library, Atlantic Monthly Press, 1973).

20. Harvey Mansfield, "The Law and the President: In a National Emergency, Who You Gonna Call?" *Weekly Standard,* January 16, 2006, p. 1; Michael Stokes Paulsen, "The Constitution of Necessity," *Notre Dame Law Review,* 79 (2004), p. 1257; Yoo, *The Powers of War and Peace.*

21. Bruce Ackerman, *Before the Next Attack* (New Haven, CT: Yale University Press, 2006); Crenson and Ginsberg, *Presidential Power, Unchecked and Unbalanced*; Sanford Levinson, *Our Undemocratic Constitution* (New York: Oxford University Press, 2006), pp. 104–107; Geoffrey R. Stone, *Perilous Times: Free Speech in Wartime* (New York: Norton, 2004).

22. David Margolis, "Memorandum for the Attorney General," January 5, 2010, p. 67.

23. Marjorie Randon Hershey, *Party Politics in America* (New York: Pearson, 2009), pp. 266–272; Sidney M. Milkis and Jesse H. Rhodes, "George W. Bush, the Republican Party, and the New

American Party System," *Perspectives on Politics,* 5, no. 3 (September 2007), pp. 461–488.

24. James P. Pfiffner, *The Modern Presidency* (New York: St. Martin's Press, 1998), ch. 4. Also see Edwards and Wayne, *Presidential Leadership,* ch. 6; James P. Pfiffner and Roger H. Davidson, eds., *Understanding the Presidency* (New York: Pearson Longman, 2009), pp. 229–232.

25. Edwards and Wayne, *Presidential Leadership,* p. 209.

26. Nathan Miller, *FDR: An Intimate History* (Lanham, MD: Madison Books, 1983), p. 276.

27. Thomas E. Cronin and Michael A. Genovese, *The Paradoxes of the American Presidency* (New York: Oxford University Press, 2004), ch. 10; Joseph A. Pika, "The Vice-Presidency: Dick Cheney, Joe Biden, and the New Vice Presidency," in Nelson, *The Presidency and the Political System.*

28. Edwards and Wayne, *Presidential Leadership,* p. 216.

29. Elizabeth Bumiller and Eric Schmitt, "In Indictment's Wake, A Focus on Cheney's Powerful Role in the White House," *The New York Times,* October 20, 2005, p. A1.

30. Stephen F. Hayes, *Cheney: The Untold Story of the Nation's Most Powerful and Controversial Vice President* (New York: Harper Collins, 2007); Barton Gellman, *Angler: The Cheney Vice Presidency* (New York: Penguin, 2008).

31. Charles O. Jones, *Separate but Equal: Congress and the Presidency* (New York: Chatham House, 1999); Roger H. Davidson, Walter J. Oleszek, and Frances E. Lee, *Congress and Its Members,* 12th ed. (Washington, D.C.: CQ Press, 2010), pp. 326–330; Roger H. Davidson, "Presidential Relations With Congress," in Pfiffner and Davidson, *Understanding the Presidency.*

32. Andrew Rudalevige, "The Executive Branch and the Legislative Process," in Joel D. Aberbach and Mark A. Peterson, eds., *The Executive Branch* (New York: Oxford University Press, 2005), pp. 432–445; Davidson, Oleszek, and Lee, *Congress and Its Members,* ch. 10.

33. Edwards and Wayne, *Presidential Leadership,* pp. 336–348; Jon R. Bond and Richard Fleisher, eds., *Polarized Politics: Congress and the President in a Partisan Era* (Washington, D.C.: CQ Press, 2000); Jeffrey S. Peake, "Back on Track," *American Politics Research,* November 2004, pp. 679–697.

34. Terry Sullivan, "Headcounts, Expectations and Presidential Coalitions in Congress," *American Journal of Political Science,* 32 (1988), pp. 657–689; Davidson, Oleszek, and Lee, *Congress and Its Members,* pp. 324–325; Hershey, *Party Politics in America,* pp. 266–270.

35. "2009 Was the Most Partisan Year Ever," *Congressional Quarterly Weekly Report,* January 11, 2010, p. 1.

36. Aaron Wildavsky, "The Two Presidencies," in Aaron Wildavsky, ed., *Perspectives on the Presidency* (Boston: Little, Brown, 1975), pp. 448–461.

37. Roger H. Davidson, "Presidential Relations with Congress," in Pfiffner and Davidson, eds., *Understanding the Presidency,* pp. 292–293.

38. Richard Brody, *Assessing the President: The Media, Elite Opinion, and Public Support* (Stanford, CA: Stanford University Press, 1991); George C. Edwards III, *At the Margins: Presidential Leadership of Congress* (New Haven, CT: Yale University Press, 1989); George C. Edwards III, "Aligning Tests with Theory: Presidential Approval as a Source of Influence in Congress," *Congress and the Presidency,* 24 (Fall 1997), pp. 113–130.

39. Edwards and Wayne, *Presidential Leadership,* pp. 348–350.

40. Jeffrey K. Tulis, *The Rhetorical Presidency* (Princeton, NJ: Princeton University Press, 1987), chs. 2 and 3, esp. p. 64.

41. Woodrow Wilson, *Leaders of Men,* ed. T. H. Vail Motter (Princeton, NJ: Princeton University Press, 1952), p. 39; quoted in Tulis, *The Rhetorical Presidency,* ch. 4, which analyzes Wilson's theory at length and expresses some skepticism about it.

42. Tulis, *The Rhetorical Presidency,* pp. 138, 140.

43. Samuel Kernell, *Going Public: Strategies of Presidential Leadership,* 3rd ed. (Washington, D.C.: CQ Press, 1997), p. 92 and ch. 4.

44. Benjamin I. Page and Robert Y. Shapiro, "Presidents as Opinion Leaders: Some New Evidence," *Policy Studies Journal,* 12 (1984), pp. 649–661; Benjamin I. Page, Robert Y. Shapiro, and Glenn R. Dempsey, "What Moves Public Opinion," *American Political Science Review,* 81 (1987), pp. 23–43; but see Donald L. Jordan, "Newspaper Effects on Policy Preferences," *Public Opinion Quarterly,* 57 (1993), pp. 191–204.

45. Lawrence R. Jacobs and Robert Y. Shapiro, *Politicians Don't Pander: Political Manipulation and the Loss of Democratic Responsiveness* (Chicago: University of Chicago Press, 2000); Jacob Hacker and Paul Pierson, *Off Center* (New Haven, CT: Yale University Press, 2005).

46. Doris Graber, *Mass Media and American Politics,* 8th ed. (Washington, D.C.: CQ Press, 2010), ch. 9; Lawrence R. Jacobs, "Communicating From the White House," in Joel D. Aberbach and Mark A. Peterson, eds., *The Executive Branch* (New York: Oxford University Press, 2005), pp. 189–205.

47. Lawrence Jacobs and Robert Y. Shapiro, "The Rise of Presidential Polling: The Nixon White House in Historical Perspective," *Public Opinion Quarterly,* 59 (1995), pp. 163–195; Jacobs, "Communicating From the White House," pp. 178–189.

48. W. Lance Bennett, Regina G. Lawrence, and Steven Livingston, *When the Press Fails: Political Power and the News Media from Iraq to Katrina* (Chicago: University of Chicago Press, 2007), ch. 5; Jacobs and Shapiro, *Politicians Don't Pander.*

49. Edwards and Wayne, *Presidential Leadership,* pp. 112–123.

50. Brody, *Assessing the President.* See also Edwards and Wayne, *Presidential Leadership,* pp. 112–123; John E. Mueller, "Presidential Popularity from Truman to Johnson," *American Political Science Review,* 64 (1970), pp. 18–34; Samuel Kernell, "Explaining Presidential Popularity," *American Political Science Review,* 72 (1978), pp. 506–522; George C. Edwards III, *Presidential Approval* (Baltimore, MD: Johns Hopkins University Press, 1990).

CHAPTER 13

1. The quote is from "The Diddle Kingdom," *The Economist,* July 7, 2007, p. 63. Other sources for this chapter-opening story include Eric Lipton, "Safety Agency Faces Scrutiny Amid Charges," *The New York Times,* September 2, 2007, p. A1; Tom Lowry and Lorraine Woellert, "More Paper Tiger Than Watchdog?" *BusinessWeek,* September 3, 2007, p. 45.

2. Lipton, "Safety Agency Faces Scrutiny Amid Charges."

3. Max Weber, *Economy and Society* (London: Owen, 1962), vol. 1.

4. See Charles T. Goodsell, *The Case for Bureaucracy,* 4th ed. (Washington, D.C.: CQ Press, 2003), p. 85; Kenneth J. Meier, "Representative Bureaucracy: An Empirical Analysis," *American Political Science Review,* 69 (June 1975), pp. 537–539; Katherine C. Naff, "Representative Bureaucracy," *Encyclopedia of Public Administration and Public Policy,* 2nd ed. (Piscataway, NJ: Rutgers University Press, 2008).

5. Wallace Sayre, "Bureaucracies: Some Contrasts in Systems," *Indian Journal of Public Administration,* 10 (1964), p. 223. For contemporary evidence in support of this claim, see Gabriel A. Almond, G. Bingham Powell Jr., Kaare Strom, and Russell J. Dalton, *Comparative Politics Today* (New York: Pearson Longman, 2010), pp. 120–124.

6. John A. Rohr, *Civil Servants and Their Constitutions* (Lawrence, KS: University of Kansas Press, 2002); Richard J. Stillman II, *The American Bureaucracy* (Chicago: Nelson-Hall, 1987), p. 18.

7. Rohr, *Civil Servants and Their Constitutions,* ch. 4; and David E. Lewis and Terry M. Moe, "The Presidency and the Bureaucracy: The Levers of Presidential Control," in Michael Nelson, ed., *The Presidency and the Political System* (Washington, D.C.: CQ Press, 2010).

8. Jay M. Shafritz, E. W. Russell, and Christopher P. Borick, *Introducing Public Administration* (New York: Pearson Longman, 2007), pp. 87–94; B. Guy Peters, *American Public Policy: Policy and Performance,* 8th ed. (New York: CQ Press, 2010), pp. 114–121.

9. Peters, *American Public Policy,* p. 116.

10. Daniel Carpenter, "The Evolution of National Bureaucracy in the United States," in Joel D. Aberbach and Mark A. Peterson, eds., *The Executive Branch* (New York: Oxford University Press, 2005), pp. 55–57.

11. Peters, *American Public Policy,* p. 118.

12. Theodore J. Lowi, *The End of Liberalism,* 2nd ed. (New York: Norton, 1979); Christian Hunold and B. Guy Peters, "Bureaucratic Discretion and Deliberative Democracy," in Matti Malkia, Ari-Veikko Anttiroiko, and Reijo Savolainen, eds., *Transformation in Governance* (London: Idea Group, 2004), pp. 131–149.

13. Roger H. Davidson, Walter J. Oleszek, and Frances E. Lee, *Congress and Its Members,* 12th ed. (Washington, D.C.: CQ Press, 2010), p. 347.

14. Charles R. Shipan, "Congress and the Bureaucracy," in Paul J. Quirk and Sarah A. Binder, eds., *The Legislative Branch* (New York: Oxford University Press, 2005).

15. Patricia W. Ingraham, "The Federal Service: the People and the Challenge," in Joel D. Aberbach and Mark A. Peterson, eds., *The Executive Branch* (New York: Oxford University Press, 2005), pp. 290–291.

16. Ibid., pp. 294–296.

17. See Samuel Krislov and David H. Rosenbloom, *Representative Bureaucracy and the American Political System* (New York: Praeger, 1981); Goodsell, *The Case for Bureaucracy;* Ingraham, "The Federal Service."

18. OECD (2005) as reported in "Public Service Careers," *The Economist* (October 31, 2009), p. 71.

19. Goodsell, *The Case for Bureaucracy,* pp. 84–90; Stanley Rothman and S. Robert Lichter, "How Liberal Are Bureaucrats?" *Regulation,* November–December 1983, pp. 35–47.

20. Office of Personnel Management, 2005.

21. Ingraham, "The Federal Service," pp. 291–294.

22. Richard P. Nathan, *The Administrative Presidency* (New York: Wiley, 1983).

23. David E. Rosenbaum and Stephen Labaton, "Amid Many Fights on Qualifications, a Nomination Stalls," *The New York Times,* September 24, 2005, p. A12.

24. Hugh Heclo, *A Government of Strangers* (Washington, D.C.: Brookings Institution, 1977), p. 103.

25. Richard E. Neustadt, *Presidential Power* (New York: Wiley, 1960); George C. Edwards III and Stephen J. Wayne, *Presidential Leadership: Politics and Policy Making* (Wadsworth, CA: Thomson Wadsworth, 2009), ch. 9.

26. Terry M. Moe, "Control and Feedback in Economic Regulation," *American Political Science Review,* 79 (1985), pp. 1094–1116; Lewis and Moe, "The Presidency and the Bureaucracy: The Levers of Presidential Control," in Nelson, *The Presidency and the Political System;* Richard W. Waterman, *Presidential Influence and the Administrative State* (Knoxville, TN: University of Tennessee Press, 1989); Edwards and Wayne, *Presidential Leadership,* pp. 295–303.

27. Richard W. Waterman and Kenneth J. Meier, "Principal-Agent Models: An Expansion?" *Journal of Public Administration Research and Theory,* 8 (April 1998), pp. 173–202; Edwards and Wayne, *Presidential Leadership,* pp. 305–307.

28. For a review of research on the presidents appointment powers see Joel D. Aberbach and Bert A. Rockman, "The Appointments Process and the Administrative Presidency," *Presidential Studies Quarterly,* 39, no. 1 (January 2009), pp. 38–59.

29. See John Yoo, *The Powers of War and Peace: The Constitution and Foreign Affairs After 9/11* (Chicago: University of Chicago Press, 2005). In contrast see Matthew Crenson and Benjamin Ginsberg, *Presidential Power, Unchecked and Unbalanced* (New York: Norton, 2007).

30. James P. Pfiffner, "Constraining Executive Power: George W. Bush and the Constitution," in James P. Pfiffner and Roger H. Davidson, *Understanding the Presidency* (New York: Pearson Longman, 2009); Andrew Rudalevige, "The Presidency and Unilateral Power," in Michael Nelson, ed., *The Presidency and the Political System* (Washington, D.C.: CQ Press, 2010).

31. Roger H. Davidson, Walter J. Oleszek, and Frances E. Lee, *Congress and Its Members,* 11th ed. (Washington, D.C.: CQ Press, 2008), pp. 336–357; Steven S. Smith, Jason M. Roberts, and Ryan J. Vander Wielen, *The American Congress,* 5th ed. (New York: Cambridge University Press, 2007), pp. 291–301.

32. Nolan McCarty and Rose Razaghian, "Advice and Consent: Senate Responses to Executive Branch Nominations, 1885–1996," *American Journal of Political Science,* 43 (October 1999), pp. 1122–1143.

33. Richard Fenno, *The Power of the Purse* (Boston: Little, Brown, 1966); Aaron Wildavsky, *The Politics of the Budgetary Process* (Boston: Little, Brown, 1964); Davidson, Oleszek, and Lee, *Congress and Its Members,* pp. 354–355, 428–432.

34. John A. Ferejohn and Charles R. Shipan, "Congressional Influence on Administrative Agencies: A Case Study of Telecommunications Policy," in Lawrence C. Dodd and Bruce I. Oppenheimer, eds., *Congress Reconsidered,* 4th ed. (Washington, D.C.: CQ Press, 1989); Davidson, Oleszek, and Lee, *Congress and Its Members,* pp. 356–357.

35. Barry R. Weingast, "Caught in the Middle: The President, Congress, and the Political-Bureaucratic System," in Joel D. Aberbach and Mark A. Peterson, eds., *The Executive Branch* (New York: Oxford University Press, 2005), pp. 322–325.

36. Cornelius M. Kerwin, *Rulemaking: How Government Agencies Write Law and Make Policy* (Washington, D.C.: CQ Press, 2003), p. 183.

37. See Derek Bok, *The Trouble with Government* (Cambridge, MA: Harvard University Press, 2001), ch. 9; Emanuel S. Savas, *Privatization: The Key to Better Government* (Chatham, NJ: Chatham House, 1987); Sheila B. Kamerman and Alfred J. Kahn, eds., *Privatization and the Welfare State* (Princeton, NJ: Princeton University Press, 1989); Lester M. Salamon, ed., *The Tools of Government: A Guide to the New Governance* (Oxford, U.K.: Oxford University Press, 2002).

38. Moshe Schwartz, "Department of Defense Contractors in Iraq and Afghanistan: Background and Analysis" (Washington, DC: The Congressional Research Service, December 14, 2009).

39. Paul Light, *The Size of Government* (Washington, D.C.: Brookings, 1999); Paul Light, "Fact Sheet on the True Size of Government" (Washington, D.C.: Brookings Center for Public Service, 2004); Ingraham, "The Federal Public Service," pp. 301–303; Patricia Wallace Ingraham, "You Talking To Me? Accountability and the Modern Public Service," *PS* (January 2005), pp. 19–20.

40. Bernard Wysocki Jr., "Is U.S. Government Outsourcing Its Brain?" *The Wall Street Journal,* March 30, 2007, p. 1.

41. Bok, *The Trouble with Government,* pp. 233–234; Roberta Lynch and Ann Markusen, "Can Markets Govern?" *American Prospect,* Winter 1994, pp. 125–134; Dan Guttman, "Governance by Contract," *Public Contract Law Journal,* 33 (Winter 2004), pp. 321–360.

42. John Cassidy, *How Markets Fail: The Logic of Economic Calamities* (New York: Farrar, Straus and Giroux, 2009).

43. David Osborne and Ted Gaebler, *Reinventing Government* (Reading, MA: Addison-Wesley, 1992).

44. Bok, *The Trouble with Government,* pp. 234–239; Joel D. Aberbach and Bert A. Rockman, eds., *In the Web of Politics: Three Decades of the U.S. Federal Executive* (Washington, D.C.: Brookings Institution Press, 2000); Lester M. Salamon, "The New Governance and the Tools of Public Administration," in Lester M. Salamon, ed., *The Tools of Government* (Oxford, U.K.: Oxford University Press, 2002); Steven G. Koven, "Bureaucracy, Democracy, and the New Public Management," in Ali Farazmand, ed., *Bureaucracy and Administration* (Boca Raton, FL: CRC Press, 2009).

45. Carpenter, "The Evolution of National Bureaucracy," pp. 63–64; Shafritz, Russell, and Borick, *Introducing Public Administration,* pp. 112–114.

46. Terry M. Moe, "The Politics of Bureaucratic Structure," in John E. Chubb and Paul E. Peterson, eds., *Can the Government Govern?* (Washington, D.C.: Brookings Institution, 1989), p. 280; John E. Chubb and Paul E. Peterson, "American Political Institutions and the Problem of Governance," in Chubb and Peterson, eds., *Can the Government Govern?,* p. 41; James L. Sundquist, *Constitutional Reform and Effective Government* (Washington, D.C.: Brookings Institution, 1986).

CHAPTER 14

1. All quotes are from Neil A. Lewis, "Bitter Senators Divided Anew on Judgeships," *The Washington Post,* November 15, 2003, p. A1.

2. Jan Crawford Greenburg, *Supreme Conflict: The Inside Story of the Struggle for Control of the United States Supreme Court* (New York: Penguin, 2007); Jess Bravin, "Top Court Hands Conservatives Victories," *The Wall Street Journal,* June 26, 2007, p. 1; Linda Greenhouse, "In Steps Big and Small, Supreme Court Moves Right," *The New York Times,* July 1, 2007, p. A1; Lexington, "Supreme Success," *The Economist,* July 7, 2007, p. 36; "Conservatives Resurgent," *The Economist,* April 21, 2007, p. 34.

3. Akhil Reed Amar, *America's Constitution: A Biography* (New York: Random House, 2005), ch. 6.

4. J. M. Sosin, *The Aristocracy of the Long Robe: The Origins of Judicial Review in America* (Westport, CT: Greenwood Press, 1989); William E. Nelson, "The Historical Foundations of the American Judiciary," Kermit L. Hall, "Judicial Independence and the Majoritarian Difficulty," and Cass R. Sunstein, "Judges and Democracy: The Changing Role of the United States Supreme Court," in Kermit L. Hall and Kevin T. McGuire, eds., *The Judicial Branch* (New York: Oxford University Press, 2005).

5. Lee Epstein and Thomas G. Walker, *Rights, Liberties, and Justice* (Washington, D.C.: CQ Press, 2010), pp. 47, 53; Mark A. Graber, "Establishing Judicial Review? *Schooner Peggy* and the Early Marshall Court," *Political Research Quarterly,* 51 (1998), pp. 221–239.

6. Robert G. McCloskey, *The American Supreme Court,* 4th ed. (Chicago: University of Chicago Press, 2005), pp. 12–13.

7. On *Marbury,* see Sylvia Snowmiss, *Judicial Review and the Law of the Constitution* (New Haven, CT: Yale University Press, 1990).

8. David O'Brien, *Constitutional Law and Politics, Vol. 2* (New York: Norton, 2008), p. 36.

9. Linda Greenhouse, "The Imperial Presidency vs. the Imperial Judiciary," *The New York Times,* March 2, 2000, Week in Review sec., p. 1; Paul Gewirtz and Chad Golder, "So Who Are the Activists?" *The New York Times,* July 6, 2005, p. A1.

10. See *Ex parte Milligan* (1866) and *Youngstown Sheet and Tube Co. v. Sawyer* (1952).

11. Robert A. Dahl, *How Democratic Is the American Constitution?* (New Haven, CT: Yale University Press, 2001), pp. 54–55. Also see Lawrence D. Kramer, *The People Themselves: Popular Constitutionalism and Judicial Review* (New York: Oxford University Press, 2004).

12. Alexander M. Bickel, *The Least Dangerous Branch: The Supreme Court at the Bar of Politics* (Indianapolis, IN: Bobbs-Merrill, 1962), pp. 16–18.

13. Robert A. Dahl, "Decision-Making in a Democracy: The Supreme Court as a National Policy Maker," *Journal of Public Law,* 6 (1957), pp. 279–295; Mark A. Graber, "Constructing Judicial Review," *Annual Review of Political Science,* 8 (2005), pp. 425–451.

14. Richard S. Randall, *American Constitutional Development* (New York: Longman, 2002), pp. 488–489.

15. Federal Court Management Statistics, 2008 (**http://www.uscourts.gov/cgi-bin/cmsd2008.pl**).

16. Ibid.

17. Neil Lewis, "An Appeals Court That Always Veers to the Right," *The New York Times,* May 24, 1999, p. A1; Deborah Sontag, "The Power of the Fourth," *The New York Times Sunday Magazine,* March 9, 2003, pp. 38–44.

18. Lawrence Baum, *The Supreme Court* (Washington, D.C.: CQ Press, 2010), pp. 6–10.

19. David M. O'Brien, *Storm Center: The Supreme Court in American Politics,* 7th ed. (New York: Norton, 2005), p. 73. Also see Joel B. Grossman, "Paths to the Bench," in Kermit L. Hall and Kevin T. McGuire, eds., *The Judicial Branch* (New York: Oxford University Press, 2005), p. 162. Also see Lee Epstein, Jack Knight, and

Andrew D. Martin, "The Norm of Judicial Experience," *University of California Law Review*, 91 (2003), pp. 938–939.

20. Greenburg, *Supreme Conflict*.

21. Robert A. Carp and Ronald Stidham, *Judicial Process in America*, 6th ed. (Washington, D.C.: CQ Press, 2004), ch. 8; Grossman, "Paths to the Bench," pp. 160–161.

22. Baum, *The Supreme Court*, pp. 27–50; Ronald Brownstein, *The Second Civil War: How Extreme Partisanship Has Paralyzed Washington and Polarized America* (New York: Penguin, 2007); Greenburg, *Supreme Conflict*; Alan Wolfe, *Does American Democracy Still Work?* (New Haven, CT: Yale University Press, 2006), ch. 5.

23. Lee Epstein and Jeffrey A. Segal, *Advice and Consent: The Politics of Judicial Appointments* (New York: Oxford University Press, 2005), ch. 3; Baum, *The Supreme Court*, pp. 27–50; Roger H. Davidson, Walter J. Oleszek, and Frances E. Lee, *Congress and Its Members*, 12th ed. (Washington, D.C.: CQ Press, 2010), pp. 376–385.

24. Charlie Savage, "Obama Backers Fear Opportunities to Reshape Judiciary Are Slipping Away," *The New York Times* (November 14, 2009), p. 1.

25. Epstein and Segal, *Advice and Consent*, ch. 3; Baum, *The Supreme Court*, pp. 123–125; Grossman, "Paths to the Bench"; Lawrence Baum, "The Supreme Court in American Politics," in Nelson W. Polsby, ed., *Annual Review of Political Science* (Palo Alto, CA: Annual Reviews, 2003), pp. 161–180; Dahl, "Decision-Making in a Democracy"; Ronald Stidham and Robert A. Carp, "Judges, Presidents, and Policy Choices," *Social Science Quarterly*, 68 (1987), pp. 395–404; Carp and Stidham, *Judicial Process in America*, ch. 9.

26. See Bernard Schwartz, *Decision: How the Supreme Court Decides Cases* (New York: Oxford University Press, 2005).

27. Jeffrey Rosen, "So, Do You Believe in 'Super-Precedent'?" *The New York Times*, October 30, 2005, p. IV. 1.

28. Jeffrey A. Segal, Harold J. Spaeth, and Sara C. Benesh, *The Supreme Court in the American Legal System* (New York: Cambridge University Press, 2005), ch. 11; Epstein and Walker, *Rights, Liberty and Justice*, pp. 57–63.

29. For details, see H. W. Perry Jr., *Deciding to Decide: Agenda Setting in the United States Supreme Court* (Cambridge, MA: Harvard University Press, 2005).

30. Ibid. For a current review of the extensive scholarly literature see Thomas M. Keck, "Party, Policy, or Duty: Why Does the Supreme Court Invalidate Federal Statutes?" *American Political Science Review*, 101 (May 2007), pp. 321–338. Also see Epstein and Segal, *Advice and Consent*, ch. 5.

31. Segal, Spaeth, and Benesh, *The Supreme Court in the American Legal System*, pp. 318–323; David Adamany, "The Supreme Court," in John B. Gates and Charles A. Johnson, eds., *The American Courts* (Washington, D.C.: CQ Press, 1991), pp. 111–112; Baum, "The Supreme Court in U.S. Politics," pp. 162–168; Glendon Schubert, *The Judicial Mind* (Evanston, IL: Northwestern University Press, 1965); Jeffrey A. Segal and Harold J. Spaeth, *The Supreme Court and the Attitudinal Model* (New York: Cambridge University Press, 1993); John D. Sprague, *Voting Patterns of the United States Supreme Court* (Indianapolis, IN: Bobbs-Merrill, 1968); Tom S. Clark, "Measuring Ideological Polarization on the United States Supreme Court," *Political Research Quarterly*, 20, no. 10 (May, 2008), pp. 1–12.

32. Walter Murphy, *Elements of Judicial Strategy* (Princeton, NJ: Princeton University Press, 1964); Lee Epstein and Jack Knight, *The Choices Justices Make* (Washington, D.C.: CQ Press, 1997).

33. Joel B. Grossman, "Social Backgrounds and Judicial Decision-Making," *Harvard Law Review*, 79 (1966), pp. 1551–1564; S. Sidney Ulmer, "Dissent Behavior and the Social Background of Supreme Court Justices," *Journal of Politics*, 32 (1970), pp. 580–589.

34. L. Epstein, J. Knight, and J. Martin, "The Supreme Court as a Strategic National Policy-Maker," *Emory Law Review*, 50 (2001), pp. 583–610.

35. Nicholas Wade, "A Mathematician Crunches the Supreme Court's Numbers," *The New York Times*, August 4, 2003, p. A21; Segal, Spaeth, and Benesh, *The Supreme Court in the American Legal System*, pp. 318–323.

36. John Harlan, "A Glimpse of the Supreme Court at Work," *University of Chicago Law School Record*, 1, no. 7 (1963), pp. 35–52.

37. Bob Woodward and Scott Armstrong, *The Brethren: Inside the Supreme Court* (New York: Simon & Schuster, 1979).

38. Lee Epstein and Jack Knight, "Mapping Out the Strategic Terrain: The Informational Role of Amici Curiae," in Cornell Clayton and Howard Gillman, eds., *Supreme Court Decision-Making* (Chicago: University of Chicago Press, 1999); Segal, Spaeth, and Benesh, *The Supreme Court in the American Legal System*, chs. 12 and 13.

39. Herbert Jacob, *Justice in America*, 3rd ed. (Boston: Little, Brown, 1978), p. 245. Also see Keith E. Whittington, "Judicial Review and Interpretation," in Kermit L. Hall and Kevin T. McGuire, eds., *The Judicial Branch* (New York: Oxford University Press, 2005).

40. McCloskey, *The American Supreme Court*. Also see James H. Fowler and Sangick Jeon, "The Authority of Supreme Court Precedent," University of California, Davis, Working Paper (June 29, 2005).

41. Carp and Stidham, *Judicial Process in America*, p. 28.

42. Ibid., p. 57.

43. Mark A. Graber, "From Republic to Democracy: The Judiciary and the Political Process," in Kermit L. Hall and Kevin T. McGuire, eds., *The Judicial Branch* (New York: Oxford University Press, 2005).

44. McCloskey, *The American Supreme Court*. Also see H. W. Perry Jr., *The Transformation of the Supreme Court's Agenda: From the New Deal to the Reagan Administration* (Boulder, CO: Westview Press, 1991); Charles R. Epp, "The Supreme Court and the Rights Revolution," in Kermit L. Hall and Kevin T. McGuire, eds., *The Judicial Branch* (New York: Oxford University Press, 2005); Sunstein, "Judges and Democracy."

45. *Hamdi* v. *Rumsfeld* (2004).

46. Nasn Aron, "Roberts Court Protects the Powerful," *Politico* (May 5, 2010), at **www.politico.com**.

47. Gewirtz and Golder, "So Who Are the Activists?" p. A29.

48. Ibid.

49. Neal Devins and Louis Fischer, *The Democratic Constitution* (New York: Oxford University Press, 2004); Larry D. Kramer, *The People Themselves: Popular Constitutionalism and Judicial Review* (New York: Oxford University Press, 2004).

50. See the discussion in Allison M. Martens, "Reconsidering Judicial Supremacy: From the Counter-Majoritarian Difficulty to Constitutional Transformations," *Perspectives on Politics*, 5, no. 3 (September 2007), pp. 447–459.

51. Epstein and Walker, *Rights, Liberty and Justice*, pp. 22–28.

52. Graber, "Constructing Judicial Review"; Thomas M. Keck, *The Most Activist Supreme Court in History: The Road to Modern Judicial Conservatism* (Chicago: University of Chicago Press, 2004); George I. Lovell, *Legislative Deferrals: Statutory Ambiguity, Judicial Power, and American Democracy* (New York: Cambridge University Press, 2003); Kevin K. McMahon, *Reconsidering Roosevelt on Race: How the Presidency Paved the Way for Brown* (Chicago: University of Chicago Press, 2004); Keith E. Whittington, *Political Foundations of Judicial Supremacy: The Presidency, the Supreme Court, and Constitutional Leadership in U.S. History* (Princeton, NJ: Princeton University Press, 2007). Also see Bruce, Ackerman, *We the People: Transformations* (Cambridge, MA: Harvard University Press, 2000); McCloskey, *The American Supreme Court.*

53. Baum, "The Supreme Court in American Politics," p. 167; Davidson, Oleszek, and Lee, *Congress and Its Members*, p. 373.

54. See Davidson, Oleszek, and Lee, *Congress and Its Members*, pp. 372–379, for a discussion of legislative checks on the judiciary.

55. Tom S. Clark, "The Separation of Powers, Court Curbing, and Judicial Legitimacy," *American Journal of Political Science*, 53, no. 4 (October, 2009), pp. 971–989.

56. Lisa A. Solowiej and Paul M. Collins Jr., "Counteractive Lobbying in the U.S. Supreme Court," *American Politics Research*, 37, no. 4 (2009), pp. 670–699.

57. Edward Lazarus, *Closed Chambers* (New York: Penguin, 1999), pp. 373–374.

58. Epstein and Knight, "Mapping Out the Strategic Terrain."

59. Dahl, "Decision Making in a Democracy," pp. 279–295; Thomas R. Marshall, "Public Opinion, Representation, and the Modern Supreme Court," *American Politics Quarterly*, 16 (1988), pp. 296–316; McCloskey, *The American Supreme Court*, p. 22; O'Brien, *Storm Center*, p. 325; Baum, *The Supreme Court*, pp. 142–144.

60. G. Caldeira, "Courts and Public Opinion," in John B. Gates and Charles A. Johnson, eds., *The American Courts* (Washington, D.C.: CQ Press, 1991); Jay Casper, "The Supreme Court and National Policy Making," *American Political Science Review*, 70 (1976), pp. 50–63; Marshall, "Public Opinion, Representation, and the Modern Supreme Court"; William Mishler and Reginald S. Sheehan, "The Supreme Court as a Counter-Majoritarian Institution: The Impact of Public Opinion on Supreme Court Decisions," *American Political Science Review*, 87 (1993), pp. 87–101; Benjamin I. Page and Robert Y. Shapiro, "Effects of Public Opinion on Policy," *American Political Science Review*, 77 (1983), p. 183.

61. Segal, Spaeth, and Benesh, *The Supreme Court in the American Legal System*, pp. 326–328; Baum, *The Supreme Court*, pp. 140–142.

CHAPTER 15

1. These and other examples of campus speech codes, as well as an extended discussion of the controversies surrounding them, can be found in Donald Alexander Downs, *Restoring Free Speech and Liberty on Campus* (New York: Cambridge University Press, 2005).

2. Nat Hentoff, "Chilling Codes," *Washington Post*, Nexis: LEGISLATE Article No. 225/226.

3. On the "contract clause" see Lee Epstein and Thomas G. Walker, *Constitutional Law for a Changing America* (Washington, D.C.: CQ Press, 2005), ch. 9.

4. James E. Ely Jr., "Property Rights and Democracy in the American Constitutional Order, " in Kermit L. Hall and Kevin T. McGuire, eds., *The Judicial Branch* (New York: Oxford University Press, 2005); Richard Fallon, *The Dynamic Constitution: An Introduction to American Constitutional Law* (New York: Cambridge University Press, 2004), ch. 3, "Protection of Economic Liberties."

5. Laurence H. Tribe, *American Constitutional Law*, 3rd ed. (New York: Foundation Press, 2000), ch. 9.

6. Morton J. Horwitz, *The Transformation of American Law, 1780–1860* (Cambridge, MA: Harvard University Press, 1977); J. Willard Hurst, *Law and the Conditions of Freedom in the Nineteenth-Century United States* (Madison, WI: University of Wisconsin Press, 1956).

7. Lee Epstein and Thomas G. Walker, *Rights, Liberties, and Justice* (Washington, D.C.: CQ Press, 2010), pp. 67–87, 93–94.

8. Adam Liptak, "A Liberal Case for Gun Rights Sways Judiciary," *The New York Times*, May 6, 2007, p. A1; Sanford Levinson, "The Embarrassing Second Amendment," *Yale Law Review*, 99 (1989), pp. 637–659.

9. Epstein and Walker, *Constitutional Law for a Changing America*, pp. 438–431; Anthony Lewis, *Freedom for the Thought That We Hate: A Biography of the First Amendment* (New York: Basic Books, 2007); John C. Domino, *Civil Rights and Liberties in the 21st Century* (New York: Pearson Longman, 2010), ch. 2.

10. See Geoffrey R. Stone, *Perilous Times: Free Speech in Wartime* (New York: W. W. Norton, 2004).

11. See Stanley I. Kutler, *The American Inquisition: Justice and Injustice in the Cold War* (New York: Hill & Wang, 1982).

12. David Stout, "FBI Head Admits Mistakes in Use of Security Act," *The New York Times*, March 10, 2007, p. A1; "FBI Underreported Patriot Act Use," *The Wall Street Journal*, March 9, 2007, p. 1.

13. See Fred W. Friendly, *Minnesota Rag* (New York: Vintage, 1981).

14. Epstein and Walker, *Rights, Liberties, and Justice*, pp. 292–295.

15. See Charles Rembar, *The End of Obscenity* (New York: Harper & Row, 1968).

16. Fallon, *The Dynamic Constitution*, p. 48.

17. Epstein and Walker, *Rights, Liberties, and Justice*, pp. 145–192.

18. Fallon, *The Dynamic Constitution*, pp. 61–67.

19. Ibid., p. 63.

20. Ibid., p. 45.

21. Eva R. Rubin, *Abortion, Politics, and the Courts* (Westport, CT: Greenwood Press, 1982), ch. 2.

22. Kristen Luker, *Abortion and the Politics of Motherhood* (Berkeley: University of California Press, 1984), ch. 2.

23. "World Prison Brief" (London: International Center for Prison Studies, Kings College, London, press release, April 22, 2008).

24. Epstein and Walker, *Rights, Liberties, and Justice*, pp. 447–448.

25. *Katz* v. *United States* (1967).

26. *United States* v. *Leon* (1984); *Massachusetts* v. *Sheppard* (1984).

27. *Nix* v. *Williams* (1984).

28. *Harris* v. *New York* (1971); *New York* v. *Quarles* (1984).

29. *Arizona* v. *Fulminate* (1991).

30. Jim Yardley, "A Role Model for Executions," *The New York Times*, January 9, 2000, p. A1, IV-5.

31. Gallup Poll, October 1–4, 2009.

32. Neil A. Lewis, "Death Sentences Decline, and Experts Offer Reasons," *The New York Times,* December 15, 2006, p. A1; **www.deathpenaltyinfo.org** (accessed March 6, 2010).

33. Stone, *Perilous Times: Free Speech in Wartime;* Fallon, *The Dynamic Constitution,* ch. 12.

34. Former Chief Justice William Rehnquist believed that each successive American war involved fewer and less serious violations of civil liberties. See *All the Laws But One: Civil Liberties in Wartime* (New York: Knopf, 1998).

35. "Security Trumps Civil Liberties," a report of a poll conducted by National Public Radio, the Kennedy School of Government of Harvard University, and the Kaiser Family Fund (November 30, 2001).

36. "FBI Underreported Patriot Act Use"

37. Barton Gellman, "The FBI's Secret Scrutiny," *The Washington Post,* November 6, 2005, p. A1.

38. Pew Research Center, "Threat of Terrorism and Civil Liberties" (December 3, 2009).

CHAPTER 16

1. Greg Winter, "Schools Resegregate, Study Finds," *The New York Times,* January 21, 2003, p. A14.

2. Gary Orfield, *Reviving the Goal of an Integrated Society: A 21st Century Challenge* (Los Angeles: University of California at Los Angeles, The Civil Rights Project, 2009).

3. Ibid.

4. Ibid. Also see Charles T. Clotfelter, *After Brown: The Rise and Retreat of School Desegregation* (Princeton, NJ: Princeton University Press, 2004).

5. Richard H. Fallon, *The Dynamic Constitution: An Introduction to Constitutional Law* (New York: Cambridge University Press, 2004), pp. 109–110; John C. Domino, *Civil Rights and Liberties in the 21st Century* (New York: Pearson Longman, 2010), pp. 2–3.

6. James MacGregor Burns and Stewart Burns, *A People's Charter: The Pursuit of Rights in America* (New York: Knopf, 1991), p. 37.

7. On why the courts were such an attractive target for people seeking to expand civil rights, see Charles R. Epp, "The Courts and the Rights Revolution," in Kermit L. Hall and Kevin T. McGuire, eds., *The Judicial Branch* (New York: Oxford University Press, 2005).

8. William H. Chafe, *The Unfinished Journey: America Since World War II* (New York: Oxford University Press, 1986), p. 149.

9. Fallon, *The Dynamic Constitution,* pp. 118–120.

10. Ibid., pp. 119–122. Also see Lee Epstein and Thomas G. Walker, *Rights, Liberty, and Justice* (Washington, D.C.: CQ Press, 2010), pp. 593–601.

11. Domino, *Civil Rights and Liberties in the 21st Century,* p. 297; Chafe, *The Unfinished Journey* pp; 79–110 .

12. Epp, "The Courts and the Rights Revolution."

13. CBS News/*New York Times* Poll (July 7–14, 2008).

14. Richard Morin and Michael H. Cottman, "The Invisible Slap," *The Washington Post National Edition,* July 2–8, 2001, p. 5.

15. For additional survey data on these issues, see "A Year After Obama's Election" (Washington, D.C.: Pew Research Center, January 12, 2010).

16. This section is based on Richard D. Kahlenberg, *The Remedy: Class, Race, and Affirmative Action* (New York: Basic Books, 1996); Fallon, *The Dynamic Constitution,* ch. 5.

17. Ira Katznelson, *When Affirmative Action Was White: An Untold Story of Racial Inequality in Twentieth-Century America* (New York: W.W. Norton, 2005), pp. 145–149.

18. Ibid.

19. Martin Gilens, Paul M. Sniderman, and James H. Kuklinski, "Affirmative Action and the Politics of Realignment," *British Journal of Political Science,* 28 (January 1998), pp. 159–184; Jack Citrin, David O. Sears, Christopher Muste, and Cara Wong, "Multiculturalism in American Public Opinion," *British Journal of Political Science* 31 (2001), pp. 247–275.

20. "Public Backs Affirmative Action, But Not Minority Preferences" (Washington, D.C.: Pew Research Center, June 2, 2009); "Trends in Political Values and Core Attitudes: 1987–2007" (Washington, D.C.: Pew Research Center, 2007).

21. George M. Fredrickson, "Still Separate and Unequal," *The New York Review of Books,* November 17, 2005, p. 13.

22. In *Hunt* v. *Cromartie* (1999), the Court ruled in favor of the redrawn Twelfth Congressional District in North Carolina, presumably because race was not the only consideration in drawing district lines.

23. Opinion of the Court, *Grutter* v. *Bollinger* (2003).

24. *Meredith* v. *Jefferson County Board of Education* (2007); *Parents Involved in Community Schools* v. *Seattle School District No. 1* (2007).

25. Epstein and Walker, *Rights, Liberty, and Justice,* pp. 686–687.

26. A. Judith Baer and Leslie Friedman Goldstein, *The Constitutional and Legal Rights of Women* (Belmont, CA: Roxbury Publishing, 2006); Chafe, *The Unfinished Journey;* Barbara Sinclair Deckard, *The Women's Movement* (New York: Harper and Row, 1975); Ethel Klein, *Gender Politics* (Cambridge, MA: Harvard University Press, 1984), ch. 2; J. Freeman, *Politics of Women's Liberation* (New York: McKay, 1975).

27. See Epp, "Courts and the Rights Revolution"; Fallon, *The Dynamic Constitution,* pp. 129–133.

28. Epstein and Walker, *Rights, Liberties, and Justice,* p. 629.

29. For sharply conflicting views on the seriousness of the wage gap, see testimony on the Paycheck Fairness Act before the House Committee on Education and Labor on September 11, 2007, by Marcia Greenberger and before the Senate Committee on Health, Labor and Pensions on April 12, 2007, by Barbara Berish Brown.

30. Sam Roberts, "For Young Earners in Big City, a Gap in Women's Favor," *The New York Times,* August 3, 2007, p. A1. The article is based on research reported by Professor Andrew Beveridge of Queens College.

31. Harris Poll, July 2007.

32. Linda Greenhouse, "Justices Give the States Immunity from Suits by Disabled Workers," *The New York Times,* February 22, 2001, p. A1.

33. Kenneth Sherrill and Alan Yang, "From Outlaws to In-Laws," *Public Perspectives,* January/February 2000, pp. 20–23; "The Agony and the Ecstasy," *The Economist,* July 2, 2005.

34. Pew Research Center, "Most Still Oppose Gay Marriage, but Support for Civil Unions Continues to Rise," October 9, 2009.

35. National Council of State Legislatures, January 2010.

CHAPTER 17

1. For general accounts see John Cassidy, *How Markets Fail* (New York: Farrar, Straus and Giroux, 2009); Carmen M. Reinhart and Kenneth Rogoff, *This Time Is Different: Eight Centuries of Financial Folly* (Princeton, NJ: Princeton University Press, 2009); Joseph E. Stiglitz, *Freefall: America, Free Markets and the Sinking of the World Economy* (New York: W.W. Norton, 2010).

2. National Bureau of Economic Analysis, "National Income and Product Accounts" (Washington, D.C.: U.S. Department of Commerce, press release, July 31, 2009).

3. Bureau of Labor Statistics.

4. U.S. Department of Labor, May 21, 2010.

5. CNN/Opinion Research Corporation Poll (February 12–15, 2010).

6. Theodore J. Lowi, "Four Systems of Policy, Policy, and Choice," *Public Administration Review,* 32 (1972), pp. 298–310. For alternative ways of classifying policies see B. Guy Peters and Jon Pierre, eds., *Handbook of Public Policy* (Thousand Oaks, CA: Sage, 2006).

7. Edward S. Greenberg, *Capitalism and the American Political Ideal* (Armonk, NY: M. E. Sharpe, 1985); Gabriel Kolko, *The Triumph of Conservatism* (Chicago: Quadrangle, 1967); Walter Korpi, *The Democratic Class Struggle* (London: Routledge and Kegan Paul, 1983); James O'Connor, *The Fiscal Crisis of the State* (New York: St. Martin's Press, 1973).

8. Thomas R. Dye, *Who's Running America?* (Englewood Cliffs, NJ: Prentice Hall, 1976); G. William Domhoff, *The Higher Circles* (New York: Random House, 1970).

9. Robert Dahl, *Who Governs?* (New Haven, CT: Yale University Press, 1961); Theodore J. Lowi, *The End of Liberalism* (New York: Norton, 1979).

10. Anthony Downs, *An Economic Theory of Democracy* (New York: Harper & Row, 1957); V. O. Key Jr., *Public Opinion and American Democracy* (New York: Knopf, 1961); Morris P. Fiorina, *Retrospective Voting in American National Elections* (Cambridge, MA: Harvard University Press, 1981).

11. The lesson-forgetting was encouraged by the work of economists Milton Friedman and his protégés, including former Fed chair Alan Greenspan, and the advocates of "efficient markets theory" in economics. Leading figures here, among many others, include Eugene Fama, Robert Lucas, Harry Markowitz, and Olivier Blanchard.

12. This discussion is based largely on B. Guy Peters, *American Public Policy: Promise and Performance,* 8th ed. (New York: CQ Press, 2010), pp. 202–213.

13. On the benefits of economic growth see William J. Baumol, Robert E. Litan, and Carl J. Schramm, *Good Capitalism, Bad Capitalism and the Economics of Growth and Prosperity* (New Haven, CT: Yale University Press, 2007), ch. 2; Gregg Easterbrook, *The Progress Paradox* (New York: Random House, 2003).

14. "Losing Faith in the Greenback: How Long Will the Dollar Remain the World's Premier Currency?" *The Economist,* December 1, 2007, p. 85; Keith Bradsher, "China Losing Taste for Debt From U.S.," *The New York Times,* January 7, 2009, p. 1.

15. Roger Lowenstein, "The Education of Ben Bernanke," *The Sunday New York Times Magazine,* January 20, 2008, pp. 36–39, 61–68.

16. See "The Keynes Comeback," *The Economist,* October 3, 2009, pp. 103–104; Noam Scheiber, "Market Riot," *Foreign Policy* (December 2009), pp.45–48. The theorist of financial crises,

17. John Cassidy, *How Markets Fail: The Logic of Economic Calamities* (New York: Farrar, Straus and Giroux, 2009).

18. Peters, *American Public Policy,* pp. 142–144.

19. The following discussion of the budget-making process is based on Roger H. Davidson, Walter J. Oleszek, and Frances E. Lee, *Congress and Its Members,* 12th ed. (Washington, D.C.: CQ Press, 2010), pp. 428–442; Mandel, "Can Anyone Steer the Economy?" pp. 130–138; Peters, *American Public Policy,* pp. 141–151

20. Irene S. Rubin, "Budgeting," in B. Guy Peters and Jon Pierre, eds., *Handbook of Public Policy* (Thousand Oaks, CA: Sage, 2006).

21. All budget numbers in this section are from the "Historical Tables," *Budget of the United States Government, Fiscal Year 2011* (Washington, D.C.: Office of Management and Budget, February 2010).

22. "Bush to Ask for More War Funding," *The Wall Street Journal,* February 3, 2006, p. 1.

23. For a concise and stimulating discussion of forms of taxation and their effects, as well as the politics surrounding them see B. Guy Peters, "Tax Policy," in B. Guy Peters and Jon Pierre, eds., *Handbook of Public Policy* (Thousand Oaks, CA: Sage, 2006), pp. 281–292.

24. *The Budget of the United States Government, Fiscal Year 2011.*

25. Peters, *American Public Policy,* pp. 229–231; "Effective Tax Rates," *The National Bureau of Economic Research,* 2010.

26. Benjamin Friedman, *Day of Reckoning: The Consequences of American Economic Policy Under Reagan and After* (New York: Random House, 1989), p. 90.

27. Jackie Calmes, "Party Gridlock in Washington Feeds Fear of a Debt Crisis," *The New York Times,* February 17, 2010, p. 1.

28. David Leonhardt, "In Greek Debt Crisis, Some See Parallels to U.S." *The New York Times* (May 12, 2010), p. 1.

29. George J. Stigler, "The Theory of Economic Regulation," *Bell Journal,* 2 (Spring 1971), pp. 3–21. Also see Kolko, *The Triumph of Conservatism;* James Weinstein, *The Corporate Ideal in the Liberal State* (Boston: Beacon Press, 1968).

30. See Richard Harris and Sidney Milkis, *The Politics of Regulatory Change* (New York: Oxford University Press, 1989); Marc Allen Eisner, *Regulatory Politics in Transition* (Baltimore: Johns Hopkins University Press, 2000).

31. See G. William Domhoff, *The Higher Circles* (New York: Random House, 1970); Greenberg, *Capitalism and the American Political Ideal;* Kolko, *The Triumph of Conservatism;* Weinstein, *The Corporate Ideal in the Liberal State.*

32. Frances Fox Piven and Richard A. Cloward, *Poor People's Movements* (New York: Vintage, 1979).

33. Marver Bernstein, *Regulation by Independent Commission* (Princeton, NJ: Princeton University Press, 1955); Grant McConnell, *Private Power and American Democracy* (New York: Vintage Books, 1966); Lowi, *The End of Liberalism.*

34. David Vogel, *Fluctuating Fortunes: The Political Power of Business in the United States* (New York: Basic Books, 1989), pp. 59, 112.

35. James Buchanan and Gordon Tullock, "Polluters, Profits and Political Responses: Direct Control versus Taxes," *American*

Hyman Minsky, also gained new adherents, given his near-perfect prediction in his 1986 book *Stabilizing an Unstable Economy* of what came to a head in 2008.

Economic Review, 65 (1975), pp. 139–147; L. Lave, *The Strategy of Social Regulation* (Washington, D.C.: Brookings Institution, 1981); Murray Weidenbaum, *The Costs of Government Regulation of Business* (Washington, D.C.: Joint Economic Committee of Congress, 1978).

36. See Thomas Byrne Edsall, *The New Politics of Inequality* (New York: Norton, 1984); Vogel, *Fluctuating Fortunes;* Kevin P. Phillips, *The Politics of Rich and Poor: Wealth and the American Electorate in the Reagan Aftermath* (New York: Random House, 1990); Thomas Ferguson and Joel Rogers, *Right Turn: The Decline of the Democrats and the Future of American Politics* (New York: Farrar, Straus & Giroux, 1986).

37. Catherine Rampell, "Lax Oversight Caused Crisis, Bernanke Says," *The New York Times* (January 6, 2001), p. 1.

38. Christopher A. Simon, *Public Policy: Preferences and Outcomes* (New York: Pearson Longman, 2007), p. 15; Christoph Knill, "Environmental Policy," in B. Guy Peters and Jon Pierre, eds., *Handbook of Public Policy* (Thousand Oats, CA: Sage, 2006); *IPCC Fourth Assessment* (New York: United Nations, 2007), pp. 249–264, available online at **www.ipcc.ch/ipccreports/ar4-syr.htm**.

39. "How the European Union Is Becoming the World's Chief Regulator," *The Economist,* September 22, 2007, p. 66.

40. For accessible descriptions of this shadow banking system and its risky practices, see Simon Johnson and James Kwak, *13 Bankers: The Wall Street Takeover and the Next Financial Meltdown* (New York: Pantheon, 2010); Michael Lewis, *The Big Short: Inside the Doomsday Machine* (New York: W.W. Norton, 2010); Roger Lowenstein, *The End of Wall Street* (New York: Penguin, 2010).

41. David Cay Johnston, *Perfectly Legal* (New York: Portfolio, 2003).

CHAPTER 18

1. Harold Wilensky, *The Welfare State and Equality* (Berkeley, CA: University of California Press, 1975); Harold L. Wilensky, *Rich Democracies: Political Economy, Public Policy, and Performance* (Berkeley, CA: University of California Press, 2002). Also see the review and discussion of research on the expansion of social welfare in the United States in Diana M. DiNitto, *Social Welfare: Politics and Public Policy* (Boston: Pearson Allyn & Bacon, 2007), ch. 2; and the classic work by Charles Noble, *Welfare as We Knew It: A Political History of the American Welfare State* (New York: Oxford University Press, 1997).

2. Wilensky, *The Welfare State and Equality;* Wilensky, *Rich Democracies.*

3. On the details of this argument, see Clem Brooks and Jeff Manza, *Why Welfare States Exist: The Importance of Public Opinion in Democracies* (Chicago: University of Chicago Press, 2007). Also see Noble, *Welfare as We Knew It.*

4. Gosta Esping-Andersen, *Politics Against Markets* (Princeton, NJ: Princeton University Press, 1985); Walter Korpi, *The Democratic Class Struggle* (New York: Routledge, 1983).

5. Francis Fox Piven and Richard Cloward, *Regulating the Poor: The Functions of Public Welfare* (New York: Vintage, 1993).

6. Paul Conkin, *The New Deal* (New York: Crowell, 1967); G. William Domhoff, *The Higher Circles* (New York: Vintage, 1971); Gabriel Kolko, *The Triumph of Conservatism* (Chicago: Quadrangle, 1967); James Weinstein, *The Corporate Ideal in the Liberal State* (Boston: Beacon, 1968).

7. "Historical Tables," *Budget of the United States Government, Fiscal Year 2011* (Washington, D.C.: Office of Management and Budget, February 2010).

8. Howard Jacob Karger and David Stoesz, *American Welfare State Policy: A Pluralist Approach* (Boston: Allyn & Bacon, 2010), pp. 260–261.

9. DiNitto, *Social Welfare,* p. 138.

10. Hacker, *The Great Risk Shift,* ch. 2.

11. *The 2007 OASDI Trustees Report* (Washington, D.C.: The Social Security Administration, 2007).

12. Roger Lowenstein, "A Question of Numbers," *New York Times Magazine,* January 16, 2005, pp. 42–47.

13. Mark Penn, *Microtrends: The Small Forces Behind Tomorrow's Big Changes* (New York: Twelve, the Hachette Book Group, 2007), pp. 31–34.

14. Benjamin I. Page and James R. Simmons, *What Government Can Do: Dealing with Poverty and Inequality* (Chicago: University of Chicago Press, 2000), ch. 3; Edmund L. Andrews, "4 Ways That Might Save the Government Trillions," *The New York Times,* February 4, 2006, p. A7; B. Guy Peters, *American Public Policy: Promise and Performance,* 8th ed. (Washington, D.C.: CQ Press, 2010), pp. 300–311.

15. Edward P. Lazear, "The Virtues of Personal Accounts for Social Security," *The Economists' Voice,* 2, no. 1 (2005), pp. 1–7.

16. Kaiser Family Foundation, press release, May 13, 2009.

17. DiNitto, *Social Welfare,* pp. 310–318.

18. Peters, *American Public Policy,* pp. 277–279.

19. "Could you live on $300 a week?" the MSN Money Team, **www.articles.moneycentral.msn.com/SavingandDebt/LearnToBudget/how-much-jobless-pay-would-you-get.aspx**.

20. DiNitto, *Social Welfare,* pp. 146–148, 262–264.

21. "U.S. Pensions Found to Lift Many of the Poor," *The New York Times,* December 28, 1989, p. A1. See also Theodore R. K. Marmor, Jerry L. Mashaw, and Philip L. Harvey, *America's Misunderstood Welfare State* (New York: HarperCollins, 1990), ch. 4.

22. David S. Johnson, "2008 Income, Poverty, and Health Insurance Estimates for the Current Population Survey," (Washington, D.C.: U.S. Census Bureau, September 10, 2009).

23. U.S. Bureau of the Census, *Statistical Abstracts of the United States, 2010.*

24. Jason Furman, *Top Ten Facts on Social Security's 70th Anniversary* (Washington, D.C.: Center on Budget and Policy Priorities, 2007).

25. Lawrence Mishel, Ross Eisenbrey, and John Irons, *Strategy of Economic Rebound* (Washington, D.C.: Economic Policy Institute, January 11, 2008).

26. Peters, *American Public Policy,* p 311.

27. "Americans Dissatisfied with Government's Efforts on Poverty," *The Gallup Poll,* October 25, 2005; "Majority Call Fighting Poverty a Top Priority," Zogby International Poll, press release, June 4, 2007.

28. Hugh Heclo, "The Political Foundations of Anti-Poverty Policy," in Sheldon Danziger and Daniel Weinberg, eds., *Fighting Poverty: What Works and What Doesn't?* (Cambridge, MA: Harvard University Press, 1986); Fay Lomax Cook and Edith J. Barrett, *Support for the American Welfare State: The Views of Congress and the Public* (New York: HarperCollins, 1990), ch 4.

29. Handler and Hasenfeld, *Blame Welfare, Ignore Poverty and Inequality;* Martin Gilens, *Why Americans Hate Welfare: Race,*

Media, and the Politics of Antipoverty Policy (Chicago: The University of Chicago Press, 1999).

30. Center for Budget and Policy Priorities, 2007; DiNitto, *Social Welfare*, pp. 240–245.

31. "From Welfare to Work," *The Economist*, July 29, 2006, pp. 27–30; Lauren Etter, "Welfare Reform: Ten Years Later," *The Wall Street Journal*, August 26, 2006, p. A9; Robert Pear and Erik Eckholm, "A Decade After Welfare Reform," *The New York Times*, August 21, 2006, p. A12.

32. Ibid.

33. Karger and Stoesz, *American Social Welfare Policy*, pp. 277–280.

34. Robert Pear, "In a Tough Economy, Old Limits on Welfare," *The New York Times*, April 10, 2010, p. 1.

35. Robert Greenstein, *Dispelling Confusion on Food Stamps, Tax Rebates, and the Stimulus Package* (Washington, D.C.: Center on Budget and Policy Priorities, January 26, 2008). Also see John E. Schwarz, *America's Hidden Success: A Reassessment of Public Policy from Kennedy to Reagan* (New York: Norton, 1988), p. 37; Karger and Stoesz, *American Social Welfare Policy*, pp. 453–456.

36. Karger and Stoesz, *American Social Welfare Policy*, p. 310.

37. Ibid., p. 311.

38. DiNitto, *Social Welfare*, pp. 302–310.

39. Kaiser Family Foundation, press release, June 12, 2007.

40. *What Is SCHIP* (Washington, D.C.: Center for Budget and Policy Priorities, 2007).

41. Peters, *American Public Policy*, p. 320; Howard, *The Hidden Welfare State*, ch. 3.

42. Robert Greenstein, *The Earned Income Tax Credit* (Washington, D.C.: The Center for Budget Priorities, September 2005).

43. Gosta Esping-Andersen, "The Three Political Economies of the Welfare State," *Canadian Review of Sociology and Anthropology*, 26 (1989), pp. 10–36; Jonas Pontusson, "The American Welfare State in Comparative Perspective," *Perspectives on Politics*, 4, no. 2 (June 2006), pp. 315–326.

44. See "OECD Social Indicators" at the "statistics portal" of the Organization for Economic Cooperation and Development at **www.oecd.org/topicsstatsportal** (February 2007). Also see Vincent A. Mahler and Claudio J. Katz, "Social Benefits in Advanced Capitalist Countries: A Cross-National Assessment," *Comparative Politics*, 21 (1988), pp. 37–50; Arnold J. Heidenheimer, Hugh Heclo, and Carolyn Teich Adams, *Comparative Public Policy: The Politics of Social Choice in America, Europe, and Japan*, 3rd ed. (New York: St. Martin's Press, 1990).

45. "OECD Social Indicators"; U.S. Bureau of the Census, *Statistical Abstract of the United States, 2008*. For a more general historical discussion of how this happened see Peter Lindert, *Growing Public: Social Spending and Economic Growth Since the 18th Century* (Cambridge, U.K.: Cambridge University Press, 2004).

46. Howard, *The Hidden Welfare State*; Christopher Howard, "Is the American Welfare State Unusually Small?" *PS*, July 2003, pp. 411–416.

47. Andrea Brandolini and Timothy Smeeding, "Patterns of Economic Inequality in Western Democracies: Some Facts on Levels and Trends," *PS*, January 2006, pp. 21–26; Lee Kenworthy and Jonas Pontusson, "Rising Inequality and the Politics of Redistribution in Affluent Countries," *Perspectives on Politics*, 3, no. 3 (September 2005), pp. 449–472.

48. Alberto Alesina and Edward L. Glaeser, *Fighting Poverty in the US and Europe: A World of Difference* (New York: Oxford University Press, 2004); Nathan Glazer, *The Limits of Social Policy* (Cambridge, MA: Harvard University Press, 1988), pp. 187–188. See also W. Sombart, *Why There Is No Socialism in the United States* (Armonk, NY: Sharpe, 1976).

49. Gilens, *Why Americans Hate Welfare*; Jeff Manza, "Race and the Underdevelopment of the American Welfare State," *Theory and Society*, 29 (2000), pp. 819–832. Also see Alberto Alesina and Edward L. Glaeser, *Fighting Poverty in the US and Europe: A World of Difference* (Oxford, U.K.: Oxford University Press, 2004); Carol A. Horton, *Race and the Making of American Liberalism* (New York: Oxford University Press, 2005).

50. Wilensky, *The Welfare State and Equality*; John Micklethwait and Adrain Wooldridge, *The Right Nation: Conservative Power in America* (New York: Penguin, 2004); Handler and Hasenfeld, *Blame Welfare, Ignore Poverty and Inequality*.

51. Hacker, *The Great Risk Shift*.

52. Michael Moran, "Health Policy," in B. Guy Peters and Jon Pierre, eds., *Handbook of Public Policy* (Thousand Oaks, CA: Sage, 2006).

53. Francis G. Castles, *The Impact of Parties: Politics and Policies in Democratic Capitalist States* (Newbury Park, CA: Sage, 1982); Esping-Andersen, *Politics Against Markets*; Korpi, *Democratic Class Struggle*; John Stephens, *The Transition from Capitalism to Socialism* (London: Macmillan, 1979).

CHAPTER 19

1. Helene Cooper, Michael Wines, and David E. Sanger, "China's Role as Lender Alters Obama's Visit," *The New York Times*, November 14, 2009, p. 1.

2. John Hawksworth and Gordon Cookson, "The World in 2050— Beyond the BRICSs" (New York: Price-WaterhouseCoopers, March 2008).

3. Benjamin I. Page with Marshall M. Bouton, *The Foreign Policy Disconnect: What Americans Want from Our Leaders But Don't Get* (Chicago: University of Chicago Press, 2006).

4. Niall Ferguson, *Colossus: The Price of America's Empire* (New York: Penguin, 2004); William E. Odom and Robert Dujarric, *America's Inadvertent Empire* (New Haven, CT: Yale University Press, 2004); Chalmers Johnson, *The Sorrows of Empire* (New York: Metropolitan Books, 2004). For a thoughtful review of a shelf of relatively recent books describing, lamenting, or celebrating American empire see Emily S. Rosenberg, "Bursting America's Imperial Bubble," *The Chronicle of Higher Education*, 53, no. 11 (November 3, 2006), p. B10. For an analysis that suggests that the United States is less of an imperial power than it once was, see Daniel H. Nexon and Thomas Wright, "What's at Stake in the American Empire Debate," *American Political Science Review*, 101, no. 2 (May 2007), pp. 253–271.

5. Statistics are from the *CIA World Factbook, 2009*, **www.cia.gov/cia/publications/factbook**.

6. Gregg Easterbrook, "American Might Moves Beyond Superpower," *The New York Times*, April 27, 2003, Week in Review Section, p. 1; The Center for Defense Information, **www.cdi.org** (2006); the Center for Arms Control and Non-Proliferation, **www.armscontrolcenter.org** (2006).

7. Johnson, *The Sorrows of Empire*.

8. Ibid.

9. "China Plans to Slow Expansion of Defense Spending in 2010," *Bloomberg News Service,* March 5, 2010.

10. "The Hobbled Hegemon," *The Economist,* June 30, 2007, pp. 29–32; David Lague, "Chinese Submarine Fleet Is Growing, Analysts Say," *The New York Times,* February 25, 2008, p. A1; Drew Thompson, "China's Military," *Foreign Policy,* March/April 2010, pp. 86–90.

11. Ibid.

12. Michael R. Gordon, "U.S. Army Shifts Focus to Nation-Building," *International Herald Tribune,* February 8, 2008, p. 1.

13. Joseph S. Nye Jr., "Redefining the National Interest," *Foreign Affairs,* July/August 1999, pp. 22–35. Also see Richard Florida, *The Rise of the Creative Class* (New York: Basic Books, 2002), chs. 3 and 14.

14. Ibid; Thomas L. Friedman, *The Lexus and the Olive Tree* (New York: Farrar, Straus, Giroux, 1999).

15. Pew Research Center for the People and the Press, "War with Iraq Further Divides Global Publics" (June 3, 2003), "A Year After Iraq War: Mistrust of America in Europe Ever Higher, Muslim Anger Persists" (March 16, 2004), and "Global Unease with Major World Powers" (June 27, 2007).

16. "Global Opinion: The Spread of Anti-Americanism," *Trends, 2005* (Washington, D.C.: Pew Research Center for the People and the Press, 2005), p. 106; "America's Image Slips, But Allies Share U.S. Concern Over Iran, Hamas," *Survey Report* (Washington, D.C.: Pew Research Center for the People and the Press, June 13, 2006); "The Great Divide: How Westerners and Muslims View Each Other," *Global Attitudes Project Report* (Washington, D.C.: Pew Research Center, June 22, 2006).

17. Pew, "Global Unease with Major World Powers," p. 20.

18. "Obama More Popular Abroad Than at Home, Global Image of U.S. Continues to Benefit" (Washington, D.C.: Pew Research Center, June 12, 2010).

19. Melvyn P. Leffler, "Bush's Foreign Policy," *Foreign Policy,* September/October 2004, p. 23.

20. Robert O. Keohane and Joseph S. Nye Jr., *Power and Interdependence: World Politics in Transition* (Boston: Little Brown, 1977); Robert Gilpin, *The Political Economy of International Relations* (Princeton, NJ: Princeton University Press, 1987).

21. Michael Mandelbaum, *The Case for Goliath* (New York: Public Affairs, 2005); Ferguson, *Colossus;* Odom and Dujarric, *America's Inadvertent Empire.* Also see Robert Gilpin, *The Challenge of Global Capitalism: The World Economy in the 21st Century* (Princeton, NJ: Princeton University Press, 2000).

22. C. Fred Bergsten, "A Partnership of Equals," *Foreign Affairs,* July/August 2008, pp.

23. John Lewis Gaddis, "A Grand Strategy," *Foreign Policy,* November/December 2002, pp. 50–57; Ivo H. Daalder and James M. Lindsay, *America Unbound: The Bush Revolution in Foreign Policy* (Washington, D.C.: Brookings Institution Press, 2003).

24. Zbigniew Brzezinski, *The Choice: Global Domination or Global Leadership* (New York: Basic Books, 2004); Al Gore, *The Path to Survival* (New York: Rodale Books, 2008); Fareed Zakaria, *The Post-American World* (New York: W. W. Norton, 2008).

25. Brian Knowlton, "Gates Calls European Mood a Danger to Peace," *The New York Times,* February 23, 2010, p. 1.

26. "The Terrorist Threat to the Homeland," *National Intelligence Estimate* (Washington, D.C.: Director of National Intelligence, press release, July 17, 2007).

27. *Arab Human Development Report 2005* (New York: The United Nations, 2006).

28. Samuel P. Huntington, "The Clash of Civilizations," *Foreign Affairs,* 72 (1993), pp. 22–49. Also see Martin Jacques, *When China Rules the World: The End of the Western World and the Birth of a New Order* (New York: Penguin Press, 2009).

29. See "Somewhere Over the Rainbow," *The Economist,* January 26, 2008, pp 27–29; "Liberty's Great Advance," *The Economist,* June 28, 2003, pp. 5–9; Jagdish Bhagwati, *In Defense of Globalization* (New York: Oxford University Press, 2004); Jagdish Bhagwati and Marvin H. Kosters, eds., *Trade and Wages: Leveling Down Wages?* (Washington, D.C.: AEI Press, 1994); Martin Wolf, *Why Globalization Works* (New Haven, CT: Yale University Press, 2004); Michael Veseth, *Globaloney: Unraveling the Myths of Globalization* (Lanham, MD: Rowman and Littlefield, 2005). Dani Rodrik, among others, disagrees. See his *Has Globalization Gone Too Far?* (Washington, D.C.: The Institute of International Economics, 1997). Also see E. Stiglitz, *Globalization and Its Discontents* (New York: W. W. Norton, 2003).

30. "Economists Rethink Free Trade," *BusinessWeek,* February 11, 2008, pp. 32–34.

31. *The United Nations Annual Report,* World Health Organization, 2009.

32. Ibid.

33. *Budget of the United States Government, Fiscal Year 2011* (Washington, D.C.: Office of Management and Budget, 2010); Organization for Economic Cooperation and Development (OECD), *International Development Statistics,* 2010.

34. For a review of the key criticism of development aid to poor countries see William J. Baumol, Robert E. Litan, and Carl J. Schramm, *Good Capitalism, Bad Capitalism, and the Economics of Growth and Prosperity* (New Haven, CT: Yale University Press, 2007), ch. 6; William Easterly, *The Elusive Quest for Growth: Economists' Adventures and Misadventures in the Tropics* (Cambridge, MA: MIT Press, 2001).

35. *No Global Climate Change Alarm in the U.S., China* (Washington, D.C.: Pew Research Center, Survey Report, June 13, 2006).

36. Matthew Crenson and Benjamin Ginsberg, *Presidential Power: Unchecked and Unbalanced* (New York: W.W. Norton, 2007).

37. On the gap in outlooks between American leaders and the American public on issues of foreign and national security policies, see Page with Bouton, *The Foreign Policy Disconnect.*

CREDITS

Text, Figures, and Tables

Page 17: By the Numbers box, Map of Freedom 2007 from Freedom House Publications. Copyright © 2007. Reprinted by permission; **p. 79:** Figure 3.4, Adapted from Morris P. Fiorina and Paul E. Peterson, *New American Democracy,* 2nd ed. Copyright © 2001. Reprinted by permission of Pearson Education, Inc.; **p. 105:** By the Numbers box (both graphs), From *Perspectives on Politics,* vol. 3, no. 3, 2005. Copyright © 2005. Reprinted with the permission of Cambridge University Press; **p. 263:** Table 9.1, "Major Political Parties in American History" from *Party Politics in America,* 12th ed., Marjorie Randon Hershey. Copyright © 2007 Reprinted with permission by Pearson Education, Inc.; **p. 457:** Figure 14.3, From *Storm Center: The Supreme Court in American Politics,* Seventh Edition, by David O'Brien. Copyright © 2005, 2003, 2000, 1996, 1993, 1990, 1986 by David O'Brien. Used by permission of W. W. Norton & Company, Inc.; **p. 536:** Figure 16.1, Center for American Women and Politics (January 2008).

Photos

Page 3: Danny Molonski/Corbis; **p. 6:** Farnood/Sipa Press; **p. 7:** James Leynse/Corbis; **p. 9:** Getty Images; **p. 12:** The Granger Collection; **p. 12:** The Granger Collection; **p. 17:** Desmond Kwando/Getty Images; **p. 20:** Bettmann/Corbis; **p. 27:** Pavlos Makridis/Corbis; **p. 30L:** The Granger Collection; **p. 30R:** Library of Congress; **p. 32:** Library of Congress; **p. 36:** The Granger Collection; **p. 39:** The Granger Collection; **p. 46:** Richard T. Norwitz/Corbis; **p. 52:** Mark Peterson/Corbis; **p. 59:** Kevin Lamarque/Corbis; **p. 61:** Getty Images; **p. 65:** Ann Johansson/AP Images; **p. 67:** Zhang Jan/Corbis; **p. 72:** Bettmann/Corbis; **p. 73:** Library of Congress; **p. 75:** Steven Helber/AP Images; **p. 80:** Ralph A. Clevenger; **p. 83:** Comstock RF; **p. 91:** Teh Eng Koon/Getty Images; **p. 95:** Tony Avelar/AP Images; **p. 105:** Pearson Education/Pearson College; **p. 106:** Chris Hondoros/Getty Images; **p. 107:** Christopher Morris/AP Images; **p. 111:** Bryan Denton/Corbis; **p. 113:** Fuji Photos/The Image Works; **p. 116:** Justin Sullivan/Getty Images; **p. 123:** John Griffiths/Magnum Photos; **p. 125:** AP Images; **p. 129:** Fuji Productions/Corbis; **p. 130:** Bettmann/Corbis; **p. 131:** Kent Meireis/The Image Works; **p. 135:** Cory Young/AP Images; **p. 136:** Jae C. Hong/AP Images; **p. 139:** Bob Adelman/Magnum Photos; **p. 142:** Ted S. Warren/AP Images; **p. 144:** Nati Harnik/AP Images; **p. 146:** David Buffington/Corbis; **p. 147:** Tim Sloan/Getty Images; **p. 152:** Mark Mainz/Getty Images; **p. 161:** Patrick Barth/Getty Images; **p. 163:** Copyright 2007 Newsday; **p. 164:** Getty Images; **p. 168:** Matt Rourke/AP Images; **p. 169:** AP Images; **p. 170:** Ron Edmonds/AP Images; **p. 173:** Superstock; **p. 176:** Ron Edmonds/AP Images; **p. 178:** Chad Hunt/Corbis; **p. 179:** Chris Nesbitt/The Image Works; **p. 181:** Alex Brandon/Landov; **p. 183:** Davis Turner/Getty Images; **p. 187:** AP Images; **p. 190:** Photofest; **p. 191:** Getty Images; **p. 192:** Jose Azel/Getty Images; **p. 199:** Getty Image News; **p. 202:** Library of Congress; **p. 205:** Zak Brian/Sipa Press/AP Images; **p. 206:** Alex Brandon/AP Images; **p. 209:** Dustin Cunningham/AP Images; **p. 210:** Chuck Bigger/AP Photos; **p. 212:** Hose Luis Magana/AP Images; **p. 217:** moodboard/Corbis; **p. 224:** David Burnett/Getty Images; **p. 231:** Bettmann/Corbis; **p. 234:** Brooks Kraft/Corbis; **p. 236:** AP Images; **p. 240:** Mui Chun Jou/Corbis; **p. 244:** Alex Wong/Getty Images; **p. 247:** Charles Pereira/AP Images; **p. 248:** Bettmann/Corbis; **p. 252:** Bettmann/Corbis; **p. 253:** Rubberball/RF/Getty; **p. 259:** Tannen Maury/Corbis; **p. 262:** AFP/Getty Images; **p. 264:** John Giles/Landov; **p. 265:** Bogdan Christe/Reuters/Corbis; **p. 267:** Brooks Craft/Corbis; **p. 269:** Bettmann/Corbis; **p. 274:** Mandel Ngan/Getty Images; **p. 277:** Spencer Platt/Getty Images; **p. 282:** Jose Luis Magana/AP Images; **p. 291:** Chris McGrath/Getty Images; **p. 295:** Bob Daemmrich/Getty Images; **p. 300:** The County Election by George Caleb Bingham 1852. The St. Louis Art Museum; **p. 302:** John Paul Pelissier/Reuters; **p. 305:** ITTC Productions/Getty Images; **p. 306:** William Thomas Cain/Getty Images; **p. 308:** Bob Daemmrich/PhotoEdit; **p. 310:** Corbis Images; **p. 313:** Brian Bohannon/AP Images; **p. 315L:** Corbis Images; **p. 315R:** Bettmann/Corbis; **p. 317:** Ray Hoffman/AP Images; **p. 327:** AP Images; **p. 337:** Matthew Cavanaugh/Corbis; **p. 343:** Michael Reynolds/Corbis; **p. 352:** Courtesy of Representative Rosa De Lauro; **p. 356:** Mike Theiler/Corbis; **p. 360:** Mark Wilson/Getty Images; **p. 361:** AP Images; **p. 367:** Scott J. Ferrell/Getty Images; **p. 372:** Jay Mallin/Getty Images; **p. 379:** Corbis/News/Corbis; **p. 381:** Washington Reviewing The Troops at Fort Cumberland Maryland by Frederick Kemmelmeyer. The Metropolitan Museum of Art. Gift of Edgar William and Beatrice Chrysler Garbish 1963 (63.20.2) Photograph c 1983. The Metropolitan Museum of Art; **p. 383:** Bettmann/Corbis; **p. 384:** AP Images; **p. 386:** Corbis News/Corbis; **p. 387:** Joe Scherschel/Getty Images; **p. 398:** Mandel Ngan/Getty Images; **p. 394:** Peter Turnley/Corbis; **p. 397:** Ann Young/AP Images; **p. 398:** Corbis News/Corbis; **p. 399:** Evan Vucci/AP Images; **p. 401:** Mohammed Obaldi/AFP/Getty Images; **p. 408:** Andrew Holbrooke/Corbis; **p. 414:** Eitan Abramovich/Getty Images; **p. 419:** Vincent Kessler/Sipa; **p. 422:** Steve Liss/Corbis; **p. 424:** Erik Lesser/Corbis; **p. 430:** Michael Reynolds/Corbis; **p. 436:** AP Images; **p. 439:** AP Images; **p. 440:** Gervaso Sanchez/AP Images; **p. 443:** Roger Ressmeyer/Corbis; **p. 449:** AP Images; **p. 451L:** Superstock; **p. 451R:** John Marshall by Chester Harding ca 1829. Washington and Lee University; **p. 459:** JRI/Gripas/Corbis; **p. 463:** David Hume Kennerly/Getty Images; **p. 464:** Art Lien/courtartist.com; **p. 471:** Larry Downing/Reuters; **p. 472:** Ann Johansen/Corbis; **p. 475:** Hank Walker/Time and Life/Getty Images; **p. 483:** Kyle Fasanella; **p. 488:** Bettmann/Corbis; **p. 490:** Nik Wheeler/Corbis; **p. 492:** AP Images; **p. 496:** Nola Tully/Corbis; **p. 498:** Frederc Noy/Newscom; **p. 500:** Stan Grossfeld/Landov; **p. 502:** Mark Peterson/Corbis; **p. 505:** Milie Simons/Corbis; **p. 512:** Jason Reed/Corbis; **p. 518:** Jim West/PhotoEdit; **p. 521:** The Granger Collection; **p. 523:** Historical Premium/Corbis; **p. 526:** Bettmann/Corbis; **p. 527:** Time and Life/Getty Images; **p. 529:** Tom Carter/PhotoEdit; **p. 536:** Lance King/Corbis; **p. 537:** Robyn Beck/Getty Images; **p. 540:** Larry Mulvehill/The Image Works; **p. 508:** Mario Tana/Getty Images; **p. 542:** Corbis News/Corbis; **p. 548:** Rick Gershon/Getty Images; **p. 552:** John Moore/Getty Images; **p. 554:** Saul Loeb/Getty Images; **p. 555:** Bloomberg/Getty Images; **p. 558:** Nicole Bengivone/NYT/Redux; **p. 561:** Yuri Gripas/Corbis; **p. 562:** Getty Images; **p. 566:** Scott Ferrell/Getty Images; **p. 568:** Lance Cheung/Getty Images; **p. 570:** AP Images; **p. 575:** Ben Stansall/Getty Images; **p. 576:** Andy Nelson/Getty Images; **p. 584:** Scott Thew/Corbis; **p. 588L:** Rolls Press/Getty Images;

INDEX